EXPLORING CULTURES
A Prentice Hall Series in Anthropology

Crossing Currents
Continuity and Change in Latin America

Edited by

Michael B. Whiteford
Iowa State University

Scott Whiteford
Michigan State University

Prentice Hall
Upper Saddle River, NJ 07458

Library of Congress Cataloging-in-Publication Data

Crossing currents : continuity and change in Latin America / edited by
  Michael B. Whiteford, Scott Whiteford.
      p.   cm. —(Exploring cultures)
    Includes bibliographical references.
    ISBN 0-13-656471-2 (pbk.)
      1. Ethnology—Latin America.   2. Social structure—Latin America.
  3. Social change—Latin America.   4. Latin America—History.
  5. Latin America—Social conditions.   6. Latin America—Economic
  conditions.   I. Whiteford, Michael B   II. Whiteford
  Scott.   III. Series.
  GN564.L29C76   1998
  306'.098—dc21   97-45892
                                           CIP

Editorial director: Charlyce Jones Owen
Acquisitions editor: Nancy Roberts
Editorial/production supervision
  and interior design: Mary Araneo
Buyer: Mary Ann Gloriande
Cover director: Jayne Conte
Editorial assistant: Maureen Diana

This book was set in 10/11 Times New Roman by
A & A Publishing Services, Inc., and was printed
and bound by Hamilton Printing Co. The cover was
printed by Phoenix Color Corp.

 © 1998 by Prentice-Hall, Inc.
Simon & Schuster/A Viacom Company
Upper Saddle River, New Jersey 07458

Printed in the United States of America

10 9 8 7 6 5 4 3 2

ISBN 0-13-656471-2

PRENTICE-HALL INTERNATIONAL (UK) LIMITED, *London*
PRENTICE-HALL OF AUSTRALIA PTY. LIMITED, *Sydney*
PRENTICE-HALL CANADA INC., *Toronto*
PRENTICE-HALL HISPANOAMERICANA, S.A., *Mexico*
PRENTICE-HALL OF INDIA PRIVATE LIMITED, *New Delhi*
PRENTICE-HALL OF JAPAN, INC., *Tokyo*
SIMON & SCHUSTER ASIA PTE. LTD., *Singapore*
EDITORA PRENTICE-HALL DO BRASIL, LTDA., *Rio de Janeiro*

Dedicamos este libro a nuestros amigos y colegas de américa latina. Gracias por su ayuda y por los años de amistad.

Contents

Part IV: Ethnicity

Part V: Gender

Part VI: Social Structure

Part VII: Religion

Part VIII: Health

Part IX: Economics, Neoliberal Reforms, and Trade Agreements

Part X: Environment

Part XI: Population Movement and Changing Cities

Preface

"Come see the village where time stood still!" beckons the colorful travel poster. So often the scene features a cobblestone street set against a crumbling brick wall, over whose sides cascade gorgeous mounds of flaming purple and red bougainvillea. Along this street are whitewashed adobe houses topped with dark orange tile roofs. If the brochure is really alluring, one can see at its end the baroque architecture of a small church. An outdoor market may be in full swing in front of it, adding more splashes of color to the scene.

Pasted on the plate glass window of the travel agency, this romanticized view is enticing, particularly on a cold January day in the Midwest. Indeed, this common backdrop could truly be in almost any country in Latin America, and it probably fits the image—reinforced by movies and television—that many outsiders have of Latin America: a region of small villages where roosters constantly crow, donkeys bray without provocation, peasants and their oxen tend fields, and where cacti, with snow-capped mountains behind them, dot the landscape.

Almost in juxtaposition is another image harbored by many outsiders. It is one of a region of enormous cities, replete with futuristic skyscrapers of steel and glass, whose occupants drive Mercedes Benzes and Porsches and where the rich own condominiums in Miami, send their offspring to schools in the United States and in Europe, and ski at Aspen during the peak season.

Around the outskirts of these metropolises are shantytowns that seem to stretch for miles. Here dwellings are made from concoctions of cardboard, pieces of plywood, and flattened-out oil tins. Tucked amidst these modest structures are more substantial houses with concrete block walls, wrought-iron grillwork covering their windows, and a television antenna or satellite dishes perched on the roofs. These settlements seem awash with children who dart in and out of the assorted dwellings and whose laughter and squeals compete with the cacophony of barking dogs and the music emanating from the myriad radios. Small housefront stores, automotive repair shops, bakeries, and cobbler shops are sprinkled throughout these settlements. Unpretentious in their appearance, they provide economic support for residents.

Latin America is an area of contrasts and conundrums. In the pages that follow, we have pulled together a collection of articles we hope will introduce the reader to this fascinating and diverse region of the world. Most of the contributions are written by anthropologists and thus give the volume a more local perspective than might be found in a collection of essays written by sociologists, demographers, economists, or political scientists.

The organization of the book follows the approach the two of us take in the courses we teach on contemporary Latin America and thus covers a wide swath of topics ranging from prehistory to contemporary issues related to urbanization and development. In assembling the materials for this tome we have tried to provide the reader with a mixture of classics, relatively unknown pieces, and materials written expressly for this volume. In all instances we hope readers will find the contributions interesting and at times provocative.

As editors and siblings, we have had a long fascination with the region. Our father, Andrew H. Whiteford, also an anthropologist, first took us to Latin America when we were children and he was doing research. Subsequent trips further cemented a bond between us and the area. We have been returning to live and do research on our own since that initial exposure more than four decades ago. We were not the only ones in the family so enamored of Latin America. One of our sisters, Linda Whiteford, works in Latin America, as does her spouse, Doug Uzzell. Friends and colleagues often wonder whether family gatherings resemble sessions of the American Anthropological Association. They don't.

Our paths toward understanding about and appreciating Latin America have been long and exciting ones. We have learned so much from so many people that it is hard to know where to draw the line in affirming input and influence. The lessons began with our parents, who took us to Popayán, Colombia, in the early 1950s and who have been continual teachers since then. George M. Foster, Richard N. Adams, and Angel Palerm were mentors in graduate school. They made sure we were rigorous in method and approach and were instrumental in helping us establish our professional directions and careers. We would not be undertaking this project if it were not for the help and assistance of our colleagues and friends in Latin America, who were (and still are) our teachers. Recognizing that our obligation to these colleagues is profound and deep, we have requested that any royalties that accrue from the sale of this book go to the Society for Latin American Anthropology, a section of the American Anthropological Association, for the purpose of bringing Latin American scholars to professional meetings in the United States. We are pleased that we can reciprocate in some small fashion for years of help and guidance.

We would also like to acknowledge the following Prentice Hall reviewers for their input: Jon Olson, California State University—Los Angeles, and Robert Alvarez, Arizona State University.

Finally, more than can adequately be expressed, we appreciate the continual support of spouses (Patty and Weegee) and offspring (Scott, Aaron, and Cindy and Ian and Chloe), who, whether they accompanied us to the field or kept things running at home during our absences, shared our interest in and fascination with Latin America.

Michael B. Whiteford
Scott Whiteford

1

Introduction to Latin America
Its Land and People

Carlos Fuentes, the noted Mexican author and diplomat, tells this story.[1] When Fuentes was a young boy, his father, who was a young lawyer with the Borders Claims Commission, took him to a place along the border. Placing one foot in Mexico and the other in the United States, he gave his son a memorable lecture on the differences between the cultures of the two neighboring nations. The apocryphal lesson the astute father delivered was important in many ways and has caused his famous son to think often of the many important and challenging differences between the cultures of Latin American and the United States.

"You are," he tells audiences in the United States, "representatives of a Protestant, capitalist, Nordic culture, and we are members of a culture that is Indo-Mediterranean, Catholic, conflictively individualistic and communitarian, a culture of syncretism and the Baroque." Fuentes notes that the cultures are very different, very dissimilar in their origins. Each is strange and challenging to comprehend by members of the other culture. He points out that people in the United States are interested in the future; Latin Americans focus on their past. He goes on, "Your past is often forgotten; ours is still doing battle with our souls." In Latin America,

grace is achieved only through mediation of a hierarchy. North Americans[2] believe in direct grace between humans and God. In the United States, people believe in the diffusion of power; in Latin America, there has been a total centralization of it. Perhaps because he is a novelist, Fuentes is also a student of human culture, and in an eloquent fashion he is able to pinpoint some of the confounding differences between Latin American and U.S. cultures.[3]

As university professors, the classes we teach on Latin America are comprised mainly of students who are natives of the United States, although there is always a sprinkling of Latin American and other international students. It is the mixture of students from diverse areas with different perspectives that enhances these classes. Because we both teach at state-supported Midwestern universities, that primarily serve students who are attending schools in their home states, we begin our courses by talking about why it is important for residents of the United States to learn more about our neighbors to the south and the historical connections between the United States and Latin America. Discussion usually moves quickly to the one-sided and paternalistic role we have usually taken in dealing with our neighbors. The Mexican students in the classes learned at a very early age that more than a century ago, over a course of two decades, the United States divested Mexico of over half the total territory it had when it became independent. Central American and Caribbean students are keenly aware of the various military incursions by U.S. forces in their countries within this century. Colombians still bristle at Teddy Roosevelt's heavy-handed "liberation" of Panama in order to build the canal, and many Latin Americans only partially believe that the United States will ultimately return full control of the canal to Panama when the time comes. Undoubtedly speaking for all of Latin America, the late Mexican dictator Porfirio Díaz is credited with uttering, "Poor Mexico, so far from God, so close to the United States."

On the other hand, our U.S. students are aware of the growing influence of Latin cultures in this country. Increasingly, restaurants serving various types of Latin American cuisine have become popular dining choices. Latin American music is found on radio stations and in music stores across the country. The number of Latin American television and movie stars is growing. In recent years, there has been a continuing discussion revolving around trade issues with Latin America and an increasing realization of the burgeoning and intractable economic interconnectedness between the two regions. Spanish classes at all academic levels enjoy robust enrollments across the country.

In the pages that follow, we offer a collection of readings that examine a variety of issues in Latin America. Although not all of them are written by anthropologists, most are, and the others generally have a perspective that is anthropological in nature—holistic, local, and in-depth.

Prior to beginning, however, we wish to set the stage by providing some introductory background material and observations. Some of what appears here will establish themes that will wind their way through readings in several of the sections.

A final bit of background discussion about the geographic setting called Latin America would be useful before commencing. The geographical area from the Río Grande, or the Río Bravo, as the Mexicans call it, to the tip of Tierra del Fuego 8,000 miles away, comprises a region of approximately 8 million square miles and is home to close to 500 million people. Within this vast territory is an ecologically diverse area unmatched by any comparable territory on the face of the earth. On a broad level, one finds one of the world's largest rain forests, as well as the largest mountain chain on the face of the earth. Impressive deserts are found in several parts of Latin America. Yet these sweeping statements mask the incredible microecological diversity found in many areas that act as host to a plethora of species of living things. For example, Costa Rica, a country of 20,000 square miles (about the size of West Virginia) has 850 species of birds, 560 species of mammals, amphibians, and reptiles, 130 species of freshwater fish, and at least 9,000 plant species. The biodiversity of this small nation is many times greater than what is found in comparative categories for all of the continental United States.

Within this region is a series of mountain chains that begins with the Sierra Madre mountains of Mexico and the volcanic peaks that accent the landscape of highland Mexico and Central America and continue with the towering Andes, the largest mountain chain on the face of the earth, stretching from Colombia to southern Chile. Rivers dissect all of the mountain chains, eroding away the steep slopes and creating verdant valleys. Between many of the mountain ranges and the coastal lowlands are transition zones of rolling grasslands.

East of the northern and central Andes stretch the vast lowlands of Amazonia, the largest rainforest on earth. Snaking west to east through the Amazonian lowlands is the world's broadest river, the Amazon. On the same continent is the Atacama desert of northern Chile, a barren land with the distinction of never having received any recorded rainfall. To the north, the white sands of the Caribbean coast are interrupted by occasional mangrove swamps. On other coasts, the jungle creeps up to the sea's edge or steep rocky cliffs drop precipitously to the ocean below. Rivers break up the coastlines, meandering to the sea, often creating vast tropical deltas. In the south, the *pampas,* extensive temperate grasslands that form the rich agricultural region of southern South America, present another contrastive landform in the region.

The landscape of each country is in a process of continual change. While humans have had a profound impact in modifying the natural systems, other processes, such as active volcanoes, climatic changes, constant erosion, and earthquakes, constantly threaten to transform some region. The chain of mountains that extends from Tierra del Fuego in the southern tip of Argentina up through Mexico (and continues up through the United States and Canada before arching across the Aleutian Islands and dropping down to the Japanese homeland) has more than two dozen active volcanoes, and they present a real threat to the contemporary human populations that continually encroach on their slopes. Thousands were killed in Colombia in the mid-1980s when volcanic eruptions resulted in mudslides that engulfed several nearby communities. Earthquakes are even more common and ultimately more destructive. Over the past three decades, as many as 100,000 people have been killed as a result of these catastrophic forces. The region's pre-Colombian residents appreciated these forces of nature and regularly beseeched the deities to intervene on their behalf.

While in many cases the indigenous peoples who populated the region before the arrival of Europeans[4] lived in harmony with nature, in other instances they profoundly altered the environment. The Inca, for example, built elaborate irrigation systems. The Maya altered their jungle environment, which allowed them to feed large urban populations.

The colonial period brought about major changes in some areas. Mining and export agriculture changed the environment, as did the introduction of a wide variety of new plants and animals. Forests were cut to plant sugar cane and coffee and to pasture cattle. Wood was used for the colonial mines of Mexico and Peru. The Spanish and Portuguese brought with them an urban-focused colonial system. Cities such as Lima, Mexico City, and São Paulo, which evolved into megapolises, were built to support the conquest and trade.

This vast and complex region shares a number of other features, as well. While one has to be very careful not to overgeneralize or fall into the trap of making unfounded stereotypical observations, at a broad level there are a number of important cultural similarities that are found throughout the region. Acknowledging that overgeneralization masks and at times distorts much of the area's cultural diversity, we can begin our discussion of Latin American cultures by looking at features or themes its residents share in one way or another.

COMMON HISTORY

A common colonial legacy and 300 years of shared history helped establish much of the cultural foundation upon which the patina of similarity today is based. Beginning with the arrival of Christopher Columbus and extending over a period of several decades, the conquering Spanish and Portuguese brought this vast area under the sway of these two European powers. The colonial period and its Iberian heritage, which (with the exception of Brazilian independence from Portugal) ended in the early decades of the nineteenth century, firmly established a series of institutions that are still in place.[5]

RELIGION

From the outset, the Roman Catholic Church has constituted one of the most important and enduring of these institutions. As the religion of the conquerors, Roman Catholicism was imposed on the region's preconquest citizens. The well-organized state religions of the Aztec, Inca, and others were forcibly incorporated into Roman Catholicism. Areas where temples once stood had their edifices replaced by churches, thus preserving the sanctity of the sites. Pre-Colombian deities, whose beneficent powers were recognized and admired by the indigenous inhabitants, found themselves now praying to Christian saints, whose capability for protection or help were similar to those of the original entity. Feast days celebrating a successful harvest or the passing of lunar phases and the widespread occurrence of naming ceremonies and confessions were incorporated into the Roman Catholic Church, often so successfully that many indigenous groups insist that their history has always shown them to be Catholic.

It is impossible to understand contemporary Latin American cultures without recognizing the omnipotent role the church has played in shaping the lives of its citizens. It is intrusive in countless ways. Not only is Roman Catholicism the principal faith, but at various times in the history of the region, the church has played an active role in everything from shaping the tenor of political dialogue to being one of the region's largest property holders. For much of the area's history, the church also operated most of the schools and hospitals. Thus, in addition to addressing the people's spiritual needs, the church also ministered to society's intellectual and health concerns.[6] While competing faiths have always existed (and the growth of evangelical Protestant groups over the past several decades is one of the most interesting social movements going on today in Latin America), the role of the Roman Catholic Church continues to be very important.[7]

CLASS, POWER, AND PRIVILEGE

As a direct consequence of the colonial process, a social class system developed in Latin America in which a relatively small group of families acquired a disproportionately large segment of the region's wealth and power. The class system was based on inequality of wealth, predicated on landownership, legitimized by the church, and supported by the power of governments constituted and controlled by the landowning elites.[8] A legacy of this process is that today Latin America has the greatest inequality of wealth of any region of the world. Within the region, there are significant differences between countries, with Mexico and Brazil among the countries with the greatest differential of wealth, while Cuba is much more egalitarian.

In contrast to what is often portrayed by sociologists as a three-tiered social class system in the United States, with relatively small upper and lower classes and a proportionately larger middle class, in Latin America those at the bottom of the social and economic pyramid occupy a much more substantial segment of the system. This was, and to a certain extent still is, a fairly rigid system in which heritage (*abolengo*) and pedigree have been almost as important in determining who you were as was the traditional caste system in the Indian subcontinent. For a variety of reasons, during the past several decades the system in Latin America has changed with the growth of middle class. This has come at the expense of the old landed gentry, which has seen its almost sacrosanct position slowly being

eroded away since the end about the end of the Second World War.

LAND TENURE

Much of the claim to wealth came from control of enormous tracts of land, and not surprisingly the privileges of social class were brought about by ownership of land and it agricultural products. From the earliest of colonial times, the crown rewarded its most faithful and loyal subjects with gifts of land, land that often included entire communities that had been there for hundreds of years. By the middle of this century, many countries had land tenure arrangements, often referred to as *latifundios*, a system in which large plots of land are owned by a very small segment of the population (*latifundistas*), while at the same time one finds small plots of land, often too small to adequately support their owners (*minifundistas*). These are literally two sides of the same coin. Although many Latin American governments are working to rectify the imbalance in property ownership that characterizes land tenure throughout much of the region, one cannot fully comprehend and appreciate the political and economics dynamics of the region without understanding something of the history of land tenure.[9]

Many of the vast tracks of land became plantations (or *haciendas*. On plantations, export crops such as sugar, cotton, henequen, and coffee were grown with slave labor or worked by people who previously had made their living independently on the land. The plantations were often highly efficient and brutal with their workers. Haciendas, on the other hand, usually produced for domestic markets or provided pasture for cattle. They needed less labor than the plantations and frequently controlled large populations by allowing people to rent land. These feudal-like estates often dominated immense regions, controlling land, jobs, and access to food and other consumer goods. The landlords, often known as *patrones*, created sets of patron-client ties with tenants, further legitimizing the inequality. Hundreds of thousands of indigenous people were relocated as a result of both the plantation and hacienda systems. Coupled with the plague of European diseases and the relocation and the hunger that they brought, the indigenous populations were decimated.[10] In spite of these incredible problems, indigenous peoples survived throughout Mexico and Central and South America.

The independence period (between 1825 and 1835) witnessed a greater linking of the Latin American economies with world economies, and this was accomplished without significantly altering internal power relations. By the end of the nineteenth century, companies from the United States began to purchase huge tracts of land for agricultural production aimed at markets in the United States and Europe. In Central America, for example, the United Fruit Company created enclaves of dominance and power for growing and exporting bananas. Other companies vied with each other for the control, production, processing, and marketing of sugar.[11] Corporate investments were encouraged by many Latin American governments, as leaders tried to gain new markets and technology. Usually, the elite families that facilitated the process also profited from them.

While the agrarian history of each Latin American country is different, the early land tenure of most countries during the early twentieth century was remarkably similar, characterized by vast inequalities of power and land. For example, in Colombia through the early 1960s, approximately 20 percent of the landowners controlled 80 percent of the land. Approximately 80 of the peasant landowners made their living from 20 percent of the land. At the onset of the Mexican revolution 3 percent of the hacienda owners controlled 97 percent of the country's land.

As the world market expanded for agricultural products from Latin America, plantations, corporations, and haciendas expanded their landholdings at the expense of the peasantry, often through force or legal manipulations. The peasantry resisted in many ways. Many stopped working, others burned crops, and, in many regions, small holders took up arms. In many cases the armed uprisings were met with massive force by the national army. In Mexico, the armed insurrection in the state of Morelos sparked a prolonged struggle for land and equality. One of the consequences of the Mexican Revolution (1910–1917) was land reform.

At different times, revolutions erupted and triumphed in Bolivia, Peru, Cuba, and Nicaragua. The promise of land reform and greater democracy were themes of these struggles. Confiscation of large landholdings was undertaken in each of these countries, and agrarian reform of different types were implemented in each. Problems of access to credit, technical assistance, and entry to markets handicapped some of these reforms.

Throughout Latin America, small rural producers continue to struggle with improving the conditions of their lives. In some regions, peasants have taken up arms over the issues surrounding inequality of landholdings, as in the Ejército Zapatista de Liberación Nacional (EZLN—the Zapatista National Liberation Army) in southern Mexico or the Tupac Amarú in Peru. In other countries, such as Argentina and Brazil, the struggle for social reform took different forms, and the land tenure system, while modified, remained intact.

AGROECONOMICS

The importance of control of land and its traditional role in determining social, economic, and political power is a reflection of the region's long dependence on an agriculturally based economy. For many years, and this is still true today, the region derives much of its foreign income from the exportation of unprocessed agricultural products like coffee, bananas, or cattle. Until the last several decades, countries like Colombia might count on coffee for two-thirds of its export earnings. For a long time, Costa Rica relied almost exclusively on bananas and coffee to generate hard currency.[12] Reliance on one or two agricultural products has made the economies of many Latin American nations vulnerable to the whims of weather (droughts, too much rain, cold snaps, and the like), pests, or diseases, which could severely threaten the economic stability of a country.[13]

To complicate matters further, many Latin American nations have not been terribly successful in establishing the price they wish to receive for a given agricultural commodity. This often has had an unsettling effect on economic planners. In a letter to the editor of *Time* magazine in the early 1980s, the president of Costa Rica openly complained about the situation in which countries like his found themselves. Responding to an article that commented unfavorably about the increase in the prices of some imported agricultural products that folks in the United States were reluctantly having to pay, President Carazo pointed out that they were still getting a comparatively good deal. He noted that the price of bananas, which Costa Rica exports in profusion, had dropped precipitously over the preceding twenty years. At the same time, the prices Costa Ricans were having to pay for machinery and other manufactured goods were continuing to creep higher and higher. He pointed out that a tractor that cost the equivalent of 3 tons of bananas in 1960 now required the equivalent of about 20 tons.

Simply getting away from agricultural production has not always provided a solution to these problems. The oil boom of the late 1970s and early 1980s resulted in billions of dollars flowing into the state coffers in Mexico and Venezuela. Monies were committed to countless projects, and excitement ran high about the resultant development prospects. But the short-term financial boom was followed by severe disappointment and economic pain when the bottom dropped out of the oil market several years later.

Some of the larger countries, such as Brazil and Argentina, have become quite successful. Not only do both countries manufacture a wide range of goods under license from other nations, both have an impressive array of local industry in which everything from computers to sophisticated military armaments are manufactured. Many other nations are trying to position themselves as sites where goods from one country arrive in raw form and are assembled into finished products for transshipment to a third site. The development of *maquiladoras* (plants for the final assembly of products ranging from television sets to the sewing together of shirts and blouses) throughout Latin America is testimony to the allure of certain aspects of economic diversification. Today there is not a country in Latin America that is not working diligently to diversify its economy.

URBANIZATION, POPULATION GROWTH, AND THE RURAL-URBAN INTERFACE

One of the most profound changes that has occurred in Latin America during the past forty years has been the transformation of most of the countries from predominately rural to predominately urban. In 1950, 41 percent of the population of the region lived in towns and cities. By 1995, more than 75 percent of the population lived in cities and towns.

While the change characterizes the whole region, again significant differences exist among countries. Some countries are heavily urban (defined as having more than 85 percent of their population in urban centers). These countries include Chile, Uruguay, Venezuela, and Argentina, with Mexico and Colombia rapidly approaching this figure. Other countries, such as El Salvador, Guatemala, Honduras, Costa Rica, and Peru, while urbanizing, were still less than 50 percent urban in 1995.

Some of the largest cities in the world are in Latin America. Mexico City is the second-largest city in the world. Buenos Aires and São Paulo are megalopolises with populations of over 12 million people.[14] Other major cities include Lima, Bogotá, Santiago, Caracas, Belo Horizonte, and Havana. These cities, and others in Latin America, are blessed with the combination of colonial architecture, new skyscrapers, and elegant malls and residential neighborhoods, but which also include sprawling low-income neighborhoods that often lack basic services.

Population growth is one of the forces contributing to urbanization. Rapid rates of population growth in rural areas, especially where landholdings are unequally held, have not generated the jobs or opportunities for education and higher standards of living perceived to exist in the cities, the centers of wealth and industrial growth. Latin America has had one of the highest rates of population growth in the world, but again, the rate has varied greatly among countries. The annual population growth during the 1990s for Argentina and Uruguay, for example, has been under 1.12 percent per year, while the population growth rate in neighboring Paraguay has been 2.75 percent per year. Significant differences also exist between countries in Central America, ranging from Panama, which has had an annual growth rate during the 1990s of 1.76 percent, to Honduras and Nicaragua, which have had an annual growth rate of approximately 2.76 percent. Within each country, significant differences often exist between the rural and urban populations and between families of different socioeconomic classes.

Despite industrialization and massive construction in major Latin American cities, few have been able to create jobs fast enough to absorb the combination of their own population growth and the arrival of new migrants. As a result, what is known as the informal economy has grown in urban Latin America. The informal economy consists of enterprises and associated jobs that take place outside of the regulation of the government and includes a range of jobs from domestic services, street vending, and odd jobs for small businesses. In some cases the informal economy has been seen as having the potential for generating growth.[15] In Colombia, Peru, Bolivia, and Nicaragua, to name just a few of the countries, the informal economy generates more jobs than the rest of the economy.

There has not been enough housing for the growing low-income population. This has led low-income people to organize invasions of unoccupied land, often held by urban land speculators, where the invaders set up temporary housing made of tin, cardboard, and scrap lumber. In some instances, the police or army forcibly remove the squatters. In other cases, people have been allowed to hold the land, and the government has helped compensate the landowners. Eventually, settlements may get electricity and water systems as the occupants become able to invest in the gradual building of more stable housing.

Migrating to cities in Latin America does not mean people cut their ties to their home communities.[16] While there is great variation, many people return regularly to their communities to see family and friends. Major community fiestas attract former residents from all over the country. Many migrants send remittances or part of their wages back to their families, and, in some countries, such as Peru, urban associations of migrants put funds together and send them back for community development projects. Equally important, urban migrants help family members and friends with information about jobs and provide housing for those who visit to either market their produce or look for employment. The social networks are dynamic ties that link people across rural-urban boundaries.

While most of the migration occurs within countries, historically Latin America has received thousands of immigrants from Europe and Asia. During the last century, this immigration has declined, replaced by immigration from the Caribbean countries and other Latin American countries. The main currents of immigration have been from Bolivia to Argentina and Brazil, Colombia to Venezuela, El Salvador to Honduras, and Guatemala to Mexico.

Movement from Latin American countries to the United States has taken place for years. Often the process is permanent with immigrants taking up citizenship in the United States. Frequently, however, the process is one of circular movement, with people moving back to Latin America after a period of time in the United States. This has caused a new sense of what it means to be Latin American to emerge. This process, coupled with changes in the media and enhanced communications across borders, has generated a new awareness of regional differences and hemispheric ties.

POLITICAL PARTICIPATION, ARMED RESISTANCE, AND THE ROLE OF THE MILITARY

Another general thread of commonality has been political systems that traditionally have been characterized by two features: relatively limited political participation and a propensity for military intervention. Limited political participation resulted from several factors. For much of its postindependence period, substantial segments of the population in Latin America have routinely been marginalized or excluded from full participation in the political process. Although this process did not occur exclusively along class lines, nonetheless indigenous people and countless others from the lower class either did not vote or were given strict instructions on how to cast their ballots by those on whose lands they lived or in whose factories they worked. In some countries, direct election of local government leaders was not regularly part of the political process. Rather, the equivalents of governors and mayors would be appointed by politicians in the national capitals.[17] Colombia, for example, did not get away from this process until the mid-1990s. Women were also excluded from full participation in the political process until well into the middle of the twentieth century. While this situation has changed greatly in the past two decades and while percentages of eligible voters who cast their ballots in presidential elections in Latin America are much higher than the percentages of such voters in the United States, Latin America has had a long history of decisions being made by a very small group of men.

Civilian resistance to the status quo has been a common occurrence throughout Latin American history. Many of these opposition movements have been violent, bloody affairs. Peasant uprisings, most of them short-lived, have taken place throughout Latin America, since the wars of independence. In the twentieth century alone, armed conflict has brought about revolutionary changes to governments in Mexico, Cuba, and Nicaragua.

Historically, the armed forces in Latin America have viewed their role as defenders and interpreters of their constitutions from a much more activist position than what has normally been the case in the United States. Generally speaking, the military has viewed itself as a conservative force for stability, not surprisingly sharing many of the same views about how countries should be run with the church and the ruling elite. There have been several interesting exceptions to this general pattern in the last several decades. In Peru, the military coup that took place in October 1968 initially brought to power a group of officers who felt that promised social changes were not taking place quickly enough. With the ousting of the civilian government, the armed forces embarked on an aggressive program of agrarian reform and nationalization of industries and made a concerted attempt to truly incorporate the country's large indigenous population into the fabric of Peruvian society. Within a couple of years of the military's takeover, however, many of the changes implemented in the late 1960s were already being reversed, and by the time the military exited from power, things had in large part returned to the way they had been. At the time of this writing, there were no countries in Latin America under direct military rule. Thirty years ago, however, this was not the case; with more than two-thirds of the population under military rule, democratically elected governments were rather scarce. Even today in many countries, while the troops may be in the barracks, the military is constantly peering over the shoulders of the civilian leaders, always reminding them of their presence.

THE ELUSIVE GOAL: SUSTAINABLE DEVELOPMENT

The goals of economic growth and raising the standards of living for its citizens has been a major theme running throughout the history of most Latin American governments since independence. Of course, rising standards of living do not necessarily follow economic growth, but the two goals are politically popular and often linked by politicians. Since the 1990s, the issue of sustainability has been incorporated into the development agenda. Sustainable development for some Latin American planners suggests that growth should be carried out in a manner that does not destroy national resources, but taps them in a renewable way, building for a better, long-term future. "Sustainable development" in some cases has become merely window dressing, whereas in others it has been incorporated into policy and enforced. Each country has pursued a variety of economic and social strategies to achieve this elusive goal of raising standards of living and sustainable economic growth, even though as a whole, countries of the region have pursued similar economic policies over the past 100 years.

From the early 1930s to the mid-1980s, countries pursued growth by linking to world markets, thereby expanding imports and exports. During this period, agricultural products were the major source of exports, and many industrial products were imported for consumption by elites and the emerging middle class. The terms of trade were inherently uneven, and the countries of Latin America found themselves increasingly dependent on the United States and Europe for capital goods and technology, with raw materials and food products streaming north at low prices.

In the 1930s, policies shifted to import substitution, in which tariffs barred importation of specific capital goods and other products made by national industry. Small domestic markets for the domestically produced products meant that a limited number of people could be employed in industry at a period when larger numbers of people were moving from the countryside to the city. By the 1970s, an economic crisis emerged because of stagnating economic growth, growing populations, and rapid urbanization. Most countries made increasingly greater investments in development projects and state-owned or managed industries in an effort to generate growth and employment. The process led to a series of foreign debt crises and economic stagnation or recession.

The response of the 1990s has been spearheaded

by the World Bank and the Inter-American Development Bank. Across Latin America, the new economic strategies called for privatization of state enterprises, the reduction of trade barriers, economic policies that reduced the role of the state in providing social services, and the reduction of the national debt as countries attempted to stimulate the private sector. New trade blocks were formed with a long-term goal, defined by the presidents of the countries at the Summit of the Americas, of an integrated economic market of the Americas. Mexico joined Canada and the United States in the North American Trade Association. The other countries of the region soon formed regional trade blocks. Meanwhile, GATT, the General Agreement on Tariffs and Trade, was signed in Uruguay, with long-term, worldwide tariff reductions.

The environmental, economic, and social impacts of NAFTA—the North American Free Trade Agreement—are just beginning to be understood, but one aspect is clear. The agreement has generated a new need for students in the United States to learn Spanish and to study the history and culture of our southern neighbors with whom we share a 2,000-mile border. As we move into the global century and new economic, cultural, and social ties link the United States with Latin America, the importance of mutual understanding will become paramount.

Unequally endowed with natural resources, population, enlightened leadership, and location, the consequences for each country in Latin America have been uneven. There are many ways that development can be defined. There are social indicators that help show the developmental differences among countries and change; these indicators over time. For example, literacy rates in Argentina, Cuba, Chile, and Costa Rica are all well above 90 percent, while the literacy rates of Haiti, Nicaragua, and Guatemala are barely above 50 percent. Life expectancy at birth for Argentina, Chile, Costa Rica, Cuba, Mexico, and Venezuela in 1995 was well above 70 years, while the life expectancy rates for the same year of Bolivia, El Salvador, Guatemala, Haiti, and Nicaragua were below 70 years. Other indicators, such as infant mortality, nutritional deficiencies, access to safe water, adequate housing, doctor-patient ratios, physical safety from violent crime, rural-to-urban distributions, and income or land distribution are important measures of development and quality of life.[18]

A different set of issues evolves when questions of political participation are raised. The countries of Latin America have, during the last decade, become almost entirely democratic, with varying degrees of freedom of expression and basic civil rights. For many countries, the transition from dictatorship to democratically elected governments is a true cause for celebration and a precious liberty to maintain.

SOCIAL MOVEMENTS, IDENTITY, AND CHANGE

Latin American contemporary history has been characterized as a period of contention and resistance. Dating back to the successful revolutions of Mexico, Bolivia, and Cuba and to the 1990s exigencies generated by the debt crisis and structural adjustment policies, Latin Americans have mobilized in many different ways to change the status quo. The roots of mobilization can be traced to alternative politics of the political left and liberation theology, which helped spark what became known as the new social movements. Traditionally strong organizations such as labor unions and peasant leagues, organized to secure resources, continued to be political actors, but a new type of social mobilization emerged. New social movements include a broad range of organizations and efforts, including those focused on human rights, indigenous power, environmental concerns, women's rights, and neighborhood associations. In all of these cases, the movements are linked to people's struggles for social recognition[19] of their existence and for political spaces of expression, without attempting to overthrow vested interests in power. Equally important, these organizations have looked to non-class-based sources of unity and identity, which at times incorporated people from multiple class positions, usually in a very democratic fashion. In these cases, collective activity is dependent on mobilizing a shared set of concerns and consciousness-raising.

New social movements emerged throughout Latin America under conditions that created political openings for broader political participation during a period of transition and negotiation of democracy. Yet the nature of the social movements in each country has been conditioned by the unique national history, class structure, and cultural composition of the population, amid other socioeconomic and political variables. For example, the Zapatista revolt in Chiapas described by Frank Cancian and Peter Brown erupted as an indigenous movement in Chiapas, Mexico, caused by a combination of local structural conditions and the incorporation of Mexico into NAFTA.[20] In Guatemala, indigenous people have been engaged in a prolonged armed struggle since the 1980s, a struggle that has witnessed entire indigenous communities being destroyed and the displacement of over a million indigenous people. In the lowlands of South America, indigenous people with a much lower population density than those in Guatemala or Chiapas have organized in different ways to defend their rights.[21]

Women's movements[22] have become powerful forces in Latin America, but the movements in each country have been different. In Nicaragua, for example, early support for the Sandinistas (FSLN) was helped by the powerful women's organization AMNLAE, which pushed for women's political rights and democratization throughout the revolutionary period. In Mexico, the Women's Council of the National Coordinating Committee of the Urban Popular Movement, CONAMUP, was organized during the early 1980s with the specific issues of economic survival, representation, and domestic violence as central to their concerns. Other women's movements have focused on issues such as access to food, the environment, and access to information.

The environmental movements in Latin America are relatively new. In Mexico, the contamination of Mexico City sparked the first major environmental mobilization. In contrast, in Brazilian Amazonia, rubber tappers mobilized in an effort to save the rain forest as an extractive reserve. In both cases, the movements were intended to save the environment, but the environments and the political processes were different as they were played out on the national and international arena, and people had very different reasons for participating.

While not all of these social movements were successful nor had they produced long-term impacts, together they represent an important step of broader political participation and engagement as people worked together to address some of the most pressing issues of their era.

ETHNIC MOSAIC

Ethnic diversity is another important similarity found throughout Latin America. Anthropologists know that humans have inhabited the Americas for approximately 40,000 years and that this hemisphere was populated in a series of waves that took place over the course of several thousand years. There is no accurate method of speculating on the size of the population of Native Americans in the New World at the time of the first contact with Europeans. It was certainly in the millions and contained everything from remote small bands of hunter-gatherers to well-organized nation states with cities that were larger and better managed than anything that existed in Europe at the time. In spite of the catastrophic declines in their populations in the first decades after contact and the several hundred years of colonial subjugation, millions of the descendants of those who crossed the Bering Straits thousands of years ago populate Latin America today. Some countries, such as Mexico, Guatemala, Peru, and Bolivia, have indigenous populations that are so substantial in number that their presence cannot go unnoticed. In Mexico and Guatemala alone, a cacophony of almost 100 indigenous languages is spoken, and large segments of the population do not speak Spanish. In Peru and in parts of Ecuador and Bolivia, various dialects of the Incan language Quechua are spoken routinely in the rural areas. Other nations, such as Argentina, Uruguay, and Costa Rica, have very small numbers of Native Americans, and their presence in those countries is not so readily apparent.

Fairly early in the colonial period, the Spanish and Portuguese crowns encouraged the importation of slaves into its colonies, particularly in the Caribbean region and across the northeastern coast of Brazil. Coming principally from West Africa, but originally from a number of different ethnic groups, African Americans formed a significant presence in shaping the cultures of colonial Latin America. Although the largest number of individuals of African descent are still found in the Caribbean region, African Americans are well represented throughout Latin America today.

Inhabitants of the Iberian Peninsula came over to the New World during the colonial period, but in terms of numbers, the process was nothing like what was taking place in the Northern Hemisphere.

With relatively few exceptions, the Spanish and Portuguese territories in the Americas were not places where the dispossessed European went to escape religious persecution or to find lands to farm. Immigration to the Southern Hemisphere began in earnest after the wars of independence. In a manner not too dissimilar to what took place in the Northern Hemisphere, the last decades of the nineteenth century witnessed the arrival of people from many parts of Europe who proceeded to settle throughout the region.

Toward the end of the nineteenth century, during the same period in which large numbers of Chinese were coming to the United States to work as indentured servants, much the same process was taking place on the west coast of Latin America. Although their numbers fluctuated in response to economic conditions in China and the anti-immigration policies of individual Latin American countries, the numbers of Chinese (and later, Japanese) continued to grow throughout the early decades of the twentieth century.

Other ethnic groups—such as the Christian Arabs, who were trying to escape the confines of the Ottoman Empire; European Jews, who were attempting to flee Nazi expansionism; and displaced refugees after World War II—have all turned to Latin America in an effort to create new lives. Although the overall numbers are fewer and the impact on individual countries is somewhat less, much of the same intermixing of cultures that has given the United States its interesting cultural mosaic can be found today in Latin America.[23]

We return to the point with which we began this essay. Latin America is a region of great contrasts and fascinating similarities. In the pages that follow, we invite the reader to join us in attempting to understand and appreciate this important area of the world.

NOTES

1. Talk entitled "High Noon in Latin America" given by Carlos Fuentes at Iowa State University, January 31, 1985.

2. In the United States, people generally refer to themselves as "Americans" or "North Americans," often without regard to the fact those titles are claimed by our neighbors as well. When this is pointed out, offense is often taken—frequently by both parties. Canadians and Mexicans correctly insist that they, too, are "North Americans," while anyone in the New World (a term that carries with it some unfortunate baggage) can rightly state they can lay equal claim to be called "Americans."

3. In their contributions in this anthology, Rodolfo Stavenhagen and Carlos Fuentes set the stage by providing the reader with some important background information on some of the similarities and significant differences.

4. The works of Anna Roosevelt, Clark Erickson, and Michael Harner provide us with some interesting perspectives on what was going on in three very diverse areas at different periods before the arrival of the Europeans.

5. The arrival of the Spaniards and the Portuguese transformed what was to become Latin America in ways that were irrevocably felt. In their contributions, noted anthropologists George M. Foster and Eric Wolf discuss the impact of conquest and colonization on both the Iberian Peninsula and the Americas.

6. Several articles examine a variety of health-related, differing methods of diagnosis and curing issues in this volume. See Linda M. Whiteford, Sidney M. Greenfield, George M. Foster, and Joseph Bastien.

7. John K. Chance's article addresses how religion, in the form of the *cargo* system, controlled the social and economic aspects of the lives of Mesoamerican villagers over time and how this institution has changed in this century. The article by Diana De G. Brown and Mario Bick looks at the role of social class and the blending and syncretism of Roman Catholicism with aspects of West African traditional religious beliefs. In the same section, Chris Smith examines the multiple impacts of Protestantism in Latin America today.

8. Social structure is investigated from various angles and perspectives by Richard N. Adams, Arthur D. Murphy and Alex Stepick, Samuel Stone, and Andrew H. Whiteford in the section of Part VI entitled "Social Structure."

9. For discussions related to issues specifically surrounding access to and ownership of land, see contributions by Frank Cancian and Peter Brown, Eliana Cardoso, and Lynn Stephen.

10. Katharine Milton examines problems encountered with the interface of indigenous tribal populations with contemporary "outside" culture.

11. See Donna Cholett's contribution on this matter.

12. Kevin Healy and Kenyon Stebbins look at issues surrounding the production of a single crop in very contrastive and poignant perspectives.

13. For discussions that address a combination of economic, political, and environmental issues, see contributions by Marc Edelman, Elizabeth Dore, and Peter Rosset.

14. See Alan Gilbert on the "Latin American city."

15. J. Douglas Uzzell addresses these issues in his contribution to this volume.

16. See Douglas Butterworth and John Chance.

17. In July 1997, the residents of Mexico City elected a mayor for the first time in more than sixty years. Previously, the mayor was appointed by the president of the country.

18. See the contribution by Arturo Escobar.

19. See Carole Nagengast and Michael Kearney.

20. See Mark Ritchie's discussion on the implications of NAFTA.

21. See Suzana Sawyer's and Frank Cancian and Peter Brown's contributions.

22. For discussions of gender see contributions by Evelyn Stevens, Norma Chinchilla, Helen Safa, and Michael B. Whiteford and Ruth Alden.

23. For several different perspectives on the concepts related to ethnicity, see the contributions by John Kicza, Charles Hale, and Conrad Kottak.

2

Challenging the Nation-State in Latin America

Rodolfo Stavenhagen

Are we Europeans? So many copper-colored faces deny it! Are we indigenous? Perhaps the answer is given by the condescending smiles of our blonde ladies. Mixed? Nobody wants to be it, and there are thousands who would want to be called neither Americans nor Argentinians. Are we a nation? A nation without the accumulation of mixed materials, without the adjustment of foundations?[1]

—Domingo Faustino Sarmiento,
Argentine writer and statesman, 1883

When most Latin American countries achieved political independence from Spain in the early nineteenth century, the ideas of nationalism and the formation of national states were just beginning to emerge as central forces in Western thinking. Under the influence of the Enlightenment and the American and French revolutions, leaders of independence movements in Latin America were clearly inspired more by concepts of liberty and sover-

From Rodolfo Stevenhagen, "Challenging the Nation-State in Latin America," *Journal of International Affairs* 45(2):421–440, 1992.

eignty than by the ideal of creating a "cultural nation-state" that fired the imaginations and struggles of the romantic European nationalists in later decades. Once independence had been obtained by force of arms (Bolivar, O'Higgins and Hidalgo), the rulers of the new states were faced with the daunting task of building new nations. Forging viable polities that might serve the interests of the new ruling groups out of the fragmented remains of the Spanish empire was no small matter, particularly in view of the highly stratified and hierarchical nature of the social system inherited from the colonial period and the ethnic and racial diversity of the population. Thus it became necessary to invent and create nations and to construct national identities. The intellectuals set this task for themselves in the nineteenth century: By some accounts it has not yet been completed, for the search for national identity is still a principal concern of Latin American intellectuals to this day.[2]

It is no wonder, then, that post-colonial Latin American elites adopted a nationalist ideology as the guiding orientation in their search for legitimation. Once the new republican political units had been established, true nations would have to be constituted as an act of state and government.

In Latin America, as in so many other post-colonial societies, the state and its intellectual and political elites created the nation; the sociological nation itself did not struggle to create its own state, as happened—and is happening again—in Europe.[3]

The purpose of this essay is not to retrace the story of nationalism in Latin America but rather to suggest that one of the unresolved issues of the nationalist debate in the region is the relationship between the model of the unitary state, which was adopted after the wars of independence and developed during the republican period, and the ethnic and cultural diversity of the societies of Latin America. This contradiction has contributed to the weakness of political institutions in the area and to persistent tension between the political structure and the various social forces, occasionally leading to protracted and sometimes violent social conflict as in Guatemala and Peru.

HETEROGENEOUS SOCIETIES: THE PERPETUATION OF A COLOR-CLASS CONTINUUM

The leaders of the independence movements recognized the importance of the various ethnic components that made up the populations of Latin America: European, African and indigenous. Simón Bolivar, the "liberator of America," realized early on the difficulties of creating unified nations out of extremely heterogeneous populations. He warned in 1819:

> We must keep in mind that our people are neither European nor North American: rather, they are a mixture of Africans and the Americans who originated in Europe....It is impossible to determine with any degree of accuracy where we belong in the human family. The greater portion of the native Indians have been annihilated; Spaniards have mixed with Americans and Africans, and Africans with Indians and Spaniards.[4]

Bolivar, himself of mixed origin, was not alone in expressing qualms about his ethnic identity and his place in "the human family." Others doubted that civilized nations could emerge at all from such

diverse racial and ethnic backgrounds, as the opening quote by the Argentine Sarmiento aptly illustrates. Bolivar, and many others after him, expected these various population groups to mesh into a new amalgam: the mixed or *mestizo* population for which Latin America is widely known. Racial mixture did take place over the centuries, but not to the extent that its early proponents had foreseen. Nor did it bring about the social and political consequences with which it has been associated in so many writings about Latin America.[5]

Since the colonial period, the various ethnic categories of the population have been related to each other within the framework of a polarized social class system based on race, color and ethnicity. Thus, racial and ethnic integration took place only to the extent that changes in the socioeconomic structure allowed. The abolition of slavery in Brazil towards the end of the nineteenth century, as in the United States, did not lead directly to a "racial democracy," although institutionalized segregation and racism were not part of the Brazilian experience. As in the Caribbean, a pervasive color-class continuum continues to exist in Latin America, in which the lighter-skinned population of European descent is at the top of the social structure and the darker-skinned people of indigenous or African descent are to be found at the bottom.

The Place of Indigenous Peoples in Latin American Society

The European invasion of the sixteenth century produced a disastrous demographic decline of the continent's indigenous peoples. Within 50 to 60 years after the first contact, it is estimated that the total population of around 100 million fell by 80 percent, due to epidemics hitherto unknown to the indigenous peoples, the breakdown of the native subsistence economies, harsh living and labor conditions imposed by the colonial overlords and, as a lesser causal factor, the casualties of war and conquest.[6] By today's standards, this would be labeled genocide, and it is considered as such by indigenous organizations of the continent. Slowly, demographic growth picked up again, and by about the beginning of the twentieth century the total population had reached the same level as three centuries before. Over the last hundred years, at least until the 1960s, overseas immigration has also played an increasingly important role in the composition of Latin America's populations.

This process of demographic growth implies the expansion of the *mestizo* population, but it has not resulted in the disappearance of indigenous peoples and communities. Despite the political, economic and cultural aggressions that the latter suffered at the hands first of the colonizers and their direct descendants, and later of the ruling classes of the independent nation-states, a deeply-rooted "culture of resistance" has ensured the survival of over four hundred distinct ethnic groups (there were of course many more in precolonial times). These groups today represent more than 35 million people, over one-tenth of Latin America's total population.[7]

The pacification of the Pampas in the South was similar to the conquest of the West in North America. Indigenous societies were practically wiped out, or reduced to the status of dependent, vulnerable minority groups whose survival depended on the generosity of a national state that had appropriated their sovereignty and land; a state that they could hardly consider as their own. Elsewhere, the *criollo* self-perception of cultural and racial superiority over the indigenous peoples led to policies designed to accelerate the disappearance of the indigenous peoples and their rapid incorporation into the so-called national mainstream, that is, into the model of the nation-state as defined by the *criollo* upper class.

The inferior status accorded indigenous peoples was most pronounced in regions such as the Andean highlands, the Antilles and Mesoamerica, where the majority indigenous peasantries and the minority *criollo* upper classes were integrated into a single economic system and where a deep social and cultural chasm separated the two groups. In these parts of the continent, a much larger proportion of the original indigenous population survived the arrival of colonizers and a majority indigenous population continued to exist alongside the European colonialists. A colonial policy established a system of economic exploitation based primarily on the concentration of landholdings and various forms of servile peasant labor. This in turn led to a highly hierarchical social structure in which vertical mobility between the horizontal strata was almost completely absent. The lowest strata were made up of the indigenous peasantries. Political independence

from Spain aggravated the situation of these peasant populations as the *criollo* elites, white upper classes of Spanish ancestry, were able to consolidate their position by concentrating land, riches and political power.

When economic growth took off again toward the end of the century, stimulated by the industrial world's demand for Latin America's cash crops and mineral exports, the situation of the indigenous peasantries deteriorated once more. Much of their remaining land was taken from them, working conditions deteriorated and the expanding monetary economy weakened the formerly self-sufficient agricultural communities and fostered an increasing flow of labor migrations out of the subsistence sector. This process lasted well into the middle of the twentieth century, at which time growing population pressure on limited resources also played a role. Contemporary analysts have long debated whether to call this system feudal, colonial or capitalist.[8] Regardless, it persisted over several centuries and was able to adjust to a number of different political regimes.

As elsewhere in the world, it was the ruling class and the intelligentsia who imagined and invented the modern Latin American nations, trying to shape them in their own image. The indigenous peoples were excluded from the "national projects" that emerged in the nineteenth century. They have remained in the background since then, shadowy figures which, like Greek choruses, step into the historical limelight during revolutions, rebellions and uprisings, only to recede again into a forgotten world.

The Argentine statesman Sarmiento and many others were convinced that as long as indigenous peoples continued to constitute any substantial portion of the population, the Latin American countries would be unable to join the civilized nations of the world. Just as the political constitutions were drawn from the American Constitution, so were the legal institutions, the educational system and varieties of cultural policies taken from European models to serve the *criollo* upper classes. While the indigenous peoples were recognized as distinct and separate cultures, their languages and their social, religious and political institutions were not incorporated into the dominant mode of governance. The indigenous cultures were at best ignored and at worst exterminated. Thus, while lip service was at times given to the indigenous roots of modern Latin American societies, the cultural and political leaders of the independent republics were reluctant to recognize the indigenous peoples as part of the new nations. Indeed, the indigenous peoples were explicitly rejected and excluded. As long as they were geographically isolated and numerically insignificant, this approach did not threaten the self-image of the elites, who first affirmed their new-found national identities against the former colonial power Spain, and later, against the upcoming continental hegemonic power, the Anglo-Saxon United States.[9]

European immigration was stimulated to further *criollo* objectives. A number of countries not only opened their doors to immigration, but sought it actively. Latin American governments sent agents to European countries in order to recruit likely prospects. Colonization and transportation companies were set up, and land grants and economic facilities offered. European immigrants were expected to contribute to economic development, bring skills and capital, teach the local populations how to improve agriculture and industry and enhance the biological stock of the country by intermarriage with the local population. Through immigration, it was held, the Latin American nations would finally be recognized as equals by their European and North American counterparts. In fact, immigration did play a considerable role in changing the demographic profile of numerous Latin American countries, in some of which Asian migrants also arrived, but in lesser numbers and under less auspicious circumstances. Immigration flows continued until after the Second World War and into the 1950s. It has fallen off during the last two decades due to military dictatorships, political instability and economic crisis. Nevertheless, it did contribute to the process of *mestizaje:* the building of a *mestizo* race.

Mestizaje: A New "Cosmic Race" and the Politics of Indigenismo

During the early colonial period, the *mestizo* population had only a slightly higher status than the indigenous peoples and was usually rejected by both the Spanish upper strata and the indigenous communities. Marginal to both cultures, the *mestizos* lacked a coherent identity of their own, a problem that has preoccupied intellectuals, psychologists and sociologists to this day. The racial theories of the nineteenth century, which Latin America's elites willingly imported from Europe and the United States, considered not only the indigenous peoples but also the mixed-breed *mestizos* as inferior human groups. What kind of a modern nation could be built upon such flimsy human material? No wonder so many intellectuals despaired of their nations and their continent. The indigenous groups were rejected outright as being passive, dependent, fatalistic, docile, stupid, incapable of higher civilization, lacking in emotions and sensitivity, impervious to pain and suffering, unable to improve their miserable conditions of living and therefore generally a major obstacle to the progress of the Latin American countries. The *mestizos,* in turn, were said to embody the worst elements of both their ancestors: They were hot-headed, violent, unreliable, dishonest, shiftless, opportunistic, passionate, power-hungry, lazy and generally considered incapable of ruling their countries.

Nevertheless, over time the *mestizos* came to occupy the economic and social space that neither the reduced *criollo* upper classes nor the indigenous peasantries were able to control. With the capitalist expansion of the economy and the growth of cities, trade, services and industry during the nineteenth century, the *mestizo* soon became identified with the national mainstream, as the driving force of economic, social and, most recently, political progress. The earlier doubts about *mestizo* biological and psychological capabilities vanished, except among some foreign observers who still carried the old stereotypes well into the twentieth century.

By now, the *mestizos* had developed their own distinct culture; they became the bearers of truly nationalist sentiments. Moreover, they became identified with the burgeoning urban middle classes and thus with progress, change and modernization. An ideological reversal had occurred. *Mestizo* intellectuals sang the virtues of *mestizaje* as not only a biological process, but rather as a cultural and political condition leading to economic development and political democracy. *Por mi raza hablará el espíritu*—"The spirit will speak for my race"—proclaimed the 1920 slogan of the National University of Mexico, coined by José Vasconcelos, Minister of Education in one of Mexico's postrevolutionary governments and standard-bearer of the *mestizos* as a new "cosmic race" in Latin America.[10]

While Europe was regressing to the myth of racial purity and superiority and while white supremacy was still legally enshrined in the United States, the idealization of the mixed-blood *mestizo* in Latin America during the 1920s and 1930s could be considered as something of a heterodox, if not a revolutionary, position. The identification of the *mestizo* population with national culture, the middle classes and economic progress soon became the ideological underpinning of various kinds of government policies designed to strengthen the unitary nation-state and the incorporation of the "nonnational" elements, namely, the indigenous peoples. By the 1940s a set of government policies, known as *indigenismo,* had been devised to carry out the "national integration" of the indigenous communities through forcing the social and cultural changes necessary for their assimilation into the *mestizo* national model. Various states established departments or institutes of indigenous affairs that promoted educational and economic development projects at the local level, designed to "integrate" the indigenous peoples. By then, indigenous cultures had already changed considerably, and many observers considered that they were no longer viable and would soon disappear of their own accord. Thus, the argument ran, government policy would only hasten their demise and accelerate a natural and inevitable process.

The supposed inferiority of the indigenous peoples was now no longer phrased in biological terms, but rather in the fashionable language of the times—culture and levels of socioeconomic development. Indigenous cultures were deemed to be underdeveloped, archaic, backward, traditional and simple rather than complex, communalist rather than individualist and parochial rather than universalist. Social-science theories were invoked to explain the differences between the indigenous communities and the national societies, providing the parameters for public policy. The writings of Durkheim, Spencer, Tönnies, Weber, Parsons, Boas and Redfield were gleaned for insights that would then justify *indigenista* policies.[11]

In 1940, after several years' preparation, the first continental Inter-American Indianist Congress was held in Mexico. Here, the governments of the Americas laid down general guidelines for dealing with their "Indian problem" and agreed to coordinate their activities in the field of Indianist policies. To be sure, respect for indigenous cultures and values was expressed, but the dominant idea was integration, incorporation and assimilation. The Congress set up the Inter-American Indianist Institute, subordinate to the Organization of American States, as a coordinating agency. Those national governments that had not already done so were invited to establish their own bureaus of Indian affairs.

Before the late 1950s and 1960s, Latin America's political parties and movements had not dealt with the Indian question to any great extent, a position that reflected the marginality of these issues in the body politic and the fact that politics itself was still the domain of a relatively small "political class."

THE "INDIGENOUS PROBLEM" AND LATIN AMERICAN DEVELOPMENT

The two principal ideological currents of the times had rather clear ideas about how to deal with *el problema indígena.* Neoliberal thinkers considered the problem of the indigenous populations as one of underdevelopment, technological backwardness, traditionalism and marginality. Within the generally accepted framework of modernization politics, conceiving economic and social development as a unilinear progression along a series of necessary stages, economists, anthropologists and politicians thought that the so-called Indian problem would disappear by way of community development, regional planning, education, technological innovations and paternalistic acculturation. The responsibility for carrying out these policies lay in the hands of the state, which played a tutelary role. Through such policies, indigenous subsistence peasants would become modern farmers. Traditional values, which were considered to be inimical to progress, would have to be changed through modern education; the virtues of individualism and entrepreneurship would have to be learned, and the bonds of the local community would have to be broken so that the outside world could penetrate and impart its bounties. For many observers during the heyday of developmentalism, the indigenous problem was an economic problem to be solved by technological change, investments, cash crops, wage labor, profit maximization and the monetarization of the local subsistence economy.

Development policies targeted at the indigenous populations had two principal justifications. First, it was thought that only by means of such policies would the quality of Indian life improve. Second, it was felt that as long as the indigenous peoples lived in poverty and backwardness, isolated from the centers of modernization and growth, the country as a whole would remain backward and underdeveloped. Such countries would be particularly vulnerable to foreign interference and interests, especially economic imperialism coming from the North. As long as the Latin American nations were internally fragmented and polarized, embodied in the concept of the "dual society," they would be weak and unable to assert their sovereignty and independence in the world.

Another point of view was put forward as early as the 1920s by Marxist-oriented writers such as José Carlos Mariátegui in Peru. They considered the indigenous peoples to be a part of the exploited peasantry, whose interests lay in making common cause with other segments of the toiling classes. Indeed, they were viewed as the most exploited and backward element of the working class, lacking in class consciousness precisely because of their community-centered, traditional world outlook. Moreover, their cultural distinctiveness in areas such as language, dress, religious organization, family and community structures—all of which set them apart from the *mestizo* population—facilitated their exploitation by the bourgeoisie and the landholding oligarchies. Through depressed wages and the retention of different kinds of forced and servile labor arrangements, such as peonage, the indigenous peoples were prevented from joining forces with the revolutionary proletariat in the class struggle. Indeed, it was held that the maintenance of indigenous cultural specificity was actually in the interests of the bourgeoisie, or at least its more backward factions, within the framework of underdeveloped and dependent capitalism for which Latin America became notorious in the 1960s.[12]

The Marxist controversy regarding the indigenous peoples—sometimes framed as "the national question" in reference to the debates among Marxists in Central and Eastern Europe before the First World War—continued well into the 1980s. While much of the debate initially took place in the academic environment, it progressively filtered into leftist political movements and the revolutionary guerrilla activities, which emerged in many parts of the continent as a consequence of the Cuban revolution. Che Guevara's attempt to spark a revolutionary uprising in Bolivia in the 1960s probably failed, among other reasons, because Guevara was unaware of, or insensitive to, the national question in that country. Revolutionary theory at that point did not find such issues relevant.

A number of revolutionary guerrilla groups in Guatemala from the 1960s onward were easily isolated and eliminated by repressive, American-backed military regimes because they had not been able to deal adequately, in theoretical or political terms, with the fact that the majority of Guatemala's population is indigenous. One of the reasons that revolutionary activity has continued despite brutal repression is that the revolutionary organizations have now revised the "class" approach of traditional Marxist analysis and have framed their struggle in terms of a national question, challenging not only class rule but also the dominant view of the nation-state. With this concept they have been able to acquire a foothold among the indigenous peoples.[13]

More widely known, because of the media attention it received, was the conflict between the Miskito Indians and the Sandinista government in Nicaragua during the 1980s. This conflict arose because the Sandinistas, basing their policies on class analysis, assumed that the indigenous peoples of the Atlantic coast had a natural interest in joining forces with them. It came as a surprise to the Sandinistas that the indigenous organizations had a different agenda, and they quickly attributed counterrevolutionary intentions to them. This unnecessary, if inevitable, confrontation had disastrous consequences in terms of lives and resources lost, and weakened the political position of the Sandinista government both at home and abroad. The Reagan administration was quick to take up the Miskito cause as a major human-rights issue in its undeclared war against Nicaragua. By the time the Sandinistas recognized their mistakes in the mid-1980s, the damage had been done.[14]

Though originating in different intellectual traditions and based on different analyses and interpretations of social and economic dynamics, the neoliberal and the orthodox Marxist approaches to the indigenous question in Latin America have held one view in common: that indigenous peoples constituted an obstacle to development and progress. Both approaches set out to devise policies to overcome such obstacles. In the former it became "acculturation" and "modernization"' in the latter, the "class struggle." In both scenarios, indigenous cultures would have to disappear eventually, and the sooner the better. These two intellectual traditions also shared the belief that indigenous peoples had not participated in the formulation of either scenario.

From the sixteenth century through the 1960s, indigenous peoples have been written about, but rarely have they been listened to. They have been the object of scholarly research, but they have yet to become the active subjects in rewriting their own history. Except for brief flashes, such as the uprising of Tupac Amaru in Peru or the Caste War in Mexico, countless localized revolts and rebellions have not found their way into official historiography. As scholars now acknowledge, indigenous opposition to domination took the form of passive resistance, of turning inward and building protective shells around community life and cultural identity. This mode of resistance enabled many indigenous cultures to survive into the twentieth century, although countless others did disappear in time.

NEW PRESSURES, NEW FORMS OF RESISTANCE

As a result of economic growth, technological changes and the increasing internationalization of the Latin American economies, social and cultural transformations accelerated during the twentieth century. The remaining indigenous peoples have been put under enormous pressure since the Second World War in their attempts to retain their traditional lifestyle and resist integration into mainstream modern life. The numerous conflicts arising in the Amazon basin illustrate these pressures profoundly: Among the world's last natural frontiers, the Amazon rain forest has increasingly become the target of massive invasions by economic and political pressures, national and international, such as giant mining or hydroelectric projects, strategic road building, deforestation and uncontrolled human settlements. Observers agree that what is happening in the Amazon is ecocide and ethnocide on a massive scale, all in the name of state nationalism, modernization and economic growth.[15]

As the indigenous peoples became the victims of renewed assaults on their lands, resources and cultures in the latter half of the present century, they began to adopt new forms of resistance and defense. Though scattered attempts at political organization had occurred before, the beginnings of a coherent and forceful indigenous political movement began in earnest in the 1970s. Various organizations began to express claims about indigenous rights that had only been stated occasionally and unsystematically before. Congresses, coalitions and federations were set up at the national and local levels, followed by international organizations advocating indigenous rights. As in other forms of social and political mobilization, factionalism, divisions and rivalries appeared. Grassroots organizations sprang up in different areas; local groups merged to structure organizations along ethnic-group lines, as in the case of the Shuar federation in eastern Ecuador. Professional interest groups were also formed for such groups as indigenous plantation workers, bilingual schoolteachers and indigenous lawyers.

Attempts to form political parties centered on the mandate of furthering indigenous rights have met with mixed success: Indigenous political parties such as *Katarismo* in Bolivia and an indigenous political party in Guatemala have not yet been able to garner large-scale support among the wider population. In other states, indigenous "sectors" of existing parties appeared: The Institutional Revolutionary Party (PRI) in Mexico organized a National Council of Indigenous Peoples. A number of organizations, particularly at the national and international levels, were structured from the top down. In the 1960s, not more than a smattering of indigenous organizations existed; by the beginning of the 1990s, dozens of such groups have been identified as established and representative associations in every country. Hundreds probably exist continent-wide. The emergence of these interest groups is due to a number of factors including:

the growth of an indigenous elite or intelligentsia out of the ranks of those who received formal schooling in official or missionary establishments; the widespread disillusionment with development policies that did not bring benefits to the indigenous peoples; the neglect by traditional political parties or class associations of issues of specific interest to indigenous peoples; and the dissemination of information about liberation struggles among colonized peoples in other parts of the world.

In all of these efforts, a newly emerging indigenous intelligentsia has played a fundamental role, aided by indigenous advocates from the social sciences, the churches and a number of political formations. In earlier years, the indigenous intelligentsia would have been siphoned off and assimilated into the dominant society. While this process continues today, indigenous professional people, intellectuals and political activists are consciously embracing their ethnic heritage and providing leadership to their communities. This new leadership is also displacing the more traditional community authority that has played a fundamental role in the period of passive resistance and retrenchment, when, as anthropologists would have it, indigenous peoples lived in closed, corporate communities. As indigenous communities are also internally differentiated according to socioeconomic criteria, so the new indigenous leaders often reflect different interests in the community itself. Whether this leadership represents the interests of the indigenous ethnic groups at large, or only those of an emerging "indigenous bourgeoisie," is currently a topic of widespread debate.

These organizations articulate various sorts of demands relating to the fundamental problems that indigenous peoples face at the present time. Heading the list, no doubt, is the land question. They demand that indigenous land rights be respected and restored, either through agrarian reform (Mexico, Guatemala and Peru), territorial demarcation (Brazil and Panama) or land-titling (Argentina, Chile and Costa Rica). In addition to land, traditional rights to natural and subsoil resources are also claimed. These demands sometimes face stiff opposition by large landholders, mining and lumber companies, the military—which sees claims for territorial demarcation as a threat to national security—and their respective representatives in government.

A second major set of claims that indigenous organizations have been pursuing relates to cultural and legal identity and deals with educational and linguistic policies. Until very recently, most Latin American countries did not recognize themselves as multiethnic. Demands for bilingual and bicultural education in indigenous communities were considered irrelevant, even subversive, by the proponents of the unitary nation-state. In the past few years this opposition has eroded, and most countries now have bilingual and intercultural educational programs that cater to an increasing number of indigenous populations. The Inter-American Indianist Congresses, which are usually held every three years, have gone on record in support of such programs and have urged their member states to take adequate measures.

The third major area that has been widely discussed by indigenous organizations concerns the questions of local and regional autonomy, respect for traditional forms of authority and government, recognition of customary alternative legal systems and, more recently, the right to self-determination. These are usually quite controversial issues, to the extent that even by raising them, the indigenous organizations are challenging the hegemonic concept of the Latin American nation-state. Some sort of local autonomy for indigenous peoples does exist in several countries, such as Panama. As a result of the ethnic conflict in the 1980s, the National Assembly of Nicaragua adopted a Statute for the Autonomy of the Communities of the Atlantic Coast, which was later incorporated into the new national constitution. The question of legal pluralism is widely discussed: Some changes have been made in the legal systems of a number of countries, but progress in this field is slow because too little is known about customary legal systems of the indigenous peoples.[16]

Self-determination, considered both a basic human right and a political issue, is a much more complex matter. Here, indigenous peoples have clashed with the state on more than one occasion. Indigenous organizations have put forward claims to the right of peoples to self-determination, as contained in the United Nations human rights conventions. Governments, which fear territorial break-up and secessionist movements, have rejected such demands outright. Generally, indigenous movements do not see the exercise of self-determination as a secessionist proposal. Rather, they see it as a move toward greater participation in the political system on an equal basis with whites and *mestizos* and, above all, as the right to decide for themselves which issues relate to their welfare and survival.[17]

International law has established that self-determination refers to a single political decision usually involving independence. As used here, however, self-determination may be seen as a process involving different levels and multiple decisions over a period of time. First, a distinction may be made between "internal" and "external" self-determination, the former referring to the economic, social and political arrangements that a people wish to abide by and the latter to the kinds of links binding a specific people to another entity, which may or may not be a nation-state of which they are a part. Generally, when the right of a people to self-determination is invoked, external self-determination is thought of. When the indigenous peoples of Latin America speak of self-determination, however, they usually refer to internal self-determination, that is, the right to preserve and develop their own cultures, the right to land and territory and the development of economic resources on their own terms, yet all within the context of existing nation-states.

INDIGENOUS POLITICAL MOBILIZATION TODAY

The extension and intensity of indigenous mobilization all over the continent in the past few years has put the indigenous question on the political agenda. A number of countries have adopted legislation relating to indigenous populations. In some cases, entirely new constitutions have been drafted that, for the first time, include the question of indigenous rights. Chapter 8 of the Brazilian constitution, entitled "The Indians," was adopted after much public debate in 1988. It recognizes the permanent rights of the indigenous peoples to their traditional lands and obligates the government to demarcate them within five years of ratification. It also acknowledges indigenous communities and organizations as legal entities. In Nicaragua, the autonomy of the communities of the Atlantic Coast has been incorporated in the new constitution of 1988. Guatemala's constitution of 1985 stipulates

the state's obligation to protect indigenous lands and cultures. In 1991, Colombia adopted a new political constitution, drafted over several months by a special constituent assembly in which several indigenous representatives took part. It also includes articles on the rights of indigenous communities. Despite the fact that Mexico has the largest indigenous population in Latin America (over 12 million) and can boast a long history of official *indigenismo,* the Mexican constitution of 1917 did not acknowledge the legal existence of indigenous peoples. From 1990 to 1991, the Federal Congress debated the text of a constitutional amendment which would finally recognize indigenous rights.

By enacting legislation that in some way establishes or acknowledges the rights of indigenous peoples, leaving behind the earlier paternalistic and tutelary legal approaches, the countries of Latin America are beginning to change their national self-image. Of course, as the experience of Guatemala shows, just changing the legislation does not by itself guarantee the effective enjoyment of indigenous peoples' rights. But it may herald changes to come.

The rights that are being reassessed through these processes in Latin America are individual and collective human rights. Due to the inferiority imposed on them by society, indigenous groups have often been the victims of human rights abuses. These have been more than occasional and regrettable excesses by over zealous agents of the state. Because they are embedded in the social structure, they should be regarded as structural violations of the human rights of the indigenous peoples. Human-rights violations in Latin America have been widely documented in recent years by nongovernmental organizations such as Amnesty International and Americas Watch, whose yearly reports and special studies constitute an important contribution to our knowledge about these issues. Also, the Department of State country reports, though sometimes acknowledged to be politically biased, have provided significant information. Reports prepared by the Inter-American Commission of Human Rights and the U.N. Human Rights Commission are also revealing.[18]

The civil and political rights of the indigenous peoples have been too readily neglected and abused precisely because the collective rights to cultural survival, identity and self-determination have been ignored and denied. Thus, the emerging indigenous movement has been placing an emphasis on the collective rights of ethnically specific indigenous peoples.

These issues have also been taken up by inter-governmental organizations, such as the United Nations, the International Labor Organization (ILO) and the Organization of American States (OAS). The U.N. Sub-Commission on Prevention of Discrimination and Protection of Minorities, a subordinate organ of the Human Rights Commission, established a Working Group on Indigenous Populations in the early 1980s. Its sessions have been attended by numerous indigenous nongovernmental organizations, and it is currently drafting a Universal Declaration of the Rights of Indigenous Peoples to be adopted, perhaps as early as 1993, by the General Assembly. The issue of collective rights, including the right of indigenous peoples to self-determination, figures prominently in these discussions. Whether the member states of the United Nations will adopt such a declaration remains an open question, but the indigenous organizations that are actively engaged in promoting the declaration are already looking ahead toward the adoption of an international convention of indigenous rights.

The Sub-Commission has also initiated a study on the situation of treaties between indigenous peoples and nation-states. North American Indians are particularly interested in this issue, because the treaties that their ancestors signed in the name of then-independent, sovereign nations were unilaterally abrogated by the U.S. government in the nineteenth century. The Indians consider this to be related to international law and of interest to the United Nations. In most of Latin America, the relations between indigenous peoples and states were never governed by bilateral treaties. Nevertheless, a number of such treaties were signed by the Spanish crown and also by some republican governments in the nineteenth century. They have been similarly ignored by contemporary governments.

In 1957 the ILO adopted Convention 107 on the protection of indigenous and tribal populations in independent states, which has been ratified by 26 states. In 1985 the ILO initiated a process of revision of this international instrument, which resulted in the adoption in 1989 of a revised convention, now known as Convention 169. The issue of land

rights and territorial rights figures prominently here also, as does the concept of indigenous "peoples" rather than populations. The ILO Convention disclaims any political intention with the use of the term peoples, but for the indigenous it represents a victory of sorts in that it is peoples, and not populations, who have the right of self-determination as set out in the two international human rights covenants.

More recently, the General Assembly of the OAS requested the Inter-American Commission of Human Rights to initiate consultations which might lead to the drafting and adoption of a new human rights legal instrument in the Inter-American system pertaining to indigenous peoples. While governments are not enthusiastic about it, this development reflects the growing concern and awareness of states regarding the issues pertaining to indigenous rights.

INDIGENOUS PEOPLES AND NATIONAL IDENTITY IN LATIN AMERICA: LOOKING FORWARD

In conclusion, the indigenous peoples are achieving a new political presence in Latin America, and this has led to a reexamination of Latin America's national societies. At the same time, they present a challenge to the traditional ideologies of nationalism and the concept of the nation-state itself.

The legal recognition of indigenous rights in the new constitutions of Brazil, Colombia, Nicaragua and other states is opening the way for new legal and political arrangements between the states and the indigenous peoples. Brazil and Venezuela have both recognized the autonomy of the Yanomami Indians on their common border. "National security ideology" does not disappear so easily; but while "hard-line" nationalists in these countries may not like the idea, such changes may be a harbinger of things to come. Public opinion has begun to recognize that earlier concepts of the culturally homogenous nation-state may no longer apply. The struggle for political democracy in Latin America now also includes the need to recognize indigenous peoples' specific collective rights and their position within the wider society. As these transformations occur, it is inevitable that the perception of national identity will also change, and that the earlier idea of the nation-state will make way for a wider concept of the multicultural, multiethnic society.

NOTES

1. Quoted in Leopoldo Zea, *Discurso desde la marginación y la barbarie* (México DF: Fondo de Cultura Económica, 1990) p. 102. Translation by the author.

2. See Pablo González Casanova, ed., *Cultura y creación intelectual en América Latina* (México DF: Siglo XXI, 1979); Hugo Zemelman, ed., *Cultura y política en América Latina* (México DF: Siglo XXI, 1990); Leopoldo Zea, *The Latin American Mind* (Norman, OK: University of Oklahoma Press, 1963).

3. See Anthony D. Smith, *National Identity* (Harmondsworth, UK: Penguin, 1991).

4. Quoted in Winthrop R. Wright, *Café con Leche, Race, Class and National Image in Venezuela* (Austin, TX: University of Texas Press, 1990) p. 27.

5. See Magnus Mörner, *Race Mixture in the History of Latin America* (Boston, MA: Little and Brown, 1967).

6. William N. Denevan, *The Native Population of the Americas in 1492* (Madison, WI: University of Wisconsin Press, 1976).

7. Latin American Center, *Statistical Abstract of Latin America,* 28 (Los Angeles, CA: University of California Press, 1990) table 658.

8. See André Gunder Frank, *Capitalism and Underdevelopment in Latin America* (New York: Monthly Review Press, 1967); Rodolfo Stavenhagen, *Social Classes in Agrarian Societies* (New York: Doubleday, 1975).

9. Zea.

10. José Vasconcelos, *La raza cósmica, misión de la raza iberoamericana* (Paris: Agencia Mundial de Librería, 1925).

11. For an assessment of *indigenismo* in Mexico, see Alan Knight, "Racism, Revolution, and *Indigenismo:* Mexico, 1910–1940" in Richard Graham, ed., *The Idea of Race in Latin America, 1870–1940* (Austin, TX: University of Texas Press, 1990).

12. Fernando Henrique Cardoso and Enzo Faletto, *Dependence and Development in Latin America* (Berkeley, CA: University of California Press, 1979).

13. See Arturo Arias, "Changing Indian Identity: Guatemala's Violent Transition to Modernity," Carol A. Smith, ed., *Guatemalan Indians and the State, 1540–1988* (Austin, TX: University of Texas Press, 1990).

14. See Carlos Vilas, *State, Class and Ethnicity in Nicaragua* (Boulder, CO: Lynne Reinner Publishers, 1989).

15. See Susana Hecht and Alexander Cockburn, *The Fate of the Forest: Developers, Destroyers and Defenders of the Amazon* (New York: Harper Perennial, 1990).

16. See Rodolfo Stavenhagen and Diego Iturralde, eds., *Entre la ley y la costumbre. El derecho consuetudinario indígena en América Latina* (México DF: Instituto Indigenista Interamericano and Instituto Interamericano de Derechos Humanos, 1990).

17. See Rodolfo Stavenhagen, *Derecho indígena y derechos humanos en América Latina* (México DF: El Colegio de México and Instituto Interamericano de Derechos Humanos, 1988).

18. See Amnesty International, *Mexico: Human Rights in Rural Areas, 1986*; Americas Watch, *Rural Violence in Brazil, 1991.* For a critique of the Department of State reports, see Lawyers Committee for Human Rights, *Critique: Review of the Department of State's Country Reports on Human Rights Practices for 1990,* July 1991.

3

The Mirror of the Other

Carlos Fuentes

The U.S.-Mexico border, some of those who cross it say, is not really a border but a scar. Will it heal? Will it bleed once more? When a Hispanic worker crosses this border, he sometimes asks, "Hasn't this always been our land? Am I not coming back to it? Is it not in some way ours?" He can taste it, hear its language, sing its songs and pray to its saints. Will this not always be in its bones a Hispanic land?

But first we must remember that ours was once an empty continent. All of us came here from somewhere else, beginning with the nomadic tribes from Asia who became the first Americans. The Spaniards came later, looking for the Seven Cities of Gold, but when they found none in what is today the southwestern United States, they left their language and their religion, and sometimes their blood. The Spanish empire extended as far north as Oregon and filled the coastal region with the sonorous names of its cities: Los Angeles, Sacramento, San Francisco, Santa Barbara, San Diego, San Luis Obispo, San Bernardino, Monterey, Santa Cruz.

Carlos Fuentes, "The Mirror of the Other," *The Nation,* March 30, 1992, pp. 408–11. Reprinted by permission of the publisher.

When it achieved independence, the Mexican republic inherited these vast, underpopulated territories, but it lost them in 1848 to the expanding North American republic and its ideology of Manifest Destiny: the U.S.A., from sea to shining sea.

So the Hispanic world did not come to the United States, the United States came to the Hispanic world. It is perhaps an act of poetic justice that now the Hispanic world should return, both to the United States and to part of its ancestral heritage in the Western Hemisphere. The immigrants keep coming, not only to the Southwest but up the Eastern Seaboard to New York and Boston and west to Chicago and the Midwest, where they meet the long-established Chicanos, the North Americans of Mexican origin, who have been here even longer than the gringos. They all join to make up the 25 million Hispanics in the United States—the vast majority of Mexican origin, but many from Puerto Rico, Cuba, and Central and South America. It is the fastest-growing minority in the United States.

Los Angeles is now the second-largest Spanish-speaking city in the world, after Mexico City, before Madrid and Barcelona. You can prosper in southern Florida even if you speak only Spanish, as the population is predominantly Cuban. San Antonio, integrated by Mexicans, has been a bilingual city for

150 years. By the middle of the coming century, almost half the population of the United States will be Spanish-speaking.

This third Hispanic development, that of the United States, is not only an economic and political event; it is above all a cultural event. A whole civilization with a Hispanic pulse has been created in the United States. A literature has been born in this country, one that stresses autobiography—the personal narrative, memories of childhood, the family album—as a way of answering the question, What does it mean to be a Chicano, a Mexican-American, a Puerto Rican living in Manhattan, a second-generation Cuban-American living in exile in Miami? For example, consider the varied work of Rudolfo Anaya (*Bless Me, Ultima*), Ron Arías (*The Road to Tamazunchale*), Ernesto Galarza (*Barrio Boy*), Alejandro Morales (*The Brick People*), Arturo Islas (*The Rain God*), Tomás Rivera (*Y No Se lo Trago la Tierra*) and Rolando Hinojosa (*The Valley*); or of the women writers Sandra Cisneros (*Woman Hollering Creek*), Dolores Prida (*Beautiful Señoritas & Other Plays*) and Judith Ortiz Cofer (*The Line of the Sun*); or of the poets Alurista and Alberto Rios. Or consider the definitive statements of Rosario Ferré or Luis Rafael Sánchez, who simply decided to write in Spanish from the island of Puerto Rico.

An art has also been created here; in a violent, even garish way, it joins a tradition going all the way from the caves of Altamira to the graffiti of East Los Angeles. It includes pictures of memory and dynamic paintings of clashes, like the car-crash paintings of Carlos Almaráz, who was part of the group called Los Four, along with Frank Romero, Beto de la Rocha and Gilbert Luján. The beauty and violence of these artists' work not only contribute to the need for contact between cultures that must refuse complacency or submission to injustice in order to become alive to one another. They also assert an identity that deserves to be respected and that must be given shape if it is not visible, or a musical beat if it is inaudible. And if the other culture, the Anglo mainstream, denies Hispanic culture a past, then artists of Latin origin must invent, if necessary, an origin. And they must remember every single link that binds them to it.

For example, can one be a Chicano artist in Los Angeles without upholding the memory of Martín Ramírez? Born in 1885, Ramírez was a migrant railroad worker from Mexico who lost his speech

and for this was condemned to live for three decades in a California madhouse, until his death in 1960. He was not mad, he was just speechless. So he became an artist, and drew his muteness for thirty years.

No wonder that the Hispanic culture of the United States must manifest itself as forcefully as in a Luján painting; as dramatically as in a stage production by Luis Valdez; with a prose as powerful as that of Oscar Hijuelos with his mambo kings; or with a beat as life giving as that of Rubén Blades in his salsa songs of city woes and streetwise humor.

This vast flow of negation and affirmation forces newcomers as well as native Hispanics to ask themselves, "What do we bring? What would we like to retain? What do we want to offer this country?" The answers are determined by the fact that these people reflect a very broad social group that includes families, individuals, whole communities and networks, transmitting values, memories, traditions. At one end of the spectrum are 300,000 Hispanic businessmen prospering in the United States, and at the other is a 19-year-old Anglo-American shooting two immigrants to death for the simple reason that he "hates Mexicans." If one proudly spouts the statistic that Hispanic-owned businesses generate more than $20 billion a year, one can also, far less proudly, report that immigrants are shot at by Anglos with the paint-pellet guns used in mock warfare games. If one records that whole communities in Mexico are supported by the *remesas,* or remittances, of their migrant workers in the United States, and that these *remesas* add up to $4 billion a year and are Mexico's second-largest source of foreign income (after oil), then one must also record that many migrant workers are run down by vehicles on back roads near their campsites. And if, finally, one realizes that the majority of Mexican immigrants are temporary and eventually return to Mexico, then one must bear in mind the persisting differences between Anglo-America and Ibero-America, as these continue to oppose, influence and clash with each other.

The two cultures coexist, rubbing shoulders and questioning each other. We have too many common problems, which demand cooperation and understanding in a new world context, to clash as much as we do. We recognize each other more and more in challenges such as dealing with drugs, crime, the homeless and the environment. But as the formerly homogeneous society of the United States faces the immigration of vastly heterogeneous groups, Latin America faces the breakdown of the formerly homogeneous spheres of political, military and religious power through the movement of the urban dispossessed.

In this movement, which is taking place in all directions, we all give something to one another. The United States brings its own culture—the influence of its films, its music, its books, its ideas, its journalism, its politics and its language—to each and every country in Latin America. We are not frightened by this, because we feel that our own culture is strong enough, and that, in effect, the enchilada can coexist with the hamburger. Cultures only flourish in contact with others; they perish in isolation.

The culture of Spanish America also brings its own gifts. When asked, both new immigrants and long-established Hispanic-Americans speak of religion—not only Catholicism but something more like a deep sense of the sacred, a recognition that the world is holy, which is probably the oldest and deepest certitude in the Amerindian world. This is also a sensuous, tactile religion, a product of the meeting between the Mediterranean civilization and the Indian world of the Americas.

Then there is care and respect for elders, something called *respeto*—respect for experience and continuity, less than awe at change and novelty. This respect is not limited to old age in itself; in a basically oral culture, the old are the ones who remember stories, who have the store of memory. One could almost say that when an old man or an old woman dies in the Hispanic world, a whole library dies with that person.

And of course there is the family—family commitment, fighting to keep the family together, perhaps not avoiding poverty but certainly avoiding a *lonely* poverty. The family is regarded as the hearth, the sustaining warmth. It is almost a political party, the parliament of the social microcosm and the security net in times of trouble. And when have times not been troubled? The ancient stoic philosophy from Roman Iberia is deep indeed in the soul of Hispanics.

What else do Ibero-Americans bring to the United States? What would they like to retain? It is obvious they would like to keep their language,

the Spanish language. Some urge them to forget it, to integrate by using the dominant language, English. Others argue that they should use Spanish only to learn English and join the mainstream. More and more often, however, people are starting to understand that speaking more than one language does not harm anyone. There are automobile stickers in Texas that read MONOLINGUALISM IS A CURABLE DISEASE. Is monolingualism unifying and bilingualism disruptive? Or is monolingualism sterile and bilingualism fertile? The California state law decreeing that English is the official language of the state proves only one thing: that English is no longer the official language of California.

Multilingualism, then, appears as the harbinger of a multicultural world, of which Los Angeles is the prime example. A modern Byzantium, the City of the Angels receives each day, willy-nilly, the languages, the food, the mores not only of Spanish-Americans but of Vietnamese, Koreans, Chinese, Japanese. This is the price—or the gift, depending on how you look at it—of global interdependence and communications.

So the cultural dilemma of the American of Mexican, Cuban or Puerto Rican descent is suddenly universalized: to integrate or not? to maintain a personality and add to the diversity of North American society, or to fade away into anonymity in the name of the after-all nonexistent "melting pot"? Well, perhaps the question is really, once more, to be or not to be? to be with others or to be alone? Isolation means death. Encounter means birth, even rebirth.

California, and especially Los Angeles, a gateway to both Asia and Latin America, poses the universal question of the coming century: How do we deal with the Other? North Africans in France; Turks in Germany; Vietnamese in Czechoslovakia; Pakistanis in Britain; black Africans in Italy; Japanese, Koreans, Chinese and Latin Americans in the United States: Instant communications and economic interdependence have transformed what was once an isolated situation into a universal, defining, all-embracing reality of the twenty-first century.

Is anyone better prepared to deal with this central issue of dealing with the Other than we, the Spanish, the Spanish Americans, the Hispanics in the United States? We are Indian, black, European, but above all mixed, mestizo. We are Iberian and Greek; Roman and Jewish; Arab, Gothic and Gypsy. Spain and the New World are centers where multiple cultures meet—centers of incorporation, not of exclusion. When we exclude, we betray ourselves. When we include, we find ourselves.

Who are these Hispanic "ourselves"? Perhaps no story better renders the simultaneity of cultures that "The Aleph," by the Argentine author Jorge Luis Borges. In "The Aleph," the narrator finds a perfect instant in time and space where all the places in the world can be seen at the same moment, without confusion, from every angle, in perfect, simultaneous existence. What we would see in the Spanish-American aleph would be the Indian sense of sacredness, communality and the will to survive; the Mediterranean legacy of law, philosophy and the Christian, Jewish and Arab strains making up a multiracial Spain; and the New World's challenge to Spain, the syncretic, baroque continuation of the multicultural and multiracial experience, now including Indian, European and black African contributions. We would see a struggle for democracy and for revolution, coming all the way from the medieval townships and from the ideas of the European Enlightenment, but meeting our true personal and communal experience in Zapata's villages, on Bolívar's plains, in Tupac Amaru's highlands.

And we would then see the past becoming present in one seamless creation. The Indian world becomes present in the paintings of Rufino Tamayo, who was born in an Indian village in Oaxaca and whose modern art includes an Indian continuity in the sense of color and the spirit of celebration, in the cosmic consciousness and in Tamayo's capacity to recreate on canvas the dream of a form that *can* contain dreams. A younger painter, Francisco Toledo, also from an Indian village in Oaxaca, gives the ancient Indian fear and love of nature their most physical and visual proximity to our urban lives, while the Cuban Wifredo Lam permits his African roots to grow in his pictures. The Mexican painter Alberto Gironella bitingly recovers the traditions of Spanish art and commerce: His Valázquez spinoffs are framed by sardine cans.

Culture is the way we laugh, even at ourselves, as in the paintings of the Colombian Fernando Botero. It is the way we remember, as when the Venezuelan Jacobo Borges imagines the endless tunnel of memory. But culture is above all our bodies, our bodies so often sacrificed and denied, our shackled, dreaming, carnal bodies, like the body of the Mexican artist Frida Kahlo. Our bodies are deformed and dreamy creatures in the art of the Mexican José Luis Cuevas. Indeed, like Goya, Cuevas offers the mirror of imagination as the only truth; his figures are the offspring of our nightmares, but also the brothers and sisters of our desires.

The union of Cuevas in the Americas with Goya in Spain also reminds us that when we embrace the Other, we not only meet ourselves, we embrace the marginal images that the modern world, optimistic and progressive as it has been, has shunned and has then paid a price for forgetting. The conventional values of middle-class Western society were brutally shattered in the two world wars and in the totalitarian experience. Spain and Spanish America have never fooled themselves on this account. Goya's "black paintings" are perhaps the most lasting reminder we have of the price of losing the tragic sense of life in exchange for the illusion of progress. Goya asks us again and again to harbor no illusions. We are captive within society. Poverty does not make anyone kinder, only more ruthless. Nature is deaf to our pleas. It cannot save the innocent victim; history, like Saturn, devours its own children.

Goya asks us to avoid complacency. The art of Spain and Spanish America is a constant reminder of the cruelty that we can exercise on our fellow human beings. But like all tragic art, it asks us first to take a hard look at the consequences of our actions, and to respect the passage of time so that we can transform our experience into knowledge. Acting on knowledge, we can have hope that this time we shall prevail.

We will be able to embrace the Other, enlarging our human possibility. People and their cultures perish in isolation, but they are born or reborn in contact with other men and women, with men and women of another culture, another creed, another race. If we do not recognize our humanity in others, we shall not recognize it in ourselves.

Often we have failed to meet this challenge. But we have finally seen ourselves whole in the unburied mirror of identity only when accompanied—ourselves with others. We can hear the voice of the poet Pablo Neruda exclaiming throughout this vision, "I am here to sing this history."

Part II
PREHISTORY

4

Lost Civilizations of the Lower Amazon

Anna Roosevelt

When Europeans first explored the Amazon mainstream, they discovered a productive floodplain inhabited by large populations of Indians. One of the first accounts is that of Friar Gaspar de Carvajal, who accompanied the Spanish explorer Francisco de Orellana in 1541–42. Carvajal was entranced by what he saw:

> Inland from the river there could be seen some very large cities that glistened white . . . the land is as good, as fertile . . . as our Spain. It is a temperate land where much wheat may be harvested and all kinds of fruit trees may be grown; the woods of this country are groves . . . the land is high and makes rolling savannas . . . and there is a great deal of game of all sorts.

The early records describe settlements of thousands to tens of thousands of people along the banks of the river. Carvajal reports that one "stretched for five leagues without there interven-

Anna Roosevelt, "Lost Civilizations of the Lower Amazon." With permission from *Natural History* (Feb. 1989). Copyright the American Museum of Natural History (1989).

ing any space from house to house, which was a marvelous thing to behold." The dwellings were large thatched structures for households of many families. Some settlements were fortified, and the greater ones had central squares and were divided into neighborhoods.

Hunting, fishing, and seed and root agriculture provided the subsistence base for these settled populations. Europeans found abundant stores of food, especially maize and dried fish. Artifacts were produced on a large scale and traded over long distances. Carvajal saw

> a village where we found very great quantities of food, of which we laid in a supply. In this village there was a villa in which there was a great deal of porcelain ware of various makes, both jars and pitchers, very large, . . . and other small pieces such as plates and bowls and candelabra, the best that has ever been seen in the world . . . because it is all glazed and embellished with all colors and so bright that they astonish, and . . . the drawings and paintings which they make on them are so accurately worked.

According to the early accounts, these societies

were organized into ranks—hereditary chiefs and nobles, commoners, and captive slaves—and marriage within rank was preferred. Descent seems often to have been reckoned in the female line, and all along the Amazon the Indians told of a society ruled by women, though no Europeans ever saw this perhaps mythical realm. From the principal seats, paramount chiefs claiming divine origin ruled over territories hundreds of miles long. The chiefdoms were warlike and expansionist, and some of the earliest explorers were pursued relentlessly by flotillas of large canoes filled with tall, robust warriors shooting poisoned arrows.

Community religion emphasized worship of the chiefs' ancestors. Mummies and large-scale painted images of the ancestors, along with ritual paraphernalia and military equipment, were housed in special structures and brought out for ceremonies. Other idols were said to represent the sun and the moon and gods of marriage, childbirth, crops, and rain. Carvajal saw settlements with very large, carved wooden sculptures in the principal square, which he reported were dedicated to "their mistress, who is the one who rules over all the land of the aforesaid women," to whom the inhabitants said they paid tribute. Tithes of crops were collected to provide beer for periodic ceremonies that honored deities with music, dancing, and singing. Specialists were in charge of the religious houses and rituals, and there were diviners and curers. Although women were not allowed to view certain ceremonies, high-ranking women served as important diviners. Both boys and girls had to go through lengthy initiation rites and ordeals, and life crises such as birth and death were celebrated.

As they did to the Inca Empire in the Andes, the Europeans set about conquering and "civilizing" this realm, the better to exploit it. As a result of new diseases, war, and enslavement, the large populations of the chiefdoms were decimated and their hierarchies destroyed. Native military resistance was defeated, and the people were gathered into missions, where their traditional social ways were disallowed and their biological distinctiveness submerged through miscegenation. Within about 150 years of Orellana's voyage, the chiefdoms of the floodplains had become extinct.

The present-day Amazonian Indians number no more than a few hundred thousand and are thinly dispersed in hinterland forests and savannas. They live in small, isolated villages of communal households, relocating frequently. They build dwellings and make tools with materials from the forest and subsist on food from shifting cultivation, hunting, gathering, and fishing. With some exceptions, people tend to be small, which has been thought to be a genetic adaptation to millennia of living in the forest. Communities have no formal political relationships with others, but intermarriage, trade, and joint seasonal feasting are common. Despite a broadly uniform way of life, languages and cultures vary greatly throughout Amazonia, and warfare and raiding are intense in some areas. Men conduct outside relations and run ceremonial life, including curing magic in which shamans go into drug trances to communicate with ancestral spirits.

Amazonian Indians were first studied systematically by professional anthropologists in the 1930s and 1940s. By then, many of the conquest-period accounts of the chiefdoms had been more or less forgotten or discounted as exaggerations. Similarly overlooked was the obscure work of nineteenth-century scholars, mainly biologists and geologists, who had explored the monumental mounds and large refuse heaps left by the prehistoric inhabitants. With the hinterland Indians as their primary source of information, anthropologists began to think of the lifestyle of these people as the characteristic Amazonian way, an ancient adaptation to the tropical rain forest, with its high heat and humidity, lush vegetation, poor soils, and scarce game. Only since World War II, through archeology and a new appreciation of conquest-period and nineteenth-century literature, have scholars widely recognized that the ancient cultures of the floodplains of Amazonia were more like civilizations than like the isolated villages of surviving Indians.

One of the best known of these societies is the mound-building culture of Marajó, a 15,000-square-mile island at the mouth of the Amazon. The art and earthworks of Marajó fascinated nineteenth-century scholars, who concluded that they represented a preconquest civilization. In 1948–49, professional archeologists Betty Meggers and Clifford Evans of the Smithsonian Institution began preliminary investigations at Marajó, and they too were persuaded that this had been a complex society. Their explanation for an apparent civilization where none was expected was that a people had invaded from the Andes, the locus of Inca and earlier civilizations. They pronounced the "Marajoara" society to have been an intrusive culture that had deteriorated rapidly in the inappropriate tropical forest environment. The discovery of related artifacts in the intervening territory, along the Amazon as far as the foothills of the Andes, seemed to reinforce this interpretation.

This view was disputed by University of Illinois anthropologist Donald Lathrap and his associates, who believed that Amazonia had actually been a center of innovation and had even influenced the early cultures of the Andes. But until recently, there has been little concrete evidence to refute Meggers and Evans's explanation. Since 1983, however, my colleagues and I have been surveying and excavating sites on Marajó and elsewhere in the lower Amazon. Our results, and the archival studies of such Brazilian scholars as José Brochado, are documenting the characteristics of Marajoara society and revising ideas about its origins.

The habitat of this prehistoric society was eastern Marajó, a broad, grassy plain flooded half the year during the rainy season and parched by drought in the dry season. Often lumped with the Amazonian tropical rain forest by anthropologists, the area in in fact a savanna and has forests only along the small, often seasonal streams and relict levees. The soil is rich alluvium, not poor leached soil, and has been used as natural pasture for a productive cattle industry for hundreds of years. Here the Marajoara built many large earth mounds and created beautiful multicolored, modeled, and incised pottery, the hallmark of their culture.

The mounds were built as platforms for villages. Oval or oblong and usually oriented parallel to a small river, they lie in the lowest, swampiest parts of the plains, where water is available year-round but where flooding is deep and extensive during the rainy season. During flooding, the mounds become islands of dry land. They may have been defensive works as well because they were built much higher than necessary just to escape flooding. Local people today often call them *fortalezas,* or "forts."

Most of the mounds are six or seven acres in area and ten to twenty feet high. The mound with the largest area is more than fifty acres; the tallest, about sixty-five feet high and twelve acres in size,

was built with more than a million cubic yards of earth. About 400 large and small mounds have been discovered so far, including several multimound centers several square miles in area. The largest known center, Os Camutins, has forty mounds along a two-mile stretch of the Anajas River. There are also small, nonmound sites in the streamside forests, possibly even more numerous than the mounds.

All the mounds investigated so far have abundant remains of habitation. The dwelling foundations suggest oblong houses of earth, poles, and thatch, oriented east to west. These were multifamily structures, a house type known in Amazonia today as *maloca.* Erected on earth foundations, they had clean clay floors spread with white sand. Garbage was swept up regularly and used to fill in the areas between houses. Troughlike hearths of baked clay were closely grouped along the center of the house. Each house had several contemporary hearths, each with room for about three large pots, sufficient for the needs of a nuclear family.

The Marajoara occupation lasted more than a thousand years, coming to an end before the arrival of Europeans. Many mounds appear to have been occupied more or less continuously for hundreds of years, and some sites, such as Teso dos Bichos, have produced radiocarbon dates ranging from 400 B.C. to A.D. 1300 (these and other radiocarbon dates have been corrected for variations in carbon 14 in the atmosphere and other factors). There are many building stages in each mound. Earthworks were repaired and augmented and buildings and facilities carefully maintained or replaced. Some mounds reveal as many as twenty superimposed house foundations.

By counting hearths per house and houses per mound, we can reconstruct the prehistoric population. The average house seems to have had about nine hearths in use at the same time. If each nuclear family had four people, most houses would then have had about thirty-six people, as is often the case among Amazonian Indians today. Five to ten or more houses were occupied simultaneously on each mound. Teso dos Bichos, for example, had more than twenty contemporary houses, arranged in an approximate oval around a central open space, a pattern similar to some present-day villages in southern Amazonia. The average-sized mounds would have had several hundred people; the larger mounds would have had almost 1,000 people; and the multimound sites, such as Os Camutins and Fortaleza, as many as 10,000 or more. By our counts, the overall population of the Marajoara society would have been at least 100,000 and probably more.

As surmised by José Brochado, Marajoara cultivation may have resembled that of recognized civilizations elsewhere in the world, emphasizing annual grain agriculture rather than the shifting root cropping typical of living Amazonian Indians. Among the food remains we have screened and filtered from the soil are abundant carbonized seeds of various kinds, including maize and other cereals, palm seeds, and possibly chenopods. Small fish were also important in the diet. Today they are by far the most abundant fauna in Amazon waters and are collected, by mass fishing methods such as poisoning, primarily with the labor of women and children. Bones from terrestrial mammals and large water fauna, usually hunted by men nowadays, are absent from Marajoara garbage dumps, although there are rare caches of them in some places. Game thus may have been restricted for special uses, such as food for ceremonies or certain groups of people.

The thirty-odd Marajoara skeletons in museum and private collections reveal traces of some ailments that have been noted among settled agriculturists, including dental disease, osteoarthritis, osteoporosis, and some nutrient deficiencies. Morphologically, the skeletons seem closer to those of living Amazonians than to Andean Indians. Many men, however, were much taller than most present-day Amazonian Indians. They were strong and well nourished, and some had highly developed muscles, possibly from such activities as wrestling and running. Such sports are popular among present-day Amazonians and help train warriors for combat. Interestingly, such men seem not to have developed the kind of arthritis caused by the hard labor of weeding, digging, and carrying crops. Possibly we are looking at elite men, likely to have been buried in the large, decorated urns favored by collectors.

The Marajoara dead, accompanied by feast dishes, musical instruments, drug paraphernalia, figurines, ornaments, and tools, were interred in covered urns. These were buried between houses in clusters of fifty to several hundred, as if in family cemeteries. The cemeteries were used and maintained for long periods, with urns laid in two or more horizontal layers. Worldwide, such orderly, localized, long-term cemeteries are often characteristic of ranked societies that emphasize unilineal descent, the tracing of a person's ancestry through either the mother's or father's line.

The most impressive burial urns are two- to four-foot-tall globular, painted jars that represent crouched humans, most often female, depicted Janus-like on either side of the jar. The images have half-closed eyes, as if dead, and protruding tongues, a metaphor for sexual intercourse in some areas of Amazonia today. Their bodies are shown in X-ray fashion, with stylized limb bones and internal reproductive organs rendered in red, sometimes with a figure shown inside the belly. They wear elaborate ear ornaments and are decorated with sinuous, geometric patterns suggestive of the abstract "spirit" designs that living Indians in the western and northwest Amazon see in drug visions and consider to be the markings or features of supernatural animals.

According to some reports, almost completely articulated, tightly flexed bodies have been found in some of these urns, with hair still present, suggesting that they were mummy bundles. Perhaps, like those observed during the conquest, bodies were used as idols in Marajoara ancestor cults. The dead, crouched appearance of the urn images suggests that the urns themselves depict flexed bodies or mummy bundles; the images are usually female, however, and so do not depict the deceased, who in contrast are usually males. Since the idols often are shown pregnant, they may represent female ancestors or, perhaps, mythical female progenitors, such as those that figure in Amazonian myths today. Today, life crises are often symbolized by rebirth rituals that recall the birth of human ancestors during creation; perhaps the transition of the dead to the spirit world was similarly symbolized.

Another common type of funerary urn held disarticulated, red-painted bones, relics that may have provided genealogical justification for, or proof of, ranking. These smaller urns, ranging in height from less than a foot to three feet high, often represent women in white, slit-necked tunics decorated with spirit designs. The women's eyes are depicted as scorpions; their arms are shown as snakes or they wear snakes as bandoliers. Both animals are important to Indian shamans today, who in drug trances call on them to search out and kill bad sorcerers. Similar slit-necked tunics are still worn today by Indian men in western Amazonia, often for ceremonies and shamanistic rituals. The Marajoara images, therefore, seem to show women in guises of shamanistic power, a rare role for them today in Amazonia, except in the myths.

Funerary effigies are the best-known Marajoara artifacts, but there are many other kinds. Stone—including quartz, metamorphic and igneous rocks, serpentine, and nephrite—was imported from hundreds of miles away on the mainland and made into axes, grinders, mashers, hammers, abraders, nutcrackers, and ornaments. Pottery was shaped into vessels for food and drink, figurines, statues, pubic covers, ear plugs, lamps, paint pots, snuffers, spindle whorls, funnels, stamps, musical instruments, stools, and miniatures. There are also numerous pottery rattles, phallic in shape but decorated to represent erotic or pregnant female figures. These seem likely symbols for human fertility. Except for the phallic rattles, there are very few male images in Marajoara art.

Throughout Marajoara art, humans are prominent, with animals usually smaller and in subsidiary roles if humans are present. Some of the most common animals depicted are turtles, armadillos, ducks, dolphins, manatees, crocodilians, and fish, considered by many groups today to inhabit the female part of the world, in the water or beneath the earth's surface. Representations of large terrestrial carnivores, such as felines, and raptors, such as hawks, considered inhabitants of the male world—the earth's surface and the daytime sky—are rare. Images of night flyers, carrion eaters, and venomous creatures may relate to the mortuary cult or to shamanistic curing. The human emphasis in Marajoara art, uncommon in Amazonia today, may have developed to glorify the ancestors of higher-ranked individuals.

Marajoara iconography is also somewhat different from that of the later prehistoric chiefdoms of the lower Amazon, which flourished from A.D. 1000 until the European conquest. Although female images predominated in such cultures as well,

males became more common than before. Some later art, such as that of the Maracá, who lived just west of Marajó, included numerous pottery statues of men or women wearing special headgear and sitting on large stools in the shape of animals or humans. Among Amazonian Indians today, such stools are often known as chiefs' stools and are considered to give authority and supernatural power to leading men. Such statues suggest that central political and ritual roles were becoming more developed. In the art of Santarém, a late prehistoric chiefdom upriver at the mouth of the Tapajós River, men's and women's symbolic roles have diverged, and only men are shown as chiefs or shamans. Santarém women are shown in more conventional female attitudes, offering food or holding babies.

The distribution of art and artifacts varies greatly within and between Marajoara sites. In the ancient houses, simple, everyday cooking and serving wares predominate; large, elaborate feast dishes and imported stone tools and ornaments are mainly found outside the domestic areas. The mounds in general contain a richer variety of artifacts than the small nonmound sites, which have mainly domestic wares. The multimound sites in particular seem to have been ritual and political centers and centers of specialized crafts. The contrasts within and between sites support the idea that there may have been at least two ranks in the society: an elite living on the mounds and fisherpeople and farmers living primarily in small villages and working as servants and laborers at the mounds. The monumental earthworks, numerous large sites, and extensive territory further suggest that the Marajoara society was a chiefdom. Still to be ruled out, however, is the possibility that the society was differentiated principally by gender and age, and that the same people simply used the different kinds of sites for different activities.

One of the fruits of recent investigations is the knowledge that this important society, "lost" as an Amazonian cultural development through its interpretation as a foreign product, was indeed native in origin. As José Brochado pointed out in 1980, the radiocarbon dates show that the earliest of the Amazonian cultures that produced multicolored pottery were on Marajó in the lower Amazon, not in the area near the Andes. Instead of decaying rapidly in the tropical environment, the Marajoara occupation was a long-term florescence, and as archeologist Joanne Magalis Harris determined, the complexity of its arts and crafts increased with time. The culture had enormous influence throughout the Amazon lowlands and spread as far as the foothills of the Andes. Although the Marajoara are now extinct, the multicolored art style is still alive among remaining Indians in the four corners of Amazonia.

Marajoara art has antecedents in earlier lowland styles, and the particular method of painting (in water-soluble pigments) and the subject matter are lowland in character, not Andean. The genetic affiliation of Marajoara skeletons seems closer to Amazonian than to Andean people. The *maloca* house type, the oval villages, and the symbolic importance of females are all Amazonian patterns, not Andean. In fact, mound-building chiefdoms with urn cemeteries are primarily lowland in distribution in South America. Such cultures existed wherever there were large expanses of fertile, seasonal floodplains: the plains of Mojos in the Bolivian Amazon, the middle Orinoco, the coastal plain of the region known as Guiana, and some tributaries of southern Amazonia. In retrospect, the idea that advanced cultures in the tropics had to come from more civilized temperate areas seems to reflect a colonial view of the relationship between industrial and Third World nations.

Our findings from different parts of Amazonia give a new picture of cultural development. We now perceive a long sequence, beginning with nomadic hunters and gatherers at least 10,000 years ago. People settled down at rivers and estuaries to exploit fish and shellfish and, according to our recent excavations, began to make pottery in the New World by 1,400 years and 3,000 years before the first pottery in Andean or coastal areas of Peru. A culture of staple tropical root cropping appeared throughout the Amazon basin by 4,500 years ago, along with complex styles of pottery decorated with geometric and animal designs. Thus efficient hor-

ticulture and ceramic art developed earlier in the lowlands than in the Andes, presumably because the tropical riverine resources fostered sedentary life.

Chiefdoms and full-scale agriculture appeared in Amazonia much later than in the Andes, however, As suggested by anthropologist Robert Carneiro, this occurred only after the vast floodplains had become densely populated and conflict arose over resources. The Marajoara culture was one such development. With time, in some of the most densely settled areas of Amazonia, chiefdoms more like states appeared, with strong central rule, well-developed military forces, and large economically and socially differentiated populations. The best known of these is the Tapajós society of Santarém, which was defeated by the Portuguese. We have documented a center with more than two square miles of middens and low mounds. The mounds have yielded large ceramic statues of rulers, caches of intricate vessels, and fine stone carvings, tools, and weapons. Santarém habitation sites extend almost continuously along the river for hundreds of miles; there are numerous public works, including wells, roads, and fortifications, and evidence of a far-flung trading system. According to the early accounts, this chiefdom was in the process of conquering the lower Amazon in the sixteenth century. Had this indigenous trajectory not been cut off suddenly by the European conquest, there is no reason to suppose it would not have continued.

The fate of the long-lived Marajoara culture itself remains a mystery. It suddenly disappeared sometime before 1300, perhaps because of ecological stresses or strains on its organizational structure as the population grew. Another possibility is than an early, unrecorded landfall from the Old World occurred, and new diseases ravaged the population. At any rate, by the time of the first written accounts, Indians with a different culture were found along the coasts of Marajó, and the interior plains had been abandoned.

5

Applied Archaeology and Rural Development
Archaeology's Potential Contribution to the Future

Clark Erickson

ABSTRACT/SUMMARY

Archaeology can play a significant role in development projects, especially those focusing on improving agricultural production. Local agricultural systems, both prehistoric and traditional, are commonly neglected by development groups seeking to introduce Western capital-intensive technologies. Although research on these systems has received only a minuscule percentage of funds compared to research on Western systems, it has been demonstrated that many of these traditional systems can be both efficient and productive. Throughout the Americas, traces of relict agricultural field systems can be found (for example, terraces, raised fields, and irrigation canals) that were part of once highly productive landscapes. Archaeology is unique in that it provides the methodology to examine such systems in a diachronic perspective. Because many systems, such as raised fields, have been completely abandoned, archaeology may be the only way to understand these technologies. Archaeological excavation of prehistoric agricultural features can provide the model for the rehabilitation of these abandoned field systems. A recent case of applied archaeology which combines raised field agricultural studies and rural development in the South central Andes of Peru is presented.

From Clark Erickson, "Applied Archaeology and Rural Development: Archaeology's Potential Contribution to the Future," *Journal of the Steward Anthropological Society* 20 (1–2): 1–16, 1992.

INTRODUCTION

The most direct contribution that the field of archaeology can make to the contemporary world and the future is in the area of rural agricultural development. Recent research interest in prehistoric human-made landscapes (e.g., Farrington 1985; Darch 1983; Denevan et al. 1987; Miller and Gleason 1995; Fedick 1996; Turner and Harrison 1983, Harrison and Turner 1978; Killion 1992) provides the basis for what I refer to as an "applied archaeology." Applied archaeology is the anthropologically informed study of the human past, primarily through material remains, with a goal of employing the knowledge gained from this research to improve

Raised fields covering the seasonally inundated plain near Huatta, Peru. The rehabilitated fields in the center (the dark areas flanked by water-filled canals) are surrounded by traces of ancient raised fields.

the human condition in the contemporary world. Quite often, past human activities and culture are embedded in and layered on the landscape in the form of field patterning and boundaries, pathways and roads, agricultural infrastructure such as canals, terraces, and farming settlements. Archaeological investigations of the landscape can provide important insights into issues such as long-term land-use, agricultural sustainability, indigenous knowledge systems, human- vs. natural-induced environmental change, and the human effect on biodiversity. I argue that this approach is particularly useful for rural development, especially in areas where the archaeological record indicates that humans successfully managed landscapes over considerable periods of time.

Groups promoting rural development in developing countries have slowly begun to realize the critical need to incorporate anthropology into their programs if they are to succeed. Much of the failure of the "Green Revolution" can be blamed on lack of understanding of local technological, social, economic, and political systems. To attempt to address this, agronomists, developers, and social scientists involved in agricultural rural development have developed their own version of cultural ecology and systems analysis known as "farming systems research" (Shaner et al. 1982).

Despite evidence that most contemporary landscapes are the product of thousands of years of changing land use practices and human transformation of regional environments, farming systems research and related approaches result in what are basically synchronic studies. Most include short-term evaluations based on questionnaires, sometimes with follow-up, but these studies rarely include data collected over a period of several years. The refusal to consider the long history of the traditional systems being studied or modeled severely hampers any attempts to understand present situations and plan effective development strategies. The integration of archaeological approaches in development studies and applied projects could help resolve this critical deficiency.

Farming systems research and the "agroecological approach" has emphasized the importance of systemic interrelationships within the agricultural context (Altieri 1983) but it is often assumed

Farmers of Huatta re-constructing raised fields during the dry season. The soil is cut and moved using *chakitaqllas* (Andean footplows), hoes, shovels, and carrying cloths.

that the ideal state of agriculture is equilibrium and stability (now commonly glossed under "sustainability"). It is doubtful that any agricultural system, past or present, has been static, and most, if not all, systems are probably inherently unstable and dynamic (Rindos 1984; Crumley 1995; Stahl 1996). Archaeology should play a key role in development because farming systems are dynamic, historically contingent, and the product of hundreds of years of intentional and unintentional human agency.

Traditionally, development workers have assumed that indigenous and past land management systems in developing countries are inefficient, backwards, and "primitive" (for critiques of this perspective, see Netting 1993; Wilken 1987). Many evaluation studies focus on how poorly the land is used today, neglecting the archaeological evidence that these same lands may have been used productively in the past. Development agencies commonly fail to recognize that no environment is "pristine"; all landscapes have been used and transformed by humans in the past, some continuously (Denevan 1992). Farming over many centuries accounts for most of the disturbances. Landscapes throughout the Americas that appear pristine or abandoned usually show evidence of human modification at some time in the past, commonly in the form of agricultural remains. Human modification of such environments appears subtle to the uninformed observer, but is often quite profound, especially when measured in terms of increased biodiversity (Stahl 1996). So far, archaeology plays no part in the planning and implementation of modern development schemes; although in many, if not all cases, it can be demonstrated that prehistoric peoples fully utilized the same landscapes, sometimes very successfully.

Extensive archaeological remains of farming such as the massive terraces lining the steep slopes of the Andes mountains are often considered to be quaint "testimony" to the accomplishments of past civilizations. These features and the sophisticated technological knowledge they represent are not considered to have any practical modern use. Indigenous agricultural practices, often based on long traditions, are rarely considered worthy of study; more often, they are more something to wipe out so "progress" can occur. The "Green Revolution" of the 1960s and 1970s resulted in the displacement of many local land races of crops by genetically "improved" varieties, the destruction

A communal farming group in Huatta, Peru, posing in front of a newly constructed raised field.

of prehistoric and traditional agricultural infrastructure through the introduction of energy- and capital-intensive mechanized farming, and an increased dependence on Western technology and markets by previously self-sufficient farming communities (Netting 1993). Unfortunately, this situation continues to the present in Latin America driven by poorly planned development programs. The post–Green Revolution strategy has been to focus on "appropriate," "alternative," or "adequate" technologies. Although not as capital intensive as the previous approaches, most emphasize Western technology (e.g., biogas production, windmill power, small water pumps, greenhouses, and small tractors) and rarely consider the potential indigenous models.

PREHISTORIC AGRICULTURAL LANDSCAPES IN THE AMERICAS

Before the arrival of Europeans in 1492, vast areas of the Americas were farmed intensively. The steep mountain slopes in the Andean region of Ecuador, Peru, Bolivia and Chile include remains of possibly tens of thousands of square kilometers of irrigated

and nonirrigated terraces (Donkin 1979). In Peru alone, there are between 500,000 and 1 million hectares of terraces, of which 50 to 75 percent now lie abandoned (Treacy and Denevan 1994; Masson 1986). Raised fields (discussed below) cover large areas of the Llanos of Venezuela, Rio San Jorge Basin in Colombia, the Rio Guayas basin in Ecuador, the Llanos de Moxos in Bolivia, highland Ecuador and Colombia, and the Lake Titicaca Basin of Peru (Parsons and Denevan 1967; Denevan 1970, 1983). There is now evidence that the Maya Civilization, once believed to have been supported by slash and burn agriculture, was based on sophisticated combinations of construction of terraces, artificial reservoirs, raised fields and elaborate agroforestry practices (Harrison and Turner 1978; Killion 1992; Fedick 1996). A conservative estimate for the area in Latin America covered by ancient raised fields is 1,000 square kilometers (Denevan 1982). On the north coast of Peru, vast networks of prehistoric irrigation canals channeled water over an area 20 to 40 percent larger than that cultivated today (Moseley 1983). Archaeological studies of many of these agricultural remains have provided a basis for understanding the origins, evolution, and abandonment of once productive farm-

Raised field platforms (10 meters wide) planted in potatoes and water-filled canals during the rainy season in Huatta, Peru. The water can be used for irrigation, for the production and capture of nutrients, for aquaculture, and/or for improved crop microclimate through the capture of solar radiation.

ing strategies (e.g., Erickson 1996; Mosely 1983; Turner and Harrison 1983).

Unfortunately, much of the research on past agricultural systems remains at a descriptive and analytical level, with little emphasis given to potential application of this knowledge to contemporary situations. Ironically, Peru and Bolivia, the countries with the most impressive abandoned remains of prehistoric intensive land use and modification, now have some of the worst problems of poverty and underdevelopment in the Americas. Applied archaeological investigation of these once productive landscapes could provide viable alternatives for contemporary rural development.

APPLIED ARCHAEOLOGY: A CASE STUDY FROM PERU

Located at 12,500 feet in the Andean Highlands, the Lake Titicaca Basin of southern Peru and northern Bolivia is a difficult environment for farming. Frequent frosts and hailstorms, irregular rainfall resulting in serious droughts and flooding, high altitude, and generally poor soils characterize this zone. Despite these environmental limitations to agriculture, the area supported dense and well-organized populations before the Spanish conquest.

The Lake Titicaca Basin is one of the most massively human-modified landscapes in the Americas where hundreds of square kilometers of terraces and raised fields were constructed. Raised fields are large elevated planting platforms designed to improve soil fertility, to provide drainage, and to improve microclimates. The adjoining canals excavated during construction conserve water for irrigation, produce "green manure" that can be placed on the fields as an organic muck for soil fertility, store heat against radiation frosts, and may have been used for raising fish and economically useful aquatic plants (Denevan and Turner 1974; Erickson 1985, 1992). As a system, the raised fields demonstrate hydraulic sophistication in the management of water resources (Lennon 1983; Kolata 1993). Some 82,000 ha. of surface remains have been documented for the basin (Smith et al. 1968).

Farmers of Huatta harvesting potatoes on community raised fields. Potato yields here were two to three times that of traditional potato fields in the community.

Soil up to two meters in depth was disturbed by prehistoric farmers to construct the raised field platforms and canals.

Our raised field research was conducted between 1981 and 1986 in the Quechua-speaking community of Huatta (Brinkmeier 1986; Erickson 1995, 1996; Erickson and Candler 1989; Garaycochea 1987, 1987). Huatta is located in southern Peru on the flat seasonally inundated plains surrounding Lake Titicaca at 3,800 meters above sea level. The Raised Field Agricultural Project combined archaeological reconnaissance, excavation of raised fields and associated occupation sites, agronomic studies, and agricultural experiments using reconstructed raised fields (Erickson 1994). The research design was directed towards investigating (1) the social organization necessary for the construction and maintenance of prehistoric raised field agriculture, (2) the overall efficiency (labor input and production output) of the fields, (3) the functions of raised fields, (4) the origins, evolution, and abandonment of the raised fields, and (5) the potential role that raised field technology could have in contemporary rural development.

The importance of archaeological techniques in understanding prehistoric agriculture technology is demonstrated in the reconstruction of raised fields for experimental purposes. Reconstructions had to be based on the prehistoric models because the system has been completely abandoned. Soil profile data on the original morphology and construction stages were used to guide the reconstruction.

Labor for the reconstruction of raised fields for experimental purposes was provided by Quechua farmers using the local traditional tools (Andean footplow, hoe, clod breaker, and carrying cloths). In exchange for potato seed and the harvest, several communities in Huatta offered unused communal land and their labor to construct large blocks of fields to expand the experiments. With the initial success of the small-scale experimental fields, the program was expanded to include other Quechua communities in the area.

The results were encouraging and demonstrated the feasibility of the reintroduction of raised field farming in indigenous communities of the Lake Titicaca Basin. Archaeological investigation showed that raised field farming has an extremely long and complex history extending back some 3,000 years (Erickson 1987, 1996). Our experiments documented how raised fields improve soil, humidity, and microclimate conditions resulting in impressive productivity two to three times that of traditional fields in the zone (Erickson 1985, 1996; Garaycochea 1987).

One major criticism leveled by development agencies at the proposed reuse of many prehistoric agricultural systems in the Americas is that the labor costs are too high and that complex social organization including centralization and administrative hierarchies are necessary. Unfortunately, archaeologists and geographers have done much to reinforce this idea by wholeheartedly adopting the model of Ester Boserup on agricultural intensification and a revival of certain aspects of Karl Wittfogel's ideas on the need for centralization in complex irrigation systems and other intensive forms of agriculture such as raised fields and terraces (e.g. Kolata 1993; Harrison and Turner 1978; Farrington 1985; Darch 1983). This may be a major misunderstanding of past agricultural systems.

In our raised field experiments we demonstrated that over the long run, raised field farming is actually very efficient (Erickson 1985, 1996; Garaycochea 1986, 1987; Erickson and Candler 1989). The long-term benefits of high continuous productivity and low maintenance easily offset labor input. Another surprising find was that raised fields do not necessarily require centralization or administration. Local communal landholding groups of farmers such as the traditional Andean *ayllu* and even individual farm families can effectively mobilize the necessary labor and organization and appear to have also done so in the past (Erickson 1993, 1996).

The present situation in Huatta and nearby communities is very favorable to the rapid adoption of raised field technology. The plains have remained little used except for limited grazing since the fields were abandoned. These marginal lands with little potential, once part of haciendas and later a failed government cooperative, were recently turned over to indigenous communities which have begun successfully to exploit them using raised field technology. This is the only means to use this land intensively without major capital investment. The positive response to raised field technology is not only at the community level. Many individual farmers who learned the technology by participating in the communal groups have transferred this knowledge to their private fields (Erickson and Candler 1989). By 1995, over 300 hectares of raised fields had been rehabilitated in Peru and Bolivia and over fifty indigenous communities had participated in various projects. Much of the work has been done using incentives (food, wages, and/or seed) provided by the development agencies and it is not certain what will happen if these incentives are withdrawn.

POTENTIAL APPLICATION OF RAISED FIELD TECHNOLOGY

How generally applicable is raised field technology to rural development? Raised fields are only effective in areas of permanent wetlands or seasonal inundation. Socioeconomic and political factors will vary in areas of potential application and must be considered in their context. In addition, there is no one single model of raised field that will work in all cases. The remains of raised fields (and some still functioning such as in New Guinea, China, and Africa) have been found throughout the world (Farrington 1985; Denevan and Turner 1974; Denevan 1970, 1982), indicating that the use of raised fields was a common response by small farmers to many wetland and seasonally inundated savanna environments. Are raised fields and other indigenous forms of past and present agriculture the panacea for all development problems? Certainly not, and I am not suggesting that raised field technology can be applied to every wetland situation in the world, or even the Andean region. We have noted above and elsewhere (Erickson and Candler 1989) that the social, political, and economic situation has (inevitably) changed considerably since the Spanish conquest and in many cases the local indigenous infrastructure (traditional land tenure, original crops, tools, social organization, and sectorial fallow systems) necessary for raised field agriculture is gone.

APPLIED ARCHAEOLOGY: ADDITIONAL CASE STUDIES

The rehabilitation of raised fields in Huatta is a case study of applied archaeology and the potential that archaeological methodology can contribute to rural development. Archaeological approaches to other

Covers of two agricultural extension booklets used by the Raised Field Agricultural Project to train local farmers in raised field agricultural technology (drawings are by Dan Brinkmeier). These manuals were used with a video program in the Quechua language.

abandoned agricultural landscapes have also shown potential. Three cases are summarized below.

Andean Terracing: The remains of ancient terracing (*andenes*) can be found throughout the Andean region, especially in Central and Southern Peru and Bolivia. In many places, these terraces extend continuously from valley bottom to the high peaks of mountains. Recent archaeological and geographical research in highland Peru (Treacy and Denevan 1994, Treacy 1989) has suggested that terrace rehabilitation may be possible where abandoned remains are found. Between 1981–1987, strong interest in terrace rehabilitation was demonstrated by the Peruvian government and various nongovernment organizations. Impressive reconstruction projects were planned with hopes of eventually putting all abandoned terraces back into use and also applying this technology to nonterraced slopes. Government ministries even competed with each other for community participation. Unfortunately little, if any, of the construction of terraces was based on archaeological or agronomic information. At first, the model for terrace construction and reconstruction was that developed by United States Soil Conservation Service and applied to Central America by the USAID more than two decades ago. The projects, although apparently successful in some situations, were fraught with social, economic, and political problems (Gelles 1988; Treacy 1989). The use of detailed archaeological and agronomic studies of the terraces such as those conducted by Denevan and colleagues for the Colca Valley, combined with long-term agronomic experimental studies could have prevented some of the problems facing terrace reconstruction projects (Treacy and Denevan 1994). Terracing probably has much potential in the Andes, it will just need more archaeological investigation to develop adequate models for reconstruction.

Chinampa Agriculture: *Chinampas,* a form of raised field agriculture, provided a major portion of the food production for sustaining the large Aztec urban center and capital of Tenochtitlán. Similar raised fields are now believed to have provided much of the support for the densely populated urban centers in the Maya lowlands (Harrison and Turner 1978; Turner and Harrison 1983). The state government of Tabasco, Mexico, attempted to implement a *chinampa* program in the late 1970s in the wetlands near Villahermosa (Gómez Pompa et al. 1982; Denevan 1982). This program, the Camellones Chontales Project, was declared a failure, despite high praise and positive publicity, and near mythical status. Continuous crop failures, high costs, lack of markets for the crops produced, and discontent with communal labor organization has been pointed to as the causes of this failure (Chapin 1988). Many of the technical problems were due to the short-sighted approach the government used (e.g., heavy machinery, which dug canals too deeply into the lake sediments, placing sterile subsoil on the raised field platforms). Many of these problems could have been avoided if archaeologists had been consulted on the project. Little of the knowledge of the contemporary *chinampa* farmers of Mexico was used in the construction and planning, nor was any of the archaeological information collected during years of excavations in prehistoric raised fields used. As an afternote, the local Chontales Maya made the *chinampas* highly productive after the government abandoned the project and they are requesting that more be constructed. Other *chinampa* projects throughout Mexico have been successful as agronomic experiments, but few have had positive impact for rural development (Gomez-Pompa 1988; Chapin 1988).

Desert Farming in the Negev: The classic example of archaeology's successful contribution to rural development is the Negev project in Israel in the 1960s, directed by Michael Evenari (Evenari et al. 1971). Here, archeologists, working closely with agronomists, ecologists, botanists, and hydrologists, were successful in applying information gained from the detailed study of the prehistoric remains of structures that were used to collect runoff after infrequent rains. The discovery of ruins of farmsteads and larger settlements with associated agricultural features in the inhospitable desert had long been an enigma for Israelis. Archaeological investigation of these remains, combined with the experimental reconstruction of several farms based on the archaeological information, provided the foundation for the development program. The success of this applied archaeology project demonstrated that development of the desert is possible using the knowledge available to the prehistoric inhabitants of the area.

APPLIED ARCHAEOLOGY: WHAT CAN BE DONE?

The failure of development projects to consider past land use is common for Ecuador, Peru, and Bolivia. Prehistoric terraces, irrigation canals, and raised fields are ignored as if they do not exist. Although the modest raised field rehabilitation project has been successful in relatively small areas around Lake Titicaca, each year thousands of raised fields are plowed under by tractors for monocropping, or bulldozed away for roads, bridges, causeways, and housing. What is remarkable about this destruction of potentially useful archaeological resources is that the policies of the Peruvian and Bolivian governments and international development agencies are responsible for much of this destruction. Examples include the USAID-sponsored irrigation project and the projects of the National Agrarian University and the Ministry of Agriculture to introduce capital intensive agriculture to Illpa, near Huatta. These projects have resulted in the destruction of large areas of prehistoric raised fields (Erickson and Candler 1989).

Capital-intensive agricultural systems, especially the crops used in such systems, have received a disproportionate amount of the research funds, whereas thousands of potentially important food crops go unstudied. We know very little about non-Western systems (precise figures of yields, efficiency, input-output, production, and sustainability) which makes it nearly impossible to compare them to modern Western systems. Agronomists often declare that traditional systems are not as efficient as modern systems, but we have so little data (especially in the long term) for comparison. Experimentation based on archaeological models derived from ancient field forms may provide viable alternatives to introduced, nonlocal systems.

What can be done to remedy the situation? Archaeologists should be included in development planning as regular consultants. The training of archaeology students in developing countries for archaeological investigation of prehistoric agricultural systems is critical. What is drastically needed is increased funding for archaeology student training and projects investigating non-Western traditional and prehistoric agricultural systems. Many of the projects, such as mapping, documentation, and basic description of past land-use sys-

tems, could be done without huge funding. Archaeology could play a part, just as cultural anthropologists play a critical role in the planning and evaluation of today's development projects.

CONCLUSIONS: THE FUTURE OF ARCHAEOLOGY IN DEVELOPMENT

Archaeology has traditionally had the problem of not being considered very relevant, with at best an indirect application (Ford 1973). Throughout the 1960s and 1970s, the "lawlike generalizations of human behavior" were regarded by many as our most important contribution to the larger world (Watson et al. 1984 and others). Now, such claims are rarely heard and statements are much more modest. Recent articles speculating on the future of archaeology have stressed the importance of conservation of archaeological resources, use of Darwinian and sociobiological evolutionary models, and the adoption of new rigorous methods and technologies for more precise data collection, especially using the recent advances in remote sensing and computer hardware and software (Fagan 1989; Nash and Whitlam 1985). If archaeology is to continue to be funded at an adequate level in the future, I suggest that we may have to demonstrate a more direct, practical application. One important contribution of archaeology is that our methods can be applied to understanding long-term landscape use, which may have implications for rural development and understanding the history of local environments. I also suggest that development agencies and planners use archaeological insight on past land use. Most areas of the underdeveloped world show evidence of previous, long-term, successful use of the land by humans, often taking the form of massive transformations of the earth through terracing, irrigation, and raised fields. Before imposing capital-intensive systems or "appropriate technology" developed in and for the Western agricultural context, development organizations should seriously consider indigenous alternatives. Archaeological techniques can provide critical information on the structure and functioning of these ancient farming systems.

Time is running out for archaeologists, agronomists, geographers, and developers as many agricultural technologies with potential for rural development are being lost. Many functioning traditional systems are marginalized or have been eradicated by the introduction of capital-based systems. Ancient and traditional landscapes are rapidly disappearing under the plow or are being replaced with monocropping and mechanized agriculture. As a result, once-productive rural populations are being displaced, causing massive migrations to urban areas. Genetic erosion of local races of important crops is severe in such areas. Many of the traditional social institutions that organized labor exchange, controlled crop fallowing cycles, and provided access to community land are disappearing.

What is being argued here is *not* a naive romantic "return to the past," but a plea for the need to investigate and experiment with past agricultural systems as potentially viable alternative models for rural development.

REFERENCES

Altierei, Miguel A., 1983. *Agroecology: The Scientific Basis of Alternative Agriculture.* Division of Biological Control, University of California, Berkeley.

Brinkmeier, Daniel A., 1985. *A Plan for Disseminating Information about Traditional Agriculture to Indigenous Farmers in the Department of Puno, Peru.* Masters Thesis, department of Journalism and Mass Communication, Iowa State University, Ames.

Chapin, Mac, 1988. The Seduction of Models: Chinampa Agriculture in Mexico. *Grassroots Development* 12(1):8–17.

Crumley, Carol (ed.), 1994. *Historical Ecology: Cultural Knowledge and Changing Landscapes.* School of American Research Advanced Seminar Series.

Darch, J. P. (ed.), 1983. *Drained Fields of the Americas.* British Archaeological Reports, International Series, no. 189, Oxford.

Denevan, William M., 1970. Aboriginal Drained Field Cultivation in the Americas. Science 169:647–654.

————, 1982. Hydraulic Agriculture in the American Tropics: Forms, Measures, and Recent Research. In *Maya Subsistence,* edited by Kent V. Flannery, pp. 181–203, Academic Press, New York.

————, 1992. The Pristine Myth: The Landscape of the Americas in 1492. *Annals of the American Association of Geographers* 82:396–385.

————, Kent Mathewson, and Gregory Knapp (eds.), 1987. *Pre-Hispanic Agricultural Fields in the Andean*

Region. British Archaeological Reports, International Series, No. 359, Part i and ii, Oxford.

————, and B. L. Turner II, 1974. Forms, Functions, and Associations of Raised Fields in the Old World Tropics. *Journal of Tropical Geography* 39:24–33.

Donkin, R. A., 1979. *Agricultural Terracing in the Aboriginal New World.* University of Arizona Press, Tucson.

Erickson, Clark L., 1985. Applications of Prehistoric Andean Technology: Experiments in Raised Field Agriculture, Huatta, Lake Titicaca, Peru, 1981–1983. In *Prehistoric Intensive Agriculture in the Tropics* edited by Ian Farrington, pp. 209–232, British Archaeological Reports, International Series, No. 232, Oxford.

————, 1987. The Dating of Raised Field Agriculture in the Lake Titicaca Basin of Peru. In *Pre-Hispanic Agricultural Fields in the Andean Region,* edited by William M. Denevan, Kent Mathewson and Gregory Knapp, pp. 373–383, British Archaeological Reports, International Series, No. 359, Oxford.

————, 1988. Raised Field Agriculture in the Lake Titicaca Basin: Putting Ancient Andean Agriculture Back to Work. *Expedition,* 30(2):8–16.

————, 1992. Prehistoric Landscape Management in the Andean Highlands: Raised Field Agriculture and its Environmental Impact. *Population and Environment* 13(4):285–300.

————, 1993. The Social Organization of Prehispanic Raised Field Agriculture in the Lake Titicaca Basin. In *Economic Aspects of Water Management in the Prehispanic New World.* Research in Economic Anthropology Supplement 7, JAI Press, Greenwich, Connecticut, pp. 369–426.

————, 1994. Methodological Considerations in the Study of Ancient Andean Field Systems. In *The Archaeology of Garden and Field.* University of Pennsylvania Press, Philadelphia, pp. 111–152.

————, 1996. *Investigación arqueológica del sistema agrícola de los camellones en la Cuenca del Lago Titicaca del Perú.* PIWA, Centro de Información para el Desarrollo, La Paz.

————, and Kay L. Candler, 1989. Raised Fields and Sustainable Agriculture in the Lake Titicaca Basin. In *Fragile Lands of Latin America: Strategies for Sustainable Development,* edited by John Browder, pp. 230–248. Westview Press, Boulder.

Evenari, Michael, Leslie Shanan, and Naphtali Tadmore, 1971. *The Negev: The Challenge of a Desert.* Harvard University Press, Cambridge.

Fagan, Brian (ed.), 1989. A.D. 2050: A 21st Century View of the Human Past. In *Archaeology* special issue, 42(1).

Farrington, Ian (ed.), 1985. *Prehistoric Intensive Agri-*

culture in the Tropics. British Archaeological Reports, International Series, No. 232, Part I and IIi, Oxford.

Fedick, Scott L. (ed.), 1996. *The Managed Mosaic: Ancient Maya Agriculture and Resource Use.* University of Utah Press, Salt Lake City.

Ford, Richard I., 1973. Archeology Serving Humanity. In *Research and Theory in Current Archeology,* edited by Charles L. Redman, pp. 83–93, John Wiley and Sons, New York

Garaycochea Z., Ignacio, 1986. *Rehabilitacion de camellones en la Comunidad Campesina de Huatta, Puno.* Unpublished thesis, Department of Agronomy, Universidad Nacional del Altiplano, Puno, Peru.

———, 1987. Agricultural Experiments in Raised Fields in the Titicaca Basin, Peru: Preliminary Considerations. In *Pre-Hispanic Agricultural Fields in the Andean Region,* edited by William M. Denevan, Kent Mathewson, and Gregory Knapp, pp. 385–398, British Archaeological Reports, International Series, No. 359, Oxford.

Gelles, Paul, 1988. Irrigation, Community, and the Agrarian Frontier in Cabanaconde (Caylloma, Arequipa), Peru. Paper presented at the International Congress of Americanists (Amsterdam).

Gomez-Pompa, Arturo, 1990. Letter to the Editor. *Grassroots Development* 14(2):49–52; also vol. 12(2):50–51.

———, 1990. Seduction by the Chinampas. *The Desfile Newsletter* 4(1):3, 6–7 (USAID Development Strategies for Fragile Lands Project).

———, Hector Luis Morales, Epifanio Jimenez Avilla, and Julio Jimenez Avilla, 1982. Experiences in Traditional Hydraulic Agriculture. In *Maya Subsistence,* edited by Kent V. Flannery, pp. 327–342, Academic Press, New York.

Harrison, Peter D., and B. L. Turner II (eds.), 1978. *Pre-Hispanic Maya Agriculture.* University of New Mexico Press, Albuquerque.

Killion, Thomas W. (ed.), 1992. *Gardens of Prehistory: The Archaeology of Settlement Agriculture in Greater Mesoamerica.* University of Alabama Press, Tuscaloosa.

Kolata, Alan L., 1993. *The Tiwanaku: Portrait of an Andean Civilization.* Blackwell, Cambridge.

Lennon, Thomas J., 1983. Pattern Analysis of Prehispanic Raised Fields of Lake Titicaca, Peru. In *Drained Fields of the Americas,* edited by J. P. Darch, pp. 183–200, British Archaeological Reports, International Series, no. 189, Oxford.

Masson M., Luis, 1986. Rehabilitación de andenes en la comunidad de San Pedro de Casta, Lima. In *Andenes y camellones en el Peru Andino: historia, presente y futuro,* edited by Carlos de la Torre and Manuel Burga, pp. 207–216, Consejo Nacional de Ciencia y Tecnología, Lima.

Miller, Naomi, and Kathryn Gleason (eds.), 1994. *The Archaeology of Garden and Field.* University of Pennsylvania Press, Philadelphia.

Mosely, Michael E., 1983. The Good Old Days Were Better: Agrarian Collapse and Tectonics. *American Anthropologist* 85:773–799.

Nash, Ronald J., and Robert G. Whitlam, 1985. Future-Oriented Archaeology. *Canadian Journal of Archaeology* 9(2):95-108.

Netting, Robert McC., 1993. *Smallholders, Householders: Farm Families and the Ecology of Intensive, Sustainable Agriculture.* Stanford University Press, Stanford.

Rindos, David, 1984. *The Origins of Agriculture: An Evolutionary Perspective.* Academic Press, New York.

Shaner, W. W., P. F. Philipp, and W. R. Schmehl, 1982. *Farming Systems Research and Development: Guidelines for Developing Countries.* Westview Press, Boulder.

Smith, Clifford T., William M. Denevan, and Patrick Hamilton, 1968. Ancient Ridged Fields in the Region of Lake Titicaca. *The Geographical Journal* 134:353–367.

Stahl, Peter, 1996. Holocene Biodiversity: An Archaeological Perspective from the Americas. *Annual Review of Anthropology* 25:105–126.

Treacy, John, 1989. Agricultural Terraces in the Colca Valley: Promises and Problems of an Ancient Technology. In *Fragile Lands of Latin America: Strategies for Sustainable Development* edited by John Browder, Westview Press, Boulder.

Treacy, John, and William Denevan, 1994. The Creation of Cultivated Land through Terracing. In The Archaeology of Garden and Field. University of Pensylvania Press, Philadelphia, pp. 91–110.

Turner, B. L. II, and Peter D. Harrison (eds.), 1983. *Pultrouser Swamp: Ancient Maya Habitat, Agriculture, and Settlement in Northern Belize.* University of Texas Press, Austin.

Watson, Patty Jo, Steven Leblanc, and Charles Redman, 1984. *Archaeological Explanation: The Scientific Method in Archaeology,* Columbia University Press, New York.

Wilken, Gene C., 1987. *Good Farmers: Traditional Agricultural Resource Management in Mexico and Central America.* University of California Press, Berkeley.

6

The Enigma of Aztec Sacrifice

Michael Harner

On the morning of November 8, 1519, a small band of bearded, dirty, exhausted Spanish adventurers stood at the edge of a great inland lake in central Mexico, staring in disbelief at the sight before them. Rising from the center of the lake was a magnificent island city, shining chalk white in the early sun. Stretching over the lake were long causeways teeming with travelers to and from the metropolis, Tenochtitlán, the capital of the Aztec empire, now known as Mexico City.

The Spaniards, under the command of Hernán Cortés, were fresh from the wars of the Mediterranean and the conquest of the Caribbean. Tough and ruthless men, numbering fewer than four hundred, they had fought their way up from the eastern tropical coast of Mexico. Many had been wounded or killed in battles with hostile Indians on the long

From Michael Harner, "The Enigma of Aztec Sacrifice," in D. Hunter and P. Whitten, eds., *Anthropology: Contemporary Perspectives,* (2nd ed.). Boston: Little, Brown and Company, pp. 237–242, 1979. Reprinted by permission of the author. For a more complete discussion of this issue, see Michael Harner, "The Ecological Basis for Aztec Sacrifice." *American Ethnologist,* vol. 4, no. 1 (Feb) 1977, pps. 117–135.

march. Possibly all would have died but for their minuscule cavalry of fifteen horses—which terrified the Indians, who thought the animals were gods—and the aid of a small army of Indian allies, enemies of the Aztecs.

The panorama of the Aztec citadel across the water seemed to promise the Spaniards the riches that had eluded them all their lives. One of them, Bernal Díaz del Castillo, later wrote: "To many of us it appeared doubtful whether we were asleep or awake . . . never yet did man see, hear, or dream of anything equal to our eyes this day." For the Spaniards, it was a vision of heaven.

Slightly more than a year and a half later, in the early summer of 1521, it was a glimpse of hell. Again the Spaniards found themselves on the lakeshore, looking toward the great capital. But this time they had just been driven back from the city by the Aztec army. Sixty-two of their companions had been captured, and Cortés and the other survivors helplessly watched a pageant being enacted a mile away across the water on one of the major temple-pyramids of the city. As Bernal Díaz later described it,

The dismal drum of Huichilobos sounded again,

accompanied by conches, horns, and trumpet-like instruments. It was a terrifying sound, and when we looked at the tall *cue* [temple-pyramid] from which it came we saw our comrades who had been captured in Cortés' defeat being dragged up the steps to be sacrificed. When they had hauled them up to a small platform in front of the shrine where they kept their accursed idols we saw them put plumes on the heads of many of them; and then they made them dance with a sort of fan in front of Huichilobos. Then after they had danced the *papas* [Aztec priests] laid them down on their backs on some narrow stones of sacrifice and, cutting open their chests, drew out their palpitating hearts which they offered to the idols before them.

Cortés and his men were the only Europeans to see the human sacrifices of the Aztecs, for the practice ended shortly after the successful Spanish conquest of the Aztec empire. But the extremity of Aztec sacrifice has long persisted in puzzling scholars. No human society known to history approached that of the Aztecs in the quantities of people offered as religious sacrifices: 20,000 a year is a common estimate.

A typical anthropological explanation is that the religion of the Aztecs required human sacrifices; that their gods demanded these extravagant, frequent offerings. This explanation fails to suggest why that particular form of religion should have evolved when and where it did. I suggest that the Aztec sacrifices, and the cultural patterns surrounding them, were a natural result of distinctive ecological circumstances.

Some of the Aztecs' ecological circumstances were common to ancient civilizations in general. Recent theoretical work in anthropology indicates that the rise of early civilizations was a consequence of the pressures that growing populations brought to bear on natural resources. As human populations slowly multiplied, even before the development of plant and animal domestication, they gradually reduced the wild flora and fauna available for food and disrupted the ecological equilibriums of their environments. The earliest strong evidence of humans causing environmental damage was the extinction of many big game species in Europe by about 10,000 B.C., and in America north of Mexico by about 9,000 B.C. Simultaneously, human

populations in broad regions of the Old and New Worlds had to shift increasingly to marine food resources and small-game hunting. Finally, declining quantities of wild game and food plants made domestication of plants and animals essential in most regions of the planet.

In the Old World, domestication of herbivorous mammals, such as cattle, sheep, and pigs, proceeded apace with that of food plants. By about 7,200 B.C. in the New World, however, ancient hunters had completely eliminated herbivores suitable for domestication from the area anthropologists call Mesoamerica, the region of the future high civilizations of Mexico and Guatemala. Only in the Andean region and southern South America did some camel-related species, especially the llama and the alpaca, manage to survive hunters' onslaughts, and thus could be domesticated later, along with another important local herbivore, the guinea pig. In Mesoamerica, the guinea pig was not available, and the Camelidae species became extinct several thousand years before domesticated food production had to be seriously undertaken. Dogs, such as the Mexican hairless, and wildfowl, such as the turkey, had to be bred for protein. The dog, however, was a far from satisfactory solution because, as a carnivore, it competed with its breeders for animal protein.

The need for intensified domesticated food production was felt early, as anthropologist Robert Carneiro has pointed out, by growing populations in fertile localities circumscribed by terrain poorly suited to farming. In such cases, plants always became domesticated, climate and environment permitting, but herbivorous mammals apparently could not, unless appropriate species existed. In Mesoamerica, the Valley of Mexico, with its fertile and well-watered bottomlands surrounded by mountains, fits well Carneiro's environmental model. In this confined area, population was increasing up to the time of the Spanish conquest, and the supply of wild game was declining. Deer were nearly gone from the Valley by the Aztec period.

The Aztecs responded to their increasing problems of food supply by intensifying agricultural production with a variety of ingenious techniques, including the reclamation of soil from marsh and lake bottoms in the *chinampa,* or floating garden, method. Unfortunately, their ingenuity could not correct their lack of a suitable domesticable herbivore that could provide animal protein and fats. Hence, the ecological situation of the Aztecs and their Mesoamerican neighbors was unique among the world's major civilizations. I have recently proposed the theory that large-scale cannibalism, disguised as sacrifice, was the natural consequence of these ecological circumstances.

The contrast between Mesoamerica and the Andes, in terms of the existence of domesticated herbivores, was also reflected in the numbers of human victims sacrificed in the two areas. In the huge Andean Inca empire, the other major political entity in the New World at the time of the conquest, annual human sacrifices apparently amounted to a few hundred at most. Among the Aztecs, the numbers were incomparably greater. The commonly mentioned figure of 20,000, however, is unreliable. For example, one sixteenth-century account states that 20,000 were sacrificed yearly in the capital city alone, another reports this as 20,000 infants, and a third claims the same number as being slaughtered throughout the Aztec empire on a single particular day. The most famous specific sacrifice took place in 1487 at the dedication of the main pyramid in Tenochtitlán. Here, too, figures vary: one source states 20,000, another 72,344, and several give 80,400.

In 1946 Sherburne Cook, a demographer specializing in American Indian populations, estimated an overall annual mean of 15,000 victims in a central Mexican population reckoned at two million. Later, however, he and his colleague Woodrow Borah revised his estimate of the total central Mexican population upward to 25 million. Recently, Borah, possibly the leading authority on the demography of Mexico at the time of the conquest, has also revised the estimated number of persons sacrificed in central Mexico in the fifteenth century to 250,000 per year, equivalent to one percent of the total population. According to Borah, this figure is consistent with the sacrifice of an estimated 1,000 to 3,000 persons yearly at the largest of the thousands of temples scattered throughout the Aztec Triple Alliance. The numbers, of course, were fewer at the lesser temples, and may have shaded down to zero at the smallest.

These enormous numbers call for consideration of what the Aztecs did with the bodies after the sacrifices. Evidence of Aztec cannibalism has been largely ignored or consciously or unconsciously covered up. For example, the major twentieth-century books on the Aztecs barely mention it; others bypass the subject completely. Probably some modern Mexicans and anthropologists have been embarrassed by the topic: the former partly for nationalistic reasons; the latter partly out of a desire to portray native peoples in the best possible light. Ironically, both these attitudes may represent European ethnocentrism regarding cannibalism—a viewpoint to be expected from a culture that has had relatively abundant livestock for meat and milk.

A search of the sixteenth-century literature, however, leaves no doubt as to the prevalence of cannibalism among the central Mexicans. The Spanish conquistadores wrote amply about it, as did several Spanish priests who engaged in ethnological research on Aztec culture shortly after the conquest. Among the latter, Bernardino de Sahagún is of particular interest because his informants were former Aztec nobles, who supplied dictated or written information in the Aztec language, Nahuatl.

According to these early accounts, some sacrificial victims were not eaten, such as children offered by drowning to the rain god, Tlaloc, or persons suffering skin diseases. But the overwhelming majority of the sacrificed captives apparently were consumed. A principal—and sometimes only—objective of Aztec war expeditions was to capture prisoners for sacrifice. While some might be sacrificed and eaten on the field of battle, most were taken to home communities or to the capital, where they were kept in wooden cages to be fattened until sacrificed by the priests at the temple-pyramids. Most of the sacrifices involved tearing out the heart, offering it to the sun and, with some blood, also to the idols. The corpse was then tumbled down the steps of the pyramid and carried off to be butchered. The head went on the local skull rack, displayed in central plazas alongside the temple-pyramids. At least three of the limbs were the property of the captor if he had seized the prisoner without assistance in battle. Later, at a feast given at the captor's quarters, the central dish was a stew of tomatoes, peppers, and the limbs of his victim. The remaining torso, in Tenochtitlán at least, went to the royal zoo where it was used to feed carnivorous mammals, birds, and snakes.

Recent archeological research lends support to conquistadores' and informants' vivid and detailed accounts of Aztec cannibalism. Mexican archeologists excavating at an Aztec sacrificial site in the Tlatelolco section of Mexico City between 1960 and 1969 uncovered headless human rib cages completely lacking the limb bones. Associated with these remains were some razorlike obsidian blades, which the archeologists believe were used in the butchering. Nearby they also discovered piles of human skulls, which apparently had been broken open to obtain the brains, possibly a choice delicacy reserved for the priesthood, and to mount the skulls on a ceremonial rack.

Through cannibalism, the Aztecs appear to have been attempting to reduce very particular nutritional deficiencies. Under the conditions of high population pressure and class stratification that characterized the Aztec state, commoners or lower-class persons rarely had the opportunity to eat any game, even the domesticated turkey, except on great occasions. They often had to content themselves with such creatures as worms and snakes and an edible lake-surface scum called "stone dung," which may have been algae fostered by pollution from Tenochtitlán. Preliminary research seems to indicate that although fish and waterfowl were taken from the lakes, most of the Aztec poor did not have significant access to this protein source and were forced to be near-vegetarians, subsisting mainly on domesticated plant foods such as maize and beans.

The commoners theoretically could get the eight essential amino acids necessary for building body tissues from maize and beans. (A combination of the two foods complement each other in their essential amino acid components.) However, recent nutritional research indicates that in order to assure that their bodies would use the eight essential amino acids to rebuild body tissues, and not simply siphon off the dietary protein as energy, the Aztec commoners would have had to consume large quantities of maize and beans simultaneously or nearly simultaneously year-round. But crop failures and famines were common. According to Durán, a sixteenth-century chronicler, poor people often could not obtain maize and beans in the same season, and hence could not rely upon these plants as a source of the essential amino acids. How did the Aztecs know they needed the essential amino acids? Like other organisms perfected under natural selection, the human body is a homeostatic system that, under conditions of nutritional stress, tends to seek out the dietary elements in which it is deficient. Without this innate capacity, living organisms could not survive.

Another Aztec dietary problem was the paucity of fats, which were so scarce in central Mexico that the Spaniards resorted to boiling down the bodies of Indians killed in battle in order to obtain fat for dressing wounds and tallow for caulking boats. While the exact amount of fatty acids required by the human body remains a subject of uncertainty among nutritionists, they agree that fats, due to their slower rate of metabolism, provide a longer-lasting energy source than carbohydrates. Fatty meat, by providing not only fat, which the body will use as energy, but also essential proteins, assures the utilization of the essential amino acids for tissue building. Interestingly, prisoners confined by the Aztecs in wooden cages prior to sacrifice could be fed purely on carbohydrates to build up fat.

In contrast to the commoners, the Aztec elite normally had a diet enriched by wild game imported from the far reaches of the empire where species had not been so depleted. But even nobles could suffer from famines and sometimes had to sell their children into slavery in order to survive. Not surprisingly, the Aztec elite apparently reserved for themselves the right to eat human flesh, and conveniently, times of famine meant that the gods demanded appeasement through many human sacrifices.

At first glance, this prohibition against commoners eating human flesh casts doubt on cannibalism's potential to mobilize the masses of Aztec society to engage in wars for prisoners. Actually, the prohibition was, if anything, a goad to the lower class to participate in these wars since those who single-handedly took captives several times gained the right to eat human flesh. Successful warriors became members of the Aztec elite and their descendants shared their privileges. Through the reward of flesh-eating rights to the group most in need of them, the Aztec rulers assured themselves an aggressive war machine and were able to motivate the bulk of the population, the poor, to contribute to state and upper-class maintenance through active participation in offensive military operations. Underlying the war machine's victories, and the resultant sacrifices, were the ecological extremities of the Valley of Mexico.

With an understanding of the importance of cannibalism in Aztec culture, and of the ecological reasons for its existence, some of the Aztecs' more distinctive institutions begin to make anthropological sense. For example, the old question of whether the Aztecs' political structure was or was not an "empire" can be reexamined. One part of this problem is that the Aztecs frequently withdrew from conquered territory without establishing administrative centers or garrisons. This "failure" to consolidate conquest in the Old World fashion puzzled Cortés, who asked Moctezuma to explain why he allowed the surrounded Tlaxcalans to maintain their independence. Moctezuma reportedly replied that his people could thus obtain captives for sacrifice. Since the Aztecs did not normally eat people of their own polity, which would have been socially and politically disruptive, they needed nearby "enemy" populations on whom they could prey for captives. This behavior makes sense in terms of Aztec cannibalism: from the Aztec point of view, the Tlaxcalan state was preserved as a stockyard. The Aztecs were unique among the world's states in having a cannibal empire. Understandably, they did not conform to Old World concepts of empire, based on economies with domesticated herbivores providing meat or milk.

The ecological situation of the Aztecs was probably an extreme case of problems general to the high population pressure societies of Mesoamerica. Cannibalism encouraged the definition of the gods as eaters of human flesh and led almost inevitably to emphasis on fierce, ravenous, and carnivorous deities, such as the jaguar and the serpent, which are characteristic of Mesoamerican pantheons. Pre-Colombian populations could, in turn, rationalize the more grisly aspects of large-scale cannibalism as consequences of the gods' demands. Mesoamerican cannibalism, disguised as propitiation of the gods, bequeathed to the world some of its most distinctive art and architecture. The temple-pyramids of the Maya and the Toltecs, and of the pre-Aztec site at Teotihuacán in the valley of Mexico, resemble those of the Aztecs in appearance and probably had similar uses. Even small touches, such as the steepness of the steps on pyramids in Aztec and other Mesoamerican ruins, become understandable given the need for efficiently tumbling the bodies from the sacrificial altars to the multitudes below. Perhaps those prehistoric scenes were not too dissimilar from that which Bernal Díaz described when his companions were sacrificed before his eyes in Tenochtitlán:

> Then they kicked the bodies down the steps, and the Indian butchers who were waiting below cut off their arms and legs and flayed their faces, which they afterwards prepared like glove leather, with their beards on, and kept for their drunken festivals. Then they ate their flesh with a sauce of peppers and tomatoes.

Gruesome as these practices may seem, an ecological perspective and population pressure theory render the Aztec emphasis on human sacrifice understandable as a natural and rational response to the material conditions of their existence. In *Tristes Tropiques,* the French anthropologist Claude Levi-Strauss described the Aztecs as suffering from "a maniacal obsession with blood and torture." A materialist ecological approach reveals the Aztecs to be neither irrational nor mentally ill, but merely human beings who, faced with unusual survival problems, responded with unusual behavior.

7

Culture and Conquest

George Foster

I now wish to consider very briefly what happens to a conquest culture—that of Spain, of course—in a new world. Conquest culture represents but a small part of the totality of traits and complexities that comprise the donor culture. Then, through a second screening process in the geographical region of the recipient peoples, conquest culture is still further reduced, in the process of playing its role as a builder of colonial culture. Two distinct but related analytical approaches help us to understand this reduction process. The first deals with the social and psychological mechanisms whereby recipient peoples, in those situations in which they are allowed choice, exercise discretion in accepting and rejecting elements presented to them. The second deals with the time dimension, with the sequence in presentation of conquest culture. It suggests a concept, which may be called "cultural crystallization," illustrating how essentially nonso-

From George Foster, *Culture and Conquest: America's Spanish Heritage*. (Viking Fund Publications in Anthropology, Number 27). New York: Wenner-Gren Foundation for Anthropological Research, Incorporated, pp. 227–234, 1960. Used by permission of author.

cial and nonpsychological factors may be very significant in determining what the final stabilized forms of an acculturated society will be. These approaches, and the conclusions they lead to, are discussed in turn.

The operation of social and psychological mechanisms both produces and is governed by the structure of the contact situation. In relation to areas of high culture, and especially to Mexico, it is well to bear in mind that, although we tend to think only in terms of Indians acculturating to Spanish ways, there were, in fact, two recipient groups in process of change: Indian and Spanish. Every Spaniard in America represented some phase of the donor culture, and thereby helped carry conquest culture. At the same time each Spaniard was exposed not only to Indians, but also to other Spaniards, who often faced him with laws and regulations, and with less formal cultural items, many of which were very strange to him. That is, the Spaniard as well as the Indian was exposed to conquest culture. Both were faced with a similar problem of selection and adjustment. The Spaniard did not have to adjust to metal tools, domestic animals, the plow, and Christianity, but he did have to come to terms with a new sociopolitical and environmental situation and to other Spaniards and their customs as well as to the Indians.

The manner in which both Indian and Spaniard and their mestizo offspring were exposed to conquest culture was structured by the social setting, and particularly by the division of society into urban and rural components. This division, as it existed in pre-Conquest times, can be thought of in terms of the familiar folk-urban continuum with, to use Aguirre Beltrán's terminology, a "ceremonial center" pole representing the elite tradition and a "community culture" representing the peasant tradition.

In the very first years of the Conquest, acculturation must have been marked by much direct transmission from Spaniards to Indians all along this continuum, and from Spaniards to Spaniards. But as Spanish cities were founded and native cities were rebuilt, the picture changed. The native urban-elite authority structure was replaced by the Spanish equivalent so that, instead of a continuum both poles of which represented variants of a single culture, there now existed a continuum for which the authority pole was Spanish. After this modified continuum was established, and after the initial culturally mixed mestizo populations came into being, the acculturation process took the familiar pattern of flow of influence downward and outward, from the urban-elite pole to lower classes and peasant. Spanish, hispanicized, and partly hispanicized peoples all along this continuum therefore continued to be exposed to new Spanish influences as they were passed along from cities, and these peoples in turn became a point of diffusion of the items they accepted, to other populations less influenced by Spain.

The sociopsychological mechanisms whereby the peoples along this continuum screened conquest culture, accepting what they perceived to be desirable and within their reach and rejecting what they perceived to be undesirable and within their ability to refuse, can be best observed in relation to Indian culture reacting to conquest culture, since this offers the maximum contrast. Without attempting a thorough study of these mechanisms, the following observations may be made:

1. In the field of material culture and techniques, Spanish forms were welcomed when they were recognized by the Indians as useful, and when there were no indigenous counterparts or when indigenous counterparts were rudimentary. New crops, agricultural implements, and domestic animals were recognized by most Indian groups as useful. And since indigenous patterns of care of the few domestic animals known did not furnish a broad enough base on which radically to modify Spanish practices of animal husbandry, these are overwhelmingly predominant in America. Where agriculture with some other tool than the digging stick was feasible, the utility of Spanish methods, especially the plow and ox, was usually apparent; hence in much of America, Spanish agricultural techniques used in preparing the ground, sowing, and harvesting (e.g., broadcast sowing of grain and the division of fields into *melgas*) predominate. With respect to heavy transportation of the Spanish solid-wheeled oxcart, the *carro chirrión*, had no native competitor in America, and it was soon widely adopted. Indigenous metalworking techniques were so limited that they offered no serious competition to European methods.

Conversely, where there were satisfactory native counterparts, Spanish influence was much less marked. This is particularly apparent with respect to food, and in the practices and beliefs associated with the life cycle. Although religious, political, and social institutions were well developed in America, and therefore might be expected to have changed less rapidly than they did, the special manner in which they were singled out for formal attention by the conquerors caused the native institutions to disintegrate at a rapid rate.

2. Again, in the field of material culture and techniques, Spanish forms set the pattern when they were recognized by the Indians as obviously superior to, or representing a significant extension of their indigenous forms. The Moorish roof tile, the primitive Iberian potter's kiln, and the Spanish carpenter's simple tools were all widely (but by no means universally) adopted. The ubiquity of Spanish-type fishing devices certainly again reflects the fact that they were recognized by the Indians as preferable to their own types. At least some Spanish costume was better than existing Indian types: outside the area of the llama, wool cloth made possible by the introduction of sheep was an enormous boon to both sexes. The fulled bayeta skirt must have brought previously unknown comfort to Indian women, and woolen blankets blouses, and jackets must have been appreciated by all wearers in cold areas. The Spanish flat-bed loom, although by no means replacing the native back-strap loom, quickly

found its place, further contributing to more adequate clothing and a more comfortable bed. (It must be remembered that the patterns of Indian clothing in parts of Colonial America were also set by decree.) And the Old World crops of wheat, rye, barley, sugarcane, and many vegetables and fruits, as well as Spanish animals—sheep, cattle, horses, the chicken, burro, and pig—represent significant extensions of indigenous content.

3. In the field of folk culture, in a somewhat limited sense of the term, the process at work in the acceptance or rejection of Spanish elements by Indian cultures are less clear than in the two foregoing categories. We are dealing here with areas of culture not of primary concern to State and Church and with areas of culture in which obvious superiority either does not exist or cannot be easily recognized. This is an area in which chance, and perhaps the personality of unusual individuals, both Spanish and Indian, seems to have played a very important role. With respect to such things as dietary patterns, superstitions, folk medicine, folklore, and music, Spanish traits found themselves in competition with indigenous traits, and often with no clear advantage. Here individual motivation is an important factor, but at this distance in time it is difficult to work out these motivations. We can assume that the motivations that are important in contemporary culture change—prestige and curiosity, to name two—were equally important in sixteenth-century America, but it is difficult to link these general motivations to the introduction of specific traits. To the extent that it can be done, it must be done with historical techniques.

Now let us turn to the second of the two approaches—that involving a time dimension—which help in understanding what happens to conquest culture in the recipient area. This approach concerns the question of the geographical origin in Spain of Hispanic American traits and complexes. The problem is whether we can find Spanish foci or distribution areas for prototypes of such things as agricultural tools, transportation devices, fishing techniques, clothing forms, beliefs and practices associated with the life cycle, and popular religious observances. If we find such distribution areas, what implications do they hold for understanding the sequence of presentation of conquest culture to America? And what do they have to do with the concept of "cultural crystallization"?

Although peninsular distribution areas for Hispanic American prototypes have not been worked out in detail, certain broad patterns, which will shortly be pointed out, do exist. That is, Spanish culture in America does not represent an equal and balanced selection from all parts of the country; some areas of Spain are much more heavily represented than others. Why is this? A common explanation is based on the theory of what may be called "proportional representation." Since we know that cultures meet through their carriers, each individual—each emigrant of a donor culture—is a potential device for transmitting something of his local culture to the new region. Therefore, it might be expected that each geographical area of such a country as Spain would be represented culturally in America in proportion to its share of the total numbers of emigrants who left the peninsula. The apparent predominance of Andalusian and Extremaduran trains in America is therefore often "explained" by saying that "a majority of conquistadors and settlers came from these areas."

If we utilize the data presented to determine whether in fact the cultures of Andalusia and Extremadura are most heavily represented in America, we come to the conclusion that this popular belief is essentially correct. Minor modifications are needed: eastern Andalusia appears less important, and much of New Castile and the southerly parts of Old Castile and León must be included in the area of greatest influence. Here are samples of the data that lead one to this conclusion:

AGRICULTURE

In America the Andalusian and Extremaduran plow is found to the apparent exclusion of all other peninsular forms. The highly useful Castilian threshing sledge (tribulum) is unknown, while the absence of the modern Andalusian threshing cart (the ancient plostellum) can be explained on the basis of its nineteenth-century reintroduction into southern Spain, so that it was not available in earlier centuries for export to America. For drawing plows and carts the north-Spanish neck yoke is uncommon or absent in America, its place taken by the central-southern Spanish horn yoke.

FISHING

American net types and terminology, especially the various parts of the jábega-chinchorro seine, suggest the Andalusian coast rather than Galicia or Catalonia. I have no explanation, however, for the puzzling fact that the term "chinchorro" appears to be used in all Spanish America to the complete exclusion of the more common Spanish term "jábega," and the near exclusion of the term "boliche." Perhaps American net forms are drawn from a very limited area of Andalusia where the term "chinchorro" predominated. In view of the great variation in terminology applied to similar nets along Spanish coasts, this is certainly a possibility.

ARTS AND CRAFTS

Spanish American folk pottery techniques of peninsular origin appear to draw most heavily on Spanish forms found from Granada west, and then north to León, while American manufacture of finer ware, such as Talavera, is due to Sevillian and Toledan influence. With respect to the textile arts, the south-Spanish horizontal spinning wheel rather than the north-Spanish upright model is found in America. Spanish American folk costume suggests south Spain rather than north Spain; for example, the garments of peasant women from Old Castile north are surprisingly different from those of women in rural America. Some specific items, like the *tapada* of colonial Peru, quite obviously come from Andalusia. Salamancan jewelry, especially such things as articulated silver fish, appears to be ancestral to many Peruvian and Mexican forms.

SOCIAL PATTERNS

To the extent that a peninsular type of *compadrazgo* is ancestral to Hispanic American variants, it is Andalusian. Negatively, the absence in America of the widespread Old Castilian-Leonese institution of bachelors' societies, and of most of the popular wedding customs and forms of horseplay of north-central and northwest Spain, is significant.

FUNERARY PRACTICES

On the basis of available data the customs of Extremadura, Huelva, and parts of New Castile are particularly suggestive of America, although the *baile del angelito* points to the southeast. At the time of the Conquest, however, this custom may well have been much more widespread. Negatively, the north-Spanish funeral orgy appears not to have characterized America, nor have paid mourners been noted in the New World. Likewise, north-Spanish inheritance patterns seem to have had little influence in America, whereas south-Spanish forms have been important.

POPULAR RELIGIOUS PRACTICES

A number of widespread central and northern Spanish activities are little known or lacking entirely in America. Among these are the pig of St. Anthony, the Candlemas torte, the festivities of Santa Agueda and the married women's *cofradia* [sisterhood], and *la maya* [a May queen or any girl who takes part in festivities connected with the month]. The "burial of the sardine" [to mark the end of Carnival], general in central and northern Spain in earlier years, was absent in Andalusia, and very rare in America.

SPEECH

Although linguistic acculturation is an enormously complicated subject, which cannot be touched upon here, in a general way it seems that southern and western Spanish variants of Castilian were more important in America than central and northern forms.

This list deals primarily with cultural elements brought to America through informal channels. It is clear that the formally transmitted categories of culture, in which Church and State policy were predominant, are Castilian rather than Andalusian-Extremaduran. This is to be expected, for the obvious reason that Castile was the kingdom of the ruling house and of the administrators and churchmen most concerned with government.

If we therefore ignore these formally transmitted categories of culture, it looks as if we have a good case for the hypothesis of "proportional representation" as it is popularly expressed: a preponderance of southern and western influences, because of a preponderance of emigrants from these areas. But we know now that the old belief in the importance of settlers from Andalusia and Extremadura is not borne out by demographic data. Sufficiently large numbers of emigrants came from nearly all parts of the country, so that we might logically expect less Andalusian-Extremaduran influence and more from Old Castile, Asturias, Navarre, Aragón, León, and Galicia. What explanation can be advanced to explain the seeming anomaly of a disproportionately large total of cultural influences stemming from Andalusia-Extremadura as compared with the numbers of emigrants from these regions?

The answer appears to lie in the *sequence* of formation and presentation of conquest culture. It is probable that at any given time undirected conquest culture (i.e., that not controlled by Church and State) was made up of elements which reflected at least a rough correlation between subcultural areas and numbers of emigrants from these areas. This means that conquest culture was not formed overnight, to remain essentially static over a long period of time. Rather, it was fluid, changing over the years as the composition of its carriers changed. At any specific time it was given shape by the culture type of the most numerous groups of emigrants, at least as far as informally transmitted elements are concerned.

In its earliest manifestation, then, it must have represented the local culture of the first waves of conquistadors and settlers. And these people, we know, did come in significant numbers from Andalusia and Extremadura. While it is true that, if we consider the entire sixteenth century or even the first fifty years of widespread emigration, nearly all parts of Spain were represented in significant quantity, it is also true that during the first two or three decades the provinces of western Andalusia, Extremadura, New Castile, southern León, and southern Old Castile were particularly well represented. This is by no means a homogeneous culture area, but there are basic similarities which stem from the fact that its northern part had recolonized its southern part several centuries earlier.

Therefore, during the very first years of conquest and settlement in America, in its unplanned

aspects conquest culture represented south-west and west-central Spain rather than the north. This initial phase was relatively short, although I hesitate to set a time span. It was a highly fluid, formative period in America in which the basic answers to new conditions of life had to be found, and a rapid adaptation to changed, conditions on the part of both Indians and Spaniards was imperative. This was the period of the blocking out of colonial cultures. Quick decisions, individual and collective, conscious and unconscious, had to be made on innumerable points. And the information on which settlers had to draw, in making these decisions, was the knowledge that characterized their particular variants of Spanish culture.

The basic outlines of the new colonial cultures took shape at a rapid rate. Once they became comparatively well integrated and offered preliminary answers to the most pressing problems of settlers, their forms became more rigid: they may be said to have crystallized. After crystallization, and during a period of reasonably satisfactory adjustments to social and natural environments, the new Spanish American colonial cultures appear to have become more resistant to continuing Spanish influence. These stabilizing cultures were then less receptive to change and less prone to accept new elements from the parent culture which had been left behind or rejected in the initial movement.

When, then, increasing numbers of emigrants from more northerly areas reached the New World, they encountered a going concern to which they had to adapt themselves. The culture they brought with them, which would have been perfectly adequate in working out solutions to new problems in America, was now less important, simply because it came later in the time sequence.

The duration of the initial period of fluid cultural conditions and hospitality to Spanish forms is difficult to determine. It varied from place to place, depending on the date of effective conquest. On the mainland this initial period began and ended first in central Mexico, whereas in South America it came some years later. Writing about Yucatán, [France V.] Scholes says that the basic pattern of Hispano-Indian society

was clearly marked out by the end of the sixteenth century or about sixty years after the Conquest. By that time a new ruling caste of foreign origin, extremely jealous of its privileges, had obtained firm control over the destinies of the Maya race; . . . and a considerable amount of fusion of culture, especially in the realm of religion, had taken place. *During the remainder of the colonial period these basic problems of provincial society remained essentially the same.* [Italics mine, G. M. F.][1]

There is evidence for the validity of the concept of cultural crystallization from other sources. [Melville J.] Herskovits, faced with the problem of reconciling the fact that slaves were drawn from a wide African area but that major Negro influences in America apparently represent a relatively restricted area on the west coast, has come to similar conclusions. He believes the answer to his problem lies in the fact that "the slaves who came late to the New World had to accommodate themselves to patterns of Negro behavior established earlier on the basis of the customs of the tribes" that preceded them,[2] just as Spaniards who came to America after the earliest phases of conquest had to adjust to prevailing circumstances.

Pursuing this line of reasoning further, he suggests that in colonial United States the early Senegalese arrivals

were overshadowed by the traditions of the more numerous Guinea coast Negroes; while as for late-comers such as the Congo Negroes, the slaves they found were numerous enough, and well enough established, to have translated their modes of behavior . . . into community patterns.[3]

I believe that similar processes explain the apparent predominance of southern and western Spanish forms in America. In the very early years of the conquest of America, Andalusian and Extremaduran emigrants were numerically superior to those from all other areas, even though well before the end of the sixteenth century this pattern had shifted drastically. Moreover, to the extent that items of material culture were carried to America—plows and nets, for example—they would certainly be objects locally manufactured near the seaports which traded with the Indies. Poor internal transportation in Spain would preclude the hauling of Castilian plows and Navarense yokes to Sevilla, when perfectly adequate local models were available.

The early decades in America were decades of decision, a time when new adjustments and colonial cultures were roughed out and the basic outlines set. To the extent that Church and State did not take charge, the customs and ways of the earliest immigrants had the best chance of surviving, of finding niches in the new societies. Equally satisfactory competing forms, which came with more northerly immigrants only a few years later, would find the functions they fulfilled already taken care of, and their carriers, like the later African slaves in the United States, had to adjust to the forms already set. After the first several decades a comparative hardening of colonial cultures occurred which, for a significant period of time, made these cultures less receptive to new items and less tolerant in their appraisal of later Spanish cultural influence.

If the concept of cultural crystallization is valid, it is clear that the common anthropological emphasis on social and psychological phenomena to explain acceptance or rejection of new elements by a subordinate people can never fully explain what takes place in an acculturation situation. The time sequence of formation and presentation of conquest culture plays an equally important role in determining the final selection of imported traits by native and colonial cultures. The sociopsychological reasons for acceptance and rejection can never be fully understood until they are placed in the perspective of time sequence and until it is recognized that new hybrid and drastically altered native cultures must make rapid decisions and then abide by most of these decisions, if they are to endure.

NOTES

1. France V. Scholes, "The Beginnings of Hispano-Indian Society in Yucatán," *Scientific Monthly*, 44 (1937), 531.

2. Melville J. Herskovits, *The Myth of the Negro Past* (New York: Harper, 1941), p. 52.

3. Loc. cit.

8

Sons of the Shaking Earth

Eric Wolf

The Indian before the Conquest had been a cultivator, a seed-planter. The conquering Spaniard
became a mining entrepreneur, a producer of commercial crops, a rancher, a merchant. The strategic
economic relationship of the pre-Conquest period
united Indian peasant and Indian lord, tribute-pro-
ducer and tribute-consumer. The goal of the Indian
noble was to consume wealth commensurate with
his social position. The Spanish colonist, however,
labored for different ends. He wanted to convert
wealth and labor into salable goods—into gold and
silver, hides and wool, wheat and sugar cane. No
Spaniard could count himself wealthy as a mere
recipient of loads of maize, pieces of jade, or cacao
beans. Wealth to him meant wealth invested in
Spanish goods, capital multiplying miraculously
in the process of exchange. He had not braved the
hardships of the Indies merely to come into the
inheritance of his Indian predecessor; he wanted
to organize and press the human resources under
his command, to pay his debts, to enlarge his estate,

From Eric Wolf, *Sons of the Shaking Earth,* University of Chicago Press, pp. 176–256, 1959. Reprinted by
permission of the publisher.

to take his place among the other men grown rich
and powerful in the new utopia.

The motor of this capitalism was mining, carried on first in the footsteps of the Indians, later in
deep deposits discovered by Spanish prospectors.
The Indians had worked gold and silver before the
Conquest, but they had obtained these elements
from small placers or shallow pits where the ore-
bearing veins are close to the surface. Spanish
exploration for placer mines began very early. Even
before the fall of the Tenochtitlán, members of
Cortés' party had located placers in the headwaters of the Papaloapan and Balsas rivers; shortly
after the Conquest, other placers were found on the
Caribbean coast of Honduras. Such mining has
remained a feature of Middle American life to this
day. Cheap, requiring no outlay for mechanical
equipment beyond the large wooden bowl or *batea*,
it has always been open to the adventurous individual willing to stake his few worldly possessions
on the hope of gaining a sudden and overwhelming
fortune.

Such small-scale mining, however, was quickly
superseded as a major source of capital accumulation. Large and deep deposits of mineral wealth
were discovered in 1543, near Compostela, just

northwest of modern Guadalajara. In 1546, Zacatecas began to produce silver; in 1548, Guanajuato; in 1549, Taxco, Sultepec, and Temalscalzepec; in 1551, Pachuca; in 1555, Sombrerete and Durango; in 1569, Fresnillo. The year 1557 witnessed the introduction of the patio process in which silver is extracted from ore with the aid of mercury. This process, invented by the Mexican miner Bartolomé de Medina, revolutionized the mining industry. It permitted profitable exploitation of low-grade ores, where the older method of smelting required high-grade ores. So successful was this procedure that it was not replaced until the introduction of the cyanide process in the late nineteenth century. This new exploitation of deep mines was also immensely more expensive than the exploitation of placers. Capital was required to pay for the construction of stamp mills and refineries, for the sinking of shafts and timbering, for the purchase of mules, labor, food, and mercury, for drainage equipment and pumps. Where placer mining remained in the hands of single individuals, laboring to enter the utopia of wealth through a small door, deep mining produced the capitalist of whom Henrie Hawks, English merchant to New Spain, wrote in 1572 that they were "princes in keeping of their houses, and bountiful in all manner of things." By the end of the sixteenth century, most of the great mining districts of New Spain had been located, and the technology of large-scale capitalist mining was firmly established.

Mining enriched some men; others took to planting and selling agricultural crops. The Indians had raised maize and amaranth for their own consumption and for tribute; but in their new habitat the Spaniards, heirs of different food habits, longed for their native wheat, to turn into their accustomed bread. Using oxen and plow, on land taken over over from a pagan temple or from the patrimony of the shattered Mexica state, or uncultivated or purloined—together with the strategic water supply—from some Indian community, new entrepreneurs set out to meet this need for wheat by growing it for the rising cities and the mushrooming mining camps. By the end of the sixteenth century, wheat farms and mills to grind wheat had spread out along the new axis of trade and control linking Mexico City with Veracruz to the east and with Guadalajara to the west, and were fast spreading northward—beyond the con-

fines of pre-Conquest agriculture—to feed the newly opened mines along the arid periphery of Middle America.

In the lowlands, on the other hand, the main crop produced for sale was sugar cane. Cane-farming could be carried on by small-scale operators, using hand-powered or animal-powered mills to grind the cane, but as output rose, sugar-raising—like mining—fast became a large-scale capitalist form of enterprise. The strategic factor in this process was the high cost of a large-scale mill needed to grind the cane. Only a person or a group of persons possessed of considerable wealth could purchase one of these *ingenios* or "engines." In the course of the seventeenth century, the entrepreneurs capable of shouldering such costs proved to be mostly religious bodies, who had accumulated wealth through donations. The output of these large-scale mills, exported in the beginning, also gave rise to the pervading Middle American taste for sweets, immortalized in innumerable shapes and kinds of candy and other confections, and to a new beverage, *aguardiente* or firewater, distilled to a high potency in the novel stills, also imported for the first time by the new lords of the land.

Another product which demanded considerable capital outlay in production was indigo, a blue dye of great natural fastness. Just as deep mining, wheat-farming, and cane-farming, it was taken over entirely by colonist entrepreneurs. Indigo is obtained from the leaves of a shrublike plant (*Indigofera suffruticosa* Mill.), varieties of which are found both in the Old and New World. The pigment is found only in the leaves. Since the amount of pigment per leaf is small, the dye is expensive. The plants are cut, then steeped in water; the sludge formed is allowed to oxidate, then heated, cooled, filtered, and made into paste, cut into bars and finally into the so-called indigo cakes. The first indigo exported came from Guatemala, but it was soon raised elsewhere in the Middle American lowlands, especially in Yucatán. By the fourth quarter of the sixteenth century, more than fifty Spanish-owned indigo "factories" were in operation in the peninsula, each equipped with its mule-driven water pump, its vats and cauldrons. As in the case of sugar production and deep mining, the cost of the mill tended to render indigo production prohibitive to small operators and furthered the emergence of capitalist entrepreneurs in the field. Indigo dye remained a viable commercial product until the advent of aniline dyes in the mid-nineteenth century.

The Spaniards thus reserved to themselves the production, processing, and distribution of all products which required high outlays of capital in processing machinery. They did, however, entrust to the Indians all raising of commercial products which did not require much capital and equipment to produce and process, retaining for themselves the handsome profits of their distribution. Such products were cotton, silk, cacao, and cochineal dye. Cotton production remained largely in Indian hands and was grown along the Pacific and Atlantic coasts of the southern highlands; Spaniards reaped the rewards of its distribution. Cotton-growing was soon supplemented by silk-raising, first upon a mulberry native to Middle America, later upon black mulberries imported from the Old World. The valley of Puebla and the southern highlands benefits especially from this new pursuit; for half a century the Mixtec-speaking highlands became the center of silk production in the New World. Many Indians grew rich in the process, though the major profits went to the Spaniards, who monopolized the spinning and weaving of the new thread. But silk-raising had only a relatively brief period of efflorescence; it was sacrificed to Chinese competition toward the end of the sixteenth century.

Cacao had served the Indians not merely as a beverage but as money, and for some time after the Conquest the cacao bean continued to serve as a ready medium of exchange. Most cacao production remained in Indian hands, with the Spaniards again playing the role of middlemen and distributors. The colonists themselves began to fancy the Indian drink *chocolatl*, prepared from the cacao bean, and soon introduced this new exotic taste into Europe. The Indians also remained the primary producers of cochineal. Cochineal is a source of red dyes produced from insects (*Coccus cacti*) which feed on a cactus (*Cactus nopalea cochinellifera*). About 70,000 dried insects produced one pound of dye. The Indians collected the insects, extracted the dye, and delivered the product to the Spanish entrepreneurs who mediated the trade with Spain. For a long time, New Spain remained the only producer of cochineal. The Spanish government guarded its monopoly jealously; and for the better part of two centuries Europeans remained ignorant of how the dye was produced. Only in the late eighteenth century were the dye-producing insects brought to Spain.

True to their Peninsular tradition, the Spaniards also took up stock-raising: cattle primarily for their hides and tallow, sheep largely for their wool. Leather was then in high demand both in Europe and in New Spain. Leather containers and cables were needed in mines and factories and leather constituted one of the chief requirements of the expanding armies of the day. Wool, on the other hand, was everywhere beginning to replace homespun linen. The Spaniards brought with them two kinds of cattle, the broad and heavy-horned dun type of general European affiliation and the black Iberians, ancestors of the Spanish fighting bull. In sheep they favored the *rasa*, which yields both wool and meat, and the *merino*, which yields fine wool but poor meat, over the hardy *churro*, which yields milk but poor wool. Introduced into an entirely new environment, unaffected by past grazing, the new herds began to multiply at an astonishing rate. Like a flood, they inundated cultivated fields and uncultivated range alike, causing severe dislocations in many settled zones of the central highland, until the crown succeeded in diverting the flood to peripheral areas, the arid north country and the lowlands of the Atlantic and Pacific coastlines. To herd the growing livestock, the Spaniards used their horse, bred to great hardihood from Barb or North African strains crossed with dun and striped indigenous Iberians. Often allowed to roam until needed, these horses formed near-wild herds. Such horses were called *mesteños*, which in the mouths of Anglo-American cowboys was to become "mustang."

Indian nobles and Indian communities quickly adopted the raising of sheep and cattle, but stock-raising as a large-scale enterprise remained in Spanish hands, partly because of laws through which the Spaniards barred Indians from owning horses and retained a monopoly of this means of transportation and warfare for themselves, partly because the Indians were unable to finance expansion into the new grazing lands beyond the old agricultural frontier. Indian stock raising remained confined to an occasional village herd and to chickens, pigs, mules, and donkeys—the minor domesticated animals introduced by the conquerors. Mediterranean breeds of chickens—Andalusians, Minorcas, Leghorns, and others—came to form an important part of

Indian household economy, along with the indigenous turkey. The pigs, driven in droves in the train of advancing Spanish armies to provide them with readily available food, were descendants of razor-backed Spanish breeds. Pork and lard quickly became staple ingredients of Middle American cooking. The donkey, derived from Andalusian breeds, grew smaller and sturdier in adapting to the Middle American environment, and together with the mule became an indispensable source of motor power in mines and mills and on the highroads. Transportation on mule-back gave rise to a whole social group of mule-skinners, or mule-drivers, who traveled from market to market, from city to city, from hostelry to hostelry, linking the country in a great network of back-country trails. Still today, the ancient craft survives in out-of-the-way places such as the Tarascan-speaking uplands of Michoacán or the eastern escarpment, where no other form of transportation provides an adequate alternative.

Together with horses, oxen, mules, and donkeys, came the wheel, long known in the Old World but unknown—or rather not utilized—in the New. The Spaniards brought with them their traditional oxcart, put together with wooden pegs and mounted upon spokeless wheels. That the Indians were acquainted with the basic principle of the wheel is clear from finds of fascinating prehistoric toys, mounted upon rollers, from coastal Veracruz. The principle had never been applied, however, to the construction of wheelbarrows or carts to ease men's burdens, or to the mass production of pottery, or to the transmission of wind and water power. Even today there are many Indian villages where the wheel remains an alien artifact and where men rely on their traditional bodily skills to balance heavy burdens upon their backs with the aid of the tumpline, a leather strap laid across the bowed head.

The newly settled towns of the realm also constituted markets for the products of Spanish craftsmen who brought not only their inherited skills but also their traditional technique of organizing craftsmen into guilds. A guild was an association of specialists who alone possessed the right to exercise a given craft; such guilds also protected members against unfair competition from fellow professionals. Detailed statutes regulated the tools and techniques to be used, the number of workers to be employed, and the salaries to be paid. Advertising was prohibited throughout New Spain. Where the craftsmen themselves did not set up such bodies, the municipality in which they resided organized them on its own initiative, with royal sanction. As in the Old World, the guilds soon competed fiercely with one another for the lesser stakes of prestige and privilege, with the merchant guild (*Consulado*) occupying top rank in status and power.

This new organization of production and distribution soon came into conflict with two opposing forces. The organization of the guild and its regulation of production was geared to an essentially static level of consumption. Strongly monopolistic, it abhorred unregulated competition by outsiders and insiders; in fact, it frowned upon all cumulative capitalist activity. Very soon, therefore, it found itself combating capitalist tendencies, especially in the weaving trades. As Spanish craftsmen settled in the accustomed grooves of life, other Spaniards organized industrial establishments, *obrajes*, for the production of wool and cotton textiles. The basic equipment of these establishments was all of Spanish origin: spinning wheel, reel, cards—the wooden paddles set with iron spikes to clean wool—the horizontal loom with pedals to manipulate the sheds. Some capital was needed also to set up the water-driven machinery (*batán*) for soaking woolens in alkaline solution and for beating them until the fibers were felted together to create a uniform surface. The water powering these fulling mills was more often than not obtained from streams which had previously irrigated Indian fields. To obtain the necessary labor force, the *obrajes* frequently made use of forced labor. Workers were prisoners condemned to work off a sentence or a debt, or simply men held against their will. They included not only Indians but also Negroes from Africa and Oriental slaves imported from the Philippines. The crown attempted to regulate these prison-like establishments and to improve working conditions, but they continued to flourish in the shadow of the law and of guild regulations, building their profits upon the outright exploitation of non-guild labor. Conditions in these prison-like mills did not change until the advent of the first steam-driven machinery in the mid-nineteenth century.

Just as the guilds could not prevent such capitalist competition on the part of their fellow Spaniards, so they also had great difficulty in maintaining their monopoly of skill against the free

Indian artisans. All the guilds' codes carried restrictive regulations, prohibiting the access to their professions of Indians or the descendants of Indian-Spanish or Negro-Spanish unions. Yet the Indians proved excellent imitators who learned the skills of the conquerors in an astonishingly short period of time. Within the confines of the cities, the guilds could perhaps maintain their restrictive covenants. But in the countryside an Indian craftsman applied his newly won knowledge to the traditional Indian crafts, especially to pottery and the manufacture of textiles.

These Spanish enterprises—mining, agriculture, stock-raising, manufacture—inevitably changed the face of the land and the relation of men to the land they inhabited. Before the Spanish Conquest, Middle America had been landlocked; what shipping there was, was confined to the coast. The Spanish Conquest bridged the oceans and linked New Spain to the Old World through the twin ports of Veracruz on the east coast and Acapulco on the west coast. Veracruz connected New Spain with Cádiz, along the most direct line of Atlantic travel; Acapulco connected the colony with Manila, over a sea route discovered in 1564–65, which was to be used without alteration for three centuries. The connection through Veracruz remained primary; it was the umbilical cord connecting the colony to the mother country.

Under the new order, Middle America was no longer allowed to follow out the logic of its past development. Now part of an empire upon which the sun never set, it was subject to the dictates of an imperial reason of state which transcended local decisions arrived at for local reasons. New Spain, like other parts of the Spanish Empire, was to be a valuable source of raw materials for the homeland, not a primary producer in its own right. Each year a fleet would carry Spanish goods to the Indies and return laden with the produce and precious metals of the colony. Spain would export iron, mercury—essential to mining operations overseas—arms, paper, fine cloth, books, wine, olive oil, and soap and receive in turn silver and gold, sugar and cacao, cochineal and indigo, leather and tallow—the varied products of commercial enterprise overseas.

There was to be no free trade; the crown regarded the link with the Indies as the power cable of its imperial system and shielded it from outside interference by force of arms and minute bureaucratic regulation. Men and goods traveling to and from the Indies could embark only at certain privileged ports. A corps of royal officials, organized in the Casa de Contratación, guarded the Spanish terminus of this imperial lifeline at Cádiz and Seville. A body of privileged merchants with judicial powers over trade, the Consulado, stood watch over the Middle American terminus at Veracruz. The entire commercial rhythm of the colony was geared to the recurrent departures and arrivals of the transatlantic fleet at the east coast port. Goods piled up on the wharves in expectation of the fleet's arrival, and merchants from all over New Spain gathered at the annual fair at Jalapa near Veracruz to receive the staples of their trade for redistribution in the colony. On the goings and comings of these merchants, on their calculations and manipulations, all the commercial enterprises of the colony depended. For it was through their mediation that the colonists acquired the goods which they deemed the proper symbols of their newly won status as lords of the land, and it was through their hands that the commercial products of the land flowed on to their destination in Spain and yielded the purchasing power required to buy the trappings of power and wealth. Similarly, once a year—to the sound of church bells imploring God's favor—the merchants of Mexico City would descend to Acapulco to await the coming of the Manila galleon, to receive from it the riches of China and to load it for the return trip with New Spanish wares.

Just as the economy of New Spain was thus geared to the requirements of the mother country, so it was circumscribed by royal regulation, to fit it as one component part into the larger empire. The crown frowned on the production of goods in the colony which could compete with products of the mother country. The production of olive oil, wine, silken goods, and textiles was therefore forbidden or inhibited. Single colonies might receive exclusive rights to the production of certain other crops; but these rights were frequently reallocated to the detriment of established plantings. Thus in the course of the century, cacao production in New Spain was halted and transferred to Venezuela, to underwrite the economic development of Caracas. This was done in spite of the fact that Middle America was the homeland of cacao and that no cacao had been grown previously along the southern Caribbean littoral. From then on, New Spain had to export silver, flour, sacking, tableware, and copper goods to acquire Venezuelan cacao. At various times, tobacco-growing in New Spain was sacrificed to promote tobacco-growing in Cuba or Louisiana. At intervals New Spanish silver and wheat flour were commandeered to supply the Antilles, where their arrival was celebrated with the joyful ringing of bells and the sound of fifes. New Spain thus took its place in a planned economy in which its economic decisions were subject to revision and censorship by a superior authority thousands of miles away.

Royal command and supervision ordered not only the relations of New Spain to Spain and New Spain to the other Spanish colonies; it also regulated the relation between conquerors and Indians, especially in the economic realm, between the entrepreneurs-to-be and their laborers. To obtain labor for their enterprises, the colonists at first had recourse to two institutions: the institution of slavery and the institution of *encomienda* or trusteeship. The Spaniards were familiar with slavery as an institution; they had but recently sold into slavery the entire population of the Canary Islands. It seemed natural to them, therefore, to brand and sell as slaves Indians captured in war or received in tribute or condemned to expiate some crime, often enough some infraction of an ill-understood new Spanish law. The Middle American Indians had known a kind of limited slavery in which slaves had been permitted to own property, call some of their time their own, and in which the children of slaves were free. They were confronted now with a new, unlimited slavery in which a human being was treated as a mere commodity, to be sold to mines, sugar mills, and farms, and to be used as an expendable resource.

To receive Indians in *encomienda*, on the other hand, meant that the *encomendero* or trustee received rights to tribute payments and unrestricted personal services from a stipulated number of Indians living in stipulated Indian villages. The institution had prototypes in Castile and perhaps in the *iktá* of Islam, as well as in the perquisites of the Indians chiefs before the Conquest. Yet, in the eyes of the colonist, it was not its medieval provenience which lent merit to the institution; it was rather the opportunity it provided for the organization of a capitalist labor force over which he alone would exercise untrammeled sway.

For this reason, both slavery and trusteeship met with royal opposition, for both threatened to raise in the New World the specter of feudalism so recently laid in the Old. The crown, wishing to stand above all men, could not countenance any social arrangement which permitted the re-emergence of power figures who held in their hands combined economic, military, judicial, and social power. In royalist eyes, as Silvio Zavala has said, the nobleman no longer represented a pillar of society, but a source of discord and rebellion. To guard against the rise of combinations of power that could rival the authority of the crown, the king divorced the right to receive Indian tribute from the control of Indian labor. If Indian labor made the wheels turn in this New Spain, then whoever was lord and master of Indians would also be lord and master of the land. With unlimited access to Indian energy, the colonists would soon have no need of Spain or king; hence the crown had to limit this access, supervise it, curtail it. The Indians were thus declared to be direct vassals of the crown, like the colonists themselves. This did not mean that the Indians were to be free to act as they liked, to pursue goals freely chosen with means freely decided upon. It did mean that no private person could lay hands on Indians without prior license from the crown. The Indians were to be royal wards; crown officers would be their tutors upon the road to civilization. These officers would see to it that no Indian remained idle, with satanic thoughts to plague his unoccupied mind. They would work, but they would perform their labor under the watchful eye of royal officers informed of the proper legal prescriptions applying to the particular case.

First, the king abolished all involuntary servitude imposed on individual Indians by individual masters. From 1530 on, Indian slavery was increasingly curtailed; in 1561 the Audiencia of Mexico heard the last cases of slaves to be set free. Only along the northern periphery of New Spain, where Spaniards encountered mobile nomad tribesmen, was slavery maintained as a weapon in the subjugation and pacification of the frontier.

Second, after 1549, the institution of trusteeship no longer included the right to Indian labor. The trustee was to be merely a passive recipient of tribute payments from a given number of Indian villages, but with this tribute—set by royal officials and supervised by the crown—went neither the right to live near his Indians nor to use their labor nor to sit in judgment over them. The trust carried no rights over land. If the crown so desired, it could—and did—allocate land pertaining to one man's Indian villages to another person who applied for a grant of land. Moreover, the grant of tribute was personal and temporary; it applied to the colonist so honored and his son. After the first filial generation, the grant reverted to the king, and the descendants of the original recipient had no claim upon it.

Third, after the middle of the sixteenth century, the crown turned increasingly to a system of compulsory regulated labor, mediated through royal labor exchanges, to fill applications for labor on the part of individuals. In one form or another, this system of regulated labor or *cuatequil* persisted up to the end of the eighteenth century. It bound the employer of Indian labor to pay his workers a standard wage. Labor was to be periodic rather than continuous, allowing workers to return to their native villages after working a stipulated period of time. No more than 4 percent of the laborers of any community were to be away on outside labor during any given period, nor were they to be taken long distances from their homes. If a trustee wanted Indian labor, he had to hire it from a royal labor exchange at the same price as other men competing for the same precious labor-producing commodity, and no trustee could interfere if a royal officer wished to assign Indians from his tributary villages to the enterprises of another.

The Spanish Conquest was not confined to the Middle America of the cultivators. The conquerors quickly pushed beyond the frontier of agriculture to the north, thus upsetting the balance of core area and periphery which had come to characterize Middle America under Mexica rule. From their capital in the valley of Mexico, the Mexica conquerors had poured eastward, southeastward, and southward. To the west, their expansion had been halted by the redoubtable Tarascans, ensconced in their pine-covered uplands. To the north lay the arid Chichimeca, abandoned to bands of roving food collectors since the collapse of the Toltec power. The Spaniards lost no time in consolidating their grip upon the Mexica possessions. They, too, built their capital in the valley, upon the ruins of the shattered Tenochtitlán. But the main force behind their conquest was the lust for gold and silver, and the main thrust of their expansion took them westward and northward, into the thirsty tableland. The main axis of their push followed the eastern foothills of the western escarpment. Like steppingstones into the great unknown, mining camps and settlements began to reach out toward the north. And where there were mines, there also grew up stock ranches and grain farms: stock ranches to provide the mules and donkeys for the mines, and to produce meat for the miners, hides for sacking and ore-sieves, rawhide for thongs and cables, tallow for candles; grain farms to raise wheat and maize. Mining, stock-raising, and grain-farming all entered the north country together and laid the foundations of Spanish enterprise in the area. By 1590, the great corridor to New Mexico was in Spanish hands.

The new possessions, however, presented a sharp contrast to the Middle America of the civilized seed-planters. The hold of the pre-Conquest urban cultures on this land had always been tenuous. The lack of water in this hot and dry tableland inhibited the growth of a dense population, the rise of cities or towns. At the time of the Conquest only small islands of cultivators survived in the area, surrounded on all sides by hunters and gatherers.

Armed with bows and arrows and stone knives, these nomad warriors were the first obstacle to permanent Spanish colonization. Launching their attacks at first on foot, they were soon riding stolen Spanish horses and raiding their enemies on horseback, often under leaders familiar with Spanish ways from earlier captivity or from childhood training among the missionaries. By the last quarter of the sixteenth century, the horse-riding Indian of the plains had made his appearance, not to be fully subjugated until the last part of the nineteenth century. Like their later North American cousins, these early raiders also scalped and tortured their captives. Traveling in small bands, they ambushed Spanish parties and raided settlements, only to vanish again into the arid steppe before the cumbersome Spanish soldiery could catch up with them.

To deal with such a mobile and scattered enemy, maneuvering against the backdrop of large open spaces, the colonists developed new techniques, many of which anticipated similar methods to be employed two and a half centuries later on the expanding United States frontier. The newly invented covered wagon came increasingly into its own after 1550. The soldiery adopted light leather armor and organized itself into flying detachments for purposes of patrols and escort. The fort or *presidio* made its appearance, alongside the mission. In addition to the use of such new methods in warfare, the Spaniards established colonies of armed Indian peasants from the urban area as strategic outposts in the hostile countryside. Tlaxcaltec colonists were established in several such settlements throughout San Luis Potosí.

The nomads presented not only a military obstacle to colonization. They also affected the nature of the labor supply in the new northern provinces. Food collectors do not lend themselves to easy pacification. When Chichimec prisoners were enslaved and put to work in the mines or on ranches and farms, they sickened and died. Nor was their number sufficient to cover the labor requirements of the new northern enterprises. Negro slaves were introduced in considerable numbers, but their high cost tended to discourage the growth of an African labor force. More important, in the long run, than either Chichimec or Negro slaves were free laborers, both Indian and Spanish, who came to live on the northern frontier of their own will and were willing to work for wages or perquisites rendered in kind. Most of them were Indians from the urban belt to the south who were attempting to escape either the burdens of tribute payment or personal services to the new conquerors, or were trying to escape the tribulations of personal and communal disorganization in the area to the south. Some were poor Spaniards, whose deeds had gone unrecognized in the distribution of rewards after the Conquest and who sought employment and adventure in the north country after the aegis of a more powerful protector. All, however, were individuals who found little to recommend in the settled and stable existence of the southern heartland; they belonged to the typically mobile men attracted by any frontier. The North would organize its communities by drawing together such individuals in associations of common self-interest. In contrast, the South would always rely upon the Indians, old upon the land long before the Conquest. The frontiersmen would lose their separate cultural heritages in the common experience of the frontier. In the South, the Indian would persist, increasingly unwilling to forego the security of living in communities of men of his own cultural kind. In the North, as later on the

frontier of the United States, the only good Indian would be a dead Indian.

The costs of exploration, warfare, imported labor, and settlement in areas so far removed from the centers of supply to the south could not be sustained by the average colonist. The northward expansion was the work of great capitalists, grown rich in mining, stock-raising, and commercial agriculture, not of subsistence farmers, patiently staking a claim for themselves and for their families, as on the later western frontier of North America. When mining output and revenues declined at the end of the sixteenth century, the advance was maintained by stock-breeders, looking for new pastures to feed their enormous herds. Stock-breeding, not cultivation, thus provided the "cutting edge" of the northward Spanish advance. Here and there communities of Spanish farmers reached into New Mexico, Arizona, or California to found irrigated oases settlements. But they remained isolated islands in a wide-open stock-breeding countryside, just as before the Conquest settlements of cultivators had constituted islands in a sea of hunters and gatherers.

By the end of the sixteenth century, the ranching frontier extended from Culiacán in the west to Monterrey in the east. As distance increased, however, between the traditional core area of New Spain—with its bases of supply—and the far-distant outposts to the north, the military threat presented by the armed nomads grew correspondingly. At the same time, further advance in strength into the north also encountered environmental barriers. Just as the Great Plains held up United States expansion until the nineteenth century, so they impeded expansion from the south. Not until the advent of a new technology, equipped with iron plowshare, barbed-wire fence, windmill, six-shooter, and repeating rifle, did the conquest of the Plains become a profitable undertaking. And this conquest was undertaken not by the Spaniards from the south but by the United States from the east. Important as the northern periphery thus became to New Spain, its northernmost edges remained shadowy and ill-defined and ultimately prey to annexation by an expanding and rapacious power from the north.

It is one of the ironies of the Spanish Conquest that the enterprise and expansion of the colonist produced not utopia but collapse. Like Tantalus reaching in vain for the fruit that would still his hunger and thirst, the conqueror extended his hand for the fruits of victory, only to find that they turned to ashes at the touch of his fingers.

All the claims to utopia—economic, religious, and political—rested ultimately upon the management and control of but one resource: the indigenous population of the colony. The conquerors wanted Indian labor, the crown Indian subjects, the friars Indian souls. The Conquest was to initiate utopia; instead, it produced a biological catastrophe. Between 1519 and 1650, six-sevenths of the Indian population of Middle America was wiped out; only a seventh remained to turn the wheels of paradise. Like the baroque altars soon to arise in the colony, the splendor and wealth of the new possessions but covered a grinning skull.

Pleaders of special causes ascribed the decimation of the Indian population to Spanish cruelty, but the Spaniards were neither more nor less cruel than other conquerors, past or present. Faced with a large and pliable native population, they perhaps grew accustomed too quickly to the lavish use of Indian services. Yet even the most senseless mismanagement of human resources cannot alone account for such hideous decimation. The chief factor in this disaster appears to have been not conscious maltreatment of the Indian but the introduction of new diseases to which the Indians were not immune. Every population is a feeding ground for micro-organisms that labor to reduce living organic substance to inorganic matter. Most populations sooner or later strike a balance in this battle against biological disintegration; they pay the price of temporary disease and death for the acquisition of more permanent immunities and fight the disease organism to a standstill along new battle lines.

Such a spread of micro-organisms and resultant immunities had gone on within both hemispheres since they were first settled by man. Up to the time of the Spanish Conquest, however, the Pacific and the Atlantic had acted as barriers against their universal extension. The disease organisms of the Old World were not those of the New, nor the immunities of the New World population those of the Old. Disease and death were thus presented with new victims. From the New World, the Spaniards returned to Europe with but one major disease—syphilis—which in its passage through the new hosts developed a virulence unknown in pre-Conquest America. But in the Indian population of the New World, the disease organisms of the Old World encountered a vast undefended pasture ground. The Spaniards introduced smallpox, which struck in virulent epidemics in 1520, 1531, and 1545; typhoid fever, which brought on epidemics in 1545, 1576, 1735, and twenty-nine times thereafter during the period of Spanish rule; measles, which exploded in a great epidemic in 1595; and—imported apparently in the hold of slave ships from Africa—malaria and yellow fever, the twin scourges of the American tropical lowlands. The Indian population possessed no antibodies against these plagues; they spread without obstruction.

Yet we must remember that such epidemics were not peculiar to the New World in this age; they were common everywhere in the Old World. Indeed, the sixteenth century seems to have been a period of open warfare between men and micro-organisms. During this time Europe experienced more disastrous epidemics than in any other century of modern history. Typhus, pox, sweating disease (1529), bubonic plague (1552–64), and influenza (1580–92) sent multitudes to their common graves. The rich art of the baroque decorated not only the insides of churches but also the "plague columns" whose agonized figures writhing in the grip of disease are still a feature of many a European market square. The Spanish conquerors noted that many Indians died; but death by epidemic disease must have been a rather more familiar sight to them than it would be to the modern observer.

Biological disaster was intensified by economic factors. It appears that at the time of the Conquest population in Middle America had begun to outgrow the available food supply. There were several severe famines in the valley of Mexico in the course of the fifteenth century and the prevalence of human sacrifice would seem to indicate that Indian society had begun to produce more people than it could integrate into its everyday life. The introduction of new economic purposes into such a tenuously poised situation easily tilted the balance against human survival. For the Spanish Conquest did not merely add the conquerors to the number of people already living upon the land. As we have seen, it also altered significantly the relationship between man and his environment. Spanish economy, indeed western European economy in general, was inimical to men upon the land. While Indian cultivation made some intensive use of land, the Spaniards used land extensively. While Indian economy massed labor in cultivation, the Spaniards massed animals and tools.

The Indians had possessed no large domesticated animals; the Spaniards let loose upon New Spain a flood of cattle and sheep. Encountering a grazing range rich in its original vegetative cover or fed with the nutriments of cultivated fields, the Spanish herds multiplied rapidly. Following suit, Indian communities and Indian nobles also filled agricultural land with livestock. Only some of this land was land cultivated by the Indian population; a great deal of new range had probably never been under cultivation. But even a small amount of land withdrawn from agriculture had a considerable effect on the distribution of the Indian population. Livestock-keeping implies a notably more extensive use of land than cultivation, which can support many more people per unit of land than pasture range. Nor did livestock-keeping affect only land in actual cultivation. In many cases, it engulfed land which the Indians did not farm during any given year but which constituted the indispensable reserve in their system of field-to-forest rotation. Occupation of this reserve imperiled the continued productivity of the field left in Indian hands and thus also the Indian population which lived off that land. Sheep produced wool, cattle produced hides; both produced meat. These products could be sold for good money; yet the wealth so obtained was won at the expense of hungry mouths. "Sheep eat men," went the saying when livestock-raising replaced farming in seventeenth- and eighteenth-century England. Sheep also ate men in Middle America.

Where the Indians had farmed land with a dibble, the Spaniards introduced a light plow drawn by oxen and capable of making shallow furrows and conserving moisture in the soil. With this new instrument, men were probably able to farm land which they had not farmed before: the plow with a metal tip is a much better tool for loosening deep sod and breaking up the tangle of roots and rhizomes than the hoe. Undoubtedly, therefore, the conquerors took under cultivation land which the Indian had not utilized and thus added to the total stock of land available for food production. But in

its net effect, the plow also upset the balance of Indian life upon the land. The plow is efficient only where land is plentiful but labor is scarce. Plow agriculture does not produce as much as hoe cultivation on any given unit of land: in modern Tepoztlán, men achieve twice the yield with hoe cultivation as with plow agriculture. Also, plow agriculture means that oxen must be fed, and some land must be devoted to their care. What the plow accomplishes is a saving in labor; the plow performs the work of the hoe cultivator in a third of the time. But it was not labor that was scarce in pre-Conquest Middle America. On the other hand, every unit of land withdrawn from Indian agriculture meant a halving of the food supply produced on that land, and thus a halving also of the population dependent on that food supply. And when that land was planted to wheat to feed the Spanish conquerors rather than the Indian inhabitants of the land, the growing imbalance between man and land was intensified.

Finally, the Spaniards also laid hands on the scarcest and most strategic resource of Middle American ecology: water. They needed water to irrigate their newly plowed fields, to water their stock, to drive the mills that ground their wheat into flour and the mills that fulled their woolens. Sons of a dry land themselves, they were master builders of aqueducts and wells; but all too often they appropriated the canals of the native population and impounded the streams behind their own dams. In a country in which a large percentage of the population had depended for their food supply on intensive cultivation made possible by irrigation, this wrecked a pattern of life precariously balanced between sufficiency and starvation. In a population ravaged by disease, such loss of land and water must have had a snowballing effect; it condemned a large percentage of the population to obsolescence and decay.

But the Conquest not only destroyed people physically; it also rent asunder the accustomed fabric of their lives and the pattern of motives that animated that life. Pre-Hispanic society and the new society established by the Conquest both rested on the exploitation of man by man; but they differed both in the means of their exploitation and in the ends to which it was directed. Under the Mexica, a peasantry had labored to maintain a ruling class with the surpluses derived from the intensive cultivation of its fields. But these rulers, in turn, were the armed knights of the sun who labored through sacrifice and warfare to maintain the balance of the universe. In the face of divergent interests, such a society possessed both a common transcendental purpose—to keep the sun in its heaven—and a common ritual idiom for the articulation of this purpose. The society produced by the Sapnish Conquest, however, lacked both a common purpose and a common idiom in which such a purpose could be made manifest. It not only replaced intensive seed-planting with extensive pursuits; it also sacrificed men to the production of objects intended to serve no end beyond the maximization of profit and glory of the individual conqueror. Moreover, each group of conquerors—ecclesiastic, official, colonist—pursued a separate and divergent utopia.

Laboring in alien field or mine or mill, bewildered by the conflicting demands upon his loyalty, the exploited Indian could perceive no universal meaning in his suffering. It was not exploitation as such that was new; it was rather that men found no sense of participation in the process to which they offered up their lives. Only the religious forms of the conquerors drew Indian loyalty; around these forms the Indians finally rebuilt their impaired morale. Yet Christianity did not bring salvation for all. Like Carlos Moctezuma, the Indian ruler of Texcoco, executed by the Inquisition for his stiff-necked adherence to the old gods, many Indians could not make the transition from a religion which assuaged fear and guilt through repeated human sacrifice to a view of the world in which salvation was to be assured through the single and unique sacrifice of Christ. Such men, orphaned by the old gods yet unsaved by the new, despaired of the world in which they had to live out their lives.

Many Spaniards, especially the friars, labored valiantly to aid and comfort the Indian sick. Yet it is likely that some of their own cultural practices, introduced into this new cultural medium, proved directly lethal rather than beneficial. The Spanish insistence, for example, that the Indians be concentrated in towns where they could receive the direct benefits of royal law and Christian religion accentuated rather than abated the danger of infection. The friars' battle against the Indian sweat bath, the *temazcalli*, also played a part. Indian use of the sweat bath was a religious rite of purification, carried out under the auspices of the earth goddess.

The friars, however, associated bathing with the paganism of the ancient Mediterranean and with the Islamic enemy whom they had just extirpated in southern Spain. They condemned the Indian sweat bath out of religious conviction and in so doing removed still another defense against attacks of germ-borne disease and death.

Yet the labor of these sick and dying Indians was to have made the wheels go round in the new utopia. Without Indian labor, there could be neither silver nor crops for the market. The mines were especially hard hit, for by 1580 they had run out of rich surface deposits. They had begun to work the less accessible ores which required ever new increments of labor. Yields declined steadily from 1600 on. Not until 1690 did mining output again attain the 1560 level. Food supplies underwent a parallel decline. From 1579 to 1700, the colonists found it difficult to obtain adequate food deliveries to towns and mines, except in an occasional bumper year. Spanish cities had to initiate mandatory deliveries from the surrounding countryside and set up public granaries to stockpile grain for resale at fixed prices during lean years. Silk production suffered and declined, as the labor needed during the peak harvesting periods also declined. By 1600 the industry was moribund. Cacao production witnessed a similar fate, as disease and death took toll of the hands required to harvest and process the bean. The decline in mining in turn affected stock-raising, which had counted upon the mines as one of the chief outlets for its multiple by-products. The country faced an emergency; increasingly it abandoned large-scale commercial enterprises in favor of restricted exchange, coupled with production for subsistence purposes. The bubble of unlimited expansion had burst, together with the utopian dream of wealth unlimited

About 1600, too, the mother country began to suffer the unforeseen consequences of its overseas expansion. Its industry swamped by the gold and silver of the New World, inflation ran rampant, raising prices for Spanish goods at the very same time that purchasing power in the colonies declined toward the vanishing point. Nor could the mother country absorb the wool, hides, and dyes which the colony was still able to supply. Spain and New Spain, linked together by an umbilical cord from which both were to take rich nourishment, found themselves trapped in common misfortune.

Had Spain sustained the cumulative development of the sixteenth century, Middle America might well have achieved a new and vital synthesis. But the depression of the seventeenth century put an end to utopian dreaming; the bankrupt dream passed into receivership. As in past periods of social and political catabolism, Middle America again retreated into its countryside. The wider galaxies dissolved once more into their component solar systems to allow for reintegration on more parochial levels.

In the course of this retreat there emerged two new patterns for such integration: the *hacienda*, the privately owned landed estate of the colonist, and the tightly knit community of the Indian peasantry, the *república de indios*, as it is often called in the colonial records. Each produced its characteristic cultural design, and each imprinted this design so strongly on its carriers that the outlines of the two patterns are visible in the Middle American fabric to this day. The purposes which animated the two institutions were clearly divergent: one was an instrument of the conquerors, the other an instrument of the conquered. Yet in their divergence they shared a common denominator. Both were institutions of retreat, both were designed to stem the tide of disorder. And both met the challenge of depression in the same way, for both brought a reduction in the risks of living at the price of progress.

The colonists had come to America in search of gold and—through the possession of gold—of liberty. But falling prices in a depressed market and the catastrophically declining labor force quickly ended the hopes of limitless wealth and untrammeled self-determination. As reality encroached upon the utopian dream, it again forced men to recognize its terms, terms which made a sack of doubloons in the hand weigh more in the balance than the hidden treasure of Moctezuma, a string of mules worth more than the waters of the Fountain of Eternal Youth. Some of course never acknowledged this confrontation and were lost in search of their personal El Dorados. Others were deprived of access to legitimate tangible claims or cheated of them: only forty years after the Conquest there were four thousand Spaniards in New Spain without visible means of support. But some there were who through guile or personal energy or bureaucratic favor shouldered aside their competitors and laid hold of the means of production required to support them in the fashion to which they wished to become accustomed. These men—recruited from all manner of men who had come from the mother country—became the members of a new colonial elite.

The characteristic cultural form through which they exercised their domination was no longer the trusteeship over Indians but the outright ownership of land in the hacienda, the large privately owned estate. The title to this land they acquired through purchase, by paying good money into an increasingly depleted royal treasury. The trusteeship had included rights to Indian produce only, and not to land; it had left the trustee passively dependent, at the mercy of royal favor. When a man succeeded in obtaining an outright grant of land, however, he became a director of property he could call his own, property to which he could add, which he might pawn, or which he could sell. To work this new property, the colonists needed labor. This they sought extralegally, by circumventing the royal labor code. The system was deceptive in its simplicity. They invited workers to settle permanently on or near their new estates. The entrepreneur would undertake to pay their tribute to the royal authorities and offer to pay them wages, usually in kind. At the same time, he would grant the worker the right to purchase goods on credit or, as needed, advance him small sums of money. The worker's account would be debited to the extent of the sums involved, in return for a promise to repay the money through labor. Such workers became known as *gañanes, laborios, naborías, tlaquehuales*, or *peones*, the system of labor use *gañanía* or peonage. Upon the twin foundations of landownership and peonage, the colonists thus erected their new economic edifice, the mainstay of their new social order.

Organized for commercial ends, the hacienda proved strangely hybrid in its characteristics. It combined in practice features which seem oddly contradictory in theory. Geared to sell products in a market, it yet aimed at having little to sell. Voracious for land, it deliberately made inefficient use of it. Operating with large numbers of workers, it nevertheless personalized the relation between worker and owner. Created to produce a profit, it consumed a large part of its substance in conspicuous and unproductive displays of wealth. Some writers have called the institution "feudal," because it involved the rule of a dominant landowner over his dependent laborers. But it lacked the legal guaranties of security which compensated the feudal serf for his lack of liberty and self-determination. Others have called it "capitalist," and so it was, but strangely different from the commercial establishments in agriculture with which we are familiar in the modern commercial and industrial world. Half "feudal," half "capitalist," caught between past and future, it exhibited characteristics of both ways of life, as well as their inherent contradiction.

Offspring of an economic depression, the hacienda was set up to feed a limited demand. With its external markets dried up by an economic downturn and by political weakness in the mother country, it relied on market within the colony. In New Spain, however, only the towns and the mining camps represented secure outlets for agricultural produce; the Indians of the countryside secured their own foodstuffs and fed themselves. And means of transportation were neither rapid nor plentiful enough to allow surpluses from an area with a good harvest to be transferred quickly to an area of food shortage. Markets were limited not only by the food habits of the Indian population and by the distribution of the Spanish settlements but also by the limited capacity of any region to absorb its own products. A glut quickly lowered prices to the point where commercial agriculture met its ruin. Thus the hacienda played safe by always producing below capacity. It never staked all or even most of its land on the vagaries of the market. In times of uncertainty, it could always fall back on its own resources and feed itself. It possessed its own defenses, which it never jeopardized.

Inefficient in its use of land, it was yet greedy for it. It needed and wanted more land, not to raise more crops, but to take land from the Indians in order to force them to leave their holdings and to become dependent on the hacienda for land and work. Once this land was in its possession, the hacienda readily let it out to the inhabitants of the deprived villages for farming and stock-raising, but at the price of a stipulated number of workdays on the cash-crop–producing lands of the hacienda. Such workers, obtained through indirect means of coercion, constituted the bulk of a hacienda's labor force. They were called *peones baldillos*, because they made use of the hacienda's *baldío* or uncultivated land.

To produce the cash crop, a hacienda would farm only a small portion of its total land resources—its best land—but would do so with an unchanging and antiquated sixteenth-century technology, based on the use of the wooden plow and oxen in the fields and on the water-powered wheel in processing. Its cash crop would be a product of many hands, laboring within the *casco* or core of the hacienda, the sum of many individual efforts each operating at a low level of productivity but considerable in the aggregate through the mere process of addition.

The greater part of this labor was drawn from the non-resident inhabitants of the hacienda's periphery, but the tempo and intensity of the work effort were sustained by a corps of resident laborers, the *peones acasillados*. An *acasillado* had both more rights and more duties than a *baldillo*. Paid in tokens, he could make advance purchases at the store owned and operated by the hacienda, the *tienda de raya*. There he could always obtain maize for himself and his family at lower than market prices. In the highlands, he was entitled to a daily ration of pulque, usually ladled out after a day's work, at the completion of the religious services which peon and owner both attended in the hacienda's chapel. Each man was given a house, and—if he proved faithful and obedient—a plot of land on which he could raise crops for himself. If a man proved properly submissive, moreover, the owner would finance his wedding or a baptism or a religious devotion, or aid him in other times of financial need. To repay these advances, such a worker would then bind himself to work for the owner until the debt was paid, an occurrence not marked by its frequency.

From 1540 on, growing numbers of Indians accepted the liabilities of peonage. Often they welcomed the system as a way of freeing themselves from the increasingly onerous bondage to Indian communities ravaged by death and disease, threatened with loss of land and water, yet all too often required to bear burdens of tribute and labor services assessed on the basis of their past number of inhabitants. Many of the newcomers were attracted also by the novel goods of Spanish manufacture, more accessible through hacienda channels than in the impoverished Indian villages. Extralegal as the system of peonage was, the new worker and his employer soon found themselves partners in a conspiracy to elude royal supervision. Crown officials, aware that they could not stem the tide of peonage, nevertheless strove to limit it by placing a ceiling of five pesos on the sums which could be advanced to any Indian, though they showed no parallel concern for the debt limit of the offspring of mixed Euro-Afro-Indian unions. But soon the new kind of life which developed on the haciendas—favorable to intermarriage and transculturation, providing shared experiences and growing kinship—bound the workers to their common place of residence as much as the accumulating debts bound them to the owner of the hacienda.

Thus the system had advantages for both owner and worker: the owner was guaranteed labor, the worker a measure of novelty, together with security. The system, however, also exacted its social and psychological costs, for—as in all systems of bondage—security was purchased only at the price of liberty. The peon was dependent on the owner, both economically and psychologically. He abrogated his right to decide his own fate; the owner of the hacienda became his guardian and judge, as well as his employer.

Such relations between owner and worker are so different from those to which we are accustomed in modern industrial society that they seem to possess the closeness of personal ties which many tend to miss in present-day life, where superiors and subordinates go their separate, impersonal ways. This has caused some writers to idealize the hacienda, as others have idealized the slaveholding plantation of the ante-bellum South. But there exists a distinction between personal relations, such as those familiar to anthropologists from the study of closely knit small primitive tribes, and personalized relations, in which the relationship bears the guise of a personal relation but serves an impersonal function. Neither hacienda nor slave plantation existed to provide satisfactory relationships between persons. They existed to realize returns on invested capital, to produce profits, functions that take no account of kinship or friendship, of personal needs or desires. The hacienda, like the slave plantation, was a system designed to produce goods by marshaling human beings regardless of their qualities and involvements as persons, an institution of the "technical order," as Robert Redfield has called it, instead of the "moral order." And yet the hacienda personalized many aspects of the relation between owner and worker where modern industrial or commercial organizations substitute the neutral mechanisms of impersonal management through a faceless bureaucracy.

There are relationships which are so basic to all human life that we remain their prisoners as well as their beneficiaries throughout our adult lives. These are the relationships which we experience in growing up in families. When an appropriate situation in adulthood reproduces our infantile condition, we react with emotions learned long ago toward father or mother or siblings, figures often now distant or dead. These emotions provide the fuel for adult institutions which manage to counterfeit the character of the original situation that first produced them. The hacienda achieved this end by elevating the hacienda owner to the role of a stern and irascible father, prepared to guide the steps of his worker-children, ready to unleash his temper and anger upon them when provoked. As long as the worker remained dependent and submissive, he received his just reward: a sum of money, a draft of pulque, a plot for growing corn. When he rebelled against authority, or provoked its anger, he was tied to the whipping post, possessed by every hacienda, and cruelly lashed. Thus the hacienda bound men not only through debts or through force but also through ties of love and hate.

Deprived of their ability to rule their own lives, the workers in turn invested the relation of owner and worker with the elements of personalization. The owner's person became the governor of their lives, their relation with this person the major guaranty of the security and stability on which depended their daily bread and a roof over their heads. Only the owner could materially raise a man's prospects in life, only he could reduce the risks to which the worker was subject. This person, clad in authority and living a life far beyond the reach of his laborers, had to be won over, placated into benevolence, by a show of humility, a pantomime of servitude. The worker not only put his labor time at his owner's disposal; he also offered himself and his family, to secure perhaps yet another advantage in the struggle for support. But each gain of benevolence was achieved only at the expense of competition and conflict with his fellow workers. Where all strive for the same goal, only a few could gain access to the generosity of the master; most remained for life outside the charmed, personalized circle. This competition for imaginary stakes, however, bound the worker with invisible bonds. He set his hopes upon the person of the master. If he succeeded in his ritual pantomime of submission, the master received the credit. If he failed, he blamed himself, or others more successful then he. At the same time, he cut himself off from others in a like condition.

No human institution, not even the most inhuman, can rely wholly on bayonets; it must build also on the motivations of its participants. On the hacienda, personal motives were harnessed to maintained the regime of labor. Given the appropriate social conditions, men make peons of themselves.

Limited in capital, the hacienda presents a further paradox in the display of power and wealth of its owner: wealth invested in the big house, with its high walls, gateways, courtyards, chapel, jail, and outbuildings; wealth invested in rich clothing and silver trappings for horses; wealth displayed in great feasts and public ostentation. This show of grandeur, however, also had its functions, functions appropriate to the context in which the hacienda arose. It underlined the owner's dominance over his workers, it enhanced his self-esteem, it impressed others. In impressing others, it enshrined an economic purpose, today served by departments of public relations or advertising. A *hacendado*'s display was a public demonstration of his credit rating, an assertion that—in the midst of an economy starved for capital—he deserved credit because his enterprise was capable of generating capital and wealth.

Moreover, such display gave him still another psychological hold over his workers, for it encouraged their vicarious identification with his splendor. Children admire and yet fear an overweening father; they also identify with him. His well-being becomes a symbol of the well-being of the entire family. Overpowered and restrained by him, they also wish to see him acknowledged as powerful by others, to make their own submission seem logical and right. Thus, on the hacienda, workers identified with the figure of the owner. His person became symbolic of the enterprise as a whole, his well-being the justification of their collective effort. Dominated by his will, they yet identified with his mastery, his ability to command respect from others. His glory became theirs; it furnished the element of drama in their earth-bound and restricted lives.

The hacienda system was here to stay. The dual nature of the hacienda—its ability to retrench in times of adverse markets, its ability to increase production if demand rose—allowed it to adapt even to conditions which differed from those that gave it birth. When the depression of the seventeenth century came to an end in the economic upswing of the eighteenth century, the hacienda, too, participated in the renewed expansion. Peonage, which at the outset had served to bind and hold a labor supply in the face of a diminishing population, became the foundation of an onerous and exploitative system of labor as population again increased. Squads of peons gave rise to peon companies, peon companies to entire armies of peons, all born within the framework of the haciendas and bound to them through debt and past condition of servitude. By the end of the seventeenth century, New Spain was securely in the hands of a class of great landed proprietors, self-made nobles, commanding thousands of dependent laborers, captains of private armies, living in splendid houses, and leading the life of a new aristocracy on horseback, with its display of equestrian skill in competitive games. In sharp contrast with Europe, where a decline of population and an improved technology had freed the feudal serf and turned him into an owner or renter of agricultural property, but much as in Russia during the late eighteenth and nineteenth centuries, the growth of capitalism in New Spain did not produce a greater measure of liberty and freedom for the laborer; instead it sharpened exploitation and increased bondage.

In the retreat from utopia, the strong sought refuge against instability in the control of men and land through the organizational form of the hacienda. But the rest of the countryside, inhabited by the submerged Indian population, witnessed a parallel movement toward consolidation. The Indian, like the Spaniard, sought security, but he had to avail himself of other means.

The Spanish colonist ultimately had access to an apparatus of power managed by others like himself. But the Conquest had deprived the Indian of access to state power. Knowingly, the conquerors had destroyed the connection between the Indian present and the pre-Hispanic past. In dismantling the Mexica state, they had removed also the cortex of the Middle American political organism and severed the nerves which bound communities and regions to the larger economic and political centers. The Indian state was not rebuilt. Royal decree carefully circumscribed the position of the Indian commoners. They were enjoined from wearing Spanish dress and forced to don "Indian" costume, a combination of Spanish and Indian articles of clothing. Indian commoners could not own or use horses and saddles and were prohibited from bearing arms. They had to pay tribute, but, because they paid tribute, they were endowed with economic personality and therefore with judicial personality. They could present their cases in special "Indian" courts and were defined as "free vassals" of the king. They were exempt from military service and from such taxes as the tithe and the sales tax, imposed on Spaniards and others. But legal rights were not accompanied by common political representation. Where Indian officials had once exercised power on the national and regional level, Spanish officials now held sway. The Indian political apparatus had been smashed by the Conquest; and the conquerors were not ill-advised enough to countenance its reconstruction.

With the assumption of power by the Spaniards, the Indian ruling class lost its functions. Some of the chiefs moved to town, adopted Spanish dress and manners, learned to speak Spanish, and became commercial entrepreneurs employing European technology and working land with Indian tributaries and Negro slaves. Spanish law abetted this process by equating them socially with the nobility of Spain and economically with the Spanish *encomenderos.* Since the new law took inadequate account of the pre-Hispanic division between nobility of office and nobility of lineage, granting to all nobles the privileges of hereditary descent, many Indian nobles even added to the pre-Hispanic perquisites of their rank and gained title to lands which had previously belonged either to a community or to a non-hereditary office. Also, the Indian noble who was treated like a Spanish *encomendero* received rights to tribute and personal services and, like other *encomenderos*, began to invest in the process of building capital through capitalist enterprise. Frequently, intermarriage with the conquerors still further dissipated their Indian identity, until they lost touch with the Indian commoners who in the midst of death and upheaval were building a new Indian life in the countryside.

Nobles who remained in the villages, on the other hand, were reduced by loss of wealth and standing to the position of their Indian fellow citizens. Because his person was still suffused with the magic of past power, a former priest or local chieftain here and there assumed a post in a local community, but he soon lost the ability to command tribute or labor-power to which his ancestors had been accustomed. The new Indian communities were communities of the poor, too overburdened to sustain a class that had lost its function.

With the disappearance of the Indian political elite, there also vanished the specialists who had depended on elite demands: the priests, the chroniclers, the scribes, the artisans, the long-distance traders of pre-Hispanic society. Spanish entrepreneurs replaced the *pochteca*; Spanish artisans took the place of Indian feather-workers and jade-carvers; Spanish priests displaced the Indian religious specialists. Soon there was no longer anyone who knew how to make feather cloaks and decorations, how to find and carve jade, how to recall the deeds of gods and ancestors in days gone by. For a brief period the Indians strove valiantly to learn the new arts of the Mediterranean, and men like Bernardino de Sahagún (1499–1590) and the scholars of the short-lived college of Santiago de Tlatelolco (1536–1606) labored to maintain and enrich the intellectual patterns of Indian culture. But the return to ruralism of the seventeenth century put an end to these hopes and endeavors.

Under the new dispensation, the Indian was to be a peasant, the Indian community a community of peasants. Stripped of their elite and urban components, the Indians were relegated to the countryside. Thus the Indians suffered not only exploitation and biological collapse but also deculturation—cultural loss—and in the course of such ill use lost also the feeling of belonging to a social order which made such poor use of its human resources. They became strangers in it, divided from its purposes and agents by an abyss of distrust. The new society could command their labor, but it could not command their loyalty. Nor has this gulf healed in the course of time. The trauma of the Conquest remains an open wound upon the body of Middle American society to this day.

The strategic unit of the new Indian life was to be not the individual but the Indian community. This the crown protected and furthered, as a double check upon the colonists—ever eager to subjugate the Indians to their exclusive control—as well as upon the Indians themselves, whose individual freedom it wished to curb. To this end, it underwrote the legal separateness and identity of each Indian commune.

Each commune was to be a self-contained economic unit, holding a guaranteed 6.5 square miles of agricultural land, land which its members could sell only after special review by the viceroy. In every commune the duly constituted Indian authorities would collect the tribute and levy the labor services for which the members of the commune were to be jointly responsible (not until the eighteenth century was tribute payment individualized). A portion of this tribute would go into the royal coffers, but part of it would be set aside in a "community chest" (*caja de comunidad*) to finance community projects. Communal officials were to administer the law through the instrumentality of their traditional custom, wherever that custom did not conflict with the demands of church and state. The officers of the crown retained the privilege of judging major crimes and legal cases involving more than one community; but the Indian authorities received sufficient power to guarantee peace and order in the new communes. The autonomy which the crown denied to the Indian sector of society as a whole, it willingly granted to the local social unit.

This model for reconstruction did not envisage a return of the pre-Hispanic community. Yet so well did it meet the needs of the Indian peasant that he could take it up and make it his own. Poised precariously on the abyss of disintegration, the commune proved remarkably resilient. It has undergone great changes since the time when it was first constituted in a shattered countryside three centuries ago, but its essential features are still visible in the Indian communities today, especially in the southern and southeastern highlands. Thus it is still possible to speak of this community in the present tense, to regard the present-day Indian community as a direct descendant of the reconstructed community of the seventeenth century.

The core of this kind of community is its political and religious system. In this system, the burden of religious worship is rotated among the households of the community. Each year, a different group of men undertakes to carry out the tasks of religious office; each year a different group of men makes itself responsible for the purchase and ritual disposal of food, liquor, candles, incense, fire-

works, and for all other attendant expenditures. A tour of religious duty may leave a man impoverished for several years, yet in the eyes of his fellow citizens he has added greatly to his prestige. This spurs men to renewed labor toward the day when they will be able to underwrite another set of ceremonies; and a man will sponsor several such ceremonials in the course of his life. Each tour of sponsorship will add to the esteem in which he is held by his fellow men, until—old and poor—he reaches the pinnacle of prestige and commands the respect of the entire community. The essential element in repeated sponsorship is therefore time: the older a man is, the greater the likelihood that he has repeatedly acted as religious sponsor. Thus old age itself becomes a source of prestige for Indians: an old man is one who has labored in the interests of the community for many years and whose repeated religious activity has brought him ever closer to the state of grace and secular wisdom.

Since all men have an equal opportunity to enlist in carrying the burdens of the gods, and thus to gain prestige, the religious system allows all households to be ranked along a scale of religious participation, prestige, and age. At one end of the scale, the Indians will place the young household which has but recently come into existence and whose head is just beginning to play his part in keeping the balance between community and universe. At the other end, he will place the households of the very old, whose moral ascendancy over the community is very great, owing to their years of faithful service and ritual expenditure.

Certainly this religious pattern has Spanish prototypes in the Iberian *cofradía* or religious sodality, a voluntary association of men for religious purposes. But it is also pre-Hispanic in origin. "There were some," says the Spanish friar Toribio de Benavente of the days before the Conquest, "who labored two or three years and acquired as much as possible for the purpose of honoring the demon with a feast. On such a feast they not only spent all that they possessed but even went into debt, so that they would have to do service a year and sometimes two years in order to get out of debt." In the reconstructed Indian community of the post-Conquest period, this religious pattern was charged with additional functions. It became the chief mechanism through which people gained prestige, as well as the balance wheel of communal economics. Each year, religious participation wipes out considerable sums of goods and money; each year part of the surplus of the community is consumed in offerings or exploded in fireworks to please the saints. The system takes from those who have, in order to make all men have-nots. By liquidating the surpluses, it makes all men rich in sacred experience but poor in earthly goods. Since it levels differences of wealth, it also inhibits the growth of class distinctions based on wealth. Like the thermostat activated by an increase in heat to shut off the furnace, expenditure in religious worship returns the distribution of wealth to a state of balance, wiping out any accumulation of wealth that might upset the existing equilibrium. In engineering parlance, it acts as a feedback, returning a system that is beginning to oscillate to its original course.

The religious complex also has aesthetic functions. The *fiesta* with its processions, burning incense, fireworks, crowds, color, is not merely a mechanism of prestige and of economic justice. It is also "a work of art," the creation of a magic moment in mythological time, in which men and women transcend the realities of everyday life in their entry and procession through the magical space of the vaulted, incense-filled church, let their souls soar on the temporary trajectory of a rocket, or wash away the pains of life in holy-day drunkenness. For the Indians, time is not linear, as it is for the citizens of the industrialized North Atlantic world, where each moment points toward a future of new effort, new experience, and new goals. The Indian scheme of life moves in an endless round, in which everyday labor issues into the magic moment of religious ritual, only to have the ritual dissolve again into the everyday labor that began the cycle. The Indian community has now forgotten its pre-Hispanic past; its past and its future have merged in a timeless rhythm of alternating mundane and holy days.

The social, economic, aesthetic, and ritual mechanisms of the religious complex do not stand alone. They are part and parcel of a larger system which makes political and religious behavior mutually interdependent. For participation in the religious system qualifies a man also for political office. In Indian eyes, a man who has won prestige for himself by bearing the burden of the community in its relations with the gods is expected and—more than expected—required to assume political office. Thus

men who have laid down their burdens as religious sponsors will be asked next to serve as community officials. Qualified for office by past religious participation, they are the ones who transact the business of the community: allocating land, settling boundary disputes, investigating thefts, confirming marriages, disarming disturbers of the peace, dealing with the emissaries of outside power. A man cannot seek political office for its own sake, nor can he bend political power to his individual end. Power is bestowed by the community, and reallocated at intervals to a new group of officeholders. It is the office that governs men, not its occupant. In this democracy of the poor, there is no way to monopolize power. It is divorced from persons and distributed, through election, among all in turn.

The Indian cannot control men; he only wishes to come to terms with them. This process of mutual adjustment has become a group concern. The group counts more than the individual; it limits individual autonomy and initiative. It is suspicious of conflict, tireless in the advocacy of "adjustment." People raised in cultures that thrive on the conflicts of individual with individual would find it difficult to fit into such a community; yet the community can be understood in terms of its context, a larger social order in which men continually fight for power and are ever willing to pay for its fruits the price of their own corruption. In this setting, the Indian community shows great consistency in refusing to play a game that will always seek its first victims among its members. For navigation in troubled waters its politico-religious system is a steering mechanism of great resilience.

As the Indian community leveled differences of class, so it obliterated other internal divisions intervening between its jurisdiction and the households that composed it. The diligent ethnologist may still find among the Otomí-speakers on the fringes of the valley of Mexico, hamlets based on common descent in the male line and enforced marriage outside the community; or patrilineal kinship units sharing a common name, a common saint, and a measure of social solidarity among the Tzeltal-Tzotzil–speakers of Chiapas, though there too they have lost their former exogamy and the common residence which they possessed in the past. But these examples remain the fascinating exceptions to the general rule that, among Middle American Indians as a whole, common territoriality in one community and common participation in communal life have long since robbed such units of any separatist jurisdiction they may at one time have exercised. This holds also for the divisions called *barrios* or sections, which some have traced back to the pre-Hispanic *calpulli* and which in many cases go back to joint settlement in one community—voluntary or enforced—of groups of different origins, in both pre-Hispanic and post-Hispanic times. In most cases these units have simply been transformed into religious sodalities, each concerned with the support of its special saint and socially amorphous in any context other than the religious, although mutual name-calling, backbiting, or slander of one another's reputation may serve to drain off some of the minor irritations of daily life.

It is the household, then, that makes the basic decisions within both the politico-religious and the economic field, the household being usually composed of husband, wife, and children. Such unions are customarily formed through monogamous marriages; polygyny, the marriage of one male to more than one female, occurs but rarely. An unmarried man or woman is not regarded as an adult member of the community and cannot take up his responsibilities in communal life. A person who has lost a marriage partner through divorce or death must remarry before the community will again ratify the social standing he enjoyed before the breakup or end of his marriage. Nor is it marriage alone that bestows full rights of citizenship. A couple must have children to validate their claim to complete adult status; a sterile marriage quickly falls prey to conflict and divorce. Marriage therefore, and a marriage blessed with children, is the common goal of the Indian men and women.

Economically, a marriage is a union of two technological specialists: a male specialist skilled in field labor and house-building, a female specialist skilled in tending the kitchen garden, caring for the small livestock, making pots and clothing, raising children, preparing the daily meal. The functions of the division of labor and of reproduction take precedence in people's minds over marriage as an outlet for sexual impulses. Marriages are often arranged by the parents of the prospective couple, through the services of a go-between. The Indian man seeks a woman to bear his children and to keep up his home: there is little romantic love. Ideally, people conform to strict standards of marital fidelity. In practice, however, there is considerable latitude for sexual adventure outside marriage, and philandering does not usually endanger the bonds of the union. Nor do Indians engage in sexual conquest as a validation of their masculinity; sexual conquest does not add luster to the reputation of the individual. Exploitation of one sex by the other encounters little sympathy, just as political or economic exploitation of one man by another is not countenanced within the boundaries of the community.

Throughout their marriage, the partners retain a rough equality, though, ideally, wives are held subordinate to husbands. Women own the movable goods which they bring with them into the marriage. If a woman owns land, her husband may farm it for her, but the proceeds from the sale of produce raised on such a field is her own, as are the proceeds from the sales of her handicraft products. If she owns livestock, she retains her rights of ownership. In case of divorce, the family herd is divided equally between the divorcing partners. When one of the partners dies, his property is divided equally among the children; the surviving partner retains his share. Women do not occupy political or religious office, but they help their husbands in making the relevant decisions and in carrying out the attendant obligations. Within the home, the woman has a great deal to say, in strongly marked contrast to her non-Indian sister.

Just as the questions of participation in religio-political life are raised and settled within the household, so the day-to-day economic decisions are also made on the household level. It is the household that plants its fields to crops, that sells its maize or chili, that buys the needed kerosene or pottery. It is the men and women of these unit households who handle the money derived from these sales and act as individual economic agents. This apparent contradiction between the behavior of the Indian as a member of his community on the religio-political plane and his behavior as an economic agent has so impressed some observers that they have lost sight of the communal involvements of the Indian and treated him in terms of capitalist economic theory. Indeed, Sol Tax has spoken of the Indians as "penny capitalists," presumably in contrast to more affluent "nickel" or "dime" or "millionaire" capitalists, thus drawing attention at once to his comparative poverty and characterizing his participation in the wider economy as an individual agent, and a capitalist to boot. Certainly the Indian is poor, and no Middle American Indian community ever existed on a desert island; it always formed part and parcel of a larger society. Its economic agents, the members of its households, are subject to a wider economy and to its laws. For instance, the value of the money they use and the prices of the commodities they buy and sell are often influenced, if not directly determined, by national conditions. The recent [article was written in 1959] inflation, to name but one case, has affected Indians and non-Indians alike.

But the Indian is not merely quantitatively different in his economic involvements from other members of society. He differs qualitatively from the poor non-Indian Mexican or Guatemalan because he is culturally different from them. Superficially, he may resemble the individual economic agent of classical economics, unrestrictedly exchanging goods in a capitalist market. But he is not a capitalist, nor free of restrictions. His economic goal is not capital accumulation but subsistence and participation in the religio-political system of his community. He handles money; but he does not use money to build capital. It is for him merely one way of reckoning equivalences, of appraising the value of goods in exchange. The Indian works first so that he may eat. When he feels that he has accomplished this goal, he labors to build a surplus so that he can sponsor a ceremony and gain prestige in the eyes of his fellow Indians. In the course of his sponsorship, he redistributes or destroys his surplus by providing displays of fireworks or dressing the saint's image in a new cloak. Clearly, the quality of his involvement in the national economy differs from that of the commercial farmer, industrial worker, or entrepreneur. Moreover, this pattern of consumption operates within cultural limitations laid down and maintained by his community. When we see the solitary Indian bent over his patch of maize, we seem to see a lone economic agent engaged in isolated production. But this man is enmeshed in a complicated web of traditional rights to land maintained by his community. Spanish rule granted each community sovereign jurisdiction over a well-defined amount of land. With the passage of time, general communal rights over land have become attenuated, usually in favor of a mixed system of ownership, where the richer bottom lands along the valley floors are now owned by individual members of the community, while the community retains communal rights over hilly land and forests. Yet the community still retains jurisdictional rights over land everywhere, rights which remove land from the category of free commodities. The most important of these rights states that members of the community may not sell land to outsiders. This is usually reinforced by a stringent rule of endogamy, which prohibits members of the community from marrying outsiders and thus endangering the man-land balance. Frequently this taboo is strengthened by other sanctions: the right allowing existing members of the community to glean or the right to graze their livestock on any land within the community after the harvest. Such rights frequently imply sanctions in their turn. A man cannot put a fence around his piece of land or grow crops that mature at variance with the crops of his neighbors. Both land and crops are thus subject to negative limitations, even though the actual process of production is entrusted to the several separate households.

Such limitations also apply to the craft products made in a given community. We may see a woman shaping a pot or a man weaving a hat, and taking pot or hat to market. Again, we apparently see an individual agent engaged in autonomous economic activity. We must however realize that the producer is not "free" to choose the object he wishes to produce and market. What looks like individual craft specialization is but an aspect of a pattern of specialization by communities. There is a general tendency for each community to engage in one or several crafts that are not shared by other communities in its vicinity. Thus, in the Tarascan-speaking area, for instance, Cocucho makes pottery, Tanaco weaves with century-plant fibers, Paracho manufactures wooden objects and cotton cloth, Nahuatzen weaves woolens, Uruapan paints gourds, and Santa Clara del Cobre produces items of beaten copper.

The Indian market is a place where the members of the different communities meet to exchange their products. Such a market brings together a very large and varied supply of articles, larger and more varied than could be sold by any permanent storekeeper in the market town, and does so at prices low enough to match the low income of the Indians. Thus, while the individual producer enters a market that is highly heterogeneous in the variety of goods offered, his particular individual contribution is homogeneous with that of other members of his community. In the characteristic Indian marketing pattern, where the sellers of similar types of objects are arranged together in carefully drawn-up rows what looks to the casual observer like a mere grouping of individuals is actually a grouping of communities.

We must conclude, therefore, that the Indian's economic involvements are different from those of other participants in the national economy. The individual Indian household is indeed *in* the economy, but not *of* it. For added to the household's general purposes of self-maintenance are the community's purposes aiming at maintaining the Indian social group intact in its possession of land and membership, despite the corrosive influences that continually surround it. A peasantry needs land, and the Indian community defends its land against outsiders through the twin weapons of endogamy and the prohibition of sale to non-members. A peasantry faces the risks of class differentiation. As soon as one man accumulates wealth and is allowed to keep and reinvest it, he threatens, in the straitened circumstances of Indian life, to take from others the instruments of their own livelihood. More seriously, wealth breeds power, and power—unless adequately checked—corrupts, stacking the political cards in favor of some men to the detriment of others. Thus the Indian community strives to abolish wealth and to redistribute power. It even frowns on any display of wealth, any individual assertion of independence that may upset the balance of egalitarian poverty. Its social ideal is the social conformist, not the innovator, the controlled individual, not the seeker after untrammeled power. It places its faith in an equality of risk-taking.

It is doubtful whether the Indian community could have achieved these ends by itself alone. Certainly, without the world beyond its confines, it could not have solved its population problem. Each new generation born to it threatens to upset again and again the balance between mouths to feed and land available to feed them. It can solve this problem only by continually exporting population. To stay in the running, it must continually sacrifice some of its sons and daughters to the outside world, thus ever feeding the forces which it attempts to resist. Increasing its own security by exporting people, it at the same time endangers the security of the larger society. Neither Indian peasant nor colonist entrepreneur, the emigrants fall into no ordered category, occupy no defined place in the social order. They become the Ishmaels of Middle America, its marginal men. Cast out into the shadows, with no stake in the existing order, they are forced to seek their own vindication, their place in the sun. If this is impossible within the social framework, then it must needs be against it. Thus the Indian community perpetually creates a body of potential antagonists, ready to invade it and benefit by its destruction.

Without the outside world, moreover, the Indian can never close the ever opening gap between his production and his needs. Robbed of land and water by the Conquest and subsequent encroachment, the Indian community can rarely be self-sufficient. It must not only export people; it must also export craft produce and labor. Each Indian who goes off to work seasonally in other men's fields strengthens his community; each hat, fire fan, or reed mat sold beyond the limits of the community adds to its capacity to resist encroachment. Each Indian who, in the past, enlisted on a hacienda as a *peón baldillo* thus benefited his community. Paradoxically, he also benefited the hacienda that used his labor. Assured of seasonal laborers who would do its bidding at the critical periods in the process of production, the haciendas welcomed the presence of Indian communities on their fringes. For such a community constituted a convenient reservoir of laborers where men maintained their labor power until needed, at no additional cost to the entrepreneur. Suddenly we find, therefore, that the institution of the conquerors and the institution of the conquered were linked phenomena. Each was a self-limiting system, powered by antagonism to the other; and yet their coexistence produced a perpetual if hostile symbiosis, in which one was wedded to the other in a series of interlocking functions.

If colonists and Indians achieved symbiosis, they did not achieve synthesis. While the great landowners secured virtual political and economic autonomy behind the walls of their great estates, they remained ideologically tied to Spain and, through Spain, to Europe. If the Conquest deculturated the conquered, it also affected the conquerors. First it narrowed the range of patterns carried by the newcomers, only to render them doubly provincial in the enforced readaptation to the ruralism of the seventeenth century. If the Conquest ended, once and for all, the isolation of America from the cultural development of the Old World, the ensuing decline of Spain left the new colonies on the margins of the new and larger world into which they had so suddenly been introduced. Here they suffered the fate of any marginal area isolated from its center of cultural productivity.

At the same time, the Conquest cut the lines of communication with the pre-Hispanic past: the conquerors could not take over the culture of the conquered. But neither could they develop a cultural configuration of their own. Communication with Europe remained formalistic and empty. The intellectual and artistic currency of the Old World was sought more for the sake of provincial display than for the sake of a new vital synthesis. Thus, for example, what is astonishing about the colonial architecture of New Spain is not the degree of indigenous influence in its construction but the virtual absence of it. Churches and palaces were built along European lines, even though greater wealth might render them more ornate or though an occasional decorative symbol might betray the hand of an Indian craftsman as yet untutored in the canons of Occidental art. Similarly, New Spain borrowed from Europe the models of sophisticated thought, first the intellectual formulas of the Counter-Reformation, later those of an Enlightenment tempered with Thomism, still later—in rapid succession—the phraseology of Jacobinism, English Liberalism, Comtean Positivism, only to see the European catchwords produce a sterile harvest in the Middle American soil. Thus the society of the post-Conquest period suffered not only from the deepening cleavage between Indian and non-Indian. It also clogged the wellsprings of autonomous cultural creativity. Product of the meeting of two cultural traditions, it should have been the richer for their encounter. But design and circumstance both reduced the capacity of each component to quicken and stimulate the other into new cultural growth, and to be quickened in turn by stimuli from outside. Instead of organic synthesis, the meeting of Indian and Spaniard resulted in a social unity that remained culturally mechanical.

Hacienda and Indian community divided the countryside between them, but, like all monopolies, they created the forces for their own undoing. For, claiming exclusive power over men and land, they left no room for a social group neither Indian nor colonist which grew rapidly after the mid-seventeenth century. This new grouping drew its recruits from the sons of Indians who had left the encysting communities because they could no longer make a living there or because they preferred a freer life outside; from the descendants of African slaves, those manumitted by their owners or runaways hiding in the shadows of the law; from the offspring of mixed Indo-Afro-European unions, often illegitimate, who found a home neither in the Indian communities nor in the precincts of the Spaniards. With the passage of time, all these were joined also by descendants of poor conquerors, men who had come off second best in the distribution of riches; by men who had staked their all and lost it in one turn of fortune's wheel; and by men who found the cards stacked against them in their search for an adequate and respectable livelihood.

There were many of these. To gain wealth, to improve his chances in life, to secure a newly won position against competitors, a man needed connections. Only royal good will could grant the merchant his license to trade, the royal official his delegated power. Only the royal signature gave the landowner title to his land or the right to keep his estate undivided upon inheritance. Only through political connections and connivance could the mighty build their armies of peons or extend their sway over lands claimed by others. In the strongly centralized government of New Spain, only a few doors led into the sanctuary of power in Mexico City; only the wealthiest and the most powerful could gain entrance, through ties of marriage or offers of profitable collusion. Inevitably, therefore, the colonists came to be divided into the well-connected, for whom all things were easy, and the unconnected, who found their paths barred by invisible hands, their holdings and wealth eroded by lack of political guaranties. Where the well-connected flourished, the unconnected had to content themselves with humbler returns on their capital. Increasingly, they found themselves edged out, pushed into provincial areas too mountainous or too far from city markets or lacking in potential labor to support large holdings. Steadily and implacably, they came to feel he narrowness of their circumstances. As holdings grew smaller, fathers found it ever more difficult to provide their daughters with proper dowries, their sons with farms adequate to maintain them. Their inability to entail their estates, to keep their wealth inviolate, forced many of the sons into the poorly paid priesthood or into petty officialdom.

Other ruling elites, in other places and at other times, have shared their power gradually and carefully with the disadvantaged. But this the colonial elite either would not or could not do. Such a step would have demanded that the favored merchant yield his prerogatives to his own best customers; that the privileged landowner relinquish the political guaranties of his stability in favor of his competitors; and that the royal official—mediating between colonist and Indian—abdicate his power to the colonist party. Rather than resign their positions, the elite families bound themselves ever more tightly to Spain, seeking in the mother country both their marriage partners and their political replacements. For the unconnected, the pattern of life descended from dignified poverty to bare existence, without title to property, without guaranties in court.

Deprived of a place in the sun, relegated to the byways and back alleys of society, all these varieties of men encountered one another in common destitution along the trail, in mining camps, in hostelries, in city taverns. Recognizing their common fate, they produced common offspring, resulting in an ever increasing number of mixed physical types. These the colonial authorities called "colored" people or *castas*, following the traditional Iberian usage of "caste" for color. Later it became fashionable to call them *mestizos* or mixed-bloods, or—harking back to the days of the Roman Empire when Spain had been Romanized—*ladinos*, a term which meant somebody Latinized and therefore wise to the ways of the world.

At first, the members of this group were relatively few. In 1650—when the Indian population of New Spain had declined to its lowest point—the mestizo element consisted of only 130,000 persons, as compared with some 1,270,000 Indians and 120,000 people socially defined as white. By the end of the eighteenth century the Indian population of New Spain had quadrupled, to a total of about 5,200,000, but the *castas* had increased more than seventeen times, to a total of 2,270,000. From the end of the eighteenth century to the present, the Indian population of what was once New Spain

has remained surprisingly stable. But during the same period, partly through steady recruitment from the Indian communities, partly through natural increase, the mestizo population of Mexico and Guatemala has increased more than a hundredfold. In numbers the Indian has held his own; but it is clearly the mestizo who represents the future of Middle America.

The terms *casta* and *mestizo* are both opprobrious, but it would be a mistake to read into them the twentieth-century prejudice against race mixture which informs similar terms in the North Atlantic world. The negative sentiment that adheres to them is social prejudice, not racial prejudice. Social prejudice, the dislike of the in-group for the out-group, the prejudice of the initiated for the encroaching stranger, is attested by the remnants of cannibalistic meals eaten half a million years ago in the Chinese cave of Chouk'outien. But racial prejudice is no older than the experience of Negro slavery in the New World and the rise of industrialism in Europe. The first European contacts with members of other races were formulated in religious and not in racial terms: all men were capable of salvation, all men were children of Adam and therefore brothers. This argument held even in seventeenth-century Virginia, where authorities still drew the legal line between "heathen" and "Christian," and not between "white" and "black," and where Negro slaves baptized in Africa were freed, equipped with dowries, and married to desirable mates. Only the rising economic importance of Negro slavery in America and the development of industrial wage labor in Europe produced the racist attempt to convert people into things by denying them a common humanity and by degrading them through various kinds of pseudo-science to the status of the burden-bearing animal.

This form of prejudice did not take root in Latin America until the nineteenth century, and then only briefly in restricted areas of the Caribbean, when the institution of Negro slavery was nearing its end. But in Middle America, the prejudice against *castas*, as indeed the prejudice against Indians, remained social prejudice. If the offspring of a mixed union gained wealth and standing, he could obtain from the pertinent authorities a legal paper that declared him to be "white" (*que se tenga por blanco*). Thus the white group quickly became a social, not a racial, group, just as an Indian was any person, whatever his parents, acknowledged to be a member of an Indian community. In like fashion, *castas* or mestizos were neither "white" nor "Indian," but embodiments of all those interstitial human elements whose social position made it impossible for them to join the other two groupings. What the colonial society feared was not the creation of mixed offspring but the growth of a large mass of unattached, disinherited, rootless people in its centers and along its margins. In their fear of the mestizo, men feared for the future of their social order.

Also, because men usually hate, dislike, or fear those of whom they avail themselves in the pursuit of socially concealed ends, feeling toward the mestizos came to be tinged with the mixed emotions of hidden complicity. This was perhaps most obvious in the sexual sphere, where men frequently claimed no responsibility for the mixed offspring they had fathered, leaving them to be raised by their usually destitute mothers. But resentment was generated also in other contacts of social life. There was little correspondence between law and reality in the utopian order of New Spain. The crown wished to deny the colonist his own supply of labor; the colonist obtained it illegally by attaching peons to his person and his land. Royal prescript supported the trade monopoly over goods flowing in and out of the colony; but along the edges of the law moved smugglers, cattle-rustlers, bandits, the buyers and sellers of clandestine produce. To blind the eyes of the law, there arose a multitude of scribes, lawyers, go-betweens, influence peddlers, and undercover agents, the *coyotes* of modern Middle America, a term that one merely designated one of the physical types produced by mixed unions. In such a society, even the transactions of everyday life could smack of illegality; yet such illegality was the stuff of which this social order was made. Illicit transactions demanded their agents; the army of the disinherited, deprived of alternative sources of employment, provided these agents. Thus a tide of illegality and disorder seemed ever ready to swallow up the precariously defended islands of legality and privilege. At the same time, just as the Masai of East Africa blame their smiths for forcing them to make war by making their weapons, the citizens of New Spain blamed the mestizo for those of their own activities that daily subverted an order of society they were formally committed to uphold.

Disinherited by society, the mestizo was also disinherited culturally. Deprived of a stable place in the social order, he could make only limited use of the heterogeneous cultural heritage left him by his varied ancestors. The Negro, bound in servitude to mill or mine, could not recreate Africa in Middle America; only here and there, in isolated pockets on the Pacific coast of the southern highlands or along the Gulf, did "Negro" or Afro-mestizo groups weave some African culture elements into their ongoing life. Similarly, the Indian had little to contribute to the new ways of city, stock ranch, mine, or factory, beyond his inventory of household arts, his techniques for curing illness, his folk beliefs about the supernatural. The heritage of Spain had already undergone the simplification of transatlantic migration and Conquest; much of it the mestizo had to jettison still further, because it was not consonant with the erratic rhythm of his new life. His chances of survival lay neither in accumulating cultural furniture nor in cleaving to cultural norms, but in an ability to change, to adapt, to improvise. The ever shifting nature of his social condition forced him to move with guile and speed through the hidden passageways of society, not to commit himself to any one position or to any one spot. Always he would be called upon to seem both more or less than what he was, to be both more or less than what he seemed.

Thus the mestizo would come to be the very antithesis of the Indian. Where the Indian was rooted in a community, he would be rootless. Where the Indian clung stubbornly to the norms of his group, he would learn to change his behavior as other men assume or doff a mask. Where the Indian remained closed in upon himself, impervious to arguments raised beyond the confines of his local universe, he would have to make himself at home in the market place of goods, ideas, and people. The Indian could turn a face to the outside world that yielded no knowledge and accepted no premise of the larger society; but the mestizo would have to operate with its premises and logic, so as to be counted among "men of reason" (*gente de razón*), as non-Indians are called in Middle America. Where the Indian valued access to land, land to work by the sweat of his brow, the mestizo would value manipulation of people and situations. Above all, he would value power, the instrument that would make people listen where society granted him no voice and obey where the law yielded him no authority. Where the Indian saw power as an attribute of office and redistributed it with care lest it attach itself to persons, the mestizo would value power as an attribute of the self, as personal energy that could subjugate and subject people.

For the mestizo, power is not an attribute of groups. The group exists to back the individual; the individual does not exist for the group. The individual wish, the individual gesture, are paramount, subject only to a man's grip upon his fellow men. The measure of success is the readiness of others to serve him, to underwrite with their services his conspicuous consumption of time and goods. The outcome of defeat is bondage or death. There is no middle ground: if a man does not wish to be victor, he must needs be loser. Ultimately, all means are legitimate in this battle for personal control of people and things, even violence and death.

This struggle for power was more than a means: as a validation of self and of one's station in society, it became an end in itself. To the mestizo, the capacity to exercise power is ultimately sexual in character: a man succeeds because he is truly male (*macho*), possessed of sexual potency. While the Indian strives neither to control nor to exploit other men and women, the mestizo reaches for power over women as over men. As the urge for personal vindication through power is continuous and limitless, so the mestizo possesses "a limitless sexual deficit" which feeds merely upon past conquests. While the Indian man and the Indian woman achieve a measure of balance in their relationship, the mestizo male requires absolute ascendance over women. Thus even familial and personal relationships become battlegrounds of emotion, subject to defeat and to victory.

As men expect hostility and aggression from others, so they rise to defend themselves with hostility and aggression. They advance upon each other, ever circumspect, ever ready to defend themselves, ever willing to take advantage of the chink in their opponent's armor. Personal encounters thus become daily dramas in which the participants transcend the limits of the workaday world through gestures of potency or submission. The ultimate gesture, however, is not the stance of the victor; it is the defiant posture of the victim who can turn defeat and death into triumph by a calm and derisive acceptance of his fate.

There are cultures which preach the acceptance of things as they are; others, seeing the reality of daily life as cold and unpleasant, exalt the wish, the longing, the play of fantasy. The Indian is reality-adjusted and reality-bound. Hard work and its fruits are his primary values; he knows that wishing does not make it so. The mestizo, in contrast, enjoys the play of fantasy. Standing on the edge of society, he has also come to stand on the edge of reality. Uncertain of backing from his fellows, he is thrown back on his own resources; propertyless and alienated, he often feels estranged from society. Wishing to escape reality, he has learned to "drown the pain of living" in alcohol or gambling, creating for himself an unreal world with unreal stakes. Despising life, he has learned to substitute the dream for unfriendly reality. He may rise suddenly on a crest of fantasy into a dream world of personal dominance, only to fall back into a trough of self-denigration, filled with feelings of misfortune and insufficiency. Rarely in tune with things as they are, he is in the words of José Iturriaga, "either above or below them." Yet, suspicious of reality, he is also suspicious of dreams. Dreams do not come true, and in a sudden reversal of moods he may pull himself back to the demands of life with a cynical joke. Thus he does not commit himself easily either to dream or to actuality. The dream may give him wings, unleash the energy for which he strives, but in the pursuit of energy the dream is but a means, the original catalyst. Dreaming, men retain a vast gift for improvisation, an ability to shift both ends and means that enables them to score a personal triumph where critics could predict only the failure of a cause.

To transcend reality, to suggest possibilities and plans that in real life remain unrealized and unrealizable, the mestizo often submerges himself in verbal fantasy that decorates truth with falsehood, falsehood with truth. Yet as he distrusts the dream, he also distrusts the promise of words. He finds their play pleasurable but does not become their captive. His slogans of the moment may be liberal or socialist or facist or capitalist. But he is not a system-builder; the use of such phrases does not make him a liberal, a socialist, a fascist, or a capitalist. Quick to change ends and means, he is also quick to change the tokens of communication. Moreover, he is often unwilling to commit himself to an unpredictable future; to this end he can use language as a strategy in which explicit meanings disguise implicit messages, and a man can speak with two contradictory tongues, to the confusion of the uninitiated. Often, language is not so much a means of communication, of "putting all your cards on the table," as the North American would have it, as it is a means of avoiding entanglement. Nothing will excite moving-picture audiences in Middle America to greater glee than the antics of their glorious clown Cantínflas (Mario Moreno), who in an eternal round of wish fulfillment steps nimbly around the traps of life with fancy footwork and hilarious doubletalk, traveling lightly through the social corridors. Owning nothing, he can lose nothing; standing neither to gain nor to lose, he lives without responsibilities or commitments.

Denied his patrimony by society, the mestizo was yet destined to be its heir and receiver. Superficially, this rise to power resembles the experience of the European middle classes and their emancipation in a series of "bourgeois" revolutions. But the mestizo mass was not a middle class, or a class at all—if class be defined in terms of differential access to the means of production. The European middle classes occupied a clear-cut position between the rich and powerful and the poor and powerless. Owning property and having traditional claims to the intermediate positions in civil and religious hierarchies, they also possessed a stake in constituted society and—based on that stake— a well-knot system of common behavior and understanding, a common subculture. The mestizos, on the other hand, comprised both men who worked with their hands and men who worked with their wits. They shared not a common stake in society but the lack of such a stake; they shared a common condition of social alienation. Relegated to the edges of society, living in permanent insecurity, their reactions were akin not to the firmly anchored, substantial European middle classes but to the groups which Karl Marx called the "Lazarus-layers of the working class" and to the rootless, underemployed, unemployable intelligentsia-in-rags of post-1929 Europe who furnished the *condottiere* of the European Right and Left. In their common estrangement from society, the petty official, the political fixer, the hard-pressed rancher, the hungry priest, found a common denominator with the Indian bereft of the protection of his community, the artisan burning his midnight oil in poverty and

religious devotion, the petty trader or cattle-rustler, the half-employed pauper of the streets, the ragamuffin of the Thieves' Market. Such men constituted neither a middle class nor a proletariat; they belonged to a social shadow-world.

Nor was industrial or commercial development in Middle America ever steady and sustained enough to recruit more than a handful from the mestizo mass into what might be a middle class or a proletariat until the advent of the twentieth century. The Industrial Revolution of North Atlantic Europe, advancing steadily both in space and time, generated middle classes and proletariats that could build, coral-like, upon the achievements of their predecessors. The problems of political order were resolved early in the course of industrial growth to insure the victory of the bourgeoisie over feudal lords and to reduce the political struggle to the niceties of parliamentary behavior. In contrast, Middle America—as indeed much of the colonial world—moved economically not in a straight line but in fits and starts, in a succession of upswings and downswings.

The sixteenth century had witnessed the establishment of the colonial utopia and the consequent flow of specie and rapidly growing transatlantic trade. The seventeenth century relapsed into rural isolation and restricted markets: the hacienda became the bulwark of colonial life in the countryside, the Indian community its ruralized Indian counterpart. The eighteenth century again witnessed an upswing in mining, trade, production for export; but independence from Spain drove Middle America back into reliance on the countryside. Thus Middle America entered the nineteenth century without a middle class and without a proletariat. The basic issue of power remained similarly unresolved. Economic power and power won by force remained similarly unresolved. Economic power and power won by force of arms remained wedded to each other. The power-seekers had to employ both together; each kind of power fed and reinforced the other.

Yet, paradoxically, the very weakness of the mestizos, their very alienation from society, spelled subterranean strength. As society abdicated to them its informal and unacknowledged business, they became brokers and carriers of the multiple transactions that caused the blood to flow through the veins of the social organism. Beneath the formal veneer of Spanish colonial government and economic organization, their fingers wove the network of social relations and communication through which alone men could bridge the gaps between formal institutions. At the same time, such informal relations drew men together and strengthened their sense of a common fate. Subterranean as they were, they depended on face-to-face relations. They owed nothing to governmental prescript; their organization depended entirely on the vicissitudes of personal power. As men fought their personal battles of loyalty and disloyalty, they unwittingly wove the new patterns of dominance and submission that would serve to organize men into common action within larger groups. Thus in the unacknowledged niches of the powerless, a new social pattern developed, a mestizo pattern, a common etiquette of signaling and receiving. Beneath the integument of Spanish power, the Middle American patterns of nationality were born.

As the mestizos filled with their own web of relationships the social void left by the Spanish overlords, they also projected into the society that harbored them a common emotional force, the passion of nationalism. Nationalism becomes a passion because it allows men to transcend the limits of the separate self and to merge that self with a social body, the nation, to which they impute a magical collective strength. As members of a nation, men need no longer feel isolated and alone; and as they gain in strength through numbers, the collectivity becomes the bearer of their secret wishes. In attacking a common national enemy, they can attack also—on the symbolic level—the inimical forces that threaten their personal well-being. To the Middle American mestizo, this symbolic enemy was inevitably first the Spaniard who had denied him his rightful inheritance; but after Independence it would be the *gringo* from north of the border, whose wealth and self-confident brashness would remain a standing irritant to Middle American pride even after the United States soldiery had withdrawn from the Halls of Montezuma.

A nation, says Ortega y Gasset, is an invitation extended by some men to others to join them in a common undertaking. To make themselves heard in such a venture and to insure continuity of purpose, men must be able to communicate. To become a nation, groups of men must learn to transact social business with one another. They need an etiquette to rule this newly discovered mutuality, a shared grammar of manners and morals and of shared emotional inflections to govern their exchanges in a common market place of goods and ideas, to channel their conflicts in a common political arena. In the hidden passageways of society, as he tightened the informal network of economic, military, and political relations, the mestizo learned just such a new etiquette of communication. Yet the gates to the citadel of power and wealth stood shut. As long as the structure of privilege persisted, his newly found idiom could remain no more than a subterranean jargon. Hacienda and Indian community discoursed endlessly over their closed circuits upon the subject of their separate identities. Trade was in the hands of the great merchants, land and men in the hands of the landowners or the protected Indian communities, craft production in the hands of guild masters, ecclesiastical power in the hands of Spanish-born priests, political power in the hands of Peninsular officials and their friends. To create the future, the mestizo had to war upon privilege, to open the sluice gates of circulation through which goods, land, labor, and power could all flow out as negotiable commodities upon an open market, to impose one grammar of manners and morals—his cultural grammar—as a national means of communication. Only as closed society gave way to open society, closed communication to open communication, could the mestizo win his place in the sun.

To become masters in the Middle American house, the mestizos had first to be apprentices. For a long time they could play no independent political or economic role. Some served their journeymen years in the armies of the large landowners who broke the grip of the Spanish bureaucracy on Middle America, not to create a new and open society, but to tighten more securely their own hold over the supply of available labor. But independence from Spain ushered in no new dawn of liberty. It merely swept away royal protection of the Indians and put an end to labor exchanges, special Indian courts, legal limits to Indian debts, laws governing the duration and kind of work open to Indians. After independence the hacienda emerged with redoubled strength. A decline of mining at the end of the eighteenth century, the disorders of war and rebellion, the sudden removal of Middle America from the economic bloc of the Spanish Empire, all favored, once again, a return to the ramparts of power in the countryside.

Everywhere, too, independence was followed by attempts to divide the Indian communal holdings among the members of the community, or to allocate them to outsiders. The language used to justify this breakup of long-established tenures was the language of economic liberalism, the ostensible aim to create a Middle American yeomanry, a sturdy class of independent property-holders, in the image of the English and French revolutions. In this invasion of the Indian communities mestizos and landowners made common cause. But when the dust of battle had cleared, the haciendas had gained all; the mestizos who had ridden in their service had gained little or nothing. The haciendas had added both land and peons, while in areas too distant or too poor to prove rewarding to the outsider, the Indians had simply withdrawn further into their communal shells, turning the dream of the sturdy Middle American yeoman into merely another political and economic chimera.

Paradoxically, however, this solidification of power on the local level opened a third gate to mestizo participation in politics and civil warfare. It created a power vacuum on the national level. A hacienda could dominate a community, a valley, even a region; but the hacienda system did not give rise to a united national planter class, conscious of its interests. The removal of the Spanish viceroy and his staff left vacant the seats of power; no committee of powerful landowners took his place. Inevitably, this lack of power on the national level drew men into a round of endless conquests for real or imaginary spoils. Sometimes the contestants fought their own battles; at other times they were the witting or unwitting agents of foreign powers taking advantage of the power vacuum to further their own interests. Yet, in the very pursuit of chaos the mestizo emerged from his shadow-world on the edges of society into the full light of day. The prevalent political and economic disorder was his school of public administration and his military academy. In the struggle for the instruments of the state, he learned how to project personal power into public power. If the retreat into the countryside solidified the power of the landowners, it also made the mestizo a force to be reckoned with, for it propelled him—weapons in hand—upon a national stage.

In the second half of the nineteenth century, this time under the stimulus of foreign capital investment, the economic balance began to shift once more away from agriculture. In Mexico, investment speeded the growth of mining, textile production, railroad construction, petroleum exploitation; in Guatemala, it flowed into the commercial cultivation of bananas and coffee. Wherever it penetrated, it quickened the economic pulse and speeded up the circulation of people and goods. Wherever if diffused, it created new hopes for the future. This was true especially of Mexico, and especially of northern and central Mexico as compared with southern Mexico and Guatemala. By 1895 Mexico had an industrial proletariat of 365,000, a rural middle class of 213,000, an urban middle class of 776,000. In comparison with the 7,853,000 living in peon families on haciendas, these represent only a fraction of the population; but their very presence indicates the direction of social and economic growth.

Yet between the possibilities offered by this growth and their realization stood a formidable array of vested interests. These included not only the traditional tenants of power in the rural areas but also foreign financiers, fearful for the fate of their investments, and—toward the end of the century—a mestizo cabal which had emerged victorious in the successive political and military eliminations and which lived by selling protection both against the increasingly restless peons and against disorders which might curtail the flow of foreign capital. Poised between past and future, these power-holders maintained an uneasy equilibrium between hostile forces by eliminating, through bribery and violence, all possible rivals from below.

Only a revolution could break through this network of interests and clear the way to an open society; and in the course of this revolution the mestizo would graduate from political apprenticeship to political mastery. The revolution came in Mexico in 1910, belatedly and abortively in 1945 in Guatemala. In these revolutions the mestizo leadership abandoned its alliance with the traditional power-holders and allied itself instead with the submerged elements of the old order, the peons of the haciendas and the Indians of the Indian communities. The economic cement of this alliance was land reform, the division of land among the propertyless; the ideological cement was Indianism, the search for roots in the Indian past.

In the course of land reform, in Mexico, successive revolutionary governments distributed—between 1910 and 1945—close to 76 million acres, including the holdings of foreigners who owned a fifth of all the cultivable land in the Republic. All this land was allocated either to independent smallholders or to communities called *ejidos,* in which the community, not the individual, retained ultimate proprietary rights. Guatemala, in the course of its belated revolution, distributed close to a million acres, including half the holdings of the United States–owned United Fruit Company. Here land remained in the hands of the government; recipients of land grants were to pay a small annual rent to validate their rights of usufruct. In both countries, legal reform accompanied the reform in land tenure, and newly promulgated laws struck at the relationship between landowner and peon. In both countries, too, agricultural workers and peasants formed organizations capable of defending their interests against the vanquished landlord class by force of arms or through recourse to the courts. In Guatemala, counterrevolution reversed these steps in 1954; but in Mexico they became the law of the land.

The ideological counterpart of this social mobilization was the burgeoning and spread of Indianism. This intellectual movement had begun in the nineteenth century as a rather self-conscious attempt on the part of a few individuals to draw moral inspiration for the new order from the legacy of the Indian past. With the coming of the revolution, their symbols and attitudes achieved a new and wider popularity. Indian themes sounded again in the music of a Carlos Chávez, populated the murals of the Mexican Neo-Realists, guided the brush of a Roberto Ossaye in Guatemala, the hand of an architect designing the new university in Mexico City. Heroes of the Indian past became national archetypes; the bloodthirsty Mexica tyrants were transfigured into champions of the new united nation. Collective scorn and pity were heaped upon a Malinche, the Indian concubine of Cortés, for the betrayal into Spanish hands of her fellow Indians. In the murals of a Siqueiros, Cuauhtémoc, the last Mexica king, tortured and put to death by Cortés, achieved a new transfiguration, rising from the dead to affirm a new and glorious future, while—in Diego Rivera's hands—his Spanish protagonist emerged as a hydrocephalic, syphilitic idiot. Transmuted into myth, the indigenous past became a golden age, the colonial period a time of trial and darkness, the mestizo present a return to the abundance and innocence of the country's golden youth. The foreigners had been expelled; now Cuauhtémoc would again be master in his own mansions.

But land reform, like Indianism, was only a halfway house to the achievement of the new society. The new order began there; yet it could not stop there. Land reform may be a prelude to solutions; but by itself alone it is incapable of solving any problem on more than a temporary basis. If a country possesses sufficient land for all now living, division of land may postpone a renewal of agrarian conflict for a generation; but population growth alone will soon reopen the question of land to the landless. If a country, like Middle America, lacks sufficient land for all, the very act of distribution will refuel the voices of discord. In Mexico, the average recipient received 10.4 acres of crop land, little of this irrigated. Such a gift would not supply the needs of a growing family for very long.

The ultimate effects of land reform, as of the Indianist movement, were therefore not those foreseen by its early advocates. Land reform solved no economic problem; nor did the archive of the Indianist contain a road map to guide the society on its future path. But land reform had transcendental political effects. It not only broke the monopoly of power of the landholding elite and freed the peons; it created new sources of power in the countryside. For in the very act of distributing land to the landless, the agents of the land reform became the new power-holders in the rural area. In the deed of land the revolutionary government paid its rural citizens an earnest of its intentions; but in the act of bestowal the new government simultaneously laid the foundations of a new political machine to replace the one overturned by the revolution. In the creation of this new political weapon the revolutionary government not only guaranteed its present stability; it also created a set of checks against the vicissitudes of the future.

For the future could no longer be built upon the past. To fulfill the goals of his revolution the mestizo had to go beyond land reform and beyond Indianism to an active transformation of society in his own image. The economic instruments of this transformation are industrialization and the mechanization of agriculture. The political instruments of this transformation are the political machines that maintain the peace of the countryside. And the ideological instrument of this transformation is nationalism, together with its concomitant desire not to return to the cultural patterns of the Indian but to put an end to his separate cultural existence. Yet industrialization, political consolidation, and nationalism have a logic of their own. They exact a price, and as that price increases, those who pay it begin to question what goods and services all this blood, sweat, and tears will finally buy. Thus, if the revolution granted the mestizo the levers of power, it also made the maintenance of this power dependent upon his ability to deliver on his promises. Those who unleash the storm must know how to ride it, or become its victims.

The "underdeveloped" countries of the world have a choice of two major patterns of industrialization. The first pattern was adopted by the Soviet Union and by China. It grants priority to the construction of heavy industry; it carries out what Nikolai Bukharin called "war-feudal exploitation of the peasantry" to generate the capital needed for this purpose; and it throttles consumer needs to a minimum. The other pattern is that of the modern capitalist world. For both external and internal political and economic reasons Mexico has followed the second pattern. It involves a combination of various types of economic effort. Some capital is built up through sales of products to the heavily industrialized countries of the world; thus Mexico sells to the outside world a number of raw materials, and snares quantities of mobile dollars through its growing tourist trade and industry. At the same time, there is a growing light industry directed toward an internal market. This industry has its roots in the textile industry of the late nineteenth century; but in contrast to its predecessor it is beginning to supply—often on the installment plan—goods which until recently were the hallmark of North American mass production: radios, gas stoves, sewing machines, watches, costume jewelry, knives and forks, television sets, aluminum pots, overalls, shoes—the cheap, quickly obsolescent, easily replaceable commodities of the "American way of life." These goods do not go into a foreign market; they are marketed in Mexico to an ever growing number of Mexican wage-earners.

This change in the pattern of consumption is a direct function of industrialization. In the narrow sense, it provides a means of fulfilling some of the promises of the revolution. Industrialization everywhere has involved people in the dilemma of "steel versus butter," between consumption now and consumption postponed in favor of continued reinvestment. In the countries of the Soviet bloc industrialization has been subsidized by restricted consumption and discrimination against the agricultural producer; in Mexico, it has been supported by the low real income of the Mexican wage-earner. While the Mexican economy as a whole has witnessed a phenomenal rate of growth, real wages have increased but slightly since 1910. The small increase in wages has not gone into a better diet or into better housing. It has gone into the acquisition of the cheap and expendable items of North American culture. Not everyone can participate in their consumption; but their "demonstration effect" makes "pie in the sky" seem increasingly available in the here and now, thus making the hidden exploitation of the industrial labor force.

The spread of the new culture pattern also symbolizes the advent, here and now, of the open society of the future. That society, like the society of the United States north of the border, will be based on the premises that mobility is open to everyone; that position in society is measured not by descent but by income and by the goods income can buy; that all elites are temporary and that the tastes and goods of the elite should be distributed among the general population as quickly and as widely as possible; and that unlimited production and ever changing consumption are values in their own right. Hence Middle America borrows in the United States not only some of its capital for economic development but also canons of taste and the goods to satisfy these tastes. As nineteenth-century France offered the world the symbols of consumption that marked off the cultivated and educated man from the boorish and illiterate, so in the twentieth century the United States provides the world with the symbolic small-change of participation in the open society. The result is a cultural hybrid which the Mexicans deride publicly as *pocho* culture, although they are unable to resist its attraction and its advance.

But the spread of *pocho* culture does more than this. Along with a politics based on land reform, it is a powerful solvent of Indian resistance to incorporation. The diffusion of its cheap and expendable goods effectively undermines the scheme of means and ends through which the Indian has hitherto defended his autonomy. Limited wants, covered in limited ways, are yielding to growing wants and to the spread of alternative means to their satisfaction. Each year brings, in this community or that, the breakdown of the ritual system of enforced expenditures which has hitherto checked individual accumulation of wealth. At the same time, each year witnesses—here and there—the abandonment of the traditional unity of secular and sacred offices, up to now the chief defense of the community against the accumulation and misuse of power by one of its members. Each year, in some community, men grown old in the service of their fellow men and of the supernatural yield to young men untried in communal administration but willing to align themselves with the new mobile men in the larger society beyond.

Yet the spread of this pattern raises as many problems as it answers. Many communities have indeed yielded to its temptations, but at the time of telling there still remain everywhere reservoirs of resistance, communities as yet unwilling or unable to open the gates to the flow of new cultural alternatives. Will all these communities eventually be integrated into the mainstream of national life? This would represent a signal triumph for the mestizo cause; yet it would imply, too, the disintegration of that local unity on which Middle America has so often relied for its defense in past times of crisis. But what if the process of integration should encounter limits, as it has so often encountered limits in the past? Perhaps there are still communities so distant from the centers of national life, so poor in resources, that they could not multiply their wants even if they had the will to do so. Perhaps there are still communities so lacking in assets possible to mobilize that any effort to make them part of the nation would outweigh the advantages thus gained. Shall we then witness the unwished-for and unenvisioned emergence of "native reserves," in which the remaining Indians will cling, hillbilly-like, to an ever more barren, ever more impoverished hinterland?

Nor is the spread of *pocho* culture an unmixed boon even for those willing and able to purchase its trappings. Perhaps Middle America can achieve integration and liberation from the dead hand of the past only by borrowing the cultural patterns of its powerful northern neighbor. Yet such borrowing involves a deeper paradox, the paradox of a social unity gained at the price of cultural indebtedness to another society. Would Middle America be willing to pay for such a solution with lowered self-esteem and valuation of its society, and would it then substitute for its hostility against itself the rituals of a nationalism exacerbated rather than attenuated by the growing similarity in the cultural field, in order to preserve its social identity? Or will Middle America eventually find its own voice? Is the great flowering of Mexican painting and architecture evidence of such a new and fruitful synthesis, or will it, too, wither away as Indianism declines in the face of the new utilitarian concerns of the new occupants of power?

Thus men still remain torn between yesterday and tomorrow; and Middle America remains in travail. There can therefore be no finis to this book [*Sons of the Shaking Earth*] nor any prophecy. The rooster has cried a coming dawn, but in the gray daybreak the shadows still lie in dark pools about doorway and alley. Somewhere, an Indian elder bows to the four directions and invokes the rain-givers, the earth-shakers in their mountainous domain. The mouth of the volcano still yawns; the future is not yet. It lies in the walk of that man, shielding his face against the cold; in the gestures of that woman, fanning the embers of her fire and drawing her shawl more closely about her sleeping child; in that lonely figure, setting a signal along a railroad track. There is still time until the sun rises, but men scan the sky; for their lives are mortgaged to tomorrow.

9

The Indian in Latin American History

John Kicza

The history of Latin America does not begin in 1492. Some tens of millions of peoples organized into distinct polities and ethnic groups had already lived in this vast region for thousands of years before Europeans reached the hemisphere. Nor are we dependent just on archaeology and oral traditions for our knowledge of the history and culture of many of these societies. The more elaborate among them—most notably, the Maya and the Aztecs—had developed writing and mnemonic systems that recorded aspects of their pasts and their beliefs. Further, soon after the arrival of the Europeans, some members of these cultures learned to write their language using the Spanish alphabet. They then composed versions both of their histories and of contemporary events in their societies, sometimes with very little Spanish intervention.

The native peoples of the Americas have dis-

From John Kicza, "Introduction," from *The Indian in Latin American History: Resistance, Resilience, and Acculturation.* Wilmington, DE: Scholarly Resources, pp. xi–xxvi. Copyright 1993 by Scholarly Resources Inc. Reprinted by permission of Scholarly Resources Inc.

played remarkable cultural resilience in the face of demographic catastrophes; loss of lands and local political autonomy; recurrent infusions of outside technologies, animals, foods, and procedures over the centuries; and disrespectful treatment of their values and ways of life by the governments and citizens of those nations into which they have been merged. To the extent possible, Indian peoples have been selective about what aspects of the outside world they incorporate into their cultures. The indigenous communities have not been without resources. They have used their internal unity, under dedicated local leaders in many cases, to incorporate the changes forced upon them on the best terms that they could muster. Nor were they cowed or passive before the impositions of colonial and national governments. Both individual Indians and Indian corporations commonly initiated petitions and lawsuits to demand remedies for perceived injustices. Local rebellions by native peoples were endemic in large parts of Latin America over the centuries; some indigenous communities had well-earned reputations for insurrection. Occasionally, these rebellions became widespread and threatened major regions and even national governments. Through a combination of selective adaptation and peaceful (or sometimes violent) resistance, the native peoples of Latin America, even those subjugated by the Europeans, have been making their own histories for five hundred years.

Latin American Indians have been so successful in drawing upon their own resources and capacities that today their numbers are growing and they constitute a majority of the population in countries such as Guatemala and Bolivia and a substantial plurality in Mexico, Ecuador, and Peru. Even in countries where they do not make up a large part of the population—Brazil, Colombia, and Chile, for example—native peoples have been able to assert their rights and claims and make the national societies come to grips with the issues of native autonomy and control over land and other resources.

Clear evidence of human habitation in the Americas dates from at least 25,000 B.C. and some findings hint at a human presence in this continent perhaps twenty thousand years earlier. Whatever the actual date of humanity's arrival in this part of the world, undoubtedly the next great transforming development was the emergence of agriculture in the centuries before 1,500 B.C. Indications are that native peoples of Mexico, Guatemala, Colombia, and Peru commenced the cultivation of crops—instead of continuing their practice of hunting and gathering—autonomously and at roughly the same time. By 1,500 B.C. villages of full-time farmers were proliferating. Maize, beans, and squash constituted the primary crops cultivated, but potatoes and manioc dominated some major agricultural zones in South America.

The intensive, permanent cultivation of crops had immense consequences for the native people's way of life. It promoted a vast increase in the population and required practitioners to remain settled in communities surrounded by their fields. This sedentary existence facilitated occupational differentiation, as farmers routinely produced food surpluses that they were willing to trade for the finished goods fashioned by local artisans. Social distinctions also emerged. With time, ruling classes, sometimes complete with royal families, appeared, as did a priesthood. In fact, religious practice became more elaborate, and large ceremonial complexes were constructed for the first time. Hundreds of ethnic groups worshiped similar sets of gods, though each group gave its local versions distinct names and, understandably, saw its own

gods as the rightful and effective ones, unlike those of the other peoples.

These hundreds of ethnic groups practicing agriculture eventually formed themselves into political entities, organized as provinces in which a head town—where the ruling dynasty resided—controlled a complex of subject villages; in turn, each village there was a set of families who governed local society. It was from among these sedentary agricultural societies, with their labor surpluses, local craft specializations, and large armies, that empires developed. These entities could be found in Mesoamerica (the sedentary zone of Central America, roughly the southern two-thirds of Mexico, all of Guatemala, and most of El Salvador, Honduras, and Nicaragua) and in the Andean highlands in the modern nations of Ecuador, Peru, and Bolivia at least a millennium and a half before the arrival of Europeans in the hemisphere. No other true empires would appear in indigenous America, for the hundreds of other ethnic groups, totaling in the millions of people, did not practice fully sedentary agriculture and hence lacked the attributes needed for the long-term conquest of other societies (although warfare was common among these peoples).

Mesoamerica and the Andean zone witnessed the rise and fall of a series of empires over the centuries. The conquerors typically demanded labor service from the subjugated peoples and, in the case of Mesoamerica, formal tribute payments also. The Incas and the Aztecs were the last examples—though certainly dramatically successful ones—of such polities, and in most aspects they replicated the institutions and practices of their predecessors. Characteristically, all of these empires permitted the inhabitants of their subjugated provinces to retain their own languages, sets of gods, local rulers, and separate ethnic identities. . . . These long-surviving empires did not destroy the ethnic distinctiveness of the subordinated peoples, who were quick to rebel whenever they saw any chance of success.

Many other peoples practiced some agriculture, but their environments were sufficiently unaccommodating that they had to move their settlements within a certain zone every few years and perhaps supplement their crops with substantial amounts of other foods. Most of the Maya of the Yucatán Peninsula and Guatemala practiced this slash-and-burn, or swidden, agriculture. Such agriculture dictated lower population densities and made enduring empires harder to attain—these peoples were more difficult to organize into large polities and had fewer surplus resources that they could transfer to an imperial power. Besides living in the southern zone of Mesoamerica, substantial numbers of semisedentary peoples resided on the major Caribbean islands and in highland Colombia, Brazil, Paraguay, and Chile.

Hunting-and-gathering peoples who practiced no agriculture remained in the desert, mountain, and tropical areas of Latin America. Organized into many small ethnic groups, they actually totaled far fewer persons than did either the sedentary or semisedentary societies. Without agriculture but with a need to migrate over considerable distances in order to gain sufficient resources to survive, these bands had to remain rather small in order to function effectively. Understandable, there was little political or craft differentiation among these peoples; the primary distinction in labor roles was based on gender. The artistic achievements of these peoples was rudimentary, and they used natural sites rather than constructed arenas as their religious centers. There were no empires among such societies, but they were especially adept fighters, utilizing ambushes and rapid retreats and advances as tactics and bows and arrows, sometimes poisoned, as weapons.

The best estimates indicate that the total native population of the Americas approached 75 million people on the eve of the Europeans' arrival. Of these native peoples, around 8 million lived in North America, more than 22 million in Mexico, some 8 million in Central America, another 8 million in the Caribbean, about 17 million along the Andes, and perhaps 12 million in lowland South America.

The vast numbers in Mexico and the Andes resulted, of course, from the dominance of agriculture and densely settled permanent villages in these areas.

It is only to non-natives that these peoples can be classified into a collective population termed "Indian." They were as distinct from each other in language and ethnic identity as their counterparts were in Europe—and often as contentious. In fact, the major differences between native Americans and the peoples of Europe, Africa, and Asia (for the peoples of these three continents shared broadly similar characteristics) were largely accidents of history and geography. The native Americans

lacked metal tools and weapons, did not have draft animals, and did not use the wheel in manual labor. They also were insulated from most of the epidemic diseases that regularly ravaged the Old World.

The Americans routinely refined gold, silver, and copper, which they shaped into ornaments. However, they had not developed industrial metals, especially iron, which are harder and thus appropriate for making tools. As a consequence, they largely relied on hard, sharp stones as tools and weapons. Flint and obsidian functioned as projectile points and were placed along the edges of swords and clubs. Overall, their lack of industrial metals led to a certain technological stagnation among these peoples. The tools of the Aztecs and the Incas varied little from those of peoples who preceded them by a millennium and a half.

The Western Hemisphere lacked horses, oxen, and other suitable beasts of burden. It also did not have cattle, pigs, goats, or chickens. The plains of North America were, of course, the home of millions of buffalo, which provided abundant meats, hides, and other necessities of life, but buffalo are totally unsuitable as beasts of burden. Llamas constituted the only useful animals of size in South America, and, although they yielded some meat and could bear some weight, they could not pull plows or wagons. Without draft animals, native Americans had little use for the wheel. They certainly knew of it and incorporated it into small implements, but they could not use it in sizable undertakings without large animals to provide power.

In most respects the Spanish resembled other European colonists of the Americas. Unlike the others, however, the Spanish rarely just established trading bases in new lands; instead, they sought to settle the lands fully and permanently. This process entailed the significant immigration of people (commonly an appreciable minority of the immigrants were women) and importation of animals, the establishment of cities, the settling up of rural enterprises to supply the urban sector, the incorporation of the local native peoples into a dependent labor force, and a rigorous effort to locate and work deposits of precious metals. These people went to the Americas not out of some compelling need for adventure but rather to make a better life for themselves and their descendants. Hardly any of them possessed a strong curiosity about Indian thought and culture. They wished merely for the native peoples to be peaceful, to provide them with unskilled labor, and to convert to Christianity. The actual conversion effort was left largely to members of religious orders with the support of wealthier colonists who financed a good bit of the process. Precious metals were pursued because they constituted the commodity that could be exported most profitably to Europe and thereby underwrite the long-term prosperity of a colony. (Eventually, in some areas in the Americas, commodities such as sugar, tobacco, dyewoods, and furs would also support elaborate colonial societies.)

The defeat of the great imperial armies of the Aztecs and the Incas by small Spanish expeditions seems quite beyond belief until systematically examined. Of course, the Spanish forces did not have to fight all of the millions of peoples who made up these massive empires. In fact, most of the subordinated peoples already within these empires welcomed the Spanish as potential liberators from the demands of their traditional oppressors. Thus Hermán Cortés and Francisco Pizarro were able to get many ethnic groups to agree either to remain outside the fight or even, sometimes, to support the invaders. The Spanish also benefited immensely from their technological superiority over the Indians. Firearms and cannon were not too important, for they were slow to fire, inaccurate, and inappropriate for the battles in open country that characterized warfare between the Spaniards and the sedentary empires. Far more decisive were the metal weapons and armor and the small contingent of horses that each expedition usually had with it. Lacking armor, the native armies could not defend themselves against the crossbow fire, swords, and lances of the Spanish. The Spanish cavalry was virtually unstoppable, able to disperse or outflank any formation assembled against it.

The technological advantage of the Spanish was maximized by the style of warfare practiced by the imperial societies. Making only minimal use of bows and arrows, imperial soldiers preferred close engagement with their opponents. They were equipped with wooden clubs commonly edged with obsidian chips, and they typically fought in the open rather than from cover, stressing capture over the killing of their opponents. The imperial armies presented themselves in tight formations in which only the front rank could actually fight, and they remained under strict hierarchies. When commanders were killed or captured, their forces would fall out of action.

Finally, the Spanish, as did all the European colonists, unwittingly brought with them virulent epidemic diseases with which the American peoples had no experience and against which they had no resistance. Smallpox, measles, and typhus seem to have had the worst impact. These diseases were so contagious that smallpox was already sweeping through the Aztec capital when Cortés had it under siege. Both an Aztec and an Incan emperor died from this disease even though no European was in their vicinity at the time.

After the defeat of their empires, the Indians tried to explain these catastrophic defeats to themselves. Because they were very religious peoples who believed that the gods determined all outcomes, they asserted that their defeats had been prefigured by omens and that they had viewed the Spaniards as returning gods. However, the evidence indicates that this perspective developed after the fact and did not affect the course of the actual conquests.

The Spanish never saw it as in their interest to destroy the structure of native society. Rather, they sought to use the structure that was already in place to govern effectively, to mobilize cheap Indian labor, to funnel resources into the Hispanic sector of the society, and to Christianize the population. The Spanish relied on indigenous systems and traditional relationships in the decades just after the conquest of Peru, but eventually the elaboration of a large-scale market economy and the declining native population brought an end to this practice.

Against native peoples who were not fully sedentary and organized into empires, the Spaniards' technological advantages faded. For example, the Spaniards faced some difficulties when pitted against the loosely confederated Maya in the Yucatán Peninsula. The Spaniards had to fight nearly every individual settlement in this region—a difficult tropical environment in which Spanish mobility was restricted and that the Maya could utilize to their advantage. Mayan settlements could withdraw into the countryside in the face of Spanish advances, and, when beleaguered, Mayan fighters could retreat into difficult country to fight another day.

There were dramatic cases of successful resistance by native peoples. The Araucanians of southern Chile remained independent of outside control until they finally were defeated by the Chilean army around 1880. Mobility, flexibility, and adaptation explain how they were able to retain their autonomy prior to their defeat. The Araucanians adopted the horse and even changed their settlement and eating patterns to enhance their ability to resist. Over the decades they studied the Spanish way of fighting and developed suitable responses. But in the late nineteenth century, the introduction of the repeating rifle and of such developments as barbed wire and the telegraph gave the Chileans the means to subdue the Araucanians. (The Araucanians who controlled southern Argentina also were defeated at this time by an Argentine army utilizing the same advances.)

The Spanish faced immense difficulties in overcoming the hunting-and-gathering peoples located in northern Mexico, at the Amazon headwaters, in eastern Bolivia, and elsewhere. Often the colonists abandoned their efforts to subdue these native groups, which fought them so effectively using bows and arrows and hit-and-run tactics. These Indians held little promise as usable labor force and generally controlled no resources that the Spanish considered lucrative. It was in this setting that the Spanish would establish missions in an effort gradually to convert the natives and to attract them to a European style of life. In northern Mexico, however, the Spaniards discovered major silver deposits and thus had to protect the region's mining towns and shipping routes from attack. During the second half of the sixteenth century their attempts either to subjugate the local peoples or to run them off were notably unsuccessful. The Spanish viceroys finally resorted to offering the local groups annual shipments of supplies to be provided by the colonial government if they would agree to cease their raids, settle in permanent villages, and accept missionaries among them. The natives generally accepted such offers because the alternative was continued warfare in which the native societies suffered losses and dislocation even when they prevailed in a particular campaign. Consequently, much of the north was opened to colonization.

Until roughly 1650 the factor that most transformed Indian life in Latin America was the collapse of the population brought about overwhelmingly by the new epidemic diseases that arrived with the colonists. As these diseases were most virulent in temperate settings where there was heavy population density, central Mexico suffered as badly as, if not worse than, any other region. In a little over a century, successive waves of epidemics reduced the native population by about 95 percent, from more than 20 million people to fewer than 1.5 million. The indigenous community in the Spanish Caribbean literally had been eliminated by 1550. Central America and the Andean region were also badly hit. It must be stressed that the Spanish neither encouraged nor understood the catastrophe. They sought to utilize local native populations, not to eradicate them.

The primary consequence of this enormous die-off was to skew the native–colonist population ratios so greatly that the surviving Indians were more fully acculturated to the European way of life and could be more closely regulated by Spanish priests and administrators and that great expanses of agricultural land that had become depopulated were thus available for cultivation by colonists. Without this demographic catastrophe, modern Latin America would more closely resemble Africa or India, where the European impact, although certainly significant, was not as transforming of native cultural, social, and political patterns as it was in the Western Hemisphere.

The introduction of Old World animals and tools affected the indigenous way of life as well. Horses, oxen, cattle, pigs, and chickens were brought to the Americas in great numbers. Overall, Indian villagers did not incorporate draft animals into their agricultural practices in a systematic fashion, but pigs and chickens became staples in their diets. Tools, pans, and knives of metal became integral parts of native existence. Firearms, however, seem to have been used rarely by Indians, even in hunting.

The Christianization of the Indians is a controversial and poorly understood development. An appreciation that there was always a shortage of Catholic priests available to work in native communities and that the Indians often were inclined to adopt major components of the religion of their conquerors—even before the arrival of the Europeans—helps to explain much of what transpired. A Spanish cleric typically set up his parish in the head town of an Indian province. He would be able to visit the many villages within the province only two or three times each year. Church marriages, baptisms, and the like thus had to wait for such occasions. Of course, the priest could teach religious doctrine, say Mass, and hear confessions only at these times also. Understandably, then, the form of Catholicism that emerged stressed community values and public celebrations, which did not require a priest's continued presence. Individual towns adopted patron saints and shrines that they promoted in their festivities. Neighborhoods and other community groups organized themselves into religious brotherhoods (*cofradías*) to sustain such activities and to provide benefits to the membership. Over time, assumption of the burden of sponsoring community religious celebrations became the primary avenue by which an individual could rise in respect and responsibility within the society, and the men who sacrificed their interests to those of the community through such endeavors became eligible to hold the highest civic offices. This set of practices had become termed the *cargo system.*

Spanish priests commonly located their churches and chapels upon sites that the Indians already considered sacred. For their part, the Indians often merged the Catholic church's spectrum of saints with their own enduring pantheon of gods. The result of such practices was a certain combining of systems of belief, called syncretism, that has lasted in many areas to the present day.

It would be misleading, however, to argue that Spanish priests—or colonial officials, for that matter—acted as the primary agents of change in native culture. Rather, that honor goes to the colonists themselves, who, by their continuing interaction with the Indians, generally in the most informal and unstructured ways, engendered new practices and relationships. For despite laws against it, Indians interacted incessantly with Spaniards in colonial towns, mining camps, and rural estates. Sometimes natives would fulfill a labor shift at such a location, during which time they would be exposed to European material culture and customs, and then would return to their home community. Other natives, however, remained and became permanent members of Spanish colonial society. Nor did Spaniards and, later, the persons of mixed blood (mestizos) who resulted from the matings between

Spaniards and Indians, stay out of Indian communities. Few of these individuals chose to live in such communities in the colonial period (though later a scattering would reside interspersed in Indian villages with regularity), but they passed through as peddlers, labor recruiters, and the like.

Early in the colonial period, Indian communities were expected to supply a portion of their adult male populations—generally around one sixth—on a rotating basis to work in the Spanish sector of the economy. Such labor gangs were organized by the villages' headmen (caciques), and they remained under the immediate supervision of their own leaders during their period of labor. But the fruit of the natives' efforts, of course, directly assisted the Spanish sector of the society. With time, as the colonial economies became more elaborate, this form of temporary unskilled labor became less useful, and, characteristically, it endured only in the more backward parts of Latin America. Instead, Spanish entrepreneurs attracted particularly skilled and industrious Indians as permanent workers in their enterprises by offering them improved terms of employment. Many natives accepted such offers because of the considerable deterioration that had taken place in their own communities from population decline and Spanish demands for labor service and tribute payments. Working for individual Spaniards provided them with a degree of security and protection from the worst of these demands. Over the long term, then, a considerable number of Indians came to reside permanently in Spanish colonial society, and their children were born to this, rather than to the traditional village way of life. As the Indians interbred with Spaniards and blacks in the cities and on rural estates, a large community of persons of mixed blood emerged with whom urban Indians interacted on a regular basis.

The eighteenth century was a time of considerable economic growth in Latin America. Previously peripheral regions were incorporated into the world market economy for the first time and prospered as a result. In already heavily settled and economically developed regions, such as Mexico and Peru, market-oriented estates proliferated throughout the countryside, occupying virtually all of the land suitable for cultivation and grazing. Indian communities were increasingly restricted to just the lands they traditionally controlled, lands that the colonial governments had recognized as theirs and now helped to protect. Both Indian communities and their individual members now enjoyed little opportunity to expand their land holdings.

This situation might not have been harmful except for the sizable growth in the indigenous population that took place during the same era. Whereas the native population in the Americas would never again approach what it had been upon the arrival of the Europeans, it did increase rapidly as the natives built up resistance to the several epidemic diseases that periodically had ravaged their population over the previous two centuries. For example, indications are that Mexico's native population roughly doubled, to a total of about 3.7 million over the hundred years before 1810. But the Spanish and mixed-blood populations were growing as well and at nearly comparable rates at this time. Heightened competition for the limited resources in these societies resulted.

As Indian communities experienced little improvement in productivity, they had to send out their members, either temporarily or permanently, to the laborers in the Spanish sector of the economy. Some natives thus lost their connections with their communities of birth and became permanent dwellers in cities or on rural estates. Others returned to their villages, using their external earnings to help their communities survive economically. (This pattern has endured to the present day, and one may inquire whether modern Indian communities could survive without the continuing outmigration of their young combined with an influx of part of the money that is earned.)

Village uprisings increased greatly in frequency in both Mexico and Peru during this period. However, these uprisings typically addressed local grievances and, therefore, rarely developed into regional or crossethnic revolts against the government. Nonetheless, in 1780, an Andean cacique named Josó Gabriel de Condorcanqui, who himself lived and operated regularly within the Spanish sector of the society, initiated a revolt that was joined by great numbers of people in the highlands. He gave himself the name Tupac Amaru II, claiming descent from the last autonomous Inca ruler, Tupac Amaru, who was executed in 1572. His movement dominated the highlands around Cuzco for some months, even attracting active support from people of mixed blood and from lower-class Spaniards, until a mil-

itary expedition dispatched from Lima defeated the insurgents. Tupac Amaru, his wife (a Spaniard who functioned as one of his primary lieutenants), and other commanders were captured and executed. But the Andean highlands remained in an unsettled state for another half century, with periodic regional revolts breaking out throughout Peru and Bolivia.

Members of Indian communities had surprisingly little involvement in the Latin American independence movements from 1808 to 1825. By and large, the leaders of these movements belonged to local elites, and their complaints simply did not address the place of native peoples in their societies, except for arguing that equality before the law should prevail in the new nations and that ethnic designations should be eliminated. Furthermore, neither the patriots nor the royalists saw a need to mobilize the Indian masses in their warfare against each other.

Although the vast number of Indians who lived in traditional villages under the authority of their ethnic leaders stayed out of the independence struggle (if anything, they seem to have favored the status quo), in Mexico that substantial minority of Indians who had left their communities to live permanently in the Spanish sector of the society strongly backed the initial uprising against the colonial order. This uprising was led by Father Miguel Hidalgo and began in the prosperous agricultural and mining region north of Mexico City. Tens of thousands of lower-class Spaniards, people of mixed blood, and acculturated Indians joined Hidalgo's army as it captured important regional centers and advanced on Mexico City. To the extent that we can determine the intentions of those Indians who participated, it seems that they resented the discrimination they endured under the prevailing social and political order as well as the requirement that they continue to pay tribute to the government even though most of them had long abandoned their association with native communities. When Hidalgo's army was crushed in a battle that took place about six months after the start of the insurrection, most of the priest's supporters tried to resume their civilian lives, but a substantial minority organized themselves into small regional gangs—often not very different from bandits—and remained active for years.

The new national governments, usually dominated by liberals, thought that Indians should lose both the special protections afforded and the obligations placed upon them during the colonial period and become full and equal citizens. They also believed that Indian lands should no longer be held in common but instead should be distributed to individual members of the communities who then would either work their private plots or sell them, as they saw fit. But these early governments were so weak and politically unstable that none could organize an effective campaign to achieve these ends. They were desperate for revenue, and some nations therefore retained the Indian tribute system for several decades after independence, renaming the impost an "indigenous contribution" in an effort to distinguish it from its colonial precedent. Residents of many Indian communities in Central America and the Andean republics were expected to contribute several days of free labor each year to maintain local roads.

Village uprisings occurred in the early national period much as they had in the late colonial, but now the Indian communities were commonly on the offensive rather than seeking to protect themselves from threatening initiatives. Encountering politically divided elites, failing national economies, and ineffective governments, many Indian communities undertook to take lands away from nearby haciendas. In Mexico, in the late 1840s, several of these movements turned into widespread regional revolts in which the Indians organized into interethnic coalitions and acted jointly to drive all non-Indians (and thus the national government) from their provinces.

The most notable and enduring of these insurrections took place in the Yucatán and was called the "Caste War." Casualties ran into the thousands, and many thousands more fled the region. The non-Indian population had to abandon virtually the entire countryside and cluster in several cities, and the Yucatán's market economy simply collapsed. Within a couple of years, the Mexican government was able to take the offensive against the insurgents, but vast parts of the peninsula remained firmly under rebel control. A belief that a divine cross located in a remote cave spoke to their leaders, directing them to continue the revolt, helped to maintain unity among the insurgents. The rebel commanders demanded heavy labor and military service from their followers but fought among

themselves, with assassinations sometimes the result. The insurrection also benefited from the rebels' ability to purchase arms from traders in British Honduras. Finally, in the first years of the twentieth century, the development of henequen plantations in the Yucatán, the fortification of the boundary with British Honduras, and the continuous deteriorating conditions in "Chan Santa Cruz," the territory controlled by the rebels, killed off the organized vestiges of the uprising. Until after World War II, however, extensive parts of the Yucatán backcountry remained in the hands of indigenous villages, which were still autonomous and sought to rekindle the revolt.

Some governments in heavily Indian countries did seek to protect their native populations in the mid-nineteenth century. Perhaps the greatest success was in Guatemala, where for more than twenty-five years starting in 1838, the conservative dictator José Rafael Carrera insulated the communal holdings of native villages from liberal demands that the collectives be broken up into small individual holdings. Carrera's government also enacted an "Indian Code" so that natives did not fall under the jurisdiction of the national legal system. Although Carrera promoted the use of indigenous languages, he still argued, nonetheless, that native peoples should eventually assimilate themselves into the larger Guatemalan nation and culture and that this should be a benign and gradual process.

The half century after about 1870 was perhaps the worst period since the initial conquest era for the Indian peoples of Latin America. Stimulated by a vastly heightened demand in the industrialized world for the commodities and minerals that they held in such abundance as well as by a tremendous influx of foreign capital and by the rapid-development of railroad and utility systems and port facilities, Latin American countries installed governments oriented toward capitalist development and friendly to the large-scale projects attractive to individual investors. An atmosphere of disdain toward native peoples and their cultures proliferated throughout the hemisphere. Newly created national armies moved aggressively against those indigenous societies that sought to protect their lands and their traditional political autonomy. One of the most enduring resistance movements was organized by the Yaquis of northwestern Mexico. This unrelenting attack on native resources, culture, and autonomy continued in most countries well into the twentieth century.

The Mexican Revolution, which took place between 1910 and 1920, marks the first distinct break in this onslaught. The struggle to regain communally owned lands that had been alienated from indigenous villages over the previous half century played a major role within this movement. By the end of the violent stage of the revolution, its leaders had committed themselves to restoring these lands. In the early 1920s, vast amounts of land in central Mexico and the Yucatán were returned to the native communities that had lost them. Establishing collectives became a central part of the revolutionary program, and their number and extent expanded each decade through the 1970s.

Land reform was not, however, without its opponents and drawbacks. Both the Indian and non-Indian populations of Mexico had increased rapidly after the revolution to the extent that the number of landless rural dwellers continued to grow in absolute terms while a vast amount of land was being distributed to millions of people. The recipients of this land often did not produce surpluses sufficient to feed Mexico's massive urban population or to be sold abroad for badly needed foreign earnings. Nor was the government's protection of native lands totally successful. Local businesspeople, often with official connections, circumvented regulations in order to gain control of communal lands or became favored suppliers and marketers to the native communities.

Beginning in the late 1930s, the Mexican government has sought to protect the diverse Indian languages and cultures of the country. Traditional caciques and village councils have had some of their authority restored. Teachers now often endeavor to provide native children with a bilingual education rather than to eradicate indigenous languages. Powerful government institutes work to preserve Indian cultures and to develop handicraft practices that may earn the natives money in the larger national economy.

Conditions for the native peoples in much of Latin America outside Mexico stayed worse longer. In countries such as Guatemala and Peru, Indian villages were required by statute to provide laborers for public works projects or large agricultural enterprises. Such laws generally were not changed until the World War II period. Even in recent times, native peoples are under duress—often with the compliance of government agencies or armed forces—to labor on plantations far from their homes. They typically are paid very low wages and may in fact owe money by the time that their obligation is over; these debts may be used to compel workers to return the following year. Wives and children often accompany the men during these periods. They live in squalid temporary housing where they are susceptible to dangerous diseases, and sometimes they too have to labor in the fields.

The native peoples of Bolivia, largely Aymara speaking, lost most of their lands early in the twentieth century to Hispanic Bolivians, who used their privileged position in the economy and in the political system to their advantage. Most of these Aymara then became retainers on the large—and typically unproductive—estates that resulted. However, the indigenous populations were not passive before these offensives against them. In their resistance, they revealed their retention of ancient native rituals and beliefs and also their sensitivity to the expectations and procedures of the national Bolivian society in which they lived.

In 1952, appreciating the opportunity afforded them by the overthrow of the government by a reformist coalition, Indian communities throughout Bolivia rose up, expelled estate owners, and reclaimed their traditional lands. Given the total collapse of the Bolivian military and government structures, the amount of violence involved was rather limited. The nascent reform government, recognizing the benefits to be gained from supporting the land seizures, passed a law the following year officially validating the land redistribution. Since that time, although Bolivia remains one of the most impoverished countries in Latin America, most rural villages have experienced an improvement in their quality of life. The villagers have been able to grow crops for urban markets, retain authority over their internal affairs, and benefit from the extension of education and public health services into their communities. They also are connected to the larger political system and to developments at the national level to an unprecedented extent.

Despite some concerted efforts at improvement over the last twenty-five years, conditions for the Indian peoples of Peru continue to be worse than perhaps they are in any other nation of Latin America. Until the late 1960s, the Indians' land and labor situation closely resembled that of the Bolivian native communities before the 1952 land reform. But even more than the Indians of Bolivia, the Indians of Peru were seen as belonging to an inferior culture apart from mainstream life; this attitude and Indian isolation were reinforced because the majority of Indians dwelled in the Andean highlands, whereas the Spanish, internationally oriented sector of Peruvian society predominated in the coastal regions. By the early 1960s, Indian communities and Indian workers on the backward estates that dominated the highlands had begun to protest and, sometimes, to revolt. The military who repressed these movements became sensitized to the plight of these people and to the primitiveness prevalent in this vast region of the country.

The opportunity for systematic change appeared in 1968, when a reformist military regime seized power in Peru. The following year it implemented a large-scale agrarian reform that affected the majority of estates in both the highland and coastal zones. Many permanent workers became members of the collectives that took over these lands. However, the cultural and economic isolation of these regions was not broken. By the mid-1970s, when the country entered a deep and persistent recession, the utility and appropriateness of these collectives were called into question.

In the early 1980s a radical and ruthless terrorist movement, the Shining Path, began to attack exposed highland communities. By the end of the decade they effectively controlled extensive regions and even could attack in cities along the coast. Cocaine production had begun to expand dramatically in this otherwise depressed economic climate, and many communities could survive only by growing coca leaf for the international drug trade.

Most native peoples of Latin America had continued contact with the Spanish sectors of their societies and in response made tremendous modifications in their cultures—often voluntarily, but sometimes forced. In fact, over time, though sometimes haltingly, the Spanish (or Western, if you will) sphere of Latin American society has tended to expand, and the portion of the economy and society that has remained Indian has shrunk. Thus the Indian population residing within modern national societies (which excludes only that small percentage of the overall Indian population that still lives along or beyond the frontiers of effective settlement by Latin Americans of European descent, such as the peoples of the upper Amazon) is so much a part of the larger culture—passing routinely from their communities into large cities and economic enterprises and bringing back to their communities new technology and practices—that some scholars question the utility of categorizing any of these traditional villages as "Indian" any longer. As vast numbers of indigenous people have become well integrated into the market economies and dynamic cultures of their national societies, they have lost, willingly or not, most the attributes that had distinguished them from peoples of European or mixed ancestry.

Even where native identify is more firmly set—as it is in the southern Mexican municipality of Zinacantan—powerful forces threaten the cohesion and cultural integrity of the Indian society. Most indigenous communities are so poor that they must send many of their youths to find work out in the larger society. Sometimes these emigrants are expected to send part of their earnings back to their home communities to help support those who remain. As these communities promote their own internal economic growth and diversification, they typically find it difficult to maintain their ethnic distinctiveness. Permitting a significant number of outsiders to marry into or to own property or establish businesses in the community also often threatens the community's distinct cultural heritage over the long term.

Thus many Indian communities in modern Latin America find themselves caught in a dilemma. If they continue their traditional agricultural, landholding, and marriage practices, their internal economies will stagnate, and they will have to export many of their young people or relegate them to increasing poverty. If they encourage integration into the national market economies, however, over time their populations are likely to lose their ethnic uniformity and their societies their cultural integrity. Either choice is unpleasant, but in the modern world the need to make such a choice seems unavoidable.

10

Inter-Ethnic Relations and Class Structure in Nicaragua's Atlantic Coast
A Historical Overview

Charles R. Hale

INTRODUCTION

From a macro historical perspective, the most salient force shaping social change on Nicaragua's Atlantic Coast has been external domination. At each critical juncture, the course of local events has been determined by the economic and geopolitical designs of an imperial power—first the British, who waged a successful struggle against Spain to control the territory, then the North Americans, whose direct presence receded only when opportunities for profits dwindled and a reliable surrogate (the Somoza family) was firmly entrenched. The system imposed by successive imperial powers underwent constant change, but it had one static feature: a sharp differentiation between white colonizers, capitalists, and imperial representatives, on the one hand, and native

From CIDCA/Development Study Unit, *Ethnic Groups and the Nation State*. Stockholm: Department of Social Anthropology, University of Stockholm, 1987. Used by permission of author. Research carried out for the two articles by Charles Hale was supported by a National Science Foundation grant, No. BNS–8510813.

inhabitants, African slaves, black and mestizo immigrants, on the other. Given the inordinate power of these white actors, their interests determined the overall direction of social change among all the dominated ethnic groups.

However, this fundamental dichotomy—center/periphery or colonizer/colonized—does not begin to capture the full extent of the historical complexity. In the first place, the dominated peoples themselves are subject to further political and economic differentiation. In multi-ethnic settings like the Atlantic Coast, the resulting hierarchy tends to occur along ethnic lines. Members of an ethnic group often have these interethnic relations as the main point of reference in their political perceptions and actions. Second, even when ethnic groups are differentiated internally, ethnic identity can unify disparate economic sectors, motivating people to act in ways that do not coincide with their strictly defined economic interests. These two factors suggest that interethnic relations—conflict, assimilation, alliance—can be an important agent of historical change, barely perceptible from the perspective of the center-periphery dichotomy.

My guiding argument, therefore, is that a focus on ethnic interactions and ethnic hierarchy can make an important contribution to understanding the history of Nicaragua's Atlantic Coast. The essay is divided into four sections. In each of the first three I examine a major transformation in the coastal ethnic hierarchy: (1) the Miskitu rise to dominance; (2) Creole ascendance and Miskitu decline; (3) entrance of mestizo elites. Important parallels in the three cases will emerge from this analysis. First, in each transformation one ethnic group (Miskitu, Creole, and Mestizo, respectively) acquired ascendance owing to active support provided by the imperial power. Second, having developed a structural advantage over the other dominated peoples, members of the privileged group tended to view themselves as culturally proximate to the whites and clearly superior to the rest. Third, the privileged group's role as intermediary meant that, directly or indirectly, it acted in alliance with the imperial power to uphold the existing order. In short, while the actions of the imperial power underlay the major transformations of the ethnic hierarchy, analysis of interethnic relations helps to demonstrate how the dominated peoples actively shaped the resulting historical change. In a fourth section I briefly examine the ethnic hierarchy under the Somoza dictatorship and point to a few implications of this legacy for ethnopolitics after the triumph of the Nicaraguan revolution.

BRITISH COLONIALISM, MISKITU DOMINANCE, AND SUMU SUBJUGATION

In pre-Columbian times, the Caribbean lowlands of present-day Nicaragua and Honduras were inhabited by numerous tribes whose members lived in small, dispersed settlements. All these subtribes belonged to the Macro-Chibchan linguistic family (Stone 1966:209); each had a distinct language though some were similar enough to be mutually intelligible (Conzemius 1932:14). They met subsistence needs by hunting, gathering, fishing, and, especially those who lived further inland, swidden agriculture. Although analysts disagree as to whether these Indians had permanent settlements on the Caribbean Coast,[1] at least some had highly developed skills as sea fishermen, a crucial factor in their subsequent interactions with Europeans. Villages consisted of a small number of multifamily dwellings, with very little internal social hierarchy. Elders took decisions on important matters affecting the whole village, including the designation of chiefs to lead intertribal warfare (Chapman 1958:120; W. M. 1732:307). This warfare may have followed ritualized, socially stipulated patterns, given that raiding and trading were known to occur in conjunction with one another (Helms 1982). Even though such interaction between tribes was frequent, the conditions of this contact did not permit one group to benefit inordinately at the expense of the others.[2]

The European presence profoundly altered this political and military equality among the indigenous subtribes by creating opportunities for internal differentiation within coast society. In this section I shall explain how, responding to these opportunities, indigenous (and later African) peoples actively shaped the emergence of a colonial ethnic hierarchy, thereby transforming the power relations between ethnic groups and the identities of each. A striking pattern in this upheaval that requires special explanation was the strong Miskitu affinity with the Europeans, in defiance of their subordinate status as a colonized people.

The Miskitu

Colonization of the Atlantic Coast was negotiated through intermediaries. By the late seventeenth century, members of one group, which acquired the name Miskitu,[3] had emerged as close allies and privileged trading partners of the European colonists. A crucial factor leading the Miskitu to enter into trade relations with the Europeans was the allure of the goods being exchanged and the enhanced social and economic status that resulted from their possession. Metal tools and implements dramatically increased the ease and productivity of subsistence tasks, and more important, they created a formidable military advantage relative to those who remained restricted to wood and stone. The latter is true even though muskets were probably not offered in trade at first, or used effectively until later.[4]

Alliance with the Europeans was also a means of self-defense. From the 1520s onward, Spanish conquistadores ravaged the indigenous population of the western highlands of the isthmus, exporting hundreds of thousands as slaves and extracting force labor and tribute from the rest. It is likely that news of this near ethnocide quickly reached the coastal Indians.[5] The known threat of Spanish domination may have made relations with other Europeans appear desirable, as a tactic for survival. Such relations occurred sporadically in the last part of the sixteenth century, but the opportunity for substantive interaction did not arise until British Puritans settled Providence Island. Founded in 1625 as an agricultural enterprise, Providence Island soon became a base for trade with coastal Indians. In the early 1630s the British set up a permanent trading post on Cabo Gracias a Dios, exchanging metal implements and glass beads for silkgrass, sarsaparilla, and other items collected by the *several nations* of Indians who lived nearby (Parson 1956:10, Holm 1978:18).

The Puritans actively sought the Indians' friendship owing to their own precarious military situation. Under constant threat of attack and expulsion by the Spanish, the settlers received strict instructions from their financial sponsors in Britain to treat the Indians with the utmost respect and to keep labor relations absolutely voluntary (Parson 1956:11). This approach, originating largely in immediate pragmatic considerations, helped to disarm the Indians' fears and lay the basis for a bond of loyalty and subservience. Furthermore, in sharp contrast to Spanish designs on the indigenous peoples, these British settlers at first sought material gain from trade relations that demanded little more from the indigenous peoples than an extension of their traditional subsistence activities. This was true not only of the trade goods that Indians gathered, but also of their fishing skills, which came to be highly appraised later in the century by pirates and buccaneers (Dampier 1968:16).

The British strategy of using chiefs as dependable trade partners also helps to explain why their relations with the Indians prospered. Although little is known about the social organization of the Indian groups who first traded with the Europeans, there are indications that trade accentuated existing patterns of differentiation, or even introduced a new form of stratification. For example sometime around 1638 the traders of Cabo Gracias singled out a *chief* and made arrangements for his son to be educated in England (Holm 1978:26–27). When the young man returned three years later, he took over his deceased father's position and enjoyed the added prestige of linguistic and cultural affinity with the English.

Since early accounts make no mention of permanent kings, chiefs, or princes, and since it is agreed that lowland Indians were nonhierarchical prior to the conquest, it seems likely that the British promoted this political differentiation as a means of assuring stable trade relations. The chiefs, who benefited disproportionately from the trade, worked to prevent others from disrupting relations. Over the next century as the Miskitu kingdom became well established, kings and chiefs took this protective role quite seriously.[6]

A final factor influencing Indian receptivity to the Europeans was their previous intermarriage with outsiders, especially Africans. Although this may have begun prior to the establishment of the Providence trading post (Holm 1978:75–76), it was probably minimal until 1641, when an African slave vessel was shipwrecked on the nearby cays and an unknown number of captives made it ashore. Holm hypothesizes that these Africans were slaves who had escaped from Providence Island when it was sacked that same year (1978:175–180). Whether or not he is correct (contradicting evidence can be found in Parson 1956:8), accounts agree that the Africans intermarried with the local inhabitants and produced offspring that assumed an Indian cultural identity. A second group of about 800 escaped African captives further swelled Miskitu ranks sometime after 1710 (Holm 1978:181–187).

Since that time, the terms *mulatto* and *sambo* were commonly applied to the local inhabitants, highlighting their phenotypic contrast with *pure Indians* (e.g., W. M. 1732; Hodgson 1757, in Helms 1982). In 1699, these mulattos lived in small settlements up the Wangks (Coco) River and on the shore west of Cabo Gracias a Dios apart from the Indians (W. M. 1732). Sometime before 1711, they had come into conflict with the Indians and by the 1720s they seem to have won the upper hand.[7] *Africanization* of the Indian population at Cabo Gracias occurred during the same period that the tribal name *Miskitu* (with various spellings) first appears in historical documents, as does the fact that these coastal Indians developed a reputation as outstanding warriors and traders. Having managed to escape the arduous conditions of slavery, these Africans must have been worldly-wise and aggressive. Intermarriage produced Miskitu offspring, but would also have transformed the ethnic identity, strengthening their orientation towards assertive relations with outsiders.

The Sumu

The remaining indigenous groups, who took on the name *Sumu*[8], bore the brunt of Miskitu ascendance. Seventeenth century accounts (especially those of W. M., portray the Miskitu as militarily dominant in relation to the Sumu. However, they describe the two groups as mutual enemies, and refer to numerous counterattacks by Sumu on outlaying Miskitu settlements. In the following years Miskitu hegemony grew. Although raids and slaving formed part of traditional intertribal relations, colonialism created conditions that made these activities immensely more fruitful. First, the Miskitu had increasing access to firearms and other manufactured goods that assured the success of their ventures. Second, they enjoyed rising economic opportunities from the sale of slaves and captured goods to the English. Third, as Miskitu gained prestige and economic status as intermediaries, they began to emphasize differences with the Sumu and affinities with the English. Taking non-Miskitu as slaves would have been an effective way to accentuate this redefinition of ethnic identity.

During the eighteenth century, Miskitu slaving expeditions reached as far south as the Chiriqui Lagoon (present-day Panama), west to Belize, and deep into Spanish territory as well. They kept Sumu slaves themselves, but sold most of them to English settlers of the Mosquito shore, and to traders who transported them to Jamaica (W. M. 1732:302; Helms 1982:16). Robert Hodgson's 1757 census of the Mosquito shore, for example, counted 300 Indian slaves (cited in Holm 1978:88). Although quantitative data are not available, there is good reason to believe that this slaving was extensive and contributed to the drastic reduction or extinction of many Sumu tribes.[9]

Once the balance of military power was tipped to such an extent that resistance was virtually impossible, Sumu responses to Miskitu domination consisted of either withdrawal or assimilation. The present-day distribution of the remaining Sumu settlements—in inaccessible areas, often at the headwaters of rivers—attests to the choice of the first option. This withdrawal reduced their military vulnerability to the Miskitu at the expense of increased economic dependence. Without access to trade with the Europeans (who lived only on the coast), the Sumu were left to rely on Miskitu intermediaries. By the nineteenth century this had

become a well-established economic pattern; Sumu exchanged local goods (e.g., canoes, net-hammocks, Indian corn, sarsaparilla, balsam) with the Miskitu for manufactured goods acquired from the British (Bell 1862:252)[10]. A combination of Miskitu military prowess and economic control of trade with the hinterland, therefore, locked the Sumu out of more advantageous direct relations with the Europeans.

Assimilation also existed as a possible response to the same oppressive conditions that generated resistance and withdrawal. In the case of Sumu slaves in Miskitu villages, who were mainly women and children, assimilation occurred by coercion. There is also evidence, however, that whole Sumu villages went through a collective process of assimilation to the Miskitu. For example, Bell describes the Toonglas (a Sumu tribe) in the 1840s as ". . . a mixed race between Smoos and Mosquito Indians, and their dialect is nearly pure Mosquito with large mixture of Smoo words" (1862:258). The Toonglas pledged obedience and paid tribute to the local Miskitu authority, which probably reduced the constant threat of warfare and led to intermarriage and other social interactions (Roberts 1827) 1978:67–73). Under these conditions, learning the Miskitu language and identifying as Miskitu would have been a means to gain access to the benefits of Miskitu relations with the British.

In sum, until 1740 the British presence on the Mosquito Shore consisted mainly of traders, buccaneers, woodcutters and a few plantation owners. They did not form part of a coherent, well-consolidated colonial program. Nevertheless, by introducing a new correlation of political and economic forces, colonization fundamentally transformed interethnic relations. The whites held primary political power and economic resources, and therefore, had unquestioned dominance. The Miskitu filled the role of intermediaries between the colonizers and other Indians, achieving limited access to more developed productive forces, the source of colonial power. This was a necessary condition for the dramatic growth of the Miskitu population, as well as for their economic and political dominance. Given their privileged position, it was in the Miskitu interest to accentuate their dissimilarity with subordinates and to emulate the British. The Africanization of the Miskitu contributed to this process of ethnic differentiation and may also have brought out cultural traits that helped to consolidate the

Miskitu proclivity for the intermediary role. The Sumu responded to Miskitu domination first with resistance, then with withdrawal and assimilation. For the same reasons that the Miskitu sought to identify with the English, many Sumu associated survival and betterment with the ability to live as Miskitu. Africans who managed to escape from slavery made a similar choice, until identification as *Creoles* became a viable option, with greater potential benefits.

During the first half of the nineteenth century, Creoles emerged as the dominant ethnic group on the Atlantic Coast and played the role of intermediaries between the white Europeans and the native coastal inhabitants. The ethnic hierarchy had essentially been inverted: Creoles acquired a structural position similar to that which Miskitu had in the previous two centuries. Imperial interests—first British and then North American—created the underlying conditions for this shift, but it became consolidated only as Creoles themselves asserted their dominance vis-à-vis the Miskitu.

Britain formally established a colonial presence on the Mosquito Shore in 1740, by creating the position of Superintendent. Robert Hodgson, the man who first filled that post, William Pitt, and a number of other Englishmen formed settlements in Black River, Cabo Gracias a Dios, Sandy Bay, Pearl Lagoon, Corn Island, and Bluefields. Claiming to have purchased land from the Miskitu king (White 1893:51), they planted cotton, cacao, and sugarcane, cut mahogany, and, most important, engaged in commerce—both with the Indians and contraband trade with the Spanish.[11] At least two successive Miskitu kings made a free and formal cession of the dominion of their country . . . acknowledging the King of Great Britain for their Sovereign . . . (White 1793:51), which in turn provided the legal rationale for the British colonial presence.[12] The wealthiest colonists owned African slaves, who totalled 500 in 1757 and 900 by 1770 (CIDCA 1982). Another group of African descent—mixed-bloods and free blacks—had a more ambiguous position. They numbered about 200 in 1770, spoke English, owned property, and had economic pursuits similar to whites, though with more limited opportunities.[13] The whites, *free coloreds*, and African slaves together formed the nucleus of the Miskitu Coast Creole ethnic group, which subsequently rose to prominence.

In 1783 Britain signed a treaty ceding its dominion on the Mosquito Shore to Spain and agreed that all British subjects would leave. By 1787, most Englishmen had left for Belize, carrying their slave and other possessions with them. Although there are quite thorough counts of the evacuees,[14] evidence of those who stayed behind is scarce. Robert Hodgson (son of the first superintendent) became at least nominally a Spanish subject, which allowed him to retain his residence and extensive holdings in Bluefields.[15] Slaveholding residents of Corn Island made similar arrangements (Conzemius 1929:5). A number of *mixed bloods* also stayed behind, forming communities that observers in the early nineteenth century described as *Creole*.[16] Immigrants from Jamaica and other Caribbean islands joined these, communities, strengthening the separate Creole identity.

The British withdrawal of 1787 created a forty-year colonial vacuum, filled principally by the Miskitu. In 1790, an internal dispute over the Miskitu governorship set off an assault on Bluefields, in which 300 armed *Miskitu-sambos* plundered Robert Hodgson's holdings and drove him from the area.[17] In 1800, Miskitu General Robinson led a contingent of *Moskuito-Zambos* to destroy the Spanish fort at Black River that had been handed over by the British (Sorsby 1972:152). The Spanish tried to make overtures of friendship to the Miskitu chiefs, and in one case were successful.[18] However, the bulk of the Miskitu forces remained hostile, which became a major factor in the failure of Spanish attempts to colonize the newly gained territory. During this period, the Miskitu also continued to dominate the Sumu, although coercive political relations gradually replaced warfare and slaving.

The position of black people during these forty years was varied and complex, in part because Miskitu Coast Creole society was still taking shape. The term *Creole*, to the extent that it existed at this time, was probably used in reference to immigrants from other parts of the Caribbean (especially Jamaica) where Creole society was well established. These immigrants were mainly mulattoes, a social group clearly distinct from the slaves, recently freed slaves, and runaways who made up most of the Atlantic coast black population. Members of this latter group occupied a lower social position than Miskitu chiefs, and probably the

Miskitu people in general. Miskitu governor Robinson, who controlled the Black River area, had African slaves as late as the 1820s, and according to one description, Miskitu chiefs oppressed free blacks in that area much as they did the Sumu (Roberts 1827:97). Observers also indicate that the pattern of African-to-Miskitu assimilation, described in the previous section, continued into the nineteenth century.[19] However, there were a few settlements of Creoles such as English Bank (Pearl Lagoon), Bluefields, and Corn Island, that remained independent from the Miskitu chiefs' authority. Blacks who lived in or near these settlements were directly subject to Creole influence and soon came to identify as Miskitu Coast Creoles. Bell (1899:17), who observed Bluefields in the 1850s, reports that ". . . coloured people (of Bluefields) call themselves Creoles. . . ."

A new set of economic and political interests motivated Britain's return to the Mosquito Shore in the 1830s, and this reentry directly strengthened incipient Creole society. The Mosquitia had gained geopolitical importance in the light of intercolonial competition to build and control a transoceanic canal. Furthermore, a group of British subjects, mainly Jamaicans and Belizian Creoles, had become involved in commerce and the mahogany export business (Naylor 1967). They settled mainly in previously established Creole towns, adding to the Creole numbers and further accentuating their cultural separation from the surrounding indigenous population.

Heightened British colonial interests and the growth of a Creole elite brought about crucial changes in the Miskitu kingdom. Although the successive kings continued to be Miskitu, chosen largely from the same family line, the political power of the kingdom came to reside solely in the hands of Creoles, under the close supervision of the British and, later, the North Americans. During Robert Charles Frederik's reign (1824:42) the King's residence moved to Pearl Lagoon and then Bluefields, towns inhabited largely by Creoles and British. In 1840, superintendent MacDonald insisted that the King establish an advisory Commission (headed by MacDonald himself), which later evolved into a ruling Council composed mainly of Creoles.[20] Whether for formal legal reasons,[21] or de facto political power, Creole rather than Miskitu constituted the kingdom's authority in its final fifty years.

Members of the Miskitu community must have experienced an increasing separation between themselves and the authorities of the kingdom, beginning in the late 1830s. Since the kings no longer resided in Miskitu communities, the Miskitu people would have seen them only during occasional visits. In addition, after 1860 many Miskitu were formally outside the government's jurisdiction. Britain signed a treaty with Nicaragua in that year, which recognized limited Nicaraguan sovereignty over the Mosquitia and reduced the domain of the Mosquito king considerable. The new Mosquito territory of *Reserve*[22] excluded nearly all the traditional centres of Miskitu population. This added to the irony of the internal shift in political power. Creoles controlled a government formally constituted to represent the Miskitu, most of whom were outside the government's territorial jurisdiction in the first place.[23]

On top of these factors, the kings were very probably culturally estranged from the members of the Miskitu community. At least from the beginning of the nineteenth century, *royal* children had been sent at a young age to Belize, Jamaica, or England to be educated. On their return they lived mainly among Creoles and hardly had the opportunity to learn Miskitu and become accustomed to their peoples' ways. Pim and Seeman (1869:269) said of King George Augustus Frederik, for example, he "spoke English perfectly . . . (but) could not speak Mosquitian so well."

Despite this *Creolization* of the Miskitu kings, it is interesting that, in the 1860s, new regulations of the Miskitu kingdom required that the king be of "pure Indian" descent (in Olien 1983:232). At the same time, after more than a century of kings described as *Sambos* and *mixed-bloods*, George Augustus Frederik and his successors apparently ceased to have African phenotypic traits. The political calculations of Creole Council members must have been influential in this shift.[24] These Creoles benefited directly from the existing political arrangement, and realized that the historical and legal foundation of the Mosquito government was the recognition of a special set of rights for *Miskitu* inhabitants of the coast. By seeking a phenotypically Indian king, and denying his African admixture, they could deflect inevitable arguments on the part of the Nicaraguan state that the Mosquito government no longer served its original purpose.[25]

The Moravian church, which became active on the Atlantic coast in the 1850s, further consolidated the new ethnic hierarchy. Working first in Bluefields and Pearl Lagoon, the missionaries educated and proselytized Creoles before they expanded their efforts to include the Miskitu communities. For this reason, and because Creoles had more education, the first "native" church leaders (lay preachers and parsons) were all Creole. The white missionaries also sent a number of Jamaican Creole Moravian parsons to work on the Atlantic Coast, adding to the Creole presence in the church structure.

By the early 1860s, the Moravians had begun to proselytize in Miskitu, having realized that the Gospel would "not penetrate into the innermost recesses of the human heart . . . unless it (could) be preached in the native tongue" (Mueller 1932:144). Despite initial setbacks, their efforts eventually proved fruitful, resulting in the massive conversion of the Miskitu population throughout the Atlantic Coast. Church historians point to the 1880s as a crucial decade when divine intervention produced a *great awakening*, more than tripling church membership (e.g., Wilson 1975:205). There has yet to be an adequate historical explanation for this dramatic change.

Conversions to the Moravian faith meant acceptance of a homogenized code of values and cultural practice, which explicitly endorsed the existing social order. White missionaries were Godlike and omniscient; Creoles were to be emulated because they spoke the white people's language and had some leadership positions in the church; Indians were at best recently converted *heathens*.[26] The missionaries' commitment to proselytize in the Miskitu language should not be mistaken for tolerance of cultural diversity. To the contrary, they made systematic and efficient efforts to eliminate manifestations of religious syncretism[27] and to introduce uniform cultural practices in most areas of daily life: eating habits, housing styles, clothing, marriage practices, work discipline, and so on. The degree of one's assimilation of these new practices determined one's standing as a *Christian*. Creoles as a group, then, were patently more "Christian" than Miskitu. Not surprisingly, the Creoles of Bluefields came to "despise" Indians and looked down on them as "ignorant and almost unreclaimable creatures" (Mueller 1932:69).

The final and definitive factor in consolidating the inversion of the ethnic hierarchy was the great influx of North American capital to the Mosquitia, beginning in the 1860s and reaching its peak by 1890. Foreign investment focused first on lumber and rubber extraction, and then on a much larger scale on mining and bananas. Numerous major trading houses also sprang up during that time, making Bluefields a commercial and productive boom town. Most of these houses were owned by foreigners, though a few Creole families accumulated sufficient capital to go into business for themselves.[28] The boom also spread to smaller towns up the coast such as Pearl Lagoon, Rio Grande bar, Prinzapolka and Cape Gracias a Dios, which served as transshipment centers for upriver production and commercial outposts linked to the major Bluefields establishments. By the 1890s, the British political presence had greatly diminished and Britain's economic involvement was even smaller. North Americans controlled 90 percent of the capital investment in the region.[29]

North American capitalists and administrators, many of whom came from the southern United States, brought with them their own racist notions of the appropriate ethnic division of labor, which they probably adapted to the existing conditions. Creoles obtained jobs as middle-level administrators, bosses, and skilled workers. Company owners sought black immigrants from the Caribbean to carry out hard manual labor (e.g., laying rails, as stevedores) because they were disciplined and well adapted to the difficult conditions (Ruiz and Ruiz 1925:55). A steady stream of black immigrants, who settled mainly in the previously established Creole towns where the companies were based, met these demands. Finally, the *bush work* and temporary labor was left for the Indians (mainly Miskitu) and the Spanish-speaking mestizo immigrants from the Pacific. This ethnic division of labor established a horizon of social and economic opportunities available to members of each ethnic group, which, in turn, acted to perpetuate the lines of differentiation.

In sum, the Creole ascendance and the resulting inversion of the ethnic hierarchy did not occur until British colonialism reentered the Mosquitia. During the previous years of the colonial power vacuum, a number of Miskitu chiefs had become wealthy and powerful and there were indications of an emerging Miskitu elite. By the early 1840s, the British colonial authorities brought the Miskitu government under their control, and physically moved its seat to a Creole population center. They also acted to promote the interests of immigrant Creole traders and capitalists, who formed the core of elite Creole society. Black immigrants and former slaves constituted a lower strum of this emergent Creole society, and by association with elite Creoles they achieved a social status uniformly above the Miskitu. The dual entrance of Moravian missionaries and North American companies reinforced this new ethnic hierarchy. They both also initiated profound changes in Miskitu communities throughout the Atlantic Coast—economic boom and mass conversion. These changes certainly contributed to Miskitu quiescence, by disguising what turned out to be a dramatic loss in Miskitu social and economic status, relative to the Creoles.

ENTRANCE OF THE MESTIZO ELITE

In February 1894, Nicaraguan government soldiers occupied Bluefields and proclaimed Nicaraguan state sovereignty over the people and territory of the Mosquito Reserve. This political act, which the Nicaraguan mestizos called *la reincorporacion* and the Creoles of Bluefields called the *overthrow*, initiated yet another fundamental shift in the coastal ethnic hierarchy. Mestizos from the Pacific took control of the local state apparatus, and this prepared the ground for mestizo economic dominance. As in the previous two cases, the imperial power played a critical role in this change. Once the United States decided to back the Nicaraguan state's expansionist policy, the Reincorporation became a foregone conclusion. Nevertheless, the real significance of the new ethnic hierarchy for Coast politics can be found in Miskitu and Creole responses to this assertion of mestizo dominance. Creole protests against the terms of the Reincorporation were more active and frequent than those of the Miskitu, both initially and in the subsequent forty years. Although more passive, Miskitu political orientations contained a latent challenge to Nicaraguan mestizo national sovereignty that was largely absent among the Creoles. A key to understanding both responses, I shall argue, is the varying positions of both groups in the coastal class and ethnic hierarchy that had existed since the mid-nineteenth century.

The mestizo inhabitants of the coast make up at least two quite distinct class groups. The first mestizos to reach the coast in large numbers were poor peasants in search of wage labor, not elites. Attracted by rubber production in the 1860s, and then by banana plantations and mining, mestizo immigrants rapidly became an important component of the North American companies' workforce. Although precise figures on ethnic composition are not available, there are strong indications that mestizo workers predominated in most of the major productive centres of the enclave.[30] These mestizos in general occupied lower positions in the company ethnic hierarchy than Creoles, but were marginally better off than Miskitu.[31]

Prior to 1894, the only important presence of a mestizo political or economic elite was in Cabo Gracias a Dios, which since 1860 had been the administrative center of the northeastern province of the same name (Alegret 1985). In Bluefields, at the time of the Reincorporation, there were at most one or two elite mestizo families.[32] However, mestizos in the liberal government of José Santos Zelaya sought a foothold in the Mosquito Reserve, hoping to benefit from the Coast's economic boom. With similar motivations, Creole advisers to the Miskitu king levied new taxes on ships and merchandise passing through the Reserve. This move provoked complaints by U.S. merchants living in Bluefields, which, in turn, convinced the United States to give Zelaya the go-ahead (Laird 1971:33–40). In February 1894 Rigoberto Cabezas occupied Bluefields and took control of the government. A mestizo political elite arose rapidly thereafter.

The immediate response of most Creole and Miskitu in the southern Atlantic Coast to Cabeza's military occupation of Bluefields was an unconditional rejection of Nicaraguan national sovereignty over the Mosquitia. Within a month a petition containing 1800 signatures had been presented to the British Consul, informing him that the continued Nicaraguan presence was unacceptable:

we will be in the hands of a government and people who have not the slightest interests, sympathy, or good feeling for the inhabitants of the Mosquito Reservation; and as our manners, customs, religion, laws and language are not in accord, there can never be a unity.

Their demand was straightforward: "We most respectfully beg . . . your Majesty . . . to take back under your protection the Mosquito nation and people, so that we may become a people of your Majesty's Empire."[33] In July a group of about thirty Creoles put these sentiments into direct action. They stormed the Nicaraguan garrison, drove out Cabezas, and reconstituted the Mosquito government. Cabezas quelled the rebellion within a month, and went on to form the new municipal and regional government. Cabezas himself became the highest authority of the region (Gobernador y Intendente de la Mosquitia), while a North American occupied the position of mayor of Bluefields (Perez-Valle 1978:225).

A steady stream of Creole protests against the Reincorporation occurred between the July uprising and the landmark speech of Senator Horacio Hodgson in 1934. At first, these protests contained the same political orientation: a rejection of Nicaraguan sovereignty, and an assertion of what might be called *Mosquitian* nationalism. The Creoles spoke on behalf of themselves and the Miskitu, referring always to the guarantees of autonomy contained in the 1860 treaty of Managua. Since the language of the treaty conferred rights only on the Miskitu, it was logical for the Creoles to posit racial arguments to justify their claim:

> It must be understood that natives are both Creoles and Indians alike, for all the Creoles before 1894 were born under the Mosquito flag, and are direct descendants of the Indians, since it can be proven that a great many so-called Creoles are full-blooded Indians, some can trace their Indian pedigree to their grand-parents and none need to go further back to do so than their great-grand-parents.[34]

However, it appears that Mosquitian nationalism never prospered. Among other reasons, Creoles must have found it distasteful for the legitimacy of their political claim to be dependent on ancestral links with members of a socially subordinate ethnic group. A second strain of Creole protest emerged during this same time and became dominant by the 1930s. Creoles began to demand their rights as specified by the Reincorporation decree, rights to political representation as an ethnic group, a reasonable amount of control over the regional economy, and assurance of benefits from economic development.

One of the first proponents of this orientation may have been Davis Ingram, a Creole who made the highly unpopular decision to serve on the Municipal Council formed by Cabezas in 1894.[35] Senator Horacio Hodgson made the paramount statement of this Creole ethnic and regionalist assertion in a speech to the National Assembly in 1934. He claimed that the coast had seen no economic or social progress since the Reincorporation, largely because returns on production had not been reinvested locally, that government posts were filled only by Nicaraguans from the Pacific, and that the government had discriminated against coastal people in granting rights to production. His attachment to the Nicaraguan nation is clear throughout, especially in the statement on education:

> La idea (de Zelaya) de poner escuelas nacionales en la Costa era muy buena, pero los procedimientos fueron mal escoginos . . . Cuando nuestro Gobierno usa las rentas de la Costa para educarlo e instruirlo entonces aprenderá la lengua española a perfección.[36]

The Reincorporation affected the Miskitu much less directly than it did the Creoles. As members of a largely rural and economically subordinate group, few Miskitu had economic interests that were threatened by Cabeza's occupation of Bluefields. Furthermore, the Miskitu had been virtually excluded from political circles in previous years. Although the Miskitu appeared at least nominally in every Creole petition, they are not likely to have played an active role in these initial protests. *Mosquitian* nationalism, like the Mosquito government itself, was a Creole-dominated political construct.

From the outset Cabezas attempted to exploit this Creole-Miskitu division, arguing for example that the Reincorporation would reclaim the Miskitu from the state of "slavery" at the hands of the Creoles. This message appeared in the preamble to the Reincorporation Decree, approved by some eighty Miskitu delegates to a Convention called by Cabezas at the end of 1894. the convention also selected a Miskitu *Jefe Inspector*, Andrew Hendy, as their chief and liaison with the central government.[37] Subsequent assertions, that the Miskitu were coerced or manipulated into signing the decree, are undoubtedly well-founded.[38] Nevertheless, that Cabezas was able to achieve his objective without incident is an indication both of Miskitu quiescence and of the effectiveness of the divide-and-rule strategy.

The most important early expression of Miskitu resistance of the Nicaraguan government involved a Miskitu leader named Samuel Pitts from the northern town of Yulu. Although he participated dutifully in the Mosquito Convention in 1894, by 1898 Pitts' name was attached to a letter of protest against the government, and a reinstitution of the Miskitu kingdom. The British Crown, the Moravian missionaries, and the Creole elite all turned a deaf ear to his efforts. By 1907 Pitts called himself the new Miskitu king, though he probably did not enjoy popular support much beyond Yulu and the surrounding communities. The Nicaraguan army killed Pitts and dispersed his followers that same year.[39] It is possible that Pitts' movements represented a first expression of *Miskitu* rather than "Mosquitian" nationalism, which would explain the cool response from Bluefields Creoles.[40]

In sum, though Miskitu and Creoles both resented the mestizo dominance imposed by the Reincorporation, their respective ethnic identities and demands developed in divergent ways. After a brief spurt of "Mosquitian" nationalism, Creoles appear to have settled for ethnic and economic demands leveled against mestizos but within the context of a common Nicaraguan national identity. Access to, or reasonable expectations of achieving, the basic comforts and privileges of the middle class facilitated Creoles' acceptance of this path. The Miskitu, in contrast, had less of the type of economic and cultural intercourse that engenders ties of national identity. Moreover, the contact they did have with mestizo (and Creole) society was from the bottom of a class and ethnic hierarchy. This produced alienation and resentment that could only be redressed by an assertion of ethnic identity. Sentiments favoring such an assertion smoldered, but until contemporary times never managed to ignite.

THE LEGACY OF ETHNIC HIERARCHY FROM THE SOMOZA DICTATORSHIP

The Somoza dictatorship reinforced the existing ethnic hierarchy, keeping regional political and economic power largely in the hands of mestizos. On the Rio Coco, mestizos controlled (along with Chi-

nese) all commerce and the local state bureaucracy, generating deep resentment among the Miskitu inhabitants (Helms 1971:174, 222).[41] Though this resentment was generally passive, it burst into active resistance against Somoza's state-owned forestry enterprise, INFONAC, which they claimed violated community land rights. Some community members went to the extreme of burning down tracts of forest to prevent INFONAC from exploiting them illegally (Jenkins 1986:149). Despite strong anti-Indian discrimination, a small number of Miskitu from the north managed to become educated and acquire middle-class jobs, mainly in Waspam and Puerto Cabezas. In the north, this upward mobility was often accompanied by assimilation toward mestizo culture.[42]

In the south, Creole-mestizo contention for dominance continued. Creoles predominated in the middle sectors of the economy—skilled workers, fishing captains, and professionals. Although Somoza allowed some Creoles to rise to high political positions, most of these were reserved for mestizos. A survey of leading heads of institutions before 1979 concludes that Creoles held only nine of the thirty-five positions (CIDCA 1984). Especially with the Somoza regime's corruption, political leadership gave people direct access to the means of wealth accumulation. It was common for Creoles to assimilate toward mestizo culture, in response both to the racism and the economic and cultural dominance of mestizos in the their midst.

The Miskitu faced domination by both Creoles and mestizos and had even fewer opportunities to reach the middle class. Outside Bluefields, Creoles controlled most commerce and means of production, and this reinforced the long-standing tendency for upwardly mobile Miskitu to assimilate toward Creole culture. Three southern Miskitu communities—Haulover, Tasbapauni, and Sandy Bay Sirpi—form today a continuum in this assimilation pattern that illuminates the historical process. Inhabitants of Haulover, a town contiguous with the Creole center of Pearl Lagoon, recognize their Miskitu ancestry but, with the exception of a few elders, speak only Creole English and identify as Creoles. Sandy Bay Sirpi, the farthest from Pearl Lagoon, is still solidly Miskitu, although it shows signs of what could be the beginnings of assimilation. Most adults speak Creole English; between five and ten Creole men who speak little Miskitu have married into the community; advantaged community members tend to speak Creole well and prefer it to Miskitu. Members of Tasbapauni, situated geographically between Haulover and Sandy Bay Sirpi, are at an intermediate stage of assimilation. Most adults over thirty speak Miskitu but use English more, while the young people speak only English and have an ambiguous ethnic identity, definitely in the process of change toward Creole.

Thus the ethnic hierarchy in place since the late nineteenth century persisted, leaving a complex legacy of interethnic relations to be inherited by the Sandinista revolution in 1979. I shall mention briefly three aspects of this legacy that have had a crucial impact on interethnic relations in the postrevolutionary period.

First, ever since 1894, mestizos controlled the state apparatus on the Atlantic Coast. The Creoles resented this control and actively contested it. The Miskitu protested less, but *Spanish* dominance reinforced their sense of ethnic disenfranchisement and their incipient desire to return to Miskitu government and hegemony. Given these conditions, the mestizo character of the revolutionary state was bound to have a deep impact on Miskitu and Creole perceptions of the revolution. By focusing on the mestizo continuity, these perceptions were bound to obscure the radical changes in the state's structure and policy after the revolutionary triumph of 1979.

Second, Creoles developed a series of strong aspirations for the maintenance of their relative economic and political privileges as an ethnic minority group within the context of the Nicaraguan nation. This had mixed implications for their reception of the revolution. On the one hand, these aspirations were apt to come into contradiction both with the overall mestizo character of the revolution and with the egalitarian vision of the FSLN. On the other hand, their education, experience in middle-level positions, and affirmation of Nicaraguan nationality have made Creoles able and sought-after recruits to positions of leadership in the party and government.

Finally, the Miskitu lived mainly in rural areas and faced a dual class and ethnic oppression which reinforced their sense of marginalization from Nicaraguan national identity. Their political demands, therefore, were conceived largely in ethnic terms and had a latent nationalist orientation. The triumph of the Nicaraguan revolution in 1979 gave rise to a burst of Miskitu political expression, which soon displayed elements of this ethnic nationalism.

CONCLUSION

In the cases presented above, I have examined three fundamental transformations of the Atlantic Coast ethnic hierarchy. In each transformation, I argued that an imperial power provided the basic conditions for ethnic interaction and change. At the same time, the case studies have demonstrated the limits of this conclusion. Only be examining the complex internal class and ethnic differentiation within Coast society can one arrive at a complete explanation of the social change and an understanding of the implications for Atlantic Coast politics.

The same insight applies to Coast politics in the present period, as I pointed out in a brief final section. However, as in each of the historical cases, an imperial power still exerts a tremendous influence on the course of inter-ethnic relations and conflicts, and the possibilities for their resolution. The Sandinista revolution is actively engaged in a struggle precisely to contest this influence and to prevent the United States from shaping the direction of national social change. It is fundamental to the revolution's very existence that this persistent feature of Nicaraguan history can and will be overcome.

NOTES

1. Using archeological evidence, Richard Magnus suggests that people fished at temporary coastal camps to supplement agricultural production in permanent inland villages. Evidence in W. M. (1732:301) supports this hypothesis. Nietschmann (1973) argues that the precolonial predecessors of the Miskitu had a primary marine focus.

2. This is inferred from the early ethnographic information on the coastal inhabitants, which gives no indication that one subtribe dominated the rest.

3. John Holm, whose research is remarkably thorough especially on sociolinguistic matters, cites 1670 as the date when the tribal name Miskitu first appears in the documents. He argues, along with most other student of the Miskitu, that a self-conscious *Miskitu* identity could not have emerged much before that time (see also

Helms 1971:228). Members of a second group, either implicitly (Parson 1956) or explicitly (Nietschmann 1973:23) contend that Miskitu existed as a discrete ethnic identity much earlier. I find the evidence for Holm's case (1978:306–309) much more convincing.

4. The Puritans of Providence Island were warned not to let gunpowder get into Indian hands (Parson 1956:11) and W. M. observed at the end of the seventeenth century that firearms were often rendered ineffective because incessant rain tended to dampen the powder (1732:292).

5. Holm presents linguistic evidence for trade relations in the sixteenth century between the coastal Indians and either the Indians of the interior or directly with the Spanish. In either case, they would have gained ample information about the hardships of those who directly experienced Spanish colonial rule.

6. King Peter (1729–1739) at the start of his reign sent a letter to the Governor of Jamaica in which he deplored the conditions of the kingdom since his predecessor died. The lapse in power, he lamented, has "given some of my people an opportunity to rise in rebellion and commit such outrages as I am ashamed to think of having robb'd the white people living near them. . . . But be assured I shalt use my utmost endeavors to settle these affairs to the general satisfaction of the white people residing amongst us, and bring all the offenders to consign punishment. . . ." (in Olien 1983:206). Another example of this action on part of Miskitu leaders appears in Irias (1853:164).

7. Evidence for the conflict comes from Uring ([1726] 1928:227): ". . . some people [of Cabo Gracias] who were not of the ancient Inhabitants, but new Upstarts, were got into the Government, and behaved themselves with so much Pride and Insolence that they [the Indians] could not bear and therefore separated from the main group." These "upstarts," he goes on to explain, were "Negroes" who mixed among the Native Muscheto People . . . and begot a Race of Mulattoes, which were the People that Society could not brook should bear any kind of Command amongst them." One Captain Hobby, a leader of these "mulattoes" became the Miskitu general (one of the three principal leadership positions) around 1739. From that time on, the subordinates of the Miskitu king and General are commonly described as *sambos* or *mulattoes* (Olien 1983:209–211). Phenotypic descriptions are not available on Kings Edward (1739–1755) or George (1755–1775). By 1777 at the latest, the Miskitu king himself was considered to be a *sambo* as well.

8. The word *Sumu*, introduced sometime in the eigh-teenth century, became commonly used to refer generically to any non-Miskitu indigenous inhabitants of the region (Stone 1966). Nevertheless, many of the specific tribal names survived into the twentieth century until the tribe itself became extinct.

9. One example of such a group is the Kukra, previously located in the vicinity of Bluefields (see Bell 1862:259). It should be noted that disease is generally mentioned as an important cause of Sumu depopulation as well.

10. The role of warfare versus trade in Miskitu/Sumu relations is not completely clear. Judging from W. M.'s observations in 1699, both were carried out sequentially, between the same groups within a relatively short period. Economic considerations (e.g., fluctuations in the value of slaves and other goods being traded) or other more circumstantial factors may have determined which form of interaction the Miskitu chose.

11. Roberts (1827) (1978:148) claims that in the mid-eighteenth century, these settlers owned twelve merchant ships with which to carry out this trade.

12. These kings were Jeremy II (1720–1729) and Edward (1739–1755), according to White (1793:120, and supplement, :7). Although British observers' interests might have led them to exaggerate Miskitu expressions of loyalty, the Miskitu king's enthusiasm for ties with the British is beyond question.

13. Some of these free persons of color had probably been born in Jamaica rather than on the Mosquito shore. As early as 1699, W. M. states that the Miskitu traded with *Jamaica men* who must have been migrants of this same social category from Jamaica.

14. Estimates of evacuees are provided by White: 1808 slaves, 414 whites (1789:34).

15. He had as many as 400 slaves and owned sawmills and commercial establishments (Salvatierra 1958 in Perez-Valle 1978:46).

16. For example, the case of Pearl Lagoon, in Roberts (1827:63).

17. Gamez (1939:159–160) gives this account, without reference to the original documents. In all likelihood, the attack had a political motivation besides mere plunder, especially since Hodgson, as a British authority, had previously enjoyed Miskitu support.

18. One Miskitu general, *Clementi*, converted to Catholicism, married a Spanish woman, and was said to espouse loyalty to the Spanish.

19. Interestingly, in the 1820's, Roberts ([1827] 1978:92) describes a colony of *negroes* near the Patook River which, despite the presence of a few Miskitu, he

assumes would develop in the same direction as Pearl Lagoon and Bluefields—toward Creole. Young (1847:80) provides a description of what has to have been the same community, around 1840: ". . . an old negro named William . . . established himself at Patook, and from being the owner of one cow, he now possesses . . . upwards of 400 heads. . . . Other negros dwell here, who have intermarried with the sambos, follow their customs, and consider themselves in all respects Mosquitian."

20. Christie, the British Consul, described the Council in 1848 as follows: "The council now consists of the four following persons: 1. Mr. Alexander Hodgson . . . his appearance is quite that of an African; he can sign his name, but can write nothing else. . . . 2. Mr. John Dixon, another man very slightly removed from the African. . . . 3. Mr. W. H. Ingram, a coloured man from Jamaica . . . a carpenter and very bad one; he is superior to the two preceding as he can read and write moderately well. . . . 4. Mr. Porter, another Jamaica coloured man. . . . None of the members ever opens him mouth in Council. I am expected to propose everything, and everything I propose is immediately assented to. . . ." (Christie to Viscount Palmerston, 5 September 1848, CIDCA-Bluefields archives).

21. During thirty-five of the last fifty-two years of the Miskitu kingdom (or chiefdom), there was either no designated king or the king was under the age of twenty-one. This information is taken from Olien (1983).

22. The limits of the Reserve were the Rio Hueso in the north, and the Rio Maiz in the south. All the inhabitants of the Rio Coco and the northern coastline between Cabo Gracias a Dio and Bilwi were excluded. A thorough historical explanation for the resulting choice of boundaries for the Reserve requires further research. Alegret (1985) suggests that internal Miskitu politics played a role, since the northern border coincides with traditional boundaries between the Miskitu king and governor. The northern bordermay also have been the intransigent demand of the Nicaraguan state representatives, whose primary interests would have focused on the geopolitical importance of the Coco and San Juan Rivers and on keeping the Reserve embedded in undisputed national lands.

23. The following description of a Convention held in Bluefields in 1861, shortly after the establishment of the Miskitu Reserve is indicative: "Altogether fifty-one headmen of 'the Mosquitos and of the mixed population' attended the convention. . . . Included in the group of headmen were nineteen individuals from Bluefields, nine of whom had the family name of Hodgson. Only eleven of the fifty-one names appear to be Indian. Out of the fifty-one headmen who attended the convention, the chief appointed forty-three as the General Council. Of these, only three of the names appear to be Indian" (Olien 1983:230).

24. This argument holds, whether or not an *actual* change in phenotype took place. Both Olien (1983) and Helms (1977) suggest that it did not. There certainly is support for the position that descriptions of the kings varied tremendously according to the observer's own interests and biased perceptions. For example, Pim and Seeman (1869:269) describe king George Augustus Frederik as a *pure Indian* whose hair was "without the slightest appearance of a curl or even waviness." Squire (1852):64), in contrast, wrote that the king was "nothing more or less than a negro with hardly a perceptible trace of Indian blood."

25. Indeed, the Nicaraguan state's eventual argument for Reincorporation of the Mosquitia was that the government had been taken over by a group of *Jamaicans* (Cuadra 1944:11).

26. Many Miskitu today refer to their state previous to the arrival of the white missionaries as *heathen.*

27. For example, necromancy, practiced by both Indians and lower-class Jamaicans (Perez-Valle; 1978:143), and certain non-Western forms of conduct inside the church were vigorously suppressed.

28. At least one of the major trading houses in 1890 was owned by a Creole (Henry Clay Ingram), according to Brautigam-Beer (1970).

29. This information and the best general description of this boom can be found in Laird (1971:25–31).

30. In reference to the Rio Escondido/Siquia banana-producing region, Vitta ([1894] 1946:29) states that inhabitants are ". . . compuesto en su mayor parte di los hijos del pais. . . ." In banana production up the Rio Grande, an elderly informant described the workforce as a mixed bag, but an account of a strike there in 1925 states that all the participants were mestizos (Brautigam-Beer 1982). According to Ruiz and Ruiz (1925:54) nearly all the "*operarios de las plantaciones de banana* [at the Bragnan Bluff company in Puerto Cabezas] *son nicaragüenses. . . .*" Conzemius (1932:7) note that ladinos "are particularly numerous at the Pis Pis mining district."

31. In Puerto Cabezas, mestizo workers presented a formal protest to the company because *negros* were receiving better jobs, housing, and preferential treatment in general from the company (Ruiz and Ruiz 1925:60). Miskitu, on the other hand, tended to receive only temporary work.

32. Vitta (1894:26) described the Bluefields population as consisting of *"negroes, americanos y zambos."* To form the Municipal Council of Bluefields on 4 October 1894, Cabezas gathered together about fifty of the *"mas honorables vecinos de la Comunidad."* Only two could conceivably have been mestizo, judging from their surnames (in Pérez-Valle 1978:225–226).

33. Confidential Print No. 6547 (Further Correspondence respecting the Mosquito Reserve Part V, January–June 1894), pp. 89–104 (London, Public Records Office).

34. Records of the Department of State relating to the Internal Affairs of Nicaragua, 1920–1929, Record Group 59, Midrofilm M–632, Roll No. 94 (National Archives, Washington D.C.). The letter was directed to the Secretary of State Charles Evans Hughes in 1924 on behalf of *Indians and Creoles of the Mosquito Reserve.* The impression given by the text is that Howell himself is a Creole, and that the argumentation is developed throughout from a Creole (rather than a Miskitu) perspective.

35. Creoles boycotted elections repeatedly and at least one subsequent Creole petition refers to Ingram (though not by name) as a traitor (Wunderich 1985:41).

36. His complete statement appears in Cuadra (1944). See also the petition submitted by the Costeno League in 1925, which contains all the same demands (in Ruiz and Ruiz 1925:181).

37. A more subtle aspect of Cabeza's strategy was to include Miskitu from outside the Reserve—about twenty-one of the total eighty, who already had lived thirty years under Nicaraguan sovereignty. They presumably would have put up less resistance to the Reincorporation. Significantly, the elected chief Andrew Hendy was also from one of these outside communities.

38. See, for example, first-hand observations cited in Wunderich and Rossbach (1985) and Samuel M. Howell to Secretary of State Hughes, ibid.

39. This information on Pitts comes entirely from Rossbach (1985).

40. Miskitu today, in their expression of incipient ethnic nationalism, tend to claim primary political and economic rights to the Mosquitia, relegating Creoles to a subordinate status.

41. It is typical of this control that, when Miskitu of the Rio Coco first formed an organization to represent their interests as an ethnic group, they met with strong resistance from ". . . non-Indian politicians, agency officials and the National Guard. The dominant non-Indian group reacted with fear and in some cases with violence."

(Report to Catholic Relief Services from country representative John Keegan, August 1974, CIDCA archives).

42. Indicative of this desire to assimilate to avoid anti-Indian discrimination, a Ministry of Education study found that *"Las poblacion no deseaba aprender a leer y escribir in su idioma vernacular . . . muchos presentation quejas por el hecho de que algunos maestros proporcionaban ensenanza en el idioma miskitu"* (Proyecto piloto de Educacion Fundamental del Rio Coco. Informe Final sobre la labor, realizada por la Organizacion Desarrollo de la Communidad. Ministerio de Educacion, 1960).

BIBLIOGRAPHY

Alegret, Juan, 1986, "La comarca de Cabo Gracia a Dios," *Encuentro*, 24–25. Managua.

Bell, Charles Napier, 1862, "Bell's remarks on the Mosquito Territory." *Royal Geographical Society J.* 32:242–268.

————1899, *Tangweera: Life and adventures among gentle savages.* London.

Borhek, Mary Virginia, 1949, *Watchmen on the walls.* Society for the Propagation of the Gospel, Bethlehem.

Brautigam-Berr, Donavon, 1970, Apuntes para una historia de nuestra Costa Atlántica. *In La Prensa* (Managau, Nicaragua). Series of 29 articles published from 19 May to 17 June, 1970.

————1982, "La masacre de Rio Grande." *Nicaraguac.* October 8: 180–184.

Chapman, Anne, 1958. *A historical analysis of the tropical forest tribes of the southern border of Mesoamerica* Ph.D. dissertation, Columbia University.

CIDCA, 1982. *Demografia costeña: notas sobre la historia demográfica y la situación actual de los grupos étnicos de la Costa Atlántica nicaragüense.* CIDCA: Managua.

————1984. *Survey on leaders of institutions.* Unpublished.

Conzemius, Eduard, 1929. "Les iles Corn du Nicaragua." *Géographie.* 52:346–362.

————1932. *Ethnographical survey of the Miskitu and Sumu Indians of Honduras and Nicaragua.* Bureau of American Ethnology, Bulletin 106. U.S. Government Printing Office, Washington D.C.

Cuadra, Chamorro, Pedro J. 1944. *La Reincorporación de la Mosquitia.* Managua.

Dampier, William, 1968. *A Voyage around the world.* New York: Dover Publications.

Gamez, Jose Dolores, 1939. *Historia de la Costa de Mosquitos.* Managua.

Grossman, Guido, n.d. *Nicaragua: Pais y costumbre y el tratado de la hermandad en Nicaragua y Hon-*

duras. Translation from German by Dagmar Petzold, for CIDCA.

Helms, Mary, 1971. *Asang: Adaptations to culture contact in a Miskitu Community.* Gainsville: University of Florida Press.

———— 1977. "Negro or Indian?" In Pescatello, A. (ed.) *New Roots: Old Lands.* Westport, CT: Greenwood Press.

———— 1982. *Miskitu slaving in the 17th and 18th centuries; Culture contact and ethnicity in an expanding population.* Paper presented at the 44th International Congress of Americanists, Manchester, England.

Hodgson, Col. Robert, 1757. *Some account of the Misquito territory, contained in a memoir written in 1757.* Edinburgh.

Holm, John, 1978. *The Creole English of Nicaragua's Miskitu Coast: It's sociolinguistic history and a comparative study of its lexicon and syntax.* Ph.D. thesis, University College, London.

Irias, Don Juan Francisco, 1853. "Rio Wanks and the Mosco Indians," *Transactions of the American Ethnological Society* 3:161–68.

Jenkins, Jorge J., 1986. *El disafio indigena en Nicaragua: El caso de los Miskitos.* Editorial Katun, Mexico.

Laird, Larry, 1971. *Origins of the reincorporation of the Miskitu Coast.* Unpublished M.A. thesis, University of Kansas. (Translated and published by the Fondo Cultural del Banco de America (Managua), 1978).

Mueller, Karl, 1932. *Among Creoles, Miskitos and Sumu. Eastern Nicaragua and its Moravian Missions.* Bethlehem PA: The Comenius Press.

Naylor, Robert, 1967. "The mahogany trade as a factor in the British return to the Mosquito shore in the second quarter of the 19th century," *Jamaica Historical Review*, 1–2.

Nietschmann, Bernard, 1973, *Between land and water: The subsistence ecology of the Miskitu Indians, Eastern Nicaragua* New York: Seminar Press.

Olien, Michael, 1983. "Miskito kings and the line of succession," *J of Anthropological Research.*

Parson, James J., 1956, *San Andres and Providencia; English speaking islands in the western Caribbean.* Berkeley: University of California Press.

Perez-Valle, Eduardo, 1978. *Expendiente de Campos Azules.* Managua.

Pim, Bedford, and Berthold Seemann, 1869. *Dottings on the roadside in Panama, Nicaragua and Mosquito.* London: Chapman and Hall.

Roberts, Orlando, 1827. *Narrative of voyages and excursions on the East Coast and interior of Central America.* Edinburgh: Constable and Co. (Translation: 1978, Banco de America; Fondo de Promocion cultural).

Rossbach, Lioba, 1985. "Ascenso y caida de Samuel Pitts (1894–1907)," *Encuentro,* No. 24–25. April–September 1985.

Ruiz and Ruiz, Frutos, 1925, *Informe sobre la Costa Atlántica.*

Sorsby, William, 1972. "Spanish colonization of the Mosquito Coast, 1787–1800." R.H.A. 72–4:145–153.

Squire, Ephraim G., 1852, *Nicaragua: Its people, scenery, monuments, etc.* New York.

Stone, Doris, 1966. "Synthesis of Lower Central American Ethnohistory," *Handbook of Middle American Indians* (pp. 209–233).

Uring, Nataniel, 1928. *The voyages and travels of Captain Nathaniel Uring.* London: Cassell and Company. (reprint of 1726 edition).

Vitta, Jose, 1894. "La Costa Atlántica," *Revista de la Academia de Geografía e Historia de Nicaragua,* VIII:2.

Von Oertzen, Elenore, 1985. "El colonialismo britanico y el reino misquito en los siglos XVII y XVIII," *Encuentro,* 24–25, Managua.

W. M., 1732. "The Mosqueto Indian and his Golden River," In Churchill (ed.) *A collection of voyages and travels.* Vol. 6, pp. 285–298.

Wheelock, Jaime, 1974. *Raíces indígenas de la lucha anti-colonialista en Nicaragua.* Editorial Nueva Nicaragua, Managua.

White, Robert, 1793. *The case of his majesty's subjects having property in and lately established upon the Mosquito Shore in America.* London.

Wilson, John, 1975. " Obra morava en Nicaragua: Trasfondo y breve historia," Paper presented to the Latin American Biblical seminar, San Jose, Costa Rica.

Wunderich, Volker, and Lioba Rossbach, 1985. "Derechos indigenas y estado nacional en Nicaragua: La convencion Mosquitia de 1894," *Encuentro,* No. 24–25, April–September 1985.

Young, Thomas, 1847. *Narrative of a residence on the Mosquito Shore.* London: Smith, Elder and Cornhill.

11

Assault on Paradise

Conrad Kottak

Conrad Kottak first went to the coastal fishing community of Arembepe, Brazil, in 1962, when he was an anthropology undergraduate student at Columbia University. Over the years Professor Kottak has returned to Arembepe, documenting the changes that have occurred in so many areas. The community, once very isolated from the mainstream of Brazilian culture, is now caught up in many of the changes that have impacted so much of the rest of Brazilian society. Since the construction of an all-weather road took place, the community has become accessible in a manner not previously possible. Today people come and go with ease. Tourists now walk the beaches and new industries have found their way into the community. Social class and social organization have been primary interests of the author. Within the context of continuity and change, this contribution addresses these themes.

Because of its relatively simple economy and social structure, Arembepe of the 1960s had differed from

From Conrad Kottak, *Assault on Paradise*, 2nd ed. New York: McGraw-Hill, 1992, pp. 47–70.

other Brazilian communities that ethnographers had studied. With a few exceptions (e.g., Johnson, 1971), anthropologists had studied Brazilian communities (usually county seats) with social class divisions. Arembepe, by contrast, had lacked class-based contrasts in wealth, occupation, education, and political power. It had been a lower-class community, with few insurmountable obstacles to achieving success locally, but with many barriers to rising out of the national lower class.

A villager's lower-class identity became particularly obvious when he or she left the community and met, most often in Salvador, members of the middle or upper class. Manners, dress, and speech provided cues that the urban elites use to identify lower-class people. Arembepeiros in the city faced discrimination as poor, powerless, "uneducated" people, and as "country bumpkins."

Within Arembepe the differences in income, inherited wealth, and life style were minuscule compared with the contrasts existing in Brazil as a whole. The local ladder of success had closely spaced rungs, and anyone could climb it. Arembepe contrasted with class-stratified towns, in which inherited wealth gives some people a head start in economic opportunities and social status. The wealth differences that did exist in Arembepe placed its residents in a graded hierarchy, not a stratified one. That is, there were no sharp differences between a poor and a rich group.

Thus, the data on 1964 household budgets (roughly equal to annual income) show a gradual increase from poorest to wealthiest household, with no large gaps. The largest budget reflects an income worth about $1,000 in 1964—far less than Brazilian middle-class households earned. In other words, Arembepe of the 1960s had a social hierarchy but no social classes. In anthropological parlance, its social system was ranked, not stratified.

The village lacked greater socioeconomic contracts than these because, ever since its founding, it had been cut off from external resources that might have brought greater wealth and power to (some of) its people. The people of Arembepe were poor because of their circumstances, not because they lacked ambition. Many villagers were very ambitious, contradicting the assumptions of those "experts" on Third World economic development who attribute poverty and "backwardness" to such factors as "low achievement motivation" or "inappropriate values."

All successful Arembepeiros were self-made entrepreneurs. Achievement in this small fishing village required exactly those personality traits that the sociologist Max Weber, in his famous book, *The Protestant Ethic and the Spirit of Capitalism* (1958), attributed to the first capitalists. Weber argued that the rise of Protestantism in Europe fostered capitalism by teaching such values as profit making, hard work, rational planning, willingness to take calculated risks, simple tastes, an ascetic life style, stability, trustworthiness, and sobriety. In Weber's view, early Protestantism, by seeing business success as a sign of divine favor, also promoted individualism—since the individual, not the household or family, would be eternally graced or damned.

Appropriate values existed in Arembepe, but economic advance by its people was limited by a combination of meager resources and social factors, known as leveling mechanisms, which kept ambitious villagers "in their place." *Leveling mechanisms* are devices that discourage people from surpassing their peers—punishing those who do, pushing them back to the common level.

Such mechanisms, according to Weber, also existed in European peasant communities before the rise of capitalism. Weber argued that peasant values (shared, he said, with the Catholic church) resisted the rise of capitalism and Protestantism. Peasants, said Weber, worked just hard enough to satisfy their immediate needs. Then they quit, mistrusting people who needlessly worked more than others. The individualism associated with Protestantism and capitalism had to surmount the collectivism of the peasant community, in which gossip and other social pressures brought deviants (including overachievers) back in line.

Anthropologist George Foster's (1965) discussion of peasants recalls Weber's description of Europe before the rise of Protestantism and capitalism. Foster notes the importance of leveling mechanisms in "classic" peasant societies throughout the world. Both Weber's and Foster's analyses apply to Arembepe, though its people were fishermen, not peasant farmers. Foster argues that peasants throughout the world share an "image of limited good," according to which all valued things are finite. Peasants regard the total amount of health, wealth, honor, or success available to community members as limited. One person can excel only at the expense of others. Unless good fortune clearly comes from outside (for example, external wage work or a lottery) and unless the fruits of success are shared with others, successful people face ostracizing techniques (leveling mechanisms). These include gossip, avoidance, insults, and physical attack.

Although it had neither peasants nor Protestants, Arembepe did have a unique mix of community collectivism, the image of limited good, and Protestant-capitalist-individualist values. This value set had emerged without religious support. Although, through baptism, all villagers were nominal Catholics, organized religion played a small role in local life. The people of Arembepe were not the devout Catholics of Mediterranean or east European peasant communities. A priest visited the village twice a year, but only women and children attended the services. "The church is a place for women," said one fisherman. "They're the ones who hold the prayer meetings and cut flowers for the saints." (The "saints" are household figurines.) Men had their doubts about priestly sanctity, particularly the ability of priests to stick to their vow of celibacy.

Arembepe's values were influenced by contacts with nearby farming villages, but they were especially molded by the attitudes and character traits evoked by the fishing economy. Like the hunting-gathering economies that existed everywhere until about 10,000 years ago, fishing is a form of foraging, rather than food production. Like other hunter-gatherers, fishermen live off nature's bounty, rather than planting, tending, and harvesting crops, or stockbreeding animals. Food production is usually more certain than foraging is. Crop yields are more predictable and more subject to human control than is a fish supply. Farmers follow a calendar of cultivation and can usually count on a harvest. Similarly, herders lead their animals through a well-trodden annual trek, as they follow seasonally available pasture.

Fishing is chancier. Seasonal fish runs are larger some years than others. Some days, fishing at a given spot at sea is productive; others, it isn't. "Sometimes the fish get smart and move away. Or they hide in the rocks. Fishing isn't a profession you can count on; everything depends on your luck," remarked Alberto, the fisherman who became my best informant, as we rocked up and down on the Atlantic one day in July 1964, waiting for the first bite.

Fishing calls for less routine and more innovation than food production does. If all fishermen have access to the same technology and territory, as was true in Arembepe, larger catches depend most clearly on harder work. Over time, the crew that works more hours can be expected to catch more fish. Arembepe's captains also pursued varied strategies, some with more payoff than others. Most successful were those who innovated. Such captains tried out new technology, looked for new fishing grounds, and sailed to familiar fishing spots out of season. They carefully evaluated costs and benefits and took calculated risks.

I had trouble getting Tomé, the most successful captain, to agree on a day to take me out fishing. "There's always the chance I'll decide to sail up to Guarajuba [15 kilometers away] to look for *guaraçain* [*Caranx latus*], and I may fish there through the night." Tomé was afraid I might not tolerate a trip lasting longer than the usual eight to ten hours. His practice was to see where the other boats were going, then to try his luck in less-fished, usually more distant, areas, and to fish longer hours.

His reward was Arembepe's largest income based on fishing.

Entrepreneurial activity (experimentation, risk taking, and innovation) was the key to productive fishing and to general economic success in Arembepe in the 1960s. The inflation that has continued to plague Brazil was severe during the early 1960s[1]; to have hoarded profits then would have been a recipe for economic disaster. Local entrepreneurs were willing to experiment with many options for reinvesting profits. They put their money in land, coconut trees, boats, new fishing equipment, and consumer goods. Because of inflation, the entrepreneurial behavior and values that were favored on the open sea found reinforcement on the land.

During the 1960s people with intelligence, ambition, and business sense could move from the very bottom to the very top of the local economic hierarchy. To rise further, to succeed in the outside world, was exceedingly difficult. The wealth generated in Arembepe was too meager to propel any native son or daughter into the national middle class. Limited educational opportunities formed another barrier. Only by studying outside could local kids hope to qualify for the greater incomes offered, for example, by Petrobrás, the national oil monopoly. Only a few natives managed to obtain such schooling and such jobs.

The other prominent dimension of Arembepe's value system (community collectivism and leveling mechanisms) acted as a brake on individual economic advance. As wealth grew, so did the obligation to share it. Villagers respected their obligations because no one could be sure that, given old age or infirmity, he or she might not have to depend on others. No pensions or social security benefits were available to lower-class rural fishermen in Brazil in the 1960s. Kinship and community formed Arembepe's only social security system.

AN OPEN, NONCORPORATE COMMUNITY

Although the scale of Arembepe's confrontation with the outside world has increased dramatically since 1965, the village had never been truly isolated from external forces. Despite its egalitarian values and unstratified social structure, Arembepe has always been an "open, noncorporate community." This is one of two basic types of Latin American peasant communities identified by Eric Wolf (1955). Arembepe had all the defining features of the open community. These include production for both cash and subsistence, reliance on external supplies, and participation in national culture through the national language. For decades the people of Arembepe have sold some of their fish to outsiders. At first the buyers were small-scale mule drivers who bought fish to resell, mainly in towns nearer Salvador. By the early 1960s buyers were arriving by jeep from Salvador and its suburbs. Coconuts, Arembepe's only other important export item, also went to market in Salvador.

Arembepeiros have long depended on items produced outside the village Most of the boats in the fishing fleet in the 1960s had been made elsewhere; only one local man still knew how to make a sailboat from scratch. Still, fishing did not yet rely on motors and fossil fuels. The fishermen of Arembepe therefore lacked the concern with costs, supplies, and repairs that accompany such dependence. Villagers bought kerosene, rice, sugar, beans, coffee, lard, matches, soft drinks, beer, rum, and soap from local storekeepers. Arembepe had twelve small stores in 1964, one for every 60 of the village's 730 inhabitants. Three of these did much more business than the others did.

The ties with the external world were mainly economic. Some people had left to study or work outside. A few men were fishing on commercial trawlers out of Salvador, Rio de Janeiro, and other major ports. Some native women worked as domestics in Salvador. A few others had studied *candomblé*, an Afro-Brazilian spirit-possession cult, at a temple in the capital. The family that owned the land on which Arembepe stands all lived outside. Except for one well-educated landowner, who was planning the subdivision of his family's estate, the sale of lots, and Arembepe's development as a resort, the landlords rarely visited the village. They had little to do with life there. Their local representative was Prudencio, an elderly man who collected the nominal rents that villagers paid for their house sites. These rents, worth between $.50 and $1.00 per year in 1964, had been legally set at a higher amount, then eroded by inflation. Prudencio also granted requests to build new houses, and he oversaw the marketing of the produce of the landowners' 5,600 coconut trees.

One fishing captain summed up the role of the landlords and their agent in local life: "Prudencio's the closest thing we have to a chief (*chefe*) here. But that's because he stands in for the landlords. They don't bother us much. They're mainly interested in their coconuts."

Despite Arembepe's economic orientation to the outside world, its people had been shielded from the power relationships that are routinely experienced by most lower-class Brazilians. The poor, seasonally impassable, road limited contacts with Salvador. People had to walk 19 kilometers to catch a bus to the city; the round trip took two days. There had been little in Arembepe's economy or placement to attract powerful outsiders. The estate of land and coconut trees on which the village is located couldn't even support the middle-class life style of the landowners, and the last one had left Arembepe in 1925. All her heirs had urban careers; they rarely visited Arembepe. During the 1960s, one of them, Jorge Camões, the first member of his family with a university education, planned Arembepe's development for tourism. Jorge's knowledge, business skills, political clout, and position in the state division of the national highway agency combined to promote Arembepe's coming encounter with economic development and the world system.

Previously, Arembepe's location—its shielding by sand, lagoons, and ocean—and its limited resources had kept it from being a center of anything. The land's productivity is low. "Nothing grows here. Not even watermelon and peanuts." People got their produce from small farms to the west, but sandy soils reduced the farming potential there, too. Throughout the municipality (county) of Camaçari during the 1960s the main economic activities were charcoal extraction, small-scale cultivation, and coconut production. Arembepe's land is suited only for the last. Its export products were fish, coconuts, and straw hats made by local women. Coconuts brought villagers, including the landowners, a total income of just $5,000 annually. The cash receipts from the entire straw hat industry didn't exceed $50 per year. Fish catches were limited by simple technology—sailboats with small crews doing day-long hook-and-line fishing. Until tourism became practicable in 1970, Arembepe had little to offer outside investors.

Like its economy, Arembepe's political structure

was also simple. The village has never been the seat of a municipality, or even of a rural "district." Arembepe's official classification was "hamlet," within one of the six districts of its municipality, with Abrantes, on the road to Salvador, as its district seat. Arembepe lacked the roster of tax collector, justice of the peace, statistical agent, postal official, and other government workers who are present in even district seats. Government jobs would have brought greater wealth contrasts into Arembepe and might have threatened the graded hierarchy. "Abrantes has a few people who are well-off because they managed to get jobs as civil servants, but there's no one like that here. All we've got is fishermen and storekeepers." Civil service positions also would have brought "the government"—with its contrasts in power and authority—right into Arembepe. But this had never happened.

Arembepe had surprisingly few political figures for a community in a large and populous country. Besides the landlords' caretaker, there was a municipally appointed policeman (*subdelegado*). He drew a small salary and was afraid to use the revolver the county had provided. No arrests were ever made; the jail stood empty, except occasional visitors who were allowed to sleep there. The policeman's father was the only villager with a federal position. Long a successful captain, this old man had become port captain, in theory overseeing fishing operations between Itapoan, to the south, and Praia do Forte, to the north. He was supposed to grant fishing permits to fishermen in this area, but few of them had such licenses.

The port captain explained: "It's hard for Arembepeiros to get to Salvador for the papers they need for fishing licenses. Most fishermen can't even read. Anyway, why do they need licenses when no one ever comes here to check." No one replaced this man when he retired, and he continued his duties informally until his death in 1973, while receiving the only federal pension in Arembepe.

The roster of local leadership ended with the officers of the Fishermen's Society and of the Saint Francis Soccer Club. The soccer club included fishermen, plus native sons employed outside who came on weekends to play against other communities. Tomé, the most successful fisherman, was the soccer captain. The Fishermen's Society organized the annual festivals held for Arembepe's patron saint, Saint Francis (February 20), and for Saint John (June 24). The top officer was the treasurer. Normally, the captain-owner with the year's largest catch was elected treasurer, as Tomé was in 1965.

Very little that was collective, communal, governmental, or even political could be detected in Arembepe. The village also differed from the typical rural Brazilian community as described by Charles Wagley (1963, p. 148), in that it was not an urban nucleus for surrounding rural neighborhoods. Arembepe had only one satellite, Big Well, with eight houses. Residents of two agricultural estates a few kilometers to the west, Açu and Coqueiros, came to Arembepe to buy fish and to sell produce. Many of the coconut trees owned in 1964 by 42 percent of Arembepe's adults were in Açu and Coqueiros, and twenty Arembepeiros rented small farms there. Their crops supplemented their incomes and diets from fishing or business.

Many villagers had been born on the western estates. After gaining their freedom in 1889, the slaves whose descendants made up most of Arembepe's 1960s population initially took up subsistence farming on these estates. Their children and grandchildren gradually left farming for seasonal, and then year-round, fishing in Arembepe.

"I remember one of my grandmothers who had been a slave," recounted Alberto. "Once she was freed she moved to Açu and took up with my grandfather. They farmed for a while; then he started fishing. Eventually they moved to Arembepe, and he became a full-time fisherman."

Arembepe's insulation from power wielders was also a result of the split between its economic orientation (toward Salvador) and its political orientation (toward Camaçari), Salvador has traditionally drained Camaçari, like Arembepe, of landowners, rural elites, and local people with middle-class aspirations (Gross, 1964). Camaçari's orientation toward the capital, instead of its own hinterland, was another reason for Arembepe's insulation from power. Because the village got its cash from one place and its political orders from another, economic and political influence did not reinforce one another. Officials in Camaçari lacked control over the marketing of fish and coconuts and could do Arembepeiros no economic harm.

THE COSTS AND BENEFITS OF KINSHIP

Several factors thus combined to shield Arembepe from the Brazilian power structure. This is why—despite the village's economic dependence on the outside and its inclusion in a nation-state—its social relations were similar to the egalitarian, kind-based societies that anthropologists have studied in many parts of the world. With no major economic gaps or marked contrasts in power dividing the people of Arembepe, they kept up the fiction that they were all relatives. The twin assertions "We're all equal here" and "We're all relatives here" were offered repeatedly as Arembepeiros' own summaries of the nature and basis of local life. Like members of a clan (who claim to share common ancestry, but who can't say exactly how they are related), most villagers couldn't trace precise genealogical links to their distant kin. "What difference does it make—as long as we know we're relatives?"

As in most nonindustrial societies, close personal relations were either based or modeled on kinship and marriage. A degree of community solidarity was promoted, for example, by the myth that everyone was kin. It's important to point out, however, that social solidarity was actually much *less* developed in Arembepe than in societies with clans and lineages—which use genealogy to include some people, and *exclude* others, from membership in a given descent group. Intense social solidarity demands that some people be excluded. By asserting that they all were related—that is, by excluding no one—Arembepeiros were actually weakening kinship's potential strength in creating and maintaining group solidarity.

Villagers were only half-serious when they claimed that everyone was related. This was clear from their other statements about kinship. Like lower-class Brazilians generally, the people of Arembepe calculated kinship more narrowly than do members of the middle or upper class, who, according to Wagley (1963, pp. 196–198), recognize kinship with hundreds of people. Despite this, kinship reckoning in Arembepe was more inclusive than that of typical middle-class Americans. For example, Arembepeiros normally called the first cousins of their parents "uncle" and "aunt," and the children of their own first cousins "nephew" and "niece."

Kinship calculation broke down with more remote relatives. Distant cousins were called either "third cousin" or "distant cousin"; this wasn't a close relationship. Villagers didn't share the anthropologist's delight in tracing genealogies and kin links. I exasperated Alberto with my questions about specific kin links among fishermen. "It doesn't mean anything if people in the same crews happen to be third cousins. Only closer relatives fish together because they're related."

Nor did villagers trace kinship very far back. Rarely did they recall the names of their great-grandparents, and then only of the ones they had known. Last names were used infrequently. Most people were known (sometimes only) by nicknames derived from, say, a physical attribute ("Little Black José"), a characteristic ability ("Breaks Coconuts with His Feet," "Farts When He Sneezes"), or place of origin ("Sergipe," a nearby state). Few villagers knew the full names of even their close kin. This was another sign of insulation from the national power structure. Full names are used in legal contexts that the people of Arembepe generally avoided.

Besides the rights and obligations based on kinship, Arembepeiros acquired others through marriage. Couples could be "married" formally or informally. The most common union (40 percent of the couples in 1964) was a stable common-law marriage. Less common (28 percent), but with more prestige, was legal (civil) marriage, performed by a justice of the peace and conferring inheritance rights. Half the estate went to the surviving spouse, the other half to the children. The union with the most prestige (10 percent of the marriages) combined legal validity with a church ceremony. A few people (8 percent) had been married in a religious service only. A civil marriage was for life, and Arembepeiros used the multiple marriage types to cope with the difficulty of getting divorced in Brazil.

"I lived with one woman for a few years," recounted a retired fisherman. "I got tired of her and left her for another one I liked better. But I still wasn't ready for a legal marriage, so we just had a church ceremony. Later, after leaving her and taking up with my wife, I finally decided I was ready for the civil."

A surplus of women (54 percent) between the ages of sixteen and forty-nine was one reason some women lacked coresident males. There were eight visiting unions, in which the "husband" simultaneously had another, principal wife. For the men, the visiting union was secondary, but some of those unions lasted several years. The women involved in them were severely stigmatized—labeled *rapariga* (village prostitute). "Those are the good-for-nothing females who live off other women's husbands" was one elderly woman's summary of a common local opinion.

There was a quantum leap in the rights and obligations that went with legal, compared with common-law, unions, even stable ones. Common-law spouses had no right to inherit. Neither did children, unless they had been registered in the parent's name. Only legal marriage created an in-law relationship. A man who married in a civil ceremony agreed to share not just with his wife and kids but also with his wife's parents and siblings if necessary. By contrast, men in common-law unions denied that they had "parents-in-law" or "siblings-in-law."

The rights and obligations associated with kinship and marriage comprised the local social security system, but people had to weigh the benefits of the system against its costs. The most obvious cost was this: Villagers had to share in proportion to their success. As ambitious men climbed the local ladder of success, they got more dependents. To maintain their standing in public opinion, and to guarantee that they could depend on others in old age, they had to share. However, sharing was a powerful leveling mechanism. It drained surplus wealth and restricted upward mobility. The correlation between wealth and obligations was one of the main reasons why Arembepe remained an unstratified, lower-class community.

How, specifically, did this leveling work? As is often true in stratified nations, Brazilian national cultural norms are set by the upper classes. Middle- and upper-class Brazilians usually marry legally and in the church. Even Arembepeiros knew that this was the only "proper" way to marry. The most ambitious local men—usually also the most successful—copied the behavior of elite Brazilians. By doing so, they hoped to acquire some of their prestige (see Kottak, 1966, p. 101).

However, legal marriage drained individual wealth, for example, by creating a responsibility to support in-laws. Such obligations could be reg-

ular and costly. Obligations to kids also increased with income, because successful people tended to have more living children. During the 1960s—and even in 1973—villagers used no birth control. Only a few women induced abortions. These were dangerous, and, besides, children were valued as companions, and as an eventual economic benefit to their parents. Boys especially were prized because their economic prospects were so much brighter than those of girls.

The average married woman in 1964 had given birth to 5.6 live children, of whom only 3.2 survived—just 57 percent. Infant and child mortality was the main check on population growth. Children's chances of survival surged dramatically in wealthier households with better diets. The normal household diet included fish—usually in a stew with tomatoes, onions, palm oil, vinegar, and lemon. Dried beef replaced fish once a week. Sawdust-like roasted manioc flour (*farinha*) was the main source of calories and was eaten at all meals. Other daily staples included coffee, sugar, and salt. Bananas, mangoes, and other fruits and vegetables were eaten in season. Diet was one of the main contrasts between households. The poorest people didn't eat fish regularly; often they subsisted on manioc flour, coffee, and sugar. Only the wealthiest people could afford the rice and beans that middle- and upper-class Brazilians view as the basis of "the Brazilian diet." Better-off households supplemented the staples with milk, butter, eggs, rice, beans, and more ample portions of fresh fish, fruits, and vegetables.

Children's distended bellies and reddish hair were among the clinical signs of malnutrition and intestinal parasites. The poorer kids were especially prone to infectious diseases, the main cause of death among them. Malnutrition also affected fetuses; most women had suffered a miscarriage or stillbirth. Like other fishermen, Alberto and his wife Carolina had lost children to malnutrition and disease, but their losses (10 out 13) were extreme.

I witnessed an especially painful one. In June 1964 Alberto asked me to drive him and his severely ill two-and-a-half-year-old son to a doctor in Itapoan. The boy was vomiting, after several days of diarrhea. He was running a fever and had been unable to sleep. The child's nonstop screams unnerved me during our long drive over the muddy road to Itapoan. We arrived to find that the doctor hadn't been seen that day. The pharmacist prescribed medication, telling Alberto that the doctor always used those pills for the boy's symptoms. I tried to persuade Alberto that we should drive on to a clinic in Salvador, but he refused. I still regret not pushing harder. The boy slept most of the way back to Arembepe, but he died that night, and Alberto, whose surplus cash had gone for the medicine, accepted my offer of a few dollars to help pay for a bare cardboard coffin.

Adequate incomes bought improved diets and provided the means and confidence to seek out better medical attention than was locally available. Most of the kids born in the wealthier households survived. But this meant more mouths to feed, and (since the heads of such households usually wanted a better education for their children) it meant increased expenditures on outside schooling. The correlation between economic success and large families (without birth control) was another siphoner of wealth that braked individual economic advance. Tomé, a fishing entrepreneur, envisioned a life of constant hard work if he was to feed, clothe, and educate his growing family. With an income three times that of Alberto, Tomé and his wife had never lost a child. But he recognized that his growing family would, in the short run, be a drain on his resources. "But in the end, I'll have successful sons to help their mother and me, if we need it, in our old age."

Arembepeiros knew who could afford to share with others; success can't be concealed in a small community. Villagers based their expectations of others on this knowledge. Successful people had to share with more kin and in-laws, and with more distant kin, than did poorer people. Successful captains and boat owners were expected to buy beer for ordinary fishermen; storeowners had to sell on credit. Any well-off person was expected to exhibit a corresponding generosity. With increasing wealth, people were also more frequently asked to enter ritual kin relationships. Through baptism—which took place twice a year when a priest visited, or which could be done outside—a child acquired two godparents. These became the coparents (*compadres*) of the baby's parents.

Unlike other parts of Latin America, where the coparent relationship is more important than godparenthood per se (Mintz and Wolf, 1950), the two relationships were equally important in Arembepe.

Children asked their godparents for a blessing the first time they saw them each day. Godparents occasionally gave cookies, candy, and money, and larger presents on special occasions. Later in life one could acquire another godparent (just one) by being confirmed by a bishop. Through formal marriage, a couple could acquire four more godparents, couples chosen respectively by the bride and groom.

For ritual kinship we reach the same conclusion as for kinship and marriage: ritual kinship obligations increased with wealth, and this limited individual economic advance. Thus kinship, marriage, and ritual kinship, as they operated in Arembepe in the 1960s, had costs and benefits. The costs were limits on the economic advance of individuals. The primary benefit was social security—guaranteed help from kin, in-laws, and ritual kin in times of need. Benefits, however, came only after costs had been paid—that is, only to those who had lived "proper" lives, not deviating too noticeably from local norms.

GENDER ISSUES: MACHISMO AND MALE-FEMALE INEQUALITY

We have seen that the main requirements for success during the 1960s were ambition, hard work, and good business and investment strategy. Another must be added: being male. It is no exaggeration to say that almost all the wealth held by Arembepeiros in 1965—through inheritance or income—had been created, ultimately, by the entrepreneurial activity of some male. I divided the village population into three groups (primary producers, secondary producers, and dependents), based on their contributions to the household's cash income and food supply. Most of the primary producers were men. The secondary producers included a few men, about half the women, and a few teen-age boys. The dependent population included half the women and most of the children.

The cash-earning options for women were limited. The manufacture of straw hats from palm fibers generated a *total* of about $50 annually. A few women were the sole owners of successful stores. Others ran businesses or did some farming with their husbands, sometimes as equal partners. Ten married women functioned as co-household heads—making major economic decisions and planning their children's lives.

The behavior of these women stood out as unusual only because of the general pattern of male dominance. Of Arembepe's 159 household heads, for example, 83 percent were males. Reflecting men's easier access to wealth were household incomes and budgets. In a sample of 118 household budgets for 1964, the female-headed households ranked at the bottom: 118, 116–111, 108, 103, 101, 97, and 67. None of the households headed by women was in the wealthier half. Their average annual expenditures were equivalent to $109, compared to $314 for the male-headed households.

There is more to the story. Only two of the twenty-eight female-headed households were self-sufficient. One was headed by an unmarried storekeeper, the other by a woman who had inherited coconut trees. Four other women depended on partial support from other households, and the remaining twenty-two relied on other households for most of their support. Eight of these twenty-two were the secondary wives of polygynous males, and their economic situation was most precarious.

The prevailing morality viewed polygyny as improper, and secondary wives were often scorned as village prostitutes. Typically, the main wife and her relatives enlisted community pressure to end the husband's philandering. When a secondary union broke up, the woman had to rely on her kin until she managed to attract another man. Arembepe had a group of such women—seen as deviants, as the lowest of the low—who were forced into a succession of unions and breakups. The woman's need to support her children left her with few options but to continue the pattern, and, without contraception, her responsibilities grew as new children were born.

A pathetic aspect of daily life during the 1960s was the sight of children from female-headed households on the beach, meeting the fishing boats as they returned in the early evening. Dora, our cook in 1962, customarily sent her oldest son each afternoon to wander from boat to boat seeking a piece of fish for their dinner. The four-year-old boy, who suffered from a congenital heart defect that killed him at age thirteen, was often successful with one of his mother's brothers, a captain. If not, he went to other maternal relatives, since his father

lived in distant Camaçari, the county seat. When the boy tired, which he did easily because of the heart condition, he would squat until his energy returned for another try at getting a fisherman's attention. One vivid memory from my early years in Arembepe involves this boy's panting and squatting on the beach, and the joy on his face when he was successful in his quest for fish.

Illegitimate boys sometimes got their fathers to recognize them with a fish. Or else they went from boat to boat, relying on other kin connections, a good day's fishing, or a fisherman's pity to cut the monotony of a diet otherwise limited to manioc flour, coffee, and sugar. Although there was no formal enforcement of the restriction, the beach was off-limits to "proper" women; so women had to send their children to beg. The psychological results of asking for food and for recognition of kinship—and of being rejected, particularly by fathers—have been varied. Some children have grown up to be alcoholics. Others, determined never to relive such childhood experiences, have developed tremendous ambition.

"The thing I hated most during my childhood," said Arembepe's most successful businessman, "was having to beg on the beach. My father was married to another woman, and he was stingy with my mother. Then she took up with another man and my brother was born. After that man left her, it was my job to get fish for them both. I'll make sure my sons never have to beg."

Although Arembepeiros asserted their mutual kinship, the village lacked the clans and lineages of many nonindustrial societies. It also lacked the formal patrilineal or matrilineal rules that determine descent-group membership in such societies. In theory, the kinship system stressed neither the father's nor the mother's side but viewed them as equal. In fact, and reflecting another aspect of local male dominance, kin links through males were more important. One reason for this was a long-term pattern of greater female migration to Arembepe. About 60 percent of the migrants to the village in 1964 were females. Most of these were between the ages of sixteen and forty-nine, the only age group in which females outnumbered males (54 percent to 46 percent). The pattern was for immigrant women—mostly from nearby agricultural estates—to seek husbands in Arembepe. As a result, 42 percent of all wives had been born outside the village, compared with 31 percent of the husbands.

The people of Arembepe have always distinguished between natives and outsiders. This was not a very significant contrast in the 1960s, since two-thirds of the population had at least one parent who had been born outside, and since only a third of the marriages involved two natives. Males and females used different strategies to enter local society. Women often came to visit relatives and stayed on. Men, too, might come because of a kin link. They might take up residence near a relative or friend, perhaps someone who farmed near the immigrant's home. Men who wanted to settle tried to find positions in boat crews. Usually they started fishing with the less successful captains, eventually asking to fish temporarily with other crews when their regular captains missed fishing because of drunkenness or laziness. As an immigrant's reputation for reliability grew he could graduate to a good boat. Some immigrants became well-to-do captains and boat owners.

Male immigrants had many more opportunities than women did to join in community life. They could meet other fishermen on the beach, bathe with other men in the lagoon, and congregate in bars and on the chapel stoop, where most of the fishermen gathered for conversation each evening. Following a general Mediterranean and Latin American pattern, men's access to public space was much wider than women's (cf. Harding, 1975; Reiter, 1975). Adult women left home to wash, fetch, water, bathe, shop, or visit neighbors and kin, but women usually met in smaller groups and spent more time indoors.

To stay in Arembepe, an immigrant woman needed to find a husband. Even then, such a woman's position was more precarious than that of a native woman. Without local kin, the migrant faced destitution if her husband deserted her. Without her family close by to offer at least moral support, the immigrant wife often had to tolerate more abusive treatment than a wife born in Arembepe did. The children of a migrant weren't as familiar with their outside kin as they were with the native parent's family. This was the main reason that kin links through males showed up more often in local life—for example, among members of a boat crew.

Thus, the contrasting opportunities of men and women showed up in the economy, in access to public space, and in networks of kin-based support. They also showed up in political life. Arembepe had few authority positions, and men held them all. Most household heads and all boat captains were males. These were just some of many manifestations of the lower value that villagers assigned to females. Parents valued boys more than girls; unhappy was the man who hadn't sired a *macho*. Boys got better food and better treatment than girls did. Discrimination against girls showed up in childhood mortality. More often neglected, girls were less likely to survive than boys were. In 1964 there were 113 boys for every 100 girls aged ten and under. No one admitted that this neglect was really covert female infanticide, one expression of an economic devaluation of females that ramified through the local social system and ideology. Villagers did recognize that boys got better care than girls did. "Boys need to eat more if they're to grow up strong."

From infancy, male freedom was encouraged; girls were fettered. Girls wore dresses from their third month of life, but boys could walk around naked until near adolescence. During a baby boy's first year, mothers commented on, fondled, and kissed his genitals. Fathers publicly grabbed the penises of older boys, stimulating them to erection, laughing at the child's reaction. Boys were encouraged to masturbate, to engage in homosexual play, and to have sexual relations with willing girls and women, and with livestock. Beginning with chickens, they might move their way up the food chain (as it were)—through turkeys and sheep, perhaps even to cows and mares.

The freedom and sexuality of maleness contrasted with the confinement of female sexuality. Arembepeiros saw virginity as a commodity. They believed that girls had to be virgins if they hoped to marry legally. In 1965 two women had preserved their virginity until their late twenties. One eventually realized her long-term plan to marry a successful man from outside and to move closer to the city. Only as a virgin, villagers supposed, could a local woman make such a match. Legal marriage meant proposal, formal engagement, and a long courting period. Common-law couples, by contrast, eloped, usually after sex on the beach or in the bush. Arembepeiros viewed virginity as a commodity that could be exchanged for the inheritance rights that came from legal marriage. Except for women with inherited estates, virginity was just about all that local women thought they had to offer a prospective husband.

RACE RELATIONS

Although gender roles were unequal, the general community pattern of egalitarianism did extend to race relations. Despite marked phenotypical (physical) variation in the population, all villagers had some slave ancestry. Most would have been considered "black" (African-American) in the United States. To study "race relations" in Arembepe, I had to work out (for reasons that will become obvious) a (five-part) scale to measure racial variation. By my scale, only 5 percent of the population was either "white" (3 percent) or "black" (2 percent). Most (45 percent) were intermediate (*mulato*). The others were either dark *mulato* (24 percent), or light *mulato* (26 percent). This scheme was my simplification, for statistical analysis, of Arembepe's far more varied and detailed treatment of racial variation.

Previous studies in Brazil had clarified certain important contrasts between race relations there and in the United States. The main difference is that the United States has a dual system of stratification, in which both "race" and class divide the population. In Brazil there is a single stratified order in which race, or phenotype, is simply one factor in determining a person's class affiliation. Other determinants are education, wealth, job, and family connections.

A second basic contrast is the rule of hypodescent, which has operated in the United States to assign—unambiguously and for life—anyone with any "black" ancestry to membership in that group (the socioeconomically disadvantaged group, or lower category in the stratified order). Brazil has no such rule. My 1962 research (Harris and Kottak, 1963) showed that even full siblings could belong to different races—an impossibility if a descent rule operates.

A third contrast is that Brazilians use many more terms than Americans do to deal with racial differences. The people of Arembepe shared with other Brazilians an extensive vocabulary of terms to describe phenotypical differences among people. In answering my questions about someone's race

(*qualidade,*) they paid attention not simply to skin color—which North Americans focus on by using such terms as "black" and "white"—but also to nose length and form, lip thickness, eye color and shape, hair type and color, and other traits. Just by asking 100 villagers the race of drawings of nine phenotypically contrasting individuals, I found that they used more than forty racial terms. My research on racial terminology (Kottak, 1967b) also showed that Arembepeiros were inconsistent in their use of the terms. Presented with the drawings, which varied skin color, facial features, and hair, there was substantial disagreement about the race of the pictured individual. For one drawing, villagers offered nineteen different racial terms, and the least number of terms for any drawing was nine.

Villagers also disagreed when classifying real people, including themselves. I occasionally asked someone to tell me again what his or her race was, saying that I had forgotten the previous answer. Often I got a different term. When I asked about my race, some people made me a *branco* ("white"), some a *mulato claro* ("light *mulato*"), some simply a *mulato*, and some a *sarará* (a term considered funny, used for someone with reddish skin, which I had when sunburned, and light curly hair). (In the United States, I am "white.") Some people called me one thing one day, another the next. There was a similar variation in their use of racial terms for other villagers. How did this behavior compare with that of other Brazilians, and what was its significance?

Unlike stratified Brazilian communities, where light skin correlates with higher economic status, the only significant association between light skin color and wealth in Arembepe involved land ownership. As more recent descendants of slaves, darker people were less likely to own land than lighter villagers were. Remember that land ownership played only a small role in the local economy. Fishing, and reinvestment of fishing profits (in such areas as coconut trees), were the economic mainstays during the 1960s. There was no correlation between skin color and success in these activities—the basis of the local economy.[2]

This is why my informants, although sharing a larger racial vocabulary with other Brazilians, used the terms ambiguously and inconsistently: racial differences had minimal significance in local society. Two equally successful boat captains, one a light *mulato*, the other a dark *mulato*, were best friends and *compadres*. They spent most of their leisure time together. Two poor widows, one "white," the other "black," often sat in front of their adjoining houses and made hats together. Officers of the Fishermen's Society and the soccer club had been men of all shades. Nor did differences in skin shade provide obstacles to marriage. None of the "whites" or "blacks" was married to another "white" or "black." All had married people from the intermediate categories. Prudencio, the landlord's agent and a former municipal assemblyman, was a light *mulato*. His wife, the local schoolteacher, was very dark. The two most successful businessmen were medium and dark *mulatos*. The kin network of any villager spanned an array of racial categories.

Social behavior and the fluid use of racial terms illustrated the lack of racial discrimination in egalitarian Arembepe. When people are sensitive to racial differences, and where phenotypical variation correlates with access to wealth and power, there is more concurrence on categories. This seems to be so in stratified Brazilian communities (see Wagley, 1952). When there is no agreement on the definitions of terms or the classification of actual people, the minimal conditions for converting racial awareness into racial discrimination are absent. They certainly were absent in Arembepe in the 1960s, and this was just one more expression of the egalitarian local social structure.

NOTES

1. The exchange rate of old cruzeiros per U.S. dollar increased from 475 in 1962 to 620 in 1963, 1,500 in 1964, and 1,800 in 1965. [It rose to 6,500 (6.5 new cruzeiros) in 1973 and had reached 60,000 (60) by 1980.]

2. Correlation coefficients (Pearson's *r*: All variables were treated as interval variables in assessing the association between coconut-tree ownership and light skin color, and between boat ownership and light skin color) were .124 and −.044, respectively. Neither coefficient was statistically significant.

REFERENCES CITED

Foster, George M., 1965. "Peasant Society and the Image of Limited Good." *American Anthropologist* 67:293–315.

Gross, Rose Lee, 1964. "Local Politics and Administration: Camaçari, Bahia, Brazil." New York: Columbia-Cornell-Harvard-Illinois Summer Field Studies Program in Anthropology. (Program Files, Columbia University.)

Harris, Marvin, and Conrad Kottak, 1963. "The Structural Significance of Brazilian Racial Categories." *Sociologia* 25:203–209.

Johnson, Allen, 1971. *Sharecroppers of the Sertão: Economics and Dependence on a Brazilian Plantation,* Stanford, Calif.: Stanford University Press.

Kottak, Conrad Phillip, 1967. "Race Relations in a Bahian Fishing Village." *Luso-Brazilian Review* 4:35–52.

Mintz, Sidney, and Eric R. Wolf, 1950. "An Analysis of Ritual Co-parenthood (*Compadrazgo*)." *Southwestern Journal of Anthropology* 6:341–368.

Wagley, Charles W., 1963. *Introduction to Brazil.* New York: Columbia University Press.

———, ed., 1952. *Race and Class in Rural Brazil.* Paris: UNESCO.

Weber, Max, 1958. (orig. 1920) *The Protestant Ethic and the Spirit of Capitalism.* New York: Scribner's.

Wolf, Eric R., 1955. "Types of Latin American Peasantry." *American Anthropologist* 57:452.

12

Machismo and Marianismo

Evelyn Stevens

"If your wife asks you to jump out the window, pray God that it's from the first floor," is a popular Latin American witticism. Does this sound like the realm of *machismo* and oppressed women? Social scientists and feminists in the North have expressed alarm over the plight of Latin American women. It is time to set the record straight: from the Rio Bravo south to Patagonia it is at least 50 percent a woman's world, even though the men don't know it.

Latin American men and women have unequivocal conceptions of their roles and they play them out, if not in harmony, at least in counterpoint. The interpersonal dynamics of the existing social structure afford each sex a complementary sphere of influence that satisfies basic personal and social needs.

The inference we draw from the available material on Latin American women is that they do not want a change of status. While they almost unanimously complain about their sad lot, their suffering

and the unfairness of male domination, they seem to enjoy their martyrdom, and make few concrete proposals for even minimal changes in the status quo. Certainly there has been no movement comparable either to the nineteenth century feminist movement or the twentieth century one in the North Atlantic industrialized nations. Such efforts as have been made were limited almost exclusively to the question of female suffrage; once that was attained, public discussion declined precipitously.

Because much of what has been written about machismo is either moralistic, fragmentary or disguised boasting, it will be helpful to present a more systematic description of its major characteristics before discussing the female attitude and behavior patterns which have developed in a parallel manner.

Mexicans like to think that machismo is an exclusively Mexican phenomenon: the country's principal product. Because Mexico is the nearest culture that exhibits the pattern and because so many Anglo-Americans have visited that country, the misconception persists. A survey of Latin American social science literature reveals that some observers in every country perceive machismo as a widespread, deep-rooted psychosocial problem. Within this general area, however, there are wide variations in the distribution and intensity of its manifestations. Differences can be accounted for in terms of the existing microcultures.

Residents of those areas where indigenous groups have been least affected by contact with "outside" cultural influences show few machista traits. Certain parts of highland Peru, of Bolivia, Colombia, Ecuador and even of Mexico fall into the machismo-free category.

In some Indian communities, matrilineal family structure prevails and women have high prestige, often exercising more authority than the men within the confines of the home. Among the Aymara Indians of Peru, complete premarital sexual freedom prevails for females as well as males. Among the Kuikuru of Brazil, extramarital as well as premarital freedom is the accepted norm for both sexes.

SEVEN DEADLY SINS

In countries populated chiefly by Europeans or their descendants (such as Uruguay, Argentina, Chile and Costa Rica), the machismo behavior pattern exists in somewhat attenuated form. This watering down is particularly interesting because it is generally agreed that the cultural roots of machismo can be traced to the Mediterranean countries, especially to Spain and Italy, from which the Latin American nations have received much of their European immigration.

Machismo seems to flourish in areas where the cultures of two or more great continents have mingled: the urbanized, mestizo sectors of the "Indian" countries as well as the countries of African-European mixture (for example, Brazil, Cuba, Puerto Rico and Venezuela). In all such countries, typical manifestations are reported for all economic classes.

Prevalence of the pattern throughout the class structure seems to contradict the unsupported assertions of recent Afro-American writers in the United States that machismo is found only in the most economically deprived social groups. As a matter of fact, the term *machismo* may be a misnomer for North American black male behavior.

As pictured by some Latin American writers, a description of machista behavior reads like an excerpt from a list of the seven deadly sins.

Pride, better translated as arrogance, heads the list. Resembling the caricature of a sixteenth century Spanish conquistador, today's Latin American male exhibits an overbearing attitude toward anyone in a position inferior to his, demanding menial services and subservience from subordinates.

BURDEN OF CIVILITY

Another manifestation of the trait is his insistence on having his own way, forcing acceptance of his views, winning every argument in which he engages, considering every difference of opinion as a declaration of enmity. For this reason, the macho is reluctant to engage in frank discussion of any important problem, because if he risks expressing an opinion, he must literally be ready to fight for it. Conversely, he must avoid eliciting opinions from other males in order not to appear to be inviting a quarrel which might have physically and psychologically dangerous consequences. Much of the conversation of Latin American male groups consists of "small talk," sparring at arm's length so that all involved can protect themselves from the hazards of conflict. The resultant impoverishment of interpersonal relations makes men lonely and somewhat wistful. Mexicans get drunk, asserts Octavio Paz, when they can no longer bear the burden of civility.

Under the pressures of the machismo ethos, the Iberian concept of *dignidad,* based on the belief that all human beings are equal recipients of grace, becomes deformed into a hypersensitivity, a touchiness, a disposition to interpret almost any remark as an insult. Men bear themselves as though they carried signs reading, "Don't trifle with me," and in smaller print, "Don't josh me, jostle me or cross my will." Almost the only area in which they permit themselves any leeway in disagreeing openly with each other is in discussions of sporting events. Soccer, football and jai alai are immensely popular, in part because betting by spectators affords a ritualized and therefore safe outlet for expressions of hostility. Unfortunately, pride often forces men to bet ruinous sums. Cock fighting and bull fighting are even more popular spectacles, but fall in a separate category, hardly classifiable as sports.

Wrath, the second of the seven deadly sins, manifests itself not only as violence but even more importantly as intransigence. Just as pride leads machos into betting sums they cannot afford, stubbornness traps them into adopting inflexible positions. Once committed to a particular point of view or line of conduct, men refuse to modify or retreat from it. With rare exceptions, Latin American politics leaves little room for accommodation of conflicting policy preferences through negotiation. *He dicho* ("I have spoken") announces that the die is cast and that the speaker is irrevocably bound to his position. For many years Mexico's dominant party, the PRI, kept its conflicts from public view, allowing politicians to contend with each other without risking the dissolution of the entire political system, but there are signs that this arrangement is now failing to contain accumulated hostilities.

LUST AND ANXIETY

Life is risky for the Latin American male. Even more than in other cultures, the man is forced to act or pretend to act aggressively at all times, yet he must take great care that this aggressiveness does not lead him into a trap, because the penalty for a false move can be death, disgrace or ridicule. For some men, business or professional activities can be nonphysical expressions of aggressiveness, but only a very small band of the social spectrum can enjoy such release. The only safe kind of aggression available to men of all classes is that which they aim at women.

Lust is the theological label for sexual aggressiveness. It is also the behavioral trait that has given machismo its bad press at home and abroad. One suspects, however, that the apparent humility and self-excoriation with which men confess their collective sinfulness to each other and to the outside world contains a thinly concealed boast.

Amorous conquests serve a double purpose. While each seduction gives a man the temporary sensation of having bested an elusive adversary, it also serves to reassure him that the supposed essence of his manhood—his sexual potency—is intact. Trapped by his anxieties, he sees manliness, potency and fertility as an inseparable trio. Because the fear of losing his potency is everpresent, the macho lives in a nightmare world; like a writer between books or an actor between plays, he is desperately unsure about whether he can produce another hit. Miser-like, he reviews his collection of sex partners, hoping to add new ones to the list.

He worries constantly that other men may not believe his boasts. *Marinerito sobre cubierta* ("cash on the line"), they may say. Anybody can appear to have slept with a woman, but where is the proof? The only effective proof, the one that will silence even the most skeptical, is to get the woman pregnant. Thus, a man's children, in and out of wedlock, becomes his insurance against the imputation of impotence.

So that there can be no doubt about the identity of the father, a man does everything possible to restrict his woman's contacts with other men. Some even forbid their women to be seen talking with another member of the opposite sex. "It is a strange kind of civilization," commented a Spanish writer, "where a man's honor depends completely on the fickle behavior of a woman." This jealous watchfulness is an illustration of the way the same behavior pattern can serve different purposes in different cultures. when a Chocó Indian of the Colombian highlands takes his wife to town, she must walk behind him without looking at or speaking with any other man. Women are fewer than men in this Indian group; a Chocó male lucky enough to secure a wife worries constantly that she may be lured away by a more attractive offer. The question for the fearful macho is not whether his wife or mistress may leave him; he worries about giving other men any kind of opening wedge to doubt his claims of potency. Unlike the members of unacculturated Indian communities, *mestizo* males cannot look forward to increasing prestige and dignity as they grow older. As a man leaves his youth behind him, another worry is added to his list: Are his sexual powers diminishing faster than they should? Will be become a *viejo inútil* ("useless old man")? Conscious of this preoccupation, a younger man who wishes to compliment him may make the sly suggestion that some small child in the neighborhood bears a strong resemblance to him.

CALLOUSNESS TOWARDS WOMEN

Among some lower-class males there exists the notion that the sex of the offspring is an indication of the degree of a man's virility; male babies prove that the father is *muy macho,* whereas females reflect a certain "weakness of seed." Particular importance is attached to the sex of the first child, since this can either establish his reputation firmly or leave it hanging in doubt.

The true macho is expected to show callousness toward women except, of course, his mother. This is the cause of women's martyrdom and lamentations, the characteristic women have in mind when they refer to a "repressive and machista society."

When he is behaving according to the stereotype, especially when he is in a group of men, the male feels obliged to express hostility toward women, including his wife and his concubine(s). He is expected to show a regal disdain for their feelings, a lack of concern for the effect his actions may have on their physical or emotional welfare; in fact, ostentatious cruelty toward women can be expected to elicit respectful admiration from male companions and friends. This can take many forms, but probably the most widespread is the practice of seduction, the purpose of which is to persuade an unwilling woman—often by trickery—to engage in sexual intercourse without the man's becoming emotionally involved with her. "To make love without loving" is the basis of the exploits of the prototype Don Juan, whose epithet is *El Burlador* ("The Trickster"), he who makes a laughing-stock of women.

LOVE AND MARRIAGE

Does this mean that a man cannot marry for love? No; he is permitted that temporary lapse into vulnerability, but he is expected to recover his callousness as quickly as possible and to demonstrate it by engaging in extramarital sexual activity and mistreatment of his wife.

Other forms of cruelty may include such petty harassment as deliberately arriving late for meals, prolonged unexplained absences from the home, gratuitous demands for menial services, brusqueness or even verbal abuse of his wife or mistress, unnecessary stinginess and unreasonable restrictions on the woman's freedom of movement (for example, forbidding her to visit with women friends). Wife-beating, although not uncommon, is mostly confined to the lower classes.

The only exception to this behavior pattern is the mother. To her children, but especially to her male children, she is an object of reverence, a royal personage whose wishes must be gratified, and the everloving, always forgiving surrogate of the Virgin Mary. Typically, a man may comment that he is going to try to make restitution to his mother for all the suffering his father has caused her. At the same time, he is acting toward his wife in such a way that his children, in turn, will see her as a martyr.

The conomics of machismo, as explained by a Puerto Rican professional, are that a middle-class man can easily afford a mistress from the working class. Poverty is so widespread that many individuals live on the border of starvation. Unemployment is widespread, as is underemployment. Peasant women flocking to cities are lucky to find jobs as shockingly underpaid, very badly treated servants. For a few dollars a month, a man can rent a room for a woman, feed her, buy her a few clothes and take her dancing occasionally to a cheap night club (thus making sure that his liaison is noticed by other men). The women who are "bought" in this fashion find at least temporary relief from the pressures of economic necessity. Many of them entertain the hope that they can somehow persuade the men to divorce their present wives and marry them. Such things do happen, though rarely. At any rate, it is more comfortable to be a middle-class man's mistress than a peasant's concubine or an underpaid abused servant. A significant upward trend in economic development would probably reduce the pool of available mistresses.

Rich and middle-income men take advantage of their superior position to recruit women from the more economically deprived strata for their displays of conspicuous sexual consumption. There is a kind of pecking order involved here; rich men usually choose middle-class women, while middle-class men customarily dip into the ranks of poor women for their extramarital partners. Economic deprivation, however, does not bar poor men from acquiring one or more concubines. With his pitifully scant income, the Puerto Rican *jibaro* ("peasant') often maintains a *casa principal* ("main house," a term used to designate the residence of either a legal or a common-law partner) as well as a *casa chica* ("little house," a phrase designating the abode of the principal concubine), and not infrequently a *casa media* ("middle house," the residence of a secondary concubine).

The sexual activity of Latin American males—their proudest claim to high status as machos—bears a curious resemblance to Mark Twain's weather: everybody talks about it, but very little research is done to clarify the point. A decade ago, an investigator commented:

> Just as it is tempting to deduce attitudes from behavior, so it is tempting to deduce a high frequency of sex relations from high fertility, since sex relations are a necessary antecedent to fertility. . . . The available evidence, while unfortunately limited, points in the opposite direction.

Ten years later, there is still no reliable way of determining whether the Latin American male who engages in extramarital sex is more active than one who does not, but researchers agree that the frequency of intercourse for both types of men probably does not vary much from the norm appropriate for their age group. It may very well be that whatever they give to one woman, they deny to another. The *mujeriego* ("philanderer") may simply distribute what he has to offer over a wider field of recipients.

NUMBERS GAME

Latin American wives cooperate in this numbers game in several ways: first by maintaining the attitude that enjoyment of coitus is repugnant to their finer natures, and again by encouraging the notion that men are incurably puerile, unable to restrain their impulses. That these attitudes operate as a self-fulfilling prophecy is confirmed by another Latin American investigator who says that the women in his study do not have organsm and their frequency of sexual relations does not add up to any more than four times per month in some carefully studied areas.

Lest Anglo-American feminists rush to the conclusion that Latin women have been brainwashed by men, fragmentary data indicate that men are more generous than women in their estimate of the latter's enjoyment of sexual relations.

It appears that in Latin America, each female member of the triangle (or quadrangle or pentagon) derives certain advantages from the male's acknowledged weakness. For this mistress, the compensation is chiefly economic. While the man needs her as visible proof of his proclaimed hypersexuality and aggressiveness, his financial support relieves her of the need to seek more distasteful employment, such as domestic servitude, if she comes from the lower class, or ill-paid drudgery in a store or office. The wife, on the other hand, is able to play on her husband's feelings of guilt at his "moral depravity" by reigning over his "legitimate" household, tyrannizing the servants, basking in the adulation of her children and receiving the approval of society.

But what about our opening epigraph that indicates a man's subservience to his wife's whims? How can that be reconciled with the arrogant, aggressive, lustful figure portrayed above? The quotation reveals men's uneasiness, their fear of being dominated by women and their suspicion that no matter how much they struggle to assert themselves, the battle is irretrievably lost; in fact, has been lost since the beginning of time.

At the core of machista behavior, observes a Mexican male, "there is the obstinate, unshakable, obsessive purpose of proving by all available means that one is free with respect to the woman and that she is absolutely submissive to him. Much of the Latine American literature on the subject reflects a sense of desperation on the part of the men. They seem to feel driven, hounded by the stereotypical prescriptions to conform to the norms of machista behavior. If they want to attain and retain the respect of other human beings, they must go through the ritual of boasting about courage and sexual prowess.

Often they are forced to validate this boasting with some kind of token behavior, which on occasion can lead them into a disastrous cul-de-sac such as the bloody Mexican game of Russian roulette, so ably satirized by the film comic, Mario Moreno ("Cantinflas") in *El Sietemachos*.

MALE HYPERSEXUALITY

Pressures to conform to the macho stereotype come as strongly from Latin American women as from the men. In women's gossip circles, a favorite topic is the shamelessness with which individual men (designated by name) engage in extramarital promiscuity or in other behavior calculated to humiliate women. A newcomer from another culture is at first shocked and pained by such recitals, until it becomes evident that the only men who are regarded contemptuously for their "pusillanimity" are those who lead blameless lives. Some years ago in Puerto Rico, a dignified justice of the Supreme Court became a candidate for the office of governor, with the support of the local Catholic hierarchy. His campaign slogan, *Vote por Don Martin Travieso; no ha tenido más que una mujer en toda la vida* ("He has had only one woman [wife] in his whole life"), made him the laughing-stock of the island. The slogan was a left-handed reference to the private life of the popular candidate, Luis Muñoz Marín, who won the election by a large majority.

Just as the myth of male hypersexuality glosses over the individual inadequacies of many Latin American men, so the idealization of spiritual love masks the range of temperaments found in women. Because inspiration for this secular cult of femininity is drawn from the adoration of the Virgin Mary, I have called it *marianismo*.

MARY-WORSHIP

Although the church has long counseled women to emulate the virtues of Mary, the excessive veneration of flesh-and-blood women has no support in dogma and in fact remains completely devoid of theological sanction. Interestingly, although Marianism or Mariology, as it is called in liturgical discussions, is a world-wide religious manifestation, only in Latin cultures have its main features been appropriated to forge a powerful lay instrument for the sanctification of all women.

Taking its cue from the worship of Mary, marianismo pictures its subjects as semi-divine, morally superior and spiritually stronger than men. This constellation of attributes enables women to bear the indignities inflicted on them by men, and to forgive those who bring them pain. Like Mary, women are seen as mediatrices without whose intercession men would have little chance of obtaining forgiveness for their transgressions. Conversely, a female cannot hope to attain full spiritual stature until her forbearance and abnegation have been tested by male-inflicted suffering. Men's wickedness is therefore the necessary precondition of women's superior status.

Because the *Mater Dolorosa* is the ideal of womanhood, socialization of female children and adolescents is directed toward appreciation of the requisite attitudes toward male members of the family. Within the family, the male ego is the center of attention; mother and sisters cater and defer to him, make excuses and pray for him, and intercede on his behalf with his father during the latter's brief, infrequent but usually harsh exercise of authority. In turn, the male treats his sisters with condescension, more or less tempered by affection, and is expected to watch over their behavior, especially when they venture out of the house. Every male member of the family acts as part of a vigilante network, charged with keeping predatory outside males from making off with the females' "honor" (virginity). A girl who is known as "wild" or "easy" brings disgrace not only on herself, but— more important—on the whole family, in that she reveals the inability of her male relatives—their lack of virile strength and courage—to "protect" her.

MATER DOLOROSA

To an outsider it might seem logical to expect that mother and sisters would be scrupulous in their insistence that the males of the family respect the "honor" of other unmarried females, but this is not the case. Sisters will often act as intermediaries for the males' amorous campaigns against their female friends, taking satisfaction in helping their brothers add to their list of conquests. Mothers show a curious lack of concern, amounting at times to spitefulness toward the females involved.

For men, unmarried females are moral and intellectual imbeciles, in need of constant supervision. How is it possible that from such unpromising material each generation produces its own quota of saintly mothers who reign supreme over the extended family or its truncated urbanized version? The apotheosis is neither facile nor swift.

For the woman, the early years of marriage are seen as an apprenticeship, a "trial by fire," in anticipation of a state of blessedness which can be attained only after middle life, when the childbearing period is past and after a woman has supposedly been divested of her specific sexuality. Menopause becomes a sign of divine grace.

Women strive not to avoid suffering but to make known their suffering, for their misfortunes are the stigmata of incipient sainthood which are further validated by the appropriate attitude of abnegation. "The test of womanhood," comments sociologist Lloyd Rogler, "is self-sacrifice." The more closely the husband conforms to stereotyped macho behavior the more rapidly his suffering wife advances toward her anticipated beatification.

It is difficult if not impossible to achieve full sainthood without having borne children. The pain of childbirth is the surest proof of martyrdom; loyalty to marianismo would prevent a woman from admitting to an easy delivery. Maternity sections of hospitals resound with the eloquent cries of the parturients, who call upon *their* mothers to help them bear the torture: *"Ay, mamá, no puedo más!"* As there can be no saint unless there are votaries, the multiparous woman provides the setting for her own future cult. Adult daughters will, after socialization, become valuable allies and vestal priestesses, but adult sons will be necessary as worshippers.

POWER OF LOVE

Mexican psychiatrist Rogelio Díaz Guerrero agrees that, "far from being victims of this dichotomous portrayal of the sex roles, Latin American women are the deliberate perpetrators of the myth." Guerrero continues:

> For one reason or another, historically, males and females in Mexico realized that whenever there are more than two people together, they will have to accommodate in regards to at least two important dimensions, the dimension of power and the dimension of love. In the Mexican family for one reason or another, it appears that it was decided that the father should have the power and the mother should have the love (and the power of love).

This is an extraordinarily perceptive appreication of the dynamics involved in the male-female relationship. For women do enjoy great power in Latin America, based on their acknowledged spiritual superiority. In the hierarchy of values of Latin American culture, matters of the spirit stand undis-

putedly above all others. In comparing themselves with members of other societies, Latin Americans stress their spirituality, their devotion to "the finer things of life," rather than to the crass materialistic objectives pursued by others. José Enrique Rodó, the revered apostle of Latin American self-affirmation, chose Shakespeare's Ariel to personify the ethereal nature of his people, likening the Anglo Americans to the coarse and brutal Prospero. There is hardly an educated Latin American who cannot quote in their entirety the relevant passages from Rodó's work.

A married woman can be lazy, bad tempered, improvident, but as long as she is not found to be sexually promiscuous, she will be regarded as a good wife and mother. Curiously, as she grows older, her children and even her husband will change the details of her real behavior for a pseudobiography that conforms to the marianismo stereotype.

Secure in the knowledge that her imperfections are immaterial, the Latin American woman wages undeclared war on her husband. Is he stingy? The children are taught to shame him by their tearful begging. Is he abusive? The children are there to comfort their mother. Is he unfaithful? The children's admiration for their mother's abnegation only increases. Does he indulge in petty harassments? The children's silent hostility can be felt. In sum, his efforts to sustain his reputation as a macho in the world outside of the home require that he relinquish his claims to respect and love within the home. He retains his titular authority, but even after he has made a decision he may have the uncomfortable suspicion that he has been manipulated into doing precisely what his wife wanted.

SYMBIOTIC RELATIONSHIP

If this attempt to set the record straight has given the impression that the role structure for men and women in Latin America is intolerably rigid, this is only due to the oversimplification made necessary by space requirements. In every country, many intelligent individuals, male and female, adopt alternative modes of behavior, sometimes in open defiance of the prescriptions but more often by developing stratagems for quiet noncompliance. It has been my observation—unconfirmed and perhaps unconfirmable by any statistical survey—that Latin American men and women are no more ill at ease with each other than are Europeans or Anglo-Americans.

The marianismo-machismo pattern of attitudes and behavior provides a stable symbiosis in Latin American culture. Within the context of nonindustrialized societies, it has provided clear-cut role definitions for both sexes. As these societies change in the direction of economic growth and development, it will be interesting to observe whether or not new patterns emerge.

13

Women's Movements in the Americas
Feminism's Second Wave

Norma Chinchilla

Under the healing rays of the sun and the salty ocean air, some 500 Central American women gathered at the beach resort of Montelimar, Nicaragua, in March of [1992] to discuss the question of power. They talked about the power Central American women have in their "public" and "private" lives, the kind of power they would like to have, and how to go about getting that power. The *encuentro* was the largest and most diverse gathering of Central American women in history, and the first to include lesbian groups and discussion of lesbianism as a formal part of the program. Black women educated conference participants about the pain and joy of the black female experience in the Central American context, and Indian women conducted a workshop comparing and contrasting Indian and mestiza women's identities and relations.

The *encuentro* was a significant milestone in Latin America's nascent women's movement. Dur-

From Norma Chinchilla, "Women's Movements in the Americas: Feminism's Second Wave," *NACLA Report on the Americas* 28(1): 17–23, 1993.

ing the 1970s and 1980s, the media, the Catholic Church and many political parties promoted pejorative caricatures of feminists as self-indulgent and egotistical, anti-family and anti-male, and divisive of community and class solidarity. Such stigmas made it difficult to imagine that a feminist movement of any significance would ever take root in Latin America.

By the end of the 1980s, however, a "second wave" of feminism—following the first surge of women's mobilization in the late nineteenth and early twentieth century—did occur. The significant role women played in popular and social movements throughout the hemisphere, the exposure to feminism and women's organizations that Latin American women got while in exile, and exchanges with North American and European feminists through solidarity movements created fertile ground for the emergence of feminism in a number of Latin American countries, in particular Peru, the Southern Cone, Brazil, Mexico and the Dominican Republic.

Feminism arrived late in Central America—with the exception of Costa Rica. In part, this was due to the overriding priorities created by war and revolution. The fierce grip on power which foreign and

133

domestic elites have traditionally had in the region also quelled new social movements and kept countries isolated from one another. Multinational corporations have historically made it easier to telephone and trade with the United States than communicate with or travel to another Central American country.

The Montelimar *encuentro* marked the first time that Central American feminists had ever tried to work together on a region-wide event. Illustrative of the tentative nature of the project, the word "feminist" did not appear in the title of the event because organizers from some countries felt that many women had not yet had a chance to explore the idea in a safe context. Feminism was, however, clearly the driving force behind the questions that framed the discussion groups and workshops, the process or *metodología* which guided them, and the *encuentro's* focus on regional strategies for increasing women's power.

Women were encouraged to discuss and organize *as women*—"for, of, and by women," as one organizer put it. The participants shared their assessments of how Central American women were faring in their daily lives, as well as their aspirations and dreams for the future. Thus the women focused on transforming social reality not only for others, but for themselves; in that way the political became personal, and the personal political. "Many women in Central America don't have an explicit name for what they think or do; that is, they can't say 'I am a feminist for this and this reason,'" said Carmen Lucíía Pellecer, a member of the Guatemalan women's organization Tierra Viva, the first group to have an explicitly feminist as well as popular movement focus. "But they start to develop a feminist perspective when they begin working with women from the point of view of women. They start out working for other women, and they end up working for themselves as well. It's at that point that the women begin to look for or demand their own spaces."

Implicit in discussion at the *encuentro* was the assumption that all women—not just poor and working-class women—share to some extent the experience of sexism and subordination, and that cross-class coalitions and alliances can be formed to work on common projects. Implicit as well, although not shared by all the women present, was the assumption that even though women's subor-dination is interrelated with other forms of exploitation and oppression—such as those based on class, imperialism or ethnicity—it must be addressed directly. The Regional Organizing Committee's statement provides a good working definition of feminism:

Our politics are feminist because feminism proposes a personal and collective way of life that rejects unequal power relations not only among the sexes but also in society as a whole. Feminism is a traditional social practice in Latin America and we Central American women are contributing our own elements to this tradition. We are a large constituency that seeks to build a kind of feminism that is rooted in our material conditions of life and from which we seek to develop proposals for overall change.

In the idyllic setting of Montelimar, many women broached potentially controversial and previously "taboo" topics, ranging from women's power in "mixed" organizations and institutions, to domestic violence, reproductive rights, sexual orientation, and sexuality. For many women, the *encuentro* not only represented a well-earned respite from years of back-breaking labor in the service of others, but also the discovery of a dormant feminist orientation that had always been repressed or put on the back burner in favor of what seemed to be (or what were said to be) more pressing priorities: war, revolution, the defense of national sovereignty, the reduction of social and economic inequality, and economic survival.

The women discussed what kind of power they have in mixed-gender organizations, and how much autonomy women's groups, caucuses, or secretariats should have. Drawing on their years of experience as Sandinista activists, Nicaraguan women—some of whom now identify primarily as independent feminists—warned Salvadoran and Guatemalan women not to equate participation with gender equality. They also advised their counterparts not to expect that dedication, sacrifice and heroism would automatically guarantee women's interests in the peace process, or women's leadership in the new civil institutions and organizations being established.

The Nicaraguan women argued that women

need to demand recognition *as women,* independent of whatever social sectors or groups they represent. They contended that women should present the state and their social, religious, educational, and political organizations with gender-specific and feminist demands, such as the right to autonomous women's spaces within and outside other sectoral and political organizations, direct representation of women's interests, and the promotion of women's leadership and women electoral candidates at the municipal and national levels.

"We have come from a very long war, a difficult process in which our needs and demands have been postponed by the war and the specific circumstance we have faced," said Morena Herrera, a Salvadoran activist and leader of Mujeres por la Dignidad y la Vida. "At his moment, the familiar argument is that national reconstruction and the upcoming elections in 1994 are important and that women's concerns should wait until after the elections. This conference has allowed us to say 'No more.' We are not going to keep postponing our needs, our demands and our struggles."

The women spiritedly debated how much and what kind of autonomy should be sought in the consolidation of Central American feminism. They agreed that autonomy is multidimensional—personal, economic, institutional, political, and ideological. For example, nongovernmental organizations (NGOs) that are focused on explicitly feminist projects may be politically and organizationally independent of the state and lefist political parties, but economically dependent on external funding, which may carry certain ideological and political conditions. Likewise, women in unions and political parties may gain the right to select their own leadership and determine their own agenda, but they may lack personal autonomy with respect to families, boyfriends, and spouses.

The women were divided over the question of whether to build autonomous feminist groups or work within existing mixed organizations. Those who favored autonomy argued that women should make a clean break with the hierarchical, male-dominated political organizations of the past, and create their own organizations in which they don't have to constantly justify the importance of their projects to men. Those who favored working for feminist agendas within mixed organizations countered that

women risk becoming isolated politically if they do not struggle for power and influence within existing political organizations. Moreover, they contended, the feminist movement should take advantage of the many women—especially working-class, poor and "minority" women—who may already be organized. They also worried that with human and material resources scarce, a dispersion of effort may concede territory to the enemies of feminism in the broader conservative political context.

This debate was a reflection of that taking place in Nicaragua where tensions have appeared between independent feminists and female political-party militants. A number of party militants feel that the independent feminists regard them as impure in their feminism and inherently subordinate to men in their political-party activities. Independent feminists, on the other hand, feel that their credentials as revolutionaries and commitment to class struggle in Latin America are being questioned. The tension between the two sides is reminiscent of that between *"las políticas"* and *"las feministas"* in the early stages of the feminist movement in the Southern Cone. The difference, however, is that in Central America, both sides have a history of feminist activism. Exacerbating the tension is the fact that many of the Nicaraguan women who line up on opposing sides of the debate were once comrades in the Sandinista Front.

In Nicaragua, as well as at the *encuentro,* there is agreement on the importance of promoting a feminist agenda within mixed organizations. Everyone agrees that women in mixed organizations should have the right to discuss and rank their priorities and choose their leadership. Autonomous women's institutions and organizations, most activists believe, play an important role by providing a safe place for women to recharge their batteries, accumulate independent resources, and unleash their creativity. Moreover, the women in autonomous organizations can also still pursue close links to women who are organized or can potentially be organized around other issues and movements—for example, human rights, class, neighborhood, religion, environment, or ethnicity.

Bridging their differences, a number of the women at the *encuentro* felt that given the diversity of women activists and the degree to which their personal as well as political lives may be in flux, women may feel comfortable in different organizational forms at different points in time, or may burn out in one organizational form but blossom in another. Some women may prefer working in all-female, explicitly feminist groups, while other women who strongly identify with a community or sector may prefer to promote a feminist agenda within mixed groups. The challenge is to link up the various organizational forms and forge a powerful collective political force.

Central American women are not alone in debating the question of how women's movements should relate to the state, to each other, and to other progressive sectors, organizations and issues. In Chile, for example, where women played a central role in resistance to the military dictatorship, the feminist movement has worked hard to push for the inclusion of women's demands in the platforms and agendas of political parties, and to generate awareness of women as a political constituency. Nevertheless, the women's movement seems to have been, to a large extent, marginalized by political parties since the transition to electoral democracy.

The Chilean government has been able to coopt the feminist agenda by creating a national women's office with ministerial rank—Servicio Nacional de la Mujer (SERNAM). SERNAM was established not only to propose and develop programs to improve the lives of women, but also to monitor other state agencies. It thus gives a public, state-legitimized face to the struggle against discrimination against women. Like any regulatory agency which is both part of and dependent upon the state while at the same time charged with monitoring the state, its position is, by definition, contradictory. While there are several well-known feminists in key positions in SERNAM, the majority of the appointees, including the director, are women who have little history or experience working in or with women's organizations. Moreover, with its conservative discourse on family preservation, SERNAM has seemed to go out of its way to antagonize the women's movement.

In part, SERNAM's ability to establish itself as the interlocutor for women is a reflection of the weakness of the women's movement itself. This weakness, in turn, is a reflection of how difficult it is to redefine and reorient a women's movement

born in unified opposition to a dictatorship in order to create a strong mass-based, cross-class movement. In the fledgling democracies of the Southern Cone, the independent feminist movement must define itself not only in relation to the state and political parties, but also in relation to well funded nongovernmental organizations (NGOs) which carry out much of the community-based, grassroots work that many predemocracy women's organizations used to do.

The question of what relationship the women's movement should establish with NGOs—even feminist NGOs—has become vital in countries experiencing the repercussions of neoliberal economic reforms. In Chile, for example, the external funding that once supported women's political activism has greatly diminished. That which still exists has largely reverted to its traditional pattern of favoring social and economic development projects, albeit with a greater gender consciousness than before.

In a time of dramatic cutbacks in state spending and heavy downward pressures on the standard of living, the importance of having paid organizers and professionals on staff at NGOs cannot be discounted. This makes it possible for a certain number of women to devote themselves fulltime to working for change on behalf of women and to promoting general projects that are "gender-conscious." But some women activists argue that in the context of a weak women's movement, NGOs can become the substitute for a broad-based, cross-class feminist movement. In this scenario, the NGOs might wrongly conflate their own desire to survive and grow with the needs of women as a whole.

The emergence of feminist and women-oriented NGOs—such as cultural projects, service centers, and independent research groups—gives Latin American feminism a stability and wealth of resources that never existed before. At the same time, the growth of these institutions results in a potentially problematic distinction between "professional feminists" who are "credentialed" by the national and international development establishments as "women's advocates," and "*militantes*" who may be "increasingly marginalized from both policymaking and funding networks." At the same time, financing for feminist institutions can be very fickle. It can vary greatly over time, depending on the political context and the momentary popularity of different causes for funding sources.

Brazilian feminists face many of the same strategic challenges as their Chilean counterparts in their relationship to the state as a result of the transition to electoral democracy. Despite the fact that feminism is less visible than it was five years ago, and some feminists are disappointed with how political parties have appropriated their claims, the Brazilian feminist movement continues to be the largest, most vital and diverse in the hemisphere.

The current expressions of Brazilian feminism are cultural as well as political. On the political front, women have fought to make government-sponsored women's police stations more responsive to women's needs, and to ensure that the municipal, state and regional governments effectively implement progressive gender laws. In the cultural realm, women have developed popular feminist film and video, and Afro Brazilian feminist aesthetics in the fields of music, dance and theater. Like Chile, Brazil has feminist newspapers, radio stations, publishing houses and bookstores, as well as women's studies programs and research centers. A number of open lesbian groups now participate in both the feminist and gay liberation movements.

The focal point of much of the Brazilian feminist movement, however, continues to be the state. During the 1980s, the Brazilian state went from being considered "women's worst enemy" to "women's best friend" as the result of the formulation of many feminist demands into public policy proposals, and the unprecedented inclusion of women's rights provisions in the new federal constitution. In addition, the national government created women's spaces, such as councils on the status of women and women's police stations.

The transition to democratic rule did not, however, abolish the essentially patriarchal and racist character of the Brazilian state. Nor did it slow down the rush to neoliberal state policies. Confronted with these limits, especially at the federal level, Brazilian feminists have continually had to think creatively and strategically about how, at what level, and in what ways to intervene in the state to ensure that their efforts to extend and redefine women's citizenship have the greatest possible impact.

Urban movements, often led by the Brazilian Workers Party (PT), have managed to successfully organize and secure political and social rights at the municipal and state levels. The overwhelming majority of participants in these movements continue to be women. As a consequence, many Brazilian feminists, while not abandoning efforts to change federal policies, have chosen to focus on influencing local levels of government that are "closer to home, potentially more permeable, and more vulnerable to citizen scrutiny and intervention." The São Paulo Council on the Status of Women, for example, last year launched a campaign for "The Year of the Implementation of Legislation on the Equality of Women." This year they persuaded São Paulo Governor Luiz Antonio Fleury Filho to promulgate a state-sponsored "Convention on the Rights of Women," to be signed by the governor and dozens of mayors in September of this year.

The Workers Party's conscious policy of pressuring for greater decentralization of state authority and resources, and its unexpectedly successful 1988 electoral victories in São Paulo and two dozen other Brazilian cities have helped to focus grassroots activism on local and regional government to a degree that is unusual in Latin America. While the states and localities are chronically underfunded, the focus on local governance deepens democratic participation in ways that mitigate the effects of structural adjustment on poor and working-class citizens. This focus on local and regional struggles, underpinned by neighborhood and grassroots organizing, cannot help but strengthen women's activism and leadership.

If there is one trend which characterizes women's organizing throughout the hemisphere, it is the growing diversity of organizational forms, strategies, and creative efforts. This diversity is both a reflection of the great vitality and strength of the women's movement in this profoundly conservative era and an enormous strategic challenge. How can women's diverse expressions of discontent and resistance be coordinated so as to expand and defend grassroots democracy? How can the movement recognize and accept, for example, that women come to feminism and gender-specific activism through a multiplicity of paths—through religious activity, in defense of their families and children, through activism around racial, ethnic, environmental or sexual orientation issues, or in response to the economic crisis? How can a feminist current be injected into other struggles without forcing them to be ranked in order of importance?

The political, economic, and cultural room within which feminism has to maneuver in the Southern Cone (as well as Mexico and Costa Rica) still seems great in comparison to the obstacles that feminists and women activists still have to overcome in Nicaragua, El Salvador and Guatemala. In the latter three countries, feminism was born out of war and revolution, with all the deprivations and sacrifices that those cataclysmic events brought with them. While, to a large extent, the disruption of the old order made feminist and genderspecific organizing possible, the rebuilding process is much greater than in the Southern Cone where a political infrastructure and culture are already in place.

Throughout the hemisphere, however, women's movements face significant challenges. The disas-trous effects of neoliberal economic policy makes this a difficult moment in history for women's struggle. "We feminists began to talk about wanting power at a very difficult moment in history, at precisely that moment when the power slipped away from our closest allies, that is, leftist men," veteran Dominican feminist Magali Piñeda observed. "At this moment in history, it seems that all societies have entered into a conservative stage, where deep [structural] changes don't appear possible. But it is better that we arrive late to the idea than not at all."

But precisely because the situation calls for imaginative responses and new visions, Latin American women are increasingly dissatisfied with promises of indirect access to power. To those who continue to underestimate the potential power of Latin American feminism to redefine power and politics, Piñeda has a warning: "If people were afraid of communism as a radical specter that would haunt the world, they should really be afraid now because the specter of feminism is the one that is really radical . . . radical because we want to change things at the root. . . ."

14

Women's Social Movements in Latin America

Helen Safa

The past decade has witnessed a marked increase in participation by women in social movements in Latin America. Latin American women are participating in organizations led by and for women, struggling for their rights as workers in trade unions, as housewives in squatter settlements, and as mothers defending human rights against state repression. While undoubtedly influenced by the feminist movements that developed earlier and were largely middle class in origin, these social movements are distinguished by the widespread participation by poor women, who focus their demands on the state in their struggle for basic survival and against repression.

While many studies trace the origin of these movements to the current economic and political crisis in the region, I believe they are indicative of a broader historical trend toward the breakdown of the traditional division between the private and public spheres in Latin America.[1] The private sphere of the family has always been considered the domain of women, but it is increasingly threatened by economic and political forces. Industrial-

ization and urbanization have reduced the role of the family and strengthened the role of the state. There have been marked occupational changes, including an increasing incorporation of women into the labor force. The importance of women as wage earners has been made even more acute by the economic crisis now gripping Latin America, while state services upon which women have come to depend have been reduced or curtailed. Authoritarian military regimes have invaded the very heart of the family by taking the lives of children and other loved ones and subjecting them to terror and state repression.

However, women in Latin America are not just defending the private domain of the family against increasing state and market intervention. They are also demanding incorporation into the state, so that their rights as citizens will be fully recognized. In this sense, these movements not only are symptomatic of the breakdown between the public and private spheres in Latin America but are themselves furthering this process. Women are demanding to be recognized as full participants in the public world and no longer wish to have their interests represented solely by men, whether as heads of household, *barrio* leaders, politicians, or union officials.

From Helen Safa, "Women's Social Movements in Latin American," 1990, *Gender and Society* 4(3):354–369.

At this same time, as Jelin notes (1987), Latin American women are insisting upon distinct forms of incorporation that reaffirm their identity as women, and particularly as wives and mothers. This form of incorporation differs from the contemporary U.S. and Western European experience, in which women seek a gender-neutral participation in the public sphere. Latin American women, in contrast, think that their roles as wives and mothers legitimize their sense of injustice and outrage, since they are protesting their inability to effectively carry out these roles, as military governments take away their children or the rising cost of living prevents them from feeding their families adequately. In short, they are redefining and transforming their domestic role from one of private nurturance to one of collective, public protest, and in this way challenging the traditional seclusion of women into the private sphere of the family.

The prominence of women in these new social movements challenges Marxist theory in at least two fundamental ways. In the first place, participation in these women's movements is based primarily on gender rather than on class, which Marxists have emphasized as the principal avenue for collective action. Most of the poor women who participate in these movements are conscious of both class and gender exploitation, but they tend to legitimize their concerns over issues such as human rights or the cost of living primarily in terms of their roles as wives and mothers rather than as members of a subordinated class. This tendency points out the weakness of Marxist theory in addressing the importance of gender, racial, or religious differences within the working class. Second, and as a consequence of their gender emphasis, the primary arena of confrontation for women's social movements in Latin America has not been with capital but with the state, largely in terms of their reproductive role as wives, mothers, and consumers of both state services and private consumer goods. The state has assumed a major role in social reproduction in Latin America, particularly in terms of the provision of basic services, such as health, education, and transportation. At the same time, the need for these services has grown with the rapid increase in urbanization and industrialization in the post–World War II period.

Women are not the only subordinated group to challenge the state, and social movements have arisen as well among youth, peasants, the urban poor, and broader-based human rights groups. Latin American women have also demanded greater participation in labor unions, political parties, and peasant movements that have attempted to make the state more responsive to their needs. They have worked with feminists in establishing day-care centers or in developing ways to cope with sexual violence and other problems. However, this article focuses on Latin American women's movements for human rights and those centering around consumer issues. It explores the factors that contributed to the increased participation of women in social movements in Latin America and why women have chosen the state as the principal arena of confrontation rather than capital, as in workplace-related issues of collective action. It also discusses how successful these social movements have been in bringing about fundamental changes in gender roles in Latin America.

THE BASES OF WOMEN'S SOCIAL MOVEMENTS IN LATIN AMERICA

Women's social movements in Latin America are commonly seen as a response to military authorization rule and the current economic crisis, both of which create particular hardships for the working class. In an attempt to address the growing debt crisis, many Latin American governments have set up structural adjustment programs designed by the International Monetary Fund. These programs have had a devastating impact on women and children, since they have resulted in increased unemployment and underemployment, a decline in real wages coupled with accelerated inflation, the elimination of state subsidies for basic foods, as well as cuts in government expenditures for social services, such as health and education (Cornia 1987). The economic crisis has reinforced the need for collective action, particularly among poor urban women who organize primarily on a neighborhood basis.

The urban poor in Latin America have a long history of collective action, as demonstrated by the squatter settlements and other neighborhood actions to improve urban services (e.g., Safa 1974). Women have always played a prominent role in these neighborhood forms of collective action, though their importance has seldom been explicitly acknowledged (Caldeira 1987, 77). At the same time, women commonly resort to informal networks of mutual aid, including extended family and neighbors, to help stretch the family income and resolve community problems. Women also add to the family income through participation in the informal economy as domestic servants, street vendors, industrial homeworkers, and other forms of self-employment. With the economic crisis, these survival strategies have been intensified and institutionalized into formal organizations, such as the *comedores populares* or *ollas comunes* (communal kitchens) for food distribution or *talleres productivos* (workshops) for making garments or doing other types of piecework. In Santiago, Chile, in 1986, there were 768 organizations dedicated to collective consumption, including consumer cooperatives (Artega 1988, 577).

The participation of women in social movements in Latin America is also a product of the changes in women's roles in Latin America in the past two decades. Fertility has been declining steadily in most countries of the region, so that by 1980–85, only three Latin American countries registered average fertility rates in excess of six children per women, while eight countries had rates of fewer than four children per woman (ECLAC 1988a, 2). Fertility decline was associated with women's higher educational levels and increased labor-force participation, as well as with greater access to contraceptives and the promotion of family-planning programs in several Latin American countries. Women's educational levels rose at a faster rate than men's as part of the enormous expansion in primary and, in particular, secondary education between 1950 and 1970. The number of women in higher education rose from 35 percent to 45 percent from 1970 to 1985 (ECLAC 1988a, 3–4). As a result, the female labor force increased threefold in Latin America between 1950 and 1980, with overall participation rates rising from almost 18 percent to over 26 percent in the same period (ECLAC 1988b, 15). Work-force participation rates for women grew faster than those for men, and while all age groups experienced growth, single women between the ages of 20 and 29 continued to have the highest level of paid employment among women.

Women industrial workers in the Caribbean are now making a major contribution to their household economies, which has resulted in a shift toward more egalitarian conjugal relationships (Safa 1990). In contrast to the assumptions of some feminist theorists (e.g., Barrett 1980), women in Latin America and the Caribbean seem to have been more successful in negotiating change within the home than at the level of the workplace or the state, where their needs are still not given legitimacy.

The increased educational and occupational levels of Latin American women also contributed to the growth of a feminist movement among middle-class women, who felt their exclusion from the public sphere even more sharply than poor women did. These feminists have devoted much attention to the poor through research and involvement in action projects, such as day care, health services, and centers for raped and battered women. These programs helped to transmit feminist concerns for greater gender equality and have stimulated poor women to challenge their traditional role. The visibility these gender issues received during the U.N. Decade for the Equality of Women through numerous conferences, publications, and projects reinformed their appeal.

Poor women in Latin America also received considerable support from the church (Alvarez 1989, 20–26). Women played a major role in the Catholic church's organization of ecclesiastic base communities (CEBs) in Brazil and other Latin American countries. The CEBs were part of the church's efforts to give more support to social justice for the poor in Latin America, emanating from liberation theology, which is now under increasing attack from the Vatican. The CEBs were also an attempt by the church to reinforce grass-roots support, which was weakening with the growth of Protestantism and the church's elitist stance. Women were organized into mothers' clubs for the provision of food, sewing classes, and other traditional domestic tasks. Many of women's collective consumption strategies, such as communal kitchens, have received church support. While based on traditional women's roles, these clubs provided an additional organizational base from which women could challenge the existing order.

Under military rule, the church often provided the only legitimate umbrella under which women and other groups could organize, since all other forms of mobilization were prohibited. In some

Latin American countries, such as Chile and Brazil, women from all class levels, with church support, organized into human rights groups to protest the disappearance or killing of their loved ones, or to seek amnesty for political prisoners or exiles. Catholic doctrine played an important role in these women's self-definition and quest for legitimacy, and they rarely questioned traditional gender roles. On the contrary, these women often appealed to Catholic symbols of motherhood and the family in legitimizing their protest—values that these authoritarian states also proclaimed but destroyed in the name of national security. Women themselves were often victims of this repression: They were systematically sought out for violent sexual torture designed to destroy their femininity and human dignity (Bunster-Burotto 1986).

In sum, many factors have contributed to the recent increased participation of women in social movements in Latin America. Women had long been active at the neighborhood level, both through informal networks and more organized forms of collective action, such as squatter settlements and *barrio* committees. With economic crisis and military rule, these activities took on added importance and also received the support of important groups, such as the Catholic church and nongovernmental agencies. Increased educational and occupational opportunities made women more aware of previous restrictions and more vocal in protesting them. Poor women became more receptive to the largely middle-class feminist movement in Latin America and began to redefine their traditional role, including their relationship to the state.

WOMEN'S SOCIAL MOVEMENTS AND THE STATE

Women's social movements have been described as a new form of doing politics (*nueva forma de hacer politica*) in Latin America, but the impetus for most of these movements has not come from traditional political parties and labor unions in the region. Most women's movements have consciously avoided partisan political connections, in part because of the weakness of these traditional avenues of political action during the period of authoritarian military rule when most of these movements

arose. The attempt of these regimes to limit legitimate political action contributed to the politicization of women and other groups who had not been participating actively in the public arena (Jelin 1987).

The other reason women's social movements took place largely outside the realm of traditional political parties is that politics is seen as men's sphere, particularly by poor women. Latin American political parties traditionally have been dominated by men and have been seen as engaged in struggles for power in which the poor are essentially clients. Poor people's loyalty to the party is exchanged for favors, such as paving a road, providing state services, guaranteeing title to land, or getting jobs. The Centros de Madres in Chile, which had begun to acquire some autonomy under the governments of Frei and Allende, were, under the military dictatorship of Pinochet, completely subverted to the needs of the state for the control and co-optation of poor women (Valdés et al. 1989). Although the Centros de Madres were privatized, they were run by a staff of volunteers appointed by the government and headed by Pinochet's wife, who offered to both rural and urban women such services as training courses that focused largely on improving their domestic role. Political participation was discouraged as "unfeminine," although members were often called upon to display their loyalty to the regime by participating in rallies and other activities. As a result, membership in the Centros de Madres declined drastically from the premilitary period, and new nonofficial women's groups arose, in the areas of both human rights and collective survival strategies, in response to Chile's severe economic crisis and rising rates of unemployment (Arteaga 1988, 573). These nonofficial groups provided the base for the women's movement against Pinochet starting in 1983.

Latin American women appear to have chosen the state as the principal arena of their collective action rather than the workplace as men traditionally have, partly because industrial capitalism transformed the organization and social relations of production and the gendered division of labor. While industrial capitalism initially drew women into the paid labor force in many areas, they were never as fully incorporated as men, who became the chief breadwinners. Women were relegated to a role as supplementary wage earners, while their reproductive role as housewives and consumers assumed new importance. Despite recent significant increases in women's labor-force participation in Latin America, this image of women as supplementary workers persists and helps explain women's comparatively low level of consciousness as workers. Most poor women are relatively recent and less-stable entrants to the formal labor force in Latin America and work primarily to support themselves and their families, obtaining little gratification or self-fulfillment from their jobs. Their primary identification, even when they are working, is as wives and mothers.

The gendered division of labor in the workplace may reinforce gender hierarchies rather than weaken them, by relegating women to inferior jobs. Even in São Paulo, Brazil, where the spectacular industrial boom of the 1970s led to a 181 percent increase in women's employment in manufacturing between 1970 and 1980, women workers were largely concentrated in exclusively women's jobs at the bottom of the job hierarchy (Humphrey 1987). These gender asymmetries in the workplace were reflected in the conflict between male-dominated unions and working women. Souza-Lobo's study (forthcoming) of the metallurgy industry found that although women formed union committees, and some individually active women were integrated into the union structure, women continued to see the union as a men's sphere that remained largely unresponsive to their demands.

As a result of their frustration in working through political parties and labor unions, the recognized channels for collective action, Latin American women presented their demands to the state directly. One of the principal demands was for the provision of public services, such as running water, electricity, and transportation, all of which are sorely lacking in the squatter settlements in which most of these poor women live. Women's reproductive role as housewives and mothers had tended to push them into the foreground as champions of these collective consumption issues, and they have been in the forefront of protests against the cost of living and for demands for programs to provide day care, health services, and even food.

One of the most successful and unique collective consumption strategies to combat the growing economic crisis is the *comedores populares* or communal kitchens organized by women in Lima, Santiago, and other Latin American cities. Groups of 15 to 50 households buy and prepare food collectively for the neighborhood, with each family paying according to the number of meals requested. Many of these *comedores* sprang up spontaneously, while others have been started or at least supported by the church, the state, and other local and international agencies. UNICEF–Peru in 1985 estimated that there were 300 in Lima (Cornia 1987, 99), while Blondet (1989) recently estimated their numbers at 1,000–1,200. Their growing number is evidence of women's collective response to the increasing severity of the economic crisis in Peru and other Latin American countries in the past decade.

In Lima, popular organizations may be the only alternative to acquire basic services, such as health, education, and food, yet the *asistencialismo* (welfare dependency) that this policy encourages may be exploited by the government, political parties, and other agencies (Blondet 1989). Traditional district and neighborhood organizations are controlled by male leaders, who attempt to usurp the popular support enjoyed by women's groups for their own partisan ends. Blondet (1989) recounts, for example, how the popular women's federation in Villa El Salvador, a large shanty town in Lima, split and was partially absorbed through pressure brought by the traditional men's organization. The political fragmentation then occurring among leftist political parties in Peru was reproduced within the women's organizations, further weakening their base of support.

Some feminists have been critical of these women's self-help organizations because they focus almost exclusively on traditional women's tasks and do not challenge the traditional division of labor. I would argue that the collectivization of private tasks, such as food preparation and child care, is transforming women's roles, even though they are not undertaken as conscious challenges to gender subordination. These women never reject their domestic role but use it as a base to give them strength and legitimacy in their demands on the state (Alvarez 1989, 20; Caldeira 1987, 97). In moving their domestic concerns into the public arena, they are redefining the meaning associated with domesticity to include participation and struggle rather than obedience and passivity.

Nowhere is their militancy more apparent than

in the demands Latin American women have placed on the state for the recognition of human rights. One of the best-known cases in contemporary Latin America is Las Madres del Plaza de Mayo, who played a decisive role in the defeat of the military dictatorship that ruled Argentina from 1976 to 1983. Composed mostly of older women with no political experience, Las Madres take their name from the Plaza de Mayo, the principal seat of government power in Buenos Aires, in which they march every Thursday, wearing a white kerchief and carrying photographs of their missing children as a symbol of protest. Although the military government attempted to discredit them as madwomen or mothers of subversives, they continued to march, publish petitions in the newspaper, organize trips abroad, and seek cooperation with other human rights groups and youth movements, with whom they organized larger demonstrations in 1981 and 1982. The publicity they received from the foreign media and the support given them by some European countries and the United States during the Carter administration contributed to their popular support (Reimers 1989). In order to maintain their legitimacy during the military regime, they refused any identification with political parties or feminism. They maintained, *"Nosotros no defendemos ideologias, defendemos la vida"* ("We don't defend ideologies, we defend life"; Feijoo and Gogna 1987, 155). Their true demands were not political power for themselves, but that the state guarantee the return of their loved ones and punish the military who had violated the sanctity of the home and family. These demands remain largely unfulfilled. Though the top military were prosecuted, most officers were granted amnesty, and even some of those imprisoned were later released.

After the end of military rule, Las Madres were weakened by internal struggles that reflected a split between those who wished to remain aloof from partisan politics and those who sought alliances with political parties, chiefly the Peronists, to achieve their goals. Although women's human rights groups similar to Las Madres del Plaza de Mayo have arisen in Uruguay, Chile, Brazil, Honduras, El Salvador, Guatemala, and other Latin American countries subject to military rule, the decline in popular support for Las Madres reflects the difficulty women's social movements have in converting political mobilization into institutional representation (cf. Jaquette 1989, 194).

THE TRANSFORMATIVE POTENTIAL OF WOMEN'S SOCIAL MOVEMENTS IN LATIN AMERICA

Most participation by women in social movements arises out of women's immediate perceived needs and experiences, or out of what Molyneux (1986) terms women's "practical gender interests." Molyneux claims these practical gender interests do not challenge gender subordination directly, whereas strategic gender interests question or transform the division of labor. As we have seen, women's social movements are often based on their roles as wives and mothers and may reinforce or defend women's domestic role. However, as these practical gender interests are collectivized and politicized, they may also lead to a greater consciousness of gender subordination and the transformation of practical into strategic gender interests.

Although neither women's movements for human rights nor collective consumption were designed as challenges to gender subordination, participation in these movements has apparently led to greater self-esteem and recognition by women of their rights, as the following statement by a Brazilian woman, leader of a neighborhood organization, underlines:

> Within the Women's Movement, as a woman, I discovered myself, as a person, as a human being. I had not discovered that the woman . . . always was oppressed. But it never came to my mind that the woman was oppressed, although she had rights. The woman had to obey because she was a woman. . . . It was in the Women's Movement that I came to identify myself as a woman, and to understand the rights I have as a woman, from which I have knowledge to pass on as well to other companions. (Caldeira 1987, 95–96, my translation)

As this statement exemplifies, women's participation in social movements has produced changes in Latin American women's self-definition. Such changes are the best guarantee that these women will resist any attempt to reestablish the old order and will continue to press for their rights. They imply a redefinition of women's roles from a purely domestic image as guardians of the private sphere into equal participants as citizens in a democratic state. However, this redefinition must occur not only in the minds of women themselves but in the society at large, so that women are no longer treated as supplementary wage earners and pawns in the political process. To achieve such goals, there must be unity within the women's movement, across class, ethnic, and ideological lines; and women must also gain support from other groups in the society, such as political parties and labor unions, whom we have seen often try to utilize women's movements for their own ends.

A glaring example of co-optation comes from an earlier period in Bolivia, when women's committees within the party then in power and the housewives' committee of the miners' union were used for partisan politics, and neither the party nor the union ever addressed demands specific to women (Ardaya 1986). Neither of these women's committees had sought autonomy, since they saw themselves serving class rather than gender interests.

Tension between the primacy of class and gender interests in women's organizations throughout Latin America produces differences between women who are feminists and those who are *políticas* (party militants of the left) (Kirkwood 1986, 196). While feminists view politics as a way of furthering their own interests, *políticas* subordinate women's needs to a political program in the hope of their future incorporation. Those who profess to uphold both feminist and partisan political goals are said to be practicing *doble militancia* or double militancy.

This tension between feminists and *políticas* has become more apparent with the end of military rule in Latin America and the reemergence of political parties, which reactivate divisions within the women's movement formerly united in the opposition. The women's movement in Chile suffered less partisan fragmentation than other social sectors opposing the military dictatorship and was an important force in the plebiscite to oust General Pinochet. A group of 12 women's organizations were able to draft the Demands of Women

for Democracy, which were presented to the opposition shortly before the plebiscite, and which included the constitutional guarantee of equality between men and women; the reform of civil, penal, and labor legislation that discriminates against women; and an affirmative action policy to reserve 30 percent of government posts for women. However, although the military and the opposition political parties have recognized the importance of women's electoral support, few have given women access to power (Valenzuela 1989). Since the newly elected democratic government in Chile has only recently taken power, it is too early at this writing to see whether women's demands will be implemented, but the small number of women elected or appointed to government office does not augur well for the future.

The Brazilian liberal, democratic state that supplanted military rule has been more successful in addressing women's needs and electing women to public office, including 26 women in the 1986 congressional elections (Alvarez, 1989, 58). The initial impetus given by the church through the development of base communities (CEBs) and by feminist groups for the women's movement was critical in building a wider base of support, even though these groups remain divided on some issues, such as family planning. Women also gained greater representation within the state through the government-appointed Council on the Status of Women in São Paulo, which was subsequently established in 23 other states and municipalities, and through the National Council on Women's Rights, which played a critical role in developing women's proposals for the new Brazilian constitution. Pressure put on the council, particularly in São Paulo, by an active grass-roots constituency operating outside the state has kept it responsive to women's needs (Alvarez 1989, 53). However, in Brazil as in Chile, the increased importance of elections rekindled old political divisions between rival political parties formerly united in the opposition. The recent election of a conservative president and the continuing economic crisis weakens the possibility of implementing women's demands, because of budgetary constraints and because of the election and appointment of women with less identification with women's interests.

Women's organizations under socialism have been accused of being imposed from above and of being instruments of state policy. Molyneux (1986) claims that although women's emancipation is officially recognized and supported by the socialist state, it is contained within defined limits. Both Cuba and Nicaragua have been eminently successful in the incorporation of women into the labor force, which is considered a key to women's emancipation, and have supported working women with education and training programs, day-care centers, ample maternity leaves, and other measures. Women's employment has helped the state to meet its labor needs but has also been costly because of the support services women require, which make women considerably more expensive to employ than men (Safa 1989). Therefore, it is hard to argue, as some critics have, that socialist states have simply taken advantage of women's labor power.

Perhaps the most controversial issue for socialist feminists is continued state support of the family, embodied in legal reforms such as the Family Code in Cuba and the Provision Law in Nicaragua. While both reforms aim at greater sharing of responsibility in the household and financial support for women and children, they are also attempts by the state to make the family responsible for needs the state at present cannot meet, given its limited resources (Molyneux 1989). Thus, the goal of these socialist states is to modify the family, to make it more egalitarian rather than to do away with it. This does not differ radically from goal of most women's social movements in capitalist Latin American countries.

The tenacity of the family in Latin American socialist or capitalist societies derives not only from the needs of the state, or Catholic doctrine, but from the strong identification and emotional gratification women feel in their roles as wives and especially mothers (Safa 1990). The family fulfills their emotional needs for giving and receiving affection, needs that men tend to deny or undervalue. Women continue to value the family because their role within it is never questioned, while they continue to seek legitimacy in the public sphere. As Jaquette (1989, 193) notes, "The feminist perception of the family as an arena of conflict between men and women directly contradicts how women in urban poor neighborhoods understand and justify their politicization—*for* the family." The strong attach-

ment to the family may be one reason why the distinction between the public and private spheres is still more prevalent in Latin America than in more advanced industrial countries like the United States.

CONCLUSION

What is the future of women's social movements in Latin America? Are we to conclude with Jelin (1987) that Latin American women participate more frequently in short-term, sporadic protest movements than in long-term, formalized institutional settings? Or does women's political mobilization represent part of a progressive longer-term trend that may suffer setbacks but not total eclipse?

I would argue for the latter perspective. Latin American women have been too incorporated into the public sphere to retreat back into the private domestic sphere. They have become increasingly important members of the labor force and contributors to the household economy; they have organized social movements for human rights and social welfare; and they are trying to voice their demands in labor unions and political parties. Even if these activities are not undertaken as conscious challenges to gender subordination, they show that women have broken out of the domestic sphere and that gender roles are changing. Latin American women's emergence into the public sphere is both cause and effect of profound cultural changes in the private sphere, in which women are demanding more "democracy in the home" as well as in the state. These changes in Latin American women's self-definition are most likely to endure and to give women the confidence to continue bringing pressure on public authorities for greater recognition of women's rights.

Despite the political and economic problems Latin American countries are facing in the transition to democracy, important gains in women's rights have been made as a result of these social movements. The new Brazilian constitution adopted in 1988 guarantees women equality before the law, including right to property ownership, equal rights in marriage, maternity leave, and the prohibition of salary differences based on sex, age, or civil status (*Debate Sindical* 1989, 24). Argentina has legalized divorce and modified *patria potestad* to give women joint custody of children and equality in other family matters (Jaquette 1989, 199–200). Despite concerted efforts by the Pinochet dictatorship to court women's support in the 1988 plebiscite, 52 percent of Chilean women rejected the continuation in power of the military government, reflecting in part the effectiveness of opposition women's groups.[2] Whether current governments in power in these countries will continue to support women's needs depends on the importance of their electoral support and on the strength and unity of the women's movement in each country.

When women's demands are confined to domestic issues like child care, communal kitchens, or even human rights, they pose less of a threat than when women attempt to gain leverage in men's power structures, such as political parties or labor unions. In short, as women move away from practical to strategic gender interests, they are likely to encounter more opposition on both gender and class lines from established interest groups who are unwilling to grant them the same legitimacy as men in the public arena.

Latin American women are attempting to establish a new relationship to the state, one based not on subordination, control, and dependency but on rights, autonomy, and equality (Valdés and Weinstein 1989). They have passed beyond the stage in which women's needs were largely invisible and ignored, to where women are now heard, even if some may be co-opted for partisan political ends. By politicizing the private sphere, women have redefined rather than rejected their domestic role and extended the struggle against the state beyond the workplace into the home and community. This shift does not invalidate the Marxist theory of class struggle but calls for its reinterpretation to accommodate these new political voices. As Kirkwood (1986, 65) reminds us, the issue is not simply one of women's incorporation into a male-defined world but of transforming this world to do away with the hierarchies of class, gender, race, and ethnicity that have so long subordinated much of the Latin American population, men as well as women.

NOTES

1. While the concept of public-private spheres has been criticized by many feminists and has been largely replaced by the notion of production and reproduction, it has validity for Latin America, the Caribbean, and Mediterranean Europe, where it has been widely used in the study of gender roles. While the reasons for its usefulness for this region lie beyond the scope of this article, it should be noted that I am using the concept of public-private spheres as poles of a continuum rather than as a dichotomy between mutually exclusive categories (cf. Tiano 1988, 40). It is this fluidity that makes possible the domination of the private by the public sphere.

2. The importance of women's labor-force participation in arousing political consciousness can be seen in a study conducted two months prior to the plebiscite, according to which a greater percentage of housewives supported Pinochet than working women (Valenzuela 1989).

REFERENCES

Alvarez, Sonia. 1989. Women's movements and gender politics in the Brazilian transition. In *The women's movement in Latin America: Feminism and the transition to democracy*, edited by Jane Jaquette. Winchester, MA: Unwin Hyman.

Ardaya, Gloria. 1986. The Barzolas and the housewives committee. In *Women and change in Latin America*, edited by J. Nash and H. Safa. Westport, CT: Bergin & Garvey/Greenwood.

Arteaga, Ana Maria. 1988. Politización de lo privado y subversión de lo cotidiano (Politicization of the private and subversion of everyday life). In *Mundo de Mujer: Continuida y Cambia* (Woman's world: Continuity and change). Santiago: Centro de Estudios de la Mujer.

Barrett, Michèle. 1980. *Women's oppression today*. London: Verso.

Blondet, Cecilia. 1989. Women's organizations and politics in a time of crisis. Paper presented at the Helen Kellogg Institute for International Studies, University of Notre Dame, Notre Dame, IN.

Bunster-Burotto, Ximena. 1986. Surviving beyond fear: Women and torture in Latin America. In *Women and change in Latin America*, edited by J. Nash and H. Safa. Westport, CT: Bergin & Garvey/Greenwood.

Caldeira, Teresa. 1987. Mujeres, cotidianidad y política (Women, everyday life and politics). In *Ciudadania e Identidad: Las Mujeres en los Movimientos Sociales Latino-Americanos* (Citizenship and identity: Women and Latin American social movements), edited by E. Jelin. Geneva: UNRISD (United Nations Research Institute for Social Development).

Cornia, Giovanni. 1987. Adjustment at the household level: Potentials and limitations of survival strategies. In *Adjustment with a human face*, edited by G. Cornia, R. Jolly, and F. Stewart. New York: UNICEF/Oxford: Clarendon Press.

Debate Sindical. 1989. *A mujer trabalhadora* (The woman worker). São Paulo: Departamento de Estudos Socio-Economicos, Central Unicas dos Trabalhadores (Department of Socioeconomic Studies, Central Workers Federation).

ECLAC (Economic Commission for Latin America and the Caribbean). 1988a. *Women, work and crisis*. LC/L 458 (CRM.4/6). Santiago, Chile.

———. 1988b. *Latin American and Caribbean women: Between change and crisis*. LC/L 464 (CRM.4/2). Santiago, Chile.

Feijoo, María del Carmen and Monica Gogna. 1987. Las mujeres en la transición a la democrácia (Women in the transition to democracy). In *Ciudadania e Identidad: Las Mujeres en los Movimientos Sociales Latino-Americanos* (Citizenship and identity: Women and Latin American social movements), edited by E. Jelin. Geneva: UNRISD (United Nations Research Institute for Social Development).

Humphrey, John. 1987. *Gender and work in the Third World*. London: Tavistock.

Jaquette, Jane. 1989. Conclusion: Women and the new democratic politics. In *The women's movement in Latin America: Feminism and the transition to democracy*, edited by J. Jaquette. Winchester, MA: Unwin Hyman.

Jelin, Elizabeth. 1987. Introduction. In *Ciudadania e Identidad: Las Mujeres en los Movimientos Sociales Latino-Americanos* (Citizenship and identity: Women and Latin American social movements), edited by E. Jelin. Geneva: UNRISD (United Nations Research Institute for Social Development).

Kirkwood, Julieta. 1986. *Ser politica en Chile: Las feministas y los partidos* (To be political in Chile: Feminists and parties). Santiago: FLACSO (Latin American Faculty of Social Science.

Molyneux, Maxine. 1986. Mobilization without emancipation? Women's interests, state, and revolution. In *Transition and development: Problems of the Third World socialism*, edited by R. Fagen, C. D. Deere, and J. L. Corragio. New York: Monthly Review Press.

———. 1989. Women's role in the Nicaraguan revolutionary process: The early years. In *Promissory notes: Women in the transition to socialism*, edited by S. Kruks, R. Rapp, and M. Young, New York: Monthly Review Press.

Reimers, Isolde. 1989. *The decline of a social movement: The Mothers of the Plaza de Mayo*. Master's thesis, Center for Latin American Studies, University of Florida, Gainesville.

Safa, Helen I. 1974. *The urban poor of Puerto Rico: A study in development and inequality*. New York: Holt, Rinehard & Winston.

———. 1989. Women, industrialization and state policy in Cuba. Working Paper no 133. Helen Kellogg Institute for International Studies, University of Notre Dame, Notre Dame, IN.

———. 1990. Women and industrialization in the Caribbean. In *Women, employment and the family in the international division of labor*, edited by S. Stichter and J. Parpart. London: Macmillan

Souza-Lobo, Elizabeth. Forthcoming. Brazilian social movements, feminism and women worker's struggle in the São Paolo trade unions. In *Strength in diversity: Anthropological perspectives on women's collective action*, edited by Constance Sutton.

Tiano, Susan. 1988. Women's work in the public and private spheres: A critique and reformulation. In *Women, development and change: The Third World experience*, edited by M. F. Abraham and P. S. Abraham. Bristol, IN: Wyndham Hall Press.

Valdés, Teresa, and Marisa Weinstein. 1989. *Organizaciones de pobladoras y construción en Chile* (Organizations of squatter settlements and democratic reconstruction in Chile). Documento de Trabajo 434 (Working Paper 434), Santiago: FLACSO–CHILE.

Valdés, Teresa, Marisa Weinstein, M. Isabel Toledo, and Lillian Leielier. 1989. *Centros de Madres 1973–1989: Sólo disciplinamiento? (Mothers' Centers 1973–1989: Only imposed discipline?)*. Documcino de Trabajo 416 (Working Paper 416). Santiago: FLACSO-CHILE.

Valenzuela, Maria Elena. 1989. Los nuevos roles de las mujeres y la transción democrática en Chile. (The new roles of women and the democratic transition in Chile). Paper presented at Conference on Transformation and Transition in Chile, 1982–89, University of California, San Diego.

15

Changing Gender Role Attitudes among Women in an Urban Mexican Neighborhood

Michael B. Whiteford and Ruth Alden

INTRODUCTION

Gender constitutes an important topic in the study of social change in Latin America (e.g., Stephen 1991). Changing attitudes toward gender roles are permeating the work place, politics, and the social structure of even the most distant and remote areas. The purpose of this paper is to contrast sex role attitudes in a Mexican neighborhood with traditional sex role attitudes reported elsewhere for that country. Using a case study approach, women's attitudes toward gender roles in Colonial Volcanes, a neighborhood of approximately 8,000 inhabitants, located on the edge of the city of Oaxaca, Mexico, are explored.

Background. There is no question that a great many factors or mechanisms affect gender role attitude changes. The encroachment of the outside world, be it by a neighboring community, by the state, or by an international entity, will almost certainly cause people to reevaluate their belief systems (Friedlander 1975; Kottak 1992). For example, Conrad Kottak (1992) describes the impact that the building of a road had on the town of Arembepe in Brazil. Among a vast array of changes were some

subtle changes in gender roles. These were reflected most notably in the style of women's dress, and the way women worked (less communally because of the introduction of modern appliances). Radio and, more recently, television have also had profound impacts on the world view of people in Mexico. As people become more and more exposed to these external influences, their faithfulness to traditional ways often lessens. Michael B. Whiteford (1989a) refers to this as the process of social urbanization and defines it as

> . . . such things as the outgrowth of rural education, improved roads better linking rural communities with regional centers, efforts of outside extension workers to bring about "development," ever greater numbers of migrants who have worked and lived elsewhere for periods of time and return home with a knowledge of things greatly extending beyond regional and state boundaries, and of course exposure to the outside world through radio and increasingly television (ibid. 1989a:84).

It has also been hypothesized that migration from rural to urban areas causes a change in gender role attitudes. The assumption is that gender role attitudes would be more traditional in the rural areas and less traditional in the urban areas. Exposure to the less traditional attitudes of the urban areas would cause migrants to change their attitudes accordingly. Shirley Harkness (1973), Michael B. Whiteford (1978) and C. H. Browner (1986) studied this hypothesis with mixed results. Harkness did not find that migration was a factor in forming gender role attitudes. Browner found that mobility (i.e., whether the woman has ever lived outside of her rural community) was a definite factor in a change in attitude toward gender roles. It is unclear whether migration from rural to urban areas can be seen as a mechanism for change in gender role attitudes. An obvious step is to study the length of residence in the city, which could then be examined as a measure of the influence of migration on role attitudes.

Social class is another factor that must be examined. Beneria and Roldan (1987) believe that the study of gender and class must go hand in hand. Studying one without the other may lead to a very distorted picture since women of different social classes will respond to different incentives for change (also cf. Stephen 1991). Therefore, in studying gender role attitudes, class must become an issue. For example, as will be discussed shortly, the women of Mexico reacted in a gender specific way to the Industrial Revolution, but within this gender based reaction, there were definite class differences (Vallens 1978).

Income change due to the market economy is also involved in gender role attitude change. As women are forced out of the agricultural economy because of mechanization of the consolidation of large farming and ranching operations, they must find new ways to maintain a level of subsistence for their families. Many women respond by migrating to the city to take on some form of wage-labor activity. As women are forced to add to the home coffers, they will gain more influence in the home (particularly in their conjugal relationships), leading to changes in their gender role attitudes (Nash and Safa 1986; Acosta-Belen and Bose 1990; Safa 1990). Such changes challenge the traditional roles in which men were the authorities in the family because they were "the providers" (Cancian, et al 1978; Lavrin 1987; Acosta-Belen and Bose 1990; Chinchilla 1990; Babb 1989; Safa 1990).

Increasing access to birth control, coupled with changing attitudes regarding the desirability of large families, is another factor that may lead to changes in gender role attitudes. As a result of consistently high birthrates and decreasing mortality rates, the population of Mexico has been rapidly rising since mid-century. Keeping in mind the traditional role attitudes in Mexico and the nation's historically slow moving policies concerning women, it is not surprising that those who adhere to the traditional role prefer to have "as many children as God sees fit." Traditionally, men see a large number of offspring as proof of their masculinity, and women recognize it as an increase in their power base. Some researchers have also suggested that more children bring a feeling of security to those who are not well off economically by adding to the potential earning power of the family unit (Riding 1984; Chambers 1987). This traditional view of fertility has recently been challenged by Mexico's population policy.

Mexico's policies are aimed at decreasing population growth by decreasing fertility. In order to do this, Mexico's government has opted to take an integrated approach to reducing the perceived need to have large families. These policies include the need to raise employment, improve income distribution, restructure the agriculture sector, provide primary health care to rural areas, improve access to family planning services, and improve the status of women by the year 2000 (United Nations Population Fund 1986–87:343). As can be seen, the last two goals in this list are an attempt to change attitudes toward conjugal and fertility behavior.

Implied here is the assumption that women with more children will have to put more time into caring for their family and thus will be more likely to adhere to more traditional means of action than women with small families. On the other hand, women with fewer children will be able to spend less time as physical caretakers and more time in other pursuits, which may include such activities as self-education, income generation, or community, state or national betterment. Thus, they will have a broader range of options to draw on in terms of health care, education, and employment. A broader range of options also means more power (personal, family, community, state, and national) for women.

Education has been found to be a prime mover in the transition to nonrestrictive and egalitarian attitude changes in Latin America. In Costa Rica, Patricia C. Whiteford and colleagues (1986) found that higher education led to more egalitarian conjugal role attitudes, which, in turn, led to less restrictive attitudes toward fertility. Whiteford and Dvorak (1984) found that media education, through radio and television, supplies most people with an idea of what contraceptives are and where they can be found. Helen I. Safa states that "increased educational and occupational opportunities [have] made women more aware of previous restrictions and more vocal in protesting them" (Safa 1990:359).

Age is another factor that must be considered. The passage of time and the changes it brings will affect the way each generation sees their roles in society. Older women will be more likely to hold true to their traditional role attitudes, whereas younger women will be more likely to be egalitarian or nonrestrictive in their attitudes as a result of some of the factors listed above, such as higher levels of education and a different worldview from that of their mothers and grandmothers (Harkness 1973; Whiteford and Dvorak 1984; Whiteford, et al. 1986).

Factors such as religion, nationalism, and oppression often play a part in changing gender role attitudes as well. Historically, the origins of many of the gender-specific roles of women in Mexico were religious. Religion continues to dictate what is proper and acceptable behavior for women. Nationalism can provide a platform from which women declare their interests; in the city of Oaxaca, it is not uncommon to see women marching with the men through the streets to take part in political activism (Higgins 1990; Safa 1990). Oppression may also collectivize women and promote changes in gender roles as well as changes in a multitude of other phases of family, community, and national life (Bunster-Burotto 1986; Acosta-Belen and Bose 1990; Safa 1990).

Picking up on several of these interrelated themes, this study[1] will provide a sense of the change in gender role attitudes occurring in the lives of the women in Colonia Volcanes and, perhaps by extension, elsewhere in Mexico. Analysis of the data may also reveal gender role attitudes to be an indicator of the social climate as well. For example, in addition to applied changes in family relationships and feelings toward reproduction, they may reflect overall changes in worldview or changes in attitudes toward women in the workforce and in politics.

Attitudes. Milton Rokeach defines an *attitude* as "a relatively enduring organization of beliefs around an object or situation predisposing one to respond in some preferential manner" (1972:112). *Beliefs* are "the knowledge and information which a person assumes to be true about the environment" and *values* are "general feelings about what is desirable or undesirable" (Schafer and Tait 1981:4). Our beliefs and values become the driving force behind our attitudes. Thus, attitudes can be altered by changing the beliefs and values behind them. It has been suggested that this may be accomplished using methods such as education, persuasion, removal of ego threats, positive reinforcement, and becoming familiar with an individual's background and the factors that affect his or her attitudes (ibid. 1981:7). External or foreign influences such as development, tourism, and various other forms of contact, have led many Mexicans in even the remotest rural areas to redefine their beliefs and their worldview (Friedlander 1975; Newbold Chiñas 1992; Stephen 1991; Kearney 1986).

Gender Role Theory. Attitude change is a central goal of gender role theory. A change in gender role attitudes indicates change in a person or society's belief system. The main goal set by promoters of change regarding gender role attitudes is the empowerment of women. They believe that women must change the way they look at themselves in order to begin to become less dependent on men. (Acosta-Belen and Bose 1990; Bourque and Warren 1981; Mies et al. 1988). For example, Steffen Schmidt (1988:31) believes that there are two different schools of thought regarding how Colombian women should change the way they look at themselves. One school of thought is modeled after the European–North American feminist movement, in which women achieve their goals in spite of the fact that they are women. The other school of thought is that in which women achieve their goals because they are women. However, both of these views involve a change in attitudes toward gender roles if women are to be successful.

Egalitarian/Nonrestrictive Role Attitudes.
Factors cited as reasons for change have led to the emergence of a set of attitudes, usually centered around and in urban areas, which have been referred to as nonrestrictive or egalitarian role attitudes (Whiteford and Dvorak 1984; Whiteford, et al. 1986). These attitudes are in opposition to the traditional authoritative or restrictive role attitudes. Cancian and associates (1978) list several ways in which the family has been affected by these attitudes. First, a parent's authority over children and a husband's authority over his wife has been weakened. Secondly, extended kin relations have been weakened as a result of the weakening of family functions. Thirdly, "companionship and affection have become the dominant emotions in relations among family members . . . thus families are said to have become increasingly isolated, nuclear and specialized in emotional gratification" (Cancian, et al. 1978:320). Shirley J. Harkness reported similar findings in respect to changing role attitudes. She noted that, in Bogotá, Colombia, the egalitarian role attitudes toward conjugal relationships were those centered on love and affection instead of obedience and service, and the attitudes toward children were based on love and education (for both girls and boys) rather than discipline (Harkness 1973:241).

COLONIA VOLCANES

The location for this study is Colonia Volcanes, a neighborhood situated on the northeastern outskirts of the metropolitan area of the city of Oaxaca, Mexico. The city is located in the center of the state in a large mountain valley about 5,000 feet above sea level. In the past, several extremely impressive civilizations developed in the valley and the surrounding mountains. To a certain extent, geographic impediments kept the region relatively insulated until well into this century. However, with the advent of paved roads, railroads, and air travel, Oaxaca is becoming more exposed to the outside world.

The area has not been so remote in the past that it was kept completely from participating in national life. Politically, the city and the state have had an influence on the Mexican political scene. The city

was once the proud home of the revolutionary hero and first Native American president of Mexico, Benito Juárez, as well as his successor, the president and dictator Porfirio Díaz.

In an economic sense, it is the source of many of the finest crafts in Mexico. The crafts include such things as wool blankets, pottery, baskets, and cotton cloth. Some of these are marketed internationally.

However, it is in the cultural sense that Oaxaca is most unique. The large number of indigenous groups, with Zapotecs, Mixtecs, and Mixes in the majority, add to Oaxaca's authenticity and charm. The richness and diversity of its cultures cannot be matched in any other part of Mexico. In the zócalo one can hear a cacophony of indigenous languages and see a variety of styles of native dress as people sell their wares. The city, which in the late 1960s had a population of about 70,000 now numbers close to 400,000. This rapid increase of population is mostly as a result of improved medical services, which have lowered the mortality rate in he city, and massive spates of rural to urban migration within the last twenty years (Murphy and Stepick 1991; Selby, et al. 1990).

One of the many destinations of people migrating to Oaxaca has been Colonia Volcanes. The population of the community consists of about three-fourths migrants (mostly in-state) and one-fourth native born Oaxaqueños. The migrants are from a variety of cultural backgrounds, although most speak Spanish, and a few are also fluent in one of the indigenous languages of the region. With a population of less than 10,000 residents, the average household size of five people is much the same as the rest of Mexico.

Community services have become well established in Colonia Volcanes as well. Electricity is readily available. However, the availability of city-supplied water was tenuous at best in most parts of the community. Even though all but the poorest or the newest homes had water piped onto the property, for many it came only every two or three days. Colonia Volcanes is also the final destination of a number of buses that go through the city. This alleviates the problem of transportation that some of the other outlying areas experience. At the end of the bus line, the community also has a fairly new, well-kept, one-story school with a large playground.

On practically every block and on many corners are small stores or homes that sell foodstuffs and various other items. These provide last-minute supplies for meals or emergency items for health care which would otherwise require a lengthy trip into the city.

While the community is essentially a low-income, working-class neighborhood, like many Latin American neighborhoods, the architecture is mixed. Looking down a dirt road in the colonia, one sees a large, beautiful home made of cement block or concrete, with one or two new cars in the garage and a satellite dish on the roof. Next door, leaning on the cement wall surrounding this fabulous home is a one-room shack with a dirt floor. The walls are made of tin cans flattened out and bolted together and topped off with more flattened cans.

The disparate lifestyles present in Colonia Volcanes would suggest that the neighborhood is representative of the city of Oaxaca and the country of Mexico as well. The study of Colonia Volcanes could, therefore, be an important contribution to research on all levels.

Since the focus of this particular study of Colonia Volcanes is the women of the community and their view of gender-specific roles, a common point of departure must be established. A characterization of gender roles in Mexico follows.

GENDER ROLES IN MEXICO

To study gender roles is to study the behavioral—as opposed to the biological—aspects of being male or female. Gender role theory thus helps us analyze how gender roles are learned or acted out. Gender roles are situational, unstructured, and an integral part of the dynamic social order (West and Zimmerman 1987).

Contemporary origins of gender roles in Mexico can be traced back to colonial times, which had a distinctly southern European flavor, with women secondary to men in status. Women's lower status can be evidenced in the lack of information about them in history and textbooks.

Because society and the church did not condone much outspokenness and aggressiveness by women, many women throughout Mexican history who exhibited such behavior risked much by doing so. The Mexican historian Carlos Bosch Garcia wrote:

> Those of us who know our national history cannot in conscience deny the profound impact that women have had in all the historical aspects of our national life. Yet despite a daily increase in the number of women who are affecting the political, economic, social and cultural life of Mexico, the public awareness of this role in the crucial events of our history has only just begun (Vallens 1978:1).

In keeping with the attitude of women as secondary citizens, women as a groups historically have been acknowledged mainly in respect to their responsibilities to their husbands and family. The nineteenth-century politician Melcho Ocampo expressed the attitudes of the times when he wrote:

> The man, whose sexual attributes are principally courage and strength, should and will give protection, food and guidance to the woman. The woman, whose principal attributes are abnegation, beauty, compassion, perspicacity and tenderness, should and will give her husband obedience, pleasure, assistance, consolation and counsel, always treating him with the veneration due to the person that supports and defends her.

This quote, which is still read in many civil marriage ceremonies (Riding 1984:241), spells out the essence of the stereotypical or traditional roles in Mexico. These cultural attitudes, which account for a large part of gender role separation, were firmly rooted in most of Latin American society during colonial and preindustrial times.

Machismo is the "belief in the natural inborn superiority of men over women in anything political, economic, or intellectual" (Biesanz, et al. 1982:90). Things important to the "macho" are virility, personal honor, demonstration of sexual prowess, and a show of antagonism toward women. Love is viewed as a conquest and sex as something women owe to men (Stevens 1973; Bustos 1980; Biesanz, et al 1982; Browner and Lewin 1982; Schmidt 1988). At home, the male expects to be served and catered to. However, he often spends a great share of his time and money away from home drinking with friends or visiting a mistress. The macho man rarely takes part in child rearing and maintains a certain sort of mystique in the eyes of his children. His position as ultimate authority and decision maker in the family is jealously guarded and must not be questioned. A macho feels that his main household responsibility is to provide food and clothing for his family (Blutstein, et al. 1970; Whiteford 1978; Riding 1984; Lavrin 1987).

Marianismo, in contrast is the "belief in the . . . natural and inborn moral and spiritual superiority of women" (Biesanz, et al. 1982:90). Women are to appear passive, submissive, long-suffering, and enduring, and to act the part of the martyr (Stevens 1973:60). They are encouraged to emulate the Virgin of Guadalupe, known to many as the Virgin Mary, who is considered to be the ideal woman (Lavrin 1978). William Taylor takes the significance of marianismo one step further to say that, in a surreal sense, the Virgin represents women as the "source of life" and "centres of sacred power." "Her purity carried the promise of redemption; her child was the source of a new beginning" (Taylor 1987:19–20). In more earthly terms, the importance of the Virgin of Guadalupe lies in her roles as mother and intercessor. Ideally, women are expected to emulate the Virgin through biological reproduction and maintaining a high standard of prescribed moral and spiritual behavior. They must be the long-suffering, selfless, spiritual intercessors for their morally inadequate macho counterpart (Stevens 1973). A further interpretation of this concept describes women as the family intercessors, mediating between husband and children. Women put a great deal of importance on the moral and spiritual aspects of their roles, especially the role of martyr (Béhar 1990; Higgins 1990). One woman said, "marriage is a cross which it is woman's highest calling to bear and through which she gains virtue in the eyes of God and society" (Biesanz, et al. 1982:90).

The recorded origins of machismo and marianismo in Mexico date back to colonial times. Catholic monks and scholarly men of the time wrote copiously about what should be the proper character and behavior of women. In her review of this literature, Asunción Lavrin (1978) found that many of these ideas were ultimately preached from the pulpit on Sunday mornings or reinforced through the confessional. The list of qualities that women should nurture is extensive. It includes: modesty, piety, subservience, chastity, orderlinesss, obedience, loyalty, and a dedication to husband and family. Bad qualities were: intemperance, garrulousness, stubbornness, inconsistency, passion, vanity, and pride.

At home women are in charge of the running of the household, all domestic matters, and childbearing. Their expertise in these matters is where they derive their real value (Bunster-Burotto 1986). Women provide the family with "strength and stability" and are responsible for the family's emotional environment as well (Riding 1984:243). Women are also responsible for the socialization of their children. Proper roles are emphasized from childhood on and are perpetuated by women. Boys are thought to be more demanding, aggressive, spoiled, and free to do as they please. Girls are presumed to be more homebound, weaker, more emotional, more vulnerable, and less intelligent than boys. These attitudes often become self-fulfilling (Biesanz, et al 1982; Béhar 1990). Using a common organic analogy, a popular saying in many parts of Latin America is "Men are the head of the family, but women are the heart."

HISTORICAL PERSPECTIVE ON WOMEN'S ROLES IN MEXICO

Roles for women in Mexico have gained in complexity through time. The first prescribed roles appear to have been those between husband and wife. As these roles evolved to fit the situation of the times, women's roles pertaining to the home and family were added as well.

Colonial Women.   During colonial times in Mexico, women from all levels of society relinquished their legal independence to their husbands upon marriage. These men, according to the times, felt it within their rights (and in many cases their duty as well) to physically punish and discipline their wives. A woman had few options concerning escape from a husband who was overzealous in this matter. She could settle a dowry on him and "pay him off" if she had the funds or was from a well-to-do family; she could opt for separation; she could appeal to the judicial system in hopes of gaining protection; or she could resort to magic or witchcraft. The last option was very popular in the eighteenth century because the means were readily available and it gave the woman a feeling of power or control over her circumstances. Women would often put potions in the food they prepared for their male victim. "Since food preparation was one domain over which women held virtually total control, their ability to use this power subversively was widely recognized and even feared by men" (Béhar 1987:39). Pacts with the devil were also ways in which women could gain control of their situation (ibid. 1987).

Characterizing the relationship between men and women in colonial times was a general feeling of distrust. One explanation may be that the Spanish men, upon arrival in the New World, often married women from the indigenous population. Since the Spaniards were "the enemy," men had to watch for signs of betrayal in their wives. Always in constant fear of betrayal form his spouse, a man would take a mistress and betray his wife before she could betray him (Riding 1984:8). This may have been the beginning of the stereotypical double standard in Mexican society that has received so much attention.

Women of the Independence.   During the time of struggle for national independence from Spain, the situation of women began to change slightly. In 1814, Article 24 of the constitution, written during wartime, granted equality to all Mexican citizens. During the chaos of the 1840s, the liberals, seeing the family as the glue holding Mexico together, began to advocate women's education. This advocacy eventually enabled some women to attain a degree of independence by achieving socially acceptable careers in the field of education (Macias 1982).

Women of the Porfiriato and the Industrial Revolution.   Women from all social classes and backgrounds gave up their assigned roles in the name of practicality during the period of the Porfiriato. Prior to the industrial revolution, women had depended on the land for their livelihood. They had worked side by side in the fields with men or had begun businesses out of their homes.

They were responsible for the bearing and raising of children and for any economic contributions they could make on the side. At this time in Mexico's history, "motherhood and family as a full-time occupation and an all consuming task was an unknown concept" (Vallens 1978:4).

The advent of the industrial revolution is often seen as the starting point for changes in the roles of women that began taking place in political, economic and social circles. Industry introduced a new path to independence for many women. Women found that the production of necessities that once took place in the home was now done in factories. Thus, many upper- and middle-class women had time on their hands. The upper-class women responded to this by becoming socialites. This role "discouraged initiative, energy, or independence" (ibid. 1978:5). The middle-class women responded by becoming more involved in child rearing. They centered their lives around their husband and children. These responses were reinforced by the men's attitudes of the times.:

> Men gained status from the fact that their spouses and offspring did not need to work. They surrounded their women with the mystique of moral purity supposedly caused by their separation from the sordid problems of the public and business world. Women became the guardians of morality and purity, elevated to a pedestal as angelic, fragile, and ethereal creatures. It became stylish for them to be considered physically delicate and unable to perform hard or heady tasks (ibid. 1978:5).

However, the situation for many poor women and families took a turn for the worse. These women were forced, by economic necessity, to leave their homes and agriculturally centered occupations to go to work in the factories. They were a great source of cheap and malleable labor for factory owners. In the factories, they ran looms, sewed shirts, and made cigars at wages one-third to one-half those paid to men. The factory owners felt them to be "reliable, industrious and rapid factory workers" (ibid. 1978:7). In 1895, there were almost 185,000 women working in the industrial labor force. This made up about 26.5 percent of the total labor force. By 1900, the number had risen to approximately 210,500 (ibid. 1978:32).

Women of the Revolution of 1910.   From its outset, women became involved in Mexico's revolution in many ways and for many reasons. During this time, women (*soldaderas*) accompanied the men to the battlefield. They cooked, washed clothes, and tended the injured and sick. Women were sometimes seen in the forces of the rebel armies, and a woman holding rank was not unknown. However, this did not end in a redefinition of women's roles as wife and mother. It was simply looked upon as a temporary adjustment of roles in a time of need (Miller 1981; Riding 1984; Meyer and Sherman 1987).

Even though women fought in the revolution and many had also worked beside the men in factories and fields for years, but the 1930s, there was still a question as to their competence for functioning in the world outside the home. Colonel Crescencio Treveño-Adame warned the president to refuse women's suffrage. He said, "women are in this world to care for the home and not to get involved in politics, neither to meddle in the affairs of men nor to work in offices, above all government offices" (Riding 1984:240).

Women in Recent Times.   Treviño-Adame's warning must have been popular thought during his time because women in Mexico did not gain the right to vote until 1953. In 1955, women finally voted for the first time in a presidential election (Leahy 1986:48). Almost forty years later, many of the stereotypes of women as submissive and docile creatures still exist and not always without reason. Most women have been socialized to think of themselves as reliant on men and so act accordingly.

Women are, however, gaining political footholds. By 1976, about 4 percent of the senators in Mexico and 7 percent of the deputies in the national legislature were women. In recent years, one woman was elected as governor of a state and others were elected to be mayors of major cities (Leahy 1986:55).

In contrast to political gains, women are still given secondary status in the work force. In factory work today women receive lower wages than men for performing equal work. Some of women's most prevalent characteristics noted by factory owners which make them such good workers are derived from the old stereotypes of women. Relia-bility and work stability are noted as "women's qualities." Women are said to have lower rates of absenteeism and are less likely to get drunk on the weekend and be ill or absent from work on Monday. They are said to be more careful with manual work and the handling of objects and more dexterous in meticulous work and handling small parts. They are perceived as possessing the discipline, patience, and ability to follow orders. Women are also said to be able to sit longer without growing restless, less likely to tinker with a machine if it breaks down, to have higher productivity than men, and to be less troublesome than men, in terms of demands about wages and working conditions. It is also felt that women are less likely to become involved in union activities. Women are perceived as being "submissive and docile workers" (Beneria and Roldan 1987:47–49).

CHANGING ATTITUDES TOWARD GENDER ROLES

Although factory owners applaud women for these superior qualities, they continue to pay them less than they pay men. Even though women have broken out of their stereotypical roles at many times and in many ways during their history, especially during times of national or personal crisis, they have reverted to the traditional machismo/marianismo gender roles in the end. However, because of changes in governmental policies toward fertility, people's changing worldviews, and economically hard times, changes have been taking place in the last twenty years in attitudes toward gender roles.

Some Previous Gender Role Attitude Studies.
In this study, two variables are used to assess gender role attitudes. The first variable is a measure of a woman's attitude toward her conjugal roles. The second variable is a measure of a woman's attitude toward fertility. These two dependent variables have been successfully used to measure and analyze role attitudes in Costa Rica, Mexico, and the United States. Whiteford and Dvorak (1984) studied 105 couples in Los Angeles de Santo Domingo, Costa Rica, to analyze the relationship between authority in the home and fertility behavior. They found that the couples whose orientation was more egalitarian were less likely to have a large

family and more likely to use contraceptives. They also found age to be a factor in that, among the older women in the sample, those with a more egalitarian orientation were more likely to use contraceptives. A subsequent study of Los Angeles de Santo Domingo was made by Whiteford, et al. (1986). The gender role attitudes of a sample of 141 women from the community were compared to those of 244 women in the community of Veintesiete de Abril, Costa Rica. The study revealed education to be the main force behind changes in gender role attitudes in both communities. First, results showed that the more highly educated the woman was, the more likely she was to have egalitarian conjugal role attitudes and nonrestrictive fertility attitudes. Secondly, they indicated that the more egalitarian a woman's attitudes toward conjugal roles were, the more likely she was to have a nonrestrictive attitude toward fertility. The researchers also found that age and the extent of a rural or urban community orientation were important factors affecting the state of gender role attitudes in the two communities.

In a study conducted in El Ocotillo, Mexico, Whiteford (1989a) used the same series of statements again to act as a measure of worldview. The purpose of the larger scale study was to gain an understanding of the sociocultural factors associated with the nutritional and dietary status of the children in the community. He found that children whose mothers held a less traditional world view were more likely to have a higher nutritional status than those children whose mothers held a more traditional worldview.

Two of the five statements pertaining to conjugal role attitudes[2] were also used in a study conducted in the United States by Sharpe (1988). The sample consisted of 360 women. The gender role statements were used to measure role attitudes, which were found to be a significant factor in the time women devoted to household tasks.

METHODOLOGY

In the present study, female heads of households in the Oaxaca City neighborhood of Colonia Volcanes were asked about attitudes towards women roles. Founded in the late 1960s, the colonia has approximately 8,000 residents today. Like many of the inhabitants living elsewhere in the city, the majority of the household heads living in Volcanes were born outside of the city, many arriving in the city of Oaxaca only within the past decade. Households are overwhelmingly nuclear in composition, perhaps reflecting an intentional migrant pattern of single individuals or young married couples leaving the countryside. Families range in size from 1 individual to 1 of 12 persons, with a mean of 5.48 individuals and a mode of 5.00 occupants per dwelling.

Sampling Procedures and Data Collection. Sampling was conducted in two states. The first state consisted of a simple random sample of blocks. To aid in sample selection, recent detailed maps were obtained from the Oficina de Obras Públicas, Obras de Recuperación in the city of Oaxaca. Using these maps, a sample of one half of the blocks was drawn. The second stage of sample selection consisted of a systematic random sample of households within the selected blocks (Babbie 1986; Bernard 1988; Whiteford 1989b, 1991).

Two hundred seven female household heads participated in the study. The interviewer identified the female household head by asking to speak to *la jefa*. *La jefa* refers to the female in the household who makes the adult decisions. In this way, the task of defining who was "the female household head" was relegated to the household itself and not left to the discretion of the interviewer. If there was no female in charge of the household, the interviewer went on to the next house.

The Variables. Two dependent and seven independent variables are analyzed and discussed in this study. The dependent variables consist of two separate scales used to assess gender role attitudes. The first measures a woman's conjugal role attitudes and the second measures her fertility attitudes. The independent variables are sociocultural characteristics of the women: age, level of education, percent of her life she has lived in the city, household size, place of socialization, income, and level of living.

Each woman was asked to reveal her attitudes about the roles of men and women by expressing her opinion regarding five statements concerning conjugal role attitudes and five statements concerning fertility attitudes.[3] The statements regarding conjugal role attitudes were as follows:

1. The man is the boss in the family and the woman is obligated to obey him.
2. Most of the important decisions in the life of the family should be made by the man of the house.
3. There is women's work and there is men's work; one should not dabble in work that belongs to the other.
4. It is perfectly okay for a man to go out alone, without his wife, whenever he wants to.
5. The man has more right to cheat on the woman than she has to cheat on him.

The statements referring to fertility attitudes were as follows:

1. People respect you more when you have children.
2. A girl becomes a woman only after becoming a mother.
3. It is not right for a couple to go against nature by limiting the number of children they have.
4. A person who does not have children can never be truly happy.[4]

The women answered "strongly agree," "agree," "indifferent," "disagree," or "strongly disagree" to each statement. Those women who responded to the statements regarding conjugal roles with "strongly agree" or "agree" exhibited traditional conjugal role attitudes and those women who responded with "disagree" or "strongly disagree" exhibited egalitarian conjugal role attitudes. Women who responded to the statements referring to fertility with "strongly agree" or "agree" exhibited traditional fertility attitudes and women who responded with "disagree" or "strongly disagree" exhibited nonrestrictive fertility attitudes.

With only two exceptions, the responses to each statement were distributed in a fairly equal fashion, with about one-half of the respondents expressing traditional gender role attitudes and about one-half expressing more egalitarian or nonrestrictive role attitudes. The first exception was the response to the statement "It is perfectly okay for a man to go out alone, without his wife, whenever he wants to." Only 20 percent of the women agreed with this statement while 80 percent disagreed. Therefore,

the majority of women in this sample have more egalitarian attitudes toward this particular aspect of conjugal role relations. The second statement receiving disproportionate responses was "It is not right for a couple to go against nature by limiting the number of children they have." Only 25 percent of the women agreed with this statement as opposed to 75 percent who disagreed. In other words, the majority of women in this sample hold more nonrestrictive attitudes toward some sort of birth control.

The statements were combined into two scales, one for conjugal role attitudes and one for fertility attitudes,[5] by summing the responses. Responses to the statements regarding conjugal roles have a range of 5 to 25 with a mean of 16.[6] Sixty-one percent of the women interviewed exhibited egalitarian conjugal role attitudes and 39 percent leaned toward traditional attitudes. Responses to the statements regarding fertility attitudes have a range from 4 to 20 and a mean of 12.3. Forty-six percent of the respondents expressed nonrestrictive fertility attitudes, 54 percent expressed traditional attitudes (see Table 15–1).

TABLE 15–1   Percentages for Variable Divisions

Variable	Percentage
Age (years)	
15 thru 39	59
40 thru 70	41
Education (years)	
0 thru 5	49
6 thru 20	51
Percent of a woman's life she has lived in the city	
0 thru 49	48
50 thru 100	52
Household size (people per household)	
1 thru 5	56
6 thru 12	44
Place of socialization	
in the city	45
outside of the city	55
Income (pesos)	
0 thru 599,999	51
600,000 thru 6,000,000	49
Level of living (scale)	
0 thru 10 (low level of living)	49
11 thru 30 (high level of living	51
Conjugal role attitudes (scale)	
5 thru 15 (traditional conjugal role attitudes)	39
16 thru 25 (egalitarian conjugal role attitudes)	61
Fertility attitudes (scale)	
4 thru 12 (traditional fertility attitudes)	54
13 thru 20 (non-restrictive fertility attitudes)	46

In order to assess the effect of social and cultural factors on gender role attitudes, seven social indicators were used in the analysis. These were the age of the woman, her level of education, the percent of her lifetime she has lived in the city, the size of her household, her place of socialization, the total monthly household income and her level of living.

Age is the first sociocultural variable. The ages of the women interviewed range from 16 to 68 with an average age of 38. Fifty-nine percent of the women are under 40 years old and 41 percent are 40 or more years of age.

Education for women in Colonia Volcanes ranges from 0 to 19 years with a mean of 5.54 years. Forty-nine percent of the women have less than 6 years of education and 51 percent have 6 or more years of education. The most common levels of education are 6 years (25%) or none (16%). One-fourth of the women have spent more than 7 years in school.

The percent of her life that a woman has lived in the city is a variable used to ascertain what effect city life has on a woman's attitudes and worldview, since most (80 percent) of the women were born outside the city. The mean percentage of 56 indicates that the average woman in this sample has lived a little over half of her life in the city. Forty-eight percent of the women have spent less than half of their lives in the city and 52 percent have lived in the city for over half of their lives.

Households in the colonia range in size from 1 person to 12. Fifty-six percent of the households consist of 5 or fewer people, while 44 percent of the households are made up of 6 or more people. About one-half of the households range in size from 4 to 7 people. The average household size, at 5.45, is not significantly different from the national average.

Place of socialization is a variable used to assess how much of a lasting effect a woman's place of upbringing has on her gender role attitudes. The place of socialization would be the city of Oaxaca if the woman was born and raised there or moved there before or during her fifteenth year. If she moved to the city after the age of 15, she would be thought to have been socialized elsewhere. Almost all (98 percent) of the women in this sample who were socialized elsewhere came from small towns or rural communities. Forty-five percent of the women in the sample were socialized in the city of Oaxaca, and fifty-five percent were socialized elsewhere.

Total monthly household income includes the income of all members of the household. The data for this variable were collected as income on a daily, weekly, bi-monthly, monthly or yearly basis and then computed to a monthly figure for each household. Incomes in this sample range from 2,000 pesos ($.80 U.S.) a month[7] to 5,575,367 pesos ($2,230 U.S.) a month and the average monthly household income is 706,568 pesos ($283 U.S.)[8] Fifty-one percent of the households have an income less than 600,000 pesos ($240 U.S.) a month and 49 percent have an income of 600,000 pesos or more per month.

An attempt was made to include informal as well as formal income.[9] Because of some of the aforementioned difficulties assessing monies brought into the household through work in the informal sector, a frequently used method of assessing the financial well-being of the household would be to establish some scale or criteria for estimating a level-of-living score as an indicator of economic status. Level of living is a computed variable that has been used to assess socioeconomic status in lieu of or in addition to household income. Many researchers feel that it gives a more complete picture of the family's resource base (Foster 1988; Danes, et al. 1987; Whiteford 1978, 1982, 1991; Winter, et al. 1989). The scale[10] includes things such as appliances, furniture, radio and television, and transportation (bicycles, motorcycles, automobiles). The range of the scale is 1 to 29, with a mean of 12. Fifty-one percent of the households have a level of living of 10 or less and 49 percent have a level of living of 11 or more.

Expected Influences of Independent Variables. Each independent variable was analyzed for its effect on the dependent variables according to the following:

1. Age.   The older the woman, the more likely she will be to have more traditional conjugal role and fertility attitudes.
2. Education.   The higher a woman's level of education, the more likely she will be to have more egalitarian conjugal role attitudes and more nonrestrictive fertility attitudes.

3. Percent of the woman's life she has spent living in the city of Oaxaca. The greater the percent of her life a woman has lived in the city, the more likely she will be to have more egalitarian conjugal role attitudes and more nonrestrictive fertility attitudes.
4. Household size. The larger the size of the her household, the more likely the woman will be to have more traditional conjugal role and fertility attitudes.
5. Place of socialization. Women socialized in an urban setting are likely to have more egalitarian conjugal role attitudes and more nonrestrictive fertility attitudes than women socialized in a rural setting.
6. Total monthly household income. The larger her household income, the more likely the women will be to have egalitarian conjugal role attitudes and a nonrestrictive fertility attitudes.
7. Level of living. The higher her household's level of living, the more likely a woman will be to have more egalitarian conjugal role attitudes and more nonrestrictive fertility attitudes.

DATA ANALYSIS AND INTERPRETATION

In addition to frequencies and reliability testing, statistical analysis was conducted via a Pearson correlation matrix, two- and three-way crosstabulations, and regressions. SPSS/PC+ was used for the execution of these tests.[11]

Age and Gender Role Attitudes. According to the Pearson correlation coefficient (see Table 15–2), the relationship between the age of the woman and her conjugal role attitudes is not significant (-.11), but the relationship between the age of the woman and her attitude toward fertility is significant (-.19). However, upon further analysis through cross-tabulations (see Table 15–3), the opposite was found to be true.

Cross-tabulations between the age of the woman and her conjugal role attitudes show a very significant chi-square, but a low gamma (-.12). The reason for this discrepancy is a curvilinear relationship, which means that women over fifty tend to hold very traditional attitudes toward their conjugal role relationships and women under thirty hold more egalitarian views of these relationships. However, women between thirty and fifty years of age tend to have attitudes even more egalitarian in nature than those under thirty. For this group of women, between thirty and fifty years of age, there seem to be other factors at play in the relationships between age and conjugal role attitudes. For instance, for women older than forty years of age, those with six or more years of education are more likely to have egalitarian conjugal role attitudes (see Figure 15–1).

Although fertility attitudes are not significantly related to the age of the woman on the basis of the chi-square, controlling for the woman's total monthly household income reveals a significant relationship between the two. Among women with a higher household income, the younger women tend to have less restrictive fertility attitudes (see Figure 15–2). A second explanation may lie in the woman's level of education. Among women with 5 or less years of education, the younger the woman, the more likely it is that she will have less restrictive fertility attitudes (see Figure 15–3).

Education and Gender Role Attitudes. Education seems to be an enormous factor in the formation of gender role attitudes. The correlations and cross-tabulations between education and the two attitudinal scales indicate that there is a very strong tendency for women with more than 6 years of education to have more egalitarian conjugal role attitudes and less restrictive attitudes toward childbearing.

Income and Gender Role Attitudes. Total monthly household income has a weaker but significant relationship with a woman's conjugal role attitudes. The higher the family's income, the more likely the woman will be to have more egalitarian conjugal role attitudes. However, correlations would seem to indicate that no relationship exists between income and fertility attitudes. Again, education helps to further explain this. Among women with more than 6 years of education, the higher her household income, the less restrictive her fertility attitudes will tend to be (see Figure 15–4).

Level of Living and Gender Role Attitudes. Level of living is another strongly significant variable affecting women's gender role attitudes. It has

TABLE 15–2   Correlation Coefficients among All Pairs of Variables

Variable	1	2	3	4	5	6	7	8	9
1. Age	—	−.49**	−.13	.17	.22*	.23*	.05	−.11	−.19*
2. Education		—	.23*	−.20*	−.29**	.09	.31**	.39**	.36**
3. Percent of life in city			—	−.06	−.70**	.04	.05	−.01	.06
4. Household size				—	.12	.17	.14	−.11	−.19
5. Place of socialization					—	.06	−.09	−.11	−.24**
6. Income						—	.41**	.21**	.07
7. Level of living							—	.33**	.23**
8. Conjugal role attitudes								—	.27**
9. Fertility attitudes									—

**Significant at the .001 level
*Significant at the .01 level

a strong relationship with both of the dependent variables. That is, women with a higher level of living tend to have more egalitarian conjugal role attitudes and less restrictive fertility attitudes than those with a lower level of living.

Conjugal Role Attitudes and Fertility Attitudes.
The correlation and cross-tabulation between a woman's conjugal role and fertility attitudes merit some attention. Both show that the relationship is strong, but not strong enough to suggest multicolliniarity. In other words, they are not parallel ideas. One cannot be predicted solely on the basis of the other. However, we would postulate that the woman's conjugal role attitude is the dominant of the two variables. That is, a woman's conjugal role attitude would be more likely to influence her fertility attitudes than her fertility attitudes would be to influence her conjugal role attitudes. In fact, this

was found to be the case in a previous study (Whiteford, et al. 1986).

Household Size and Gender Role Attitudes.
Two surprising results occur in this analysis. The first is that household size and fertility attitudes are not significantly correlated. However, control variables have again been entered into the analysis to further dissect the relationship and offer an explanation for this.

That there would be a relationship between household size and fertility attitudes seems to be a natural assumption if, in fact, attitudes do affect behavior. In searching for an explanation to this seeming "nonrelationship," first of all, it was found that, among women under forty, the larger the woman's household, the more traditional her fertility attitudes tend to be (see Figure 15–5).

Second, among women with 6 or more years of

TABLE 15–3   Gammas[a] for All Pairs of Variables

Variable	1	2	3	4	5	6	7	8	9
1. Age	—	−.66	−.22	.09	.46	.35	.05	−.20	−.35
2. Education		—	.31	−.22	−.47	−.03	.45	.55	.44
3. Percent of life in city			—	−.16	−.93	.11	.03	.07	.20
4. Household size				—	.32	.25	.15	−.06	−.35
5. Place of socialization					—	.03	−.05	−.16	−.42
6. Income						—	.53	.33	.08
7. Level of living							—	.59	.39
8. Conjugal role attitudes								—	.51
9. Fertility attitudes									—

[a]A gamma of +/− .20 or greater indicates that the relationship is strong enough to be of importance

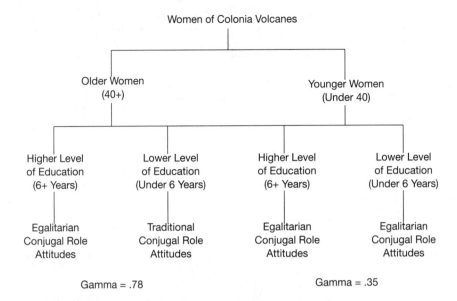

FIGURE 15–1   Relationship between education and fertility attitudes when controlling for the age of the woman.

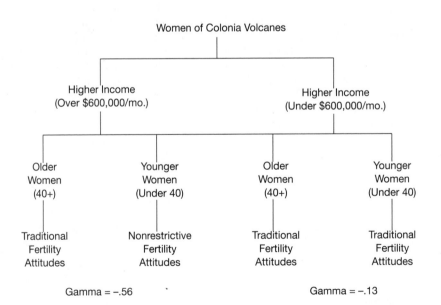

FIGURE 15–2   Relationship between age and fertility attitudes when controlling for household income.

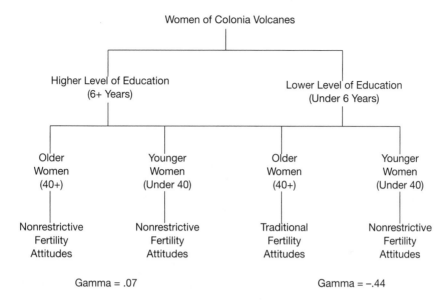

FIGURE 15–3   Relationship between age and fertility attitudes when controlling for the education of the woman.

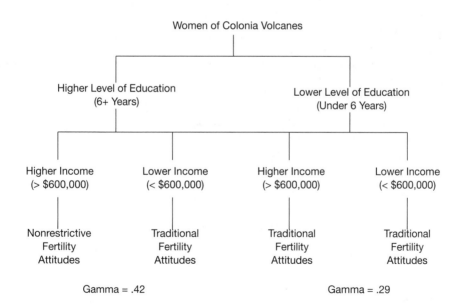

FIGURE 15–4   Relationship between income and fertility attitudes when controlling for the education of the woman.

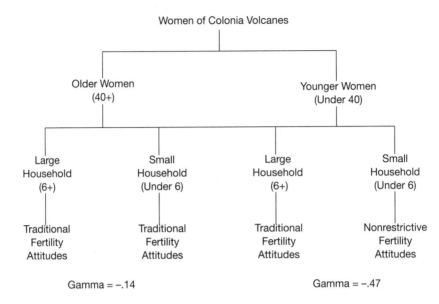

FIGURE 15–5   Relationship between ihousehold size and fertility attitudes when controlling for the age of the woman.

education, the larger her household, the more traditional her fertility attitudes are likely to be (see Figure 15–6).

A third finding was added to this by controlling for a woman's conjugal role attitudes. It was found that, among women with more egalitarian conjugal role attitudes, a woman with 5 people or fewer in her home is more likely to have nonrestrictive fertility attitudes than a woman with more than 5 people in her home (see Figure 15–7). This may be because women with lower levels of education are those who tend to have more traditional fertility attitudes. Or it may be due to factors such as the woman's age, the place of her socialization, or lack of knowledge pertaining to contraception.

The fourth finding does, in fact, reveal a partial relationship between household size and fertility attitudes due to a woman's place of socialization. Among women who were socialized in Oaxaca, those with more than 5 people in the household are more likely to have more traditional fertility attitudes (see Figure 15–8).

A fifth and similar finding that may explain the relationship between household size and fertility attitudes is that women's attitudes may change due to the influence of city life. As women spend more time in the city they may become less faithful to their traditional ways. This hypothesis is supported by the finding that among women who have lived in the city for more than half of their lives, those with 5 or fewer members in their household will tend to have more nonrestrictive fertility attitudes than those with more than 5 members in their household (see Figure 15–9).

Percent of Life in the City and Gender Role Attitudes.   The second surprising finding is that the percent of a woman's life she has lived in the city is not related to either her conjugal role or fertility attitudes. This finding may also be explained by introducing control variables into the cross-tabulation. An explanation surfaces once more in the woman's level of education. Among women with fewer than six years of education, those who have lived more than half of their lives in the city tend to have more egalitarian conjugal role attitudes (see Figure 15–10).

Furthermore, among women with more egalitarian conjugal role attitudes, those who have lived more than half of their lives in the city tend to have less restrictive fertility attitudes (see Figure 15–11). Conversely, among women who have lived more

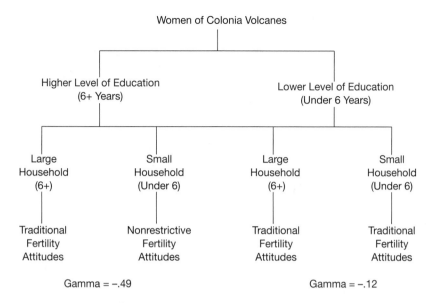

FIGURE 15–6   Relationship between ihousehold size and fertility attitudes when controlling for the education of the woman.

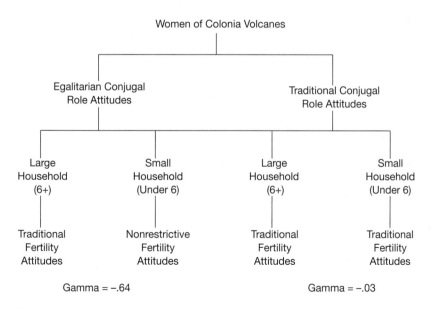

FIGURE 15–7   Relationship between ihousehold size and fertility attitudes when controlling for the conjugal role attitudes of the woman.

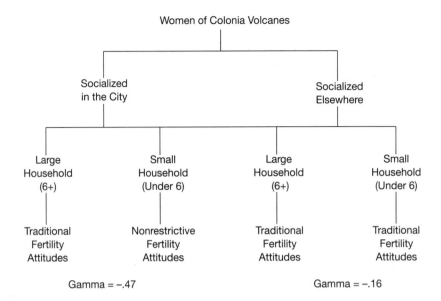

FIGURE 15–8   Relationship between ihousehold size and fertility attitudes when controlling for the woman's place of socialization.

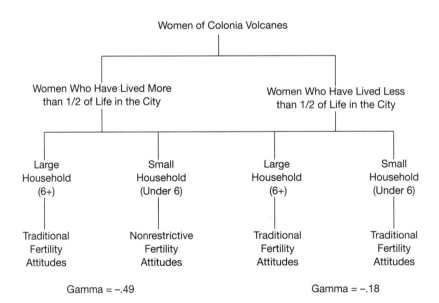

FIGURE 15–9   Relationship between ihousehold size and fertility attitudes when controlling for the percent of her life a woman has lived in the city of Oaxaca.

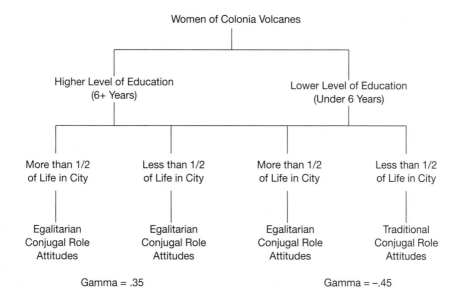

FIGURE 15–10　Relationship between ithe percent of her life a woman has lived in the city of Oaxaca and her conjugal role attitudes when controlling for the education of the woman.

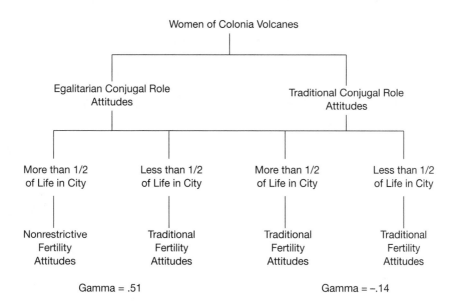

FIGURE 15–11　Relationship between percent of her life a woman has lived in the city of Oaxaca and fertility attitudes when controlling for conjugal role.

than half of their lives in the city, the more egalitarian their conjugal role attitudes, the more likely they are to have non-restrictive fertility attitudes (see Figure 15–12). In fact, within this subset of women, conjugal role attitudes and fertility attitudes are so strongly related (gamma =.72) that they become synonymous.

Place of Socialization and Gender Role Attitudes.

The last variable, place of socialization, is significantly related to a woman's fertility attitudes. That is, women socialized in the city of Oaxaca are more apt to have nonrestrictive fertility attitudes than those socialized elsewhere. However, a curiously unexplainable finding is that her place of socialization is in no way related to her conjugal role attitudes. Perhaps this is indicative of the process of social urbanization that Whiteford (1979 and 1989a) describes. Those whose conjugal role attitudes are likely to change as a result of outside influences have already changed or established different attitudes before coming to the city. The exposure to the "outside" from radio, television, trips to the city, or visitors to the countryside or village may have already affected their attitudes toward conjugal roles as much as living in the city would have.

SUMMARY AND CONCLUSIONS

The purpose of this study was to gain insight into the nature of changes taking place in women's gender role attitudes in Colonia Volcanes and the possible causes of these changes. Several findings are of particular interest.

Major Findings. A majority of the women in Colonia Volcanes have egalitarian attitudes toward conjugal roles. Fertility issues, however, are fairly well divided between traditional and nonrestrictive attitudes. Slightly more than half of the women have traditional fertility attitudes and a little less than half have nonrestrictive fertility attitudes. One aspect of reproduction on which a majority of women agree, however, is that it is acceptable behavior for a couple to practice birth control.

The configuration of influences causing changes in women's conjugal role and fertility attitudes seems to be somewhat complex. However, it is quite clear that a woman's level of education is the best predictor of her gender role attitudes. That is, both her conjugal role and fertility attitudes are very strongly influenced by her level of education. The higher her level of education, the more likely she

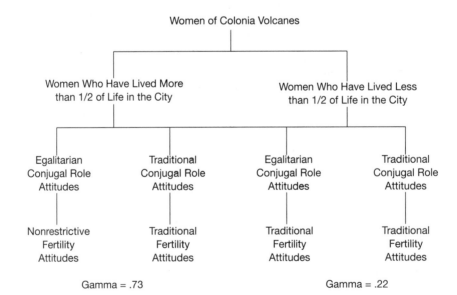

FIGURE 15–12   Relationship between conjugal role attitudes and fertility attitudes when controlling for the percent of her life a woman has lived in the city of Oaxaca.

will be to have egalitarian conjugal role attitudes and nonrestrictive fertility attitudes.

In addition to education, a woman's level of living and family income may influence her conjugal role attitudes. The higher her level of living and family income, the more likely she will be to have egalitarian conjugal role attitudes. In some cases, conjugal role attitudes may also be influenced by the woman's age and by the proportion of her life she has lived in the city.

The influence of sociocultural factors on fertility attitudes is far more intricate. In addition to a woman's level of education, fertility attitudes are shaped to a significant extent by a woman's level of living. They are also clearly influenced by a woman's place of socialization. Women socialized in the city tend to have less restrictive fertility attitudes. Fertility attitudes are also influenced somewhat by a woman's age. In general, the women with nonrestrictive fertility attitudes are those under forty years of age. In conjunction with other sociocultural factors (age, education, place of socialization, percent of her life a woman has lived in the city, a woman's conjugal role attitudes), fertility attitudes may also be predicted on the basis of the size of a woman's household. Last of all, of a woman has lived more than half of her life in the city and has egalitarian conjugal role attitudes, she will be likely to have nonrestrictive fertility attitudes as well.

Theoretical Implications. All of these partial explanations surrounding the formation of a woman's gender role attitudes might lead to the conclusion that women's attitudes are indeed changing. Support for this stems from the fact that many of these explanations are cited as mechanisms or causes of social change. These findings, then, lend support to theories of the causes of social change. In particular, social urbanization, socioeconomic status, and education are highly influential causes of changes in gender role attitudes.

The first suggestion of a possible cause of changing gender role attitudes is that of social urbanization. This mechanism of social change is obvious in its influence on conjugal role attitudes, but not in its influence on fertility attitudes. In this study, the concept of social urbanization was encompassed by two variables: the woman's place of socialization and the percent of her life she has lived in the city.

The results of the study suggest that social urbanization, in this area of Mexico, is at work but is not as straightforward a catalyst of change as other factors seem to be. As a cause of changing attitudes, social urbanization does appear to be especially relevant in relation to conjugal role attitudes. Conjugal role attitudes are not influenced by a woman's place of socialization; however, fertility attitudes are. Therefore, woman may already have been sensitized to egalitarian conjugal role attitudes before moving to the city. Furthermore, the percent of a woman's life she has lived in the city affects a woman's conjugal role attitudes as well as her fertility attitudes. These findings indicate change taking place in women's conjugal role attitudes and fertility attitudes.

In order to study the causal relationship between a woman's socioeconomic status and her gender role attitudes, the woman's level of living was examined. This variable proved to be a clearly significant determinant of the woman's gender role attitudes. Women with a higher socioeconomic status tended to have nonrestrictive or egalitarian role attitudes. This finding supports the theory that change in socioeconomic status acts as a mechanism for social change and, in this case, as a source for change in women's gender role attitudes.

This study also supports the theory that education is another source of social change. In fact, it shows education to be the single most important factor in changing gender role attitudes in Colonia Volcanes. Women with higher levels of education are those who will tend to have nonrestrictive and egalitarian role attitudes.

These three theoretically and statistically supported causes for social change constitute a large part of the explanation for changing gender role attitudes among women in Colonia Volcanes. This study clearly reveals evidence in support of theories of social change cited earlier in this document.

ACKNOWLEDGEMENTS

This paper is based on research data gathered in Oaxaca, Mexico, between May and August 1989. The authors would like to thank Iowa State University for several small grants that provided support for this project. Special thanks go to Paola Sesia-Lewis, Alejandro de Avila, and Maria Teresa

Pardo at the Grupo de Apoyo al Desarrollo Etnico (GADE) for personal and institutional support in the field. In addition, we appreciate the work of our assistants in Oaxaca: Zenón Ramirez, Lourdes Cornoa, Virginia Jurado, Julia Esther Rios, Catalina Solano, Alfonso Pacheco, and Antoineta Solano. John Bower, Patricia Whiteford, and Mary Winter read earlier drafts of this paper, and the authors appreciate their comments and acknowledge their input. Most importantly, special thinks go to the women in Colonia Volcanes whose cooperation and participation made this project possible.

NOTES

1. In this study, some of the factors specifically examined as possible causes of changing role attitudes are age; levels of education; among migrants from rural areas, the amount of her life she has lived in an urban environment; household size, and household income (or some measure of family financial well-being). In addition, the gender role attitudes of the female household heads will consist of two computed scales that will measure whether the woman holds a traditional authoritative or a nontraditional egalitarian view of her role with respect to conjugal relationships, and whether she holds a traditional restrictive or nontraditional nonrestrictive view of her role with respect to fertility and reproduction.

2. The two statements were: 1. Most of the important decisions in the life of the family should be made by the man of the house. 2. There is women's work and there is men's work; one should not do work that belongs to the other.

3. These five statements were created by the Instituto de Estudios Sociales en Población (IDESPO) at the National University, Heredia, Costa Rica. They were first used in a national study of women administered by the National University of Costa Rica and Cornell University.

4. A fifth statement about fertility was also given during interviews which seemed to cause some confusion on the part of the respondent. The statement was: "A couple should think seriously about the inconveniences of having children before they have them." During data analysis, the five fertility attitude statements were submitted to reliability testing. The responses to the fifth statement were not consistent with the responses to the other four. Therefore, that statement was omitted from the scale for the analysis. The reliability including responses to all five statements was Alpha = .43. By removing the fifth statement, the reliability became Alpha = .49.

5. The reliability of this scale is Alpha = .69.

6. The low end of the scale represents traditional conjugal role or fertility attitudes and the high end represents egalitarian conjugal role or nonrestrictive fertility attitudes.

7. The rate of exchange used for these computations is $2,500 (Mexico): $1 (U.S.).

8. Missing data on income was recoded in a different manner than the other data. The frequency distribution of the household's monthly income was divided into four equal sections, each section containing 25 percent of the responses, and the mean was computed for each of these divisions. Responses were then recoded to the mean of one of the divisions on the basis of the respondent's level of living. In other words, if monthly household income was missing and the reported level of living for that household was 7 or less, the income was recoded to the mean of the lowest income division. If the level of living was greater than 7 and less than 11, or greater than 10 and less than 15, the monthly household income was assigned to the respective mean of the next two income divisions. If the level of living was 15 or greater, the monthly household income was recoded to the mean of the highest of the four income categories (Babbie 1986).

9. However, an exact report on total monthly household income is often difficult to ascertain. The difficulty of collecting information on income may be caused by several factors. A woman's husband may not put her in charge of all of the family's funds or even inform her of the exact amount of income he generates. It is also possible that the family's income may be of a sporadic nature. Income may vary depending on how business goes that month, or it may depend on the particular season (agricultural, tourist, or holiday) in which the interview was conducted. In some cases, it may vary depending on how much her husband or kinfolk are able to send her at any given time from Oregon or Southern California or any other number of points north of the border. Another possibility may be that she may discount the informal income that she or her husband makes as not truly "income." A further possibility may be that she may be shy about reporting the family's income to strangers for fear that they may be government officials or officials from her husband's place of employment checking up on the financial status of the family.

10. The reliability of this scale is Alpha = .80.

11. Pearson correlation matrix and cross-tabulations was to establish the significance, strength, and direction

of the relationships among gender role attitudes and the sociocultural variables. The cross-tabulations were done using two variables, one independent and one dependent. When results were not as expected, a control variable was added and three-variable cross-tabulations were computed in order to discover whether or not the variables would be related under certain circumstances. The three-variables cross-tabulations are not an attempt to assess causal relationships, but rather an attempt to determine what set of circumstances or variables surround traditional or egalitarian, nonrestrictive role attitudes.

BIBLIOGRAPHY

Acosta-Belen, Edna, and Christine E. Bose, 1990. "From Structural Subordination to Empowerment: Women and Development in Third World Contexts," *Gender and Society* 4 (No. 3):299–320.

Babb, Florence, 1989. *Between Field and Cooking Pot: The Political Economy of Marketwomen in Peru.* (Texas Press Sourcebook in Anthropology, No. 15). Austin: University of Texas Press.

Babbie, Earl. 1986. *The Practice of Social Research.* Belmont, California: Wadsworth Publishing Co.

Béhar, Ruth, 1987. "Sex and Sin, Witchcraft and the Devil in Late-Colonial Mexico," *American Ethnologist* 14 (No. 1):34–54.

Beneria, L., and M. Roldan, 1987. *The Crossroads of Class and Gender: Industrial Homework, Subcontracting and Household Dynamics in Mexico City.* Chicago: University of Chicago.

Bernard, H. Russell, 1988. *Research Methods in Cultural Anthropology.* Newbury Park, California: Sage Publications, Inc.

Biesanz, Richard, Karen Zubria Biesanz, and Mavis H. Biesanz, 1982. *The Costa Ricans.* Upper Saddle River, New Jersey: Prentice-Hall, Inc.

Blutstein, Howard I., Lynne C. Andersen, Elinor C. Betters, John H. Dombrowski, and Charles Townsend, 1970. *Area Handbook for Costa Rica.* Washington, D.C.: U.S. Government Printing Office.

Bourque, Susan C. and Kay Barbara Warren, 1981. *Women of the Andes: Patriarchy and Social Change in Two Peruvian Towns.* Ann Arbor: The University of Michigan Press.

Browner, C. H., 1986. "Gender Roles and Social Change: A Mexican Case," *Ethnology* 25 (No. 2):89–106.

Browner, Carole, and Ellen Lewin, 1982. "Female Altruism Reconsidered: the Virgin Mary as Economic Woman," *American Ethnologist* 9 (No. 1):61–75.

Bunster-Burotto, Ximena, 1986. "Surviving Beyond Fear: Women and Torture in Latin America." Chapter 15 in J. Nash and H. I. Safa (eds.), *Women and Change in Latin America.* South Hadley, Massachusetts: Bergin and Garey Publishers, Inc.

Bustos, Jorge Gissi, 1980. "Mythology About Women, With Special Reference to Chile." Chapter 2 in J. Nash and H. I. Safa (eds.), *Sex and Class in Latin America: Women's Perspectives on Politics, Economics and the Family in the Third World.* Brooklyn, New York: J. F. Bergin Publishers, Inc.

Cancian, Francesca M., Louis Wolf Goodman, and Peter H. Smith, 1978. "Capitalism, Industrialization, and Kinship in Latin America: Major Issues," *Journal of Family History* (Winter):319–335.

Chambers, Robert, 1987. *Rural Development: Putting the Last First.* New York: Longman.

Chinchilla, Norma Stolz, 1990. "Revolutionary Popular Feminism in Nicaragua: Articulating Class, Gender, and National Sovereignty," *Gender and Society* 4 (No. 3):370–397.

Danes, Sharon M., Mary Winter, and Michael B. Whiteford, 1987. "Level of Living and Participation in the Informal Market Sector among Rural Honduran Women," *Journal of Marriage and the Family* 49 (No. 3):631–639.

Foster, George M., 1988. *Tzintzuntzan: Mexican Peasants in a Changing World.* Prospect Heights, Illinois: Waveland Press, Inc.

Friedlander, Judith, 1975. *Being Indian in Hueyapan: A Study of Forced Identity in Contemporary Mexico.* New York: St. Martin's Press.

Harkness, Shirley J., 1973. "The Pursuit of an Ideal: Migration, Social Class, and Women's Roles in Bogota, Colombia." Pp. 231–254 in Ann Pescatello (ed.), *Female and Male in Latin America: Essays.* Pittsburgh: University of Pittsburgh Press.

Higgins, Michael James, 1990. "Martyrs and Virgins: Popular Religion in Mexico and Nicaragua." Chapter 10 in L. Stephen and J. Dow (eds.), *Class, Politics, and Popular Religion in Mexico and Central America,* vol. 10. Washington, D.C.: Society for Latin American Anthropology Publication Series.

Kearney, Michael, 1986. *The Winds of Ixtepeji: World View and Society in a Zapotec Town.* Prospect Heights, Illinois: Waveland Press, Inc.

Kottak, Conrad P., 1992. *Assault on Paradise: Social Change in a Brazilian Village,* 2nd ed. New York: McGraw-Hill, Inc.

Lavrin, Asunción, 1978. "In search of the colonial woman in Mexico: the seventeen and eighteen centuries." Chapter 1 in A. Lavrin (ed.), *Latin American Women: Historical Perspectives.* Westport, Connecticut: Greenwood Press, Inc.

———, 1987. "Women, the Family, and Social-Change in Latin America," *World Affairs* 150 (No.2):109–128.

Leahy, Margaret E., 1986. *Development Strategies and*

the Status of Women: A Comparative Study of the United States, Mexico, the Soviet Union and Cuba. Boulder, Colorado: Lynne Rienner Publishers, Inc.

Macías, Ana, 1982. *Against All Odds: The Feminist Movement in Mexico to 1940.* Contributors in Women's Studies, Number 30. Westport, Connecticut: Greenwood Press.

Meyer, Michael C., and William L. Sherman, 1987. *The Course of Mexican History.* New York: Oxford.

Mies, Mariz, Veronika Bennholdt-Thomsen, and C. von Werlhof, 1988. *Women: The Last Colony.* London: Zed.

Miller, Barbara, 1981. "Women and Revolution: The Brigadas Femeninas and the Mexican Cristero Rebellion, 1926–29." Pp. 57–66 in Sandra F. McGee (ed.), *Women and Politics in Twentieth Century Latin America*, vol. 15. Williamsburg, Virginia: Studies in Third World Societies.

Murphy, Arthur, and Alex Stepick, 1991. *Adaptation and Inequality: Political Economy and Cultural Ecology in a Secondary Mexican City.* Philadelphia: Temple University Press.

Nash, June, and Helen I. Safa (eds.), 1986. *Women and Change in Latin America.* South Hadley, Massachusetts: Bergin & Garvey.

Newbold Chiñas, Beverly L., 1992. *The Isthmus Zapotecs: A Matrifocal Culture of Mexico*, 2nd ed., Fort Worth, Texas: Harcourt Brace Jovanovich.

Riding, Alan, 1984. *Distant Neighbors: A Portrait of the Mexicans.* New York: Random House.

Rokeach, Milton, 1972. *Beliefs Attitudes and Values: A Theory of Organization and Change.* San Francisco: Jossey-Bass, Inc.

Safa, Helen Icken, 1990. "Women's Social Movements in Latin American," *Gender and Society* 4 (No.3):354–369.

Schafer, Robert B., and John L. Tait, 1981. *A Guide for Understanding Attitudes and Attitude Change.* Ames, Iowa: North Central Regional Extension Publication 138.

Schmidt, Steffen W. 1988. "The Origins of Gender Values: Notes on the Colombian Case," *Journal of Popular Culture* 22 (No. 1):17–36.

Selby, Henry A., Arthur D. Murphy, and Stephen A. Lorenzen, 1990. *The Mexican Urban Household: Organizing for Self-Defense.* Austin: University of Texas Press.

Sharpe, Deanna Lee Black, 1988. "Time devoted by women to selected household tasks, 1975–1981: Implications for assessing change in standards." Ph.D. dissertation, Iowa State University, Ames, Iowa.

Stephen, Lynn, 1991. *Zapotec Women.* (Texas Press

Sourcebook in Anthropology, No. 16). Austin: University of Texas Press.

Stevens, Evelyn P., 1973. "Machismo and Marianismo," *Society* 10 (No. 6):313–321.

Taylor, William B., 1987. "The Virgin of Guadalupe in New Spain: An Inquiry into the Social History of Marian Devotion," *American Ethnologist* 14 (No. 1):9–33.

United Nations Population Fund, 1986–87. *Inventory of Population Projects in Developing Countries around the World.* New York: United Nations.

Vallens, Vivian M., 1978. *Working Women in Mexico during the Porfiriato 1880–1910.* San Francisco: R & E Research Associates, Inc.

West, Candace, and Don H. Zimmerman, 1987. "Doing Gender," *Gender and Society* 4 (No.3):125–151.

Whiteford, Michael B., 1978. "Women, Migration and Social Change: A Colombian Case Study," *International Migration Review* 12 (No. 2):236–247.

———, 1979. "Social Urbanization in the Cauca Valley, Colombia." Urban Anthropology 8 (No. 3/4):351–363.

———, 1982. "The interface of cultural factors with nutritional well-being: the case of Moroceli, Honduras." Medical Anthropology 6:221–330.

———1989a. "The Household Ecology of Malnutrition: The Case of El Ocotillo, Mexico," *Journal of Developing Societies* 5:82–96.

———, 1989b. "Como Se Cura: Patterns of Medical Choice Among Working Class Families in the City of Oaxaca, Mexico." Paper prepared for the 88th Annual Meeting of the American Anthropological Association, November 15–19, Washington, D.C.

———, 1991. "The Patient as Diagnostician: Intracultural Differences in Illness Etiology in a Mexican Neighborhood," *Journal of Developing Societies* 7:256–268.

Whiteford, Michael B., and Suzanne Dvorak, 1984. "Conjugal Relationships and Fertility Behavior: Determinants of Family Size in a Costa Rican Community," *The Rural Sociologist* 4 (No. 1):44–50.

Whiteford, Patricia C., E. W. Morris, and M. B. Whiteford, 1986. "Education and Changing Roles in a Transitional Society: The Case of Rural Costa Rica," *Journal of Developing Societies* 2:89–102.

Winter, Mary, Earl W. Morris, and Arthur D. Murphy, 1989. "Food Expenditures, Food Purchases, and Satisfaction with Food in the City of Oaxaca." Paper prepared for the Annual Meeting of the Society for Applied Anthropology, April 7, Santa Fe, New Mexico.

16

Brokers and Career Mobility Systems in the Structure of Complex Societies[1]

Richard N. Adams

The purpose of this paper is to relate career mobility systems and power brokers with two analytical notions that concern the structure of complex societies, power domains and levels of articulation. Three generally familiar concepts are first reviewed; some modifications are then suggested; finally, interrelations are proposed among them. The proposals are speculative and stem from analyses of the national social structure of Guatemala (Adams 1970).

LEVELS OF INTEGRATION, BROKERS, AND CAREER MOBILITY SYSTEMS

The concept of levels in human society has been used in many contexts and for many centuries. In contemporary anthropology, however, it is especially associated with the work of Steward (1955), and Wolf (1967) has added further thoughts on the subject. While Steward used the concept to refer

From *Southwestern Journal of Anthropology,* XXVI (1970), 315–327. Copyright 1970 by The University of New Mexico. Reprinted by permission of the author and publisher.

specifically to "national" and "local" levels, Wolf expanded this to seven "levels and sublevels" for Middle America. But neither author, so far as I know, has directed his attention to a rather central problem: What *is* a level of integration? That is, how do we know when we are dealing with one? How do we know that one may exist, be coming into existence, or possibly be changing? How do we then account for the possible fact that there may be different numbers of such levels in different societies, or in different parts of a single complex society? If these questions cannot be answered, then the concept can never be a satisfactory analytical tool.

"Brokers" has been used to refer to individuals who occupy linkage roles between sectors of a society. "Marriage brokers," as well as "stock brokers," serve to articulate two clients in order to effect an exchange of approximate equivalence. Until a few years ago, this exchange of equivalencies seemed to imply that brokers worked between social equals. Wolf (1956) suggested that this kind of articulatory role could be seen operating in individuals who related social elements which were clearly not equals, where the things being linked were on different levels of the society and, therefore, stood in relatively different positions of power. This extension of the concept has facilitated the conceptualization of the connections and linkages between local levels of a society and the larger system. A problem in the use of the concept, however, is that we have little notion why these "cultural brokers" seem less congenial in some societies than in others and what conditions lead to their appearance or disappearance. A further question is whether the cultural contact between two different levels afforded by a broker is of relevance structurally and, if so, under what circumstances.

"Career mobility systems" refers to a phenomenon that has received little elaboration beyond the case that was presented by Leeds (1965) in Brazil, and the model of spiralism proposed by Watson (1964) for Great Britain. Obviously, in dealing with levels we are also interested in the process of mobility, the devices whereby an individual or party succeeds in moving from one level to another. Societies clearly differ in the degree to which mobility during one's career is possible; and in those societies where mobility is feasible, it usually can be described rather systematically. It is possible, therefore, to speak of career mobility systems as those patterned processes within a given society whereby one moves up or down.

What is sometimes overlooked about these systems is that they are more than merely ways for individuals to move up or down; they also establish linkages between the different levels. Whereas brokers translate the interests of one level into responses at another, in mobility systems those with interests at one level can attempt to move to the next level and to assess their own interests there. In one respect, therefore, career mobility systems parallel the activities of brokers, and the problem posed concerning brokers is equally applicable to them: i.e., under what conditions do these systems come into operation or fall into disuse? Further, do they specifically have some relation to the presence or absence of brokers?

POWER DOMAINS, LEVELS OF ARTICULATION, AND CONFRONTATIONS

The conceptual relations I wish to explore here are derived from trying to understand a series of events covering a twenty-five year period in Guatemala and include matters such as relationships between rural community dwellers, changing national governments, associations of national scope, and the role of foreign powers, specifically Germany, the United States, and Cuba.

Of the concepts central to this discussion, that of the power domain has been discussed elsewhere (Adams 1966). It should be kept in mind that the concept of power used here is not derived from Weber (1964:152–153); i.e., it does not include the totality of influences that make people obey the wills of others. It refers to control over the environment; the environment encompasses any set of events external and relevant to the persons doing the controlling. We are concerned, however, with a particular phase of control, that which one individual may have over the environment of another. Thus, the concept of power being used here diverges from the Weberian in that power is only one of the totality of influences that may exist between two individuals or players. Moreover, we also use a generalized concept of player, one that can include any kind of social operating unit that is coping with the environment. (Adams 1970:39–53 contains an extended treatment of these concepts.) Thus, a family, a community, a political party, a military establishment, a government may all be operating units, and hence players. A power domain, then, is a relationship wherein one player has greater control over the environment of a second than the second does over that of the first. The domain concept is useful in organizing and examining the dynamics of inequalities in systems of power.

To this, I want to add a remodeling of the notion of levels. To avoid confusion with earlier usages, I am referring to this as "levels of articulation" (see Adams 1970:53–70 for a detailed treatment). A level of articulation comes into being when two players meet in a confrontation. A confrontation takes place when two players find that successfully coping with the environment brings them into a situation where either may stand as an obstacle to the further exercise of power by the other. Confrontations may occur randomly, but they are more commonly foreseen and often actually planned by at least one of the parties. In terms of power, success in a confrontation means that one so uses his power tactically that he eliminates the other or superimposes himself in a domain over the other. This then places them at different levels. Confrontations may, however, be continuing and fairly stabilized, without either party winning. In this case, the parties remain in articulation, to some degree intentionally keeping each other under stress. It is the condition of the continuing presence of balanced confrontations, and the repetition of similar confrontations, that serves to provide some permanence to levels.

It is probably worth noting that the term "confrontation" here is not being used in quite the same manner as in international and local U.S. politics in recent years. This latter usage suggests that a face-to-face meeting necessarily implies a potential conflict and a necessarily violent resolution; e.g., to say that two nations wish to "avoid a confrontation" has become almost synonymous with saying that they wish to avoid a war. In the context of this essay, "confrontation" refers to the fact that two parties are in articulation because one or both are obstacles to the other; it does not imply that they will choose to fight over the issue nor, indeed, that these issues will necessarily ever be resolved.

Levels of articulation become increasingly explicit and important as confrontations become more durable, as more of them occur between parties of equivalent power, and, therefore, as the perception of relative power becomes institutionalized within the society. As such, levels are more than merely loci of confrontations; they also provide a place for many kinds of relationships between parties, ranging from confrontation and competition to cooperation and assimilation. Individuals may find themselves operating at different levels, depending upon which of their various roles they occupy at the moment. Consequently, a consistency tends to emerge among levels of articulation. Instead of ranging over a broad undifferentiated continuum, players tend to bunch where those of roughly equivalent power are maintaining their positions and, consequently, where those who wish to confront them must also congregate. To this should be added the recognition that real players operate in real space. This means that topography and other external features will influence the possibility of confrontations taking place. Because of this, levels in one locale or region need not precisely correspond to those elsewhere. Anything which promotes isolation, be it cultural or physical, may differentiate systems of levels.

In spite of this, however, most complex societies have sets of levels that approximate the following: (1) sub-communal (possibly identified around kin, households, etc.); (2) local (possibly neighborhoods, communities, or sets of small communities); (3) regional (possibly large towns or cities and hinterland, sets of communities, etc.); (4) national (sets of regions or a collectivity of small national scenes); (5) clearly supranational, the maximal level at which the more powerful nations operate.

The concepts can be illustrated in the Guatemalan cases as follows. Guatemala itself is in a power domain of the United States; its economy is heavily dependent upon actions taken by the United States government, and its political system is explicitly aligned with the policy decisions of the United States and against those of socialist countries. The government of Guatemala, in turn, exercises domain over all Guatemalans in various aspects. And within Guatemala, there are lesser domains of businesses, the church, agrarian enterprises, industries, corporate communities, etc. Levels of articulation can be identified within Guatemala by taking note of the confrontation articulations between individual family heads, of town officials dealing with like officials elsewhere, of ministers of government negotiating with leaders in business and industry or with political figures of distinction, and so forth. They are also evident in the dealings between the Guatemalan government and other governments and in the fact that the United States clearly exercises more power over Guatemalan decisions than the reverse. In this paper, however, we are concerned with the lower levels of articulation, those that operate within the nation.

It is important to recognize that domains and levels are two different ways of conceptualizing the consequences of power operations within a single society. The presence of domains can be examined to see how players with roughly equivalent access to power are aligned horizontally; and the manifestation of levels indicates that the relationship between domains has become somewhat institutionalized. However, the two concepts need differentiation because confrontations may produce domains which are not clearly aligned within a set of levels. The notion to be explored in this paper is that societies, or subsegments of societies, will from time to time place special emphasis on either domains or levels, and that this differential emphasis has consequences for our understanding of brokers and career mobility systems.

APPLICATION OF THE CONCEPTS

Let us now return to the concepts mentioned at the outset. "Levels of articulation" obviously refers to much that is contained in Steward's (1955) and Wolf's (1967) "levels of integration." The new notion, however, is more precise in its referent, allows for cross-cultural correlation of varying forms, indicates the dynamics of the levels, how they come into being, and how they may change. Since they are products of potential conflicts, their locus and systematization must reflect the adaptation to the total environment. Because of these advantages, however, there are some cautions which must also be observed. Since one cannot, a priori, assume that levels found in one locale will necessarily be present or operative in another, they must be sought out empirically. The study of different regional power structures in Guatemala made this quite clear (Adams 1970:219–237). Just as kinship, locality, and political and economic organizations may be assumed to exist in some form, so may levels. But their specific forms must be discovered and described; they cannot be assumed.

The concept of brokers, as a linkage or articulation between levels, has principally been applied in the literature on Latin America to relations between local and national levels. The material from the Guatemalan study suggests that the concept of broker should be modified in two ways. First, it is a term that refers to two quite different kinds of linkages; second, it is a form which seems to be important principally when domain structures are emphasized over levels.

As linkages between local and national levels, various authors have cited instances such as caciques, school teachers, political agents, military recruiting agents, tax collectors, lawyers, labor recruiters, etc. Emphasis generally has been laid on such matters as whether the individual had his origins at the local rather than the national level or whether he represented the interests of one over the other. If it is asked whether brokers act as channels through which power is exercised, however, then we find we must differentiate between two quite different kinds of intermediaries.

Classically in Guatemala, and in many other Latin American countries, the school teacher is a cultural representative of the national system working in a culture different from that within which he is used to operating. While the teacher may serve to make national traits available, he usually has no power himself. he cannot expect firm support from his own Ministry of Education and consequently has little to offer or deny the members of the local group beyond whatever may be inherent in his role. The teacher's weakness at the national level means that he is of little interest to them in any except his specialized capacity. The same may be said for the public health doctor and the agricultural extension agent.

The situation of essential weakness is quite different from that of the cacique, an individual who classically plays the role of intermediary through utilizing his controls at each level to the advantage of the other. He can offer support by the local population to regional or national figures only if he can then be sure that they will respond to his calls for support. His actual control over either sphere depends upon his success in dealing with the other; his controls in one level of articulation provide a basis for controls in another. In addition to the classic cacique, brokers in this sense include political party agents, mass organization leaders, labor union leaders and agents, industrial foremen, local and regional marketeers and credit agents, labor recruiters, lawyers, etc.

It is clear that these "power brokers" differ from those of the first category, for whom we may retain the label "cultural broker." The cultural broker is an individual from one level who lives or operates among individuals of another level. Whatever influence he may have on the other level depends basically not on the power that he can wield but on his own skill and personal influence. Even flamboyant success at one level may have absolutely no effect on his role at the other. The school teacher who is a favorite in a rural school is not necessarily going to be the favorite in the Ministry; and he who "politicks" around the Ministry may fail to gain a following in his own school.

The power broker, on the other hand, specifically wields power at each of two levels, and his power in one level depends upon the success of his operations at the other level. He controls one domain only by virtue of having access to derivative power from a larger domain. It is interesting that so many Latin American governments have, from time to time, attempted to use cultural broker roles in a context where they really needed power brokers. Few governments, however, allow their school teachers or agricultural agents access to power.

The conditions under which each of these brokers appears within a complex society necessarily differ. Cultural brokers are usually sponsored through upper level decisions and are destined to act at lower levels. Their tasks, however, are seldom of first priority, since a failure to realize them is not felt to be a threat to the relative position of power of the parties sponsoring them. Classically, a Minister of Education does not lose his job because he fails to improve national education but because he becomes a political liability. The increase of teachers, public health agents, and agricultural agents varies with changes in national government policy about the importance of these particular areas of life for the government or for the nation. The increase of traveling agents of breweries, shoe salesmen, and wholesale agents depends upon how and when commercial houses decide to improve business operations. In general, I would assume that the importance of cultural brokers varies with the state of the national economy and the particular efforts being made to promote the spread of a national culture.

The incidence of power brokers answers to a different structure. Power brokers link units or actors at different levels, where the difference in power is such that the inferior has no real chance to confront the superior. The 19th-century Guatemalan Indian dealt through the elders or cacique because little could be gained by going directly to officials at the national level. Political party agents operate at the local level to gain voting support for their candidates because it is impossible for the candidate himself to do all the organizing, traveling, and convincing necessary for his election. The military establishment keeps local agents to undertake recruiting because it cannot afford to take up the time of colonels and generals in such a menial task.

In all, the power broker holds an important place in the power structure of the country and particularly in the region within which he works.

Since a major feature of the role of power brokers is to mediate where confrontations do not occur, it follows that they should be especially important where domains are dominant. If someone low in a domain wishes to obtain something that is available only to superiors in the domain, he may attempt a confrontation, or he may try to do it through a broker. If he attempts a confrontation, he makes the levels more flexible; if he operates through a broker, he strengthens the domain. Power brokers are important, then, where domains are strong and, correlatively, where levels tend to be rigid. In prerevolutionary Guatemala (prior to 1944) dictator Ubico allowed no confrontation; similarly, no coffee farmer would allow a show of organized power on the part of his laborers. The major means of handling problems were through elders, caciques, town *intendentes* (government-appointed town mayors), farm administrators, and others who stood in power brokerage positions. At the same time, there was no question as to what levels existed, and each person knew where he stood. Domains were strong and levels were rigid.

During the 1944–1954 revolutionary period, new sources of power opened up, and multiple access to power was made possible by organizing political parties, mass organizations, labor unions, and the like; concomitant with these changes, the incidence of confrontations between organizations and domain superiors increased. As a result, the system of levels became much more flexible, and domains weakened. By the same token, the role of the power broker became ambiguous. As it became increasingly possible for the lower sector to get what it wanted through various new channels, the broker was by-passed if he was not effective. The outstanding case was the manner in which young, politically oriented individuals began to take over control of local governments through the elective process and thereby ignored the traditional channels of local political authority. Indian elders, local *ladino* (mestizo) upper strata, and large farm operators could all be confronted or by-passed completely by virtue of the new access to power of the political party and labor union. (See Adams 1957 for case histories.)

The change bringing about the new emphasis on levels, and the concomitant de-emphasis on domains, did not stop with the end of the revolutionary period in 1954. The increase in confrontations was reduced in important ways, but the new power sources and new channels opened by the revolution began to be used in different ways. Labor courts continued in operation, and, although under severe practical constraints, they were more effective in dealing directly with a farm administrator in extreme instances. Labor unions, while weakened, nevertheless continued to operate, particularly in the capital city.

A contrary case, which tends to demonstrate the proposition here suggested, is that of the labor recruiter. Seasonal migrant labor, which probably numbers as high as 400,000, did not have effective access to new power under the revolution. The labor laws and unions could do little to influence their situation. The means of contracting labor had traditionally been through individuals who would act as brokers between the farm administrations and the laborers of particular towns or villages. These *habilitadores* and *enganchadores,* perfect examples of power brokers, continue to operate up to the present. They serve a purpose for which no readily devisable means of confrontations have been invented. It may be predicted, however, that if and when the labor needs of farms outstrip the availability of the rural population for seasonal labor, then confrontations will begin to take place and the broker will disappear.

Just as rigidity of levels is an aspect of a strong domain system, so flexibility of levels is a concomitant of the weakening of domains. And whereas brokers have a real role in the former situation, this role is replaced by mobility in the latter. In systems where brokers operate, upward mobility is very difficult. Individuals at the lower levels, in the absence of access to derived power, depend upon brokers to provide what little they may get. The weakening of domains and disappearance of brokers is simultaneous with an increase in mobility. Aggressive lower sector individuals reach directly for power themselves; intrasocietal patterns develop whereby confrontations may be made, and the cleverer and luckier individuals and groups will gain more power for themselves and thereby move to higher levels. As was indi-

cated earlier, we are faced with a painful shortage of studies of the mobility processes that have evolved in different societies. Leeds' (1965) description of the career system in Brazil was an important innovative study because here it was made perfectly clear that mobility is considerably more than a set of sociological statistics and that it probably manifests the same diversities that are to be found elsewhere in sociocultural systems.

The replacement of brokerage by mobility suggests that the latter is more than a means of bettering the lot of individuals within the society, that it is also a structural linkage within the system as a whole. Both mobility and brokers enable a social system to continue on its course with only gradual structural change. The difference, quite obviously, is that one keeps people in their appointed roles, whereas the other allows them to change. In both, the role system remains much the same. The increase of confrontations, however, means that individuals and groupings accomplish this mediation by moving out of the lower levels and by obtaining direct access to power (whether derivative or independent).

Another way to look at the contrast between the two situations is to see the broker system as static and the mobility system as dynamic. A broker does not change his position within the total structure by virtue of his activities as broker. Since his power in each level depends upon maintaining his control over resources in both areas, he generally cannot move without losing control over one or both sources. (I say "generally," because there are occasional individuals who are successful in moving out of the brokerage position into higher levels through confrontations. The classic case of the provincial *caudillo* who takes over the central government, as Rafael Carrera did in Guatemala in 1838, does occur. But they are relatively few when compared with the number of brokers in operation.) Consequently, the broker accomplishes linkage within the society by not moving. In a career mobility system, on the other hand, the linkage is accomplished by the individual occupying one position in one part of the society at one point in his career and another position later. He may retain relations at the different levels, but his roles change as he moves up. Time does not change the broker's position, but it extends the roles of the mobile person across various levels of society, and it is the very movement over time that provides the linkage.

THE PROCESS OF WEAKENING AND STRENGTHENING OF DOMAINS

There remains a question as to the reasons that domains vary from weakness to strength and levels of articulation from flexibility to rigidity. Basically a domain may be said to be strong when it has sufficient power within its control to keep subordinates in an inferior position. The circumstances which may affect the relative control of domain superiors are too varied to permit even a cursory review here. They may be illustrated, however, in terms of recent Guatemalan history.

Since levels are defined by the presence of confrontations, it follows that an increased flexibility in levels depends upon an increase in confrontations. Some of the more obvious conditions that produce this include population increase, economic development, and political expansion. Population growth brings about competition over land and other resources, and it results in confrontations which may appear at any level, from the family to the international. Economic development, entailing as it does an increased extraction of resources and production, is inherently a competitive process, both internally and internationally. It, too, may breed confrontations at any level, although they are perhaps better known at higher levels. Political expansion refers mainly to the expansion of nation states or to political movements within nations. These, also, are apparent at higher levels, but they occasionally occur in the form of urban demonstrations and of peasant or Indian movements. Even within the community, the expansion of a family or kin group may be seen in this light.

Because we live in an age where both national growth and economic development, as well as population growth, seem to be in evidence almost everywhere, it may seem harder to find cases where there is a shift from flexible to rigid levels. Indeed, the three processes just described constitute three phases of the major course of contemporary social evolution. Their conjunction is not a convergence of independent variables but a complex whereby each

affects the other, and feedback from one increases activities within another.

Given this picture, and assuming reasonably that the course of evolution is unidirectional, it would be easy to assume that flexibility of levels regularly increases. This, however, is erroneous. The changing flexibility of levels and strength of domains is a mechanism within the evolutionary process, not an outcome of it. A major unidirectional change is to increase the number of domains, to increase the amount of power at the top, and, therefore, to increase the importance of larger domains. This inevitably leads to more confrontations and, consequently, to a more complex structure of levels. The specificity of real situations, however, will inevitably lead to a periodic or fluctuating relative isolation of domains; and this relative isolation leads inevitably to fewer confrontations at those points and to a concomitant strengthening of the domain.

To return to the recent history of Guatemala, under the pre-1944 government, the country was a somewhat isolated domain, characteristically a unitary domain, under the general external power of Germany and the United States. Germany was eliminated by World War II, and the United States remained the sole external power of any importance. During the revolutionary period of 1945 to 1954, the internal structure of the country began a drastic reorganization such that internal multiple domains became common and, with this, a sharp increase in confrontations. Levels became flexible, and the internal domains weakened. As the United States became frightened of activity in Guatemala that it considered to be "communistic," it began to provide support to encourage a confrontation between the government and the elements working against the government, a process which culminated in a counterrevolution in 1954. This, in turn, coupled with a steady process of economic development and population increase, led to a severe strengthening of the upper sector, with a concomitant strengthening of and reemphasis on domains and rigidity of levels. In this the United States provided important derivative power crucial to the process. The gradual regeneration of a more virile revolutionary movement in the 1960s, following the Cuban Revolution, led the conservative elements of Guatemala to align themselves (not by any means always to their taste) with United States demands, so that confrontations became parallel at various levels. Not only was the United States in confrontation with Cuba and the socialist world, but the government of Guatemala was in confrontation with some fairly agile guerrilla groups, and in both rural and urban populations there were frequent politically related assassinations. In this way, the increasing activity at various levels initiated a new series of specifically political confrontations. Over the past thirty years, then, Guatemala has shifted from a period of strong domains (pre-1944), to a weakening (1945–1954), back again to strength (1954–ca. 1961), and now again to signs of weakening (ca. 1961 to the present).

Nation states essentially attempt to strengthen their own domain structures. But the fact that they are undergoing economic development and that their populations are usually growing means that inherently the frequency of confrontations increases. Concurrently, levels reassert themselves and become more flexible through confrontations, promoting the appearance of career mobility systems and putting power brokers out of business.

FINAL COMMENT

The intent of this essay has been to relate the process of brokerage and mobility to more inclusive conditions of the total society. It has done this through relating the modes of handling power within a society to the shape and emphasis of the larger social system; it has further suggested that the condition of the larger system sets constraints on the kind of linkages that will emerge within it. As stated at the outset, it has been speculative, and, as such, I hope it will serve to stimulate further inquiry into the relations of the unit activity within a complex society to the world society and to the social evolution of which it is a part.

NOTE

1. This is a revised version of a paper read at the 1968 American Anthropological Association Annual Meetings. The Guatemalan work on which it was based was supported by the Ford Foundation and the Institute of Latin American Studies, the University of Texas at Austin.

BIBLIOGRAPHY

Adams, Richard N., 1957. *Political Changes in Guatemalan Indian Communities: a Symposium.* Tulane University, Middle American Research Institute, publication 24, pp. 1–54.

———,1966. "Power and Power Domains," *América Latina,* ano 9, no. 2, pp. 3–21.

———,1970. *Crucifixion by Power: Essays in the National Social Structure of Guatemala, 1944–1966.* Austin: University of Texas Press.

Leeds, Anthony, 1965. "Brazilian Careers and Social Structure: a Case History and Model," in *Contemporary Cultures and Societies of Latin America* (ed. by D. B. Heath and R. N. Adams), pp. 379–404. New York: Random House.

Steward, Julian, 1955. *The Theory of Culture Change.* Urbana: University of Illinois Press.

Watson, William, 1964. "Social Mobility and Social Class in Industrial Communities," in *Closed Systems and Open Minds* (ed. by Max Gluckman), pp. 129–157. Chicago: Aldine.

Weber, Max, 1964. *The Theory of Economic and Social Organization* (trans. by A. M. Henderson and Talcott Parsons. Ed. with an introduction by Talcott Parsons). Glencoe, Ill.: The Free Press.

Wolf, Eric, 1956. "Aspects of Group Relations in a Complex Society: Mexico," *American Anthropologist* 58:1065–1078.

———,1967. "Levels of Communal Relations," in *Handbook of Middle American Indians* (R. Wauchope, general ed., and M. Nash, vol. ed.), vol. 6, pp. 299–316. Austin: University of Texas Press.

17

Social Inequality in Oaxaca

Arthur D. Murphy and Alex Stepick

The colonial city of Oaxaca, an urban center of approximately 350,000, is situated approximately 200 miles south of Mexico City. Since the early 1970s anthropologists Murphy and Stepick have been studying the city's social class system. The following contribution examines the lives and survival strategies of two families representing very different socio-economic backgrounds.

In this chapter we present the life history of a household in two different income groups in Oaxaca, Mexico. These life histories typify the dynamic strategies Oaxacans employ to cope with their changing environment. While these life histories serve as the culmination of our description of the city, in our personal experience they provided the inspiration and final reference for our work. As anthropologists, fundamental social reality lies for us in the concrete struggles and joys of individuals and families. María Teresa, her daughter Elodia, and Abel, as well as others, have been our teachers in the field. In many ways watching them over time helped us develop the ideas we present here. Their range of incomes is great, and they are unlikely to meet on an informal social level, but these families exemplify the common bond among all households in an intermediate Mexican city: one must struggle to survive. The interviews for these life histories were conducted in the late 1970s, after Oaxaca had begun to suffer the economic shocks from the 1976 devaluations. In a few cases we added information to update them to the 1980s economic jolt. Each life history begins with a description of the family's house and then discusses migration, employment, the dynamics of family and household structure, gender relations, and political involvement.

From Arthur D. Murphy and Alex Stepick, *Social Inequality in Oaxaca,* Philadelphia, PA: Temple University Press, 1991, pps. 171–180, 201–208. Reprinted by permission of Temple University Press.

MARÍA TERESA AND ELODIA: A VERY POOR HOUSEHOLD

María Teresa and her daughter Elodia are residents of one of the mid-1960s squatter settlements. Our focus on them admittedly violates our definition of

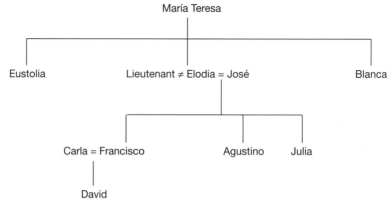

Kinship diagram—María Teresa and Elodia

households as cohabiting individuals. Although María Teresa lived for an extended period with her daughter, Elodia, she has since moved to the house of one of her other daughters, Eustolia. We nevertheless consider them together because they illustrate the struggles of a female-headed household and the daughter's transition to a traditional nuclear-family household. As in the three other cases presented in this chapter, mother and daughter are migrants to the city. Theirs is a clear example of the "push factor" in migration: the death of a parent early in María Teresa's life left her in the care of grandparents. While she claims life was not hard in the village, her grandmother clearly felt it necessary to push María Teresa into an early marriage rather than invest time in education, which in the grandmother's eyes could only have a negative payoff.

This story also demonstrates the link between urban wages and rural villages. Although María Teresa insists life was easier when she was a young woman, she was forced to send her two daughters to work in Oaxaca City to help support the family back in the village. This decision is a version of a strategy common to many Mexican households and reflected in the second life history, that of Samuel: sending family members to the United States in hope of receiving remittances sufficient to enable the rest of the family to remain intact in their present location (Roberts, 1973; Selby and Murphy 1982). Throughout María Teresa's and Elodia's story, one is struck by the strength of character and will in these two women who, despite tremendous hardship and obstacles, continue to struggle for the future of their children.

María Teresa's and Elodia's family participated in the massive squatter invasion [in 1975] that produced Colonia Santa Rosa. Elodia's son, Francisco, was part of the first wave of invaders. While Elodia and her mother continued living above the invasion in Colonia Benito Juarez, they did travel down the hill to the invasion site to attend the organizational meetings with the invaders. The rhetoric and arguments of the student organizers convinced them of the justice of the invasion and their right to land and services. Later, when the government decided to build a site-and-services project in response to the invasion, both mother and daughter were selected in the lottery for new lots. María Teresa has now moved to that project, where she lives with her other daughter, Eustolia. Elodia and her family remain in Colonia Benito Juarez, not because they prefer it to the site-and-services project, but because they have not been able to purchase materials to begin building there.

Elodia's lot in Colonia Benito Juarez has a couple of trees that provide some shade from the usually hot afternoon sun. Typically the family keeps a few chickens, which run freely through the lot and frequently out into other parts of the neighborhood. The house, a single room about three by five meters (about ten by sixteen feet), is of adobe bricks with a fiberglass roof, the latter donated by INDECO after one particularly harsh rainy season. The door, made from scraps of discarded wood and metal, hangs somewhat loosely from the hinges and has no lock. A small opening in the adobe about half a meter square and covered by a particle-board shutter hinged on the inside constitutes the only window.

Inside, darkness prevails even at midday, because the one bare electric light bulb is used only in the evenings. The floor is packed dirt. Furniture consists of one bed with an old metal frame and planks supporting a thin, sagging mattress, and a kitchen table with three chairs of rough-hewn wood. On one wall is a portable metal cupboard with two sliding glass doors on the top and an open shelf in the middle. Behind the glass doors is the family's best ware, opaque glass dishes, bowls, and dinner plates. On the shelf is a plastic flower arrangement and miscellaneous important papers, such as birth certificates and school report cards. The small family altar sits atop a small table in the corner. It consists of several religious pictures of saints, some candles, a cross, and an inexpensive glass vase filled with now-dried flowers that are replaced by fresh ones on special occasions.

This is María Teresa and Elodia's story—how they explain and interpret their lives when given an opportunity to reminisce freely. María Teresa speaks first:

MARÍA TERESA: I was born in 1914 in Santa Marta Chichihualtepec, a village a little below Ejutla. When I was eight days old my mother died. My father had died a few days before. They both were killed by what was called the fever.

My grandmother raised me. Now I don't even want to remember those things. Everything was cheap; and as people from a village, we had much to eat. Whatever was in season we could eat—vegetables, nopales. We didn't have to buy things, and what we did buy was cheap. Then a peso was a lot! When we wanted to buy a piece of cloth to make a dress, with a peso we could do it—twenty-five centavos a meter, a whole dress for a peso.

We had goats, nearly a hundred. My grandmother sent me to herd the goats in the mountains. There I ate nopales, herbs, whatever there was, because when I got back to the house at night it was always very late. I just wanted to grab my blanket, lie down, and sleep.

I wanted to go to school, but my grandmother wouldn't let me. There were things to do, work to be done, and school would teach me to be lazy. I wouldn't want to do what needed to be done. But one day when the teacher came to the house to enroll students, my grandmother wasn't there, and I signed up. When the first day of class came, I said I was going to school. Oh, she was angry. She wouldn't let me go. The whole first week, she wouldn't let me go. But after a week the teacher came to find out why I hadn't come.

My grandmother said that she had not wanted me to sign up for school, but the teacher responded that I was on the list. My grandmother got angry with me and said, "Why did you put yourself on the list? Do you always do things on your own?" "No," I said, "I wanted to go to study. If I just stay with you I won't be able to learn anything. Who knows what would happen to my head?" So, I went to school for a year. I could only go for a year and study the first book. But I learned how to read and write.

Then everything in school was free. It didn't cost us anything because the government gave us the notebooks, paper, pencils, pens, ink. Everything they gave us. The teacher just said, "Here, take this and tell me when you need more." The children then were very careful. They didn't draw monkeys and things like that in their books. If you didn't do your lesson, you couldn't leave for the midday meal. You just had to stand there, quiet, with your stomach growling.

After a year in school, I left to get married. My grandmother gave me what I needed. I didn't want to leave school, but my grandmother said I should get married. On the twenty-first of June I turned thirteen, and on the twenty-second of July I got married. I barely knew my husband. He had asked my grandmother for my hand. I knew who he was, but I had never talked with him.

My husband was an orphan, too. He had been raised by his aunt and uncle, and they gave him his herd of goats. Whenever we were hungry, we could kill a goat and have a barbecue and eat cheese, too. Then goats were cheap, three pesos each. Now [the late 1970s] they're worth five hundred or six hundred pesos. Cheese was cheap, too, fifty centavos each. Now they're fifty or sixty pesos each. Things were O.K. then.

But when Eustolia was seven years old and Elodia four, and the youngest just eighteen months, my husband was killed. He had gone to a fiesta in a neighboring village. He liked to drink and got in an argument there, and they beat him. I wanted the police to do something, but we didn't have any money. My uncle advised me that if I tried to do anything, I would just make enemies and would have to leave the village to live somewhere else. "Why fight more?" he said. "You can't bring him back to life."

After my husband died, there was nothing we could do. We were all women, myself and three young daughters. We couldn't do all the work. I had to sell the land and animals in order to survive. The land we had was ejido land. It wasn't private property, but communal. We only got five hundred pesos for all of it.[1] My daughters were in school, but they had to leave to earn money. The two oldest went to Oaxaca to become domestics. There they stayed, living and working in the houses of rich people, while I stayed in the village and made tortillas for people who didn't want to make their own.

Eventually, after my daughters were grown and had families of their own, I moved to Oaxaca, too. I've lived with both Elodia and Eustolia, whichever one has more room for me. I can't work any more, but I can help out around the house. I can still wash clothes, cook, take care of the kids, and go look for firewood. Finding firewood is more difficult here in the city than it is back in the village. You have to walk sometimes for miles and miles to find abandoned wood. But I prefer tortillas made over a wood fire and *comal* to those machine-made ones.

Now I sit back and watch my grandchildren. I'm glad their life is not as difficult as mine or even their mothers'. They can go to school and at least finish elementary school. Of course, one needs more education now, but at least they have a chance. They'll never be rich. They'll never live in a fancy house nor will they ever have servants. But they have a chance, if they can finish their schooling, to suffer a little less than we have.

ELODIA: I was ten years old when my mother sent me and my sisters to Oaxaca to work. I had been in school for only a year. I worked in a house here in Oaxaca. I swept, mopped, washed, and things like that. They paid me three pesos fifty centavos a month. My sister was in another house. They paid her seven pesos a month. They treated me very badly. They were always admonishing us for not working hard enough, but they never gave us any time off. Even on Sundays we couldn't leave the house. Seven days a week we had to work. We couldn't even go to the corner store. While the family ate meat and other things, we were given only beans and tortillas. After three months both of us changed to another house where they paid us a bit more. They paid me fifteen pesos and thirty to my sister.

All this time my mother and other sister stayed back in the village. One month our money would go to them, and another month we would keep it. We worked like that for three years. Then, my sister, who was fifteen years old, said she was going to visit our mother and she would come for me on Sunday. "I'm going to see my mother, too," I said to myself. And there I was, waiting and waiting for my sister. But she didn't come. And there I was worrying about her. She said she was going to come on Sunday, but she didn't come. So I said to the woman I worked for, "I need permission to leave to go to my village because my sister said she was going to come and she hasn't come. I'm afraid something has happened to her." The señora said, "No, you can't go. She'll get here." But I wanted to go. I wanted to see my mother, too. So I left, and when I got to my village, my mother told me that my sister had left with a man. She had gone with her boyfriend. I said to myself, "Who's going to go with me to Oaxaca?" My mother said to me, "Your sister has left Oaxaca. You shouldn't go back, either. You're still young, and you shouldn't go by yourself. I worry about you a lot because you're still small. It would be better if you don't go."

So I stayed in the village with my mother and my other sister. My mother made the tortillas, and we carried the firewood and the water so she could make the tortillas. But life was hard in the village. We couldn't survive. Eustolia and her husband had moved to Ocotlán, and her husband said all of us could come and live with them. So we moved to Ocotlán (thirty minutes south of Oaxaca City by car), and we lived there eight years. There we made *empanadas* to sell at the Estrella del Valle bus station. Times were pretty good then. Although we sold the *empanadas* for only twenty centavos each, we sold a lot of them, and everything was cheap. Life was better in Ocotlán than back in the village. Sometimes we would drink milk and have meat for breakfast.

There was a lieutenant there who wanted to marry me. I was only thirteen years old, and he was about thirty. But he wanted to marry me, and he spoke to my mother and my mother said to me, "Why don't you want to get married?" And I replied that I was too young. I hadn't thought about marriage. Later the lieutenant died. I never wanted to marry. But when I was twenty-one, I met the father of my children, José. We lived together. But then I was older, twenty-one.

He took me to the lowlands, to the coffee *fin-*

cas where we worked for a while. He and others picked coffee, and I helped them. Things were pretty good there. It's sort of like being in a village. One doesn't have to buy wood for cooking. If you want to have a little coffee, you don't have to buy coffee. It's just lying there on the ground, and the bosses said we could just pick it up if we wanted to use it. There was no mill, so we ground it ourselves with a hand grinder. I used to get up at five in the morning to grind four or five kilos each day.

We didn't really suffer there. Not like back in my village. They gave a little piece of land to us to grow things on, and it was very productive. The corn ripened in August, and there was enough to sell.

A while later the cotton harvesting began, and the same *patrón* took us to where the cotton plantations were. He took us in a truck, and we didn't have to pay. Where the cotton was, there was a lot of fruit, too—avocados, bananas. We didn't suffer. Whenever we were short of anything, we just made a list and gave it to the *patrón,* and he would bring it to us. We were never able to save anything. We had to spend everything we had, but we always had something to eat. Food was very cheap. Whenever we had to buy meals, it was only five pesos for all three meals.

But eventually, we came back to Oaxaca. The *patrón* told us there was no more work and took the little piece of land away from us. We came to where my mother lives in Oaxaca City.

When I got here, I said to my mother I was going to work. My husband had not worked in Oaxaca before, and it's hard to find work without having *conocidos* to help. He does somewhat better now, but still there are times when he can't find work. Even when he does work, the pay of a peon is not enough for a family. So I had to work, and I went to look up a comadre I have over in the Colonia Alemán, and I went to work for her. And my husband began working as a construction worker. After some months my comadre said she was going to Mexico [City] and, if I wanted to continue working, I could go with her to Mexico. But I had my children here in Oaxaca. I have three, two boys and a girl, Francisco, Agustino, and Julia. I couldn't go to Mexico. So I went to another comadre. These others were good people. I didn't suffer because I didn't have to work that hard. I just had one room and the kitchen to clean, and I

had to go to the market and buy things and make the food. The woman didn't have much to do, and she treated me well.

But my daughter, Julia, was getting older, and my mother didn't want to take care of her all the time. So I had to leave that job and begin doing day work so I could take my daughter with me. That was harder, because lots of people don't like you to bring your children along.

Finally, I decided to try something else. I decided to look for clothes I could sell. I knew someone who did that, and I asked her if she could give me some of her clothes and I would sell them. So I went door to door selling clothes—usually here in the valley, or even in this colonia. But sometimes I would go way out into the country, like back to my village and other villages. But I didn't like traveling that far in those places, and they like to barter. Rather than giving you money, they give avocados, beans, squash, or peas—something like that. Many times I would trade for those things and bring them here and sell them and keep some to eat for my family.

But then as the kids started growing, I couldn't afford to leave the house so much. I had to stay here to take care of them. I have to worry about what's going to happen to them now. I want them to get as much education as possible. It's only by way of education that one can get ahead.

We still don't have enough really to save and get ahead. We don't have any skill or training that will allow us to get ahead, to get a steady job. When there's work, my husband works; but when there's not, he doesn't. Then we have to ask for a loan from someone. Then when there's work, we're working to pay back the loan.

That's why I want my children to go to school. Here in the city there are schools. Back in the village there aren't any schools, and the children suffer. They don't have much chance of preparing themselves. Here, even the poorest can go to secondary school. I would like them to learn a business or at least be teachers so they won't suffer. I don't want them to have to move all over like I had to do in search of work. I don't want them to have to work for others like I did, work for rich people who mistreat you and then fire you when you speak up for your rights. I wish I could go back to school, be young again, so I could learn a trade that would make me rich. I wonder what kind of work I would have been able to get if I had kept on going to school. I think I could have become a teacher.

I have one child, Agustino, who is like I was. He's very restless, but he doesn't forget things. The others are more forgetful. Francisco, the oldest, dropped out after finishing elementary school. I wish he could have continued, but he wanted to work, to earn some money. Now he's a construction worker like his father. His father helps him find work; so it's not as difficult for Francisco as it was for my husband when he first started working in Oaxaca. He's got his own wife, Carla, already started a family, one son, David. I'm a grandmother.

They lived with us for awhile, but that didn't work out very well. We have only one room and it was a bit crowded, so he found a place to rent in another neighborhood. But it doesn't look like he's going to be any better off than we are. Even though he finished elementary school, it's not enough anymore. You need secondary or even preparatory nowadays, and the poor can't afford to send all their kids to school forever.

My daughter, Julia, she's in the secondary school studying to be a secretary and working, too. She works as a clerk in a store downtown. She works hard because the señora doesn't have any other employees. But she still has a lot to learn. They are only paying her two hundred pesos [\$10 U.S. in 1977] a week. When she gets enough experience, she can look for work somewhere else. I just hope she can finish school and learn a trade. But it's hard now. Every time you turn around the schools are asking for money—money for this, money for that. Who knows what for? And there goes the money. There's not enough to go around, and it's hard to keep the children in school, especially the girls— they almost never finish. I don't know if Julia will make it or not.

But I have hopes for Agustino. I think he may not have to suffer as much as we have. But he will have to work. The poor always have to struggle for everything. No one gives us anything. Look at our housing problems. In the village, everyone has a place to live, but here in the city there aren't any places. You have to pay for everything, and they don't pay you enough to afford it. That's why we have to fight for our housing. We took part in the squatters' invasion in 1975, the one where thousands invaded and the army came and pushed us out. The government was against us all the way, but the students helped. They organized us and kept the pressure on the government. The capitalists were against us and forced the government to kick us off the land. But we workers have to stick together and fight them. With the students' help we were able to do that. We got this new colonia, Santa Rosa, because we stuck together and didn't give in. Once the government said they would build the colonia, they still dragged their feet and didn't deliver. But we kept up the pressure and finally got out colonia. But even then we couldn't stop. We had to keep up the pressure to get our services, to get the water, electricity, and school that had been promised. If we stick together, then we can get something out of the government. Otherwise they don't give the poor anything. They just ignore us.

María Teresa and Elodia have battled continuously against the ravages of poverty. The tragic death of María Teresa's husband dissolved her economic base, producing and reinforcing poverty while revealing the absence of economic opportunities for female-headed households in rural Oaxaca. María Teresa's husband's land was communal land, which is legally controlled by the community, but she was able to sell the rights to use it, although at lower than normal market price. The push from rural roots initiated a persistent family and household dynamic structure as individual members migrated to and from the city, between various rural locations, and in and out of particular households. For both generations, María Teresa and Elodia, working conditions have been harsh and remuneration minimal. The conditions of domestic child labor confronted by Elodia can only be described as superexploitation. While she made no mention of the sexual abuse or beatings frequently mentioned by others, she clearly suffered.

Oaxaca's contemporary reintegration with the nation has brought little noticeable improvements for this family. Their gender and lack of skills have excluded them from the emerging formal sector. They must rely solely upon their family and informal social networks. When in need of work, they look first to comadres and friends.

In spite of this domestic flux and struggle, firm family ties have endured. María Teresa's and Elodia's family has been and remains the primary institution in their lives. One of the primary adaptive responses of the very poor is to maintain small households. María Teresa and Elodia each had only three children and everyone moved in and out of households in search of employment and to keep expenses as low as possible. Reintegration has materially affected them first in a way they only indirectly realize. María Teresa fondly recalls her youth as a time when everything was cheap and she did not need to struggle so strenuously and ceaselessly. Nevertheless, she is materially somewhat better off now than she or her grandparents were. The number of consumer items in her life has increased: María Teresa's housing is somewhat better in the government site-and-services project, which has more readily available water and electricity. The family has a radio. Others in their class have television sets and, a few, a gas stove. Yet, as we shall see from the other life histories, María Teresa's and Elodia's material well-being has not improved as much as others in Oaxaca. A refrigerator is unlikely for anyone in this income group; a car, impossible.

The most obvious impact of reintegration upon this family is in politics and housing. The 1975 squatter invasion permeated their lives and consciousness. They not only participated in the invasion and subsequently received lots from the federal agency involved, but they henceforth articulated a radical critique of their own conditions and society. This vision, however, is limited by structural realities. They did obtain a lot with services much more quickly than other colonias populares, but the government's violent suppression of the student movement deterred them from expanding their political battles into, for example, the area of employment. The other consequence of reintegration is ideological but less radical. The hopes of these women for a better life reside primarily in their children, and their faith in education is impressively strong. The descriptions of the very poor in the previous chapter, however, reveal the limits of that hope. Elodia's children have already confronted rising credentialism. They have more schooling than their mother, but her eldest is only an unskilled construction worker and her daughter is a store clerk. The poor recognize that despite a strong will to succeed, they and their children have a limited future. We have witnessed many others who begin working while still completing their studies. Despite the ideals expressed concerning education, for many young people among the poor, work and family become greater commitments than finishing school.

Abel is the youngest member of one of the city's wealthier families, a family typifying Oaxaca's most recent manifestation of an externally oriented elite. Unlike the locally oriented elite, he does not have family roots in the area's Spanish colonial past or the old commercial elite class. Rather, his father was a skilled technician who anticipated Mexico's post–World War II expansion. He moved from rural Oaxaca to the city to provide an education for his sons and thus prepare them for the new era. He saw to it that his sons were ready to take advantage of Mexico's growth when it did occur.

One of Abel's brothers is a medical doctor; one, a civil engineer; another was a captain in the military and now runs a business in Oaxaca; Abel runs an automobile service station that serves the external transportation business in both the public and private sectors.

Abel's living conditions reflect the success of his business. He recently moved to a new home in the northern part of the city. The house, started but not completed by one of the city's physicians, is a typical example of new upper-middle-class and elite housing in the city. It fronts the street with imposing wooden doors to the garage and front entrance. The garage has two cars, each less than five years old: a Dodge sedan for his wife and a Jeep Wagoneer for himself. Inside the house there is a large kitchen, living room, dining room, family room, and patio. Upstairs there are four bedrooms (even though Abel's children live out of the city) and two baths. Flooring is either wood or polished concrete with new, coordinated furnishings in every room, including a stereo system and the latest kitchen appliances. The living area is dominated by a large china cabinet where Abel and his wife display the gifts they have received at special times in their life cycle, for example, their wedding and the baptisms of their children. Abel is particularly happy about the fact that he is on the same water system as the government's INFONAVIT development and therefore will have fewer water problems than friends who live farther into the heart of Oaxaca.

Abel enjoys the fruits of success. He is a frequent vacationer at the beach resorts of Mexico and during the late 1970s boom he paid cash for a second home in one of the fastest growing university cities of the south-western United States. The house, a three-bedroom tract dwelling in a suburb of the city, is currently being used by his children as they attend college. It is Abel's inten-

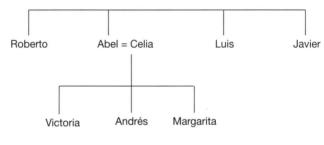

Kinship diagram—Abel

tion to retire there when he gives up his current business.

ABEL: I was born in the city of Oaxaca in October 1928, approximately one year after my father came down from the northern mountains in order to educate the family. My father was a mechanic, or what today would be an engineer, working for one of the mining companies in the mountains. At that time, there were only four years of school in those places, and my father had to educate himself using a correspondence course from the United States. He decided to bring the family to Oaxaca in order to make it possible for us all to get a better education.

When we came down there were four children—all of them boys. About a year after they came down, I was born here, over on the street of Morelos where we were living at the time. When I was growing up, my father had to travel a lot in order to do his work. He went back to the mountains for a while, and after spending a few years there, he went to Taxco to work in the mines. He was there for ten years. Then after that, he went up to work in Durango for another ten years, and then he went to Chihuahua to work for five more years. But by then his lungs were giving out, because in those days they didn't use any kind of breathing devices or filters. And so my father, who had been a very strong man, came back to Oaxaca a weak and disabled man.

He did all that work in order to educate us kids so that we could do well in life. One of my brothers is now a doctor up in Guerrero and another is a civil engineer. My other brother was a pilot and captain in the military for several years and is now back in Oaxaca and has his own business. I was also studying medicine. In Mexico City, I went through two years of preparatory school in the med-

ical program, but my marks weren't very good or not as good as my other brother. I was also the youngest. So my parents decided that since they probably couldn't afford to send everybody to school, and since my marks were the lowest, that my other brother would stay in school.

So I came back to Oaxaca in 1951 and went back to work at the service station up on García Vigil Street. I worked real hard, and the owner and I got along really well. I was his right-hand man. But then one day the owner was killed in an automobile accident. That was about 1953. And shortly thereafter, his family and his children told me they wanted me to turn over the shop to them. So I cleared up all the paper work and turned it over to them.

I then went to work for another gasoline station. All that time—or I should say, we—were saving money to buy land to open our own service station. I had gotten married in October 1952. My wife, Celia, and I both worked and saved. Celia is also from Oaxaca and she has worked as hard as I have at getting our business going. We didn't have any children during that time. Then, because of people I met while running the first service station, in 1957 we bought this land here, where the service station is, right by the highway. We then worked for another two years to buy the things we needed to put in—an automobile lift and a lubrication pit—so we could begin work. In 1957 when we bought the land, it cost us thirty-five thousand pesos, and to put in the lift and the basic things we needed to be in business cost another twelve thousand pesos. All in all, it took about fifty thousand pesos to get started here. But we had saved, and we got some help from my family.

That's one of the things you find even today in Oaxaca. You find that the people who come from the outside are the ones who do most of the investing and are making this city grow. The old families of Oaxaca, or the Spaniards as we call them around here, don't really invest much. They save their money and put it in banks and let the banks do the investing for them. They don't want to take risks. That's one of the problems we have in Oaxaca. If the city is going to advance, we need some people here who are willing to invest their money and take risks—not silly risks, but calculated risks—things like the plastic container factory over by Tule or the plant to build the trailers out by Ocotlán. That trailer plant is part of a Mexico City firm, but it was started by Oaxaca money. It builds commercial trailers, everything from flatbeds to semis. It's a small plant by Mexico City standards. It employs somewhat less than two hundred workers, but that's very big and important here in Oaxaca. And it's been a big success for those who invested in it. That and the plastic factory are rather risky businesses, since they have to bring all the material down and transport the finished product out. But those people are making good money right now. You know, we don't even have our own eggs in Oaxaca. We have to import all those from Tehuacan. Why doesn't somebody open up a major egg-producing plant? It's hard to understand sometimes.

Celia and I, we don't have any of our money that isn't invested. It's all working in something, and very little of it is in the bank. If you look around, you'll find that the old families and the Spanish families who came in the mid 1930s own all the land and a lot of the commercial establishments, but nothing productive—nothing that brings in new money from the outside.

Anyway, Celia and I opened this business in 1959 with ourselves and two helpers. Today we have eight. My wife has worked here with me the whole time. A year after we opened up, our first child was born. That was Victoria, in 1960. A year later Andrés was born. Our third child, Margarita, was born in 1962. They're all just a little over a year apart. We planned our family, because we knew we had to save, and we couldn't afford to take care of them while we were getting the business started. Then we decided three was plenty, because we wanted to raise them and educate them well, and we didn't think that if we had more we would be able to do it. My brother who is a doctor also planned his family. He only has two children. My other brother, the pilot, has six. He's more of a macho than the rest of us. It's probably a good

thing that we haven't had any more children, because things are getting much more difficult economically now.

All of our kids have gone to the United States for at least some of their university education. We bought a house so they could all live comfortably and my wife, Celia, moved up there to be with them while they were going to school. It was kind of difficult for me to see them all leave and go to the U.S. We are a very close family, but we felt that we had to do it for economic reasons, to give the children the most opportunities.

And, even though I'm alone, I'm not really alone. I still have my brothers and their families here. We see each other every day. One of my brothers owns a tire shop right next to my station and so we see each other in the course of our work. And on the weekends we are always together. That's one of the things about Mexican families. They always stick together. Eat together, play together, have fun together. If it weren't for my family, I would be nowhere. Our father sacrificed so that we would get a good education and after that we each help each other out. My brothers helped me put the money together to get this business started and they helped me pay for the house in the United States. And, I, of course, help them when they need it.

All three of our children are in the United States now. The eldest, Victoria, was studying hotel management. She married a gringo and now she's a reservations manager in a Hyatt. The youngest, Margarita, is also in the United States studying to be a travel agent. Andrés is in the United States studying mechanics. He wants to open up his own service station, and we'll probably help him do that. But he's not going to do it here. He's going to Guadalajara, because he wants to open up a specialized shop, and you can't do that in Oaxaca. If you opened up a specialized shop in Oaxaca, you'd go broke, because there aren't enough cars. Andrés will have a much more difficult time opening his shop than I did. He'll probably need at least a million pesos to get his shop open.

We used to do much better than we do now, especially with the tourists. I used to be able to put together two to three hundred dollars a week, in dollars, from what I would bring in here from the automobile tourists who came through. But now it's much different. I'm lucky if I get a hundred dollars in U.S. dollars a month. What's happened is that the whole tourist industry has changed in Oaxaca. It used to be that we would get people coming down in their automobiles traveling around. But with the new emphasis on foreign tourists coming by airplane to the big hotels on package tours, we just don't get the kind of business we once did. It's good for the big hotel chains, but it doesn't do us medium-sized merchants very much good. That's one reason my son wants to open up his shop in Guadalajara.

Now Victoria, we may open our own hotel for her when she comes back. But we'll have to see how that goes—see how tourism is gong in Oaxaca at the time and decide whether we want to invest in that. Tourism is a real problem here, because the people in Oaxaca are not used to dealing with outsiders. They still really don't know how to run good tourist facilities. You compare the best hotels in Oaxaca with the best hotels in Cancún, for example. In Cancún they're no more expensive than in Oaxaca, but they treat you a whole lot better. Margarita will have her own travel agency here in the city, because the travel agencies are going well, and we've been here long enough to have enough connections to help them.

But it's going to be tough, because things are getting much more expensive here in Oaxaca. Oaxaca is a really expensive city to live in. I travel a lot, and I can tell you that it's much more expensive in Oaxaca than in other places—even like Mexico City or Cancún, especially for the traveler. And that's one of the problems in Oaxaca. They're trying to make too much quick money off the tourist and not taking care of long-term trends.

However, I think my kids will do fine, because we've been able to educate them very well, and they've been able to go to the United States and learn English, and they interact very well with North Americans, which, if they're going to live in Oaxaca and make any money, they're going to have to do.

But we're going to have problems right here in Oaxaca because things are getting much more expensive, and most people are not willing—or can't—raise the wages of the workers as fast as prices are going up. The only solution is for the owners of establishments to make a little less money. And that would be all right, except that you don't see the government or anybody in the big establishments doing the same thing, and they're just causing the prices to keep going up and up faster and faster. At some point there's going to be a problem here, and I don't know when it's going to be. But I hope my children are well established so that they can take care of it when it comes.

Abel has benefited from Oaxcaca's reintegration with the broader economy. As a mechanical engineer working for a mining company, Abel's father used his income and status to send his children to school in Mexico City. Abel and his brothers obtained much more education than María Teresa or Elodia, although Abel admits that he was not a particularly distinguished student. The intrafamily cooperation, along with Oaxaca's reintegration, allowed Abel to benefit from his brother's education and turned him into a highly successful businessman.

Much like the small business person of North American legend, Abel feels he has pulled himself up by his bootstraps. His reconstruction of his own history tends to ignore a number of critical factors. Although he acknowledges that his family contributed to the capital that started the business, his brother helped by seeing to it that Abel got important contracts taking care of trucks for the ministry of tourism and the state police vehicles. His contacts with prominent Oaxacans, at least partially a result of family ties, provided him with the opportunity to purchase the propitious site for his business. And he was certainly much luckier in the timing of his business venture, which coincided with Oaxaca's reintegration with the national and international economies, than Alfonso had been with his weaving enterprise. Most important among all these factors was the location of the business. Situated on the Pan American Highway near two of the larger tourist hotels, he had ready access to Mexican and North American traffic when tourists started driving to Oaxaca in great numbers. In addition, the experience of his father working for a North American mining firm gave Abel some inkling as to how North Americans like to see such service businesses run. He was there when the market opened and provided a service the clients recognized as similar to what they were used to back home. The result was a steady flow of U.S. dollars into Abel's hands.

Abel's experience with and benefits from Oaxaca's reintegration have oriented him to a much broader world. The profits from the business made it possible for him to purchase his house in the United States and send his children there to school. He also anticipates helping his son establish a business in a city, Guadalajara, that is more integrated with the national and international economies than is Oaxaca. Abel's experiences have also taught him the limits of integration. He recognizes that the more Oaxaca becomes integrated, the easier it is for large-scale, Mexico City capital to displace people like him. Air transport has already begun to dislodge him indirectly since fewer tourists come in cars. His experiences are reminiscent of what happened to local traditional artisans displaced by the importation of modern mass goods via the Pan American Highway.

Abel's household composition has been the most consistently nuclear of any of the families. He also explicitly gives credit to his wife in contributing her labor to the success of his business. They also delayed having their family in order to build resources. When he and his wife subsequently had children, they stopped at three. Yet, as already observed, the extended family's economic importance has not declined. While the household may be small, the extended family of all three brothers' nuclear families remains the most important social unit.

Abel appears to engage in the least political activity of anyone we have discussed. He has apparently stayed out of public life and done well. Yet, this impression is deceiving. His older brother, Roberto, fulfills the family's political needs. Roberto attended Mexico City's polytechnic university and became a civil engineer. He worked for several years on the construction of the metro system in Mexico City, after which he returned to Oaxaca as the director of a federal agency's state office. When a new federal administration came to power, Roberto left that post and started a private construction business. Roberto's capital came from some family friends who were officers in one of the branches of a national bank that had recently moved to the city. His first contracts were for public works contracted by a bureaucrat who had been

his friend when Roberto held a public office. The construction business did well and Roberto became one of the technical advisers to the state office of the PRI. He helped Abel obtain contracts to service the trucks and automobiles of government agencies. Roberto is now in the process of refocusing his construction company. He believes the Oaxaca market is virtually saturated, and that the new opportunities are on the coast where a new highway and improved air links have opened the area to tourism. Roberto's ties with the government will provide him with the inside track when exploiting this new market.

Both men see the husbanding of resources in anticipation of future opportunities as an important quality present in the new Oaxacan entrepreneurial class, but lacking, they believe, in the old, locally oriented elite families. This may be ideological self-justification and their opinions are undoubtedly tempered by the 1980s economic calamity. In the midst of crisis, they must struggle to maintain what is a developed nation's middleclass lifestyle. Nevertheless, within Oaxaca they are undeniably much better off than anyone in the income groups below them and even in crisis they are unlikely to forfeit that advantage.

NOTES

1. Dennis 1987:39–42 described typical land tenure patterns in Oaxaca.

BIBLIOGRAPHY

Dennis, Phillip A., 1987. *Intervillage Conflict in Oaxaca.* New Brunswick, NJ: Rutgers University Press.
Roberts, Bryan, 1973. *Organizing Strangers.* Austin: University of Texas Press.
Selby, Henry A. and Arthur D. Murphy, 1982. *The Mexican Urban Household and the Decision to Migrate to the United States.* ISHI Occasional Papers in Social Change, No. 4. Philadelphia: Institute for the Study of Human Issues.

18

Aspects of Power Distribution in Costa Rica

Samuel Stone

The most important factor in the economic development of Costa Rica has been coffee cultivation. This activity was first undertaken on a large scale by a small group of planters shortly after Independence from Spain in 1821. By mid-century their entrepreneurial ability had stimulated progress to a degree where the country emerged from having been the most miserable economic quagmire on the continent to a position of prosperity far surpassing the other nations of the Central American isthmus. Coffee has allowed subsequent growth to a point ranking high on any scale designed to measure economic development in Latin America.[1]

Tracing the ancestries of the first members of this planter group to the beginning of the Spanish Conquest makes it evident that they were descended from a colonial political and economic elite; following their lines of descent into the twentieth century reveals a significant portion of those who have occupied political posts even to this day. In fact the ascending and descending lines of consanguinity and affinity among the planters from the beginning of the colonial period to the present reveal a political class[2] whose members have exercised the functions of government in the executive, legislative, and judicial branches to a far greater extent than any other group in Costa Rican society.

The foregoing gives rise to a number of questions. One of these concerns the circumstances which permitted the class to survive the transition from colony to independent republic without losing its dominant position. Another has to do with the basis of power during the various stages of the nation's social evolution. A third and more general problem is the relationship between political power and economic preponderance in Costa Rica. The continuing importance of coffee in the economy, however, leads to the more immediate issues surrounding the role of the planters in society today and poses an important question regarding the present status of the political class within the national social structure.

Samuel Stone, "Aspects of Power Distribution in Costa Rica," pp. 404–421. Reprinted by permission of Waveland Press, Inc. from D. Heath (ed.), *Contemporary Cultures & Societies of Latin America: A Reader in the Social Anthropology of Middle and South America, 2E.* (Prospect Heights, IL: Waveland Press, Inc., 1974 [revised 1988]). All rights reserved.

The following pages attempt to provide an insight into this aspect of Costa Rican society through an examination of the relationship between kinship and political power. The method used is that of a genealogical analysis; the subjects are the presidents and congressmen, a significant portion of whom appear in the lineage of a few important families who settled in Costa Rica during the first century following the Spanish Conquest. The lines of consanguinity and affinity among the descendants of those six "first families" are presented within the context of the social setting in which their class emerged and developed. While this approach is useful in casting light on the emergence of the planter group from the class after Independence, its greatest value lies in discovering the significance of the many divisions which have been taking place within the ranks of the class during the nineteenth and twentieth centuries. This in turn allows the formulation of a hypothesis concerning the structure of modern national society.

THE SPANISH CROWN AND THE BIRTH OF THE POLITICAL CLASS

During the sixteenth and seventeenth centuries Spain created a pattern of power distribution which still continues to determine the nature of Costa Rican politics. It reserved access to political posts to *Conquistadores* and *hidalgos* (nobles),[3] thus giving control of the province to a small group of families by virtue of their descent. This monopoly of power, enhanced in many instances by wealth, enabled the elite also to monopolize cacao cultivation, the most profitable activity of the colonial period. The group stood in contrast with the rest of the population, which subsisted on a primitive type of agriculture.

Two factors account for the organization of an almost exclusively agricultural economy. At the same time, they help explain the presence of a population consisting primarily of small farmers under the political tutelage of a landed gentry instead of ambitious and avaricious fortune-seekers such as existed in many other parts of Latin America. One of these factors was the absence of sufficient Indians to constitute an important labor force. This consideration alone seriously limited the scale of any type of activity and practically restricted the choice

to agriculture. As a result, a majority of the settlers, who had been attracted (principally from the working classes of Andalucia[4]) by the idea of becoming landowners under special incentives offered by the Crown during the seventeenth century, had arrived with the intention of working their newly acquired lands by themselves. The other factor was the scarcity of gold, which not only ruled out mining but also had the effect of attracting farmers of both noble and plebian stock instead of ambitious adventurers. Even before undertaking the journey to Costa Rica, all the settlers had known that the province of their choice offered neither glory nor riches.

This evokes an irony of history arising from the origin of the name of Costa Rica. On his fourth voyage, Columbus discovered the area which actually comprises the northeastern section of Panama and southeastern Costa Rica. Upon seeing the natives' display of golden objects his dreams were fulfilled and he baptized his paradise with the name of Veragua. People thus came to talk of the entire east coast of the Isthmus as the *costa rica*—the rich coast—of Veragua,[5] until it became necessary to distinguish the region which forms the present Republic of Costa Rica from the territory of Veragua claimed by the Admiral's heirs.[6] In reality, the riches of meridional Central America are still part of Columbian mythology. Early in the Conquest the legend of the *costa rica* attracted a few ambitious Spaniards, but they soon left and in their footsteps followed the farmer.

The elite continued as a small group of closely related families during the colonial period, inheriting power from generation to generation. Its predominance was greatly facilitated by the small size of the society[7] and by the isolation of the territory. Approximately three months were required to travel by horse from Costa Rica to Guatemala, the seat of its colonial government. The effect of such isolation on the population can be appreciated by considering that the bishop in charge of the province, who resided in Nicaragua, was able to pay only 11 visits to the unfortunate territory between 1607 and 1815, the intervals between visits ranging up to 33 years.[8] Such seclusion kept the inhabitants unaware of social and political trends which in other parts of the isthmus defied the positions of ruling classes.

By the eighteenth century the policies of the Crown and Guatemala had resulted in complete economic stagnation to the point where even cacao had to be abandoned. The Church and piracy are also to be blamed. The *hidalguía*, or elite, while retaining its political power, was forced to lower its standard of living, thus leading to a discrepancy between its modest manner of life and its high social and political rank. Even governors had to work their own land.By Independence, this economic leveling had favored an approaching of the social categories to a point where society presented a notably equalitarian aspect. The elite was there, however, and thanks to its political power would soon become the motor of economic expansion, finding its fuel in coffee. The group was to become, after Independence, that of the coffee planters.

The considerations have an important bearing on modern national society. The resulting land distribution into small parcels has been closely related to political stability. For lack of Indians to convert, the territory had a small clergy. It is not by coincidence that the Church has never been the focal point of violent political struggles as in other parts of the continent. For lack of Indians to conquer, the province never had a significant army (which may in part account for the continued absence of enthusiasm for the military). Finally, there could never have existed feudal structures such as the ones that developed in other parts of Central America where there were large autochthonous populations—powerful aristocracies, equally powerful clergies, classes of functionaries, and the like. The simple needs of a simple society never even gave rise to a class of artisans in colonial Costa Rica.

EMERGENCE OF THE ENTREPRENEURIAL PLANTER GROUP

In 1821, with Independence, the colonial political class inherited the leadership of the new nation and began to concentrate on finding an activity which would allow its members to raise their standard of living to a level in keeping with their political and social positions.[9] Among the many agricultural products tried was coffee. This had been cultivated since the first half of the eighteenth century but, as with other crops, the absence of an accessible market had limited production to an almost insignificant scale. An opportunity came in 1833 when a German immigrant was able to effect a small shipment

to Chile,[10] thus allowing many to foresee the possibility of further exports. Land was taken by assault and many members of the class took advantage of their positions of power to acquire the best areas of the fertile central plateau. Costa Rica, however, was on no important trade route, nor was it a regular port of call, and for these reasons exports could not be relied upon. Furthermore, coffee was processed in Chile and shipped to Europe, where it was sold as Chilean coffee at prices which appeared exorbitantly high to the Costa Rican planters. The disillusionment brought on by their not having direct access to European markets was aggravated by being obliged to work through intermediaries. The group therefore began to neglect cultivation until, quite by chance, a British shipowner gave them direct access to the English market in 1845.[11]

From this time on, national society began to undergo a transformation. The first exports had been financed by the wealthier planter families; but, as the volume of business increased following the opening of the London market, these sought credit in England on future crops. This accentuated the division of labor between modest coffee farmers from the lower social category and the growing export planters from the political class. The latter, by negotiating the sale of their own crops as well as coffee purchased from the former, soon came to control the situation. A new social category arose when partnerships of export planters began offering credit to small producers. When these could not meet their obligations their lands went to their creditors, thus giving birth to the large plantation as well as to the social class of peons, or former landed peasants who had lost their holdings.[12] The small property disappeared only in terms relative to the colonial agrarian structure, however, for the great majority of landowners continued to be humble farmers. The large plantation in Costa Rica was (and still is) quite small by comparison with large properties in other parts of Latin America. It never developed beyond certain limits because of the markedly limited supply of capital and labor.

The coffee complex that developed in this way around the elite export planter consisted of a small independent farmer and a laboring class of peons, with a strong interdependence between them. On the one hand, the success of the enterprise was subject to the productivity of the peon, and this to the paternalistic rapport which the planter could maintain with his scanty labor force. If the peon depended on the planter for his salary and home, the planter depended on the peon for good production, which was the basis of both his wealth and his prestige within his own class. The relationships which developed between the two as a result of this mutual dependence reflected the society's equalitarian values that remained from the colonial experience. All the events around which contact between them took place were of a social nature and revealed a reciprocal respect which could not have developed between similar counterparts in societies with feudal traditions. Just as the small planter depended on the export planter for the sale of his coffee, the latter depended on the former for quality.

This interdependence can still be seen in the processing system and in production financing, which at different times for over a century has come from foreign, private, and nationalized sources with no significant alterations in form. The complex was well integrated, but the traditional aspects which allowed it to function were not compatible with the concept of modernization or with that of balanced development. One of the consequences of this was monoculture, which became increasingly acute because of the high profitability of coffee. Exports soon raised the economic position of the planters, however, and the entire society was able to emerge from the stagnation which it had known since the end of the eighteenth century. The planters made possible this important first step in the economic development of Costa Rica.

The transition from colony to independent nation, then, saw a change in the type of production with no alteration in the political and administrative organization. This experience, rare in Latin America, was similar to that of the Brazilian planters, an elite which survived the passage from subsistence agriculture to slave-based and then free-labor-based agriculture, to industry, and finally to finance, all because the group possessed both political power and economic means.[13]

DIVISIONS OF THE PLANTER ELITE

As coffee production furnished growing prosperity, the first planter families increased their investments. This led to rivalries among them, and the group began to divide into factions belonging to the same families but vying for political power. The twentieth century marked the arrival of several new forces for change, not the least of which was the United Fruit Company, whose effort to attract manpower to the coastal banana zones severely depleted the already inadequate coffee labor force. Many of the coffee peons, however, were unable to tolerate either the hot climate or the new relatively impersonal type of labor-management relationship with the foreign company, and they soon returned to the coffee plantations, despite the inferior salary; this wage differential became a source of resentment, nevertheless. The peons obtained a certain degree of political autonomy with the introduction of the secret ballot; in 1929 came the Depression and with it the Communist Party. These events, and a growing rate of literacy, made the peon even more aware of possibilities of change. Such awareness spread especially fast in a society with three-quarters of the population concentrated in a small area around the capital city, allowing the demonstration-effect to readily influence consumption demands. At the same time such a situation conditioned a readily accessible segment of the population for mobilization and for active participation in the political process.[14]

This situation obligated the different groups of the political class, including the coffee factions, to pay attention to the needs of the lower strata, and it was precisely for this reason that after the Depression they began to form parties concerned with reform. They committed themselves to a redistribution of wealth; and, speaking in general terms, social legislation in Costa Rica has been stimulated by practically all political tendencies since the Depression, and the personalism which predominated until World War II has begun to wane.

During the process of subdivision of the coffee elite, which began toward the middle of the nineteenth century and continues today, its factions have tended to diversify their economic activities. Coffee is still important, but its preponderant position in the national economy has made it particularly vulnerable to taxation designed to finance much of the social legislation mentioned above. In addition, with the exception of the 1970 increase in demand and price boom resulting from Brazil's temporary decrease in production, the world market has been steadily deteriorating. Planters, then, have tended to lose their dominant role in the economy. Furthermore, all groups in the political class have tended to lose power, due in part to the social legislation which has been in the process of creating a powerful government bureaucracy that is not effectively under the control of any single group.

The foregoing is a sketch of the evolution of the political class that has played a dominant role in the development of Costa Rica. The changes it has undergone are clear: during the colonial period its members were united and engaged in cacao cultivation; during the nineteenth century many of them became coffee planters but prosperity led to divisions; today they have diversified into fields including cattle, law, medicine, and the like, and are extremely divided. The power of the class, the effects of the decentralization of its influence, and the present-day significance of the class within the context of modern national society can best be appreciated, however, by tracing and analyzing the lines of descent of several important families who settled in Costa Rica during the early part of the colonial period.

FAMILIES OF THE PLANTER CLASS

Speaking in general terms, the first *Conquistador* and *hidalgo* families constituted the political class. Some were more influential than others, and money was undoubtedly a factor which contributed to enhancing status within the class. An example of an opulent *hidalgo* who settled in Costa Rica in 1659 and whose descendants have played a most important role in the political life of the country is Don Antonio de Acosta Arévalo. The presidents and the equivalent chiefs of state in his lineage are listed in Table 18–1. Nine of these presidents have held office during the twentieth century, the most recent being Mario Echandi Jiménez, president between 1958 and 1962 and candidate in 1970. A few other important families, but by no means all of them, were those of Nicolás de González y Oviedo, Juan Vázquez de Coronado, Jorge de Alvarado Contreras (brother of Pedro de Alvarado, *Conquistador* of Guatemala), Juan Solano, and Antonio Alvarez Pereira, often called Antonio Pereira. In their lines of descent are to be found many people who have occupied the presidency or the equivalent. In those of Acosta Arévalo, González y Oviedo, and Vázquez de Coronado, for example, there are 33 of the 44 presidents in the history of the Republic, with 25 descended from Acosta Arévalo alone, as can be seen in Table 18–1.

The political class can also be seen at the level of the Legislative Assembly, where fully 220 of the 1300 deputies the Republic has had since Independence are descended from Juan Vázquez de Coronado, 150 from Antonio de Acosta Arévalo, 140 from Jorge de Alvarado, and 40 from Nicolás de González y Oviedo, to mention only a few.[16] Other aspects of the class will be discussed below,

TABLE 18–1   Presidents* Descended from Don Antonio de Acosta Arévalo

Generation	Name	Generation	Name
4th	Manuel Fernández Chacón		Vincente Herrera Zeledón
	Juan Mora Fernández		José J. Rodriguez Zeledón
	Joaquín Mora Fernández		Juan Rafael Mora Porras
5th	José Maria Castro Madríz		Julio Acosta García
	Próspero Fernández Oreamuno		Aniceto Esquivel Sáenz
	J.M. Montcalegre Fernández	7th	Rafael Yglesias Castro
	Bruno Carranza Ramírez		Mario Echandi Jiménez
	Braulio Carrillo Colina		Rafael Calderón Muñóz
	Manuel Aguilar Chacón		Teodora Picado Michalski
	José R. Gallegos Alvarado		León Cortés Castro
6th	Demetrio Yglesias Llorente		Juan B. Quirós Segura
	Bernardo Soto Alfaro	8th	Rafael A. Calderón Guardia
	Federico Tinoco Granados		

*Presidents, chiefs of state, and vice-presidents or the equivalent who actually exercised the highest post of the executive branch.
Source: See note 15.

but there is a point which should be emphasized here: Only six founding families of the class have been mentioned. While these constitute an important part of the nucleus of first families from which the class developed, there were others who for obvious reasons cannot be dealt with here.

THE PLANTERS AND THE POLITICAL CLASS

The fact that the planter families emerged from the political class is reflected in the fact that about one-third of the first 100[17] were descended from Antonio de Acosta Arévalo and one-third from Juan Vázquez de Coronado; many are to be found in both lineages. These two families alone generated 51 of the first 100 planters, and practically all of the 100 can be found in the six families mentioned above. Predictably, almost three-quarters of them held important political posts just prior to the commercialization of coffee or during the first years of its boom; in fact, nine of them exercised the presidency of the Republic.

CLASS ENDOGAMY

An interesting aspect of the political class is that, in the lineages of almost any combination of an equal number of the aforementioned families, there can be found roughly the same number of presidents and deputies—who are, moreover, generally the same people. This is an indication of a high degree of class endogamy. The list of the first 100 planter families reveals an extraordinary number of marriages between members of the class, and in many instances between cousins. Endogamy can be even better appreciated at the level of the Legislative Assembly. While the four families mentioned above would appear to have generated 550 of the total 1,300 deputies in the history of the nation, marriage between their descendants has been so frequent that many are to be found in two, three, or all of these lineages. Furthermore, in many instances a single deputy descends from the same forefather through several branches. An example of this is Vázquez de Coronado, from whom 44 descend through two branches, 9 through three, and 1 through four. Such is the degree of endogamy,

in fact, that if each deputy who appears in more than one lineage or more than once in the same lineage is counted only once, the total number generated by the collectivity of the four families is only 350 rather than 550.

POWER OF THE POLITICAL CLASS

The foregoing allows an understanding of the basis of power of the political class at the level of the Legislative Assembly. By a conservative estimate, if the number of deputies descended from five or six other families were added to the 350 descended from the four families mentioned in the preceding paragraph, it would be found that nearly half of the 1,300 have been recruited from the class. The others have been people relatively unknown in the capital area and have represented families from smaller cities and rural zones, where power transmission has followed much the same pattern. There are some instances of kin ties, consanguineal or affinal, between the national political class and the other families, but these are not common. The power of the national political class during the past century was based on the fact that the families comprising it came principally from only two cities (San José and Cartago) and generally constituted a majority in Congress. The deputies from secondary and rural zones, while important numerically speaking, represented groups whose influence did not extend beyond regional limits in dispersed areas.

THE DECENTRALIZATION OF POWER

The decentralization of power can best be seen in the Legislative Assembly, which has grown from roughly 25 to 60 members since Independence.[18] The graph in Table 18–2 demonstrates the evolution of the numerical influence of the deputies descended from Juan Vázquez de Coronado, measured against the evolution of the total number of deputies in Congress. To understand the decline of this family shortly after the turn of the century it is necessary to go back to the first Legislative Assembly. This consisted of groups of intimately related families, most of whom descended from the colonial elite. One such group in this first Con-

TABLE 18–2   Deputies Descended from Juan Vázquez de Coronado Measured against Total
Deputies in Legislative Assembly

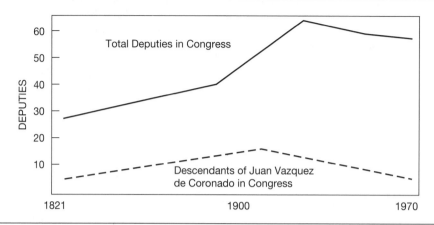

Source: See note 19.

gress, comprising 8 out of the 28 deputies, can be seen in Table 18–3.

In the same Congress there were other groups of families, and six deputies descended from Juan Vázquez de Coronado. Until early in the twentieth century, Legislative Assemblies were constituted in a similar manner, with power following family lines for many generations. This can be appreciated through tracing the lineage of one of the first congressmen, Ramón Jiménez Robredo, a descendant of Vázquez de Coronado, who appears in the second generation of Table 18–3 and many of whose descendants appear in Tables 18–4, 18–5, and 18–6. It is obvious that successive generations proliferate to the point of being unwieldy to describe, but an illustrative example is Table 18–5, showing the descendants of *only one* of Ramón Jiménez's children. Carrying this further, although again through *only one* of the five relevant lines, Table 18–6 shows the third and fourth generations of Ramón Jiménez Robredo.

These tables clearly show how the composition of Legislative Assemblies has followed lines of descent even to the present. During the nineteenth century the elite group played a very important role in Congress, with descendants of Juan Vázquez de Coronado alone occupying 21 of a total of 49 deputies' chairs in 1859.

Shortly after the beginning of the twentieth century, however, an event occurred which changed the relationship between the national political class and the other groups that had previously participated in political life. This was the campaign of Ricardo Jiménez Oreamuno (son of Jesús Jiménez Zamora: see Table 18–4, generation II), elected president in 1910. A member of the national political class, Don Ricardo was considered by some of his contemporaries to have espoused leftist views while others regarded him as excessively aristocratic. In order to obtain the electoral support necessary to defeat his opponent he turned to rural zones and sought the backing of groups which until then had not participated in the political process. This he accomplished through rural community leaders (*gamonales*) of the *Meseta Central* (the Central Plateau, where roughly three-quarters of the population are concentrated). His strategy, which appears in his party's platform, was to encourage the establishment of a strong municipal governmental system, independent of the executive branch.[23] It was through the municipal structure, then, that members of families prominent in small communities throughout the country began to get access to the Legislative Assembly after 1910. In this respect, Don Ricardo's advent to power appears to have marked the beginning of the decline in his own class; reasons for this will be discussed below. Suffice it to say that, since his campaign, there has been a greater participation in the Legislative Assembly of groups not connected with the families we have analyzed.

TABLE 18–3 Kin Ties among 8 of 28 Deputies in the First Congress

Generation I	*Generation II*	*Generation III*
	Joaquina Zamora Coronado	
	D ┌─ Ramón Jiménez Robredo	
		D Joaquín Hidalgo Muñóz
		┌─ Ana J. Oreatmuno Jiménez
	└─ Florencia Jiménez Robredo	
	D ┌─ Joaquín Oreamuno Muñóz	
		D └─ Félix Oreamuno Jiménez
		┌─ Ramona Carazo Alvarado
	D └─ Salvador Oreatmuno Muñóz	
Francisco Carazo B. (see note below)		
┌─ Ana Alvarado Baeza		
D ├─ P. J. Alvarado Baeza		D └─ Nicolás Carazo Alvarado
		┌─ Escolástica Peralta López
	*José M. Peralta Vega	
└─ J. A. Alvarado Baeza	┌─ 1) Ana Alvarado Oreamuno D	└─ Manuel M. Peralta López
Bartola Oreamuno	2) Ana B. López	Ana Echavarria Fajardo

Note: Ana Alvarado Baeza and Francisco Carazo Barahona were mother and father of Ramona and Nicolás Carazo Alvarado. What might appear to be a "generation gap" in Generation II can be explained by the size of Costa Rican families, especially during the colonial period. Francisco Carazo had 17 children; in such a family, there was a difference of "a generation" (in terms of relative age) between the oldest and the youngest of brothers. With respect to names, remember that hispanic usage combines the paternal and maternal surnames, although the latter is not always used; thus the son of Francisco Carazo and Ana Alvarado was Nicolás Carazo Alvarado.
D = Deputy in First Congress.
*Deputy during subsequent congressional periods.
Source: See note 20.

DIVISIONS OF THE POLITICAL CLASS

The significance of the divisions of the political class can be understood through an analysis of present-day party affiliations in both the executive and legislative arms of government. Since 1948, the year of the last important revolution, Costa Rica has known two major political trends. One has been that of the *Partido Liberación Nacional*, of liberal ideological tendency and closely associated with the name of President Figueres (elected in 1970), who, being of recent Spanish ancestry, does not have close blood ties with the traditional political class. He does have the support of many of its members, however, and some members of his family are related by blood to people in the class. The other is that of the *Partido Republicano*, less liberal and organized around the person of ex-President Rafael Angel Calderón Guardia.[24] There have been other significant parties, generally conserva-

TABLE 18–4　Deputies Descended from Ramón Jiménez Robredo

Generation I		Generation II
	D	┌ José Manuel Jiménez Zamora
		Dolores Oreamuno Carazo
	D	├ Agapito Jiménez Zamora
		Inés Sáenz Carazo
	D	├ Jesús Jiménez Zamora
		Esmeralda Oreamuno Gutiérrez
D　Ramón Jiménez Robredo		├ Ramona Jiménez Zamora
Joaquina Zamora Coronado	D	│ Mauricio Peralta Chavarría
		├ Dolores Jiménez Zamora
	D	│ Félix Sancho Alvarado
		└ Juana de Dios Jiménez Zamora
	D	Pedro García Oreamuno

Note: the direct (consanguineal) descendant is above the line.
D = Deputy.
Source: See note 20.

TABLE 18–5　Deputies Descended from Ramón Jiménez Robredo (continued)

Generation II		Generation III
	D	┌ Manuel Vicente Jiménez Oreamuno
		Juana Ortiz Garita
	D	├ José María Jiménez Oreamuno
		Micaela Sánchez Oreamuno
D　José Manuel Jiménez Zamora	D	├ Francisco Jiménez Oreamuno
Dolores Oreamuno Carazo		Mercedes Muñóz y Capurón
	D	├ Nicolás Jiménez Oreamuno
		Emma Valverde Carranza
		└ Matilde Jiménez Oreamuno
	D	Carlos Volio Llorente

Note: the direct (consanguineal) descendant is above the line.
D = Deputy.
Source: See note 21.

TABLE 18–6   Deputies Descended from Ramón Jiménez Robredo (continued)

Generation III		Generation IV
	D	┌─ Arturo Volio Jiménez
		1) Zoila Guardia Tinoco
Matilde Jiménez Oreamuno	D	├─ Claudio Maria Volio Jiménez
D Carlos Volio Llorente	D	├─ Jorge Volio Jiménez
		└─ Matilde Volio Jiménez
	D	Carlos Volio Tinoco

Note: the direct (consanguineal) descendant is above the line.
D = Deputy.
1) = first wife.
Source: See note 22.

tive, formed around ex-Presidents Otilio Ulate Blanco and Mario Echandi Jiménez. During the last decade a coalition called the *Partido Unificación Nacional* was formed among the more conservative parties for the purpose of presenting a united front against Figuere's *Partido Liberación Nacional*. Thus the major political blocs can be grossly called "liberal" (*liberacionista*) and "conservative" (*unificacionista*).

Within the context of these liberal and conservative trends, the divisions of the political class can be appreciated through an analysis of the party affiliations, since 1948, of the deputies descended from Juan Vázquez de Coronado. Table 18–7 shows the principal parties, their ideological tendencies,

and the number of deputies in this family belonging to each organization.

One very recent example of an important division within this same family is that of José Joaquin Fernández (*unificacionista*), who won the presidency in 1966 against Daniel Oduber Quirós (*liberacionista*). Trejos and Oduber can both trace their ancestry to a common great-grandfather, Pedro Quirós Jiménez, a brother of Ascensión Quirós Jiménez, great-grandfather of ex-President Francisco José Orlich Bolmarcich (*liberacionista*) by marriage. Orlich, in turn, who is in the sixteenth generation of Juan Vázquez de Coronado, lost the 1958 elections to Mario Echandi Jiménez (*unificacionista*) of the thirteenth generation.

TABLE 18–7   Party Affiliations of Deputies Descended from Juan Vázquez de Coronado (since 1948)

Party	Ideological Tendency	Deputies
Partido Unión Nacional	Conservative	15
Partido Unión Civica Revolucionaria	Conservative	2
Partido Republicano*	Center Right	14
Partido Liberación Nacional*	Center Left	14
Partido Vanguardia Popular	Communist	1

*Note: It is extremely difficult to classify the ideological tendencies of the *Partido Republicano* and the *Partido Liberación Nacional*. At different times they have both had membership of liberal and conservative tendencies. The most that can be said about them today is that the former is slightly more conservative than the latter.
Source: See note 19.

THE POLITICAL CLASS AND MODERN NATIONAL SOCIETY

National society is often characterized by an arbitrary division of the population into an upper, a middle, and a lower class. This generalized pattern is applicable to the situation in Costa Rica. If we were to identify at any moment in history all the living descendants, either direct or by marriage, of the first *Conquistadores* and *hidalgos*, we could see that this group holds a majority of the important political offices. In any subsequent change of government resulting from elections or even revolution we would see those in power replaced with other people from the same group. The people in power at any given time constitute the political elite of the moment, but the point is that the elite, regardless of party affiliation, are always recruited principally from the same group. This group is the national political class and, with a few notable exceptions, is also the upper economic class. Within it there exists a certain horizontal and vertical mobility, but a person born into it will continue to form part of it regardless of economic or other adversities. Changes of position within the class are due to changes (which are always temporary) in the economic status of the individual, and to marriages contracted with members of other social strata. Generally speaking, the class is inaccessible, except by marriage, to those not born into it.

Several characteristics distinguish the middle class from the political upper class. While education and occupations are similar at both levels, members of the middle class generally occupy secondary positions, especially in government and commerce. In professions such as law or engineering, they often look toward government or autonomous institutions for employment. By contrast, members of the political upper class tend to establish their own firms or join existing firms belonging to others of that class. In medicine, the only difference between the two would be the clientele: middle-class doctors would seldom have access to upper-class patients. In agriculture and particularly coffee, middle-class farmers have smaller holdings and tend to live on their farms more frequently than upper-class farmers, who often reside part of the week in the capital area and manage their lands through an administrator.[25] The outstanding characteristic differentiating the middle class from the upper, however, is the former's virtual lack of kin ties with the six named families. In rare cases where such ties do exist, they are indirect and remote, and they have little or no instrumental value to the individual concerned.

Members of the lower class are also employed in government, commerce, and agriculture, but their lower levels of education relegate them to menial administrative labor positions or manual labor. They occasionally find an opportunity through the national education system to study professions such as law and medicine, which are their principal means of mobility toward the middle class. Most members of the lower class dispose of very scanty economic means.

Three additional comments are relevant to national society. There are several minority groups who do not fit into any of the aforementioned categories. One of these consists of Poles of Jewish origin engaged largely in commerce. Many are extremely wealthy, but two characteristics are to be noted: They rarely hold political office and their kin ties with the aforementioned families are very unusual [Stone's note: Costa Rica also includes significant Negro, Chinese, and other minority populations, who play little role in politics.]. The second comment concerns the relationship between occupation and class. While the foregoing is a sketch of the usual types of occupations for different classes, it is not uncommon to find daughters of families in the political upper class holding jobs as secretaries in government ministries or salesgirls in commerce. Under no circumstances, however, can they be considered members of a lower class for this reason. The last comment is merely to point out the existence of a stratification within each class.

A word should be mentioned about values. These do not differ significantly from the values found in other Latin American societies, except in what concerns the tensions between "elitism," as manifested by the presence of the political class, and the equalitarianism resulting from the colonial experience. The general orientation of values is particularistic, diffuse, and ascriptive, but the equalitarian tendency gives rise to a concern with personal security closely associated with the welfare ideology[26] which has made itself increasingly patent in national policies. In this sense the colonial period, which endowed the society with its equalitarian aspects, also gave it a propensity to welfarism similar to that of Uruguay.

FINAL CONSIDERATIONS ON THE POLITICAL CLASS

In considering the retention of power by the political class, the small size of Costa Rican society must not be overlooked; the present population is slightly over a million and a half. This is not so small, however, as to preclude the existence of a pluralistic society or the emergence of rival groups to defy the position of the dominant class.

Another factor which helps explain how the elite class has been able to maintain its preponderance is the role of the capital city in the life of the country, for it is the only important economic, political, and social center. This has prevented the emergence of rival groups in other zones and from other lineages. Marriage has also been important in the retention of power by the class. As has been pointed out, class endogamy has been a striking feature. A similar instance, the predominance of the Hohenstaufen family in Germany during the twelfth and thirteenth centuries, is attributed by Joseph A. Schumpeter to this same factor of continuous intermarriage within a group.[27]

An important question arises concerning the extent to which it is still meaningful, in mid-twentieth century, to talk of the political dominance of this small class. An examination of its influence at the level of the executive branch during the four campaigns between 1958 and 1970 show that of the ten presidential candidates representing the major parties, seven were descended from Juan Vázquez de Coronado alone. At the level of the vice-presidential candidates in the 1966 and 1970 elections, three of the seven were descended from Vázquez de Coronado. In the Legislative Assembly, however, there would appear to have been a decline in the power of the class; details of this apparent decline cannot be properly judged without a full genealogical analysis. It is clear, however, that a striking feature of modern political life is that a great many of those in positions of responsibility (at the level of the presidency, the Legislative Assembly, autonomous institutions, ministries, embassies, the higher courts, and other government branches) are members of the class.

A hypothesis could be advanced to explain the situation: Until the twentieth century, when other groups came to participate in the political process, most administrative levels of government were dominated directly by the class. Since 1910 the participation of new groups in Congress has been stimulated by rival factions within the class, and this sharing of power has lessened its direct control over this and many other branches of government. What appears to have happened is that the new arrivals, representing diverse interests from widely scattered geographical regions, have come under the domination of the national political class from the capital area. The class, then, appears to have changed from "owner" of power during the last century to "leader" of power during the present. However, it must be remembered that these new groups have given their support to the contending factions of the national political class in exchange for a participation which will undoubtedly acquire greater proportions in the future.[28]

Those who belong to the national political class continue to have access to political posts; and, since it is a relatively small class, there is a constant interaction among its members, which in turn facilitates the retention of power. This factor is extremely important and may explain the phenomenon of the role of kin relationships in the political process. The difficulty of access to the class has meant that its members have had a relatively limited circulation within national society, a fact which can be appreciated at the level of its social and even economic organizations, where family considerations are still prime criteria for participation. The same applies to the political domain where the access to positions of power is limited, to an important extent, to people in the aforementioned lineages.

Within these processes of power the greatest unknown in terms of power is the relatively new and rapidly proliferating state bureaucracy. Its growth may soon pose new problems to the traditional political class and effect significant changes in the distribution of power in Costa Rica.[29]

NOTES

1. Costa Rica's gross national produce per capita in 1968 was $570, which puts the country in seventh place after Argentina, Chile, Mexico, Panama, Uruguay, and Venezuela. The 1968 increase in GNP was 8.1 percent,

the highest in Latin America. For the same year literacy was estimated at 84 percent, ranking third in Latin America along with Chile, after Argentina and Uruguay. These data were taken from "Anexo Estadistico," *Progreso* (Enero/Febrero de 1970), pp. 89–104.

2. For a similar concept of political class, see Raymond Aron, "Social Class, Political Class, Ruling Class," in Reinhard Bendix and Seymour Martin Lipset, eds., *Class, Status and Power.* London: Routledge & Kegan Paul Ltd., 1967, pp. 201–210.

3. Norberto de Castro y Tosi, "La Población de la Ciudad de Cartago en los Siglos XVII y XVIII," *Revista de los Archivos Nacionales*, XXVIII (Segundo Semestre 1964), San José, pp. 153–154.

4. It has often been argued that certain unique traits of Costa Rican society can be attributed to the "fact" that the settlers during the colonial period were primarily of Galician extraction. This is a misconception which has been clearly laid to rest by Monseñor Victor Sanabria Martínez, late Bishop of San José, who studied the origins of all the settlers in Costa Rica after the Conquest and traced their lineages to 1850. His monumental work, which was accomplished through baptismal records, was 14 years in preparation and was published in six large volumes. Among other things, Monseñor Sanabria shows that the settlers of Costa Rica came primarily from Andalucia. (See his *Genealogías de Cartago hasta 1850*, San José: Servicios Secretariales, 1957, esp. pp. LIX–LXII.).

5. Carlos Meléndez Chaverri, *Juan Vázquez de Coronado*, San José: Editorial Costa Rica, 1966, p. 21.

6. Ricardo Fernández Guardia, *Cartilla Histórica de Costa Rica*, San José: Librería e Imprenta Atenca (Antonio Lehmann), 1967, p. 30.

7. At the beginning of the nineteenth century Costa Rica had fewer than 53,000 inhabitants. For the demographic evolution of the province during the colonial period, see Bernardo Augusto Thiel, "Monografía de la Población de la República de Costa Rica," In Bernardo Thiel, et al., *Costa Rica en el Siglo XIX*, San José: Tipografía Nacional, 1902, p. 8.

8. Bernardo Augusto Thiel, "La Iglesia Católica de Costa Rica durante el Siglo 19," in Thiel, et al., op. cit., pp. 303–306.

9. For an interpretation of the significance of such a quest as a force of change in traditional society, see Everett E. Hagen, *On the Theory of Social Change*, Homewood, Ill.: The Dorsey Press, 1963.

10. Samuel Z. Stone, "Los Cafetaleros," *Revista de Ciencias Jurídicas*, Universidad de Costa Rica, 13 (June 1969), p. 178.

11. Ibid., p. 180.

12. Rodrigo Facio Brenes, *Estudio de Economia Costarricense*, San José: Editorial Surco, 1942, pp. 23–30.

13. Warren Dean, "The Planter as Entrepreneur: the Case of Sao Paolo," *The Hispanic American Historical Review*, XLVI, No. 2 (May 1966), p. 139.

14. For a description of such a process, see Karl Deutsch, "Social Mobilization and Political Development," in Jason Finkle and Richard Gable, eds., *Political Development and Social Change*, New York: John Wiley & Sons, 1968.

15. Julio E. Revollo Acosta, "La Ilustre Descendencia de Don Antonio de Acosta Arévalo," *Revista de la Academia Costarricenses de Ciencias Genealógicas* (San José), No. 8 (May 1960), pp. 17–32. For the exact way in which each president descends from Don Antonio de Acosta Arévalo, see Samuel Z. Stone, *Los Cafetaleros: Une Etude des Grands Planteurs de Café au Costa Rica* (unpublished Ph.D. dissertation, University of Paris, 1968), pp. 181–190.

16. In what concerns the deputies in all of these lineages, the number descended from each family is a rounded figure. In the case of Vázquez de Coronado, for example, 219 have been found. However, in all cases, more will undoubtedly be found in the future. The sources from which these data were obtained are given in note 19.

17. For a list of the first 100 planter families from the political class, see Stone, 1969, op. cit., pp. 185–188.

18. These are rough figures. The number of deputies has fluctuated greatly from year to year and has reached 80. In recent years it has remained stable at 57.

19. Tables 2 and 7 were prepared from data obtained through research conducted in San José, Costa Rica, between 1967 and 1970. Data concerning families from the colonial period to the twentieth century were obtained primarily from Victor Sanabria Martínez, op. cit. (see note 4) and the National Archives in the Section of Protocolos of San José, as well as from numerous publications of the *Revista de la Academia Costarricense de Ciencias Genealógicas* (San José). Data concerning families during the twentieth century were obtained primarily from interviews, over the years mentioned, with many older members of the community.

20. Victor Sanabria Martínez, op. cit.

21. Ibid. Also interviews with many older members of the community. See note 19.

22. Interviews with older members of the community. See note 19.

23. Mario Alberto Jiménez, *Obras Completas* (2 vols.), San José: Editorial Costa Rica 1962, I, pp. 103–106.

24. Dr. Calderón Guardia died in 1970.

25. Data concerning the tendency of landowners to live on their farms was taken from Ministerio de Economía y Hacienda, Dirección General de Estadística y Censos, *Censo Agropecuario de 1963*, San José: Dirección General de Estadística y Censos, 1965.

26. Where the general orientation of values is ascriptive, particularistic, and diffuse and there is an equalitarian tendency, there tends to be a special concern with personal security closely associated with welfare ideology. For a discussion of this point, see Lipset, "Values, Education and Entrepreneurship," in Seymour Martin Lipset and Aldo Solari, eds., *Elites in Latin America*, New York: Oxford University Press, 1967, p. 32.

27. Joseph A. Schumpeter, *Imperialism and Social Classes: Two Essays*, Cleveland: World Publishing Company, 1968, p. 116.

28. For a discussion of this idea see Gino Germani, "Clases Populares y Democracia Representativa," in Joseph A. Kahl, ed., *La Industrialización en America Latina,* México: Fondo de Cultura Económica, 1965.

29. This article is based on Stone, op. cit., 1968, Stone, op. cit., 1969, and on further research soon to be published in *Cahiers des Amériques Latines*, University of Paris (publication data not yet available). The author gratefully acknowledges the permission of all concerned to use this material.

19

Changing Life Patterns
The Elite of the Valle de Pubenza, Colombia

Andrew Hunter Whiteford

The upper Cauca Valley, in the region of Popayán, has been the seat of an established aristocracy since the time of its settlement in the early sixteenth century. For more than three centuries, social eminence coincided with economic wealth and political power. Many of the original land holdings were acquired as rewards for service during the conquest or as officers of the crown during the early colonial period, to be enlarged or reduced as fortunes changed during the subsequent years of revolutionary and civil warfare. Throughout the centuries of turmoil, the predominant families retained their positions in the society and cultivated a way of life that was the epitome of a Latin American provincial aristocracy. A substantial number could demonstrate relationship with various branches of the Spanish nobility and the possession of *abolengo* (lineage) with *pergamino*, literally a certificate of noble descent, was a prerequisite for social acceptance in the highly stratified society.

This paper was presented at the 73rd Annual Meeting of the American Anthropological Association, November 19–24, 1974. The support of the Wenner-Gren Foundation for Anthropological Research is gratefully acknowledged.

In spite of the geographic isolation of this region, until the third decade of this century at least, the members of the elite families traveled to Europe and occasionally to the United States, and the men played important roles in the national government. As I said in an earlier report (Whiteford, A. H. 1964) "Sixteen presidents of Colombia came from Popayán, its families produced numerous archbishops, bishops, ambassadors and other diplomats, and generals—sometimes for both sides—in the civil wars of the nineteenth century." They imported ideas and furniture from France, cultivated their literary talents as poets, essayists, and historians; and sent their sons to the universities. They built large houses around the central plaza and raised large families, after marrying their schoolmates' sisters or cousins. It was a vigorous, inbred, tightly interrelated social class which managed to maintain itself and its basic ideology remarkably intact for a long period of time.

When I first came to Popayán in 1947 and returned to begin research in 1949, the city was slowly and reluctantly entering a period of growth and change. It was connected to the outside world when the railroad arrived from Cali and an increasing number of young people were going away to school and to live, temporarily or permanently, in the larger cities. The early airlines flew into Popayán, but the roads connecting it with Cali, or anywhere else, were miserable. The community was still isolated. There were no factories or other productive units larger than the local brick-making *galpones* and the departmental plant, which produced aguardiente. In 1949–50, the country was tense under a state of siege following the assassination of Gaitán, the Bogotázo, and the growing *Violencia*, but little social change was discernable in Popayán. The basic pattern of life, and its variations among members of the different segments of the society, have been described in *Two Cities of Latin America* (A. H. Whiteford 1964) and need not be repeated here except for purposes of comparison.

Twenty-five years later, it is apparent that changes have occurred in the Valle de Pubenza. To those who live there and who see the explosive growth and exciting (or threatening) changes that have taken place in Cali and Bogotá, it seems that "everything changes, but Popayán is always the same." Comparatively, this is true, but viewed over a span of years and separated from emotional desires for a "new world" the transformations are quite obvious. The city still lacks some of the major symbols of modernity: there are no large factories with smoking chimneys and extruding effluents, there are no elevated freeways or even a major highway cutting through the center, there is not a single high-rise office or apartment building, a large Sears store, a shopping center, or a complex of condominiums; there are not very many billboards or electric signs. Nevertheless, there are changes. New highways now facilitate transportation to Cali and to Pasto in the south and, as a result, the number of automobiles, trucks and buses in the city has increased enormously. At noon and in the late afternoon the main streets are filled with traffic, a major change from the past when there were so few autos that evening strollers walked in the streets apprehensive only of horse-droppings.

The city has grown, in area and in population. The figures from the last census are not yet available but the number is considered to have doubled, from 35,000 in 1950 to ± 75,000 today. To accomodate this growth, the city has expanded with a multiplicity of housing developments and subdivisions. Because of surrounding hills on the south and west, growth has moved in the other directions with a concentration of lower-class mass housing to the west and middle and upper-class subdivisions to the north, along the highway to Cali. The enlarged expanse of the city and the increased concentration of people are apparent. Popayán shares with other cities the problem of providing not only living accommodations, but also jobs for the increased population, a problem that is acute here because there are practically no industries or other large-scale enterprises to employ the growing number of unskilled laborers. (For treatment of this problem see, Michael B. Whiteford, "Barrio Tulcán: Fieldwork in a Colombian City," in Foster and Kemper 1974). As a result of recent developments, greatly increased hydroelectric resources are now available, so future industrialization may take place, but at the moment it is apparent only in improved municipal lighting and the once-common fading of domestic and entertainment lights to the equivalent of flickering candles no longer occurs.

People often say that the *ambiente* of the city is still the same and this is certainly true early in the morning and after dark, when the streets become quiet and empty. At those hours, Popayán is very much as it was twenty years ago, but during the daylight hours the tone and feeling of the city is obviously different. As in all the world, styles are much more informal and colorful: men of all ages are often without coats and ties and almost every woman wears pants. Sex can be sold, and the colored magazine covers on the stands exhibit bare breasts and nearly-bare females with articles on the prolongation of copulation. These occurences reflect major changes in attitudes within a short period. During more than a month of the past summer the major theater in the center of the city (one of three) did not exhibit a single film that was not censored for those under eighteen. The fact that some censorship does exist in movies makes acceptance of the magazine and record covers an even greater contrast with the past. Old residents decry such changes and attribute the "breakdown in morals" and the disappearance of manners and courtesy to the influx of newcomers who know nothing of the city's cultural tradition and care very little. The old pattern of formal courtesies and personal relationships still exists, but it is obscured and hidden by the impersonality of the mass of unknown faces in the streets.

The central market has been replaced with a modern but rather bleak Centro Comercial, and women do their shopping at three markets located on the edges of the city, or in a *super mercado* with self-service such as has long existed in the larger cities. Furthermore, the women of almost every social stratum now do their own shopping and members of the most elite families can now be seen wearing pants, haggling with vendors, and even carrying their own baskets or shopping bags. There are more shops than before but most of them are rather small and are different from the shops of an earlier era in the greater variety of their goods, the better quality, and more sophisticated styling. There are appliances such as televisions, stoves, and refrigerators available now, and two striking additions are the large hardware stores that sell construction materials and repair parts for machinery, and the several large, handsomely modern bank buildings. At least four such financial temples have been constructed within the past five or six years and they are clearly the most imposing contemporary monuments in the city: well designed, sumptuous in their offices and board rooms, and decorated with large murals, sculpture, and fountains.

Within this slowly evolving and modernizing society the people of Popayán struggle to maintain themselves and their families, to improve their life conditions, and to secure the future for their children. Some do better than others. Some are poor and some are rich, but qualified observers have noted that the poor of this city live in conditions that are far better than the slums of the large cities, and here the rich do not exhibit anything like the opulence of the wealthy in Cali or Bogotá. If the elite families of Popayán possess great fortunes, their effect is difficult to discern: there are no mansions, no limousines, no fabulous parties, or clumps of glittering jewels. Some of them live very well: at a level comparable to the upper middle class in a North American community. They send their children to universities and sometimes abroad for further study, they occasionally travel abroad themselves, they dress well, have a car or two, and often have a vacation house in the country. This is both more and less than their grandfathers had, and more than most other people have now.

The large, two-story houses surrounding the central plaza, which once belonged to elite families, have almost all been divided into stores and apartments, or turned into institutional buildings for government offices. Many families still live in ancestral houses a block or two from the center, but others have constructed modern houses further out and their sons and daughters are building even more modern houses still further out: in the edging subdivisions or in the surrounding hills. Some of the houses are relatively modest ($40–45,000 level in the central United States) others are quite large ($60–70,000 level). Most are well designed by local architects. The corps of servants that existed in the past has been replaced by automatic household machines; the larger families now have a cook, a maid, maybe a girl or a nurse if there are young children, and perhaps a yard man as occasional help. The cars driven by members of the family are usually Fiats, Toyotas, Renaults, and occasionally Jeeps or pick-up trucks.

It is still typical of elite families that a part of their income is derived from landholdings, and both men and women are interested in matters of cattle breeding and agricultural productivity. Division through inheritance and government land reform, or threat of reform and redistribution, have changed the relationship to the land. Very few families now possess holdings that are large enough or productive enough to provide adequate income. Some land in the more level sections of the valley has been converted to the production of fique fiber and a large number of *fincas* (farms) have turned from beef cattle to the development of dairy herds. Both of these enterprises require more investment and much more careful planning and supervision than was needed for the traditional sprawling, semiwild cattle hacienda. Changes in modern transportation have made the change possible. Some men now visit their *fincas* regularly twice a week to check with the mayordomo on milk production, breeding, feeding schedules, and other details of an operation located on land that was once so remote that their fathers and grandfathers inspected them only two or three times a year. Pure-bred stock has been mixed with the native *criollo* cattle for many years, but it is only in recent years that some *fincas* have specialized in fine Holsteins or Brown Swiss for pure dairy purposes, and Normans, Charolais, milking Shorthorns, and other breeds for both milk and beef. Wild pastures have been plowed and planted with improved grasses such as Kikuyu and Miquai, and breeding and production records are carefully noted. Some of the changes have been forced by actual or pending agrarian reforms, others have been stimulated with the assistance of the national Cattlemen's Association, the Cattlemen's Bank (Asociación de Ganaderos, Banco Ganadero), and many have been made possible through the increased knowledge of the owners and the increasing number of sons who have acquired advanced education in animal husbandry. Some of these trained younger men would like to become full-time cattle or dairy men, but most of them feel that they are forced into other activities because they do not have access to sufficient capital, enough secure land, and adequate credit. Some of their grandfathers were able to "retire on their investments" and live like landed gentry, but almost all members of the present generations work for a living.

"Working for a living" almost always means a professional career. Higher education is regarded as a necessity for men, and increasingly for women also; an increasing proportion of elite women attend the university and their brothers are sent to Europe and the United States or Mexico for advanced graduate study in medicine or engineering or agronomy. In earlier generations the men from these families all took university degrees in the "liberal professions." Many of them never practiced, but turned their attention to politics, participating actively in the organization of the two major parties and serving as governors, senators, ambassadors, and presidents. With a few exceptions, the men of the present senior generation and their sons have shown much less interest in political office. Some have held departmental and national positions, but their general association with government has recently been as hired professionals: trained agronomists with INCORA, engineers with the department of public works, doctors with the department of public health or the municipal hospital. Those in private practice take an interest in local and national affairs and are enthusiastically concerned with their *fincas* but, first and foremost, they are professional doctors, dentists, architects, engineers. Most of them spend long hours at their work, they make an effort to keep up with new developments in their field, and their sons frequently join them in their professions.

As administrators and professionals, the present elite earn relatively high incomes, they occupy positions of respect and prestige, and they continue to have access to power and influence at the local and national level. When information is needed or "special attention" is required, a member of the elite is usually able to proceed through personal channels by contacting a brother who is the manager of the bank, a cousin who is in charge of the departmental roads, another cousin who is an assistant minister of education, a sister who is a senator in the national legislature, a brother-in-law who is rector of the university, and another who is the ambassador to Mexico. The list of relatives is very long and nepotism is still regarded as a virtue and a duty. Even without special concessions, the access to privileged information constitutes an important advantage in making decisions and in exercising leadership. The leaders of the elite families are certainly much less visible and less recognizable now than when Popayán was quieter and smaller, and everyone recognized and greeted maestro Guillermo Valencia and Dr. Rafael Obando as they strolled through the streets. But those who belong to the upper class today still know each other and their lives are intertwined at many levels.

The network of social and business relationships tends to coincide with kinship; this is one of the life-ways that seems to be relatively unchanged across the span of three generations. The upper class has always been regarded as exclusive, aloof, and inbred. These traits persist and tend to be sustained by the nature of the community. Members of the elite do not confine their contacts largely to each other because of any conscious feeling of superiority or an active desire to exclude others. The crucial factors are the relatively small number of people in the city with whom they have much in common, and the large numbers of relatives with whom they have social obligations. A gathering of any single family constitutes a party; with the addition of a few affines and collaterals, it becomes a major fiesta. It is very difficult to find time and space for unrelated outsiders. Members of these families interact frequently and intensively. Married sisters meet frequently at their mother's home to chat and sew, sisters and cousins belong to the same church organizations and cooperate in their programs. Daughters-in-law who are not native Payanés cluster around their husband's family and Payanés daughters who have married outside the city return for frequent weekends and for long vacations at the family *finca*. Summer at the *finca* is a tradition that is made easier by improved transportation. The women of the family often move to the country as soon as school is out in July, taking the children and various servants with them. Married daughters and daughters-in-law join the entourage with their children and the swollen household becomes a family camp. The men generally commute to the city if the distance and roads permit, or they remain in town and spend weekends at the *finca*. In most cases, the women are able to drive back and forth to town with little inconvenience.

Vacation on the *finca* constitutes an important element in forging the strong bonds of sentiment between the Payaneses and the land; it is also a most effective force in welding the immediate family together and bringing cousins and affines into a sense of intimacy that is rarely broken in later life. The pattern of life in the country is simple. Some *fincas* retain the old hacienda houses that were part of the original landholding; new *fincas* resulting from land divisions have more modern houses of recent construction. The old houses are usually rambling single-story constructions with a series of bedrooms arranged around the central patio, a large *sala* in the front, and often a railed veranda. Rooms have been added at various times and usually some effort has been made to bring the kitchen and bathroom facilities up to the twentieth century. The old houses are picturesque, but they tend to be dank and rather bare when they are not filled with noisy children and their laughing relatives. A few new *finca* houses are quite elaborate, but most are simple, modern reflections of the traditional model. The houses are rarely symbols for prestige. They tend to be functional, utilitarian constructions that serve the needs of the expanded family and usually allow for some decorating arts and crafts by the women who live there. They are colorful, attractive, fairly comfortable—and not much more.

The pattern of activities is also simple. There is sometimes a pool, a pond, or a nearby stream for paddling and swimming; horses are always available and even the small children ride. The children chase each other, build things, have contests, walk on stilts, and play innumerable games, often with the adults. The women decorate the house, do needle-point, knit, paint, play some cards, and discuss.

When the men arrive they sometimes ride together, swim, or go for walks. A favorite pastime is sitting on the veranda together, reading the Bogotá Sunday paper, napping in the hammock, occasionally watching television, and discussing. For a big occasion, such as a birthday, a lamb or a joint of beef will be barbequed and relatives will ride in from neighboring *fincas* for an evening of singing and dancing to the music of guitars and tiples. Both young and old take turns on the *columpio*, a maypole affair which is usually on a steep bank so the swingers twist and turn high above the ground. The most obvious changes from an earlier time are the presence of a television and/or radio, electric lights, and the greater ease in getting to and from the city; in most other respects, the pattern is relatively unchanged.

For the upper-class women in Popayán, lifestyles have changed substantially during the past twenty years. At the beginning of this period, women were beginning to enter the universities and a few were making their way in the professions. Although the women are still wives and mothers, many have attended the university and are working as physicians and dentists as well as in many other positions. Styles have changed drastically and the former emphasis upon white gloves, high heels, and Paris fashions has given way to slack-suits. As always, upper-class women are much more circumspect about wearing tight pants and revealing their bare midriffs than are the women of some other segments of the society, but what they wear is colorful, stylish, and definitely modern. There have always been strong women in this class and some of them have moved forward by serving in the national legislature as senators, filling the position of *alcalde* in the city, and managing offices and other enterprises. What changes, if any, these new roles have brought about in the families concerned, I do not know.

Twenty years ago the only commercial or industrial building one would notice in Popayán was the malt plant of the Bavaria brewing company. Although the building was quite large the operation had little effect upon the city because it employed a small number of workers. When it closed down a few years ago, the plant was taken over and organized as the first factory in the community: a weaving mill to produce sacks from the locally grown fique fiber. Although owned by companies outside of Popayán, the factory has been under the supervision of managers from the city. In the past three years, three additional factories have come into the community. One is another "foreign-owned" enterprise: a clean, precise plant that employs some 350 white-smocked women to assemble children's books and a variety of games, gift candles, and greeting cards. These items are all produced to be shipped to publishers and distributors in the United States. The factory is owned by a large company in Cali; the plant manager is a young member of the local elite. This factory may be especially significant in presaging the kind of development that can be organized here to make use of the many skilled hands available in the area.

Another important development is a much more loosely organized plant next door that is operated for the production of metal furniture for schools and offices. In the large, open shed, various operations are carried out, from forming metal tubes and sheets, to cutting and finishing wood forms, and stuffing and fitting upholstery. Some of the workmen are trained on the job; others come with some welding and machine skills, which they have acquired in the departmental trade schools. Here is another example of the development of a light industry that utilizes local workers who have acquired some skills. Formerly, there was little opportunity for such workers in Popayán, and it is important to note that this is not an imported industry but entirely a local development.

The founders and owners of this plant, and also of another small plant on the opposite side of the city, are a group of young men from elite families who have decided to pool their resources and their skills to accomplish a number of objectives: to make a profit, to provide jobs in the city, to gain some control over industrial development before outsiders move in, to apply their personal training in work that they enjoy. Not only are the organizers related as members of the traditional elite, they are also brothers and cousins. Among them they number two or three trained engineers with graduate training in Europe and the United States; two bankers, both with graduate training; and two others who are working in unrelated professions. One of the engineers is the plant manager who is responsible for the design of the products and their production, the rest of the group have their own jobs elsewhere but they meet to discuss all aspects of

the enterprise and to lend their particular expertise to the various problems that arise. At this point the factory is doing well, they are ready to expand operations, and the committee is considering new prospects for development.

This particular case is of special interest because it illustrates so precisely the classic interlocking between the old landowning elite of Latin America and the newer industrial urban elite that has been described in many instances. Gustavo Polit describes the situation in Argentina in the following paragraph:

> The industrialists of Argentina started out linked to the land; this has been the distinguishing characteristic of this class from the beginning. Both sectors, industrialists and landowners, are intertwined; the vague boundaries that separate them are attenuated through the investment of agrarian rent in industry and the investment of industrial profit in agriculture, converting the landholders into industrialists and the industrialists into landowners. (Gustavo Polit 1968, pp. 399–400)

Frederick B. Pike (1968, pp. 209–210) describes the same situation for Chile: "By the turn-of-the-century period, then, urban and rural interests were crossed and criss-crossed to such a degree that the distinction was often meaningless." In the same publication (Petras and Zeitlin, eds., 1968), the relationship between these two powerful social elements is similarly described for Peru by Aníbal Quijano Obregón:

> The sectors of the bourgeoisie involved in agricultural production for export as well as for domestic markets and those that are primarily involved in financial, mercantile, and industrial activities, share the same class interests. They are inseparably interconnected economically, and through close family and social ties. (1968, p. 315)

These writers all regard the coincidence and commonality between the urban industrial elite and the landowning aristocracy as a major obstruction to social and economic progress in Latin America. Havens and Flinn share this view regarding Colombia specifically:

. . . there is no real conflict between the industrial elite and the landholding elite. Rather, these supposed conflicting elites constitute the same elite that has emerged to fill the gap left when the Spanish elite was evicted. The effect of their control over the allocation of resources has been the same as if the Spanish colonial government was still existent. (1970, p. 10)

Perhaps so! It may bode ill for the future development of the Valle de Pubenza, but the fact is that young members of the traditional landed elite have taken the first steps in the industrialization of the area. If it goes well, jobs will be created, the productive base of the region will be diversified, job security will be increased, and, of course, their own fortunes and hegemony will be solidified. And what are the alternatives? What else could these men be expected to do with their talents, training, and ambition once they had decided to remain in their homeland and raise their families there? Who else except possible outside interests might have access to the resources and experience to do the same? There are few alternatives, but it should be pointed out that the "demonstration effect" is already at work and some enterprising artisans are enlarging their *talleres* in miniature emulation of the new factories. Given some time and a bit of financing, some of these may develop into factories themselves.

Regardless of the ultimate outcome, the present picture shows the young adult generation of the traditional elite in this area developing trained professional skills and turning to the management of utilities, financial institutions, and nascent industries as their family cattle lands diminish. In returning to the quiet life and the future challenges of the Valle de Pubenza, after having lived in other parts of Colombia and the outside world, these young people have made a conscious choice. They have chosen the quiet life of Popayán and its intimacy with family and nature over the excitement of the big cities and their greater potentials for material rewards. There are many other factors involved in the decision to return and they are expressed clearly with no qualifications. They know what they are doing, and they make it clear that the option to make their homes and careers in the Valle de Pubenza is in no manner a retreat or a withdrawal from the problems which exist in Colombia today.

Their experience and their educations have made them acutely aware of changing social conditions, of the need for agrarian reform, of poverty in the cities, of the importance of both developing and conserving natural resources, of fumbling government bureaucracies, and the threats and promises of conflicting political ideologies. Some of them have been university radicals, others have worked at one time or another with INCORA, INDERENA, and other government programs in which they believed; and most of them have come to share a suspicion of political programs and a growing belief that vigorous private enterprise of some kind is also necessary in dealing with the problems. Personal survival is an element of such enterprise, but these people see their personal careers as completely intermeshed with the fortunes of Popayán and the Valle de Pubenza. Jaime and Jeanne Posada said of the aristocrats in the top echelons of the CVC in Cali that, "They consider their positions as civic duties and opportunities to exercise their training and talents, as least as much as for ways of furthering their long range economic interests." (Posada and Posada, 1966, p. 209). This element of devotion to the region and the people with whom their families have lived for several hundred years should not be discounted because they take it seriously themselves.

They fear government confiscation of their lands and move to avoid it by dividing it among members of the family and intensifying its use. They also develop profit-sharing programs and other incentives with their mayordomos and help to build schools and houses for their farm workers. They generally recognize that peasant land seizures and redistributions are inevitable and many of them take it for granted that major reforms are necessary for the survival and welfare of the country. They do not have either the power or the interest to resist social and economic change, but they feel that they possess the necessary knowledge and enterprise to guide its direction to some degree. They are neither paranoid about the threat of communism nor blind to the conditions which make it seem a desirable solution for some people: a prospect that is unlikely as long as these people retain their present vitality and solidarity. Whether their influence on the development of the area will be "exploitative and repressive" or ultimately beneficent will be apparent in the not very distant future.

APPENDIX: RESIDENCE AND MARRIAGE

In an attempt to obtain some measure of the extent to which members of the upper class in Popayán married local people and continued to live in (or returned to) the city, we examined the geneologies of three major families. The total number of individuals in the four living generations exceeds 200. For those in the Ego Generation (approximately 45 to 65 years of age) data was available on 44 individuals with the information that 63 percent of them (28) married spouses from Popayán, and 47 percent (21) continued to live in the city, or returned to it. Data on 51 individuals for the First Descending generation (25 to 45 years of age) was extended by adding information regarding the present situations of people who had attended an upper-class children's party in 1951. Data were thus available for 146 people: 68 were known to be married and their professions and present locations were also known, 56 percent (30) of them had married spouses from Popayán, and 28 percent (42) were presently living in the city.

These figures show that approximately half of the Older Adult generation of the upper-class married and live in Popayán. More than half of the Young Adult generation married in the city, but the proportion still living in Popayán is smaller than that of the previous generation. Interview data indicate that a substantial number of these younger people are still in graduate studies in other cities or are "experiencing life in the larger world" before returning to the Valle de Pubenza to settle down and raise their families. This is only to say that the figure is incomplete.

How these figures may compare with those from another community or another class is unknown. Considering the large size of elite families, the limited opportunities for career or pleasure in a traditional provincial city, and the broad experiences and opportunities available in nearby cities (Cali) or far parts of the world, it is interesting that so many have elected to remain or return.

REFERENCES

Havens, A. Eugene, and W. L. Flinn, *Internal Colonialism and Structural Change in Colombia.* Praeger Special Studies in International Economics and Development. New York: Praeger, 1970.

Pike, Frederick B., "Aspects of Class Relations in Chile, 1850–1960." In J. Petras and M. Zeitlin (eds.), *Latin America: Reform or Revolution?* New York: Fawcett, 1968.

Polit, Gustavo, "The Industrialists of Argentina." In J. Petras and M. Zeitlin (eds.), *Latin America: Reform or Revolution?* New York: Fawcett, 1968.

Posada, Antonio J., and Jeanne de Posada, *The CVC: Challenge to Underdevelopment and Traditionalism,* Collection: Aventura del Desarrollo 9, Tercer Mundo, Bogotá.

Quijano Obregón, Aníbal, "Peruvian Development and Class Structure." In J. Petras and M. Zeitlin (eds.), *Latin America: Reform or Revolution?* New York: Fawcett, 1968.

Whiteford, Andrew H., *Two Cities of Latin America: A Comparative Description of Social Classes.* New York: Anchor Books, Doubleday & Co., 1964.

Whiteford, Michael B., "Barrio Tulcan: Fieldwork in a Colombian City." In George M. Foster and R. V. Kemper (eds.), *Anthropologists in Cities.* Boston: Little, Brown & Co., 1974.

20

Changes in Twentieth-Century Mesoamerican *Cargo* Systems

John K. Chance

INTRODUCTION

During the last 50 years, ethnographers of Mesoamerica have placed special emphasis on the civil-religious hierarchy or *cargo* system as key to understanding indigenous communities and their relationships with the national societies of Mexico and Guatemala. In sheer volume, more pages of ethnographic description and analysis probably have been devoted to *cargo* systems than to any other aspect of village life. The so-called "traditional" or "classic" form of the system as described ethnographically consists of a hierarchy of ranked offices that together comprise a community's public civil and religions administration. The civil offices articulate the community with regional and national political systems, while the religious *cargos* are associated with the worship of the local

From John K. Chance, "Changes in Twentieth-Century Mesoamerican Cargo Systems." In Lynn Stephen and James Dow (eds.), *Class, Politics, and Popular Religion in Mexico and Central America.* Society for Latin American Anthropology Publication Series, Volume 10. Washington, D.C.: American Anthropological Association, 1990, pp. 27–42.

saints (and normally are only tenuously linked to the external church hierarchy). Individuals or couples representing different households ascend this ladder of service during their lifetimes, alternating back and forth between civil and religious posts. Men with the resources and longevity to make it to the top join a select group of *principales*, or elders, who often are very influential in local politics. A central feature of the system is the private sponsorship of fiestas in honor of the saints by holders of religious *cargos*. Considerable amounts of wealth may thus be expended as an individual or couple ascends the hierarchy in search of influence and prestige in the eyes of fellow villagers.[1]

The vast majority of contemporary ethnographic descriptions of Mesoamerican civil-religious hierarchies come from the Oaxaca region and the Maya highlands of Chiapas, Mexico and Guatemala (see DeWalt 1975:88 and Table 20–1 below). Michoacán has not yielded any examples in the twentieth century, though there may have been civil-religious hierarchies there in the past (Carrasco 1952). Tzintzuntzan, one of the most thoroughly studied of all Mesoamerican communities, had a *cargo* system prior to 1925, but it lacked a civil component and was comprised entirely of religious offices (Foster

1967; Brandes 1988). The Yucatan peninsula likewise seems to be lacking in civil-religious systems, despite the interesting account by Grant Jones (1981) of a "fiesta system"—which is not the same thing—in nineteenth-century northern Belize.[2] Equally anomalous is the dearth of civil-religious systems in Nahuatl-speaking central Mexico, where *cargo* systems today are usually religious in structure (Table 20–1, but see also Montoya Briones 1964). Explanation of this regional variation must await future ethnohistorical research.

In this paper I will confine my attention to the central and southern highlands and argue that in twentieth century indigenous communities which still maintain functioning *cargo* systems, civil-religious hierarchies are being transformed into religious hierarchies. Supporting data come from 23 ethnographic case studies published since 1965, the year that marked the appearance of Frank Cancian's landmark study of the religious *cargo* system of Zinacantan, Chiapas. As William Taylor and I have previously noted (Chance and Taylor 1985: 20), analytical gains can be made by breaking down the civil-religious hierarchy into its three component parts—the civil hierarchy, the religious hierarchy, and the practice of fiesta sponsorship by individuals or couples (as representatives of households). The analysis that follows builds on this lead, and takes the primary defining characteristic of a *cargo* system to be the existence of a hierarchy of ranked public offices through which individuals are expected to pass in a certain order. It also assumes that ascending this ladder brings prestige. The nature of the offices themselves (civil or religious, etc.), whether or not they involve celebration of fiestas, and the practices surrounding fiesta financing are all secondary characteristics.

Discussions of the factors that promote change and breakdown in *cargo* systems are nearly as voluminous as the descriptive literature on the system itself. Many ethnographers, faced with faded or defunct *cargo* systems, have alluded to the local events which led up to their demise. Frank Cancian (1967:293–296) and Waldemar Smith (1977), on a more general level, posit that weakening or breakdown of *cargo* systems may be brought about by "*ladinoization*," direct political action by national governments, increasing poverty, increasing prosperity, and a reduction or increase in population. Billie DeWalt (1975:95, 100–102) stresses increasing "contact with the outside world"[3] and occupational specialization as correlates of the process of breakdown. James Greenberg (1981:159) singles out changes in modes of production and changing metropolis-satellite relations as causative forces. In this paper I neither endorse nor dispute any of these accounts, but rather take up the issue of *structural* change in the system. Despite the extensive debates over the origins and functions of the hierarchies (see Chance and Taylor 1985 for a summary), relatively little attention has been paid to the formal shape of *cargo* systems and the kinds of offices they contain. DeWalt (1975) offers a useful fourfold typology of forms, but fails to connect it convincingly with a theory of systemic change. In contrast, in this paper I utilize a broader typology and attempt to sketch a general process of change that has surfaced in many communities since the 1920s. To understand this process, it is necessary to place it in historical perspective and relate it to other changes in Mesoamerican *cargo* systems which have occurred during the last three centuries.

FROM CIVIL TO CIVIL-RELIGIOUS HIERARCHIES

In a previous paper, Taylor and I (Chance and Taylor 1985) challenged the long-held assumption that the civil-religious hierarchy has its origins in the early colonial period. We argue that such an assumption errs in projecting a twentieth-century ethnographic present back into the colonial past. Drawing on primary and secondary sources for Jalisco, Michoacán, the central Mexican highlands, the Valley of Oaxaca, the Sierra Zapoteca of Oaxaca, and Chiapas, we have suggested that the earliest form of the *cargo* system was a *civil* hierarchy, that it emerged in the sixteenth century, and that it was comprised of the political offices making up the municipal *cabildo* (town council). While some of the lower offices had indigenous names and probably dated from pre-Hispanic times, the higher *cargos* all carried Spanish titles and were filled by annual elections as required by colonial law.

Religious offices in colonial indigenous towns were centered in *cofradías*, religious sodalities founded to organize support for the cult of local saints and pay for its expenses. These sodalities, however, were a relatively late colonial development—most were founded in the seventeenth and eighteenth centuries. Furthermore, the evidence indicates that for most of the colonial period, these religious offices existed separately from the civil *cargo* systems, that is, that there were no unified civil-religious hierarchies. The custom of household sponsorship of fiestas, so important to twentieth-century *cargo* systems, was more the exception than the rule during colonial times when most fiestas were sponsored corporately by the *cofradías* themselves. Proceeds from their own cornfields or cattle herds were a primary means of financing fiestas. The civil-religious *cargo* system of the type recorded by ethnographers first emerged in the late eighteenth century and proliferated during the nineteenth, due to expropriations of *cofradía* property by the church and prohibition of communal support of religious fiestas by some Spanish political officials. These pressures brought about a shift from collective to household fiesta sponsorship. At the same time, the colonial status differences between indigenous nobles and commoners were being dismantled and there was growing concern in the villages that each household should help shoulder the burden of maintaining the cult of the saints. The historical outcome of these factors was the "classic" form of the civil-religious hierarchy.

If our ethnohistorical analysis is correct, major structural changes in village *cargo* systems can be expected to occur at times when direct political interference and external pressure on local resources are high. Civil *cargo* hierarchies arose initially in the sixteenth century as a local response to Spanish efforts to impose political control on indigenous communities via a European-derived model of town government. Likewise, the transformation from a civil to a civil-religious system came at a time when the corporate holdings of *cofradías* were under attack from external powerholders. Here I extend this line of reasoning into the twentieth century and argue that another structural change has been brought about by new external political pressures.

FROM CIVIL-RELIGIOUS TO RELIGIOUS HIERARCHIES

In reference to Guatemalan *cargo* systems in the 1950s, Manning Nash (1958:67) noted that the twin political and religious ladders

are tied together by common symbols, and in virtue of the fact that men in office alternate between posts in each of the ladders. The difference between the two ladders is conceptual. Indians tend to think of them as one system. And the term civil-religious hierarchy recognizes this fact of interrelation.

A decade later, following his fieldwork in Zinacantan, Chiapas, Cancian (1967:284) claimed that

In other communities—apparently where national governments have recently imposed a new system of civil offices—the differentiation is clear, and the civil offices may even be excluded from the formal hierarchy of service.

Such is the case in Zinacantan, and Cancian (1965) subtitled his study of the hierarchy in that community *The Religious Cargo System in Zinacantan*. Table 20–1 lists published case studies since 1965 that provide evidence of functioning *cargo* systems. I make no claims for completeness; a number of works had to be excluded because they failed to provide sufficient data on the relationships between the civil and religious components of the hierarchies. But I believe the cases in Table 20–1 stand as a reasonably accurate representation of accumulated ethnographic knowledge between 1965 and 1986.

On the whole, these 23 examples show that while the old colonial civil hierarchies have passed from the scene (no cases are reported), civil-religious hierarchies are now themselves in the minority. The most prominent trend in recent ethnography is the proliferation of *religious cargo* systems, which are now twice as common as those of the civil-religious type. (The five "transitional" systems will be discussed below.) I define religious *cargo* systems as those which maintain a hierarchy of public offices for the manifest purpose of serving the local saints. Such hierarchies may consist of sodalities (*cofradías*), or as is common today in Mexico, single positions (*mayordomías*), but in either case offices are usually ranked hierarchically in a more or less clear-cut order.[4] In communities with religious *cargo* systems, the civil offices have become in large measure formally divorced from the traditional prestige hierarchy. This is, I would argue, the most fundamental structural change in twentieth-century *cargo* systems.

TABLE 20–1   Ethnographies of Mesoamerican *Cargo* Systems, 1965 to 1986

Community and Type of System	Ethnolinguistic Group	Source
Civil-Religious Systems:		
Sta. María Yolotepec, Oaxaca	Chatino	Bartolomé and Barabas 1982
Yaitepec, Oaxaca	Chatino	Greenberg 1981
San Mateo del Mar, Oaxaca	Huave	Signorini 1979
San Pedro Yolox, Oaxaca	Chinantec	Gwaltney 1970
Chinautla, Guatemala	Pokomam	Reina 1966
Momostenango, Guatemala	Quiché	Tedlock 1982
Transitional Systems:		
Tlalchiyahualica, Hidalgo	Nahua	Schryer n.d.
Xalpatláhuac, Guerrero	Nahua	Dehouve 1976
Tlacoapa, Guerrero	Tlapanec	Oettinger 1980
Tlahuitoltepec, Oaxaca	Mixe	Kuroda 1984
Amatenango, Chiapas	Tzeltal	J. Nash 1970
Religious Systems:		
Atempan, Puebla	Nahua	Buchler 1967
Tlaxcalancingo, Puebla	Nahua	Olivera 1967
Chignaula, Puebla	Nahua	Slade 1973
Eastern Morelos region	Nahua	Warman 1980
Tlayacapan, Morelos	Nahua	Ingham 1986
San Bernardino Contla, Tlaxcala	Nahua	Nutini 1968
San Rafael Tepetlaxco, Tlaxcala	Nahua	Chick 1981
Santa Monica, Hidalgo	Otomí	Dow 1977
Ihuatzio, Michoacán	Tarascan	Zantwijk 1967
Jamiltepec, Oaxaca	Mixtec	Flanet 1977
"San Miguel," Oaxaca	Zapotec	Mathews 1985
Zinacantan, Chiapas	Tzotzil	Cancian 1965

Before proceeding to examine this change in more detail, DeWalt's (1975) alternative typology deserves consideration. He surveyed 26 published case studies dating from the 1930s to the mid 1970s and sorted them into four types: civil-religious (10 cases), ornate religious (3), acephalous (5), and faded (8). DeWalt's "ornate religious" type is the same as that which I call "religious." By acephalous hierarchies he means those in which the "highest civil offices no longer require passage through the rest of the system as a prerequisite" (DeWalt 1975:91). Shortcuts are available for those who are literate in Spanish and possess other desirable skills, causing the civil side of the hierarchy to break down at the top. I regard such systems as "transitional." DeWalt's "faded" hierarchies are those in which only individual *mayordomos* remain. They may still sponsor fiestas, but are no longer part of a clear-cut hierarchy of religious offices. In my analysis, these cases do not qualify as functioning *cargo* systems, since the key defining element—a hierarchy of public offices—is no longer present.

In DeWalt's survey, more cases are of the "traditional" civil-religious type than any other. Yet it is significant that the data in six of the ten cases were obtained in the 1930s and 1940s. (And, not surprisingly, eight of the ten cases come from Oaxaca and Guatemala.) In contrast, all three of his "ornate religious" cases derive from studies done in the 1960s. These three appear in my Table 20–1 (Atempan, Contla, and Zinacantan), along with nine more, seven of which have appeared since DeWalt's survey. Clearly, the trend is away from a civil-religious to an essentially religious structure. This direction of change is also reflected in DeWalt's typology itself. His fourfold classification masks the fact that all 16 of his cases that deviate from the "traditional" civil-religious structure (i.e., the 3 ornate religious, 5 acephalous, and 8 faded) are similar in that they display either a weakening, breakdown, or sloughing off of the civil rungs of the older system. In all of these instances, community government has come to operate partly, if not entirely, outside the confines of the hierarchy.

There are, of course, other sorts of changes and other possible outcomes. Indeed, the most common variant of all is the collapse of the entire system, as the local prestige hierarchy gives way to more cosmopolitan modes of status seeking and status validation. Indigenous villages which support active *cargo* systems of any kind now comprise a dwindling minority. Quite frequently, what DeWalt terms "faded" systems may survive by replacing household fiesta sponsorship with a church committee or a collection of voluntary contributions (DeWalt 1975; Smith 1977; Brandes 1988). But in such cases the local prestige hierarchy may cease to function effectively, at least in the ritual context.

Yet a third response is well documented by Stephen (1987, *intra*) for the Zapotec town of Teotitlán del Valle in the Valley of Oaxaca. Here the religious hierarchy associated with the *mayordomías* has declined, but the ritual content and form of the system, instead of disappearing, have been relocated to the life cycle rituals. By transferring fiestas from *mayordomías* to occasions such as baptisms, confirmations, and birthdays, Teotiecos have, Stephen argues, "transformed domestic rituals into public celebrations" (*intra*). This adaptation may well prove to be widespread among the more open communities which are highly integrated with the market system through commercial agriculture and craft production for export. But while the continuities in such cases may be striking, whether they can be regarded as *cargo* systems is an open question. To view them as such, it would have to be shown that household-based fiestas for life cycle events can support a recognized community prestige hierarchy. This question lies beyond the scope of this paper. The present analysis is intended to apply only to the more closed, conservative communities which still maintain functioning *cargo* hierarchies.

Fundamentally, the structural shift from a civil-religious to a religious hierarchy is symptomatic of increasing community integration into the structures of state and national government. As the legally appointed town governments come to operate more independently of the *cargo* systems, the

hierarchies themselves become more occupied than before with internal ritual activities and less concerned with representing the community to the outside. The political pressures that bring about the change from a civil-religious to a religious system are most evident in the transitional cases listed in Table 20–1. These are communities where (using the ethnographic present) the civil and religious sides of the hierarchy are in tension and growing further apart, but have not yet been sundered. A good example is Danièle Dehouve's (1976:220–239) analysis of the increasing power of the Mexican state in the affairs of the Nahuatl-speaking village of Xalpatláhuac, Guerrero. New political *cargos* resulting from government reforms after 1930 have not been incorporated into the hierarchy, but exist outside of it and have stimulated considerable factionalism. A similar situation can be found in Amatenango, Chiapas where a civil-religious hierarchy still exists, although the high political *cargos* of *presidente, síndico*, and *secretario* are excluded from it and filled by young men who are literate in Spanish. As for the lower civil *cargos*, they are mainly ceremonial and ambitious individuals may bypass them altogether (J. Nash 1970:159–196). In the Tlapanec community of Tlacoapa, Guerrero, civil and religious affairs are also becoming estranged. The civil-religious hierarchy is no longer well defined and there is little alternation between civil and religious posts (Oettinger 1980:99–104). A further example of how the civil-religious hierarchy is bifurcated is succinctly summarized by Frans Schryer (n.d.:317) for Nahuatl-speaking Tlalchiyahualica, located in the *municipio* (township) of Yahualica, Hidalgo:

> Most civil posts (beyond the lowest rank of *topile*) are highly regulated by the national system and all top posts (*juez* and *comisariado*) must be confirmed by the *presidente municipal* or the Land Reform bureaucracy. In contrast, the religious posts represent a parallel but unofficial structure which provides prestige, but little real power.

The transition to a full-blown religious *cargo* system has important implications not only for the administration of political affairs and the exercise of power, but also for cultural integration in the community. One of the fullest accounts available is Doren Slade's (1973) description of the religious *cargo* system in Chignautla, a Nahuatl-speaking town in Puebla's Sierra Norte. Here the distinction between civil and religious administrations—the *ayuntamiento municipal* and the *autoridad eclesiástica*—is the most basic principle in the organization of public life. According to Slade:

> To Chignautecos . . . the most significant differentiation of *cargos* is on the basis of which authority appoints the individuals who hold them and controls their activities, and not on the basis of duties performed. In essence, there are two systems, a moral system and a legal system paralleling a difference between religious life and civil life which does not always coincide with the administration process, but operates in terms of the ultimate locus of authority in each system.
>
> At the basis of the moral system is a belief that God created the ideals and norms for human behavior. . . . in the legal system, the ultimate authority is the legal code of the state which may be manipulated and to which one must answer only if caught (1973:194–196).

I suggest that the growing estrangement between the formal civil and religious ladders in the transitional systems described above is the first step in the evolution of an explicitly religious *cargo* system of the type found in Chignautla. There are, of course, a host of local factors that have a bearing on the direction of change in each case, but the evident commonalities in the ethnographic record indicate that there are also more general socio-historical processes at work. The principal factors involved in the emergence of religious *cargo* systems are not at all mysterious, but they acquire a special significance when we consider the history of the institution and that the first *cargo* systems were *civil* systems which linked indigenous communities to the colonial Spanish regime. Only in the twentieth century have state and national governments acted to replace colonial forms of local government with new systems more in line with national priorities. The nineteenth century is the least understood period in the ethnohistory of Mesoamerican village politics, but if Ronald Spores's (1984) work on Oaxaca is at all representative, there was surprisingly little change in the structure of local level

government during the turbulent years following Mexican Independence. He says:

> What may be most remarkable is that despite the great political upheavals of the [nineteenth] century, local level government and relations between local, state, and national levels ended essentially as they began. A practical and basically effective system which evolved during the colonial period survived and persisted through a series of experiments in government (1984:168).

All this began to change significantly following revolutionary movements in the twentieth century. Drawing on a number of case studies, Richard Adams (1957) has shown that the pivotal events in Guatemala followed on the heels of the Revolution of 1944. The promotion of political parties and competitive local elections brought fundamental changes in community government, among them the weakening and destruction of many civil-religious hierarchies. The corresponding triggering event in Mexico came earlier, in the form of the Revolution of 1910. One of the most important revolutionary products was the Mexican Constitution of 1917 that called for a new system of local political offices, subject to regulation by individual state laws, to replace the older colonial forms.

Especially important were the attempts of the Mexican government to apply the new constitution between 1920 and 1940. Despite the revolutionary rhetoric supporting the concept of the *municipio libre* (the free municipio, or township), the Obregón, Calles, and Cárdenas governments actively sought to limit the autonomy of the local community and integrate it in new ways into national society (see Greenberg *intra*). The formation of a national revolutionary political party in 1929 (The Partido Nacional Revolucionario, precursor of today's Partido Revolucionario Institucional, or PRI) had important repercussions at the local level, even in seemingly remote areas. A federal school system by the state was begun and the anticlericalism of the Calles administration posed a threat to many local ritual traditions. These penetrations into local community spread to different regions of Mexico at different rates, but the general trend is clear and few, if any, villages appears to have remained unaffected. Despite some communities' ability to incorporate the newer political offices into their civil-religious hierarchies (see Table 20–1), many others have failed to do so effectively. Such failure may lead to a total breakdown of a preexisting *cargo* system or to the formation of a religious hierarchy which excludes the new political offices. A common result in either case is a decrease in local level autonomy and an increase in community dependency on state and federal governments. Political brokering by local officials becomes an important source of community income, and individuals who are literate in Spanish and equipped to deal with outsiders respond to these demands. In the process they frequently violate the rules of the civil-religious hierarchy by going quickly to the top of the civil ladder instead of passing through the ranks in the traditional way. Such activity is a sign that tension between the civil and religious spheres of public life has begun to build in addition to the transitional cases discussed above, see also Kuroda (1984:63; Mathews 1985:291–292; Signorini 1979:93–121; and others cited in DeWalt 1975:95).

Certainly there are exceptions to this trend toward decreasing local autonomy. Lynn Stephen's work (1987; 1988; n.d.) in Teotitlán del Valle suggests that a relatively affluent community able to fund public works projects is less in need of political brokers than are poorer communities. Teotitlán can *afford* to fill civil *cargo* posts with people who are more concerned with local priorities than with external political affairs. Commercial development in this town (centered around the tourist-oriented weaving industry) has led to class tensions between merchant and weaving households, but class-based criteria for prestige must still compete with those based on community ethnic solidarity. This slower growth of class relations may be due to the fact that Teotitlán's development as a weaving town explicitly builds on its indigenous cultural heritage. Stephen (n.d.) points to a dual ethnic identity in the community: one identity produced for outside consumers of Teotitlán's textiles and indigenous culture (tourists, importers, state officials, etc.), and another defined from within, accessible only to those who participate in local social networks and institutions. This analysis perhaps could be extended to other economically successful tourist and craft communities, but there are not many of them. Overall, the number of indigenous communities able to retain this sort of quasi-independence from government funding is decreasing.

Most twentieth-century civil-religious hierarchies, when confronted with state interference, have adapted by retrenching, by transforming themselves into more overtly religious hierarchies, and by turning inward and emphasizing local ritual matters. Communities that choose this path give up some of their political autonomy, but are turning inward and emphasizing local ritual matters. Communities that choose this path give up some of their political autonomy, but are apt to retain strong local identities. In other cases, of course, civil-religious hierarchies have failed to adapt to internal political pressures and have collapsed altogether.

A number of ethnographers have noted that the *cargo* systems in the villages they studied began to unravel in the 1920s (see, for example, Acheson 1970:245; Foster 1967:194–211; J. Nash 1970:230). The timing is significant, given the pressure exerted on municipalities by the revolutionary governments, as discussed above. Not only does state encroachment drive a wedge between the civil and religious spheres of traditional hierarchies, but it also can polarize them and place them in competition with each other. Kate Young (1976) gives a vivid account of political struggles in a highland Zapotec village in Oaxaca between 1920 and 1940, in which progressive and conservative factions mirrored the civil and religious sides of the *cargo* system. She shows how the PRI, its precursor parties, and the Oaxaca state government, working through local officials, effectively polarized the community for twenty years and ultimately destroyed its civil-religious hierarchy:

> The President at the beginning of the 1920s was always an elderly man (usually near 60); nowadays he is generally in his thirties. The streaming of *cargos* . . . has also had the effect of channelling the important posts in the village administration to men who tend on the whole to be more oriented toward the national culture. They are also possibly more malleable, that is they are less likely to reject out of hand improvements such as installing a telegraph office. At the same time there is no longer a single system of ranking with which the allocation of prestige is articulated; rather the emphasis on youth, education and wealth is in direct opposition to

the former emphasis on age, service to the gods and the fulfillment of obligations to the community.

By taking political power away from the elders, the local administrative apparatus was restructured in such a way as to be more responsive to pressure from the centre—either the state or the federal government. The undermining of the elders' authority also played an important part in freeing people from the bonds of the previous system so that they could participate in the new type of social and economic relations which were developing throughout the period (Young 1976:260-261).

It is important to note that the process Young describes was not an unplanned consequence or by-product of national government reforms, but rather the outcome of deliberate efforts by particular Oaxaca politicians to destroy the traditional hierarchies in this and other villages. Stephen (1987; *intra*) recounts a similar chain of events that unfolded in Teotitlán del Valle during the same period, and further shows how the decline of the *mayordomía* system there was linked to the anti-church policies of the Calles presidency. While Teotitlán's status as a craft village and higher level of market integration make it different in many respects from the poorer highland community described by Young, the exogenous forces penetrating each town in the 1920s were quite similar.

Another significant, if less dramatic, example of polarization between civil and religious sectors comes from Arturo Warman's work in several towns in eastern Morelos. Religious *cargo* systems prevail there, but they are on the defensive—they are important only in small satellite villages which have few civil officials to challenge their authority. *Cabeceras* (municipal head towns) with a full complement of civil officials, and frequently a resident priest as well, have weak religious *cargo* systems. Thus the hierarchies are being driven out of the nodes of formal power in eastern Morelos, and are taking refuge in smaller places where they can partially and informally fill the political vacuum. In some towns, community *mayordomos* have been replaced by committees and the religious hierarchies have retreated to the level of the *barrio* (neighborhood). In these instances, autonomy is sacrificed at the community level, but retained at

lower levels through fragmentation (Warman 1980:291–293).

While the Oaxaca and Morelos examples have overtones of conflict between church and state, the fundamental contradiction is really between the state and the local community. In Young's highland Zapotec case, the community lost the battle when its religious hierarchy collapsed in 1940 and out-migration began its upward spiral. But this is, after all, just a single village. Teotitlán, more favored economically, has been able to hold its own. Warman's Morelos study shows that at the regional level the confrontation may proceed slowly and perhaps more gradually.

One of the most elusive aspects of the rise of religious hierarchies is its relationship to the changing distribution of power, both within particular communities and between those communities and the state. The divorce of civil positions from a *cargo* system does not mean that local power will be concentrated entirely in the hands of the formally constituted civil authorities. The balance of power may indeed tilt toward the civil administration (see Flanet 1977:42–49; Schryer n.d.: 317; Olivera 1967:70; Warman 1980:291–293), but some can be expected to remain in the hands of the religious *cargo* holders. The problem lies in determining how the balance is struck. In Chignautla, Puebla, for example, Slade (1973:221) shows that as far as the indigenous community members are concerned, civil *cargos*—held by *mestizos*—carry authority, but very little legitimacy. Power in this community is shared by mestizo civil authorities and indigenous community members of high ritual status who have participated in the religious *cargo* system, though Slade does not assign them a relative weighting.

More revealing of trends over time is June Nash's assessment of the balance of power between *principales* and civil officials in Amatenango, Chiapas, in the 1960s. Amatenango retains a civil-religious hierarchy, but it should be understood as "transitional" because there have been important changes. According to Nash, the *principales* have been rendered nearly powerless in the face of strong support for an independent civil authority. While the overt form of political organization—the civil-religious hierarchy—remains the same, there has been a shift in the balance of power "from leaders whose authority rested on guardianship linked with the ancestors to leaders who can deal with the external power structure" (J. Nash 1970:266).

I would hypothesize that the shift from a civil-religious to a religious *cargo* system can be expected to carry with it a decrease in the power and functions of the *principales*. The extent of the decrease, and whether or not the *principales* will come to share power with other groups, will vary from town to town, as the comparison of Chignautla with Amatenango suggests. Another case in point comes from the District of Jamiltepec in Oaxaca, where Mixtec communities support civil-religious hierarchies and powerful groups of elders (De Cicco 1966:372). In the head town of Jamiltepec itself, however, civil offices are controlled by *mestizos* and the indigenous community members maintain a *cargo* system with a much weaker array of elders (Flanet, 1977:42–49).[5]

I would further suggest that the replacement of civil-religious hierarchies with religious hierarchies and separate civil offices entails a fragmentation of local power centers and an overall loss of community power vis-à-vis the state. Guillermo de la Peña (1981:240) notes the significant fragmentation which has occurred in Tlayacapan, Morelos (a town with a religious *cargo* system; see Ingham 1986:92–95). Most striking is the multiplicity of agencies in Tlayacapan (and many other Mexican villages) concerned with the maintenance of order, administration of justice, and implementation of public goals. In addition to the *ayuntamiento* (municipal council), there are the *ejido* land committee, the communal land committee, the village auxiliary officers, the public works committee, and the PRI committee. There is also considerable interference by district level officials, including the police, the courts, the district deputy, and the tax collector. According to de la Peña:

> All these agencies compete with one another for control of local environments; and it is only through the dependence on patrons in higher political spheres that a partial (never a total) control over environments is achieved. . . .
>
> Loyalty and the perception of their own powerlessness are related to the participation by the local authorities in a series of activities which further reinforce their subordination and dependence (1981:240, 245).

Tlayacapan may well represent one extreme on a continuum of local dependency on state and regional structures. It is difficult to say whether de la Peña's analysis would apply to southern communities with religious hierarchies such as Zinacantan. June Nash (1970:265) argues convincingly that while Amatenango has experienced an internal shift in power groups, the town as a whole has ceded little autonomy to external political authorities. But Amatenango is a transitional community, and it is clear that a major instrument for the maintenance of its autonomy is the preservation of its civil-religious hierarchy.

Another possible method of preserving local power, of course, is *cacique* rule. Henning Siverts (1981:53) describes how in Chiapas powerful *caciques* sometimes emerge in communities where parallel indigenous and ladino administrative systems are in conflict. James Dow (personal communication) suggests that *caciquismo* is best adapted to times of war and that a community may oscillate between a *cacique* system and a *cargo* system as conditions change. These are important issues, but necessarily remain beyond the scope of this paper.

It would be erroneous to view religious *cargo* systems in purely expressive terms and deny them a role in village political life. They can perhaps most accurately be seen as part of the process of fragmentation of local power alluded to above. In this sense a religious hierarchy is likely to be just one of several local groups competing for power. From the external point of view, however, it is also clear that the political spoils to be had in such communities are meager. Religious *cargo* systems thus simultaneously constitute a recognition of decreased village autonomy and power relative to the state, as well as an attempt to prevent yet further losses.

CONCLUSION

Preservation of a local *cargo* system of any kind is a conservative strategy, an attempt to assert local autonomy and community identity in the face of external pressures. As national governments penetrate more deeply into community political life, religious *cargo* systems may form to stave off further erosion of village autonomy. Religious hierarchies are at best compromise solutions, at once products of the political penetration of community boundaries and weapons with which to combat further penetration.

Linking ethnography to ethnohistory, it is now possible to sketch the trajectory of structural change in Mesoamerican *cargo* systems over four centuries and observe how they have responded to historical episodes when communities were under particularly heavy pressure from external political and religious authorities. Early *civil cargo* systems, I have argued, were a direct result of the imposition of the Spanish model of town government in indigenous communities in the sixteenth century. They amounted to a reshaping of Spanish offices by indigenous community members to make them fit their own circumstances. These civil hierarchies facilitated colonial economic exploitation from the outside and rechanneled indigenous status aspirations on the inside. At the same time, they helped maintain the indigenous social strata of nobles and commoners that were recognized by the Spanish colonial legal system.

The change from a civil to a *civil-religious* structure was an adaptation to nineteenth-century attacks by government and the church on the corporate property holdings that had supported local religious ceremonies. During this period, household sponsorship of fiestas became institutionalized, while civil and religious offices were fused into a unified ladder of *cargos*. Economic burdens rested more directly on individual households, and the old colonial stratification between nobles and commoners crumbled. This civil-religious structure entailed a new emphasis on internal activities. These systems were more inward-looking, more involved with local ritual and local identity, and less concerned than their civil predecessors with representing the community to the outside (Chance and Taylor 1985).

Finally, in the twentieth century, revolution and political reforms for the first time opposed the whole concept of the politically autonomous indigenous community, and state and federal governments have attempted to incorporate local leadership into higher level bureaucratic and party hierarchies. Where these efforts have been successful, local civil hierarchies have become divorced from religious offices and in a sense have left the community

and become appendages of higher-level systems. This process has effectively destroyed many civil-religious hierarchies, but a significant number have adapted by transforming themselves into primarily religious systems. Such changes have meant yet another step inward and a renewed emphasis on internal ritual affairs.

NOTES

Acknowledgments. This is a revised and expanded version of a paper presented at the 86th annual meeting of the American Anthropological Association, Chicago, November 18–22, 1987, as part of a symposium on "The Political Economy of Religion in Mexico and Central America." I wish to thank Frans Schryer for generously providing me with his unpublished manuscript and Frank Cancian, Pedro Carrasco, James Dow, Stephen Gudeman, and Lynn Stephen for their comments on earlier drafts of this paper. Any errors that remain are entirely my own.

1. In some communities, fiesta sponsorship is undertaken not by individuals, but by male and female pairs, often, but not always, consisting of husband and wife (Mathews 1985; Reina 1966; Stephen 1988). This pattern may well represent the norm. I believe most anthropologists would agree, however, that whether sponsorship is undertaken by individuals or by couples, they act as representatives of households.

2. I find it useful to distinguish between a *cargo* system, a hierarchy of ranked offices which individuals or couples ascend, and a fiesta system in which prestige is attained through ceremonial sponsorship in the absence of any fixed hierarchy of positions. *Cargo* systems often involve fiesta sponsorship, especially in the twentieth century, but Taylor and I have argued that colonial civil *cargo* systems lacked this feature (Chance and Taylor 1985).

3. As measured by a high degree of geographical mobility, location near a large city, economic and social ties with large cities, supplementary wage labor in other regions, and variety of transportation facilities (DeWalt 1975:95).

4. Some studies note that the rank order of offices is not well defined or even nonexistent (Chick 1981:227; Dehouve 1976:220–239; Oettinger 1980;99; Slade 1973:106–113). The importance of these observations

is unclear. Perhaps a muddled ranking is linked to the growing bifurcation of civil and religious positions.

5. The District of Jamiltepec also seems to exhibit the same sort of polarization between civil and religious authority noted above for eastern Morelos (Warman 1980).

REFERENCES

Acheson, James, 1970. "Where Opportunity Knocked: Social and Economic Change in the Tarascan Pueblo of Cuanajo, Michoacán." Ph.D. dissertation, University of Rochester.

Adams, Richard N., 1957. "Changing Political Relationships in Guatemala." In *Political Changes in Guatemalan Indian Communities*. Richard N. Adams, editor, pp. 48–54. Middle American Research Institute Publication 24. New Orleans: Tulane University.

Bartolomé, Miguel A. and Alicia M. Barabas, 1982. *Tierra de la palabra: historia y etnografía de los chatinos de Oaxaca*. Mexico City: INAH. Colección Científica No. 108.

Brandes, Stanley, 1988. *Power and Persuasion: Fiestas and Social Control in Rural Mexico*. Philadelphia: University of Pennsylvania Press.

Buchler, Ira R., 1967. "La organización ceremonial de una aldea mexicana." *América Indígena* 27(2):237–263.

Cancian, Frank, 1965. *Economics and Prestige in a Maya Community: The Religious Cargo System in Zinacantan*. Stanford: Stanford University Press.

———, 1967. "Political and Religious Organization." In *Handbook of Middle American Indians*, Volume 6. Robert Wauchope, general editor, pp. 283–298. Austin: University of Texas Press.

Carrasco, Pedro, 1952. *Tarascan Folk Religion: An Analysis of Economic, Social, and Religious Interactions*. Middle American Research Institute, Publication 17. New Orleans: Tulane University.

Chance, John K. and William B. Taylor, 1985. "Cofradías and Cargos: An Historical Perspective on the Mesoamerican Civil-Religious Hierarchy," *American Ethnologist* 12(1):1–26.

Chick, Garry E., 1981. "Concept and Behavior in a Tlaxcalan Cargo Hierarchy," *Ethnology* 20(3):217–228.

De Cicco, Gabriel, 1966. "Systems of Civil Authority in the Mixteca Baja: Patterns and Conflicts." In *Summa anthropologica en homenaje a Roberto J. Weitlaner*. Mexico City: Secretaría de Educación Pública and INAH, pp. 371–374.

Dehouve, Danièle, 1976. *El tequio de los santos y la competencia entre los mercaderes*. Mexico City: Instituto Nacional Indigenista.

de la Peña, Guillermo, 1981. *A Legacy of Promises*. Austin: University of Texas Press.

DeWalt, Billie R., 1975. "Changes in the Cargo Systems of Mesoamerica," *Anthropological Quarterly* 48:87–105.

Dow, James, 1977. "Religion in the Organization of a Mexican Peasant Economy." In Rhoda Halperin and James Dow (eds.), *Peasant Livelihood: Studies in Economic Anthropology and Cultural Ecology*. New York: St. Martin's Press, pp. 215–226.

Flanet, Veronique, 1977. *Viveré si Dios quiere*. Mexico City: Instituto Nacional Indigenista.

Foster, George, 1967. *Tzintzuntzan: Mexican Peasants in a Changing World*. Boston: Little, Brown.

Greenberg, James B., 1981. *Santiago's Sword: Chatino Peasant Religion and Economics*. Berkeley: University of California Press.

Gwaltney, John L., 1970. *The Thrice Shy*. New York: Columbia University Press.

Ingham, John M., 1986. *Mary, Michael, and Lucifer: Folk Catholicism in Central Mexico*. Austin: University of Texas Press.

Jones, Grant D., 1981. "Symbolic Dramas of Ethnic Stratification: The Yucatecan Fiesta System on a Colonial Frontier." *University of Oklahoma Papers in Anthropology* 22(1):131–155.

Kuroda, Etsuko, 1984. "Under Mt. Zempoaltépetl: Highland Mixe Society and Ritual." *Senri Ethnological Studies*, No. 12. Osaka, Japan: National Museum of Ethnology.

Mathews, Holly F., 1985. "We are Mayordomo: A Reinterpretation of Women's Roles in the Mexican Cargo System," *American Ethnologist* 12(2):285–301.

Montoya Briones, José de Jesús, 1964. *Atla; ethnografía de un pueblo náhuatl*. Mexico City: INAH.

Nash, June, 1970. *In the Eyes of the Ancestors*. New Haven: Yale University Press.

Nash, Manning, 1958. "Political Relations in Guatemala," *Social and Economic Studies* 7:65–75.

Nutini, Hugo G., 1968. *San Bernardino Contla*. Pittsburgh: University of Pittsburgh Press.

Oettinger, Marion, 1980. *Una comunidad tlapaneca*. Mexico City: Instituto Nacional Indigenista.

Olivera de V., Mercedes, 1967. *Tlaxcalancingo*. Mexico City: INAH, Departamento de Investigaciones Antropológicos, Pub. No. 18.

Reina, Ruben E., 1966. *The Law of the Saints*. Indianapolis: Bobbs-Merrill.

Schryer, Frans J., n.d. "Class Conflict and Ethnicity in Rural Mexico: Peasant Revolt in a Nahua Region." Unpublished manuscript. University of Guelph, Canada.

Signorini, Italo, 1979. *Los Huaves de San Mateo del Mar*. Mexico City: Instituto Nacional Indigenista.

Siverts, Henning, 1981. "Stability and Change in Highland Chiapas, Mexico," *University of Bergen, Occasional Papers in Social Anthropology*, No. 4 Bergen, Norway.

Slade, Doren L., 1973. "The Mayordomos of San Mateo: Political Economy of a Religious System." Ph.D. dissertation, University of Pittsburgh.

Smith, Waldemar R., 1977. *The Fiesta System and Economic Change*. New York: Columbia University Press.

Spores, Ronald, 1984. "Multi-Level Government in Nineteenth-Century Oaxaca." In Ronald Spores and Ross Hassig (eds.), *Five Centuries of Law and Politics in Central Mexico*. Nashville: Vanderbilt University Publications in Anthropology, No. 30, pp. 145–172.

Stephen, Lynn, 1987. *Weaving Changes: Economic Development and Gender Roles in Zapotec Ritual and Production*. Ph.D. dissertation, Brandeis University. Ann Arbor: University Microfilms.

———, 1988. "Zapotec Gender Politics: The Creation of Political Arenas by and for Peasant Women." Paper presented at the 87th annual meeting of the American Anthropological Association, November 16–20, Phoenix, Arizona.

———, n.d. "Culture as a Resource: Four Cases of Self-Managed Indigenous Craft Production." *Economic Development and Cultural Change*. In Press.

Tedlock, Barbara, 1982. *Time and the Highland Maya*. Albuquerque: University of New Mexico Press.

Warman, Arturo, 1980. *We Come to Object*. Baltimore: Johns Hopkins University Press.

Young, Kate, 1976. "The Social Setting of Migration." Ph.D. dissertation, London University.

Zantwijk, R.A.M. Van, 1967. *Servants of the Saints*. Assen, The Netherlands: Van Gorcum.

21

Religion, Class, and Context
Continuities and Discontinuities in Brazilian Umbanda

Diana De G. Brown and Mario Bick

The period of Brazilian slavery provided all the ingredients for a classic encounter between Western and non-Western religions, as Portuguese Catholic slaveholders exercised almost total power over African and African-descended slaves. According to virtually all Western models of change, such an unequal encounter would result in the demise, or at best the marginalization, fragmentation, or secular folklorization of the religions of the slaves (M. Herskovits, 1941; Thomas 1971:663–668). The diaspora status of the Brazilian slaves, effectively cut off from contact with Africa after the closing of the slave trade in the 1850s, together with the conscious deculturative and acculturative policies of the slaverarchy and the brutal realities of slave life, should have made this process particularly rapid.

Diana De G. Grown and Mario Bick, "Religion, Class, and Context: Continuities and Discontinuities in Brazilian Umbanda." Reproduced by permission of the American Anthropological Association from *American Ethnologist* 14: 1, 73—93, February 1987. Not for further reproduction.

Despite these apparently ideal conditions for the triumph of Western civilization and Christianity over the religious traditions of the African slaves, Brazilian history has not conformed to these expectations. The African religious heritage was not displaced by Catholicism, nor was it reduced to a condition of fragmentation, marginalization, or "mere superstition" disarticulated from everyday life and relegated to the status of secular folklore. On the contrary, it has endured and has become an increasingly vital part of Brazilian religious life. More than 350 years after the inception of slavery, and a decade after its abolition, in 1888, Afro-Brazilian religions flourished within the African-descended populations and were spreading throughout the popular urban classes. Observers in the 1930s and 1940s reported their continuing popularity and further spread in Brazil's major coastal cities, and in the 1950s, a new Afro-Brazilian religion, Umbanda, was observed to be gaining a major following in the southern industrial centers, and spreading throughout the nation.

Umbanda, the religion on which we will focus in this paper, carries on the Afro-Brazilian form of collective spirit possession and celebrates the spirits and deities of earlier Afro-Brazilian traditions.

It places Afro-Brazilian religious vigor and creativity at the very center of the advanced capitalist development in Brazil. Moreover, since its beginnings in the 1920s and early 1930s, Umbanda has appealed to a wide spectrum of Brazilian urban society, drawing its adherents, including leaders and mediums, from the affluent to the very poor, from the university educated to the illiterate. Members of all of Brazil's major racial and ethnic groups participate, and it retains its popularity among Brazilian blacks.[1] Umbanda is now estimated to have as many as 30 million practitioners in a population of 120 million. Its success has brought it recognition as a major competitor of Catholicism, and some followers and observers view it as the emerging national religion of Brazil. It is practiced in Brazilian immigrant communities in Uruguay (Moro and Ramirez 1981) and in the United States, in Los Angeles, Washington, New York, and Newark (Brown 1980a).

Umbanda represents an extreme, but not unique, example of the changes that Afro-Brazilian religions have undergone over the past century in their identification with the African heritage, the class locus, size, and composition of their memberships, and in their acceptance into the mainstream of Brazilian culture. Transformations since the 1930s have only recently begun to receive serious attention (Bastide 1978; Brown 1974, 1986; Dantas 1982; Fry 1982a; Ortiz 1978). Most scholars have focused on religious continuities and purity at the expense of discontinuities and recombination, on class segregation rather than the interplay of classes, and have failed to study these religions within the context of the historical processes that shape them and of which they are a part.

This paper explores the complexities of contemporary Afro-Brazilian religious change through an examination of Umbanda. We argue that an understanding of Umbanda is a historical and sociological phenomenon requires an examination of Brazilian class formation and interaction, race and racial identities, national political institutions and ideologies, as well as national and international reevaluations of the image of Africa and its peoples. We draw upon other examples to show that comparable changes have also occurred in other Brazilian religions. Our analysis emphasizes that the processes by which the African heritage in Brazil has undergone dilution and reconstitution

are both flexible and protean. We argue against any necessary unilineal and unidirectional process governing the history of these religions, and present evidence that while they continue to provide important ties for Brazilian blacks, among themselves and toward Africa, they have also gained an independent existence in the broader Brazilian cultural repertoire, constituting an important ideological component of the dominant classes and the state.

Following a brief historical sketch of the origins and spread of Afro-Brazilian religions, we identify major sources of error and bias in this literature. We then give an account of Umbanda as currently practiced and as it has developed from its beginnings in Rio in the 1920s and 30s, locating its development in the political, economic, cultural, and racial changes in Brazilian society. Finally, we suggest ways in which our own analysis of Umbanda informs an analysis of other Afro-Brazilian religions.

HISTORICAL BACKGROUND

A review of the major features of Brazilian slavery and slave society provides a basis for understanding the strength of the African-derived cultural forms first described in the 1890s. Throughout the entire period of the slave trade (approximately 1530–1850), Brazilian slave owners continued to rely principally on slaves imported from Africa rather than on the reproduction of the native slave population as occurred, for example, in the United States (Cunha 1985; Harris, 1964). The continuous steam of African peoples Brazil absorbed into its resident slave population through the mid-19th century ensured an undiminished African cultural presence. By at least the 18th century, and through the mid-19th century ensured an undiminished African cultural presence. By at least the 18th century, and through the mid-19th century, the Brazilian slave population significantly outnumbered the free population, and this disparity is considerably increased when African-descended freedmen (*libertos*) are added to the slave population (Cunha 1985:18–22). In the large urban centers where slave populations were most concentrated, the colonial regime adopted a form of social control which contributed to the preservation rather than to the suppression of many African cultural traditions

(Bastide 1971; Moreno Fraginals 1984). This took the form of divide and rule. Slaves were organized into "nations" (*nações*), based on broad similarities of origin, language, and culture. Within these "nations," which constituted ethnic groups rather than "pure" traditions of any specific African culture (Bastide 1971; Cunha 1985; Nina Rodrigues 1977), religious as well as secular African practices and beliefs were tolerated, protected, and even institutionalized (Bastide 1971).[2]

The Catholic Church, while succeeding in the nominal conversion of the slaves, failed to suppress their religious practices. Under the direct control of the Portuguese Crown throughout the Colonial period and until the end of the Empire in 1889, the Church in Brazil depended on the state for funds. Extreme limitations on its personnel further reduced its sphere of action in the Brazilian colony, and made the Church weaker in Brazil than in South America. Religious lay brotherhoods (*irmandades*) provided the main source of Catholic religious influence over the Brazilian slave populations. In their memberships, the *irmandades* often reproduced the Crown's division of the slave population into nations. While encouraging Catholic belief and practice, they also tolerated forms of African cultural expression, thereby sustaining African religions during the colonial period, and acting as a locus for the blending of African and Catholic traditions, called "syncretisms," which have continued to mark these religions (M. Herskovits 1937; Bastide 1971, 1978; Cardozo 1947; Russell-Wood 1982:128–160). Significantly, the appearance of the first autonomous Afro-Brazilian churches during the 19th century coincided with the period of decline of the brotherhoods (Bastide 1971).

By the 19th century, Afro-Brazilian religions were visible and flourishing in all major coastal cities and some rural areas. Traced back to 1830 in Salvador (Bastide 1978), to the mid-19th century in Recife (Ribeiro 1952:34–35) and São Luis (Costa Eduardo 1948:47), they were already widespread in the lesser studied southern region, in Rio by 1900, and in Vitória in the state of Espirito Santo during the late 19th century (Nery, quoted in Nina Rodrigues 1977:255–260). During the 20th century they have spread throughout Brazil, acquiring distinct regional forms and identities: *Candomblé* (in Bahia), *Xangó* (in Pernambuco, Alagoas, and Sergipe). *Casa das Minas* (in Maranhão), *Batuque*

(in Belém and Manaus), *Macumba* (throughout the southeast, but especially in Rio), and *Batuque* (in Porto Alegre). Broad regional differences have also been noted: a stronger Amerindian influence in the Amazon area, greater emphasis on the "orthodoxy" of African forms among denser concentrations of blacks in northeastern cities, and the prominence of more "syncretic" forms in the industrializing south.[3]

THE AFRO-BRAZILIAN LITERATURE

The voluminous literature on Afro-Brazilian religions produced by various scholars over almost a century is rich in ethnographic description, and short on sociological analysis. Some distortions and biases date back to the late 19th century and reveal these scholars' failure to critically examine the positions of their contemporaries or predecessors. The major biases, which assume the inferiority of Afro-Brazilian religions and the mental inferiority or ignorance of practitioners, were expressed in the overt racism of two influential early interpreters, Nina Rodrigues, writing at the turn of the century (1935, 1977) and Ramos, in the 1930s (1934, 1939). Both derided these "primitive," "barbaric," "fetishistic" religions of Africa and the ignorance, superstition, prelogical, and pathological mentality of their practitioners which was said to render them largely impervious to the civilizing influence of Catholicism (Nina Rodrigues 1935:182; Ramos, 1934:295). They feared the religions would jeopardize Brazil's capacity to modernize and, along with other educated Brazilians of the time, they placed their hopes for Brazil's progress in the whitening process (*embranquecimento*), which predicted the eventual domination of the culturally and biologically superior Euro-Brazilians over the inferior Afro-Brazilians.[4]

Though in attenuated form, these prejudices continued to haunt the literature through the 1950s and they still provide the language for criticism and denunciation by the press, the Catholic Church, and unsympathetic members of the Brazilian public.[5] A more subtle form of this same bias is found in the convention of referring to the religions as "cults," in contrast to Catholic and Protestant "religions,"[6] and in the pronounced tendency to emphasize the ritual aspects of Afro-Brazilian religious practice and neglect, and thus implicitly call into question, their theological content (see Dos Santos and Dos Santos 1984).

The work of Herskovits and his students (see F. Herskovits 1966; Ribeiro 1952; Costa Eduardo 1948), and of Landes (1947), and Carneiro (1936, 1937, 1940, 1961), which stressed the dignity, complexity, and social value of Afro-Brazilian religions, helped to counter their negative image. At the same time, their focus on cultural contact and the acculturation process distanced their studies from the realities of class and racial group interactions, and from the political and economic processes within which they were embedded.[7] It also fostered another persistent bias that the religions with the greatest number of African "survivals," which were referred to as "orthodox," or "pure," were superior to and more worthy of study than the more eclectic of "syncretic" forms. These latter came to be referred to as "tainted," "diluted," or "disintegrative," and received only cursory attention.[8] This bias has obscured the fact that all of these religions were adapted and blended within their Brazilian context, and that the categories "orthodox" and "syncretic," represent social constructs (Dantas 1982b) that are themselves worthy of study. Moreover, while the more "orthodox" forms have been seen as relatively unmodified, fossilized cultural survivals of an earlier period, they in fact reflect a form of change which has occurred during the present century, and involves the active pursuit of African orthodoxy. The research preference for "orthodox" religions has privileged the study of what is only a tiny fraction of the many thousands of Afro-Brazilian churches, and has led to the neglect of the vast majority that have become more eclectic. In Rio, viewed as the center of the syncretic tradition, as Bahia was considered the center of orthodoxy, lack of research interest in its "adulterated" Afro-Brazilian traditions has obscured Umbanda's origins and its relationship to older traditions known collectively as "Macumba."[9]

First attempts to place these religions within a wider framework of socioeconomic change (Pierson 1942; Costa Pinto 1952) continued to view them as inferior religions, products of ignorance and poverty, lingering remnants of incompletely assimilated African populations (Pierson 1942:237–274), or of an agrarian past (Cost Pinto 1952:238). Under the impact of modernization,

education, and upward mobility, these holdovers of the traditional sector, although portrayed as flourishing, were confidently expected to dissipate and lose their appeal, assimilating into Catholicism (Pierson 1942:305–317) or being relegated to the status of secular folklore (Costa Pinto 1952:257). This argument stressed class, rather than racial factors, and these researchers uniformly insisted that upwardly mobile blacks and mulattos would abandon their religious heritage (see also Hutchinson 1957; Wagley 1952). As Pierson concluded, quoting a white Brazilian informant, "when a Black man puts on a tie and shoes and learns to read and write, he loses his interest in the *candomblé*" (1942:316). That this did not represent social reality (though it may have been a cultural ideal) is clearly indicated in another contemporary study in the same city (Landes 1947), and may be inferred from the insistent tone with which the black press of the period exorted its readers to abandon Afro-Brazilian religions (Rolnik 1986, personal communication).

A more recent version of this class and race bias emerged in the period after 1945, when evidence of Umbanda's expansion in the heart of the urban industrial south forced the recognition that an Afro-Brazilian religion could be a part of, rather than apart from, contemporary industrial change. The first interpretations of Umbanda (Bastide 1978; Camargo 1961; Willems 1966), while recognizing its multiclass and multiracial composition, continued to interpret it as a creation and collective representation of the lower classes, of the proletariat (Willems 1966), or of a colored proletariat in formation (Bastide 1978). On the basis of these analyses, Umbanda entered the wider literature as a religion of the Brazilian oppressed (Lanternari 1963; Lewis 1971; Wilson 1973). This view assumed homogeneity and cohesiveness within Umbanda, denied differences of interest or conflicts among different class sectors, and assumed middle-class participation to be of peripheral importance. It thus presented an essential static view, which failed to explore the significance of middle-sector participation, and its important creative and co-optive role in the formation and development of Umbanda (Brown 1986). This same static view is perpetuated in the work of Ortiz (1978) who recognizes the importance and influence of he middle class in the formation of Umbanda, but sees it, within the industrial urban setting, as gradually converging with the lower-class practice of Umbanda through a process of mutual cultural osmosis involving the simultaneous "blackening" (Africanizing) of middle-class Spiritism and the "whitening" (de-Africanizing) of lower-class Afro-Brazilian traditions. As in earlier interpretations, the dynamics of class domination and conflict, power and politics, remain unexplored.

The legacy of these studies has been to obscure many crucial aspects of these religions' changing significance within Brazilian society. The work of the 1970s and 1980s, which has begun to explore these issues, will be discussed later.

UMBANDA

We now turn to an examination of Umbanda, taking as our focus the form originally known as Umbanda Pura (Pure Umbanda), or Umbanda Branca (White Umbanda),[10] more often known simply as Umbanda. Umbanda Pura was organized by the middle class in the last 1920s and early 1930s, and came to have a decisive influence over Umbanda as a whole (Brown 1974, 1977, 1986; Ortiz 1978). Yet the dynamism and flexibility in practice and belief which characterize Umbanda, and which we wish to highlight in this paper, preclude any neat characterization of its form or its boundaries. Umbanda has so far resisted various efforts at unification and codification, and thus a large range of ritual forms may be identified as Umbanda. Its adherents now accept it as a heterodox religion, although this has not always been the case.

Umbanda Pura shades off both toward more Spiritist and occult-influenced forms of Umbanda, and toward Umbanda forms that place greater emphasis upon African-derived practices and deities. These may also be identified simply as Umbanda, or by the use of such qualifiers as Umbanda Kardecista (Kardecist or Spiritist Umbanda), Umbanda Africana (African Umbanda), Umbanda Culto de Nação (referring to the African "nations"), Candomblé, Quimbanda,[11] or "Macumba," now a pejorative term used principally by detractors to refer to many Afro-Brazilian religious practices, including Umbanda.

The contemporary practice of Umbanda Pura

takes place in churches called *centros* or *terreiros*. Located in specially designed buildings, backyards, or private living rooms, *centros* consist of a large central ritual area, with an altar at the back, facing which is a seating area for the congregation. Ceremonies are public affairs that take place two or three times a week in the evenings. At these ceremonies, leader and initiates dressed in white nurses' uniforms, first appear in the ritual area to begin the service with homage to the Umbanda deities and spirits in the form of hymns, accompanied by hand-clapping and sometimes by drums. Gradually they become possessed, exchange ritual greetings, and dance, each adopting the persona of the spirit received. The second part of the ceremony is devoted to *consultas*, spiritual consultations in which the spirits still act and speak through mediums and give assistance to members of the congregation, most of whom have attended for this reason. Clients consult about illness, unemployment, family conflicts, and other practical concerns. The spirits give spiritual cleansings (*passes*), prescribe ritual remedies involving herbal baths, the lighting of candles, and often offer practical advice. The diagnosis of client's problems, and their treatment, may also induce possession in the clients. Spiritual aid through *consultas* is the principal form of the practice of *caridade* (charity), a central and defining precept of this form of Umbanda. They are an important attraction and a basis of recruitment to more active participation in Umbanda and to initiation as a medium. Umbanda churches encourage membership, demanding only nominal monthly dues, and sometimes small fees for *consultas*.

Umbanda theology is founded on the belief that spiritual beings intervene in the daily lives of humans, and that participation in Umbanda rituals is necessary to ensure that this intervention is beneficial. The Umbanda cosmos is composed of a vast spiritual hierarchy ordered in levels of spiritual evolution, which humans, who occupy its lower levels, ascend through successive reincarnations, assisted by various superior spirit patrons. The upper ranks of the hierarchy are occupied by God, who has both a Christian and an African identity, and below him, figures with dual identities as African deities and Catholic saints. Though powerful, these supernaturals are otiose figures, whose presence is expressed mainly through iconic representations on the altars and in paintings. The public ceremonies that are the heart of Umbanda are dominated by the less powerful, but more accessible, spirits who possess the initiates. These spirits are *Caboclos*, spirits of unacculturated Brazilian Indians, proud, arrogant, virile, and *Pretos Velhos* ("Old Blacks") spirits of Africans enslaved in Brazil, elderly, humble, and patient. Both are considered to be equally benevolent and efficacious in ministering to human woes. They act as intermediaries between more powerful spirit patrons and human clients within a vast spiritual patronage system, and as patrons of Umbanda ritual and curing.

Umbanda churches are autonomous units, organized around the figure of a charismatic leader, the medium, ranked according to their spiritual talents, and the lay members. An additional administrative body legally responsible for *centro* activities may have little practical significance in smaller, poorer churches, but is very active in larger, more affluent ones. In addition to their bureaucratic activities, which concern membership and finances, Umbanda churches often combine secular forms of charity with spiritual ones, as leaders redistribute the resources of the participants to those in need. Churches may also offer more formal social welfare services, ranging from child care, dental and medical clinics, and cut-rate medicines, to distributions of food and clothing, and the maintenance of an orphanage.

While most Umbanda churches remain autonomous, many choose to join Umbanda federations, whose leaders have close associations with local politicians and figures from the mass media. The federations mediate between the churches and the city bureaucracy, solve legal problems, and often seek to influence the organization, ritual, beliefs,, and voting behaviors of the member churches. Although the federations have never affiliated more than a minority of churches, they have exercised a disproportionate influence over the development of Umbanda.

A rather different social as well as ritual emphasis may be seen in the more African forms of Umbanda practice. Drums form an essential, rather than an optional aspect of ritual, and songs, sung in Portuguese in Umbanda Pura, are in part or entirely in African languages. Costumes are more elaborate and brightly colored. Possession may be chiefly, or even entirely, by African deities; and

Exús—African deities transformed within a Brazilian and Catholic context into devil figures, and marginalized in Umbanda Pura—often have central roles. Consultations customarily are held outside of the public ceremonies, and their greater privacy lends itself to accusations of exploitative fees and of services rendered for dubious moral ends. Rituals are less frequent and more elaborate, placing greater emphasis on affect than on the instrumentality associated with the *consultas* of Umbanda Pura.

Umbanda Pura thus distinguishes itself as a religion of spirit possession, with a thaumaturgical emphasis, and rituals that are sedate and tempered in contrast to the more African forms of Umbanda. Umbanda Pura emphasizes the practice of charity, especially through spiritual healing, and is organized for accessibility and compatibility with the work week, with expenses minimized and initiation curtailed.

Umbanda rituals of the type just described derive their core structure of collective spirit possession from Afro-Brazilian religions. From these come the dual figures of African deities and Catholic saints and the *Pretos Velhos* and *Caboclos*.[12] The Catholic influence in Umbanda is apparent in the figures of the Saints in the pantheon, Catholic prayers, which may be offered during ceremonies, the use of incense, and genuflection by members of the congregation upon entering the ritual area. As in other Afro-Brazilian religions, many practitioners of Umbanda are also Catholics, though many now declare themselves converts to Umbanda.[13]

Spiritism, or Kardecism (*Espiritismo, Kardecismo*)[14] another major influence in Umbanda, came to Brazil in the mid-19th century from France, and by the end of the century had spread throughout Brazil. Popular chiefly among the more educated and affluent sectors, its influence has also been noted within the lower classes. Spiritism, influenced by Comtean Positivism, professes spiritual evolution through reincarnation and the law of Karma, to be achieved through charity. At Spiritist rituals, mediums, seated at a table, receive spirits of the dead who give lengthy testimonials to their past lives and discourse on diverse themes, and practice spiritual healing in the form of spiritual cleansings (*passes*). Spiritists are noted for their intellectual activities and their charity, including the founding or orphanages and hospitals.[15] Umbanda's early organizers were former Spiritists, and its influence in Umbanda Pura can be seen in its cosmological system, the form of its spiritual consultations, and its emphasis on charity. Umbanda cosmology has also been influenced by Rosicrucianism, Theosophy, and the Kabbala.

Umbanda's innovativeness, however, did not derive from its eclecticism. Various blends of Spiritism and Afro-Brazilian traditions had been noted since the 19th century. What was new in this religion was that its early leaders organized the Afro-Brazilian churches of Rio and other southern cities in a relationship of classes, through religion, and brought new values, ideology, and organizational forms to it.

The activities which led to the prominence of Umbanda Pura in Rio, and throughout Brazil, began in the late 1920s and early 1930s in Niteroi, across the bay from Rio (Brown 1986).[16] A group of middle-class whites, disenchanted Spiritists who had taken to frequenting Afro-Brazilian churches, constructed from the two traditions a religion which they called Umbanda,[17] whose practices bore some resemblance to descriptions of prior Afro-Brazilian practices (Brown 1986:35–36). Our concern, however, is not with the originality of their results, but with the emphases and meaning given to them by the social groups who practiced them, and the organizing activities through which these groups sought to publicize, promote, and legitimize Umbanda.

These early Umbandistas included small scale businessmen, government bureaucrats, military officers, journalists, teachers, and lawyers. They represented the upwardly mobile, white middle sectors, and included several descendants of European immigrants. Through 1945, they devoted themselves to discussions of ritual and doctrine and to the organizing of networks of churches in Niteroi and Rio. The organizers also founded the first Umbanda federation, and issued the first volumes in what has now become a voluminous Umbanda literature. Of particular significance was their convening in 1941 of the First Congress of the Spiritism of Umbanda, a major effort to codify practices.

Umbanda's initial growth was limited mainly to the Rio area. These were the years of the Vargas dictatorship (1930–45), and Umbanda churches,

as well as those of the older Afro-Brazilian traditions, were subjected to considerable repression by the police.[18] The fear of repression provided an important stimulus for organizing Umbanda federations, which emphasized legal protection for their member churches.

The first Umbanda Congress (Anon. 1944), provides many insights into the leaders' intentions and concerns, revealing the class and racial attitudes that lay behind their beliefs and practices. They denied Umbanda's African origins and claimed descent from the "high" civilizations of India and Egypt. It was after Umbanda's diffusion via Lemuria to Africa, they asserted, that it had become debased to the level of fetishism, in which state it traveled to Brazil. These leaders wished to rescue Umbanda from its primitive past, and *purify* it of "barbaric" African practices such as animal sacrifice, and from associations with black magic (*magia negra*), evil, immorality, and exploitation. They sought to *whiten* Umbanda, and to stress its dedication to benevolent and charitable white magic (*magic branca*). These goals were expressed in the qualifiers, "pure," "clean," and "white" added to the term Umbanda, which contained racial overtones so obvious as to concern even some of the congress participants (Anonymous 1944:267). All of the negative, "primitive," and "barbaric," qualities and practices from which these leaders wished to disassociate themselves, and which in fact represented what we have shown to be a common stereotype of Afro-Brazilian practices, were attributed to another religion they identified as Quimbanda.[19]

These efforts to codify Umbanda, which continued within Umbanda literature, reflected the ideology and values of its middle-sector founders. They revealed a preoccupation with whitening the Afro-Brazilian heritage, and with its rescue and recuperation from its "primitive" origins. Umbanda thus became a religious metaphor for the acculturation of the African, encoded within Umbanda ritual and cosmology. The explicitly African deities were displaced by *Pretos Velhos*, domesticated, acculturated Africans who were even referred to in the contemporary literature as having "black skins and white souls" (Freitas 1939:44). Umbanda's early leaders thus manifested extreme ambivalence toward Africa, on the one hand embracing the African cultural contribution, and on the other seeking to de-Africanize that tradition.

After 1945 Umbanda began a burst of organizational activity, which resulted in expansion, increasing visibility, political representation, and in its transformation into a nationally popular and legitimate Brazilian religion. The end of the Vargas dictatorship in 1945 reestablished electoral politics, enfranchised the lower and middle classes, and saw a massive rural migration to the cities. Repression of Afro-Brazilian religions also ended. New Umbanda churches flourished, together with new federations, while Umbanda newspapers and radio programs advocated the rituals and ideas of Umbanda Pura. Umbanda attracted new members from all sectors of the population, and drew many older Afro-Brazilian churches into its orbit of influence and its organizational networks. As it spread throughout Brazil, it began to influence, fuse with, and accommodate local and regional Afro-Brazilian traditions. Its expanding associations, patronage networks, and its growing lower-class constituency, also attracted politicians who championed its political rights. It gained its own census category in the yearly religious census (1965), its place in city and state religious calendars, and became a popular topic in the news media. An enormous literature and a lively commerce in the sale of ritual articles grew up around Umbanda.

Umbanda's relationship to ongoing Afro-Brazilian religions has been complex. In the period after 1945, many churches, attracted to Umbanda federations by Umbanda's increasing legitimacy and promises of political protection, modified and "whitened" their own rituals and merged with Umbanda Pura. Some articulate Afro-Brazilian church leaders opposed Umbanda Pura for its middle-class and racist emphasis, and during the early 1950s formed their own, rival, Afro-Brazilian federations (Brown 1977, 1986), only to be drawn, later in the decade, into relations of political patronage with middle-class leaders of the Umbanda Pura tradition. Umbanda's ritual heterodoxy and tolerance have now come to be accepted by all sectors of the Umbanda spectrum, but the ongoing and creative nature of this heterodoxy are reflected in the re-Africanizing of some churches in both São Paulo (Negrão 1979) and in Rio (Bandeira 1985 personal communication), perhaps linked to the rising interest among Brazilian blacks in expressions of African pride and black consciousness (Negrão 1979).

Historically, then, Umbanda represents a reinterpretation of Afro-Brazilian religions by the white middle sectors, which gained legitimacy and, by remaining open to a wide range of beliefs and practices, was able to confer that legitimacy upon Afro-Brazilian churches that had developed independently of it. Analysts have often portrayed Umbanda as constituting a "new," "Brazilianized," "autochthonous," "endogenous" religion (Brown 1986; Ortiz 1978), or as constituting an appendage of Kardecism rather than of Afro-Brazilian religious traditions (Bastide 1978; Simpson 1978; 147–170). We wish to emphasize that white Umbanda Pura represents a reformulation of an Afro-Brazilian religious heritage, it does not break with it. The African heritage is specifically acknowledged and preserved in Umbanda, and this fact is recognized by the majority of Umbanda churches. Moreover, Umbanda's protean quality has allowed not only for an initial process of whitening, but also for the counter process of re-Africanizing, as seems to be occurring in recent years among some Umbanda churches and federations, without causing fission. The question of what particular aspects of Afro-Brazilian religious traditions will be utilized in individual churches appears to be in a constant state of negotiation that does not threaten their ability to identify with, or be identified as, Umbanda.

While Umbanda continues to represent for Brazilian blacks a continuity with their own ethnic religious traditions, it has the same time transcended that identification, becoming incorporated into national culture as an aspect not only of ethnic or class identity, but as a diacritic of Brazilianness (Fry 1982a:47–53).

INTERPRETATION

We now turn to an analysis of the political, economic, and cultural processes which underlie Umbanda's emergence and growth, and of which it forms a part.

The Socioeconomic and Political Context. Umbanda's development coincides with a radical disjunction in Brazil's economic and political history during which a largely rural, commodity exporting, politically decentralized and bimodal society was transformed into an increasingly urban; industrializing, politically centralized and multiclass society. Umbanda's success, and its very existence, are related to its ability to mediate between and provide a vehicle for the new classes that emerged within this process. These changes, like Umbanda, originated and took form in the southeastern states, especially Rio de Janeiro and São Paulo, from which they spread to the south, and more recently, to the urban centers of the northeast.

The economic, urbanizing, and political transformations of the 1920s and 1930s created new opportunities for the middle class, historically small, fragmented, and identifying with the dominant sectors. The spread of commerce, the creation of white-collar service jobs, and the burgeoning of state and federal bureaucracies, particularly in the city of Rio, which formed the Federal District, led to a rapid increase in the middle sectors, which were recruited largely from native and immigrant whites. With growth, this sector began increasingly to develop an identity separate from that of the upper classes and partially defined through its alignment with the state (Chauí 1978). Excluded from political power prior to the Vargas regime, this class sector began to openly support nationalist movements such as Integralism, to fight for the expansion of the franchise as an instrument of its own class interests, and to adopt nationalist forms of cultural expression and identity.

Getúlio Vargas and the authoritarian regime that he created in the Estado Novo (1937–45), responded to emerging middle-sector pressures, and to middle- and dominant-sector fears of the militant labor movements in Rio and São Paulo, and of the growing urban masses. Vargas suspended the electoral process, centralized power in the state, initiated state support of industrialization, co-opted the unions within a paternalistic state apparatus, and vastly increased the size of the bureaucracy. The middle sectors were rewarded with jobs, and the masses controlled through direct coercion and patronage. Patronage, previously a mechanism of elite control, was institutionalized within the state apparatus where it became accessible to middle-sector functionaries. Rio, as the locus of the state bureaucracy, was the center of this process.

The black population in Rio and São Paulo remained within the poorest and least proletarianized sectors of the lower classes (F. Fernandes 1969). This was due in part to the success of European immigrants in establishing virtual control over the most desirable forms of employment in the expanding industries, based on their urban and industrial skills and experience in forming trade unions and voluntary associations. But the most important source of blacks' continuing low economic status was Brazil's entrenched racism. It is now widely acknowledged that Brazil is not the racial democracy its apologists have claimed, and that prejudice and discrimination against blacks (the latter illegal since 1951) are systemic. Various black social movements in the period between 1917–40 had little effect in ameliorating the economic conditions of this race/class sector. Residential dispersal, the failure of black elites to identify with the poor, and discrimination against blacks by both native and immigrant whites all combined to undermine collective efforts and activities among Brazilian blacks (Degler 1971; Dzidzienyo 1979; F. Fernandes 1969; Hasenbalg 1979). Blacks were thus disproportionately represented among the urban poor in Rio and especially in São Paulo, although they represented a minority within this sector. They intermixed with other, similarly disadvantaged ethnic populations, with whom they shared similar conditions of economic and political oppression. All lacked effective mechanisms for economic, political, and social mobilization.

The beginnings of Umbanda in the period around 1930 thus represented the articulation of a new religious identity from within the middle sectors, one which was distinct from that of the dominant sectors and which, in its choice of a religious idiom, identified with the traditions of the urban poor. This identity, together with its clientele structures, drew the lower classes into relations of dependency upon the middle sectors. The latter gained a power base; in addition, their efforts suggest a recognition of the threat posed by the urban masses, and the wish to bring them under control through patronage and charity. The Afro-Brazilian religions should have come to serve as the basis for such an alliance seems related to their prevalence within the lower-class milieu.

While the literature on associational activities in urban Brazil denies significant associational activity among the urban poor at this time, such associations were widespread within the working classes (Conniff 1981; F. Fernandes 1969; Mitchell 1983). Afro-Brazilian churches (which these authors ignore) must have represented an important form of lower-class organizational activity as well as a source of Afro-Brazilian cultural identification. This would account for their rapid proliferation throughout urban Brazil, and their presence in more or less eclectic forms among Afro-Brazilian populations as well as in lower-class urban environments. During this period they served (see M. Herskovits 1945), as they do today, as sources of mutual aid for people lacking any form of social welfare other than occasional private sector and Catholic Church charity. The more affluent sectors of Brazilian society may have feared these religious centers as manifestations of the "primitive masses" and as sources of social contagion, yet it is clear from repeated references dating from the 19th century that wealthy clients were attracted to these churches and sought out their powers. Thus, in addition to sources of mutual aid for the lower classes, these churches served as meeting places for the rich and poor.

The fall of the Estado Novo in 1945 reopened the electoral process, extending the vote to the middle sectors and to a large percentage of the working classes and the urban poor. Politicians quickly recognized the new political realities, and the period from 1945 to the military coup of 1964 was marked by an expansion of populist politics. While negotiation with the largely white, urban proletariats of São Paulo and to a lesser degree of Rio, could take place through their labor and associational structures (Conniff 1981), the masses, including most of the urban, black population, constituted an important new, and untapped, political resource. It was no coincidence that the most stable form of organization found within this sector, its religious centers, became targets for middle-sector politicians. Umbanda centers were cited by political analysts as one of the few sources of access to lower-class voters (Singer 1965).

Patronage and clientelism were not limited to electoral politics during this period, but were a feature of Brazilian society, permeating all social relations (Leeds 1964). The strong patronage orientation in Umbanda thus replicated an aspect of daily experience which was attractive to Afro-Brazilian churches, and more widely to the urban poor. Patronage, charity, and populist politics combined within Umbanda to create a vertical alliance between the middle sectors and the urban poor.

For many members of older Afro-Brazilian churches that had suffered police repression during the 1920s and 1930s, promises of legal protection of Umbanda federations offered an irresistible attraction. The continuities of Afro-Brazilian religious identity could be maintained within a context of increased legitimacy.

Recent shifts of the political pendulum have had little effect upon Umbanda. The military coup of 1964 and the military government that followed temporarily suspended the electoral advantages of Umbanda's multiclass clienteles, and ended the political careers of a few leftist Umbanda politicians. However, many of Umbanda's legal gains and its legitimacy were consolidated under the military dictatorship, during which Umbanda continued to enjoy benign tolerance. This was facilitated by the new prominence of Umbandista military officers in leadership positions in Umbanda federations and churches. Their presence was a signal of the political conservativism represented in Umbanda's ideological emphasis on individual destiny and fate, and its ritual and cosmological focus on patronage relations, which did little to threaten the state. Umbanda's cosmological articulation of Brazilian racial democracy, especially through its central spirits, *Caboclos* and *Pretos Velhos*, complemented government strategies of nationalism, while bread and circus tactics of class diversion (Lever 1969) sometimes resulted in overt government support. Umbanda's relationship to the Brazilian military regime contrasts sharply to that of the Catholic Church, which shifted sharply to the left during this period, placing many Brazilian church leaders into direct conflict with the state. Umbanda may even have been the beneficiary of worsening church/state opposition. The Catholic Church's relations with Umbanda throughout this period varied from attacks launched against it in the media by some Catholic leaders in the 1950s, to a position of greater tolerance under the influence of Vatican II. The Church's recognition of Umbanda's success in gaining adherents among the urban poor and working classes has acted as a stimulant to its own organizational efforts within these same sectors in recent years.

The period of *abertura* and redemocratization

since 1976 has done little to change the form or direction of Umbanda. The financial crisis and increasing impoverishment of both middle and lower classes in Brazil has served to maintain the structures of patronage and clientism upon which the religion was founded.[20] Particularly in Rio, the populist political forms of the past have reemerged (Diniz 1982), and Umbanda clienteles have once again become targets and political bases for politicians involved in patronage politics (Silverstein et al. 1982).

Thus the continuities in Brazilian society which have fostered the continuing dependency of the urban poor and of the middle sectors upon forms of patronage and populism as modes of economic, political, and social survival, have also fostered the continuing growth and development of Umbanda, and its spread from its origins in Rio and the south. Its growing national dimensions, and its tendency to fuse with local and regional traditions reproduces the centralizing tendencies of the Brazilian state seeking to transcend regional divisions and differences through the creation of a national Brazilian culture. Yet this process seems clearly destined to remain incomplete, since Umbanda churches continue to resist unification, preserving their autonomy, dynamism, and creativity.

The Cultural and Religious Context.   There remains the question of the ready acceptance of Umbanda's occult and African aspects by sophisticated, educated urban populations. An examination of the cultural and religious climate within which Umbanda developed indicates that major aspects of its beliefs were widespread within the educated as well as poorer sectors of the Brazilian population well before Umbanda began, many since at least the 19th century.

Brazilian Catholicism unquestionably created acceptance for many aspects of Umbanda. The more orthodox, Roman-oriented form of Catholic practice, which gained ascendancy within the Brazilian Church at the end of the 19th century did not supplant entrenched forms of practice that had developed earlier in relative isolation from Rome and in the absence of a strong clergy. These more relaxed, nationalistic, and social forms during the colonial period owed much to the more mystically oriented Portuguese Catholic traditions (Bastide 1951:334–355; Warren 1968a), which emphasized

the worship of the Catholic saints. This "cult of the saints," the focus of "popular," or "folk" forms of Catholicism, is centered in the belief in their miraculous powers, particularly their ability to cure illness, and in their willingness to answer individual petitions. While this form of Catholicism has been analyzed primarily as a lower-class and, above all, as a rural phenomenon, with close affinities to Afro-Brazilian religions (deKadt 1967; Willems 1966; Bastide 1951), the literature hints at a more widespread acceptance among all social classes. (T. Azevedo 1968; Bastide 1951, 1978; Freyre 1946). This is corroborated by recent fieldwork among the upper classes of a large, industrial city, who were found to regularly visit *benzedeiras* (Catholic blessers) and Catholic priests widely known for their abilities as exorcists, diviners, and curers (Brown 1976; Lemos Fiho 1975). For affluent as well as lower-class practitioners of Umbanda, then, Popular Catholicism may be seen as legitimizing the individual quest for supernatural forms of assistance, and thus providing a basis for belief in the curative powers of the *Caboclos* and *Pretos Velhos* in Umbanda.

A constant flow of competing religious and philosophical beliefs and practices, which has challenged Catholic hegemony and produced a climate of great cultural and religious diversity since the early 19th century, has also created a basis for belief and practice of Umbanda. The literate sectors have been particularly active in pursuing these new ideas, but the ideas have also diffused through the lower classes. Spiritism entered Brazil from France in the mid-19th century, bearing the strong mark of Comtean Positivism, which was already popular among the educated elite (Renshaw 1969). Spiritism carried the Positivist emphasis on rationalism, evolution, and progress into the middle and lower classes, and eventually into Umbanda. But perhaps the most important contribution of Spiritism to the acceptance of Umbanda was the fact that it, too, was a religion of spirit possession. While Spiritism did not escape attacks by Catholic intellectuals and the medical profession, often in the same terms used to denigrate Afro-Brazilian religions,[21] the social and intellectual status of leading Spiritists, and their extensive sponsorship of charitable activities established Spiritism's acceptability as a religion, and in turn helped to legitimize its rituals and beliefs within the upper sectors of the Brazilian population. Moreover, like Spiritism, many other occult and mystical religions and philosophies that flourished among the educated sectors in late-19th century Brazil, including Theosophy, Rosicrucianism, and Swedenborgianism (see Borges 1985; Rio 1951), created a climate of belief in the existence of spirit and astral worlds that directly interact with our world, and that are worthy of human attention.

The medical context within which Umbanda developed gave support to many of its curing activities. Brazilian science, and the biomedical forms of medical treatment which developed slowly through the 19th and early 20th centuries in Brazil (Stepan 1976) competed with a multitude of alternative medical forms (Borges 1985), without establishing hegemonic control within Brazil. Homeopathy, which entered Brazil in the late 19th century, quickly gained popularity, especially among the elite, and homeopathic medical schools, doctors, and pharmacies proliferated. Spiritism, too, claimed a curative function, and offered spiritual curing and spiritual surgery (Greenfield 1984). Thus, problems of health and curing never became the sole domain of official medicine, treatment being shared among the medical establishment, homeopathy, and religions, including Spiritism and Catholicism, as well as Umbanda. It is not uncommon to find Brazilian doctors who combine in their practice both official medicine and various forms of spiritual healing, (Brown 1976; Perelberg 1980) and Spiritist and Umbanda hospitals also combine biomedical and spiritual forms of treatment.

Prior to the middle sector's participation in Umbanda, then, the practice and belief in spirit possession, spiritual curing, miracles, spiritual interventions, and reincarnation were widely accepted by educated Brazilians. What was new in the middle sector's involvement with Umbanda did not lie in its adoption of new religious forms, but in its public identification with the Afro-Brazilian religious heritage, and its active promotion of a cultural tradition it had previously denigrated.

This striking reversal in attitude toward the Afro-Brazilian heritage by middle-sector whites formed part of a broader cultural valorization of the African heritage, integrally connected to the development of Brazilian nationalism. This process, which promoted the creation of a unique Brazilian identity, began after Independence (1822) with the literary romanticization of the Brazilian Indian, and after abolition came to include the African as well. Nationalist sentiment reached a crescendo with the Modernist movement in the 1920s, which had a wide effect throughout the arts and contributed to Vargas' brand of political nationalism.

Cultural nationalism, especially the valorization of an African heritage, gained its major expression in the work of Gilbert Freyre, whose bestselling book. *The Masters and the Slaves* (1933), set forth the thesis that Brazil's distinctive cultural identity lay in its unique biological and cultural blend: Iberian (Portuguese), Indian, and African. This Luso-tropical people, molded through conquest, the plantation system, and miscegenation into a racially harmonious nation was said to incorporate the traditions of all of its racial groups. Freyre and those he influenced explicitly recognized the important contribution of African culture to Brazil's identity. Significantly, early Umbandista literature often directly paraphrased Freyre, declaring that since Umbanda drew upon the contributions of the three races and cultures—Catholic, Indian, and African— it could justly claim to be the only "genuinely Brazilian religion" (see Macaia 1968; Anon. 1944).

During the 1930s, then, Brazil began to be defined positively as possessing its own syncretic culture, rather than as an extension of European culture in the New World. Cultural and intellectual expressions of nationalism converged with the agenda of the Vargas government which was promoting a national identity that would override class and region differences, and would appeal to and strengthen a sense of national unity and purpose. The regime encouraged research and artistic production on African and indigenous themes.[22]

The valorization of the African heritage within Brazil found additional support in the changing image of Africa and elsewhere in the world. During the 1920s, the Negritude movement in the Caribbean and in Africa had in important impact on Brazil via French intellectual and artistic circles (F. Fernandes 1969; 187–233); Nascimento 1978). In the post-World War II period, black nationalism and the civil rights movement in the United States and independence movements in Africa provided new political status for Diaspora and African Blacks. The earlier transformation of African and other so-called "primitive" arts from objects of scorn to high art helped precipitate the modern art movement in Brazil as well as Europe, and raised the general prestige of African and Afro-Brazilian cultural forms. This spurred the Brazilian upper classes to explore and to begin to appropriate for their own uses a variety of African cultural forms: the *escolas de samba*, (samba music), *capoeira* (an African-derived martial art and dance form), black forms of *carnaval*, and Bahian foods (see Brown 1986; Dantas 1982b; Fry 1982b; Rodrigues 1984). In the period since the 1920s, these, together with *futebol* (soccer) and Umbanda, have become defining features of Brazilian national culture.

Placed within this context, the appropriation of African culture by the middle sectors, represented in Umbanda, can be seen to be part of a larger process. It is only when viewed apart from its wider cultural and political context (as in the work of Herskovits, Bastide, and so on) that middle-sector participation in Umbanda appears to be anomalous. However, it is important to note that Umbanda differs somewhat from these other examples in its valorization of the African heritage. While other movements glorify Africa, Umbanda provides for the apotheosis of the Brazilian African slave. The *Pretos Velhos*, Umbanda's central symbols of Africa's contribution to Brazil, are domesticated, deculturated, Brazilianized Africans. Umbanda thus appears to express in extreme form the deep ambivalence that Brazilian whites still feel toward the African presence in Brazil. This ambivalence serves to deny and mask, and thus to perpetuate the realities of racial prejudice and discrimination.

DISCUSSION

We have argued that the development of Umbanda should be understood as having formed in response to a complex process of class interplay, the role of the state, the political, economic, and cultural conditions, rather than representing a response to a unidirectional, acculturative, and modernizing process. A similar processual complexity may be seen to have shaped other Afro-Brazilian religious phenomena. We will illustrate the extension of our analysis through a brief comparison with Candomblé.

Bahian Candomblé offers the opportunity for a closer examination of the issue of African "orthodoxy." As already noted Candomblé has been regarded as the least acculturated of Afro-Brazilian religions, the most faithful to it African religious roots. This "orthodoxy" has been a source of great prestige and status within the relatively closed Afro-Brazilian religious community of Salvador (capital city of the State of Bahia), and has sustained that city's reputation as the center of African culture in Brazil. Candomblé is a source of local and regional pride, and of the city and region's appeal as a major center for national and international tourism.

Candomblé is often spoken as having "preserved" its "orthodoxy" of African tradition. This "orthodoxy," however, represents a social and historical construct (Dantas 1982a, 1982b) which has evolved through a process of accommodation between Yoruban African origins and Catholicism, and has been continually reconstituted through the 20th century (Dos Santos and Dos Santos 1984). Candomblé leaders have made frequent pilgrimages to the Yoruba religious homeland in Africa for that purpose (Landes 1947; Pierson 1942). Moreover, the Bahian intellectual elite, through their ritual patronage roles as *ogans* (a status created in Brazil), has served as a source of political protection and financial support for Candomblé, helping groups to maintain long, costly, and elaborate ritual initiations—considered the linchpin in the maintenance of orthodoxy—which could not have survived without some substantial source of support. These intellectuals have used Candomblé as the inspiration for their writing and art (the novels of Jorge Amada are the best known), for the most part ignoring the far more prevalent "eclectic" Afro-Brazilian religions of the area. Moreover, recent work by Dantas (1982a) suggests that more than simply supporting "orthodoxy," intellectuals and other members of the elite have influenced the very content of what is defined as "orthodox." A comparative analysis of orthodox Yoruban traditions in Sergipe (the site of Dantas' own fieldwork) and in Salvador, indicates that what both communities consider to be "pure" Yoruba traditions differs radically in each case influenced by their respective elite's interpretations, as well as by that of the more active adherents.

Umbanda's emphasis on whitening the Afro-Brazilian heritage, in contrast to Candomblé's emphasis on African orthodoxy, may be related to differing regional elite interests, each attempting to rationalize its regional racial composition (predominantly white in Rio; predominantly black in Bahia [Dantas 1982b:155–162]). These differences also appear to be affected by different class structures in the two areas. Within the bimodal class structure of the northeast, upper-class elites act primarily as patrons, rather than as adherents of Candomblé and other orthodox traditions, supporting the maintenance of African orthodoxy. In Rio and the south, the middle classes, as full participants in Umbanda, have sought to whiten Afro-Brazilian practices within the framework of a new religion. That is, in the south, Umbandista leadership has come from an emergent and increasingly important class sector whose interests are consonant with the formation of political and economic alliances with the poor, though these are clearly asymmetric and exploitative ones. Whitening occurred in conjunction with the maintenance of recognizable Afro-Brazilian religious elements. Umbanda thus represents a compromise between the symbolic and ritual identifications of both the poor and the emergent middle sectors, creating a religion open to both, and to blacks as well as whites. In the northeast, the elite's advocacy of Afro-Brazilian religious orthodoxy reinforces a bimodal class structure threatened by the class-integrated, mediating religious forms of the areas and in Umbanda. Here the elite emphasis on purity reinforces the link between race and class, and the distance between patronized African and its white elite patrons. In this political setting, the more orthodox religions gain status and influence with the poor, at the same time benefiting from elite patronage. Local economic conditions and class structures thus aid us in understanding the divergent histories of Afro-Brazilian religions in the two areas.

The creative and dynamic nature of Afro-Brazilian religions leaves them open to shifts in their identification with Catholicism as well as with Africa. This is dramatically illustrated by Bahian Candomblé, especially in the events that occurred at the Second World Conference of the Tradition of the Orixás (Yoruban deities) held in Salvador in 1983 (Birman 1984; Fry 1984; Veja 1983). Leaders of the religion, most from West Africa, had met to discuss the formation of a world Yoruban religion. They complimented Bahian Candomblé leaders on their orthodoxy and fidelity to Yoruba practice (noting that Bahian Candomblé had even preserved practices now lost in Africa) and then supported a proposal by a leading faction within Bahian Candomblé that all elements of Catholicism should be eliminated from Candomblé practice, most particularly the worship of Catholic saints and the identification of saints with the Orixás. This suggestion generated a furious and ongoing debate over the merits of newly defined "syncretic" forms of Candomblé, that is, formerly "orthodox" houses which continued to include Catholic practice, versus "orthodox" houses who wished to delete those practices.[23] The debate illustrates the degree to which Catholicism has become an integral component of "orthodox" Afro-Brazilian practice and belief, and the openness and flexibility of Afro-Catholic "syncretisms" to the same shifts in definition that occur in Brazilian attitudes toward the African heritage. The two may even work together. In the present case, the strengthening of ties with African forms of Yoruba religion gains support from the politics of the black consciousness movement, as Candomblé practitioners aim to eliminate Catholic practices and beliefs from their religion.[24] However, these efforts have been met by strong resistance from many major leaders within the Candomblé community. It is clear in other words that like African identity in Brazil, religious "syncretism" is not fixed and immutable, nor subject to simple forms of unidirectional change, but responds continually to changing political, social, and religious conditions.

Umbanda presents the paradox of a 20th-century religion, urban in origin, codified and led by Brazilians of European descent, its practices and ideology drawn from Europe and from the religious creativity of African slaves and their descendants. Umbanda's adherents represent almost all class and ethnic sectors of Brazilian society, and its spread and success challenges the dominance of the Catholic Church. Umbanda's protean history speaks directly to the questions of religious encounter and change that we have addressed here. Our examination of Umbanda, in relation to other Afro-Brazilian religions and to the Catholic Church points to the fallacy of arguments that see the encounter between the religions of dominant and dominated groups as simply unidirectional. As Umbanda's early leaders sought to whiten the Afro-Brazilian tradition, like some practitioners of Candomblé, elements of Umbanda today seek to re-Africanize it. In no simple sense has any religion established hegemony in Brazil. Instead, Brazilians move freely among religions, seeing themselves as adherents of more than one religion at the same time. To whatever degree models of unidirectional change in the realm of religion apply elsewhere, such models clearly do not apply to Brazil.

The history of religions and of their interactions in Brazil seem best interpreted in relation to a specific class and cultural history, and to class and race relations as they unfold in the context of economic and political conditions. As we have pointed out, the dynamics of interaction change through time, and may differ at any point in time among different social classes, and in different regions of Brazil. We have demonstrated the creativity of all class sectors in this realm. Where Church and State have neither the will nor the ability to impose absolute cultural and ideological hegemony, as has been the case in Brazil, religious innovation becomes a major factor in the negotiations between classes and class factions for access to power and status, health and spiritual well-being.

NOTES

Acknowledgements. We would like to thank Shirley Lindenbaum, Jane Schneider, and our anonymous reviewer for their invaluable editorial assistance.

1. We have largely avoided the morass of Brazilian racial taxonomy, merging variations within the opposed and polar categories, black (*preto*) and white (*branco*), as is increasingly the practice in Brazil (F. Fernandes 1979:98). We categorically reject any implication that these socially constructed categories are biologically meaningful.

2. That the state was quite capable of repressing the religions of the slaves is clear from their elimination, though deportation and execution, of the leaders of the Islamic-led slave revolt of 1815, and the subsequent rapid demise of a flourishing Islamic religious community (Bastide 1978:146).

3. The distinction between "orthodox" and "syncretic" forms has also frequently been assumed to correlate with differences in the slave origins. For example, it has been noted that "orthodoxy" has been greatest among Yoruban and Dahomean "nations," from which the Candomblé derived, while the practice of other "nations," which adopted and further modified its basic form have been seen as more "syncretic." While ethnic factors have certainly had some influence upon degrees of syncreticism, our own interpretation will stress other factors.

4. Both shared in the scientific racism that permeated Brazilian intellectual thought at the time (Correa 1982; Skidmore 1974). *Embranquecimento* was to occur in three ways: through an absolute decline in the black population through lower fertility; through the encouragement of massive European immigration; and through miscegenation, which would dilute the biological contribution of blacks (see Skidmore 1974:64–77).

5. All these terms, for example, may be found in the denunciation of Umbanda by a Catholic prelate, now a bishop, which was published as a full-length book by the major Brazilian Catholic press (see Kloppenburg 1961a).

6. While the term *"culto"* in Portuguese is used in censuses to apply to all religions—as in "Culto Umbandista" and "Culto Católico"—it does not affect the significance of the contrasts common in the literature between *cultos* Afrobrasileiros and *"a religião Católica."*

7. Herskovits' students were sensitive to demographic issues, equating "purity" or "survival" of African cultural traditions with densely concentrated urban Afro-Brazilian populations, and greater syncretism and eventual attentuation and loss as the Afro-Brazilian population dispersed beyond urban ethnic enclaves. However, this approach denied other class or ethnic sectors any role in maintaining African orthodoxy.

8. This distinction had been first developed in Brazil by Nina Rodrigues, based on studies of African societies by the French ethnographer Letourneau (Nina Rodrigues 1935:163–164), and was then adopted by Ramos. The widespread adoption among Afro-Brazilian churches of a form of collective spirit possession derived from West Africa was seen as a result of the cultural superiority of "Sudanese" (West African) over "Bantu" (Central and South African) peoples and their culture. These authors praised the practices of what were labeled "Sudanese" groups, chiefly Candomblé, as true, though primitive, polytheistic forms of religion, possessing integrated collective rituals and theology. However, those thought to be of "Bantu" origin (especially Rio "Macumba") were seen as inferior forms, fragmented, individualistic, exploitative forms of fetishism and magic rather than religion, which because they lacked integrated ritual and belief systems, were given to eclecticism (Nina Rodrigues 1935:1622–1624; Ramos 1934:755–776; see also Dantas 1982b).

9. Referred to by the generic term "Macumba," Afro-Brazilian religions in Rio were categorized as "adulterated" (Ramos 1939:92), "unwholesome and in a state of disintegration" (Pierson 1942:305), representing the "disintegrative phase" of Afro-Brazilian religious development (Bastide 1978:285–303).

10. Both terms are still in use. The form of Umbanda which we refer to as Umbanda Pura (see also Brown 1977, 1979, 1986) is the same as that which Ortiz (1978) refers to as Umbanda Branca.

11. These terms are often used loosely in Rio. *Culto de nação* (cult of "nations") refers to the various ethnic groupings formed during colonial times. *Candomblé* may means the Bahian form, or simply denote a more "African" form of Umbanda practice. Quimbanda is discussed in a later section of the paper.

12. *Caboclo* spirits appear to derive from the northeastern practices known as *Candomblés de Caboclo*, already popular in Bahia in the late 19th century (see Carreiro 1964; Landes 1947:37; Nina Rodrigues 1977:221–222), and to represent an indigenous influence, though their form is highly romanticized. The origins of the *Pretos Velhos* are more obscure. However, they appear to have originated in southern Brazil. For one origin myth of the *Pretos Velhos* see Brown (1986:61–72).

13. A survey conducted in Rio in 1969 based on structured interviews with 403 individuals in 14 Umbanda churches indicated that of the former Catholics surveyed, 44 percent still considered themselves Catholic as well as Umbandista, while 56 percent now declared themselves converts to Umbanda (see Brown 1974, 1986:133–137).

14. For discussions of Spiritism (also known as Kardecism) in Brazil (see Brown 1986:15–27; Renshaw 1969; Warren 1968a, 1968b).

15. See Brown (1986:21–23). According to a 1958 census, Spiritists in the state of São Paulo provided more charitable services than the Catholic Church.

16. For a more extensive discussion of Umbanda's origins and criticism of Ortiz's (1978) theory of its multiple origins, see Brown (1986:37–41, 212–214).

17. The term Umbanda was not new in Afro-Brazilian circles although it appears not to have previously referred to a religion (see Brown 1986:42).

18. Police repression of Afro-Brazilian religions was extensive through Brazil from the 19th century through the period of 1945 (see, for example, Bastide 1978:136–42/ Nascimento 1978:103–106). For the period of the 1930s and early 1940s, it is not clear to what degree the repression and harassment exercised against Afro-Brazilian religions by the police (which was particularly harsh in the northeast) was directed at these religions, or was more a result of generalized political repression directed against all lower-class organizations.

19. While the origins of the term "Quimbanda" and its putative practices are as obscure as those of Umbanda (see Brown 1986:44–46), it is clear that for these early Umbandistas, Quimbanda represented a repository for all the opprobrious associations from which they wished to escape.

20. The most substantial change, the emergence of strong working-class solidarities and a worker's political party (the P.T.), has developed largely within the industrial proletariat of greater São Paulo. This organized urban proletariat appears not to have been an important source of Umbanda supporters, though data is lacking on this question.

21. See F. Azevedo, quoted in Amorim (1965); Brown (1974:21–63, 1986; 15–25); Kloppenburg (1961b, 1964).

22. One example is provided by Vargas' encouragement of figures such as a composer Hector Villa Lobos to incorporate Brazilian folk themes into a national Brazilian music (see Squeff and Wisnick 1982). The Vargas government also supported the first major series of publications on the Negro in Brazil, which was published by the Biblioteca da Divulgação Cientifica. Between 1934 and 1940, 20 volumes were issued in this series, among them the major publications of Nina Rodrigues, Ramos, and Carneiro.

23. This desyncretizing faction dominated the Brazilian delegation at the Third World Conference of Orisa Tradition and Culture held in New York in 1986 (M. Azevedo 1986).

24. At the Third World Conference an alliance between the Bahian black consciousness movement and the desyncretizing Candomblé leadership was apparent (Bick 1986).

REFERENCES

Amorim, Deolindo, 1965. Caracteristics da Doutrina Espirita *Anais do Instituto da Cultura Espirita do Brasil* 2:69–81.

Anonymous, 1944. O Culto de Umbanda em Face da Lei. Rio de Janeiro.

Azevedo, Maria Estela de, 1986. Sincretismo. Unpublished paper presented at the Third World Conference of Orisa Tradition and Culture, New York, 8 October 1986.

Azevedo, Thales de, 1968. Popular Catholicism in Brazil:

Typology and Function, *In Portugal and Brazil in Transition.* Raymond Sayers, ed. pp. 175–178. Minneapolis: University of Minnesota Press.

Bastide, Roger, 1951. *Religion and the Church in Brazil.* In *Brazil: Portrait of a Half a Continent.* T. Lynn Smith, ed. pp. 334–355. New York: Dryden.

———, 1971, *African Civilizations in the New World.* New York: Harper and Row.

———, 1978 [1960]. *The African Religions of Brazil.* Baltimore: John Hopkins.

Bick, Mario, 1986. Unpublished notes on the session, Traditional Belief Systems in Brazil. Third World Conference of Orisa Tradition and Culture, New York, 8 October 1986.

Birman, Patricia, 1984. Comentários à propósito da II Conferéncia Mundial da Tradição dos Orixás. Comuniçaões do ISER 8:47–54.

Borges, Dain, 1985. Medical Ideas, Class and Race in Brazil, 1830–1930. Paper presented at the XII International Congress of the Latin American Studies Association, Albuquerque, NM, Mimeo.

Brown, Diana, DeG., 1974. Umbanda: Politics of an Urban Religious Movement. Unpublished Ph.D. dissertation. Columbia University, Ann Arbor: University Microfilms.

———, 1976. Unpublished field notes Rio de Janeiro.

———, 1977. Umbanda e Classes Sociais, *Religião e Sociedade* 1:31–42.

———, 1979. Umbanda and Class Relations in Brazil. In *Brazil: Anthropological Perspectives, Essays in Honor of Charles Wagley.* Maxine L. Margolis and William E. Carter, eds., pp. 270–304. New York: Columbia University Press.

———, 1980a. Illness and Income: The Utilization of Official and Alternative Health Resources by Rich and Poor Brazilian Women. Unpublished paper presented to the Columbia University Seminar on Brazil, Mimeo.

———, 1980b. *Umbanda in Newark: Alternative Healing in the Brazilian and Portuguese Communities.* Working Paper No. 24. Resource Center for Multicultural Care and Prevention. Newark: New Jersey Medical School Press.

———, 1986. *Umbanda: Religion and Politics in Urban Brazil.* Ann Arbor: UMI Research.

Burns, E. Bradford, 1980. *A History of Brazil,* 2nd edition. New York: Columbia University Press.

Camargo, Cándido Procôpo Ferreira de, 1961. *Kardecismo e Umbanda.* São Paulo: Livraria Pioneira.

Cardozo, Manoel, 1947. The Lay Brotherhoods of Colonial Bahia, *The Catholic Historical Review* 33(1):12–30.

Carneiro, Edison, 1936. *Religões Negras.* Rio de Janeiro: Editoria Civilização Brasileira.

———, 1937. *Negros Bantus.* Rio de Janeiro: Editoria Civilização Brasileira.

———, 1940. The Structure of African Cults in Bahia, *Journal of American Folklore* 53:271–278.

———, 1961. *Candomblés de Bahia* 3rd edition. Rio de Janeiro: Editora Conquista.

———, 1964. Os Caboclos de Aruanda. In *Ladinos e Crioulos: Estudos Sobre o Negro no Brasil.* Edison Carnerio, ed. pp. 143–158. Rio de Janeiro: Civilização Brasileira.

Chauí, Marilena, 1978. Apontamentos para uma Critica da Ação Integralista Brasileiro. In *Ideologia e Mobilização Popular.* Marilena Chauí and Maria Sylvia Carvalho, eds. pp. 17–149. Rio de Janeiro: Co-edições CEDEC/Paz e Terra.

Connif, Michael L., 1981. *Urban Politics in Brazil: The Rise of Populism, 1925–1945.* Pittsburgh: University of Pittsburgh Press.

Correa, Mariza, 1982. As Ilusões da Liberdade: a Escola Nina Rodrigues e a Antropologia no Brasil. Unpublished Ph.D. dissertation. Universidade de São Paulo.

Costa, Eduardo, Octávio da, 1948. *The Negro in Northern Brazil.* Monographs of the American Ethnological Society No. 15. Seattle: University of Washington Press.

Costa Pinto, Luis A., 1952. *O Negro no Rio de Janeiro.* São Paulo: Companhia Editora Nacional.

Cunha, Manuela Carneiro da, 1985. *Negros, Estrangeiros:os Escravos Libertos e sua Volta à Africa.* Sáo Paulo: Editora Brasiliense.

Dantas, Beatriz Gois, 1982a. Repensanda a Pureza Nagô. *Religião e Sociedade* 8:15–20.

———, 1982b. Vovó Nagô e Papai Branco: Usos e Abusos da Africa no Brasil. Unpublished MA thesis. Universidade Estadual de Campinas.

Degler, Carl N., 1971. Neither Black nor White: Slavery and Race Relations in Brazil and the United States. New York: Macmillan.

deKadt, Emmanuel, 1967. Religion, the Church and Social Change in Brazil. In *The Politics of Conformity in Latin America.* Claudio Veliz, ed., New York: Oxford.

Diniz, Eli, 1982. *Voto e Máquina Politica: Patronagem e Clientelismo no Rio de Janeiro.* Rio de Janeiro: Paz e Terra.

Đos Santos, Juana Elbein, and Deoscoredes M. Dos Santos, 1984. Religion and Black Culture. In *Africa in Latin America: Essays on History, Culture and Socialization.* Manuel Moreno Fraginals, ed., pp. 61–82. Lenor Blum, transl. New York: Holmes and Meier.

Dzidzienyo, Anani, 1979. The Position of Blacks in Brazilian Society. In *The Position of Blacks in Brazilian and Cuban Society.* Anani Dzidzienyo and Lourdes Casal, eds. pp. 2–11. Minority Rights Group Report No. 7. London.

Fernandes, Florestan, 1969. *The Negro in Brazilian Society*. Phyllis B. Eveleth, ed. Jacqueline D. Skiles, A. Brunel, and Arthur Rothwell, transl. New York: Columbia University Press.

———, 1979. The Negro in Brazilian Society: Twenty-Five Years Later. In *Brazil Anthropological Perspectives, Essays in Honor of Charles Wagley*. Maxine L. Margolis and William E. Carter, eds. pp. 96–113. New York: Columbia University Press.

Fernandes, Rubem Cesar, 1982. *Os Cavaleiros do Bom Jesus: Uma Introdução as Religiões Populares. São Paulo: Brasiliense.*

———, 1984. *Religiões Populares: Uma Visão Parcial da Literature Recente.* BIB 18:3–26.

Freitas, João de, 1939. *Umbanda*. Rio de Janeiro: Editora Moderna.

Freyre, Gilberto, 1946[1933]. *The Masters and the Slaves.* Samuel Putnam, transl. New York: Alfred A. Knopf.

Fry, Peter H., 1982a. Feijoada e Soul Food: Notas Sobre a Manipulação de Símbolos Étnicos e Nacionais. In Para Inglês Ver. Peter Fry. pp. 47–53. Rio de Janeiro: Zahar.

———, 1982b. Para Inglés Ver: *Identidade Política na Cultura Brasileira.* Rio de Janeiro: Zahar.

———, 1984. De um Observador não Participante . . . *Communicaçõs do ISER* 8:37–45.

Greenfield, Sidney, 1984. *Spirit Healing in Brazil.* Latin American Center. Milwaukee: University of Wisconsin Press. Film.

Harris, Marvin, 1964. *Patterns of Race in the Americas.* New York: Walker.

Hasenbalg, Carlos A., 1979. *Discriminação e Desigualdades Raciais no Brasil.* Rio de Janeiro: Graal.

Herskovits, Frances, ed., 1966. *The New World Negro.* Bloomington: Indiana University Press.

Herskovits, Melville, 1937. African Gods and Catholic Saints in New World Negro Belief. *American Anthropologist* 39:635–643.

———, 1941. *The Myth of the Negro Past.* New York: Harper and Brothers.

———, 1945. The Social Organization of Candomblé. *Congresso Internacional de Americanistas* 31:505–532.

———, 1966. The Contribution of Afroamerican Studies to Africanist Research. In The New World Negro. Frances Herskovits, ed. pp. 12–23. Bloomington: Indiana University Press.

Hutchinson, Harry William, 1957. *Village and Plantation Life in Northeastern Brazil.* Seattle: University of Washington Press.

Kloppenburg, Boaventura O. F. M., 1961a. *Umbanda: Orientação para os Católicos.* Rio de Janeiro: Editoria Vozes.

———, 1961b. *Ação Pastoral Perante o Espiritismo.* Petropólis: Editora Vozes.

———, 1964. *O Espiritismo no Brasil: Orientação Para os Católics.* Petropólis: Editora Vozes.

Landes, Ruth, 1947. *City of Women.* New York: Macmillan.

Lanternari, Vittorio, 1963. *Religions of the Oppressed.* New York: Alfred Knopf.

Leeds, Anthony, 1964. Brazilian Careers and Social Structure: A Case History and Model. *American Anthropologist* 66:1321–1347.

Lemos Filho, Arnaldo, 1975. Padres que Curam: Uma Análise Antropológica de Medicina Popular. Unpublished paper. Mimeo.

Lever, Janet, 1969. Soccer: Opium of the Brazilian People. *Trans-Action* 7(2):36–43.

Lewis I.M., 1971. *Ecstatic Religion: An Anthropological Study of Spirit Possession and Shaminism.* Baltimore: Penguin.

Macáia, 1968. Monthly Newsletter. Rio de Janeiro: Tenda de Umbanda Luz, Esperanca, Fraternidade. October. No. 10.

Mitchell, Michael, 1983. Race, Legitimacy and the State in Brazil. Unpublished paper presented at the Latin American Studies Association Annual Meeting. Mexico City. Mimeo.

Moreno Fraginals, Manuel, 1984. Cultural Contributions and Deculturation. In *Africa In Latin America: Essays on History, Culture, and Socialization.* Manuel Moreno Fraginals, ed. pp. 5–22. Leonor Blum, transl. New York: Holmes and Meier.

Moro, America, and Mercedes Ramirez, 1981. *La Macumba y otros Cultos Afro-Brasileros en Montevideo.* Montevideo: Editora Oriental.

Nascimento, Abdias do, 1978. *O Genocido do Negro Brasileiro: Processo de um Racismo Mascarado.* Rio de Janeiro: Paz e Terra.

Negrão, Lisias, 1979. A Umbanda Como Expressão Religiosidade Popular. *Religião e Sociedade* 4:171–180.

Nina Rodrigues, Raymundo, 1935. *O Animismo Fetichista dos Negros Bajanos.* Rio de Janeiro: Civilização Brasileira.

———, 1977. *Os Africanos no Brasil.* São Paulo: Companhia Editora Nacional.

Ortiz, Renato, 1978. *A Morte Braca do Feitçeiro Negro.* Petropólis: Editora Vozes.

Perelberg, Rosine, 1980. Umbanda and Psychoanalysis as Different Ways of Interpreting Mental Illness. *Journal of Medical Psychiatry* 53:323–332.

Pierson, Donald, 1942. *Negros in Brazil.* Chicago: University of Chicago Press.

Ramos, Artur, 1934. *O Negro Brasileiro.* Rio: Editora Civilazação Brasileira.

———, 1939. *The Negro in Brazil.* Washington: Associated Publishers.

————, 1951. The Negro in Brazil. In *Brazil: Portrait of Half a Continent*. T. Lynn Smith and Alexander Marchant, eds. pp. 125–146. New York: Dryden.

Renshaw, J. Parke, 1969. A Sociological Analysis of Spiritism in Brazil. Ph.D. dissertation. Gainesville: University of Florida Press.

Riberiro, René, 1952. *Cultos Afrobrasileiros do Recife*. Recife: Boletim do Instituto Joaquim Nabuco.

Rio, João do (Paulo Barreto), 1951[1904] As Religióes no Rio. Rio de Janeiro: Ediçóes da Organização Simóes.

Rodrigues, Ana Maria, 1984. *Samba Negro: Espoliação Branca*. Sáo Paulo: HUCITEC.

Russell-Wood, A.J.R., 1982. *The Black Man in Slavery and Freedom in Colonial Brazil*. New York: St. Martin's.

Silverstein, Leni, P. Birman, and Z. Seiblitz, 1982. Os Saravás da Umbanda: Um Estudo das Federaçóes Umbandistas no Grande Rio. Report prepared for the Ford Foundation. Mimeo.

Simpson, George E., 1978. *Black Religions in the New World*. New York: Columbia University Press.

Singer, Paulo, 1965. A Politica das Classes Dominates. In *Politica e Revoluçã Social no Brasil*. Octavio Ianni, et al., eds. pp. 65–125. Rio de Janeiro: Editora Civilização Brasileira.

Skidmore, Thomas E., 1974. *Black into White: Race and Nationality in Brazilian Thought*. New York: Oxford University Press.

Squeff, Enio, and José Miguel Wisnick, 1982. *Música. Coleção o Nacional e o Popular na Cultura Brasileira*. São Paulo: Editora Brasiliense.

Stepan, Nancy, 1976. *Beginnings of Brazilian Science*. New York: Science History Publications.

Thomas, Keith, 1971. *Religion and the Decline of Magic*. New York: Charles Scribner.

Veja, 1983. Festa Nagóo. No. 777, (27 July):49–50.

Wagley, Charles, ed., 1952. *Race and Class in Rural Brasil*. Paris: UNESCO.

Warren, Donald, 1968a. Portuguese Roots of Brazilian Spiritism. *Luso-Brazilian Review* 5(2):3–33.

————, 1968b. Spiritism in Brazil. *Journal of Inter-American Studies* 10:393–405.

Willems, Emilio, 1966. Religious Mass Movements and Social Change in Brazil. In *New Perspectives on Brazil*. Eric Baklanoff, ed. Nashville: Vanderbilt.

Wilson, Bryan, 1973. *Magic and the Millenium: A Sociological Study of Religious Movements of Protest Among Tribal and Third-World People*. New York: Harper and Row.

22

The Spirit and Democracy
Base Communities, Protestantism, and Democratization in Latin America

Christian Smith

This article seeks to evaluate the present and potential impact of two important Latin American religious movements on the strengthening of political democracy in Latin America. Specifically, it addresses the questions: do the base ecclesial communities (*communidades eclesiales de base* or CEBs) associated with liberation theology and the rapid spread of Protestantism, particularly pentecostalism in Latin America represent forces that are either supportive of, inimical to, or irrelevant to the consolidation of democracy in Latin America, and why?[1] The analysis is based on a critical reading of the literature on the subject and on the author's own studies of CEBs in Chile, Peru, Guatemala, and Nicaragua conducted as part of a larger research project on the history of the emergence of Latin American liberation theology (Smith 1991).

I will argue that *in the short run* CEBs represent a significant force helping to strengthen democ-

racy in Latin America, while Latin American Protestantism, for the most part, does not. Indeed, CEBs in a variety of political settings have already demonstrated their ability to mobilize political activism in the struggle for a more egalitarian, participatory world. I will also argue, however, that *in the long run* it is not unlikely that the political influence of these two religious movements will be reversed. That is, there are reasons to believe that, with the passage of time, CEBs will increasingly encounter significant limitations in their ability to contribute to the strengthening of democracy, while in contrast, Latin American Protestantism will emerge as a significant positive force helping to foster genuine democratization.

DEMOCRACY AND ITS OBSTACLES IN LATIN AMERICA

For our purposes, "democracy" denotes a form and practice of government that (1) entails genuine competition between rival political programs and parties in which incumbents may actually lose and surrender their power, (2) involves broad participation by the public in the political process, and

Chris Smith, "The Spirit and Democracy: Base Communities, Protestantism, and Democratization in Latin America," *Sociology of Religion* 55(2):119–143, 1994. © Association for the Sociology of Religion, Inc.

(3) honors the fundamental human and civil rights of its citizens (Lipset 1981; Huntington 1984; Touraine 1991). I will regard CEBs and Protestantism as helping to strengthen democracy in Latin America, then, to the extent that they (1) encourage genuine political competition, (2) mobilize sustained, popular participation in the political process, and (3) promote an expectation and practice of governmental accountability to civil society for the respect of human and civil rights.

Historically, achieving sustained, genuine democracy in Latin America has been difficult. Pro-democracy forces in Latin America find themselves facing an abundance of seemingly intractable obstacles—internal and external, cultural and structural—to the process of genuine democratization.[2] Primary among the *cultural* obstacles is Latin America's half-millennium old dominant political culture of "monistic corporatism." This political culture is grounded in the pre-Enlightenment, pre-scientific-revolution, precapitalist, aristocratic, patrimonialist, monolithically Catholic, and structurally semifeudal world of the Iberian Peninsula of the sixteenth century, which made a deep impression on the Iberian colonies through conquest and colonization (Rossi and Plano 1980; Erickson 1977; Malloy 1977; Stepan 1978; Pike and Stritch 1974; Wiarda 1973, 1974, 1976, 1977, 1981; Wagley 1992).[3]

Monistic corporatism maintains, in short, that humans find true fulfillment in a well-ordered, organic community, the components of which are harmonized by a central authority to achieve the collective goal of the common good. In this view, a good society does not check and balance opposing social and political factions through competition, but integrates or eliminates them in the name of collective harmony. Accordingly, a well-ordered society is regulated from the top down by a centralized, partimonialist state that structures the community, horizontally, as a hierarchy of class and caste and, vertically, as a coordinated arrangement of pillared social sectors corresponding to the traditional estates of Church, army landowners, universities, organized labor, and so on. Particular interests, social diversity, cultural pluralism, religious nonconformity, and disrespect for tradition and authority are all viewed as detrimental to the common good. Rights do exist, but they are conceived as group rights, not individual rights. Societies shaped by this Iberian-derived monistic corporatism tend to be characterized by authoritarianism, elitism, clientelism, patrimonialism, familism, hierarchy, *caudillismo, machismo*, minimal socioeconomic mobility, double standards of sexual morals, reverence for military and political authority, and an aristocratic ethos of disdain for manual labor and high regard for formal etiquette (Rossi and Plano 1980; Wiarda 1986, 1992; Dealy 1985; Martz and Meyers 1992; Willems 1975).[4]

The monistic-corporatist political tradition represents one of the greatest obstacles to the strengthening of authentic, sustained democracy in Latin America (Rossi and Plano 1980:76). Without overemphasizing cultural factors to the exclusion of social-structural ones, we can, nevertheless, acknowledge that monistic corporatism's tendencies tend to make the establishment of democracy difficult if not impossible. When democracies are established, they usually take the highly centralized and paternalistic forms of "guided" or "tutelary democracies" (Wiarda 1992:324–26). Our exploration of the potential of CEBs and Protestantism to advance democracy in Latin America, therefore, must ask the questions: Do CEBs or Protestantism represent a decisive break with monistic corporatism? Or are their political ramifications congruous with that legacy?

BASE ECCLESIAL COMMUNITIES

CEBs are fundamentally religious, not political, organizations. They exist primarily to enable their members to live out their Christian faith more fully in the world. Yet the boundary between personal and group empowerment and public political activism is quite porous. What begins as a spiritual insight can easily have consequences—intentional and unintentional—in the world of public discourse and collective decision-making (see Reilly 1986:43). Hence, we may observe a number of interrelated features of CEBs that tend to strengthen democratic institutions and practices.

First, *CEBs create "open spaces" in civil society.* Healthy democracies require vibrant civil societies that facilitate rich public associational life relatively free of state interference. Such social environments encourage the formation of a panoply of intermediate-level groups that provide information bridges and communication bridges between masses of individuals and bureaucratic states. These "mediating structures" both help bring stability to private life and transfer meaning and value to the mega-institutions of public life. They help to provide the strong organizational and moral fabric that underlies any genuinely democratic polity (Berger and Neuhaus 1977). Such groups are particularly important for the strengthening of democracy in societies—such as many in Latin America—with histories of social monism and authoritarian dictatorships. Fortuitously, then, for pro-democracy forces in Latin America, "CEBs have been significant in providing a basically democratic, participatory space in a generally elitist society" (Mainwaring 1986:127; also see Bruneau 1979:227–28). According to CEB observer J.B. Libânio (1976:1),

> the Base Ecclesial Community becomes a place of *personalization*. In a world of racial and cultural oppression and discrimination . . . it is highly justifiable that people should be able to find a place where they can feel like people; where they can speak; where they can sense that they are being respected; where their voices are heard in decisions and actions. The dehumanization of society around us, especially around those who have been stepped on, justifies the existence of such groups united by primary relationships.

This creation of open spaces in civil society appears to further the process of Latin American democratization in that its work of social differentiation generates associations free from the paternalistic state control inherent in monistic corporatism. In this way, it also indirectly promotes the kind of political pluralism stipulated in the working conception of democracy stated above.

Second, *CEBs foster an attitude of "engaged criticism."* Latin American democracies suffer from widespread "cosmological fatalism" and "passive criticism" (Krischke 1991:201; Ireland 1989). Many of Latin America's poor—which is to say, of its majority—remain disengaged from politics because they believe their involvement would make no difference. They endure their lot in a state of resignation, incapacitated by what Forman (1975) calls a "culture of despair" and Huizer (1972) calls a "cul-

ture of repression." Equally disengaging is the cynicism about politicians and political processes widespread among Latin America's majority poor. These attitudes do have some basis in fact. But they also help to perpetuate the reality they condemn by inducing Latin Americans to abandon the "dirty" world of politics to selfish and corrupt forces. Such a situation is lethal to the process of democratization.

CEBs, however, have proved themselves able to overcome this disempowering fatalism and passive criticism, not by promoting a social and political involvement inspired by naïve idealism, but by fostering in their members an attitude of "engaged criticism." CEB participants commonly retain a critical attitude toward the violations and injustices of politics, yet channel their critique and the indignation it generates into social-change activism (Stokes 1991). Crucial in the cultivation of this attitude of engaged criticism, which overcomes both fatalism and passive criticism, is the process of "conscientization" developed by Brazilian educator Paulo Freire in the 1960s and adopted by many Latin American CEBs in the 1970s. Through conscientization, CEB members gradually come to see many of their own troubles and society's ills not as the results of God's will or an unalterable fate, but as human social products created by a minority who benefit from the social status quo. And if social structures are humanly formed, so the insight goes, they can be humanly transformed through collective political action (see Adriance 1986:109–10).

Conscientization and the engaged criticism it produces helps to generate active political involvement for justice and freedom characterized by "relentless persistence" (*firmeza permanente*), a slogan popular among many Latin American progressives (McManus and Schlabach 1991). And the cultivation of the attitude of engaged criticism tends to strengthen civil society's demands that governments be accountable to their citizens for the respect of human and civil rights—a convention which, according to our working definition advanced above, is fundamental to the existence of any authentic democracy. Furthermore, engaged criticism challenges the unity and elitism of monistic corporatism, in that the posture itself represents an expression of social nonconformity, ideological diversity, and political dissent springing up from the grassroots.

A third way that CEBs appear to contribute positively to the consolidation of democracy in Latin America is that *CEBs develop their members' organizational, communication, and leadership skills.* Democracy, by definition, requires that a nation's people participate in the political system that governs them. But without a minimal level of political skills, organizational know-how, and proficiency in communication, political participation is difficult and unlikely. The more people comprehend the dynamics and mechanisms of electoral processes, political parties, legislative procedures, bureaucratic systems of complaint and redress, lobbying, and demonstrating, the greater political efficacy they feel and the more likely they are to participate politically and to do so in a consistent and informed manner (Milbrath and Goel 1977:35–42; Conway 1985:38; McAdam *et al.* 1988:708–9).

CEBs enhance political efficacy in their members by providing protected opportunities for them to develop within their groups their abilities to speak, organize, negotiate, compromise, recruit, lead, challenge, cooperate, plan, and assess relationships, programs, and social systems. In this way, CEBs help to demystify the state's organization of power and collective decision making, rendering local, regional, and national political systems more psychologically accessible (Levine 1988). In other words, CEBs often operate as micro-level "proto-democracies" that help prepare their members for subsequent macro-level political participation and so provide a training ground for democratic politics (see Pottenger 1989:141). Such grassroots education promises to contribute significantly to a profound, bottom-up process of democratization in Latin America (see Levine 1990a:73).

Fourth, *CEBs often cultivate in their members a sense of responsibility for the condition of society and history.* In O'Gorman's words (1983:4), through their involvement in CEBs, participants come to realize the imperative of becoming "the subjects and not the objects of history." This realization spawns a new appreciation of their own human dignity, empowering the CEB members for political involvement (see Romero 1989:267). This empowering realization of dignity and responsibility is evident in this 1981 statement of the CEBs of Minas Gerais, Brazil: "What we are doing in

our communities may seem almost like nothing, but it is one of the most important works of the Church today in Brazil and throughout Latin America. . . . We are forming an immense chain and we have the task of trying to reach our liberation" (quoted in O'Gorman 1983:11). This orientation only strengthens democracy in Latin America by discouraging the paternalistic and "assistentialistic" tendencies of monistic corporatism, and instead promoting the self-starting political initiative and participation that are required in healthy democracies (see Hewitt 1988:150–51).

Fifth, *CEBs directly mobilize political participation.* Genuine democracy requires widespread and sustained public participation in the political process. By fostering an attitude of engaged criticism, by developing their members' organizational, communication, and leadership skills, and by cultivating in their members a sense of responsibility for the conditions of society and history, CEBs *indirectly* encourage such political participation.

The importance of organizational ties in facilitating political activism, including ties to officially nonpolitical organizations, is well documented (Barnes and Kaase 1979; Milbrath and Goel 1977; McAdam *et al.* 1988:708; Conway 1985; Verba and Nie 1972). And, by most accounts, that correlation is confirmed by the experience of CEBs in most Latin American countries (e.g., Jeffrey 1991; Levine and Mainwaring 1989:216; Smith 1991; Van Vugt 1991; LADOC 1976; Cook 1985; Bruneau 1986; Smith 1986; Romero 1989; Krischke 1991; Cáceres Prendes 1989; Doimo 1989; Kincaid 1987:492; Adriance 1991). CEB members tend to participate more than equivalent non-CEB members in both electoral and nonelectoral politics as a result of their CEB involvement (see Adriance 1986:159). CEBs encourage their members to participate in both CEB-sponsored community and political activities as well as in the political activities of other organizations, such as labor unions, pressure groups, political parties, neighborhood associations, and other popular movements (see Mainwaring 1986:147).[5]

In some times and places, these political activities take the form of standard, institutionalized politics. Elsewhere, they take more confrontative and disruptive forms—which, depending in part on one's politics, may or may not be seen as promoting democracy (see Stoll 1990: 142). According to Berryman, in Central America in the 1980s, for example, "the church's pastoral work was responsible for the rise of militant organizations during the 1970s. . . . Pastoral work, particularly in the CEBs . . . intersected with the rise and growth of those movements" (Berryman 1986:58). In general, however, given the importance of public participation in politics to liberal democracy, to the degree that CEBs raise, in these ways, the proportion of Latin American citizens who are engaged in multiple forms of political activism, CEBs strengthen the process of Latin American democratization and likely weaken the cultural influence of monistic corporatism (see Adriance 1986:160).

Sixth, and finally, CEBs appear to support Latin American democratization in that the *CEBs represent a power-base for organized influence on political parties*. Monistic corporatism would have Latin America's populace paternalistically overseen and coordinated by unified centralized states controlled by elites. By creating an organized mass-base of power that is socially engaged and relatively politically independent, CEBs present a challenge to the traditional dominance of oligarchy- and elite-controlled regimes. In this way, they help to create the preconditions for a more bottom-up, less top-down model of democracy. CEBs, for example, could potentially provide an important element of a new power-base that would support genuinely democratic reformist political parties. Indeed, inklings of that potential have already expressed themselves in Brazil (see Cook 1985:249).

Thus, in at least six distinct ways, CEBs in Latin America appear to represent a force fortifying the process of democratization. By creating open spaces in civil society, fostering attitudes of engaged criticism, developing their members' organizational and leadership skills, cultivating in their members a sense of responsibility for society and history, directly mobilizing political participation, and furnishing a power-base for an organized influence on political parties, CEBs serve functions that help to strengthen democracy. That is, they appear to erode the cultural influence of monistic corporatism, advance political pluralism, foster political participation, and promote an expectation and practice of governmental accountability for human and civil rights. Such processes, generated by CEBs, have been at work for two decades and still largely remain in effect today.

DOUBTS ABOUT THE FUTURE

All of this having been said, however, there are some reasons to doubt whether in the future CEBs themselves will continue to develop in a direction that will significantly help to sustain Latin American democratization. Indeed, an honest appraisal of CEBs reveals what appear to be a number of nontrivial constraints on their democratizing potential. To begin, the Roman Catholic Church, to which most CEBs belong, is itself a profoundly nondemocratic institution, based on centralized hierarchy, top-down authority and orthodoxy-through-discipline. This models for Latin America's faithful an inescapable contradiction between Church social doctrine and actual Church practice, begging the question why if democracy is promoted by Rome as such a choice system of social relations outside of the Church it would not also be a choiceworthy system for the Church itself (Levine 1986; for another perspective, see Sigmund 1987). In fact, CEBs and their apologists have never been able to escape the incongruity of their own participatory and egalitarian ecclesiology operating in the larger context of a powerful ecclesiastical hierarchy and authority. Indeed, serious attempts to address the matter directly have been met with heavy-handed correctional censureship, as in Leonardo Boff's disciplining by the Vatican for his book, *Church: Charism and Power—Liberation Theology and the Institutional Church* (1985; also see Boff 1986), which eventually resulted in Boff resigning from the priesthood (see Cox 1988).

Another factor that may curtail the CEBs long-term democratizing potential is the palpable lack of immediate results of most of their attempts to transform the structures of society beyond the community level (Pottenger 1989:141ff.). While CEBs can have a significant effect in transforming their local worlds, jumping to the level of national and international structural change is another matter. Most of the CEB's potential for political change described above, in fact, involves gradual transformation, often based on cultural changes, the effects of which would take years and sometimes decades to appreciate fully. Relentless persistence notwithstanding, however, the ongoing apparent inability to transform macro-social structures significantly can have a discouraging effect. Indeed, many of the Nicaraguan CEBs, which once appeared to have the most to show fore their political activism, are now struggling and discouraged (Rehberg 1992; Serbin 1992; also see Peña 1992). This situation is not helped by the sometimes ephemeral nature of many CEBs, compared at least to many Latin American pentecostal churches, noticed by many observers (e.g., Cook 1990:1178). Some even doubt the magnitude of the CEBs' presence. Serbin (1992:405), for example, claims that, "evidence indicates that the renowned CEBs probably number a fraction of the tens of thousands claimed by the church. Nor is it clear how successfully they have been in attracting the poor."

Furthermore, the exact depth of the participatory, egalitarian, and activist commitments of many CEBs is not entirely certain. Recent studies have revealed some antiactivist and antidemocratic tendencies developing in CEBs which contrast with portrayals in earlier literature written largely by enthusiastic proponents of CEBs (e.g., Barreiro 1982; Barbé 1982; Torres and Eagleson 1981). Some have recently suggested, for example, that CEBs tend to become both smaller and decreasingly active politically as they age (e.g., Hewitt 1988, 1990). Others claim that, compared to pentecostal churches, the style and attitudes of at least some CEBs exclude poor speakers, illiterates, those with little free time, dark-skinned members, and women abused by their husbands (Burdick 1992). Yet others point out the continuing patronizing and disempowering communication- and organization-styles of many church personnel officially responsible for leading CEBs (e.g., Van Vugt 1991; Ireland 1989). Many prospective members, too, eventually choose to avoid participating in CEBs because they fear the violent state repression that CEBs' liberationist activities have in the past so often provoked (Martin 1990:290). Finally, the political involvements of even the best of CEBs can often be thwarted by the frequent lack of community recognition, interference from government and church officials, and enduring religious traditionalism among CEB members (Levine 1990a:73; Hewitt 1986). Each of these problems can, in its own way, constrain the potential of CEBs to strengthen democracy in Latin America.

Perhaps most important, there is reason to doubt whether the democratizing tendencies of CEBs may not, in the end, be coopted or domesticated by the legacy of monistic corporatism. Such an outcome is possible both because of the proven adaptability and durability of monistic corporatism and because of inherent ambiguities in the very project of CEBs and many of their leaders. The CEBs' emphasis on community and cooperation, for example, cuts in two directions. On the one hand it serves to empower, dignify, and mobilize people for social-change activism. On the other hand, however, it opens the door for a collectivist mentality which *may*—not certainly will, only may—feed directly back into monistic-corporatist solutions to perceived problems. Indeed, in one survey of 479 Brazilian Catholics, CEB members were *more-* likely than nonmembers to look to "patron and government" to solve their social problems (Bruneau 1986:121). While many Latin American social problems clearly call for major *structural* reforms, it is equally clear that they do not call for solutions devised and delivered by patrons.

Furthermore, vestiges, if not themes, of monistic corporatism appear to remain in much of the thought of liberation theologians and other leaders of the CEB movement. In the early 1970s, many liberation theologians viewed electoral democracy as a fraudulent mechanism of bourgeois rule (Sigmund 1988:41). It is true, however, that today, "an evolution toward cautious political positions is visible among Church progressives" (Mainwaring and Wilde 1989:27). McGovern (1989:589) notes that "Liberation theologians have . . . modified their politico-economic views in recent years. The new political context in many parts of Latin America has led liberation theologians to talk about building a 'participatory democracy' from within civil society." Hugo Assman, for example, "long considered the most Marxist of the liberation theologians . . . spoke in the mid-1980s of the 're-democratization of Latin America' as an essential priority" (McGovern 1989:186). According to Sigmund, "Assman seems now to equate revolution with democracy" (1988:40). And Roth observes that "Assman has apparently become much more concerned to consider how democracy can work on behalf of the poor" (1988:239). Nevertheless, one should not automatically project a Lockean-liberal spin on this increasingly favorable view of democracy among these progressive church leaders (see Mainwaring 1989:181). Thus, although it is certainly not inevitable, it also is not unimaginable that the CEB movement, whether intentionally or not, would end up reinforcing rather than eroding the antidemocratic cultural legacy of monistic corporatism.

None of these stated doubts about the CEBs' future contribution to democratization necessarily negates any of the arguments advanced in the previous section about the CEBs' positive democratizing effects. They merely highlight the danger of simply extrapolating the future from the past and the present. In years past and even today, CEBs do appear to represent a force strengthening democracy in Latin America. Nevertheless, the antidemocratic nature of the Catholic Church, the short-term inability of CEBs to effect major social changes, certain antiactivist and antidemocratic tendencies within at least some CEBs, and the apparent potential for ultimate cooptation by monistic corporatism may significantly restrict the CEBs' future capacity to reinforce democracy. Indeed, it is not entirely unlikely that the CEBs' democratizing effects will be superseded in the long run by those of a now rapidly spreading Protestantism.

LATIN AMERICAN PROTESTANTISM

We want to know whether Latin American Protestantism has in the past, does in the present, or might in the future encourage political competition and pluralism, mobilize sustained public participation in the political process, promote an expectation and practice of governmental accountability to civil society for the respect of human rights, or generally help to diminish the cultural influence of monistic corporatism. Assessing Latin American Protestantism's impact on democratization using these four criteria, I will cautiously conclude that Protestantism does possess the *potential* to help advance democracy in Latin America, that this potential is thus far largely unrealized, but that in the long run it would be unlikely for this democracy-strengthening potential to remain substantially unfulfilled.[6]

Admittedly, the term "Latin American Protestantism" suggests a homogeneity that is grossly oversimplistic. In fact, "Protestant" (*evangélico*) in Latin America refers to all non-Catholic Christians and, as such, comprises an immense multiplicity of dissimilar religious phenomena. These include transplanted mainline United States Protestant denominations (e.g., Presbyterian, Methodist, Episcopalian), transplanted United States non-

charismatic fundamentalist and evangelical "faith-mission" churches (e.g., Southern Baptist), the churches of European immigrants (e.g., German Lutherans in Brazil and Chile), transplanted United States Mormon, Jehovah's Witness, and Seventh-day Adventist churches, and a huge variety of indigenous and transplanted pentecostal churches (Stoll 1990:4; Montgomery 1979; Paredes 1992). And, within these types of churches can be found a great variety of theological, social, and political perspectives. Indeed, Latin American Protestantism includes an entire spectrum of theological and political positions, from conservative reactionaries to moderate reformists to flaming radicals. My analysis, then, will unfortunately but unavoidably be dealing with overgeneralizations. Since three-quarters of Latin America's 40 million Protestants are pentecostals, however, my analysis will primarily focus on these pentecostals and the second largest group, the noncharismatic fundamentalists and evangelicals. The mainline Protestants, European immigrant churches, Mormons, Jehovah's Witnesses, and Seventh-day Adventists are distinctive enough to merit their own separate analyses.

Latin American Protestantism is by now well known in popular and scholarly circles for apolitical, right-wing, authoritarian tendencies. There exists no shortage of Latin American liberation theologians, social scientists, Catholic church officials, and radical Protestants, nor of North American liberal theologians, academic scholars, and researching Ph.D. students to point out and often decry the alleged otherworldly, reactionary, and dogmatic proclivities of Latin American Protestantism. These proclivities are, in fact, often very real. Many studies do reveal in Protestantism a rejection of political participation, the reproduction of clientistic patronage relations, a refusal to confront social injustices, contempt for "worldly" social involvements, authoritarian church leadership, reductionistic individualism in social analysis, frequent endorsements of repressive military dictatorships, and theological and ideological narrow-mindedness (e.g., Willems 1967; Bastain 1986; Lalive d'Epinay 1969; Hoffnagel 1978; Stoll 1990; Alves 1985; Martin 1990). Certainly, none of these tendencies, when and where they do exist, qualifies Latin American Protestantism as a leading nurturer of liberal democracy.

To avoid a stereotyped caricature of Protestantism, however, we would do well to clarify three points. First, it is untrue that Latin American Protestants are disinterested in effecting social and political change, but their approach to social change, like that of their conservative North American counterparts (Hollinger 1983), is radically individualistic—that is, nonstructuralist. In other words, Latin American Protestants generally believe that one changes society by converting the individual members of society. When enough people get saved, it is thought, a new morality will emerge that will eventually infiltrate the institutions of society and induce needed reforms (see Stoll 1990:2–3). At issue, therefore, is not the end—namely, social, economic, and political improvement—but the means to that end. And there is nothing about the Protestants' current individualistic understanding of the proper means that is either immune to the potential incorporation of a more structuralist approach or intrinsically inimical to a contribution to political pluralism and democratic participation, as Protestants become more established and sophisticated. Indeed, historically, individualism has been strongly associated with the functioning of liberal democracy.

Second, Latin American Protestants' contempt for worldly affairs, including political struggles, does not automatically make them radical separatists. For in Christian scripture, "worldly" (*kosmikós*) does not mean everything in the natural and social world, but those ideas and systems which are positively hostile to God and in the service of evil (Bromiley 1985:363–65). Yet nothing inherent in Protestantism—including the Wesleya-Methodist American holiness movement, from which pentecostalism was derived—defines direct involvement in secular political systems as innately worldly.[7] What is forbidden is not involvement itself, but the sins of corruption, injustice, lying, oppression, and so on that might attend political involvements. If and when they do abstain from political participation, that is a conditional position shaped by particular social circumstances, not the inevitable outworking of their theological tradition. Thus, changes in their social environment could easily and quickly shift their orientation toward heavy political involvement, similar to, for example, the decisive shift toward activism made by Jerry Falwell and many other North American fundamentalists in the late 1970s and early 1980s.

Third, we ought to be careful to distinguish the views of Protestant ministers and church spokesmen (almost always men) from the views and actions of the Protestant laity. Ideological rhetoric and actual life practice do not always correspond (Burdick 1992). Mariz (1992:64) rightly observes: "There are limits on [Protestants'] abilities to put their official ideologies into effect. . . . The very process of attempting to live by [their] precepts . . . generates behavior that does not entirely reflect the values expressed in their official systems of discourse." Thus, Protestant ministers may preach abstention from politics, but the preachers themselves may simultaneously curry favors from local politicians, and members of their congregations may become involved in social reform when their interests are threatened (e.g., Stoll 1990:111, 212). Likewise, virtually all Latin American pentecostals, evangelicals, and fundamentalists repudiate liberation theology in public, yet church investigations have sometimes discovered covert sympathy for liberation theology among some members (Stoll 1990:21). Our analysis, therefore, needs to attend not only to what leaders say, but also to how the mass of laity in fact think and behave, which is ultimately more important.

Returning to our main argument, Latin American Protestantism today, it must be conceded, is characteristically conservative, politically withdrawn, and structurally authoritarian. But we should not allow these conspicuous traits to obscure a number of other less obvious but important features of Latin American Protestantism whose effects should, theoretically at least, directly or indirectly assist the process of Latin American democratization. Some of these features may be facilitating democratization even now, though without much recognition. Others may be having their more immediate democratizing effects neutralized, *for the time being*, by the more primary antidemocratic characteristics of Latin American Protestantism noted above—a contingent neutralization, however, subject to change in the future.

The first feature that should assist the process of Latin American democratization is that at a basic level *the rapid spread of Protestantism in Latin America represents a decisive structural break with the religiously unified social pattern of monistic corporatism*. Latin America's traditional, primary political culture, we have observed, presumes and promotes a harmonious society in pursuit of a common good, where social sectors are integrated by a centralized state and bound in religious unity by a single Catholic culture. Social diversity, religious nonconformity, and cultural pluralism are eschewed as detrimental to the common good. Protestantism's expansion and entrenchment, however, represents a definitive rupture in this sociocultural "organic solidarity," a driving wedge cleaving apart monistic corporatism's social-structural unity. For this reason, Montgomery (1979:90–91) has argued that "Protestantism . . . has [already] played a critical, if minor, role in the overthrow of traditional society by introducing new norms, values, and institutions contrary to the existing ones." Martin (1990:265–66) explains:

> Catholicism symbolizes integration into a complete socio-religious system. . . . For Protestants [this] is . . . part and parcel of a society they decisively reject. Whatever their political attitudes, Protestants desire (and express) a process of social differentiation in the direction of personal choice and egalitarian participation. From their standpoint, Catholicism still appears as involved in hierarchical forms, in priestly mediation through controlled channels, and in comprehensive organic integration. . . . Protestantism initiates the era of the individual in his (or her) specifically religious incarnation, and the obverse of that is a view of society not easily amenable to holistic and structural understandings.[8]

We know of at least one historical instance of the Protestant rupture in Latin America's sociocultural unity facilitating radical political change. According to Deborah Baldwin (1990), Protestants prior to and during the Mexican revolution championed the so-called "radical liberals" and Francisco Madero's race for the presidency (also see Bastain 1983). Baldwin observes that, rather than being politically conservative, Protestants during the Mexican Revolution eagerly embraced radical change. Because they had already disengaged from traditional religion, they found it easy to break with the established political arrangements. As Protestantism continues to spread throughout Latin America, it may be that, given the right conditions, the break with Latin America's religious tradition will help to facilitate a more decisive break with Latin America's longstanding undemocratic political tradition.

Second, *Protestant churches, like CEBs, create "open spaces" in civil society, as relatively politically independent intermediate-level organizations.* Martin (1990:267–68; also see Stoll 1990:321) elaborates on the inescapably political dimension of these potentially democracy-sustaining open spaces:

> Evangelical religion . . . passes through periods of social latency before trying to generalize peace and reconciliation from the interior of the group to the wider social world. During these periods of latency, the social changes initiated by religious faith, above all universal participation, operate at the level of culture and of symbolism. Protestantism creates a "free space," though the free space reverberates with echoes from a patriarchal past. That "free space" is temporarily protected by an apolitical stance, setting up a boundary with a dangerous, corrupt, and amoral outside world. Nevertheless, the creation of any space in the conditions inherent in Latin America remains inherently political.

The third feature of Protestantism that should foster the process of Latin American democratization is that *Latin American Protestant church structures are not unambiguously authoritarian—they also encourage the development of lay leadership and participation in ways that partially cross-cut standard dimensions of social stratification.* According to Mariz (1992:68; also see Stoll 1990:36):

> The experience of revealed knowledge and the assumption that any member can relate directly to God allows the development of a lay leadership. . . . [P]entecostal churches consist of relatively independent small groups that are mainly led by ordinary people who have ample opportunities to develop organizational skills, including the ability to mobilize themselves for collective action.

The very religious character of Protestantism itself seems to foster in believers the development of important relational and communication skills:

The importance of the written word and the theoretical elaboration of the faith has, as a consequence, encouraged people to become literate for the purpose of reading the Bible and to develop speaking skills for expounding scripture and discussing it with others. . . . The stimulus for reading, speaking, and forming opinions can be useful both for individual social mobility and for the organization of political movements (Mariz 1992:65; also see Stoll 1990:175–79).

According to observers, the opportunities for leadership development and shared participation afforded in most Protestant churches partially undermine the broader culture's bases of social stratification, helping to erode further the horizontal social divisions sustained by monistic corporatism. Burdick (1992:180), for example, notes:

Pentecostalism's vision of transformation forges the possibility for negros [dark-skinned Brazilians] to be treated as equals—even better than equals—with light-skinned *crentes* [Protestant believers]. Pentecostal doctrine proclaims that the Holy Spirit is no respecter of persons. In fact, *crentes* commonly claim that the lower and humbler one is in the world, the more open one is likely to be to the power of the Spirit. Based in this principle . . . negroes discover that Pentecostalism allows them to develop a degree of authority impossible in any other social arena.

Likewise, although Protestant churches usually do not actually allow women to become formal preaching authorities, they do typically afford environments where women experience more relational empowerment than ever before.[9] Coleman (1991:60; also see Stoll 1990:317–18), for example, suggests that "Pentecostalism appeals to women by offering them a public place where they can experience independence, self-esteem, and power by taming in their men the abuse of drink and cult of *machismo*" (also see Burdick 1992:177–78).[10] To the extent that hundreds of thousands of Latin American Protestant churches provide relatively open opportunities for a wide range of believers to gain leadership skills, organizational experience, and moral authority, they function, like the CEBs described above, as "proto-democracies," forging personal changes at a small-group level that could

have potential political ramifications at the regional and national level (see Martin 1990:284–85).

Fourth, *Latin American Protestantism contains a nascent rational individualism that should function—in the long run, at least—to support political democratization.* Stoll (1990:318) suggests: "If we are looking for a religious movement that promotes the kind of rationalization associated with bourgeois and socialist revolutions, then pentecostalism is an interesting beast. . . . Pentecostalism places authority in a single godhead, creates universal ethical standards, and promotes individual responsibility." And, according to Mariz (1992:65), "Pentecostalism, [even] with its otherworldliness and its respect for constituted authority, fosters a critical, non-fatalistic outlook on life that can work against the movement's official posture of avoiding involvement in 'worldly affairs." Rational individualism adheres in Latin American Protestantism—even if only latently—in many ways. Religious conversion, for example, central to the Latin American Protestant world view, is understood as a matter of individual choice, made in a state of free will, that responds to a message containing propositional truths.

This emphasis on achieved rather than ascribed status contrasts sharply with traditional Catholicism's Christendom notion, where all members of society are automatically Christians by virtue of their parents' faith and their own sacramentally operative infant baptism. In addition, the very experience of Protestant conversion, not to mention of the pentecostals' "second blessing" or "baptism by the Spirit," involves a dramatic shaking-up of the taken-for-granted world and the embrace of a new way of seeing reality itself that explicitly devalues the prior state of perception and the reality it formed. ("Once I was blind, now I can see; once I was dead, now I am alive.") Furthermore, the Protestants' stress on personal sanctification, on changes in personal morality to achieve a righteous lifestyle, is cast in a rational and individualistic mold. The spiritual introspection, methodical self-discipline, application of faith to everyday experience, means-end mentality, and personal responsibility involved in the conservative Protestant sanctification experience all engenders an ethos of rational individualism. In these and other ways, Latin American Protestantism carries and inculcates a complex of beliefs and practices that are much more compatible with and supportive of democracy than the collectivism, fatalism, mysticism, and traditionalism found in much of Catholic, monistic-corporatist Latin America.

Fifth, *Latin American Protestantism fosters in its members a respect for the rule of law*. Latin American Protestants' law-based understanding of God's will for human behavior and their focus on certain obvious political teachings in Christian scripture (Romans 13:1–7; 1 Peter 2:13–17) compel them conscientiously to obey the laws of the state. In the Latin American context, this can and often has translated into passive or active support for authoritarian regimes, thus undermining some of Protestantism's other pro-democracy potential. But even this religiously grounded respect for the rule of law can cut against nondemocratic polities in two ways.

First, the New Testament passages that command submission to existing political authorities also define the ruler as being "God's servant, an agent of justice to bring punishment on the wrongdoer" and as "sent by [God] to punish those who do wrong and to commend those who do right" (1 Peter 2:14). Ironically, this establishes a divine standard by which rulers themselves can be judged. This opens up the potential to conclude, when rulers violate that standard, as they often do, that political authorities have forfeited their God-bestowed legitimacy. Hence, the command to obey contains its own potential nullification, and an invitation to critique the performance of—and for some, such as many Calvinists, to revolt against—abusive political regimes.

Second, the Latin American Protestants' respect for the rule of law, at least in theory and sometimes in practice,transfers the object of obedience from the specific ruler or regime to the system of laws that transcends the ruler or regime. Ultimately, it is the law itself that must be obeyed, not the person who wrote it. In the Latin American Protestant mind, in other words, no political authority is above his or her own law. Practically, this mentality functions both to undermine the personalistic *caudillismo* of monistic corporatism and to hold political authorities accountable for their own legal violations. According to Mariz (1992:68) pentecostals' respect for law-based, instead of person-based, authority and their insistence that authority figures obey God's law has freed them from the traditional submissive-authoritarian elements of Brazilian pop-

ular culture and religion. All of this promotes among Protestants a certain critical distance from the state, a moral autonomy that contains the potential for a governmental accountability that was lacking in most of Latin America's traditional Catholicism. Thus, according to Stoll (1990:319–20):

> Despite the flagrant romances between pentecostal patriarchs and right-wing regimes, congregations tend to retain considerable autonomy in their dealings with the state and society. They conform to outer constraints yet maintain a degree of independence, in a paradoxical way that critics have not captured when they accuse pentecostals of isolating themselves from society.

Finally, despite widespread perceptions of a totally apolitical Protestant character, in fact, *Latin American Protestants—pentecostals, evangelicals, and fundamentalists—have already begun to engage significantly in democratic political involvements*. The notion that all Protestants shun political participation is simply misinformed. In fact, there exists a dynamic internal struggle in Latin American Protestantism about how to interact with the secular world (Stoll 1990:19). This is not surprising, given the biblical ambiguities in the very concept "worldly" and the immense variety within Latin American Protestantism itself. According to Martin (1990:236), "all [political] options have been explored by some Pentecostals. There is no route which Pentecostal doctrine absolutely precludes, except adherence to a movement which is doctrinally atheist." Mariz (1992:68), too, notes that the "Pentecostals' . . . ideology does not encourage political participation, but when personal, class, or religious interests of pentecostals are at stake, many of them do become involved in politics."

This involvement includes participation in electoral politics, both as voters and candidates. Protestants, for example, were active in Peru's 1990 presidential election. "In Peru, although Protestants still make up only 3% to 5% of the population, they helped to get out the vote for [the victorious candidate] Alberto Fujimori" (Ryser *et al.* 1990:79). Indeed, "Protestants in Peru . . . were credited with rallying key support for Alberto Fujimori in the 1990 presidential election." (Burnett 1992:219). And in Brazil, "Protestants have emerged [as elected officials] in considerable numbers in state politics. They number up to forty deputies and clearly they are beginning to constitute a distinct Protestant political presence" (Martin 1990:259). Countering both the perception that Protestants avoid all political involvements and that the Protestant laity automatically follow the directives of their leaders, Martin (1990:239–40) asserts:

> Pentecostals *do* vote and not so much below non-Pentecostals in their electoral participation. . . . [According to surveys of Chilean pentecostals in the early 1970s] the sympathies of the great mass of Pentecostals did not correspond to those of their leaders. The distribution of their votes accorded with their social position or, at any rate, with the distribution among comparable non-Pentecostals. More than that, 80 percent of Pentecostals preferred [socialist candidate Salvador] Allende to [Christian Democrat Eduardo] Frei, compared with 60 percent of non-Pentecostals.

At the same time, occasionally, Protestant church *leaders* also promote political participation for social and political reform. Brazilian Pentecostal revivalist Manoel de Melo, for example, campaigned in the early 1970s for democracy, social justice, and religious freedom, claiming that pentecostal churches often became "marshalling grounds for the entry of . . . new persons into political life" (Frase 1975:567). Also, a consortium of theologically conservative Protestant theologians, the Latin American Theological Fraternity, has struggled since the early 1970s to promote in the churches social engagement and an understanding of sin as structural as well as personal (Stoll 1990:131–32; also see Berryman 1987:43).

Protestant political participation also sometimes has taken the form of opposition protest. In Nicaragua in the 1980s, for example, conservative Protestants became involved in political opposition to the Sandinista regime, even at the cost of provoking government retaliation (Crahan 1989:50; also see Montgomery 1979:92–94). On another occasion, however,

> even conservative Protestants began to speak against the [United States-sponsored "Contra"] war. A Campaign of Fasting and Prayer for Peace and Justice, organized by CEPAD [Evan-

gelical Committee for Aid to Development], culminated in an October 1986 all-night vigil in Managua, in which over 10,000 Christians, most of them Pentecostals, prayed energetically for peace (Jeffrey 1991:166).

Furthermore, in Guatemala, conservative Presbyterians have been forced to protest gross government violations of the human rights of Indians, many of whom were Presbyterian converts (Stoll 1990:22, 212). Latin American Protestantism has also at times fed personnel into popular, sometimes even leftist, political organizations (see Mariz 1992:68; Cáceres Prendes 1989:144).

Hence, we see that the idea of total political withdrawal by Latin American Protestants is a misnomer. Protestants have the capacity and inclination, under the right conditions, to become active in electoral, protest, and social-movement politics. Indeed, examination of those instances of involvement demonstrates, on some occasions, specific religious motivations for political participation and, on other occasions, the power of the class interests of believers to override any apolitical tendencies in their belief systems.

Thus, in at least six different ways, Latin American Protestantism appears to possess the potential to act as a social force in support of democratization in Latin America. By breaking the social unity of monistic corporatism, creating open spaces in civil society, developing leadership and participation skills in a wide range of believers, promoting rational individualism, fostering a respect for the rule of law, and demonstrating the capacity to mobilize political participation, Latin American Protestantism displays an incipient capacity to advance democracy in Latin America. Whether that capacity eventually overrides Latin American Protestantism's current undemocratic tendencies appears to depend on future developments within Protestantism and changes in the social, economic, and political conditions that Protestants will have to negotiate.

A PRODEMOCRACY FUTURE FOR PROTESTANTISM?

The political future of Latin American Protestantism depends in large measure on the political future of Latin American Catholicism, for a major determinant of Protestant identity is the effort to escape and invert Catholic identity. Whatever Catholics are, Latin American Protestants do not want to be—which is understandable, given their social and historical context. Thus, when, in the early twentieth century, Latin American Catholics were staunchly conservative and traditionalist politically, Protestants tended to be politically progressive, liberal, and even sometimes revolutionary. Then, as Catholicism grew more socially engaged, politically progressive, and sometimes revolutionary in the late 1960s and 1970s—precisely at the time of Protestantism's major growth spurt—Latin American Protestants defined themselves as apolitical and socially conservative. The 1980s and early 1990s, however, have witnessed a backing away from progressive politics in the Catholic Church, particularly from the project of liberation theology (Smith 1991:222–33). If the Catholic Church in Latin America were to continue to head in a politically conservative direction, emphasizing spiritual devotion over social engagement, this would open the door for Protestants increasingly to explore political participation and democratic social reform without threatening the anti-Catholic dimension of their identity.

A second factor that might encourage the pro-democracy potential of Latin American Protestantism would be a blockage of Protestant upward mobility. Many, especially enthusiastic champions of capitalism echoing themes of Weber's *Protestant Ethic* (e.g., Kamm 1991; Ryser *et al.* 1990; Marcom 1990), have acclaimed Latin American Protestantism's promise of lifting its members into middle-class prosperity through personal virtue, thrift, and hard work. Unfortunately, Latin America's peasants and urban laborers do not face the same favorable macrostructural conditions enjoyed by the rising bourgeoisie of early modern Europe. Hence, observers have found little evidence of upward social mobility among the rank and file of grass-roots evangelicalism (Cook 1990:1178; 1985:280–81). It is not entirely unlikely, in other words, that if and when the majority of Latin American Protestants discover the avenue of individual upward mobility through marketplace achievement to be blocked, they will head in the direction of group mobility through political activism. This would serve both to introduce a more structuralist approach to Protestant social analysis and to mobilize sustained, reformist Protestant political participation.

Third, it is probable that, as Protestantism in Latin America continues to grow into significant national minorities and, possibly, majorities (in Guatemala, for example), new and existing political parties will increasingly court the Protestant vote. Protestants often do vote, and consequently, in many countries they increasingly represent a potential political goldmine for politicians and parties who could successfully tap into the Latin American Protestant *Weltanschauung*. Were Protestants to become a publicly recognized political prize, this would animate the Protestants' awareness of their own political influence, decrease their sense of the inherent futility of politics itself, and further encourage their participation in democratic political processes At the risk of drawing close parallels between very different worlds, the response of the so-called New Christian Right to the political attention paid to it by Republican party coalition-builders prior to the 1980 United States Presidential election serves as a model for such a process.

Fourth and related to the previous point, if Latin American Protestants were for a host of possible reasons increasingly to perceive the world of politics as less spiritually corrupting, less physically dangerous, and more efficacious in matters of value to them, they would likely become more comfortable with expanded involvement in reformist democracy. Indeed, I hypothesize that the conditions of political life have an antithetical effect on the political involvements of Protestants and CEBs. That is, the more unjust and unscrupulous politics are, the more CEBs, whose historical strengths are resistance and protest, appear to become politically engaged and the more Protestants become politically withdrawn. Conversely, the more politics become honest and equitable and the more CEBs appear to shift into charity and devotional activities, the more Protestants do and will become politically active.

Matters of safety and survival are greatly relevant here. The period of Latin American Protestantism's greatest surge in numbers coincided with the sweeping emergence of repressive bureaucratic authoritarianism. Many liberation-theology oriented Catholic CEBs challenged repressive military regimes and paid dearly in lives and official political status (Smith 1991:189–221). Protestantism's strategy of safety and survival, in contrast, was to declare apolitical withdrawal, while often offering de facto support for the authoritarian regimes. To use Stoll's grim image, liberation theology was very effective in filling graves, while Protestantism was effective in filling church buildings. As political participation has become and may increasingly become more safe and open, however, Protestants may be more prepared to shift into a more politically active strategy. Thus, the emergence of healthy, honorable democracies and Protestant political participation may well have mutually reinforcing effects.

Finally, the coming of age of a "second generation" of Latin American Protestants in the next two decades will likely alter the political posture of Protestantism. Stoll (1990:329) reminds us that "the history of social movements is replete with shifts from a redemptive (saving one's soul) to a transformative (changing the world) emphasis, or vice versa, often after the first generation." Latin American Protestantism, we have seen, actually possesses many features that could potentially work to bolster democratization. As Protestantism becomes more entrenched, stable, self-confident, routinized, and sophisticated, a second generation of Protestants could very well turn its attention to matters quite different from those that occupied the first generation.[11]

Again, without straining resemblances drawn from very different contexts, North American evangelicalism provides an example of such a dynamic. Arising in the 1940s out of the fundamentalist movement, the relatively homogeneous evangelicals of Billy Graham and Carl Henry's generation maintained an individualistic reductionism in social analysis and a low political profile. By the early 1970s, however, after three decades of growth and institution building, a new generation of evangelicals emerged who challenged first-generation assumptions and opened up new possibilities of theological, social, and political engagement (Fowler 1982; Quebedeaux 1974). Thus, in the words of a Presbyterian missionary to Latin America: "You have to take a long perspective, because in the short term, yes, evangelical religion is reactionary. But a lot of the second and third generation lose their spirituality and start asking different questions of the Bible" (in Stoll 1990:330–31).[12] And if the second generation does begin to search

for religious legitimations for social and political engagement, it will find and rejuvenate the activism-justifying themes that always resided in its own theological tradition and scripture (Cook 1985:280–81).

Taken in this light, Protestantism's current relative political passivity could conceivably represent a long-term gain for democracy in Latin America—to the extent that Protestantism could ever encourage democracy. For it may afford Protestantism the undistracted opportunity to grow numerically, build stable institutions, establish an alternative culture, and gain the collective self-confidence necessary for a future broadening of perspectives and engagements. Taking this line of thought, Martin (1990:287) argues that these kinds of self-enclosed protections,

> constitute the paradoxical precondition of any serious revision of consciousness and social practice. A very large number of the models of change which have gone to make up our modern world were set in motion in precisely this way. . . . Religious groupings construct advanced platforms in consciousness, and test their viability in enclosed protected environments. They send out signals about what may be possible, and the wider society in time picks these up.

Does Latin American Protestantism, then, have a pro-democracy future? If Protestants were to become more politically aware, might they become a potent force for democratic change? Perhaps. But only under propitious conditions. A conservative and traditionalist retrenchment by the Catholic Church, the obstruction of individualistically-oriented Protestant upward mobility, the confidence-building courting of the Protestant vote by politicians and parties, and the emergence of a more socially and intellectually restless second generation of Protestants would all go a long way toward helping Latin American Protestantism realize its democracy-strengthening potential.

CONCLUSION

To put this entire discussion into perspective, we must acknowledge two points. First, the prospects for robust, sustained democracy in Latin America do not appear to be great. Certainly, at least, we lack the grounds for the optimism that characterized much writing on the subject during the early- to mid-1980s. Even as this article was being drafted, the president of Guatemala, Jorge Serrano, suspended the nation's constitution, ruled by decree for one week, then was deposed by the army. Meanwhile, Peru is entering its second year under a regime that has dissolved parliament, suspended the constitution, and rules by Presidential decree—all with a 66 percent approval rating among Peruvians (Constable 1993). Democracy's prospects in both countries, as in much of Latin America, remains tenuous (Roniger 1989; also see, e.g., Ribadeneira 1993). Second, the political ramifications of Latin American CEBs and Protestantism for shaping the outcome of the process of Latin American democratization will not, in all likelihood, ultimately be decisive. A host of other identifiable macroeconomic and political factors, as well as any number of unpredictable historical contingencies, will almost assuredly determine democracy's fate more than either of the religious movements analyzed here.

At the same time, we ought not to underestimate the actual and potential democratizing influences of CEBs and Protestantism. Just because they are not decisive does not mean they are unimportant. CEBs have already demonstrated many characteristics that are best understood as democracy-strengthening. On the other hand, whether CEBs continue in the future to serve the interests of democracy in Latin America remains, in my judgment, uncertain, if not doubtful. Moreover, Latin American Protestantism, when probed beyond its democracy-undermining traits, also evidences features that reflect the potential, at least, to nurture democracy. Under the right conditions Protestantism may prove in decades ahead to be a powerful force advancing the cause of democracy in Latin America.

NOTES

1. Space considerations prohibit detailed descriptions of these two religious phenomena. Briefly, however, base ecclesial communities, which began springing up in Latin America in the early 1960s as supplements or alternatives to standard Catholic parish churches, are small, neighborhood- and family-based gatherings of fifteen to forty members for scriptural study, prayer, mutual aid, and cooperative social action. Their members are mostly poor peasants, rural wage workers, and urban slum dwellers. Base ecclesial communities are said to number between 150,000 and 200,000 in Latin America (see Adriance 1986; Cook 1985; Levine 1990b; Hewitt 1986, 1987, 1989; Bruneau 1979; and Mainwaring 1986). The spread of Protestantism in Latin America has been remarkable, growing from 15 million in the late 1960s to more than 40 million (10 percent of Latin America's population) in the early 1990s. Approximately three-quarters of Latin American Protestants are pentecostals. "Since 1960, Protestantism . . . has tripled its numbers in Argentina, Nicaragua, and the Dominican Republic; quadrupled in Brazil; quintupled in El Salvador, Peru, and Costa Rica; and grown six-fold in Ecuador and Colombia and seven-fold in Guatemala" (Coleman 1991:59; also see Kamm 1991). Brazil, Chile, Guatemala, El Salvador, and Honduras are reported to have Protestant populations that exceed one-quarter of their general populations (Burnett 1992). In Brazil, 600,000 Catholics leave the Church annually (Kamm 1991), and full-time Protestant pastors outnumber Catholic priests, 15,000 to 13,176 (Ryser et al. 1990:79; see Stoll 1990; Montgomery 1979; Martin 1990; Mariz 1992; Burnett 1992; Der Spiegel 1991).

2. These include a historical legacy of fractions and divisive political violence (Rosenberg 1991); dualistic socioeconomic structures generating vast inequalities of wealth that produce polities dominated by the narrow interests of oligarchies (Brockett 1990); widespread political alienation and fatalism among popular classes that spawn political passivity; recurrent United States military interventions and intermittent impositions of democratic forms that lack the spirit and substance of democracy (Carothers 1991; Robinson 1992); the excessive political autonomy of Latin American militaries, which habitually infringe on processes of civilian rule (e.g., Brazil in 1964, Chile in 1973); the difficulty of fragile political regimes making politically popular economic-development policies in the context of world-system dependency; and a deep Latin American ambivalence toward democracy itself (Castillo-Cardenas 1993; Silvert 1977:58; also see Brockett 1990; Cammack 1985; Grugel 1991; Karl and Schmitter 1991; Lechner 1991; Pastor 1989; Rial 1991; Stepan 1986; Whitehead 1992; on the role of culture in political democratization, see Berntzen and Selle 1990; Eckstein 1988; Inglehart 1988; Shin *et al.* 1989; Wildavsky 1987).

3. Monistic corporatism is rooted, philosophically and socially, in ancient Greek social theories of organic solidarity, Roman hierarchical systems of law and governance, medieval Catholicism's sectoral and compartmentalized structuring of society, the Thomistic theological tradition, the Iberian system of medieval guilds, the absolutist scholasticism of the Spanish Inquisition, the reconquest mentality of the prolonged struggle to expel the Moors from Iberia, and the organicist and patriarchal political theory of Spanish Jesuit theologian and jurist Francisco Suárez (Martz and Meyers 1983; Wiarda 1986).

4. Although Latin American political culture is fundamentally and primarily informed by monistic corporatism, it is not exclusively so. Two other political traditions have been subsequently fused into Latin America's legacy of monistic corporatism. Enlightenment liberalism—republican, egalitarian, and often secular and rationalist—was superimposed upon monistic corporatism in the nineteenth century. And socialism, was, in turn, superimposed on the first two in the twentieth century (Wiarda and Kline 1985:16; also see Lambert 1969). Thus, liberalism and (to a lesser extent) socialism both represent significant, subordinate ideological challenges to monisitc corporatism. Yet, it would be a mistake to underestimate monistic corporatism's continuing influence by overestimating the impact Enlightenment liberalism has had on Latin American culture.

5. Counter to a long-standing theory in the literature that grassroots pressure impedes the consolidation of stable democracy (e.g., Stepan 1986:78–79; Rial 1991), a number of recent studies on Latin America conclude that popular pressure from below can facilitate democratization (see, e.g., Stokes 1991; Grugel 1991; Ignacio Leiva and Petras 1986; Foley 1990; Seligson and Booth 1979).

6. Some, in contrast, have argued more pessimistically that Protestantism has already "missed its historical mission," that Latin American politics are simply too patromonialist and authoritarian for Protestantism to have significantly changed them (e.g., Bastain 1986:173–78).

7. Indeed, John Wesley, the American holiness movement's taproot figure, was himself a postmillennialist whose influence on nineteenth-century revivalism helped produce Christian involvement in legal, prison, slavery, education, and political reform.

8. Martin continues elsewhere (1990:285): "The growing network of chapels represents a walkout from society as presently constituted. The evangelical believer is one who has symbolically repudiated what previously held him in place, vertically and horizontally. He cannot overturn the actual structures and is, in any case, committed to nonviolence, but he can emigrate from the ecclesiastical symbol of its all-inclusive claims: Catholicism."

9. Interestingly, if theological lineages matter, the North American churches involved in the nineteenth-century holiness movement and the pentecostal movement that sprang from it, were among the few Protestant churches of their day to allow women to participate fully in evangelistic, preaching, and leadership roles.

10. Burdick (1992) also notes how Protestant churches open up participation and leadership opportunities for those who have difficulty reading and speaking as well as those with little free time in their schedules because of work and family responsibilities.

11. I presume that Protestantism has a long-term future, in part, because of the stability that results from its family- and kinship-based recruitment and retention structure (Stoll 1990:318).

12. Thus, "the 'full . . . effects' of religion, Weber wrote in his seminal *Protestant Ethic and the Spirit of Capitalism*, emerged in Europe 'only after the peak of the purely religious enthusiasm was past' " (Marcom 1990:64).

REFERENCES

Adriance, M. 1986. *Opting for the Poor*. Kansas City, MO: Sheed and Ward.

———. 1991. "Agents of change." *Journal for the Scientific Study of Religion* 30:292–305.

Alves, R. 1985. *Protestantism and Repression*. Maryknoll, NY: Orbis.

Baldwin, D. 1990. *Protestants and the Mexican Revolution*. Urbana: University of Illinois Press.

Barbé, D. 1982. *La grâce et le pouvoir*. Paris: Cerf.

Barnes, S., and M. Kaase. 1979. *Political Action*. Beverly Hills, CA: Sage.

Barreiro, A. 1982. *Basic Ecclesial Communities*. Maryknoll, NY: Orbis.

Bastain, J.P. 1983. *Protestantismo y Sociedad en Mexico*. Mexico City: Casa de Publicaciones Unidas.

———. 1986. *Breve Historia del Protestantismo en América Latina*. Mexico City: Casa de Publicaciones Unidas.

Berger, P., and R. Neuhaus. 1977. *To Empower People*. Washington, DC: American Enterprise Institute for Public Policy Research.

Berntzen, E., and P. Selle. 1990. "Plaidoyer for the restoration of the concept of political culture or bringing political culture back in." *International Journal of Comparative Sociology* 31:32–48.

Berryman, P. 1986. "El Salvador," pp. 58–78 in D. Levine, *q.v.*

———. 1987. *Liberation Theology.* New York: Pantheon.

Boff, L. 1985. *Church: Charism and Power.* New York: Crossroad.

———. 1986. *Ecclesiogenesis.* Maryknoll, NY: Orbis.

Brockett, C. 1990. *Land, Power, and Poverty.* Boulder, CO: Westview Press.

Bromiley, G. (ed.). 1985. *Theological Dictionary of the New Testament.* Grand Rapids, MI: Eerdmans.

Bruneau, T. 1979. "Basic Christian communities in Latin America," pp. 225–37 in D. Levine, *q.v.*

———. 1986. "Brazil," pp. 106–23 in D. Levine, *q.v.*

Burdick, J. 1992. "Rethinking the study of social movements," pp. 171–84 in A. Escobar and S. Alvarez (eds.), *THe Making of Social Movements in Latin America.* Boulder, CO: Westview Press.

Burnett, V. 1992. "Protestantism in Latin America." *Latin American Research Review* 27:218–30.

Cáceres Prendes, J. 1989. "Political radicalization and popular pastoral practices in El Salvador, 1969–1985," pp. 103–48 in S. Mainwaring and A. Wilde, *q.v.*

Cammack, P. 1985. "Democratization." *Bulletin of Latin American Research* 4:39–46.

Carothers, T. 1991. *In the Name of Democracy.* Berkeley, CA: University of California Press.

Castillo-Cardenas, G. 1993. "Christian ethics in Latin America, 1970–90," pp. 89–109 in D. Hessel (ed.), *The Church's Public Role.* Grand Rapids, MI: Eerdmans.

Coleman, J. 1991. "Will Latin America become Protestant?" *Commonweal* 118 (Jan. 25):59–63.

Constable, P. 1993. "Peruvian gives authoritarianism a boost." *Boston Globe* (June 21):1, 12.

Conway, M. 1985. *Political Participation in the United States.* Washington, D.C.: Congressional Quarterly.

Cook, G. 1985. *The Expectation of the Poor.* Maryknoll, NY: Orbis.

———. 1990. "The evangelical groundswell in Latin America." *Christian Century* 107 (Dec. 12):1172–79.

Cox, H. 1988. *The Silencing of Leonardo Boff.* Oak Park, IL: Meyer-Stone.

Crahan, M. 1989. "Religion and politics in revolutionary Nicaragua," pp. 41–63 in S. Mainwaring and A. Wilde, *q.v.*

Dealy, G. 1985. "Pipe dreams." *Foreign Policy* 57 (Winter):281–94.

Der Spiegel, 1991. "A quiet revolution in Latin America," *World Press Review* 38 (March):30–31.

Doimo, A.M. 1989. "Social movements and the Catholic church in Vitória, Brazil," pp. 193–273 in S. Mainwaring and A. Wilde, *q.v.*

Eckstein, H. 1988. "A culturalist theory of political change." *American Political Science Review* 82:789–820.

Erickson, K. 1977. *The Brazilian Corporative State and Working Class Politics.* Berkeley: University of California Press.

Foley, M. 1990. "Organizing, ideology, and moral suasion." *Comparative Study of Society and History* 32:455–87.

Forman, S. 1975. *The Brazilian Peasantry.* New York: Columbia University Press.

Fowler, R. 1982. *A New Engagement.* Grand Rapids, MI: Eerdmans.

Frase, R. 1975. "A Sociological Analysis of the Development of Brazilian Protestantism," doctoral dissertation, Princeton Theological Seminary.

Grugel, J. 1991. "Transitions from authoritarian rule." *Political Studies* 39;363–68.

Hewitt, W.E. 1986. "Strategies for change employed by communidades eclesiais de base (CEBs) in the archdiocese of São Paulo." *Journal for the Scientific Study of Religion* 25:16–30.

———. 1987. "The influence of social class on activity preferences of comunidades eclesiais de base (CEBs) in the archidocese of São Paulo." *Journal of Latin American Studies* 19:141–56.

———. 1988. "Myths and realities of liberation theology," pp. 135–55 in R. Rubenstein and J. Roth, *q.v.*

———. 1989. "Origins and prospects of the option for the poor in Brazilian Catholicism." *Journal for the Scientific Study of Religion* 28:120–35.

———. 1990. "Religion and the consolidation of democracy in Brazil." *Sociological Analysis* 51:139–52.

Hoffnagel, J. 1978. "The Believers," doctoral dissertation, Indiana University.

Hollinger, D. 1983. *Individualism and Social Ethics.* Lanham, MD: University Press of America.

Huizer, G. 1972. *The Revolutionary Potential of Peasants in Latin America.* Lexington, MA: Lexington Books.

Huntington, S. 1984. "Will more countries become democratic?" *Political Science Quarterly* 99:193–218.

Ignacio Leiva, F. and J. Petras, 1986. "Chile's poor in the struggle for democracy." *Latin American Perspectives* 13:5–25.

Inglehart, R. 1988. "The renaissance of political culture." *American Political Science Review* 82:1203–30.

Ireland, R. 1989. "Catholic base communities, spiritist groups, and the deepening of democracy in Brazil," pp. 224–50 in S. Mainwaring and A. Wilde, *q.v.*

Jeffrey, P. 1991. "Nicaragua," pp. 153–73 in P. McManus and G. Schlabach, *q.v.*

Kamm, T. 1991. "Evangelicals, stressing, 'cures' for

masses' misery, make inroads in Roman Catholic Latin America." *Wall Street Journal* (Oct. 16):A12.

Karl, T.L. and P. Schmitter, 1991. "Modes of transition in Latin America, southern and eastern Europe." *International Social Science Journal* 128:270–84.

Kincaid, A.D. 1987. "Peasants into rebels." *Comparative Study of Society and History* 29:466–94.

Krischke, P. 1991. "Church base communities and democratic change in Brazilian society." *Comparative Political Studies* 24:186–211.

LADOC. 1976. *Basic Christian Communities*. Washington, DC: Latin American Documentation.

Lalive d'Epinay, C. 1969. *Haven of the Masses*. London: Lutterworth Press.

Lambert, J. 1969. *Latin America*. Berkeley: University of California Press.

Lechner, N. 1991. "The search for lost community." *International Social Science Journal* 129:541–53.

Levine, D. (ed.). 1986. *Churches and Politics in Latin America*. Beverly Hills, CA: Sage.

——— (ed.). 1986. *Religion and Political Conflict in Latin America*. Chapel Hill, NC: University of North Carolina Press.

———. 1988. "Assessing the impact of liberation theology in Latin America." *Review of Politics* 50:241–63.

———. 1990a. "The impact of Medellín and Puebla," pp. 64–74 in E. Cleary (ed.), *Born of the Poor*. Notre Dame, IN: University of Notre Dame Press.

———. 1990b. "Popular groups, popular culture, and popular religion." *Comparative Study of History and Society* 32:718–64.

——— and S. Mainwaring. 1989. "Religion and popular protest in Latin America," pp. 203–40 in S. Eckstein (ed.), *Power and Popular Protest*. Berkeley: University of California Press.

Libânio, J.B. 1976. *Communidade Eclesial de Base*. Rio de Janeiro: PUC.

Lipset, S. 1981. *Political Man*. Baltimore, MD: Johns Hopkins University Press.

Mainwaring, S. 1986. "Brazil," pp. 124–55 in D. Levine, *q.v.*

———. 1989. "Grass-roots Catholic groups and politics in Brazil," pp. 151–92 in S. Mainwaring and A. Wilde, *q.v.*

——— and A. Wilde (eds.). 1989. *The Progressive Church in Latin America*. Notre Dame, IN: University of Notre Dame Press.

Malloy, J. 1977. *Authoritarianism and Corporatism in Latin America*. Pittsburgh: University of Pittsburgh Press.

Marcom, J. 1990. "The fire down south." *Forbes* 146 (Oct. 15): 56–71.

Mariz, C. 1992. "Religion and poverty in Brazil." *Sociological Analysis* 53:S63–70.

Martin, D. 1990. *Tongues of Fire*. Oxford: Blackwell.

Martz, J., and D. Meyers, 1992. "Understanding Latin American politics." *Polity* 16:214–41.

McAdam, D., J. McCarthy, and M. Zald. 1988. "Social movements," pp. 695–737 in N. Smelser (ed.), *Handbook of Sociology*. Newbury Park, CA: Sage.

McGovern, A. 1989. *Liberation Theology and its Critics*. Maryknoll, NY: Orbis.

McManus, P., and G. Schlabach (eds.). 1991. *Relentless Persistence*. Philadelphia: New Society.

Milbrath, L., and M.L. Goel. 1977. *Political Participation*. Chicago: Rand McNally.

Montgomery, T.S. 1979. "Latin American evangelicals," pp. 87–107 in D. Levine, *q.v.*

O'Gorman, F. 1983. *Base Communities in Brazil*. São Paulo: FASE NUCLAR.

Paredes, T. 1992. "The many faces of los Evangélicos." *Christianity Today* 36 (Apr. 6):34–35.

Pastor, R. 1989. "Securing a democratic hemisphere." *Foreign Policy* 73:41–60.

Peña, M. 1992. "The Sodalitium Vitae movement in Peru." *Sociological Analysis* 53:159–73.

Pike, F., and T. Stritch (eds.). 1974. *The New Corporatism*. Notre Dame, IN: University of Notre Dame Press.

Pottenger, J. 1989. *The Political Theory of Liberation Theology*. Albany: SUNY Press.

Quebedeaux, R. 1974. *The Young Evangelicals*. New York: Harper & Row.

Rehberg, W. 1992. "Nicaragua's base communities now." *Christianity and Crisis* 52 (May 11):152–54.

Reilly, C. 1986. "Latin Americas's religious populists," pp. 42–57 in D. Levine, *q.v.*

Rial, J. 1991. "Transitions in Latin America on the threshold of the 1990s." *International Social Science Journal* 128:285–300.

Ribadeneira, D. 1993. "Instability deepens in Nicaragua." *Boston Globe* (Aug.25):1, 15.

Robinson, W. 1992. *A Faustian Bargain*. Boulder, CO: Westview Press.

Romero, C. 1989. "The Peruvian church," pp. 253–75 in S. Mainwaring and A. Wilde, *q.v.*

Roniger, L. 1989. "Democratic transitions and consolidation in contemporary southern Europe and Latin America." *International Journal of Comparative Sociology* 30:216–30.

Rosenberg, T. 1991. *Children of Cain*. New York: Penguin.

Rossi, E., and J. Plano (eds.). 1980. *The Latin American Political Dictionary*. Santa Barbara: ABC-CLIO.

Roth, J. 1988. "The great enemy?," pp. 225–46 in R. Rubenstein and J. Roth, *q.v.*

Ryser, J., S. Baker, M. Day, and S. Anderson. 1990. "Latin America's Protestants." *Business Week* (June 4):79.

Seligson, M., and J. Booth (eds.). 1979. *Political Participation in Latin America*, vol. 2, New York: Holmes and Meier.

Serbin, K. 1992. "Latin American Catholicism." *Christianity and Crisis* 52:403–7.

Shin, D.C., M. Chey, and K. Kim. 1989. "Cultural origins of public support for democracy in Korea." *Comparative Political Studies* 22:217–38.

Sigmund, P. 1987. "The Catholic tradition and modern democracy." *Review of Politics* 49:530–48.

———. 1988. "The development of liberation theology," pp. 21–47 in R. Rubenstein and J. Roth, *q.v.*

Silvert, K. 1977. *Essays in Understanding Latin America*. Philadelphia: Institute for the Study of Human Issues.

Smith, B. 1986. "Chile," pp. 156–86 in D. Levine, *q.v.*

Smith, C. 1991. *The Emergence of Liberation Theology*. Chicago: University of Chicago Press.

Stepan, A. 1978. *The State and Society*. Princeton, NJ: Princeton University Press.

———. 1986. "Paths toward redemocratization," pp. 64–86 in G. O'Donnell, P. Schmitter and L. Whitehead (eds.), *Transitions from Authoritarian Rule*. Baltimore, MD: Johns Hopkins University Press.

Stokes, S. 1991. "Politics and Latin America's urban poor." *Latin America Research Review* 26(2):75–101.

Stoll, D. 1990. *Is Latin America Turning Protestant?* Berkeley, CA: University of California Press.

Torres, S., and J. Eagleson (eds.). 1981. *The Challenge of Basic Christian Communities*. Maryknoll, NY: Orbis.

Touraine, A. 1991. "What does democracy mean today?" *International Social Science Journal* 128:259–68.

Van Vugt, J. 1991. *Democratic Organization for Social Change*. New York: Bergin and Garvey.

Verba, S., and N. Nie. 1972. *Participation in America*. New York: Harper & Row.

Wagley, C. 1992. "A framework for Latin American culture," pp. 25–30 in H. Wiarda, *q.v.*

Whitehead, L. 1992. "The alternatives to 'liberal democracy'." *Political Studies* 60 (Special Issue):146–59.

Wiarda, H. 1973. "Toward a framework for the study of political change in the Iberic-Latin tradition." *World Politics* 25:206–35.

———. 1974. "Corporatism and development in the Iberic-Latin world." *Review of Politics* 36:3–33.

———. 1976. "The corporative origins of the Iberian and Latin American labor relations systems." *Studies in Comparative and International Development* 13:3–37.

———. 1977. *Corporatism and Development*. Amherst, MA: University of Massachusetts Press.

———. 1981. *Corporatism and Development in Latin America*. Boulder, CO: Westview Press.

———. 1986. "Social change, political development, and the Latin American tradition," pp. 197–218 in P. Klarén and T. Bossert (eds.), *Promise of Development*. Boulder, CO: Westview Press.

——— (ed.). 1992. *Politics and Social Change in Latin America*. Boulder, CO: Westview Press.

——— and H. Kline. 1985. "The context of Latin American politics," pp. 633–42 in H. Wiarda and H. Kline (eds.), *Latin American Politics and Development*. Boulder, CO: Westview Press.

Wildavsky, A. 1987. "Choosing preferences by constructing institutions." *American Political Science Review* 81:3–21.

Willems, E. 1967. *Followers of the New Faith*. Nashville, TN: Vanderbilt University Press.

———. 1975. *Latin American Culture*. New York: Harper & Row.

23

Sembrando El Futuro
Globalization and the Commodification of Health

Linda M. Whiteford

INTRODUCTION

Global processes play out differentially based on the cultural, historical, and political contexts in which they occur. This chapter addresses how national and transnational economic agreements directly and indirectly affect the health of people living in two Caribbean islands, the Dominican Republic and Cuba. I selected the Dominican Republic and Cuba for this analysis because they share similar colonial histories; indigenous, disasporan, and colonial populations; and physical environments. However, following the overthrow of Batista and Trujillo—the Cuban and Dominican dictators who controlled the islands during the middle third of the twentieth century—the political directions of two islands have diverged. As their political histories diverged, there emerged in each country national identities grounded in individual political and economic realities and reflecting citizens' relations with their government and with each other. I suggest that in the health arena, national geopolitical and ideological identities, in concert with global political and economic processes, influence how health experiences are commodified. That is, the set of rights, responsibilities, and obligations

associated with individual, community, and national health provision is shaped not only by global economic forces, but also by local responses. Those local responses are, in turn, a reflection of negotiated cultural identities. Furthermore, I suggest that global forces, national responses, and local identities transform health experiences into forms of commodification. Investigating these forms of health commodificaiton can provide insight into the process of globalization as well as the process of culturally negotiated identities.

The primary emphasis of this chapter is a political economic analysis of the process of health commodification in the Dominican Republic. The analysis is intended to demonstrate how ideological seeds sown in national and global politics and mediated by local identities are harvested, having both immediate and long-term repercussions in the area of health. Data from Cuba are used to provide a limited contrast to the Dominican experience. Both my data from, and experience in, Cuba is far more limited than that in the Dominican Republic, but the contrast is offered here to exemplify how an analysis of the commodification of health offers us insight into the complex interplay among local, national, and global forces.

In this chapter, I rely on Kearney's definition of globalization as the "social, economic, cultural and demographic processes that take place within nations but also transcend them, such that attention limited to local processes, identities and units of analysis yields incomplete understandings of the local" (1995:548).[1]

The commodification of experience, in this case of health, is the conceptualization of a particular type of occurrence in terms of its social as well as economic costs (Taussig 1980), by embedding it in the economic and cultural conditions of contemporary global capitalism. It may be that one of the consequences of globalization is the commodification of health. If this is true, as I suspect it is, then the investigation of contemporary health experiences takes on added significance similar to the increased interest in the construction of identity as a reflection of the dispersion, decentering, interpenetration, and general complexity of globalization.

In the following pages, I explore some of the relationships between global geopolitics, economic conditions, and health by examining demographic, economic, epidemiological, and anthropological data, as well as hundreds of personal interviews taken during a period of five years of intermittent field research. I am particularly interested in the symbolic and accumulated capital in health accrued by Dominicans and Cubans between 1980 and 1992, a period of intense economic change in each country.

Mala Unión and *Sembrando el Futuro* are two key concepts used in the Dominican Republic and Cuba, respectively, that reflect differential identities created in response to culturally determined ideological and material strategies. In the Dominican Republic, people used the phrase *mala unión* to explain their perception of lack of political will on the part of the government to improve lives of ordinary Dominicans (Whiteford et al. 1991a; 1991b; Whiteford 1997). The symbolic capital of such a phrase as a powerful deterrent to community-based activities such as mosquito control is evident even though Dominicans suffer from a variety of debilitating, painful, and potentially fatal mosquito-borne diseases such as malaria and dengue fever (Whiteford 1993; 1997).

In contrast, Cuban health was made a central focus of postrevolutionary reforms and was sym-

bolized by the phrase *sembrando el futuro*, or sowing the seeds of the future, suggesting a relationship between current acts and future rewards. *Mala Unión* and *Sembrando el Futuro* are powerful symbolic images of expectations, reflecting social relations between citizens and their government based on a combination of material reality and social promise. The commodification of health occurs in both contexts. In the Dominican Republic, the commodification is played out in the loss of primary health care, the unequal distribution of human and fiscal resources, and the increase in infectious disease at the same time as the Dominican government continues to pay a relatively large percentage of its GDP for the declining health of its people.

The commodification of health in Cuba is expressed in both symbolic and material forms as well. Symbolically, health is a public and international success for Cuba both at home and abroad. Its success is also a symbol commodified for international distribution. And, as the following data show, health commodification for Cuba translates into more than symbolic successes.

In order to show how health becomes commodified as a result of local identities, national ideologies, and global pressures, I will discuss some of the economic forces that have prevailed in the Dominican Republic and Cuba in the last two decades, describe how responses to those pressures are expressed in changed health conditions, and analyze how accumulated symbolic and material capital are the result of both the process of globalization and constructed identity.

THE ECONOMIC CRISIS

Triggered by increases in world oil prices, the global recession of the late 1970s forced the Dominican Republic into a debt crisis from which every effort to extricate itself saddled it with crippling economic agreements. The International Monetary Fund (IMF) imposed perilous structural adjustments on the Dominican economy as part of lending agreements, while simultaneously U.S. trade policies dealt a serious blow to Dominican sugar exports with the development of the U.S. Economic Recovery Act (ERA). In the early 1980s, international economic policies resulted in the loss of Dominican revenue from sugar exports, a reduction of gross domestic product (GDP) which resulted in a severe decrease in government expenditures on health. Even when the percentage of the GDP dedicated to health increased in the mid-1980s, li8ttle was available for discretionary costs. Most was committed to the maintenance of the administrative and infrastructural fixed costs.

The economic crisis attacked the Dominican quality of health from several directions. For instance, loss of personal income led to increasingly crowded living conditions, deteriorating sanitation, declining nutritional status, and increased exposure to infectious disease. Simultaneously, as more women entered the workforce to supplement the decreased incomes of male wage earners, child care became more problematic as it was more dispersed and less adequate. Meanwhile, at the very moment of increased health risk and need for services, the economic crisis forced the Dominican government to withdraw support from its already ailing primary health system (Whiteford 1990).

In Cuba, the thirty-year-old U.S. trade embargo not only continued, but was strengthened (Santana 1992:1). The U.S. government continued to attempt to economically isolate Cuba through sanctions against other countries trading with Cuba. Of equal if not of more significance, was the loss of the Soviet Union as both a trading partner and provider. Before 1989, the Soviet Union and its trading system provided Cuba with food, medical supplies, and fuel; its loss meant increased food, medical, and energy shortages for the Cuban population. As a result of the loss of that trading partnership, shortages became so common in Cuba in the early 1990s that one could evaluate if a shop had food by the presence of a line of people waiting: "No line, no food." Bread, always a staple in the Cuban diet, became expensive and difficult to obtain; bakeries were unable to make enough bread because of the shortages in raw materials (Deere 1991:62).

Paradoxically, the epidemiological data from neither Cuba nor the Dominican Republic indicated staggering increases in mortality rates. Upon close investigation of the Dominican data, however, Dominican rates of maternal and infant mortality, infectious disease, and severe malnutrition are seen to have increased since the onset of the economic crisis. Those increases are, however, difficult to attribute *exclusively* to the economic crisis. The stagnation of the Dominican public health system, the reversal of a twenty-year-trend of health

improvements, the cessation of effective community and rural health interventions, and the exacerbation of mala unión, however, are the direct consequences of decisions politicians and policy analysts made in the commodification of Dominican health (Whiteford, 1990, 1992, 1993).

PRE-CRISIS HEALTH INDICATORS

Following the death of Trujillo in 1961, Dominican health statistics show a steady improvement. For almost twenty years, fertility rates in the Dominican Republic decreased, and, with them, mortality rates. Between 1970 and 1983, fertility rates fell from 6.1 per 1,000 to 4.1 per 1,000 (Gomez, Cedno, and Tatis 1987; Ramirez, Duarte, and Gomez 1986; Molina and Gomez 1991; Mendoza 1991). Fertility rates in the urban areas were most responsive to family planning and decreased from 4.6 to 3.6 (per 1,000). Rural fertility rates also fell a remarkable 2.5 (from 7.4 to 4.9 between 1970 and 1983). Gross general mortality rates decreased between the years of 1950 and 1980. Overall mortality figures for the general population fell from 20.3 per 1,000 to 8.4 per 1,000 (Ceara 1987).

The rate of decrease, however, slowed dramatically with the approach of the 1980s. Between 1960 and 1980, maternal mortality dropped from 10.1 to 7.2 (per 10,000 live births) Bustillo 1989); neonatal mortality fell from 41 to 23 (per 1,000 live births) (Hay 1990); the rate of abortions decreased from 140 to 65 (Mendoza 1991); prenatal care coverage increased to reach almost 80 percent by 1975 (Mendoza 1991).

As a general trend, Dominican mortality and morbidity levels have decreased since the 1950s. The trend was clear and unidirectional until the early 1980s, when early effects of the economic crisis on health status appeared with increases in the reported levels of infectious disease and severe malnutrition increased (Ramirez, Duarte, and Gomez 1986). Between 1970 and 1984, rates of syphilis rose from 206.9 to 280.9; rates of gastroenteritis soared from 714.8 to 2,530.2, and rates of lung tuberculosis more than doubled from 14.8 to 49.4 (Ramirez et al. 1986). Malnutrition, always difficult to measure consistently, decreased in incidence of those suffering from moderate levels (Ceara 1987), while the incidence of severe malnutrition increased.

The relation between malnutrition and illness is complex; however, the synergistic effects of the two cannot be ignored. Often child mortality indices reflect only a primary cause of death, while the secondary or contributing factors are not recorded. Yet poverty and undernutrition clearly contribute to child death. According to Ceara in 1977, 71.4 percent of the children hospitalized in Santo Domingo's largest children's hospital were suffering from malnutrition (1987). In 1986, the percentage was reduced to 56.2 percent, yet the levels of severe malnutrition *doubled* during the same period. Simultaneously, 67.0 percent of child deaths due to pneumonia in 1986 were among undernourished children (Bustillo 1989).

Dominican maternal mortality, infant mortality by infectious disease, incidence of neonatal tetanus, rate of miscarriage, and stillbirth all have increased since the onset of the economic crisis in the 1980s. Between 1970 and 1980, maternal mortality at the national maternity hospital decreased to 7.2 (per 10,000 live births). In the five years between 1980 and 1985, the maternal mortality rate more than tripled when it rose to 23 (per 10,000 live births). The national maternal mortality rate also increased sharply. In 1978, it was 56 per 100,000 live births; by 1987 it had increased to between 100 and 200 (Hay 1990). Infant mortality rates in 1978 had decreased to between 31 and 65 (reflecting rural-urban differences). Following the onset of the economic crisis, that rate almost doubled to 70 to 100 (AID 1987; SESPAS 1986; Whiteford 1990). A reversal of the 1960s and 1970s trend toward increased birth weights also came with the crisis; the percentage of low birth weight neonates born increased from 14 to 16 percent, and the rate of prematurity almost doubled (Hay 1990). Even accepting the estimated 40 to 60 percent underreporting of Dominican health statistics, these data point toward the degradation of health after the onset of the economic crisis.

THE DECADE OF LOSS: CHANGES IN HEALTH STATUS AS INDIRECT CONSEQUENCES OF THE CRISIS

Infant Mortality. Evaluations of infant mortality both by age and cause of death suggests that poor maternal health and nutritional status during pregnancy contribute heavily to the high infant death rate. The women also were at risk; maternal mortality was twenty times higher in the Dominican Republic than in more developed countries. Dominican health status was compromised by lack of a stable food supply and lack of reliable access to potable water. In 1985, the three leading causes of the high infant mortality were diarrheal diseases, nutritional deficiencies, and respiratory infections. This common medical picture was complicated by the parasitic load carried by the population. Sixty percent of the Dominican population carried a parasitic load capable of consuming as much as 25 percent of the already scarce calories and nutrients ingested by their human hosts (SESPAS 1986). During this period, as many as 40 percent of all the reported perinatal infant deaths may have been caused by intestinal infections exacerbated by protein-calorie malnutrition (Johnson 1988).

During the early 1980s, 10 percent of infant deaths in the Dominican Republic occurred on the day of birth, one-third of recorded infant deaths happened during the first week of life; and, cumulatively, more than 50 percent of infant deaths occurred in the first thirty days of life (SESPAS 1986). Infant mortality rates increased as a result of increases in maternal undernutrition, which contributes to low birth weight and the provision of little resistance to disease; these conditions suggest that health became a commodity that only the wealthy could afford. Infants born in public hospitals in the 1980s were at high risk of an early death. They were often born to undernourished women, in hospitals without supplies, and returned to living conditions without potable water, sufficient food, or the support of a community.

There are no accurate records of infant deaths; infant mortality figures in the Dominican Republic have always been seriously underreported (PAHO estimates an underreporting of approximately 50 percent) (PAHO 1996). It is striking that, underreported though the rate remains, the Dominican infant mortality rate in the mid 1980s of between 70 and 100 per 1,000 births (urban and rural areas) was eight times higher than infant mortality rates in developed countries. The Dominican national infant mortality rate was officially listed as 80 to 84 per 1,000. The national average combines the rates from areas of low infant mortality such as upper and middle-class neighborhoods in the capital city, with rates from impoverished rural communities, where infant mortality rates stand between 90 and

103 per 1,000, thus masking the trend within particular groups (AID 1987). In 1980, the infant mortality rate in rural areas was about 20 percent higher than in urban areas (National Office of Health Statistics 1982).

In 1982, the Dominican national child mortality rate was officially listed as 18 per 1,000, but ranged to highs of 22 to 24 per 1,000 in some regions of the country. The Dominican Republic has historically had high levels of malnourished children and high rates of infant death attributed to malnutrition. In the mid-1970s, it was reported that more than 76 percent of infant deaths occurred among malnourished infants (National Office of Health Statistics 1982). Often unreported, undernourishment alone rarely kills, it increases a child's susceptibility to infectious diseases that do. Therefore, the nutritional status of children becomes a significant indicator of overall child health.

In Cuba, infant mortality rates continued to fall straight through the pan-Caribbean economic crisis of the 1970s. Infant mortality in 1983 was 17.3 (per 1,000) (Ubell 1983:435), by 1988 it had fallen to 10.6 (personal interview). Data available in 1993 from the Population Reference Bureau listed the infant mortality rate in Cuba as 11.1 (per 1,000). Regardless of the intensification of the Cuban economic situation, by 1997 the Pan American Health Organization (the Latin American arm of the World Health Organization) listed the infant mortality rate in Cuba at an all-time low of 9.1 (per 1,000) (PAHO 1997).

Maternal Mortality.   Maternal mortality in the Dominican Republic in the mid-1980s was reported as 13 per 10,000, although some regions in the southwestern part of the country averaged maternal mortality rates as high as 18 per 10,000. In the capital, the rate of maternal mortality soared as high as 22 per 10,000 (SESPAS 1987). According to Dominican Republic public health documents, the leading causes of maternal mortality are categorized as "ill-defined states," frequently influenced by socioeconomic variables such as lack of access to adequate prenatal care, inappropriate diet, and exposure to infection during labor and delivery, conditions that often contribute to maternal death caused by toxemia, hemorrhage, sepsis, or complications following abortion (SESPAS 1987).

In Cuba, maternal mortality declined in parallel with infant mortality, with rapid and precipitous reduction following 1959 and continued progress in improving maternal health status. Maternal mortality in 1959 was 12.5 (per 10,000), dropping to 11.8 in 1990 (Vidal and Pardon 1991). While Cuban infant mortality rates have continued to fall, maternal mortality rates rose slightly during the early 1990s (Santana 1992:3).

Public Hospital Conditions.   Even with adequate medical care, without electricity it was impossible to maintain antiseptic conditions in large public Dominican hospitals. During the 1980s, electrical blackouts became so common that most of the time hospitals had no lights, no access to running water, and no flushing toilets, and patients, clinicians, and janitors had no water with which to clean themselves, their equipment, or buildings. Many hospitals had alternative generators that were so overworked they frequently broke down, causing, for instance, emergency Cesarean sections to be performed by the light from open windows. A recent report suggested that 91.5 percent of maternal deaths occurred because of complications in the woman's condition and deficiencies in her obstetrical care (Molina and Gomez 1991). This was an increase from 89.2 percent of maternal deaths over the previous year. Hospital conditions and lack of adequate prenatal care in the Dominican Republic also account for the increase in neonatal tetanus, which more than doubled between 1985 and 1988 (from 6.0 to 14.0), after having been successfully reduced from 23.0 to 6.0 in the period immediately preceding the crisis (Molina and Gomez 1991).

The commodification of health is also seen in the lack of hospital supplies such as sheets, pillow cases, towels, or diapers and blankets for babies. Hospitals did not supply medications, and patients' families were expected to supply the required medications and bring them to the hospital. If the patient was unable to purchase them herself, or if the medications were too expensive and the family could not afford them, then the patient did without.

Until the late 1980s, Dominican families were allowed to bring meals for family members who were patients. Hospital administrators, however, decided that families made too much noise, brought in too much dirt and germs and cluttered up the halls, so families were barred from bringing food into the hospital. Hospital kitchens, often without electricity or refrigeration, and with personnel costs cut were also unable to provide food for patients. As a result, postpartum women, for instance, sometimes went without food or drink for the 12 to 24 hours immediately following labor and delivery. Some pregnant women were given nothing except a cup of watery hot chocolate between the times they entered and left the hospital.

But, most dangerously, hospital medical instruments were in poor repair. In one hospital, the only autoclave was broken and not repaired until two women died and five others became seriously ill, all linked to the broken autoclave. In the mid-1980s, 90 percent of the incubators in the entire country were out of order, and the largest maternity hospital in Santiago (the second-largest city) had but one fetal monitor, which had been in disrepair for two years (personal interviews). In short, in the early 1980s, the commodification of health in the Dominican Republic meant the maintenance of a hospital-based system that failed to provide patients with the basic necessities while also failing to offer them the tools of prevention.

In Cuba, the hospitals I observed had no luxuries but were spartan and clean. I had greater access, and therefore observed more hospitals in the Dominican Republic than in Cuba and the data reflect that difference. However, other sources support the observations reported here. Cuban physicians used herbal remedies to supplement the loss of biomedical medicines, and homemade soap substituted when no soap could be purchased. During the 1960s and 1970s, Cuba decentralized medical care, establishing community-based primary health care clinics. These clinics were staffed with medical professionals but required little medical equipment or complex technology. Physicians and nurses often lived above or near the community health center where they worked. This alternative to centralized medicine was a crucial ideological decision and one that deflects some of the most costly effects of the economic crisis. In addition, the commitment of community-based health workers continually supported the sense of a shared group struggling against the odds for a better future.

By the early 1990s, the economic crisis in Cuba resulted in a loss of medical support services and supplies. In 1990, there were 2,000 ambulances in the country. This number was reduced to 1,350 by the mid-1990s (Reuters 1996). Surgical operations decreased by 45 percent in the first three years of the 1990s; provision of eye and dental care was also cut back. Nonessential hospital procedures were limited, yet health continued to be given priority funding by the Cuban government, continuing to support its medical infrastructure with almost 8 percent of its gross domestic product in the mid-1990s (Reuters 1996).

Maternal mortality is a reflection of access to adequate resources. Women die because they have limited access to adequate prenatal care, are undernourished, and are exposed to infection and unsanitary conditions during labor and delivery. The Cuban community-based commodification of health demonstrates a response predating the 1980s crisis and distinctive from that of the Dominican government, each engendering distinctive results.

Nutrition. The deterioration of the Dominican economic situation was manifest by an increased number of people struggling with decreased access to food. In the late 1980s, some foods were not available because they were exported in response to the IMF agreement, while inflation or loss of price subsidies placed other foods beyond peoples' ability to purchase them. Malnutrition is chronic in the Dominican Republic, but as the government's health budget decreased, the public agencies' already inefficient food supplement programs reached fewer and fewer people. According to UNICEF studies on the impact of the economic crisis, changes in Dominican consumption and dietary patterns occurred, showing declining intakes of protein-rich commodities such as milk, eggs, and meat, and an increased consumption of cheap sources of calories such as rice, potatoes, and yuca (SESPAS 1987). Even before the most recent economic crisis, 90 percent of the Dominican population consumed less than the recommended minimum of 2,300 calories and 60 grams of protein per day (Ramirez et al. 1986). During the crisis, Dominicans' level of consumption of proteins and calories fell t what it was in 1959 at the end of Trujillo's devastating dictatorship (Ceara 1987).

The highest rates of malnutrition occurred among the five- to eight-month old age group (Safa n.d.). This is attributed to a variety of causes, including the abrupt cessation of breastfeeding as mothers were forced by economic conditions to work away from their children, the dilution of infant feeding formulas, and the lack of potable water used in infant feeding (SESPAS 1987). Estimates of the proportion of children suffering from malnutrition in poor urban neighborhoods and in rural communities of sugar workers range from 30 to 75 percent of respective populations. An estimated 165,000 children nationwide were thought to be severely malnourished; an additional 150,000 pregnant or nursing mothers were malnourished, contributing to high rates of infant mortality (Ramirez et al, 1986). The most disturbing information came from one of the private voluntary organizations involved in food supplement programs. Their data showed that the number of children suffering from the most severe degrees of malnutrition was no longer decreasing at the rate it had been before the economic crisis. Instead, the rate was increasing, reflecting the continuing difficulties poor families experienced in the provision of even minimal quantities of food for their children.

In a 1986 survey conducted by the Dominican Ministry of Public Health, 29 percent of all children under the age of five years were weighed and fully 40 percent of those children showed evidence of malnutrition (Tufts Report 1987). While diagnosis of malnutrition vary and national averages distort the severity of the problem by masking the extremes, some regions presented a clearer picture of nutritional distress. Two national public health regions showed that more than 50 percent of the children living there were malnourished. Of those malnourished, almost one-third were at level I malnutrition, between 11 and 13 percent were level II, and, in some areas, 3 percent of the malnourished children were suffering from the most extreme degree (level III) malnutrition (Johnson 1988).

A 1987 nongovernmental nutritional survey found that a higher percentage (than previously reported) of Dominican children were malnourished and that the percentage was rising (Safa n.d.). Malnutrition, unsanitary living conditions, and inadequate and inaccessible medical services reflect a pattern of commodification of short-terms investments, ignoring their long-term future repercussions.

Cuba, like the Dominican Republic, in the late 1980s and early 1990s was increasingly deprived of the food staples on which its populace depends.

Recent Cuban statistics showed a small increase in the number of low birth weight infants and a large increase in elderly and maternal mortality, even as infant mortality continues to fall (Santana 1992:3), Data suggest that Cuba's loss of its primary trading partner and provider of its petroleum products resulted in serious food shortages engendered both through the lack of important foods and also through harvest reductions caused by lack of fertilizer and pesticides (Santana 1992:2). In 1990, Cubans ate 3,000 calories a day and 80 grams of protein. By 1991, Cubans ate only 2,700 calories and 60 grams of protein (Santana 1992:2). Both personal observations and first-hand accounts suggest the reality of food shortages and that Cubans were eating considerably less in 1993 than in 1991. In 1992, the Cuban government instructed people to plant vegetable gardens in their front yards. The green spaces in front of public buildings like clinics also were planted in edible gardens. Deere reports that the Cuban government was increasingly turning to food substitution and community-based self-sufficiency programs (Deere 1991:5) that rely on a sense of *sembrando el futuro*. One result of the dietary restrictions was that 30,000 Cubans suffered partial or total loss of vision because of an optic nerve disorder caused by a lack of vitamins in the diet in 1993 (Kirkpatrick 1994).

The Public Health System. The Dominican Ministry of Public Health is responsible for the provision of low-cost medical care to those who cannot afford private health care. The Ministry was the single source of health care for roughly 80 percent of the population. However, a 1986 estimate showed that the Ministry was providing coverage to only 40 percent of those in need (Whiteford 1992; SESPAS 1987; Musgrove 1987). The state social security system (responsible for providing medical care to wage earners) is financed through combined contributions made by employees, their employers, and the state. However, in the 1980s, the state failed to maintain its contributions and this failure resulted in further erosion of the public health system and (Musgrove 1987) a reification of the community's sense of *mala unión*.

Prior to the economic crisis, the Dominican public health infrastructure was in a state of crisis caused by structural barriers such as overcentralization of administration, overdependence on physicians, patronage-based staffing, lack of a civil service system, and underutilization of graduate nurses (Whiteford 1992). Public hospitals in the Dominican Republic operated at less than half their capacity, were open only until midday, and provided little or no follow-up care, and their physical plants were in disrepair and without electrical light, running water, flushing toilets, many medicines, or other supplies (Whiteford 1990).

The crisis in the Dominican commodification of health is exacerbated by a history of administrative centralization, a hierarchy of private/public facilities, and an emphasis on curative, not preventive, medicine that deprives Dominicans of even the most basic health care. There is little symbolic or material accumulated capital in the Dominican Republic because the form of commodification instigated by global pressures furthers a perception of *mala unión* as a result of the government's failure to provide basic necessities in either the hospital or the community. By the mid-1980s, the Dominican government had demolished or allowed to lie fallow a system of rural primary health facilities and community health workers (Whiteford 1990). Since that time, health has been transformed into an urban-based system that provides little room for members of communities to work with the government to provide for basic health and sanitation needs. There are no potable water systems in the country, sanitary excreta and solid waste disposal are not routinely taken care of by the government, and less than 40 percent of the population has access to public sector health care (PAHO 1997).

The Cuban government, on the other hand, decentralized its medical care, relying instead on a network of public health clinics that were community-based and nontechnologically dependent. Public health nurses and physicians were encouraged to live in the (urban or rural) community in which they worked. Their jobs were theirs for life, their education and housing were provided, and their obligation to the community was explicit. Each doctor was assigned 120 families, or about 750 people, for whom she or he would be responsible (personal interview). Along with community responsibility for the clinic, clinic personnel were expected to be responsive to other needs in the community.

Cuba reduced its infant mortality rate between 1960 and 1990 primarily through effective and free community-based preventive health care. This care laid groundwork for the shared sense of a community preparing for a better future and its accumulated and symbolic capital. Women were provided prenatal care and extensive (as compared with U.S. policies and practices) postpartum and well-baby care. This level of care was provided exclusively by the primary health care/community-based health personnel. In 1992, well-baby home visits were provided to women daily for the week following the birth, weekly for the first month, and twice per month visits during the first year. What to some might appear to be "excessive" follow-up and well-baby care in actuality served a multiplicity of purposes. Health personnel employed those opportunities to come to know the family and their neighbors (and the neighborhood), and check on the health of various members of the household. As one young physician told me, "After all, I am going to be their doctor for a long time; the more I know about them the better I can help them stay well. So, when I check on the baby I also find out how grandma is doing. It helps all of us." And, this system strengthens the perception of a shared identity and investment in the future.

GLOBAL ECONOMIC PRESSURES AND DOMINICAN RESPONSES

What were the global pressures that, combined with Dominican history and politics, brought about the commodification of health, resulting in an overall decline in Dominicans' health? How did the Caribbean economic crisis reverse twenty years of steady improvements in Dominicans' health? In the following pages, the case of the economic crisis in the Dominican Republic is traced in detail. The Dominican case is but an example of the types of global forces that constrain national decision makers and how they intersect with national priorities and local identities to create patterns of commodification that transform health.

The Dominican economic crisis can be traced from the late 1970s and early 1980s. A pan-Caribbean economic period of instability and debt was generated by the 1970s oil crisis. One consequence for the Dominican Republic was the negotiation of a IMF loan for $466 million in 1983. In response to the IMF structural adjustment requirements, an austerity program was implemented requiring currency changes, the elimination of government subsidies for basic foods and subsidized credits to farmers, the freezing of real wages, further cuts in government spending for social programs, and the encouragement of export-dominant production.

In 1984, in response to the structural adjustment policies, the Dominican government introduced price increases of over 80 percent on basic items and of 300 percent on import tariffs. These increases led to violent public protests, and the government response left more than 60 people dead or injured. A month later, negotiations with the IMF were suspended after the government rejected the IMF's proposed program of further financial austerity and refused to comply with the IMF's insistence that the government immediately transfer all imports to the "parallel" exchange rate of 2.95 pesos per dollar, and increase the price of petroleum products and electricity between 20 and300 percent (Europa Year Book 1988:916–917).

The Dominican economy was further depleted by the U.S.–imposed sugar import quotas. As a result in the 1984–85 fiscal year, Dominican earnings from sugar exports decreased by 63 percent. In an attempt to offset the revenue losses, the government negotiated an IMF–approved loan in November 1985 for $15.5 million, bringing the country's total external debt to $3,800 million by 1986 (Sunshine 1985).

In 1985, the value of Dominican sugar exports again plummeted, this time to 41.7 percent less than the previous year. This drastic drop was due to the decline in both unit value and volume exported. In one fiscal year alone, there was a loss of 63 percent of the total income generated by the sale of sugar in the Dominican Republic (U.S. Department of State 1988). The sharp downward trend in exports of this critical product in the years between 1981 and 1985 was reflected in a more than 70 percent reduction of all exports during that period (UN Doc. 1987). In 1982, earnings from the export of sugar amounted to 34.6 percent of the value of total exports, bringing into the government $266 million (U.S.) (Europa Year Book 1988). In less than three years, the earnings from sugar dropped to an estimated 21.5 percent of the total value of exports. Export earnings derived from the sale of raw sugar fell from U.S. $272 million in 1984, to an estimated

U.S.$134 million in 1986, almost half of what they were in 1982 (WRH Report 1986).

These losses were particularly significant for the Dominican Republic. The tariffs on sugar imports precipitated a major crisis in the Dominican sugar industry. The United States not only bought less sugar from the Dominican Republic, it also bought it at cheaper prices than it had previously. In 1983–84, the Dominican Republic was allowed to sell to the United States 535,383 short tons of sugar at 17 cents per pound. In 1984–85, the United States bought only 302,016 short tons of sugar at the protected price; the rest sold at 5 cents per pound (EIU Country Report 1988:11). The reduction in sugar exports to the United States continued throughout the years of the Reagan administration.

The direct effects of these economic and political changes were serious losses of government revenues and, concomitantly, decreased governmental expenditures on health, decreased employment opportunities, decreased equitable distribution of income, decreased purchasing power, and widespread food shortages. The indirect effects were no less substantial: an increased number of Dominicans at nutritional risk, women and children suffering from increasing rates of infectious disease, and an ever-deepening sense of loss of political will, or *mala unión* (Whiteford 1993).

Employment.   Unemployment, underemployment, malnutrition, and maldistribution of resources each reflect the direct social consequences of the economic crisis. Each are chronic problems in the Dominican Republic; each has been made more difficult to recover from by the losses incurred during the crisis. During much of the twentieth century, Dominican unemployment hovered around at 25 percent. Following the key years of the economic crisis, the devaluation of the peso and the loss of U.S.–protected sugar quotas, the unemployment rate rose to more than one-third of the total labor force, one of the highest rates in Latin America (Ramirez et al. 1986). By 1986, unemployment and underemployment were exacting heavy costs from the Dominican people, affecting about 1.4 million people, or 56 percent of the total labor force. Inflation, controlled during the Trujillo years and maintained with the parallel exchange rate, was at 6.3 percent in 1986. By 1988, it had reached an unprecedented 58.9 percent, and was estimated to grow to 70 percent (Kurlansky 1989).

Distribution of Income. The unequal distribution of income was exacerbated following 1977. According to a survey conducted by the Dominican Banco Central for the period of 1976–77, 86 percent of Dominican families had a monthly income below 400 pesos and received only 56 percent of the total income of the country. At the same time, the four percent of the population who were receiving 22 percent of the income of the country had monthly incomes of over 800 pesos (Ramirez et al. 1986). "Peasants, workers and merchants have all seen the standard of living plummet. In 1986 a quarter of all Dominicans lived below the Government's absolute poverty line . . . today, as many as half of them do" (Kurlansky 1989:24).

In the countryside, the situation of chronic inequitable distribution of income was even worse. Seventy-five percent of the families lived on only 45 percent of the total national income, subsisting on monthly incomes below 200 pesos (approximately U.S.\$30 in 1988). The income gap continued to widen. The most conservative estimates showed the percentage of families living on a monthly income of less than 200 pesos increased from 23 percent to 27 percent between 1977 and 1984 (Ramirez et al. 1986).

According to the results of a 1983–1984 household budget survey, significant changes in the distribution of income occurred since the previous survey in 1976–77. The changes showed an increased inequality in the distribution of income, with more people subsisting in poverty (Musgrove 1987). The number of Dominicans living below the government's absolute poverty line continued to increase and in the two years between 1986 and 1988 increased by 100 percent (Kurlansky 1989). The greater the concentration of the crisis on the poor, the more powerful its effect is on their health experience (Musgrove 1987). The rich can afford alternative sources of food, medical supplies, and employment; the poor have fewer choices. "Even small economic losses may have significant consequences for health if they hurt primarily the poor, whereas greater income losses will have little impact if they are more equitably shared or affect mostly the nonpoor" (Musgrove 1987:423).

Real Wages. Between 1970 and 1984, the average Dominican real wage decreased by 51 percent (*Listin Diario* 1987). Since then, real wages continued to fall; between 1980 and 1985, real minimum wage earnings decreased by 80 percent (Gomez 1987:1534). The average real monthly wage paid by the public sector in 1970 was DR\$3,075. In 1984, the average real monthly salary was DR\$1,573. While economic deterioration of real wages and purchasing power occurred throughout the economic crisis, the initial losses reduced the possibility of economic recovery. Even with the nominal increases in minimum wage secured through strikes by physicians' unions and transportation unions, real wages were unable to keep up with increases in the price index.

While unemployment continued to rise and real wages fell, the prices paid for housing and food soared. In the eight years between 1978 and 1986, the cost of housing in the Dominican Republic increased by almost 300 percent (297.12 percent). During the same period, the prices of food, beverages, and tobacco increased by 315.85 percent, and the general price index rose by 317.35 percent between 1978 and 1986. The most radical increase in the price index occurred between 1984 and 1985, the years of most significant loss in sugar revenues, when the food price index increased from 196.61 to 282.20 percent. One year later, it continued its increase to reach 315.85 percent of what it had been eight years before. The price increases were felt particularly by the poor who had few resources to fall back on, and for whom there was no margin of safety.

Food Costs. In the five years between 1980 and 1985, the food prices increased by 84 percent, even as real salaries decreased to 80 percent of their 1980 value (*Indicadores Basicos* 1986). These increases were due to an increased dependence on food imports and the removal of subsidies and controls on the prices of food (Safa n.d.).

Analysis of the growth index of the main agropecuarian products (based on gross production values) showed continued slow growth. Outdated agricultural techniques, increased costs for fertilizers (based on petroleum products), soil depletion, and the high cost of importing raw materials combined to prevent the Dominican Republic from producing enough food to feed its people. It was not only that there was not enough food, or that it was too expensive to buy, but also that access to foods was unevenly distributed within the population. Sixty percent of the poorest households were at serious risk of not getting enough to eat (resulting in deficient caloric intake), compared to only 8.4 percent of the members of households in the highest economic quartile (Rogers and Swindale 1988:ii).

During the time of the most severe impact of the economic crisis (1984–85), the price of food increased by 42.9 percent, while the purchasing power of the peso decreased (Indicadores Basicos 1986), thereby exacerbating the inability of many sectors of the population to meet basic food needs. Between 1979 and 1984, the cost of living rose by 17.1 percent and average real wage declined by 3.8 percent. In 1969, food prices were 31.9 percent of family costs, but by 1976–77, food costs consumed 38.9 percent of a family's income. As food prices continued to increase, they continued to take a larger percentage of the household's income. In the six months between April and September of a single year (1988), the price of beans and rice each doubled. Tomatoes, another constant in the Dominican traditional diet, tripled in cost in six months (*Listin Diario* 1987). During July and August 1988, widespread food shortages were common. Increasingly, high-protein, traditional foods became too expensive or unavailable for many people.

Price increases, dependence on imported foods, reduction of state price subsidies, and reduction in domestic production resulted in the changed availability of products. Commercial chicken feed, for instance, was imported and its price increased to more than 200 percent of its pre-crisis costs (Murphy 1987;241–259). As a result of the increases, chicken eggs disappeared from the grocery shelves. Eggs did not generate enough revenue to cover the increased cost of imported chicken feed to make it beneficial for producers to supply eggs for local consumption. During the same period, the price of infant formula, heavily relied on as an infant food source, rose 200 percent compared to its price the previous year (Murphy 1987), thereby removing two staples in households with infants and young children.

During the summer of 1988, shortages of milk, sugar, eggs, and meat were common. When women recovering from childbirth were interviewed about what foods were best for the healthy fetal development, they replied "fruits, vegetables, meat, eggs and milk." When asked what they ate before they came to the hospital to have the baby, they said only "*sospua*," a weak soup made with plantains, yuca, sweet potatoes, and guandules. Asked to explain why they ate so little of what they believed were good for their developing child, their replies were straightforward: they ate what they could find. They either could not find eggs, milk, or meat in the stores, or when they did locate the foods, they could not afford them. The women's descriptions of food scarcity were confirmed by neonatal statistics. An estimated one-fourth of all babies born in the Dominican Republic were born to malnourished mothers (SESPAS 1986).

GLOBAL ECONOMIC PRESSURE AND CUBAN HEALTH COMMODIFICATION

The Cuban economic crisis is also a reflection of its geographic and geopolitical position. An island like the Dominican Republic, it is limited in its natural resources, and, like the Dominican Republic, is affected by global political and economic forces. Therefore, it is valuable to see how the commodification of health and accumulation of both symbolic and medical capital in Cuba is distinctive from health commodification in the Dominican Republic. The loss of Cuba's trading partners inversely affected the supply of medical equipment, medicine, and raw materials for Cuba's pharmaceutical industry (Benjamin and Haendel 1991:6). The shortage of medical and food supplies led to a decrease in the high standard of health provision to which Cubans had become accustomed and a slight increase in diarrheal diseases (deaths caused by acute diarrhea increased from 378 cases in 1990 to 417 cases in 1991) and other health problems (Reuters 1996). While the infant mortality rate continues to fall (PAHO 1997), there were slight increases in the incidence of certain infectious diseases, such as TB (Eberstadt 1986:7). Tuberculosis, long associated with poverty and unsanitary living conditions, is often seen as a harbinger of dangerous changes in living conditions.

In addition, the energy shortage caused by the U.S. embargo against Cuba led to rationing and the halt of construction projects. In 1990. Cuba suffered a 25 percent reduction in oil imports (Deere 1991:56) when it lost the $4 billion previously annually provided by the Soviet Union in an oil-for-sugar exchange (Reuters 1996). The housing crisis worsened and the loss of petroleum necessary for construction was manifest. The withdrawal of $3 to $5 billion annually in aid from the previous Soviet Union forced Cuba into a situation of extreme shortages. Even in light of those shortages, the Cuban government continued to support its health infrastructure. In 1994, health represented 8 percent of the gross domestic product, supporting 312,000 people employed in the health sector (Reuters 1996). While 8 percent is a decrease from previous years, it remains considerably higher than any of its Caribbean neighbors (and higher than many developed countries as well).

While almost all babies are born in hospitals in both the Dominican Republic and in Cuba, and official statistics for each country suggest that the majority of women receive prenatal care (Ubell 1983:438; Benjamin and Haendel 1994:4; Whitefore 1990), the similarity is less than it first appears. Cuba and the Dominican Republic share history, geography, proximity to the United States, and the economic crisis. In terms of child survival, one of the greatest differences between the two islands is that Cuba transferred its vision of *sembrando el futuro*—planting the future—by creating an island-wide primary health care network, a community-based health care system, while the Dominican Republic allowed to lie fallow its rural health, primary-care system and turned its resources instead to urban-based hospitals. Because of its emphasis on community and preventive health, the Cuban public health system appears to be withstanding the current economic challenges by reliance on the accumulation of both symbolic and medical capital, while the Dominican commodification of health remains costly for its poor results.

In the 1960s and 1970s. Cuba developed a system of community health centers, family health providers, public health education, potable water, and collection of human and solid wastes each dependent on the central government and on the good will and participation of the community. Had the economic crisis not occurred, and had development according to Cuba's Public Health Plan, by 1995 Cuba would have been the first country

to have comprehensive family practice coverage for 100 percent of its people (Nelson 1991). The economic crisis made that an impossible goal to achieve by 1995. However, even failing to reach its 1995 goal, Cuba's health accomplishments are significant. In 1991, Cuba had 38,000 physicians and a physician-to-population ratio of 1 to 534, compared to the 1-to-2,320 physician-to-population ratio in the Dominican Republic, making total coverage a realistic possibility (Nelson 1991). In addition, by 1992, Cuba had achieved a life expectancy rate within two years of that for the United States, an infant mortality rate within 1 percentage point of that in the United States, and had reduced low birth weight births to within 2 percentage points of the U.S. (*New York Times* 1994). While the Cuban trends in infant mortality, birth weights and deaths from infectious disease, each relatively sensitive indicators of changes in health status, showed small increases in the number of low birth weight babies born and number of deaths from infectious disease, the overall infant mortality rate continued to drop (*New York Times* 1994).

In light of the economic restructuring that Cuba has endured, the question must be asked; "how were they able to do so much?" In the early 1960s, Cuba set four national health goals: "(1) increased emphasis on preventive medicine; (2) improvements of sanitation and related areas; (3) raising of nutritional levels for the disadvantaged social groups; and (4) education of the public regarding health matters" (Diaz-Briquets 1983:105–106). To accomplish those goals, they provided free access to medical care, increased the number of trained health workers, increased the number of medical facilities in rural areas, increased chemical treatment of water, eradicated malaria, began food rationing to allocate food to those most in need, and began aggressive early intervention strategies to treat both problem pregnancies and diarrheal diseases (Diaz-Briquets 1983:107–112).

In so doing, Cuba made equity and access a central focus of both their policy and practice. They built an accumulation of symbolic and medical capital that served them during the economic crisis. Both Dominicans and Cubans face conditions that challenge their survival—shortages of food, housing, and medical supplies. However, Dominicans also struggle with little health education, restricted access to health care, inadequate services within the health system, a centralized, urban based medical infrastructure, the lack of access to clean water and waste disposal, and the lack of political will to improve health.

CONCLUSION

Global and transnational economic pressures on the Dominican Republic resulted in increased external flows of capital and labor. Labor migration and remittances became increasingly significant as a survival strategy for Dominicans. More than 700,000 Dominicans have emigrated since the 1970s, most of them during the decade of the 1980s, and especially since 1985 (PAHO http://www). Dominican health became commodified by reducing financial costs incurred in the provisions of services by refusing to fund long-term preventive measures such as clean water and waste disposal, thereby reducing the accumulated medical capital, and restricting equity and access to public health programs. "The connection between income and health depends not only on current flows but on the stock of capital—including medical capital as well as safe water supplies and sanitation—accumulated from the past" (Musgrove 1987:421).

For the Dominican Republic, the issue of accumulated capital is particularly critical because there was little medical capital previously accumulated, and what little there was does not serve to reverse community sentiment of mala union. Cuba on the other hand, showed real gains in accumulated and symbolic capital particularly in the area of public health, equity and access, and community identity.

Antrobus has pointed out how global trade and lending policies have a severe effect on the living conditions of the poor by "(1) reducing income through increased unemployment and a reduction in real wages; (2) price increases on basic necessities, resulting from the removal of food subsidies as well as from the increasing costs of food imports due to devaluation; and (3) shifting the level and composition of government expenditure away from the social services to debt servicing and military expenditures" (Safa n.d. p.3). The case of the Dominican Republic shows the effect of just such lending and trade policies on social conditions and their consequences in once again reifying the community perception of the *mala unión* of the government.

These global pressures commodify Dominican health in "quick fix" immunization campaigns while ignoring the long-term health needs of communities. This loss of support for communities further erodes Dominicans' belief in their government and, even in their own abilities to participate in the alleviation of shared problems. *Mala unión* expands to permeate not only relations between the national government and individuals, but also between individuals, defeating community-based solutions.

Furthermore, because the Dominican Republic, unlike Cuba, had not made prevention, health education, and equity and access to health care a major thrust of their public policy, there is more at risk. While the direct effects of the crisis can be measured, it will be the indirect effects that kill peoples' will. Even when the economic crisis recedes, the costs may be irrecoverable not because of the crisis, but because of the construction of an identity and a pattern of reciprocal relations that place Dominicans in a *mala unión* with their government, when they might be better served to be part of a future harvest.

NOTES

1. Based on Glick, Schiller N., L. Basch, and C. Blanc-Szanton. 1992. *Towards a Transnational Perspective on Migration: Race, Class, Ethnicity, and Nationalism Reconsidered*. New York: NY Academy of Science.

REFERENCES

AID, 1987. AID Child Survival Paper, Project No. 517-0239. USAID/Dominican Republic September 9.

Benjamin, Medea, and Mark Haendel, 1991. "A Health Revolution?" *Links: Health and Development Report* 8(3):3–6.

Bustillo-Hernandez, M., 1989. "Differential Child Mortality in the City of Santo Domingo, Dominican Republic, 1976–1981. "Unpublished Master's thesis. University of Florida.

Ceara, M., 1987. *Debate Nacional Sobre la Situación de la Niñez y la Mujer Dominicana*. UNICEF, Santo Domingo, 28.

Deere, Carmen O., 1991. "Cuba's Struggle for Self-Sufficiency." *Monthly Review* July/August, pp. 55–73.

Diaz-Briquets, Sergio, 1983. *The Health Revolution in Cuba*. Austin: University of Texas Press.

Eberstadt, Nicholas, 1986. "Did Fidel Fudge the Figures? Literacy and Health: The Cuban Model." *Caribbean Review* 15(2):4–7, 37–8.

The Europa Year Book, 1, 916–917, 1988.

Gomez, C., 1987. *Consideraciones Sobre la Situacion Nutricional de la Poblacion Dominicana*. Poblacion y Desarrollo, Enero-Marzo, 1534.

Gomez, C., M. Q. Cedno, and A. Tatis, 1987. *Poplacion Rural y Ecosistemas*. Poplacion y Desarrollo, Enero-Marzo, pp. 3–14.

Hay, S., 1990. "Prenatal Care Utilization in a Public Hospital in the Dominican Republic." Unpublished master's thesis.

Indicadores Basicos, 1986. Secretariado Tecnico de la Presidencia. Oficina Nacional de Planificación. Fondo de la Naciones Unidas para la Infancia. Santa Domingo, R.D.

Johnson, C., 1988. *Nutritional Adequacy in the Dominican Republic*. Tufts University, Medford, MA.

Kearney, Michael, 1995. "The Local and the Global: The Anthropology of Globalization and Transnationalism." *Annual Reviews in Anthropology* 24:547–65.

Kirkpatrick, Anthony, 1994. "Disease Plagues Cuba," *St. Petersburg Times*, July 17, p. 8D.

Kurlansky, M., 1989. "The Dominican Republic: In the Land of the Blind Caudillo." *New York Times*, August 6, p. 24.

Listin Diario, 7/9/87. Dominican Republic.

Mendoza, H., et al., 1991. Unpublished field report.

Molina, M. and C. Gomez, 1991. Unpublished Report on Changes in Dominican Health Status Indicators.

Murphy, M. 1987. "The International Monetary Fund and Contemporary Crisis in the Dominican Republic." In *Political Economy of the World-System Annuals*, vol. 9, R. Taranico (ed.) 241259. Sage Publications.

Musgrove, P., 1987. "The Economic Crisis and Its Impact on Health and Health Care in Latin America and the Caribbean," *International Journal of Health Services* 17:411–441.

National Office of Statistics, 1986. *Statistical Report on Dominican Health Status*. Santo Domingo: Ministry of Health.

Nelson, Harry, 1991. "Overmedicated? An Excess of Success May Ail Cuba's Top Flight Health Care System," *Los Angeles Times*, July 22.

Newfarmer, R.S., 1985. Economic Policy Toward the Caribbean Basin: The Balance Sheet. *Journal of Interamerican Studies* 27(1):63–90.

Oficina Nacional de Estatísticas y Centro Latinoamerica de 1982 Demografíca.

PAHO, 1996. http://www.paho.org/english/cuba.htm

PAHO, 1996. http://www.paho.org.english/dominican republic.htm

Ramirez, N., 1986. Población y Desarrollo, Boletín 16:1–44.

Ramirez, N., I. Duarte, and C. Gomez, 1986. Poplación y Salud en la Republica Dominicana, Estudio No. 5. Poplación y Desarrollo, Octubre-Diciembre.

———, 1987. Sintesis del Estudio: Población, Producción de Alimentos y Nutrición en la Republica Dominicana. Población y Desarrollo, 1–4.

Reuters, Wire Service, 1996. Cuba Health System Strained. *St. Petersburg Times,* May30:8a.

Rogers, B.L. and A. Swindale, 1988. Determinants of Food Consumption in the Dominican Republic, Vol. 1. Tufts University School of Nutrition.

Safa, H.I., 1988. Women and the Debt Crisis in the Caribbean. (Draft used with permission of the author).

Santana, Sarah, 1992. Cuba-Trends and Conditions in Health, Food and Nutrition. Paper Presented at the Annual LASA Meeting, Los Angeles, September.

SESPAS Politicas de Salud, 1983–86, 1987. Grafíco No. 50, 62.

Sunshine, C., 1985. The Dominican Republic: Society without Solutions. In The Caribbean: Survival, Struggle and Sovereignty. Boston: EPICA publication, South End Press, MA.

Taussig, Michael T., 1980. The Devil and Commodity Fetishism. Chapel Hill: University of North Carolina Press.

Tesh, Sylvia Noble, 1988. Hidden Arguments: Political Ideology and Disease Prevention Policy. New Brunswick: Rutgers University Press.

Tufts University School of Nutrition/USAID Nutritional Survey. 1987. Nutritional Status in the Dominican Republic. A Report to USAID, Santo Domingo.

Ubell, Robert N., 1983. Twenty-five Years of Cuban health Care. *New England Journal of Medicine* 309(23):1468–72.

Ugalde, A., 1989. The Delivery of Primary Health Care in Latin America During the Times of Crisis: Issues and Policies. Unpublished paper.

United Nations, 1987. Economic Commission for Latin America and the Caribbean Economic Survey of Latin America and the Caribbean, 1985.

U.S. Department of State, 1988. Report U.S. by Department of State on the Caribbean Basin Initiative (CBI): Progress to Date. Bureau of Inter-American Affairs, March.

Vidal, Manuel Limont and Guillermo Padron, 1991. (Translated by Margaret Gilpin). The Development of High Technology and Its Medical Applications in Cuba. Latin American Perspectives 69:118 #2 (101–113).

Whiteford, L.M. and J. Coreil, 1991. The Household Ecology of Dengue Fever. Unpublished monograph.

Whiteford, L.M., 1990. A Question of Adequacy: Primary Health Care in the Dominican Republic. *Social Science and Medicine* 30:221–226.

———, 1992. Contemporary Health Care and the Colonial and Neo-Colonial Experience: The Case of the Dominican Republic. *Social Science and Medicine* 35(10):1215–1223.

———, 1993. Child and Maternal Health and International Economic Policies. *Social Science and Medicine* 37(11):1391–1400.

———, 1997. The Ethnoecology of Dengue Fever. *Medical Anthropology Quarterly.* June.

———, 1997. Economic Restructuring and Child Health: The Dominican Republic. In Small Wars: Child Survival Revisited (ed.s) Nancy Scheper-Huges and Carolyn Sargent, University of California Press.

24

German Spirit Doctors in Spiritist Healing in Urban Brazil

Sidney M. Greenfield

THE PROBLEM OF GERMAN SPIRIT-GUIDES

Elsewhere (Greenfield 1984, 1986, 1987a, 1987b; Greenfield and Gray 1988) I have described and examined the work of Edson Queiroz and Brazilian Spiritist healing. In this paper I am interested in the ethnic and social backgrounds of the spirit guides of Brazilian healer-mediums, among whom early twentieth-century German doctors are considerably overrepresented.

From at least the middle of the twentieth century, Brazil has been the home of healers who at times perform spectacular acts of healing that have not been adequately examined by Western science and medicine. José Pedro de Freitas, more commonly known as Zé Arigó, John Fuller's (1974) "surgeon of the rusty knife," is perhaps the best

Sidney M. Greenfield, "German Spirit Doctors in Spiritist Healing in Urban Brazil," in D. Posey and W. Overal (eds.), *Ethnobiology: Implications and Applications*. Belem, Brazil: Proceedings of the First International Congress of Ethnobiology, 1988, pp. 241–256. Reprinted by permission of publishers.

known of these healers, both to Brazilians and to foreigners. In the small town of Congonhas do Campo in the interior of the states of Minas Gerais during the 1950s and 1960s he is reported to have removed tumors and performed delicate eye operations with a paring knife and without the use of antiseptics and anesthesia (Comenale n.d.; Fuller 1974; Jorge 1963; Pires 1963; Puharich 1974; Rizzini 1961). The belief common to Brazil, transmitted to foreign audiences both lay and academic, was that Arigó was a medium whose body was used by the spirits of deceased physicians. Spiritism, based on the writings of Allan Kardec (n.d., 1975, 1980), is the belief system that both orients and informs what Arigó and other Spiritist healers did and continue to do.

Spiritists believe that there are two planes of reality, the material, or visible and the spiritual, or invisible, with continual communication between the two (Cavalcanti 1983; Greenfield 1986, 1987a, 1987b). Spirits, the vital force in the universe, who live in the invisible between incarnations, may return to the material world—without reincarnating, assuming they have no need or desire to do so— and do good works through mediums whose bodies they may use for short periods of time.

For believers in Spiritism, Spiritist healers are able to effect extraordinary cures, because a spirit, bringing knowledge and power from the spiritual plane, heals. This belief explains the reports of tumors being removed without blood or pain, the lame walking, the blind seeing, cancers being cured, and other extraordinary acts.

Arigó is reported to have been the medium for a team of spirit doctors and healers headed by one who answered to the name of Adolph Fritz. While Arigó was in a trance, Fritz claimed to have last lived on earth in Germany during the First World War.

Although the first, Arigó was not the only Brazilian medium through whom the now famous Dr. Fritz is reported to have healed. Within a year of Arigós death in an automobile crash in 1971, the spirit of the German doctor was reported back in Brazil, being received by the medium Edivaldo Oliveira Silva, a second-grade teacher in the small town of Vitoria da Conquista in the northeaster state of Bahia. Edivaldo, however, after but a few years of service as a healer-medium, was also killed in an automobile crash (Alves Netto n.d.: 65–74).

Then Dr. Fritz is reported to have appeared again, this time using as his medium Edivaldo's brother, Oscar Wilde Oliveira Silva. Oscar Wilde, however, then also was killed in an automobile crash.[1]

A few years later Dr. Fritz was back again, now using as his medium Edson Cavalcante de Querioz, a resident of the city of Recife in the state of Pernambuco. In contrast with Arigó, Edivaldo, Oscar Wilde, and the vast majority of healer-mediums in Brazil who are poorly educated, Edson is a trained and licensed physician, a graduate of the Medical School of the Federal University of Pernambuco who earns his livelihood as a gynecologist and surgeon. One a week, however, and more often when he visits Spiritist centers throughout Brazil and at times overseas, he serves as medium for Dr. Fritz and his team of spirit healers at the *Fundação Espírita Dr. Adolph Fritz* in Recife.[2]

Healers-mediums usually receive teams of spirits composed of specialists in the various fields of medicine. The teams are composed of spirits who have lived in different nations and cultures in diverse historical periods. Indians from Asia are popular, as are Brazilians in lesser numbers, other Europeans, and North Americans. Japanese and Chinese appear but in still smaller numbers. Occasionally an Amerindian or an African might appear. Most members of these healing teams, however,

and invariably the leaders, are Germans, most of whom were last incarnate during the first half of the twentieth century.

Adolph Fritz, although the most famous, was not the first nor only spirit of a German doctor reported to be received by a Brazilian healer-medium. Alves Netto (n.d.: 30–32), for example, cites reports in the Brazilian press of Dr. Frederick Kempler, who also last lived in Germany during the First World War, who performed surgeries through a medium by the name of Waldemar Golvin in Recife in the early 1950s. He also tells us of the medium Severino Paz de Lira in São Lourenço de Mata in the state of Pernambuco who since 1954 has been healing under the guidance of a team headed by a Dr. Adolph Fritz Dutzold (Alves Netto n.d.: 9–11). Severino was still receiving the German doctor and his team and healing when I visited him in 1984. I have visited and/or been told of many other healer-mediums working under the guidance of spirits of German doctors in such distant and diverse parts of Brazil as Rio Grande do Sul, São Paulo, Minas Gerais, Bahia, Goiãs and Rio de Janeiro. Alves Netto also tells us of Dr. Hans Friedrich Goldmann, who came to the medium Milton Nonato Junior in the state of Alagoas in the 1960s (n.d.:37), and Drs. Josef Gleber and Otto Kurtz, who oriented the healings of the medium Antonio José de Sales from Caratinga in Minas Gerais in the 1960s (n.d.:50–52). More recently, Rocha Lima (n.d.) describes in detail Dr. Frederick Von Stein, who is still healing through the medium Frei Luis in Jacareipagua in Rio de Janeiro. The medium Antonio de Oliveira Rios, whom I visited in Palmelo, Goiás, receives Dr. Ricardo Stams, and Edu in Porto Alegre receives yet another Dr. Fritz. In addition, informants have told me of still German spirit guides, at least some of whom were known in Brazil before Fritz and Arigó came to prominence.[3]

Healing spirits, I should note, are not like most spirits received by Brazilian Spiritist mediums. The general pattern, introduced by the earliest Spiritists in the nineteenth century and still practiced by the usually well educated nonhealing mediums, is to receive spirits of well-known personages in the history of the Western literary-educational tradition. That is, the spirits received are usually "household names" (to the educated and to the followers of Spiritism) from a previous era who were usually of high moral repute. Famous political leaders of the past, literary figures, artists, philosophers, and others come to and/or send messages through mediums. Alternatively, the spirits of obscure Indians or other exotic enough to teach about reincarnation and life in the invisible world also are received. Healer-mediums, by contrast, receive doctors and other spirits whose names and reputations usually are not known to the medium, the patient, or the educated public. As was the case with Arigó and Dr. Fritz, Waldemar Golvin and Dr. Kempler, Antonio and Dr. Ricardo, and Severino and Dr. Adolph Fritz Dutzhold, the credentials and information about the previous incarnations of the spirit guide was made known only after a reputation for successful healing had been established.

One might expect unknown spirits to become the guides of Brazilian healer-mediums to be French. Spiritism was brought to Brazil from France and was greatly influenced by French medical figures.[4] Furthermore, in the late nineteenth and early twentieth centuries, when Spiritism was taking form, Brazilian medicine was strongly influenced by French medicine and French-trained medical figures.[5] So by the dominance of Germans among the spirit guides received by Brazilian Spiritist healers?[6]

After examining the data on Spiritist healing in the context of contemporary Brazilian social structure, in the remainder of this paper I wish to propose an explanation for the disproportionally large number of spirits of German doctors presently healing in Brazil through a large and growing number of Brazilian healer-mediums. In the following pages I develop an hypothesis relating aspects of Brazilian social structure, specifically traditional relations of patronage and clientele and their extension into networks, to the stereotypes Brazilians hold about Germans. This, I propose, will explain the selection of Germans, as opposed to the spirits of doctors of other nationalities and cultures, by so many Brazilian healer-mediums.

THE CONTEXT: THE SOCIAL TRANSFORMATION OF BRAZILIAN SOCIETY

In the four decades since the Second World War Brazil has undergone a major social transformation. The population has increased dramatically while the society has urbanized and modernized.

The total population has increased three and one-half, to more than 140 million in 1989. Large numbers of former rural dwellers have migrated from the interior to the cities (Merrick and Graham 1979). According to the 1941 census, Brazil's population of almost 41 million was two-thirds rural. According to the 1980 census, however, two-thirds of the more than 120 million people counted were urban dwellers. Ten cities and more than a million inhabitants, with São Paulo, one of the largest cities in the world, presently exceeding 15 million in its greater metropolitan area and Rio de Janeiro exceeding 8 million.

As is the case in so many other developing nations in the twentieth century, Brazil's newly founded capital-intensive industries are unable to provide jobs for the large numbers of migrants streaming into the cities from the interior. In addition, the cities themselves are unable to provide the most basic facilities for most of the immigrants. Many migrants, who live with their numerous offspring by squatting in the shanty towns for *favelas*,[7] are not served with water, sewage, electricity, public transportation, and other basic facilities. Large numbers live in dwellings assembled from materials found in other people's trash, on land that is not theirs and whose ownership often is in dispute. Unemployment rates are high and underemployment is a fact of life. One-third of Brazilian workers, for example, according to a report in *Fortune Magazine* (Main 1986), earn less than the minimum wage. Two-thirds of the population consumes less than the 2,400 calories considered a minimum daily requirement. And health experts report rising rates of infant mortality and such communicable diseases as malaria, tuberculosis, dengue fever, and polio.

As with any combined demographic explosion and social dislocation of this magnitude, large numbers of Brazilians living in São Paulo (the industrial capital of a country that now ranks eighth amongst the free world's economies), Rio de Janeiro, Belo Horizonte, Porto Alegre, Salvador, Belém, Manaus, Recife, or Fortaleza are not only poor, but must struggle just to survive each day. There are few, if any, institutions, public or private to help them solve the countless problems they face daily. In the urban setting, of course, their old rural ways are believed to be no longer effective. But the cities have not provided new means to help them satisfy their most basic needs.

TRADITIONAL BRAZILIAN SOCIAL STRUCTURE

Although most of today's urban dwellers, or their parents, were poor and dissatisfied with their conditions in the interior, the major reason for the large-scale migration, they were able to survive there. Survival, however, is something many are finding themselves less and less able to do in the cities today lest they turn to theft, robbery, assault and other forms of crime (Zaluar 1985). The survival of those at the bottom of the heap in Brazil's traditional rural economy, which was and still is characterized by a land tenure system in which a small percentage of the population owns almost all of the land, was a system of social relations dominated by patronage and clientele (Boissevain 1966; Eisentadt and Roniger 1984; Gelner and Waterbury 1977; Greenfield 1968, 1972. 1977, 1979; Kaufman 1974; Roninger 1981; Schmidt, et al. 1976; Strickon and Greenfield 1972; Weingrod 1968; Wolf 1966). The terms refer to a system of exchange that forms the basis for social relations in which people in different positions in a hierarchically ordered society exchange goods and services. Since those at different places in the social hierarchy have access to different kinds of goods and services each may offer what he (or she) has in exchange for what he (or she) needs. The key is to find someone who needs or wants what any *ego* has to offer, and then to keep the exchange going.

The paradigm for the system is the historical relationship between a landowner and any of the many laborers living on his property. The two, of course, are of unequal status and located in different places in the socio-economic hierarchy. Both, however, have needs which differ significantly from those of the other. The laborer, who is landless, of course needs access to the means of production, which in this case is the land owned by the other. He also needs a place to live and someone to whom he can turn to in the event of illness or other emergency. The landowner also has needs. Given the long standing practice of Brazilian elites to eschew manual labor, he minimally needs someone to work his land for him, and to do the daily tasks that call for physical labor.

The unequal parties were brought together by means of an exchange in which the landowner, the *patrão* or patron, provided access to his land and a dwelling to the other; in return his social and economic inferior provided his labor, both on the land and contingently elsewhere, should his *patrão* request it. The two parties then shared in the crops produced on the land, the split varying from fifty-fifty to 75 percent to the landowner and 25 percent to the laborer, depending on the crops planted, the availability of laborers in the area, and other factors.

The relationship between the parties was open ended in that subsidiary exchanges could be added to the primary one. That is, the landowner was free to call on the laborer, his client-dependent, should he need him for any other activity that may or may not have called for physical effort. Likewise, the laborer-dependent was able to turn to is landowner-patron when he was faced with an emergency outside the normal range of daily activities.

The patron-client exchange, the basis for patron-client relationships in traditional rural Brazil, was both strengthened and elevated to a new dimension when electoral legitimacy was instituted as the basis for public office and political control with the establishment of the Old Republic at the end of the nineteenth-century. In addition to his labor and miscellaneous services, the worker on a rural estate could offer his vote in support of the candidate designated by his landowner-*patrão*.

The landowner was able to extend the range of his transactions into the political realm with the development of the system students of Brazilian politics refer to as *coronelismo* (Carone, 1971, 1978; Castelo Branco 1979; Cintra 1979; Nunes Leal 1949; Pang 1979). In exchange for the votes of his multiple dependents the rural landowner was able to obtain a range of "favors" from those he helped to elect. The value of these favors in a society in transition, in turn, enhanced the value of and the need for large numbers of client-dependents by the traditional landed elite. Given the continuing needs of the mass of poor, undernourished, endemically ill laborers in the interior, patron-client exchanges, extending out into interrelated networks of such exchanges, dominated the social structure of traditional rural Brazil (Greenfield 1977).

From the perspective of the rural laborer, no matter how bad things got for him, he knew that in desperation he could turn to his *patrão* and, although there were no guarantees, expect help, which more often than not grudgingly was forthcoming. In brief, no matter the problem, its solution was to be arranged for the poor laborer by his landowner-patron, usually through the network of relationships—often built on the basis of the votes, labor, and other contributions of dependents—his socially and economically superior exchange partner was able to develop.

PHYSICIANS AS TRADITIONAL PATRONS

Although serving as the paradigm for the system, landowners were not the only ones to head networks of patron-client exchanges in the traditional society of rural Brazil. Doctors, as I have shown elsewhere (Greenfield 1977, 1987), also were important heads of patronage networks.

In a study of patronage relations conducted in the mid-1960s in the Zona da Mata of the state of Minas Gerais (Greenfield 1968, 1972, 1977, 1979), I had been surprised by the high level of participation in the political-electoral process by the small number of doctors in the area. The doctors did not have lucrative medical practices, because most of their patients, like most people in the area, could not afford to pay for medical services.

The doctors in the Zona de Mata, whose wealth came from other sources, were rich and powerful, members of the local elite. Each, however, devoted himself conscientiously to attending patients, even those who could not pay his fees. Long lines waited each day outside each of their clinics. A doctor permitted himself to be interrupted by patients at all hours of the day and night. What I wrote of one doctor, that "He gave of himself . . . ,generously and without complaint, almost at times, as some of his loyal followers reported, in the image of a saint performing a spiritual calling" (Greenfield 1977: 148), was true of many of them.

I went on to explain that by providing his services to the patient who could not pay his fee, the doctor and his patient entered into a patron-client relationship in which the latter was indebted to the former. Patient-clients then would try to reciprocate whenever they were able, and especially when called upon to do so in a specific way by their doctor-patron.

During election campaigns politicians contesting for office, or their representatives, would court the medical practitioners in the region. In return for their support—and the support of their patient-dependents—for example, the doctors would be promised clinics or hospitals, to be built with state or federal funds, from which they would be paid a salary (as administrator) and other benefits. They also would be offered free medical supplies, to be paid for from government grants, low or interest free personal loans, construction contracts—for the doctor or his designate—or other benefits that would increase the personal wealth and power of the doctor. The expectation, of course, was that the doctor would "inform" his patient-clients of his preferred candidates and they, as a means of satisfying their indebtedness to him, would vote for them. The doctor, as a result, served as an intermediary between state and national level politicians who, in return for being elected at least in part by the votes of dependents he controlled, would provide him access to the resources controlled by the government.

Central to the extensive networks of patronage and clientele that articulated the institutions of the state and national bureaucracies with local communities throughout the country were individuals who accumulated debts by performing services most recipients could not afford to purchase in the market at the prevailing rate. In this way services like health care were made available to the poor rural masses. Doctors, among others, performed services, and even redistributed material wealth, as patrons and brokers in the traditional system.

PATRON-CLIENT NETWORKS IN THE CITIES

When the poor from the interior migrated to the cities they found no counterparts of the landowner, doctor, or other patrons to whom they could turn for help with new problems. And, since jobs were often hard to find, if they existed at all, and therefore material resources were difficult to come by, and conditions differed so greatly from what they were used to, the number of problems with which they needed help increased far beyond what most migrants had experienced in their traditional rural settings. This condition, that at times approached a hopelessness and desperation that has been likened to a state of anomy (Fontenelle 1985), is the social context in which the question of the disproportionate number of spirits of German physicians being received by Spiritist healer-mediums in Brazilian cities must be understood.

Elsewhere (Greenfield 1987) I have suggested that Spiritist healers, like their Umbanda (Brown 1986; Prust 1985; Greenfield and Prust in press), Xango (Motta and Scott 1983; 95 and 96), and other religious counterparts are developing networks of social relationships based on patron-client exchanges that incorporate and provide services— material and spiritual—for, among others, some of the most destitute of the urban poor. In contrast with most urban politicians who seek their votes with promises that rarely if ever are fulfilled (Dinz 1982; Zaluar 1985), the founders and leaders of the numerous and diverse alternative religious groups actually satisfy some of the needs of those who come to them with problems (see Greenfield and Prust in press).

Edson Queiroz, for example, has built a network of client-dependents for whom he is patron in much the same way the rural doctors in Minas Gerais in the 1960s had done. As did the rural doctors, Edson, as medium for Dr. Fritz, treats large numbers of sick and suffering individuals who seek him out; and consistent with Spiritist beliefs, he does so without charge.[8] Once treated, the patients, because they have not paid for the service, owe a debt to the healer,[9] as the rural patient owed his doctor.

The patients treated by Edson Queiroz and other Spiritist healers, however, are not just the poor and the destitute. Reports of spectacular cures of illnesses for which modern medicine offers little hope have convinced many middle- and upper-class Brazilians who are not necessarily believers in Spiritism to avail themselves of the services of Spiritist healer-mediums. Often they come after have exhausted all other options. Some are cured, or, at least in their own perceptions, helped. When they are, they often show their gratitude by giving gifts to the medium. There is no Spiritist stricture against the giving and acceptance of gifts. Prominent healer-mediums, those who treat wealthy clients, therefore, may themselves accumulate considerable material wealth. In addition, recipients of fluidic healing at a distance[10] are sent the name of a bank and an account number, should they wish to "assist" in the charitable work of the medium and the center.

Elsewhere I have shown that Spiritist healer Edson Queiroz (Greenfield 1987) and Umbanda cult leader Sr. Zé (Greenfield and Prust in press) both receive gifts of material goods and services that at times are of considerable value. More importantly, they each have a number of client-dependents of substantial wealth and influence. Having healed them, or otherwise helped them, and not accepted a fee, the patient-clients, even though they may have given gifts, remain in their respective debt. They find it difficult to refuse should the healer (or his spirit guide) turn to them with a request for assistance. For example, one day while in trance Edson announced to a group of his more affluent followers that they should do something to help the poor. Under the leadership of a couple who owned several restaurants, a soup kitchen was organized. The restaurateurs provided the cooking utensils and staples. Others contributed money while yet others donated ingredients.

Several women who do volunteer work at the *Fundação* then went out to a nearby *favela* to invite the residents to come to the *Fundação* on a specified day of the week to obtain bread and soup for their families. Once the program was started, bread and soup were prepared and distributed one day each week. Edson and his wife contributed time, money, and materials. In this instance the medium was primarily a middleman brokering the redistribution of the resources of other people. Although he contributed some of his own funds, he was more the catalyst than the traditional patron. But because he articulated the network of people who prepared and distributed the food, he appeared, especially to the recipients of the largess, as a patron.

Among Edson's Sr. Zé's, and other Spiritist and Umbanda leader's patient-clients there also are individuals who have access to and control over jobs, medicines, and other valuable and scarce resources. When treating or otherwise helping a client who is suffering, for example from malnutrition because he/she does not have work, Edson (Fritz), Sr. Zé (Xango), etc. may suggest that they go see one of his more affluent client-dependents (see also Brown 1986). The name of the healer-medium then serves as did an introduction to a merchant or pharmacist from a landowner-patron in the rural past. The present day businessman or merchant, as an extension of his relationship with the healer-medium, in partial repayment of his outstanding debt, might then help the poor fellow dependent of their common patron. The medium-cult leader also may direct other client-dependents to others in his network with the resources needed to help them with their particular problems.

While the medium can and does combine the resources flowing directly to him, such as those given as personal gifts, or in the case of Edson (Fritz), those sent to the numbered bank account, and use them to help those in need, he also can put together individuals in need with others who have, or have access to the resources that can help them. In brief, the medium acts as a middleman broker-ing people and resources. Through his healing activities, and perhaps because of them, he has become the center of a network through which resources and needs are brought together and resources redistributed to help satisfy the needs of a growing number of individuals. Another way of saying this is that healer-mediums like Edson Queiroz, Sr. Zé, etc. have become patrons who broker resources through expanding networks of individuals who come from the various classes and strata that make up present-day urban Brazilian society.

Successful healer-mediums then, whether or not they wish it or are conscious of it, have become patrons. In the urban setting they are developing, in terms of the paradigm of patron-client exchanges and patronage networks, a clientele. This group of dependents then turn to them for help with the many needs for which urban society in Brazil has not provided solutions.

My argument then is that Spiritist healer-mediums, Umbanda mediums, and other leaders of newly emergent urban religious groups in Brazil are creating what at one level appears to be a new social system in response to the pressing demands of the numerous, dislocated, anomic poor, while at another level they are recreating the traditional social structure of rural Brazil with its patron-client exchanges and networks of patronage and dependence.

In the rural setting patrons invariably came from the upper socio-economic classes. For the most part they were landowners, or the sons of landown-ers who had entered the liberal professions. Their position and prestige rested on their control of the society's primary productive resource. Their ability to establish themselves as patrons negotiating networks of client-dependents rested in great part

on the authority that went with their social and economic position.

In the urban centers, however, the vast majority of the Spiritist healer-mediums, Umbanda cult leaders, and heads of other religious healing groups are poor. Many, especially in Umbanda and other African-derived religious groups, also are black.[11] They are very different socioeconomicially—and often phenotypically as well—from traditional rural patrons.[12] In a society that values hierarchy, and still associates authority and control over resources with social position, these new healer-medium, religious leader-patrons are not easily accepted as leaders and heads of patronage networks, especially in the early stages of their careers.

Umbanda mediums and heads of other African-derived spirit possession cults, however, have less of a problem than do Spiritist healer-mediums. When they begin to heal and/or otherwise help potential follower-dependents, they receive, or are possessed by, an *orixá*, or saint, a deity from the African past who has been syncretized with a Roman Catholic saint, or by one of the new spirits generally recognized for their supernatural abilities. The medium then takes on attributes of his (her) spirit guide, giving him (or her), as medium from Xango, the *Caboclo Sete Flechas*, etc., prestige, authority, and power.

Spiritism, however, does not have a pantheon of deities whose characteristics, power, and authority are well known in the society at large as is the case with Umbanda and the African-derived religions. Spiritist mediums receive spirits of the dead, once-living individuals who may or may not have been important, respectable, and prestigious. Needless to say, being the intermediary for a Gandhi, a Churchill, or some other well-known leader from the past could help a young medium just beginning a career. But there are not that many world leaders who have become household names in Brazil. Furthermore, Spiritism's primary activity, on which its public acclaim and acceptance to a considerable degree is based, is the doing of charity; and Spiritist charity in Brazil has come to focus more than anything else on healing (Renshaw 1969; St. Clair 1971; Greenfield 1987). What a young Spiritist healer-medium beginning a career would need would be a spirit guide who was a respected, prestigious healer in the past whose name and memory would provide him with authority. How many healers, as opposed to political leaders, artists, writers, and other figures from the past have become household names in Brazil? How many could provide a medium who receives them with the status and authority needed to gain the respect of potential followers?

GERMAN STEREOTYPES AND THE NEW URBAN HEALER-MEDIUM PATRONS

It is here that the stereotypes Brazilians hold of Germans, and specifically of German doctors, come into play. In the popular mind, Germans are characterized as being efficient and authoritative. German culture is viewed as being technologically advanced and Germans are assumed to be technically proficient—in marked contrast, for example, with Brazilians. German science and medicine are seen as the standard for organization and efficiency; and doctors represent the high point of this German technological advancement and proficiency. German doctors, therefore, are believed to be technologically proficient, able, and efficient. These characteristics give them prestige that enable them to be dominating and to exercise authority. They are assumed to be able to resolve problems, much as did the still remembered *patrão* of the rural past.

As with most stereotypes, truth and reality are less important than imagery and belief. Germans in fact may be efficient and authoritative. There are a large number of descendants of German immigrants living in Brazil, especially in the southernmost states. Many are said to manifest at least some of the characteristics of the stereotype. But the contemporary Brazilian stereotype of Germans is not based on the behavior and attributes of any actual Germans, either in Brazil or elsewhere. It is taken from the movies, especially from Hollywood's portrayal of Germans in films made about the period from World War I to World War II. In the movies, and reinforced in the popular press, Germans, and especially the doctors, were portrayed as authoritarian, prestigious, dominating, and technically efficient. They were individuals who had the ability to get done what had to be done, no matter the task at hand. In this respect they shared many of the characteristics Brazil's urban masses associate with traditional elites and former patrons.

Brazilians, as I said earlier, do not know very much about Drs. Adolph Fritz, Frederick Kempler, Hans Frederich Goldman, Josef Gleber, Otto Kurtz, Frederich Von Stein, Ricardo Stams, Fritz Dutzhold, and the other Germans who heal through Spiritist mediums. They do not have to. The spirits are German doctors, and given the stereotype, this means that they are believed to be strong, able, and authoritative. When these spirits of German doctors come to this world and incorporate in Brazilians, they are able to provide even lower class, poorly educated, minority mediums with the prestige and authority needed to start a career and develop a following. They provide the prestige and authority that convince many potential clients that the medium is able to heal them, or do whatever else is necessary to help them with their problem. But there is more. German spirits highlight the Spiritism theme of moral decadence and advancement.

In the movies and in the popular press—Germany during World War I and especially World War II represented a high point of moral decadence. Although we know little of the details of the lives of the spirit doctors who return to cure through Brazilian mediums, we do know that almost all worked in one capacity or another for regimes that perpetrated some of the gravest of moral crimes and injustices known to mankind. As collaborators with those regimes, they shared in the immorality.

Spiritists believe that the vital forces that animate the universe are spirits, each set out on a path towards moral perfection. Possessed with free will, they come periodically to the material world to experience trials from which they can learn. When during the courses of a lifetime they make what by Judeo-Christian standards are the morally correct choices and behave appropriately, they advance; when they do not progress. Over the millennia each spirit accumulates a combination of moral pluses and minuses that shape its future both in the spirit world and in the future incarnations. Unless it wipes out the minuses with good works—charity—it will not be able to achieve the cosmic goal of perfection.

German doctors who were incarnate during either the First or the Second World War are assumed to have negative moral balances that they must work off before they can get back on the path of moral advancement. This is usually done by reincarnating. However, according to Spiritists, a number have chosen to return through mediums to help redeem themselves by applying the healing skills they learned—both in previous incarnations and in the spirit world—and/or otherwise helping the living who are in need. To do this charity they need mediums. Healer-mediums who receive German doctors then benefit both from their generally accepted prestige and authority and from the redemptive experience which associates them directly with the cosmic process of doing good.

By adopting a German spirit guide, members of even the lowest social classes, racial, ethnic and gender categories in the seemingly disorganized, anomic, and fast-growing urban sector of Brazil, who traditionally are without economic, political, or moral authority and power, are able to attract follower client-dependents. Starting usually with healing, many of these new urban patrons in-the-making are able to accumulate resources that they redistribute to poor and needy by means of patron-client exchanges and networks thereof. With the help of the authority provided them by the stereotypical image of the German doctor and his struggle for redemption, they are reconstructing, in modified form, the system of social relations that dominated the traditional past of the nation. And as was true in the rural areas, these networks of patron-client exchanges are making available to the new urban poor solutions to at least some of their more pressing survival needs.

NOTES

1. Lucia Silva Monteiro, a sister of the family, is reported to have healed with Dr. Fritz as her spirit guide, at least until she, too, was killed in an automobile crash.

2. There, using only a tweezers and a pair of scissors, he will remove a growth from the eye of a patient. With a scalpel he will make an incision in some part of another patient's body. With his unwashed fingers he will then go in to remove a tumor using only a piece of gauze to control the bleeding. He will combine the insertion of needles along a patient's spinal column with the vigorous scraping of a vertebrae with the same uncleaned scalpel. In all cases he uses no visible antiseptics and does not anesthetize his patients. The patients, however, do not report experiencing excessive pain and few, if any, complaints of infections and/or other complications have been reported (Greenfield 1984, 1986, 1987a, 1987b; Greenfield and Gray 1988).

3. Otherwise the disproportionate number of spirits of German doctors found today might be explained as diffusion, based on the copying of Adolph Fritz' extraordinary successes when working through Arigó. See also Laplantine (1989).

4. The most notable was Franz Anton Mesmer, whose concept of animal magnetism and model of curing was adopted by Allan Kardec and incorporated as part of the Spiritist belief system.

5. Perhaps the most famous example from Brazilian medicine was Dr. Oswaldo Cruz, the French-trained Brazilian doctor who led the fight to eradicate yellow fever in the early years of the twentieth century. And as far as stereotypes, the examples of Pasteur and the Curies are household names more familiar to most Brazilians than the Germans believed to come back to heal (see Stepan 1976).

6. I asked Edson Queiroz while he was in trance one day during one of visits to Recife why there were so many German spirits healing through Brazilian healer-mediums. His answer, that Brazilians were a poor, undeveloped people who needed help, and that he (Dr. Fritz, and by implication the other Germans) was helping them in order to redeem himself for misdeeds committed in a previous lifetime, was far from satisfying. It might be consistent with Spiritist philosophy, but I was convinced, there had to be more.

7. Adriano Murgel Branco, Secretary of Housing for the state of São Paulo, for example, has estimated that "one-third of the country's entire population lives in precarious conditions" (*New York Times*, May 24, 1987). In São Paulo alone, he goes on, there are an estimated one million people living in 1,200 squatter communities with an additional 3.5 million renting slum dwellings and a similar number living in homes built on plots with disputed titles.

8. Spiritists believe that since healing is the work not of the healer but of God and the spirits, it is improper and immoral for them to accept payment for healing (Greenfield 1987a, 1987b; see also Greenfield, in press, for some of the reactions of the Brazilian medical establishment to this practice).

9. This is especially true for those in the most dire circumstances because in addition to giving them an opportunity to reciprocate for services already rendered, it also enables them to return to the healer-medium with traditional requests for help in the future.

10. One of the five healing modalities used by Spiritist healers (see Greenfield 1987a, 1987b).

11. Edson Quieroz is one of a small number of excep-

tions. As the son of a middle-class family who went to the university and is a practicing physician, he comes closer to being a traditional patron than most healer-mediums and others establishing patronage networks as heads of Spiritist centers, Umbanda groups, and other religious groupings in Brazilian cities today.

12. It may be argued that by functioning as patrons, even though they are redistributing the wealth of others rather than giving what is theirs—as did the traditional patrons of the interior—they are inverting the social order (see Greenfield 1988).

REFERENCES

Alves Neto, A. n.d. *Extraordináias Curas Espirituais* Rio de Janeiro, Editors Mandarino Ltds.

Boissevain, J. 1966 Patronage in Sicily. *Mari* n.a.: 18–33

Brown, D. 1986.Umbanda: Religion and Politics in Urban Brazil *Ann Arbor, Michigan, University of Michigan Press*

Carone, E. 1971 Coronelismo: Definição Histórica e Bibliográfica. *Revista de Administração de Empresas* 3: 85–92.

———. 1978 *A Republica Velha I: Instituiçoes e Classes Socias* Rio de Janeiro and São Paulo, Difel.

Cavalcanti, M.L.C. 1983 *O Mundo Invisivel: Cosmologia, Sistema Ritual e Noção de Pessoa no Espiritismo* Rio de Janeiro, Zahar Editores.

Cintra, A.C. 1979. Traditional Brazilian Politics: An Interpretation of Relations between Center and Periphery. In: N. Agular (ed.) *The Structure of Brazilian Development* New Brunswick, NJ: Transaction Books.

Comenale, R. n.d *Zé Arigó, a Oitava Maravilha* Belo Horizonte, Editors Boa Viagem.

Costa L.C.B.F. 1979. *Arraial e Coronel. Dois Estudos da Históoria Social* São Paulo, Cultrix.

Diniz, E.L. 1982. *Voto e Mâquina Politico* Rio de Janeiro, Terra e Paz.

Eisenstadt, S.N. & L. Roniger, 1984. *Patrons, Clients, and Friends Interpersonal Relations and the Structure of Trust in Society* Cambridge: Cambridge University Press.

Fontenelle, L.F. R. 1985. *Um Mundo Dividido* Fortaleza: Universidade Federal do Ceará.

Fuller J. 1974. *Arigó, The Surgeon of the Rusty Knife* New York: Thomas Y. Crowell.

Gelner, E. & J. Waterbury, (eds.) 1977. *Patrons and Clients in Mediterranean Societies* London: Duckworth.

Greenfield, S.M. 1968. Patronage Networks, Factions, Political Parties, and National Integration in Contemporary Brazilian Society. Discussion Paper No.

12, Center for Latin America, The University of Wisconsin-Milwaukee.

———, 1972. Charwomen, Cesspools and Road Building: An Examination of Patronage, Clientele and Political Power in Southeastern Mines Gerais. In: Arnold Strickon & Sidney M. Greenfield (eds.) *Structure and Process in Latin America*. Albuquerque, New Mexico: University of New Mexico Press, pp. 71–100.

———, 1977. Patronage, Politics and the Articulation of Local Community and National Society in Pre-1968 Brazil. *Journal of Inter-American Studies and World Affairs* 19 (2): 139–172.

———, 1979. Domestic Crises, Schools and Patron-Clientele in Southeastern Minas Gerais. In: Maxine Margolis & William Carter (eds.) *Brazil: Anthropological Perspectives* New York: Columbia University Press, pp. 362–378.

———, 1984. *Spiritist Healing in Brazil* Video Documentary Produced at the Educational Communications Department, University of Wisconsin-Milwaukee.

———, 1986. Espiritismo Como Sistema de Cura. In: R. Parry Scott (org.) *Sistemas de Cura: As Alternativas do Povo* Recife, Mestrado em Antropologia.

———, 1987a. The Return of Dr. Fritz: Spiritist Healing and Patronage Networks in Urban, Industrial Brazil. *Social Science and Medicine* 24 (12): 1095–1108.

———, 1987b. The Best of Two Worlds: Spiritist Healing in Brazil. In: A. Retel Laurentin (ed.) *Etiologie et Perception de la Maladie*. Paris: L'Harmattan.

———, 1988. The Elderly in Brazil: Some Contrasts and Comparative Insights. In: Enid Gort (ed.) *Aging in Cross Cultural Perspective: Africa and the Americas* New York: Phelps Stokes Fund.

———, in press. O Corpo Como Uma Casca Descartável: O Médium-Curador e Seus Críticos. In: Antonio Mourão Cavalcante (org.) *Corpo de Saúde: Corpo de Fé. Fortaleza: Fundo Estadual de Desenvolvimento Cientifco e Tecnológico do Estado do Ceará-FUNDETEC.*

Greenfield, S.M. & J. Gray, 1988. *The Return of Dr. Fritz: Healing by the Spirits in Brazil* Video Documentary Produced at the Educational Communications Department, University of Wisconsin-Milwaukee.

Greenfield, S.M. & R. Prust, in press. Popular Religion, Patronage, and Resource Distribution in Brazil: A Model of an Hypothesis for the Survival of the Economically Marginal. In: M. Estelle Smith (ed.) *Making Out and Making Do: The Informal Economy in Cross-Cultural Perspective*. Washington: University Press of America.

Jorge, M. 1963. *Arigó a Verdade que Abalo a Brazil*. São Paulo: EDICEL.

Kardec, A. n.d *The Spirit's Book*. A. Blackwell (transl.). São Paulo: Livraria Allan Kardec.

———, 1975. *The Medium's Book* A. Blackwell (transl.) São Paulo, Livraria Allan Kardec.

———, 1980. *The Gospel According to Allan Kardec*. Brooklyn: T. Gaus.

Kaufman, R. 1974. The Patron-Client Concept and Macropolitics: Prospects and Problems. *Comparative Studies in Society and History* 16: 284–308.

Laplantine, F. 1974. Therapeutic Mediumnity and Artistic Mediumnity in Contemporary Brazilian Spiritism. Paper presented at the Annual Meetings of the American Anthropological Association, Washington, D.C.

Main, J. 1986. Brazil's Tomorrow. *Fortune*, September 15.

Merrick, T.W. & D. H. Graham, 1979. *Population and Economic Development in Brazil, 1800 to the Present*. Baltimore and London: Johns Hopkins University Press.

Motta, R. & P. Scott, 1983. *Sobrevivéncia e Fontes de Renda: Estratégias das Familias de Baixa Renda no Recife*. Recife: Fundação Josquim Nabuco, Editora Massangana.

New York Times. 1987. Sunday, May 24, p. 11

Nunes Leal, V. 1949. *Coronelismo, Enxada e Voto*. São Paulo, Alfa Omega.

Pang, E.P. 1979. *Coronelismo e Oligarquias, 1889–1934*. Rio de Janeiro: Civilização Brasileira.

Pires, J.H. 1963. *Arigó–Vida, Mediunidade e Martfrio* São Paulo: EDICEL.

Prust, R. 1985. *Brazilian Umbranda: An Urban Resource Distributional System* Unpublished Doctoral Dissertation, University of Wisconsin-Milwaukee.

Puharich, H.K. 1974. Psychic Research as the Healing Process. In: Edgar D. Mitchell (ed.) *Psychic Exploration* New York: G. P. Putnam's Sons.

Renshaw, P. 1969. *A Sociological Analysis of Spiritism in Brazil* Unpublished doctoral dissertation. Gainesville: University of Florida.

Rizzini, P. 1961. *José Arigó, Revolução no Campo de Mediunidade*. São Paulo: Edições Kardequino.

Rocha, Lima, L. n.d *Medicina dos Espíritos*. Rio de Janeiro: Educanário Social Lar Frei Luiz.

Roniger, L. 1981. Clientelism and Patron-Client Relations: A Bibliography. In: S.N. Eisenstadt & R. Lemarchand (eds.) *Political Clientelism, Patronage, and Development*. London: Sage Publications.

Schmidt, S.W. et al. 1976. *Friends, Followers and Factions* Berkeley: University of California Press.

St. Clair, D. 1971. *Drum and Candle* Garden City, N.Y.: Doubleday and Co.

Stepan, N. 1976. *Beginning of Brazilian Science: Oswald Cruz, Medical Research and Policy, 1890–1920*. New York: Science History Publications.

Strickon, A. & S. M. Greenfield, 1972. The Analysis of Patron-Client Systems: An Introduction. In: Arnold Strickon & Sidney M. Greenfield (eds.) *Structure and Process in Latin America*. Albuquerque, N.M.: University of New Mexico Press, pp. 1–17.

Weingrod, A. 1968. Patrons, Patronage and Political Parties. *Comparative Studies in Society and History* 10: 377–400.

Wolf, E. 1966. Friendship and Patron-Client Relations in Complex Societies. In: M. Banton (ed.) *The Social Anthropology of Complex Societies*. London: Tavistock.

Zaluar, A. 1985. *A Máquina e a Revolta: As Organizaçóes Populares e a Significado da Pobreza*. Rio de Janeiro: Editors Brasiliense.

25

How to Stay Well in Tzintzuntzan

George M. Foster

INTRODUCTION

Ethnomedical accounts if the health beliefs and practices of traditional peoples overwhelmingly deal with causation and cure.[1] Remarkably little attention is paid to the preventive practices that are followed, and to the beliefs that provide the rationale for these practices. Yet in many societies—most, or even all, I suspect—people are just as concerned to avoid illness as to cure it, and a substantial part of their health-related behavior falls into the category of preventive medicine. In the following pages I am concerned to describe and analyze the major causality concepts of the ethnomedical system of Tzintzuntzan, Mexico, and to relate these concepts to the forms of behavior believed to minimize the likelihood of illness.

Tzintzuntzan lies on the shores of Lake Pátzcuaro in Michoacán State, about 230 miles

From George M. Foster, " How to Stay Well in Tzintzuntzan." Reprinted with permission from *Social Science and Medicine*, Vol. 19, No. 5, pp. 523–533, 1984, Elsevier Science Ltds., Oxford, England.

west of Mexico City, at an elevation of 7,000 feet.[2] A village of considerable antiquity, at the time of the Spanish Conquest of Mexico it was the capital of the Tarascan Indian Empire. When I began research in Tzintzuntzan in 1945, and for a number of years thereafter, it conformed closely to the models of peasant society that were formulated by anthropologists following World War II. Today, because of rapid change during recent years, the appelation "peasant" no longer fits. Thanks to dollar earnings of migrant laborers in the United States, to a vast expansion of production of traditional arts and crafts, to the development of a class of middlemen engaged in buying, distributing and selling arts and crafts and to the relatively high incomes of a new professional class (especially school teachers). Tzintzuntzan now has one of the highest standards of living of villages its size (2,600 in 1980) in the state of Michoacán. Almost all homes have electricity and running water, more than half have television and propane stoves; a quarter have trucks or cars and some have telephones, flush toilets, automatic hot water and sewer systems.

Despite its relative modernity, Tzintzuntzan's dual Tarascan Indian and Spanish colonial heritage continues strongly to influence customs and beliefs in many aspects of culture, including religion, marriage, the *compadrazgo* complex and health and illness. Thus, the "traditional" ethnomedical system that has flourished for the past four centuries is a folk variant of Graeco-Romano humoral pathology brought to the New World from Spain in the fifteenth and sixteenth centuries, slightly influenced by native American ideas. Latin American humoral pathology, and particularly those aspects that have come to be known as the "hot/cold syndrome," has been more exhaustively described than any other traditional medical system.[3] As is now well known, in much of Latin American foods, beverages, herbs and a number of nonherbal remedies and other items are marked by non-thermal "qualities" of heat or cold that conform to a metaphoric domain first described by Hippocrates and later elaborated upon by Galen. People who subscribe to the tenets of humoral pathology believe that much illness is caused by the effect of metaphoric heat or cold on the body, and that therapies must be based on the "principle of opposites" in which metaphorically cold remedies are used to treat illnesses caused by heat, and vice versa.

Collectively the published accounts of Latin American humoral pathology tell us a great deal about the system, and its local variants. Yet with the exception of that of Orso[4] no single account is comprehensive. Some authors discuss hot and cold largely in terms of dietary beliefs and practices. at the expense of wider health implications.[5] Others, by concentrating on the metaphorical dimensions of hot and cold, fail to give adequate weight to the role of real, sensory thermal heat.[6] And, in stressing the curative aspects of medicine, almost all authors have given the impression that the "principle of opposites" is what is unique about the system. Preventive medicine, however, as was first pointed out by Orso[7] and noted by Logan[8] operates according to very different rules, which Orso has called the "principle of the avoidance of opposites." This principle explains much, but not all preventive behavior in Tzintzuntzan. In order to make comprehensive the full range of behavior that is believed to make it possible "to stay well in Tzintzuntzan," it will be necessary to describe in some detail humoral causality as it is understood today.

HEALTH BEHAVIOR IN TZINTZUNTZAN

Because of effective immunization programs, fairly good environmental sanitation and public and private sector health services, health levels have improved dramatically in Tzintzuntzan in recent years. Physicians, including a native son who practices in the village, are now first choice for almost everyone for illness deemed to be serious. Only one *curandera* remains, a woman approaching 80, and she limits her practice to such "folk" illnesses as *caida de la mollera* (fallen fontanelle), *bilis* (hepatitis?) and *empacho* (obstructed intestinal tract). As knowledgeable old people die off, young people learn less and less of the formal structure of humoral pathology. Nonetheless, an astonishingly high percentage of illness episodes, including most treated by physicians, continue to be explained in terms of hot and cold, and health precautions, knowingly and unknowingly, are based on the dictates of humoral pathology. Herbal teas are widely used as remedies, plasters are stuck to temples for headaches, potters refuse to bathe for 36 hours after firing their kilns, and in many other ways, traditional beliefs and practices flourish. People are continually aware of such threats as cold *aire*, or the heat of the sun following a bath, and they constantly give health advice, solicited and unsolicited: "Don't drink that cold water; you are *fogueado*" (very hot): "Don't take off those heavy boots; your feet haven't yet cooled"; "No, it isn't safe for you to go to the wake; you are menstruating and *el cáncer* [heat exuded by the corpse] will harm you." Even among the young and educated, most steps taken (apart from immunization) in the belief that they will prevent illness more nearly conform to traditional beliefs than to those of modern medicine. (In the following pages the first letter of words used for metaphoric temperature are capitalized; lower case first letters indicate thermal temperature.)

METHODOLOGICAL PROBLEMS

The beliefs and practices that make up a medical system, and particularly one in a state of transition and acculturation to scientific medicine, do not conform to a simple and obvious model, one to which all members of a community subscribe.

Opinions differ as to the metaphoric "qualities" of many foods and herbs and, in fact, the same informant will give contradictory answers on different occasions[9]. A single informant will also give contradictory answers as to what one should, and should not do to remain healthy. For example, sleeping is a heating experience, and a person upon awakening must be careful to avoid cold air and cold beverages for a half hour or so, until the body has cooled. On one occasion a friend's 5-year-old granddaughter was napping in a bedroom off the porch, where we were seated. Upon awakening she emerged from the room, rubbing her sleepy eyes, and reached for a banana lying on a table. Her grandmother was shocked. "The banana is Cold," she told her granddaughter; "don't you know it will make you ill unless you wait for a while?" Twenty years later I asked the same grandmother if Cold foods should be avoided immediately after sleeping. She categorically denied that they represented a danger.

In describing a fiesta, particularly if witnessed on several occasions, an anthropologist can give a fairly accurate account of what has happened, the degree of variation from one year to the next, and the interpretations of the participants. The same is not true in describing a medical system, where only a tiny fraction of illness episodes can be witnessed, and where one is much more dependent on what informants say. Hence, in attempting to formulate the principles which I believe underlie health behavior in Tzintzuntzan, I see the problem as analagous to a jig-saw puzzle. The discrete bits of health behavior I have observed and the answers to questions I have asked, must be examined in relation to all other comparable bits of behavior and answers, to find those that fit together to form small "islands" or clusters of pieces, which in turn are fitted together until the full picture emerges. The process is inductive, and it leads to major generalizations. These generalizations, following structural principles, then suggest additional conformities for which one must search. Sometimes they appear; other times they do not, for no cultural system or subsystem is perfectly symmetrical.

These generalizations, however, lend themselves to an empirical test; they can be "fed back" to informants who accept, partially accept, or reject them. Disagreement calls for additional investigation, until the formulation elicits general compliance. What I am saying is that, while no informant could begin to outline the picture that follows, I believe that most villagers—and particularly the older villagers—would subscribe to the broad outline of what is presented.

BASIC PRINCIPLES OF THE ETHNOMEDICAL SYSTEM OF TZINTZUNTZAN

In broad outline, the system is based on the following beliefs:

1. There are *two* domains of temperature that constantly interact with each other; a *thermal* domain that can be sensed and measured and a *metaphoric* domain characterizing all foods, medicinal herbs and many other substances, to which *calidades* or "qualities" of heat and cold are assigned. The qualities of specific items are determined largely, but not entirely, by their perceived heating or cooling effect on the human body.
2. The healthy body is marked by an evenly distributed thermal warmth that represents an equilibrium between the forces of heat and cold.
3. This equilibrium is upset when the body's temperature is raised by exposure to either thermal or metaphoric heat or to a combination of both.
4. The equilibrium is also upset when the body temperature is lowered by exposure to either thermal or metaphoric cold or to a combination of both.
5. A person subjected to *substantial* heat can expect to fall ill.
6. A person subjected to *moderate* heat will not fall ill, but during the period of above-normal heat he will be significantly at risk from cold, and somewhat at risk from additional heat.
7. A person subjected to *substantial* cold can expect to fall ill.
8. A person subjected to *moderate* cold will not fall ill, but during the period of below-normal heat he will be significantly at risk from heat, and somewhat at risk from additional cold.

In the following pages I will elaborate upon these rules to illustrate the rationale for the actions Tzintzunteños take to stay well.

THE TWO DOMAINS OF TEMPERATURE

Although a number of authors have noted in passing that thermal temperature plays a role in Latin American humoral pathology, none fully explicates this point; all concentrate on metaphoric temperature. In Tzintzuntzan thermal temperature is regarded just as seriously as metaphoric temperature, as a threat to health, and as a force to be manipulated in the treatment of illness. Thermally hot beverages have one effect on the body, and thermally cold beverages another. Exposure to a heated pottery kiln heats the body, as does a hot bath. A cold bath chills the body, as does a cold drink of water or an ice cream cone.

In addition to their thermal temperature, all foods, beverages, herbs, minerals and many other things are marked by a *calidad* or "quality" of Heat or Cold conceptually quite different from thermal temperature. For example, whatever their thermal state at a given moment, beans, garlic and mole sauce are always metaphorically Hot, while papaya, carrots and the meat of spring lambs are always Cold. Although a person may not know the *calidad* of an item, or two people may disagree, no one doubts that (with rare exceptions) it has a metaphoric temperature.

Although the two domains of temperature are conceptually quite distinct, they do not maintain their integrity as they effect the human body; there is a continual interdigitation of the two systems, crossings over from one to the other. Thus, a person who has been thermally heated by exposure to the sun will, if wise, avoid eating metaphorically Very Cold foods until his body regains its normal equilibrium. And a recently-baptized infant, metaphorically Hot from the holy oil, is protected against thermal cold by careful bundling up. Thermal heat can produce metaphoric Heat; maize, usually described as Temperate (neither Hot nor Cold) becomes Hot from toasting and grinding the individual grains to make *pinole*, while sardine-size *charrales*. Cold when taken from the lake, become Hot after sun-drying. Metaphoric Heat can also produce thermal heat, as when a massage with Ben-Gay ointment or alcohol (both Hot) thermally heats the body. Metaphoric Cold also produces thermal chill, as when a body is cooled by the "refreshing" effect of a thermally-hot bath.

Since the two systems so thoroughly intertwine in speech and practice, it is sometimes difficult and occasionally impossible to know whether a speaker refers to thermal or metaphoric temperature. Two types of evidence help clarify meaning: the choice of adjective, verb or noun used to indicate degree of heat or cold; and the form of the verb "to be" that is used, *ser* for permanent, unchanging characteristics and *estar* for temporal, changing states.

Although the basic contrast in both domains of temperature is that between hot and cold, four degrees of intensity, plus a mid-point of temperate (or neutral) are recognized semantically; very hot, hot, temperate, cold and very cold. In describing these points, or degrees of intensity, eight adjectival, three verbal and two nominal forms customarily are used. The adverb *muy* ("very") is often used to express the greatest degree of heat, and only by its use can the greatest degree of cold be expressed. Nominal adjectives many also be used to express great heat, heat and cold.

The adjectives *irritante, muy caliente, cordial, fresco* and *muy fresco*, the verb *irritar* and the nominal adjectives *lo irritante, lo caliente* and *lo fresco* usually but not invariably apply to metaphoric temperature. The adjectives *cálido* and *frío* and the nouns *calor* and *el frio* most frequently are used in a thermal sense, as is the adjective *tibio*, largely limited to qualifying water temperature. To emphasize extreme metaphoric cold, *frio*, and especially *muy frio* are used more often than *muy fresco*. The adjectives *caliente* and *templado* and the verbs *calentar* and *enfriar* apply equally to both domains. Except for *irritante* and *irritar* ("irritating," "to irritate"), *cordial ("cordial"), fresco ("fresh," "cool")* and cálido *("hot"), all words are used in the standard Spanish sense.*

"Temperate" is an anomalous concept, a residual category used to cover the ambiguous area between Hot and Cold. Of a sample of 6,000 answers from 31 people to the question, "What is the *calidad* of———?", only 0.033 ($n = 201$) are Temperate. Nine informants never used the Temperate category, and for others who did, the true answer obviously was "I don't know." No item was classified as Temperate by a majority of informants. Temperate answers were given most frequently for a handful of staple items about which there is little consensus as to quality: maize, tortillas, bread, beef, hen and the *perón* chile. The words *templado* and *cordial* are used especially to classify prepared foods and herbal remedies that combine Hot and Cold items. Bread, for example, is Temperate for many people because wheat flour (generally considered to be Hot) is neutralized by Cold yeast.

With a high degree of frequency—perhaps 90% of the time—metaphoric *calidades*, which do not fluctuate, are indicated by the *ser* form of "to be," while thermal temperatures, which fluctuate, are indicated by the *estar* form.[10] Thus, when speaking of *calidad* one says *El café ES caliente* ("Coffee is Hot"), while when speaking of temperature one says *La tasa de café ESTÁ fría* ("The cup of coffee is cold"). Again, *Los frijoles SON calientes* ("Beans are Hot") vs *Estos frijoles ESTÁN fríos* ("These beans are cold"). Often I have recorded both usages in the same sentence: e.g. *Por su calidad las habas SON muy fríos, aunque ESTÉN calientes* ("For their 'quality,' broad beans are Very Cold, even though they may be hot"). And as for ice, "In reality [i.e. thermally] it is cold, but for its effects, it is Hot."

BODY ORGANS AND THEIR FUNCTIONS

To understand the rules for staying well in Tzintzuntzan, it is essential to know beliefs pertaining to the principal body organs, their functions and the ways in which they are affected by heat and cold. Knowledge about the inner organs is based on a variety of sources, including oral transmission of colonial beliefs for one generation to the next, observation of the entrails of slaughtered animals, witnessing surgical operations such as appendectomies, looking at X-rays and consulting physicians. In spite of, or perhaps because of, these varied sources, many ideas about the working of the human body belong in the realm of folklore rather than human anatomy.

From the throat, say informants, the *tongollo* (esophagus) descends to the *boca del estómago* (pit of the stomach), to which it is attached. Adjoining the *tongollo* to the right is the *hígado* (liver), in which nestles *la pajarilla* (pancreas). Some, but not all, informants say that the *vesícula* (gall bladder) is also attached to the liver. Just behind this complex lie the *pulmones* (lungs). On the left side, symmetrically balanced with the liver, is the *corazón* (heart), and below it, at the point the elbow touches the side, the *bazo* (spleen). Some informants say that beneath the spleen lies the *bejiga* (bladder). Other informants believe that *bazo* and *bejiga* are words for the same organ, the former used for humans, the latter for animals. The stomach is described as an oval, horizontally-placed, container somewhat above the navel. Some informants say it has two outlets; the *tripas* (large intestines), through which solid wastes pass, and a duct leading to the *bazo,* into which all liquids flow, prior to urination. Other informants insist that all liquids flow directly into the *bazo,* entirely bypassing the stomach.

The critical organs, in the sense of being intimately related to health, and most affected by thermal and metaphorical temperature, are the stomach, the spleen and the liver—gall bladder complex. All food passes to the stomach, where it is "cooked," the term used to describe digestion. Opinions differ as to the source of heat in the stomach. Some say that it comes from *la sustancia*, the "substance" of the food itself. Others say that bile (*hiel*) forms in the gall bladder or the liver and, under normal conditions, falls drop by drop into the stomach where, because of its great Heat, it "cooks" the food. In a healthy body food solids give up their *nutrimento* or *sustancia*, their nourishing qualities, while "cooking" in the stomach, and then pass into *las tripas*, where the last bit of nourishment is extracted, leaving—as one informant put it—*bagazo* or "pressed pulp," i.e. excrement. The digestive process for liquids is given little thought. Soup and broth are recognized as having nourishing qualities, and many people say they pass through the stomach on their way to the *bazo*. Others say nourishment is extracted directly in the *bazo*.

The function of the womb (*matriz*) is known, but only recently have people heard of ovaries, about which most know nothing. Traditional anatomical beliefs have no explanation for the functions of the heart, although today one hears that "it makes the blood work," i.e. circulate. As for the kidneys, all of the "suffering" from hard work collects there, making them vulnerable to attacks of pain-causing cold. *Me duelen los riñones* ("My kidneys hurt") is the customary way to say one has lower back pains. The lungs, visualized as lying under the shoulder blades, and exposed to cold through the upper back, help produce a nursing mother's milk, and give strength to men.

The stomach, gall bladder–liver complex, and

the spleen are delicately balanced organs, easily upset, and much illness is explained in terms of excess heat in the stomach and excess cold in the spleen. When a person experiences an emotional shock such as fright, anger or envy, *se derrame la hiel*, i.e. there is a great overflow of Hot bile from the gall bladder–liver which floods the stomach with Heat, producing that most common of Mexican folk illnesses, *bilis*, as well as Hot diarrhea. In contrast, *bazo resfriado* (chilled spleen) results from drinking too much cold water, or eating ice cream or popsicles when the body is heated. The result is *cólico* (stomach ache) and Cold diarrhea.

THE HEALTHY BODY

The healthy body thermally is slightly warm, heated by its blood. Although all living human bodies are warm, their individual "normal" temperatures are not identical. Men are believed to have more heat than women, and the young more than the elderly. Newborn infants are the hottest of all. Women with many children have lost a little heat with each birth, so that by the menopause their bodies are colder than those of their age-mates who have had few or no children. In spite of these age and sex differences, the metaphoric and thermal hot–cold forces that govern health and illness work in the same way for everyone: it is simply that the base-lines vary. Hence, everyone has what may be considered an ideal body temperature, a personal hot–cold equilibrium representing optimum health and minimal exposure to illness threats.

Opinions differ as to whether the heat of blood is thermal or metaphoric. About half of the people to whom I put the question say that it has a *calidad* (i.e. its heat is metaphoric), while the others, including my most knowledgeable informants, say that it does not have a *calidad* (hence, its heat is thermal). Whatever their view on blood, informants agree that body temperatures are thermal. *Calidades*, it will be recalled, are constant; rarely they may be changed, but they do not fluctuate. In contrast, body temperatures fluctuate almost constantly, in response to various heating and cooling experiences. Body temperatures are also judged to be thermal on a second count. Animals, like humans, have thermal heat. The flesh of all those eaten also has a *calidad* of Hot, Temperate, or Cold, as the

case may be. The ethnologist finds out by asking, "What is the *calidad* of turkey?" (or hen or lamb or pork). The answer is based on how the informant believes the meat affects the human body. But, since human flesh is not eaten, it can have no effect on the body, hence, it can have no *calidad*. The question, "What is the *calidad* of the human body?" strikes informants as ridiculous.

THE EFFECTS OF HEAT AND COLD ON THE BODY

Paradoxically, the "normal" hot/cold equilibrium of a human body rarely prevails; almost continually it is subjected to heating and cooling experiences that upset this equilibrium, thereby causing one of two things to happen:

1. a *substantial* heating or cooling experience leads directly to illness;
2. a *lesser* heating or cooling experience raises or lowers the normal body temperature but does not cause illness.

How does one distinguish between a substantial and lesser heating or cooling experience? Obviously, if when the body is at equilibrium illness follows a known heating or cooling experience, that experience was substantial; if illness does not ensue, just as obviously it was lesser. The principal hot causes of illness to a person at equilibrium are internal metaphoric, especially Very Hot foods, including alcohol (which cause Hot diarrhea), and Hot bile (which leads to *bilks*) produced by such strong emotions as anger, fright and envy. In lesser degree exterior thermal heat is believed to cause illness; smallpox (the last case occurred more than 60 years ago) was blamed on playing in the sun, and sunstroke today is attributed to prolonged exposure to the sun.

Cold leading directly to illness is also both metaphoric and thermal. The principal metaphoric form is Very Cold food (which causes stomachache) while, oddly, the principal thermal form works by producing heat. Thermal cold from a tile floor enters bare feet and, like a heat piston, compresses the normal body heat upward, causing *calor subido* ("risen heat"), which leads to inflamed tonsils, sore throat, abscessed teeth, pneumonia and other ailments of the head and upper torso. Treatment for hot/cold induced illnesses conforms to the "principle of opposites"; metaphoric and/or thermal heat for an illness stemming from cold and cold for an illness caused by heat.

A substantial heating or cooling experience obviously is cause for alarm. Lesser experiences, which raise or lower body temperatures, while no cause for alarm, do require precautions as long as the body is out of equilibrium. These precautions are the heart of preventive medicine in Tzintzuntzan. Almost always lesser temperature fluctuations are temporary, self-correcting episodes that require no treatment; after an interval of from a few minutes to a day or so, the body regains its equilibrium without harm. But during these periods of imbalance the body is "at risk," vulnerable in greater degree than when at equilibrium, to further loads of illness-causing heat and/or cold.

TEMPERATURE DIFFERENTIAL

In other words, heat and cold insults, unless substantial, are most apt to cause illness when a person has already lost his normal hot/cold equilibrium, when his body temperature is already above or below normal. At first thought it seems odd that a body in an above-normal heat state, while threatened primarily by cold, in lesser degree is also threatened by more heat. Similarly, a body at below normal equilibrium, while threatened primarily by heat, in lesser degree is also threatened by more cold. The answer to this apparent paradox lies in the concept of "temperature differential." The body, as we have just seen, can absorb modest heat and cold insults without harm; what it cannot absorb are *major* heat and cold insults that create a substantial temperature deviation from equilibrium, or from the prevailing "at risk" temperature levels. A differential of threatening magnitude can occur in either of two ways:

1. with the body in equilibrium either a single massive heat or cold insult, or smaller incremental insults that build up to the critical point, create the differential;
2. with the body at either above-normal or below-normal "at risk" points, modest insults of cold for the former or heat for the latter, that would

not threaten a body in equilibrium, produce the critical differential.

To illustrate, a man who fires his kiln becomes moderately hot from proximity to the fire. A man with a hangover is also moderately hot, from the effects of the Hot alcohol. Both conditions place a person at risk from additional heat but do not themselves lead to illness. If, however, a man with a hangover fires his kiln, he thereby exposes himself to *two* moderately heating experiences which, taken together, add up to a major heat exposure. *Tapiado de los orines* (inability to urinate) is the price he pays for his indiscretion. Similarly, when a person is *fogueado* (i.e. moderately hot and sweaty from working in the sun) he is likely to suffer diarrhea if he eats Very Hot food such as *mole*. Neither moderate exposure to the sun, nor eating *mole* in moderation, harms a person who starts out at equilibrium. It is the cumulative effect of two moderately heating experiences in sequence that produces a very hot bodily state that induces diarrhea.

Two moderately cooling experiences work in the same way. If a menstruating woman, whose body temperature is believed to be below-normal from loss of blood, drinks cold water or eats Cold food, she is apt to suffer menstrual cramps known as *dolor de ijada*. The combined cooling effects of blood loss and cold water or Cold food, none of which threatens a person at equilibrium, produce the critical temperature differential that leads to pain.

An equally threatening temperature differential can also be obtained by swinging from a hot "at risk" point to a cold "at risk" point. To return to the man with a hangover, not only is he vulnerable to more heat, but also to cold; he must not bathe because of the cooling effect of the water, an effect which, were his body at equilibrium would not harm him. Yet because the temperature differential between hot and cold "at risk" points is equivalent to that between equilibrium and a very cold point, he is likely to come down with a bad cold or pneumonia. Similarly, a person moderately cold in body from bathing is threatened by exposure to the sun or a kiln. A moderately cooling plus a moderately heating experience, neither of which alone is a threat, add up to a major temperature differential that is apt to cause skin eruptions.

AIRE AND FRÍO

Before discussing in greater detail the sources of heat and cold that cause illness, or put a body at risk, it is necessary to clarify the meaning of two words that occur continually in discussions of health and illness: *el aire* ("the air") and *el frío* ("the cold"). The terms are related, but not identical, *El frío* is a thermal characteristic of a number of substances and places: cold water (which is metaphorically Hot); a tile or cement floor, especially if freshly laid or recently mopped, and hence still damp; the ground beneath a shady tree, which is thought to be humid; damp shoes or shoes unworn for some time; *el sereno,* believed to be the dew falling from the sky; and *aire. El frío* is present both outdoors and indoors; in contrast, *aire* usually is found only outdoors. Sometimes it can be felt, as a breeze; at other times, especially at night, when it carries a greater cold load than during the day, it cannot be felt, but it is known to be there. *El frío* is thus a more comprehensive, pervasive concept than *el aire.*

As a health threat, *aire* and *frío* differ largely as to how and where, they strike. *Aire* radiates, while *frío* enters the body through direct contact. *Aire* always, and *frío* never, strikes the head, causing such things as *punzadas* (shooting pains in the eyes), earache and headache. Some toothaches are caused by the entry of *aire* into the mouth; this is one reason people are careful to cover their mouths and noses with rebozos or serapes at night and in the early morning. *Aire* strikes the lungs through the shoulder blades, causing pneumonia, and it may strike the bare stomach of a recent diner, causing a stroke, if he is so incautious as to change his clothing or lower his trousers to defecate. In all these cases it is cold that causes the damage, but *aire* is the vehicle of the cold.

On all other parts of the body *frío* strikes directly, in the form of cold water on the skin, as ice water to be drunk, as ice cream to be eaten, or from stepping on a tile or cement floor in bare feet. For aches and pains in the limbs and trunk, one says "it's from cold." But for most pains in the lungs and head, the culprit is *aire.*

El frío, as just pointed out, is a thermal characteristic; hence, it can have no *calidad.* Opinions differ as to whether *aire* has a *calidad,* but most informants after pondering the direct question,

decide that it does not. The fact that they must think before replying is further evidence to this effect.

SOURCES OF HEAT

With the general principles thought to govern health and illness in Tzintzuntzan in mind, we now turn to the specific sources of heat and cold that cause illness or put the body at risk. It would gratify the ethnologist's sense of structural symmetry to be able to divide heating and cooling experiences into distinct categories corresponding, say, to the two domains of temperature, or to those directly causing illness versus those that put the body at risk. Unfortunately, the picture is not that neat; the two domains almost continually intertwine, and many sources of heat and cold may cause illness or, in lesser strength, simply put a body at risk, I have therefore found it most convenient to describe in turn all heating and cooling experiences, indicating with each whether they are thermal, metaphoric or mixed in nature, and whether they cause illness or merely place a body at risk. For expository purposes I classify both heating and cooling experiences as internally generated, externally generated, and as due to exposure to metaphoric temperature.

Internally-Generated Heat

The most common internal bodily processes believed to heat the body are eating, sleeping, exercise and work, "heat buildup," emotional experiences, illness and pregnancy.

Eating. As earlier pointed out, opinions differ as to whether the heat of digestion comes from the Hot bile that falls, a drop at a time, into the stomach, or from the "substance" of the food itself. Whatever their views about causality, everyone agrees that eating heats the stomach, and to a lesser degree the entire body, causing it to *trasudar,* to perspire lightly, placing it at risk for an hour or so from both heat and cold. Metaphorically Hot foods, such as honey, chocolate or pork and thermally hot foods, such as soup, may contribute to, but are not essential to, the heating effects of eating. The cold threats are water, principally bathing and swimming and *aire,* especially if it strikes the hot stomach. Recent diners also avoid additional heat by not engaging in physical exercise, including the use of the eyes for close work. They justify the latter by quoting the aphorism, *Despues decomer, ni un sobre escrito leer* ("After eating, don't even read the address on an envelope"). The act of eating places a body at risk, but does not in itself cause illness.

Sleeping.   The heat from sleeping appears to be purely thermal, from blankets, and from the warm bodies of others who may share the bed. A sleeping person, although warmer than usual, is at risk only upon arising and going outside where *aire* may lurk. When possible, upon awakening people linger in their rooms a short time to avoid this danger. Recent sleepers do not bathe or wash their faces, drink cold water or eat cold foods such as ice cream. In the recent past Cold foods such as fruit were seen as a danger by some people, but this stricture no longer carries much weight. As with eating, the heat from sleeping does not directly cause illness; unlike eating, it imposes no restriction on exercise.

Exercise.   Physical exertion, including normal work and *agitándose*, i.e. scurrying around and "working up a sweat," heat the entire body. Hands are heated by such activities as writing, sewing and milking cows, while eyes are heated by any kind of close work, including reading, writing, embroidering and watching TV. Feet are heated by walking, particularly in heavy shoes. People hot from exercise should neither bathe nor ingest cold things such as water or ice cream. Since most close use of the eyes occurs indoors, people who have been reading or watching TV like to wait a few minutes before exposing themselves to outside *aire*, while men whose feet are hot from walking wait until they cool before removing their shoes, thus avoiding exposing their feet to the dangers of a cold floor or to cold shoes. People with heated hands wait to wash until they have cooled off.

The heating effect of exercise belongs to the thermal domain and, as with eating and sleeping, it puts a body at risk but does not directly cause illness.

Heat Buildup.   The exertion of work, exposure to the sun, hot kilns and cooking fires and the ingestion of Very Hot foods—the everyday experiences that cannot be avoided—gradually raise body temperature levels, thus placing a person at

increasing risk from cold threats. Regular bathing, which cools the body, whatever the thermal temperature of the water, keeps this heat load from rising to the danger point. Bathing, therefore, is looked upon as preventive medicine, not because of cleanliness but because it keeps body temperatures within safe limits. As prevention, bathing should be done before body temperatures reach the point where the cooling effect of water might cause harm.

Emotional Experiences.   Strong emotional experiences such as *córaje* (anger), *susto* (fright) and *envidia* (envy) are thought to heat the body by producing an overflow of Hot bile from the liver–gall bladder into the stomach and blood. Following such an experience blood is often said to be "irritated." Moderate degrees of anger and fright place the body at risk from cold, in the form of bathing and drinking cold water, and from additional heat from Very Hot food, including alcohol. Extreme anger and fright lead directly to that well-known Mexican folk illness, *bilis*, whose symptoms suggest hepatitis.

The heat of envy works in a different fashion, in that the object of envy, and not the envier, is threatened by it. Some people who admire a child, particularly if they *acariciar* it (caress it, pinch its cheeks fondly), radiate the heat of their envy, in the form of *mal de ojo*, the evil eye. Unless they symbolically disavow their envy by slapping the child on the cheeks, it is believed the child will fall ill.

Illness.   All illness raises body temperatures above normal. Consequently, a sick person is at further risk primarily in the sense that violating the rules pertaining to a healthy body at an above-normal temperature will aggravate the illness. Most illness proscriptions are to protect the sufferer from thermal and metaphoric cold: Don't bathe, don't get wet, stay away from cold, humid places, don't drink cold water or eat ice cream, don't risk *aire* by changing clothes, don't sew (a steel needle is Cold) and avoid Very Cold foods. Thermal heat appears to be no threat to a sick person, but Very Hot food, especially chile peppers, are prohibited. So strict is the usual rule against bathing that the traditional way a patient has assured friends that he is fully recovered is to say, *Ya me bañé* ("I have bathed"). (For exceptions to the no-bathing rule, see "Pregnancy" following).

Parts of the body may also be heated by injury and illness. Broken bones and strains and sprains must be protected against cold. Strains and sprains are bandaged, not primarily for support, but to keep out *aire*. If broken bones cool, knitting is believed long delayed. Hence, in addition to splints a broken bone is bound up in a Hot poultice of such things as turpentine, cloves, pepper and rosemary to keep out the cold and to keep the break warm, so that it will heal quickly. In contrast to these, heat, and not cold, threatens *llagas* (infected sores and skin ulcers) which are locally hot. If exposed to the sun or to the heat of *el cáncer* (see below) they are further irritated.

Pregnancy.   A pregnant woman's temperature rises above normal, due to retention of hot blood normally lost during her menses, and from the Hot foetus which owes its *calidad* to the father's Hot semen. Oddly, and unlike other hot bodily states, cold is not a threat to a pregnant woman. Heat is, however, and to keep her temperature within safe limits she bathes frequently and avoids additional increments of heat by not sleeping too much, nor getting too close to a hot kiln. A pregnant women also stays away from a wake, for fear of the heat of *el cáncer*, exuded by the corpse (see below), which will cause fever sores and an irritated vagina. Formerly, at least, pregnant women bound a small piece of steel (Cold)—often a key or safety pin—in their abdominal sash to protect against the heat of an eclipse, which otherwise might "eat" the foetus, causing it to be born with a harelip.

Although avoidance of bathing when the body is in an above normal state of heat is a fundamental rule of preventive medicine, there are exceptions in addition to pregnancy care. Patients with high fevers are bathed, as are sufferers from *bilis*, a condition described as "terrific heat." Patients taking such Very Hot herbal remedies as *cauchalalate* bark, *espinosilla* and *prodijiosa*, as well as those receiving hypodermic injections, thought to be Very Hot, also regularly bathe. The apparent anomaly of prescribed bathing when the body is above normal in heat is resolved when we remember that illness is treated by the "principle of opposites," and when we examine the meaning of the word "bathe." In a generic sense "to bathe" means to apply water to all or a major part of the body. For a healthy person a bath means washing the body from head to toe, either in a shower, or standing in a basin and pouring water on the head from a dipper. For a person with fever, however, water is *never* applied above the neck. In discussing fever treatments informants usually say, *hay que bañarse* ("one must bathe"), failing to distinguish between a general bath and a therapeutic bath. When pressed to describe a fever bath they use the term *asientos y baños*. The patient sits (*asentarse* = to sit) in a shallow basin of warm water, his feet in a second basin of hot water. Lukewarm water is then poured over his stomach and low back. Cold herbs sometimes are added to the warm water, to augument the refreshing effect of the metaphorically Cold water.

Pregnancy is anomalous in that, like eating and sleeping it is, for adult women, a normal experience that results in above-normal body temperatures. But, unlike eating and sleeping, pregnancy is classed as *una enfermedad*, an illness. This is convenient, for it provides an "out," an acceptable rationalization for bathing. One may go for 2 or 3 weeks, or even a month without bathing, but 9 months is too long. By invoking the rule of the "principle of opposites" to permit bathing of the "ill" pregnant woman, the dilemma is resolved.

Externally-Generated Heat

This heat is thermal, not metaphoric. Heat radiated by the sun, a hot kiln, a truck engine or a cooking fire raises body temperatures, but with one exception (*fogueado*) does not cause illness. Illness may directly result from other forms of external heat assaulting the body: *el cáncer*, an eclipse, *humores* and *vapores*.

Exposure to the radiant heat of the sun, a hot kiln and the like places a person at risk from *aire* or *frío* in any of their usual forms, such as bathing, drinking cold water, eating ice cream or going into a cold room with a freshly-mopped and hence humid floor. A person thermally heated is also at risk from metaphoric heat and cold: Very Hot food, including alcohol, is believed to cause typhoid fever, while *pulque* (Very Cold) may lead to pneumonia. *Fogueado* is the term generally used to refer to this thermal overload, although it must be noted that a person can *foguearse* metaphorically from ingesting alcohol and other Very Hot foods, from hypodermic injections (Hot) and from commercial oral medicines (most of which are deemed Hot).

Although a *foguenado* person usually is only at risk, in extreme cases the condition is viewed as so threatening that it must be treated as an illness, requiring a stomach poultice of Cold substances such as lard, ashes, bicarbonate of soda, and the herb *tepuza* and/or an enema of cold water in which Cold herbs have been steeped. Both treatments, which conform to the "principle of opposites," are believed to draw out the heat, which is thought to have concentrated in the stomach.

El Cáncer.   A corpse is considered to be very dangerous because of the heat it exudes. This heat, called *el cáncer* (which is unrelated to tumors), is described by many informants as the normal body heat of a living person that is now *despidiéndose*, i.e. saying goodbye, to the body that has sheltered it. To protect those who come to a wake a chilacayote squash (Very Cold) is opened and placed under the bier to draw the contagion of the heat, and to protect the mourners. *El cáncer* does not place a person at risk by raising body temperatures; it directly attacks. Healthy people are not in great danger; at most they feel a burning sensation around the mouth. But people who have, or who recently have had, blood on the surface of their bodies, are in great danger of irritation and infection of the places where blood emerges: menstruating women, people recently operated upon, a person with a surface ulcer or recent nosebleed or a new mother. Some informants say that pregnant women, especially in the last months, are in danger from *el cáncer*. Bathing also places a person at risk, since cooling the body in this fashion opens the pores, making the individual susceptible to the heat and contagion of *el cáncer*. So strong is the belief about bathing and death that traditionally people have not bathed during the last 3 days of Easter Week, when the *Santo Entierro*, the larger-than-lifesize image of Christ crucified, lies on an open bier in church, threatening worshipers with its *cáncer*.

Most informants say that *el cáncer*, while very hot, does not have a *calidad*. The fact that it radiats, rather than touches its victims, suggests thermal heat as well. Use of the metaphorically Cold chilacayote to counteract *el cáncer*'s thermal heat nicely illustrates the way the two domains may interact.

Humores and Vapores.   Humors are described as body heat that builds up as a person goes longer and longer without bathing. A man who visits a prostitute also may exude humors. Not surprisingly, in view of long stretches between baths, humors are also described as body odors, an explanation that semantically confuses *olor* ("odor") with *humor*. By some *humor* is also confused with *calor* (heat) as, for example, when barley water (Cold) baths were used to "lower the heat or humor of the body" of smallpox sufferers.[11]

Vapores (vapors) are analagous to humors in that they represent natural but pestiferous heat leaving a body, in this case that of mother nature. By the end of the dry season the earth has become very hot from the heat of the sun. With the first rains this heat begins to be released, continuing until the earth is completely cold. One informant described vapors as *el calor encerrado que está debajo de la tierra* ("enclosed" or "cooped up" heat beneath the earth), a perfect analogy to *calor encerrado* that may accumulate in the human body. A person exposed to the steaming effects of rain on parched earth risks fever, asthma, pneumonia and similar ailments. *Humores* and *vapores*, like *el cáncer*, do not put a person at risk by raising body temperature; they directly cause illness. Most informants say that, while hot, they have no *calidad*.

Exposure to Metaphoric Heat

Metaphoric heat affects the body only by direct contact, of which the following are the most common forms:

Ingestion of Very Hot Food and Drink. *Comida irritante*, such as chocolate, peanuts, honey, wheat tortillas and hard liquor is likely, when consumed in moderate quantities, to *foguear el estómago*, i.e. heat the stomach until the diner is at risk from both heat and cold and even, in case of a very great heat overload, directly to cause illness. The cold threats are *aire* striking the stomach, bathing, cold (especially iced) drinks, and very Cold foods such as watermelon or pineapple. A person *fogueado* by Hot food or drink is also threatened by additional heat, either more Hot food, or; the heat of the sun or a kiln. Specific rules specify the dangerous combinations of Very Hot foods. Among those most commonly cited are chile peppers or chocolate with honey and chocolate or pork with avocados.

Medicines. Most physician's prescriptions, both oral and injected, and most over-the-counter drugs, such as aspirin, are thought to be Hot; they put the body at risk both from cold and additional heat. For example, hard liquor (Very Hot) is avoided when one is taking medicine. So rigorous and widely understood is this proscription that the standard way of refusing a drink without insult is to say "I am taking medicine."

External Contact with Metaphorically Hot Substances. A Woman who massages another person with Hot substances such as alcohol, Ben-Gay ointment or the herbs *altamisa* or *chicalote*, must not wash her hands for some hours. The person massaged must also avoid exposure to cold, particularly bathing, for 24 hours or more. People who make bees wax candles, or weave wheat straw figurines, likewise cannot wash, since both substances are Very Hot.

Smoking. Tobacco is Hot. Opinions differ as to whether cigarette smoke therefore has the same *calidad*, but everyone agrees that it heats the bronchial tubes and lungs, putting a smoker at risk from *aire*, cold water or ice cream. Asthma, a cough or bronchial congestion known as *pecho pasmado* may result from exposure to these risks. If a person smoking must go out into the night air, it is deemed best to continue to smoke rather than to stop. The heat, although dangerous, protects against the even worse danger of cold *aire*.

THE SOURCES OF COLD

The experiences that cool a body, far fewer than those that heat it, can be grouped into the same three categories:

Internal Processes

Since a good supply of blood is believed to maintain body warmth, quite logically loss of blood during menstruation and childbirth and from accidents, disease and surgery, is assumed to cool the body. Loss of blood puts a person at risk for a number of threats but it does not *per se* cause illness, short of bleeding to death. A menstruating woman does not bathe during her period lest the additional chill cause *frío en la matriz*, a cold womb, generally thought to be the reason a woman does not conceive. The only heat that threatens menstruating women is that of *el cáncer* and, as we have seen, they avoid going to wakes.

Informants describe childbirth both as a cooling and a heating experience: cooling from loss of blood and heating "from the perspiring of labor." Since all of the care of a post-parturient is heating, it is clear that cold is seen as the greater threat. New mothers are well bundled up, and they do not bathe—formerly at least for a week, today for 2 or 3 days. Nor do they eat Very Cold foods such as pineapple, uncondimented turkey and most fish. Prescribed foods are Hot (but not Very Hot) such as hen's broth, chocolate tempered with Cold milk and sugarcane water. Very Hot foods including peanuts, avocados and wheat tortillas are proscribed, not because they might harm the mother, but because they heat her milk to the point where it gives her nursing infant *chincual* (diaper rash).

External Assaults

All bathing, whether in cold water (metaphorically Hot) or in hot water (metaphorically Cold) "refreshes" the body, placing it at risk from heat, especially the sun. Almost all "breaking out" illnesses, whether on the skin or in the mouth and throat, such as hives, warts, erysipelas, sties, fever sores and tonsillitis, are attributed to exposure to the sun after bathing. The interplay of metaphoric and thermal temperature is particularly well illustrated by bathing in hot water. Bathing in hot water thermally heats the body, and for half an hour or so, a bather is at risk from *aire*. I once had a cold explained as due to my carelessness in emerging from a hot shower and failing, while en route to my room, to wrap my head in the towel. I had been struck by *un aire*. Yet the same bath cools for several hours. Presumably had I, an hour later, gone out into the hot sun I would have fallen victim to a skin eruption.

To be soaked by rain, or simply to be outside lightly clad on an overcast, raw day, will also cool the body, putting a person at risk from heat insults. Other forms of cold, while most threatening to a person in an above-normal temperature state, may also directly cause illness even if a body is at equilibrium. *Aire* strikes the head, causing *punzadas*—

throbbing pains in the ears, eyes and even teeth—and it directly invades the ears, nostrils and mouth, to cause other inner pains. Cold enters the lower part of the body when a person gets his feet wet or steps barefoot on a cold floor, to cause *calor subido*.

Excessive quantities of Very Cold food, such as pineapple, watermelon and peas, are believed to cause stomachache and sometimes diarrhea. An excess of thermally cold foods, such as iced drinks and ice cream, and simply foods at room temperature, which have cooled after cooking, are also considered dangerous. The major part of *every* meal must be not only cooked, but hot, and left-overs from earlier meals, including meat dishes, vegetables and tortillas, are always reheated prior to serving.[12] With both metaphorically and thermally cold foods it is feared that the natural heat of the stomach will be insufficient to "cook" what has been eaten. Diners who fear they have been indiscrete in eating Cold or unwarmed food may drink teas of Hot herbs to boost the heat of the stomach, thereby aiding digestion.

El sereno (dew) is thought to be one of the most deadly forms of cold. It is assumed to fall from the sky, even though it cannot be seen until it appears on vegetation. People who must sleep outside are careful to shield their eyes, lest the cold cause cataracts or blindness. Opinions differ as to whether the cold of *el sereno* is thermal or metaphoric.

Contact with Metaphorically Cold Substances

Metaphorically cold substances tend not so much to place the body at risk as to lead directly to illness particularly, as just pointed out, from consumption of Very Cold food. In one situation, Cold threatens a body already cool: menstruating and post-partum women do not sew, since the steel needle (Cold) is believed to produce hand cramps. *Greta* (lead glaze) is Very Cold; grinding it on a metate chills a woman's hands and body, and the fine dust invades her lungs, cooling her milk if she is nursing. But the nursing child, and not the mother, is at risk. Before picking up the infant the potter mother should scrub her hands carefully and rub them with alcohol so her touch will not chill the baby's body. Nursing potter mothers formerly drank chocolate mixed with rue (both Very Hot) to warm their milk.

Failure to do so was believed to cause *alferecía*, epilepsy-like attacks that struck nursing children. Since today glaze is purchased already ground, and mothers are spared several hours of close contact with the dust, *alferecía* is said to be rare.

CONCLUSIONS

We now return to the title of this paper, "How to stay well in Tzintzuntzan." The basic rule is for the individual to be aware of his temperature level at all times, and to be alert to the heat and cold threats known to lie in wait for him. These rules can be summarized as follows:

1. When one's body is at equilibrium, avoid excessive doses of thermal and/or metaphoric heat and cold, but don't be preoccupied by moderate heating and cooling experiences.
2. When one's body is at above-normal temperature, avoid
   (a) Heat insults that will make the body even hotter.
   (b) Cold insults of sufficient magnitude to create an illness-provoking temperature differential.
3. When one's body is at below-normal temperature, avoid
   (a) Cold insults that will make the body even colder.
   (b) Hot insults of sufficient magnitude to create an illness-provoking temperature differential.

Not all rules for healthful living relate to hot and cold. Some foods, for example, are classed as *pesada* ("heavy"). These include most meat, milk, eggs, rice and potatoes. *Comida pesada* is a good, nourishing food, proper for the midday meal when people are working hard, but dangerous in the morning or evening. People interested in their health remember this, as well as the aphorism, *Almuerza mucho, come más, cena poca, y vivirás* ("Breakfast well, dine more so, sup lightly, and you will live [a long time]").

In Tzintzuntzan, health and illness beliefs and practices are not a consistent response to a finely-honed humoral theory. Rather, they have accrued over generations. Most, I think, are European in origin but some clearly are native American. Often the latter have been reinterpreted within the hot–cold framework. In native American belief *susto* (fright) causes illness because of soul loss; in Tzintzuntzan *susto* causes illness because of the Hot bile it produces. Native American belief attributes an eclipse to a fight between heavenly bodies, the sun and moon or a bear that tries to eat the sun. The sun–moon fight explanation is known to elderly Tzintzuntzeños, but the danger of the eclipse is now explained in terms of celestial anger which, like earthly anger, is a heating experience.

Over the years, I have violated practically all of the rules here described. I have showered on a full stomach, wandered over my tile floor in bare feet, simultaneously drunk milk (Cold) and eaten avocado (Very Hot) and risked my eyes, Hot from reading, by going into the night air. Harm rarely has come to me. Although I doubt that the rules really have much to do with health, I see much of psychological value in the system. First and foremost, people have—or believe they have—a *degree of control* over their health, and *an understanding of what is going on*, that far exceeds that of those of use who subscribe to the tenants of scientific medicine. Theoretically, at least, by rigorously following all of the rules believed to prevent illness, a person can stay well indefinitely. That one cannot always do so is because of human fallibility; with the best intentions in the world, one slips or becomes careless. Not for nothing is the "cause" of an illness the patient himself, who has brought his conditions upon himself by failing to follow known rules.

Humoral theory likewise provides an explanation for what has happened, as well as a rationale for what must be done. It is a marvelously flexible instrument that can be manipulated to give almost any desired result. In contrast to many traditional medical systems, in which divination of cause is the primary role of the curer, in Tzintzuntzan illness customarily is self-diagnosed. When illness strikes, the sick person, usually added by family members, thinks back to recent events: bathing, exposure to sun or kiln, sleeping behavior and foods eaten. When an episode that the system says can lead to illness is hit upon, that diagnoses the problem, simultaneously indicating therapy. Diarrhea?

If upon searching the past it develops that the patient was so injudicious as to eat honey with chile peppers or chocolate with avocado (all Very Hot), the triggering event is evident. But then, perhaps it was milk (Cold) with avocado. Milk, oddly, not only can be mixed with chocolate, but it is prescribed to temper the extreme Heat of chocolate to make it safe for those who otherwise could not support it. The point is not that the system is perfectly consistent, but that it *always* provides an explanation, that is deemed acceptable.

When asked why they have given particular answers to health questions informants with great frequency cite specific cases. Almost all nonviolent deaths are diagnosed by the community at large, and are cited on innumerable occasions as justification for why certain forms of behavior are threats to health. Why are *vapores* dangerous? Although he died over 50 years ago, the case of Don José María is still cited. At the end of the dry season, with the ground cracking from heat, he swept his patio, and then to lay the dust, sprinkled it with water. From the hot *vapores* that rose from the ground and entered his lungs, he developed pneumonia and died. Why can ice cream be dangerous? Don Francisco had suffered from *bronquitis* for some time. One hot afternoon, while still slightly ill, he was so injudicious as to eat an ice cream cone. He developed pneumonia, and died the next day. Hot hands should be kept away from water? Don Plácido wove wheat straw (Very Hot) during the last 25 years of his life, constantly dipping the straw into water to keep it flexible. Toward the end of his life his hands were crippled from arthritis and from this, in some way, he died. In similar fashion, any remembered illness episode cited to substantiate a health belief of action. Does Very Cold food obstruct urination? Don Genaro was *very* fond of broad bean soup (Very Cold). He downed one bowl in the evening, and asked for a second. During the night he became surfeited, then he couldn't urinate, and he died. Hence, the answer to the question is "yes."

Because of the degree of control over health and illness that Tzintzuntzeños believe their traditional medicine provide, because of its ability to answer the questions "what happened," and "what am I suffering from," and because of its ability to specify acceptable therapies, I suspect that humoral pathology will continue to play an important role in their health beliefs and behavior for a long time to come.

NOTES

1. The notable exception to this generalization is Colson A.C. *The Prevention of Illness in a Malay Village*. Wake Forest University, Developing Nations Monograph Series. Series II, No. 1, Winston-Salem, NC 1971.

2. For a general account of Tzintzuntzan see Foster G.M. *Tzintzuntzan: Mexican Peasants in a Changing World*. Revised Edition Elsevier, New York, 1979.

3. e.g. Logan M.H. Selected references on the hot-cold theory of disease. *Med. Anthrop. Newslett.* 6, No. 2, 8–14, 1975.

4. Orso, E. *Hot and Cold in the Folk Medicine of the Island of Chira, Costa Rica*. Louisiana State University, Monograph and Dissertation Series, No. 1, Baton Rouge, 1970.

5. e.g. Mazess R. B. Hot–cold foods beliefs among Andean peasants. *J. Am. Diet. Ass.* 53, 109–113, 1968;

Molony C. H. Systematic valence coding of Mexican "hot"–"cold" food. *Ecol, Fd Nutr.* 4, 67–74, 1975.

6. e. g. Logan M.H. Anthropological research on the hot–cold theory of disease: some methodological suggestions. *Med. Anthrop.* 1, No. 4, 87–112, 1977.

7. Orso E. *op cit.*, p. ii.

8. Logan M.H. *op. cit.*, p. 89, 1977.

9. For a discussion of this problem in Tzintzuntzan see Foster G. M. Methodological problems in the study of intracultural variation: the hot/cold dichotomy in Tzintzuntzan. *Hum. Org.* 38, 179–183, 1979.

10. Orso E. *op. cit.*, was the first to note this important point.

11. The term *humor* is also used in the sense of "predisposition." Of a person who suffers frequent recurrences of an illness, such as inflamed tonsils, it is said *el tiene humor para las anginas* ("He is predisposed to tonsillitis").

12. Friends have expressed amazement to me that Americans routinely make entire meals of salads and cold sandwiches; they wonder why we do not fall ill because of this dangerous diet.

26

Adaptive Strategies of Bolivian Herbalists to Biomedicine

Joseph Bastien

The process of integrating ethnomedicine and biomedicine involves opposition and adaptation by their practitioners. This process is best illustrated by examining ethnomedical practices of three Kallawaya herbalists in Bolivia and their relationships with doctors. Florentino Alvarez utilizes both ethnomedicine and biomedicine; Mario Salcedo has sanitized herbal practices to make them more biomedicinal; and Nestor Llaves has modified ethnomedicine to treat a clientele dissatisfied with biomedicine. Essential to the practice of ethnomedicine is that it be flexible, adapting to changing political, economic, social, and cultural conditions, more so than in biomedicine with its costly technology, political affiliations, and structured practice through licensing procedures and conventional medical schools (Foucalt 1975). Kallawaya herbalists exhibit this required flexibility by their adaptation to the geographical, social, political, and economic environment of Bolivia.

From Joseph Bastien, "Adaptive Strategies of Bolivian Herbalists to Biomedicine." In *Drum and Stethoscope: Integrity Ethnomedicine and Biomedicine in Bolivia*, 1992.

The Kallawaya ethnic group has about 128 herbalists who employ more than a thousand medicinal plants 25 to 30 percent of which provide effective cures (Girault 1984:22; 1987). Effective here means according to measurements using biomedical methodology. Another 30 percent are likely "effective" using another yardstick and may be important in healing. These herbalists are renowned throughout Argentina, Bolivia, Peru, and Chile as very skilled healers. They employ elaborate rituals in their healing (see Bastien 1978; Girault 1988; Oblitas Poblete 1978; and Rosing 1990).

Although Kallawayas speak Quechua, Spanish, and some Aymara, the herbalists use a secret language for curing, *machaj-juyai*, which means language of colleagues (Girault 1989; Oblitas Poblete 1968). Although this language is rapidly disappearing, it had an estimated 12,000 words. Herbalists speak it principally to exclude outsiders and in curing rituals. *Machaj-juyai* is a hybrid language formed from a lexicon mostly of Puquina words and a Quechua grammar (Stark 1972). As Puquina disappeared in the seventeenth century, Kallawayas continued to use Puquina words with a Quechua grammar to talk about plants and medicinal paraphernalia.

In 1969 I began research among the Kallawaya and have continued until the present (Bastien 1973, 1978, 1982, 1985, 1987; Bastien et al. 1990).

The Kallawaya live in Province Bautista Saavedra, Department of La Paz. Bolivia, which borders on Peru, northwest of Lake Titicaca. Charazani is the provincial capital. Approximately thirteen thousand Kallawayas live in Bautista Saavedra (975 square miles), an area the size of the state of Delaware. Population density is 13.3 people per square mile. Although many Kallawayas have moved to cities, the population has not decreased much due to improved health and birthrates. Bautista Saavedra is located north of the Cordillera Real (Oriental) in the foothills of the Apolobamba mountains, also called the Carabaya mountains. Water from Lake Titicaca and glaciers in the Apolobamba mountains feed Río Charazani and Río Calaya, which flow east to join the Mapiri and Beni rivers of the Amazon. The Charazani and Calaya rivers form a system of high and medium valleys where the Kallawaya live at elevations between 2,700 and 5,000 m, above the rain forests of the Yungas area and below the regions of permafrost. Their proximity to high mountain and tropical ecological zones provides access to many plants, animals, and minerals used in their curing procedures.

These rivers and valleys create natural boundaries for an *ayllu*, an ecological, cultural, and social unit of Kallawaya society. Tributaries flowing into the Charazani and Calaya rivers and form triangulated land masses with various ecological levels. The Kallawaya, and many other Andeans as well, distinguish their communities according to the mountain on which the community is located. The mountains are the *ayllus* and each one has three major levels: low, central, and high, where basically corn (cereals), potatoes, and llamas are produced. After the Bolivian Agrarian Reform (1954), the *ayllu* system was diminished, with prominence given to separate communities and Bolivian political units (cantons, provinces, and peasant syndicates). The Kallawaya have nine *ayllus*; Amarete, Chajaya, Chari, Chullina, Curva, Inca, Calaya, Kaata, and Upinhuaya.

The Kallawaya are horticulturists and herders. A family lives in three small adobe buildings (5 m by 4 m), one for cooking, one for sleeping, and one for storage. The buildings form three sides of a courtyard, which is enclosed by a wall with a gate and is where family members weave, raise chickens and guinea pigs, and congregate. Burros, pigs, and sheep are kept in open corrals behind the sleeping quarters. Within each *ayllu*, people in the lower communities grow maize, wheat, barley, peas, and beans on the lower slopes (3,200 to 3,500 m); those in central communities cultivate *oca* (*Oxalis crassicaulis*) and potatoes on rotated fields of the central slopes (3,500 to 4,300 m); and those of highland communities herd alpacas, llamas, and sheep on the highlands (4,300 to 4,000 m). Traditionally, *ayllu* members from the three levels exchange produce and provide each other with the necessary carbohydrates, minerals, and proteins to maintain a balanced subsistence.

Herbalists live in *ayllus* Chajaya (28); Chari (15); Curva (37); which also includes Lagunilla (13); and Inca (15). There are also herbalists in Charazani (8) and Huata Huata (12). These *ayllus* and communities have specialized in herbal medicine and are complementary to *ayllus* that have other specialties. Amarete and Upinhuaya provide potters and tool- and hatmakers for the province. According to a division of labor, the communities on each mountain specialize in some profession. The *ayllus* exchange services and supply each other as well as other parts of the central Andes with necessary resources.

For Kaatans, their *ayllus* also has metaphorical meanings: they believe their mountain has three resource areas and communities that are analogous to the human body. In brief, Kaatans relate Apacheta, Kaata, and Niñokorin—the high, central, and low communities—to the head, trunk, and legs of a human body.

The mountain-body metaphor is the unifying and holistic principle for *ayllu* Kaata. Judy, my wife, and I participated as members of the Marcelino Yanahuaya family in twelve rituals that dealt with sickness, death, lineage, and land (Bastien 1973). In some ways, every ritual centered around the mountain metaphor. Sickness, for example, is cured by symbolically putting the body of the mountain together. Marriage rituals gather together people and produce from three levels of the mountain to symbolize that marriage unites the people of the mountain. Metaphorically, then, agriculture, health, and social principles correspond to a mountain seen as a human body with its three parts (Bastien 1978:xix).

An *ayllu* and its relationships are bases for cognitive and cultural understandings of how Kallawayas perceive their bodies and how they deal with sicknesses. Most important, ethnomedical practitioners perform rituals that are enacted, shared, and negotiated discourses concerned with the integration (health) or disintegration (sickness) of bodies, communities, resources, and mountains (see Bastien 1978:129–70; 1987:67–76). An ethnological comprehension of this system provides a basis for not only understanding Kallawaya ethnomedicine per se but also seeing how it functions within an ecological and cultural context. This contextual knowledge is necessary for incorporating ethnomedicine with biomedicine in Bolivia and in other countries as well.

THE TRAVELING HERBALISTS

Kallawaya herbalists, many of whom now live in cities, serve community members by bringing them medicines and produce from other places. Reliance on the exchange of goods between urban herbalists and rural peasants is important as a buffer in a region of unpredictable weather and frequent crop failure. Only one-quarter of the adult male population in Chajaya and Curva are herbalists; other individuals provide them with a support system: gathering herbs, repairing roads, proving food, and maintaining their animals, land, and households. Women take care of the animals and farm while men are absent on herbal trips, usually during the nonproductive part of the agricultural year. Children herd sheep and work in the fields soon after they begin to walk.

For centuries, Kallawayas traded medicinal knowledge among themselves and other Andean groups. Various villages had assigned trade routes for their herbalists: those from Curva traveled to Cochabamba, Oruro, Potosí, and Sucre in Bolivia; Arequipa, Peru; and northern Argentina. Those from Chajaya and Kanlaya traveled through the Central Highlands of Peru to Lima and up the coast to Ecuador, at times reaching the Panama Canal. *Ayllu* Calaya harvested coca in the Yungas and marketed it in the densely populated areas of the Puna. This international trade has decreased because of difficulties crossing borders, settlement in urban centers, and changing markets.

THE LONG HISTORY OF HERBALISTS

Kallawaya herbalists follow a long history of healing and are part of an Andean ethnomedical system (Bastien 1985). Kallawayas were purveyors of medicines during the Tiahuanaco cultures (A.D. 400–1145), Mollo culture (1145–1438), Inca Empire (1438–1532), Spanish Conquest (1532–1825), and the Bolivian Republic (1825–present). As early as the Tiahuanaco period, Kallawayas practiced trephination, reshaped craniums, and used enemas, snuff trays, and medicinal plants from lowland regions (Wassén 1972). Throughout Mollo culture, Kallawayas built elaborate cisterns as burials for their ancestors who were prominent in ritual and herbal powers (Arellano López 1978). During the Inca Empire, they carried the chair of the Inca (Guaman Poma de Avala 1936:331), traveled up and down the Andes, and learned the pharmacopoeias of many Andean groups. After the Spanish conquest, Kallawayas lost large parts of their land and were moved to villages. Covertly, they continued worshipping their ancestors and earth shrines, but they also learned about European medicinal plants (Saignes 1984). After independence in 1825, the Republican period ushered in the rise of the mestizos in Charazani, who considered themselves a class apart from the peasants of the surrounding *ayllus*. Some of these mestizos became herbalists and competed with peasant herbalists. To avoid their influence and competition, Kallawayas from communities of Curva and Chajaya traveled long distances throughout Argentina, Chile, Ecuador, and Peru. The herbalists of each *ayllu* had distinct trade routes that they protected by mutual agreement among the elders. Through this widespread travel, they had become world famous by the turn of the twentieth century.

During the first half of the twentieth century, there were few doctors and clinics in rural Bolivia. Native practitioners healed the sick and there was little competition between them and doctors. Synthetic drugs were unavailable to peasants, who used medicinal plants. In 1904, for instance, Paloma, an herbalist from Achacachi, performed trephination on Francisca Calderon, who had her skull fractured in a fight (Bandelier 1904). With a pocketknife, Paloma cut an oblong hole in the temporal ridge, released the fluid, and sewed the skin over the wound. Learning of this successful surgery with rudimentary instruments, doctors from La Paz presented Paloma with a surgical kit that he never used, preferring his pocket-knife. This is an *early* example of attempts to collaborate between practitioners of ethnomedicine and biomedicine. Even though Paloma practiced with outdated techniques, he and other herbalists, such as the Kallawaya, were the only medical practitioners available to Andean peasants at the time.

During the nineteenth and early twentieth centuries, the Kallawaya acquired notoriety for certain cures. For example, Fawcett relates how Carlos Franck's daughter was cured by a Kallawaya, Pablos Alvarez (Oblitas Poblete 1969:19). She was crippled, and German doctors in Lima who had performed four hip operations had failed to cure her. Alvarez was successful in a week with a treatment of compresses and medicinal plants. Cures such as this one fostered the reputation of the Kallawaya to such a degree that they were sent to the Panama Canal to cure workers of yellow fever, which they did with *quina cascarilli* (quinine bark). In 1889, Kallawaya herbalists got worldwide attention when they sent a list of their pharmacopoeia to the Eighth World Exposition of Paris. Doctor Nicanor Iturralde and Eugenio Guinault studied the list and classified the plants according to botanical species and pharmacological uses by Kallawayas. Commenting on their work, Carlos Bravo (1918:167–72) wrote that this was a profound study that included many native plants and information needed for world health. Bravo criticized the authors for not readily accepting the medicinal qualities of these plants: "If the lowly, ignorant Indians are cured by these plants, what more evidence do we need?"

Kallawaya acclaim became so widespread during this period that people came from other countries of South America and Europe to be treated for diseases that had been diagnosed as incurable. Kallawaya herbal medicine assumed legendary dimensions, partially because of the herbalists' mysterious practices, transient activities, and knowledge of medicinal plants. Moreover, herbalists employed magic, ritual, and prayers in their healing sessions, which gave them an aura of shamanism. These factors made it difficult to validate the authenticity of reputed cures. Incurables thought of them as their healing saviors. Realistically, however, the Kallawaya refused to treat patients who

were likely to die or could not be cured by their methods. Consequently, their success rate was higher than that of doctors who accepted patients on their deathbeds. The herbalists' trademark was, and still is, an elaborately woven shoulder bag for herbs neatly wrapped in cloths to distinguish them. Kallawaya herbalists were called *Qolla Kapachayuh* (Lords of the Medicine Bag) and their *ayllus* were called *Qollahuaya* (Place of Herbs). (Kallawaya is an alternative spelling for Qollahuaya.)

SUPPRESSION OF LORDS OF THE MEDICINE BAG

Toward the second half of the twentieth century, doctors and pharmacists campaigned against the "backward" practices of herbalists, depicting them as obstacles to scientific medicine. Doctors, nurses, and auxiliary nurses started serving peasants after the Bolivian Agrarian Reform in 1954. Herbalists were prohibited from practicing medicine in many places. Some were arrested, tried, and imprisoned for short sentences. Others were classified as *brujos*, witches. In order to avoid these criticisms, some herbalists, such as Mario Salcedo of La Paz, used only empirical cures and discontinued prayers, symbols, and rituals in healing sessions. Others practiced covertly. This persecution brought a decline in the number of herbalists, because as one old herbalist told me, "Why should I educate my son to be an herbalist, a profession of Gypsies."

Another factor for the decline of herbalism during the 1940s and 1950s was the advent of synthetic medicines, the "miracle drugs." Antibiotics such as penicillin and streptomycin cured syphilis and tuberculosis, both common in Bolivia, much faster than did *cola de caballi* (shavegrass) and *salvia grande* (sage). The emerging classes of Westernized Bolivians believed that modern medicine had replaced their remedies from the countryside. Pharmaceutical companies, which previously had relied on herbs and herbalists for their prescriptions, now imported synthetic drugs at greater costs and much greater profits. They became competitors with herbalists, who lacked the advantages of packaging public endorsement, and advertisement. In fact, pharmaceutical companies, such as Vita and Inti, in Bolivia had developed about forty pharmaceutical products from herbal recipes of Kallawaya herbalists, providing no patent rights. Although this appears to have legitimized the use of herbs, pharmaceutical products from herbs were given new names, references to plant sources were omitted, and herbal suppliers were minimally paid. Because of this exploitation, herbalists refused to collaborate with pharmaceutical companies in research. The lesson learned is that compensation is necessary for herbalists whose plants are used commercially. Patent rights need to be extended to herbalists.

An example of infringement of property rights for commercial gain happened recently. The musical group Kaoma stole a song, "Llorando se Fue," from another musical group, Los Karkas, and made millions from it. They had changed the lyrics to Portuguese and given it a lambada rhythm. Nonetheless, Los Karkas won the lawsuit as having prior rights to the song and received compensation. Relevant here is that pharmaceutical companies are violating intellectual property rights of many herbalists who continue to own rights to discoveries of herbal remedies. Unless these herbalists are compensated, lawsuits will be forthcoming.

By the middle of the twentieth century, many Kallawayas had moved to cities and abandoned their craft; those who did continue practicing medicine dressed in Western clothing, forgot their language, and accepted biomedicine. There was a sharp decline in the number of medicinal plants used in curing. Old-time herbalists used an average of 300 medicinal plants, whereas younger herbalists were by 1960 using around 80 plants. Herbalists made fewer trips and many illnesses were dealt with more effectively by synthetic drugs. When I visited herbalists from 1963 through 1985, they were cautious and reticent about disclosing their practice for fear that they would be persecuted by the Ministry of Rural Health. In 1979 Pastor Llaves, a noted Kallawaya herbalist in Cochabamba, said that he had been refused permission to visit his patients in the hospital and had also been arrested for herbal practices.

RENEWAL OF HERBALISM

During my fieldwork from 1985 until the present, Kallawaya herbalists were less reticent, and proudly talked about their practices. The waning herbal tra-

dition began waxing in 1985 when Bolivians and others throughout the Western world began rediscovering the value of medicinal plants. Bolivians, especially peasants, could little afford synthetic drugs and feared their side effects. First-generation Aymara Indians received penicillin injections with high rates of success and few reactions, but second and subsequent generations had lower rates of success and substantial reactions.

Moreover, there was a growing hostility to Westernization and capitalization of Bolivia. Before Victor Paz ascended to the presidency in 1985, cocaine cartels had brought corruption, and either bought or opposed regimes. Tin mines were closed in Oruro by 1985, vastly increasing unemployment, and inflation had reached 29,800 percent. Effects on the poor and middle classes were great, with their salaries light years behind the rate of inflation. As soon as workers were paid, they rushed to buy merchandise before their money devaluated at 80 percent a day. Merchants stopped buying and selling goods, many closing shop to move to other countries, as also did members of the professional classes.

Bolivians became disillusioned with the high cost of biomedicine and its dependence upon international economic forces. The price of imported pharmaceutical products rose with inflation: in 1984 the cost of a penicillin injection was upwards of U.S.$10, several days' wages for peasants. Doctors and nurses were frequently on strike. These economic factors forced Bolivians to develop appropriate technologies from internal natural resources. Bolivians began looking more to their own traditions for solutions and less to products from the industrialized countries. Bolivians resorted to herbs, herbalists, and other ethnomedical practitioners.

Herbal medicines increased in demand, as did herbalists and herbal vendors. Although the population of La Paz tripled between 1965 and 1985, the number of herbal stalls in La Paz increased form 30 to 130. The herbal market in Oruro is one of the largest business endeavors in the Department of Oruro, estimated as a multimillion dollar operation (Greg Rake, pers. com. 1986). One female herbal vendor travels to China to trade Bolivian medicinal plants for Chinese herbs (Oscar Velasco, pers. com. 1986). An international exchange of folk remedies brings medicinal plants from Africa, Asia, Europe, and other parts of Latin America to Bolivia, which can be purchased from herbal vendors throughout the country. Estimates of 60 percent to 70 percent of the Bolivian population rely on natural remedies.

Another reason for the increase in herbalism is the growing resentment of Bolivians toward doctors who perform surgery, are sometimes unsuccessful, and charge excessive fees. For years, in Bolivia the two routes to gentlemanliness and legitimacy were medicine and law. Now, doctors in Bolivia no longer have this prestigious and wealthy role compared to doctors in the United States and Europe—one reason why many doctors have emigrated to these countries—nor do they monopolize medicine now that herbalists are popular.

Certain problems arose with the rising popularity of herbal curing. Improperly trained herbalists tried to cash in on the booming trade. Claiming to be Kallawayas, these impostors cheated the sick with concoctions of narcotic and toxic plants. The Kallawaya Mario Salcedo observed that peasants come to La Paz to be treated by doctors who are unable to cure them, so they resort to poorly trained city herbalists who deceive them with plants and magic. They finally return to their villages to be treated by country herbalists.

Unemployment also contributed to the increase in the number of herbalists. Out of work, some adopted the herbal profession which, unfortunately, because of its esoteric nature, could easily be manipulated to "con" already desperate and vulnerable patients. Furthermore, the number of herbal books increased, and courses in traditional medicine were offered by members of the Escuela Nacional de Salud Pública and the Sociedad Boliviana de Medicina Natural (SBMN). Mario Salcedo lectured on uses of plants (see Bastien 1987:10–11, 29–32). Walter Alvarez, M.D., son of a Kallawaya herbalist, discussed pathology and herbal cures. And Jaime Zalles, a homeopathologist, and Jaime Mondaca, a medical student, trained participants in certain aspects of biomedicine. These courses lasted four days, two hours each evening, and were attended by around fifteen people. Participants were charged five bolivianos (U.S.$1 = B. $2.05 = day's meals). Inappropriately, some participants considered themselves herbalists after attending one course.

The integration between herbalists and doctors in Bolivia has also improved with the increased interest in ethnomedicine. Doctors and herbalists collaborated with Servicios Múltiples de Tecnologías Apropiadas (SEMTA) in organizing several herbal and biomedical courses, one within the Kallawaya region and two outside the region. SEMTA also helped erect two buildings in the Kallawaya region, which were to become schools for aspiring herbalists, but has since abandoned the program. Herbalists and medical doctors jointly staff clinics in La Paz, El Alto, and Oruro, and plan to staff a hospital for Kallawayas of *ayllu* Amarete. Finally, there was a national symposium on ethnomedicine and biomedicine in Oruro, Bolivia, in 1985.

LEGITIMACY AND LICENSING

Mario Salcedo and Walter Alvarez suggested, as a measure to control the quality of herbalists in Bolivia, that expert herbalists should provide aspirants longer courses with qualifying exams and licenses to practice. Although they are correct in calling for measures to discriminate against unqualified herbalists, they also advocate that herbalists be licensed by the Ministry of Health (MPSSP), which is doctor controlled. As legitimacy and status become the means to control herbalists, the diversity of practices among Kallawayas will be lost. Herbalists follow a folk tradition that is subject to change and experience: it is not codified into set formulas, such as medical books, which are compilations of empirical facts and generalizations, scientifically verifiable. Kallawaya folklore is passed along from father to son and learned by practice. The effort to formalize this folklore with herbal institutes, manuals, exams, and licenses might make herbalists more uniform in their practice, but it might also inhibit the dynamic aspects of a living tradition. Herbalists would also be less flexible. Bolivia has many ethnic groups and classes of people. For Kallawayas to be effective, they must adapt their practice to these differing cultures, politics, and economics.

Doctors object to this by replying that if degrees and licenses are not required of these practitioners, how are Bolivians to know who is qualified or not. For foreigners and strangers, this is a problem, but it is not for most Bolivians, who select ethnomedical practitioners as well as biomedical practitioners, according to reputation. The Kallawaya slowly build up their practice by successful curing rates. They also establish social ties with patients and their families. Among Kallawayas, herbalists are ranked according to expertise, so that, if asked, they will tell you who is the most noted healer, such as when they nominated Florentino Alvarez to be in charge of the ethnomedicine display in La Paz in 1956.

As a folk system, ethnomedicine has its own criteria of expertise. In the integration of herbalists, criteria found in the community can be used for evaluating their practices. The communities of Chajaya and Curva exert a controlling influence on the quality of herbalists from these villages. Elders of Chajaya require that an aspirant herbalist serve as an apprentice before curing alone. When herbalists gather at fiestas to compare herbs and cures, they criticize the less skilled so they can protect their reputation and income. Some Kallawaya herbalists offer a guarantee in the sense that they do not charge if a patient is not cured. If, however, a patient dies, they may not charge for fear of reprisals. Where members of the community do not exert much influence over ethnomedical practitioners, associations of healers may serve a similar function of regulating their practice.

For Kallawayas, an apprenticeship used to last as long as eight years, which contemporary youths consider too long for too little reward. One solution is to combine apprenticeship with book learning to facilitate the dissemination of herbal knowledge. One disadvantage of this is that more emphasis is placed on abstract information than on observation, experience, and personal contact. No known herbal study is able to contain the experiences, insights, and knowledge of a practitioner such as Florentino Alvarez. To carry on the Kallawaya tradition, long-term apprenticeships are necessary. Another disadvantage would be the structure imposed to disseminate such knowledge should the state want to control it by licensure (Libbet Crandon-Malamud, pers. com. 1990).

SYNCRETIZEOR: FLORENTINO ALVAREZ

Popularity and profiteering pose problems for older Kallawaya herbalists, who fear their tradition is losing its quality. A major concern of these herbalists is that their children do not want to spend long apprenticeships learning their craft. Consider how Florentino Alvarez, a very famous Kallawaya herbalist, learned how to cure (Bastien 1987:27–29). In 1924, when Florentino was thirteen, he served as an apprentice to Damian Alvarez, an accomplished herbalist who specialized in ailments of the kidneys, lungs, liver, and those related to childbirth. Damian became like a father to Florentino, teaching him the art of herbal curing. They spent months combining the countryside from their native village of Chajaya to Lima gathering plants and then visiting hamlets up and down the valleys of the Andes and across the deserts of Peru curing the sick.

When Damian died in 1926, Florentino continued his education with another famous herbalist, Manuel Redondo. Together, they traveled thousands of miles up and down the north coast of Peru and across the Andes to Kanlaya. They cured all classes of people; Indians, mestizos, Europeans. According to Florentino, Manuel cured crippled people by making them sweat with *chilca*, eucalyptus, and nettle leaves boiled in water. He cured pain in the lungs by rubbing the chest with a lotion made from animal fat, and he treated yellow fever with enemas made from quinine bark. Relatives provided Florentino and Manuel with food and lodging during the cure, which lasted from a few days to several weeks. They cured in the home and were well paid.

Florentino oscillated between ethnomedicine and biomedicine, an ambiguity that enabled him to examine and criticize both systems. At different times, he adopted nature curing with water therapy, and at others he resorted to biomedicine. Florentino frequently used elements from several alternative medicines, and was described by Doctor Harold Haley (pers. com. 1982) as being like someone who after the introduction of the belt could not abandon the security of suspenders and so wore both. This metaphor captures the insecurity of herbalists, such as Florentino, who act as bridges between traditional ethnomedicine and revolutionary biomedicine.

In 1940, Florentino temporarily abandoned the use of herbs for chemotherapeutic products from Inti and Vita. As their representative he traveled the southern route from La Paz to Santa Cruz, Argentina. He soon observed that synthesized drugs cost more and caused more side effects than did medicinal plants.

In 1942 Florentino quit his job with the pharmaceutical companies and served as an apprentice of Professor Reyes, a natural healer. Reyes had recently come from Santiago, Chile, to set up a clinic in La Paz. He taught Florentino the uses of water in healing: baths, saunas, and massages. That same year, Florentino returned to Chajaya, where he established a clinic of natural healing (*clínica naturista*). He constructed an adobe Turkish bath and built cabinets for medicinal plants. He also operated a small store with basic supplies of rice, sugar, soft drinks, kerosene, and candles. When he was not farming, he would sit behind a blue wooden counter and sell his supplies or discuss cures with people.

Florentino continued to travel several times a year until 1960, when he fell from a cliff and broke his foot. After this, people traveled from Argentina, Chile, Peru, and other parts of Bolivia to Chajaya to be healed by him. They made long and difficult journeys: the trip from La Paz to Chajaya is ten hours riding in the back of a large truck loaded with supplies and people. Nonetheless, ten to fifteen people visited Florentino annually to be cured. they believed that he was able to heal the incurables.

Unlike some other herbalists, Florentino was not presumptuous about his skills; he was deeply humble and admitted many failures in curing. There was no magic involved. Essentially, he was a very compassionate healer, who, if he was unable to cure someone, at least helped the person deal with his or her sickness. He also told the truth to sick people, careful not to mislead them about his abilities. This is contrary to some herbalists who claim to cure any disease, only to deceive the clientele temporarily. Florentino's humility and desire to heal diseases motivated him to continually search for cures.

As a result, Florentino enhanced the general reputation of all Kallawaya herbalists. In 1956, Victor Paz Estenssoro, president of Bolivia, commissioned him to prepare a display of Kallawaya medicines for the Museo Casa Murillo in La Paz. Victor Paz wrote him a letter of commendation for his contributions to Andean medicine. This beautiful collection, titled *Botica Antigua*, is one tribute to Florentino and other Kallawayas. Florentino practiced in his clinic until 1981, when

he died of a cerebral hemorrhage. He was survived by one adopted son, Vicente, who now farms Florentino's land. he is not an herbalist.

Florentino, the last of the great Kallawaya herbalists, stood on the threshold of the merging of ethnomedicine and biomedicine: his unique role was to be between ethnomedicine and the advance of biomedicine. He continually tried to incorporate the use of synthesized drugs with that of medicinal plants and to convince herbalists to use antibiotics (penicillin and streptomycin) for curing syphilis and tuberculosis. Once when I was suffering from a urinary infection, Florentino suspected syphilis and suggested that I have a blood test in La Paz. He also warned me, "Drugs are expensive. They calm the symptoms, but have many side effects." Florentino gathered sacks of rue (*Ruta chalapensis*) in the Chajaya region to sell to the Vita and Inti companies in La Paz, which used it for lotions to treat rheumatism (Bastien 1978:148–149). He complained that they paid him the same price as for a sack of corn—a minimal payment.

I was with Florentino in his store in Chajaya in 1980 when a commission of government officials and doctors visited him to announce that they wanted to start an herbal college and name him instructor. They complained that the villagers were not present to receive them. Florentino told them that the people were working in the fields and had not time to attend to formalities. He wanted to show them the new hospital in Charazani, but they refused to visit it and said they were primarily interested in herbal medicines of the Kallawaya. Walter Alvarez, M.D., who led the commission, was remotely related to Florentino, who considered him politically ambitious. Instead of learning herbal medicine, Walter had studied biomedicine in Cuba. Upon his return to Bolivia, he led a movement to incorporate Kallawaya ethnomedicine with biomedicine, somewhat for ethnic reasons but also to market herbal remedies once they became legitimate. After the commission left, Florentino was little impressed and astutely commented, "*palabras no más*" ("only words"). Although Florentino never explicitly expressed it, he communicated to me that to heal the sick he would share his knowledge with doctors, pharmacists, and anthropologists, but that they would benefit the most and provide him with very little in return.

Recalling how Florentino had received little in return for his knowledge, I gave him my binoculars, which he used to see the jagged, snow-crested peaks of Aqhamani, his earth shrine. He had suffered a stroke. I was somewhat able to help him by massaging his muscles, but he remained partially crippled. With the binoculars, his eyes could travel the distances he once had walked as an herbalist. Bolivian peasants have seldom gained from the exploitation of their country for medicines and drugs, such as quinine and cocaine. In return for information provided me, I have published an herbal manual in Spanish that is being used by promoters in the Department of Oruro (Bastien 1983a).

In 1984, Kallawaya herbalists acknowledged the contributions of Florentino Alvarez by dedicating an herbal book to him (SEMTA 1984). In an attempt to continue Kallawaya herbal tradition, Walter Alvarez started herbal colleges in *ayllus* Chajaya and Curva, but by 1989 these colleges were discontinued for lack of funds. Many herbalists continue the tradition, but there is a decreasing number of youths who are willing to spend years of apprenticeships learning by practice and oral traditions. There is a need for herbal colleges, books, and courses to replace some of the oral tradition that is being discontinued. Walter Alvarez was instrumental in helping the Kallawaya of *ayllu* Amarete get an integrated clinic with an herbalist and a doctor, supported by the Ministry of Health, which they had petitioned.

Florentino represents the ethnomedical practitioner that is first rejected, then exploited, and finally exonerated with honor. Walter represents the biomedical practitioner and descendant of herbalists that first rejects his tradition but then embraces it. Kallawaya herbalists, as well as scores of other ethnomedical practitioners, experience similar rejections and acceptances, depending on popularity, politics, economics, and nationalism.

Popular acceptance of ethnomedicine increases when there is a growing ethnic identity coupled with a lessening involvement with public institutions, especially those with international interests. Ethnomedical practitioners realize this and are suspicious of administrators' and politicians' motives. They are suspicious of attempts to integrate them into the biomedical system, not because they are unscientific but because they recognize exploitative relationships. Herbalists know that past endeavors to integrate them have either failed or resulted in further exploitation. The lesson learned is that for integration ethnomedical practitioners need surety of their rights and resources. Their practices need to be protected and not referred off to doctors, and patents should be given to them for new medicines.

Throughout the developing world, many doctors and nurses are similar to Walter in that running through their blood are ethnomedical traditions which they have been taught to reject and suppress. These doctors and nurses need to repair the damages they have done to themselves and to ethnomedical practitioners: disparagement of reputations, taking away of clients, and relegation to inferior roles. Herbalists like Florentino may be humble, but they are also sensitive and very proud. They resent being looked down on by a new breed of "technocrats." Biomedical knowledge, which brings power to doctors and nurses, oppresses herbalists when wrongly used. Aware of this, Kallawayas used a secret language for centuries to guard their precious herbal knowledge, but now that they are willing to share this knowledge with doctors, they want status, recognition, and recompense in return.

SANTIZER: MARIO SALCEDO

Another way that Kallawaya herbalists have adapted to biomedicine is by trying to act like doctors and nurses, as illustrated by Mario Salcedo. Mario is a Kallawaya herbalist who moved to La Paz, became a mestizo, and established a "respectable" clinic for middle- and upper-class Bolivians. Whereas Florentino represents a "belt and suspenders" type of integration, Mario represents a Kallawaya who tries to "sanitize" or legitimize ethnomedicine to make it scientific so it fits into biomedicine. Although he achieved respectability and legitimacy, he remained peripheral to the herbalists of Chajaya, who rejected his advice and never named him sponsor (*preste*) for the fiesta, and to doctors, who never permitted him to practice in the hospitals of La Paz. Like Florentino, Mario was an orphan and liminal figure; the former was firmly rooted as a peasant making overtures to biomedicine, and the latter became a mestizo emulating middle-class doctors. Bolivians classify people as mestizos when they have become Westernized or Europeanized by speaking Spanish fluently, wearing suits or dresses, being educated (or at least giving airs as such), and considering themselves superior to *compesinos* (peasants) and *cholos* (urbanized peasants). As herbalists attempt to integrate with doctors, they encounter questions of identity, as well as those of ethnicity, class, and domination.

Literacy has reduced the reliance that ethnomedical practitioners have had on oral traditions passed along as inheritance through the lineage. As a result, ethnomedical practitioners can learn from books, exhibit individuality in practice, and be less dependent upon or free of controls by relatives. Mario was basically a self-taught herbalist. Born in 1908, Mario accompanies Domingo Flores on two trips, each four months long. This apprenticeship was short, so Mario began to study on his own. He learned to read and write and expanded his knowledge of curing by reading herbal books that contained popular herbal remedies from Europe and South America. At this time, vegetal drugs were the common form of treatment, so these manuals were important to Bolivian medicine. Throughout the 1930s and 1940s, Mario traveled alone and remained apart form other Kallawaya herbalists because of his knowledge and sophistication. He built up a clientele in La Paz and later remained in his La Paz clinic except when he traveled to the Kallawaya region to gather plants.

Adapting to the status of an early twentieth-century doctor, Mario exhibited self-confidence and a dogmatic view of curing. He tried to stimulate the role of the medical doctor—wearing a white smock and being authoritarian, which might have given him legitimacy but which also separated him from his clients and colleagues. He attempted to legitimize his practice scientifically by debating doctors and writing articles in the newspapers. He has been instrumental in establishing cooperative clinics between doctors and herbalists in La Paz and El Alto. He avoided and openly criticized Kallawayas for curing with magic and ritual because he advocated an ethnoscience of Kallawaya healing. Kallawayas in Chajaya resented his superior attitude and ignored his criticism, which they associated with the oppressive class of mestizos in Charazani. Moreover, peasants who were tenants on his land in Chajaya harvested plants for him at low wages.

Doctors respected Mario as an old-time herbalist with professional expertise, different from other Kallawayas, especially the itinerant ones of Calle Sagarnaga in La Paz. Doctors mentioned Mario as an example of how herbalists could be integrated into health programs by a redefinition of the herbalist's role to become more technical, professional, and scientific. However, this modification increased the impersonality and aloofness between him and his patients. Although this change communicates professional skills to clients, it also gives them a sense of powerlessness and lessens their participation in the therapeutic process. Moreover, Mario might have thrown out the baby with the bath water when he discarded the magical and ritual paraphernalia of herbal curing that may have had more indirect curative effects than the active ingredients of plants.

Donald Joralemon (1986) points out in his study of Peruvian *curanderos'* curing rituals in two distinct communities that the contrast between active engagement and passive participation is attributed to the social context of the ritual location from which patients are drawn. Patients as well as specialists contribute to the modification of folk-healing practices in changed social and cultural circumstances. But, in regard to Mario's case, patients have not transformed his transactions with them as much as have his efforts to appear "professional." Herbalists I interviewed had a lower image of their profession that did doctors, with the exception of Mario, who thought he was better than most doctors and had to prove it by acting like a doctor.

Pressures for herbalists to be more "scientific" and to act like doctors may work to bring them closer to the dominant medical establishment, but it also may limit what they have to offer to total health care. A vital contribution of herbalists to biomedicine is personalized therapy and communication with their patients, involving them in the healing process if only by manipulating symbols and performing rituals. Elsewhere I have shown that there are two interrelated systems at work within Kallawaya ethnomedicine: the empirical effects of medicinal plants and how these physical factors fit into body concepts, which I have described as a topographical-hydraulic ethnophysiology (Bastien 1985). Herbalists most effectively can cure with the cultural context of how plants are understood and related to their ethnophysiology. An analogy would be if a biomedical practitioner with an office lined with diplomas, expensive equipment, and technicians diagnosed a patient by using coca leaves and prescribed some herbs. Conversely, when herbalists act like doctors, patients are confused because they have other expectations for herbalists. There is a surplus of doctors in La Paz and many more reasonable than Mario Salcedo.

When herbalists and doctors diagnose and treat the same illness, there is frequently a problem because they do not agree as to the cause of nature of the illness, and even less to the treatment. Illnesses take on social, cultural, psychological, as well as biological meanings, which are discussed between practitioners and patients. Mario checks the urine and pulse and questions the patient about behavior and diet, which he considers important causes of illnesses. A close follower of hot/cold etiology, Mario attributes the causes of diseases to imbalances of diet and temperature. For example, he diagnosed a case of Bell's palsy, with which I had been sick years before, to have been caused by eating cold cuts of pork and lying on damp ground after playing tennis. Even though this had happened in 1959 and I had been treated by doctors and physical therapists, Mario claimed that he could cure my residual paralysis with herbs, diet, and physical therapy. Unfortunately, I did not have time to pursue the cure. Ethnomedical practitioners advertise cures for illnesses, which biomedical practitioners cannot because the former assume different causes of sickness and health from the latter. Differences in diagnosis and treatment between ethno- and biomedicine need to be understood and respected by doctors and herbalists for an integrated health program. This approach enhances both practices by including more aspects in the therapeutic process.

Granted that some of the Kallawaya practice is "scientifically sound" and founded on material and efficient causality, a large part is not, such as divinations for discussing social conflicts, rituals for relieving mental illnesses, and amulets for recovering losses. These techniques affect psychological and social factors that are important for healing. An important conclusion is that in order to collaborate with doctors, herbalists should not be pressured to use only medicinal plants, to defend the validity of their cures, and to abandon ritual cures.

TRADITIONALIST: NESTOR LLAVES

Another way that ethnomedical practitioners have adapted to biomedicine is by filling in aspects of health care that biomedical practitioners do not include. As in many parts of the world, Bolivians depend upon herbal, ritual, divinatory, and group therapeutics. Although Mario legitimized the role of Kallawaya herbalist, he discarded some therapeutic practices. Herbal curing is a complex art that includes a combination of physiological, psychological, spiritual, and symbolic factors. Herbalists frequently cure not because of their medicine but because of their overall influence on the patient's well-being.

Nestor Llaves, however, has extended the role of herbalist to include aspects of *espiritistas* and diviners. Nestor is a Kallawaya herbalist and ritualist from *ayllu* Curva who has a clinic in La Paz. By having a small stature and protruding stomach and engaging in magical activity, he resembles Ekeko, the dwarf divinity of good fortune in the Andes. In reality, Nestor is about as rich as Ekeko, being the owner of a six-ton Toyota truck, a school bus, two homes, and a large farm in Curva. More than Mario and much more than Florentino, Nestor has built a thriving business of healing the sick in La Paz. All classes of people consult with him concerning spiritual, psychological, and physical ailments. He deals with witchcraft, theft, depression, hatred, unrequited love, divination, burial of the dead, séances, and diseases. Nestor has a flexible style: treating physical symptoms with natural remedies, supernatural disharmonies with rituals, and psychological upsets with a combination of psychoanalysis and counseling. He treats forty patients a day. The success of his practice demonstrates that people want to be treated by psychological, supernatural, and cultural techniques along with empirical methods of curing.

Nestor was born in 1913 in Curva to Manuel Llaves and Matiasa Pérez. His father traveled as an herbalist to Argentina, Brazil, Chile, Ecuador, and Peru. He died from a heart attack when Nestor was thirteen. The following year, Nestor began learning the herbal profession from his great-grandfather, Lorenzo Llaves, and his grandfather, Andres Llaves. Nestor, as well as other Kallawaya herbalists from Curva, traveled frequently to Argentina between 1929 and 1944. The people from Curva traveled this trade route, whereas those from Chajaya traveled mostly through Peru and up the coast to Colombia. Herbalists made contacts along these routes, establishing a network of resource exchange between the various regions. This was one way Kallawayas increased their herbal knowledge.

In 1945 Nestor stopped traveling to Argentina, and in 1946 started a clinic in La Paz near the crowded market section of Calle Buenos Aires after he purchased, through connections, a license from the Municipality of the City of La Paz—but not from the Ministry of Health as had Mario—to operate a business. Around the same time, other Kallawaya herbalists moved to La Paz, abandoned their profession, and became jewelers, merchants, and truckers (see Bastien 1987:22–26). They established a powerful *cholo* network in La Paz connected with the Kallawaya region (see Bastien 1987:36–37 for urban/rural ties). Also differing from Mario, who aspired to be a member of the hispanicized mestizo class, Nestor fit into the large *cholo* class of La Paz.

Cholos(as) are peasants who have moved to the city, still speak Aymara or Quechua, and whose men wear pants, shirts, jackets, and occasionally a poncho to keep warm and whose women wear the traditional skirt, *pullera*, and hat (either the derby or Puritan stove). *Cholos* are a broker mercantile class who do business with *campesinos* (peasants) in the countryside and mestizos in the city. Like Nestor, *cholos* have made some interesting adaptations to the class system in La Paz: *cholo* truckers have built houses in upper-class neighborhoods that are similar in outside architecture to other houses in the area, but inside, the houses are arranged like a peasant's hut with very little furniture, stacks of supplies, and animals and children everywhere. Although not legitimately recognized as members of the mestizo class, *cholos* control a large part of the Bolivian economy, especially contraband, transportation, and trucking, and are a significant political force.

At first, Nestor's clinic was a one-room adobe hut near the crowded streets of Buenos Aires where peasants and *cholos* do business. Nestor walked the streets wearing his poncho and medicine bag, advertising himself as a Kallawaya. Slowly, people began coming to his house, sometimes only two or three a week, to consult about spiritual and physiological matters. These people told other people, and his reputation spread. By 1970, he had built a two-story apartment with reception rooms for his clients on Calle Pioneros de Rochdale.

He works ten hours a day, with all classes of people consulting him for superstitious, supernatural, psychological, and physiological reasons. He heals the warts of peasants and the headaches of generals. When the Pope was ill in 1982, some *cholos* wanted to send Nestor to Rome. He charges "Whatever you can afford," and receives whatever is appropriate because he is good at shaming cheapskates as well as generous to the poor. Rooms of his house are loaded with goods, from Swiss army knives to guinea pigs. Until recently, he drank excessively, being intoxicated for days at a time. Although this inconvenienced patients, it apparently did not discredit his practice, because they would wait until he sobered up. On several intoxicated occasions, he confided to me that he drank because he dealt with so much suffering in people's lives, continually listening to their problems. When I last visited Nestor in 1990, his wife had just died, and he had stopped drinking several years ago. He was very sad and together we prayed for his wife. He then began seeing patients: it was 7:00A.M. and already a line had formed to visit him.

In his medical practice, Nestor combines several roles: spiritist, diviner, and herbalist. According to him, spiritists (*ch'amakani* in Aymara) cure with prayers that intercede with the powers of the sacred places or earth shrines (*mallkus*). Spiritists enter into a trance to negotiate an exchange with the dead so that, instead of taking the life of the sick person, the dead will be satisfied with the life of a chicken or llama. The number of talented spiritists and diviners has decreased in Bolivia, perhaps because these roles require an intuitive and mystical lifestyle that has become less important with modernization. The best spiritists are found in remote highland villages, where they live apart and spend long periods meditating about mountains, streams, the sun, and stars.

Because *cholos* still seek diviners to predict and deal with their earth shrines and spiritists to uncover unknown facts, ambitious Bolivians have adopted this practice with a limited amount of skill. Nestor has adopted some spiritist practices. He has a small chapel with a skull where he performs intercessions. Although he conducts wakes for the dead, he does not attempt to converse with them. he also tries to figure out the psychic causes of bad fortune, but says he lacks the psychic intuitions of a spiritist. As a diviner, Nestor diagnoses the patient by reading coca leaves and tarot cards. he does this principally to examine the possibilities and to authenticate his diagnosis. If the coca leaves, a divine plant, agree with his diagnosis, then the patient more readily accepts Nestor's opinion: there is a cultural validity to his opinion and treatment.

The intermingling of cultural symbols and clinical techniques is important for curing peasants, and Nestor is skilled at this. Nestor, however, like a diviner for agricultural rituals, uses his empirical skills to figure out what is wrong. He reads the pulse in an elaborate way, determining whether the blood is fast, slow, wet, or dry. He also examines urine and has a long list of questions concerning the person's well-being. He is a skilled counselor. For example, he employs fright to scare people out of depression and reinforcement to relax severely anxious people. He uses rosaries, holy pictures, holy water, crucifixes, incense, and amulets.

Mario Salcedo criticized Nestor and said that herbalists should dedicate themselves exclusively to the use of natural means to avoid the accusation that they are magical curers. The paradox is that Mario is a victim of cultural imperialism, yet proudly adheres to the fact that he is a Kallawaya herbalist. Whereas Nestor—also a very skilled herbalist—uses the devices of spiritists and diviners to cure his patients in a cultural context. Nestor realizes the importance of cultural context and claims that this is what the *cholos* want him to do. They ask him to pray over them, to perform rituals to feed the earth shrines, and to divine their fortune. He is smart enough to adapt to the clinical needs of the *cholo* class. Adapting to the needs of his clients, Nestor treats urban migrants: people rooted in Andean culture and befuddled by the urban industrial poverty of La Paz. *Cholos* are more concerned than mestizos in looking for links with their Andean heritage. Nestor is a mediator between the old and new ways.

In regard to class, Nestor is more realistic than Mario. Nestor admits that legitimizing his herbal trade to fit into the dominant biomedical system and mestizo class limits his practice and provides less economic gain than adapting Andean ethnomedical roles. As a result, he is wealthier than most doctors in La Paz. He treats clientele from other ethnic groups and classes. If he had tried to become a mestizo herbalist like Mario, he would have been a small fish in a big pond. Nestor, however, no longer wants to be associated with the *campesino* class of Curva as did his wife, who, when dying, asked to be buried in Curva, near the land she had farmed and her earth shrine. A *Paceño* and *cholo*, Nestor purchased a funeral plan and will be buried in the cemetery wall of La Paz.

DIFFERENT STROKES FOR DIFFERENT FOLKS

The diverse styles of Florentino, Mario, and Nestor represent how Kallawayas have integrated their herbal practices with biomedicine. For all classes, Florentino oscillated between biomedicine and ethnomedicine, finally concentrating on natural cures and using biomedicine only when necessary. For upper- and middle-class mestizos, Mario tried to adopt the "scientific" empirical style of professional biomedicine to validate his herbal cures. For peasants and *cholos*, Nestor modified empirical practices to include more magic and ritual to administer to patients without the coldly clinical practices of biomedicine. For different classes and in their own fashion, they articulated their practice with biomedicine by adopting cures from it, by using it to sanitize ethnomedicine, and by complementing it. Their diversity of practices illustrates that Kallawaya herbalists, as well as other herbalists throughout the world, are part of a dynamic, living tradition.

Herbalists are necessary links for urban peasants in that their curing art combines traditional and modern features. They are part of the inventive aspects of culture emerging from people leaving the traditional countryside for settlement in the industrial city.

REFERENCES

Arellano López. Jorge, 1978. "La Cultura Mollo: Ensay de Síntesis Arquelógica." *Pumapunki* 12:87—113.

Bandelier, Adolf, 1904. "Aboriginal Trephining in Bolivia." *American Anthropologist* 6:440–46.

Bastien, Joseph W., 1973. *Qollahuaya Rituals: An Ethnographic Account of the Symbolic Relations of Man and Land in an Andean Village*. Ithaca: Cornell University Latin American Studies Program.

———, 1978. *Mountain of the Condor: Metaphor and Ritual in an Andean Ayllu*. American Ethnological Society Monograph 64. St. Paul: West Publishing Company. (Reissued by Waveland Press, 1985).

———, 1982. "Herbal Curing by Qollahuaya Andeans," *Journal of Ethnopharmacology* 6:13–28.

———, 1983. "Pharmacopeia of Qollahuaya Andeans," *Journal of Ethnopharmacology* 8:97–111.

———, 1983a. *Las plantas Medicinales de los Kallawayas*. Oruro: Proyecto Concern.

———, 1985. "Qollahuaya-Andean Body Concepts: A Topographical-Hydraulic Model of Physiology." *American Anthropologist* 87:595–611.

———, 1987. *Healers of the Andes: Kallawaya Herbalists and Their Medicinal Plants*. Salt Lake City: University of Utah Press.

Bravo, Carlos, 1918. "El Callahuaya." *Boletín de la Sociedad Geográfica de La Paz* 47:167–72.

Foucault, Michel, 1975. *The Birth of the Clinic: An Archaeology of Medical Perception*, translated by A. M. Sheridan Smith. New York: Vintage/Random House.

Girault, Louis, 1984. *Kallawaya: Guírisseurs Itinérants des Andes*. Paris: Mémoires ORSTOM.

———, 1987. *Kallawaya: Curanderos Itinerantes de los Andes*. La Paz: UNICEF.

———, 1988. *Rituales en las Regiones Andinas de Bolivia y Peru*. La Paz: Don Bosco.

———, 1989. *Kallawaya: El Idioma Secreto de los Incas*. La Paz: UNICEF.

Guaman Poma de Ayala, Felipe, 1936. *Nueva Corónica y Buen Govierno*. Travaux et Mémoires de l'Institut d'Ethnologie, vol. 23. Paris.

Joralemon, Donald, 1986. "Performing Patient in Ritual Healing." *Social Science and Medicine* 23 (9):841–45.

Oblitas, Poblete, Enrique, 1968. *La Lengua Secreta de los Incas*. La Paz: Editorial "Los Amigos del Libro."

———, 1969. *Plantas Medicinales en Bolivia*. La Paz: Editorial "Los Amigos del Libro."

———, 1978. *Cultura Callawaya*. La Paz: Imprenta "Alba."

Rosing, Ina, 1990. *Introducción al Mundo Callawaya*. La Paz: "Los Amigos del Libro."

Saignes, Thierry, 1984. "Quines Son los Callahuayas? Nota sobre un Enigma Histórico." In *Espacio y Tiempo en el Mundo Callahuaya*, edited by T. Gisbert and P. Seibert, 111–29. La Paz: Universidad Mayor de San Andrés.

SEMTA (Servicios Múltiples de Tecnologías Apropiadas*)*, 1984. *Plantas y Tratameintos Kallawayas*. La Paz: SEMTA.

Stark, Louisa, 1972. "Machaj-juayai: Secret Language of the Callahuayas." *Papers in Andean Linguistics* 1:199–227.

Wassén, Henry, 1972. *A Medicine-man's Implements and Plants in a Tiahuanacoid Tomb in Highland Bolivia*. Goteborg: Goteborgs Etnografiska Museum.

27

Tobacco or Health in the Third World

A Political Economy Perspective with Emphasis on Mexico

Kenyon Stebbins

Transnational corporations affect the health and well-being of great numbers of people in the Third World in a variety of ways: by extracting cash and other valued resources, by causing environmental degradation, and by reducing available acreage for health-promoting crops. Transnational *tobacco* conglomerates are especially detrimental to well-being in underdeveloped nations, because in addition to all of the above (1, p. 20; 2, p. 483; 3, p. 61; 4, p. 172; 5, pp. 281, 288), they also vigorously promote the consumption of unhealthy products for consumers who are at best only vaguely aware of the health risks associated with cigarette smoking. From a political economy perspective (6), the author examines the impact on human health of transnational tobacco corporations operating in the Third World, with special emphasis on Mexico.

It is estimated that in the world as a whole, more than 2.5 million premature deaths each year can be

attributed to cigarette smoking. While the number of smokers in the developed world is leveling off as concerns about health risks become more widespread, increasing numbers of people in the developing world are taking up the habit. The World Health Organization (WHO) calls cigarette smoking the number one preventable cause of death in the United States, and it will be so in the Third World if present trends continue. The people of the Third World comprise more than half of the world's population, most of whom are inadequately prepared to make informed decisions concerning smoking. Along with the already difficult problems of malnutrition and communicable diseases, underdeveloped countries are facing the probability of a smoking epidemic that is directly related to the penetration of capitalist tobacco interests into new markets.

FACTS AND FIGURES ON SMOKING

Kenyon Stebbins, "Tobacco or Health in the Third World: A Political Economy Perspective with Emphasis on Mexico," *International Journal of Health Services* 17(3): 521–536, 1987. © 1987. Reprinted by permission of Baywood Publishing Co., Inc.

Tobacco was first domesticated in the New World, and all scientific evidence indicates that the customs of smoking and chewing tobacco were first practiced by Native Americans for ritual and "medicinal" purposes (7). The usage of tobacco products quickly spread throughout the world following Sir Walter Raleigh's introduction of tobacco to England in the late 16th century (8, p. 6). Originally an occasional upper-class luxury, tobacco usage became a "working-class necessity" in the 17th century (9, p. 36). However, the use of tobacco in the form of cigarette smoking only became affordable for the masses with the invention of labor-saving cigarette machines about 100 years ago (10, p. 1337), and world cigarette consumption has increased dramatically ever since.

Presently, about 1 billion people smoke (an estimated 50 percent of the world's males and 5 percent of the world's females) (11, p. 269), consuming almost 5 trillion cigarettes per year (1, p. 6). Worldwide, tobacco consumption has increased 73 percent in the past 20 years (1, p. 20), and worldwide consumer expenditure on cigarettes is said to be equal to one-fourth of the global military budget (8, p. 33). China, with 20 percent of the world's population, accounts for 25 percent of total consumption (1, pp. 7, 9). The United States (with roughly 6 percent of the world's people) is the second largest consumer of tobacco (15 percent of the world total), and Japan is third (8, p. 15). Third World nations account for 54 percent of the world's population, and now consumer about 25 percent of the world's tobacco,[1] having accounted for nearly one-third of the global increase in tobacco consumption over the past 10 years (1, pp. 9, 39).

Tobacco production is extremely important to the economies of many socialist, capitalist, and dependent capitalist nations. China leads the world in tobacco production, with the United States second (tobacco being its sixth most important cash crop). India is the world's third largest producer, the Soviet Union is fourth, and Brazil is fifth (1, p. 7). The global nature of tobacco is reflected in the fact that tobacco is the most widely grown non-food crop in 120 countries (5, p. 281). Significantly, about 90 percent of the countries that now grow tobacco commercially are in the Third World, and the World Bank estimates that these Third World countries now account for 63 percent of world tobacco production (12, pp. 7, 17).

During the first half of the 20th century, growth in domestic cigarette consumption was so strong that none of the world's leading cigarette companies showed any real interest in pursuing foreign markets (13). For example, the 50 million Americans who smoke purchase about 950 packs of cigarettes every second of every day (14, p. 1). However, cigarette sales in the United States have dropped 7 percent during the first half of the 1980s (15). In order to bolster stagnating cigarette sales in the United States and Europe in the 1960s and 1970s, transnational tobacco conglomerates have increasingly turned to underdeveloped nations to expand their markets (8, 12, 16–20). Evidence of the success enjoyed by the tobacco transnationals is seen in the fact that over the past 20 years, only four countries—Great Britain, Norway, Zambia, and Zimbabwe (21, p. 1003)—have reported a decline in cigarette smoking, while 63 countries have reported increases. These increases are most profound in Third World nations; cigarette consumption rose 33 percent in Africa and 24 percent in Latin America between 1970 and 1980 (17, p. 168).

These figures raise an important question: why are the people who can least afford cigarettes (both financially and in terms of health risks) so rapidly beginning to smoke? While the tobacco companies are quick to suggest that people who smoke are exercising their "free choice" as consumers in an "open marketplace," I suggest in this article that political and economic forces go much further in explaining this question. The powerful influence of multinational tobacco conglomerates (in promoting their products and in influencing the tobacco-related policies of Third World governments), along with the addictive properties of nicotine (22, p. 997; 23, p. 1052), certainly are much more important factors in understanding the increase in cigarette smoking in the Third World.

Curiously (but not surprisingly, given the power of the cigarette industry in the United States), tobacco is not considered a food, or a drug, or a cosmetic by U.S. regulatory agencies, and thus escapes regulation. If it were subject to scrutiny by the Food and Drug Administration or the Consumer Products Safety Commission, for example, its sale would almost certainly be prohibited because of the risks associated with its use (24, p. 278; 25, p. 130).

TOBACCO OR HEALTH: THE EVIDENCE IS IN

Cigarette smoking has been called the single most important preventable adult health problem in the world and the biggest cause of avoidable morbidity and premature mortality by WHO (11, 26, 27), the U.S. Surgeon General, the American Medical Association, and the British Medical Association, among others. This greatest of public health problems is responsible for between 350,000 and 500,000 premature deaths in the United States each year (4, p. xiii; 28), or approximately 1,000 deaths per day (the equivalent of three jumbo jets crashing daily in the United States) (25, p. 127). Stated differently, one in every seven deaths in the United States is attributable to cigarette smoking (4, p. 10).

Worldwide, tobacco's toll is more difficult to measure, but Worldwatch Institute estimates that nearly 2.5 million smokers die each year from heart disease, lung cancer, and emphysema (all tobacco-related ailments) (1, p. 12), far in excess of the deaths caused by AIDS, automobile accidents, famine, war, or terrorism. The debilitating effects of tobacco are of great concern to international health organizations, especially for many Third World nations which are well on their way to adding a formidable epidemic of smoking-related diseases to their already overwhelming health problems (especially malnutrition, communicable disease, and general unsanitary conditions) (3, 29, 30). The World Health Organization, for example, has stated that tobacco is "demonstrably a cause of avoidable mortality and morbidity on a scale unmatched by any other product currently available for human consumption" (31).

Even though tobacco-related illnesses are already on the rise in Third World countries, the greatest health damage from smoking appears only after years or even decades of exposure to smoke. Because of this, smokers (especially young smokers) have no idea of the price they will pay later for their current habit (28), and the health planners in underdeveloped countries, facing limited resources and more immediate problems, are almost totally unprepared for the consequences of the coming smoking epidemic.

The World Health Organization has condemned tobacco use in all of its forms as "incompatible with the international goal of improved health for all of the world's people by the turn of the century" (31), and WHO is calling cigarette smoking the most unnecessary of modern epidemics (26, 27). However, despite WHO's public comments on the health hazards of tobacco, the agency has committed less than one percent of its budget for the mid-1980s to actively combating tobacco (1, p. 36). Ironically, while WHO tries to discourage tobacco,

its sister United Nations body, the Food and Agriculture Organization (FAO), continues to be actively involved in the *promotion* of tobacco production in Third World countries (32, p. 242).

In many developed nations, concern about the ill effects of cigarette smoking are increasingly evident. For example, the U.S. Surgeon General, perhaps influenced by WHO's goal of "health for all by the year 2000" (33), has recently called for the United States to become a "smoke-free society by the year 2000" (34).[2] However, for the United States to attain this goal, it will be necessary to overcome the activities of giant tobacco conglomerates, many of which are based in the United States. In contrast, in the Third World there is virtually no opposition to smoking, and the associated health risks are rarely presented. In such an environment, WHO's goal of improving health for all by the year 2000 is being overwhelmed by multinational tobacco firms whose collective goal might be characterized as "cigarettes for all by the year 2000."

FACTS AND FIGURES ON TOBACCO CONGLOMERATES

The world tobacco industry is the second most highly concentrated of all manufacturing industries, with only the automotive industry being more concentrated (10, p. 1332). In this extremely oligopolistic industry, the seven biggest firms account for 90 percent of the world's processed tobacco (35, p. 630). The world's largest tobacco entity is the Chinese state monopoly. The second largest is the British-based British-American Tobacco Co., third is the [former] Soviet Union's tobacco monopoly, fourth is the Japanese government monopoly, and fifth and sixth are the U.S.–based firms, Philip Morris and RJ Reynolds. Removing the Chinese and [former] Soviet monopolies from these statistics does little to reduce the industry's concentration; over 80 percent of the "free world's" cigarettes are produced by just seven tobacco conglomerates (18, p. 17).

The tobacco industry in the United States is similarly concentrated. Over two-thirds (67.5 percent) of the U.S. cigarette market is controlled by Philip Morris and RJ Reynolds, and the 10 top-selling cigarette brands account for 71.7 percent of all cigarette sales (14, p. 66). The enormous size of the U.S.–based tobacco conglomerates is best appreciated by considering the size of some of their components. Philip Morris, for example, includes Marlboro (number one in U.S. sales with 23 percent of the U.S. cigarette market), whose 1985 sales exceeded $4 billion (aided by a $100 million advertising budget). This sales volume would place Marlboro (if it were not part of Philip Morris) among *Fortune* magazine's top 100 companies in the United States (36). The top four cigarette brands in the United States account for nearly 50 percent of the U.S. cigarette industry's sales. The United States' fifth best-selling cigarette (Philip Morris's Benson & Hedges) had sales in excess of $1 billion (with 5 percent of the U.S. market) in 1985, and even the 10th best-selling brand (RJ Reynold's Vantage, with sales of more than $600 million in 1985) would crack the Fortune 500 biggest corporations (36).

Given the enormous size of these tobacco conglomerates, it is perhaps surprising that the U.S. Surgeon General has recently predicted that the U.S. cigarette industry will vanish within the next 20 years. The recent decline in cigarette consumption in the United States is unlikely to drop to zero in the next two decades, but the Surgeon General's prediction is already true in one sense. Diversification in all of the top U.S. tobacco firms in the 1980s has resulted in the word "tobacco" being eliminated from their corporate names. RJ Reynolds Tobacco Co., for example, recently acquired Nabisco (as well as Sea-Land, the world's largest container shipping company, and other companies, including Del Monte), and is now known as RJ Reynolds Nabisco. American Tobacco Co. now also sells crackers, bourbon, toiletries, and more, and goes by the name of American Brands. Philip Morris now includes among its holdings Miller Brewing Co. (second-largest U.S. beer producer) and General Foods, making it the largest U.S.-based consumer products company. Brown & Williamson (the American subsidiary of British-American Tobacco Industries) is part of an international business empire (Batus, Inc.) that includes major department store firms (including Saks Fifth Avenue, Marshall Fields, and Gimbels). Finally, Liggett & Myers is involved in pet foods, distilled spirits, and wine, and is now known as The Liggett Group (24, 37–39).

The extent of this diversification can be considerable. For example, RJ Reynolds, by acquiring Nabisco, in 1985 had nontobacco sales that exceeded tobacco revenues for the first time in its history (by 58 percent to 42 percent). However, the profit margin on tobacco is so much greater than it is on nontobacco products that tobacco contributed 58 percent of RJ Reynolds Nabisco's earnings from operations, compared with 42 percent of earnings from food and beverages (40, p. 298).

These recent significant developments by the tobacco conglomerates may be seen both as a reaction to the health issues surrounding tobacco products in the developed world, and as a logical expansion of capitalist tobacco enterprises which seek to expand their spheres of influence (and profits) whenever and wherever possible (10, 41).

U.S.–based tobacco companies have also already "disappeared" in another sense, because these corporations are expanding into foreign markets so rapidly that they are much less concerned with domestic cigarette markets than they were just a few years ago. In fact, none of the six major U.S. cigarette firms is more than 40 percent dependent upon the domestic cigarette market, since foreign cigarette sales of the leading firms now exceed the volume of domestic sales (24, pp. 284, 287). With domestic cigarette sales stagnating, the U.S. tobacco industry admits that "much of the future for world cigarette sales lies in finding a market away from home" (42, p. 57).

So powerful are the tobacco transnational conglomerates that many developed and underdeveloped countries have been completely marginalized in many ways. The recent interest of the United States' "big three" cigarette manufacturers (Philip Morris, RJ Reynolds, and Brown & Williamson) in expanding their operations in Japan and South Korea illustrates their ability to manipulate favorable trade arrangements. U.S. cigarettes presently account for only 3 percent of the 310 billion cigarettes sold each year in Japan, the world's third-largest market (64 percent of Japanese men presently smoke). However, U.S. tobacco interests have successfully persuaded the Reagan administration to pressure Japan into eliminating its tariff on U.S. cigarettes beginning in 1987. This will make U.S. cigarettes more competitive with Japanese brands and is expected to "bring a dramatic increase in the U.S. share of [Japan's] $30 billion market" (43).

Similarly, in South Korea (14th in the world in

cigarette consumption), it was illegal to possess U.S. cigarettes until September 1986 (15). U.S. senators representing tobacco states threatened to withdraw duty-free status on Korean exports to the United States if Korean officials refused to allow U.S. tobacco products to have access to their lucrative markets, where tobacco use has doubled in the past 10 years (44). In response to this pressure, South Korea has agreed to allow U.S. tobacco products to be sold in South Korea (45). Most recently, in late 1986, Taiwan opened up its $1 billion-a-year trade market to U.S. cigarettes, in response to U.S. government threats of retaliation (46, p. 3).

Cigarettes have been smoked in underdeveloped countries throughout the 20th century, but in the past decade there has been a marked upswing in consumption, directly related to the arrival of the cigarette transnationals in the Third World. This rapid increase in consumption is largely the result of increases in "demand creation," primarily advertising and other promotional techniques (discussed below) (47, p. 96). An indication of capitalism's interest in the Third World is seen in the fact that the British-American Tobacco Co. sells its cigarettes in more than 180 countries (more than 300 brands) and Philip Morris covers more than 170 countries (with more than 160 brands and more than 40 manufacturing and/or marketing affiliates in the Third World) (8, p. 22). Not only international health groups, but obviously tobacco companies as well recognize the susceptibility of Third World nations to the smoking habit, where between 1980 and 1984, consumption increased 3.9 percent, more than triple the increase reported for developed countries (5, p. 283).

In fact, tobacco interests in the United States have been "donating" their products to Third World nations for more than 30 years, purportedly in pursuit of "peace." In a curious interpretation of the word "food," tobacco was included in the U.S. Food for Peace program beginning in 1955. In the 1960s this accounted for nearly 20 percent of all U.S. tobacco exports, but by 1980 tobacco's contribution to Food for Peace was negligible (32, pp. 262–263). This cynical use of tobacco in a supposedly humanitarian aid program served tobacco interests by unloading unwanted surplus domestic tobacco and by exposing millions of foreigners to U.S. tobacco—a huge potential new market (16, p. 264). Not coincidentally, politically favored gov-

ernments in the Third World enjoyed financial aid derived from the donated tobacco. While serving these purposes, these tobacco "donations" have also increased the chances for a smoking epidemic in underdeveloped countries.

THIRD WORLD GOVERNMENTS' POSTURE REGARDING TOBACCO

Many underdeveloped countries have a contradictory policy of simultaneously promoting tobacco production (for economic reasons) and discouraging tobacco consumption (for health reasons). For example, China has revolutionized the health care of its people, and yet leads the world in tobacco production and consumption (18, p. 19).[3] In many Third World countries (including Mexico), cigarette advertising and promotions overwhelm poorly funded anti-smoking efforts that go virtually unnoticed by the general public.

Relationships between the transnational tobacco conglomerates and Third World governments often exacerbate these problems (48). Given the great need for cash in the poor countries of the world, the ruling elites in underdeveloped countries are attracted by (*a*) the promise of substantial revenues from taxes on tobacco products (18, p. 19); (*b*) prospects of becoming tobacco exporters, thereby improving their balance of trade (4, p. 168); and (*c*) possible bribes and kickbacks. Tobacco export revenues are unlikely to be realized, however, because as Whelan notes (4, p. 173):

> Every Third World country entering into tobacco production dreams of being able to export tobacco. But there is actually little chance of improving their balance of trade in this manner because Third World countries themselves are the intended consumers of the tobacco they produce. Tobacco companies did not venture into the Third World because they lacked the land or resources for tobacco production at home, but because they lacked a sufficient market.

Bribes and kickbacks, however, are not unusual. A 1976 report filed by Philip Morris with the Securities and Exchange Commission indicates that $2.4 million in "questionable payments" were made by Philip Morris and its subsidiaries over the previous five years, including monthly payments to the president of "a Latin American state" by Philip Morris's 43 percent–owned affiliate. This affiliate "made payoffs to all major political parties, but particularly to the dominant ruling party" (10, p. 1343). The payments were explained as necessary for corporate survival and profitability, and to ensure that favorable legislation was enacted (10, p. 1343). Such practices are not unique to Philip Morris (32, pp. 264–273).

Economic incentives offered by tobacco manufacturers to political leaders in the Third World encourage the growth and consumption of tobacco, while at the same time making the eventual health consequences of developing a national tobacco habit seem small and distant. Many underdeveloped countries have highly regressive cigarette taxes, which provide up to 15 percent of a country's total revenues (often the country's single largest source of internal revenue). The money that these taxes take from consumers is rarely returned to them in the form of useful public services (47, p. 102).

It is clear that public health has not counted for much when money and politics are weighed against it (32). Given the economic difficulties of Third World nations, the multinational tobacco conglomerates have enormous control over their operations. One indication of this is suggested by the fact that only 24 percent of the underdeveloped countries have laws pertaining to cigarette marketing and health warnings, while 95 percent of the developed nations have such regulations (4, p. 170). Another powerful influence used by the transnational tobacco companies to promote their products in underdeveloped countries is advertising, to which we now turn.

ADVERTISING AND PROMOTION OF CIGARETTES IN THE THIRD WORLD

Tobacco is the most heavily advertised product in the world (49, p. 1062), with tobacco companies annually spending $4 billion globally, according to the United Nations Council on Trade and Development (50, p. 636). These huge sums of money spent on cigarette advertising serve the interests of cigarette companies in at least three ways. First, they recruit new users (thus increasing general consumption); second, they distract smokers from their anxieties about the health consequences of smoking; and third, they present smoking as socially acceptable and desirable (4, p. 182).

With the leveling off of cigarette sales in many developed countries, the tobacco corporations have increasingly turned to the Third World where massive advertising and promotional campaigns meet with few restrictions (5, p. 282; 47, p. 103; 51, p. 93). Prohibitions against advertising in various media (e.g., television) are very rare sales restrictions (e.g., to minors) are rarely encountered, and tar and nicotine contents are rarely declared. Cigarettes sold in the Third World by transnational tobacco companies often have much higher tar and nicotine contents than the identical brands sold in the developed world, where regulation is greater (2, p. 483; 11, p. 269; 47, p. 111). By smoking cigarettes with more nicotine, the consumer is all the more exposed to its addictive properties, thus increasing the likelihood that the user will "be back for more." Also, health warnings on cigarette packages and in advertisements are often not required. The health warnings that do occur in some countries are largely ignored because (*a*) large segments of the smoking population are illiterate, (*b*) the warning is printed so small and insignificantly that it does not carry much impact, and (*c*) there are rarely campaigns concerning smoking as a health hazard. Also, many consumers in underdeveloped countries purchase their cigarettes one at a time from sidewalk vendors, and thus never see the health warning on the package (52).

Tobacco transnational conglomerates employ a variety of methods by which to promote their products, including advertising through television, radio, magazines and newspapers, posters and billboards, and point of sale displays. In addition, they sponsor sporting and cultural events, produce gift articles and clothing items imprinted with their brand names/logos, and promote new brands by giving away free samples (often cartons). An indication of the extent to which cigarette conglomerates rely on advertising to stimulate sales is seen in Kenya, where the British-American Tobacco Co. is the fourth largest advertiser in the nation, despite having no competition (4, p. 182)!

Cigarette advertisements associate smoking with good health and youthful vigor, and suggest that smoking goes with social and financial success.

Advertising, for all its influence in developed countries, is even more powerful in the underdeveloped countries where consumers are "even more vulnerable to the encroachments of the value systems inherent in the consumption ideology" (10, p. 1341). In Third World countries, where illiteracy is widespread, the impact of such messages associating cigarette smoking with "the good life" is reported to be far greater than elsewhere (30, p. 87).

The advertising efforts of the tobacco transnational conglomerates have been enormously successful in encouraging people in underdeveloped countries to purchase their products. In spite of (or perhaps because of) the ongoing serious economic difficulties in the Third World, a cigarette remains one of the least expensive ways to "buy in" to the Western world.

FOCUS ON MEXICO

Having presented global information concerning health and tobacco, we now focus on the particular case of Mexico, which has much in common with other underdeveloped nations facing the "tobacco or health" dilemma. While Mexico is larger than many Third World nations, and is somewhat better off than many of them in terms of certain economic indicators, it is not an extreme example. Mexico, with about 48,525 hectares (119,908 acres) in tobacco, is Latin America's third largest tobacco producer, behind Brazil and Argentina (12, p. 17). This area of land amounts to approximately 0.2 percent of all of Mexico's "arable and permanent croplands" (12, p. 7), and reflects a 24 percent increase in land devoted to tobacco from 1984 to 1985 (53, p. 325). The majority (70 percent) of Mexico's tobacco is used for domestic manufacture, where demand is reported to be increasing on average 4 percent per year—Mexican smokers spent an estimated U.S.$1.68 billion on cigarettes in 1985 (54).

Transnational corporations are attracted to Third World countries because of the opportunity to realize profits. Return on investment is often greater in underdeveloped countries than in the developed world. In Mexico, for example, transnational corporations returned 36.2 percent, compared to 5.2 percent for national firms in the same industry subsector (between 1970 and 1975) (55, p. 332).

Tobacco is exceptionally profitable in Mexico. Tobacco's ratio of pre-tax profit to total gross fixed assets in 1975 was 136.5, almost double that of the next closest industry (the beverage industry's ratio was 69.6) (56, p. 730).

Prior to 1972, independent subsidiaries of several foreign tobacco firms (including British-American Tobacco and Philip Morris) were operating in Mexico. On November 4, 1972, these subsidiaries were nationalized, and tobacco production in Mexico has since been regulated and controlled by TABAMEX (Tabacos Mexicanos), a state-controlled company (57). The transnational tobacco conglomerates operating through Mexican subsidiaries totally dominate TABAMEX (58, p. 158; 59), which "strictly controls all aspects of production, from the production and marketing of seeds to the distribution of tobacco to industrial consumers" (60). While this nationalization of the tobacco-*processing* industry in Mexico has served corporate interests well, it has had little effect on the exploitation of tobacco growers and cutters by commercial and foreign tobacco firms, whose interests align with those of TABAMEX (57; 58, p. 201).

Relations between tobacco conglomerates and host governments in underdeveloped countries are often clouded in secrecy, and information available to the public may be misleading. Corporate annual reports suggest that transnational corporations (including those in the tobacco industry) with extensive foreign investment are associated with a rapidly expanding and modernizing agricultural sector, but the reality is usually quite different (61). Tobacco-*processing* operations in Mexico have indeed modernized dramatically, but this has had little effect on agricultural production or on the technological level of tobacco agriculture. While the multinational tobacco companies derive great profits from their investments, the Mexican peasant farmers who produce tobacco "continue to obtain low yields per hectare and use few modern inputs, despite the incentive of increased industrial demand" (55, p. 336). Not surprisingly, relations between producers and processors are not always cordial. In the Oaxaca Valley, where some 1,750 hectares of prime agricultural land are devoted to small-leaf tobacco (the aromatic leaf that is blended with large-leaf tobacco), peasant cultivators occasionally protest TABAMEX's prices by collectively reducing their tobacco production dramatically.

While smoking is on the rise in Mexico, there are 35 million Mexicans who cannot meet their basic nutritional needs (55, p. 335). They are mostly illiterate, and largely young. Many of them are exposed daily to pro-smoking propaganda in a variety of ways, including free samples donated by the cigarette manufacturers. The Mexican government's ambivalence about tobacco or health is seen in its ongoing contradictory policies of encouraging home consumption of tobacco products while also trying to discourage smoking (54). In fact, Mexico's Minister of Agriculture recently stated that the government would use a "light touch" in its regulation of tobacco production and sales, and would "give prompt and positive attention to proposals for tobacco-industry expansion projects and requests for price increases" (62).

Mexico, like most Third World nations, is reluctant to jeopardize the valued tobacco revenue. Mexico's enormous external debt, rampant inflation, chronic food shortages, and rising expectations on the part of the people (with the accompanying threat of political unrest) all contribute to tobacco's strength in Mexico. The fact that TABAMEX is presently one of the few Mexican government enterprises operating at a profit reinforces its value in the eyes of the government (62).

Very little research has been done on cigarette smoking in Latin America, and even less in Mexico (63–65), and those studies that do exist ignore the rural sector and pay scant attention to people's awareness of health consequences of smoking. During the summer of 1986, I conducted surveys in a rural and an urban setting in southern Mexico concerning people's smoking habits and their perceptions of health risks associated with smoking. Although the data were not gathered from a truly random sample, they nevertheless provide important information concerning cigarette smoking and health beliefs in Mexico. In-depth interviews with 102 middle-class urban Oaxaca residents (in the state capital) revealed that 45.1 percent currently smoked cigarettes, almost equally divided between males (46.8 percent) and females (43.6 percent). In contrast, in the rural sample of 90 men from a highland Chinantec Indian community (66–69) in the Sierra Juarez (some seven hours by bus from the state capital), only 2.2 percent ($n = 2$) smoked more than four cigarettes per day, and only one woman smoked at all. An additional 5.6 percent (n

= 5) of the rural men smoked two to four cigarettes per day, but most men smoked infrequently, primarily during ritual occasions throughout the year.

Except for a very small and innocuous health warning printed on cigarette packages ("This product may be harmful to health"), there is almost no anti-smoking information provided for the average Mexican. Although two major health care institutes in Mexico do have some anti-smoking propaganda, health officials in Oaxaca reported that they have far more pressing immediate health problems, and that their limited resources do not afford them the luxury of a meaningful anti-smoking campaign.

There is virtually no anti-smoking information in the broadcast media or print media to counterbalance the pro-smoking propaganda in Mexico (which includes free cartons of cigarettes given away by manufacturers when introducing new brands). Thus it is somewhat surprising to learn that the overwhelming majority of both rural (83.5 percent) and urban (98 percent) Mexicans interviewed during the summer of 1986 felt that cigarette smoking *can* be harmful to one's health.

To elicit this information, people were asked if they had any information from any source about cigarette smoking being harmful to one's health. They were then asked about having received any such information from each of the following possible sources: official health personnel (including doctors, nurses, auxiliaries, and health promoters), school teachers, radio, television, newspapers, and magazines. While virtually all of the urban sample had heard some anti-smoking message from at least one of these specific sources, 60.5 percent of the rural sample had heard about negative health consequences *only* from friends. Furthermore, while 70.6 percent of the urban sample knew of someone whose health had been damaged by cigarettes (mostly lung and respiratory damage, along with seven deaths), the rural sample had much less familiarity with these problems, with only 21.4 percent claiming to know anyone adversely affected by cigarettes.

Despite their general understanding of cigarette smoking being potentially harmful to health, however, most people are only "aware" of the health hazards in a rhetorical sense, and are unaware of the enormity of the dangers involved in smoking. An indication of the confusion concerning the effects of cigarette smoking on health is reflected in the fact that nearly one quarter (24 percent) of the rural Mexicans interviewed thought that tobacco can help *alleviate* or *cure* certain ailments (such as coughs, colds, and rheumatism), and 13 percent of the rural sample thought that cigarettes help to combat cold, tiredness, and hunger. On the other hand, rural Mexicans reported that they knew of people who suffered "cancer of the feet," "cancer of the teeth," and "kidney damage" as a result of cigarette smoking.

Other studies have found that smokers in the Third World are not well informed about the health risks in smoking (29, p. 18; 30, p. 86). For example, less than 10 percent of the adult population in Nigeria is aware of the potential dangers of smoking (70), and only 8.5 percent of 12,000 Ghanaians surveyed knew that tobacco was addictive (71). The relations between cigarette smoking and cancer, heart disease, and other life-threatening ailments are very rarely understood (72, p. 50). The same observation has been made among Americans, in a country where it is often erroneously assumed that "everyone already knows" that smoking is harmful to health (25, p. 141; 73). Whelan writes (4, p. 144):

Although over 90 percent of Americans are aware of the general adverse health consequences of smoking, relatively few people know about the specific cigarette-disease links. Furthermore, there is considerable confusion about the relative safety of various forms of tobacco today—filters versus non-filters, low- versus high-tar and nicotine cigarettes, pipes, cigars—and chewing tobacco.

Most Mexican smokers would like to quit the habit, as would most smokers in developed countries. [For example, about 60 percent of U.S. smokers have seriously tried to quit, and an additional 30 percent say they would try if there were an easy method (4, p. 212).] Among the urban smokers surveyed in Oaxaca, 84.5 percent reported that they have considered quitting, and 62.2 percent have tried. Of those who have tried to quit, 82.2 percent stated that attempting to quit was difficult, and fully 80 percent said that they would definitely or probably be interested in quitting if there were an easy way to do so. (There were too few smokers in the rural sample to provide significant data about their

quitting smoking.) These findings reinforce what Joly (74, p. 904) found in his survey of smokers in eight Latin American cities. However, given the overbearing presence of multinational tobacco conglomerates in Mexico, and the government's unwillingness to discourage their operations, it is likely that the social, economic, and political climate will continue to be far more conducive to smoking than to quitting the unhealthy habit.

SUMMARY

This article has provided an analysis of the impact of transnational cigarette conglomerates on people in the Third World. Data from Mexico support other studies that have found high rates of cigarette smoking among Third World urban populations, and low levels of awareness of the seriousness of the health risks associated with smoking. Faced with economic difficulties and widespread malnutrition and infectious diseases, health programs in many underdeveloped countries (including Mexico) are unwilling to prioritize anti-smoking campaigns (75, p. 608). This "trade-off" is a costly one in the long run. The eventual response to smoking-related diseases will involve expensive diagnostic and treatment efforts, in contrast to the relatively inexpensive prevention-oriented programs for malnutrition and infectious diseases (5, p. 283).

What minimal efforts are made are overshadowed by pro-cigarette propaganda that portrays smoking as wholesome and desirable. Very few people in the Third World are aware of the health risks of smoking, and cigarette consumption is rapidly rising, as are health problems associated with smoking (4, p. 171). Until greater emphasis is placed on anti-smoking (pro-health) propaganda, underdeveloped countries are increasingly likely to be facing a major avoidable public health problem of enormous proportions—namely, a smoking epidemic.

The susceptibility of the peoples of underdeveloped nations to the smoking habit is widely recognized not only by health groups, but also by enormous transnational tobacco companies. These companies see great growth potential in the Third World, where more than half of the world's peoples reside, most of whom are illiterate, and the overwhelming majority of whom are inadequately prepared to make informed decisions concerning smoking.

An individual's "choice" to begin smoking cigarettes is made within social, political, and economic contexts. In the Third World, individuals are influenced by specially designed advertisements and promotions (including free cigarettes) provided by transnational tobacco companies, whose self-interests require the sale and continued use of a product that causes premature death for millions of people around the world. With the compliance of Third World governments, the health of their citizens is being sacrificed for the financial health of the tobacco industry. This is explained by Taylor (32, p. 246) as follows:

> Warnings of epidemics still to come tend to fall on deaf ears as governments struggle to survive in the present. Few are disposed to bite the hand that feeds them. This is why the Third World not only affords the international tobacco companies the new soil and markets they need, but the political and economic climate in which to make the most of their opportunities.

Third World governments are ambivalent about the tobacco industry and its products. On the one hand they value the economic benefits associated with tobacco sales, but on the other hand they have an obligation to reduce disease and prevent death (18, p. 19). Cuba, where per capita cigarette consumption is among the world's highest, in 1985 instituted an energetic campaign involving social pressures and economic disincentives to discourage tobacco consumption (76, p. 94). While sugar exports bring in about 50 times more revenue than tobacco exports (76, p. 96), Cuba continues to grow and sell tobacco on the international market, with 19 percent of its arable land being devoted to tobacco (12, p. 7).

Despite the rapid growth in cigarette smoking in underdeveloped countries, it is still a relatively recent phenomenon. Because the typical Third World smoker presently consumes an average of only 300 cigarettes a year (compared to 2,500 a year for Western smokers), the World Health Organization believes that there is still time to take avoiding action to prevent the new epidemic (32, p. 254; 47, p. 110).

International health agencies and planners are urging Third World countries to adopt a variety of anti-smoking campaigns (26; 27; 29, p. 80; 47, p. 109; 77, p. 84). Others have suggested that a boycott of products made by the transnational tobacco conglomerates be organized along the lines of the recent Nestlé (infant formula) boycott (78).

What is most needed to combat the coming smoking epidemic, however, is the political will to sacrifice immediate tobacco revenue for the long-term well-being of the population (50, p. 639). As long as the narrow class interests of the upper- and upper-middle class take precedence over the well-being of the population as a whole, then tobacco use will continue to be encouraged in the Third World, making a mockery of the World Health Organization's goal of improved health for all by the year 2000.

NOTES

1. Corresponding figures for industrial Western nations are 16 percent of the world's population consuming 37 percent of the world's tobacco, and for Eastern block nations (including the Soviet Union), 8.5 percent consuming 16 percent (1, p. 39).

2. Health risks associated with smokeless tobacco products have caused this goal to be revised to a "*tobacco*-free society by the year 2000." This article's focus on cigarette smoking is not intended to minimize the health risks associated with other forms of tobacco use, including cigars, pipes, and smokeless tobacco products.

3. The same schizophrenic posture is seen in developed countries as well, but these contradictory policies are at a standoff in the United States, for example, where anti-smoking propaganda (despite being enormously outspent by pro-smoking propaganda) has resulted in a slight decline in cigarette consumption.

REFERENCES

1. Chandler, W.U. *Banishing Tobacco.* Worldwatch Paper 68. Worldwatch Institute, Washington, D.C., 1986.

2. Jacobson, B. Smoking and health: A new generation of campaigners. *Br. Med. J.* 287;483–484, 1983.

3. Muller, M. *Tobacco and the Third World: Tomorrow's Epidemic?* War on Want, London, 1978.

4. Whelan, E.M. *A Smoking Gun: How the Tobacco Industry Gets Away with Murder.* Stickley, Philadelphia, 1984.

5. Yach, D. The impact of smoking in developing countries with special reference to Africa. *Int. J. Health Serv.* 16(2): 279–292, 1986.

6. Baer, H. On the political economy of health. *Med. Anthropol. Newsletter* 14(1): 1, 2, 13–17, 1982.

7. Robicsek, F. *The Smoking Gods: Tobacco in Maya Art, History, and Religion.* University of Oklahoma Press, Norman, 1978.

8. Eckholm, E. *Cutting Tobacco's Toll.* Worldwatch Paper 18. Worldwatch Institute, Washington, D.C., 1978.

9. Mintz, S. W. *Sweetness and Power: The Place of Sugar in Modern History.* Viking, New York, 1985.

10. Clairmonte, F.F. World tobacco: Dynamics of oligopolistic annexationism. *Economic and Political Weekly* 14:1331–1344, 1979.

11. Crofton, J. The gathering smoke clouds: A worldwide challenge. *Int. J. Epidemiol.* 13(3): 269–270, 1984.

12. Steele, I., Third World tobacco growing scorned in West, not Third World. *Tobacco International* 186(4): 7, 11, 13, 17, 1984.

13. Shepherd, P.L. Sold American!!! A Study of the Foreign Operations of the American Cigarette Industry, pp. 862–864. Doctoral dissertation, Vanderbilt University, 1983.

14. Gloede, W.F. Lotsa smoke, no fire: Ban tobacco ads? Marketers stay cool. *Advertising Age.* August 4, 1986, pp. 1, 66.

15. Nesbitt, R. Trade pacts may be boon for burley. *Lexington (KY) Herald-Leader*, October 27, 1986, pp. D-1, D-16.

16. Eckholm, E. The deadly pleasure: Can the world kick the tobacco habit? *The Futurist* 12(4): 261–269, 1978.

17. Finger, W.R. *The Tobacco Industry in Transition.* Lexington Books, Lexington, Mass. 1981.

18. Ledwith, F. Smoking policy and the tobacco industry: A multi-national problem of economic development. *HYGIE [Int. J. Health Educ.]* 2(1): 17–21, 1983.

19. Sangenito, P. P. Latin America tobaccos: It's up . . . it's down . . . it's the same. *Tobacco Reporter* 108(10): 30–33, 44, 46, 47, 50, 52, 54–56, 58, 60, 62, 1982.

20. Warner, K. E. Toward a global strategy to combat smoking: The 5th World Conference on Smoking and Health. *J. Public Health Policy* 5:28–39, 1984.

21. Goldsmith, M.F. Dark days predicted as Third World lights up. *JAMA* 255(8): 1000, 1003, 1986.

22. Goldsmith, M.F. Tobacco-addiction-death link shown but labels don't tell it. *JAMA* 255(8): 997–998, 1003, 1986.

23. Lundberg, G.D., and Knoll, E. Tobacco: For consenting adults in private only. *JAMA* 255(8): 1051–1053, 1986.

24. Sapolsky, H.M. The political obstacles to the control of cigarette smoking in the United States. *J. Health Polit. Policy Law* 5(2): 277–290, 1980.

25. Walsh, D.C., and Gordon, N.P. Legal approaches to smoking deterrence. *Ann. Rev. Public Health* 7: 127–149, 1986.

26. World Health Organization. *Smoking Control Strategies in Developing Countries.* Report of a WHO Expert Committee, Technical Report Series 695. WHO, Geneva, 1983.

27. World Health Organization. *Controlling the Smoking Epidemic.* Report of a WHO Expert Committee, Technical Report Series 636. WHO, Geneva, 1979.

28. Ravenholt, R.T., and Pollin, W. Tobacco addiction and other drug abuse among American youth. *Proceedings of the 5th World Conference on Smoking and Health.* Vol. 1, pp. 183–189. Canadian Council on Smoking and Health, Ottawa, 1983.

29. Wickstrom, B. *Cigarette Marketing in the Third World: A Study of Four Countries.* University of Gothenburg, Department of Business Administration (Marketing Section), Göteborg, Sweden, 1979.

30. Willard, N. Tobacco: Third World warning. *WHO Chronicle* 37(3): 86–90, 1983.

31. Gunby, P. Who says tobacco's bad for health? WHO! *JAMA* 255(8): 1000, 1986.

32. Taylor, P. *The Smoke Ring: Tobacco, Money, and Multinational Politics.* Pantheon Books, New York, 1984.

33. Mahler, H. Health for all by the year 2000. *WHO Chronicle* 29: 457–461, 1975.

34. Ockene, J.K. Toward a smoke-free society. *Am. J. Public Health* 74(11): 1198–1200, 1984.

35. Smoking and the Third World. *S. Afr. Med. J.* 65: 630–631, 1984.

36. Gloede, W.F. Top smokes spending big bucks: Promotions gaining favor to heat up cool market. *Advertising Age*, August 25, 1986, p. 28.

37. American Cancer Society. *Facts and Figures on Smoking: 1976–1986*, p. 13. American Cancer Society publication, 1986.

38. Neuber, D. A year of change for the U.S. cigarette industry. *TJI [Tabak Journal International]*, January 1986, pp. 29–30.

39. Neuber, D. A year of change for Philip Morris. *TJI [Tabak Journal International]*, June 1985, p. 458.

40. A good year for the leading U.S. cigarette companies. *TJI [Tabak Journal International]*, April 1986, pp. 296, 298.

41. Miles, R. H. *Coffin Nails and Corporate Strategies*. Prentice Hall, Inc., Englewood Cliffs, N.J., 1982.

42. Shelton, A. Tobacco tomorrow: Cigarette sales and markets. *Tobacco Reporter* 111(4): 54, 56–57, 1984.

43. Nesbitt, R. Japan to repeal tariff on tobacco. *Lexington [KY] Herald-Leader*, October 4, 1986.

44. Rugeley, C. Senators want Korea to permit tobacco imports. *Lexington [KY] Herald-Leader*, April 5, 1986.

45. South Korea to allow sale of U.S. tobacco products. *Lexington [KY] Herald-Leader*, December 19, 1986.

46. Asian markets open to U.S. cigarettes. *Tobacco Observer* 12(1): 1, 3, 1987.

47. Shepherd, P.L. Transnational corporations and the international cigarette industry. In *Profits, Progress, and Poverty: Case Studies of Internationa Industries in Latin America*, edited by R.S. Newfarmer, pp. 63–112. University of Notre Dame Press, Notre Dame, Ind., 1985.

48. Gereffi, G., and Evans, P. Transnational corporations, dependent development, and state policy in the semiperiphery: A comparison of Brazil and Mexico. *Latin American Res. Rev.* 16: 31–64, 1981.

49. Iglehart, J.K. Health policy report: The campaign against smoking gains momentum. *N. Engl. J. Med.* 314(16): 1059–1064, 1986.

50. Swartz, J. Winnipeg conference declares international war on smoking. *Can. Med. Assoc. J.* 129(6): 636–641, 1983.

51. James, J., and Lister, S. Galbraith revisited: Advertising in non-affluent societies. *World Development* 8: 87–96, 1980.

52. Nath. U.R. The experts meet the media. *Proceedings of the 5th World Conference on Smoking and Health*, Vol. 1, pp. 337–342. Canadian Council on Smoking and Health, Ottawa, 1983.

53. Mexico: Tobacco industry expanding. *TJI [Tabak Journal International]*, April 1986, pp. 325–326.

54. Mexico: Cigar plans. *WT [World Tobacco]*, September 1985, p. 38.

55. Rama, R. Do transnational agribusiness firms encourage the agriculture of developing countries? The Mexican experience. *Int. Soc. Sci. J.* 38(3): 331–343, 1985.

56. Weiss, J. Alliance for production: Mexico's incentives for private sector industrial development. *World Development* 12(7): 723–742, 1984.

57. Jáuregui, J., Kuschick, M., Itriago, H., and Garcia Torres, A.I. *TABAMEX: Un caso de integración ver-*tical de la agricultura. Editorial Nueva Imagen, Mexico City, 1980.

58. Cockcroft, J.D. *Mexico: Class Formation, Capital Accumulation, and the State*. Monthly Review Press, New York, 1983.

59. Mattelart, A. *Transnationals and the Third World: The Struggle for Culture*. p. 94. Bergin & Garvey, South Hadley, Mass., 1983.

60. Esteva, G. *The Struggle for Rural Mexico*. p. 183. Bergin & Garvey, South Hadley, Mass., 1983.

61. Gereffi, G. *The Pharmaceutical Industry and Dependency in the Third World*. Princeton University Press, Princeton, N.J., 1983.

62. Tobacco is Mexico's "Flavor of the month." *WT [World Tobacco]*. June 1986, p. 84.

63. Joly, D.J. Cigarette smoking in Latin America—A survey of eight cities. *Bull. Pan Am. Health Organ.* 9: 329–344, 1975.

64. Joly, D.J. and Sarmientos Acosta, M.R. The cigarette-smoking habit among preuniversity students in Havana, Cuba, in 1980. *Bull.Pan Am. Health Organ.* 17(2): 158–163, 1983.

65. Chaieb, J.A. et. al. An epidemiologic survey of smoking patterns and chronic obstructive bronchopulmonary disease in Porto Alegre, Brazil. *Bull. Pan Am. Health Organ.* 18(1): 26–42, 1984.

66. Stebbins, K.R. Second-class Mexicans: A Political Economy Perspective on Health Status and Health Services in a Highland Chinantec Municipio in Oaxaca. Doctoral dissertation, Michigan State University, 1984.

67. Stebbins, K.R. Politics, economics, and health services in rural Oaxaca, Mexico. *Hum. Organ.* 45(2): 112–119, 1986.

68. Stebbins, K.R. Curative medicine, preventive medicine, and health status: The influence of politics on health status in a rural Mexican village. *Soc. Sci. Med.* 23(2): 139–148, 1986.

69. Stebbins, K.R. Do improved health services guarantee improved health status? The case of a new rural heath clinic in Oaxaca, Mexico. In *Case Studies in Medical Anthropology: A Teaching and Reference Source*, edited by H. Baer, Gordon & Breach, New York, in press.

70. Fielding, J.E. Smoking: Health effect and control. *N. Engl. J. Med.* 313(9): 555–561, 1985.

71. Femi-Pearse, D. Smoking in developing countries. *Proceedings of the 5th World Conference on Smoking and Health*. Vol. 1. pp. 59–69. Canadian Council on Smoking and Health, Ottawa, 1983.

72. Whelan, E.M., and Sheridan, M. Cigarette colonialism. *USA Today*, May 1981, pp. 50, 51.

73. Chandler, W.U. *Improving World Health: A Least Cost Strategy*, p. 42. Worldwatch Paper 59, Worldwatch Institute, Washington, D.C., 1984.

74. Joly, D. J. Organizing for action in Latin America: A proposal. *Proceedings of the 3rd World Conference on Smoking and Health*. Vol. 2. pp. 903–906. U.S. Department of Health, Education, and Welfare, Washington, D.C., 1975.

75. Milio, N. Health policy and the emerging tobacco reality. *Soc. Sci. Med.* 21(6): 601–613, 1985.

76. Tesh, S. Health education in Cuba: A preface. *Int. J. Health Serv.* 16(1): 87–104, 1986.

77. Gray, N. The social and economic implications of tobacco use. *Proceedings of the 5th World Conference on Smoking and Health*. Vol. 1. pp. 77–92. Canadian Council on Smoking and Health, Ottawa, 1983.

78. Peng, M.K.K. The urgent need to control the smoking epidemic in the Third World. *Proceedings of the 5th World Conference on Smoking and Health*. Vol. 1. pp. 561–566. Canadian Council on Smoking and Health, Ottawa, 1983.

28

Free Trade versus Sustainable Agriculture
The Implications of NAFTA

Mark Ritchie

Two competing visions have emerged of the future of agriculture. The first, often referred to as sustainable agriculture, calls for social and economic initiatives to protect the environment and family farms. This approach emphasizes the use of public policy to preserve soil, water and biodiversity, and to promote economically secure family farms and rural communities. It calls for farming practices which are less chemical-and-energy-intensive, and marketing practices which place a high priority on reducing the time, distance and resources used to move food between production and consumption. Another goal is to improve freshness, quality and nutritional value by minimizing processing, packaging, transportation and preservatives.[1]

An opposing view, often referred to as the "free market," "free trade" or "deregulation" approach, pursues "economic efficiency" in order to deliver crops and livestock to processors and industrial buyers at the lowest possible price. Almost all social, environmental and health costs are "externalized,"

ultimately to be paid for by today's taxpayers or by future generations. Basing their arguments on neo-classical economic theories dating back over two hundred years, the proponents of this approach maintain that any government intervention in the day-to-day activities of business diminishes economic efficiency. They seek to scale back or eliminate farm programmes such as price supports and supply management, as well as land-use provisions designed for environmental protection. In world trade, they support the opening of state and national borders to unlimited and deregulated imports and exports. These policies are heavily promoted by agribusiness corporations involved in the trading and processing of farm commodities, which want to pay as low a price as possible, and by suppliers of farm inputs, who want to sell a maximum amount of chemicals, fertilizers and other products.[2]

The differences between these two conflicting views lie at the heart of the debate over modern agricultural policy. Recently the controversy has been given particular prominence by the trade negotiations taking place under the auspices of both the North American Free Trade Agreement (NAFTA) and the General Agreement on Tariffs and Trade (GATT).

From Mark Ritchie, "Free Trade versus Sustainable Agriculture: The Implications of NAFTA," *The Ecologist*, 22 (S): 221–227, 1992.

A MONEY-LAUNDERING SCHEME

The "free trade vs. sustainable agriculture" debate has a long history, but in the 1970s and 1980s, it took on a new importance as presidents Nixon and Reagan, with the help of the Republican-controlled Senate, implemented the most free-market-oriented U.S. farm policy since the 1920s. Legislative changes, culminating in the 1981 and 1985 Farm Bills, adapted, undermined and finally sabotaged the farm support system that had been elaborated in the 1930s to protect farmers from the vagaries of the economic system.

The policy of minimum farm prices for grain was first established in F.D. Roosevelt's presidency, through the U.S. Department of Agriculture's Commodity Credit Corporation (CCC) crop loan programme. Under this system, Congress established an annual minimum price per bushel—the CCC loan rate—roughly equivalent to the average cost of production. If the price offered by the grain corporations at harvest time fell below this price floor, farmers had the right to borrow an amount of money equal to the CCC loan rate for every bushel they produced; this was intended to tide them over until the following summer, when prices would normally rise. If the grain corporations still refused to offer prices to farmers above these minimum levels, then farmers could forfeit this grain to the government without repaying the loan. This system worked well: in most years, the grain companies offered prices above the minimum level in order to get farmers to sell, and there was very little forfeiting of grain.

However, the system was bitterly opposed by agribusiness corporations who resented the fact that the government intervened to keep prices at production costs levels. Grain traders wanted to build up a surplus of cheap grain to export, while petrochemical companies and farm machinery manufacturers saw this as a way of increasing sales. In 1971, President Nixon began to panic about rising U.S. trade deficits, and agribusiness spotted an opportunity to get rid of the Roosevelt programmes. They suggested to Nixon that if he lowered the loan rate to below the cost of production it would give them an international price advantage, making it possible for them to squeeze other countries, especially France, out of world markets.

U.S. farmers, unwilling to see prices fall below the cost of production, fought back, Nixon struck a compromise, allowing prices to fall to satisfy the grain exporters, while promising farmers direct payments from the government to cover their losses. The administration set the floor-price paid to farmers, or loan rate, at a very low level—the level, in fact, that the corporations advised was competitive. It then guaranteed security for farmers by setting a "target price," roughly equivalent to the costs of production. The loan rate was the price the corporations wanted, the target price was the price the farmers said they needed to survive, and the difference was made up by the taxpayer in the form of direct payments to farmers, called "deficiency payments." It was a cunning policy, because these payments appeared to be direct subsidies to farmers; but the purpose of the payments was to support farmers who were selling their crops to corporations at prices far below the costs of production, which in fact meant that the real subsidies were going to agribusiness. It was, in essence, a money-laundering scheme.

During the first years of this programme, the combination of the market prices and the deficiency payments covered basic costs. But the budgetary crisis created by the Vietnam war led to cutbacks in every sector, including farm programmes. By the end of the 1970s, Congress was no longer asking how high the target price needed to be set to insure that farmers survived, but how low it needed to be set so that deficiency payments stayed within a limited budget. The combination of low prices and falling deficiency payments meant that most farmers no longer received enough income to cover their costs.

In consequence the past decade has been one of crisis for the U.S. farmer. According to the U.S. Department of Agriculture, the average cost of production for corn (maize) in the U.S. has been around $3.10 per bushel, roughly $125 per tonne, over the last decade. Farmers receive $1.50 per bushel in market prices and $1.00 per bushel in deficiency payments, leaving them about $0.60 short on every bushel.[3] For many farmer, especially younger ones still buying their land and machinery, their total income is not enough to cover all costs. Many have been forced into bankruptcy and foreclosure: the U.S. has lost nearly 30 percent of its farmers since 1980.[4]

Some farmers have found ways to produce corn

for less than the average price, but often at a high long-term cost. For example, many have taken full or part-time work outside the farm to subsidize their farming operations. The stress upon families and communities has been serious, with large increases in marital problems, spouse and child abuse, and suicides. Many farm families have stopped paying health insurance so as to reduce monthly expenses by $500 to $1,000 per month.[5]

But perhaps the most common way of reducing short-term costs of production has been to intensify production methods, by abandoning soil and water conservation practices and using greater quantities of fertilizers and pesticides. Aside from the adverse environmental effects, this intensification has created enormous surpluses, forcing the Reagan administration to impose one of the largest, most expensive and most environmentally damaging land set-aside programmes in U.S. farm history, known as the Payment in Kind (PIK) system.

THE EFFECTS ABROAD

The creation of a surplus of cheap grain to sell on the international market was, of course, one of the main objectives of the agribusiness lobby. Agribusiness economists convinced Congress that lower prices would "drive other exporting countries out of the world market." Former Senator Boschwitz, a ranking Republican on the Agriculture Committee, stated this as an explicit goal: "If we do not act to discourage these countries now, our worldwide competitive position will continue to slide and be much more difficult to regain. This should be one of our foremost goals of our agricultural policy and the Farm Bill.[6] Economist promised a huge growth in export volume, enough to offset losses due to low prices.

Contrary to the computer projections, although the volume of exports rose, lower prices meant that their value fell from the late 1970s level of $40 billion per year to less than $30 billion by 1985.[7] In constant dollars, farm exports in 1990 reached only half the 1981 level, even though the number of bushels shipped was higher. This low price/high volume policy required a significant increase in U.S. imports of oil, fertilizer, tyres and machinery

imports, all of which became more costly over the same period, ultimately increasing the trade deficit.

The flaw in the agribusiness logic was that other countries cannot simply stop producing or exporting farm products just because the U.S. wants them to and sets low world prices to try to drive them out of the world market. The debts servicing obligations of countries such as Brazil, Argentina and Thailand make them dependent on food exports for hard currency earnings. When the U.S. drops its prices, other countries simply lower theirs to match, or try to boost the volume of their exports in hopes of making up for the lowest prices.

Great as the costs have been for U.S. farmers and taxpayers, the costs to the rest of the world have been just as high. Confronted with extremely low-priced grain imports in their local markets, making it impossible for them to sell their own crops at a profit, many Third World farms have been wiped out as a direct result of these deficiency payment programmes. Deficiency payment schemes have been described as "death warrants" for Third World farmers.

The European Community, similarly, has kept pace with the U.S. by creating its own agricultural surpluses, through a system of price support mechanisms. Within the framework of the current GATT negotiations, multinational grain corporations have persuaded the EC Commission, under Ray MacSharry, to switch to a deficiency payment programme similar to that used in the U.S. It is reasonable to expect that the scenario that unfolded in the U.S. will be repeated in Europe. The combination of prices and payments will be tolerated for a few years, and then budget cuts will be used to reduce payments, bankrupting many of Europe's struggling farmers. The eventual human, environmental, and budgetary costs of the MacSharry proposals, both in Europe and in the Third World, are incalculable.

REACTION TO FREE MARKET FARM POLICIES

Reagan's free market policies in the U.S. were not introduced without resistance. Farmers and small-town residents blocked foreclosure auctions and occupied government offices and banks. In 1984 and 1986, voters threw out numerous incumbent Senators and Representatives, including Republican Senators in the farm states of Iowa, North Dakota, South Dakota, Georgia, and Illinois. Rural America demanded an end to the destruction of their farms, families, livelihoods and communities.

The protests came not only from farmers and small town residents. Consumer and environmental groups began to express concern over the safety of food and the ecological impact of chemical-and energy-intensive production methods being encouraged by free market policies. The national Toxics Campaign, for example, launched a nationwide campaign to introduce farm programmes which would set farm prices at levels equal to the full cost of production, including all the environmental costs, while limiting production to the amount needed to balance supply with demand.[8] A number of family farm groups and rural citizens' organizations also advocated this approach, as a way to restore economic vitality to rural America.

Agrochemical companies began to fear that many of these new proposals could lead to stricter pesticide regulations. Laws were passed that greatly increased companies' financial liability for harm done to workers, farmers and communities through the manufacture, storage or application of their products. To avoid these regulations and liabilities, many chemical companies began to move the production of the most dangerous products overseas. Corporate farm operators also moved abroad their most chemical-and labour-intensive operations, such as cotton, fruit and vegetables.

Reacting to this sharp increase in overseas production of U.S. food supplies, a number of states and the federal government imposed progressively stricter pesticide residue regulations on imported foods. By 1989, as much as 40 percent of imported food items inspected by the Food and Drug Administration (FDA) were rejected for reasons of unsafe chemical residues, contamination levels or other violations of U.S. standards.[9] However, due to budget cuts, the FDA now inspects only two percent of all the imports. This has prompted a number of states, including California, Minnesota and Wisconsin, to implement additional food safety regulations at the state-level in response to intense consumer lobbying.

COUNTERING THE BACKLASH

Agricultural corporations feared that a political backlash might result in Reagan's free trade legislation being dismantled, especially if a Democrat were elected to the White House. They therefore began to explore ways to prevent this happening. The strategy they devised was to move policy-making on these issues out of the hands of state legislatures and Congress, and into the arena of international trade negotiations.

In U.S. trade policy, the government executive has the opportunity to overrule Congress and preempt local and state governments. Trade negotiations, for example, are conducted in secret by the White House. It is extremely difficult, even for most members of Congress, to get information about what is being negotiated until it is too late to analyze implications or to affect the outcome. Furthermore, special rules govern the approval of trade agreements. Under the "fast track" approval process, Congress cannot amend in any ways the proposed agreement. Time for debate is very limited, Congress can only rubber-stamp the final text, either "Yes" or "No."[10]

In this legislative context, social and environmental regulations in the form of farm policy reforms or food safety standards could be termed "trade barriers" and then dismantled under the guise of "liberalizing trade." New rules for international trade could even roll back pesticide and other environmental regulations, while prohibiting restrictions on imported foods. Agribusiness companies have therefore joined with other business interests, such as financial services, drug and chemical companies, and computer manufacturers, in pressuring the Reagan administration to spearhead an international drive to deregulate trade.

The principal global framework for trade negotiations is the General Agreement on Tariffs and Trade (GATT). This worldwide agreement, which more than 100 countries have signed, was drafted in 1947 with a brief to establish rules for the conduct of international trade. There is currently an effort to re-write these rules as part of the Uruguay Round, named after the country where these talks were launched in 1986.

One of the most important features of the Uruguay Round proposals is to demand that nations should no longer be able to limit the volume of agricultural or other raw material imports. Existing import quotas should be subjected to a process called "tariffication," in which import controls are converted into import taxes, called tariffs, and then phased down or out within five to ten years. This would be a disaster for sustainable agriculture in both the poor countries of the South and in the North.

If accepted, this proposal would alter the rules governing world trade in food, natural fibers, fish and forestry products and would seriously limit the right of GATT member nations to implement a wide range of natural resource protection laws at local, provincial and national levels.[11] Many poor countries now use improper controls, often in the form of quotas, to protect their local agriculture and fisheries from being wiped out by cheap imports from industrialized countries such as Australia, Canada, the U.S. or Europe. If these countries are prohibited from imposing import quotas, their own local farmers will be forced to use ever more intensive and environmentally damaging methods of production in an attempt to survive. Those farmers who are not able to intensify will eventually be pushed off their land, leading to the consolidation of small holdings into huge corporate-style farms. this is exactly what has been occurring in the U.S. with the support and encouragement of the Department of Agriculture over the last 20 years.

U.S.–CANADA FREE TRADE NEGOTIATIONS

Aside from the GATT negotiations, the U.S. has been involved in various bilateral trade talks, The first of these to promote extensively the free trade agenda of agribusiness were those between the U.S. and Canada, concluded in 1989. The agreement opened the U.S.–Canada border to greatly increased shipments by multinational food companies in both directions. The talks were used to weaken or repeal food safety and farm security laws, opposed by agribusinesses on both sides of the border.[12] Canada, for example, had to loosen its stricter regulations on pesticides and food irradiation. And there have been moves to weaken the Canadian Wheat Board and to alder drastically the system of supply management used to protect Canadian

family farmers in the poultry, egg and dairy business.

Besides blocking efforts to achieve a more sustainable agricultural system, the U.S.–Canada agreement was a setback for environmental protection in general. It almost eliminated Canadian government spending on ecological efforts such as wetlands protection and forest replanting. These types of government subsidies were labelled "trade distorting" and essentially banned. In fact, only two types of government subsidies are allowed under the U.S.–Canada deal: to help expand oil and gas exploration, and to subsidize companies and factories producing military weapons.[13] The U.S. is guaranteed long-term low-cost access to Canadian oil, gas and uranium resources, encouraging continued dependency on non-renewable fuels.

Among the wide range of environmental protection measures that have been challenged as unfair trade barriers are U.S. laws banning asbestos, Canadian rules to protect ocean fishery stocks from depletion, state-level laws in the U.S. to encourage small-scale factories through tax incentives, and requirements that newsprint must contain recycled paper. In each case, the challenging country considered that the social or environmental policy of the other country placed their own domestic industry at a competitive disadvantage.

An important lesson to be learned from the U.S.–Canada Free Trade Agreement is that there were negative effects for family farmers and the environment on both sides of the border. Deregulated trade is not an equation that benefits one country or the other, according to the skill of their respective negotiators. On the contrary, both countries pursue the interest of their transnational corporations rather than the interests of the general public. The U.S.–Canada deal is a good example of how family farmers, consumers and the environment on both sides of the border can lose under "free trade."

THE NAFTA AGREEMENT

But for the agribusiness and agrochemical countries that pushed it through, the U.S.–Canada Free Trade Agreement did not go far enough. Almost before the ink was dry, the very same corporations began to pursue the extension of the trade agreement to Mexico. This they see as the next step in their plan for a free trade zone encompassing the whole of the Western hemisphere, the "Enterprise of the Americas Initiative."[14]

There are two main threats to sustainable agriculture in the North American Free Trade Agreement (NAFTA). The first is the stated objective of increasing the "scale of production."[15] A number of specific provisions in the text will lead to both increased corporate concentration in the processing sector and the further expansion of large scale "factory farms" in all three countries.[16]

The second is the stated goal of eliminating each government's ability to regulate the importing and exporting of goods. If local, state and national governments can no longer regulate the flow of goods across their borders, as a result of the NAFTA talks, farmers consumers, workers and the environment will suffer.

The pursuit of these objectives will have grave effects for farmers in Mexico. One of the major demands of the multinational grain companies based in the U.S. is unlimited access for their exports of corn and other grains to Mexico. At present, almost three million Mexican peasants grow corn and sell it at price levels set high enough by the government to ensure that they have enough cash income to survive. This system requires that the Mexican government regulate imports very carefully so that this price level is not undermined.

Economists in both Mexico and the U.S. predict that if the grain companies are successful in their efforts to force open the Mexican corn market, the price paid to Mexican peasants will fall dramatically, forcing one million or more families off their land. Most of these families have worked at some time in the United States, so it is assumed that many will head north in search of either farmworker jobs in the countryside or service sector work in the major cities. Others will move to Mexico's urban areas, such as Mexico City and Guadalajara, already dangerously polluted.

DESTROYING FAMILY FARMS IN THE U.S.

The United States, too, has used import regulations to sustain a domestic agricultural sector. For example, Congress has established strict controls on the level of beef imports allowed into the country in the Meat Import Act of 1979. But fast-food hamburger retailers have pushed the Bush Administration hard to make sure that any NAFTA agreement will abolish or weaken these controls, allowing them to import more hamburger meat. Since beef can be produced cheaper on cleared rainforest land in southern Mexico, a sharp increase in U.S. beef imports from this region would cause an acceleration in the destruction of the rainforest. Mexico has also started to trans-ship beef raised on destroyed rainforest regions in Central and South America.[17]

Unlimited beef imports would also lower the income of family-sized cattle producers in the U.S. whose share of the market would be cut and who would have to sell at a lower price to compete. With more beef coming in from overseas, there would also be a smaller market for U.S.–grown hay, corn and other feeds.

This could create serious environmental problems in parts of the United States, quite apart from those affecting Mexico's rainforests. The state of Minnesota, for example, has generally poor soil in the northern region, often hilly with a thin topsoil. The only agriculture production suited for this land, and indeed needed to maintain it, is beef and dairy cattle grazing. If Minnesota's diversified, family beef operations were put out of business by imports from Mexico, the fragile land would most likely be put into row crops, soya beans or corn. On these hillsides, such crops would cause the topsoil to wash away at a non-sustainable rate, destroying the productivity of the land.

The U.S. meat-packing industry is also looking to Mexico for lower wages, weaker occupational health regulations and less strict environmental standards. Cargill Corporation, for example, has already relocated part of its meat-packing operations to Mexico in anticipation of the North American Free Trade Agreement. Over time, cattle and hog production will move closer to these meat-packing facilities, since livestock cannot be shipped over long distances without serious loss. Again, workers, their communities and the environment will suffer.

U.S. fruit and vegetable production is also threatened by the agreement. U.S. producers currently operate under substantial regulations concerning chemicals and worker rights. They pay higher taxes and extend more worker benefits than producers in Mexico. Even if U.S. and Mexican produce growers had the same pesticide regulations on paper, there is little chance that violators of food safety regulations would be caught, because the Food and Drug Administration inspects only two percent of the food coming across the border. Consumer confidence could be seriously damaged by a few isolated incidents of poisoning.

As well as weaker environmental laws, low wages give Mexico a competitive advantage. Edward Angstead, president of the Growers and Shippers Association of Central California, estimates the cost of farm labour in Mexico at $3 per day, compared with $5–15 per hour in California—an attractive proposition for many companies. Pillsbury Company's Green Giant division, for example, is moving a frozen-food packing factory from Watsonville, California, to Mexico in anticipation of NAFTA. The company believes the agreement will allow it to bring cheaper products formerly produced in Watsonville back into the U.S. without tariffs and with few food safety controls,[18] The move means that the farmers in the area who grew crops for the factory will lost their market, and the farm workers and cannery workers will lose their jobs. This impact on the community will be catastrophic.

A similar trend in the textile and clothing industry, where many factories are closing and moving to Mexico, is reducing markets for U.S. produced cotton. Such factories are often a source of off-farm employment for many farm families, providing an extra income to supplement low farm prices. They serve as the economic backbone of many small towns, and their loss will further undermine rural communities.

REDUCING CONSUMER CONFIDENCE

Increased food trade between the U.S., Mexico and Canada is likely to reduce consumer confidence in the safety and quality of food. Food processors will need to over-process, over-package and alter their produce genetically, for it to survive long trips and periods of storage. Quality, taste and nutritional value will be diminished. In the absence of uniform food-safety laws or country-of-origin labelling regulations, consumers cannot be sure about their food. If U.S. farmers cannot use DDT or Alar while imports with residues of these chemicals are allowed, there competitiveness will be threatened, forcing them to support a weakening of domestic standards. On the other hand, efforts to "harmonize" such regulations under the auspices of the free trade agreement are likely to be simply an underhand attempt to weaken them.

For example, some Mexican milk now comes from cows treated with Bovine Growth Hormone (BGH), a milk-production drug banned in Minnesota and Wisconsin in response to consumers' and dairy farmers' demands. U.S. consumers have expressed their grave concerns about this product's potential human health effects, especially when they found out that experimental milk from BGH test-herds here in the U.S. was being mixed with commercial milk. Over a dozen surveys have shown that consumers will buy fewer dairy products when there is a chance that they might contain BGH.[19] U.S. dairy farmers face a potential loss of markets and lower prices if Mexican milk containing BGH is allowed into the country.

This erosion of consumer confidence has already occurred as a result of the U.S.–Canada Free Trade Agreement: evidence of serious problems posed by the lack of proper regulations for the inspection of imported meat set off a storm of publicity which increased consumer fears about the safety of meat. At a time when cooperation is needed to solve major environmental problems, the NAFTA appears to be creating new conflicts between farmers, environmentalists and consumers.

At the same time organic farmers on both sides of the border are under threat. In the U.S., the general lowering of prices on commercially grown fruits and vegetables will make it hard to charge the prices needed to cover organic growers' additional costs. Meanwhile, expansion of fruit and vegetable production in Mexico will increase the overall use of chemicals, further disrupting nature pest-control patterns. Organic farmers cannot use pesticides to control pests driven to their fields by their neighbours's spray. Since they are dependent on natural predators for their own biological pest management, any increase in chemical spraying on neighboring farms will disrupt their efforts to use biological pest management.

LONG-TERM ENVIRONMENTAL IMPACT

The U.S.–Mexico–Canada free trade proposal is likely to have a serious long-term impact upon the environment. In three respects it will lead to increased petroleum use, adding more carbon dioxide to the atmosphere and therefore increasing global warming. First, food products will be transported over even longer distances. U.S. food already travels an average of 2,000 kilometers before it is consumed.[20] Second, more energy will be required to process and package foods for long-distance shipping and long-term storage. And third, farmers will intensify their production methods to boost yields in response to lower prices, leading to increase use of petrochemical fertilizers and pesticides, and petroleum-fuelled machinery.

The U.S., Mexican and Canadian governments have begun laying plans for accommodating the sharp increases in truck and rail shipping that they believe will take place under the free trade agreement. Some of their plans could significantly raise the costs of farming. At a meeting of transportation ministers from all three countries, for example, former U.S. Secretary of Transportation Samuel Skinner praised Mexico's recent encouragement of private ownership of formerly public roads. Calling toll-roads "the way of the future," Skinner predicted that they would become more common in the U.S. too, substantially raising the cost of transporting food products and causing an added burden for the farmers.

There is also a threat to biodiversity. In an overview of environmental dangers posted by NAFTA, the U.S. National Wildlife Federation (NWF) highlighted the dangers to nature conservation and genetic diversity.[21] Modern agricultural production depends on the continued evolution of crop varieties that not only yield high output but also resist diseases, pests and drought. NWF warns that free trade could threaten the survival of diverse genetic resource pools, leaving society without the genetic raw materials needed to protect our food security.

TOWARDS SUSTAINABLE TRADE

Agriculture is the main human activity on Earth and the principal influence on our planet's ecology. Over half the inhabitants of our planet are farmers. But since the Second World War, world market forces have turned much of agriculture upside-down—changing it from a life-giving activity to a life-threatening one. DDT sprayed in Mexico shows up in Canadian fish. Destroying rainforests to product beef eliminates habitat for thousands of endangered species. More than 80 percent of the water in many desert regions, including California and Saudi Arabia, is used for agriculture. By consciously driving down crop prices, agribusiness has driven 27 million U.S. farmers off the lands since 1940,[22] forcing the four million who are left to become increasingly dependent on poisonous chemicals and giant machinery. Overcrowded cities, polluted water supplies, and overburdened tax systems are among the many serious by-products of this massive dislocation.

The current debates surrounding both the GATT and the NAFTA offer a unique opportunity to being addressing these problems. In order to regenerate a sustainable, family-based system of agriculture, it is necessary to defeat the concept of global deregulation and the "new world order" currently being promoted by the Bush Administration. However, we must go beyond mere opposition, and forge a positive vision for economic, political and trading relations among nations. A positive "trade and development agreement" would address the problems caused by varying food-safety standards; if would set minimum standards or "floors" for regulations, rather than the "ceilings" proposed by the Bush Administration; it would outlaw the dumping of goods by U.S. and European corporations; and it would ensure that the full costs of production, including environmental costs, are considered in the setting of farm prices. If these things are not done, we will almost certainly find one day that global food stocks are no longer sufficient to handle the emergencies which will inevitably occur.

As a consensus evolves, we must organize to turn these ideas into policies. Agriculture groups from the U.S. must work with their colleagues from around the world to establish a common set of basic demands and solutions. This common agenda must then be promoted aggressively to all governments and to the public. The controversy and debate created by the current trade negotiations must provide the momentum for establishing new and more just relations among all nations. The survival of future generations depends upon our success today at achieving a sustainable agriculture, that in Wendell Berry's words, "depletes neither the people nor the land."

NOTES

1. For additional views on sustainable agriculture, see: Jackson, W., Berry, W. and Coleman B., eds. *Meeting the Expectations of the Land*, North Point Press, San Francisco, 1984; and Benson, J.M. and Yogtmann, H., eds., *Towards a Sustainable Agriculture*, Verlag Wirz, AG, Oberwill, Switzerland, 1978.

2. For additional views on free trade from the perspective of corporate agribusiness see: Runge, C., et al. *Liberal Agricultural Trade as a Public Good: Free Trade Versus Free Riding Under GATT*, Center for International Food and Agriculture Policy, University of Minnesota, June 1987.

3. These figures are averages. Exact yearly figures are available from Agricultural Statistics, Economics Research Service, U.S. Dept. of Agriculture.

4. U.S. Census Bureau, 1990 Census.

5. League of Rural Voters, telephone interviews with farmers in Kentucky, 1992.

6. *Time Magazine*, 18 March, 1983.

7. *World Agricultural Trends and Indicators*, Statistical Bulletin No. 781, Economics Research Services, U.S. Dept. of Agriculture.

8. O'Connor, J., *Shadow on the Land*, National Toxics Campaign, Cambridge Massachusetts, 1988.

9. *Hard to Swallow: FDA Enforcement Program for Imported Food*, Staff Report by the Subcommittee on Oversight and Investigations of the Committee on Energy and Commerce, U.S. House of Representatives, July 1989.

10. See Wallach, L. and Hilliard, T., *The Consumer and the Environment Case Against Fast Track*, Public Citizen's Congress Watch, Washington, D.C., 1991.

11. For a complete review of all ecological concerns related to GATT, see Shrybman, S., "International Trade and the Environment," *The Ecologist*, 20 (1), Jan./Feb. 1990; Ritchie, M., *Environmental Implications of GATT*, Institute for Agriculture and Trade Policy, 1990; and Ritchie, M., "GATT Agriculture and the Environment," *The Ecologist* 20 (6) Nov./Dec. 1990.

12. For more information, see: Barlow, M. and Campbell, B., *Take Back the Nation*, Key Porter Books, Toronto; and Ritchie, M., "Environmental Impact of Canada–U.S. Free Trade Agreement," *Review of European Community and International Environmental Law*, March 1992.

13. Coop, J., *Free Trade and the Militarization of the Canadian Economy*, Lawyers for Social Responsibility, Toronto, August 1988.

14. For more information on the Enterprise of the Americas Initiative, see statement by Stephen Hellinger of the Development Group for Alternative Policies before House Subcommittee on Western Hemisphere Affairs, 27 February, 1991.

15. North American Free Trade Agreement, Draft Text Article 501, May 1992.

16. For an analysis of the NAFTA Draft Text, see: *North American free Trade Agreement Draft Text: Preliminary Briefing Notes*, Action Canada Network, Canadian Center for Policy Alternatives and Common Frontiers, Toronto, April, 1992.

17. See *GATT Tropical Timber Trade, and the Decline of the World Tropical Forests*, Natural Resources Defense Council Issue paper, November 1990.

18. For information about Watsonville, see *The Nations*, 5 November, 1990, p 514.

19. *Consumer Reactions to the Use of BST in Dairy Cows*, National Dairy Promotion and Research Board, April 1990.

20. U.S. Dept. of Defense, *U.S. Agriculture: Potential Vulnerabilities*, cited in Durning, A., *How Much Is Enough*, Norton, New York and London, 1992, p. 73.

21. National Wildlife Federation Study, *Environmental Concerns Related to a United States–Mexico–Canada Free Trade Agreement*, November, 1990.

22. Bureau of the Census, *Current Population Reports, No. 439*, U.S. Dept. of Commerce.

29

Who Is Rebelling in Chiapas?

Frank Cancian and Peter Brown

Townships in Chiapas differ substantially in ethnic composition, economy, and ecological situation. Within townships significant differences exist between people who are rich and powerful and those who are poor and weak. We believe that all these differences have become more pronounced in recent decades, and that they have a lot to do with where the Zapatista rebellion began.

The rebellion comes out of two decades of rapid economic change: first there was widespread prosperity based on expanded government activity. Then, after the economic crisis of 1982, government spending contracted, opportunity decreased, and there was a severe pinch during the de la Madrid administration (1982–88) and the current Salinas de Gortari administration. Such times of rapid change often spell extra trouble for poor people. While tales of entrepreneurship, success, and economic mobility dominate accounts of economic upswings, most poor people stay poor. And they may find "opportunity" scant compensation for the threat posed by expanding entrepreneurs to their already small share of the economic pie. During downswings, they are often the first to suffer.

By looking at two "snapshots" of Chiapas we hope to better understand those who did and those who did not form the core of the Zapatista rebellion. The first snapshot describes the dynamic economic expansion in the 1970s and the early 1980s—and the political conflict that grew along with the economy. The second contrasts two townships: one where Indian peasants have been in control for decades, the other where Indian peasants have fought for centuries to get political and economic control away from a ladino (non-Indian, mestizo) minority. Given the persistent importance of ethnic statuses (Indian and ladino) and economic differences through this entire story, in the conclusions we will consider the rebels' Indianness and their poverty as sources of their actions.

ECONOMIC CHANGE BEFORE 1982

From Frank Cancian and Peter Brown, "Who Is Rebelling in Chiapas?" *Cultural Survival Quarterly* (Spring 1994): 22–25.

Government spending in Chiapas rose greatly during the populist presidency of Luis Echeverría (1970–76). In 1976 it was roughly ten times what it was in 1970 (in constant pesos). In the early 1970s the Echeverría government spent heavily to promote employment. Later, exploitation of the state's hydroelectric potential by the Federal Electric Commission and of petroleum resources by Pemex (the national petroleum monopoly) heated up the economy even more.

A few simple facts will give some idea of how dramatic these changes were and how important they were to local people. In 1970 all the roads in Chiapas totaled about 3,000 kilometers; by 1975 that figure had doubled, with almost two-thirds of the new roads officially completed in one year: 1973. That year the roads budget for the highlands region would have paid for all the corn needed to feed the roughly 300,000 families living there.

Three new dams harnessed the hydroelectric potential of the Grijalva River as it flowed from southeastern Chiapas to the Gulf of Mexico—the westernmost was built in the 1960s, the easternmost in the middle 1970s, and the third, at Chicoasén, in the late 1970s. When it was built, the Chicoasén dam was the fifth highest hydroelectric dam in the world. In 1960 the state was a rural backwater that had 3 percent of the nation's population and .5 percent of its electric generating capacity. By 1980 it had 50 percent of the national hydroelectric generating capacity and supplied 20 percent of the nation's electric power from all sources.

The discovery of petroleum reserves in north Chiapas during the mid-1970s brought huge investments by Pemex. During 1975 Pemex was responsible for 45 percent of all government expenditures in Chiapas—an amount which itself was three times what all branches of government spent in Chiapas in 1970.

This intense economic activity made the Echeverría (1970–76) and the López Portillo years (1976–1982) prosperous for many people. The expanding economy created many jobs outside of agriculture and offered many new opportunities, especially for Indian peasants from the highlands who gained entry to economic activities that had been ladino preserves—for example, lucrative transportation businesses and skilled construction trades.

At the same time, in those dozen frenzied years before the crisis of 1982, peasants lost land to the

activities that fed the prosperity. Cattle and milk production were made more attractive to large landowners by the new roads that brought their land closer to markets. Lakes flooded land as they formed behind the dams, and Pemex took land for petroleum development projects. Many peasants who found wage work an attractive alternative during the expansion of the 1970s gave up farming and made themselves more vulnerable to economic change than they had been previously.

Political troubles multiplied during the years before the economic crisis. A major congress of Indian leaders co-sponsored in October 1974 by the Catholic Church (led by Bishop Samuel Ruíz) and, perhaps reluctantly, by the state government, increased the coherence and communication of Indians' feelings of injustice and of their demands for change. It helped mobilize people who had suffered systematic social and economic oppression for their entire lifetimes. The next decade saw the formation of many independent and increasingly militant peasant organizations in the state.

Mounting political instability was also reflected in the governor's office. During López Portillo's term (1976–1982), Chiapas had three governors, rather than the normal one. The first resigned to take an important national cabinet post. The second struggled with increasing trouble in the countryside, made dramatic shifts in government aid away from the population concentrated in the highlands to areas of conflict in the lowlands, and finally resigned. The third took office in 1980 with the goal of controlling widespread dissatisfaction through an innovative program of large block grants that decentralized public works spending to the townships. These grants so focussed and magnified existing internal splits in the townships that almost 40 of the state's 110 mayors had resigned before the end of their three-year terms (1980–1982).

Thus, the period of difficult cutbacks since 1982 began with simmering discontent in the countryside. While prosperity in the 1970s brought higher average income, it also made more people ready and able to mobilize around their dissatisfaction. The government's reaction came late, and just before it was enveloped by the economic crisis and international pressure to restructure the economy. Since the early 1980s peasant organizations have grown and became more militant (see George Collier's article in this issue).

TWO TOWNSHIPS

The dynamics of the 1970s and 1980s meant different things to different people. We can best illuminate these differences and the roots of the Zapatista rebellion by contrasting two predominantly Indian townships: Zinacantán (studied by Cancian in the 1960s and the early 1980s, and by many others since the late 1950s), and Pantelhó (studied by Brown in 1990 and 1991).

Zinacantán borders San Cristóbal de las Casas and is bisected by the paved Pan American Highway that was completed in the 1950s. Even before the arrival of the Spaniards early in the 16th century, Zinacantán was on the main trade route that connected the area with central Mexico. Its present population of about 22,000 lives in about two dozen hamlets scattered across mountain valleys and hillsides. The people of Zinacantán are almost all Indians, speakers of Tzotzil, a Mayan language. They have chosen the Indian mayors (Presidentes Municipales) of their township for many decades. In the 1960s Zinacantecos lived by corn farming, mostly in the Grijalva River Valley on land rented from ladinos, by trading, and—in the case of young men—by wage work on road construction. Zinacantán is one of the richest of highland Indian townships; land reform and purchases of private land by Indian residents caused virtually all ladinos to leave the township decades ago. Almost all its people were reached by electrification and piped water systems by the 1970s.

Pantelhó presents a sharp contrast with Zinacantán. Located at the end of a dirt road, it is several hours travel from San Cristóbal. It sits on the northern edge of the highlands, near to Ocosingo, one of the townships important in the rebellion. Like Ocosingo, it has a significant ladino population—about 1,000 of the 14,000 residents in 1990. The remainder are Tzotzil and Tzeltal-speaking Indians in about equal numbers, giving Pantelhó an ethnic mixture rare in the highlands. Much of Pantelhó's land is temperate slopes favorable for coffee production and valley floors ideal for cattle. Throughout much of this century Indians in Pan-

telhó have lived and worked as peons on ladino-owned ranches. Though the last two decades have brought many changes, most Indians still live in small hamlets, unconnected to roads, and without running water and electricity. Pantelhó's much poorer than Zinacantán.

The recent economic and political histories of the townships illustrate how different by the dynamics of rural life in Chiapas can be. In Zinacantán the corn farming that was a central part of economic life in the 1960s was replaced by a diversity of occupations in the 1970s. For example, in Nachig, a hamlet of Zinacantán that straddles the Pan American highway 15 minutes from San Cristóbal, more than 90 percent of adult men had rented plots in the lowlands in 1967. By 1983 things had changed radically: of the 315 men in the hamlet, only 30 percent depended on corn farming for most of their income. Another 30 percent were unskilled laborers on construction (some maintaining small corn fields as well), and another 30 percent were traders, skilled craftsmen and full-time government employees. Twenty men, most of them young relative to those in other occupations, had purchased trucks and used them to transport people and goods. One of the most wealthy had several trucks and the Pepsi-Cola distributorship for the township. Another had two trucks and the Coca-Cola distributorship.

In 1982 PRI was unable to contain political divisions in Zinacantán. Old splits were fueled by internal competition over control of transport and by growing feelings of polarization over economic inequality. One faction was labeled the Truckers, thereby associating them with wealth and price gouging. Though led by a rich vehicle owner, the other faction took on "Peasants" as its label, thus associating itself with the poor, and efforts to control transport prices. In the election for mayor in Fall 1982 the Peasants, most of them regular PRI members in the past, voted for the candidate of the tiny PAN (National Action Party) in Zinacantán. He won by a small majority. As one of two non-PRI mayors among more than 100 mayors in Chiapas, he was constantly challenged by the large PRI opposition in Zinacantán. Before the end of his term, he renewed his membership in PRI.

The split in Zinacantán developed from old and complex power struggles, and the voting displayed hamlet coalitions as well as economic differences. Thus, Zinacantán, a relatively wealthy township whose politics were controlled by its Indian population, found itself in turmoil.

The history of Pantelhó is very different; it is dominated by a struggle between relatively wealthy ladinos and poorer Indians that has continued for centuries. Indians were expelled from Pantelhó in 1713 for their participation in the Tzeltal rebellion of 1712, and allowed to return only at the end of the century—at approximately the same time that ladinos from San Cristóbal began to acquire large ranches there. Changes begun after the revolution of 1910–17 came slowly to Pantelhó: ladinos still owned 80 percent of the land in 1944, when Zinacantán had 32 percent ladino ownership. While ladinos soon left Zinacantán and sold their land or lost it to land reform, as late as 1980 the ladinos who constituted only 14 percent of Pantelhó's population owned more than 50 percent of the land, dominated local politics, and controlled commerce—especially the lucrative coffee trade.

The pace of change in Pantelhó accelerated in the 1980s. A charismatic Indian leader who had sought to be mayor in the 1970s was assassinated, but in 1982 the first Indian mayor was elected, and only Indians have held the office since. By 1990 Indians constituted 93 percent of the population, and had gained control of 90 percent of the land—both through land reform and through sales made by ladinos under the threat of increasing Indian militancy. Nonetheless, most plots were small and many Indians remained completely landless. In 1991, shortly after a ladino who had murdered an Indian was not brought to justice, a large block of Indians deserted what they saw as the ladino-dominated PRI and voted for the Frente Cardinista, the left-wing party that made the strongest showing in the contested 1988 election of Salinas de Gortari. Relations remained strained.

Major inequalities continued. Ladinos controlled transportation and commerce. While in the early 1980s there were 20 truck owners and roughly twice that many trucks among the 2,000 Zinacantecos in the hamlet of Nachig, only local ladinos owned the vehicles that connected Pantelhó to San Cristóbal. By 1991 there were four trucks owned by Indian cooperative groups—but they all worked routes internal to the township. Ladinos still controlled transportation to San Cristóbal and through

it controlled commerce—both commerce in imported consumer goods, and the export of coffee, the township's most important economic resource. Still there was hope among Indians in Pantelhó: responding to what they interpreted as an opportunity to be offered by NAFTA, they began forming a marketing cooperative to export their coffee directly to the United States.

CONCLUSIONS

Zinacantán and Pantelhó both have internal economic differences that led to political conflict in the 1980s. But their situations are very different, because Zinacantán has long been Indian-controlled, both politically and economically, while Pantelhó was politically dominated by ladinos until a decade ago, and remains to some degree economically controlled by ladinos.

We would like to briefly interpret the differences, and on the basis of knowledge of other times and other places, speculate about their importance in understanding the Zapatista rebellion.

The story we tell about Zinacantán is that it was for many decades before the 1970s an Indian-controlled defensive refuge that excluded ladino and non-Zinacantecos as much as possible. Such communities are labeled "closed corporate peasant communities" by anthropologists. They are known for their strict control of internal conflict and their efforts to moderate internal economic inequality. Thus the conflicts in Zinacantán need to be explained. We see two important causes: first, the general prosperity of the 1970s lowered Zinacantecos' need to take a defensive posture that suppressed internal inequality, and second, the competition of the 1970s brought out different economic interests within the township. Anthropologists studying other periods in Mexico and other parts of the world have observed similar internal conflict in times of national prosperity.

Recent reports are that no incidents of rebellion took place in Zinacantán, and that, apparently, no residents of Zinacantán took part in the rebellion. We believe this is connected to the fact that their economic conflicts were internal to their township (and their ethnic group), and to the fact that they are wealthier than other Indians.

The stories we tell about Pantelhó and by analogy about Ocosingo are quite different. There, the prosperity of the 1970s, the new roads and the better transportation for cattle and coffee, also led to greater inequality—inequality that was more clearly connected to ethnic differences. Nevertheless, in the 1980s, as conflict between Indians and ladinos intensified, Pantelhó saw a major transition in economic and political power. Thus, we believe, Pantelhó was not one of the hot spots in the recent rebellion—only because Indians there had just made great gains. In Ocosingo and other townships in eastern Chiapas, on the other hand, Indians and many other diverse migrants were still fighting for land reform when the Salinas government ended the program in 1992. They were left with long-established ladino/Indian political and economic disparities, and with a competition between ladino cattlemen and Indian farmers much like those observed in other places and during earlier periods in Chiapas history. Their fight to establish themselves is still in progress.

All this brings us back to the summary question: Who is it that is rebelling in Chiapas? Are they Indians or are they poor people? The Zapatista Army declared war on the Mexican government on behalf of Chiapas' indigenous peoples. Press reports say that most of the Zapatistas are Indians. Indianness has been and probably will continue to be important to the movement's mobilization. But may ladinos (especially poor ones), in Chiapas and elsewhere in Mexico, have declared their identification with the Zapatista cause. And some Indians (for example, rich Zinacantecos) are less inclined to support its demands. So, the question becomes more complex.

It is hard to separate ethnicity from class in Chiapas, because economic conflicts are often phrased in ethnic terms like those in Pantelhó, where Indian meant poor peasant or laborer and ladino meant rich landowner or merchant. There class and ethnicity formed a single identity that manifested itself in diverse ways. Yet, in Zinacantán, rich meant rich and poor meant poor. Given what we know of [recent] events . . . , it is important to keep in mind the possibility of separating ethnicity from class—for the Zapatista rebellion seems to represent particularly poor and particularly oppressed people, not particularly Indian people.

30

Privatization Fever in Latin America

Eliana Cardoso

The race is on between Eastern Europe and Latin America to reach the promised land of free markets, private enterprise, and prosperity. Countries compete to show who is best at rejecting the past. In the wild swing of the pendulum, yesterday's truth is today's heresy. Yesterday, pervasive public control of the economy was thought to be essential for social progress and decentralization of power, as well as to keep out foreign domination. Today's recipe is just the reverse. Large public sectors entail inefficiency, corruption, and misallocation of resources. Joint ventures and foreign ownership, the sooner the better, will undo three decades of mistakes and lead to prosperity.

In Latin America, state management and public ownership of key sectors have come under sharp scrutiny. Reagan, Thatcher, the debt crisis, and the collapse of the socialist economies of Eastern Europe have spurred a return of interest in free market economics throughout the region. Privatization fever has risen with the perceived failure of state interventionism and import substitution, as well as with the stagnation of most of Latin America's insurmountable budget deficits. State-owned enterprises, formerly the beachheads of social program are now seen as a major source of political patronage and corruption.

The case for privatization is twofold: It enables governments both to unload loss-leading companies and to bolster efforts to rationalize economic relations. Nonetheless, except for unprofitable public enterprises (*parastatals*), which can be simply liquidated, the fiscal benefits of privatization are not clearly defined. If efficient *parastatals* are sacrificed to cover current budget shortfalls, the state may be faced with future cash flow problems. Similarly, hasty privatization might merely transfer monopolistic entities from public to private control unless such entities are regulated. Additionally, privatization carries social costs that derive from the redistribution of income and the potential variation in employment patterns implicit in ownership change. Finally, privatization is not an automatic process; it requires a stable regulatory and economic environment to encourage private investors' participation. The rules of the game must be clear enough to instill sufficient confidence that

From Eliana Cardoso, "Privation Fever in Latin America," *Challenge* (September/October) 35–41, 1991.

privatization will not be reversed or be subject to bureaucratic meddling.

In Latin America, commitment to free market rhetoric has varied widely by country. Most countries have offered lip service to the privatization process: few have actually reformed the public sector.

As part of their overall economic reform packages, both Chile and Mexico appear to have had the greatest success in privatizing large segments of their public sectors. Argentina has also experienced important successes despite fierce labor opposition and a relatively poor economic situation. The pace of privatization under Carlos Menem has been impressive, with the recent sales of ENTel, Aerolineas Argentinas, and other entities. Nevertheless, efforts to reshape the fiscal base through tax reform have borne little fruit and some skeptics question the sustainability of the current process.

In Bolivia and Brazil, rhetoric has far outstripped action. Bolivia's efforts have been stymied by the usual coalition of bureaucratic and political forces, which view privatization with alarm. In essence privatization in Bolivia has amounted to little more than a reorganization of the mechanics of state control over the economy. Brazil's large state-run sector has likewise been slow to disappear. The governments of José Sarney and Fernando Collor have offered a menu of privatization schemes in a bid to keep the fiscal deficit down and thus contain inflationary pressures. But the net result has been modest, chiefly limited to the reprivatization of firms that had been originally in the private sector. Collor's promise to "privatize one enterprise a month" has not engendered any meaningful reduction in the size of the state.

The successes of the Chilean and Mexican privatization programs demonstrate that privatization is merely one act in a larger play, a lesson that Argentina has been slow to grasp. The reversal of decades of statism in Chile by the regime of General Pinochet has created the basis of arguably the healthiest economy in the region. Bold policy initiatives such as the privatization of the national pension fund and the "Popular Capitalism" campaign designed to offer workers ownership stakes in newly privatized companies have invigorated the domestic capital market and muted labor criticism of the process. Nonetheless, policy errors that required the government bailout of financial institutions in the recession of 1982, underline the need to undertake a gradual approach to privatization. Although not as far-reaching as Chile's program, Mexico's privatization scheme stands as a more rational and well-conceptualized method of reducing the size of the state. Central to Mexico's return to free market economics has been the reform to tax administration and a gradual liberalization of trade restraints.

Privatization, in conjunction with tax reform and trade liberalization, offers Latin American countries the possibility of reducing their fiscal imbalances through reliance on the market as the most efficient way to organize production. Yet in order for the process to be successful, governments must ensure that private investors can provide the needed capital, management expertise, and technology that each case requires. Furthermore, the rules of the game must be clear, enforceable, and impervious to political interference. A credible and stable legal and economic environment is key to the ultimate success of the privatization process.

THE CASE FOR PRIVATIZATION

Few economists would be willing to deny the need for reform in Latin America. In addition to the original import substitution bias of the 1950s, Latin America suffered from an asymmetric opening to the world economy in the 1970s, marked by vast financial flows with limited trade penetration. Those capital flows allowed countries to sustain overvalued exchange rates and to finance a bloated public sector. Fiscal distortions caused huge deficits, and prodigal subsidies impaired market signals. High-cost public enterprises figured prominently among government failures.

Disillusioned economists today reject government intervention. This new disposition contrasts sharply with the views of development economists in the 1950s, when state involvement was seen as the essential ingredient in the economic reconstruction of Latin America. The intellectual tradition of Keynes, Prebisch, and Rosenstein Rodan wholly encouraged the belief that government coordination of private decisions and the big push were at the heart of successful economic development. Today, models of increasing returns and endogenous growth vindicate those earlier beliefs.

Nonetheless, presidents such as Sarney and Garcia make us question the benevolence of government. Many studies have successfully detailed the failure of government. The more important reason for government failure results from the less efficient resource allocation associated with protective regulation, especially in trade. When regulation and barriers to trade distort the price mechanism, artificial political advantage guides economic decision-making. When profits depend on policy, not markets, greater returns can be obtained by devoting more effort to interacting with policy-makers than to attending to efficient production. When economic policies allocate resources at less than their value, resources are used merely to capture the right to obtain them. The result is a system of patronage that allows the government to extend economic favors in exchange for political allegiance.

By the early 1980s, unworkable economic policies plagued governments in Latin America. Failures included high-cost public enterprises engaged in manufacturing and other activities, such as luxury hotels, traditionally associated with the private sector. Significant costs derived from managerial problems associated with public sector enterprises because bureaucrats lack clearly defined objectives, proper incentives to ensure economic efficiency, and operational autonomy.

Economic reform suggests the removal of controls. Government must shrink and move away from activities that are better performed by the private sector. Public enterprises must be privatized.

The fiscal benefits of privatization are less obvious than the sale of a state enterprise might suggest. Transfer of assets from the public sector to the private sector does not affect the government's fiscal position because it does not change either its net worth or expenditures. For instance, the sale of a profitable enterprise is often used to mask a current liquidity problem. The current fiscal deficit is reduced by the value of the sale, but the absence of a future stream of profits means higher deficits in later years. But, if the private sector is more efficient, the government might expect to sell the enterprise for a higher price than the expected discounted flow of future profits. In reality, however, efficiency gains from privatization may only be modest. Nonetheless, a case has been made for closing unprofitable public firms thereby enabling governments to suspend current transfers or subsidies made to the enterprise.

In principle, privatization is justified on the grounds that private ownership is more efficient in terms of resource allocation than public ownership because of different incentive structures. But privatization is unlikely to generate major gains in efficiency unless accompanied by other reforms. Moreover, if businessmen doubt a country's stability or fear regulatory reversals, they will refuse to play the game. Countries that cannot guarantee stable rules will find their privatization efforts sharply restricted.

The transaction costs of selling public enterprises are high, even in countries with well developed capital markets. If domestic resources are insufficient for privatization and the home capital market is underdeveloped, the remaining alternative is foreign direct investment. National hostility to foreign investment has faded over the past decade, and most Latin American countries are currently modifying their investment regulations in a bid to attract foreign capital.

As a political issue, privatization is contentious because it redistributes income and changes employment patterns. Issues of regulation and competition play a central role in successful privatization. A regulatory environment must be in place to prevent privatized concerns from exploiting a monopolistic position.

But privatization in Latin America still will be an easy task compared with the effort required in Eastern Europe. The public sector in Eastern Europe represents 80 to 90 percent of GDP. In contrast, even in Mexico, where until the mid-1980s public ownership was widespread, it amounted to only 17 percent of GDP. Problems arising from privatization in Latin America, where a large group of successful private businessmen already exist, are also simpler than those of Eastern Europe. In Latin America, companies can be privatized one by one, while in Eastern Europe most public enterprises, unless they are in the export sector, have to be privatized simultaneously to enforce competition.

EXPERIENCE IN LATIN AMERICAN COUNTRIES

Privatization in Latin America has created less furor at home and abroad than nationalization did in the past. Table 30–1 outlines how much has happened on the privatization front in Latin America.

TABLE 30–1   Overview of Privatization in Latin America, 1970–1991

ARGENTINA
Despite his efforts, Raul Alfonsin (1983–89) privatized few enterprises, but Carlos Menem's administration has already raised $3,232 billion through privatization.

BOLIVIA
Since 1985, state enterprises have been decentralized or transferred to regional bodies, but no companies have been privatized.

BRAZIL
Government raised $200 million in revenues through privatization in the period 1981–89. No companies have been privatized since 1989.

CHILE
Between 1973 and 1975, the restitution of 360 companies provided government with a revenue of $1 billion. Between 1975 and 1980, the sale through public auction of 90 companies and 16 banks produced $1 billion. The Implementation of the "Popular Capitalism" program in 1985 through 1988 raised $1,564 billion.

COLOMBIA
Timid program. The State development bank sold its holding in the local car assembly plant to Renault.

COSTA RICA
State holding company has been dismantled and revenue raised through privatization was approximately $3,850 million and $15 million in equity.

DOMINICAN REPUBLIC
Eight privatization projects have been approved and the Companía de Electricidad Puerto Plata has been privatized. Revenue raised through privatizations has not been published.

HONDURAS
Government raised $32 million in revenue and debt reduction through privatization.

MEXICO
Government raised $2.31 billion through February 1991 with the privatization of Telemex, Compania Mexicana de Aviacion, and Macocozac, S. A. These companies make up the bulk of the privatizations to date and another 124 smaller companies were privatized in 1989 and 1990.

NICARAGUA
Studies are being conducted to determine the feasibility of privatizing the Sector de Industria Agropecuaria Nacional, a conglomerate of companies dealing with aquaculture.

PANAMA
Government raised $567,000 through privatization.

PERU
Until 1989 privatization was limited to a few cases where plants were handed over to employees. In 1989–90, government raised approximately $6 million through privatization.

URUGUAY
Government raised approximately $30 million paid through external debt using privatizations.

VENEZUELA
Plans have been announced but no companies have yet been privatized.

Sources: Privatization of Public Enterprises in Latin America, William Glade, ed., International Center for Economic Growth (1991); *Latin Finance, Supplement on Privatization in Latin America* (March 1991); and John Williamson, *The Progress of Policy Reform in Latin America*, Institute for International Economics (1990).

Bolivia.   The exception to generalized privatization efforts in Latin America is Bolivia. Although Bolivia was one of Latin America's first countries to reform its economy according to the neoliberal model, it is among the slowest to privatize its companies. The creation Bolivian *parastatals* began in the 1940s and 1950s as part of the general trend sweeping Latin America at the time. The influence and direct presence of the gov-

ernment in the economy became more pronounced with the nationalization of the mines following the revolution of 1952. By 1985 the number of state-owned companies had increased to roughly 150.

In 1985, the decision was made to transfer the retail trade of hydrocarbons and their derivatives to the private sector. The same decree decentralized the Bolivian Mining Corporation and dissolved the Bolivian Encouragement Corporation. Nonetheless, privatization in Bolivia is not imminent. Political parties and the state administration have traditionally used public companies to distribute favors, a scheme that has yet to be overcome. Moreover, the government must first turn to the Congress to introduce a special law permitting the sales to the private sector. No law has yet been introduced to the Congress for this purpose, and to make matters worse, the government does not enjoy an absolute majority in Congress, making the approval of such a law difficult.

Argentina. During the last decade, episodes of hyperinflation have alternated with failed attempts at stabilization in Argentina. Although losses of state-owned companies (which numbered 353 companies in mid-1980s) have traditionally been an important component of the budget deficit, the privatization experience was limited by an inadequate legal framework, an inhospitable investment environment, and union opposition.

President Carlos Menem's primary goal since he took office in July 1989 has been to reduce the federal deficit to stop inflation. He has tried to increase tax revenues and cut tax evasion by reshaping the federal tax system and by imposing criminal penalties on tax evaders. Efforts have also been made to eliminate public subsidies and tax incentives under several industrial promotion programs. As of December 1990, a variety of activities and state-owned companies have already been totally or partially transferred to the private sector. These include several radio stations, road repair and maintenance, the national airline, the national telecommunication company, railway cargo services, the exploration and exploitation of oil fields, the exploitation of two new electricity power plants, and several petrochemical plants.

Brazil. Until now, privatization in Brazil has moved slowly, although rhetoric about it is as fashionable today as direct state intervention was in the 1950s. Between the 1960s and the 1980s, hundreds of public enterprises were created, numbering more than 300 by the mid-1980s. In the last decade privatization appeared on the Brazilian government's agenda. In 1981 the government initiated a debureaucratizaiton plan which contained some rules for the transfer of state-owned companies to private control, and in 1985 President Sarney launched a privatization program. Its net result was small.

Of the seventeen publicly owned firms privatized between 1980 and 1989, only one of the privatized companies had more than 1,000 employees. The majority consisted of firms that originally had been taken over by the state in bankruptcy proceedings.

Fernando Collor assumed the presidency in March 1990 promising to privatize one company per month. One year later no companies have been privatized. But sound privatization procedures (such as ensuring appropriate bidding conditions and realistic valuation of the assets) have been established setting the stage for a program that could go far. The federal government will use privatization proceeds to reduce the federal public debt. Supporters of privatization in Brazil associate asset sales with the restructuring of the public sector's consolidated balance sheet, reducing its overindebtedness. This would make the public deficit less vulnerable to fluctuations of domestic and foreign interest rates.

Chile. The landmark interventionism in Chile was the creation of CORFO (Corporación de Fomento) in 1939. Throughout the 1950s, CORFO's involvement expanded, creating myriad entities. In 1971 President Allende nationalized the copper companies with congressional backing. By 1973 there were 498 publicly held companies: 277 were CORFO subsidiaries; 223 were intervened companies; 19 were nationalized banks; and there was a single state-owned copper conglomerate.

In September 1973, a military junta took over and proceeded to free all prices, devalue the exchange rate, control wages, and impose restrictive fiscal and monetary policies. Most activities in the public sector were returned to private hands. Furthermore, trade was opened up. The privatization process was originally designed to return those companies seized by the government to their deprived owners. Between 1973 and 1975, 360 companies (with an aggregate book value of $1 billion) were returned to their previous owners. Between 1975 and 1980, ninety companies and sixteen banks were sold through public auction with a collected value of $1 billion (all sales at market value). The 1982–1983 financial crisis and the fragile condition of financial institutions forced massive rescue operations and liquidations. It brought the privatization process to a halt and caused the government to increase its role in the economy as a consequence of bank bailouts and intervention. Soon after, however, the government resumed the privatization process by selling the intervened banks and companies and other public enterprises. It also established a program known as "Popular Capitalism," which consisted of giving taxpayers the option to buy shares in the intervened banks at favorable credit terms.

Chile undertook a major privatization of its national pension fund in 1980. The new pension funds replaced the bankrupt state-run pension and retirement system. Under the new system, private firms collect payments, manage funds, and supervise distributions. Pensions have markedly increased. At the same time, payments to the disabled and to widows and orphans are more than twice their previous level.

Mexico. In the early 1970s, President Echeverria expanded the state's role in the Mexican economy. With the oil discoveries of the late 1970s, growth surged and with it surged government enterprises. President Lopez Portillo's interventionism culminated with the expropriation of banks in 1982. By the mid-1980s however, President Miguel de la Madrid initiated the economic reforms that President Carlos Salinas would improve subsequently.

Between 1983 and 1991 remarkable reforms took place on the fiscal and trade fronts. Privatization played a key role in the reduction of the budget deficit. It included not only the sale of companies, but also their liquidation, merger, and transfer to local governments. The antiquated Funditura Monterrey steel mill was simply shut down altogether, with a loss of nine thousand jobs. The total number of *parastatals* dropped from 1,155 in 1982 to approximately 536 in 1990. The biggest sale has been that of Telefonos de Mexico (Telmex), which will amount to $8 billion. Telephone workers voted unanimously for privatization in return for job preservation agreements. The funds generated from sales are to be used in social service projects such as housing and education.

UNRESOLVED ISSUES OF PRIVATIZATION

Two important questions have been raised concerning the prerequisites for selling public enterprises. First, should firms be restructured before being offered for sale? Second, what are the macro and market reforms as well as the regulatory homework the government needs to do prior to any sale?

Firm restructuring involves decisions about plants and products, management operations, and personnel. In this area, government is likely to command far less expertise than prospective buyers. The government must make a decision whether to close a plant or to offer it for sale, but once the decision to sell has been reached, there is little logic in trying to improve the price by devoting time and expertise to a restructuring task better accomplished by a new buyer. Of course, measures such as eliminating subsidies and solving legal problems (labor contracts, for instance) must be taken before a case is ready for privatization.

Because firms destined for privatization have to be modernized, governments should accept a lower asking price and allow more flexibility for new owners. In countries such as Argentina, most of the assets to be privatized have suffered a prolonged process of disinvestment. Only after new investments are made will it be possible to obtain a better infrastructure and more efficient industries. If the new owners of the privatized companies do not satisfy the investment needs that the government cannot afford to make, then the process merely transfers rights from the governments to private groups.

The price of the assets being privatized cannot be the sole factor determining the government's choice among bidders. The government has to ensure that privatization is made to consortia with the capacity to attract capital, management, and technology. The conflict between auctioning to the highest bidder and the need to ensure that firms are acquired by sound investors can be solved in a two step-procedure: unacceptable bidders are sorted out according to qualitative criteria before the public auction is held. Mexico routinely evaluates bidders, and the possibility of barring certain candidates from a given sale is already established in Brazil.

Unviable enterprises must be closed in order to allocate public sector resources rationally. Going through formal bankruptcy procedures with layoffs helps credibility. To ensure that the bidding conditions are appropriate, that the regulatory framework for the postprivatization period will be consistent with the current experiences of other countries; that the valuation of the assets is realistic, and that reliable information on financial markets is given due consideration when establishing the financial conditions, privatization requires both recognized international industry specialists and financial advisers. For example, the most controversial issue surrounding Chilean privatizations was the value of the sales themselves. Suspicions still remain that the shares were sold at less than their "true worth." Shares were sold at their market values quoted in the Stock Exchange, as opposed to their book values. Book values were deemed irrelevant, while market values responded (1) to the present value of future flows associated with the assets, and (2) to the risk implicit in the line of business of the company. Because sales prices always become subject to public debate and political controversy, the government needs to assure the objectivity that comes from using the services of independent experts.

A theme not mentioned frequently enough among the good reasons for privatization, but recognized by Mexican policymakers, is that privatization relaxes the credit constraint faced by governments. Today in Latin America, the public sector still faces credit rationing with virtually no access to world capital markets and high domestic borrowing costs. As a result, maintenance and capacity expansion in the public sector have not taken place. This lack of investment leads to a lack of infrastructure that impairs the profitability and competitiveness of private investment. Neither the private sector nor, of course, foreign investors face credit rationing and therefore are much better placed to conduct those operations that require major investment in the most profitable way even from the social point of view. Examples most conspicuously include airlines and telecommunication businesses but also ports and highways.

Labor has resisted privatization with good reason: the logical first step in cutting losses is to cut the payroll. A small number of worker ownership schemes have been set up in Chile and Costa Rica. The main challenge is financing such programs because few workers can raise sufficient capital. Throughout the region, unions have taken the lead in fighting privatization. When Aeromexico was privatized in 1988, the three affected unions managed to obtain substantial severance pay and a 64 billion peso indemnity for their workers. Because public sector workers form an important part of the ruling party's constituency in Mexico, they have

been able to negotiate concessions as *parastatals* are sold.

An argument could be made against allowing employees to buy shares at discounted prices because it could be seen as a giveaway of public assets to better-off workers. Despite this distributional inequity, the sale of a given percentage of shares to workers on favorable credit terms overcomes workers' opposition. It helps to bring about the productivity increases associated with restructuring.

GRADUALISM VS. "SHOCK THERAPY"

A comparison between Chile and Mexico's experiences leads us to favor the gradualist approach chosen by Mexico. From 1983 to 1985 the Mexican government closed down nonviable enterprises; from 1986 to 1988, it privatized small and medium-sized firms; it only undertook to privatize the large projects in 1988. Learning from the experience of privatizing smaller firms first reduces errors and costs when privatizing larger companies.

Chile by contrast did it the hard way. Fiscal correction created massive unemployment. Of course, adjustment was made more difficult by two bad terms of trade shocks in 1974 and in 1982, but the drawbacks of the Chilean approach appear in its two-stage process. During its first phase, financial liberalization took an extreme form and ignored prudent regulation. Credit demand was biased toward high-risk firms, and banks took risky lending strategies. Furthermore, policymakers underestimated the complexity of each transaction and, as a consequence, the rapid sale of state-owned enterprises between 1974 and 1981 had to be reversed. The Chilean process was improved after 1983 through efforts to diffuse ownership and to screen prospective buyers.

Politicians like to get instant credit by announcing pervasive, far-reaching, and quick reforms. But to interest foreign bidders, privatization involves difficult technical problems from accounting to finance. It is difficult to assess the timetable at the outset. The recent Brazilian experience shows that it is inexpedient to announce an unrealistic timetable. Privatization is a prolonged process that has made it impossible for Collor to fulfill his promise of privatizing one company per month. An anticipated process, which drags out, creates uncertainty and political friction. This it is more expedient, before announcing each privatization, to get the case ready by adjusting product prices, eliminating subsidies, and solving legal problems such as labor contracts.

Macroreform is an essential prerequisite to successful privatization. Privatization can only achieve its ends if the marketplace is a stable, unfettered, economic system. Thus, the mechanism of reform necessarily includes liberalization. Moreover, buyers of public enterprises need to know the economic environment in which they will have to operate, what tax structure they will have to face, and how the trade regime will affect profits. Barriers to entry in an industry and access to intermediate goods in world markets are among important prior considerations that affect the anticipated profitability of firms and thus the price that could be realized on sale.

Finally, managers must be granted autonomy from political interference and receive the right incentives. This can happen only if the economic environment is stable and businessmen have the confidence to make long-term investments without fearing that their decisions are liable to be overturned for political reasons.

Legal rules are a common good allowing coordination of individual actions. Erratic, discretionary rules and privileged access to public officials limit the ability of economic entities to contract, and thus produce economic losses. An impartial enforcement mechanism of explicit legal rules is essential to facilitate private contracting. Neutrally enforced legislation presumes a stable government committed to the existing laws and to the strict enforcement of these laws.

31

Accommodation and Resistance
Ejidatario, Ejidataria, and Official Views of Ejido Reform

Lynn Stephen

INTRODUCTION

On January 1, 1994, the Zapatista Army of National Liberation (EZLN) composed primarily of indigenous peasants from six Mayan ethnic groups took over four country seats and opened a new epoch in agrarian political history in Mexico. In the names of Emiliano Zapata and Pancho Villa they called for "work, land, housing, food, health, education, independence, liberty, democracy, justice, and peace." Their later and more specific demands focused on democratizing the political process in Mexico, respect for the rights of indigenous peoples, and land. In many of their communiques the Zapatistas suggested the dismantling of recent changes made in Article 27 of the Mexican constitution.

A cornerstone of Mexico's 1990s policy encouraging privatization and foreign investment is ending redistribution of land to peasants and allowing the 54 percent of Mexican national territory held in ejidos and indigenous communities to be privatized. *Ejido* refers to agrarian reform communities granted land taken from large landholders after the Mexican revolution. Until the change in Article 27 in the Mexican constitution made in 1992, ejido land was held corporately by the group of people constituting the ejido. This corporate group elected their own officials who governed the ejido and interacted with government offices such as the Agrarian Reform Ministry (Secretaría de Reforma Agraria, SRA) and the Ministry of Agriculture and Water Resources (Secretaría de Agricultura y Recursos Hydraulicos, SARH). Heads of households had use rights to the land that could be inherited by their offspring and many families have consistently worked the same parcels of land through several generations, Ejido land could not be legally sold or rented. Indigenous communities, legally called agrarian communities, did not receive land, but had their landholdings legally recognized and titled under the 1942 agrarian reform law. Land in agrarian communities is communally held land and does not necessarily follow the same pattern of land use as ejido land. Rotation of plots and the assignment of different plots at different points in time to community members has characterized the

From Lynn Stephen, "Accommodation and Resistance: Ejidatario, Ejidataria, and Official Views of Ejido Reform," *Urban Anthropology* 23 (2–3): 233–265, 1994.

use of collective land in some indigenous communities. Here I will use the term indigenous community to refer to *comunidades agrarias*, to recognize their cultural legacy as well as land-use patterns.

Modifications to Article 27 of the Constitution grant ejidatarios the ability to sell, buy or rent land ejido, to hire labor or to associate with other producers and third parties, and to hold contracts with or establish joint-venture schemes with domestic and foreign private investors. Most significantly, it allows individual ejidatarios who have had use rights to land, the possibility of holding an individual title to land after going through a certification and titling program known as PROCEDE or the Program for Certification of Ejidal Rights and Titling of Urban House Lots.

This article looks at the reactions of what might be termed "the silent majority" of Mexican rural workers and peasants who have entered into the government's certification and titling program. Their viewpoints are contrasted with those of government officials, many of them young, who have been recruited to carry out a land reform program which is eventually predicted to result in the displacement of up to 15 percent of Mexico's population from the countryside. While the policy was written for a unitary *campesino* population, in its initial phases it is already apparent that it has variable impact on people living in the countryside in relation to age, gender, class, and also ethnicity.

While most of the rural men and women included in this research voluntarily entered the government's certification program, most express a contradictory position about the policy's ability to improve their lives. Much of the frustration, historical connections with the land, and doubts about the government expressed in the communiques of the Zapatistas can be seen in the words and actions of the people highlighted here. On the other side are optimistic government workers who began wit a firm belief in their project and are facing never-ending obstacles to the certification process. Research for this article was carried out in December, 1992, and July and August of 1993. The fundamental change in Mexican agrarian politics brought about by the Zapatista rebellion and the response to it by peasant and indigenous organizations has changed the context in which ejido reform efforts must now progress.

This article begins by describing the structure and functions of the Procuraduría Agraria (Agrarian Ombudsmen's Office) created to administer the ejido reform, the certification process, and the perspectives of employees of the Procuraduría about the program they are administering. Then contrasting views on the ejido reform held by men and women and older and younger generations of ejidatarios from three ejidos in Oaxaca, Mexico, are highlighted. The article concludes by discussing future implications of the land reform, the relationship of ejidatarios' behavior to theories of accommodation and resistance to state-imposed economic change, and the implications of the Zapatista rebellion and its aftermath for the future of the ejido reform program.

CREATION OF THE PROCURADURÍA AGRARIA

In February, 1993, President Salinas de Gortari spoke to a large meeting attended by representatives of both official and independent peasant organizations. He stated:

> We have reformed article 27 of the constitution so that it now explicitly protects the ejidos and agrarian communities, opens new opportunities for these entities to associate with other producers and parties, explicitly prohibits latifundios and at the same time, fixes ejido forms of production, and gives ejidatarios the decision-making power that allows them to behave like legitimate owners of their land.
>
> . . . In its time, Mexico's Agrarian Reform succeeded in provided land and with that inheritance an income source for 3.5 million families in the countryside. Today with the constitutional reform and new laws, we are able to solidify the inheritance that rural men and women gained through their struggle for land (Salinas de Gortari 1993).

To accommodate the dramatic changes in the constitution referred to by President Salinas a new government office was created, the Procuraduría Agraria. This office is charged with eventually incorporating all of Mexico's 28,058 ejidos and indigenous communities into the certification and titling program which is at the heart of ejido reform.

Nationally, the Procuraduría employs more than 3,000 people, most of whom are not the usual bureaucrats. Instead of coming from a history of government employment, many are fresh out of the university. In an effort to wipe the slate clean of previous government-farmer interactions, a new culture is being projected for ejidos: one which is to limit paternalism and center decision-making in the ejido, empowering people to make their own decisions about what to do with their land. Officials at the higher levels of the Procuraduría Agraria believe that in many communities elected ejido officials acted more or less as *caciques* or political bosses. They are believed to have ruled ejidos as little fiefdoms and to have allowed little true participation from ejido members. While this may be true in some cases, it is not uniformly the case. In addition, officials correctly perceive that most rural inhabitants of Mexico viewed the government as a last resort in resolving land disputes through the Ministry of Agrarian Reform and as occasionally offering small handouts and projects to help out poor farmers. By and large rural men and women were treated as passive recipients of government projects and judged incapable of knowing what they needed to improve their lives or of governing themselves. The intentions of the certification program are to empower peasants to make their own decisions. This is an interesting proposition given the fact that very few peasant organizations participated in the design of the certification program nor were they consulted about its implementation.

The language of the Procuraduría suggests that the program is concerned with men, women, and families and their future in the countryside. The certification program of the Procuraduría is built around protecting the rights of ejidatarios through providing them with certificates specifying that particular plots of land belong to them as individuals. The possibility of holding individual title to a piece of land, however small, has motivated ejidatarios to formally enter the government's certification program. Upon signing up, they receive an onslaught of information, official visits from lawyers and agronomists, advice, teams to measure their community boundaries and individual plots, invitations to participate in programs to "help" peasants and a pile of paper to document the entire process. This is described below.

The Procuraduría has a structure of regional offices (*delegaciones*) and local districts (*residencias*). The state of Oaxaca, for example, is one regional office and has ten local districts. Each regional office has a director. Because the national head of the Procuraduría, Dr. Arturo Warman, was formerly the head of the National Indian Institute (INI), other INI employees have been tapped to staff the Procuraduría office throughout the nation. The head of Oaxaca's Procuraduría is a former INI employee. His background in agrarian issues came primarily through historical research and working in defense of indigenous land rights.

Below the regional director are three levels of employees. Each local district is overseen by a *residente* who acts as a coordinator and overseer. Below this person are *visitadores*, literally "visitors," young professionals who have completed an intensive three-week training session on the new agrarian reform law. Below them, but working closely with them are *becarios campesinos/auxiliaries* or auxiliary "peasant fellows." These are also young people, supposedly from rural backgrounds, who work with the *visitadores* in researching legal issues and organizing and training ejidatarios as they go through the certification process. In August, 1993, there were 89 *visitadores* and 170 *becarios campesinos* in the Oaxaca regional office.

Interviews with seven *visitadores* in the state of Oaxaca revealed consistent profiles of these government ambassadors. Most are recent college graduates in law and agronomy, and a few have degrees in social science. Many were recruited directly from their universities by the Procuraduría. Most are in their twenties and have relatively little experience working professionally in peasant communities. There were a few exceptional *visitadores* who have worked five to ten years in a variety of grassroots level development programs. Most of the *visitadores'* knowledge about the history of agrarian reform in Mexico and its consequences for rural inhabitants comes primarily from the three week intensive course they completed before beginning their work for the Procuraduría.

All but one *visitador* interviewed expressed a high level of confidence in the certification program, indicating their belief that they were helping to preserve the ejido and assisting people in obtaining their basic rights as individual property owners. Few were concerned with issues of privatization or its potential consequences to the social organization of the ejido. One of the few indigenous *visitadores* in Oaxaca of Mixe origin stated:

> I think the certification program is good. It will reinforce and strengthen everything, especially the rights of ejidatarios. . . . The process cannot undermine an ejido that has clear internal bylaws and strong customs. The ejidos are capable of preserving their way of life and unity.

He refers to an important part of the certification program which is helping each ejido create its own set of internal bylaws for decision making. There is no one pattern that must be followed. Most ejidos are presented with the same model, however. By preserving customs he may be referring to varied patterns of land-use such as rotating land of varying quality among community members and working collectively to farm certain areas as a part of *tequio* or reciprocal labor obligations.

Another *visitador* with an unusual amount of experience working with peasants and urban poor people commented that the training course emphasized all the wonderful things that certification would do to preserve the rights of ejidatarios, but failed to mention some of the negatives.

> I do think that people will privatize. If we don't strengthen the ejidos as units then they will privatize. This program does give legal security to ejidatarios, but it also offers security for the investor. A lot of people working here don't recognize this. In the training courses we received, they didn't want to really acknowledge the dangers of privatization. It wasn't dealt with. I think most people who work here don't really see both sides of the coin.

While language promoting the certification program promotes its positive impact on rural families, few employees of the Procuraduría ever spoke of the program in terms of its impact on family members. At a number of levels, information about its potential impact on women and young people had to be explicitly solicited. When questions were answered, it was almost always seen as beneficial to women as reflected in this interchange with the director from Oaxaca.

> The law will restore democracy and give legal security to women. For example, when a woman is an ejidataria, and she starts to get old and weak, the president of the ejido would often give her parcel to someone else on the assumption that she couldn't work it. With this new certification program, the president of the ejido doesn't have the right to do that. Now conditions exist so that the woman can defend her rights and hang onto her land.

He was then asked to comment on the law's effect on married women who were not named as ejidatarias.

> Well, they could participate in a UAIM. They could also negotiate access to the land through someone else.

A UAIM refers to an Agro-Industrial Unit for Women. A change in the Agrarian Reform law in 1971 allowed women who were not ejidatarias to receive a plot of land (as a group) for a productive project such as planting corn and beans, an orchard, a chicken hatchery, vegetable gardening, tortilla factories, or bakeries. As a group the women had the vote of one ejidatario.

At present there are no plans in the Procuraduría to instruct ejidos in how to structure internal bylaws to better include the participation of women and young people. In the official literature of the Procuraduría Agraria, women are noted only in reference to how the program will benefit "hombres y mujeres del campo mexicano" (men and women in the Mexican countryside) and how the program will coordinate with the National Solidarity Program "which is taking on the situation of those groups that require special attention: residents, women, indigenous people, and workers affected by the most severe social problems" (Warman 1993:5). Women are periodically named as social actors who will benefit from the program, but there is no consideration of the fact that most women do not have a formal role in the ejido political structure. Only those individuals formally named as ejidatarios can vote in ejido meetings. In most ejidos, men form 70–95 percent of the voting body. Overall, employees in the Procuraduría express a sincere belief that the program will help save the Mexican ejido, promote democratic processes in ejido assemblies, and guarantee individual property rights that will benefit everyone in the family unit.

THE CERTIFICATION PROCESS

To receive an individual certificate for their piece of land, (which under a separate process can be converted to a title) ejidatarios must go through a formal series of meetings, measuring procedures, and dispute resolutions with officials from the Procuraduría, from The Institute of Statistics, Geography and Information (Instituto de Estadística, Geografía e Informática-INEGI) and from The National Agrarian Registry (Registro Agrario Nacional, RAN). The process begins by visits from a *visitador* and one or two *auxiliares* from the Procuraduría to "inform" and "sensitize" people in the ejido. They usually meet several times with ejido officials (president, secretary, treasurer, security commission, and their alternates). In the process of meeting with ejido officials and small groups of ejidatarios unofficially, *visitadores* and *auxiliares* gather data about the ejido for a diagnostic questionnaire and are supposed to assess the viability of the ejido being successfully incorporated into the certification program.

The internal structure of the ejido is as follows: *comisariado ejidal* (ejido commissioner, head elected official), *secretario* (secretary), *tesorero* (treasurer), *Consejo de Vigilancia* (Security Council) consisting of *presidente* (president) and four to five members. Each of these offices also has an alternate (suplente). The *Consejo de Vigilancia* is in charge of maintaining the security of the ejido's boundaries with neighboring communities, private property and with other ejidos as well as resolving internal disputes. They also play key roles in any land disputes through interacting with officials from the Secretary of Agrarian Reform.

Once initial meetings have taken place and the ejido is perceived as "ready," an official meeting for "information and announcing" the certification program is held. All ejidatarios are highly encouraged to come to this meeting in which officials from the Procuraduría together with employees of INEGI outline the program. Fifty percent of the ejidatarios are supposed to be present at this meeting where a decision is made about whether or not to formally enter the certification program. At this same meeting an "Auxiliary Commission" is created which then is supposed to be the primary group of people responsible for carrying out the certification process in conjunction with elected ejido officials. The creation of a second set of ejido authorities through the "auxiliary commission" often ends up in subtle conflict as they take over the role of elected ejido officials. In most cases both this "auxiliary commission" and elected ejido officials end up working with and/or opposing the certification process. All the steps which are gone through tus involve a group of 16 ejidatarios who go to a never-ending round of meetings, discussions, and measurements.

After an ejido formally enters the certification program, an information meeting is supposed to be held by the auxiliary commission to get approval from the ejidatarios in drawing up a list of those who have rights to land, creating a hand-drawn map which shows the distribution of individual plots within the ejido, and to clarify any internal conflicts. There are three categories of individuals with rights to land: (1) *Ejidatarios con derechos* possess a certificate that recognizes their ejido grant. (2) *Posesionarios con derechos* have parcels of land that they work, but do not have a certificate that recognizes their right to that land. They have the most to gain from the certification and titling process. (3) *Avecindados* do not have land to work, but possess land for housing and are eligible to receive titles for that land. To be included on the list of those who have rights to land, ejidatarios have to present the following documents: birth certificate and certificate of individual agrarian rights if they have it, or a letter certifying their rights from the ejido commissioner. Those who are named as inheriting ejido rights also must present documents. Gathering all of the documents is a very time-consuming process.

The most labor intensive part of the certification program then begins. INEGI officials arrive in the community and begin measuring all of the individual ejidatarios' plots. Measuring requires the presence of the comisión auxiliar, ejidatarios whose plots border one another, and elected ejido officials come along as well. Often people do not appear for the measuring of their plots and it has to be repeatedly rescheduled. And disagreements which have been laid aside take on new life as ejidatarios argue over whether a neighbor has slowly encroached on their plot or if putting in a road through the ejido is penalizing them. Boundaries must also be clarified with all surrounding communities, other ejidos, and all private landowners. In many Oaxacan ejidos this can involve a series of meetings with up to seven or eight other communities and ejidos as well as dozens of private land holders.

INEGI officials and ejido officials must walk to the far corners of the ejido and communal boundaries to verify where the land of one ejido or community ends and that of another begins. This process brings to light historical community battles over land, past measuring and mapping errors, and disagreements that were officially resolved between communities in the Secretary of Agrarian Reform, but remain unofficially unresolved as ejidatarios remember that their grandfathers and grandmothers were not in agreement with past decisions. Most of the ejidos that have begun the certification program remain stuck in this phase because of internal and external land disputes.

If all disputes have been resolved, then a formal meeting is held to approve the list of all who have rights to land, to approve the boundaries of the ejido and the measurements and assignments of individual plots of land. The ejido assembly also has to approve the designation of land assigned to common use and as urban house plots. If this has all been agreed upon, then RAN provides certificates of individual ejido plots, certificates showing land designated for communal use, and titles for urban house plots.

CASE STUDY COMMUNITIES

The state of Oaxaca has between 1,325 and 1,480 ejidos and indigenous communities. Different agencies have published different numbers (see Fundación Oaxaca, A.C. 1992, INEGI 1988; Procuraduría Agraria 1993:10). Seventy percent of Oaxaca's territory is held in ejido or communal status. There are approximately 330,000 ejidatarios

and comuneros who make up 43.7 percent of the economically active population of the state (Fundación Oaxaca, A.C. 1992: 4). These 330,000 individuals are the targets of the Procuraduría's certification program. This study focuses on three ejido communities that entered the certification and titling process in 1993.

1. Santa María del Tule

Santa María del Tule is one of the oldest ejidos in Oaxaca, located in a community of Zapotec indigenous origin. Formed in 1917, the ejido has a total of 599 hectares. As the population of the ejido increased and the original ejido land was divided up among the children and grandchildren of the original ejidatarios, each person received an increasingly smaller piece of land. By the 1960s and 1970s, many ejidatarios received only one to two hectares of land (2.47–4.94 acres), not enough to live from. Ejido land is planted in corns, beans, and squash with some of it dedicated to commercial vegetable production. Most of the corn and beans produced are for subsistence,but some are sold in local markets. Because of its proximity to Oaxaca, many younger ejidatarios or sons and daughters of ejidatarios began working full-time in Oaxaca as laborers, maids, market vendors, and with increasing education as clerks and secretaries. By the 1980s, there were two distinct generations of ejidatarios: those ages 40–80 who still worked full-time in the fields and those in their 20s and 30s who were more oriented toward working in the urban wage labor force.

By 1992 there were 308 people claiming ejidal rights in El Tule. Of these, 79 or 25 percent are women, primarily widows and single mothers. El Tule entered the certification process in May of 1993 and in August, 1993 was involved in clarifying internal boundary disputes between ejidatarios.

2. Unión Zapata

Located about 45 kilometers from Oaxaca, Unión Zapata is one of the poorest communities found in the central valleys of Oaxaca. It was cobbled together from five surrounding communities to produce the requisite 20 families needed to form an ejido. Most people in the community are of mestizo origin. Ejido land is dedicated to corn, beans, and squash for local consumption with some production of tomatoes and other vegetables for local markets. A majority of women produce milk and cheese products sold in local markets. While older ejidatarios in Unión Zapata continued to work their land in the 1980s, their sons and daughters began to work increasingly outside of the ejido. A chicken-hatching plant employs 10–15 young men and another ten are working in a PEMEX gas station in nearby Tlacolula. Others work in Oaxaca or have begun to migrate to the United States. Interviews revealed a migration flow beginning in the mid-1980s of people now in their twenties and thirties. Seventy-four people are currently recognized as having ejidal rights. Four of them or 5.4 percent are women. In 1990, Unión Zapata had a population of 696, with approximately 106 households.

3. San Dionisio Ocotlán

Located a few kilometers from the market center of Ocotlán de Morelos, San Dionisio has a population of about 900. San Dionisio once had a large number of Zapotec speakers, but now most people identify as Spanish-speaking. Corn, beans, squash, and soybeans are grown on ejido land. Many younger men work in wage labor jobs in construction or in light manufacturing and women sell milk and cheese products in Ocotlán. About 20 women in the community also produce embroidery on a piecework basis for merchants in nearby San Antonio. The 384 hectare ejido has a total of 93 members, 20 of whom or about 21 percent are women. A UAIM (Agro-Industrial Unit for Women) was established in the community in 1984.

San Dionisio entered the ejido certification program in May, 1993. In August, 1993, ejidatarios faced a number of problems. They have a border dispute with the neighboring Zapotec community of Santa Lucía. In addition, some members of the ejido want to take away the land allotted to women in the UAIM because of their internal conflicts. Two different groups of women are now fighting to be recognized as official members of the UAIM so that they can receive title to the land. Finally, many people in San Dionisio have been renting their land *a medias* to farmers from Santa Lucía.[1] In some cases this arrangement has existed for

many years, giving those in Santa Lucía long periods in possession of ejido land from San Dionisio.

THE VIEW FROM THE EJIDO: MEN AND WOMEN, OLD AND YOUNG

Age and Generation

Observers of ejido assemblies are struck by one obvious social characteristic: most ejidatarios are middle aged and elderly, between the ages of 40 and 80. The sight of young men and women from the Procuraduría Agraria running meetings made up of white-haired men and women with sun-drenched skin is a striking sight. In central Oaxaca, age is a major factor in how the ejido certification program is being received and how ejidatarios see their future. Age is particularly important in relation to attitudes about selling land and the future of the ejido.

All 20 ejidatarios (10 men and 10 women) between the ages of 45 and 90 interviewed in depth exhibited a strong sense of history. They had very vivid memories of how difficult life was before their ejido was won and the sacrifices made to obtain and keep the land. Almost all identify as the offspring of *peones* (landless laborers) who worked for local *hacendados* (large landowners).

After the creation of the ejidos and some initial help offered in several communities by Lázaro Cárdenas after a visit in the 1930s, the opinion of those interviewed regarding the government and its programs quickly becomes negative. In several cases, suspicions of the government were so high that questions about events that took place in the 1920s and 1930s regarding the formation of ejidos and their use were viewed by some people as dangerous. Older and middle-aged ejidatarios in all three communities had numerous experiences with government programs and agencies that didn't deliver what they had promised. The current certification program is the most aggressive government effort they have seen, in some cases, since the establishment of their ejidos.

Middle-aged and older ejidatarios stated that they had reluctantly supported their ejidos entering the certification programs to protect their land rights, but they were worried about the consequences, particularly hidden taxes and future generations selling the ejido land. The constant presence of workers from the Procuraduría exacerbated these concerns. One ejido president expressed his doubts about the certification program even though his ejido is billed by the Procuraduría as one of their cases that is "progressing nicely."

> They are going to tax people in the ejidos. Now they say that it will be the same tax, but what about the next president after Salinas? He doesn't have much time left. . . . When the people came from the Procuraduría the ejidatarios were brainwashed, "Se lavó el cerebro." . . . Look at how much money the government is spending on this program. The young lady who is our visitador comes here three times a week. Every time she comes I sign her papers to prove that she was here so that she can get paid. They are spending a lot of money on her and other people like her. Don't tell me the government isn't going to get that money back.

The historical links between the original struggle for ejido land and the current danger that it may be privatized and disappear are best reflected in the remarks of Manuel Hernández an 80-year-old ejidatario from El Tule. Manuel demonstrates an acute awareness of both history and current events as he compares the Porfiriato period with the negotiations over the North American Free Trade Agreement which were in the headlines on a daily basis during the summer of 1993.

> All the land that is now part of the ejido used to be private property. Before, people in El Tule were really poor. All they could do was to sell their labor. They also sold their land if they had any. If someone was sick and they died, where were the poor people going to go to get money to bury them? They would go to the rich and borrow money from them. Then the rich would buy their land. In Lachigoloo they lost all of their land this way. Here too. Then they passed a law to take away all of the land from the hacienda. We got our ejido. Now they still want to take it away. Even after we got the land, the hacendados still tried to take it away.
>
> We would find them with their oxen work-

> ing on our ejido land. We had to run them off the land. We suffered a lot getting rid of these people. The people from the hacienda had the federal forces on their side. Zapata was the one who helped the poor. He had to force the hacendados out. All of the poor were on the side of Zapata. The hacendados were with the rich. They killed a lot of poor people to hang onto their land. . . .
>
> Probably the government of the United States is speaking with the Mexican government. That's what they say. The Mexican government doesn't know anything about what it's like to be poor. The government is interested in our land.
>
> The government of the United States wants to expand its territory. The United States has a lot of people and it needs more land. They are going to come here from the United States to buy our land. And who isn't going to sell to them? If they pay a high enough price then people will sell. Little by little, they will buy up the ejido, just like the hacendados did before. That is what is going to happen.

A majority of older ejidatarios interviewed expressed fears that the ejido would eventually fall apart because younger people would sell the land or put houses on it rather than continue to work it as farmland. To some degree these fears are well-founded. Twelve younger people ages 20–35 (six women and six men) interviewed in depth in the three case study communities expressed a great deal of uncertainty about whether or not they would continue to farm ejido land if given the chance. Most have been socialized as part of the wage labor force and have worked in the urban informal labor market, in light industry, and only part-time in the countryside aiding their parents. Six of the twelve had recently spent time in the United States and had siblings and cousins who also migrated. Those most interested in continuing to farm were a few young men in Unión Zapata who had begun to produce commercial vegetables in the past few years.

Francisco Ruíz is the 24-year-old son of an ejidataria who is named as a legal successor. He has doubts not only about the certification program, but about whether or not he wants to be a farmer.

I don't think this certification process is so great. They have been here measuring and writing down how much land each of us had. They are going to charge us money, like private property. Maybe it better if they just leave well-enough alone. . . . I don't even know if I would want to farm any land. Right now I work over in the chicken-hatching factory. I don't like being out in the hot sun. I would rather just earn cash.

Jorge Santiago of Unión Zapata, age 25, who plants some of his father's land, is more enthusiastic about the prospects of farming with commercial vegetables. He plants alfalfa, tomatoes, onions, and garlic twice per year on land irrigated with a well and an electric pump.

When tomatoes do well, you can earn a lot of money. When the price for tomatoes is high, people will even come right here to the town to buy them from us. I will keep farming the land with commercial vegetables.

Several others listening to the conversation noted, however, that this year's tomato crop had been miserably small and many people had lost a lot of money.

Most of the younger people interviewed expressed less interest in the history of their ejidos in contrast to their elders but did provide stories about the founding of their ejidos. They did not receive the same historical orientation that their parents had either as original ejidatarios or as children of original ejidatarios. Their weaker historical consciousness and knowledge coupled with socialization in the urban wage labor force has significantly affected the younger generation's visions of themselves and of the ejido. They have a contradictory vision of the ejido's future. On the one hand they appreciate the significance of its history for their parents and for their community, but on the other they have a pragmatic realism about their inability to make a living off the land, as much as they might like to.

An important ingredient in the pragmatic side of their world view is the size of the plots most of them will inherit. While the people currently designated with ejidal rights have between one-half and three hectares, many of their children will receive plots of minuscule size that are insufficient

for farming. Younger people consistently point out that if they inherit one-half to one-quarter hectare of land, the most they can do with it is build a house or sell it to someone who wants to farm. In San Dionisio, land inheritance patterns seem to reflect a consciousness about not breaking up land into minuscule pieces. The result there, however, is that one or two siblings inherit and the others do not, leaving them to find their fortunes elsewhere.

Gender

In 1990, more than eleven and a half million women were living in Mexico's countryside. They constituted 49.76 percent of a total rural population of 23,289,924 (Robles et al. 1993:26). Of these more than 23 million rural inhabitants, more than 3.5 million have individual communal and ejidal rights (Procuraduría Agraria 1993:10). While no one has counted the total number of women with ejidal rights, estimates range from 15 to 30 percent of ejidatarios (Botey 1993).

The increasing number of women who have become ejidatarios, particularly as widows, has resulted in some notable changes in ejido political culture. In communities such as El Tule, women now have some opportunities to participate in what was previously an all-male political arena. Here women make up well over 25 percent of ejido assembly participants. They tend to sit in gender-segregated sections and to have a different style of participating in meetings than men. Ejido assemblies periodically break down into informal discussion for five to ten minute periods. During these periods, participants turn to one another and discuss the point at hand. In El Tule, women discuss issues with other women sitting nearby as did men. When the meeting assumes a formal tone with people raising their hands to speak, men reflect back to the larger for group their points of discussion. Women seldom do this, only occasionally shouting agreement with someone else. They do, however, thoroughly discuss things with other ejidatarias in the informal discussion periods and vote on all matters. Because of their tradition of attending ejido meetings, women also go to municipal assemblies, a somewhat rare occurrence in most Oaxaca communities.

While women clearly participate less in the formal part of ejido meetings, they are present at the meetings and speak with one another. This style of participation is consistent with other cultural models of female politics observed in Yalelog and in women's political discussions at fiestas in Oaxaca valley communities (Stephen 1991). The gender-segregated space of the meeting is also consistent with gender segregation of most public spaces in Oaxaca valley communities. Women who attend the meetings clearly feel that they are participating and that their presence is important. Lucía Moreno Lázaro, a 59-year-old ejidataria from El Tule, describes her feelings at ejido assemblies.

Well, the women go more to listen, to be there and to know about anything that comes up. For example, from the meeting last Sunday, we know that they are going to fine us if we don't show up while they are doing the measuring. . . . If women have problems then they speak up. But mostly it is the men who are speaking up in public meetings. But they respect us. I think they respect women even more than men.

The increasing presence and participation of women in ejido meetings is an important change in the rural political culture of many communities. The problem comes, however, for those women who are not ejidatarias and who have others making decisions for them. A majority of rural women who live and work in ejidos do not hold use rights. And even those who participate in UAIMS (created to enhance women's participation in the ejido) are limited in their political clout.

The Federal Agrarian Reform Law passed in 1971 contained some potentially important changes for women in ejidos. The law demanded equal treatment of men and women in questions of land inheritance, allowed women to hold any position of authority (*cargo*) within ejidos, and called for the creation of Agro-Industrial Units for Women (UAIMS). These units allowed groups of women to collectively hold use rights to ejido parcels equivalent to those of one ejidatario. In 1993 only 15 percent of Mexico's ejidos have registered UAIMS and an even smaller number are actually functioning (Robles et al. 1993:32). Among Oaxaca's 732 ejidos, only about 50 are listed as having active UAIMS. As seen below, the creation of UAIMs within ejidos and the plot of land they are allocated to work has become a part of the internal conflicts associated with the certification and titling process.

Article 27 most directly affects the majority of peasant women who live and work on ejido land, but who are not currently named as ejidatarios or successors. Because the certification process converts land from a family resource to individual property, women and children who are not directly named as successors will be left with what is referred to as "el derecho de tanto" (Botey 1991). This consists of the rights of family members to have the first shot at buying land if the title holder decides to sell it (Robles et al 1993:32). The only route for women who are not ejidatarias to own land is through purchasing it from their husbands and other family members. Given an average rural wage of $4.00 per day, most women are unlikely to be able to purchase land.

Women interviewed in the case study communities discussed three primary issues relating to the new law. First, those who were ejidatarias viewed the new law as partially positive because it secured their legal rights to ejido land. Several, however, were engaged in disputes with different family members about their parcels. Secondly, those women who were not ejidatarias noted that they can only benefit if their husbands died. Most hoped their husband would consult them if they wanted to sell land, but pointed out that there was no guarantee that they would do so. Finally, the case of the UAIM in San Dionisio reveals that women's land can be contested within ejidos both by other ejidatarios (men) and other women.

Through periods of Bracero migration to the United States, good harvests, and bad harvests, women and children have labored on ejido land. Their investment and maintenance of the land, however, does not translate into ownership rights under the current law.

Women ejidatarias have also found that the certification process can accelerate disputes about their rights to land. In a few interviews, ejidatarias mentioned that their brothers were trying to take away some of their land. Julia García Vásquez explains:

When my father was really old and tired, my brother started going *a medias* with him on the land and then he just kept occupying it. That is how he got the land. I got called in by the Agrarian Commission in 1990. We resolved the dispute. I received 3 pieces of land and he got five pieces. I have 2 *almudes* and one little piece with alfalfa.[2] My brother got most of it. Now he wants to try and get more of my land because I can't always work all of it. It never stops.

Because women often have to pay someone to do plowing for them, they may not be able to afford to work all of their ejido land. They may loan it out to brothers or other male relatives to work for them. Since consistent occupation of land gives someone the upper hand in declaring certification under the new law, some women have been deprived of land. The certification process may be accelerating this type of conflict.

The certification process is not only accelerating land conflicts between men and women, but among women as well. In San Dionisio Ocotlán during the summer of 1993, a large group of women led by an interim UAIM president was fighting with four women led by a former UAIM president for titling rights to several pieces of land. Some women in the larger group were sure that the contestation was provoked by the new law. Their collective farming was stalled by the process and they were disappointed that they were unable to plant [that] year.

While the 18–20 women united in the larger UAIM began a dialogue with the Ministry of Agrarian Reform to resolve who the legitimate president is, male ejido authorities treated the whole dispute as a joke. After women in the large group had received confirmation from the Agrarian Reform Ministry that their president was legitimate, they tried to organize a meeting with the larger ejido to get this recognized internally and voted on in an assembly. Their request was ignored by the ejido leadership. Two of the ejido authorities openly made fun of the women in the UAIM as being too disorganized to ever do anything, despite their successful harvest six months earlier.

Ultimately the decision about who to recognize as the legal president of the UAIM and whether to allow one group of women to receive title to their land as a UAIM will lie with the ejido assembly. Decisions about whether or not to revoke an individual or a UAIM of access to a plot of land they have been assigned to use are made by a majority vote of ejido members. In this case, the women would have to receive formal recognition of their use rights to the land before it could be titled to them. The women in the UAIM only receive one vote as a block in the ejido assembly. A majority

of people in the assembly are male. Women in the UAIM will depend on primarily on male ejidatarios to vote in their favor. Some men feel that neither group of women should be granted the land and it should be given to a more deserving male ejidatario.

While the law is supposed to protect the rights of ejidatarias, women in UAIMS and married to ejidatarios have no decision-making power to guarantee their rights.

CONCLUSIONS: THE VIEW FROM THE ANTHROPOLOGIST

The creation and maintenance of the Procuraduría Agraria and the other agencies it works with in administering the new agrarian reform law has resulted in a new generation of bureaucrats whose career advancement is pegged to the success of the certification and titling program. They are among the top recipients of government resources and support and because of lack of previous involvement are different from other rural bureaucrats. They sincerely believe in the program and seemed assured of a long period of employment before the Zapatista rebellion threw the reforms to Article 27 open to serious questioning. Predicted completion dates for the program are always changing as administrators of the Procuraduría continually run into historical land battles between communities, family feuds, and past measuring and mapping errors. Many indigenous communities still lack basic legal maps (*carpetas basicas*) outlining their boundaries.

The Zapatista rebellion, the formation of new coalitions of indigenous and peasant organizations such as the CEOIC in Chiapas (State Council of Indigenous and Peasant Organizations) and movements towards doing the same in Oaxaca and other states have produced an entirely different climate for the certification and titling program of the Procuraduría Agraria in 1994. In January 1994, only two of Oaxaca's approximately 1,488 ejidos and indigenous communities had completed the certification process. Most had not begun and those that had encountered major obstacles and multiple forms of resistance from within. The aftermath of the Zapatista rebellion has produced a climate in which peasant and indigenous organizations and individuals are establishing their rights and negotiating hard with the government to receive significantly more resources and support.

In the fall of 1993, the government announced a new program titled PRO-CAMPO (pro-countryside). It is perceived by many *ejidatarios* as part of the certification process. This program offers Mexican farmers of corn, beans, wheat, rice, soy beans, sorghum, and cotton a subsidy of about $US 100 per hectare (2.47 acres) per year over the next 15 years. Guaranteed price supports for these crops will be phased out by autumn and winter seasons of 1994–1995, pitting Mexican producers against cheaper U.S. imports and aligning crop prices to international prices. The announcement of this program by the government was evidence of a certain amount of backpeddling in the structural adjustments being carried out to facilitate NAFTA. PRO-CAMPO will clearly soften the blow of being "eased" out of the rural sector for the three million ejidatarios (and their families) the Mexican government is predicting will eventually have to be absorbed into other sectors of the economy (Mogel 1993).

The quiet dumping of resources on impoverished and often discontented populations has not proven to be sufficient in recent times, however. The state of Chiapas received approximately 56 million dollars in Solidarity aid dispersed to areas that are now Zapatista strongholds after government soldiers discovered a rebel training camp last year. But this did not stop the emergence of the Zapatistas and the nonstop declarations of solidarity with their demands from people throughout Mexico.

The precedent set by indigenous and peasant organizations in the state of Chiapas in 1994 in terms of resolving land disputes, demanding more land redistribution, access to credit, and much more sophisticated and inclusive programs for dealing with the future of rural populations than those offered by the PROCEDE and PROCAMPO is affecting the implementation of the certification program throughout the country. In many cases, Procuraduría officials have slowed down their work and are waiting to see what the outcome of the August 1994 elections will be. Whether or not the program will go forward at all will depend on who the next president is and what his model of rural development will be. With the assassination of Luis Donaldo Colosio in March 1994 and a great deal of uncertainty about the outcome of the elections, progress in the PROCEDE will be minimal if any.

Beyond the political future of the certification program in Mexico, what does its reception in the three ejidos examined in Oaxaca tell us about the future of the ejido and those people in and around it? What does it tell us about the ways in which people interact with, subvert, resist and/or accommodate to state imposed programs of economic and social change?

Gramsci's theory of hegemony is perhaps the most detailed discussion of the subtle ways in which states co-opt their subjects through culture, values and ideology (1972). This co-optation results in people subtly replicating dominant ideology in their daily activities and thoughts and blinding themselves to their own subordination. In a challenge to Gramsci, James Scott (1985) decries ideological determinism and argues that most subordinate classes and marginalized groups are perfectly capable of penetrating and demystifying prevailing ideology. They do not require vanguard intellectuals or political parties to see things as they are. The second piece of his argument is that most resistance to dominant ideology is not found in overt manifestations of oppositions but in "hidden transcripts" and everyday acts of defiance such as footdragging, dissimulation, false compliance, pilfering, feigned ignorance, slander, arson, and sabotage (1985:29). Scott's emphasis on the hidden transcripts of resistance and their importance in providing a seedbed for structural change have been both embraced (Colburn 1989; Tutino 1986) and debated (Gutmann 1993: Roseberry 1989).

The debate over the importance of overt resistance strategies versus more subtle forms of resistance is useful in analyzing the reaction of ejidatarios to the Mexican government's certification program initially and in the changed political context of the Zapatista rebellion. While many ejidatarios are captivated by the possibility of private ownership and enthusiastically entered the program, many have simultaneously engaged in subtle acts of resistance as the full implication of the program set in. Within the three case study communities, a wide range of resistance has been observed. This ranges from repeated cancelation of meetings due to an ejido president drinking to celebrate any event that occurred on the same day as meetings with the representatives from the Procuraduría, people not presenting themselves when their plots are being measured, noncompliance in presenting identification documents, misrepresenting the dimensions of plots, constant cancellation and rescheduling of ejido meetings with the Procuraduría, calling ejido meetings and not informing the Procuraduría, and lack of quorums at meetings (see Pisa 1994). Acts of subtle resistance are directed not only at the Procuraduría representatives, but at the steps that need to be carried out to complete the process.

Acts of resistance are also carried out in relation to other ejidatarios as one person tries to take advantage of another in the certification process. More than anything, internal conflicts have been fanned by the act of measuring and certifying individual parcels. At some level every ejidatario participating in the process is engaging simultaneously in multiple acts of resistance within a framework of accommodation. All three case study communities voted to enter the certification process and on the surface are going through the motions of completing it while simultaneously resisting its completion. As a group, ejidatarios and their families do not have a uniform response to the certification program. Generation, gender, class, historical consciousness, migration experience, and urban/rural location have all influenced people's perspectives on their role as ejidatarios and the future of the ejido.

Given the political uncertainties in Mexico at the point of writing this article it is difficult to predict the future impact of the certification program or even its continuation. Based on the fieldwork carried out in 1993, however, the following tentative conclusions can be drawn about the three communities studied and others similar to them.

1. The program seems to be speeding up what may have been an inevitable change in ejido social organization. Major differences in the identities and ejido strategies of present and future ejidatarios suggests that even without the certification program, the ejido would be unlikely to continue as it has since the 1920s and 1930s. New forms of peasant organizing and coalition building taking place in the wake of the Zapatista rebellion, however, may provide new forms of local organization and/or reinvigorate ejidos in the struggle to make the government pay attention to the fate of Mexico's rural population.

2. The program may be further fracturing the social organization of ejidos by highlighting multiple levels of conflict as borders between communities and individual parcels are measured, in some cases for the first time. Internal conflicts within ejidos and even between family members are a predictable outcome of entering the process. If the program fails to move forward, these conflicts may eventually diminish in some communities.

3. The most important factor to consider in individual responses to the certification program is generation. Older ejidatarios seem more likely to retain their land and continue working as farmers than younger ejidatarios and their offspring. Younger ejidatarios have a weaker connection to the history of the ejido, were socialized as wage laborers, and have increasing interest in migration as an ongoing economic strategy.

4. While the new law offers some legal protection to those 15 to 20 percent of ejidatarias who are women, for the majority of rural women the certification process continues the tendency to limit their access to land. This will encourage their continued entrance into the rural wage labor force and the urban informal economy where their participation grew considerably during the 1980s. This will be particularly true for younger women. Rates of migration of rural women will certainly increase.

5. Major shifts in local land holdings are unlikely to be visible for ten to fifteen years. When they are, those ejidatarios who have more land and resources to begin with will be more likely to take advantage of land freed for sale, particularly within families where most transfers will be.

Most importantly the contradictions seen in the responses of rural men and women to the certification program alert us to the complex identities of rural Mexicans who are no longer subsistence farmers, but also wage workers and migrants as well. While most are not revolutionaries like the Zapatistas, they have a long-standing suspicion of change imposed from above and subtly resist such impositions even while appearing to cooperate. The changed political climate brought about by the Zapatista rebellion and the torrent of peasant and indigenous organizing and negotiating that has followed in its wake highlights the ways in which subtle acts of resistance within the framework of accommodation can become significant on a larger level given the appropriate circumstances. The variation in the certification program's acceptance and its different meanings for different sectors of the population by age, gender, and class (not discussed in detail here) have now become significant political openings which are likely to result in a range of bargaining strategies carried out by people within ejidos. The example of the Zapatistas has brought all kinds of disenfranchised groups of people back into the Mexican political process. As ejidatarios saw a piece of themselves move into a central position of power through the actions and demands of the Zapatistas, their own relationship to the government and the national political process may also be fundamentally changed.

ACKNOWLEDGMENTS

I gratefully acknowledge the support of the Ejido Reform Project of the Center for U.S.–Mexican Studies and the National Science Foundation for funding the research written about here. I have also greatly benefited from my collaborative work with Rosaria Pisa and Veronica Wilson in the writing of this article.

NOTES

1. *A medias* refers to a form of land rental in which the person renting pays half the harvest to the owner. It is quite common both within and between communities in the Oaxaca valleys.

2. An *almud* is a dry measure that if filled with corn is equal to two kilos. It also refers to the amount of corn required to plant a piece of land, indicating its size. One hectare is equal to four *almudes* of corn. Two *almudes* is thus one-half hectare.

REFERENCES

Botey Estapé, Carlota (1991). La parcela ejidal es un patrimonio familiar. *Uno mas uno*, suplemento. November 18, 1991, p.3.

———— (1993). La Proletarización de la Mujer en la Ultima Decada del Siglo XX. Paper presented at the 13th International Congress of Anthropological and Ethnological Sciences, Mexico City, July 29–August 4, 1993.

Colburn, Forrest (1989). *Everyday Forms of Peasant Resistance*. Armonk: M.E. Sharpe.

Fundación Oaxaca, A.C. (1992). *Situación Agraria*. November, 1992.

Gramsci, Antonio (1971). *Selections from the Prison Notebooks of Antonio Gramsci*. Edited and Translated by Quintin Hoare and Geoffrey Nowell Smith. New York: International Publishers.

Gutmann, Matthew (1993). Rituals of Resistance: A Critique of the Theory of Everyday Forms of Resistance. *Latin American Perspectives* 20(2):74–92.

INEGI (Instituto Nacional de Estadística Geografía e Informática) (1988). *Atlas Ejidal del Estado de Oaxaca, Encuesta Nacional Agropercuario Ejidal 1988*. Mexico, D.F.

Mogel, Julio (1993). Procampo y la Via campesina de desarrollo. *La Jornada del Campo*, 26th of October, 1993, 2(20): 8–9.

Pisa, Rosario (1994). Preliminary Popular Responses to the Reform of Article 27 From the Oaxacan Countryside. A Preliminary Report. Center for U.S.–Mexican Studies, Ejido Reform Project. University of California, San Diego.

Procuraduría Agraria (1993). PROCEDE: Programa de Certificación de Derechos Ejidales y Titulación de Solares Urbanos, Documento Guía.

Robles, Rosario, Josefina Aranda, and Carlota Botey (1993). La mujer campesina en la época de la modernidad. *El Cotidiano* 52, marzo–april 1993: 25–32.

Roseberry, William (1989). *Anthropologies and Histories: Essays in Culture, History and Political Economy*. New Brunswick: Rutgers University Press.

Salinas de Gotari, Carlos (1993). Palabras del Presidente de la Republica, Lic. Carlos Salinas de Goatri en la reunion efectuada en el salon" Adolfo Lopez Mateo" en la residencia oficial de los pinos. Programa de Apoyos Al Campo, 1993 (24 de Febrero). Mexico, D.F.

Scott, James (1985). *Weapons of the Weak: Everyday Forms of Peasant Resistance*. New Haven: Yale University Press.

Stephen, Lynn (1991). *Zapotec Women*. Austin: University of Texas Press.

Tutino, John (1986). *From Insurrection to Revolution in Mexico: Social Bases of Agrarian Violence, 1750–1940*. Princeton: Princeton University Press.

Warman, Arturo (1993). Primer Informe de Labores. *Espacios* (Boletín Informativo de la Procuraduría Agraria) 2:2–6 (Mayo–Junio, 1993).

32

Culture, Sweetness, and Death
The Political Economy of Sugar Production and Consumption

Donna L. Chollett

On November 2 each year, Mexicans celebrate the Day of the Dead, that day in which the dead rise up from their graves and enjoy a meal brought to candle-lit gravesites by their living relatives. The boundaries between life and death, symbolized by thousands of molded sugar skulls (*calaveras*) sold for the occasion in shops throughout Mexico, are transcended. The feast, complete with sweet bread— *pan de los muertos* (bread of the dead), sweet tamales, and sweetened *atole*, expresses the cultural consciousness, as well as the cultural-material conditions that define one's place in the economic and political structure of the nation. Sugar skulls simultaneously connote death and humor, mourning and celebration, tragedy and optimism, contempt and irony, and presented as a gift on the Day of the Dead, form a paradoxical association between sugar and death (Crespo 1990). Octavio Paz laid bare the cultural nature of the Day of the Dead in his *Labyrinth of Solitude:* "Ritual death promotes a rebirth" (1967:51). The celebration of life provokes rebirth, but becomes a context in which to ridicule life. According to Paz, the Mexican " . . . is familiar with death, jokes about it, caresses it, sleeps with it, celebrates it. . . ." (1967:57).

Sugar skulls, an element of the culture of sweetness, form part of a tradition of popular art represented in miniature. Folk culture, through the art of sugar, intrinsically links the death theme with the multifarious dimensions of Mexico's political economy. Miniature skeletons appear not only on November 2, but throughout the year to ridicule political personalities and events. Masuoka (1990: 265) illustrates the caricature of a skeletonized individual that appeared in a national newspaper with the quote, ". . . in this world, to live is to continue being in debt . . . there is no such thing as a debt that dies." The symbolism of death alludes to the economic crisis that affects the majority of Mexicans since economic restructuring, as does the depiction of Uncle Sam, complete with death skull, which represents the major banks that hold the Mexican debt. Political figures such as past presidents Salinas de Gortari and López Portillo satirically take the form of *calaveras* to symbolize disparagement with political process in Mexico (Masuoka 1990). Through representations such as these, sugar and its fabrication into commodities and symbols of national culture permeate daily life.

SUGAR AS CONSUMPTION

Sugar, with its symbolic links to sweet comestibles, political culture, and death, has deep historical roots in Mexico. Originally considered an exotic spice and used for medicinal purposes, sugar constitutes one among many stimulants (tea, coffee, cocoa, tobacco, opium) that inserted itself into the world commodity market on increasing scale in the nineteenth century (Mintz 1979; Wolf, 1982). Mintz explains that its use as a food became common as ". . . its potency as a source of profit gradually increased" (Mintz 1985:95). Sugar began as a luxury commodity that graced the tables of the European nobility and gradually became a necessary component of the working class diet. As such, it provided low-cost food and quick energy to an emergent proletariat and favored the industrialization of Europe. The diffusion of sugar consumption from the wealthy to the masses was ". . . one of the truly important economic and cultural phenomena of the modern age" (Mintz 1979:59).

Differences in status and power similarly distinguished patterns of sugar consumption in colonial Mexico. Whereas Mexico produced a significant amount of sugar, it became a commodity for popular mass consumption only in the nineteenth century. Until then, fruits and honey remained the primary sweeteners. At the time of the conquest, hot chocolate—beaten till frothy with a *molinillo* (an ornately carved, wooden beater), was drank only by the rich and the noble, generally at the end of great feasts. It percolated down to the masses over time and today Mexicans can buy kilos of cacao beans, sugar, and almonds, which are ground and molded into disks for the preparation of the chocolate drink. If one is poor, he or she buys fewer cacao and almonds and proportionally more sugar. Tamales, the ceremonial food offered in honor of the dead, were eaten by Aztec rulers before the Spanish conquest. They are consumed in various forms today, from the *uchepos* of Michoacán, made with amaranth seeds and ground cherries, to the sweet *tamal* spiced with sugar and cinnamon sticks, and served with hot chocolate or *atole*—a drink of corn gruel and raw sugar (Kennedy 1972).

Influenced by Spain, France, and Italy, desserts, breads, sweets, and other Mexican dishes underwent a "culinary revolution" during the colonial period. Initially, innovative dishes prepared for royal tables—cake making, and the fabrication of birds, animals, and palaces from sugar—resulted in a new culture of sugar in Europe, and especially, Spain. The diffusion of these recipes and innovations to the New World was to have a tremendous impact on Mexican food and cooking (Crespo 1990). During the colonial period, nuns from Spain concocted sweetmeats and desserts that still remain in the culinary repertoire. *Mole de guajolote,* for example, originated in the convents of Puebla. The *mole,* or sauce, served with turkey, is a concoction in which mingle the sundry flavors and textures of chilies, cloves, cinnamon, anise, sesame seeds, garlic, almonds, pumpkin seeds, and chocolate. Two popular tales furnish different accounts of its origin. According to one version, the sister superior invented this dish for the Archbishop, blending ingredients for the sauce with ingredients brought from the Old World and those available in the New World. The sauce came to symbolize the mestizo, a mixing of conqueror and conquered, of Spanish and Indian. A second story relates that Fray Pascual was preparing a banquet for the Viceroy, Don Juan de Palafox y Mendoza, when a wind swept through the kitchen, blowing the strange mixture of spices into the *cazuelas,* or cooking pots. The dish became a national tradition, served at Christmas and other festive occasions (Kennedy 1972).

On visiting one colonial era convent in the 1800s, Frances Calderón de la Barca remarked, ". . . a very elegant supper . . . greeted our astonished eyes; cakes, chocolates, ices, creams, custards, tarts, jellies, blancmanges, orange and lemonade and other profane dainties . . ." (Calderón de la Barca 1966:317). Nuns in the convents of Mexico contributed to the elaboration and regional specialization of confections (e.g., bizcochos de Puebla, cajetas de Celaya, jarochas michoacanas). Travelers, visiting the Dominican convent in Oaxaca, described these accompaniments: "Here are also two cloisters of nuns which are talked of far and near, not for their religious practices, but for their skill in making two drinks . . . the one called chocolate and the other *atole,* which is like unto our almond milk . . . which they so confection with spices, musk and sugar that is not only admirable in the sweetness and smell, but much more nourishing and comforting to the stomach" (Kennedy 1972:347).

After independence, sweet confections in Mexico continued to manifest both indigenous and foreign influences. In 1838, a French pastry shop even became the focus of international war. Revolts persisted after independence, causing damage to the property of foreign nationals. France made claims for damages of ". . . a French pastry cook whose delicacies were appropriated and consumed by a group of hungry Mexican soldiers. . . ." (Meyer and Sherman 1979:328). *La Guerra de los Pasteles* (the Pastry War) ensued after the French king demanded $600,000 in compensation and Mexico ignored the demand. When a French fleet blockaded the port of Veracruz, Mexico agreed to pay the damages, but the French had raised the damages to $800,000. Mexico again refused to pay, whereupon the French bombarded the fort of San Juan de Ulua, forcing Mexico to declare war on France. Santa Ana and his troops forced the French to retreat and the pastries were compensated at the original price of $600,000. But the injuries Santa Ana suffered in the battle caused the amputation of his leg; subsequently:

> Santa Ana ordered the disinterment of his amputated leg from its quiet repose on his hacienda of Manga de Clavo. The mummified member was transported to Mexico City and, after an impressive procession through the streets of the capital in which the presidential bodyguard, the army, and the cadets from the Chapultepec Military Academy all participated, it was taken to the cemetery of Santa Fe where it was placed in a specially designed urn and set atop a huge stone pillar (Meyer and Sherman 1979:332).

More than a century and a half after the Pastry War, the fame of Mexican pastry shops is renown. The *panaderias* (bakeries) of Mexico display mounds of breads, roles, and a dizzying array of pastries; on entering, customers take a round metal pan and a pair of tongs to select the items that will satisfy their cravings for sweets. Mexican desserts are also noted for their variety: *flans,* or custard with carmelized sauce; *buñuelos,* the crisp-fried sheets of pastry drizzled with *piloncillo* (raw sugar) syrup; and the sweetest of all, *chongos zamora-*

nos, custard-like curds of goat's milk in a hypersweet syrup of sugar and whey. In Mexico City, the *Dulces de Celaya,* a family-owned candy shop dating from 1874, sells crystallized fruit, *gaznates* (pastry filled with pineapple and coconut paste), disks of chocolate ground on the metate with almonds and sugar, miniature shapes formed from almond paste, tamarind candies, and fudge rolls covered with pecans. Sweetened drinks range from the alcoholic—sugarcane alcohol (also used to pickle peaches and quinces), *teshuino* (maize fermented with raw sugar) from Chihuahua and Nayarit, and *tuba* (a drink made from the sap of coconut palm or from sugar cane) from Colima and Guerrero, to nonalcoholic stimulants—coffee is always taken with heaping tablespoons of sugar (Kennedy 1972).

Sugar is ubiquitous as a component of breads, pastas, meals, snacks, and sweetens popular drinks such as coffee and cocoa. The sheer number and variety of sweet dishes and drinks testifies to the importance of a culture based on sugar, their luxury status (e.g., *rosca de reyes*), and the fate of all humans (e.g., *pan de muerto*) (Crespo 1990). Not only are sugar-coated novelties incorporated into the diet, but they play a significant role in myth and ritual, a fact exemplified by the Day of the Dead fiesta. Among certain ethnic groups, sugar in the form of a soft drink, accompanied by *aguardiente* (sugarcane alcohol) serves as a ritual cure for susto and soul loss, and *torta de cielo* (cake of heaven) is served at important rites of passage—weddings and first communion. Community fiestas, family celebrations, and rites of passage are incomplete without soft drinks and sugar-laden snacks. Sugar was consumed in yet another way in the summer of 1996 when the popular *telenovela* (soap opera), *Cañaveral de Pasiones* (Canefield of Passions) ran for several weeks, captivating television audiences with the drama of love and hate that enveloped a family of sugar mill owners.

SUGAR AS PRODUCTION

Whether for ritual, political, or edible consumption, the use of sugar is imbued with cultural meaning. Nevertheless, the political and economic connections between the consumption of sugar and its production is seldom made. The appearance of sugar in the New World, of course, is a product of colonialism. A period of 300 years demarcates a political economy that linked increasing demand with the production of sugar as a commodity in the colonized territories. Originally domesticated in New Guinea, sugar cane was first processed for consumption in India, diffused across the Mediterranean, and was brought to the New World by Columbus in 1493. Cortés introduced sugar cane to Mexico in 1523, two years after the fall of Tenochtitlán, the Aztec capital. The substitution of sweeteners such as honey and fruits with cane sugar required satisfying the conditions for a complex technological process. In Mexico, the Spanish crown encouraged sugar production by granting lands to those who desired to install mechanized sugar mills. Crown support allowed sugarcane production to expand rapidly in the colony; sugar was exported from Veracruz to Spain as early as 1539. The Cortés family established mills on their estates, Tlaltenango and Axomulco, Morelos, in 1536, and Cortés' son built the first sugar hacienda at Atlacomulco in 1568 (García 1987; GEPLACEA 1990; von Wobeser 1988; Wolf 1982).

As the demand for sugar expanded in Europe, the sugar industry became a cornerstone in the triangular trade. Increasing sugar consumption toward the end of the sixteenth century caused sugar prices to rise, and, in turn, contributed to further expansion of sugar estates. Fueled by the slave trade, sugarcane production came to dominate the economies of the Caribbean islands in the seventeenth century (Crespo 1988; von Wobeser 1988). African slaves were also introduced to Brazil and Mexico in areas where the indigenous population crashed, largely due to European diseases. Goods flowed from Europe to Africa, to be exchanged for slaves, who in turn, labored to produce sugar—initially for the tables of the elite in Europe, and later for the consumption of an urbanizing working class (GEPLACEA 1990). It was this trade in human cargo and sugar that contributed to capital accumulation in Europe.

The exigencies of land, labor, and capital for sugarcane production transformed the political economy of the colonies as they reshaped the nature of social relations, cultural patterns, family composition, and community structures (Wolf 1982). The production of sugar as a commodity required exten-

sive land cultivation, control of a large labor force, and investment of significant amounts of capital. Initially, the conquistadors assumed their role as rulers of land and labor through a system of *encomienda,* a grant of rights to Indian tribute and labor. The *encomienda* of Cortés gave him rights over 100,000 Indians (Winn 1992). As the colonial period evolved, the hacienda emerged in the seventeenth century as a symbiotic system that tied campesino communities to sugar mills. The *hacienda* was a fundamental institution involving a complex set of social arrangements. According to Tannenbaum, "The hacienda . . . is an entire social system and it governs the life of those attached to it from the cradle to the grave" (1968:80). ". . . The hacienda is, however, not merely an economic enterprise. It is also a social, political, and cultural institution" (1968:85). Yet its roots were Iberian: ". . . the landed estate also reflected long-standing Iberian values, which viewed land ownership as a sign of status, a cultural bias that has endured over time" (Winn 1992:48). Haciendas came to represent a complex configuration of agricultural land, mechanized sugar mills, and systems of coercive labor that functioned through the exercise of social, economic, and political power.

In their hunger for land, sugar haciendas encroached on and appropriated lands and irrigation systems of campesino communities, and, in the process, freed those who could no longer support themselves for labor on the hacienda (Wolf 1982). Haciendas were frequently the only source of wage labor. Whether as *acasillados* (resident peons) or inhabitants of nearby campesino villages, rural residents engaged in various types of labor relations with the hacienda owner, or *patrón.* These included payment for labor in kind, sharecropping, and loaning hacienda land in exchange for labor. Provision of goods through the company store ensured that campesinos remained tied to the hacienda in a system of debt peonage. But paternalism also characterized the relationship between the patrón and campesinos. The landowner could be called upon for aid in emergencies and times of need, and the campesino, in turn, owed loyalty to the patrón. These relationships frequently were forged into a system of *compadrazgo* (fictive kinship) that, through baptisms and other rites of passage, established the mutual obligations of fictive kinship.

The hacienda endured into the twentieth century in many areas. Campesinos in western Mexico recalled their life on the hacienda in these early years. Workers, at the sound of the church bell, lined up each morning to be assigned their work by the mayordomo. Those who labored in the cane fields worked from 6:00 A.M. to 6:00 P.M. Wages were 50 centavos per day. Two or three dozen workers labored in the *trapiches* (small-scale, labor intensive mills) in three six-hour shifts—the work was difficult and hazardous. The *trapiche* made alcohol, *panocha* or *piloncillo*—an unrefined sugar shaped into round bars or small cones—and *cachasa,* an inexpensive, dark sugar product made from the foam of the boiled sugar juice. The *tienda de raya* sold supplies such as corn, beans, chilies, rice, lard, and clothing. On Saturdays tokens for purchasing these items were distributed, based on the number of days worked, each value being represented by a different color. Meat was available only on Saturdays when a cow was slaughtered. The *hacendado* (hacienda owner) gave workers rations of corn and beans and provided them with houses constructed of pole and cane leaves. Haciendas also rented out a portion of hacienda land to local campesinos. The landowners made loans for expenses, medical care, and so forth, perpetuating a system of debt peonage. Campesinos experienced an ambivalent blend of exploitation and paternalism, made all the more salient by the conspicuous consumption and lavish dwellings of the hacienda owners.

Independence in 1810 and the period of Porfirian economic liberalism from 1876 to 1910 reinforced the economic and political disparity between hacienda owners and campesinos. Intent on industrialization, export production, and stimulating foreign capital investment, the Mexican state fortified the power of hacienda owners, facilitated extensive acquisition of land and resources, and allowed *hacendados* to earn enormous profits (Landázuri and Vázquez 1988). These liberal policies contributed to the conversion of sugar mills into capitalist enterprises. But the Porfirian success carried seeds of its own destruction. As Wolf points out, ". . . as in all systems of bondage, security was purchased only at the expense of liberty" (1959:207). If the hacienda was an instrument for colonial masters to control labor, it was a relationship wrought with exploitation and ambivalence. The hostile

symbiosis forged a community identity in rural villages around which its members rallied to resist encroachment on their lands and the displacement of subsistence crops by sugar cane. Land invasions and destruction of cash crops by campesinos were frequent and attest to their resistance to the hegemonic power of the patrón (von Wobeser 1988). As *hacendados* promoted expansion and modernization of capitalist sugar mills, they simultaneously fomented the development of an antagonistic peasantry that would join forces with other social groups to overthrow the *hacendados* in the Mexican revolution. The campesino wing of the revolution, led by Mexico's cultural folk hero Emiliano Zapata, centered on the sugar-producing zone of Morelos.

In 1910, one percent of Mexico's population owned 97 percent of the land; haciendas held 113 million hectares (Esteva 1983). The state or Morelos, the heart of the Zapatista movement for agrarian change, had 37 haciendas and 24 sugar mills. Emiliano Zapata's Plan de Ayala called for a return of plundered communal lands, expropriation of *latifundios* (large land holdings), and autonomy and freedom for campesino villages. Following the bloody revolution, the Plan de Ayala was incorporated into Article 27 of the Mexican constitution. Land redistribution—largely delayed until the 1930s—subdued the power of the landed oligarchy and granted half of Mexico's cultivable lands to campesinos (Warman 1980). In western Mexico, a common response of hacienda owners was to oppose the granting of *ejidos* (agrarian reform land). Their tactics ranged from dividing their lands among relatives (*prestanombres*) to give the illusion of small landholdings, to hiring assassins who would rid campesino communities of land petitioners. Numerous *ejidos* are named for the martyred leaders who were murdered in the struggle over land. Entire communities, armed with rifles provided by the government, shared in guarding and protecting their villages from attack by the landowners. Once they acquired land, those campesinos who had not fled in fear for their lives turned to maize and bean production.

By the mid-1930s, land, water, and cane fields were in the hands of campesinos. But sugar mills required centralized control of factory and field, and herein lies the contradiction: campesinos, recipients of *ejido* land, lacked both resources for, and interest in, cane production. This structural breakdown in the unity of field and factory is a significant factor, since control of the productive land base was separated from the sugar-processing facility. When sugar production declined and Mexico was forced to import sugar, a 1943 government decree delineated supply zones around sugar mills, within which sugarcane growers were obligated to cultivate and supply sugar cane to mills. The decree, aimed at meeting national and U.S. demands for sugar, provided an effective means to convert campesinos who grew corn and beans for family consumption into producers for capitalist sugar mills. Soon after, in 1944, the Mexican state asserted its increasing control over sugar production by setting the price for sugar, keeping it suppressed as a low-cost wage good for urban workers, and providing credit to cane growers, effectively tying them into a system of neo-debt peonage (Crespo 1990; Jiménez 1986).

The constitution of this economic partnership between cane growers and the state takes on political dimensions as well. The Mexican state buttressed its tightening relationship with cane growers through their union organization. The largest cane growers' union, UNPCA (Unión Nacional de Productores de Caña de Azúcar), forms one level of political organization incorporated into the CNC (Confederación Nacional Campesina), which in turn, is a structural branch of PRI (Partido Revolucionario Institucional). One *cañero* (cane grower) offered this perspective on the relationship of the union to the federal government and the sugar mill:

> The government was the one that supported the *hacendados*. It set the price [of cane] for the rich. From here, the unions were born, to support the campesino. If we aren't affiliated with the union, we aren't going to have any support from the government. In Mexico we began to open our eyes that we could have the same support as the rich. Someone went to the CNC in Mexico and said, We're going to start a union to deal with the sugar mill.

Cañeros have utilized this union organization in their struggle and have achieved significant goals: health insurance, retirement benefits, and price increases, among others. The relationship between the cane union "family" and the government, however, is one of unbalanced power; the government utilizes the vertical incorporation of UNPCA into the CNC and the PRI to control the union organization. When the union has taken an active role—through strikes and other forms of protest—to defend the interests of *cañeros*, the state has alternated between manipulation of union leaders and political repression to control social unrest. In front of the national UNPCA headquarters in Mexico City stands the gilded statue of Roque Spinozo Foglia, a national union leader who was assassinated in 1985. Spinozo had led union movements and strikes in the 1970s and rejected affiliation with the CNC. This threat to state hegemony was resolved in 1977 when Spinozo reconciliated, and along with other *cañero* unions that had operated outside the fold of the CNC, unified into a single organization under the umbrella of the national campesino union. Spinozo's memory lives on as the martyred leader through whom the union achieved its historical conquests. Since his assassination, faith in the union has declined and it suffers a crisis of credibility, reflected in the words of cane growers. "The national leader doesn't serve for anything. There no longer are good leaders; they already killed the true leader that defended us, Roque Spinozo Foglia."

Historically, as the state increased its hegemony over cane union organizations, it created for itself a major role in economic control over the sugar industry. The Cuban revolution and subsequent blockade of its sugar exports led the United States to search for new sugar markets; as Mexican sugar exports soared in the next two decades, sugar became Mexico's third most important export crop and accounted for 15 percent of the value of agricultural exports (del Villar 1976; Jiménez 1986). Despite favorable sugar prices and increasing demand on the world market, the Mexican government, in an effort to control inflation, froze the price of Mexican sugar. Sugar mills across the country fell into decline as mill owners transferred their investments to more lucrative ventures and cane growers rebelled against the threat to their economic status brought about by economic instability of the sugar industry (Purcell 1981). To ensure continuing revenues from sugar exports and to control rural unrest, the Mexican government began to assume control and ownership of private sugar mills.

The state thus became the primary owner of sugar mills throughout the 1970s and 1980s. State-owned sugar mills, like other parastatals in Latin America, have been instruments for not only economic, but also social and political ends: to provide employment, ensure social welfare, and to correct the social disparities created by "the free hand of the market." The dominant role played by the state involved a culturally embedded tradition of protectionism, regulation of labor, and defense of nationalism. In state-owned sugar mills, *cañeros* benefited from government subsidies and accommodated to the dual control of the state over cane production and their union organization. Nonetheless, during this period the operation of sugar mills was beset by price controls, lack of investment, inefficient production, an overemployed work force, corruption, and its own brand of paternalism. State mills required tremendous government subsidies for loans, subsidized sugar prices, and for underwriting inefficient production, all of which overwhelmed the economy. The advent of economic crisis in 1982 brought profound changes for cane growers. The state-campesino alliance, buttressed by state paternalism, came to an abrupt end with Mexico's adoption of neoliberal policies to promote free markets, private investment, and an end to state subsidies.

In compliance with this new direction, NAFTA was passed in 1994, sugar mills were sold to private capitalists, provisions were made to privatize agrarian reform land, and support prices for campesino production were phased out. These changes were to affect the production, distribution, and consumption of sugar. Sugar is an important ingredient in the NAFTA agreement. For the first six years of NAFTA, Mexico's sugar exports to the United States are limited to 7,258 tons. However, if in any two consecutive years Mexico reaches net exporter status, it is allowed to export up to 25,000 tons. In year seven, Mexico is allowed to ship up to 150,000 tons of sugar, increasing this amount 10 percent annually over the remainder of fifteen years; after fifteen years, no quotas will be applied to exports. The political nature of trade in sugar is clear in an Executive Agreement that modified NAFTA; in determination of Mexico's net surplus status, production of sugar must exceed its consumption of *both* sugar and HFCS (high fructose corn syrup). Rules of origin prevent Mexico from importing raw sugar, refining it, and exporting it to the United States. Contingent with government withdrawal of support prices to campesino production, which lowered the value of agricultural products on the market, state control of sugar prices ended in 1995.

NAFTA changed the nature of sugar distribution, while privatization affected production and consumption patterns. The privatization of sugar mills resulted in the sale of mills to private investors, many of whom hold franchises with soft drink companies such as Coca-Cola and Pepsi-Cola. Most of these corporate interests entered the sugar sector to access a cheap raw material—sugar. Moreover, not all had an equal chance at purchasing mills. Cane growers, for example, had long aspired to become owners of their own mills. Back in 1988, during ceremonies marking the purchase of the El Higo and Mahuixtlán mills by the union, this speech commemorated the event:

> An old dream of the CNC family throughout its history, was always to convert ourselves into industrialists of our own product. Today, this vehement longing is a total reality, with the acquisition of Ingenios El Higo and Mahuixtlán by our UNPCA–CNC" (translated from *Tumbando Caña* 1989 [14]:2).

Three mills owned by the union—El Higo, Mahuixtlán, and Melchor Ocampo—were declared bankrupt and resold to Grupo Zucarmex during privatization of the industry. Grupo Escorpión purchased one of the two producers' cooperatives, Emiliano Zapata, and the other, El Mante, was sold to the long-time sugar industrialist and owner of Grupo Sáenz. The sale of the Emiliano Zapata mill, established in the heart of the Zapatista region after the revolution, is historically significant. President Lázaro Cárdenas founded the mill in the 1930s as a campesino-owned cooperative. These sales brought to an end the involvement of cane growers as associates in the ownership of mills.

Four mills were declared "inefficient" and closed after they were privatized. The Foreign

Agricultural Service of the USDA estimated that rationalization of production would eliminate forty of Mexico's sugar mills by the year 2000 (Kessel et al. 1993). One of these mill closings raises alarm about this projection. Located in the state of Michoacán, this mill was originally slated to be sold to the CNPR (Confederación Nacional de Productores Rurales), forming a partnership between the industrialist and cane growers. But the union was forced to cede its share to the private investor, who owned Empresas Gamesa (a Mexican cookie and food-processing conglomerate), whose majority shares were subsequently sold to Pepsico.[1] At the end of the first harvest season, the owner closed the mill, claiming that it was unprofitable. A total of 3,774 cane growers, mill workers, and other employees directly depended on this mill for their source of livelihood; in addition, 36,050 inhabitants of the region were indirectly affected by the loss of economic activity the mill had stimulated in the region. Unemployment, malnutrition, school dropouts, and business failures played havoc in a community formerly knit by cultural traditions extending back to the colonial period. Even community members who did not produce cane or labor in the factory recalled that they were raised and educated with the earnings of their parents who procured their livelihood from the mill. Drawing on their shared culture and community organization, cane growers, mill workers, and townspeople illegally occupied the mill and reopened it for the processing of sugar cane. They were violently repressed by local police, who arrested the usurpers, jailed and beat them, and killed one mill worker.

In other areas in which mills continued to function after privatization (1988–1992), *cañeros* found themselves in an entirely new relationship. In contrast to the traditional guarantees under state ownership, they were suddenly subjected to the vagaries of a competitive, profit-driven production system. The majority of Mexico's sixty-four sugar mills belong to twelve corporate groups owned by individuals of immense wealth and power. *Cañeros,* conditioned to traditional relations of paternalism with the state, resented the changes brought by privatization; nonetheless, they continued to apply notions of paternalism to their relationship with the new mill owners:

It is not easy to manage a sugar mill. It is like a family; if [the owners] aren't strict, all the children will be bad. With the private owners, we are all going to want to get something out, but we aren't going to get anything. And this is the real truth. It would be better if the federal government took it over. These [owners] are against the *cañeros*. They are the owners and they have no commitment to the *cañero*. The government had a different way of treating us [*cañero*].

Following the sale of sugar mills, subsidies were slashed, market opening glutted the sugar market with imported sugar, access to credit—essential for cane production—was restricted, and modifications to Article 27 of the Constitution allowed rental and sale of *ejido* parcels, and hence, ended a state-campesino alliance that had traditionally guaranteed land rights to rural producers. In 1992, fourteen sugar mills were on the verge of bankruptcy, and cane growers, who once profited from the sale of cane, found themselves indebted to sugar mills in a system of neo-debt peonage. In recent years, however, mill owners have begun to invest in their mills once again and cane growers with extra capital have improved cane yields and profits. At one mill, the manager stated: "We changed the mentality of the cane grower—now he is like a businessman." "Inefficient" *cañeros* who lacked resources to improve production, however, were denied credit, excluded from association with the sugar mill, and forced to turn to other crops or wage labor, effectively terminating a historical relationship distinguished by unequal power.

THE CULTURE OF SUGAR

The symbiotic relationship between campesino communities and sugar mills, control of land and mobilization of labor, the accumulation of capital by mill owners, and the myriad laws passed to govern the production of sugar are incalculable purely in terms of consumption and production. The role of sugar as an object of production and consumption suggests its colonial origins, reminds of the exploitive systems for control of land and labor, and recalls events that shaped the cultural life of contemporary Mexico.

Sugar production, from the era of haciendas to the development of a capitalist industry, molded forms of family organization, community structure, and ideologies premised upon campesinos' relationship with the sugar mills. This historical process gave dynamic form to the culture of sugarcane production:

> The cultivation of cane has been a culture here in Mexico. It is the most social of crops because in reality, that is where the society is—cane production maintains many families. It is a culture; it has endured 300 years. The *cañero* works, produces, and passes the land on to his sons [sic]. The rest of the family works in the planting, cultivation, and harvest—they have a hand in the raw material. What gives life to many people and villages in cane zones is precisely the cane. But to be a *cañero* is to suffer. We have relied on our own family in our struggle. Our strikes have been repressed, but this is our patrimony, our form of living. To be a *cañero* is a culture." [cane grower, Michoacán].

Sugar consumption was just as much influenced by historical forces as was sugar production. The diffusion of sugar into the multitudinal dimensions of culture coincided with the evolution of power relationships that characterized colonialism and neocolonialism. The product of a long history of changing land and labor relations in Mexico, sugar forms an ever-increasing component of contemporary lifestyles. Sugar, according to Mintz, ". . . has to be viewed in its multiple functions, as a culturally defined good" (1985:207). Octavio Paz suggests that sugar and its incorporation into national gastronomy symbolizes Mexican culture; its foods "exalt the eye and confound the taste" (1988:236), flavors and textures clash, and pleasure "tends to propagate and extend itself through taste and savoring" (1988:235) punctuated by an "insurrection of spices" (1988:240). Today, however, the culture of sugar is being nourished by the rite of passage of the sugar industry—from state capitalism to a capitalist culture premised on neoliberal ideology and wealth accumulation founded on creation of demand for vacuous calories. Eating habits have changed significantly, as individuals eat out more often, consume more processed foods, and snack more frequently. In the United States, from 1955 to 1965, per capita sugar consumption rose significantly; consumption of frozen desserts increased 31 percent, baked goods 50 percent, and soft drinks 78 percent. These consumption patterns are reproduced south of the U.S.–Mexican border. Mexico has one of the highest per capita levels of sugar consumption in the world; at 45 kg. per capita, it ranks third in the Western Hemisphere.[2]

The commercialization of sweetness, no longer restricted to elite consumption, today creates demand for vacuous calories among the poor. "The food industry has been and continues to be the principal agent in the degradation of taste, and it has now become a threat to public health" (Paz 1988:242). The industrialization of soft drinks (e.g., Coca-Cola, Pepsi-Cola), breads (e.g., Bimbo), and snacks (Tia Rosa, Sabritas, Gamesa) permeates the market and fills the shelves of city supermarkets and village *tiendas,* in addition to the ubiquitous street vendors who pedal all manner of sweets. Food industries absorb 67 percent of Mexico's sugar production; soft drink manufacturers, sweet snacks, and breads make up 80.9 percent of industrial consumption of sugar (Crespo 1990:1030). Coca-Cola (with 50 percent of the market), Pepsi-Cola (30 percent), and national brands (20 percent) share the second-largest soft drink industry in the world. Added to these corporate interests, the United States exports $222 million in food products containing sugar or HFCS to Mexico on an annual basis (Kessel et al. 1993). These industries provide the bulk of calories to Mexican consumers, even determining standards of gastronomic pleasure.

These consumptive patterns are embedded in a political economy historically marked by conflicts between actors with unequal power over land, labor, and resources. Mexico's traditional cuisines proclaim these conflicts of interest, from conquistadors to capitalist entrepreneurs, from haciendas to modernized agroindustries; the clashing of flavors, textures, and sensations symbolize the exploitative relations that traditionally linked campesinos to sugar mills. This hostile symbiosis is today being discarded as inefficient producers and mills are excluded in the name of efficiency and profit. Simultaneously, traditional foods, desserts, drinks, and sugared delicacies are giving way to junk foods promoted by this new breed of sugar mill owners.

It is through making the historical connection between production, labor relations, and sugar commodities that the power of culturally expressed meanings is elucidated. From *calaveras* to cokes, ". . . (sugar) was symbolically powerful, for its use could be endowed with many subsidiary meanings. No wonder the rich and powerful liked it so much, and no wonder the poor learned to love it" (Mintz 1985:186).

NOTES

1. Empresas Gamesa is a consortium comprised of numerous enterprises: Promotora Agropecuaria Gamesa, Productos Gerber, Ingenios Gamesa, and Grupo Gamesa. Grupo Gamesa includes Nabisco Famosa, Harinera Santos, Dulces Lady Baltimore, Mareas Alimenticias Internacionales, Galletera Palma, Gamesa Comercial, Desarrollo Industrial Gamesa, Almacenadora Gamesa, Desarrollo Inmobiliario Gamesa, Pastas Tepeyac, Inmobiliario Jalisciense, Corporativo Gamesa, and Acrosantos. Gamesa recently embarked on a pilot project with ejidatarios of Nuevo Leon to turn 10,000 acres of ejido land into wheat farming to supply wheat for Gamesa's cookies (Poole 1991).

Pepsico, Inc., purchased 72 percent of Empresas Gamesa in 1990 at a cost of $320 million. Pepsico's annual sales were $15.419 billion in 1990; it realized profits of $901 million (Ortega 1990). Pepsico bought Frito Lay, Taco Bell, Pizza Hut, and Kentucky Fried Chicken. A Mexican group that produces chicken for Tyson Foods initiated a project in Mexican *ejidos* to establish chicken farms to produce chickens for Kentucky Fried Chicken outlets in Latin America (Poole 1991). Pepsico had planned to expand the number of Kentucky Fried Chicken restaurants in Mexico from 53 to 200 (Bouleau 1990).

2. Per capita consumption of sugar declined from 1990 (54.5 kg. per capita) to 1994 (46.8 kg. per capita) because of a decrease in purchasing power and the use of high fructose sweeteners (GEPLACEA).

REFERENCES

Bouleau, Cecilia, 1990. Unilever, Pepsi Invest in Mexico. *Advertising Age,* November 19, P. 26.

Calderón de la Barca, Frances, 1966. *Life in Mexico.* New York: Doubleday.

Crespo, Horacio, Ed., 1990. *Historia del azúcar en México,* Vol. 2. México, D.F.: Fondo de Cultura Económica, S.A. de C.V.

———, 1988. *Historia del azúcar en México,* Vol. 1. México, D.F.: Fondo de Cultura Económica, S.A. de C.V.

del Villar, Samuel I., 1976. Depresioòn en la industria azucarera mexicana. *Foro Internacional* 16(4): 526–585.

Esteva, Gustavo, 1983. *The Struggle for Rural Mexico.* South Hadley, MA: Bergin and Garvey Publishers, Inc.

García Campos, Ezequiel, 1987. *Ella se llamaba dulce: Crisis y estatización azucarera.* México, D.F.: Ediciones Nueva Sociología.

GEPLACEA, 1990. *Handbook on International Sugar Marketing,* 3rd edition. México, D.F.: Group of Latin American and Caribbean Sugar Exporting Countries.

Jiménez Guzmán, Lucero, 1986. *La industrial cañero-azucarera en Mexico.* México, D.F.: Universidad Nacional Autónoma de México.

Kennedy, Diana, 1972. *The Cuisines of Mexico.* New York: Harper and Row.

Kessel, Fred, Peter Buzzanell, and Ron Lord, 1993. Mexico's Sugar Industry—Current and Future Situation. Washington, DC: Import Policy and Trade Analysis Division, Foreign Agricultural Service, USDA.

Landázuri Benítez and Verónica Vázquez Mantecón, 1988. *Azúcar y Estado (1750–1880). México, D.F.: Fondo de Cultura Económica, S.A. de C.V.*

Masuoka, Susan, 1990. *Calavera* Miniatures: Political Commentary in Three Dimensions. *Studies in Latin American Popular Culture* 9:263–278.

Meyer, Michael C., and William L. Sherman, 1979. *The Course of Mexican History.* New York: Oxford University Press.

Mintz, Sidney W., 1979. Time, Sugar, and Sweetness. *Marxist Perspectives* 2(4):56–73.

———, 1985. *Sweetness and Power: The Place of Sugar in Modern History.* New York: Viking Press.

Ortega Pizarro, Fernando, 1990. El porvenir de la industria mexicana, ser devorada por trasnacionales, dice Alberto Santos. *Proceso* 728:10–15.

Paz, Octavio, 1967. *The Labyrinth of Solitude: Life and Thought in Mexico.* New York: Grove Press.

———, 1988. Eroticism and Gastrosophy. *Daedalus* 117(3):227–249.

Poole, Claire, 1991. Land and Life! *Forbes,* April 29, pp. 45–46.

Purcell, Susan Kaufman, 1981. Business-Government Relations in Mexico: The Case of the Sugar Industry. *Comparative Politics* 13(2):211–233.

Tannenbaum, Frank, 1968. *Mexico, the Struggle for Peace and Bread.* New York: Alfred A. Knopf.

Tumbando Caña, 1989. Editorial. *Tumbando Caña* 14(9).

México, D.F.: Unión Nacional de Productores de Caña de Azúcar, C.N.C.

von Woebeser, Gisela, 1988. *La hacienda azucarera en la época colonial.* México, D.F.: Secretaría de Educación Pública and Universidad Autónoma de México.

Warman, Arturo, 1980. *We Come to Object: The Peasants of Morelos and the National State.* Baltimore: The Johns Hopkins University Press.

Winn, Peter, 1992. *Americas: The Changing Face of Latin America and the Caribbean.* Berkeley: University of California Press.

Wolf, Eric R., 1959. *Sons of the Shaking Earth.* Chicago: University of Chicago Press.

———, 1982. *Europe and the People Without History.* Berkeley: University of California Press.

33

Mixed Strategies and the Informal Sector
Three Faces of Reserve Labor

J. Douglas Uzzell

INTRODUCTION

During the past decade, a number of development economists and other scholars have investigated the role of what is often called the "informal sector" in the economies of developing countries. Although the meaning of the term "informal sector" is not always clear, it generally refers to economic activities that normally fall outside the purview of economic analysis (see ILO 1972; McGee 1979; Santos 1972; Sethuraman 1976, 1977; Tokman 1976, 1977). Usually, the informal sector is described as existing in the urban economies of Third World countries, and for those concerned with the absorption of labor into national (formal) capitalist economies, the question has arisen as to whether those employed in the informal sector constitute a reserve labor pool

From J. Douglas Uzzell, "Mixed Strategies and the Informal Sector: Three Faces of Reserve Labor," *Human Organization* 39 (1): 40–49, 1980. Copyright © 1980 by the Society for Applied Anthropology.

for the formal sector (see Cardoso 1971; Nun 1969; Quijano 1974).

In this paper, I examine three populations that I have studied in the field, whose members engage in informal sector economic activities. On the basis of these cases, I conclude that:

1. Informal sector activities are not confined to urban places or Third World countries;
2. Informal sector activities differ from formal sector activities primarily in the way that they are linked with the dominant institutions that support the capitalist system;
3. An actor's participation in informal sector activities may or may not be part of a mixed economic strategy made necessary by the actor's inability or unwillingness to follow a single economic strategy in either sector;
4. For many such actors, the mixed strategy includes nonmarket work, which in some cases resembles the peasant mode of production; and
5. Workers who divide their economic activities among formal and informal sectors and nonmarket work provide an elastic labor pool for both sectors and subsidize both.

THE THREE POPULATIONS

I have described the economic strategies of the Mexican and Peruvian populations elsewhere (Uzzell 1972, 1974a, 1974b, 1974c, 1976a for Peru: Uzzell 1976b; Dennis and Uzzell 1978 for Mexico) and L. Whiteford has discussed the economic strategies of the United States population (1979a, 1979b). Here, I will simply outline the characteristics of some of the economic choices of each.

Lima.   The population I studied in Lima lives in four *pueblos jovenes* (most commonly referred to as a kind of "squatter settlement"). Although the patterns of economic activities of residents vary from one locality to another—and within localities—many of the activities could be placed within the informal economic sector. Many enterprises (manufacturing, construction, repair, and wholesale and retail marketing) fall outside the government's control, although identical enterprises also operate legally, alongside the illegal ones. Informal institutions have developed parallel to their official counterparts, institutions for obtaining credit, housing, education,a nd urban services. These institutions have increasingly numerous links with the formal institutions. Since 1968, the government has attempted to gain control of these institutions by promoting cooperatives of various kinds, and since the early 1950s, various governments have aided the formation and development of *pueblos jovenes* (Collier 1971). At the same time, other formal institutions, including the news media, the entertainment industry, chain retail outlets, banks and the church, have sought to establish or reestablish connections with these populations.

Although members of my sample include professionals, wage laborers with established jobs, successful businessmen, and bureaucrats, as well as casual laborers, and vendors and artisans who barely subsist, virtually all residents pursue mixed economic strategies. These include a variety of activities ranging from gradual home construction done either by the owner or by informal sector builders (some of this housing is illegally rented), to household gardening and animal husbandry, and full-time, part-time, or occasional secondary employment. The supplementary strategy most pursued is engaging in adventitious (usually petty) entrepreneurial activities: buying small lots of goods wholesale and retailing them, investing in businesses, and the like.

The Oaxaca Villagers.   The population in the Oaxaca Valley is basically engaged in peasant agricultural and craft production, with most of the craftsmen also engaging in farming and husbandry. Many of their supplementary economic activities are the same as those of the Lima population: owner construction of housing and utilities, household gardening and husbandry, and secondary employment. Secondary employment, in which most male heads of households engage, regularly takes householders outside the home village to other villages in the region and to other rural regions as far away as the United States, as well as to both local and distant cities.

Their economic activities vary annually and seasonally, depending on rainfall, opportunities for obtaining use of land, condition and number of their livestock, social obligations, local work projects, and knowledge about the ability to obtain jobs outside the local area. Generally, and especially during the past ten or fifteen years, increased participation in the formal capitalist economy has required that they go farther and farther afield seeking wage employment.

Seco County, Texas.   The population in Seco County (a fictitious name) is the least likely of the three to have a single economic strategy. During periods of peak demand for rural labor, workers take any of a variety of jobs in or related to agriculture in the county, elsewhere in the state, or as far away as the Midwest or the west coast of the United States.

During the off-season they work at whatever becomes available in local businesses, farms, and ranches, occasionally taking jobs in cities in other parts of Texas. They also supplement their incomes with household gardening and husbandry, and with owner construction of housing. Some income is available from smuggling, though smuggling tends to be done by family firms, not individuals. Also many families supplement their income by taking advantage of government welfare programs and special programs for migrant workers.

These skeletal descriptions, intended only to introduce the three populations, will be supplemented by illustrative material as required in the discussion that follows. Now I turn to some of the theoretical issues and concepts that have prompted the writing of this essay.

ISSUES AND CONCEPTS

In this section, I introduce some of the basic concepts from the economics literature that are germane to my discussion: the informal sector, nonmarket work, and reserve labor. Then I introduce the notion of separating actor from role and the concept of linkages among institutions and between individuals and institutions. In the following section I attempt to bring these concepts to bear on the empirical data.

The Informal Sector. As I have said, the term "informal sector" or "lower circuit" (Santos 1975) refers to economic activities normally overlooked in economic analysis. It is difficult to define such activities precisely by any other criterion. Generally, informal-sector activities are of a lesser scale than formal activities. One may contrast a street vendor with a store owner, a cobbler with a shoe manufacturer, a person who runs a neighborhood lottery with the organization that conducts a national lottery, a neighborhood savings cooperative with a savings and loan corporation. Usually, not only does the informal enterprise have smaller volume and profits and fewer employees, but also its degree of capitalization is less: informal-sector enterprises tend to be labor intensive rather than capital intensive. Because of their scale, informal-sector enterprises tend to be family operations. None of these criteria however, provides an absolute distinction.

In a talk at the Burg Wartenstein Symposium Number 73 on "Shantytown in Developing Nations" in July 1977, Alejandro Portes suggested that a critical characteristic of informal-sector activities is that they are intrinsically illegal. That suggestion is valid if one expands it to the notion that such activities lack official recognition and sanction (though unofficially, they may enjoy both). In other words, the informal sector may be defined in terms of the nature of its linkages with formal institutions, both economic and otherwise.

This does not mean that informal-sector enterprises are not linked with institutions, but that they are not linked with an institution that is recognized

by the government, or are not linked in officially recognized ways. A clandestine manufacturer in Lima may have standing contracts with formal-sector shops, while he employs workers below the minimum wage, does not contribute to the national social security fund, and does not pay taxes on his earnings. He probably cannot secure loans from officially recognized lending institutions; but he can raise capital from his neighborhood savings cooperative or from his network of friends and relatives. His records are not submitted through official channels and data from his economic activities are not available for standard economic analysis. He deals with legal institutions in illegal ways, and he relies on other institutions that are not recognized officially.

By remaining outside formal institutions, the entrepreneur escapes taxation and legal strictures. However, in many cases, this amounts to making the best of a bad situation. Many informal-sector merchants engage in the kind of activities they do because they lack the capital, social connections, or formal training (which is institutionalized, too) to operate in the formal sector.

Economic variables in a given sector are affected by conditions in that sector's institutions. However, the two sectors are by no means isolated from one another. In fact, they are interdependent. Producers in one may be consumers in the other. A clandestine manufacturer in Lima may buy cloth from a large textile mill, manufacture clothing in his home, and sell his product (in part) to formal-sector retailers. Santos (1975:345) estimates that 60% of shoppers in Lima buy in informal-sector markets. Many of these people are employed in the formal sector.

Nonmarket Work. A major component in the economic strategies of the three populations under discussion is nonmarket work. This is similar to the notion of self-exploitation, developed by Chayanov (1977) as a partial counterpart of wages in the economy of peasant producers. For peasants, according to Chayanov, it applies to all forms of nonwage labor, and, he says, "The degree of self-exploitation is determined by a peculiar equilibrium between family demand satisfaction and the drudgery of labor itself" (1977:262). Nonmarket work, on the other hand, as it is used by modern labor economists (see Perlman 1969; Morgan

1970), includes all work not performed for wages, profits, or rents, including housework and even commuting to work. Following this definition, the part of a peasant's "self-exploitation" that goes into producing a cash crop would not be considered nonmarket work.

The connections between nonmarket work and the informal sector are complex. A good case in point is housing that is not produced by the local formal-sector housing industry. Members of all three of the populations either build their own houses (or parts of them), or hire informal-sector craftsmen and contractors to build them. These houses are usually built in increments as the owner can afford them. The degree of the owner's nonmarket work in this case depends on a number of factors, not the least of which is his skills. At one extreme, the owner may contract to have the entire structure built at once by an informal-sector contractor. At the other, he may build the entire structure himself (or with the help of friends and kinsmen), one room at a time. Intermediately, the owner may do the labor for which he has appropriate skills and contract for work such as wiring, plumbing, or plastering, which require special skills that he may not have.

There is, on the surface, no reason why the owner should not conduct business with individuals who operate in the formal sector, and certainly many owners do. However, in the three populations discussed here, there are good reasons why self-exploitation and participation in the informal sector go hand in hand. First of all, each population lives in a locality that is beyond the reach of formal institutions that prescribe construction standards. Second, with a few exceptions, neither of the three populations is in a position to borrow money for construction costs from a formal lending institution. This is not to say that quality of construction is not important, but that quality control is left to the consumer. And in the case of funding, there is no need to present a finished house, or the prospect of one, for mortgage. In this case, owners are free to pick and choose among artisans and contractors, seeking the best price and filling in with their own labor where they can, must, or want to.

Thus, house building, and many other activities, can be accomplished through some mixture of nonmarket work and participation in the informal sector in situations where the control of formal-sector

TABLE 33–1   Informal Sector Share of Gross National Product in Peru*

Year	Percent of GNP
1950	73.3
1961	65.3
1970	61.9

*Based on data given in Santos 1975. Figures include peasant agriculture.

institutions is weak or inapplicable. The two sectors and self-exploitation are interdependent economic systems. The degree of contribution by each to the local economies varies; but Santos (1975) gives estimates (see Table 33–1) of informal-sector contribution to the Peruvian economy. Santos estimates that 50% of the urban contribution to the GNP came from the informal sector in 1970 (1975:340). The direct contributions of the informal sector are probably somewhat lower in Mexico, and are certainly lower in the United States. However, it is important to remember that even nonmarket work often involves the use of manufactured goods, and, more important, serves as a supplement to wages. As such, nonmarket work increases profits of employers who otherwise might be pressed to pay higher wages. The practice of Peruvian governments of tolerating *pueblos jovenes* in Lima (or recently, of encouraging their formation) may be seen as a kind of wage subsidy. At the same time, it has stimulated formal-sector markets. In one large *pueblo joven* where I worked, I estimated that some $30 million had been spent on building materials between 1955 and 1970.

The Informal Sector and Reserve Labor. Many aspects of the debate about whether those who participate in informal-sector economic activities constitute an "industrial reserve," a peasantry, or a "protoproletariate" (McGee 1974), hinge on a fundamental confusion between actors and the roles that actors choose to perform. Leeds (1977) sets out a series of arguments for distinguishing between economic actors and the "roles" they occupy. It is unsound, on empirical grounds, to identify a person strictly in terms of an activity in which the person happens to be engaged at a particular time. That is, a person may undertake an informal-sector activity today, join the industrial labor force tomorrow, become a peasant producer next week, and engage in nonmarket work in the meantime. Keeping the definitions of role and actor separate, one may analyze the conditions under which the choice of informal-sector activities plays a part in making an actor a reserve laborer for formal-sector employers.

The three populations I treat in this paper do not just engage in informal-sector activities; they engage in them partially, as part of a mixed economic strategy that includes other activities: peasant, rural proletarian, and urban proletarian, among others. Engaging in informal-sector activities allows the actor to labor elsewhere, though not necessarily in the formal sector. Hence the term "reserve labor" denotes the choice of reserving one's labor, rather than the person who makes the choice.

The "Marginality" of the Informal Sector. Informal-sector activities are normally spoken of by economists as "marginal" to formal capitalist economies, whose "centers," particularly in Third World countries, are in urban places. The general explanation for the existence of informal sectors is that they occur where the formal sector is unable to provide subsistence for the entire population. If such activities are found in an industrialized country and in rural areas, questions arise about the simplicity of the concept. I suggest that these activities exist where the dominant mode of production is inadequate to meet the perceived needs of the population, whatever that mode of production may be. It is only when the population choosing these activities treats them as "second best" activities that the activities become marginal in a general sense. (However, see McGee 1979, p. 6, as well as Chayanov 1977; Boeke 1980; van Leur 1950; Polanyi 1957 and others on the historical development of two-sector capitalism.)

DISCUSSION

Mixed Economic Strategies. Members of the three populations meet their economic needs through mixed economic strategies. In each population, the unit of survival is usually the family (whether nuclear or extended). That is, the labor of all family members of working age is used to meet the family budget. In the Lima sample, an average of 30% of family income comes from family members other than the head of the household (and although I do not have comparable data, I am sure that the percentage is much higher in the other two populations). This, of course, only treats cash income. The value of nonmarket work involved in building one's own house is measured in terms of reduced expenses rather than increased income, although the effect on the family's economy is the same. The same is true of making the family's tortillas or clothes instead of buying manufactured ones. Such work has the same effect on the family's economy, and the choice involves the same factors: balancing demand satisfaction against the drudgery of the labor. Of course, where the alternative exists (or is perceived to exist) of selling one's labor for cash and paying that cash to escape the drudgery, the act of choosing a course of action becomes more complex. One is then forced to consider the relative unpleasantness of various kinds of work, as well as the nonmonetary rewards (e.g., time, relationships, prestige) of each.

What I am describing is a set of choices faced by most economic actors in the world. And many people who are not considered economically marginal pursue mixed economic strategies. Taking short-term jobs involving manual labor, "moonlighting," and household gardening are common among the populations I am describing: grantsmanship, consulting (for a fee), and speaking for honoraria are common among the population of which I am a member. We all know of writers who teach so that they can afford to write, and of teachers who take all manner of extra jobs so that they can afford to teach. The differences involve the amount of labor, the drudgery of the labor, the extremity of the economic need, and the number and kind of economic alternatives that are available. It is one thing to engage in some kind of drudgery in order to afford a particular lifestyle or the leisure to fulfill's one's vocation. It is quite another to engage in several kinds of drudgery in order to survive (see Liebow 1967:29–70 on this point).

It is tempting here to put the Oaxacan population in the same class with artists, athletes, and teachers, saying that their secondary employment is undertaken so that they can afford to live as peasants, and, in a certain sense, it is true. But it is possible to turn this statement upside down. By retaining their places in the village, the Oaxacans insure themselves of a place to live, of assistance during adverse times, of access to certain kinds of resources (both material and social), and of a basic supply of food for their families. Actually, they are caught in a cycle: selling their labor so that they can remain in the village—so that they can sell their labor. Dinerman (1978) makes a similar analysis of some groups in Michoacan.

Not all those who engage in informal-sector activities employ mixed strategies, nor are all poor. The resident of a *pueblo joven* in Lima who, with the profits from his illegal factor, hires a contractor to build his house and maids to do the household drudgery is identical to his formal-sector counterpart, from this point of view. Similarly, the full-time smuggler in Seco County may be conspicuously wealthy, and if he diversifies his economic activities, it may be in the direction of formal-sector activities, a genteel avocation, or a "cover" business.

Mixed Strategies and Dominant Activities.

Where people define the locally dominant mode of production as inadequate to meet their needs, they adopt mixed strategies to supplement the dominant mode. Inadequacy may or may not manifest itself as unemployment or underemployment in the formal sector. It does in Seco County, where the dominant activity is agricultural labor. In rural Oaxaca, however, the dominant activity may be said to be peasant production. Nevertheless, one of the things that makes this kind of activity inadequate to meet the needs of those who engage in it is the intrusion of consumer goods—and notions of their desirability—from the formal sector. At the same time, expansion of formal-sector transportation has made a wider variety of economic activities possible for the villagers. An interesting case is presented by several teachers in the village school, who are also agriculturalists. Each of the two roles—teacher and peasant—enhances their position in the other, and it would be difficult to say which is dominant for these actors.

For the Lima population, among whom unemployment and underemployment are quite high, it would be difficult to say whether formal or informal activities are dominant (though, of course, both are included in a capitalist mode of production). Not only is the informal sector significant in the city's economy (see Santos 1975), but for many members of the population discussed here, wage labor is looked on somewhat dubiously. As I have said elsewhere,

> We should keep in mind . . . that in Peru large-scale industry is a creole institution, and like the rest, it is structured in such a way as to exploit cholos. In Lima, employment even in a highly skilled blue collar job is a dead end, both socially and economically. By contrast, the small clandestine manufacturer produces relatively cheap consumer goods for cholos, while avoiding taxes and other creole devices for reducing his income, and the cholo merchant may sometimes distribute those goods. In contrast to blue collar jobs, these activities are *not* necessarily dead ends, however great the odds may be against one's becoming wealthy. Cholos do, in fact, become wealthy, and those who do are not wage laborers [Uzzell 1974a].

Obviously, when we speak of the dominance of a mode of production or a sector, we need to specify what we mean by "dominant," or at least make clear the point of view from which the definition is being made.

Social Activities as Economic Activities.

The mixed economic strategies chosen by members of the three populations under discussion include constellations of activities that are inseparable from the obviously economic ones and that condition decision making. Selby has noted (Selby and Hendrix 1976) that in allocating their available time, Oaxacans for whom peasant production is a dominant activity leave themselves a considerable number of free days in their work year. Much of this time is spent in forming and strengthening their interpersonal relationships, as well as in strengthening their position in the village (performing duties of municipal offices, working in church or village communal projects, etc.). A social network, for this population, makes mixed strategies possible, because through it an actor learns of the availability of work, as well as the opportunity for receiving aid (transportation, temporary housing, influence with potential employers). Of course, the expense of entertaining friends and relatives increases one's need for earnings, but these expenses are as much job related as the purchase of tools—whatever noneconomic motives may also be involved. Many of these activities also assure one of social security. It is through one's social network that one receives such benefits as emergency loans and other aid, support in old age, and child care while one is working.

Among the Peruvian population, there is a marked tendency to spread one's social network as widely as possible and then to select out for intensive interaction those individuals most likely to be useful economically. At the same time, many members of this population retain ties with natal towns and villages, where they raise capital through sale of village land or invest capital in village land, meanwhile maintaining the social relationships that make such transactions possible.

Among the Seco County population, many of the same considerations seem to be used. Social security (in addition to government programs) is provided by the extended family (see Dinerman 1978). And one's standing in the community has more than psychological value. Beyond the community, personal contacts provide information about available temporary jobs and other windfalls. A person who has contracted with a farm manager to supply a work crew on a particular date recruits among his kinsmen and friends. It is to one's advantage to have worked in a great number of places, establishing contacts along the way, because this broadens one's field of choice in time of need.

The same network may also be activated by parents on behalf of their children so that the children may learn skills. Most skills in agricultural labor are learned through apprenticeship. The parent who can arrange for a son to learn to drive a truck or a forklift is not only aiding the child by increasing the child's potential ability to earn money, but also improving the chances that the child will be able to provide for the parents in their old age.

A recent development in Seco County involves learning about how to take advantage (legally and illegally) of welfare programs and other government programs that aid the poor and the migrant. These programs provide supplementary income, special educational benefits, free medical care, and clothing. Becoming acquainted with these alternatives and with how to exploit them also involves the development of the appropriate social network (one that includes those who have special knowledge), as much as it involves reading and understanding government pamphlets. Taking advantage of these programs also conditions—and is conditioned by—one's other economic choices. For example, the family that in a given year decides not to migrate until the children have completed their special course of instruction for the children of migrants is modifying its economic choices in order to accommodate other activities, which may have long-range economic implications (L. Whiteford 1979b).

Breaking out of this system implies not only psychological cleavages, but economic considerations as well (ibid.). Of approximately three hundred people who received special training in a government-sponsored job training program between 1974 and 1977, virtually all who made use of their new skills or specialties were forced to leave the county to find employment. Local demand for their skills simply does not exist. But in deciding to move elsewhere, those who moved had to take into account their considerable social (and hidden economic) losses, as well as their gains in terms of increased wages. Where extensive cultural systems that supplement income have developed over time, the amount of savings provided by noneconomic activities may be surprisingly large.

Beating the Prevailing System. In a sense, members of each population "beat the system" through their mixed strategies, and this may involve defining activities in nonstandard ways. For most men in the Oaxaca population there is a constant assessment of alternatives—wage labor, land available to rent, the likelihood of rainfall, a cow that is producing milk. Though considered peasant villagers, the eight most prosperous men in the village I studied made their "fortunes" outside the village.

In the Peruvian population there are almost as many strategies as there are actors. However, we may look at some particularly desirable combinations. Holding a job that gives one access to bribes or rebates and does not take all of one's time is a particularly lucrative starting point. Thus, the government clerk who deals with the public, the policeman, or the salesman of building materials (who recommends craftsmen in return for a percentage of their fees) is in a good position. If one must perform wage labor, it is best to have a job that leaves one time to make business deals on the side. This must include time to be seen in the right places. It also requires at least enough money to buy a suit of clothes and an occasional round of beer. In short, one must establish a reputation for being a businessman. The amount of working capital required varies. If one is on good enough terms with a clandestine manufacturer, the manufacturer may provide goods on consignment. Whether the goods are wholesaled or retailed depends again on social contacts. Acquaintance with store owners or proprietors of market stalls enables one to turn over goods more quickly and at a higher volume than if one must peddle them on the streets.

Many houses in the *pueblo jovenes* are built with storefronts, whether or not the resident has a store. When circumstances permit, a family may decide to sell food, beer, soft drinks, or ices from these storefronts. Usually, these operations bring very little profit (because of their size), but they do permit members of the family who would not otherwise be economically productive—children too young to work or a wife who must stay at home to care for small children—to make some contribution to the family's income.

For the Seco County population a major strategy is maximizing wages. Wages have risen dramatically in Seco County during the past decade (while the number of full-time jobs available to males has decreased). Whereas a farm worker may have earned $.80 per hour in 1968, that worker now earns the national minimum wage in most places in the county. (In 1978, the national minimum wage was $2.65 per hour.) *If a person should happen to find a year-round job that paid the minimum wage*, and worked 40 hours per week for 50 weeks per year, annual earnings would be $5,300, or $442 per month. The average household earns less than this according to official reports, but much income is not reported. At the very least, a person can expect to pay $75 per month (actually, anywhere from $20 to $150) for housing and utilities, and $200 per month for food, if, say, there are three dependents. This leaves some $165 per month for all other expenses, clothing, medical expenses, and transportation. Transportation is a major problem in Seco County. It is a rural county, and there is no public transportation. Even the poorest family must maintain some kind of automobile or pickup truck just to be able to get to the job. That can easily take up half the remainder of one's income.

But the fact is that very few people live on minimum wage alone. In the first place, the jobs are not available. In the second place, few families have only a single breadwinner. Many of the large agribusinesses now pay time and one-half for overtime labor. If a person can arrange to work for two weeks, 18 hours per day, seven days per week at minimum wage, plus time and one-half for overtime, earnings will total $897, an amount that would take eight and one-half weeks to earn under normal conditions at the same wage. Even if exhaustion results and requires a week's recovery, the person is over five weeks ahead of the game. Of course, 125-hour weeks are rare, taking their place, in the tales of workers, alongside 12-point buck deer and jobs that pay union wages. But that is what one strives for and the desirability of a job is measured in those terms. This, of course, is making the best of a bad situation, because most agricultural jobs in the county last only a few weeks anyway.

During periods between jobs, one may use one's labor to supplement wages by repairing or improving shelter, clothing, or automobiles, or one may use one's leisure time to strengthen or expand the equally essential social network. In Seco County, many people go on welfare at this time. And they search for the next short-term job.

Linkages with Institutions.   Thus far, the discussion has focused on the mixed economic strategies of workers whose subsistence comes from work in the informal sector, the formal sector, and from nonmarket work. Now the question arises: What kinds of cultural systems permit or encourage such strategies, and how does the choice of such strategies affect the cultural systems?

Discussing rural-urban relationships, Schaedel (1972) specifies five types of "linkages"—ecological, economic, juridico-political, socio-religious, and culture-informational—between institutions in rural and urban places. I should like to expand his concept to include intraurban as well as rurla-urban linkages, and to include linkages between individuals and institutions. If we think of a cultural system (of any population) as containing economic, political, social, religious (etc.) subsystems, we may think of the linkages as connections between subsystems and among parts of the subsystems. Through the linkages flow power, wealth, and information, each of which may be transformed into the others. Some of the parts of the subsystems are institutions, and when we speak of the formal economic sector we refer to certain recognized institutions and the economic linkages among them, all of which provide economic options for at least some members of the population.

When the options provided by the recognized institutional linkages become inadequate (because of changes in any part of the cultural system), certain members of the population must set about creating their own linkages. This process may lead to the formation of new institutions, as seemed to be happening in Peru in 1970. When this occurs, those choosing options within the new institutions may individually disengage from the old "formal" institutions and reengage with them indirectly through the newly formed linkages between institutions. Where the individually created linkages do not become institutionalized, they remain at the level of individuals and between individuals and institutions. This is generally the case for those members of the three populations described above who pursue mixed economic strategies.

Migration. Options available to the actor who follows a mixed strategy may be densely (urban) or sparsely (rural) distributed in a given geographic space. (Where transportation is slow, the separations of contacts in time is also significant.) These options are made available through the idiosyncratic social and informational linkages forged by the actor, and may be mapped onto the actor's social network. If these linkages are geographically dispersed, the physical movements required by the mixed strategy may come to be defined as migration, although, except for the cost of transportation, the activities may be functionally identical to those of another actor who happens to be in a dense concentration of options (see also Roberts 1975). (Schaedel [personal communication] considers the aggregation of geographically dispersed elements into a single strategy to constitute a new linkage mechanism in formation.)

Mixed Strategies and Formal Insitutions. Mixed strategies often (perhaps usually) bring individuals into contact with formal institutions. The situation of the Seco County population makes a good case in point. They have many direct connections with the United States government, through welfare and special programs for migrants. This direct and indirect economic aid enables the workers to pursue their mixed strategies as a partially employed rural proletariat. The federal programs are, in effect, as much a subsidy for the agribusiness as for the workers, because without the wage supplements, employers might be forced to restructure their production techniques and/or raise wages. The production system of the agribusinesses, at the same time, allows workers to concentrate their wages selectively. The nature of their linkages with these two institutions both allows and requires the workers to perform nonmarket work and to engage in informal-sector activities. It is this set of conditions that makes the population a pool of reserve labor. Actually, the linkages are much more complex than this, in part because many valley farm owners are connected into the Mexican economic subsystem as producers, investors, and buyers, because part of the labor force comes from and returns to Mexico, and because workers in the United States make purchases and maintain social contacts in Mexico (see L. Whiteford 1979a; Uzzell in press). This situation may change following any of a number of institutional developments, for example, strengthening of the Mexican-American political lobby or unionization of workers.

Among the Oaxacan population, the government subsidizes peasant production through the *ejido* (land reform) program. (The village where I worked has communal village land, but no *ejido*.) Wage labor is provided both by government projects—mostly road construction—and by private employers. Other supplementary economic activities chosen by this population may be called nonmarket work. Whether to classify many of their activities as "peasant" or not is of only academic interest, because the activities are identical, whether performed in a village or in an urban squatter settlement. What is important is that in the mix of economic choices wage labor is a partial strategy. This again renders the population a pool of reserve labor.

Eckstein (1975) gives another example of linkages between the government and the informal sector in Mexico City. Of small-scale cobblers, she says, "They thus far have managed to survive as a class because the government protects the inefficient but labor-absorbing sector from competing shoe manufacturers" (1975:127). Nevertheless, only a portion of the cobblers are steadily employed in this activity, the remainder apparently pursuing mixed strategies (Eckstein 1975).

The Peruvian case is distinct because many of the "informal sector" activities have become institutionalized and many of the linkages are now between formal and informal institutions, rather than between individuals and institutions. As the population in the *pueblos jovenes* began to grow in the late 1950s and thereafter, a succession of governments actively courted them, in some cases giving effective permission to settle on government land or private land in return for political support. Private landowners also manipulated the squatters to their own advantage (Collier 1971). In the larger settlements, banks have installed branches and retailers have established branch outlets, the effect of which is to siphon off capital gained through wages in both sectors into the formal sector. Government co-optation (in this case, tacit or explicit permission to occupy land and build homes) amounts to wage subsidy for those who are employed full time, either in the formal sector on in the informal sector, or part time in both. The *pueblos jovenes* have provided geographic nuclei around which constellations of informal-sector activities have clustered, all linked to formal institutions in 1970. These include the church, banks, retailers, transportation enterprises, manufacturers of building materials, and the entertainment industry.

Choice of economic strategy in this context affects both the flows of capital among sets of institutions and the amount of reserve labor available in the population for use in the formal sector. Through those who choose steady employment in the formal sector, supplementing their wages through nonmarket work, capital moves into the informal institutions from the formal institutions in the form of local purchases. Those who mix steady employment in informal institutions with nonmarket work redistribute capital among the informal institutions, while channeling some of it into formal institutions. Neither of these populations can properly be considered a pool of reserve labor. It is those whose mixed strategies involve employment among formal institutions, as well as nonmarket work, who provide a pool of reserve labor. Their labor is in reserve because they are not committed to a single full-time activity in either sector.

Their lack of commitment to a single source of income is an adaptation to prevailing wages, hiring practices, and the social and political position of the workers. The adaptation is precarious at best. S. Whiteford vividly describes the position of one such population, Bolivian peasants who migrate to Argentina, among whom

> . . . individuals and their families employed a variety of tactics including patron-client relationships, multiple job holdings, small scale entrepreneurial efforts, seasonal work during the post-*zafra* [sugar cane harvest] season, and active social networks to keep informed of jobs. The assumption underlying these tactics is what I call the strategy of least vulnerability [S. Whiteford in press].

It is the inadequacy of the prevailing economic systems to provide such workers a living wage that forces them to engage in mixed economic strategies; either to survive, or to reduce their vulnerability to forces in the system over which they have no control. It is the extremity of their need, the necessity of taking, if not the willingness to take, any wage labor that may become available, that renders them a pool of reserve labor.

CONCLUSION

One thing that becomes clear as one considers informal-sector activities in terms of institutional linkages is that most definitions of the informal sector are made from the point of view of a limited set of recognized institutions. Because of that we may misleadingly classify as "informal" (i.e., marginal) a number of equally viable, extensive, and well-organized institutions, treating them as marginal when they are in fact quite central, both in the cultural system as a whole and in the economic subsystem. Some forms of clandestine manufacturing in Peru are an obvious example, and a similar case could even be made for the Seco County smugglers. If they are marginal economically or otherwise in the region, then Sir Francis Drake was marginal in Elizabethan England.

Be that as it may, it seems obvious that mixed economic strategies of a population allow that population to act as a pool of reserve labor, not informal-sector activities per se, although options in the informal sector may make mixed strategies possible. The population set that constitutes a labor reserve intersects the population set that chooses informal-sector activities where institutional linkages are inadequate (impelling individuals to forge their own linkages), and where nonmarket work in addition to wages is required for one to meet one's needs. The configuration that this makes depends not on urbanness, nor on the degree of industrialization of the economic system, but on the distribution of wealth, power, and information flowing through institutional linkages in the cultural system. Where these flows are inevitably apportioned or where, for whatever reason, there are inequities of distribution in the system, individuals, in the extremity of their need, take up the slack: invent, make do, get along. When the system returns to a new state in which their labor is again needed—however temporarily—they are available, be they peasant or proletarian, having survived by their own devices—a pool of labor in reserve.

REFERENCES

Boeke, J.H., 1930. Dualistiche Economie. Leiden: E.J. Brill.

Cardoso, F.H., 1971. Comentarios sobre los conceptos de sobrepoblación relativa y marginalidad. Revista Latinoaméricana de Ciencias Sociales 1–2 (June–December).

Chayanov, A.V., 1977. On the Theory of Non-Capitalist Economic Systems. In Peasant Livelihood: Studies in Economic Anthropology and Cultural Ecology. R. Halperin and J. Dow, eds. Pp. 257–68. New York: St. Martin's Press. Originally published 1925.

Collier, David, 1971. Squatter-Settlement Formation and the Politics of Co-optation in Peru. Ph.D. dissertation, Department of Political Science, University of Chicago.

Dennis, Philip A., and Douglas Uzzell, 1978. Corporate and Individual Inter-Village Relationships in the Valley of Oaxaca. Ethnology (July) 17(3):313–24.

Dinerman, Ina R., 1978. Patterns of Adaptation Among Household of US–Bound Migrants from Michoacan, Mexico. International Migration Review 12(4):485–502.

Eckstein, Susan, 1975. The Political Economy of Lower Class Areas in Mexico City: Societal Constraints on Local Business Prospects. In Latin American Urban Research, Vol. 5. W.A. Cornelius and F.M. Trueblood, eds. Pp. 125–45. Beverly Hills: Sage.

International Labour Office, 1972. Employment, Incomes and Equality. A Strategy for Increasing Productive Employment in Kenya. Geneva:International Labour Office.

Leeds, Anthony, 1977. Mythos and Pathos: Some Unpleasantries on Peasantries. In Peasant Livelihood: Studies in Economic Anthropology and Cultural Ecology. R. Halperin and J. Dow, eds. Pp. 227–56. New York: St. Martin's Press.

Liebow, Elliot, 1967. Tally's Corner. New York: Little, Brown.

McGee, T.G., 1974. Rejoinder. Human Organization 33(Fall):258–60.

———, 1979. Conservation and Dissolution in the Third World City: The "Shanty Town" as an Element of Conservatism. Development and Change. Vol. 10. London and Beverly Hills: Sage.

Morgan, Chester A., 1970. Labor Economics, Third Edition. Austin: Business Publications, Inc.

Nun, J., 1969. Superpoblacion Relativa, Ejercito Industrial de Reserva y Masa Marginal. Revista Latino-Americana de Sociologia 5. (January):2.

Perlman, Richard, 1969. Labor Theory. New York: Wiley.

Polanyi, Carl, 1957. The Great Transformation. Boston: Beacon.

Portes, Alejandro, 1977. Personal Communication.

Quijano, Anibal, 1974. The Marginal Pole of the Economy and the Marginalised Labour Force. Economy and Society 3 (November): 356–78.

Roberts, Brian R., 1975. Center and Periphery in the Development Process: The Case of Peru. In Latin American Urban Research, Vol. 5. W. Cornelius and F. Trueblood, eds. Pp. 77–106. Beverly Hills: Sage.

Santos, Milton, 1972. Los dos Circuitos de la Economia Urbana de los Paises Sub-Desarrollados. In La Cuidad y la Region para el Dessarrollo. J.C. Funes, ed. Pp. 67–99. Caracas: Comision de Administration Publica de Venezuela.

———, 1975. The Periphery at the Pole: Lima, Peru. In The Social Economy of Cities, Vol. 9. Urban Affairs Annual Reviews. G. Gappert and H.M. Rose, eds. Pp. 335–60. Beverly Hills: Sage.

Schaedel, Richard P., 1972. Variations in the Patterns of Contemporary and Recent Urban-Rural (Hierarchical) Linkages in Latin America. Revised Version of the Paper Presented at the IV Symposium on Urbanization in Latin America from Its Beginning to the Present Time. Rome.

Selby, Henry A., and G.G. Hendrix, 1976. Policy Planning and Poverty: Notes on a Mexican Case. In Anthropology and Public Policy Formulation. P. Sanday, ed. Pp. 219–44. New York: Academic Press.

Sethuraman, S.V., 1976. The Urban Informal Sector: Concept Measurement and Policy. International Labour Review 114 (July–August): 69–81.

———, 1977. The Urban Informal Sector in Africa. *International Labor Review* 116 (November–December): 343–52.

Tokman, Victor E., 1976. *Dinamica del Mercado de Trabajo Urbano: el Sector Informal Urbano en América Latina*. Santiago: Organizacion Internacional del Trabajo, Programa Regional del Empleo para América Latina y el Caribe. (second version).

———, 1977. *An Exploration into the Nature of Formal-Informal Sector Interrelationships*. Santiago: Organizacion Internacional del Trabajo, Programa Regional del Empleo para América Latina y el Caribe. (second version).

Uzzell, J. Douglas, 1972. Bound for Places I'm Not Known to: Adaptations of Migrants and Residence in Four Irregular Settlements in Lima, Peru. Ph.D. dissertation, University of Texas at Austin.

———, 1974a. A Strategic Analysis of Social Structure in Lima, Using the Concept of "Plays." *Urban Anthropology* 3(1):34–46.

———, 1974b. Interaction of Population and Locality in the Development of Squatter Settlements in Lima. In *Latin American Urban Research*, Vol. 4. W. Cornelius and F. Trueblood, eds. Pp. 113–34. Beverly Hills: Sage.

———, 1974c. Cholos and Bureaus in Lima: Case History and Analysis. *International Journal of Comparative Sociology* 15(3–4):23–30.

———, 1976a. From Play Lexicons to Disengagement Spheres in Peruvian Society. Rice University Program of Development Studies Paper No. 71. First Presented at the XLI Congreso Internacional de Americanistas, Mexico, D.F.

———, 1976b. Ethnography of Migration: Breaking out of the Bi-Polar Myth. In *New Approaches to the Study of Migration*. D. Guillet and J.D. Uzzell, eds. Rice University Studies 62 (Summer):3, pp. 45–54.

———, in press. Which Region? Whose Context?: Problems of Defining the Regional Context of Frontera, Texas. In *Urban Anthropology: Cities in a Hierarchical Context*. T. Collins, ed. Athens: University of Georgia Press.

van Leur, J.C., 1950. *Indonesian Trade and Society*. The Hague: Mouton.

Whiteford, Linda M., 1979a. THe Borderland as an Extended Community. In *Migration Across Frontiers: Mexico and the United States*. F. Camera and R.V. Kemper, eds. Pp. 127–40. Albany: State University of New York Press.

———, 1979b. Family Relations in Seco County: A Case Study of Social Change. Ph.D. dissertation. University of Wisconsin, Milwaukee.

Whiteford, Scott, In press. *Migrant Labor, Urbanization, and Urban Development: Bolivian Workers in North Western Argentina*. Austin: University of Texas Press.

34

Rethinking the Hamburger Thesis
Deforestation and the Crisis of Central America's Beef Exports

Marc Edelman

Since the early 1970s, growing numbers of tropical ecologists, anthropologists, and other social scientists have linked developed-country demand for Latin American beef to a host of environmental and social ills, including forest destruction (Buschbacher 1986; DeWalt 1983; Heckadon and McKay 1984; Nations and Kromer 1983a, 1983b; Parsons 1976; Shane 1986; Partridge 1984; Uhl and Parker 1986a), decreased rainfall (Hagenauer 1980; Fleming 1986), soil erosion (Myers 1981; Nations and Nigh 1978), replacement of food crops by pasture (Boyer 1986; Feder 1980; DeWalt 1983; Sanderson 1986; Spielman 1972), reduced developing-country protein consumption (Buxedas 1977; Caufield 1985; Dickinson, 1973; Holden 1981; Roux 1975), rural unemployment (Brockett 1988; Williams 1986), and concentration of land, credit, and other resources (Aguilar and Solís 1988; Da

From Marc Edelman, "Rethinking the Hamburger Thesis: Deforestation and the Crisis of Central America's Beef Exports." In M. Painter and W. Durham, *The Social Causes of Environmental Destruction in Latin America*, 1995, University of Michigan Press, Ann Arbor, MI.

Veiga 1975; Edelman 1985; Guess 1978; Keene 1978; Rutsch 1980; Slutsky 1979).[1] Articles have appeared with great frequency in normally staid scientific publications, with uncharacteristically catchy titles referring to the "hamburger connection" (Myers 1981), "hamburger society" (Nations and Kromer 1983a), "cattle eating the forest" (DeWalt 1983), and "our stead in the jungle" (Uhl and Parker 1986a).[2] One recent book on the Central American environmental crisis labels the region's countries "hamburger republics" (Hedström 1985:41). Headlines of journal commentaries inquire rhetorically "Is a quarter-pound hamburger worth a half-ton of rainforest?" (Uhl and Parker 1986b) and "Is the rainforest worth seven hundred million hamburgers?" (Matteucci 1988).

This equation of export beef production with environmental destruction has also taken on a life of its own in the popular imagination and in the mainstream communications media, in part because of newly urgent concerns about global warming, declining species diversity, and an eroding land base (Durning 1991). Advocacy groups, conjuring up images of cattle stampeding through fragile rainforests (EPOCA n.d.), have launched boycotts of fast-food chains, staged sit-ins at the World Bank to protest the negative environmental impact of lending policies, and urged major cutbacks in herd sizes and beef consumption (RAN 1989; Beyond Beef Coalition, The Goal: A 50% Reduction of Beef Consumption by 2002, *The New York Times*, 23 April 1992: B7). Editorial writers who for years proclaimed the advantages of the Brazilian "economic miracle" now decry "the rape of Rondônia" and rail against the "murder" of Alaska's temperate rain forest, proclaiming that "Tongass Trees Aren't Cheeseburgers" (Forest Murder: Ours and Theirs, *New York Times*, 20 September 1989: A26).[3]

The widespread fetishization of the hamburger-deforestation relation could be considered a successful diffusion of scientist's concerns to a broader public. But although not inaccurate *grosso modo*, like most fetishes it both reveals and conceals. As a focus for anxieties about the global environment, it is appealingly direct and suggests possibilities for effective personal action that are attractive in the individualistic and depoliticized yet health-conscious United States of the late 1980s and 1990s (boycotting Burger King, for example). As a framework for social scientific analysis, however, the by-now familiar allusions to ground-beef-for-gringos emerging from tropical pastures sometimes obscure more than they elucidate. Furthermore, oversimplifications about the "hamburger connection" may give rise to erroneous environmental policy recommendations and political strategies.

This chapter argues that the demand-based understandings of the beef export-deforestation relation that underlie the prevailing wisdom—popular and/or scientific—are no longer valid for Central America in the period of livestock sector stagnation that dates to the early 1980s. Even when applied to the deforestation that occurred during the beef export boom of the 1960s and 1970s, such explanations frequently require significant qualification, because they ignore or downplay both other factors that fueled the beef boom and other causes of forest destruction. Cattle ranching has been associated with deforestation; this chapter suggests that the relationship is a historically specific one and is, in any case, more complex than has sometimes been appreciated.[4] Adequate policy prescriptions must be based on an understanding of that complexity (Allen and Barnes 1985; Rudel 1989; WRI 1985).

Central America has been the United States' third most important source of imported beef, after

Australia and New Zealand, since the mid-1950s.[5] This chapter examines: (1) the diminishing role of foreign demand as a stimulus to livestock production in Central America, the principal source of U.S. tropical beef imports; (2) the causes of the crisis in the Central American livestock sector, especially in Costa Rica, the region's main exporting country and one much admired for its innovative conservation programs (Tangley 1986; Thrupp 1989); and (3) the extent to which the crisis in the Central American livestock sector creates political and physical space for environmentally and economically sound alternatives to pasture development and forest destruction.

FOREIGN DEMAND AND SOCIAL SCIENTIFIC MANICHAEANISM

Social scientists concerned with change in the developing world are only beginning to recover from the Manichaean excesses of dependency and world-system theory that were so fashionable in the 1960s and the 1970s.[6] In their worst manifestations, these demand-based or circulationist paradigms posited an all-powerful metropolitan "capitalism" as the explanation for underdevelopment in the periphery and in effect denied that "local initiative and local response" (Mintz 1977) had any significant role in making history. Now that historical process and human agency again occupy their deserved, privileged place in social scientific investigation (Ortner 1984), it is perhaps surprising that dualist, dependency-type determinisms remain dominant in certain areas of inquiry, such as in discussions of the beef exports-deforestation relationship.

It is ironic that rising public concern about export-oriented ranching and tropical forest destruction coincides not only with diminishing interest in dependency-type paradigms in the social sciences—an esoteric consideration understandably of no concern to environmental policymakers and activists—but more importantly also with significant declines in the foreign demand for beef that is supposed to be the root of the problem. Indeed, in Central America, a key beef-producing zone that sends most of its exports to the United States, the cattle sector has been in a serious crisis since the early 1980s (see Figures 34–1 and 34–2). In Costa Rica, the severity of the situation is such that the

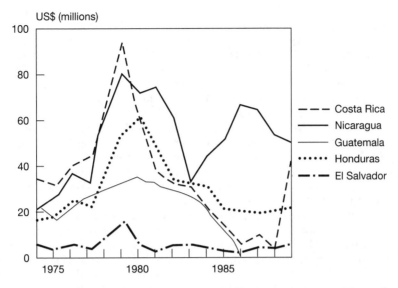

FIGURE 34–1   Central America: value of beef exports, 1974–89. (Data from FAO, Trade Yearbooks.)

Federation of Chambers of Cattle Ranchers (*Federación de Cámaras de Ganaderos*) successfully petitioned in mid-1985 to have the Minister of Agriculture declare a "state of emergency" for the livestock sector. Central Bank experts concurred, noting that for cattle production "the rate of return was negative" (Realidad 1988:8). "When there's no meat," the president of the Cattle Ranchers Federations warned in 1988, "we'll see the politicians coming to the producers, trying to correct their errors" (Montenegro 1988:9)

This rancher pessimism, even if hyperbolic at

FIGURE 34–2   Central America: volume of beef exports, 1974–89. (Data from FAO, Trade Yearbooks.)

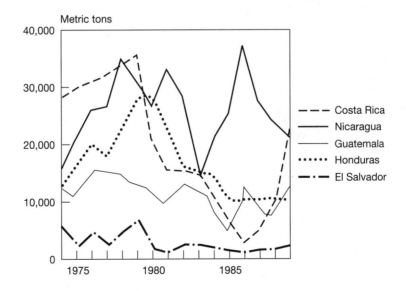

times, hardly conforms to the popular image of voracious, avaricious cattlemen bulldozing ever-greater expanses of virgin forest. The livestock "emergency" is real, although its origins are diverse and are only partially attributable to contraction of U.S. demand. Few recent analyses of the "hamburger connection" recognize the crisis (Annis 1990 is one exception), and some that do erroneously attribute it solely to the 1979 Nicaraguan revolution, when pro-Somoza ranchers drove their herds to neighboring Costa Rica and Honduras (Nations and Leonard 1986:83).[7] In fact, the crisis has both foreign—that is, U.S.— and domestic Central American roots. Both point to the need for political-economic analyses of how forces of supply and demand are mediated and shaped by the U.S. market and political system and by domestic Central American institutions, interest groups, and economic actors.

Given the intense anxiety aroused among Central American ranchers and foreign trade ministers, it is surprising that hardly any recent discussions of the "hamburger connection" mention the U.S. curbs on beef imports that went into effect at the end of 1979. Technically a "countercyclical" amendment to the 1964 Meat Import Act (P.L 88–482), this measure (P.L. 96–177) provided for decreasing import quotas during expansive phases

of the U.S. cattle cycle and increasing them during periods of contraction.[8] P.L. 96–177 has meant that the U.S. market is unlikely to absorb any significant increases in Central America's exportable beef surpluses.[9] Domestic U.S. livestock producers, concerned about low-priced beef imports, fought long and hard for passage of P.L. 96–177. They were opposed by lobbyists for the fast-food industry and consumer groups that feared higher beef prices, as well as by representatives of Central American and Caribbean beef-exporting nations. The details of this battle are beyond the scope of this discussion, but it should be sufficient to indicate that, at the very least, the strength of demand itself, rather than being determined either by capitalism or by North American hamburger hunger, is inseparable from processes of political struggle between contending interest groups. And—also rarely mentioned in the "hamburger" literature—per capital North American beef consumption has also been dropping since 1976 (see Figure 34–3), even though the proportion derived from cheap grass-fed beef, like that exported from Central America, has been on the rise.

The crisis in the Costa Rican cattle sector in the 1980s is not only the result of rigid U.S. demand codified by the 1979 countercyclical legislation. Ranchers who sold fattened cattle to export pack-

FIGURE 34–3   Costa Rican and U.S. beef consumption, 1961–90. (Data from U.S. Department of Agriculture.)

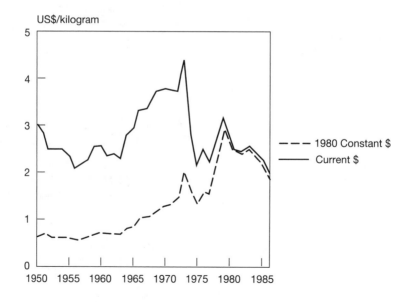

US$/kilogram

- - - 1980 Constant $
——— Current $

inghouses traditionally had paid rather little in taxes: a one percent tax on the value of each steer, eleven colones in various municipal levies, five colones for a stamp to finance the Rural Guard, and similarly symbolic assessments based on the weight of the on-hoof animal and the meat extracted.[10] In December 1981, following the previously stable colón's plunge from 8.6 to 38 per dollar in little more than a year, the Legislative Assembly, responding to importer's calls for relief, established a tax intended to limit exporters' windfall profits. In the case of the cattle sector, the law provided for a ten percent tax on "the difference between the exchange rate at which hard currency from export earnings is sold and the total that the same sale would have produced had it been realized at 8.60 colones per U.S. dollar" (CLD 1981, Laws 6707 and 6696). Suddenly, in 1981–83, cattlemen who historically had scarcely considered export taxes (or other taxes for that matter—see Edelman 1992:251) a cost of doing business were facing payments of 500 to 1,000 colones (approximately $12.50 to $25.00 in early 1982) for each steer sold to the packing plants. While this represented only about five percent of the value of an average steer, it cut dangerously into the narrow 6.5 percent average profit margin for beef producers that had been established in agreements with the export packers (FCG 1983:16). By the mid-1980s, some ranchers claimed that the total tax burden for each exported steer had risen to over 30 percent of the animal's value (Realidad 1988).

Just as ranchers had little experience with taxation, they were similarly unaccustomed to operating in genuine financial markets, in spite of the growing disaffection of many in the 1970s and 1980s with the costs of Costa Rica's social democratic development model and a consequent infatuation with pro-laissez-faire rhetoric. The unprecedented inflation of the early 1980s brought a steep rise in interest rates that represented a major additional burden to producers with low profit margins and few sources of working capital. Costa Rican ranchers had long taken for granted that the National Banking System would provide credit at negative real rates of interest, allowing them a hedge against inflation or funds that could be diverted, albeit without authorization, to more lucrative activities. While the high inflation of 1981–82 initially produced a sharp drop in real interest rates,

by 1983–84 most loan rates had recovered to the point where ranchers, now also beset by soaring costs for veterinary and other inputs, registered a mounting number of defaults. By early 1987, nearly two-thirds of Costa Rican banks' cattle loans were in arrears (Annis 1990).

International beef prices, measured in constant dollars, have also declined precipitously since the early 1970s, hardly an incentive for expanding herds or carving more pastures out of the forest, even if the costs of land clearing and grass planting are absorbed by peasant colonists or tenants. Indeed, as Figure 34–4 indicates, by the 1980s beef prices were at or below the levels prevailing during the first years of the beef boom in the 1950s and early 1960s.

DEFORESTATION TRENDS

Date on forested and deforested area must be taken with some caution, since the methods and definitions employed by different agencies and in different time series may not be consistent (Allen and Barnes 1985). Figure 34–5 provides three estimates of deforestation trends in Costa Rica, as well as data on pasture expansion and cultivated area. The destruction of Costa Rica's forests over the past five decades is alarming by any measure (see Figure 34–6).[11] Nevertheless, the "least pessimistic" estimate, derived from the last five agricultural censuses, suggests that rates of deforestation and pasture growth have slowed in the latest period.[12] This estimate would suggest that pasture expansion approached (and indeed exceeded) natural limits (in the 1963–73 intercensal period) and then slowed with the recent lack of dynamism in the livestock sector (in the last years of the 1973–84 period).

The other two deforestation estimates are based on differing interpretations of maps derived from similar sets of aerial photographs and satellite (Landsat) data; they employ a stricter definition of "forest" and a broader one of "forest clearing."[13] Sader and Joyce's estimate for the 1977–83 interval, the only departure from otherwise remarkably linear long-term trends, bears special examination both because it is extremely alarming and because it received prominence in a recent highly publicized report (WRI, UNEP, and UNDP 1990). These authors suggested that tiny Costa Rica lost an aver-

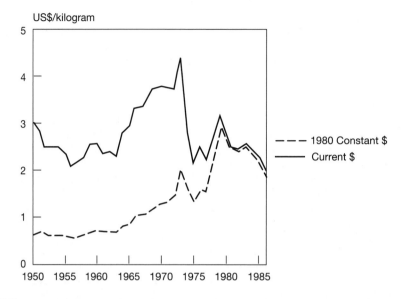

FIGURE 34–4   World market beef prices, 1950–86. (Data from World Bank Commodity Trade and Price Trends, 1987).

age of 124,000 hectares of primary forest each year during the seven-year period. But they also conceded that their editing of the 1983 data "may have resulted in an overestimation of forest clearing in the [1977–83] period" (1988:17), a caveat that passed unnoticed by both the authors of the WRI, UNEP, and UNDP report and media alarmists who accorded Costa Rica the dubious honor of "first place for deforestation in Latin America" (La Nación 1990a). The findings that caused such shock

FIGURE 34–5   Costa Rican land use, 1940–87. (Data from *Dirección General Forestal* and *Censos Agropecuarios* [pasture and crops].)

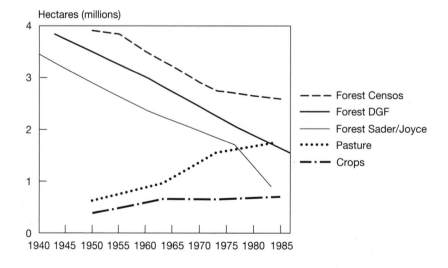

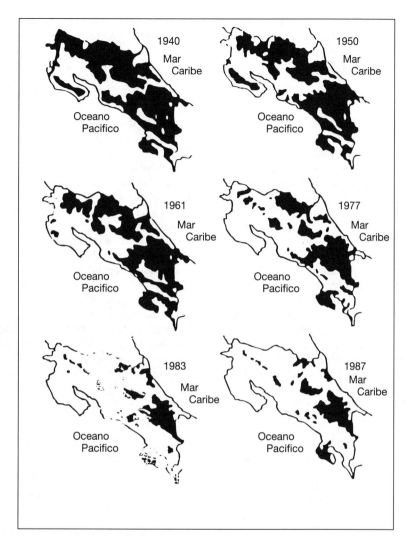

FIGURE 34–6   Costa Rica: area of closed canopy forest. (Data from *Dirección Forestal*.)

in 1990 were based on Sader and Joyce's estimate for 1977–83 (WRI, UNEP, and UNDP 1990:102–3, 292–93).

This estimate is approximately twice as high as the most extreme on-the-ground measures and was very likely (as the authors' proviso indicates) influenced by map editing procedures. Ground-based measures are hardly free of problems, but they do suggest some slowing of deforestation in recent years. During 1950–83, deforestation averaged 53,382 hectares per year (this still represents defor-

estation of approximately one percent of the national territory and three percent of remaining forested area each year, an extremely high rate compared to other developing countries);[14] in 1984, a total of 41,875 hectares were cleared (16,785 of which were authorized by the state); by 1985, estimates of deforestation by different government agencies ranged from 13,000 to 29,250 hectares (of which 10,750 hectares were authorized) (SEPSA 1986a, 1986b). In 1990, Raúl Solórzano, president of Costa Rica's Tropical Science Center, recognized that "the country is now in a transition stage. Wood [not cattle] is becoming the most important factor in deforestation" (David Dudenhoefer, Forest Crisis Nears, *Tico Times* 23 February 1990:10).[15]

DOMESTIC SUPPLY AND DEMAND

In Costa Rica, the crisis in the cattle sector has been so pronounced that during much of the 1980s ranchers slaughtered the herd faster than it could reproduce.[16] Sluggish export demand, higher taxes and indebtedness, and soaring interest rates and veterinary input costs have made cattle ranching a losing proposition for most investors (more on this below). The only ranchers able to endure are those who do not require bank financing, who obtained land and herds at little or no cost through inheritance, who specialize in breeding expensive exhibition bulls, or who in effect subsidize cattle operations with profits from other production lines. These tend to be the largest haciendas, rather than the small- and medium-sized producers. Figure 34–7 illustrates the dramatic increase since the early 1980s in the slaughter of cows and calves (note that on a semilogarithmic graph, lines with simi-

lar slopes indicate similar proportional rather than similar absolute changes). This is indicative of ranchers' interest in liquidating existing investments, but it is distinguished from their traditional reactions to cyclical downturns in beef markets by a new indifference about maintaining breeding stock for future expansion.[17]

The notion that export beef production was a scheme foisted on naive and vulnerable developing countries by international lending institutions (occasionally, one hears, in cahoots with U.S. fast-food chains) is only partially correct. Developing-country governments have been understandably reluctant to refuse offers of credit, but the recurrent dependency-type interpretations of this phenomenon ignore the extent to which cattle interests in each producing country organized, pressured, and adopted new technologies, all with the objective of entering international markets. Once this was achieved—in the 1950s for most of the region, earlier for Nicaragua, later for El Salvador—ranchers' lobbies have been among the most active political pressure groups, working to widen access to foreign markets and to secure favorable pricing, credit, and land tenure policies from regional governments. In Costa Rica, for example, leading ranchers articulated a vision of their country as a

FIGURE 34–7 Costa Rican cattle slaughter by age/sex, 1980–89 (semilogarithmic scale). (Data from *Consejo Nacional de Producción.*)

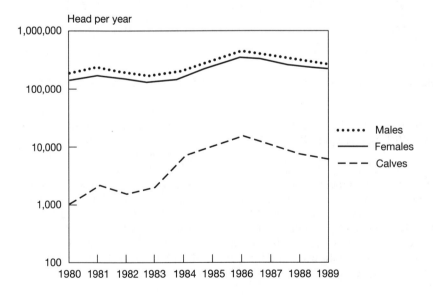

beef exporter à la Texas or Argentina even in the 1930s, when domestic needs still had to be satisfied with large imports from Nicaragua and more than two decades before significant shipments were sent abroad.[18] In the post-1955 period, the cattle lobby has been a constant presence in national politics (Edelman 1992:chap. 10; Annis 1990). Its more prominent members have also significantly diversified their interests in other economic sectors, including export agriculture, agroindustry, retail commerce, tourism, and communications media (Aguilar and Solís 1988).

While it is true that the advent of the beef export economy in Central America was associated everywhere with plummeting per capita beef consumption, the expansion of herds to meet foreign demand eventually reversed this decline in most of the region (Williams 1986).[19] Until the crisis of the mid-1980s, when even heifers began to be liquidated, only steers were sent to the export slaughterhouses. But to breed more steers, ranchers had to acquire increasing numbers of cows, and it was these that supplied much of the domestic demand and brought per capita consumption back up to near earlier, preexport boom levels (see Figure 34–3). In Costa Rica, with sluggish exports and stagnant international prices, domestic demand is increasingly important as a proportion of the total slaughter (see Figure 34–8).[20] This reflects both herd liquidation, taking place for reasons noted above, and a convergence since the late 1970s between domestic and world beef prices that reduces tendencies to channel as many head as possible to export packinghouses (see Figure 34–9).[21]

Domestic demand has received insufficient attention in the "hamburger connection" literature, something that is particularly unfortunate in a period when it is of much greater relative weight as a stimulus to cattle production in Central America, Brazil, and elsewhere. It has long been recognized that meat is a product with a very high income elasticity of demand; in other words, small increases in income levels produce proportionally greater increases in demand. In the absence in many countries of per capita real income increases during the economic crisis of the 1980s, population growth and urbanization are still producing rapidly rising demand for beef. Growth rates for domestic demand now exceed those for production even in many traditional exporting countries, such as Brazil, Mexico, El Salvador, Guatemala, Nicaragua, and Panama (Jarvis 1986). Normally, such a situation might be expected to produce rising prices and profits. To understand why such conditions have not been sufficient to rescue the livestock sector from crisis, it is necessary to consider how cattle enterprises differ from other types of production and why ranchers do not always appear to behave as rational economic actors operating in a perfect market with various types of investment options.

FIGURE 34–8   Costa Rican beef production, domestic consumption, and exports, 1969–89. 1973 data is for six months. (Data from *Consejo Nacional de Producción*.)

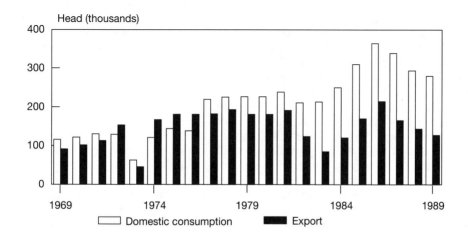

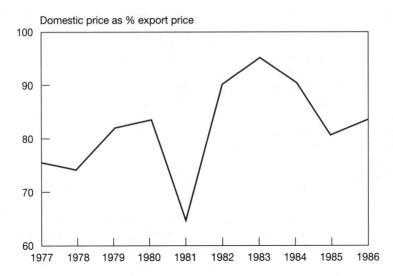

Domestic price as % export price

FIGURE 34–9   Costa Rican export and domestic beef prices, 1977–86. (Data from *Banco Central de Costa Rica*, Cifras sobre producción agropecuaria.)

SUBSIDIES FROM NATURE, SUBSIDIES FROM THE STATE

Tropical ranching has always depended on a heavy subsidy from nature, whether the availability of low-cost land, the one-time extraction of nonlivestock forest resources such as timber, or the "production" of semiferal cattle on vast estates (Bunker 1985; Edelman 1985, 1992). In mixed crop-livestock enterprises, cattle have traditionally served as insurance against higher risks inherent in cash crop cultivation. Increasingly, the economic rationality of ranching has hinged as well on significant state subventions, including favorable fiscal, land titling, and road-building policies; artificially low interest rates; price controls and duty exonerations for inputs; and government technical assistance programs (Annis 1990; Binswanger 1989; Browder 1988; Hecht et al. 1988). Usually, it has been based on extracting these diverse income streams—ground rent, speculative rent, and institutional rent (de Janvry 1981; Edelman 1985)—rather than on high profitability according to accepted accounting conventions. The illegal diversion of subsidized cattle production credit to more profitable sectors of the economy and the use of ranches principally as collateral for bank loans are only two of the most common scams that prolifer-

ate in tropical America. In some countries—notably Brazil—planting grass on untitled state land is considered a demonstration of the effective occupation required to establish secure claims and eventual private property rights; elsewhere, such "improvements" on the land protect owners from expropriation under agrarian reform laws, especially if a few cattle are grazing the newly planted pasture.

Latin American governments have rarely established significant legal sanctions against deforestation. The 1990 Forest Law in Costa Rica provides maximum prison terms of three years for those engaging in illegal forest felling on public land and one year for those doing so on private property. It also creates financial mechanisms that assure the continued existence of an enforcement and oversight apparatus (La Gaceta 1990). Most of the region's legal codes, however, do not even define deforestation, and resources for enforcement are nearly nonexistent (Porras and Villarreal 1986).[22]

The debt crisis and inflation of the 1980s have affected the complex system of subsidies for livestock in a variety of ways. In many countries, the most direct institutional rent streams—artificially low interest rates, price supports, and various kinds of tax privileges—have been cut significantly with the imposition of new neoliberal models of economic development. Even where—as in Costa Rica—concerted struggle by cattle interests has succeeded in maintaining some access to below-inflation-rate loans, this frequently has not been sufficient to cure past defaults or to offset soaring input costs and land prices that augment the opportunity cost—in nonfrontier areas—of using expensive properties for grazing.[23] Throughout the continent, high indebtedness has reduced states' capacities for providing direct subventions to uneconomic productive sectors, even if they are politically influential.[24] Especially when the foreign exchange generated is not commensurate with resources invested or land area occupied, austerity-conscious policymakers have been less and less inclined to submit to the demands of cattle lobbies and their allies. And the leading ranchers, long adept at converting rent income into capital, have diversified to the point where their coherence as a distinct, unified interest group can no longer be taken for granted. Indeed, many have embraced "eco-tourism" and new nontraditional exports (cf. Bulmer-Thomas 1988), and all the associated incentives, with the same ardor with which they earlier pursued low-cost cattle loans.

ENVIRONMENTAL CONSERVATION IN A PERIOD OF CRISIS

The crisis in the Central American livestock sector could, under certain conditions, be a blessing in environmental terms. If a changed economic climate is no longer impelling ranchers to destroy forest, political and economic space could conceivably be opened for the discussion and implementation of sustainable development and conservation measures. Several difficulties exist, however. First and most obvious is the extreme lack of resources for funding sustainable development and conservation programs (a problem not unrelated, as indicated below, to stagnation of the beef cattle sector itself). Second is the assumption—explicit or implicit in much of the "hamburger" literature—that forests are destroyed to produce cattle per se, rather than to generate income whatever the source. Third, commonly proposed solutions, such as debt-for-nature swaps or labor-intensive, sustainable exploitation of remaining forest resources, are likely to be of relatively limited scope, especially—in the latter

case—in Central America. And finally, reforestation efforts, spurred by generous fiscal incentives, have sometimes tended to reinforce the skewed resource and income distributions that were characteristic of the cattle economy and that have contributed indirectly to environmental degradation in the first place.

Livestock specialists have long known that it is technically feasible to produce considerably more beef per hectare with relatively small additional investments in pasture management, breeding, veterinary inputs, and human care and administration (León et al. 1981; Leonard 1985; Parsons 1976). Indeed, in Costa Rica, holdings of less than 20 hectares already produce an average of 383 kilograms of beef per hectare per year, while those over 200 hectares produce 162 kilograms (Hartshorn, Hartshorn, Atmella et al. 1982:6). In seasonally dry tropical environments, such as Central America's Pacific coastal plain, the better pastures can—even with investments like those presently made by many small ranchers—sustain greater grazing densities than the one-head-per-hectare level that has remained virtually unchanged since at least 1950 (León et al. 1981).

Yet even during the beef boom the latifundist land tenure system in most cattle zones has encouraged extensive land use, as ranchers seeking to extract natural capital in the form of grass- or brush-fed beef expanded into unused portions of their estates or surrounding land. Many of these landowning families acquired properties decades or even centuries ago and are thus under little pressure to modernize production or to consider the opportunity cost of land in their profit-loss calculations (Edelman 1985, 1992). The structure of incentives that has shaped modern cattle production does little or nothing to distinguish between high quality and marginal pasture. It fosters neither grazing intensification on existing pastures in areas where this would be feasible nor the abandonment and reclamation of suboptimal grasslands. In the absence of such stimuli, the landscape of Central America's depressed cattle zones will continue to have the haunting, semiabandoned quality that has become increasingly typical in the late 1980s, with mixed brush and pastures stretching as far as the eye can see, and only scattered small animals that will be slaughtered before reaching full finished weight.

Restructuring incentives would require not only the political will to confront what is, in Costa Rica at least, a still resilient cattle lobby, but financial resources that are simply no longer available in an era of economic adjustment and retrenchment. Ironically, demand-based explanations of the "hamburger connection" and their "logical" correlates, demand-reducing policy prescriptions, have an unintended and potentially damaging role in exacerbating this resource scarcity. In a trenchant denunciation of hamburgerist reasoning and activism. Daniel Janzen, whose conservationist credentials hardly brook criticism,[25] argues that North American consumers should buy, not boycott, Costa Rican beef (Janzen 1988). Refusing to buy beef (or any other tropical product) from Central America, Janzen reasons, will simply lead to more of it being purchased from other tropical zones, accelerating deforestation there. Just as important, the damage to developing countries' foreign trade balances reduces "the tax and resource base that is picking up the bill for the national parks and other kinds of reserves" (Janzen 1988:258).[26] While Janzen's argument is perhaps most compelling as regards Costa Rica, the nation with the strongest commitment to environmental conservation (and the least acute social crisis), all other Central American beef exporters, including even tiny El Salvador, have taken significant steps towards establishing protected natural areas.

Though much of the "hamburger" literature notes that pasture development is usually the last and most drastic of a series of exploitative uses of forest (or former forest) land, discussion has often taken on an almost teleological tone, assuming that beef rather than money is the ultimate goal of those destroying the tropics. Were more attention devoted to logging, artisanal and industrial gold mining, peasant squatting, and plantation agriculture, it would perhaps become clear that the natural capital of the forest can be used to subsidize a variety of activities. In the absence of strict enforcement of forest reserve boundaries and, even more importantly, of economic opportunities for those displaced by, among other things, extensive grazing and capital-intensive agriculture and industry, the pressure on remaining natural capital is not likely to abate. Moreover, the relative intensity of distinct pressures on forest resources can and does vary considerably even within a small geographic area,

such as Central America. Rather different policy tools are likely to be required for addressing the destruction caused by logging in Guatemala's Petén, gold mining in Costa Rica's Osa Peninsula, or smallholder squatting on the Nicaraguan or Honduran agricultural frontiers. The success of such policies needs to be appraised not only by the purely "physical/biological criteria" (Thrupp 1989) on which conservationists typically rely but also by socioeconomic measures that consider the well-being of rural populations, particularly in the areas of year-round income and employment generation and assuring access to land for cultivation.

EXTRACTIVE RESERVES

Recent efforts (Allegretti 1990; Clay 1989; Peters et al. 1989) to demonstrate that sustained yield gathering of nonwood forest products in the Brazilian and Peruvian Amazon can produce economic benefits per unit of area greater than swidden agriculture or ranching have excited considerable interest among environmentalist (and among ice cream enthusiasts, with the marketing by Vermont manufacturer Ben and Jerry's of a new line of products flavored with exotic jungle fruits and nuts). But in spite of promising dessert recipes and the best of intentions, this labor-intensive, forest-sensitive strategy would probably confront some formidable obstacles if implemented on a large scale, especially in Central America. Unlike the Amazonian Indians, *caboclos*, and *ribereños* that have long included petty commerce in gathered forest products (nuts, fruits, resins, etc.) as one among several complementary survival strategies, Central America's forest or near-forest peoples are—with few exceptions—thoroughly "peasantized" in terms of their productive experiences and traditions, knowledge, and expectations.[27] Reconstructing and diffusing the forest lore necessary to make large-scale commercial gathering economically viable for marginal peasant families in Central America would require resources and time, neither of which are widely available, as well as demonstrating to policymakers and to skeptical and unskilled potential participants the feasibility of prompt returns. Cooperative management of forest resources, well developed in some regions of the Amazon and a necessary concomitant of such schemes, is basically unknown in Central America outside of the few remaining indigenous forest peoples. Few cultural models exist for resolving tensions between individual accumulation and the common good in favor of the latter.[28]

Commercial gathering of nonwood resources as a means of conservation has some significant inherent limits. Much depends on the physical characteristics of the gathered product, on who controls the initial stages of commercialization and processing, on the strength of demand, and on the availability or lack of alternative sources of supply. Perishability or essential processing by monopsonistic, non-gatherer-controlled agro-industries may affect negatively the prices paid to collectors. This in turn may lead some, in the absence of strong social controls, to compensate for low unit prices by extracting greater, perhaps unsustainable, volumes.[29] If significant social controls are present, they may be adequate to prevent overharvesting, but not to confront unfavorable market conditions or asymmetrical power relations between those at different points on the chain of commercialization.[30]

To have a genuine environmental impact, gathering and extractive reserve formation must be carried out on a large scale.[31] But unless demand expands as fast as supply, high output volumes are likely to bring falling prices.[32] This may tempt collectors once again to harvest the forest's capital individually rather than just the "interest" cooperatively. If demand and prices do increase in a sustained fashion, the emergence of alternative sources of supply—perhaps based on laboratory fabrication or plantation production of previously gathered products—cannot be discounted.[33] Precedents for such a scenario are notorious, such as pharmaceutical giant Eli Lilly's synthesis of a drug for Hodgkin's disease from the rosy periwinkle, a native plant of Madagascar, or the dramatic, early twentieth-century expansion of Malayan rubber cultivation with seeds exported from Brazil.

Successful gathering projects, then, must ideally be based on nonperishable, preferably uncultivatable products that can be harvested on a sustainable basis and that have reliable markets yet few alternative sources of supply. Extraction projects must involve substantial gatherer control over initial processing and marketing. They must also be carried out by peoples with traditions of communal resource management that in effect control against unsustainable individual exploitation of the environment. Regrettably, the very specificity of these conditions does not augur well for the generalization of an extractive reserve model on a scale that would permit it to have a major environmental effect.

DEBT-FOR-NATURE SWAPS

Other mechanisms for stemming forest destruction that are now much in vogue, such as debt-for-nature swaps, are also, unfortunately, feasible primarily on a small scale. Such deals are, ironically, the bogey of the security-obsessed Brazilian right and the Central American left, both of which are suspicious of the implications for sovereignty.[34] In spite of having the appearance of "free" debt reduction, Latin American finance ministers, too, tend to regard these and other debt-equity trades with caution, fearing the inflationary consequences of the large injections of local currencies that widespread buy-back deals would entail (Patterson 1990:10). Such effects may be mitigated by issuing bonds in local currency with long amortization periods instead of simply printing more money (Sevilla 1990: 148–154). But debtor governments using locally borrowed funds to pay foreign purchasers of their debt paper may ultimately face greater budget deficits and financial costs, since developing country interest rates tend to be higher than international levels in order to discourage capital flight (Hedström 1990:188).

These formidable political obstacles obviously do not preclude occasional successes, such as the swaps that have contributed to strengthening Costa Rica's exemplary system of parks and reserves. But the very infrequency of such experiences—and their concentration in a country with an unusual political culture, a tiny territory, and a unique history of indulgence by foreign creditors, and aid agencies—suggests that swap schemes, while more than a drop in the bucket, are very far from being a panacea for the problems of either deforestation or debt.

REFORESTATION

Increasingly, in the semiabandoned savannas of Costa Rica's devastated cattle zones, one sees large, well-fenced plantations of uniform pochote (*Bam-*

bacopsis quinatun) saplings, a high-priced hardwood, and occasionally other species such as melina (*Gmelina arborea*), madero negro (*Gliricidia sepium*), and teak (*Tectona grandis*). The reforested area is still pathetically small in relation to what is needed, however, although the rate of growth is high (Ugalde and Gregersen 1987). In 1979–1984, official date indicate that a total of 8,865 hectares were reforested, 5,562 hectares with fiscal incentives that permitted landowners an income tax deduction of approximately U.S.$1,000 per reforested hectare (SEPSA 1986b). In as little as ten years, the owners of the pochote farms in particular, after benefiting from generous tax breaks and low-interest loans, stand to reap a veritable bonanza, marketing the timber in central Costa Rica or abroad.

Between 1979 and 1988, the economic benefits of reforestation incentives accrued primarily to medium- and large-size enterprises, in part because the lowest income groups simply did not pay income tax and therefore did not seek such deductions. Moreover, larger investors, unlike most smallholders, tended to have sufficient collateral for bank loans and were able to survive the lean years between planting and harvesting (Porras and Villarreal 1986; Brenes 1988). The large farmer bias in reforestation policy often had counterproductive environmental consequences, in addition to problematical implications for social equity. "Once the procedure was established," a report sponsored by the U.S. Agency for International Development notes, "an interesting phenomenon occurred:

> the 51 applications covering an area of 11,234 hectares were presented by businessmen who were looking for ways to lower their taxes. The reforestation companies that appeared overnight started businesses whereby they offered to lower taxes for persons by selling them one or more reforested hectares and charging them for technical assistance, administration and the value of the land—almost like a real estate business. These projects did generate employment for workers, technicians and professionals as well as salesmen but the reforestation value is dubious. The projects are generally centrally located in areas suited to livestock and agriculture and have begun to compete with food production. In some cases, natural forests were cut to be later

replanted under the program. Of the total area (11,234 hectares) included in the reforestation program up to 1981, 1,638 hectares or only 14 percent has been reforested. (Hartshorn, Hartshorn, Atmella et al. 1982:34).[35]

Since 1988, the policies that facilitated this type of corruption—what Costa Ricans term "sausages" (*chorizos*)—have been significantly modified, and smallholders have increasingly joined reforestation efforts. The major change was the creation of a "forestry bond" (*Certificado de Abona Forestal*), a negotiable instrument provided to reforesters (and worth, in 1991, approximately U.S. $1,000 for each hectare planted in trees, about half of initial production costs). Financed initially by the Dutch government through a U.S.$5 million debt swap with the Costa Rican government, this program was added to the existing program of tax write-offs, but it differed from the earlier system in that it provided "bonds" not only to well-off investors but to organized groups (e.g., cooperatives, peasant unions, cantonal agricultural centers) composed of individuals wishing to plant seedlings on up to 15 hectares each.[36] In order to maintain a rotating credit fund for continuing reforestation, beneficiaries are required to repay the bond after twenty years, approximately the time that they harvest the trees; they receive a seven-year grace period and pay an annual interest rate of only 8 percent, well below prevailing inflation levels (Sevilla 1990:151). In 1990, this system accounted for approximately 8,000 reforested hectares, 3,340 of which (42 percent) were planted by small producer's groups. Approximately 15,000 hectares are needed to meet Costa Rica's annual consumption of wood products (Se reforestará 15 mil hectáreas en 1991, La Nación, 2 October 1991).

Official statistics, however, may understate the actual extent of reforestation, just as they may obscure the variety of motives impelling smallholders to plant trees. Even with the advent of forestry bonds, current policy continues to encourage the planting of dense single-species stands and official date reflect this preference. Peasant tree farming of mixed stands of native or exotic species (for wind barriers, fuel, posts, shade, nuts, and fruit, as well as for lumber) represents a significant environmental factor, albeit one that is difficult to administer or measure precisely (Jones and Price

1985). Small-scale tree farmers, by conserving high biotic diversity, also reduce the risk, inherent in official reforestation schemes, of host-specific pests and pathogens devastating single-species stands.

Heavily indebted smallholders—and there are many, given the crisis in Costa Rica's agrarian sector—have also found that reforestation (or preservation of existing woods) is one of the few ways of emerging from default and regaining access to production credit. Increasingly, peasants whose properties are subject to bank liens and potential foreclosures have negotiated arrangements in which they use trees as collateral for old debts or new loans. Sometimes a smallholder divides a property and consolidates debts on a section with remaining timber, allowing the rest of the farm or the trees themselves to serve as a guarantee for a new crop production loan. In other cases, part of the farm may be reforested, with future lumber harvests functioning as security.[37] These innovative initiatives, without parallel elsewhere, may well increase in the future, as smallholders become better acquainted with the practice and as banks develop relevant procedures.[38]

One need not be overly sanguine about the ultimate environmental effect of smallholder involvement in agroforestry, whether tree plantation style or indigenous style, to recognize that in a relatively brief period Costa Rica has taken some significant strides. Before the establishment of smallholder reforestation programs, conservationists had to trade off a potentially salutary environmental impact against significant social costs. Because they incorporated previously excluded sectors of the rural population into reforestation efforts, they have reforested a larger area each year, and at least some of the negative distributional and employment effects of the 1979–88 programs have been mitigated. Importantly, such effects, like those of the beef cattle boom, were among the factors that contributed to building pressure on Costa Rica's resource base in the first place.

CONCLUSION

This chapter has examined the "hamburger-deforestation" literature in light of the crisis in Central America's (and especially Costa Rica's) beef exports during the 1980s. It argues that both social

scientific analyses and the popular awareness to which they have contributed have lagged behind current realities in failing to take note of the inadequacies of demand-based explanations of the beef export-deforestation relation. Indeed, the "hamburger-deforestation" literature is among the last bastions of a simplistic version of dependency theory that ignores the extent to which political contention influences the strength of U.S. demand for foreign beef, the important role that Central American political actors have had in shaping the conditions in which cattle producers operate, and the complexity of the deforestation process itself.

The severe crisis in the Costa Rican cattle sector in the 1980s resulted not only from lower international prices and politically influenced contraction in U.S. demand, but also from new fiscal, pricing, and credit policies that to a large degree reflected outcomes of domestic Costa Rican political processes. The crisis in beef exports coincided with strengthened domestic demand, an increasingly important factor in many beef-producing countries that has received no attention in the "hamburger" literature. But domestic demand did not usually generate the revenue traditionally produced from exports; increased domestic consumption was essentially opportunistic, deriving instead from the liquidation of herds by bankrupt, disillusioned ranchers. Whatever the causes of the crisis, however, a stagnant cattle export sector, even if buoyed by opportunistic domestic demand, is unlikely to be a major force behind further forest destruction. Much of Costa Rica's pasture land has, in fact, been abandoned in recent years, suggesting that if deforestation continues (as it has, though at a reduced rate), other types of explanations and solutions must be sought.

This requires rethinking not only the fundamental premises of the "hamburger" literature, but also those of some of the more popular policy remedies now frequently raised in discussions of environmental degradation in Central America. These include demand-reducing beef boycotts, extractive reserve models derived from different historical and cultural contexts, reforestation incentive programs for large farmers, and the debt-for-nature swaps that, as indicated above, are only feasible on a very small scale that permits little more than a highly localized environmental impact. The beef export economy was fueled by a massive subvention from nature and wasteful transfers of public resources to a relatively modest number of large ranchers who long enjoyed favorable fiscal policies, as well as subsidized credit, inputs, and technical assistance, and privileged access to the centers of political power. This skewing of income and wealth distribution, and the accompanying distortions of otherwise democratic political processes, led a wide range of actors—from rich ranchers to poor, displaced squatters—to reproduce themselves on the basis of a natural capital that lasted approximately one generation. Some of these actors had (or could have found) viable alternatives; others did not have other options. The challenge for this and future generations is to find environmentally sound measures that permit reclaiming a damaged land base, while ensuring that equity and social welfare are not sacrificed in the process.

NOTES

1. Since 1989 when I presented a draft of this chapter to the American Anthropological Association in Washington, several authors have advanced similar arguments about deforestation and cattle (e.g., Harrison 1991; Lehmann 1991, 1992) or about extractive reserves (Browder 1992). I am reassured, as any researcher must be, that in considering similar data they arrived at basically parallel conclusions. I wish to express my appreciation to Claudia Alderman, William Durham, Ricardo Godoy, Angelique Haugerud, Jeffrey R. Jones, Michael Painter, Juan Pablo Ruíz, and Robert G. Williams for their constructive criticisms of the manuscript and to Jayne Hutchcroft and César Rodríguez for assisting with the research. Obviously, I alone am responsible for any factual or analytical errors.

2. For the author's own modest contribution to this genre, see Edelman 1987.

3. Alarm about cattle and deforestation has also been utilized to demonize national enemies. In hearings on Brazil's role in Iraq's military buildup, Senator Albert Gore claimed erroneously that "the biggest single customer for beef coming out of the Amazon is—has been Iraq" (U.S. Congress, Transcript of Hearings on the Subcommittee on Science and Technology on the Joint Economic Committee, 21 September 1990, cited in Sanderson and Capistrano 1991:39).

4. Harrison (1991:90), analyzing Costa Rican agricultural census data from 1950–84, found a very strong correlation at the cantonal level between forest loss and pasture expansion. It is unlikely, for reasons outlined in this chapter, that this association would be very strong for the latter half of the 1973–84 intercensal period or subsequent years. In the absence of true time-series data or a more recent census, however, this is a difficult relation to test.

5. South American countries have not been permitted to export fresh or chilled beef to the U.S. market because of the presence of *aftosa* (hoof-and-mouth disease). Traditionally, they had their major markets in Europe, but EEC protectionism has increasingly limited this source of foreign earnings. Separated from South America by the Darien Gap forests, *aftosa*-free Central America, Mexico, and the Caribbean are the only suitable sources of imported fresh beef in the hemisphere, according to the U.S. Department of Agriculture.

EEC subsidies have, in recent years, permitted the continent to enter the ranks of exporters, and even Brazil has occasionally imported large quantities of European beef (LACR 1987), suggesting that foreign beef demand is no longer a major force behind the continuing destruction of the Amazon. Certainly U.S. demand is irrelevant in this respect: Browder (1988:115) points out that the Brazilian Legal Amazon supplied 1,700 metric tons of beef to the United States in 1982, a typical recent year, accounting for a whopping seven one-thousandths of one percent (.00007) of U.S. consumption. Clearly, at the very least, the widespread notion that North American meat lust is fueling the destruction of the Amazon cannot be sustained. Brazil, however, had a very rapidly growing domestic demand for beef until the 1988 economic collapse (LACR 1988).

6. Representative works are Frank (1969) and Wallerstein (1974). Much ink has been spilled in polemics about this approach, based in many cases on textual exegeses of Marx's writings on capitalism. Mintz (1977) provides a concise, historically based critique that, unlike much of the literature, does not descend into either undue abstraction, quasi-scriptural appeals to the authority of Marxist texts, or turgid prose.

7. One might ask why Costa Rica's and Honduras's beef exports did not rise with this new influx of *somocista* cattle. In Costa Rica, at least, the herd declined significantly by the mid-1980s, making the significance of Nicaraguan imports as an explanation for dropping exports all the more problematical. The decline in Nicaragua's exports was due to particular circumstances:

liquidation of herds by pro-Somoza ranchers in 1979 and the early 1980s, a reflection of political fears and artificially low prices; and the 1985 U.S. trade embargo. One year after the Reagan administration's imposition of trade sanctions, the U.S. Department of Agriculture proposed removing Nicaragua from the list of countries eligible to export meat to the United States, ostensibly because the "dangerous situation" there prevented inspection of local ranches (LACR 1986b). Political instability in El Salvador also had a devastating effect on the cattle sector, with the herd declining from 1.2 million head in 1979 to 600,000 in 1983, the lowest level in fifty years (CAR 1984).

8. On the U.S. cattle cycle's effects in Central America, see Edelman (1987:543–44). For more detailed analyses, see Jarvis (1986:55–64) and Sanderson (1986:156–64).

9. An additional U.S.-imposed obstacle is the institution in 1983 of tougher quality control standards for meat imports. These had a particularly devastating impact on Honduras, the least-developed Central American economy (LACR 1986a), though several other producing nations were affected as well.

10. These were used to finance the Livestock Department of the National Production Council (*Consejo Nacional de Producción*—CNP), the Animal Health Section of the Ministry of Agriculture, the *Federación de Cámaras de Ganaderos* and the regional *Cámaras*, and the Veterinary Medicine Faculty of the National University. An additional 1 percent was withheld to guarantee payment of income tax.

11. It is worth noting that most export beef production and associated deforestation has been centered in traditional livestock zones along the seasonally dry Central American Pacific coastal plain and—in Nicaragua—in the Chontales region east of Lake Nicaragua. Technically, this did not involve rainforest destruction, the bugaboo of much current discussion, but rather the felling of dry or semihumid tropical forest and the replacement of natural (or ancient derived) savanna with African grasses. If there is to be sustainable development of a grass-fed cattle sector, it is most likely to occur in these zones (Daubenmire 1972a, 1972b, 1972c). Pasture expansion in rainforest areas (e.g., Guatemala's Petén, eastern Nicaragua, and eastern Costa Rica) has sometimes occurred to supply domestic needs as traditional areas shifted to export production. Often, though, ranching expansion into humid forest zones is the second or third stage of more complex processes of colonization that have involved squatter activity, road

building, logging, and plantation agriculture (Carrière 1990; Repetto 1990).

12. This estimate was derived by adding the total forested land in private holdings to the total of untitled state lands (which were assumed to be forested). Obviously, this has limitations. Much forested land on farms is likely to be somewhat degraded or intervened in; similarly some untitled land undoubtedly consists of secondary growth or degraded primary forest.

13. Sader and Joyce (1988:123) define "forest clearing" as a removal of 20 percent or more of the upper canopy. The criteria employed in the DGF estimates are not specified with such precision; the DGF states that "forested area" refers to "closed canopy forest."

14. Estimates of the area in closed canopy forest in the late 1970s vary from 34 to 41 percent of the national territory of 50,900 square kilometers (Porras and Villarreal 1986; 20–21). Sader and Joyce's 1983 satellite imagery analysis claimed that only 17 percent of the country was covered with primary forest (Sader and Joyce 1988). For deforestation rates in other third world countries, see Allen and Barnes (1985) and WRI, UNEP, and UNDP (1990).

15. Similarly, in Honduras, a 1992 government report on deforestation found that livestock raising was not an important factor. The three most significant reasons for forest destruction were cutting for firewood (the source of 70 percent of the country's energy consumption), forest fires caused by swidden cultivators, and industrial logging (La integridad del bosque y la política forestal, *El Tiempo*, August 1992:6). Utting (1991) provides an insightful discussion of the many causes of deforestation in different countries in the region.

16. The CNP, the state commodities agency, estimated in 1985 that for the herd to maintain its size, no more than 30.7 percent of male animals, 10.5 percent of cows, and 0.7 percent of calves ought to be slaughtered. The actual figures were 36.1 percent of male animals, 16.9 percent of females, and a 1.8 percent of calves. The female and male animals weighed, on average 6.4 and 8.6 percent less, respectively, than those slaughtered the previous year (SEPSA 1986a:16).

17. In 1982, it was estimated that, of Costa Rica's bovine population of 2.3 million, 46.2 percent consisted of beef cows, 9.8 percent "double-purpose" (dairy and beef) cows, and 11.2 percent dairy cows. Males (beef and dairy) accounted for only 32.8 percent of the total. Almost all of these were beef steers; only 1.8 percent of the total population were stud animals and 0.7 percent oxen (SEPSA 1983).

18. This is discussed in more detail in Edelman 1992:chap. 5.

19. This has not prevented some analysts (e.g., Caufield 1985; Hedström 1985) from implying that this trend continued long after it in fact had been reversed.

20. In Figure 34–8, data before 1974 refer to twelve-month "cattle years" from July to June of the following year; 1973 data are for the second half of 1973. After 1973, years are calendar years.

21. With the exception of 1981, when major devaluations occurred that brought exporters extraordinarily high colón prices. Without this outlier, 54 percent of the 1977–86 variation in the domestic price/international price ratio is explained by the linear trend.

22. "Deforestation" is, as Hamilton remarks, a "horribly ambiguous word" that has referred to "fuelwood cutting; commercial logging; shifting cultivation; fodder lopping; forest clearing for conversion to continuous annual cropping, to grazing, to tree crops (foods, extractives, beverages), to forest plantations; and burned or grazed areas that are still essentially in forest" (1991:5).

23. In 1988, for example, the Ministry of Agriculture and Livestock (MAG) agreed to subsidize for three years the cost of cattle loans granted by the Banco Nacional, the principal lender. Rates for small, medium, and large producers were set, respectively, at 9, 12, and 18 percent—in a year when the overall inflation rate was 25 percent (MAG y BNCR Formalizan Subsidio para Ganaderos, *La Nación*, 25 August 1988). Ultimately, the difference almost certainly must be financed by foreign borrowing (or by the Central Bank printing more currency).

24. Where—as in Brazil—governments have long mouthed support for market economics (even while implementing Keynesianism for the rich), the rationality of pasture expansion appears to be tied most closely to the need to establish possession rights, rather than to continuing flows of subsidized credit, which have been substantially reduced in recent years. Nevertheless, the tax advantages that come with possession and the hedge it represents against inflation are still important (Binswanger 1989; Fearnside 1989; Hecht et al. 1988).

25. Janzen has been a prime mover behind the establishment of the Guanacaste National Park (GNP) in northwestern Costa Rica, an innovative conservation area, much of which is on former cattle land (Janzen 1986; McLarney 1988). Even so, the project has been assailed as an "appropriation of a huge area of land by a privileged North American who, even though good-hearted and well-intentioned, is perpetuating inequitable patterns of development and privatization [which] . . . conflict with the interests of the land-hungry poor" (Thrupp 1989:8).

Thrupp's contention that GNP represents a "private acquisition" is a variant of the suspicion many Latin Americans feel about foreign conservationists and their goals. In the case of the GNP, this likely derives from the role of the Nature Conservancy and similar organizations in raising funds of purchasing land and for an endowment to cover operating costs. Both title to park land and control of the endowment will belong to the Costa Rican National Park Foundation (*Fundación de Parques Nacionales* or FPN). Critics have charged, however, that the nongovernmental FPN constitutes a "parallel" structure that undermines sovereignty, since it duplicates functions of the state-run National Park service (*Servicio de Parques Nacionales* or SPN) but does not enjoy the FPN's access to foreign financial resources (Vargas 1990: 14). For a sophisticated, balanced discussion of foreign conservationists' involvement in Latin America, see Sevilla (1990).

26. Jagels (1990) argues in a similar vein that consumer boycotts of tropical forest hardwoods are counterproductive.

27. The exceptions, often members of indigenous groups or corporate peasant communities with common land, include *xate* palm harvesters, allspice gatherers, and chicle tappers in Guatemala's Petén (Nations 1992) and resin tappers in Honduras (Stanley 1991). Even the rural Amazonian groups that rely on extraction as one part of their survival strategy also engage in more destructive activities (gold panning, livestock raising, swidden agriculture, hunting, overharvesting of extracted resources) and are only arguable defenders of tropical forests (Browder 1992).

28. Harvester inexperience and laziness can also be obstacles to sustainable management of forest resources (Nations 1992:216). For a rich discussion of the complexities of managing communal resources, see McCay and Acheson (1987).

29. In Costa Rica, the extraction of edible "hearts" (*palmito*) from the *pejibaye* (*Guilielma utilis*) and similar palms led to their virtual disappearance in some zones. Not surprisingly, given high foreign and domestic demand, this once-wild species is now widely cultivated.

30. Few studies of extractive reserves or "tolerant forest management" practices have benefited from studies of markets distant from project zones, even though export of gathered products is often a key goal. This

introduces an element of significant uncertainty into project planning, in addition to weakening the antideforestation arguments of reserve advocates.

31. The environmental impact of extractive activities has, however, received little attention. Pearce (1990:47) suggests, for example, that harvesting Brazil nuts "can have a devastating effect on the birds and animals that would otherwise have eaten them."

32. After the creation of widely publicized extractive reserves in the Brazilian state of Acre, "prices for natural rubber and Brazil nuts have dropped sharply, jeopardizing the people's livelihood" (IDB 1992). Part of the rubber price drop was due to the removal of tariffs that kept the domestic price of rubber at roughly three times the world level. This raises the question of whether any renewable tropical forest resource can provide a basis for sustained economic activity without external subsidization (Browder 1992:176). Brazil nut collectors, even in 1990, received only 2 to 3 percent of the New York wholesale price of their nuts (Pearce 1990:1046). This share may rise to as much as 10 percent if producers are able to bypass intermediaries and transport the nuts to the local processing factory (Clay 1992:403–4), though it is uncertain if such steps will be sufficient to offset price declines.

33. Brazil nuts, for example, are now a wild forest product, the seeds of a tree (*Bertholletia excelsa*) that are sometimes propagated on a small scale by far-sighted gatherers. The success of such informal propagation efforts and the creation of relatively dense single-species stands (by Amazonian standards, at least) suggest that the tree might be suitable for plantation cultivation if economic conditions warrant.

34. This lack of symmetry in the way different groups on the political spectrum have reacted to the debt-for-nature concept in Brazil (where it is supported by important elements of the left) and in Central America and Bolivia (where its backers tend to be rightist or centrist) obviously cries out for further analysis. Sevilla (1990) argues that in the Bolivian, Costa Rican, and Ecuadorian cases, governments and local conservation organizations have been important participants in negotiations (and later in administration of protected areas) and that the fears regarding sovereignty are groundless.

35. Much of the remaining 9,596 hectares (86 percent) likely consisted of land on which planted seedlings did not survive. See Thrupp (1989) and Annis (1990) for similar descriptions of the distortions produced by reforestation tax incentives.

36. Holland acquired U.S. $33 million of Costa Rican debt from U.S. banks for U.S.$5 million. In return for retiring this obligation, the Costa Rican Central Bank supplied U.S.$10 million in colones for use in reforestation programs.

37. Interviews in Guácimo de Limón, July 1990.

38. Costa Rica's 1990 Forest Law established that standing trees may guarantee loans from public sector banks, but it left to the banks the job of drawing up pertinent regulations (La Gaceta 1990:5).

REFERENCES

Aguilar, Irene, and Manuel Solís, 1988. La Elite Ganadera en Costa Rica. San José: Editorial de la Universidad de Costa Rica.

Allegretti, Mary Helena, 1990. Extractive Reserves: An Alternative for Reconciling Development and Environmental Conservation in Amazonia. In *Alternatives to Deforestation: Steps toward Sustainable Use of the Amazon Rain Forest*, ed. Anthony B. Anderson, 252–64. New York: Columbia University Press.

Allen, Julia C., and Douglas F. Barnes, 1985. The Causes of Deforestation in Developing Countries. *Annals of the Association of American Geographers* 75 (2):163–84.

Annis, Sheldon, 1990. Debt and Wrong-Way Resource Flows in Costa Rica. *Ethics and International Affairs* 4:1–15.

BCCR (Banco Central de Costa Rica), 1988. Cifras sobre Producción Agropecuaria. San José: BCCR.

Binswanger, Hans P., 1989. Brazilian Policies that Encourage Deforestation in the Amazon. Environment Department working paper no. 16. Washington, D.C.: World Bank.

Boyer, Jefferson, C., 1986. Capitalism, Campesinos, and Calories in Southern Honduras. *Urban Anthropology* 15 (1–2):3–24.

Brenes Castillo, Carlos, 1988. ¿Desarrollo Forestal Campesino? in *La Situación Ambiental en Centroamérica y el Caribe*, ed. Ingemar Hedström, 163–74. San José: Departmento Ecumenénico de Investigaciones.

Brockett, Charles D., 1988. *Land, Power, and Poverty: Agrarian Transformation and Political Conflict in Central America*. London: Unwin Hyman.

Browder, John O., 1988. The Social Costs of Rain Forest Destruction: A Critique and Economic Analysis of the "Hamburger Debate." *Interciencia* 13(3):115–120.

———, 1992. The Limits of Extractivism: Tropical Forest Strategies beyond Extractive Reserves. *BioScience* 42 (3):174–182.

Bulmer-Thomas, Victor, 1988. The New Model of Development in Costa Rica. In *Central America: Crisis and Possibilities*, ed. Rigoberto García, 177–196. Stockholm: Institute of Latin American Studies.

Bunker, Stephen G., 1985. *Underdeveloping the Amazon*. Urbana: University of Illinois Press.

Buschbacher, Robert J., 1986. Tropical Deforestation and Pasture Development. *BioScience* 36(1):22–28.

Buxedas, Martín, 1977. El Comercio Internacional de Carne Vacuna y las Exportaciones de los Países Atrasados. *Comercia Exterior (Mexico)* 27 (2):1494–1509.

CAR (Central America Report [Guatemala]), 1984. Beef Exports Earn Fewer and Fewer Dollars. Central America Report 11 (34) (31 August):270.

Carrière, Jean, 1990. The Political Economy of Land Degradation in Costa Rica. *New Political Science* 18/19:147–163.

Caufield, Catherine, 1985. *In the Rainforest*. New York: Knopf.

Clay, Jason W., ed., 1989. *Indigenous Peoples and Tropical Forests*. Cambridge, Mass.: Cultural Survival.

Clay, Jason, 1992. Buying in the Forests: A New Program to Market Sustainably Collected Tropical Forest Products Protects Forests and Forest Residents. In *Conservation of Neotropical Forests: Working from Traditional Resource Use*, ed. Kent H. Redford and Christine Padoch, 400–415. New York: Columbia University Press.

CLD (*Colección de Leyes y Decretos 1981*. San José: Imprenta Nacional.

Daubenmire, R., 1972a. Some Ecological Consequences of Converting Forest to Savanna in Northwestern Costa Rica. *Tropical Ecology* 13(1):31–51.

———, 1972b. Standing Crops and Primary Production in Savanna Derived from Semideciduous Forest in Northwest Costa Rica. *Botanical Gazette* 133 (4):395–401.

———, 1972c. Ecology of Hyparrhenia Rufa in Derived Savanna in Northwestern Costa Rica. *Journal of Applied Ecology* 9:11–23.

Da Veiga, José S., 1975. A la Poursuite du Profit: Quand les Multinationales Font du "Ranching." Le Monde Diplomatique September:12–13.

de Janvry, Alain, 1981. *The Agrarian Question and Reformism in Latin America*. Baltimore: Johns Hopkins University Press.

DeWalt, Billie R., 1982. The Big Macro Connection: Population, Grain and Cattle in Southern Honduras. *Culture and Agriculture* 14:1–12.

———, 1983. The Cattle Are Eating the Forest. *Bulletin of the Atomic Scientists* 39 (1):18–23.

Dickinson, Joshua C., 1973. Protein Flight from Latin America: Some Social and Ecological Considerations. In *Latin American Development Issues*, Proceedings of the Conference of Latin Americanist

Geographers, ed. David Hill, 3:127–132. East Lansing, Mich.: CLAG Publications.

Durning, Alan B., 1991. Fat of the Land. *World Watch* 4(3):11–17.

Edelman, Marc, 1985. Extensive Land Use and the Logic of the Latifundio: A Case Study in Guanacaste Province, Costa Rica. *Human Ecology* 13 (2):153–185.

———, 1987. From Central American Pasture to North American hamburger. In *Food and Evolution: Toward a Theory of Human Food Habits*, ed. Marvin Harris and Eric B. Ross, 541–561. Philadelphia: Temple University Press.

———, 1992. *The Logic of the Latifundio: The Large Estates of Northwestern Costa Rica since the Late Nineteenth Century*. Stanford, Calif.: Stanford University Press.

EPOCA (Environmental Project on Central America), n.d. Central America: Roots on Environmental Destruction. San Francisco: EPOCA.

FCG (Fereración de Cámaras de Ganaderos de Costa Rica), 1983. *Problemática de la Ganadería Bovina y Propuestas para su Reactivición en el Corto Plazo*. San José: FCG.

Fearnside, Philip M., 1989. A Prescription for Slowing Deforestation in Amazonia. *Environment* 31 (4):16–20, 39–40.

Feder, Ernest, 1980. The Odious Competition between Man and Animal over Agricultural Resources in the Underdeveloped Countries. *Review* 3(3):463–500.

Fleming, Theodore H., 1986. Secular Changes in Costa Rican Rainfall: Correlation with Elevation. *Journal of Tropical Ecology* 2:87–91.

Frank, André Gunder, 1969. *Capitalism and Underdevelopment in Latin America*. New York: Monthly Review Press.

La Gaceta, 1990. Ley No. 7174: Reforma a La Ley Forestal. *La Gaceta Diario Oficial* 112 (133) (16 July):1–7.

Guardia Quirós, Jorge, 1987. *La Politica de Precios en Costa Rica*. San José: COUNSEL.

Guess, George, 1978. Narrowing the Base of Costa Rican Democracy. *Development and Change* 9 (4):599–609.

Hagenauer, Werner, 1980. Análisis Agró-Metereológico en la Zona de Cañas y Bagaces (Guanacaste) en los Años 1921 a 1979. *Informe Semestral* [Instituto Geográfico Nacional], July–December:45–59.

Hamilton, Lawrence S., 1991. Tropical Forest Misinterpretations. *Journal of Forestry* 89 (1):5–6.

Harrison, Susan, 1991. Population Growth, Land Use and Deforestation in Costa Rica, 1950–84.. *Interciencia* 16 (2):83–93.

Hartshorn, Gary, Lynne Hartshorn, Agustín Atmella, et al., 1982. *Costa Rica Country Environmental*

Profile. A Field Study. San José: Tropical Science Center—U.S. Agency for International Development.

Hecht, Susanna B., Richard B. Norgaard, and Giorgio Possio, 1988. The Economics of Cattle Ranching in Eastern Amazonia. *Interciencia* 13 (5):233–240.

Heckadon Moreno, Stanley, and Alberto McKay, eds., 1984. *Colonización y Destrucción de Bosques en Panamá.* Panama: Asociación Panameña de Antropoligía.

Hedström, Ingemar, 1985. Somos Parte de un Gran Equilibrio. La Crisis Ecológica en Centroamérica. San José: Departmento Ecuménico de Investigacioines.

———, 1990. ¿Volverán las Golondrinas? La Reintegración de la Creación desde una Perspective Latinoamericana. San José: Departmento Ecuménico de Investigaciones.

Holden, Robert H., 1981. Central America is Growing More Beef and Eating Less, as the Hamburger Connection Widens. *Multinational Monitor* 2 (19):17–18.

IDB (Inter-American Development Bank), 1992. Brazil: New Programs for Environment. *The IDB* 19 (5):11.

Jagels, Richard, 1990. Sooting the Conscience: Tropical Forest Exploitation Revisited. *Journal of Forestry* 88 (10):27–34.

Janzen, Daniel H., 1986. *Guanacaste National Park: Tropical Ecological and Cultural Restoration.* San José: Editorial Universidad Estatal a Distancia.

———, 1988. Buy Costa Rican Beef. *Oikos* 51:257–258.

Jarvis, Lovell S., 1986. *Livestock Development in Latin America.* Washington, D.C.: World Bank.

Jones, Jeffrey R., and Norman Price, 1985. Agroforestry: An Application of the Farming Systems Approach to Forestry. *Human Organization* 4(4):322–31.

Keene, Beverly, 1978. La Agroindustria de la Carne en Costa Rica. San José: Confederación Universitaria Centroamericana. Mimeo.

LACR (Latin American Commodities Report [London]), 1986a. Meat / Honduras. Latin American Commodities Report CR-86-08 (25 April):8.

———, 1986b. Meat / Nicaragua. Latin American Commodities Report CR-86-13 (10 July):8.

———, 1987. Little Cheer for Beef Markets, says FAO Latin American Commodities Report CR-87-04 (26 February):4–5.

———, 1988. Brazil Cattlemen Oppose Import Request. Latin American Commodities Report CR-88-14 (15 August):14.

Lehmann, Mary Pamela, 1991. After the Jungleburger: Forces behind Costa Rica's Continued Forest Conversion. Latinamericanist (Center for Latin American Studies, University of Florida) 26 (2):10–16.

———, 1992. Deforestation and Changing Land-Use Patterns in Costa Rica. In *Changing Tropical Forests: Historical Perspectives on Today's Challenges in Central and South America,* ed. Harold K. Steen and Richard P. Tucker, 58–76. Durham, N.C.: Forest History Society and IUFRO Forest History Group.

León, Jorge S, Carlos Barboza V., and Justo Aguilar, 1981. *Desarrollo Tecnológico en la Ganadería de Carne.* San José: Consejo Nacional de Investigaciones Cientificas y Tecnológicas. Mimeo.

Leonard, H. J., 1985. *Natural Resources and Economic Development in Central America: A Regional Environmental Profile.* Washington, D.C.: International Institute for Environment and Development.

Matteucci, Silvia Diana, 1988. Is the Rain Forest Worth Seven Hundred Million Hamburgers? *Interciencia* 12 (1):5.

McCay, Bonnie J., and James M. Acheson, eds., 1987. *The Question of the Commons: The Culture and Ecology of Communal Resources.* Tucson: University of Arizona Press.

McLarney, William O., 1988. Guanacaste: The Dawn of a Park. *Nature Conservancy Magazine* 38 (1):11–15.

Mintz, Sidney, 1977. The So-Called World System: Local Initiative and Local Response. *Dialectical Anthropology* 2 (4):253–270.

Montenegro, Esther, 1988. El Hombre Que Ha Visto Morir el Hato Nacional. *Realidad* 4 (18):9–10.

Myers, Norman, 1981. The Hamburger Connection: How Central America's Forests Become North America's Hamburgers. *Ambio* 10 (1):3–8.

———, 1990a. Primer Lugar en Deforestación en Latinoamérica: Costa Rica Destroza Sus Bosques, 23 September.

Nations, James D., 1992. Xateros, Chicleros, and Pimenteros: Harvesting Renewable Tropical Forest Resources in the Guatemalan Petén. In *Conservation of Neotropical Forests: Working from Traditional Resource Use,* ed. Kent H. Redford and Christine Padoch, 208–219. New York: Columbia University Press.

Nations, James D., and Daniel I. Kromer, 1983a. Rainforests and the Hamburger Society. *Environment* 25 (3):12–20.

———, 1983b. Central America's Tropical Rainforests: Positive Steps for Survival. *Ambio* 12 (5):232–238.

Nations, James D., and H. Jeffrey Leonard, 1986. Grounds of Conflict in Central America. In *Bordering on Trouble: Resources and Politics in Latin America,* ed. Andrew Maguire and Janet Welsh Brown, 55–98. Bethesda, Md.: Adler and Adler.

Nations, James D., and Ronald B. Nigh, 1978. Cattle, Cash, Food, and Forest: The Destruction of the American Tropics and the Lacandón Maya Alternative. *Culture and Agriculture* 6:1–5.

Navarro, Carlos, and Carlos E. Reiche, 1986. *Análisis Financiero de una Plantación Familiar de Gliricidia Sepium en Guanacaste, Costa Rica.* Turrialba, Costa

Rica: Centro Agronómico de investigación y Enseñanza. Mimeo.

Ortner, Sherry B., 1984. Theory in Anthropology since the Sixties. *Comparative Studies in Society and History* 26 (1):126–166.

Parsons, James J. 1976. Forest to Pasture: Development or Destruction? *Revista de Biología Tropical* 24 (supp. 1):121–138.

Partridge, William L., 1984. The Humid Cattle Ranching Complex: Cases from Panama Reviewed. *Human Organization* 43 (1):76–80.

Patterson, Alan, 1990. Debt for Nature Swaps and the Need for Alternatives. *Environment* 32 (10):4–13, 31–32.

Pearce, Fred, 1990. Brazil, Where the Ice Cream Cones From. *New Scientist* 127 (July 7):45–48.

Peters, Charles M., Alwun H. Gentry, and Robert O. Mendelsohn, 1989. Valuation of an Amazonian Rainforest. *Nature* 339:655–656.

Porras Zúñiga, Anabelle, and Beatriz Villarreal Montoya, 1986. *Deforestación in Costa Rica*. San José: Editorial Costa Rica.

RAN (Rainforest Action Network), 1989. Hamburger Connection Update—June 1989. San Francisco: RAN. Mimeo.

Realidad, 1988. Piden Que Salve de la Ruina a los Agricultores. *Realidad* 4(18):7–9.

Repetto, Robert, 1990. Deforestation in the Tropics. *Scientific American* 262 (4):36–42.

Roux, Bernard, 1975. Expansion du Capitalisme et Développement du sous Développement: L'Integration de l'Amérique Centrale au Marché Mondial de la Viande Bovine. *Revue du Tiers Monde* 16:355–380.

Rudel, Thomas K., 1989. Population, Development, and Tropical Deforestation: A Cross-National Study. *Rural Sociology* 54 (3):327–338.

Rutsch, Matilde, 1980. *La Cuestión Ganadera en México*. Mexico City: Centro de Investigación para la Intergración Social.

Sader, Steven A., and Armond T. Joyce, 1988. Deforestation Rates and Trends in Costa Rica, 1940–1983. *Biotropica* 20 (1):11–19.

Sáenz Maroto, Alberto, 1981. *Erosión, Deforestación y Control de Inundaciones en Costa Rica*. San José: Universidad de Costa Rica.

Sanderson, Steven E., 1986. *The Transformation of Mexican Agriculture*. Princeton, N.J.: Princeton University Press.

Sanderson, Steven E., and Ana Doris Capistrano, 1991. The Tyranny of the External: Links between International Economic Change and Natural Resource use in Latin America. Paper presented at the Latin American Studies Association, 4–6 April, Washington, D.C.

SEPSA (Secretaría Ejecutiva de Planificación Sectorial

Agropecuaria, Costa Rica), 1983. Encuesta Nacional de Ganado Bovino 1982. San José: SEPSA.

———, 1986a. Comportamiento de las Principales Actividades Productivas del Sector Agropecuario Durante 1985. San José: SEPSA.

———, 1986b. El Sector Agropecuario. San José: SEPSA.

SEPSA et al. (Secretaría Ejecutive de Planificación Sectorial Agropecuaria, Instituto Interamericano de Ciencias Agrícolas, Ministerio de Agricultura y Ganadería, Banco Nacional de Costa Rica, Federación de Cámaras de Ganaderos, Oficina Nacional de Semillas), 1985. Programa de Reactivación de la Ganadería Bovina en Costa Rica. Mimeo.

Sevilla, Roque, 1990. El Canje de la Deuda por Conservación. Los Casos de Bolivia, Ecuador y Costa Rica. In *Diálogo con Nuestro Futuro Común: Perspectivas Latinoamericanas del Informe Brundtland*, ed. Günther Maihold and Victor L. Urquidi, 139–161. Caracas: Fundación Friedrich Ebert-Editorial Nueva Sociedad.

Shane, Douglas R., 1986. *Hoofprints on the Forest: Cattle Ranching and the Destruction of Latin America's Tropical Forest*. Philadelphia: Institute for the Study of Human Issues.

Slutsky, Daniel, 1979. La Agroindustria de la Carne en Honduras. *Estudios Sociales Centroamericanos* 22:101–205.

Spielman, Hans O., 1972. La Expansión Ganadera en Costa Rica: Problemas de Desarrollo Agropecuario. *Informe Semestral* [Instituto Geográfico Nacional] July–December, 33–57.

Stanley, Denise, 1991. Demystifying the Tragedy of the Commons: The Resin Tappers of Honduras. *Grassroots Development* 15 (3):27–35.

Tangley, Laura, 1986. Costa Rica—Test Case for the Neotropics. *BioScience* 36 (5):296–300.

Thrupp, Lori Ann, 1989. The Political Ecology of Natural Resource Strategies in Central America: A Focus on Costa Rica. Paper prepared for the Latin American Studies Association Conference, 3–6 December, Miami, Fla.

Tosi, Joseph A., n.d. *Los Recursos Forestales de Costa Rica*. San José: Centro Científico Tropical. Mimeo.

Ugalde Arias, Luis A., and Hans M. Gregersen, 1987. *Incentives for Tree Growing in Relation to Deforestation and the Fuelwood Crisis in Central America*. Turrialba, Costa Rica: Centro Agronómico Tropical de Investigación y Enseñanza. Mimeo.

Uhl, Christopher, and Geoffrey Parker, 1986a. Our Steak in the Jungle. *BioScience* 36 (10:642.

———, 1986b. Is a Quarter-Pound Hamburger Worth a Half-Ton of Rain Forest? *Interciencia* 11 (5):210.

Utting, Peter, 1991. The Social Origins and Impact of Deforestation in Central America. Discussion paper

24. Geneva: United Nations Research Institute for Social Development.

Vargas Mena, Emilio, 1990. Ecología y Deuda Externa. *Aportes* 66:12–14.

Wallerstein, Immanuel, 1974. *The Modern World-System: Capitalist Agriculture and the Origins of the European World Economy in the Sixteenth Century.* New York: Academic Press.

Williams, Robert G., 1986. *Export Agriculture and the Crisis in Central America.* Chapel Hill: University of North Carolina Press.

WRI (World Resources Institute), 1985. *Tropical Forests: A Call for Action.* Washington, D.C.: WRI.

WRI, UNEP, and UNDP (World Resources Institute, United Nations Environment Programme, United Nations Development Programme), 1990. *World Resources 1990–91.* New York: Oxford University Press.

35

Capitalism and Ecological Crisis
Legacy of the 1980s

Elizabeth Dore

Since the 1980s the ecology question has occupied a prominent position in Latin American political debates. This reflects the importance of the global environmental movement as much as regional preoccupation with environmental conditions. Discussion of ecological issues centres on two questions: how to achieve sustainable development, and how imperialism conditions environmental change. In practice, however, the two approaches overlap to form a rich, if sometimes eclectic, debate.

RADICAL ENVIRONMENTALISM IN LATIN AMERICA

In the 1960s and 1970s progressive Latin Americans embraced dependency theory to explain underdevelopment. They held that Latin American

From Elizabeth Dore, "Capitalism and the Ecological Crisis: Legacy of the 1980s." In H. Collingson (ed.), *Green Guerillas: Environmental Conflicts and Initiatives in Latin America and the Caribbean,* pp. 8–19, 1996, The Latin American Bureau, London.

countries were poor because advanced industrial countries appropriated their economic surplus. Leading Latin American environmentalists have elaborated a theory of eco-dependency in which surplus extraction takes the form of ecological pillage. They argue that companies earn a higher rate of profit in Latin America than in the U.S. or Western Europe because there they can despoil the environment far more than would be tolerated "at home." This devastates the region's resource base and reduces long-term potential for capital accumulation.[1] A variant of eco-dependency is that underdevelopment is caused by the use of 'foreign' technologies. In this view, European methods of production are incompatible with the tropical climate and soils found throughout Latin America. Over time inappropriate technologies degraded the fragile ecosystems of the region. For example, cattle-grazing and mono-crop agriculture are sustainable in Europe and the United States but not in Latin America, where they were introduced after the Conquest causing long term, irreversible erosion.[2] An explicitly anti-modern strand of Latin American radical environmentalism stresses the sustainability of indigenous production systems, and the unsustainability of European ones. Writers of this persuasion hold that small-scale production is inherently good, and large-scale bad; that traditional technologies are always green, but never modern industry.[3]

There are compelling aspects of this antimodern critique. Yet, judgements about the environmental impact of production techniques when they are divorced from analysis of the social system are problematic. Small-scale production may or may not be ecologically preferable to large-scale. The central issue is not the size of the production unit, but who controls it and for what purposes. In so far as Indian and peasant communities practice more sustainable forms of natural resource use it is because they are not driven by capitalist competition. The challenge is not to do away with industrialization, but to de-link industrialization from profitmaking.

SUSTAINABLE DEVELOPMENT

In the 1980s *sustainable development* became a catch-all term widely used to frame environmental issues. It has come to mean "development that meets the needs of the present without compromising the ability of future generations to meet their own needs."[4] As this definition is both malleable and moral, sustainable development has become the broad church of environmentalism. Advocates of sustainable development offer an array of proposals, from liberalizing markets to expanding the power of the state, concentrating on how to manage the economic system to make it less polluting and less wasteful of resources. The concept is particularly favoured by policymakers because it obscures ideological differences about the causes of ecological destruction and what should be done about them. A hallmark of this eclectic approach is the assumption that countries face a trade-off between growth and environmental degradation. Sustainable development is not about transforming capitalism; it is about reforming the status quo to make capitalism more eco-friendly.

Despite its reformist character, sustainable development marks a significant advance in environmental politics in Latin America. Historically ecology movements in the region campaigned to protect any endangered species except endangered homo-sapiens. Environmentalists lobbied to pre-serve rainforests, watersheds, birds and animals, but not people. Instead of targeting the system that drives the poor to overexploit their environment, often ecologists saw poor people as the enemy. Sustainable development made the environment into a human issue by linking the protection of people and ecosystems.

Two problems with the sustainable development approach stand out. First, while tropical rainforests, especially Amazonia, monopolise the attention and funds of advocates of sustainable development, the vast majority of Latin Americans live in areas which attract minimal international interest. Second, the notion that economic growth inevitably causes ecological destruction prevents ecologists and policymakers from exploring the connections between property relations, political power and environmental destruction.

In the 1980s the multilateral lending agencies adopted sustainable development. Institutionalization turned it into the latest in a long parade of development fads: growth with equity, integrated rural development, basic needs, appropriate technology, and women in development. Each began as a critique of the orthodoxy of the development establishment. Then each was appropriated by those agencies as a way of defusing opposition, leaving the traditional agenda of the development community virtually unchanged. Sustainable development suffered the same fate.[5]

An environmental critique of development practice briefly altered the rhetoric and bureaucracies of the major lending agencies. For example, in its 1992 World Development Report the World Bank announced that "working for a better environment" was its major policy goal. Quickly sustainability rose to a prominent place within the development establishment.[6] Speeches and working papers heralded the new policy. New programme departments and professional specializations created vested interests in sustaining the fashion. The World Bank appeared to have assumed the mantle of environmentalism, but it was form over essence. Environmentalism made little impact on the Bank's core activities: adjustment lending and project aid. Despite high profile pronouncements about the importance of sustainability, concrete measures to improve the environmental impact of the Bank's activities were negligible. In the energy sector, where specialists agree that huge power schemes are neither ecologically nor economically sustainable, the World Bank continues to fund large dams and conventional power plants instead of alternative energy policies.[7]

In the end, environmental conditionality in project aid proved less significant than the ecological impact of the neoliberal economic policies that lending agencies fostered.[8] The International Monetary Fund and the World Bank imposed adjustment programmes designed to ensure that countries increased their foreign exchange earnings to service the debts they accumulated in the previous decade.[9] To this end, the agencies required that countries increase their trade balances, which meant promoting exports. This was disastrous for poor people and for the environment.

To comply with the agencies' ground rules, governments sought private investment to expand exports. As Latin American countries simultaneously were trying to attract capital, they competed over which could provide the most favourable conditions which included, among other things, low wages, a submissive labour force and few environmental restrictions. The policy was successful on its own terms. Exports of natural resources rose spectacularly. In the 1980s the value of Latin American fishery exports was almost four times greater in the previous decade. Forestry exports rose as well, and the production of iron and cooper was higher than in the 1970s.[10] Exports of selected agricultural products also grew significantly over the same period.[11] A few countries in the region succeeded in attracting low wage, high pollution industries, most notably Mexico. With pressure to export and generally to comply with IMF and World Bank economic conditionality, Latin American governments implemented development strategies which were antithetical to environmental sustainability.

Natural resource destruction accompanied the drive to export; damage was compounded by the economic orthodoxy of the development establishment. Free market economics became an article of faith in the multilateral lending agencies in the 1980s, as in the economics profession at large. Free-marketeers argue that private sector cost-benefit calculations will result in environmental improvements, that the costs to capital of ecological deterioration and natural resource depletion will compel firms to reduce pollution and take measures to conserve ecosystems. In this world view, market liberalization, free enterprise and reduction in the role of the state will improve ecological conditions.[12]

But contrary to World Bank statements, the environmental impact of liberalization was no positive in Latin America. Weak environmental regulations encouraged entrepreneurs to adopt production methods which ensured large profits in the short term with little regard for natural resource preservation. Industries were attracted to Latin America because they could pollute, dispose of toxic wastes, and extract resources with minimal state interference. Where governments introduced environmental regulations, often responding to pressure from the lending agencies themselves, their monitoring capacity was negligible. With pared budgets and reduced staffs, state agencies charged with implementing environmental regulations were unable to enforce their mandate. Environmentalism became yet another avenue for market liberalization and reduction in the ambit of the state.

Few professionals challenged the way the development establishment framed environmental debates. To retain credibility and access to the corridors of power, environmentalists raised issues of sustainability in terms acceptable to the agencies. Ironically, instead of the environment movement transforming the priorities of the multilateral agencies, the reverse occurred. The agenda of the World Bank and the IMF—export promotion, free markets, a small state—became central tenets in the ecology debate.[13]

By the 1990s it was clear to progressives in the environmental movement that the international development establishment had wrapped itself in the rhetoric of environmentalism to legitimate a structural adjustment agenda that was a barrier to sustainability and human development. As well as directly fomenting irrational resource use, structural adjustment intensified poverty throughout Latin America. In 1980, 35 percent of the population of the region lived below the poverty line. Ten years later the figure was 50 percent.[14] Poverty is intensifying pressure on the environment in numerous ways. In the countryside people are cultivating land that had been considered too eroded for agriculture, accelerating soil depletion. In urban areas reductions in subsidies and incomes have put the price of fuel beyond many people's means. As a result they cut firewood in zones surrounding cities, denuding those regions of trees.

SOCIALIST ENVIRONMENTALISM

The motor force of capitalism is the production of profits. What to produce, how to organize production, and how to distribute commodities are determined neither by social needs nor ecological sustainability, but by profitability. As growth is key to raising profits, the system continually engenders the expansion of production, consumption—and of waste.[15]

While ecological destruction is inherent under capitalism, there is scope for environmental reform. In the past decade environmental movements have forced politicians to address issues of ecological change. Local resistance to extreme contamination and natural resource destruction is common in Latin America. Wary of denunciations by national and global groups, governments of the region are beginning to pay attention to the environmental impact in their policies. Sometimes this has resulted in curbing ecological damage and its social effects. Frequently, however, official attention takes the form of paying lip service to natural resource protection. The track record of Latin American governments on environment issues is not good. Bowing to pressures from national and international capital, official policies that protect profits usually take precedence over those that protect ecological sustainability, as demonstrated by the following case studies of Amazonia and Mexico City.

AMAZONIA

The bread and butter of popular environmentalism in the United States and Europe is the myth of the destruction of the Amazon. It is a tale of rapid, irreversible deforestation and species extinction, and of global warming. While not without truth, this emphasis hides the social and political struggles that will determine the fate of the forest and its fifteen million people.[16]

For more than a century competing groups have fought over the Brazilian Amazon. Each had a different vision of how the natural resources of the region should be used.[17] A volatile mix of farmers, ranchers, miners, land speculators, indigenous tribes, rubber tappers, politicians, multinational companies and international banks all have laid claim to the resources of the region. In the last ten years the terms of those struggles have changed dramatically. In 1970 the debate was about how to modernize the region: how to turn the 'empty' forest into a productive resource. By 1990 the discourse was green; all claimants cast their demands and interests in an environmental framework. Nevertheless, optimism may be premature. Environmental sustainability and social justice are key words in the debates on the future of Amazonia. But deforestation and social violence continue. Subordinate groups who loudly press their claims are intimidated, repressed and silenced much as before.

In the early 1970s the military regime in Brazil embarked on an ambitious project to open up Amazonia. The rainforest, like tropical forests elsewhere, was seen as a vast empty space which called out for development. Development meant building roads, bringing in settlers, promoting economic activities, and taking out products. At that time all sides in the public debate over the future of the region favoured clearing the forest. One goal of the first scheme to develop the Amazon was to resettle landless families, particularly from the impoverished Northeast, on plots of 100 hectares. Official propaganda declared that the advancing Transamazonica highway would relieve problems of poverty and landlessness; it would connect "people with no land to a land with no people."[18]

As the road advanced into the jungle, people settled along the highway and cut down trees to stake their claim. Land titles and loans were available to settlers who could show that they were using land productively. The easiest way to do this was to graze cattle. Then the early populist development model fell from favour in Brasilia and government policy changed, clearly favouring large private enterprise in the modernization of Amazonia. With a few years large investors and land speculators began crowding out the settlers. Lured by the tax rebates, subsidies and soft loans originally meant to encourage small farmers to colonize the region, finance capital from southern Brazil invested in landed property. When inflation soared in the 1970s and 1980s, and investors clamoured to put their money into safe assets such as land and gold, the property market in Amazonia thrived. As large capital entered the region, first-wave settlers either moved to the edge of the frontier, clearing new lands for themselves, sought work as wage labourers on larger ranches, or returned from whence they came, often poorer than before.

Cattle-grazing created an environmental and a social disaster in Amazonia, as it did throughout Latin America. The infamous burning of the forest, the first step in clearing land, had global and local implications. Although there is no scientific consensus that reduction of the tropical rainforest produces global warming, forest burning produces considerable quantities of carbon. This heats the earth's atmosphere and contributes to the "greenhouse effect." Locally, clearing the land of trees and plants for grazing initiated rapid decline in soil fertility. Even after it became known that clearing the forest would turn the area into a waste land within five to ten years, government policy and financial incentives continued to promote the expansion of pasture land.

Profits in ranching did not derive primarily from beef production. The cattle industry became a vehicle for entrepreneurs to acquire land, subsidized credit and tax reductions. Therefore, destruction of the natural resource base of the industry did not constrain profitability. Rather, it accelerated speculation in land and capital accumulation. In short, there were few economic incentives to exploit the ecosystem in a sustainable way. Quite the contrary, profitmaking promoted the wanton and unsustainable use of land. The abuse of natural resources in the region was so flagrant that it gave cattle raising a bad name, but not because banks and ranchers made a rational appraisal of the economic, social and ecological costs and benefits of the industry. It was communities in Amazonia opposed to ranching and international environmental organizations who exposed the consequences of cattle grazing.

Ranchers and small farmers were joined by others who competed to claim the valuable resources of the forest. Mining was second to cattle in transforming the region. Brazil's Grande Carajás Project, begun in the 1980s, is the largest mining complex in the world. Everything about Carajás was mammoth, including its potential to alter the region's ecosystem. The project converted one-quarter of Amazonia into the world's largest industrial and agro-livestock centre.[19] At the hub of the enterprise are massive deposits of iron ore and manganese which reputedly enjoy the lowest production costs in the world. It was estimated that Carajás alone could produce ten percent of the world's supply of iron ore.

Grande Carajás became the heart of a vast integrated development project that includes a string of open-cast mines which produce bauxite, copper, chrome, nickel, tungsten, cassiterite and gold, in addition to iron ore and manganese. Radiating from the mines are processing plants, steel and aluminium mills, agro-livestock enterprises, hydroelectric dams, railroads and deep-water river ports. Together these cover an area of 900,000 square kilometres, the size of France and Britain combined. The complex served as a giant magnet, drawing farmers, ranchers, gold prospectors, and enterprises of all kinds into Amazonia.

The project has serious ecological implications, which, because of its scale, were difficult to predict. Soon after building began at Carajás, significant ecological changes became evident. The project involves massive deforestation. 1.6 million acres of timber was cut annually to stoke the pig-iron smelters and provide lumber for construction. The state-owned company which runs the project pays lip-service to conservation and implemented some reforestation. Nevertheless, large areas of the tropical forest were reduced to scrub land. By the time the first iron ore rolled out of Carajás in 1985, rapid deforestation had altered the climate. Less rainfall, combined with soil erosion, siltation and flooding of the region's rivers caused widespread desertification. Extinction of plant and animal species signalled great changes in the ecosystem.

Large as they were, Carajás and other corporate ventures did not monopolize mining in Amazonia. After a steep rise in the price of gold in 1979, *garimpeiros,* or small-scale miners, flocked to Amazonia. The roads, railroads, and services installed for Carajás and for the cattle industry facilitated migration. It is estimated that almost one million garimpeiros panning in and around the rivers of Amazonia produced more than 90 percent of Brazil's annual output of gold.

From the beginning grazing and mining encroached on lands used by indigenous tribes and rubber tappers. At first their rights to the resources of the forest were ignored because politicians dismissed them as primitives, soon to be swept away by progress. By the mid-1980s the struggle over the fate of the forest appeared, at least on the surface, considerably different. Indigenous groups and tappers were considered legitimate participants in the debate.[20] Their persistent resistance to expropriation and to felling the forest, combined with their links to national and international organizations, converted them from pariahs to legitimate actors in the unfolding drama.[21]

In 1970 there was no legitimate voice calling for preservation of the forest. In 1990 no group that sought legitimacy could oppose it in words. Even ranchers and loggers had to recast their claims in environmental terms. This has been called the greening of the discourse.[22] In 1970 cattle ranching was almost universally promoted as the best way to develop the Amazon. In 1990 it was a symbol of destruction. The struggles of a constellation of forces, led by rubber tappers and indigenous tribes, to claim their rights to the resources of the forest shifted consciousness and politics. That they were moderately successful reflected the influence of environmental movements worldwide over the development debate. Nevertheless, despite the greening of the discourse, and the creation of extractive and indigenous reserves (see Anthony Hall), the main thrust of Brazilian policy in the Amazon continues to promote large capitalist enterprises. Sustainable resource use remains a low political priority.

URBAN CONTAMINATION AND CORPORATIVIST MOBILIZATION: THE CASE OF MEXICO CITY

By the end of the twentieth century more than seventy percent of Latin Americans lived in cities. Nevertheless, problems of urban environmental degradation tend to be ignored by ecologists in the United States and Europe. They do not lend themselves to the simple morality of saving the rainforest.

Mexico City is infamous for air pollution. At an altitude of 2,300 metres above sea level, sprawling across a valley of 9,600 square metres, surrounded by mountains on two sides, and occupying the salty, dry beds of what once were a series of lakes, Mexico City is poorly placed for an industrial metropolis. The zone is prone to thermal inversions where lack of wind allows contaminants to accumulate in the atmosphere. Despite these geographic peculiarities, Mexico City's severe environmental problems are little different from those of other Latin American cities.

The capitalist transformation of agriculture, which accelerated in Latin America in the 1950s, set in motion a process of rural-urban migration. Facing a dual process of concentration of land in large capitalist farms and decline in the viability of small-scale production, many peasants abandoned their land, others were evicted. With the Green Revolution machinery, pesticides and fertilizers transformed agricultural production and processing, so only a small proportion of the rural poor found permanent work in the countryside. To survive people migrated to urban centres in search of work. The capital cities of Latin America, with their concentration of industry, commerce and government, became magnets for the dispossessed rural poor. Mexico City exemplified that process. Its population doubled in each decade from 1940 to 1970, a trend that was repeated in many metropolitan cities in the region.

The 1960s and 1970s, the decades that witnessed the urban demographic boom in Latin America, were also decades of industrial expansion. Subsidies and tax incentives promoted the spatial concentration of industry in the region's capitals. Whereas the pattern of urban environmental decay in Mexico City was similar to, though greater than, that found in many Latin American cities, the response of the Mexican government was unique. In keeping with its corporativist character, the Partido Revolucionario Institucional (PRI) created an ecology movement organically linked to the party and the state.[23] In the 1980s growth of the political opposition made it evident that the PRI was losing its legitimacy. One issue that focused discontent, especially among the urban middle classes, was the deplorable quality of life in the capital. The government perceived that opponents might channel this disaffection into a broad movement that could threaten the party's control. To prevent this the PRI launched an environmental campaign to reconquer the political initiative. Party leaders perceived that ecology could be a safe and at the same time popular issue which would enhance the PRI's national and international image.

By commiting the government to improving the environment, the PRI established ecology as a legitimate area of debate. It created a network of supposedly grassroots groups and encouraged their activities. As usual, the PRI used this network to channel rewards, financial and otherwise, to people who emerged as leaders, and to inform on opposition activities. In short, the PRI sought to turn critics into clients of the state. The PRI had some momentary successes nonetheless. Its politics of mobilizing ecology groups undermined the influence of independent organizations that were calling attention to the PRI's obeisance to private enterprise at the cost of environmental degradation.

The government found it could not always control the movement it created. The PRI's pledge to improve the environment, especially in the capital, clashed with the government's neoliberal economic strategy. In practice, market liberalization and fiscal austerity took precedence over environmental reform. The government encouraged investment by removing barriers to profitability and was loath to impose environmental regulations which might be viewed negatively by the private sector. In addition, by reducing the government budget it curtailed the state's regulatory capacity. As a result, the government was less able to enforce those environmental standards it legislated.

When the government reneged on its public commitment to environmental reform, tensions mounted within the environmental movement. It became apparent that the Mexican government was prepared to undertake only token reforms to alter patterns of natural resource use and abuse. When reform implied a cost to capital or to the state, as they inevitably did, the PRI shed its green veneer.

WHAT MIGHT BE

Environmentalism has emerged as one of the main forms of opposition politics in Latin America at the end of the millenium. As in other parts of the world, ecology struggles in the region have tended to concentrate on ameliorating particular examples of environmental degradation, rather than confronting its social causes. Ecological disasters in the former socialist countries of Eastern Europe demonstrated that socialism can be as environmentally devastating as capitalism. Radical transformation in the relationship between society and the environment requires conscious critiques of current norms in natural resource use, as well as of the dominant relations of property. The ecology movement has facilitated the former by creating mass consciousness of the consequences of environmental destruction. If that were joined to an ecological critique of capitalism it could provide the framework for a powerful movement for social and environmental change.

NOTES

1. Enrique Leff, "Estudios Sobre Ecología y Capital," *Estudios Sociales Centroamericanos,* 49 (enero–abril 1989) pp. 49–78; *Ecalagía y Capital: Hacia una Perspectiva Ambientol del Desarrollo.* Universidad Nacional Autónoma de México, 1986. For a Marxist critique of dependency theory see Elizabeth Dore, *The Peruvian Mining Industry: Growth, Stagnation and Crisis,* Westview Press, Boulder, 1988, Cap 1. For a more sympathetic account of dependency theory see Cristóbal Kay, *Latin American Theories of Development and Underdevelopment,* Routledge, New York, 1989.

2. Stéfano Varese develops a variation of this theme. He argues that technologies developed for and by foreign cultures were implanted in Latin America with the Conquest. Therefore, he calls the use of these inappropriate technologies "internal colonialism" as they are no longer foreign to the region. Cited in Fernando Mires, *El discursa de la naturaleza: ecologia pollrica en América Latina,* DEI, San José, Costa Rica, p. 65.

3. Victor Toledo, "Utopia y Naturaleza: El Nuevo Movimiento Ecológico de los Campesinos e Indigenas de América Latina" *Nueva Sociedad,* 122, Nov–Dec 1992, pp. 72–85; Stéfano Varese cited in Fernando Mires 1990, op cit. For a critique of this position see Elizabeth Dore, "Una interpretación socio-ecológica de la historia minera latinoamericana" *Ecología Políticu* 6 April 1994.

4. World Commission on Environment and Development (WCED), *Our Common Future,* Oxford University Press, New York, 1987.

5. Ann P. Hawkins and Frederick H. Buttel, *The Political Economy of "Sustainable Development"* n.d., ms.

6. The World Bank, the International Monetary Fund, the Inter-American Development Bank and the United

States Agency for International Development form the heart of the development establishment.

7. Bruce Rich, *Mortgaging the Earth: The World Bank, Environmental Impoverishment and the Crisis of Development,* Beacon Press, Boston, 1994.

8. John Weeks, "Contemporary Latin American Economies: Neo-Liberal Reconstruction in Sandor Halbsky and Richard L. Harris (eds) *Capital, Power and Inequality in Latin America,* Westview Press, Boulder, 1995.

9. Dore 1992, op cit, pp. 79–85.

10. Food and Agriculture Organization (FAO) *Country Tables 1989: Basic Data on the Agricultural Sector,* p. 327, Rome 1989; Ministerio de Ohras Publicas y Urbanismo (MOPU), *Desarrollo y Medio Ambiente en America Latina y el Caribe,* Mexico, 1990.

11. FAO 1989, op cit.

12. The World Bank, *World Development Report 1992.* Oxford University Press, New York, 1992, p. 10.

13. Hawkins and Buttel, op cit, pp. 4–5.

14. MOPU, 1990, op cit, p. 157.

15. This gives rise to a tension in the capitalist system: the production of profits undermines the sustainable reproduction of the physical world, which itself is necessary for the continued expansion of capital. See John Weeks, *Capital and Exploitation,* Princeton University Press, Princeton, N.J. 1981.

16. D. Faber, *Environment Under Fire: Imperialism and the Ecological Crisis in Central America* Monthly Review Press, New York; 1993; Peter Utting, *Trees, People and Power: Social Dimension and Forest Protection in Central America,* Earthscan, London 1993.

17. Much of the argument that follows is drawn from Marianne Schmink and Charles H. Wood, *Contested Frontiers in Amazonia,* Columbia University Press, New York 1992.

18. Schmink and Wood, 1992, op cit, p. 2.

19. Anthony Hall, *Developing Amazonia: Deforestation and Social Conflict in Brazil's Carajás,* p. 20. Manchester University Press, 1989.

20. The plight of the Yanomami Indians of Brazil received particular attention from survival International. For the impact of mining on the Indians of Brazil see D. Treece, *Bound in Misery and Iron: The Impact of the Grande Carajás Programme on the Indians of Brazil,* Survival International, London, 1987.

21. Hall, 1989, op cit.

22. Schmink and Wood, 1992, op cit, p. 16.

23. This argument is inconsistent with that presented in Stephen P. Mumme, "System Maintenance and Environmental Reform in Mexico" *Latin American Perspectives* 19:1, Winter 1992, pp. 123–124; and in David Barkin, "State Control of the Environment: Politics and Degradation in Mexico," *Capitalism, Nature, Socialism* February 1991, 2, pp. 86–108. It also reflects prevailing wisdom within that part of the ecology movement in Mexico which considers itself in the left opposition.

36

The Greening of Cuba

Peter Rosset

The manager of the state farm at the end of the dirt road in Villa Clara province appeared the perfect technocrat. He told me how he had fought against using oxen to prepare the land on his farm. Eventually he had no choice but to give in, since petroleum, tractor parts and tyres have virtually disappeared from the Cuban countryside in the past four years. Now he grudgingly admits that oxen have their benefits. "Before we could only fit two planting cycles into the rainy season," he said. "For more than a month each year, we couldn't prepare the land because the tractors got stuck in the mud. But an ox doesn't have that problem. You plough the day after it rains, or even while it's raining if you want." As a result, he said, the farm harvests three crops a year instead of two. Although the yield per cycle is lower, the annual yield is higher. The switch to oxen wasn't easy. Though ploughing with an ox team goes back hundreds of years in

From Peter Rosset, "The Greening of Cuba." *NACLA Report on the Americas;* Vol. 28:3, pp. 37–41. Copyright 1997 by the North American Congress on Latin America, 475 Riverside Dr., #454, New York, NY 10115-0122.

Cuba, none of the farm workers or agronomists had ever farmed with oxen themselves. "We had to hire some old *campesinos* from nearby villages as consultants to teach us how to hitch up an ox team and plough with them," the state-farm manager said. "It's amazing how much those old guys know about farming."

The 1989 collapse of trade relations with the former socialist bloc, together with the ongoing U.S. embargo, have meant that Cuban farmers now have to get by with a tiny fraction of the imported machinery and agrochemicals that they once depended upon. National sugar production, for example, which in the recent past averaged about eight million tons annually, has plummeted by a half in the past two years. This comes from a decrease in acreage planted because of machinery problems, and a drop in average yields from about 64,000 *arrobas* per *caballería* to around 50,000.[1] The state farms that supply the bulk of the cane to the Héctor Molina Sugar Mill, just south of Havana, experienced just such an enormous reduction in yields the last two years. Yet a number of small farmers from whom the mill also buys cane did not.[2]

Several independent farmers who use organic

farming techniques have turned in yields ranging from 100,000 to 150,000 *arrobas*. Another peasant who practices a traditional rotation of sugarcane with food crops and cattle pasture, though not organic, harvested about 85,000 *arrobas* last year, and was the largest supplier of food crops to the local marketing board as well. Farmers like these passed unnoticed when eight million tons of sugar were the norm, but they have recently captured the attention of agronomy experts who hope to disseminate their farming methods throughout Cuba. Since these peasant producers never used large quantities of the no longer available chemical inputs, they have been better able to weather the present crisis than the state sector has.

Times are changing so fast in the Cuban countryside that the only thing you can be certain of is that what is true today will no longer be true tomorrow. Since the 1960s three things characterized Cuban agricultural policy: sugar, state farms, and a fanatical love affair with the chemical and petroleum-intensive technologies of conventional modern agriculture. Yet since the 1989 collapse of imports, the Cuban government has had to give priority to food crops, and has turned the state farms over to the workers in an attempt to stimulate productivity.[3] Cuba has also embarked upon the first national transformation in history from conventional modern agriculture to large-scale organic and semi-organic farming.[4] Cuba's farmers and substantial scientific infrastructure—both physical plant and human resources—have been mobilized to substitute autochthonous technology for the foreign agricultural inputs. Cuban-made biopesticides and biofertilizers—the products of the country's cutting-edge biotechnology—are being combined with traditional peasant practices as well as ecological pest control, large-scale earthworm rearing, waste composting, and other environmentally rational practices.

This process has not stopped Cuba from falling into the worst food crisis in its history. Some estimates of the drop in average protein and calorie intake over the past three years are as high as 30 percent, to the point where Cubans are eating better than only Haitians and Bolivians. Because of innovations in the agricultural sector, it seems that food production is going up—though not yet by enough to compensate for the drop in imports.[5]

From the Cuban revolution in 1959 through the collapse of trading relations with the socialist bloc at the end of the 1980s, Cuba's economic development was characterized by rapid modernization and a high degree of social equity and welfare. Cubans arguably had the highest standard of living in Latin America. Yet Cuba never achieved truly independent development, as the island depended upon its socialist trading partners for petroleum, industrial equipment and supplies, agricultural inputs such as fertilizer and pesticides, and even basic foodstuffs for the population. By some estimates, as much as 57 percent of the total calories consumed by the population were imported prior to 1989.

Cuban agriculture was based on large-scale, capital-intensive monoculture, more akin in many ways to California's Imperial Valley than to the typical Latin American *minifundio* or small-scale farm. Agrochemicals and tractors replaced human labour, leading to a rural exodus, just as had occurred in the U.S. and other countries with industrialized agricultural systems. This production model has been showing sings of strain everywhere—including Cuba—as soil erosion and pesticide resistance lead to rising costs, and stagnant or falling yields. In Cuba, more than 90 percent of fertilizers and pesticides, as well as most of the ingredients to formulate them locally, were imported from abroad.

When trade relations with the socialist bloc collapsed, pesticide and fertilizer imports dropped by about 80 percent, and the availability of petroleum for agriculture dropped by a half. Food imports also fell by more than a half. Suddenly, an agricultural system almost as modern and industrialized as that of California was faced with a dual challenge: the need to essentially double food production with less than half the inputs, and at the same time maintain export-crop production so as not to erode further the country's meager foreign-exchange holdings.

In some ways Cuba was uniquely prepared to face this challenge. With only 2 percent of Latin America's population but 11 percent of its scientists and a well-developed research infrastructure, the government was able to call for "knowledge-intensive" technological innovation to substitute for the now unavailable inputs. Luckily an alternative agriculture movement had taken hold among Cuban researchers as early as 1982, and many promising research results—which had previously remained relatively unused—were available for immediate and widespread implementation.[6]

ORGANIC FARMING

Most of Cuba's agricultural soils have suffered a high degree of fertility loss and depletion of organic matter due to the past intensive use of pesticides and fertilizers. To rebuild healthy soils, Cubans are now using green manure crops as part of crop rotations, composting municipal garbage and other waste products, and undertaking the industrial-scale production of high-quality humus, using earthworms as composting agents.[7] In 1992, 172 vermicompost centres produced 93,000 tons of worm humus.[8]

Waste recycling is high on the new agenda. All kinds of waste products are being converted into animal food, energy and fertilizer. These organic by-products are collected from sugarcane processing, cattle and sheep ranches, poultry and pig farms, food and coffee processing plants, crop residues, and municipal garbage. Liquid wastes help irrigate the agricultural fields. Sugarcane stalks are being recycled into particle board and paper, as well as into fuel for the mills' boiling pots. Integrated pig production is a good example of how complex this recycling can become. The process begins with the collection of food scraps from workplace cafeterias, restaurants and schools. Theses scraps are fed to the pigs as a feed supplement. Farmers may also mix in waste from slaughterhouses, which is a good protein source. Next, the liquid and solid waste from the pigs is recycled to be used in vermiculture, in biogas generation, and even as a feed supplement for the same pigs. The stated goal is to reach zero nonrecycled waste.

Cuba has a unique system of pest management in sweet potatoes—a staple of the local diet. Predatory ants are mass-reared in banana stems and introduced into the fields at the point where tuber formation begins. The ants then build their nests around the sweet potatoes in the soil, protecting them from the ravages of the sweet-potato weevil. A similar method is used in plantain plantations. Cuba now has fourteen centres for ant production scattered around the country.[9] Other centres mass-rear other insects that prey upon or parasitize various species of crop pests.

Empirical evidence from the U.S. and elsewhere demonstrates that organic-farming methods can take between three and seven years from the initiation of the conversion process to achieve the levels of productivity that prevailed beforehand.[10] That is because it takes time to restore lost soil fertility and to re-establish natural controls of insect and disease populations. Yet Cuba does not have three to seven years; its population must be fed in the short term. Because of the urgency of the crisis, Cuban scientists and planners are bringing sophisticated biotechnology to bear on the development of new organic farming practices.

BIOTECHNOLOGY

In the U.S. we are unused to hearing the words *biotechnology* and *organic farming* in the same sentence. We tend to think of all biotechnology in terms of releasing genetically engineered organisms into the environment, a process which poses ecological and public-health risks that are not consistent with the goals of organic farming. What the Cubans are doing is different. They are collecting locally occurring strains of micro-organisms that perform useful functions in natural ecosystems. These range from disease microbes that are specific to certain crop pests, and thus non-toxic to other forms of life, to micro-organisms that convert atmospheric nitrogen into a form that crop plants can use. These micro-organisms are then massively reproduced in order to be used as biopesticides and biofertilizers in agro-ecosystems.[11] Some of these products are available commercially in the U. S. as well, but Cuba is way ahead in terms of the diversity of such biological preparations that are in widespread use.

Located on agricultural cooperatives, 222 artisanal biotechnology centres produce these biotech products for local use. These products are typically made by people in their twenties, who were born on the cooperative and who have some university-level training. In a sense, Cuba is demystifying biotechnology for developing countries by showing that biotechnology does not have to rely on multi-million-dollar infrastructure and super-specialized scientists. Rather, the sons and daughters of *campesinos* can make and use biotechnology products in remote rural areas. Industrial production of these biopesticides will soon be under way for use in larger-scale farming operations that produce for export. The labour-saving methods of biotechnology are particularly appropriate for Cuba because like the U.S., Cuba faces labour shortages in agriculture. Eighty percent of the Cuban population lives in urban areas and only 20 percent lives in the countryside, while in other countries with widespread alternative agriculture such as China, this ratio is reversed. At the same time, the Cuban government is going to great lengths—such as constructing high-quality housing and entertainment centres—to make relocating in the countryside an attractive option for city dwellers.[12]

LINKING PEOPLE WITH THE LAND

Cuba is also radically reorganizing its production in order to create the small-scale management units that are essential for effective organic farming. This reorganization has centred on the privatization and cooperativization of the state sector.[13] Under conventional systems, a single technician can manage several thousand acres on a "recipe" basis by simply writing out instructions for a particular fertilizer formula or pesticide to be applied with machinery on the entire area. Not so for organic farming. Whoever manages the farm must be intimately familiar with the ecological heterogeneity of each individual patch of soil. The farmer must know, for example, where organic matter needs to be added, and where pest refuges and entry points are.

In Cuba this scaling back of production units has coincided with the issue of production incentives. Several years ago planners became aware that the organization of work on state farms was profoundly alienating in terms of the relationship between the agricultural worker and the land. Large farms of thousands of acres had their work forces organized into teams which would prepare the soil in one area, move on to plant another, weed still another, and later harvest an altogether different area. Almost never would the same person both plant and harvest the same field. Thus no one ever had to confront the consequences of doing something badly or conversely, enjoyed the fruits of his or her own labour. In an effort to recreate a more

intimate relationship between farmers and the land, and to tie financial incentives to productivity, Cubans began several years ago to experiment with a programme called *"Vinculando el hombre con la tierra,"* or linking people with the land. This system made small work teams directly responsible for all aspects of production in a given parcel of land, allowing remuneration to be directly linked to productivity. The new system was tried on a number of state farms, and rapidly led to enormous increases in production.

The process of linking people with the land culminated in September 1993, when the Cuban government issued a decree terminating the existence of state farms, and turning them into Basic Units of Cooperative Production (UBPCs), a form of worker-owned enterprise or cooperative. The 80 percent of all farmland that was once held by the state, including sugarcane plantations, has now essentially been privatized into the hands of the workers. The UBPCs allow collectives of workers to lease state farmlands at low rent, in permanent usufruct. Property rights remain in the hands of the state, and the UBPCs must still meet production quotas for their key crops, but the collectives are owners of what they produce. Perhaps most importantly, what they produce in excess of their quotas can now be freely sold on the newly reopened farmers' markets.[14] Members elect management teams that determine the division of jobs, what crops will be planted on which parcels, and how much credit will be taken out to pay for the purchase of inputs.

The pace of consolidation of the UBPCs has varied greatly in their first year of life. Today one can find a range from those where the only change is that the old manager is now an employee of the workers, to those that truly function as collectives, to some in which the workers are parcelling the farms into small plots worked by groups of friends or *socios*. It is still too early to tell toward what final variety of structures the UBPCs will evolve.

Even before the percent crisis began, Cuba had been trying to move closer towards self-sufficiency in food crops.[15] Under the National Food Program, which began in the mid-1980s, sugar estates have been required to plant food crops and raise livestock in uncultivated areas. The goal was for each farm to supply the food needs of its workers and their families. The cultivation of beans, plantains, and root crops has increased as a result, although exact figures are hard to come by.

DYNAMIC DEBATE

This process of downsizing and conversion to organic farming is, of course, not taking place without controversy and setbacks. A dynamic debate is underway inside Cuba which cuts across the agricultural sector, from government ministries, universities and research centres, to farmers and association of producers. One side argues that what is taking place should be seen not precisely as a process of conversion, but rather as a temporary substitution during a period of crisis. This viewpoint holds that once trade conditions change, agrochemical inputs should once again be vigorously used. The opposite point of view, put forth by the Cuban Association for Organic Farming among others, holds that the previous model was too import-dependent and environmentally damaging to be sustainable. People in this camp argue that the present change was long overdue, and that further transformations are needed to develop truly rational production systems.[16]

The Organic Farming Association is a nongovernmental organization (NGO), a rare phenomenon in Cuba.[17] The association is playing a pivotal role in what might be called the institutionalization of the alternative model. Members are ecological agriculture activists ranging from university professors and students, to mid-level government functionaries, farmers and farm managers. They are struggling on a shoe-string budget to carry out an educational campaign on the virtues and indeed the necessity of maintaining and reinforcing the alternative model.

Opponents of such institutionalization point to the recent collapse of Cuban attempts at massive implementation of so-called Voisin Pasture Management as evidence of the inadequacies of organic farming technologies. The Voisin system was supposed to maintain dairy productivity without the widespread use of chemical fertilizers on pastures. The basic principle is as old as animal husbandry itself—the rotation of paddocks in such a way that manure is supplied to growing grasses at the precise moment when it is most needed. The Voisin system failed in Cuba, however, because it required

portable electric fencing that was both in short supply and susceptible to the ubiquitous power cuts, and because the density of cattle per acre was too high. Advocates of an alternative model for agriculture point out that it was not the principle of rotational grazing that failed, but rather the way in which it was applied.

Such debate aside, what may be most remarkable about the recent changes in Cuban agriculture is the rediscovery of the traditional values and knowledge of farmers. The Ministry of Agriculture has launched a national programme to recover traditional farming knowledge, recognizing that peasants have always practiced low-input, agroecologically sound agriculture. Mobile seminars and workshops are taking place around the country, where farmers can meet to trade their farming secrets and to share them with researchers and government officials.

If a silver lining to the current crisis exists, it is surely the new integration of socialist values with environmental consciousness and greater individual responsibility. Roberto García Trujillo, an assistant dean at the Agricultural University of Havana (ISCAH), is the founder of the Organic Farming Association. On the weekends, he practices what he preaches, working his tiny organic farm on a patch of land inherited by his wife. While he and his son turned the compost pile one Sunday morning, he mused:

> Many people think that farming is a simple and mundane act, but they are wrong. It is the soul of any great culture, because it requires not only a great deal of accumulated knowledge, but also putting this knowledge to use every single day. Knowledge of the weather, the soil, plants, animals, the cycles of nature; all of this is used every day by a farmer to make the decisions that have to be made in order to produce the food that we eat. To us it may seem like food comes from a factory, but in reality it comes from a culture that, generation after generation, has been created to produce that food.[18]

CONCLUSION

It is clearly too soon to tell if the transformation of Cuban agriculture will be permanent, or even if it will help Cuba survive its present crisis. Nevertheless, Cuba may turn out to be a model for the rest of us. Whether we live in Latin America, the U.S., Asia, Africa or Europe, we are all facing the declining productivity of modern conventional agriculture. As soils are progressively eroded, compacted by heavy machinery, salinized by excessive irrigation, and sterilized with chemicals, and as pests become ever more resistant to pesticides, crop yields are in decline. Meanwhile, aquifers and estuaries are being contaminated with agrochemical run-off. Organic farming and other alternative technologies are intensively studied in laboratories and experimented plots worldwide, but examples of implementation by farmers remain scattered and isolated. Cuba offers us the first large-scale test of these alternatives. Before we are all forced to make this transformation, this island nation offers us perhaps our only chance to see what works and what doesn't, what the problems are and which solutions will emerge.[19] Cuba is also carving out a path back from the de-skilled work process of large-scale industrial farming, toward a more human endeavor, engaged equally with traditional knowledge and modern ecological science.

NOTES

1. Cuban measurements for weight and area. 1 *arroba* = 25 pounds and 1 *caballería* = 33 acres.

2. Until late 1993, 80 percent of arable land was in State Farms. 11 percent in peasant cooperatives, and 9 percent in the hands of small independent farmers.

3. In 1989, Cuba devoted three times as much land to sugar as to food crops, or about 53 percent of non-pasture arable land.

4. For a fuller discussion of the issues (as well as data sources) presented in this article, see Peter Rosset and Medea Benjamin, *The Greening of the Revolution: Cuba's Experiment with Organic Agriculture*, Ocean Press and Global Exchange, available for $11.95 plus $2.50 postage and handling from Food First by calling 1-800-888-3314. Also see Peter Rosset and Shea Cunningham, "The Greening of Cuba: Organic Farming Offers Hope in the Midst of Crisis," *Food First Action Alert*, Spring, 1994.

5. Reliable figures are not available for two reasons. First, the compilation and release of national statistics have been curtailed during the economic crisis, and second, official figures record only that food sold through government channels, ignoring the burgeoning black market.

6. Richard Levins, "The Ecological Transformation of Cuba," *Agriculture & Human Values*, Vol. 10, No. 3, 1993, pp. 3–8.

7. Green manures are legume plant species that can be planted as cover crops to supply nitrogen to the soil.

8 See Paul Gersper, Carmen Rodríguez-Barbosa and Laura Orlando, "Soil Conservation in Cuba: A Key to the New Model for Agriculture," *Agriculture & Human Values* Vol. 10, No. 3, 1993, pp. 16–23.

9. Nicolas Lampkin, *Organic Farming*, Farming Press, UK, 1990.

10. Beatriz Díaz and Marta R. Muñoz, "Biotecnología agricola y medio ambiente en el período especial cubano." paper presented at the XVIII Meeting of the Latin American Studies Association, Atlanta, Georgia, 10–12 March, 1994.

11. Jeff Dlott, Ivette Perfecto, Peter Rosset, Larry Burkham, Julio Monterrey, and John Vandermeer, "Management of Insect Pests and Weeds," *Agriculture & Human Values* Vol. 10, No. 3, 1993, pp 3–9.

12. Peter Rosset and Medea Benjamin, "Two Steps Back, One Step Forward: Cuba's National Policy for Alternative Agriculture," International Institute for Environment and Development Gatekeeper Series No. 46, London, 1994.

13. For a discussion of the conversion of state farms into UBPCs, see Carmen Diana Deere, Niurka Pérez and Ernel González, "The View from Below; Cuban Agriculture in the Special Period of Peacetime," paper presented at the XVIII Meeting of the Latin American Studies Association, Atlanta, Georgia, 10–12 March, 1994.

14. Cuba experimented with these markets in the early 1980s, but they were shut down because of concerns about the creation of a class of middlemen. See Joseph Collins and Michael Scott, *No Free Lunch: Food & Revolution in Cuba Today*, Food First Books, San Francisco, 1984. They wee just reopened in September of this year in an attempt to stimulate production through price incentives. See "Cuba Will Allow Farmers to Sell on Open Market," *The New York Times*, September 18, 1994.

15. Laura J. Enríquez, *The Question of Food Security in Cuban Socialism*, University of California Press, Berkeley, 1994; Carmen Diana Deere, "Socialism on One Island: Cuba's National Food Programme and its Prospects for Food Security," Institute for Social Studies, Working paper Series No. 124, The Hague, 1992.

16. Roberto García Trujillo, *La conversión hacia una agricultura orgánica*. Asociacíon Cubana de Agricultura Orgánica, Havana, 1993.

17. To contact the association, please write to: Asociación Cubana de Agricultura orgánica, Tulipón No. 1011, entre Loma y 47, Nuevo Velado, CP 10600, Havana, Cuba.

18. Interview in "The Greening of Cuba," a documentary being produced by the Institute for Food & Development Policy.

19. See John Vandemeer, Judith Carney, Paul Gersper, Ivette Perfecto, and Peter Rosset, "Cuba and the Dilemma of Modern Agriculture," *Agriculture & Human Values,* Vol. 10, No. 3, 1993, pp. 3–8; Miguel A. Altieri, "The Implications of Cuba's Agricultural Conversion for the General Latin American Agro-ecological Movement," *Agriculture & Human Values*, Vol. 10, No. 3, 1993, pp. 91–92.

37

Political Ascent of Bolivia's Peasant Coca Leaf Producers

Kevin Healy

During the past decade, Bolivia's peasant coca-leaf growers have made impressive strides in political development.[1] This development is demonstrated by their almost mercurial ascent within the national political system, a climb which parallels the upward economic mobility of many growers. Organized through a network of unions (*sindicatos*), and determined to resist state policies and programs which threaten their local economies, Bolivia's peasant coca-leaf producers have learned to improve their political skills, including the building of alliances with other key political actors.

The theses advanced here holds that not only has the peasant *sindicato* movement blocked attempts of the state to both reduce cocoa production and control cocoa-leaf marketing, but that those same state policies have actually strengthened the Left-of-Center labor unions and opposition political parties. Moreover, while the international war on drugs has thus far proved only

From Kevin Healy, "Political Ascent of Bolivia's Peasant Coca Leaf Producers," *Journal of Interamerican Studies and World Affairs* 33(1): 87–122, 1991.

minimally effective in curbing the flow of drugs from the Andean region, it has succeeded in antagonizing the *sindicato* organization of coca-leaf growers to the point that anti-U.S. sentiment is widespread throughout the Bolivian countryside.

To describe this development, the first section will outline the organizational characteristics of the coca-growers movement and how it employs its power at the local level. The second section examines the increase in the coca producers' political power in relation to the broader, national network of other peasant *sindicatos* in Bolivia—the *Confereración Sindical Unica de Trabajadores Campesinos de Bolivia* (CSUTCB). The third section then looks at the relations of the coca growers with the national union organization that represents Bolivian labor as a whole—the *Central Obrere Boliviano* (COB). Next, the fourth section describes the relationship that has begun to emerge between the coca growers and those political parties in the Left-of-Center opposition. The fifth section discusses how effective the coca-leaf growers have been, over the past decade, in their quest to influence state-directed policies and programs designed to control coca-leaf production/distribution. Finally, the sixth, and concluding, section attempts to evaluate the impact of these peasant resistance strategies on national political changes.

1. THE COCA-LEAF GROWERS MOVEMENT

Those *SINDICATOS* which have proved to be the most activist are located in the Chapare, a tropical coca-leaf producing area in the department of Cochabamba. Peasant *sindicatos* were first organized in Bolivia in 1953 as part of the national agrarian reform program; they subsequently become institutionalized in all the regions (and most of the communities) in the Bolivian countryside—including the Chapare. The local Chapare *sindicatos* were created not only to enable new settlers to establish their claims to virgin forested farmlands, but also to address a wide range of community development needs.

The Chapare resettlement zone incorporates parts of the provinces of Chapare, Carrasco, and Tiraque. However, the seats of government of all of these provinces are located in their respective mountain, rather than tropical, areas. During the 1960s, the first peasant federation of *sindicatos* emerged in the Chapare to represent the interests of the area's peasant colonists before the state, other public and private agencies, and within the Bolivian labor movement. Today, peasant farmers (representing 40,000 families) in this area belong to 160 local community-based *sindicatos*, under the umbrella of 30 sub-federations (*centrales*) which, in turn, are organized into 5 federations.[2] Approximately 85% of the Chapare *sindicatos* come under the jurisdiction of two of these federations: the *Federación Especial de Trabajadores Campesinos del Trópico de Cochabamba* (FETCTC] and the *Federación de Carrasco* (CIDRE, 1989b).[3]

The Chapare federations discussed here have their roots in two organizations which have been active since the late 1970s: the *Federación Especial Agraria Tropical* and the *Federación Especial de Colonizadores de Chimore* (Canedo Ovellana and Canelas Zannieb, 1983). The first was under the tutelage of successive Bolivian governments, and the second organization was an autonomous peasant social force. With the restoration of a civilian democratic government and civil liberties in 1982, the government-dominated federation became more active and free-wheeling, and other federations subsequently emerged to play a local political role. Although *sindicatos* have been active in local political conflicts since the 1960s, they only acquired their national reputation in the 1980s through their opposition to, and mobilization against, those state policies designed to control coca-leaf production.

Similar to prevailing patterns throughout rural Bolivia, the *sindicatos* are a form of local government in this resettlement area. They possess the authority, legitimacy, and power to establish private land boundaries for new colonists, to influence transport fares, and to manage and tax coca-leaf markets in the towns of the Chapare, with the funds so raised to be used for local, small-scale public works programs (roads, schools, health clinics, and so on).[4] *Sindicatos* have the authority to hold members accountable for participation in collective-action protests through sanctions such as fines. Various factors—increasing income, harsh treatment, constant threats from Bolivian law-enforcement agencies, and state efforts to reduce their coca-leaf fields—have combined to convert them into some of the most conscientious, dues-paying members of Bolivia's rural *sindicatos*. Members typically subscribe $1 per month per household to pay for the organizational expenditures/activities of their leaders at all (local, *central*, and regional) levels. Chapare peasants participate in frequent *sindicato* meetings at the local level, and they send their delegates to the congresses of the *centrales* and federations to devise their political strategies, exchange information about government activities, and choose direct-action tactics to thwart state efforts to control their means of livelihood. Routine local congresses frequently receive major coverage in Bolivia's national news media.

During the 1980s, a decade of restored democratic rule in Bolivia, Chapare *sindicatos* have maintained a comparatively high level of political activism. They have resorted to organized action at the grassroots level in an effort to counter the unrelenting pressure, both national and international, to reduce the production, and control the distribution, of the coca leaf on which they depend. This pressure comes from their own national government, from the U.S. State Department (pushed by the U.S. Congress), and—more recently—from the governments of Western Europe. Political pressure on the Chapare producers escalated during the second half of the 1980s due to both (a) the ineffectiveness of government drug-interdiction programs and (b) the enormous expansion of coca-leaf production (Healy, 1986; Henkel, 1989; Craig, 1987; Lee, 1990).

Among the Andean countries, Bolivia was perceived as a place in which it would be fairly "easy" to wage a war on drugs due to its stable, "peaceful" environment, free from those armed conflicts among guerrilla armies, para-military squads, and the military which make crop-substitution and/or interdiction programs so difficult to implement in Peru and Colombia. However, the conflict between the state and peasantry over this issue intensified when a new anti-coca law (the *Ley de Régimen de la Coca y Sustancias Controladas*) was first proposed and then passed by the Bolivian congress in 1988. The thrust of this law was to spell out a plan to eradicate coca-leaf production in the Chapare over a 10-year period (Healy, 1988c: 110).

In establishing a timeframe by which coca production in the Chapare would become progressively illegal, the *Ley de Régimen de la Coca* would not only convert a formerly legal activity into an illegal one but, by extension, the peasant cultivators of the coca leaf into societal delinquents. Peasant antagonism toward the state on this issue derives from (1) the threat of eradicating an essential crop and (2) the demonstrated inability—between 1975–1989— of state-directed, rural-development programs to provide cash-crop alternatives to coca-leaf growing in the Chapare.[5]

The Chapare *sindicatos* have established themselves as Bolivia's most effective, consistently active peasant groups engaged in exerting political pressure to influence changes in national policy. While complying with a democratic commitment to eschew violence in pursuit of their goals, they have employed a variety of direct-action tactics which have invariably compelled the state to give consideration to their economic and political interests. Over the past 7 years, they have galvanized hundreds of local *sindicatos* (including tens of thousands of members) to organize 6 major roadblocks, numerous hunger strikes (involving dozens of peasant leaders), and mass marches and public-protest rallies (in the small towns of the Chapare and the cities of Cochabamba and La Paz), and at least a half dozen sit-ins and occupations of local government offices. These forms of collective protest have led to a number of negotiated agreements with the state which have modified official efforts in various areas, like market control, local rural development, and programs for coca-leaf eradication (Healy, 1988c).[6]

These activist tactics have been mostly defensive in nature, a bona fide show of resistance to state efforts at control. The Chapare *sindicatos* have protested such issues as military occupations of the Chapare, congressional passage of new anti-coca laws, the state's allegedly experimental spraying of coca-leaf bushes, new land-tax policies, and the state's failure to comply with agreements that had been negotiated to protect Chapare interests. In addition, the coca producers have, upon occasion, taken the offensive in pushing alternative views via public actions. These have included advancing cultural values associated with the use of the coca leaf and proposing alternative legislation and programs for rural development.

Early in the 1980s, the Chapare *sindicatos* proved themselves to be audacious agrarian reformers. In 1983, under the protection of a Center-Left governing political coalition, the *Unidad Democrática Popular* (UDP), and with the assistance of the government's National Institute of Colonization, the Chapare *sindicatos* carried out a mini-land reform in their area. Local *sindicatos* organized, in a rapid, and ad hoc manner, the invasion of land owned by professionals, government employees, military officials, and commercial groups. Dozens of properties, generally ranging from 100–1,000 hectares, were carved up, either in toto or in part, by the peasant reformers.[7] Although their registered titles designated them to be used for "agro-industrial" purposes, the landholdings, which were grossly underutilized, had been acquired as government land grants. Consequently, the absentee owners had less legal ground to stand on in defending their rights to private property. This extensive amount of underutilized land became, therefore, a prime target for takeover by *sindicato*-led peasants who were, at one and the same time, fleeing the drought-ridden highlands and seeking to cash in on the rising coca-leaf-related income.[8] This was the only local land reform in Bolivia during the 1970s and 1980s.

As part of the their strategy to resist the state's attempts at control, the Chapare federations defended their economic interests by forging alliances with private human rights organizations, nongovernmental organizations (NGOs) engaged in social development and research, civic organizations, the clergy, social scientists, and European solidarity organizations. For example, the principal leader of the FETCTC traveled to Europe for 6 weeks to locate markets for substitute crops and to present project proposals for rural development financing to donor agencies. He also met, and planned conferences, with Peruvian coca-leaf growers in order to forge Andean alliances to resist efforts to eradicate coca-leaf cultivation. With the held of Bolivian technical advisors, peasant federations drafted their own rural development plan for the Chapare. In recent years, they have also lobbied the Catholic Church to support their cause.

2. THE COCA-LEAF GROWERS AND NATIONAL PEASANT UNIONS

At the start of the 1980s, the *Federación Especial de Chapare* was an obscure federation of peasant *sindicatos*, a grassroots organization far removed from the national political spotlight. By the end of the decade, several Chapare *sindicato* federations have entered the vanguard of the peasant organizations for the whole country, even, arguably, for the entire national trade union movement. By 1985, the Chapare federation had displaced the Aymara *Katarista* (formerly the *altiplano*'s most politically and socially active *sindicato*) and has subsequently increased its labor *sindicato* power through mobilization actions and other political strategies.[9]

The *Federación Especial de Trabajadores Campesinos del Trópico de Cochabamba* (FETCTC) is a member of the *Confederación Sindical Unica de Trabajadores Campesinos de Bolivia* (CSUTCB), Bolivia's most representative peasant-labor organization,[10] which was founded in 1977 during the opening toward civilian rule and constitutional democracy. The organization reaches down to the smallest Bolivian hamlet to incorporate peasant households into its multi-tier organizational structure, linking the smallest communities, provinces, and regions with the national executive leadership in the capital city.

The FETCTC has increased the influence of the coca-leaf growers within the CSUTCB in a variety of ways.[11] Every two years, the CSUTCB holds national congresses that bring *sindicato* delegates together from the seven regions of Bolivia. The congresses draw up an agency (*plataforma de lucha*) that addresses major peasant concerns, i.e., their social and economic grievances with the state and market—in short, their bona fide interests as peasant farmers in Bolivia. In 1987, some 1,400 delegates attended the CSUTCB congress, representing 900,000–1,000,000 peasants nationwide. At the insistence of the Chapare federations, a *Comisión de Coca* has become one of the permanent working committees of this congress, as a way to keep the coca-leaf issue in the forefront of discussion. To underscore its importance further, Chapare delegates to the 1987 congress also succeeded in placing this issue on the agendas of the "political" and "economic" commissions as well.[12] Such persistent, adroit promotion of this issue has elevated the defense of the coca-leaf, and its multiple uses, into a major rallying cry for the small farmers of Bolivia.

Representatives of the Chapare federation have adopted the argument that protecting coca protects Bolivian culture in order to convince those CSUTCB delegates and leaders from non-coca-growing regions to support their position that coca cultivation should continue and efforts to eradicate it should be opposed. For several thousand years, the coca leaf has been an essential part of a rural lifestyle (medicinal, ritual, social) for the indigenous majority in various regions of the Andes. This enables the Chapare federations to make the case that (1) coca is synonymous with Andean culture and (2) that eradication by foreign powers will destroy their way of life and cultural heritage. This cultural perspective has enabled them to attract support from traditional coca-chewing (as opposed to producing) regions, such as Chuquisaca, Potosí and Oruro. Upon return from the national congresses, union leaders carry this political message back to their home regions, where subsequent meetings and local congresses then discuss external threats to the "sacred leaf." Although the new anti-coca law contains clauses which stipulate that 12,000 hectares be reserved for the growing of coca to meet the consumption needs of the native-Andean majority, the Chapare federations have construed the law, in their presentation to peasant congresses, as one that would totally eradicate the leaf, thus suppressing consumption (and, by extension, the interests of the chewers) as well as cultivation, which is the interest of the producers.[13]

Chapare activists have introduced overtones of emotional nationalism into their argument by representing the role of the U.S. government to assist in (if not oversee) eradication efforts as a violation of national sovereignty. They point to the activities of the U.S. Drug Enforcement Agency (DEA) and its agents in Bolivia, to the various joint Bolivia–U.S. military maneuvers in Cochabamba (during the 1980s), to Operation Blast Furnace (1986), to the anti-coca leaf law (1988) and various government decrees, to UMOPAR (*Unidad Movile de Patrullaje Rural*), which is the U.S.–financed, Bolivian law-enforcement agency in the coca-leaf-growing zones, and to the apparent threat of aerial spraying of coca-leaf fields as tangible evidence of their "anti-imperialist" argument.[14] The Chapare federations take credit for being the most aggressive of Bolivia's grassroots labor organizations in protecting the country's national sovereignty, a role which—they argue—entitles them to a position of greater leadership within the national organizations.

To dramatize the need to resist "foreign intervention" and to emphasize the legitimacy of the coca leaf as central to Andean cultural values, the Chapare producers recently organized the first of what is to become an annual event, the *Día de Acullico* (day of coca-leaf chewing, or "chew-in"), to celebrate traditional uses of the coca leaf. Delegates from the various regions were bused in to the Chapare to join the multitudes representing local federations and *centrales*. The unprecedented event, involving thousands of participants, consisted of both a mass rally and a parade—with coca-leaf costumes, militant speeches, marching bands, *sindicato* banners, anti-U.S. chants, avid coca-leaf chewing, and displays of colorful textiles.

The cultural-defense argument advanced by the Chapare *sindicatos* has found a receptive audience in Bolivia due to the fact that the coca leaf has indeed been a centerpiece of Andean society from time immemorial. Thus, despite external pressure from the international community, the coca cultivators are able to marshall a domestic support for their position which would not be available to them if some other illicit crop, such as marijuana, were involved.

For example, for several decades the United States government has adhered to a self-serving policy that creates disincentives for Bolivian peasants to grow wheat. Cheap U.S. imports and food aid donations have adversely affected prices and, therefore, the incentive for local growers to produce, thereby undermining any prospects for small farmers to expand their wheat production. However, not only are wheat producers a minority among the small farmers in the highlands, but they also lack any similar cultural appeal that might enlist the support of national producer interests. Wheat growers are just unable to marshal the degree of national political clout to resist state policies, through the CSUTCB, which the coca-leaf growers have achieved.

Both to add legitimacy as well as to garner support from various peasant *sindicato* groups, the Chapare federations have recently begun to make their case in terms of economic benefits, within the context of a national recession.[15] The existence of other coca-leaf growing zones outside the Chapare-Cochabamba zone—within the department of La Paz (the Yungas provinces) and the department of Santa Cruz (Yapacane area)—makes this argument appealing to the corresponding CSUTCB peasant delegations and their peasant allies within each region. Efforts to create organizational solidarity with these other peasant groups has enabled the Chapare federations to organize the first national association of coca-leaf growers: Asociación Nacional de Productores de Coca (ANAPCOCA). This operates as a political force parallel to the national *sindicato* organizational structure and has galvanized the national *sindicato* association of peasant colonists, the *Confederación Nacional de Colonizadores de Bolivia* (or CNCB), to render multiple forms of support as well.

Leaders of the Chapare federations claim that the coca-leaf economy has positive employment effects while the national economy, caught in a prolonged recession, produces few such gains.[16] Peasant leaders are well aware of the steady stream of Bolivian highland peasant youth to the Chapare in search of employment as another factor which swells support for Chapare positions within the CSUTCB and other regional federations. Anywhere from 50,000–100,000 peasant youth from poor mountain communities to the west of the Chapare make short-run trips to work as day-laborers in coca-leaf production and as *pisacocas* in the clandestine pits where coca-paste is processed. This number increases during times of natural disasters, such as droughts and frosts in the highlands, and worsening economic conditions. This temporary employment represents an important source of income for impoverished peasant families strapped for cash in the department of Cochabamba, Potosí, Oruro, La Paz and Chuquisaca. Since 1985, the need for this extra cash has only increased, due to the devastating effects which the International Monetary Fund's (IMF) structural adjustment program have had on peasant agriculture.[17]

The Chapare peasants have also exhibited their political skill in exploiting other issues, particularly vis-à-vis the environmental consequences that flow from the political solutions prescribed to halt production of coca leaf and its processing into cocaine. The Chapare federations have made aerial spraying of the coca-leaf fields with toxic herbicides into "the ecology issue," by posing this potential state action as the *only* problem, while glossing over other serious ecological hazards. Hence, on the one hand they have been in the forefront of the campaign against the forced eradication of coca-leaf fields by chemicals while, on the other hand, they ignore the environmental damage caused by the dumping of cocaine-processing chemicals into the rivers and streams of the Chapare, not to mention overproduction of the coca leaf itself, which destroys rain forests and depletes soil nutrients, eventually leading to desertification. It was the incessant hammering on this ecology issue by the Chapare federations which lay behind the *Ley de La Régimen* article which bans herbicidal spraying. In fact, the platforms of both the Chapare federations and the CSUTCB laud the coca leaf as conveying an environmental benefit on society, due to its classification as a "renewable resource."

The combination of forging alliances and developing more sophisticated political skills have enabled the leaders and activists from the Chapare federations to increase their influence within the CSUTCB. For one thing, their activism of the 1980s, which challenged state policies and programs, has enabled them to orchestrate an unprecedented (for a single micro-region) increase in the number of their delegates to the national congress.

In Bolivia, the national peasant organizations hold congresses every two years to elect new officers and plan political strategies. At the 1987 congress in Cochabamba, the Chapare federations were able to increase their delegates from 19 to 80 (CEDOIN, 1988). The congress coincided with a time when the political mobilization of the Chapare groups was reaching its peak, which the other peasant federations were going through a period of disarray, experienced as partisan divisions, political apathy, and a falloff in their own activism, both social and political.

To some extent, this situation reflected widespread disillusionment with the government in office and its inability to rescue the economy. The government was in the hands of a Left-of-Center coalition, the *Unidad Democrática Popular* (UDP) (1982–85), which, though entering power with considerable peasant support, had failed to respond to their grievances effectively. At the same time, its policy fostered de-capitalization in the countryside by means of a record-breaking hyperinflation. Thus, across the spectrum of Bolivian peasant activism, the Chapare federations appeared united and strong by comparison.

The Chapare area had also gained strength due to its growth in population, a product of the peasant migration associated with the coca-cocaine boom, enabling their leaders to claim that this demographic change had gone underrecognized in their previous delegate representation. As their political activism brought them attention on the national scene, so the increase in the number of their delegates enabled them to make themselves heard, and carry more weight, within the congresses. They commanded a formidable bloc of delegates to advance their basic economic and political interests, particularly as these related to coca production and the state policies affecting it.

One example will give an indication of their use of this clout. From 1977, when the CSUTCB was founded, its principal executive officer had been Genaro Flores, a founder and Bolivia's most veteran peasant leader at that time. Despite the fact that Flores had supported the cause of the coca-leaf growers on many occasions, the Chapare leaders felt that his removal would bring them more influence with the CSUTCB. Consequently, since the Chapare delegates voted as a bloc and contributed financial resources to the parent organization, they were able to play a major role at the 1987 congress in the *sindicato* opposition to his continued leadership. With the support of the Chapare federations, the opposition to Flores was able to divide the congress sufficiently that a follow-up (or "extraordinary") congress was mandated to be held the following year (1988) in Potosi, at which Genaro Flores, and his *Katarista* followers, were finally unseated.

During this "extraordinary" congress in Potosi, Chapare federation representatives seized the opportunity to place their members on the key commissions (political, economic and even, health) to insure that the coca-leaf issue assumed a high priority on the agendas of the main working committees. In the national CSUTCB congress of 1989, a Chapare federation candidate competed for the highest position of the newly elected officers, while other of their members were elected to the executive offices of secretary and *sindicato* training coordinator, respectively.

A measure of the political development of these federations has been their ability to garner support and aid for their high-pressure tactics from those peasant federations from non-coca-growing areas. In 1987, the Chapare federations staged a major roadblock along the main roads of Cochabamba, particularly those between Cochabamba and the cities of Oruro and Santa Cruz, which were key supply routes as interregional transport arteries, in an effort to force the government to sign decrees for the *Plan Integral de Desarrollo y Sustitución* (PIDYS).[18] However, the success of this pressure tactic hinged upon participation by allies from the neighboring regional *sindicatos*, who resided in the non-coca-growing mountain areas along the road.

Examples of this kind of reciprocal protest-action among *sindicatos* date back to the early 1980s. In 1983, the *sindicato* federations from the departments of La Paz, Oruro, and Potosí, together with the CSUTCB, organized to block the road between the cities of La Paz and Oruro for almost a week. As a result, they were able to pressure the state into signing numerous decrees which favored peasant interests, including "free marketing of the coca leaf." Also in 1983, a roadblock was set up in the town of Mizque (western Cochabamba) to focus attention on the low price of wheat and to protest government subsidies to non-producers; the "free marketing of coca" was included on the protest agenda at the time. Both cases bear witness to the precedent of peasant groups outside a given zone of operations reciprocating with support for one another, as subsequently happened on behalf of the Chapare *sindicatos*.

This alliance between the coca-leaf growers and peasants from other regions was once again in evidence when peasant leaders throughout the country went on a hunger strike, in January 1989, to protest the government's announcement of its new coca-leaf law (the 1988 *Ley de la Régimen de la Coca y Sustancias Controladas*), which set forth the conditions by which coca-leaf acreage would be reduced over time (10 years). Peasant leaders from various non-coca-leaf-growing regions participated. By joining the strike, they were able to add their own specific grievances (such as new land taxes in indigenous communities) and petitions to the peasant agenda to be presented to the national government.[19] Not only did the broader peasant participation in this direct action tactic add clout to the protest of the coca-leaf growers, but it ultimately generated benefits for the other non-coca grievances as well. For, in order to end the strike, the government not only agreed to give the coca-leaf growers a direct role in decision making for the planning and implementation of the PIDYS program, but it also agreed to repeal the unpopular land taxes.

The mechanism designed to implement this joint government/coca-grower decision-making was the *Comisión Nacional de Desarrollo Alternativo* (CONADAL), which is comprised of 6 representatives from the government ministries and 5 representatives from coca-grower *sindicatos* and their overarching national organizations, such as the CSUTCB. This new decision-making role involves monitoring foreign-aid funds earmarked for Chapare-based government programs. It also gives the peasant *sindicatos* some leverage over state planning/implementation of new rural development investments. If fully enacted, this could enable them to serve as watchdogs for peasant interests in overseeing the "crop substitution" or alternative development, programs.

3. CHAPARE *SINDICATOS* AND NATIONAL TRADE UNION POLITICS

As the prime movers and shakers within the CSUTCB, the influence of the coca-leaf growers carried into the *Central Obrero Boliviano* (COB) as well, which, until recently, had incorporated, the national peasant *sindicato* movement within its larger organizational structure. Founded during the social revolution of 1952, the COB is Bolivia's national confederation of trade unions, representing labor groups of all kinds, not only peasants but also miners, factory workers, petroleum workers, school-teachers, bank employees, and so on. For almost 40 years, it has been the most militant, representative voice of the Bolivian working class and, as such, has been a tremendous opposition political force for the state—whether civilian or military—to reckon with. Although the peasantry is the largest single labor group in the country, historically the peasants have been treated as second-class union members by the leading COB labor leaders and affiliated groups. One peasant leader complained that "we are the spare tire, rather than one of the four main wheels of the COB," by which he meant that other labor groups—miners, oil, railway, and factory workers—were considered the main actors of the labor movement.

However, through the activism of the Chapare federations, the CSUTCB has been able to lay claim to a greater decision-making role within the COB. The Chapare federations, despite having only four delegates to the COB, have wielded influence disproportionate to their numbers, gaining the respect and attention of these labor leaders as a consequence of the activities of the peasant *sindicatos* in the 1980s. As their self-confidence has grown, so has their political development and ambition. At a recent local congress, Chapare federation leaders stated that each of their 30 *centrales* should be represented in the COB by one delegate. Though they remain far short of that goal, the influence of their *sindicato* can be measured in other ways.

The fact that activism has generally declined in Bolivia's most powerful labor groups has led the COB leaders to take a new interest in the mobilized, and apparently radicalizing, peasantry of the Chapare. For example, the last few years have seen COB leaders become part of the team bargaining with various government ministers over the legislation and executive decrees related to coca-leaf production and alternate rural development in the Chapare. Filemon Escobar, a veteran labor leader and prominent COB spokesman for many decades, has become a highly visible negotiator with government ministries on behalf of the coca-leaf grow-

ers and a dynamic orator at the mass rallies and marches in the Chapare and city of Cochabamba. Juan Lechín, Bolivia's most well-known labor leader over the past 40 years, has also become a paid professional advisor to the Chapare federations in recent years.

By the same token, the entire COB executive committee attends protests organized by the Chapare federations, evincing an interest in a rural *sindicato* federation from the hinterlands that would have been unheard of a decade ago. Because the ability of the coca growers to mobilize politically (its *poder de convocatorio*) has become so strong, perhaps the strongest of any labor group in Bolivia, the COB leadership is anxious to lend support to, and become visibly associated with, their collective-action protests.

Given their own brand of radical *sindicato* politics, COB leaders find the anti-U.S. discourse of the Chapare federations both appealing and familiar. Thus, when peasant growers charge the United States with "imperialist intervention" for advocating that coca be eradicated, this stance is consistent with the COB's own political traditions and it is easy for such leaders as Filemon Escobar to embellish such charges with polemics of their own. Throughout its history, COB leaders have allied themselves with that part of Latin America's political culture of the Left which criticizes U.S. "intervention" and U.S. support of economic and military elites at the expense of the needs of the poor majority. Consequently, it is easy for the coca-leaf growers to borrow from the "anti-imperialist" rhetoric and slogans of the COB, and for the two groups mutually to reinforce one anothers' political biases.

The political ascent of the Chapare federations within the COB has been helped by their demonstrated ability to enlist the support of other COB member groups or regional trade unions, such as the *Central Obrero Departmental* (from Cochabamba), for their protest events. In a march held in July 1987 to protest the draft proposal for the anti-coca law (which eventually became the *Ley de la Régimen de la Coca y Sustancias Controladas*), the Chapare federations managed to enlist the participation of university students and employees, miners, factory workers and school teachers.

Similarly, at the 8th COB Congress (in 1989), the *Comisión de la Coca* included workers from a wide variety of labor groups—a graphic arts worker, school teachers, miners, factory workers, and construction workers—in addition to the 7 peasant delegates. The report of the *Comisión* began with the statement that

> Our Aymara and Quechua ancestors knew the virtues of the coca leaf and, for this reason, it was considered a gift of nature for the happiness of men (Comisión de la Coca, 1989) [author translation].

However, building solidarity and alliances with non-peasant labor groups remains in an incipient stage, considerably less than the solidarity shown toward the Bolivian mine workers in their heyday (of many decades) of organizing antigovernment activities. Nonetheless, the emerging alliances, no matter how tenuous, offer good indication of the increased political sophistication of the coca-growers movement.

The rapid rise of the Chapare federation influence within the COB owes something to the decline in activism by the *Federación Sindical de Trabajadores Mineros de Bolivia* (FSTMB), at one time the single most active and radical labor organization in the country, with a history of militancy dating back to 1944 (Nash, 1979). The FSTMB was devastated when the state-owned COMIBOL (*Corporación Minera Boliviana*) mines were closed by government decree in 1985, and 23,000 out of 28,000 mineworkers were laid off. Closing the state mines was one of the harshest, as well as most socially dramatic, steps taken by the Paz Estenssoro government in implementing its new program to privatize the economy and dismantle the model of state capitalism which had been put in place as part of the 1952 social revolution.

No longer able to depend upon a militant FSTMB, and with similar economic and political changes affecting the unionized factory workers, the COB became somewhat moribund. Social analysts have argued that it has sunk to its lowest level of social protest and political pressure in years, even including periods of military repression (Rodríguez, 1989a). A labor organization known throughout Latin America for its aggressive actions and effectiveness in securing wage increases and social benefits for its members, and whose national strikes often threatened to destabilize national governments, has become only a pale image of its former self.

It was during the 1989 COB congress that the CSUTCB demanded that the peasant sector become the "second force"—after the miners—in this organization. This demand could only be made, and receive serious consideration, as a result of the demonstrable increase in Chapare political militancy that took place in the latter half of the 1980s. Due to its staunch defense of Andean culture and sovereignty, the CSUTCB felt empowered to petition for greater peasant representation within the COB. When the latter denied this request, the CSUTCB withdrew from the COB. It took this course for two reasons: (1) to avoid any open rupture within the congress, which would have weakened the labor movement at a critical juncture in national politics, when a new Right-of-Center government had just arrived on the scene; and (2)—and of equal importance—to demonstrate its strength by challenging the COB. Could the latter maintain its ability to mount effective political protests (upon which its negotiating power depended) without CSUTCB activists, led by their most militant group, the Chapare federations? Thus, the relatively recent empowerment of the Chapare federations was a critical factor in enabling the CSUTCB to withdraw from the COB, at least temporarily, on the hope, if not expectation, that it might enlarge its participation and leadership role in that body at some future time.[20]

4. COCA GROWERS AND THE NATIONAL POLITICAL PARTIES

Various pressures—foreign and domestic, political and police—have pushed these provincial peasants into the wider national political arena of multi-party organizations. At the same time, the political parties of the Left (just like the leaders of the larger labor organizations) have also been pushed toward allying themselves with the peasants by their own diminishing domestic social bases and the need this has inspired to look for ways to "beef up" their own constituencies. Since the political debâcle of the *Unidad Democrática Popular* (UDP) government (1982–85), Bolivia's Left-wing parties have witnessed a dwindling of electoral support. However, by taking up the coca-leaf cause, Leftist parties could not only enhance their popularity and influence with the Chapare producers, but also with one of their most coveted constituencies—i.e., CSUTCB delegates from all over the country, who have embraced the issue with great fervor.

As the government increased its pressure on the coca-leaf growers over the past decade, the Chapare federations were forced to seek access to power by establishing links with national political parties. Opposition parties became the most likely allies in their campaign of protest and resistance to state programs, laws, and policies aimed at the control or reduction (if not outright elimination) of coca-leaf production. During the latter 1980s, these allies have come mainly from the political Left, given the Right-of-Center stance of the *Movimiento Nacional Revolucionario* (MNR) government (1985–89), which has pursued coca-reduction with greater vigor than its predecessors (Healy, 1988). Although famous as the party responsible for Bolivia's social revolution of the 1950s, the MNR of the 1980s embraced a program of structural adjustment (privatization, trade liberalization, etc.) which has served to undermine central features of the very economic structures which they themselves created during that earlier incarnation.

In recent years, such political parties as the *Movimiento Bolivia Libre* (MBL) and the *Partido Socialista* have served as vehicles for articulating the interests of the coca-growers within the halls of parliament in its debates on pending legislation and other state measures (Healy, 1988c). the MBL is a splinter group which broke off from the *Movimiento Izquierda Revolucionario* (MIR) when the latter rejoined the UDP coalition government in 1984. Led by a prominent Leftist, Antonio Aranibar, the MBL retained a Left-of-Center political stance faithful to the social democratic principles which its organizational parent subsequently abandoned. The *Partido Socialista* is a small Left-of-Center party which emerged in the 1970s around the influential, charismatic personality of the late Marcelo Quiroga Santa Cruz, who was assassinated by the Bolivian military in 1980 (without his charismatic leadership, it has experienced a significant decline in popularity). By forging ties to the parliament via these political groups, the Chapare federations have opened another arena in which to protect and defend their interests from incursions by the state.

For example, the *Eje de Convergencia*, a coalition of small Leftist parties (including the Communists, the *Bloque Popular Patriótico*, *Alianza Patriótica*, and *MIR-Masis*), recently issued a formal statement declaring that the coca-leaf producers should be considered the vanguard of the Bolivian labor movement since their interests conflicted most directly with those of the U.S. government (*Eje*, 1989). Prior to a national peasant congress held in 1989, another political coalition, the *Izquierda Unida* (organized in 1988, the IU was made up of the MBL, its strongest member, plus the Communist Party and *MIR-Masts*, another MIR splinter group), stated the conflict over the future of coca-leaf production as follows:

> In addition to the North American thesis that, in order to have no cocaine in Bolivia, there should be no coca leaf in Bolivia, there should be added another thesis, far more alarming than the former. They say that in order that there be no more coca in Bolivia, we must extinguish the Andean culture for, to the extent that this culture exists, there will always be coca (IU, 1989).

Similar to its efforts among workers in Bolivian mining districts in the past, Left-wing parties have targeted the Chapare as an important area in which to recruit members, given the radicalizing effects of Chapare opposition to both state and U.S. policies (Rodríguez, 1989b). Not surprisingly, many federation-sponsored protests held in the Chapare and the city of Cochabamba give center stage to such representatives of *Izquierda Unida* as Antonio Aranibar (IU candidate for president in 1989) along with various leaders of the COB.

The evolution of voter preferences in the tropical zones of Chapare, Carrasco, and Tiraque also show this trend toward support of opposition parties and/or the political Left and a corresponding drop in support for the governing MNR party, sponsor of the anti-coca law and related eradication programs. These electoral trends reveal a radicalization of Chapare political attitudes and of new political allegiances, both of which are likely a response to state efforts to control coca-leaf production.

The changes in voter preferences are evident from the analyses of the relative percentages for the major political parties/fronts in the presidential election of 1985, municipal elections of 1987, and presidential election of 1989, respectively. For example, in the zone under discussion, support for the MNR party, which won a plurality in 1985, dropped precipitously from 31.25% [in 1985] to only 14% [in 1987] and then to 7% [1989] (CIDRE, 1989). The *Acción Democrática Nacionalista* (ADN) Party, which co-governed with the MNR, rose from 11.20% to 21.75% between 1985 and 1987 but then fell to only 8.3% in the 1989 presidential election (CIDRE, 1989). Former dictator Hugo Banzer Suárez (1971–78) created the ADN as a Right-of-Center party to represent the interests of the agro-industrial elite and large ranchers from the Santa Cruz region, along with other economic elites from the commerce and banking sectors. In recent years, Banzer has been effective in obtaining votes from large sectors of the middle-class as well as from low-income groups employed in the informal sector in urban areas.

The electoral performance of the *Izquierda Unida* (IU) has been the mirror opposite of the MNR. From a base of only 1.76% in 1985, support for the IU rose to 10.17% [in 1987] and then to 33.16% [in 1989] (CIDRE, 1989a).[21] In the Chapare's tropical zone, which has the greatest number of coca-leaf producers and the most militant *sindicato* federation, the IU garnered 42.33% of the vote. This is the highest percentage of the vote received by any political party in any of the three elections in this region and is particularly remarkable given that the IU obtained only 7% of the national vote. In addition, the IU had more votes annulled for minor technicalities by local judges representing the ADN, MNR and MIR parties than any of the other participating fronts and parties.

The rise in popularity of the *Movimiento Izquierda Revolucionario* (MIR) during this period (1985–1989) also presents an interesting case for examination. In spite of supporting (1) the unpopular U.S. intervention of troops to destroy cocaine factories (1986), which outraged Chapare producers because it eliminated their markets for coca leaf, and (2) the new anti-coca law in congress, the MIR campaigned in the Chapare on an astute, but vague, platform that defended the rights of the coca-leaf producer. Jaime Paz Zamora, the eventual president, even issued his presidential proclamation in the Chapare while draped with a wreath of coca leaves.

It is probable that peasant voters for the MIR did so from a perspective of political realism since, unlike the IU, it possessed a genuine chance to win the presidential election. In the past (1970s and early 1980s), the MIR had run on fairly progressive platforms (opposing military government and advocating social equity for small farmers) so that some peasant growers most likely perceived the MIR to have a residue of sympathy for the labor struggles of their group. In search of rural votes and with a short-term electoral perspective, the MIR sought to project itself in opposition to prevailing national laws and policies. During the 1985–89 period, Chapare support for the MIR climbed from 14.45% in 1985, to 21.6% and 25.05%, respectively (CIDRE, 1989). Thus, over the past few years, the IU and MIR in effect changed places with the ADN and MNR as the leading political forces and vote-getters in this area. Chapare federation endorsements of the political parties they preferred also reflected this opposition pattern: the FETCTC endorsed the *Izquierda Unida*, and the *Federación de Carrasco* supported the MIR.

However it is necessary to qualify the above-mentioned figures by acknowledging the extremely low voter turnout in the Chapare provinces: less than 20% of the eligible voters took part in the 1989 election. Rather than expressing voter apathy, it appears that voter participation was kept to a minimum by placing obstacles in the way of voting, such as making it difficult to obtain government documents required for identification purposes and by providing only a small number of provisional local voting stations to serve the large, widely dispersed population (personal communications with federation leaders). In addition, since vehicles are prohibited from operating on election day (a standard practice during Bolivian elections), many Chapare residents were compelled to walk dozens of kilometers—which also adversely affected the voter turnout. The fact that the MNR and ADN set up so few voting stations permitted the IU, as well as more objective observers (Rodríguez, 1989), to perceive this as a tactic designed to undercut the apparent groundswell of IU support which could have changed the election outcome substantially, particularly for the department of Cochabamba. The lack of total votes prevented the Chapare area from sending its own peasant coca-leaf grower representative to the Bolivian parliament on the IU ticket. They only earned an alternate position for use in the event an elected candidate from Cochabamba is unable to assume office.

5. POLITICAL EFFECTIVENESS

What has this newly acquired political power meant for the federations of peasant *sindicatos* in terms of protecting their interest in growing, and freely marketing, the coca leaf? During the 1980s, various programs and laws to reduce production of the coca leaf were instituted by the government. The Bolivian government's *Plan Trienal de Lucha contra al Narcotráfico*, which was another serious effort to reduce coca-leaf production in the Chapare, established a timetable by which 50,000 hectares of coca would be eradicated over a 2-year period. In 1988, this plan was supplanted by the *De de la Régimen de la Coca y Sustancias Controladas*, which set a 10-year timetable to eradicate production in the Chapare. Nevertheless, neither program has made significant progress in achieving its ambitious goals.

The corresponding rural development plans sponsored by the U.S.-AID, plus weak implementation strategies, have contributed to the poor results. Note that, for a number of years, the U.S.-AID made 70% reduction in coca-leaf production a requirement to participate in programs that would grant credit to produce substitute crops. When this drew little response from the peasant farmers, the cut-off amount was subsequently reduced to 10% of an individual's production. The Bolivian government did try to implement alternative programs for rural development, but these have repeatedly met with failure for a variety of reasons—technical, political, and economic. Thus, rather than reducing—or reversing—itself, coca-leaf production has tended to increase during the 1980s.

Since 1982, the amount of land devoted to coca-leaf cultivation has increased from 35,000 to 80,000 hectares (CEDIB, 1989). This expansion took place due to the superior prices earned by coca via illicit markets in a context—national as well as regional—of difficult agricultural conditions. Despite stronger laws on the books and greater diplomatic and political pressure to reduce production, from both the United States and Western Europe, a mere 3,000 hectares had been eradicated in the Chapare area by the end of 1989.[22] Not only that, but some of this eradication took place in fields of old bushes which were about to cease production anyway. The Chapare federations did begin to reduce cultivation in a significant way in 1988, but this effort was subsequently suspended when it became apparent that the Bolivian government was failing to implement alternative development programs. Thus, in that same year the U.S. State Department reported that coca-leaf production in the Chapare increased by 20%.

Other gains achieved by the growers are equally important. Because of the persistent militancy and political activism of the Chapare federations, voluntary—rather than compulsory—reductions have been the order of the day, according to both the new laws and the PIDYS (*Plan Integral de Desarrollo y Sustitución*) development plan. The mobilized *sindicatos* also played an important role regarding the issue of aerial spraying of their fields with toxic herbicides as a means of eradication, both in preventing the Bolivian government from supporting this initiative as well as in preventing any actual attempts to do so.

The new *Ley de la Rígimen* also recognizes the legitimacy of traditional uses of the coca leaf in Andean society, thereby protecting some 12,000 hectares of this crop produced in the Yungas mountain valley region for domestic consumption. This constituted a major victory for peasant forces in view of the growing determination of the Bolivian government to enforce the Single Convention, a 1961 international treaty which called the eradication of the coca leaf over a 20-year period.

However, in other areas there were serious setbacks. First, despite peasant protests, they were unable to prevent passage of the law. Second, they were unsuccessful in modifying key articles in the *Ley de la Régimen de la Coca y Sustancias Controladas* which defined coca as a "controlled substance" (Healy, 1988c). Third, since constituents from those communities affected by Bolivia's growing internal drug consumption problem (i.e., drug abuse) have not yet mobilized (as have the coca leaf growers) to translate their concern into a political issue, the most powerful lobby for the passage of this new law was the U.S. Embassy. Drug policy has been a high priority on the U.S. foreign policy agenda. The U.S. government has enormous leverage to implement this priority in Bolivia given its foreign aid program, ministerial ties, and influence on decision-making in multilateral financial institutions. The lobbying power of the Chapare federations, despite their new political skills, have been no match for that of this powerful adversary.

Neither do the spokesmen in the Left-wing opposition have sufficient influence in the congress to overturn the new laws. In 1989, the MBL introduced a new bill which, if passed, would have effectively annulled the *Ley de la Régimen*. However, it had little resonance within a parliament dominated by conservative parties who supported the new anti-coca/cocaine legislation.

At the beginning of the 1980s, military governments attempted to establish state-controlled wholesale centers for the commercial distribution of the coca leaf in the Chapare. The peasant federations initially resisted these commercial centers because of their controlled low prices, corruption, and—perhaps—in reaction to the military's self-interest in the international drug trade. However, under pressure from the U.S. government, the first freely elected civilian government in decades, the *Unidad Democrática Popular*, also insisted on adopting government programs and decrees to exert state control over coca-leaf marketing (Healy, 1988c).

In view of government efforts to control the raw material for processing cocaine, it is noteworthy that, by the end of the decade, peasant *sindicatos*, rather than the state, control several of the legal coca-leaf markets in the Chapare. Various *centrales* in the zone have assumed this function in several of the small towns, such as 14 de September, Eterrazama, and Shinahota. This is an interesting precedent in light of the difficulties and failures encountered by Bolivian peasants in other regions to secure influence, and control, over the markets for other cash crops.

Ironically, this switch of institutional roles, from the state to local peasant-controlled *centrales*, was facilitated by the state's "free trade" approach to economic management, established by the government's sweeping decrees, of 1985, to affect structural adjustment and economic stabilization. By instituting the new decrees, the state not only abolished the government's role in marketing, but also inadvertently facilitated the takeover of this commercial institution by the strongest local governing organization in some of the Chapare towns—the peasant *sindicato*. However, the significance of this role is moot since most of the coca

leaf passes directly from the farm into hidden coca-paste-making pits on rural farm sites.

CONCLUSIONS

It is clear that, during the 1980s, the Chapare federations have become a major force within Bolivia's national political system. They have shifted the locus of the peasant movement back to the region of Cochabamba, the area which gave the initial impetus to Latin America's second major agrarian reform via the national social revolution of 1952. Rather than emerging as a social force from the Upper Cochabamba Valley, however, the *sindicato* federations have their center of gravity in that department's tropical rainforest, a reception point for peasant migrants from the various regions of Bolivia. A significant factor that stimulated peasant activism in the area was provided, in 1982, by the return of democratic civilian rule and the restoration of civil liberties in Bolivia.

Chapare peasant activism grew in response to increasingly strong pressure—economic, financial, military—from national as well as foreign (now including Western Europe) governments to find a supply-side solution to the worldwide problems of cocaine consumption and drug trafficking. In order to defend the interests of their coca-leaf growing constituents, the Chapare *sindicatos* have had to engender their own political development within Bolivia's democratic, constitutional government of the 1980s.

This newly-acquired power derives from their influence over a major political issue which affects the drug-consuming industrial nations of the North. The Bolivian government, highly dependent on its foreign aid life lines is under pressure from Western industrial nations, especially the United States, to show a demonstrable reduction in coca-leaf production. To achieve such results some measure of cooperation from the two principal Chapare federations is a sine qua non.

The high priority, both national and international, accorded this focus on drugs has been a major factor in encouraging the growers to acquire the sophisticated political skills needed to defend their interests and interact with other interest groups in the Bolivian democracy. Such skills include winning national attention through organized activities (i.e., mass rallies, marches, hunger strikes, road blockades), sponsoring cultural events (coca chew-ins), occupying government offices, developing *sindicato* organizations (and expanding their influence through strategic alliances with other political interest groups, such as labor *sindicatos* and political parties), as well as bargaining with government officials regarding issues important to peasant development. The degree of improvement in their negotiating skills can be measured in both the number of new agreements favorable to their interests as well as in the subsequent enforcement of he terms of those agreements.

At the same time, the Chapare federations have failed to achieve other of their objectives, such as blocking the passage of the anti-coca law and having a peasant representative in the national parliament. For the most part, these failures have resulted from two main factors: (1) a national congress and executive branch dominated by conservative political parties, and (2) the countervailing power of the United States government, which pursues a widely-supported foreign policy goal in a small, dependent Third World nation. The Chapare federations have also failed to secure the most powerful leadership position in the CUSTCB (Executive Secretary), nor have they been able to increase the number of their delegates to the COB, despite having gained remarkable influence within both national and labor organizations during the 1980s.

The Chapare federations were assisted in their political ascent by the decline in Bolivia's labor movement elsewhere in the country, which left a void to be filled by new activist labor sectors. The Chapare federations were able to gain ground within the two major national labor organizations, the CSUTCB and the COB, as a result, first, of peasant disillusionment with the political policies of the UDP Center-Left government and, second, the MNR government's displacement (*relocalización*) of miners to other occupations and regions. The political interests of the national labor organizations with the peasant *sindicato* federations were mutually reinforcing, as the former sought to stimulate labor movement dynamism within their own ranks and the latter sought strong political allies, advisors, and broader support for peasant issues. Opposition parties of the Left, suffering from electoral decline at the polls, also turned to the Chapare federation in search of both votes and compatible ideologies.

As the regional peasant movement became revitalized and gained new allies, it demonstrated its effectiveness by its ability to retard, though not eliminate, the programs designed to reduce, if not eradicate, coca-leaf cultivation. Although eradication might have been slowed even in the absence of this grassroots *sindicato* opposition, in Bolivia—as opposed to Colombia or Peru—the conflicts are being played out in terms of this nonviolent, peasant-led movement.

The campaign waged by the coca-leaf growers to protect their perceived interests has been a politicizing, and radicalizing, collective experience for many members. Likewise, the anti-U.S. sentiment of their leadership has spread throughout Bolivia through the broad *sindicato* organizational network of the CSUTCB. A kind of siege mentality has been fostered by a combination of factors: external pressure (through law enforcement agencies in the Chapare); the spread of crime and vice within a drug-trafficking sub-culture; a constant barrage of new laws, decrees, and policies; as well as by disjointed, ineffective rural development programs aimed at replacing the income derived from the coca leaf (Healy, 1988). The challenges to the source of the producers' high income have impelled them to improve their political skills, including the forging of alliances and becoming engaged actors within the national political process. This experience in national politics and in resisting programs to eradicate the coca leaf may lead to a broader, more active social base for Bolivia's struggling Leftist political parties and to new power configurations which will bring relatively greater political power for the CSUTCB and peasant participation within the COB, Bolivia's faltering national trade union.

ACRONYMS

ADN	Acción Democrática Nacionalista
ANAPCOCA	Asociación Nacional de Productores de Coca
AP	Alianza Patriótica
CNCB	Confederación Nacional de Colonizadores de Bolivia
COB	Central Obrero Boliviano
COMIBOL	Corporación Minera Boliviana

CONADAL   Comisión Nacional de Desarrollo Alternative

CSUTCB   Confederación Sindical Unica de Trabajadores Campesinos de Bolivia

DEA   U.S. Drug Enforcement Agency

FETCTC   Federación Especial de Trabajadores Campesinos del Trópico de Cochabamba

FPU   Frente del Pueblo Unido

FSTMB   Federación Sindical de Trabajadores Mineros

MBL   Movimiento Bolivia Libre

MIR   Movimiento Izquierdo Revolucionario

MNR   Movimiento Nacional Revolucionario

PIDYS   Plan Integral de Desarrollo y Sustitución

PS   Partido Socialista

UDP   Unidad Democrática Popular

UMOPAR   Unidad Movile de Patrullaje Rural

NOTES

1. The groups of *cocaleros* described in this paper are from the Chapare area of the department of Cochabamba. According to official estimates, 90% of the coca leaf produced in Bolivia is from the Chapare.

2. There are approximately 600,000 peasant families in Bolivia. It is also important to point out that there are many coca-leaf growers who farm in the Chapare as sharecroppers, but who are not counted among the union members. The author estimates that this group, together with the producers from the Las Yungas region, would bring the totals up to some 60,000 coca-leaf producers, or 10% of the national peasant population.

3. The federations are not monolithic, however, as various attempts at their unification have failed. Over the years, several of them (the *Federación de Yungas del Chapare*, the *Federación unica de Centrales Unidas,* and the *Federación de Colonizadores de Chimore*) have been more trusting and cooperative with the various government agencies in their alternative development programs than others. However, the federations mentioned have a much smaller social base among the Chapare peasantry than the principal *sindicato* organizations identified in the text. There are also differences in their national organization affiliation since many lowland peas-

ant *sindicatos* in Bolivia belong to a separate organization than their highland counterparts. The federations from Carrasco and Chimore are affiliated with the *Confederación Nacional de Colonizadores Campesinos de Bolivia*. The other federations belong to the *Confederación Sindical Unica de Trabajadores Campesinos* (CSUTCB) which is the largest peasant *sindicato* organization in Bolivia.

4. Expenditures for grassroots public works are not impressive in absolute amounts, especially in light of the vast infrastructure needs for this rapidly growing micro-region. In recent years, the most substantial financial investments have been for dumptrucks and a road grader. In the town of Eterazama, coca-leaf revenues were employed to construct a rustic Catholic Church.

5. The U.S. Agency for International Development (U.S.-AID) has worked, since 1976, through a variety of Bolivian government programs attached to the Ministry of Agriculture and Peasant Affairs to finance and administer coca-substitution or alternative development in Chapare. Initially, more emphasis was placed on research for alternative crops, of which the Agricultural Development in the Coca Zones Project (1975) and the Chapare Regional Development Project (1983) are examples (U.S.-AID, 1986). According to evaluations of these programs, however, they failed to achieve their objectives due to numerous difficulties, such as unfavorable marketing conditions, bureaucratic and technical ineptitude, and limited agricultural development potential in the tropical rainforest (Tropical Research, 1986). There was also the *Proyecto de Desarrollo y Sustitución*, funded by the U.S. State Department's Bureau of International Narcotics Matters (BINM), in 1977.

6. One example of an effective protest action took place in early 1987, sparked by the Bolivian Senate's proposed law to eradicate cultivation of the coca leaf in the Chapare. The federations mobilized some 12,000 peasants to block the roads in Cochabamba (Hoy, 1988). The government had to call out both the military and the police to break up this well-organized protest. Although several peasants were killed in this action, subsequent negotiations with the high-ranking government officials led to the signing, by both parties, of the *Plan Integral de Desarrollo y Sustitución* (PIDYS). This plan reaffirmed the social benefits, and legitimacy, of the coca-leaf plant (by not defining it as a "controlled substance") and guaranteed that peasant participation in both decision making and financial and economic investments in socio-economic development in the Chapare would be a precondition for voluntary eradication. The new investments

were to be earmarked for road building, potable water, rural electrification, sanitation systems, and agricultural credits.

7. The evidence for this figure are documents from a so-called "federation of agro-industrialists" which was spontaneously created by groups and individuals to protect their properties from invasion by coca-leaf growers. Conversations with peasants served as additional confirmation of this peculiar mini-land reform phenomenon.

8. During the 1982–83 growing season, Bolivia experienced one of its worst droughts of this century, impacting the highlands with particular severity. Because the Chapare area was unaffected by the drought, many peasants were motivated to migrate there in search of employment and land. The area served as a safety valve for this natural disaster.

9. Based on the *altiplano*, the *Katari* peasant union organizations formed a clandestine organization organized under military rule in the early 1970s. Later in the decade, they helped to spearhead the return to civilian democracy and to create the *Confederación Sindical Unica de Trabajadores Campesinos* (CSUTCB), which was the first confederation of peasant unions in Bolivia free of dependence upon either the state or a political party (Rivera, 1983; Albo, 1984). Eventually the *Kataristas* became racked by corruption and clientelism in their top executive leadership and were also adversely affected by the shift in state politics from Left to Right. By 1985, this combination of circumstances had severely circumscribed their influence within the national organization and, shortly thereafter, the activism of their federations became almost nonexistent.

10. The *Federación de Carrasco* belongs to the *Confederación Nacional de Colonizadores de Bolivia* (CNCB) and uses its influence in that body similar to the way the FETCTC channeled dissent through the CSTUCB during the 1980s.

11. During the 1980s, the CSTUCB has functioned as a strong opposition group to Bolivia's democratic regimes, which has made it into a natural ally of the FETCTC. For example, the CSUTCB has been an unswerving critic of the programs for structural adjustment because of their adverse effect on peasant agriculture.

12. For example, when political commission discussed internal political divisions among union organizations, it considered the issues which gave rise to them, such as differences over political parties, international food aid, land disputes, and other factors.

13. However, one could argue that, since the new law would completely eradicate coca cultivation in the Chapare and substitute some form of alternative development instead, while only the Yungas region (department of La Paz) would be allowed to cultivate coca for domestic consumption, there is some truth for the Chapare position in this political argument.

14. Operation Blast Furnace was the name given to a U.S. military operation which invaded Bolivia in 1986 to destroy cocaine-processing plants in the eastern Beni region. Some 170 U.S. army personnel, using Black Hawk helicopters, took part in this 5-month operation which destroyed dozens of cocaine processing labs. Although the military action was not deployed in the Chapare area, the U.S. offensive caused coca-leaf prices to fall as buyer/traffickers fled (or went into hiding)—giving rise to peasant protests.

15. The Bolivian economy experienced negative economic growth and record-breaking hyper-inflation during the first half of the 1980s. In the second half of the 1980s, under the economic stabilization programs, economic recovery was very slow, less than the growth in population. The social costs of this economic development strategy have also been high, due to the rise in unemployment from 9% in 1981, to 25% in 1988 (Iriarte, 1989). Meanwhile, during this same timeframe, coca leaf rose in value from 10% of the national agricultural product (NAP) to 28.7%, and cocaine generated more earnings than any legal export (UDAPE, 1990).

16. Author interviews with FECTCT leaders Eva Morales and David Herrera, in the Chapare, August 1989.

17. A recent World Bank report on Bolivia, after 4 years of structural adjustment, had this to say:

> Bolivian agriculture is in crisis; agricultural production in 1988 was 4% below the 1985 level. With the exception of soybeans (and possible coca) there has been no significant increase in yield over the last decade (World Bank, 1990a).

Another report states:

> These factors have resulted in a decline in the real price and quantity of agricultural products, particularly affecting production by *campesinos*. A price index of agricultural products declined by 29% from the stabilization to the end of 1988, relative to overall consumer prices. From 1985 to 1988, total agricultural production fell by 17% in terms of volume and remained 15% below the 1980–1985 average in 1988 (World Bank, 1990b:32).

18. Road blocks in rural areas are a common tactic used by Bolivian peasant unions to express outrage for, and to exert pressure for the redress of, their economic and political grievances, both local and national. During 1982–83, the road blockade was frequently used by many different peasant federations and local unions in various regions of the country (Healy, 1989). To end one blockade, the government signed 5 executive decrees and 4 ministerial decrees to favor peasant interests over a whole range of social and economic issues. However, since 1985, the Chapare federations have employed this tactic more frequently than any other peasant union organizations in Bolivia.

19. A key component of the 1985 structural adjustment program was major tax reform. The Bolivian peasantry was to be included in this reform via land taxes. Other than coca-leaf-related issues, the land tax was the issue which generated the most peasant protest in Bolivia in the second half of the 1980s.

20. Despite the fact that the peasant *sindicatos* do not technically belong to the COB, they have continued to coordinate actions and meetings to push their common interests in dealing with government representatives and their member bodies.

21. The *Frente del Pueblo Unido* (FPU), comprised the MBL and the *Partido Comunista*, is used as a proxy here to measure the strength of the *Izquierda Unida* (IU) in the 1985 election and, for the 1987 election, the reference to the MBL and the *Alianza Patriótica*. Left-of-Center coalitions are known for their fragility and propensity to dissolve once the elections have passed.

22. In 1989, coca-leaf fields were reduced in the Yapacane area (department of Santa Cruz) rather than in the Chapare. Since the Yapacane is not a traditional area for raising coca, there is less legitimacy for growing it there than in the Chapare and Yungas regions. In 1990, however, over 5,000 hectares of coca were uprooted in the Chapare because the prices for the coca leaf hit rock bottom, and the peasants needed the cash which they received in compensation. Despite these favorable conditions, the alternative development programs remain ineffective.

REFERENCES

Albo, X. (1984) (1987) "De MNRistas a Kataristas a Katari," pp. 379–420 in Steve Stern (ed.) *Resistance, Rebellion, and Consciousness in the Andean Peasant World, 18th to 20th Centuries.* Madison, WI: University of Wisconsin Press.

Canedo Ovellana, A. and J. Canelas Zannieb (1983) *Bolivia: Coca, Cocaine.* La Paz, Bolivia: Los Amigos del Libro.

Centro de Documentación e Información (CEDOIN) (1988) El tercer congreso de la CSUTCB: Un congreso inconcluso. La Paz, Bolivia: CEDOIN.

Centro de Documentación, Información y Biblioteca (CEDIB), (1989) Realidad Nacional, Todo sobre la Coca-Cocaina-1. Cochabamba, Bolivia: CEDIB.

Centro de Investigación y Desarrollo Regional (CIDRE) (1989) Unpublished figures on election data.

Comisión de la Coca (1989) Working document of the 8th Congress of the Central Obrere Boliviano (COB). 24 September, Oruro (Bolivia).

Craig, R. (1987) "Illicit Drug Traffic: Implications for South American Source Countries," *Journal of Interamerican Studies and World Affairs* 29, 2 (Summer): 1–34.

Eje de Convergencia (1989) "21060, Las elecciones generales; perspectivas del movimiento campesino; congreso CSUTCB y COB; la coca y los cocaleros; tareas." Oruro, Bolivia.

Healy, K. (1986) "The Boom within the Crisis: Some Recent Effects of Foreign Cocaine Markets on Bolivian Rural Society and Economy," pp. 101–145 in D. Pacini and C. Franquemont (eds.) *Coca and Cocaine, Effects on People and Policy in Latin America.* Cambridge, MA: Cultural Survival, Inc.

———, (1988) "Coca, the State, and the Peasantry in Bolivia, 1982–88," *Journal of Interamerican Studies and World Affairs* 30, 2–3 (Summer–Fall): 105–126.

———, (1989) *Sindicalismo, campesino y desarrollo rural.* La Paz, Bolivia: Instituto de Historia Social de Bolivia (HISBOL).

Henkel, R. (1989) "The Cocaine Problem," in Center for Latin American Studies (ed.) *Bolivia after Hyperinflation, The Restructuring of the Bolivian Economy* (forthcoming). Tempe, AZ: Arizona State University.

Hoy (1988) (June 8).

Iriarte, G. (1989) *Análisis crítico de la realidad, esquemas de interpretación.* La Paz, Bolivia: Servicio Nacional Pastoral Social/Comisión Episcopal Boliviano (SENPAS-CEB).

Izquierda Unida (IU) (n.d.) "La unidad para avanzar hacia la victoria" (unpublished political declaration, mimeo). Tarija, Bolivia: IU.

Lee, R. (1980) *The White Labyrinth: Cocaine and Political Power.* New Brunswick, NJ: Transaction Publishers.

Nash, J. (1979) *We Eat the Mines and the Mines Eat Us: Dependency and Exploitation in Bolivian Tin Mines.* New York, NY: Columbia University Press.

Rivera, S. (1983) *Oprimidos pero no venicidos: luchas del campesinado aymara y quechua 1990–1980.* La

Paz. Bolivia: Instituto de Historia Social Boliviana/Confederación Sindical Unica de Trabajadores Campesinos de Bolivia (HISBOL-CSUTCB).

Rodriguez, G. (1989a) "La COB, mas preguntas que respuestas," *Cuarto Intermedio* 11 (May): 33–47.

———, (1989b) "Las elecciones en el trópico Cochabamba," *Presencia* (May 21):2.

Tropical Research and Development, Inc. (1986) "Evaluation of Chapare Regional Development Project." Gainesville, FL: Tropical Research and Development, Inc.

Unidad de Análisis de Políticas Económicas (UDAPE) (1990) Estrategia Nacional del Desarrollo Alternativo (February). La Paz, Bolivia: UDAPE (Bolivian government planning unit).

United States. Agency for International Development (U.S.-AID) (1986) *A Review of AID's Narcotics Control Development Assistance Program.* Washington, DC: AID.

World Bank (1990a) Bolivia Poverty Report (No. 86430-BO). Washington, DC: World Bank.

———, (1990b) "Bolivia, Updating Economic Memorandum" (unpublished document for internal use). Washington, DC: World Bank.

38

Civilization and Its Discontents

Katharine Milton

For more than a decade now, I have led a double life. I spend part of my time in the United States, living in an apartment in Berkeley and teaching anthropology classes at the University of California. The rest of my time is spent in the Amazon Basin, where I live in the company of recently contacted Indian groups, studying their traditional ecology and features of their tropical forest environment. On returning to the United States after one of these extended stays in the jungle, I always experience culture shock as I strive to regain control of my possessions, which I have totally forgotten about.

Usually my first act is to retrieve my dust-covered car, which as languished for some six to eighteen months in a garage. The battery must be charged, and then I must wash and vacuum the car, fill it with gas, and check out its many parts. Once I am mobile, I rush to a large supermarket to stock up on cleaning supplies and food. My first few days are completely taken up with chores; there never

From Katharine Milton, "Civilization and Its Discontents," *Natural History* 101:36–43 (March), 1992.

seems to be a moment when I am not contemplating some type of home repair or new purchase.

And then there is my body. What a job it is to live up to what is expected of the average American. I must visit the dentist—often more than one kind of dentist—to be sure my teeth are performing at top level. The doctor must be seen for a checkup; my eyes must be examined,, glasses and contact lenses adjusted, and so on. I begin to wonder how my friends in Berkeley manage to have any free time in all, since I have fewer possessions than they do—I own no television set, no stereo or compact disk player, no video machine, home computer, food chopper, or any number of other items my friends seem to dote on. I don't even own my apartment.

Plunged back into life in Berkeley, I see myself as a slave of material possessions, and I notice that I deeply resent the time and energy required to maintain them. Nothing could be more different from the life I have been leading with hunter-gatherers deep in the rain forests of Brazil, where people have almost no possessions, and those that they do have are made from local forest materials and are entirely biodegradable.

The groups I have visited live far from any cities, towns, or commercial enterprises. They include the Mayoruna and Maku from Amazonas State; the Arara, Parakana, and Arawete from Pará State; and the Guaja from Maranhão State—peoples so remote and little known that few outside their immediate geographic area have heard of them. Often I am one of the first nonindigenous females many members of the group have ever seen. With my pale skin and hair I am a truly terrifying apparition to younger children, who sometimes scream with fear when they first see me.

All these peoples have been recently contacted: only a few months or, at most, years have passed since the Brazilian Indian Bureau (FUNAI) managed to establish a formal relationship with them. Previously, these groups avoided or were strongly hostile to outsiders, but with contact, they have permitted a few Indian Bureau employees to live with them, to assist them, and at times, protect them in dealings with other Indian groups or members of the wider Brazilian society. Living with these people has given me the chance to see how even modest changes in their traditional lifeways—the introduction of something as innocent in appearance as a metal cooking pot or ax, a box of matches or some salt—can be the thin edge of a wedge that will gradually alter the behavior and ecological practices of an entire society.

These people typically live in small villages of fewer than a hundred inhabitants, in some cases in groups of only fifteen or twenty. Most practice slash-and-burn agriculture on a small scale, complementing crop foods with wild game and fish, forest fruits and nuts, and occasionally, wild honey. For some months life may revolve around the village, but sooner or later every group I have worked with leaves, generally in small parties, and spends weeks or even months traveling through the forest and living on forest products.

Throughout the forest there are paths that the Indians know and have used for generations. They travel mainly when wild forest fruits and nuts are most abundant and game animals are fat, but families or small groups may go on expeditions at other times of year as well. They trek a few miles, make a temporary camp, and then hunt, gather, and eat several meals in the area before moving on to a new site. At certain times of year, many groups relocate to the borders of large rivers, where they obtain turtle eggs or other seasonal river foods.

The accumulation of possessions would be an impediment to this seminomadic life style. Whenever individuals go on a trek, they carry everything they need. Leaving possessions behind in a thatch-and-pole hut, to be retrieved later, is not an option, since the humid climate and voracious insects would quickly destroy them. Great numbers of insects often live inside Indian dwellings, principally jungle cockroaches that hide in the roof thatch by day but come out by the thousands at night. Indians seem oblivious to them, letting them run about on their bodies and even crawl on the food so long as they are not perched on the next bite.

Granted, these are generally soft-bodied, small jungle cockroaches and not the tough, large roaches of our urban areas, but even so, I found it difficult to adjust to them. My frantic efforts to remove cockroaches from my body and clothes were regarded as strange by my Indian hosts. At one site, I resorted to storing my clothing each night in a heavy plastic bag, which I sealed shut and suspended from a piece of plastic fish line tied to a roof pole. Otherwise, at night, the roaches covered my shirt and pants so thoroughly that often the fabric could not be seen. Although the roaches would be gone the next morning, they would leave a musty smell; further, just the idea of wearing garments that I had seen coated with cockroaches gave me a squirmy unclean feeling.

On the forest treks, the women are invariably the most burdened, something Western observers often find difficult to understand or accept. A woman will walk for hours carrying a toddler, a large palm basket containing fifty or more pounds of animal or plant foods, hammocks, a cooking utensil or two, a machete, and the family pets, such as parrots, monkeys, and young puppies. In all the groups I have observed, the women's legs and feet are deformed by the pigeon-toed walk they adopt to give them added traction and stability on the slippery, narrow forest trails. The feet of adult men turn in only slightly, because men usually carry nothing heavier than a bow and arrows (ostensibly to be free to take advantage of any hunting opportunities).

The most important possession the Indians carry with them, however, is knowledge. There is nothing coded in the genome of an Indian concerning how to make a living in a tropical forest—each individual must become a walking bank of information on the forest landscape, its plants and animals, and their habits and uses. This information must be taught anew to the members of each generation, without the benefit of books, manuals, or educational television. Indians have no stores in which to purchase the things they need for survival. Instead, each individual must learn to collect, manufacture, or produce all the things required for his or her entire lifetime.

Because people differ in their talents, the pool of community information and abilities is far greater than its component parts. Individual men and women have their own areas of expertise, as well as their share of general knowledge. Members of the group know whom to consult for special information on hunting practices, the habits of particular game animals, rituals, tool manufacture, crop varieties, and the like.

Tropical-forest Indians talk incessantly, a characteristic I believe reflects the importance of oral transmission of culture. When I lived with the Maku, I slept in a hammock inside a small communal palm shelter. If a Maku awoke in the middle of the night, he usually began to talk or sing in a very loud voice—apparently without any thought that anyone might object to this behavior. It was considered normal, what you do when you wake up in the middle of the night and aren't sleepy. Others learn, as I did, to sleep through it or, if they aren't sleepy, to listen to it. Vocal expression apparently is expected and tolerated in Maku culture, no matter what the hour, an indication to me of how much it is valued.

Unlike our economic system, in which each person typically tries to secure and control as large a share of the available resources as possible, the hunter-gatherer economic system rests on a set of highly formalized expectations regarding cooperation and sharing. This does not mean hunter-gatherers do not compete with one another for prestige, sexual partners, and the like. But individuals do not amass a surplus. For instance, no hunter fortunate enough to kill a large game animal assumes that all this food is his or belongs only to his immediate family.

Quite the reverse is true; among some forest peoples, the hunter cannot eat game he has killed or is restricted to eating only one specific portion of his kill. Game is cut up and distributed according to defined patterns particular to each group and based in large part on kinship and marriage obligations. A hunter may have amazing luck one day, moderate luck on another, and no luck at all on a third. But he can usually expect to eat meat every day because someone bound to him in this system of reciprocity may well make a kill and share the meat.

Despite the way their culture traditionally eschews possessions, forest-living peoples embrace manufactured goods with amazing enthusiasm. They seem to appreciate instantly the efficacy of a steel machete, ax, or cooking pot. It is love at first sight, and the desire to possess such objects is absolute. There are accounts of Indian groups or individuals who have turned their backs on manufactured trade goods, but such people are the exception.

When Cândido Rondon, the founder of the Indian Protection Service in Brazil, began his pacification efforts in the early 1900s, he used trade goods as bait to attract uncontacted Indians. Pots, machetes, axes, and steel knives were hung from trees or laid along trails that Indians frequented. This practice proved so successful that it is still employed (see "Overtures to the Nambiquara," by David Price, *Natural History*, October 1984).

Whether they have been formally contacted or not, forest-living groups in the Amazon Basin are probably well aware of steel tools and metal cooking pots. After all, such goods have been in circulation along trade routes in these regions for centuries, and an Indian does not have to have seen a non-Indian in order to acquire them. However, such manufactured goods are likely to be extremely scarce among uncontacted groups. When the Arara Indians were first approached in 1975, they fled their village to escape the pacification party. Examination of their hastily abandoned dwellings showed that stone tools were still being used, but a few steel fragments were also found.

Since they already appreciate the potential utility of manufactured goods, uncontacted Indians are strongly drawn to the new and abundant items offered to lure them from isolation. Once a group has been drawn into the pacification area, all its members are presented with various trade goods—

standard gifts include metal cooking pots, salt, matches, machetes, knives, axes, cloth hammocks, T-shirts, and shorts. Not all members of the group get all of these items, but most get at least two or three of them, and in a family, the cumulative mass of new goods can be considerable.

The Indians initially are overwhelmed with delight—this is the honeymoon period when suddenly, from a position in which one or two old metal implements were shared by the entire group, a new situation prevails in which almost every adult individual has some of these wonderful new items. The honeymoon is short-lived, however. Once the Indians have grown accustomed to these new items, the next step is to teach them that these gifts will not be repeated. The Indians are now told that they must work to earn money or must manufacture goods for trade so that they can purchase new items.

Unable to contemplate returning to life without steel axes, the Indians begin to produce extra arrows or blowguns or hunt additional game or weave baskets beyond what they normally need so that this new surplus can be traded. Time that might, in the past, have been used for other tasks—subsistence activities, ceremonial events, or whatever—is now devoted to production of barter goods. In addition, actual settlement patterns may be altered so that the indigenous group is in closer, more immediate contact with sources of manufactured items. Neither of these things, in itself, is necessarily good or bad, but each does alter traditional behavior.

Thus, the newly contacted forest people are rapidly drawn into the wider economic sphere (even into the international economy: for example, the preferred glass beads for personal adornment come from Czechoslovakia). The intrusion of every item—mirrors, cloth, scissors, rice, machetes, axes, pots, bowls, needles, blankets, even bicycles and radios—not only adds to the pressure on individuals to produce trade goods but also disrupts some facet of traditional production.

Anthropologist Paul Henley, who worked with the Panare, a forest-based people in Venezuela, points out that with the introduction of steel tools, particularly axes, indigenous groups suffer a breakdown in the web of cooperative interdependence. In the past, when stone axes were used, various individuals came together and worked communally to fell trees for a new garden. With the introduction

of the steel ax, however, one man can clear a garden by himself. As Henley notes, collaboration is no longer mandatory nor particularly frequent.

Indians often begin to cultivate new crops, such as coffee, that they feel can be traded or sold easily. Another is rice, which the Indian Bureau encourages forest peoples to plant because, of course, all "real" Brazilians eat rice every day. Rice is an introduced crop both to Brazil and to forest Indians. Traditional crop foods, the successful cultivation of which has been worked out over generations in the forest environment and which are well suited to soil conditions in particular regions, may become scarce, with the result that the Indian diet becomes unbalanced.

Indians who traditionally plant manioc as a staple crop may be encouraged to increase the size of their fields and plant more manioc, which can then be transformed into *farinha*, a type of cereal that can be sold in the markets. Larger fields mean more intensive agricultural work and less time to hunt—which also affects the diet. The purchase of a shotgun may temporarily improve hunting returns, but it also tends to eliminate game in the area. In addition, shotgun shells are very expensive in Brazil, costing more than U.S.$1 apiece. Dependence on the shotgun undermines a hunter's skill with traditional hunting weapons, such as blowguns and bows and arrows, as well as the ability required to manufacture them.

Clearing larger areas for fields can also lead to increased risk from diseases such as malaria and leishmanaisis, because cleared areas with standing water of low acidity permit proliferation of disease-bearing mosquitoes and flies. New diseases also appear. Anthropologist-epidemiologist Carlos Coimbra, Jr., for example, has shown that Chagas disease, which is transmitted to humans by trypanosome-carrying assassin bugs, apparently does not yet affect Indian Populations in lowland areas of the Amozon Basin. Only when Indians cease their seminomadic way of life and begin to live for prolonged periods in the same dwellings can Chagas-carrying bugs adjust their feeding behavior and begin to depend on human hosts rather than small rodents for their blood meals.

The moment manufactured foods begin to intrude on the indigenous diet, health takes a downward turn. The liberal use of table salt (sodium chloride), one of the first things that Indians are given, is probably no more healthful for them that it is for Westerners. Most Indians do not have table salt; they manufacture small quantities of potassium salts by burning certain types of leaves and collecting the ash. Anthropologist Darrell Posey reports that the Kayapo Indians of Brazil make salt ash from various palm species and use each type for specific food.

Sweets and other foods containing refined sugar (sucrose) are also given to Indians, whose wild fruits, according to research by botanists Irene and Herbert Baker, contain primarily other sugars, such as fructose, Indians find that foods containing sucrose taste exceptionally sweet, and they tend to crave them once sampled. While a strong, sugary taste in the natural environment might signal a rare, rich energy source, the indiscriminate consumption of canned foods, candies, and gums containing large amounts of refined sugar contributes to tooth decay and can lead to obesity and even health problems such as diabetes.

Results of dietary change are often difficult to anticipate. Anthropologist Dennis Werner found that the Merkranoti of central Brazil, who did not make pottery, traditionally roasted most of their food. But the introduction of metal cooking pots allowed them to switch to boiled foods. This, in turn, allowed nursing mothers to provide supplemental foods to their infants at an earlier age. Werner found that the average nursing period in the Mekranoti had dropped steadily from 19.7 months prior to 1955 to 16 months in recent years, which corresponded to the period of steady increase in the use of metal cooking pots in the village.

One of the first things the Indian Bureau doctors generally do after contact is try to protect the Indians from the Western disease that may be communicated to them during their first prolonged interaction with outsiders. The doctors give them immunizations and may also hand out drugs to prevent or eradicate dangerous malarias. Pregnant women, infants, and preadolescents often receive massive doses of antibiotics. Antibiotics and antimalarial drugs, although helpful in some respects, may also have detrimental effects. For example, individuals exposed to antibiotics in utero or when young generally have teeth that are abnormally dark and discolored. Some drugs are reputed to interfere

with fertility among women in recently contacted groups. If this lack of fertility combines with a drop in population size due to deaths from new diseases, a population can fall to a precarious low.

Perhaps the most critical disruption suffered by these groups, however, concerns how detailed information on features of the forest environment is diluted and forgotten. This is the pool of shared knowledge that traditionally has been the bedrock, the economic currency, the patrimony of each of these nontechnological forest societies. Manuel Lizarralde, a doctoral student at the University of California, Berkeley, who has done ethnobotanical work with the Bari of Venezuela, reports that in just a single generation there was a staggering loss of information about the identity of forest trees and their uses.

Despite this tale of disruption, disease and destruction, many of the indigenous forest cultures are proving to be far more resilient than might be expected. The indigenous peoples remaining today in the Amazon Basin are true survivors who have successfully resisted the diseases, explorers, missionaries, soldiers, slave traders, rubber tappers, loggers, gold miners, fur traders, and colonists who have persistently encroached on them during the past five centuries.

Anthropologist Bill Balée, for example, has found that the Ka'apor Indians of Maranhão State, in peaceful contact with outsiders since 1928, still maintain many features of their traditional economy, social organization, and ritual life. He attributes this to the continued integrity of the nuclear family and the persistence of specific ritual duties between husband and wife that prohibit certain foods at different seasons or life stages. Such ritual practices have not only spared red-legged tortoises and other wild resources from being overharvested but have also diffused hunting pressures over a large area, thereby contributing to the persistence of the traditional economy.

Unfortunately, cultural persistence will do indigenous peoples no good if their tropical forest habitat is destroyed. Deforestation is primarily the result of outside influences, such as lumbering, cattle ranching, and colonization, that are permitted by government polices. Some estimates suggest that all remaining tropical forests will be destroyed by the year 2045.

Once the technological roller coaster gets moving, it's hard to jump off or even pause to consider the situation. Some say, so what? We can't all go back to the jungle, we can't all become forest-living Indians. No, we can't. But as I stand in my apartment in Berkeley, listening to my telephone's insistent ring and contemplating my unanswered mail, dusty curtains, dripping faucets, and stacks of newspapers for recycling, I'm not sure we wouldn't be far happier if we could.

39

Mixtec Ethnicity
Social Identity, Political Consciousness, and Political Activism

Carole Nagengast and Michael Kearney

Culture, according to one anthropological formulation, is "the structure of meaning through which people give shape to their experience" (Geertz 1973, 312). Clifford Geertz's definition necessarily implies consideration of struggles over the politics of that meaning. Implicit and explicit in such struggles are political efforts to impose upon others a particular concept of how things really are and therefore how people are obliged to act (Geertz 1973, 316). During the process of nation building, history and the structure of meaning that it gives to contemporary "culture" are often manipulated so that socially, politically, and economically opposed groups are merged into putative harmonious "imagined communities" whose reality enters into public consciousness and social discourse as the authentic past (Anderson 1983). But consciousness of shared identity and common discourse centered upon that identity are not

From Carole Nagengast and Michael Kearney, "Mixtec Ethnicity: Social Identity, Political Consciousness, and Political Activism," *Latin American Research Review* 25(2): 61–91, 1990.

uncontested. In Mexico competing images of indigenous "tradition" entail just such a political struggle over meaning, a struggle over the definition of what constitutes indigenous culture—"real" ethnic identity, as it were—and a consequent struggle over what actions, if any, need to be taken (and by whom) to combat the second-class status of most of the country's indigenous peoples.

The central question that will be addressed here is how social consciousness is generated and expressed in different contexts in Mexico, in this case how indigenous consciousness of imposed ethnicity is transformed into social protest and resistance to exploitation and repression. Our concern is first to examine the historical processes and the bases of the definitional duality between *mestizo* and *indio* through which the indigenous peoples of Mexico and particularly Mixtecs from the western part of the state of Oaxaca have been defined as "ethnic groups" by others.[1] In these processes, they have been objectified, categorized, and provided with distinctive social identities, in some circumstances a positive identity as the survivors of a mythologized pre-Columbian past, the only true bearers of Mexican culture and history. In other circumstances, indigenous peoples have been furnished with an equally mythologized but decidedly inferior social identity that divides them conceptually from other social groups along ethnic lines but also justifies their repression and exploitation.

The second and related issue that we will address is the highly contingent emergence of a self-conscious and deliberate elaboration of ethnicity by Mixtecs themselves as they migrate north from Oaxaca to the agricultural fields of Sinaloa and Baja California Norte, to U.S.–Mexico border cities, and across the border to work in commercial agriculture in California and Oregon.[2] In their homeland in the Mixteca,[3] ethnicity is not usually a form of self-identification, but in the frontier, it has become the basis for political activism and a means of defending themselves socially, economically, and politically.

It should be clear that we take ethnicity not as an ontological given, a natural fact of life, but as a social construction formed from the interface of material conditions, history, the structure of the political economy, and social practice. In other words, we contend that there is nothing automatic about ethnicity; it is one way (among others) in which people define themselves and are defined by others who stand in opposition to them. Ethnicity can be a mode of expressing consciousness, of defending the status quo, or (potentially) of organizing social protest (Comaroff 1987).

Before elaborating these ideas further, the ethnographic research on which our analysis is based requires some description. Since 1979 the authors have spent three periods of about three months each and have visited more briefly on several other occasions in the Mixteca Baja,[4] primarily in the mountain village of San Jerónimo Progreso in the *municipio* and district of Silacayoapan. The Mixteca, is inhabited primarily by Mixtec-speakers surrounding some enclaves of Triquis. Mestizos are found predominantly in the district and municipio centers and in the few cities. While residing in San Jerónimo, we were both participants in and observers of daily life in most settings, including political meetings, ritual events, and fiestas. We recorded agricultural statistics, oral histories, and migration and work histories. We were also given access to the village's historical archives, from which we copied or photographed many documents. We have witnessed numerous public political meetings held at the *palacio municipal* and have also recorded many accounts of political events that we did not actually witness.

While carrying out our research in San Jerónimo, we have also conducted intensive and extensive research with migrant workers from San Jerónimo and surrounding villages living in the U.S.–Mexico border city of Tijuana, occasionally in Nogales and Mexicali, in the San Quintín Valley of Baja California Norte, and in numerous counties in California including Riverside, San Bernardino, San Diego, Venture, Kern, Tulare, Fresno, Madera, and Sonoma. Some aspects of our research have already been reported (Kearney 1986a, 1988; Sutart and Kearney 1981; Kearney and Nagengast 1989; Nagengast, Stavenhagen, and Kearney n.d.), and others are still in progress. It has been a rare week in the past ten years that we have not had some contact in one of these locations with persons from San Jerónimo or from nearby Mixtec villages. At present (1989), we are sharing a household in California with a family from San Jerónimo, a practice we have followed for several extended periods in the past, the longest being ten months in 1984–85. Thus in some respects, we have become incorporated into the transnational network of many households from San Jerónimo. We participated actively in many of the political activities of Mixtecs on the border and in California that are described in this article. We have also observed the transformation of old "traditions" and the gestation and birth of new ones as ethnicity has been defined and redefined by Mixtecs themselves and by those in structural and political opposition to them.

GLORY AND DEGRADATION

The positive ethnic image of indigenous peoples, that of ancient glory, has been articulated in the celebration of military, artistic, scientific, and (reconstructed) architectural achievements of the pre-Columbian empire. This image has also been enshrined in Mexico's archaeological monuments and ethnographic museums as well as symbolized in the everyday use of indigenous motifs in murals, emblems of state, and tourist items. Moreover, it is encapsulated in the annual festival of the Guelaguetza in the city and state of Oaxaca, which is attended by numerous municipal and state bureaucrats, tens of thousands of Mexican and foreign tourists, but few nonperforming indigenous peoples. According to Heladio Ramírez, Governor of Oaxaca, whose greetings to visitors are included in the program distributed at the 1987 Guelaguetza festival,

> Oaxaca is the richest expression of the country's ethnic majority, with its 16 ethnic groups and its 92 dialects, keeping with great pureness many of its cultural characteristics, seen in the color and beauty of its regional costumes, in the exquisite variety of its gastronomy, in its deep music spirituality, in the multiplicity and joy of its feasts and traditions, in the notable sensibility of its craftsmen, but above all, in the resumed wiseness of its philosophy before life.

The program goes on to eulogize "authentic folklore" and "age-old tradition" in setting the tone for two consecutive July weekends of "traditional" ethnic dances, songs, costumes, and food.

The glorious image of the pre-Columbian past, rehearsed and celebrated in the Guelaguetza festival, contrasts with the second version of indigenous tradition, which transcends special occasions and defines and organizes the interaction of the "ethnic groups" with the majority. This image is a negative one that evokes backwardness or primitivity as a basic trait of indigenous peoples. In 1915 Mexican novelist and revolutionary Martín Luís Guzmán wrote of the indigenous peoples of his country: "Since the Conquest or even from pre-Hispanic times, the Indian has been prostrate, submissive, indifferent to good or ill, without conscience, his soul reduced to a rudimentary grain, incapable of even hope. To judge by what we see now, the Indian has not taken a step forward in centuries. Without idealism, hope, or aspiration, feeling no pride in its race, overcome by some mortal and irritating docility, the Indian mass is for Mexico a weight and a burden."[5]

The pervasiveness of Guzmán's atavistic characterization of indigenous peoples is reflected in the everyday use of the epithet *indio* throughout Mexico to denote ignorance or stupidity by the same citizens who point with pride to the pre-Columbian ancestry of the nation, visit the archaeological ruins and anthropological museums, and idolize the murals of Diego Rivera, Pascual Orozco, and David Siqueiros. Reprehensible though racist epithets may be, they are the surface manifestation and audible representation of underlying economic and political oppression.

In El Campo de las Pulgas (Flea Camp), a labor camp located just south of the town of Lázaro Cárdenas in the San Quintín Valley of Baja California Norte, thousands of farmworkers live in squalor. Most of them are Mixtecs, one of the larger of the sixteen ethnic groups native to Oaxaca and western Guerrero that are featured in the Guelaguetza. Tens of thousands of Mixtecs have become migrants and temporary sojourners in this valley, where they are employed by vast export-oriented tomato ranches. One of these is Los Pinos, the enterprise to which Las Pulgas is attached.

Las Pulgas consists of long sheds of corrugated sheet-metal that have been divided into some 250 windowless, dirt-floored rooms about sixteen feet square. These cubicles constitute the living quarters for Mixtec farmworkers and their children, each room housing at least one family of six persons or more. Here the inhabitants cook over open fires (the only source of heat), eat, sleep, and rest from the rigors of the day. The rooms are furnished, if at all, with discarded packing boxes, boards, and tattered blankets and are almost always filled with acrid, lung-searing smoke. One central faucet serves the needs of the entire camp, and the sanitary facilities consist of a half a dozen holes in the ground enclosed with plastic sheeting. Living conditions for farmworkers at Las Pulgas are typical of the San Quintín Valley, and some camps are even worse.

In contrast, the packing-shed employees of Los Pinos, all of them mestixos, are provided with small row apartments located apart from Las Pulgas. Although extremely rudimentary, these apartments have standard facilities, and these employees take their meals in a spacious, well-appointed cafeteria. Startled by the contrast with the quarters of the Mixtecs, we asked the manager of Los Pinos about the living conditions of the fieldworkers. He replied, "That's the only way those people [the Mixtecs] know how to live. I know it looks bad to us, but they cook over wood fires in their villages; there aren't any toilets there. If I gave them stoves, water, they wouldn't know what to do with them. If I put windows in their huts they would just cover them up. They're used to the heat and smoke. It doesn't bother them. Why, they have lived like that for centuries. They like the way they live; it's their tradition." This statement reflects more than bigotry mediated by the pragmatics and exigencies of labor costs and management. It encapsulates the second rendition of "tradition," one much closer to the daily lived experience of Mixtecs than the first. But this image attributes abysmal living and working conditions to conscious choice ("They like the way they live") as well as to a certain primitiveness or backwardness, traits supposedly as timeless and innate, if less charming, than those consecrated in the Guelaguetza festival.

To some degree, the negative stereotype of indios is believed by Mixtecs themselves Most do not know themselves as accomplished artisans, superb agriculturalists, the builders of the once-great civilizations of the preconquest (Spores 1967, 1984). Rather, they know themselves as speakers of a language they refer to as *tu?un nda?vi* ("poor words"), as non-Spanish speakers who are often forced by the dominant mestizo majority to pay more for what they buy and to receive less for what they sell, as inferiors from whom bribes are extorted as they make their way north to work on the ranches of Sinaloa and the San Quintín Valley, in the border towns of Tijuana and Nogales, and across the border to pick fruit and vegetables in California and Oregon. They know themselves as those who originate in *lugares tristes* (sad places), villages in the Mixteca where food is often scarce, a decent living is difficult to obtain, and children die of preventable diseases complicated by malnutrition. But even though the negative myth reflects their daily lives in the Mixteca and on both sides of the U.S.–Mexico border with sad accuracy, the Mixtecs do not glamorize their poverty by claiming that it is traditional.

Myths are not necessarily false—they can be partial fictions implying prescriptions for action or nonaction to believers and can embody a deep symbolic truth. All peoples take myth as reality to a certain extent. Rather than being philosophical questions, such "fictions" may become what Michael Taussig terms "a high-powered tool for domination and a principal means of political practice" (Taussig 1984, 492). One essential ingredient of myth noted by Roland Barthes is "inoculation":

"One immunizes the contents of the collective imagination by means of a small inoculation of acknowledged evil; one thus protects it against the risk of a generalized subversion" (Barthes 1972, 150). Taussig discusses alternative and partially mythical early-twentieth-century accounts of relations between the indigenous Putumayo of Colombia and European colonists who established rubber plantations there by means of Putumayo labor power (Taussig 1984). These myths dealt with the real or imagined cannibalism of the Putumayo and the European punishment of it. In Taussig's view, they provided the "cultural space" for the torturing, terrorizing, and killing of Putumayos—macabre rites of European solidarity intended to serve notice of the fate that continued resistance would bring those who defied the establishment of civilization (the appropriation of Putumayo land and labor power). In this instance, one example of cannibalism and retribution was sufficient to "inoculate" the Putumayos, that is, for Europeans to justify to themselves their extermination of an entire people without further reflection and to compel the Indians to accept the interlopers' definition of civilization. Thus do myths reconcile contradictions and justify social action.

Historically similar events and processes of inoculation occurred in Mexico during the conquest, profoundly shaping the economic and political subjugation of the indigenous population through direct coercion. Torture and killing of those who oppose the status quo is scarcely unknown today: witness the discovery of the tortured and manacled bodies of prisoners in the rubble of the headquarters of the Attorney General of the Federal District after the 1985 Mexico City earthquake, the reports of police brutality and torture in the jails of Tijuana, the disappearance and killing of peasant leaders in Chiapas and Oaxaca, and what are widely believed to be political killings in the period surrounding the elections of July 1988. But such methods have not been publicly or officially practiced, acknowledged, or condoned in Mexico for a long time.[6]

Power does not proceed only from the official arm of the state downward, however, as considerable recent research suggests (Foucault 1970, 1973, 1980). The effective exercise of power depends as well on disparate sources of "social knowledge" that become a part of public discourse. Following the centuries of direct coercion of the indigenous population of Mexico, exercised first by the conquistadores and colonizers and then by the Mexican state, the social knowledge embodied in public discourse inoculated and continues to inoculate popular opinion, thus providing a space for exploitation. This space, then and now, depends on invoking the dualistic version of "indigenous traditionalism" that emphasizes devotion to the "backwardness" of the past to justify and explain contemporary exploitation while the "positive" aspects of tradition are glorified in a manner that denies the continuing exploitation. The political meaning and irony of both partially mythical images echo Raymond Williams's description of tradition as a highly selective reading of history, an ideological device invoked to justify the status quo (Williams 1975).

INDIGENOUS PEOPLES AS OBJECTS

The dual image of complexity and accomplishments in the past but simplicity, backwardness, and passivity in the present is widely shared and articulated by ordinary Mexican citizens as well as by many social theorists and agencies of social change, Mexican and foreign alike. Theorists and agencies, however, usually express this image in more subtle terms. Tradition is invoked to account for indigenous culture, with some aspects regarded as negative (such as the inability or unwillingness to adopt behavior or technology characterized as "modern") and a few as positive (handicrafts, costumes, "traditional agriculture," and "wiseness of philosophy"). The task often set for themselves by social planners, applied anthropologists, and agencies of the state dedicated to "indigenous affairs" is to devise means of overcoming the negative traditions while not injuring the positive. But indigenous peoples are more often the object of theoretical and applied research and development projects than they are subjects who have played an active role in their own past and have a voice in their present and future.

The dual vision of indigenous peoples was encoded in the earliest Spanish renditions of the "Indian other" (Todorov 1984), a duality that has taken on added dimensions in recent social theory. Todorov, for example, seeks to foster communication between the contemporary "self" and "other" by making an exemplar of the outcome of the Spanish and Mesoamerican encounter and the ease with which the conquistadores overcame and subjugated the indigenous peoples. But as Coronil has noted, an undifferentiated West is the unambiguous "self" and an equally undifferentiated Third World is the "other," analogs to "the Spanish" and "the Mesoamericans" of the sixteenth century (Coronil n.d.). Despite good intentions, Todorov reduces a complex historical reality inextricably bound up with the exercise of power to a set of predetermined binary oppositional characteristics attributed to Spanish and "Indian." In the final analysis, indigenous peoples are reduced "to enactors of a single pre-constituted code [which] denies them selfhood and reproduces a view of them as 'others'" (Coronil n.d., 3). This process has historically entailed their reification, ranking, and mythologizing as a social group vis-à-vis the Spanish and later the more generalized mestizos or Latinos: it eventually resulted in the control of the less powerful by the more powerful (Foucault 1980). Indigenous peoples thus remain objects of study, and Todorov has enshrined duality by making it part of social theory.

More insidious in some ways than abstract social theorizing are the federal and international development projects designed for remote villages, with their immediate and concrete consequences on indigenous peoples' lives. From its inception in 1948 through the 1970s, the Instituto Nacional Indigenista (INI), the major Mexican state institution charged with overseeing projects intended to implement social change in indigenous villages, promoted Spanish-language education, vaccination programs, "modern" farming techniques, and closer commercial ties with mestizo towns. The underlying rationale came directly from the then-dominant, but now mostly discredited, modernization theory of development. This theory essentially hypothesized that indios are poor because they are backward and tradition-bound, and what they therefore need is to become more like "modern" people.

Since the mid-1970s, the INI has responded to criticisms that its earlier program was not only paternalistic but promoted internal colonialism in the interests of advancing capitalism. The INI has since begun to emphasize bilingual education and bilingual media, to promote projects to bring drinking and irrigation water to villages in order to help them become self-sufficient, and to subsidize grain, fertilizers, and pesticides. Nonetheless, indigenous persons and other critics allege that corruption and paternalism continue to characterize the INI.[7] Similar criticism has also been directed toward applied anthropologists, Mexican, and U.S. alike, and foreign and domestic agencies of social change, past and present (Riding 1986, 291–99). For example, the much-vaunted "green revolution" of the 1960s and 1970s, which was also predicated on the principles of modernization theory and was supported by U.S. foreign aid and the Rockefeller Foundation, actually intensified rural inequities and widespread poverty while contributing to the concentration of economic resources (Hewitt de Alcántara 1978, 1984; Griffin 1974, 1987; Stavenhagen 1978).

More recent efforts to bring "progress" to the Latin American countryside through projects originating in the metropolis, while formulated differently, have often had similar effects, actually creating hunger where it did not exist before (Lappé and Collins 1979; 1986). Critics note further that few locally initiated projects have sufficient support to thrive.

Thus although the pre-Columbian past has been mythologized and glorified in the interests of the Mexican state and nation, the economic and social conditions of the indigenous present, while widely recognized and discussed, remain unaddressed in any meaningful way. Indios remain objects of research, a population that poses problems requiring solutions devised by institutions of the wider society, especially those of the state, rather than subjects who experience problems resulting from structural and historic processes and their position within the dominant society. Michel Foucault has demonstrated the relationship between the "official" discourse of the state and political practice and control. This discourse is constantly legitimated by the state and by academic institutions and has become part of daily societal practice, linguistic forms, and ideas about the norms of everyday life (Foucault 1980). Within this framework, it follows that any attempt by minorities or ethnic groups to manifest opposition to their subordinate position not only will be resisted by the forces of the state but will also be labeled as "deviant" or "subversive" (Kearney and Nagengast 1989, 3).

THE TRADITION OF SURVIVAL

Most of the farmworkers employed at Los Pinos and other agribusiness enterprises in the San Quintín Valley come from the Mixteca, as do the Mixtec performers in the Guelaguetza. The largest unit having everyday political and social saliency within the Mixteca (as elsewhere in indigenous Mexico) has been the "closed corporate community" described by Eric Wolf (1957). Political and social singularity from one commune to the next has been inscribed in a set of distinctive cultural, religious, and linguistic symbols. For example, the male-dominated civil and religious complex organizes commune affairs and serves as the primary vehicle of political activity. Religious festivals are organized around reverence for a particular saint or saints who contrast with those of neighboring communes. Mixtec is the language of everyday life, although many men and some women and children speak Spanish with varying degrees of competency (few speak it well). Although linguistic differences from one village to another do not always render Mixtec dialects mutually unintelligible, they underscore separateness, as do distinctive variations in women's costumes. Marrying within the village population is the rule, and reciprocal suspicion of those from neighboring villages the norm. Thus within the Mixteca, individuals identify themselves as being from a given village. The primary political opposition emerges between villages, and ethnicity is only occasionally salient. For example, Mixtecs and Triquis may invoke their ethnicity to distinguish themselves from each other in market towns. To urban and semi-urban mestizos, however, all indigenous peoples are usually perceived simply as "indios."

San Jerónimo Progreso is a rather remote Mixtec village located high in the mountains of the Mixteca Baja. Until fifteen years ago, no road existed between San Jerónimo and its municipal and district center of Silacayoapan, and no more than twenty years ago, the sixty miles between Silacayoapan and Huajuapan de León on the Pan American Highway (the only major north-south road) required a four-day trek.[8] Today, in the dry season (November through April), a daily bus negotiates the narrow, ungraded road that winds the four miles between San Jerónimo and Silacayoapan. The road was built and is maintained by means of the communal labor obligation known as *tequio*, which is organized and enforced in San Jerónimo by elected village officials.[9] Regular bus service is also available between Silacayoapan and Huajuapan.

At present, San Jerónimo has a population of some two thousand inhabitants in 250 households. All the available land, most of it divided into tiny plots, has long been under cultivation, leaving none for growing families. In most crucial respects (the form of the domestic economy, social structure, and relations), San Jerónimo resembles hundreds of other indigenous villages in the Mixteca. A Mixtec dialect is spoken by all, and older women wear clothes identifying them as from that village. San Jerónimo is a commune rather than an *ejido*, that is to say, all land is communally held and apportioned among individual households on a more or less permanent usufruct basis. All households, even those of the few store owners, cultivate corn, beans, and squash for domestic use by means of family labor and rudimentary farming technology (machete, hoe, plow, and oxen). The division of labor is determined by age and sex, with little deviation. The civil hierarchy is staffed solely by men, and the main religious complex is organized around reverence for San Jerónimo. While women participate actively in the religious festivals, their role is decidedly that of housewives: they prepare and serve the food, arrange flowers for the altar and the processions through the village, and fulfill similar functions. Like so many closed corporate communities in rural Mexico, San Jerónimo has been engaged for decades in boundary disputes with neighboring villages. Thus to all outward appearances, San Jerónimo is a "traditional" community.

What is it exactly that is "traditional" in villages like San Jerónimo? During the first hundred years of the conquest, the native population of Mesoamerica (which was far from politically, economically, or ethnically homogeneous) declined by some 90 percent due to Spanish practices of domination but also to the ultimately more devastating diseases introduced inadvertently by Europeans. Yet despite the depredations of the conquest, much of south-

ern Mexico 350 years later—especially the states of Oaxaca, Guerrero, and Chiapas—maintains the appearance of and is celebrated as being "ethnically diverse" or "Indian." What appear to be indigenous cultural and social forms are presumed survivals of the pre-Columbian past.

During the first century of the conquest, the economy and society of the Mixtecs were profoundly transformed via the introduction of Spanish agricultural technology, forced conversion to Catholicism, and the imposition of Spanish social and cultural forms. Most of the previously dispersed population was forcibly concentrated into Spanish-planned settlements to facilitate more effective government, conversion, and (most important) extraction of wealth—all under the tutelage of priests who were largely responsible for incorporating the native peoples into the administrative structure of the colonial society and economy. Each commune was given semi-autonomy and was in fact enjoined from interacting with other communes to prevent banding together and resisting Spanish rule (Spores 1967, 1984). In time the communes became socially and culturally separate worlds in which new "traditions" developed from a syncretism of local practices and the imposed Spanish culture. One of the few genuine survivals of the pre-Columbian past is the array of indigenous languages, and these cultural traits invest all others with apparent authenticity.

Unlike their less-fortunate kin directly in the path of the Spanish, the people of the Mixteca Baja in the newly isolated communes were partially insulated by the generally inhospitable mountain terrain and by the lack of mineral riches from the most direct and severest forms of exploitation (like forced labor). They were also insulated from outright appropriation of their land by outside interests—first by the *conquistadores, caciques*, and regional land barons; then by the crown, the church, and the Mexican state; and most recently, by national and international capitalist enterprises. But these peoples were not protected from appropriation of value produced in the villages. While wealth was extracted in the forms of taxes to the crown, tributes to the local *caciques*, tithes to the church, and migratory labor, villages were still able to reproduce their numbers and the means of their existence and to define themselves collectively vis-à-vis the forces surrounding them by fusing their cultural resources and cosmology with the Spanish colonial culture forced on them.

The coalescence of ancient religious systems with Catholicism, a syncretism that owes more to indigenous forms than to Rome is but one example (Greenberg 1981). It has been widely argued that the Catholic religious complex involving the veneration of specific saints (every village has it own saints) by staging elaborate and costly fiestas in their honor actually funnels enormous sums out of the villages into the control of nonindigenous middlemen, priests, and merchants and is thus a disguised extraction of wealth from the community (Diener 1978; Wolf 1957). Endorsing this view, James Greenberg has also pointed out that while the largest share of money expended on the religious fiestas flows out of the village into the coffers of the church, mestizo merchants, and the state, the fiestas also redistribute some food to the poorest villagers (Greenberg 1981). He hastens to add that this redistribution is not ordinarily a consciously articulated intent of the religious fiestas and the amount involved is not large. Greenberg argues nevertheless that in the absence of even the most rudimentary social services (a circumstance related to the imposed isolation of most communes), the poorest might not otherwise survive. Unable to resist actively the incursions of the Catholic Church and its demands on resources, communes have managed to fulfill some of their own internal needs as well, while not incidentally reenforcing their perceptions of isolation in a hostile world.

Antipathy between adjacent communes has also reenforced village singularity, directing hostility laterally rather than vertically. Armed conflict between villages has been common in the Mixteca, as elsewhere in southern Mexico. Its endemic cause has been boundary disputes among neighboring communes, all of which suffer land shortages resulting from population pressure, soil erosion, and land grabs by those who are politically and economically more powerful. Dialect differences from one village to the next as well as differences in collective representations, no doubt intensified during the centuries of imposed isolation, continue to be seized upon as icons of village singularity, symbolizing imputed insider-outsider status.

Philip Dennis has argued convincingly that inter-village conflict over land between closed corporate communities in Oaxaca has been actively promoted for centuries by the state (first Spanish and then Mexican) to enrich its coffers and facilitate central control over the communities and their inhabitants (Dennis 1987). Such tactics have also preserved the closed nature of communities and prevented horizontal solidarity and collective action among those who have unrecognized interests in common. The perennial tension created by the dialectic of insider-outsider is experienced locally and has reinforced villagers' sense that their communities need defending and that neighboring villages they fight with over boundaries (rather than distant outside interests) are the enemy. This is the perceived reality that motivates their actions.

In short, new "traditional" forms continued to develop in response to oppression, forms that diverged from one village to the next and from those emerging in mestizo communities. Thus the perpetuation of local identity has facilitated and justified a collective closing of ranks against outsiders. It is our contention that this closing has historically constituted passive resistance to outside dominant forces and has meant that in the Mixteca, villagers ordinarily identify themselves as being from their particular village, rarely as Mixtecas, and almost never as indios.

The contemporary closed corporate communities with their diverse customs are thus not necessarily indigenous "traditional" forms left over from the pre-Columbian past. Many of them first emerged from the tension between Spanish and Mexican, the powerful and the powerless. Their isolation has been further reinforced by the economically and politically more powerful in the century and a half since independence. Even the traditions celebrated in events such as the Guelaguetza festival are not unambiguously indigenous. In the 1987 festival, for example, a dance performed by a group of Zapotecs from a pueblo in the Sierra Juárez was billed as an ancient tradition of that village. It was instead an unmistakable rendition of an eighteenth-century minuet, probably derived from Spanish court ritual. Relatively superficial traits like costumes aside, indigenous strategies for survival surely have not been preserved in their "new" sixteenth-, seventeenth-, or eighteenth-century "traditional" forms but are constantly undergoing transformation in response to changing conditions.

If *tradition* is an elusive concept, that of *indio* is equally amorphous. Given village endogamy, the relative lack of spatial mobility, and imposed commune status that dates back at least to the conquest, the inhabitants of any particular village clearly constitute a gene pool, as do those of the Mixteca Baja when contrasted with, say, the Zapotecs of the Sierra Juárez. Genes, however, may be the least salient of the criteria variously cited as defining indios. In actuality, a minuscule percentage of contemporary Mexicans (primarily elites) have no indigenous ancestors at all, and Spanish-speaking urban mestizos are often genetically indistinguishable from the Mixtec-, Zapotec-, or Mayan-speaking indios whom they despise. The most important element in the identification of indios is how the rest of Mexican society treats them, which is to say, how it exploits and represses them.

When using the term *exploitation*, we are referring explicitly to any economic, political, social, cultural, or ideological conditions and practices that enable one class, class fragment, or ethnic group to extract net value from another (Kearney 1988). Appropriation of land is an extreme form of exploitation, and repression is any practice that furthers exploitation. Thus the murder or "disappearance" of those who protest too loudly is not only repression but an extreme form of exploitation.[10] Indirect exploitation and repression are more subtle, and their sources are not immediately apparent. An example would be the historic circumstances that resulted in closed corporate communities and, more recently, the lack of alternatives to migrating from one's village and family because of having insufficient land to feed a family and being consequently forced to deliver oneself cheaply to employers in distant labor markets.

Resistance is defined as whatever enables peoples to retain value that would be otherwise taken from them, and it can be either active or passive. The form taken is shaped by the kind of exploitation or repression to which it responds. When repression is indirect (not immediately perceivable), resistance is most likely passive. As such, it is embodied in the cultural forms and cultural content that are often defined and described as "traditional." In other words, much of what is regarded as the inwardness, stoicism, passivity, and "traditionalism" of the indigenous pueblo may actually constitute a subtle and not immediately perceived resistance to repression.

We therefore suggest that the "closed" nature of the corporate commune, which is emblematic of indigenous culture, results from a political structure literally forced on indigenous peoples combined with their own resistance (albeit passive) to outside forces—a recursive dialectic of insider-outsider. This dialectic generates distinctive local social forms and symbolic systems or gives new meaning to existing ones, such as the civil-religious complexes that form the backbone of community political organization and identity and linguistic variations from commune to commune.

By the same token, to describe resistance as "active" is to imply that it is a conscious response to the immediately experienced and directly perceived relations of exploitation and repression inscribed in the realities of everyday contemporary life. Only under specific conditions have Mixtecs, as a defined social group, engaged in active resistance. This response has occurred as Mixtecs have left their natal villages in Oaxaca and become more obviously incorporated into the national and international political economy of capitalism.

DOMESTIC ECONOMY AND CAPITALISM

On the surface, San Jerónimo appears to be made up of "traditional" noncapitalist subsistence farmers engaged in domestic production solely for household use. But just as other traditions have been shown to be illusions, so too is the vision of "peasant economy." San Jerónimo is integrally articulated with national and international capitalist production through relations of domination, exploitation, and repression (Kearney 1986a).

Unlike most communes in the Mixteca, San Jerónimo's origins are relatively recent. According to village archives, it was founded in 1879 by a half-dozen families who were pushed from their former village by soil depletion and land shortages onto previously unoccupied territory higher in the mountains. The extraordinary steep slopes that constitute most of the land of San Jerónimo render it generally unsuitable for intense cultivation. Not surprisingly, the village land, like virtually all the land of the Mixteca that has been cultivated far longer, has become severely eroded after a century of being farmed with plow and oxen. Mario Ortiz Gabriel has demonstrated that the high rate of permanent out-migration from the Mixteca in general is attributable primarily to ecological deterioration at the local level (Ortiz Gabriel n.d., 112–17).

Few households in San Jerónimo have enough land to feed their inhabitants. Stuart and Kearney (1981) have calculated that collectively, the village can raise no more than 20 percent of the corn and beans necessary to feed its population. Posed somewhat differently, the typical household can eat for less than two and a half months on its yearly harvest. Thus most families would face starvation without some other form of income.

Only a few households are tied to the local capitalist economy through their contact with regional markets. For example, among the elite who are able to sustain themselves year round in San Jerónimo are four landowners who also have small retail stores in the village. They import necessities like corn, beans, salt, and matches, and "luxuries" like soft drinks, beer, and canned goods—all sold at prices considerably higher than in the nearest town. Macario T., easily the wealthiest person and the largest landowner in the village, speculates in corn and beans in addition to selling retail goods in his store. Households buy from him on credit after their own reserves are depleted, usually months after harvest time, when the prices are high. After the next harvest, they are forced to sell their corn at low prices to pay the debt. In recent years, Macario T. has purchased several cargo trucks in which he transports supplies for his store. He also rents space on his trucks to neighbors for transporting building supplies and fertilizers, to elected religious functionaries for transporting the oxen, extra food, and ceremonial items needed for the numerous fiestas (purchased mostly in the mestizo town of Juxtlahuaca), and to migrants traveling to Huajuapan on the first stage of their journey north. The other store owners, some of the few larger landowners, follow suit but on a smaller scale. It is no accident that Macario T. and the other merchants have been leaders in religious and political hierarchies and have helped arrange the *tequios* needed to maintain and improve the new road to the village.

Macario T. is also the village's primary moneylender, and he finances many migrations north at an interest rate of 15 or 20 percent per month.

The only means for the rest of the population to supplement their living in San Jerónimo itself is to weave palm hats, which are sold to merchants for about ten cents each. Two can be made in a day if every spare moment is devoted to the task. The merchants market hats to a factory in Puebla, where they are "finished" and sold for about a dollar and a half in U.S. currency. In the mid-1980s, some villagers began to concentrate on making *tenates* (tortilla baskets) rather than hats because they can be more easily stockpiled, transported, and sold directly to tourists in metropolitan areas for seventy-five cents to a dollar. Almost everyone—men, women and children—weave hats or *tenates* as a source of cash income, and for some households, it is the only source.

Erosion, the unavailability of arable land, population growth, and the absence of opportunities for wage employment mean that almost all households must send some members away from the village for part of every year in order to survive. After the spring planting, fewer than 25 percent of the men of working age can be found in San Jerónimo at any one time until the most important fiesta of the year (that of the patron saint) brings many of them back at the end of September. By the beginning of the harvest in October, the population swells further and temporarily peaks.

By and large, the neighboring town of Huajuapan has offered little in the way of employment to workers from San Jerónimo. Men now in their late seventies and eighties report having traveled to the Gulf Coast to work as cane cutters on sugar plantations from the 1920s to the 1950s. Their sons migrated to the commercial agricultural fields of Sinaloa on the Pacific Coast, and some grandsons still go there because long-established networks of kin and neighbors can provide the crucial initial support. Since the late 1960s, however, migrants from San Jerónimo have established new networks, first in the border cities of Tijuana, Nogales, and Mexicali and since 1978–79 in the San Quintín Valley, after unusually heavy rains raised its water table and made the formerly arid land attractive to agribusiness. A few pioneers crossed the U.S. border in the late 1960s, beginning what is now a large and growing U.S. network. Substantial numbers of

San Jerónimo residents regularly find employment in California and Oregon agriculture, and some now go to Florida as well.

Most San Jerónimo households have some members working as migrant wage workers for part of every year, or even all of every year on a rotating basis. The remittances they send home are vital to maintaining the local economy. Between January and May 1987, almost 875,000,000 pesos were transferred to the Silacayoapan telegraph office. OF this amount, two-thirds came from other parts of Mexico, primarily the border region, and the rest from the United States.[11] According to one study, the value of remittances sent by migrants to the Mixteca as a whole exceeds the total value of all agriculture produced there (Ortiz Gabriel n.d., 28). In 1987 almost twenty billion pesos were sent to the Mixteca from the United States alone (Ortiz Gabriel n.d., 61).[12]

There is no land available for purchase in San Jerónimo and few opportunities for capital investment (the village has all the merchants it can support).[13] Consequently, wage income from the north that is not spent on food or fertilizer and pesticides is put into consumer goods (beds, radios, an occasional refrigerator, and other furnishings) and especially into house construction. Houses in San Jerónimo are now built from cement block and have poured cement floors and glass windows (contrary to the remarks of the Los Pinos manager). The round houses made of poles set into the earth with conical thatched roofs, which we observed on our first trips to San Jerónimo ten years ago, have now disappeared, although adobe structures with dirt floors are still common. Because few villagers can afford to live in the village permanently, some of the new concrete block houses stand empty for years while others are occupied sporadically.

Most migrants can be described as "circular," that is, they spend only a portion of each year engaged in wage labor on either side of the U.S.–Mexican border, returning to their villages for planting, harvesting, and the major fiestas as well as to rest from the rigors of agricultural wage labor. Generally, a migrant worker's optimum years are those between the ages of seventeen and thirty-five. Those younger and older lack the strength and endurance for the work, and they say that they lack the speed and agility to evade unscrupulous Mexican officials or *la migra*, as the U.S. Immigration

and Naturalization Service is usually called by migrants. Raised and nurtured by the village economy, they retire back to it at an early age. In the interim, their adult years have been expended in the service of capitalist production, and the village and its putative domestic economy have suffered the loss of net value.

The village subsistence minifundios are today's source of cheap labor power for Los Pinos and other commercial agriculture in Baja California Norte, Sinaloa, and across the border into California, Oregon, and Florida. The minifundios were a similar source of labor power for the cane plantations of the coast a generation ago. Thus despite the surface appearance of a "traditional" community and a largely domestic economy divorced from the national culture, the national economy, and capitalist production, the economy of San Jerónimo and other villages in the Mixteca is an inextricable part of the encompassing political economies of Mexico and the United States.

NEW IDENTITIES, NEW ETHNICITY

Village identification in the Mixteca has historically prevented or at least retarded collective inter-village action and has handicapped Mixtecs in efforts to defend themselves in the modern world of capitalist production into which they have been thrust. Yet Mixtecs from all over the Mixteca have subsumed their differences to band together in northern locations. They have formed associations and joined labor unions dedicated to defending their interests. Their political activism in the border region has been partially structured and defined in terms of the ethnic identity that is alternately glorified and despised by the majority population. Mixtecs themselves, however, are seizing neither the positive nor the negative myths of existing images but are constructing a new identity based on both that enables them to understand their experiences and attempt to make changes. Mixtecs are beginning to define their own reality in a highly contested struggle over the meaning of ethnicity, amidst the conditions of their daily lives. In light of what is generally known about the difficulties of forming cooperative associations across the linguistic and social barriers of diverse and historically closed village organization and identity, let us now examine the specific conditions that are fostering Mixtec consciousness of direct oppression.

During the early years of migraiton to the frontier and into the United States, women and children remained in villages in the Mixteca, as they had when husbands and fathers migrated to the Gulf Coast and returned only to plant, harvest, and participate in the ceremonial cycle. The border, however, is fifteen hundred miles away, ninety-six hours on the bus, and consequently, a trip north from the Mixteca requires a substantial financial investment. Staying north less than six months makes no sense. But in six months' time, corn and bean reserves in the village are depleted, and the money orders that families depend on to survive do not always arrive because the men have suffered bad luck, robbery, or worse.[14] As a result, during the late 1970s and early 1980s, entire families began migrating to the border region, thus initiating a new social and economic strategy: the satellite or "daughter" community. Families from San Jerónimo set up temporary, subsidiary households in enclaves within neighborhoods in border communities. Adjacent enclaves were populated by families from other Mixtec villages. At this point, a new economic pattern began to emerge among Mixtecs, whose women had not previously played a significant economic role outside the household. Now Mixtec women and children sell trinkets, *tenates*, or hats made the previous year in the village on the streets of frontier cities, or they beg to supplement the family's subsistence while men seek employment in the informal economy, working as casual laborers if they are fortunate, peddling handicrafts or scavenging if they are not.

The membership of such households in border towns shifts constantly as some return to the village to cultivate or harvest, cross the border seeking employment, or move south to the San Quintín Valley. At first, enclaves replicated the corporate separateness of the Mixteca, but as border cities grew with the increasing migration from the interior, well-defined geographic barriers began to break down. Marriages now occur occasionally between inhabitants of different villages, making endogamy less the rule than in the Mixteca. To the degree that migrants return to their natal villages, spouses from other places are beginning to become part of everyday life in the Mixteca.

As difficult as life in frontier cities often is for Mixtecs, conditions in the agricultural fields of the San Quintín Valley are far worse. Here, men, women, and children plant, tie, prune, weed, spray, irrigate, hand-pick, and stack vine-ripened tomatoes for ranches like Los Pinos, while living in labor camps like Las Pulgas. Although Los Pinos is a family-owned company, other similar enterprises, like the much larger ABC Ranch, are transnationals with substantial shares owned by U.S.–based corporations. Whether Mexican or internationally owned, all employ primarily Mixtecs interspersed with small numbers of other indigenous persons from Oaxaca and Chiapas, as well as some Salvadorans, Guatemalans, and other Central Americans. The vast majority of field laborers, however, continue to be Mixtecs.

All commercial ranches in the San Quintín Valley produce mainly for the export market, selling to U.S. grocery and fast-food chains. Together, these ranches house and employ between thirty and forty thousand field-workers who earn about three dollars a day for eight to ten hours of stoop labor.[15] The short-handled hoe, outlawed in California, is legal in Mexico and is used daily at ABC, Los Pinos, and elsewhere in the valley and on similar plantations in the coastal state of Sinaloa, where Mixtecs are also employed under virtually identical circumstances.[16] Farmworkers in both locations routinely apply pesticides that are controlled or banned in the United States with few or no safety precautions,[17] and some are known to have died from acute pesticide poisoning. Doctors in the valley report that the infant mortality rate is especially high and that the incidence of respiratory ailments is extraordinary.[18]

When feasible, Mixtec migrants seek better working conditions and higher wages by crossing the border into the United States. But even under the best of circumstances, border crossings are fraught with peril. As indios, Mixtecs are especially vulnerable to extortion and exploitation by border guards, municipal and state authorities, and gangs of ordinary criminals (Nagengast, Stavenhagen, and Kearney n.d.). Daughter communities on the Mexican side, especially in Tijuana, serve as launching pads for those about to attempt a border crossing and places for refuge and rest after capture and repatriation by the INS.

Daughter communities also have been established in California and Oregon and, like their counterparts in Mexican border towns, often serve as temporary places of refuge for groups of lone men from the Mixteca. Childless women sometimes enter the United States with husbands or brothers to work, but they are often subjected to attacks that range from verbal abuse to rape (Juffer 1988). Only occasionally do women with children cross the border, although the practice has become more frequent since 1984–85.

Of the uncounted thousands of Mixtecs in the United States,[19] almost all are "illegals," never having had the opportunity to obtain "green cards." They consequently seek employment, with few exceptions, in agricultural enterprises where they can more easily hide from the INS and where technical skills are not required. They typically work in citrus or strawberry fields, generally at minimum wage or a piece rate. The work is almost always in secondary and tertiary labor markets, often temporary, and usually offers few, if any, benefits (Kearney and Nagengast 1989).[20]

Although wages in U.S. agribusiness are higher than in Mexican counterparts in Baja California and Sinaloa, living and working conditions are sometimes equally bad (Nagengast, Stavenhagen, and Kearney, n.d.). Because Mixtecs speak little Spanish and no English and are usually undocumented, they live in double jeopardy in the U.S. labor market, exploited even more viciously than mestizo undocumented workers by unscrupulous labor contractors and coyotes (those who smuggle workers across the border for a fee), who are ironically Mexicans themselves in most cases (see Conover 1987). Farm-labor contractors typically charge for all services performed for "their" workers: taking them to the market or to cash their paychecks, bringing them what few medicines they can afford (Vaupel and Maretin 1986). In this setting, Mixtecs are stigmatized as indios as often as they are in Mexico.

Despite state and federal regulations requiring U.S. growers to provide living quarters for workers that meet certain minimal standards, Mixtecs are often forced to seek abandoned vehicles, shacks constructed of cardboard, or even holes dug in the side of riverbanks or canyons in which to sleep. The only alternative, if any, may be to pay seventy-five to one hundred dollars a week per person for crowded, unheated, unfurnished, filthy rooms that lack water or toilets.

Few Mixtecs qualified for amnesty under the provisions of the 1986 Immigration Reform and Control Act (IRCA). Our preliminary research suggests that those who do not qualify for legalization but remain in the United States are being subjected to even more extensive exploitation and human rights abuses than before, especially (although not exclusively) at the hands of legal and illegal labor contractors, who are proliferating and replacing direct by growers (Nagengast, Stavenhagen, and Kearney n.d.; see also Cornelius 1988; Vaupel and Martin 1986).

To these hardships may be added others: exposure to dangerous pesticides; minimum and below-minimum wages for back-breaking work; no job security; the need to be constantly on the move following jobs; inadequate or nonexistent housing, education for children, and health care; constant fear of repatriation; and the everyday discrimination experienced by minorities. The total picture that emerges reveals life conditions that make it especially difficult to realize human dignity.

In all the locations outside the Mixteca that have been discussed (tomato plantations on the west coast of Sinaloa and in the San Quintín Valley, urban enclaves in Mexican border cities, and commercial agricultural fields in California and Oregon), Mixtecs are more directly incorporated into capitalist production than in the villages where their articulation is less immediately perceivable. In all these new settings, they experience the most direct exploitation possible: they are paid starvation wages; they are forced to compete with each other to be the most docile and willing laborers; and they often must live in subhuman conditions. The sense of oppression that results cannot be displaced to neighbors from adjoining villages. It is ironically in these conditions in the north, far from their homeland, that Mixtecs are discovering that they are indeed Mixtec. A new political consciousness and activism has coalesced into an emerging pan-Mixtec ethnic identity, an ethnic awareness that transcends commune and even district identification and manifests itself in the form of Mixtec associations and labor-union activity in the border area of the Californias and Sonora and in Oregon. This new identity as Mixtecs, which was latent in the Mixteca, has become the raw material for new cultural, ideological, and substantive resources in altered circumstances. Significantly, this new elaboration of ethnicity is also causing Mixtecs to become the target of political and economic repression as Mixtecs.

CONSCIOUSNESS AND ACTIVISM

Let us examine the situation of Mixtecs in the San Quintín Valley as a case in point. As noted above, between thirty and forty thousand Mixtecs from all over the Mixteca have migrated to the valley to work in transnational agriculture. Since 1984 the indigenous Mixtec leaders of the Central Independence de Oberos Agrícolas y Campesinos (CIOAC), an independent national labor union, have been supported by the main leftist political parties, first by the Partido Socialista Unificado de México (PSUM) and then by its successor, the Partido Mexicana Socialista (PMS). These groups have been trying to organize this work force into a union opposing that belonging to the Confederación de Trabajadores Mexicanos (CTM).[21] The latter confederation is administered by the federal government and is closely aligned with the Partido Revolucionario Institucional (PRI), which has ruled Mexico for more than four decades. The PRI has historically held a virtual monopoly on municipal, state, and federal offices. Neither the PRI nor the CTM had shown any particular interest in Mixtec farmworkers until the CIOAC began to form a local in the San Quintín Valley.

Since the CIOAC became active in San Quintín, it has been subjected to well-orchestrated repression by the combined forces of the growers and the Mexican state at all levels. For example, according to Mixtec eyewitnesses, a Mixtec organizer was deliberately run down and killed in 1984 by a driver for one of the major growers. No investigation of what was perceived by farmworkers and union activists as a political killing was launched publicly by any state agency, despite large demonstrations and mass appeals. In the summer of 1987, the body of another Mixtec CIOAC leader was found by the side of the road, apparently the victim of a hit-and-run accident. Although the man had received several death threats in the weeks prior to the incident, the police claimed they were unable to find any evidence of foul play (*Boletín Mixteco* 1987, 6). Other less dramatic but repressive incidents—including numerous death threats directed

at leaders and nonlethal attacks—punctuated the three years between these deaths.

Given the ethnic composition of the work force, the confrontation in the San Quintín Valley has become a conflict of Mixtecs versus a coalition of growers and the state. The last two groups view the situation as not only a major labor conflict on their hands but also a rather embarrassing *problema indígena* in Baja California Norte, one of the most "mestizo" parts of Mexico.[22] Mixtec leaders have repudiated the PRI and the CTM and thrown their lot in with the political opposition. Unlike the Mixteca, where there is no direct non-Mixtec political oppression against which to define Mixtec identity, in San Quintín the growers are confronting labor unrest and workers not as workers but as Mixtecs. Thus ethnicity has emerged as a noticeable theme of political consciousness and political action on both sides.

Similar scenarios are unfolding in Tijuana, Nogales, and Mexicali. Mixtecs are subject to the same dangers in these cities as other poor urban workers—crime, violence, high unemployment, low wages, and dismal living conditions—but they alone are targeted for harassment and police extortion as indios. For some years, they were referred to by the derogatory epithet of "*los oaxacas*" (a corruption of *los oaxaqueños*), but now one increasingly hears "*los mixtecos*." Mixtec women street-vendors are referred to derisively as "*las Marías*." In border towns that had been homogeneously mestizo for generations, racism now poisons public space.

As a result of police mistreatment and extortion of women street-vendors, several spokespersons from the Mixtec community in Tijuana publicly confronted municipal authorities in 1984, demanding that harassment of the women cease. These events were well-covered by the media on both sides of the border. During an embarrassing scandal, a police commandant was forced to resign, and abuses of the women subsequently decreased. Heartened by this victory, the Asociación de los Mixtecos Residentes en Tijuana (ASMIRT) was founded. It was patterned after the indigenous town council, but with two important differences: first, the association was open to any Mixtec living in Tijuana, an indication of an emerging pan-Mixtec identity; and second, unlike the make-up of the town councils, women were encouraged to take active roles and to be officers. These innovations have now become "traditions" in the association.

ASMIRT immediately declared its independence from the PRI and all other political parties and soon began to forge links with the CIOAC in San Quintín, just to the south. Perhaps because of the novel presence of indios in border cities, the media—especially newspapers opposed to the Mexican government—began to cover regularly what soon developed into the "Mixtec story." Although the Tijuana Mixtecs lacked the numbers of the San Quintín population, where the CIOAC could turn out eight to ten thousand marchers, the Tijuana group has mustered a thousand or more for demonstrations. On several occasions, they confronted the state governor in what was characterized by the local media as embarrassments for the PRI and the state. At one of these events, representatives of ASMIRT presented the governor with a jar of *mole*, a traditional Oaxacan dish said to predate the conquest, to remind him of the presence of "*indígenas*" in the city. On yet another occasion, a copy of the Mexican Constitution was ceremoniously presented to the governor on the steps of the new cultural center, a museum and auditorium complex that pays homage to the pre-Columbian ancestry of Mexico. The unmistakable message conveyed was that Mixtecs, who are celebrated in other contexts as the original inhabitants of Mexico, were not being accorded the basic civil and human rights of citizens—a calculated rebuke to the governor, to the PRI that he represents, and to the state. Such activities and public discourse about them have strengthened the Mixtecs' sense of themselves as Mixtecs, primarily in opposition to the state in its various guises, and have conversely caused the state, the media, and the public to define and treat them as Mixtecs.

The political independence of the Mixtec Association in Tijuana and the CIOAC in San Quintín has been their greatest strength but in retrospect also their biggest liability. Just as growers and state government have succeeded in stalemating the organizing efforts of the CIOAC in San Quintín, so have outside interests (apparently emanating from the PRI) intervened in the internal affairs of the Mixtec Association in Tijuana in efforts to neutralize it and bring it into the PRI fold. In fact, the independent Tijuana association has fallen into disarray as a political organization since 1986, and

some of its non-Mixtec political allies have been forced to curb their activities because of unproved and almost certainly unfounded charges leveled against them by local authorities. But although the state has successfully curtailed the association's political activism through overt repression and the co-opting of some Mixtec leaders, it has nevertheless been forced to direct increased social services to the residential enclaves of the Mixtecs. Yet in attempting to crush Mixtec political opposition, the state has actually objectified what had been only a latent pan-Mixtec identity. Ethnic awareness in these circumstances of overt repression and exploitation is beginning to offset the negative self-image that Mixtecs had internalized during centuries of less apparent oppression. For example, the everyday use of the Mixtec language now thwarts the agents of growers and the state who attempt to monitor meetings and public demonstrations of CIOAC and ASMIRT, thus giving "ugly words" a previously unrealized value to Mixtecs.

As economic conditions in rural Mexico continue to deteriorate, incentives for migrating to California and other parts of the United States to work will increase. Associations of mestizo migrants, typically made up of members from the same community in Mexico, are now common in the United States, including several founded since the mid-1980s by Mixtec migrants in California and Oregon. Like mestizo associations, they promote self-help and collect money and other resources for community projects in their home villages. But unlike mestizo groups, Mixtec associations cross-cut community of origin and base themselves instead on shared ethnicity. Moreover, they are dedicated to defending, their members from the kinds of human and civil rights abuses described above.

Although the living and working conditions of foreign migrant workers in the United States have always been harsh, they have not been uniformly so, fluctuating over the decades with the vagaries of U.S. immigration policy and the economic and political contexts that shape it (Cockcroft 1986). Adding to the conditions noted above, the passage and implementation of the 1986 Immigration Reform and Control Act (IRCA) has increased concern among human and civil rights activists in Mexico, the United States, and elsewhere over the plight of migrants to the United States. Much of this concern centers on the large numbers of Mixtecs and other undocumented workers currently in California and neighboring states who do not qualify for immigration amnesty under IRCA. Indications already suggest that such individuals and their families are being subjected to unusually extreme hardships and abuses because of this heightened vulnerability (Nagengast, Stavenhagen, and Kearney, n.d.; Cornelius 1988).

The Asociación Cívica Benito Juárez (based in Fresno and Madera, California, and in Salem, Oregon) is a pan-Mixtec transnational association based on shared ethnicity that has arisen to defend Mixtecs in their new circumstances in the United States. Members of ACBJ promote village development projects in Oaxaca but also increasingly concern themselves with discrimination, exploitation, health, and human rights abuses in Mixtec enclaves in California and Oregon, regardless of the member's village of origin. They are now attempting to transform one aspect of their organization into a labor contracting association in which Mixtec farmworkers would sell their labor directly to growers, thereby avoiding the usually exploitative labor contractors now depended on by most workers. Concern is also focusing on gathering and publicizing testimonies of human rights abuses through independent human rights organizations. The ACBJ participated in a transactional conference in Mexicali on human rights violations suffered by migrants on both sides of the border in January 1989 and in a seminar on international human rights law and its applicability to them in Los Angeles in May 1989. Overall, the ACBJ is working toward forming a transnational league of Mixtec associations that will incorporate Mixtec groups on both sides of the border. Mixtecs in the United States say that there is "more space" to organize north of the border than in Mexico, meaning that overt political oppression in the United States is less intense.

Like its counterpart organizations in Mexico, the ACBJ has taken care not to affiliate itself with any organs or institutions of the Mexican state. But since the July 1988 elections, in which the PRI probably suffered a major (although unacknowledged) defeat at the hands of Cuauhtémoc Cárdenas and the Frente Democrática Nacional, the PRI is taking unprecedented steps to woo Mixtecs (and others) back to the fold. Historically, the PRI has been able to count on the votes of most Mixtecs in

national, state, and local elections.[23] According to a political leader from San Jerónimo, village authorities in the past more or less delivered all the votes of the inhabitants in a block to the PRI. The July 1988 returns thus represented a notable departure from this routine, according to many observers. Although no accurate figures exist (nor are there likely to be any), the popular perception is that Mixtecs in the Mixteca as well as those in the frontier voted overwhelmingly for the Cardenistas—a major blow to the PRI and especially to Heladio Ramírez López, the PRI governor of Oaxaca and a self-identified Mixtec.

Ramírez López made an extraordinary visit to California in April 1989 to meet with Mixtec migrant workers living there, the first time a governor of Oaxaca ever met with constituents outside the state. At two meetings in Watsonville and Madera, he heard grievances and demands from Mixtec leaders of the ACBJ and other Mixtec organizations and from independent Mixtecs. All complained about extortion by government officials when traveling north, dishonest telegraph officials who appropriate portions of remittances sent to families in the Mixteca, and economic conditions in the Mixteca iteslf. One political leader from San Jerónimo solicited Ramírez López's intervention with the governor of Sonora to stop police harassment of Mixtecs in Nogales.

Corn prices, the costs of fiestas, and other expenses in villages in the Mixteca have all been driven up by Mexico's economic crisis, the huge inflation since 1982, and the influx of cash income. Other problems requiring attention are the inexorable soil erosion that takes more land out of production every year and reduces the yield of the rest, contaminated water, malnutrition, and the lack of even basic medical facilities. The character of the response of the Consul General of Mexico in Los Angeles to the demands of the Mixtecs is instructive: he suggested that it would be less expensive for migrants to fly from Oaxaca to the border than to pay the bribes extorted from them on the road; he further suggested that Mixtecs telegraph Oaxacan state officials in advance when large sums of money are about to be sent to the Mixteca. Governor Ramírez López, however, pledged his administration's help in better "policing" of authorities and in implementing additional local projects in the Mixteca.

What will come of the promises of Ramírez López remains to be seen. It is tempting to characterize this politician's efforts as yet another effort to "objectify" Mixtecs—an attempt to define the "problems" of indigenous migrants in terms of the official discourse and within the parameters of existing institutions of the state. In any case, the significance of Ramírez López's encounter with Mixtec immigrants lies not in his promises but in the fact that the political activism of Mixtecs qua Mixtecs in the border region is profoundly affecting the conduct of politics in the interior of Mexico, an outcome that further reinforces Mixtec ethnic identity and activism in both locations.

It is ironic that Mixtecs' hitherto unrecognized identity as mixtecos has become an icon of their new-found solidarity, both to themselves and to others. As Mixtecs go north to border towns seeking wage work and encounter more direct forms of repression, they are actively resisting exploitation and repression by invoking some of the "traditions" that previously served them in a more passive form. Group activism through ASMIRT and CIOAC in Baja California, ACBJ, and other Mixtec groupings is not simply a desperate response to stress. By claiming adherence to the "traditions" of their people and devising new ones when appropriate, they are struggling to control the politics of meaning given to the identity of Mixtec. Simultaneously, they are establishing the legitimacy of Mixtec workers as Mixtecs in altered circumstances and are transforming passive resistance to indirect and direct repression into active resistance.

TRADITION COMES FULL CIRCLE

While a few families from San Jerónimo have settled more or less permanently in daughter enclaves in Mexican border towns, California, and Oregon, most migrants are circular and most daughter settlements remain subsidiary to major residence in and identification with San Jerónimo. There they own land, albeit insufficient to provide subsistence, there parents live and grandparents are buried. And there also they will "retire" when they are too old, too sick, or too worn-down to withstand the rigors of border crossings, stoop labor, and miserable living and working conditions everywhere. In San Jerónimo, they invest their discretionary earnings and build permanent residences. Most Mixtecs feel insecure about long-term residence in the border region, especially in the face of uncertainties about IRCA and the precariousness of employment on the Mexican side. Moreover, one possible liability of prolonged absence is loss of membership in one's natal commune and the reassignment of one's land to others. Consequently, both temporary and long-term residents on both sides of the border make special efforts to reaffirm their commune membership on a regular basis. This strategy involves periodically returning to fulfill ceremonial and civil duties as well as remitting money to communal projects. In recent years, as a result of dollar income, the money expended by migrants on civic and religious obligations in San Jerónimo and other Mixtec communes has increased dramatically. Civil and religious ceremonial complexes in San Jerónimo and throughout the Mixteca have been enhanced, and the construction of migrant-financed public works has boomed in the form of new municipal buildings, churches, and chapels. Thus while Mixtecs are being expelled greater distances from their homeland in increasing numbers by economic conditions, one effect of migration is to revitalize some of the symbolic and collective expressions of commune identity in the Mixteca. Yet awareness of a new pan-Mixtec ethnic identity is also being transferred to daily life in the Mixteca and is beginning to undermine some of the results of their centuries-long oppression. The situation is now fluid, but Mixtecs are beginning to talk about intercommune projects that in time may break down the most deleterious effects of the "closed corporate" structure of villages. Ramírez López's attention to Mixtec demands may lend additional impetus to an emerging political and economic solidarity in the Mixteca that will transcend the oppressive aspects of the "traditional."

CONCLUSION

The most salient identity in the Mixteca—that of village—is negated as individuals leave their communes, especially as they leave Oaxaca for the north and find themselves collectively identified by the predominantly mestizo population in Mexico as "other," members of a minority and a despised one at that. This enforced duality between themselves and others has prevented Mixtecs from developing a common class consciousness with mestizo workers who share their everyday experience of poverty and exploitation. In the north, however, a new ethnic identity has been set into motion as a result of a dialectic relationship between the direct incorporation of Mixtecs into the capitalist organization of production, their collective exploitation and identity by others as a minority, and their own social actions. The fact that they are experiencing exploitation not as anonymous individual workers or isolated *campesinos* but as a cohesive social unit based on their ethnicity, defined by themselves and others, has led to the emergence of ethnic consciousness and political activism. Mixtec ethnicity is consequently a social creation brought into being by social actions.

Members of indigenous groups like the Mixtec who are forced to migrate into the hostile social, political, and economic environments of the wider society, whether in Mexico or in the United States, often become permanent members of an economically and politically marginalized underclass. To varying degrees, they experience "ethnocide," defined by Stavenhagen (1986) as the systematic negation or even destruction of what is described as indigenous culture. This process occurs through deliberate policies of dominant groups controlling state power but also through "unofficial" repression, economic and political exploitation, and denial of a group's positive ethnic and cultural identity. Mixtecs, however, are resisting ethnocide by distinguishing between oppression and culture and by preserving their positive cultural identity thus far with extraordinary success.

We have argued that tradition is what peoples do today (and perhaps did yesterday) and that peoples transform their traditions and their culture in the face of unique political, social, and economic conditions in ways that help them resist repression and exploitation. Thus history, social and political structures, and human agency constitute each other in the formation of new configurations. A new tradition—Mixtec ethnic identity, political consciousness, and activism—has been created and is contesting in the arena of politics the very meaning of tradition.

NOTES

1. Although the term *mestizo* implies persons of mixed European and indigenous stock, we use it here in a cultural rather than a genetic sense.

2. The movement of persons between three separate locations spanning as much as three thousand miles and an international border raises questions of an appropriate "unit of analysis." Kearney (1986a) addressed this problem by theorizing the "articulatory migration network," a unit encompassing persons in all three locations. Large Mixtec enclaves also exist in Mexico City, and smaller ones in other Mexican cities including Oaxaca, Chihuahua, and Hermosilla. On Mixtec migration to Mexico City, see Butterworth (1975).

3. The Mixteca region lies in western Oaxaca and adjacent areas of Guerrero and Puebla and is broken into three more or less ecologically distinct zones: the Mixteca Alta, the Mixteca Baja, and the Mixteca de la Costa.

4. The Mixteca Baja comprises seven of the thirty administrative districts of the state of Oaxaca, namely, Coixtlahuaca, Huajuapan, Juxtlahuaca, Nochixtlán, Silacayoapan, Teposcolula, and Tlaxiaco.

5. See Martín Luís Guzmán, *The Eagle and the Serpent*, quoted in Riding (1986, 290).

6. Amnesty International has documented the incident in Mexico City as well as similar cases of the apparent brutalizing and torture of political opponents by the state or those presumed to be operating with the tacit approval of the state. See Amnesty International, *Annual Report 1988* (London: Amnesty International, 1988), p. 176, as well as earlier *Annual Reports* for details, particularly Amnesty International's special report on Mexico, *Mexico: Human Rights Violations in Rural Areas* (London: Amnesty International, 1986). Torture and other human rights abuses in Baja California have been documented in the archives of the Tijuana-based Centro Binacional de Derechos Humanos. The Academia Mexicana de Derechos Humanos in Mexico City holds extensive documentation of human rights violations in Oaxaca and elsewhere in Mexico. See also Nagengast, Stavenhagen, and Kearney (n.d.).

7. O. Luis, an undergraduate at the University of California, Santa Cruz, the child of Mixtec and Zapotec parents, spent six months in 1987 working as an intern in the Secretaría de Educación Pública in Oaxaca. He reports widespread corruption in the department in terms of bribery and chicanery and also an often-expressed contempt for the department's indigenous clients and

the needs they cite (O. Luis, personal conversation, December 1987).

8. Romney and Romney (1966) report that the trip from Huajuapan to Juxtlahuaca, a town not far from Silacayoapan, took twelve hours by four-wheel-drive jeep in the 1960s.

9. *Tequio* is nonpaid communal work for projects such as constructing and maintaining public roads and buildings. It is an ancient system of obligation that has been utilized by the Aztecs and Mixtecs for community projects.

10. See Amnesty International, *Mexico: Human Rights Violations in Rural Areas*, which focuses on the repression, disappearance, and murder of Mixtec, Triqui, and other indigenous activists in the rural areas of Oaxaca and Chiapas.

11. This estimate is based on an examination of records of the telegraph office in Silacayoapan, Oaxaca, in July 1987. The figure includes remittances from about ten villages in the municipio of Silacayoapan, including San Jerónimo.

12. This figure was cited by the manager of the telegraph office in Oaxaca.

13. Kearney (1986b) reviews migration literature and concludes that the impact of remittances and the international experience of migrants on economic development in home locations is typically negative or neutral at best.

14. We first encountered workers from San Jerónimo in 1978 in Riverside, California, where, in the course of a robbery committed against them, one had been murdered, a second had been shot, and twelve others were being held in the Riverside county jail as material witnesses to the crime.

15. The value of the peso against the dollar has declined rapidly since 1982, when it stood at 12.5 to 1. By fall 1987, it had dropped to 2,300 to 1.

16. ABC, for example, is one of the major growers in Sinaloa. Mixtec farmworkers employed by this company in the San Quintín Valley report being bussed by ABC between the two locations according to the needs of the different growing seasons.

17. In 1985 we surveyed every store that sells pesticides in the several towns of the San Quintín Valley. Not one clerk knew what safeguards should be used when employing pesticides nor did any of the stores sell the protective clothing suggested on the pesticide containers. One doctor in the valley reports that the foremen of field crews sometimes carry syringes of atropine (a stimulant) in their trucks in case a worker goes into convulsions. See also Kistner (1986) and Wright (1986, n.d.). The use of pesticides on crops imported into the United States is beginning to concern U.S. legislators because of the potential long-term dangers being posed to U.S. constituents, but none of this official concern is directed toward the Mexican workers who are exposed to daily doses of acutely toxic and sometimes lethal pesticides. U.S. growers are the apparent proximate stimuli of the pesticide concern, although consumer concern is growing. While pesticides are undoubtedly a serious long-term hazard to U.S. consumers, newspapers and television reports suggest that competition from Mexican growers, with their decidedly lower production costs (including labor costs), is causing the dialogue. See, for example, "Crackdown Sought on Imports of Tainted Food," *San Francisco Chronicle*, 19 May 1987, p. 23.

18. Based on interviews with doctors at the Buen Pastor Clinic and the state clinic in Lázaro Cárdenas in 1985.

19. Estimates vary, but there are probably at least ten thousand Mixtecs living in the United States at any one time.

20. A full description of secondary and tertiary labor markets and the place undocumented workers occupy within them can be found in Kearney and Nagengast (1989).

21. In 1987 the PSUM was incorporated into a coalition party, the Partido Mexicano Socialista (PMS), which also supported the CIOAC. In 1988 the PMS threw its support to the Frente Democrática Nacional (FDN) led by Cuauhtémoc Cárdenas and has since been absorbed into his new party, the Partido de Revolucíon Democrática (PRD).

22. The autochthonous peoples of Baja California are at present few in number and politically insignificant.

23. Exceptions generally occur at the local level. For example, the Mixtec town of Alcozauca in Guerrero elected representatives of the PSM to the municipal government in the mid-1980s (Sidman 1988).

REFERENCES

Anderson, Benedict, 1983. *Imagined Communities: Reflections on the Origin and Spread of Nationalism*. London: Verso.

Barthes, Roland, 1972. *Mythologies*. Translated by Annette Lavers. New York: Hill and Wang.

Boletin Mixteco, 1987. "Malas noticias de San Quintín." Volume 2, no 2. (Fall).

Butterworth, Douglas, 1975. "Rural-Urban Migration and Microdemography: A Case Study from Mexico," *Urban Anthropology* 4:265–83.

Cockcroft, James, 1986. *Outlaws in the Promised Land: Mexican Immigrant Workers and America's Future.* New York: Grove Press.

Comaroff, John, 1987. "Of Totemism and Ethnicity," *Ethnos* 52, nos. 3–4:301–23.

Conover, Ted, 1987. *Coyotes: A Journey through the Secret World of America's Illegal Aliens.* New York: Basic Books.

Cornelius, Wayne, 1988. "Migrants from Mexico: Still Coming—and Staying," *Los Angeles Times*, 3 July, pt. v, pp. 1–2.

Coronil, Fernando, n.d. "Mastery by Signs, Signs of Mastery." Manuscript, University of Chicago.

Dennis, Phillip, 1987. *Intervillage Conflict in Oaxaca.* New Brunswick and London: Rutgers University Press.

Diener, Paul, 1978. "The Tears of St. Anthony: Ritual and Revolution in Eastern Guatemala," *Latin American Perspectives* 5, no. 3:92–115.

Foucault, Michel, 1970. *The Order of Things: An Archeology of the Human Sciences.* London: Tavistock Publications.

———, 1973. *Madness and Civilization.* New York: Vintage Books.

———, 1980. *Power/Knowledge: Selected Interviews and Other Writings, 1972–1977.* Edited by Colin Gordon. New York: Pantheon Books.

Geertz, Clifford, 1973. "The Politics of Meaning." In Geertz, *The Interpretation of Cultures.* New York: Basic Books.

Greenberg, James, 1981. *Santiago's Sword: Chatino Peasant Religion and Economics.* Berkeley and London: University of California Press.

Griffith, Keith, 1974. *The Political Economy of Agrarian Change: An Essay on the Green Revolution.* Cambridge, Mass.: Harvard University Press.

———, 1987. *World Hunger and the World Economy.* London: Macmillan.

Hewitt de Alcantara, Cynthia, 1978. *La modernización de la agricultura mexicana, 1940–1970.* Mexico City: Siglo Veintiuno Editores.

———, 1984. *Anthropological Perspectives on Rural Mexico.* London: Routledge and Kegan Paul.

Juffer, Jane, 1988. "Abuse at the Border," *The Progressive*, 14 Apr., pp. 14–19.

Kearney, Michael, 1986a. "Integration of the Mixteca and the Western U.S.–Mexico Region via Migratory Wage Labor." In *Regional Impacts of U.S.–Mexican Relations,* edited by Ina Rosenthal-Vrey. 71–102. La

Jolla: Center for U.S.–Mexican Studies, University of California, San Diego.

———, 1986b. "From the Invisible Hand to Visible Feet: Anthropological Studies of Migration and Development," *Annual Review of Anthropology* 15:331–61.

———, 1988. "Mixtec Political Consciousness: From Passive to Active Resistance." In *Rural Revolt in Mexico and U.S. Intervention,* edited by D. Nugent. Monograph Series, Center for U.S.–Mexican Studies, University of California, San Diego.

Kearney, Michael, and Carole Nagengast, 1989. "Anthropological Perspectives on Transnational Communities in Rural California." Working Group on Farm Labor and Rural Poverty, Working Paper no. 3. Davis, Calif.: California Institute for Rural Studies, University of California.

Kistner, William, 1986. "Scrutiny of the Bounty," *Mother Jones* 11, no. 9 (Dec.):28–35, 58.

Lappé, Frances Moore, and Joseph Collins, 1979. *Food First: Beyond the Myth of Scarcity.* New York: Ballantine Books.

———, 1986. *World Hunger: Twelve Myths.* New York: Grove Press.

Nagengast, Carole, Rodolfo Stavenhagen, and Michael Kearney, n.d. "Human Rights and Indigenous Workers: The Mixtecs in Mexico and the United States." In *Neighbors in Crisis: A Call for Joint Solutions,* edited by Lorenzo Meyer and Daniel Aldrich. Boulder, Colo.: Westview, forthcoming.

Ortiz Gabriel, Mario, n.d. "Deterioro y crisis de la economía campesina de la Mixteca de Oaxaca." Manuscript, Colegio de México.

Riding, Alan, 1986. *Distant Neighbors: A Portrait of the Mexicans.* New York: Vintage Books.

Romney, Kimball, and Romaine Romney, 1966. *The Mixtecans of Juxtlahuaca.* New York: Wiley.

Sidman, Deborah, 1988. "A Project in Alcozauca, Guerrero, Mexico." Senior thesis, University of California, Santa Cruz.

Spores, Ronald, 1967. *The Mixtec Kings and Their People.* Norman: University of Oklahoma Press.

———, 1984. *The Mixtec in Ancient and Colonial Times.* Norman: University of Oklahoma Press.

Stavenhagen, Rodolfo, 1978. *Current Problems of Mexico.* San Diego, Calif.: Institute of Public and Urban Affairs, San Diego State University.

———, 1986. "Ethnodevelopment: A Neglected Dimension in Development Thinking." Reprint from *Development Studies: Critique and Renewal.* Leiden: E.J. Brill.

Stuart, James, and Michael Kearney, 1981. *Causes and Effects of Agricultural Labor Migration from the Mixteca of Oaxaca to California.* La Jolla: Program in

U.S.–Mexican Studies, University of California, San Diego.

Taussig, Michael, 1984. "Culture of Terror—Space of Death: Roger Casement's Putumayo Report and the Explanation of Torture," *Comparative Studies in Society and History* 26, no. 3:467–97.

Todorov, Tzvetan, 1984. *The Conquest of America.* New York: Harper and Row.

Vaupel, Suzanne, and Phillip Martin, 1986. "Activity and Regulation of Farm Labor Contractors." Giannini Information Series no. 86–3, Division of Agriculture and Natural Resources. Oakland, Calif.:

Giannini Foundation of Agricultural Economics, University of California.

Williams, Raymond, 1975. *The Country and the City.* St. Albans: Paladin.

Wolf, Eric, 1957. "Closed Corporate Peasant Communities in Mesoamerica and Java," *Southwestern Journal and Anthropology* 13:1–18.

Wright, Angus, 1986. "Rethinking the Circle of Poison," *Latin American Perspectives* 13, no. 4:26–59.

———, n.d. *The Death of Ramón Gonzales: The Modern Agricultural Dilemma.* Austin: University of Texas Press, forthcoming.

40

Phantom Citizenship and the Prosthetics of Corporate Capital
"Maria Aquinda et al versus Texaco, Inc. USA"

Suzana Sawyer

In November 1993, a Philadelphia law firm filed a $1.5 billion class-action suit against Texaco, Inc. in a New York federal court on behalf of 30,000 Ecuadorian citizens. Plaintiffs sought reparations for health and environmental degradation resulting from over twenty-five years of Texaco petroleum activity in the Ecuadorian Amazon. The suit alleged that Texaco, Inc. made strategic decisions in its White Plains headquarters to maximize corporate profits by using substandard technology for oil operations in Ecuador. Negligent industrial practices and deteriorating equipment dumped toxic wastes into water and soil systems throughout the region, plaintiffs claimed, severely contaminating the environment and endangering local people. Texaco, Inc. USA claimed complete exoneration, motioning that the case be dismissed from U.S. courts. A subsidiary-of-a-subsidiary-of-a-subsidiary was liable for operations in Ecuador, the multina-tional contended, not the "parent" company. This Texaco subsidiary three-times-removed was legally based in Quito (Ecuador's capital) and it was there that Ecuadorian citizens would have to prove wrong-doing and seek restitution.

Inspired by Diana Nelson's fabulous knack for splicing together the uncommon, this paper appropriates notions of phantom and prosthetic limbs to explore how rights and accountability are produced and erased in a transnational arena. I probe how bodies severed from, or denied, citizenship at "home" phantasmically claim rights afar and how multinationals, circumscribed by codes of behavior at home, perfect their corporate performance through a detachable, and contingently disavowed, prosthetics of subsidiaries abroad. Intriguingly, a discourse on sexuality served as one realm (among others) for contesting national identity and transnational hierarchies. Gender provided a grid of social reference through which to chart and subvert the exercise of power, citizenship, and sovereignty in transnational space (cf. Scott 1986: 1069).[1]

As one might expect, the class-action suit against Texaco received notable press in Ecuador. At the time, I was doing fieldwork on petroleum politics in the rainforest approximately 50 miles south of

Paper presented at the American Anthropological Association Meetings at panel organized by Diane Nelson entitled "Phantom Limbs and Invisible Hands: Bodies, Prosthetixs, and Late Capitalist Identities," San Francisco, November 1996.

where Texaco worked. Public attention escalated, however, when the Ecuadorian ambassador in Washington, D.C., wrote a letter to the U.S. State Department demanding that it intervene in judicial process and have the Texaco case repealed from U.S. courts.[2] In his letter, the ambassador claimed that it was an affront to Ecuador's national sovereignty for a U.S. court to accept jurisdiction for a lawsuit concerning activity within Ecuadorian territory. The Ambassador questioned the "alleged" citizenship (that is, national allegiance) of the plaintiffs and warned the State Department that acceptance of the case would negatively affect the Ecuadorian economy. Hearing the case in New York would create "serious disincentives to U.S. companies" thinking of investing in Ecuador precisely as the country "attempt[ed] to attract [foreign] investors."[3] Via its diplomatic corp, the Ecuadorian regime championed the interests of a multinational corporation under the pretext of national sovereignty while simultaneously disavowing responsibility for the health and safety of its own citizens.[4]

As intimated in the ambassador's letter, the class-action suit against Texaco coincided with attempts to implement further neo-liberal changes in Ecuador. Since oil revenues accounted for 50 percent of the state's budget, the petroleum sector was a prime focus of structural adjustments. Conservative President Sixto Durán Ballén sought to boost oil exploration and production by luring foreign investment to Ecuador with more attractive fiscal arrangements.[5]

Neo-liberal reforms to "modernize"—that is, intensify—oil operations in the rainforest sparked heated debate. Indigenous and environmentalist organizations were among the most vocal opposing increased petroleum activity. Specifically, controversy centered around the extent to which Durán Ballén's regime placed the rights of multinational corporations over and above the rights of Ecuadorian citizens. Under the guise of "modernization," the administration auctioned state resources to multinationals—popular groups charged—irrespective of the deleterious effects on local people and the environment. Yet, ironically, precisely at the moment when Ecuador was embracing economic globalization with wanton fervor and championing its insertion into more integrated markets, the Executive self-righteously postured its defense

of national sovereignty, labeling those who challenged its agenda as unpatriotic and unworthy citizens. The very ambiguity globalization engendered incited the state to reaffirm and reinstantiate its sovereign will. Yet, "neo-liberal sovereignty" rang politically oxymoronic—a sign of political incoherence and anxiety.[6]

Attempts to hold multinationals legally accountable for their actions in foreign lands have been notoriously unsuccessful. The deaths of thousands from a gas leak in Union Carbide's Bhopal plant is perhaps one of the more tragic failures. Filed in the same New York district court, the Bhopal case was summarily dismissed on grounds of unsuitable jurisdiction; the court ruled (erroneously according to many) that Indian courts were an adequate alternative forum for action.[7] U.S. courts widely conclude that torts alleged to occur on foreign lands, under foreign laws, and toward foreign subjects are best arbitrated on foreign territory, regardless of who allegedly perpetrated what action.

The class-action litigation pursued by Ecuadorian plaintiffs, however, sought to obviate such ruling. Tort (or wrong-doing), they claimed, occurred on U.S. soil in Texaco's New York headquarters among multinational executives and board members. Corporate decisions had direct repercussions on how oil operations were to be carried out in Ecuador, but industrial contamination issued from investment strategies codified in New York executive chambers. Texaco's practices of dumping toxic crude, industrial solvents, and formation waters into the environment—and thereby exposing lowland residents to the long-term carcinogenic effect of heavy metals—resulted from decisions made in the United States.[8] By decentering the locus of wrong-doing from its effects, plaintiffs instantiate an alternative tactic for exercising rights, asserting a phantom-like citizenship. Collapsing boundaries in a transnational arena, the class action suit dis-articulated the space of liability from places of contamination ad thereby exercised phantom rights.

Multinationals, on the other hand, have legally exonerated themselves from culpability in foreign affairs through a prosthetics of subsidiaries. While crucial to perfecting corporate mastery, subsidiaries—as prostheses—are detachable, separable, and hence dispensable appendages of the corporate body. Eminently malleable for strategic penetration and accumulation, detachable prostheses constitute the legal loopholes whereby the "parent" company (or what Ecuadorians call the *matriz*, the "womb") maintains its immunity from exploits abroad.[9] The class-action lawsuit against Texaco challenged the impunity with which multinational petroleum capital could build up and contingently dismember its portfolio through firm prosthetics.

In public discourse, plaintiffs in the class-action suit were consistently referred to as *indígenas* (Indians); "Maria Aquinda," an indigenous female, represented the "class" of plaintiffs, as the title of this essay notes. While the notion of Amazonian Indians suing the third-largest oil conglomerate in the United States conjured up exotic images, and perhaps more international sympathy, (indeed Cofan Indians dressed in "traditional" garb filled the CNN coverage of the filing of the suit), such an angle excluded the majority who made up the "class"— tens of thousands of lowland poor *mestizo* homesteaders. Furthermore, literally and figuratively encoding plaintiffs feminine *and* Indian opened space for many state representatives to disparage their claims, now doubly denigrated. White male elites systematically infanticized and feminized lowland Indians as primitive, irrational beings whose claims could easily be dismissed. Relegated anachronistic relics of Ecuador's past, Indians were barriers to state modernization. State representatives conveniently ignored poor *mestizo* plaintiffs as their recognition only attested to the state's failures to modernize. While Indians and *mestizos* were formally granted equal rights under Ecuadorian law, the articulation of unequal race, class, and gender relations preempt the ability of the marginalized to become full citizens in practice (cf. Hall & Jacques 1990). Thus, asserting phantom rights abroad exposed the wounds left from the severing of Subalterns' citizenship at home.

In Ecuador, *patria* (often erroneously translated as fatherland) is uniquely gendered and sexed. *La Patria* in Ecuador is coded female and often referred to as the *Señora* (as noted in the national anthem)—for example, a married, heterosexual female. Above all, however, she is the cherished possession of the *pater, padre*, father. Thus, in Ecuador, a masculinist state staunchly defends the honor of any violation to the *patria*—by outside males (namely other states) or internally by devious females (namely Indians and environmentalists).

On a radio show in the spring of 1994, the Ecuadorian ambassador engaged in a debate over the Texaco suit with an Ecuadorian environmental activist who—over the previous five years— had worked to document the social and ecological effects of Texaco operations in the Northern Amazon. In the course of the debate, the ambassador incriminated, "well look *Señorita*, or is it *Señora*, I don't know what you are; though they tell me you have children"—in response to accusations of the Executive aligning itself with a U.S. firm. Implicitly the ambassador sought to undermine Paulina's credibility by questioning her sexuality. At the time, she was going through a turbulent separation from her spouse, a member of a prominent Quito family. In a country in which divorce was uncommon and female sexuality vigilantly guarded, a woman's character largely hinged on her sexual virtue—or, at least, could be slandered via her sexuality. Around the same time, rumors circulated in the Oriente that the women who worked for the same radical environmental organization were *perras* (bitches) or *putas* (whores) "seducing" Indians with foreign ideas. In more than one public meeting I attended, the Minister of Energy and Mines referred to the "*manoseo*"— the "fingering," (man-"handling" of Indians by dubious women. The feminine of questionable sexuality threatened the sovereignty of *la patria*. Many elites labeled radical women and subversive Indians ecological terrorists in a larger international green conspiracy.

Sexuality was likewise turned variously on its head. Among indigenous organizations, a long-standing joke in protest of the neo-liberal privatization of land went as follows: "They say that land is our *pacchamama* (mother earth); well, you bloody hell don't sell your mother!"[10] With increased indigenous resistance to intensified petroleum drilling—or *perforaciones* in Spanish— through the 1990s, the same joke was redeployed with a sexual innuendo: if land were the *pacchamama*, the joke enjoined, "well, you bloody hell don't screw your mother!"[11]

This analogy between petroleum drilling and heterosexual penetration acquired further currency through the imagery of another highly publicized court case in the U.S. between Ecuadorian and North American bodies—that of Lorena Gallo de Bobbitt and her emasculated, ex-Marine spouse

John Wayne Bobbitt. Pleading to have severed her husband's penis in momentary madness after years of sexual abuse and torture, Lorena Bobbitt (an Ecuadorian citizen though long-term U.S. resident) came to symbolize for many in Ecuador a critique of a phalocentric economic regime of power. Prominently situated on more than one Quito wall, read the large graffiti lettering : "Don't Urinate Here Or We'll Call Lorena."[12] Ingeniously appropriating the adage, Ecuadorian supporters for the class-action suit against Texaco rallied: "Well, Don't Contaminate Here Or We'll Call Lorena."[13] The class-action filed in New York threatens to castrate corporate capital at the source from which its prothetic subsidiaries emerged. Challenging both the neoliberal state's and multinational's political and economic virility, the suit threatened to undermine the gender, race, class, sexual hierarchies upon which their success depended.

The Texaco case was not simply a judicial matter; it embodied a long-standing effort by the marginalized in Ecuador to vindicate political rights that they claimed were systematically denied since the sixteenth century. It coincided with an emerging global discourse on the environment and the sanctity of the Amazon. Its appeal resided in a liberal discourse in which "we" are all phantom planetary citizens, responsible for our common phantom global patrimony. In April 1994, the New York district court allowed the case to enter the discovery phase and that Texaco's filed be opened to plaintiffs' lawyers for further scrutiny. Without accepting jurisdiction, the judge subpoenaed records on grounds established in the 1992 Rio Declaration on Environment and Development. While the Rio Declaration recognized the "sovereign" rights of states over their own resources (as the Ecuadorian Ambassador insisted), it likewise mandated that resource exploitation not cause damage to the environment outside "national jurisdiction." The case could potentially be heard in New York, the judge ruled, if Texaco was found negligent along these lines. Three years after the initial filing, a new judge dismissed the Texaco case from federal court precisely at the moment when the multinational faced an onslaught of racial discrimination charges at home. Ecuadorians will appeal the case in superior court. Regardless of future events, the class action pursued by Ecuadorian citizens represents a formidable challenge whereby phantom citizenship has challenged the prosthetics of corporate capital at its source.[14]

NOTES

1. I explore the gendered valences of citizenship and sovereignty as the Executive Branch of the Ecuadorian government strategically feminized as it vilified those opposed to its interests.

2. The ambassador's letter became public when, a month after plaintiffs filed the suit, Texaco, Inc. presented it to the New York judge as supporting evidence for having the case be dismissed and reverted to Ecuador.

3. Ecuadorian Ambassador to the United States of America, Edgar Terán Terán, in a letter to the United States State Department, December 3, 1993.

Specifically, Terán Terán was referring to the fact that Ecuador was one of the first Latin American countries to sign the Convention of Intellectual Property with the U.S. and was a recipient of the Andean Trade Preference Act aimed to stimulate the economy of those Andean countries vigilant in their interdiction of drug trafficking. Were "the U.S. Courts [to] accept jurisdiction" of the Texaco case, Terán Terán concluded, these benefits and guarantees would be "significantly eroded"—including, perhaps, Ecuador's war on drugs.

Two months later, the Ecuadorian Executive submitted a statement to the New York District Judge claiming that accepting jurisdiction of the class-action suit would violate "Ecuador's sovereign right to exploit and regulate its natural resources" *and* "create tension in the friendly relations between Ecuador and the U.S." (reprint in *Hoy*, March 7, 1994).

4. Widely published in Ecuadorian newspapers and disseminated among human rights, environmental, and indigenous groups, the diplomatic declarations further triggered an intriguing debate on citizenship, national sovereignty, and corporate activity within a state aspiring for neo-liberal economic change.

5. Since assuming office in August 1992, conservative President Sixto Durán Ballén sought to establish sweeping legislative changes for enacting structural adjustments. Not surprisingly, Euro-American multinationals, as well as multilateral institutions, applauded the administrations' efforts. Principally, amendments to the Hydrocarbon Law granted oil companies greater autonomy and profit-sharing—what one former president referred to as "succulent incentives" (*Energia*, Nov/Dec 1993:21). More enticing arrangements were made ready for a new

round of multinational bidding for rights to explore and produce oil in ten new Amazonian concessions—of 200,000 hectares each.

6. Doubly ironic, a broad-based national coalition of Indians, environmentalists, workers, and peasants opposed to neo-liberal change coalesced in an alliance they christened "Front for the Defense of Sovereignty and Against Privatization." See dissertation for explication of this phenomenon.

7. Deposition by Lalit P. Naithani, Senior Advocate before the Supreme Court of India and the State High Court of Allahabad, India, February 23, 1994.

8. The class-action charged that "the damage to the plaintiffs is a consequence of the following:

a. Texaco's failure to pump unprocessable crude oil and toxic residue back into wells as is the reasonable prudent industrial practice.

b. Texaco's discarding of toxic substances by dumping them into oil pits, streams, rivers, and wetlands.

c. Texaco's burning of crude oil without any temperature or pollution control.

d. Texaco's spreading of oil on the roads.

e. Texaco's design and construction of oil pipelines without adequate safety features resulting in spills of millions of gallons of crude oil.

f. Texaco's intentional decision for its own economic gain to dump unprocessed oil into the environment, thereby exposing plaintiffs and the class to toxic crude oil, benzene, arsenic, lead, mercury, and hydrocarbons, knowing that such substances are toxic to humans.

g. Texaco's practice of disposing untreated crude oil and waste products has contaminated the rivers, streams, groundwater, and air with dangerous levels of known toxins.

h. Many times more oil has been spilled in the Oriente than was spilled by the Exxon Váldez disaster in Alaska.

i. Plaintiffs and the class have suffered severe personal injury and are at an increased risk of cancer.

j. Water used by plaintiffs is contaminated with Polycyclid Aromatic Hydrocarbons.

All the charges described in a. to f. are related to corporate decisions made in Texaco's headquarters in New York or in other parts of the United States. None of these decisions was made in Ecuador. All the expert witnesses who will testify on behalf of plaintiffs live in the United States or Canada. All experts who will testify on behalf of plaintiffs and defendants as to customary oil industry practices live in the United States or Canada" (Deposition by chief lawyer for plaintiffs, Cristóbal Bonifaz, March 8, 1994, pp. 9–10).

9. Such flexible regimes of accumulation in the petroleum industry did not emerge with the advent of late capitalism; pliable configurations of subsidiaries have been prominent in the industry since the turn of the century—probably beginning in 1911 with the Supreme Court break-up of the Standard Oil of New Jersey monopoly.

10. Spanish joke: "*Se dice que la tierra es nuestra pacchamama; pues, la madre no se vende, carrajo!*"

11. Spanish joke: "*Se dice que la tierra es nuestra pacchamama; pues, la madre no se jode, carrajo!*"

12. Spanish graffiti: "*No orine aquí; llamamos a Lorena.*"

13. Spanish graffiti: "*Si contamine aqui, llamamos a Lorena.*"

14. By traversing state borders, both citizens and corporate capital extended the effects of their phantom and prosthetic reach and in the process realign understandings of belonging, accountability, and rights.

41

Latin American Urbanization

Douglas Butterworth and John Chance

DEFINITIONS AND CONCEPTS IN MIGRATION

Migration is one of the three major components of population change; the others are births (fertility, natality) and deaths (mortality). Like being born and dying, the phenomenon of population movement is as old as mankind itself, yet it is the least understood of these processes. Difficulties of definition and conceptualization, and lack of a general theory, have, at least until recently, left migration analysis to those who are mainly interested in compiling tables of figures. Such tables, while impressive in quantity, usually tell us little about migration as a process.

In his presidential address to the Population Association twenty years ago, Dudley Kirk observed:

> The study of internal migration is the stepchild of demography. Too little attention has been given by the leadership of our profession to the

From Douglas Butterworth and John Chance, *Latin American Urbanization,* pp. 33–50, 1981, Cambridge University Press, New York.

theory and measurement of migration, despite its role as the chief determinant of differences in population change and structure among local populations. . . . In the words of one leading authority in their field, the majority of recent migration studies are "planlessly empirical and trivial in content." [Kirk 1960: 30]

P. A. Morrison notes that prior to about 1960 "studies of migration did little more than describe net migration patterns." For analytical purposes, these net figures were, he adds, little more than statistical fictions: "There are not 'net migrants'; there are, rather, people who are arriving at places or leaving them. Why they are doing so is central to understanding the dynamics of urban growth and decline" (Morrison 1977: 61).

Even a cursory examination of the literature on migration soon indicates why this situation arose: Migration is a complex phenomenon embracing aspects of many disciplines:

> Migration is a demographic problem: it influences sizes of populations at origin and destination; it is an economic problem: a majority of shifts in population are due to economic

imbalances between areas; it may be a political problem: this is particularly so in international migrations where restrictions and conditions apply to those wishing to cross a political boundary; it involves social psychology insofar as the migrant is involved in a process of decision making before moving and that his personality may play an important role in the success with which he integrates into the host society; it is also a sociological problem since the social structure and cultural system both of places of origin and of destination are affected by migration and in turn affect the migrant. [Jansen 1969: 60]

Migration is often a major symptom of basic social change. Demographer Donald Bogue maintains that every region and every nation that has undergone extensive industrial development has simultaneously undergone redistribution of its population (Bogue 1959: 486). Nevertheless, as Arriaga has noted, the reverse is not necessarily true. In less urbanized Latin American countries such as the Central American nations, urbanization is occurring without any industrialization (Arriaga 1968: 241).

It has been said, facetiously no doubt, that middle-class people move but lower-class people migrate. There are some subtle implications behind this aphorism. Most microstudies of movements of people in Latin America, particularly from rural to urban areas, have dealt with the poorer elements of society. Perhaps linked to this is an unconscious value judgment: "moving" implies a degree of permanency; "migrating" may suggest a kind of shiftlessness or temporary change of residence.

Population movements may be permanent or temporary, they may occur over long distances or short, and they may involve individuals or groups of various socioeconomic levels. Some writers consider any movement of populations, no matter what the distance or time involved, to be migration. Probably what most of us have in mind when we think of migration, however, is what Petersen (1975: 41) defined as "the permanent movement of persons or groups over a significant distance. But Petersen admits that this definition is ambiguous. Does "permanent" mean forever, or just for a long time? How many miles or border crossings make a movement "significant?" "We know whether someone has

been born or died, but who shall say whether someone has migrated?" (1975: 41).

Other scholars would include in their definition of migration not only geographical mobility of slight distance and duration but also social mobility:

If geographical mobility is taken to refer to the movement of people in space, and if we are interested in assessing its social and cultural concomitants, then our model [of migration] must be expanded to include social variables, such as social mobility, and micro-movements, such as visiting and hosting, for it is during these latter activities that information about geographic mobility is exchanged. [Weaver and Downing 1976: 11]

These authors concede, however, that most sociologists would exclude social mobility and microtemporal and microspatial moves such as visiting from a definition of migration. "Social mobility," they acknowledge, "in the sociological and anthropological sense, does not generally refer to physical movement, but rather to social movement: a person moves from a lower socioeconomic class to a higher or from a higher to a lower class. The physical movement of people is migration: the social movement of people is social mobility" (1976: 11). Petersen, however, concurs with Lacroix's assessment that since "no objective, natural criterion exists on the basis of which migrants distinguish themselves from travellers . . . one should not expect to arrive at a unique criterion or definition of migration" (Lacroix 1949: 73; Petersen 1975: 41).

However true that may be, we shall adopt in these chapters an operational definition of migration—whatever the ambiguities and shortcomings of such a course—based upon a composite of definitions set forth by Lee (1966) and Mangalam (1968). We will define migration as a permanent or semipermanent change of residence of individuals, families, or larger collectivities from one geographical location to another that results in changes in the interactional systems of the migrants. As Mangalam states, migration involves an implicit or explicit decision-making process carried on by the migrants on the basis of a set of values, presumably arranged hierarchically; and, as in Lee's definition, no restriction is placed on the distance of the move or upon the voluntary nature of the act and no distinction is made between external and internal migration, although visiting, migratory labor, and habitual nomadism are excluded (Lee 1966: 49, Mangalam 1968: 8).

GENERAL THEORY AND METHODS

Mangalam and Schwartzweller have observed that scholars from various disciplines agree that progress in migration studies is hampered by serious inadequacies in theories about migration; migration theory tends to be time-bound, culture-bound, and discipline-bound; and migration cannot be understood without a comprehensive grasp of the interplay among demographic, economic, social, psychological, and other relevant factors that converge in the process of migration (Mangalam and Schwartzweller 1969: 4).

It is generally recognized that the first systematic attempt to generate "laws" of migration was made by E. G. Ravenstein in a paper presented before the Royal Statistical Society in 1885. The original paper, based upon an analysis of the British census of 1881, was expanded in 1889 to include data from other nations. Both papers bore the title "The Laws of Migration." Their conclusions may be briefly summarized: (1) Most migrants move only a short distance and the number of migrants from any one place decreases in proportion to distance. Migrants going long distances generally move to large centers of industry and commerce. (2) Consequently, there occurs "a universal shifting or displacement of the population," producing "currents of migration" in the direction of these centers. The inhabitants of the countryside surrounding a town of rapid growth flock into it; the gaps thus left in the rural population are filled up by migrants from more remote districts. Thus there is a step-by-step migratory process whose influence emanates from the largest cities. (3) Each main stream of migration produces a compensating counter-stream. (4) The natives of towns or cities are less migratory than those of the rural areas (Ravenstein 1885: 198–9). (5) Females predominate among short-journey migrants. (6) Technological development stimulates migration. (7) "Bad or oppressive laws, heavy taxation, an unattractive climate, uncongenial social

surroundings, and even compulsion . . . are still producing currents of migration, but none of these currents can compare in volume with that which arises from the desire inherent in most men to 'better' themselves in material respects" (Ravenstein 1889: 286–8).

Everett S. Lee (1966: 48), reviewing Ravenstein's work some eighty years after its original publication, observed that this century has brought no comparable excursion into migration theory. The various historical and behavioral sciences have attempted to develop their own theories and models to explain, predict, and understand human migration. The demographic approach describes the data via historical or cross-sectional associations. Both demographers and economists employ statistical models to describe relationships between variables. There are also formal quantitative models based on those developed in physics and mathematics, such as the "gravity model," multiple regression models, and computer simulation models. A discussion of these is beyond the scope of this work, but a few words should be said about the most influential of these attempts, the so-called equilibrium model.

Lee has commented that "with the development of equilibrium analysis, economists abandoned the study of population, and most sociologists and historians are reluctant to deal with masses of statistical data. A crew of demographers has sprung up, but they have been largely content with empirical findings and unwilling to generalize" (Lee 1966: 48). The major components of the equilibrium model have been stated by Bogue (1959: 487):

Migration is a necessary element of normal population adjustment and equilibrium. . . . By siphoning off excess population into areas of greater opportunity, internal migration becomes a mechanism of personal adjustment for the citizen. For the nation it is a device for maintaining a social and economic balance among communities; if migration were suddenly to be stopped, only a very short time would be required for population to "pile up" in areas of rapid growth but of low opportunity for earning a livelihood. Thus, migration is a process for preserving an existing system. Migration is an arrangement for making maximum use of persons with special qualifications. The special abilities of a particular person are useful to the nation only at certain sites, and persons who possess or acquire special abilities are not necessarily born or educated at the site where their talents are needed. Migration moves these specialized persons to the communities where their services can be used effectively.

We see here a strong tendency, perhaps inherent in the model itself, to view migration as a force independent of people. The model approaches human migration "as one would approach the study of migration of birds or the dispersion of insects from a common source" (Bogue 1959: 348; Mangalam and Schwarzweller 1969: 12–13; Goldscheider 1971: 2746). Individuals, families, and other groups are, in fact, the ultimate focus of the decision to move or not to move. Equilibrium theory tends to be static and mechanistic, while decision-making models can and ought to be dynamic, considering process and meaning, contexts, linkages between micro- and macrolevels of analysis, and the integration of migration with other cultural phenomena (Guillet and Uzzell 1976).

DECISION-MAKING PROCESSES

Unless a person or group is forced to move to a certain place at a specified time under stated circumstances, migration must involve some kind of decision on the part of the individuals who go from one place to another: when, where, and why to go; perhaps how long and with whom. It is wise to keep in mind that it is people who move and people who make the decisions. Goldscheider (1971: 2747) reminds us that whether migration is conceived of as sociodemographic behavior or sociodemographic process, we must account not only for decisions to move but also for decisions not to move; not only for rates of population movement but also for the general stability of populations.

The problem of population stability has been addressed by demographers, sociologists, and geographers, many of whom rely on statistics of net change rather than gross movement. This has led to what Jackson has referred to as one of the myths or underlying assumptions regarding the human condition and the decision-making process that studies

of population movements quite unconsciously constructed (Jackson 1969: 3). One such myth is the idea that migration is usually a "once and only" phenomenon, a notion that grew out of the emphasis on net population change. The most obvious of these assumptions, however, is the myth of the static society. This implies, by calling up the idea of a preexisting rural utopia, "that the natural condition of man is sedentary, that movement away from the natal place is a deviant activity associated with disorganization and a threat to the established harmony of *Gemeinschaft* relationships which are implied by a life lived within a fixed social framework."

This seemingly Rousseauistic view of a once-upon-a-time paradise in which harmony prevailed among people intimately involved in face-to-face relationships was in reality an ideal point on a theoretical folk–urban continuum postulated by Robert Redfield a generation ago (1947: 293–308). This ideal folk society was isolated and its members were conceived of as remaining always within the small territory they occupied. Members were bound by religion and kinship ties and the motive of commercial gain did not exist. There was neither money nor any common measure of value. The distribution of goods and services was part of the conventional and personal status relationships that made up the structure of the society: goods were exchanged as expressions of good will and largely as incidents of ceremonial and ritual activities. Quoting Raymond Firth, Redfield concludes, "On the whole, then, the compulsion to work, to save, and to expend is given not so much by a rational appreciation of the [material] benefits to be received as by the desire for social recognition through such behavior" (Redfield 1947: 305–6).

However, as cities came into being, tribal peoples lost their isolation and, according to this line of reasoning, new relationships developed and the relations between peasant and town or city were expressed in part through financial institutions: "Gain is calculated; some crop or other product is sold, in the village or elsewhere, to a buyer of a more urbanized community who pays money" (Redfield 1953: 31–2). The source of money—the city—acts as a magnet and the quest for Mammon drives people from village to metropolis, from one region to another. "Thus the expansion of civilization results in vast and complex migrations of peoples" (Redfield 1953: 46).

Assuming that Redfield's analysis represents a rough approximation of what occurred on the advent of cities and civilizations, we might expect that individuals and groups would have had to decide where, when, and if to move and that these decision-making processes would have repeated themselves through the millennia. But the imponderables—the human errors of judgment, faulty assessments, intervening variables that go into a determination of whether or not to move—went relatively unheeded by migration analysts. With economists in the fore, the equilibrium model became the standard explanation of population movements.

An economic analysis of the causes of internal migration begins with the basic hypothesis or assumption that "the redistribution of people is a purposeful way in which a population responds to its perception of changing economic opportunities" (Carvajal and Geithman 1974: 105). The most influential model attempting to cast rural–urban migration motivations in an economic straitjacket was published by Todaro in 1969, in which he underlined "the fundamental role played by job opportunities and probabilities of employment in the actual migration decision-making process" (1969: 140). In Todaro's model, the decision to migrate from rural to urban areas is functionally related to two principal variables: the rural–urban real income differential and the probability of obtaining an urban job (1969: 139). This way of looking at decision making, at "man, the rational economic creature," perforce ignores such variables as individual tastes, habits, prejudices, loves, and hates—in short, all those noneconomic factors that influence the day-to-day decisions of our lives.

Even when economic factors are an overriding consideration, as in many land-poor villages in Latin America, the decision to migrate may be less important than determinations that must be made in the wake of that decision. In their investigation of San Jerónimo, an impoverished community in the Mixteca region of Oaxaca, Mexico, Stuart and Kearney (1978: 7) state that "in the absence of other viable alternatives, it is meaningless to talk of a household's decision whether or not to send some of its members outside the community to work. The focus of decisions is where to go, who to send, and when to send them: decisions that must be made each year by most households."

In summary, however interesting decision-making processes on the individual, family, or household level may be, scholars are becoming more convinced of the far greater need to examine external constraints and structural-relationships in general as the main determinants of migration behavior.

REPULSION AND ATTRACTION: THE PUSH AND THE PULL

Clifford Jansen (1969: 65) observes that perhaps the question most asked and least understood about migration is "Why do people move?" He believes—and our experience and that of many other researchers confirm that belief—that in most cases the migrants themselves do not know the answer to this question. When asked, they usually give vague and general reasons, such as "work," "family reasons," "education," which help little in the study of the processes involved in the decision-making process. Jansen also commented that one attempt to cover all moves under a general heading is the so-called push–pull hypothesis (Jansen 1969: 65). As we have already noted, it suggests that migration occurs due to socioeconomic imbalances between regions, certain factors "pulling" migrants to the area of destination, others "pushing" them out of the region of origin.

The push–pull hypothesis is only one aspect of the great dichotomy that has pervaded the literature on migration. Guillet and Uzzell suggest that it is to a large extent part of the legacy of the Redfieldian continuum and the sociological tradition of Durkheim, Tönnies, and earlier European scholars. The terms rural-urban, Gemeinschaft-Gesellschaft, and others color our understanding by introducing an unnecessary and misleading polarization of what is essentially a continual interaction over time and space within particular contexts (Guillet and Uzzell 1976: 3).

In short, the polar view of migration considered as a simple push–pull mechanism is "at best confusing, at worst misleading, and in need of considerable revision in light of current research" (Guillet and Uzzell: 4). Nevertheless, most writers concerned with migration, including the most vociferous disclaimers of the bipolar view, continue to utilize it. The reason for this is clear. Simplistic as the push–pull view may be, it is a convenient tool for organizing and analyzing data. We use the push–pull scheme in this book for that reason. It is one, but only one, of the ways of looking at forces causing people to move, and we do not limit ourselves to this kind of analysis. We are aware that there is almost always a combination of factors involved; therefore, we use the push–pull model as one of our main tools for analyzing the masses of data on migration in Latin America.

THE PUSH

Most studies of internal migration (mostly rural to urban) have something to say about the forces that work upon a given population to encourage its movement from the country to the city. The most commonly mentioned push factors are lack of sufficient or productive land; alternative economic opportunities; absence of sanitation and medical services; poor educational facilities; and, in some place, lack of security and natural disasters.

Insufficient and poor land and lack of economic alternatives are usually cited as primary reasons for out-migration from rural communities.[1] In general, evidence supports the contention that growth of the rural population and decreasing fertility of the land, combined with fragmentation of plots by inheritance practices, create an imbalance between the population and its available economic resources. The result is an increasing shift of population from its traditional agricultural base to an urban economic foundation. This process is attested to throughout Latin America in various degrees of importance and is one of the salient demographic facts of our time. Unfortunately, some of the inferences drawn from this movement are hasty and based on insufficient and outdated information.

Many current notions are based upon ideas put forth almost a generation ago. For instance, Corrado (1955: 356) reported that people who tend to migrate are those who feel most strongly the disequilibrium between population and economic resources. "Consequently, it is the poor, rather than those who enjoy a certain welfare, who leave." Similarly, Eder (1965: 27) concluded that the raquitic economic situation of the small farmer in Latin America "has caused thousands to flee to the cities." Benitez (1962: 697) maintained that "in general, it can be said that rural urban migration is the result

of abandonment of the land because of the impossibility of subsisting on it." This rather simplistic relationship between rural poverty and migration to cities was summed up by George Hill and his colleagues: Faced with the depressed standard of living in the countryside, and ". . . . desperately seeking better opportunities for them and their children, *the rural populations feel forced to migrate. . . .* Better conditions *would undoubtedly induce* many of the young men to stay with their agricultural pursuits and to attract others [to the rural areas]" (quoted in Poblete Troncoso 1962: 44, his emphasis). More recent studies by Martínez (1968) in Peru and by Diéquez (1970) and Martine (1975) in Colombia tend to reinforce this opinion.

Certainly there is no question but that rural poverty has resulted in mass population movements out of the country to the city, and that the poorest sector of the rural population is well represented in the migrant group. Nevertheless, it is clear that there is no mechanical cause-and-effect relationship between poverty and migration.

Perlman (1976: 11) cites evidence that when rural areas of Brazil are divided into zones of varying degrees of poverty and economic/climatic depression, the rates of out-migration are fairly constant from each. No greater migration is evident from areas where push factors should be strongest. She notes that there may be land pressure without migration and there may be rapid urban growth without land pressure (Perlman: 67).

In Chile, Herrick (1965: 70) found little variation in migration to Santiago accompanying fluctuations in unemployment rates; in Costa Rica, Carvajal and Geithman (1974: 118) show that unemployment rates in towns and cities in that nation are not an important factor in migration. Germani (1969: 15–48) observed that although job opportunities for migrants are often related to urban industrial development, in many developing nations massive population movements to cities come about even when new and better employment opportunities are scarce or absent. In such cases there is a combination of forces in which the weight of the pull factors to urban areas is greater than the expulsive factors from rural zones. Analogous mechanisms can be used to describe not only the existence and intensity of rural-urban migration, but its absence as well.

Germani (1965: 74) contends that under desperately bad conditions people do not emigrate. On the other hand, in the face of rather acceptable situations people do leave. What happens is that so-called objective factors are filtered through attitudes and decisions of individuals. Impersonal decisions do not decide migration. Decisions are personal and conditioned by the attitudes of individuals. Furthermore, it is fruitless to contend that the push off the land is more important than the pull of the city, and that the attraction of the city would not exist but for the difficulties of rural life. There is a continual interaction between the rural pole and the urban pole, and there is no clearly definable boundary between some locality labeled "urban" and a rural hinterland.

Perlman (1976: 63) and others have spoken of "poles of attraction." To reintroduce the regrettable but virtually unavoidable use of labels, there is not only rural–urban migration, but urban–rural, rural–rural, and urban–urban migration as well. We repeat, however, that until very recently most research has been concerned with the first.

Earlier studies in the emerging field of urban anthropology generally took the "peasant in the city" as their central concern, focusing upon adjustment to the urban milieu and assuming, often without empirical evidence, that the push off the land was the reason the migrant had moved to the metropolis. Personal decisions were (and still are) stressed in explanations of the migration experience.

Here we are confronted with several problems. By studying the migrant in the city, the anthropologist was largely dependent upon the informant's recall of the socioeconomic, political, and personal situation in his place of origin prior to departure. Few of these earlier studies worked both ends of the continuum—the folk and the urban. As we have said, individuals and families—and perhaps other small groups—are the ultimate locus of the decision-making process concerning migration. But these decisions are made within the structural constraints of village, state, and nation. In their study of a community in Colombia, Romero and Flinn (1976) indicated that the chief underlying postulate of their investigation was that the commercialization of the agricultural sector of Colombia, resulting in changes in the socioeconomic structure of the countryside, had brought about migration, as one response by the peasantry of the community, which was impoverished in all its resources except labor (p. 37). They continue:

> Based on this premise it is hypothesized that structural variables—relationship to the means of production—will be significantly related to migration and will be better predictors of migration than the personal characteristics of the migrants. It is also hypothesized that in economically declining communities migration will be forced rather than "pulled" or self-selective as reflected in the objective measures of the relationship to the means of production. [Romero and Flinn 1976: 37]

In general, these hypotheses were confirmed. On the other hand, it was found that individual characteristics were also important in predicting migration (1976: 57). Thus structural and personal or individual factors are, except for analytical purposes, never entirely separable. For example, uneconomical exploitation of resources is widespread throughout Latin America and is frequently named as an agent in out-migration from rural areas. But is this a structural or personal factor? Consider the mechanization of agriculture. This may be based on personal decisions at some level and result in structural changes in a region or nation. Usandizaga and Havens (1966: 27) note that manpower displaced by mechanization of agriculture in Colombia has found its way to cities in that nation (and we might add to other countries, including the United States). Similar findings have been reported throughout much of Latin America.

Camargo (1960: 65–94, 115) found a relationship in Brazil among technical advances in agriculture (including better means of transportation), natural increase in rural population, and out-migration. He considers them interdependent phenomena, the first two bringing about the last. National industrialization, he believes, is the preponderant cause of the rural exodus and "deruralization" of Brazil. Referring to Camargo's analysis, Ianni (1970: 32) states that the relative retardation in the agrarian sector should not be considered indicative of the absence of progress or even of significant changes. The rural exodus, he believes, is not a unilateral fact arising from the attraction of the city and its industries, but is also related to the changes in the technical and social conditions of production in several of the agricultural regions.

Roberts (1978: 98–9) has examined some structural considerations in population movements. He refers to the work of Douglas Graham (1970), which contrasted patterns of internal migration in Brazil in the period 1940–50 with the period of 1950–60. In the earlier period, despite the poverty of the northeastern region of that nation, fewer migrants left this region than left Minas Gerais, which, while poorer than the southern area to which the migrants went in search of work, was wealthier than the northeast. It is only in the period 1950–60 that outmigration from the northeast became greater in volume than outmigration from Minas Gerais.

Graham explained the change in migration patterns between the two periods by the greater rate of economic growth in the later period, with industrialization proceeding faster than the expansion of agricultural production. He also pointed out the improvements in road networks and in transport that facilitated long-distance migration.

Graham's analysis suggests that in the first stages of urban-industrial expansion it is not necessarily the poorest areas in a nation which have the most substantial outmigration rates but those areas close to the expanding economic centers. The costs of transport and the risks of seeking work far from home counter the attraction of substantially higher incomes. Studies in Chile, Colombia and Mexico show that most migrants come from the areas close to the expanding centers (Herrick 1965; Simmons and Cardona 1972; Balán, Browning and Jelin 1973). This migration pattern is similar to that of England during her industrialization where, also, there was little long-distance migration of poor farmers from the south to the north of England. [Roberts 1978: 99][2]

Paradoxically, two apparently opposed types of land holding in Latin America—*latifundios* (large, sometimes corporate estates) and *minifundios* (small, usually family-owned plots)—have each been considered "structural determinants" of migration of almost equal importance. *Latifundios* generally absorb little manpower if they are efficient or mechanized, and *minifundios,* even where there is

high productivity, cannot employ all available manpower (Muñoz et al. 1974: 18).[3]

Another structural factor in migration is the existence of external markets. In varying degrees of importance, these impose conditions on the kind of production a nation or region puts out. They may require an expansion, a decrease, or even a substitution of crops. Migration from rural areas increases when international prices or market conditions stimulate a type of production that requires little manpower (see, for example, Muñoz *et al.* 1974; Margulis 1967; Margulis 1968; Rivarola 1967; Diéguez 1970; Martínez 1968; Martínez 1969).

Table 41–1 gives a brief overview of some of the push–pull, structural–individual forces in migration. Although these structural causes of migration often point out factors crucial to the migration process, they do little to explain the existence of these causes; such things must be explained in terms of particular national and regional contexts. Migration in Venezuela, for example, has been largely influenced by the demands of the petroleum industry (Dipolo and Suárez 1974: 184), and population movements in Argentina are related to the role of that nation as a supplier of beef and agricultural products (Testa 1970: 99).

These national and regional contexts are in large part a consequence of historical antecedents: Countries in different phases of development and with different types of economic development will have dissimilar forces acting to bring about internal (or international) migration. For example, the *latifundios, minifundios,* and feudal structure of the rural economy described by Mejía (1963: 184–6) as of primary importance in out-migration from Peruvian villages in the 1950s and early 1960s are largely absent in, say, contemporary Mexico, but similar phenomena exist in other countries such as Ecuador, and even in such economically more advanced nations as Argentina (Viale 1960: 110).

Political factors, particularly civil wars and revolutions, have stimulated large-scale population movements in Latin America. This was the case, for example, during the Mexican Revolution of 1910–21. Oscar Lewis (1951) mentioned that large numbers of people fled Tepoztlán during the Zapatista movements and subsequent battles, and doubtless the same thing occurred in many other Mexican villages. Rivarola (1967: 4–5) recalls the mobile atmosphere created in Paraguay by the

TABLE 41–1   Structural and Individual Forces in Migration

Force	Structural	Individual
Push	Type of land holding (*latifundio, minifundio*) Insufficient or poor land; uneconomical exploitation of resources Lack of alternative employment Absence of sanitation and medical facilities Lack of transportation improvements	Lack of skills Bordeom, loneliness
	Violence	
	Poor educational facilities Rudimentary communications Mechanization and commercialization of agriculture External markets	
	Poverty	
Pull	Employment opportunities Health and medical services Transportation	Chance of advancement Presence of relatives
	Educational facilities	
		Bright lights and adventure
	Rising expectations (all categories)	

Chaco War (1932–5), giving peasants more opportunities to make contact with urban life and creating new attitudes and forms of behavior among the peasantry. Similarly, the revolution of 1936 and the civil war of 1947 in Paraguay stirred significant population movements. The effects of natural disasters, such as the 1966 earthquake in Guatemala, on population redistribution are obvious. Wars and natural disasters may be considered examples of "forced" migration.

Rural insecurity is endemic in large areas of Latin America. *La violencia* (killing and other forms of violence by marauding bands) in the countryside of Colombia has resulted in important population movements, not only from country to city but from village to village. Flinn and Cartano made a comparison of the migration process to an urban barrio and to a rural community in that nation. They reported that 44 percent of the immigrants to Granada (a rural community) listed *la violencia* as a motivating factor in their decision to migrate, while only 13 percent of the residents of El Carmen (a shantytown) gave it as a reason for their move to the city (1970: 38–9).

Michael Whiteford (1976b: 17) wrote that only a few migrants in *barrio* Tulcán gave *la violencia* as a cause for movement. "In fact, in most cases migrants came from areas not badly affected by

the violence." He cites a report by McGreevey (1968: 213–14) stating that although it is often mentioned as one of the principal causes of rural–urban migration, rural violence has with few exceptions not played a significant role in interdepartmental movement of people.

It is not only such well-publicized sanguinary violence that may create sufficient insecurity to cause people to leave their villages and small towns. The aura of distrust and fear that pervades numerous rural communities has, at least until recent years, received but scant attention from social scientists investigating migration motivations. One apparent reason for this is the continued vitality of the folk model of social relations, in which the presumed idyllic nature of rustic existence is corrupted through contact with the urban way of life. In his study of La Rioja, Argentina, Margulis (1967: 78–93) describes how the economic life and belief system of the villagers were compatible until influences of the city created conflict. Roberts (1973) relates some of his experiences with informants in two neighborhoods in Guatemala City:

The one aspect of provincial life that migrants constantly refer to more than any other, favorably and unfavorably, is the slow tempo of life in the villages and small towns from which they come. In responding to a survey question about the possibility of returning to the provinces, the reason most frequently cited in favor of returning was the peace and quiet of the countryside. It is . . . a longing that is a constant theme of their conversations, and it affects their recreational activities. To go to the countryside with the family is the preferred recreation of this sample. Many choose to take vacations there, fishing or visiting relatives, as well as going on shorter day trips from the capital. In the tape-recorded life histories, the respondents were most nostalgic about the leisure activities of rural life, about the picnics, the fishing, playing by the rivers, or dancing to a small band on the balcony of the village hall. There is an evocation of tranquility and relaxation that undoubtedly does not reflect the reality of every rural day, but which is an evocation that brings up common memories among a group of men and women chatting in the street of a city neighborhood. [Roberts 1973: 50–1]

There is, then, an obvious discrepancy between people's ideals and the reality of the countryside.

As for the "reality of every rural day," we can no more generalize about that than we can about the average day in an urban metropolis. There are, to be sure, serene, antiviolent communities (see Paddock 1975), but there is abundant evidence that rural life in Latin America is often characterized by inter- and intracommunity strife, familial tension, and personal isolation. Viale (1960: 94) observed that far from enjoying intimate social contacts, the Argentinian peasant suffers from isolation from his fellow human beings and that this isolation is cause for innumerable cases of outmigration from rural areas. Margulis (1967: 93–4) described the people who remained in the village that he studied in Argentina as passive, skeptical, and resigned. Lewis (1951), Friedrich (1962), G. Foster (1967), Maccoby (1967), Butterworth (1969), and Romanucci-Ross (1973) have noted that suspicion, distrust, and uncooperativeness are characteristic of Mexican villagers.

Caciquismo (rule by a political boss or bosses) is common in much of Latin America. In Tilantongo, the community in Mexico studied by Butterworth, *caciquismo* takes the form of terrorism by one or more individuals who are not necessarily

in recognized positions of authority, although they may hold political office. By virtue of their brutality and unscrupulous dealings through bribery and deceit, they may not only keep the ordinary citizen in a state of trepidation but also intimidate the authorities into inertia. An illustration from Butterworth's fieldwork is the career of Amadeo Sánchez (a pseudonym).

Always a ruthless opportunist with a notable lack of scruples, Amadeo arrogated the presidency of Tilantongo and lost little time in establishing his personal *cacicazgo* (rule by a *cacique*) in the community. Fines were leveled at the citizenry for minor or nonexistent infractions of the law and complaints were answered by incarceration, physical beatings, and even assassination. No one is certain how many murders can be attributed to Amadeo Sánchez, but there are at least four cases where sufficient testimony is available to indict Amadeo. While he was president, he openly preempted all fines and municipal income for his personal use, stole cattle, and abused women.

Amadeo eventually was stabbed and killed in the plaza of the community. During his reign as *cacique* (political boss), however, Amadeo had caused numerous individuals and families to leave their village in search of a more secure environment—another village or an urban center. The push factor here is obvious. The pull is not so clear. Why do some people go to another rural village while others choose the city?

THE PULL

The conditions that draw members of rural communities to urban centers—the attractive or pull factors—are for the most part the complements of the conditions that obtain in the countryside. Employment and educational opportunities are generally ranked foremost among urban attractions, followed by the presence of health and recreational facilities and the excitement of urban living. Nowadays the presence of relatives in the city may be a prime factor in migration. This will be discussed in the next chapter.

The "bright city lights" explanation of migration motivations has been heavily criticized of late, but there is sufficient evidence that it is indeed a contributing (although certainly not usually a decisive) factor in rural–urban migration. Butterworth (1975b: 195–6), Usandizaga and Havens (1966: 42), and Michael Whiteford (1976b: 15) are among those who have mentioned the lack of *ambiente* (atmosphere) reported by informants about their place of origin and the *movimiento* (movement, "life") in the city. In discussing the residents of Tulcán, a *barrio* in the southwest corner of the city of Popayán, Whiteford (1976b: 15) relates that often the economic situation of the peasants before they moved to the city was not desperate. Many moved to the city because they saw it as an opportunity for a better life rather than because such a move was the only possible solution to a problem. Such peasants generally are young men and women without families, who have less at stake than family men who have been pushed off their land. In the city, the former group hopes to find high-paying jobs that will bring them closer to obtaining the good life.

Thus, although few studies of migration to urban centers in Latin America (or to other regions) fail to mention the pull of employment opportunities, both researchers and informants differ about the relative weight to give to the economic pull. Usandizaga and Havens (1966: 42) list the usual reasons given by informants for going to the city: work, education, health care. But a number of reasons are less concrete: "*más ambiente*," friends and relatives in the city, and similar noneconomic motivations. In such cases, "the wish to move refers more to an adventurous spirit than to a criticism of the situation in which the migrant finds himself" (Usandizaga and Havens: 42).

Jobs in the city are of course limited, and the influx of unskilled laborers into the urban complex often creates strains upon the national and municipal economies. Nevertheless, many Latin American countries have shown a remarkable lexibility in handling the migrant masses. Unskilled or semi-skilled labor is still very much in demand in many parts of Latin America. Second, many migrants display an admirable ingenuity in carving out an economic niche for themselves. Third, the very presence of a multitude of new city dwellers expands the economic opportunities by generating its own needs, including housing, transportation, services, entertainment, and consumer goods.

The desire for education—for oneself, or, more commonly, for one's children—ranks high among the motivations for migration to urban centers. In his landmark study, Oscar Lewis (1952: 32–3) noted that even prior to the Mexican revolution young men were leaving Tepoztlán to get a higher education, a motivation still active today. Butterworth (1962: 267), Kemper (1977: 91–3) and Browning and Feindt (1971: 50) have also commented upon the importance of educational goals in attracting peasants and their families to urban centers in Mexico. Simmons and Cardona (1968: 10) and M. Whiteford (1976b: 15) have done the same for Colombia, and Elizaga (1966: 353) for Chile. Elizaga points out that although the principal motive given for moving to Greater Santiago was work, education was the second most commonly cited reason. Among those coming from rural and semi-urban places, an overwhelming majority claimed work to be the principal motive, while those coming from urban settings were more inclined to report education as the prime motivating force.

Browning and Feindt (1971: 50) report that older family men give education very high priority for moving, but the authors observe that this clearly is education not for the respondents but for their children. Métraux (1956: 402) related how Aymara Indian families in Peru often place their children as servants in urban homes, asking in return only that the patron family send the children to school. In Colombia, M. Whiteford (1976b: 15) tells us that Tulcaneses regard education as an important way to obtain the better life. Some individuals are able to combine the desires of educating children and maintaining life in the country. They keep their landholdings but move the family into town, and the husband divides his time between city and country.

When asked for a list or ranking of motives for moving to the city, informants almost invariably list medical facilities or other reasons involving health. The medical facilities available in urban centers are absent in villages, although migrants often mention the salubrious climate of the countryside. M. Whiteford (1976b: 16) mentions that some informants migrated to Popayán because they feel that the latter has a "healthier" climate than their previous home.

While the broad outlines of what motivates peasants to abandon their rural birthplace for urban settings are fairly well understood, the relative importance of the various motivating factors is difficult to measure. A generation ago, investigators were more sanguine about the possibility of weighing the why's of migration than are their more skeptical counterparts today. Studies such as those of Matos Mar (1961), which used Peruvian census data to break down reasons for migration of household heads to Lima, attempted to give precision to this aspect of demography, yet to state that 61.05 percent of families migrate for economic reasons, another 22.85 percent for social reasons, and so forth, presents an artificial view. Even so, investigators continue to utilize these kinds of statistics to analyze push-pull motives (see Cardona 1968: 63). Such studies do provide some idea of the weight given to various factors in the move away from the countryside, and the economic factors appear to be foremost. However, as Perlman (1976: 67–8) wrote:

> According to migrants themselves, economic considerations are not the only factor in their decisions. Less than half (46 percent) mention an economic concern as the reason for their move. We found most migrants unable to describe their decision to migrate with any precision. It was clear that specific decisions involved complex factors.[4]

A word of caution may be added. Educational, health, and recreational facilities have always been negligible in most villages in Latin America, and rural poverty is by no means a modern phenomenon. However, only in relatively recent times have these been put forth as important reasons for the rural exodus. One reason for this seems to lie in the rising expectations of ruralities—a result of increased national prosperity and availability of modern conveniences in urban areas, plus better communications between the city and its hinterlands. Roads, television sets, telephones, and schools help make the peasant realize that there is a better world beyond his village, thereby adding impetus to migratory flows.

It is therefore presumptuous to assume that improving rural conditions would, at least at first, limit out-migration. To be sure, the problem is a complicated one, involving the interplay of local and national priorities. Dovring (1968: 25) comments that many people concerned with economic development seem convinced that one of the foremost requisites for underdeveloped countries is a reduction in the agricultural sector of the population. This proposition contains two elements: first, reducing the *relative* role of agriculture in the industrial or occupational structure of a country, which is the direct corollary of increasing the role of other industries that are evolving. Second, and most important, the plan consists of trying to achieve an *absolute* reduction in agricultural workers as one of the conditions to raise the productivity of those who remain on the land as well as that of the community as a whole.

Looking at the problem from the urban point of view, Benítez (1962: 97) contends that in spite of the difficulties industry has in absorbing unskilled laborers, the cities still attract ruralities, because of government policy of putting more schools, better doctors, and so forth in cities rather than in the country. The chances of eliminating migration depend on the creation of similar conditions in the countryside, including adequate employment.

Todaro (1969: 147) thinks that the most significant policy implication emerging from his model of rural–urban income differentials is the great difficulty in substantially reducing the size of the urban traditional sector without a concentrated effort at making life more atractive:

> Instead of allocating scarce capital funds to urban low cost housing projects which would effectively raise urban real incomes and might therefore lead to a worsening of the housing problem, governments in less developed countries might do better if they devoted these funds to the improvement of rural amenities. In effect, the net benefit of bringing "city lights" to the countryside might greatly exceed whatever net benefit might be derived from luring more peasants to the city by increasing the attractiveness of urban living conditions. [Todaro 1969: 147]

There are obvious difficulties, not to say inconsistencies, in trying to reduce the number of agricultural workers and at the same time attempting to induce the peasant to stay on the land. The solution proposed by most national planners in Latin America is diversification and decentralization of industry—moving the factories to the fields. Most of these plans remain on the drawing boards. When they have been implemented, the results, as Miller (1973) has shown for a new twon in Mexico, are not always what was intended. One of the problems is the selective nature of who remains at home, who goes to a new town, and who becomes a city dweller.

NOTES

1. Among those consulted are Arias and Alcalá 1973: 3; Bradfield 1973: 360-1; Browning and Feindt 1971: 49; Butterworth 1962: 260-1; Butterworth 1969: passim; Campiglia 1967: 66; Chen 1968: 167; Cornelius 1976b: 3; Doughty 1963: 115; Elizaga 1966: 352; Elizaga 1970: 88; Feindt and Browning 1972: 49; Flinn 1966: 8; Germani 1961: 212; Herrick 1965: 42; Kemper 1975: 228; Kemper 1977: 51, Lomnitz 1973: 60, López 1968: 83: Margulis 1967: 78; Margulis 1968: 101; Matos Mar 1961: 183; Métraux 1956: 392; Molina 1965: 12-13; Perlman 1976: 67-8; Preston 1969: 282; Recaséns Siches 1955: 365; Rivarola 1967: 10-13; Romero and Flinn 1976: 37; Solari 1958: 526; Usandizaga and Havens 1966: 42; Van Es and Flinn 1973: 16; Viale 1960: 141-8, M. Whiteford 1976b:15; and Wilkening 1968: 692. A cross-cultural review of the literature is contained in Connell et al. 1976.

2. In this connection, see the articles in the volume on internal migration in Brazil edited by Manoel Augusto Costa (1971). Of special interest is the contribution in that volume by Douglas Graham, "Algunas consideraçiões econômicas para a policítica migratória no meio brasileiro," (13-43).

3. Shaw (1974: 123-8) has attempted an empirical test of a model relating land tenure to migration in Latin America. Briefly, the model applies to Latin American economies with a high rate of rural natural increase, a large proportion of the rural agricultural population in minifundia or landless employee class, and a large share of the agricultural land held by latifundistas. A basic premise is that the nature of productive organization on latifundias has conditioned the cost, use, availability, and development of land to the extent that social and economic opportunities for the majority of the rural agricultural population have been stifled. Accordingly, a large proportion of rural agricultural laborers likely to be subjected to limit employment opportunities owing to the institutional system of land tenure, and, in combination with rapid population growth, conditions of economic stress are likely to evolve, followed by high rates of rural emigration.

Based mainly on statistical analysis at the rural provincial level for Chile, Peru, and Costa Rica from periods from the 1940s to the 1960s, Shaw found that chile and Peru had an extremely unequal distribution of labor to land resources. Costa Rica had one of the most even. Therefore, one would expect much higher rates of rural emigration in Chile and Peru than in Costa Rica. The empirical results generally accorded with this expectation.

4. See Rojos and de la Cruz 1978: 49-66.

REFERENCES

Arriaga, E. E. "Components of city growth in selected Latin American countries," *The Milbank Memorial Fund Quarterly* 46 (1968), no. 2, part 1, 237-52.

Benítez Zenteno, R. "La población rural y urbana en México," *Revista Mexicana de Sociología* 24 (1962), 689–703.

Bogue, D. J. "Internal migration," in *The study of population: an inventory and appraisal,* ed. P. M. Hauser and O. D. Duncan, Chicago, 1959c.

Bradfield, S. "Selectivity in rural-urban migration: the case of Huaylas, Peru," in *Urban anthropology: cross-cultural studies of urbanization,* ed. A. Southall, New York, 1973.

Browning, H. L. and Feindt, W. "The social and economic context of migration to Monterrey, Mexico," in *Latin American urban research,* vol. 1, ed. F. F. Rabinovitz and F. M. Trueblood, Beverly Hills, Cal. 1971.

Butterworth, D. S. "A study of the urbanization process among Mixtec migrants from Tilantongo in Mexico City," *América Indígena* 22 (1962), 257-74. "Factors in out-migration from a rural Mexican community." unpublished Ph.D. thesis, University of Illinois, 1969.

Chen, C. Y. *Movimientos migratorios en Venezuela,* Caracas, 1968. "Migración interna y desarrollo regional," in *Actas de la conferencia regional Latinoamericana de población,* vol. 1, México, D. F., 1972.

Connell, J. et al. *Migration from rural areas. The evidence from village studies.* Delhi, 1976.

Cornelius, W. A. *Mexican migration to the United States: the view from rural sending communities,* Cambridge, Mass., 1976b.

Corrado, G. "Acerca de las migraciones internas," in *Estudios sociológicos,* vol. 1, México, D.F., 1955.

Costa, M. A., ed. *Migracoes internas no Brasil,* Rio de Janeiro, 1971.

Diégues, M. "Causas y problemas del caso brasileño," *Aportes* 15 (1970), 146–57.

Dipolo, M. and Suarez, M. "History, patterns, and migration: a case study in the Venezuelan Andes," *Human Organization* 33 (1974), 183-95.

Doughty, P. L. "El caso de Huaylas: un distrito en la perspectiva nacional," in *Migración e integración en el Perú.* ed. H. F. Dobyns and M. C. Vázquez, Lima, 1963.

Dovring, F. "El papel de la agricultura dentro de las poblaciones en crecimiento. México, un caso de desarrollo económico reciente," *El Trimestre Económico* 35 (1968), 25-50.

Eder, G. J. "Urban concentration, agriculture, and agrarian reform," *The Annals of the American Academy of Political and Social Science* 360 (1965), 27-47.

Elizaga, J. "A study on immigrations to Greater Santiago (Chile)," *Demography* 3 (1966), 352-77.

———*Migraciones a los areas metropolitanas de América Latina,* Santiago de Chile, 1970.

Feindt, W., and Browning, H. L. "Return migration and its significance in an industrial metropolis and an agricultural town in Mexico," *International Migration Review* 6 (1972), 158-65.

Flinn, W. L. "Rural to urban migration: a Colombian case," Madison, Wis., Land Tenure Center Reprint No. 19, 1966.

———and Cartano, D. G. "A comparison of the migration process to an urban barrio and to a rural community: two case studies," *Inter-American Economic Affairs* 24 (1970), 37-48.

Friedrich, P. "Assumptions underlying Tarascan political homicide," *Psychiatry* 25 (1962), 315-27.

Germani, G. "Inquiry into the social effects of urbanization in a working-class sector of Greater Buenos Aires," in *Urbanization in Latin America,* ed. P. M. Hauser, New York, 1961.

———"Emigración del campo a la ciudad y sus causas," in *Sociedad, economía y reforma agraria,* ed. H. Gilberti et al., Buenos Aires, 1965. *Sociología de la modernización: psicología y sociología,* Buenos Aires, 1969.

Goldscheider, C. "An outline of the migration system," in *International union for the scientific study of population,* vol. 4, London, 1971.

Graham, D. "Divergent and convergent regional economic growth and internal migration in Brazil 1940-1960," *Economic Development and Cultural Change* 18 (1970), 362-82.

Guillet, D. and Uzzell, D. "Introduction," in *New approaches to the study of migration,* Houston, Tex., 1976.

———and Uzzell, D., eds. *New approaches to the study of migration,* Houston, Tex, 1976.

Herrick, B. H. *Urban migration and economic development in Chile,* Cambridge, Mass., 1965.

Ianni, O. *Crisis in Brazil,* New York, 1970.

Jackson, J. A. "Introduction," in *Migration,* ed. J. A. Jackson, Cambridge, Eng., 1969.

Jansen, C. "Some sociological aspects of migration," in *Migration,* ed. J. A. Jackson, Cambridge, Eng., 1969.

Kemper, R. V., "Social factors in migration: the case of Tzintzuntzeños in Mexico City," in *Migration and urbanization: models and adaptive strategies,* ed. B. M. DuToit and H. I. Safa, The Hague, 1975.

———*Migration and adaptation: Tzintzuntzan peasants in Mexico City,* Beverly Hills, Cal., 1977.

Kirk, D. "Some reflections on American demography in the nineteen sixties," *Population Index* 26 (1960), 305-10.

Lacroix, M. "Problems of collection and comparison of migration statistics," in *Problems in the collection and comparability of international statistics,* New York, 1949.

Lee, E. "A theory of migration," *Demography* 3 (1966), 47-57.

Lewis, O. *Life in a Mexican village: Tepoztlán restudied,* Urbana, Ill., 1951. "Urbanization without breakdown: a case study," *Scientific Monthly* 75 (1952), 31-41.

Lomnitz, L., "Supervivencia en una barriada en la ciudad de México," *Deografía y Economía* 7 (1973), 58-85.

López, J. E. *Tendencias recientes de la población venezolana,* Mérida, Venezuela, 1968.

Maccoby, M. "Love and authority: a study of Mexican villages," in *Peasant society: a reader,* ed. J. Potter, M. Díaz, and G. M. Foster, Boston, 1967.

McGreevey, W. P. "Causas de la migración interna en Colombia," in *Empleo y desempleo en Colombia,* Bogotá, 1968.

Mangalam, J. J. *Human migration: a guide to migration literature in English 1955-1962,* Lexington, 1968.

———and Schwarzweller, H. K. "General theory in the study of migration: current needs and difficulties," *International Migration Review* 3 (1969), 3-18.

Margulis, M. "Análisis de un proceso migratorio rural-urbano en Argentina," *Aportes* 3 (1967), 73-128.

———*Migración y marginalidad en la sociedad argentina,* Buenos Aires, 1968.

Martine, G. "Volume, characteristics, and consequences of internal migration in Colombia," *Demography* 12 (1975), 193-208.

Martínez, H. "Las migraciones internas en el Perú," *Aportes* 10 (1968), 136-60. *Las migraciones altiplánicas y la colonización del Tambopata,* Lima, 1969.

Matos Mar, J. "Migration and urbanization—the "barriadas" of Lima: an example of integration into urban life," in *Urbanization in Latin America,* ed. P. M. Hauser, New York, 1961.

Mejía, J. V. "Sumario sobre factores sociales en la migración," in *Migración e integración en el Perú,* ed. H. F. Dobyns and M. C. Vázquez, Lima, 1963.

Métraux, A. "Las migraciones internas de los indios Aymara en el Perú contemporáneo," in *Estudios antropológicos públicados en homenaje al doctor Manuel Gamio,* México, D. F., 1956.

Miller, F. C. *Old villages and a new town,* Menlo Park, Cal., 1973.

Molina, J. *Las migraciones internas en el Ecuador,* Quito, 1965.

Morrison, P. A. "The functions and dynamics of the migration process," in *Internal migration: a comparative perspective,* ed. A. A. Brown and E. Neuberger, New York, 1977.

Muñoz, H., and de Oliveira, O. "Migraciones internas en América Latina: exposición y crítica de algunos análisis," in *Las migraciones internas en América Latina: consíderaciones teóricas,* ed. H. Muñoz, O. de Oliveira, P. Singer and C. Stern, Buenos Aires, 1974.

Paddock, J., "Studies on antiviolent and 'normal' communities," *Aggressive Behavior* 1 (1975), 217-33.

Perlman, J. E. *The Myth of marginality: urban poverty and politics in Rio de Janeiro,* Berkeley, Cal., 1976.

Petersen, W. *Population,* 3rd ed., New York, 1975.

Poblete Troncoso, M. "El éxodo rural, sus orígenes, sus repercusiones," *América Latina* 5 (1962), 41-9.

Preston, D. A. "Rural emigration in Andean America," *Human Organization* 28 (1969), 279-86.

Ravenstein, E. G. "The laws of migration," *Journal of the Royal Statistical Society* 48 (1885), 167-227.

———"The laws of migration," *Journal of the Royal Statistical Society* 52 (1889), 241-301.

Recaséns Siches, L. "El problema de la adaptación de las gentes de orígen rural que migran en las grandes ciudades o centros industriales," in *Estudios sociológicos,* vol. 1, Mexico City, 1955.

———*The primitive world and its transformations,* Ithaca, N.Y., 1953.

———and Milton Singer. "The cultural role of cities," *Economic Development and Cultural Change* 3 (1954), 53-77.

Rivarola, D. M. *Migración paraguaya,* Asunción, Paraguay, 1967.

Roberts, B. R., *Organizing strangers: poor families in Guatemala City,* Austin, Tex., 1973.

———*Cities of peasants: the political economy of urbanization in the Third World,* London, 1978.

Rojas, E., and de la Cruz, J. "Percepción de oportunidades y migraciones internas: revisión·de algunos enfoques," *Revista Latinoamericano de Estudios Urbanos Regionales* (EURE) (1978), 49-66.

Romanucci-Ross, L. *Conflict, violence, and morality in a Mexican village,* San Diego, Cal., 1973.

Romero, L. K. and Flinn, W. L. "Effects of structural and change variables on the selectivity of migration: the case of a Colombian peasant community," *Inter-American Economic Affairs* 29 (1976), 35-58.

Shaw, R. P. "Land tenure and the rural exodus in Latin America," *Economic Development and Cultural Change* 23 (1974), 123-32.

Simmons, A. B., and Cardona Gutiérrez, R. "La selectividad de la migración en una perspectiva en el tiempo: el caso de Bogotá (Colombia) 1929-1968," in *Las migraciones internas,* ed. R. Cardona Gutiérrez, Bogotá, 1968.

Solari, A. E. *Sociología rural nacional,* 2nd ed., Montevideo, 1958.

Stuart, J. and Kearney, M. "Migration from the Mixteca of Oaxaca to the Californias: a case study," paper presented in the symposium "Migrations into the Californias: conservatism and change in retrospect and perspective," anual meeting of the American Anthropological Association, Los Angeles, Cal., November, 1978.

Testa, J. C. "Las migraciones internas en el contexto del desarrollo social latinoamericano," *Aportes* 15 (1970), 96-109.

Todaro, M. P. "A model of labor migration and urban unemployment in less developed countries," *American Economic Review* 59 (1969), 138-48.

Usandizaga, E., and Havens, E. *Tres barios de invasión: estudio de nivel de vida y actitudes en Barranquilla,* Bogotá, 1966.

van Es, J. C., and Flinn, W. L. "Note on the determinants of satisfaction among urban migrants in Bogotá, Colombia," *Inter-American Economic Affairs* 27 (1973), 15-28.

Viale, J. O. *Exodos campesinos en la Argentina,* Santa Fe, Argentina, 1960.

Weaver, T., and Downing, T. E., eds. *Mexican migration,* Tucson, Ariz., 1976.

Whiteford, M. B., *The forgotten ones: Colombian countrymen in an urban setting,* Gainesville, Fla., 1976b.

Wilkening, E. A. et al. "Role of the extended family in migration and adaptation in Brazil," *Journal of Marriage and the Family* 30, (1968), 689-95.

42

The Latin American City

Alan Gilbert

BACK IN TIME

The Latin American city is very old. The Aztecs, Mayas and Incas had all created impressive urban forms as much as a thousand years before the Iberian invasions of the eixteenth century. The remains of Cuzco in Peru, Tiahuanuco in Bolivia and Monte Albán, Tenochtitlán, Teotihuacán and Xochicalco in Mexico are eloquent testimony to the presence of urban civilisations well before the arrival of Europeans.

This pre-Columbian heritage is almost completely absent from the contemporary urban scene because the Spanish demolished the indigeous cities that they found. While they used the capital of the Sun God as foundations for the new city of Cuzco, elsewhere few remains are visible. Conquest meant the building of new cities, indeed whole new urban systems. Together with the Portuguese in colonial Brazil, the Spanish constructed an intricate administrative system based on a well-connected network of new towns and cities. As Jorge Hardoy (1975:

25) points out: "This spatial structure constitutes the basis of the present-day scheme of continental urbanization." Most of today's cities were founded by the Spanish or the Portuguese during the sixteen and seventeenth centuries.[1]

The Portuguese and Spanish Empires were run from the cities which were centres of conquest and administration rather than market places. According to Fernando Henrique Cardoso (1975: 169):

> The city that dotted the Iberian empire in the Americas, Lusitanian as well as Hispanic, was more a city of officials than a city of burghers. Neither the market nor local councils had the power to oppose the King's courts, colonial regulations, and the interests of the Crown, or to resist the colonial exploitation that cast Iberian royalty and bourgeoisie into the rigid mold of mercantile capitalism. At the opposite pole was the owner of land, Indians, or slaves. The official and the lord were the social types that gave life to the cities.

While some of the erstwhile "giants" of the Spanish and Portuguese urban systems are now merely small towns, most of the really important admin-

From Alan Gilbert, The Latin American City, pp. 23–36, 1994, Russell Press, London.

istrative centres developed into today's major cities. Lima and Mexico City, the capitals of the viceroyalties of Peru and New Spain, retain an all-dominant position within their modern national boundaries.[2] Similarly, nearly all of the twenty current capital cities were key administrative centres during the colonial period. In this sense, Latin America's urban system is rather old.

Similarly, the past is responsible for an important ingredient in the design of today's city. Both the Spaniards and the Portuguese laid out their cities according to a set plan based on practice at home. While the Portuguese were much less rigorous in their planning and allowed more local variation than did the Spanish, the influence of the colonial city is clearly recognisable throughout the region. The central square, around which were located the church or cathedral, the main administrative offices and the homes of the elite, remains at the centre of most Latin American cities. Equally, the grid-iron street plan which spreads out from the central square remains, topography permitting, the basis of most modern road layouts (see Figure 42–1).

But, if the Latin American city is in one sense very old, it is very new in another. In 1900, most Latin Americans lived in the countryside and only three cities had more than half a million inhabitants. By 1930, the total urban population of the whole region had still not reached 20 million. By comparison with Mexico City's current population of around 18 million and the present Latin American urban total of some 300 million, the 1930 total pales into insignificance. Even by 1950, there were still only six cities—Buenos Aires, Lima, Mexico City, Rio de Janeiro, Santiago and São Paulo—with more than a million people; today, there are

FIGURE 42–1   Plan of Santo Domingo
Source: Recreated from *Montanus Arnoldus,* De Nieuwe en Onbekende Weerld (Amsterdam 1691)

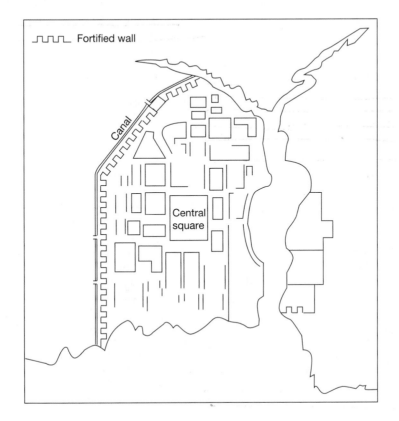

TABLE 42–1 Urban population (percent) in Latin America, 1940–90

Country	1940	1960	1980	1990
Argentina	na	74	83	86
Bolivia	na	24	33	51
Brazil	31	46	64	75
Chile	52	68	82	86
Colombia	29	53	68	70
Cuba	46	55	65	75
Ecuador	na	36	44	56
Mexico	35	51	66	73
Peru	35	47	65	70
Venezuela	31	63	79	91
Latin America	33	44	64	72

Urban population is defined as those living in settlements of more than 20,000 inhabitants.
Source: Wilkie et al. (1990)

arguably 39 (see Table 42–4). The speed of urban growth in Latin America in recent years is undoubtedly very impressive.

Urbanisation is also new in the sense that the look and shape of the cities have been greatly modified. While the central square and the grid-iron street plan can still be seen in most large cities, and while they still dominate smaller urban places, the bus, the car, the skyscraper and improved forms of electricity and water provision have transformed the city over the last fifty years. Add large-scale industrial development to the recipe and it is clear that in many respects the form of the Latin American city is very new.

FROM A RURAL TO AN URBAN SOCIETY

Until comparatively recently, most people lived in the countryside. Only Argentina, Chile, Cuba and Uruguay contained an urban majority in 1950 and as Table 42–1 shows, less than one-half of Latin Americans in 1960 lived in urban areas.

Since 1940, of course, urbanisation has been rapid and in a period of fifty years Latin America has been transformed. While the numbers of people living in rural areas has only recently begun to fall in absolute terms, the proportion of rural inhabitants has been in constant decline. As a result of cityward migration, most Latin American cities

have grown extremely quickly and, for short periods at least, some have grown at quite spectacular rates. During the 1940s, for example, Caracas grew by 7.6 percent annually, Cali by 8 percent and São Paulo by 7.4 percent; during the 1950s, Guadalajara grew annually by 6.7 percent. If these percentage figures are insufficiently impressive, during the 1970s Mexico City's population increased by 5.1 million people and that of São Paulo by 4.0 million.

Latin America was transformed from a rural to an urban region by a combination of falling mortality rates, rapid internal migration, economic development and changing technology. In 1930, Latin America had just over 100 million inhabitants; sixty years later, its population had passed the 425 million mark. Control of the worst diseases such as malaria, the introduction of drugs to treat pneumonia and tuberculosis, and immunisation campaigns against widespread killers such as measles, diptheria and typhoid led to a spectacular decline in mortality rates. Average life expectancy almost doubled from an average of 34 years in 1930 to 65 years by the early 1980s.

With death rates plummeting, fertility continued at a very high level in most of the region. Excluding Argentina and Uruguay, where average birth rates per thousand population were in the low 20s, fertility rates in the 1960s averaged around 4.5. It was not until the 1970s and 1980s that fertility rates in most of the region began to fall substantially, with average birth rates dropping from 42 per thousand in the early 1960s to 33 per thousand in the early 1980s and 27 per thousand in the early 1990s. In the meantime, Latin America's population boomed.

There is a clear link between rates of urban growth and national population growth. Argentina became an urban country at the turn of the century as immigration from Europe boosted its population. Similar patterns of growth occurred in Uruguay and southern Brazil around the same time. Elsewhere, rapid urbanisation only took place when mortality rates began to decline during the 1940s and 1950s. With fertility remaining high, rural populations began to increase and people began to move to the cities in large numbers. As Table 42–2 shows, it was only in the 1970s that population growth began to slow in most countries.

Since most of the population were living in the countryside, it was the rural areas which bore the

TABLE 42–2   National Population Growth Rates, 1920–75

Country	1920–25	1930–35	1940–45	1950–55	1960–65	1970–75
Argentina	3.2	1.9	1.7	2.1	1.6	1.3
Brazil	2.1	2.1	2.3	3.0	2.9	2.6
Chile	1.5	1.6	1.5	2.4	2.5	1.7
Colombia	1.9	2.0	2.4	3.1	3.3	2.2
Ecuador	1.1	1.7	2.1	2.8	3.6	2.9
Mexico	1.0	1.8	2.9	2.9	3.5	3.2
Peru	1.5	1.7	1.8	2.0	3.1	2.7
Venezuela	1.9	2.3	2.8	4.0	3.3	3.6
Latin America	1.9	1.9	2.2	2.7	2.9	2.6

Source: Wilkie et al (1988:109)

brunt of the increase. Rapid growth created a problem insofar as Latin America's land tenure system was very unequal and few families had ever had sufficient land to feed their children. Although rural populations continued to grow in absolute terms up to the 1970s, huge numbers moved to the cities.

That the cities could absorb this flood of migrants was due to economic growth. While jobs were always scarce, the absolute increase in urban employment was impressive. In places, manufacturing jobs increased rapidly. In Mexico City, the number of industrial jobs grew from 271,000 in 1950 to 477,000 in 1960 and 698,000 in 1970. Commerce and finance expanded enormously, creating a whole range of new jobs for shop assistants, street vendors, bank clerks and insurance workers. More people were also absorbed by the growing public sector. Whether or not they were all productively emplyed, the numbers of school teachers, bureaucrats, health workers, street cleaners and electricity workers increased dramatically. If far too many newcomers were required to work for very low pay, few were unemployed and even fewer were worse off than if they had stayed in the countryside.

While the expansion of employment helped absorb the newcomers, new forms of technology helped to house them. The introduction of bricks, cement, concrete blocks and new kinds of roofing eased the process of urban expansion, even for the majority who were increasingly living in self-help housing. New forms of transportation allowed the development of suburban housing. Despite the fast rate of urban growth, the population was kept relatively healthy; few cities suffered from the epidemics that had plagued urban life in the early twentieth century.[3] If living conditions were often squalid, they were no worse than conditions in the countryside. And, unlike the rural situation, economic growth promised to gradually improve the quality of urban life.

THE SHAPE OF THE CITY

As I have argued, Latin America's cities share many common features. Buenos Aires and Mexico City are very much larger and more sophisticated than Asunción or Tegucigalpa, but notwithstanding variations caused by differences in climate and relief, what is surprising about Latin America is how similar its cities look.

Several factors lie behind this apparent uniformity. Not only were their colonial cores built to a similar urban plan, but the processes directing their subsequent expansion have also been remarkably similar. First, every Latin American country has long formed part of the international production system. Indeed, as industrialization, foreign investment, the commercialisation of agriculture, technological adaptation and alien cultural practices have swept through the region, its cities have naturally taken on a similar look, not only to one another, but also to those of the principal source of new technology, investment and culture: North America. The transnationalisation of production and technology influenced the development of urban employment and production structures. Differences are apparent but, apart from the writing on the signs, it is sometimes difficult to distinguish the streets of Caracas from those of Los Angeles, those of São Paulo from those of New York.

Second, most Latin American countries have followed a similar kind of development path. From the sixteenth century to the middle of the twentieth, every country relied principally on mineral or agricultural exports to sustain its economy. From the 1930s every country began to industrialize, protecting itself carefully behind high tariff walls and complicated import-licence schemes. From the 1940s to the late 1970s, import-substituting industrialisation produced slow but sustained economic development. During the 1980s, practically every economy was affected badly by the debt crisis which led to a decline in per capita income in all but a handful of countries.

Third common forms of urban development are due to the increasing internationalisation of consumer tastes. Latin America's affluent suburbs featured English-style housing during the 1940s and California-style housing during the 1950s and 1960s. Today, most elite residential areas feel much like North American suburbs. Indeed, the whole suburban lifestyle is increasingly imitative of the United States, based on the car and its associated retail structures such as the supermarket and shopping and entertainment malls. Bogotá's Unicentro and Guadalajara's Plaza del Sol shopping centres are almost pure North American transplants. Even the restaurants are the same: McDonald's, Denny's and Kentucky Fried Chicken. Latin America's self-help suburbia has also adopted international consumer goods from Coca-Cola to designer labels and personal stereos. Television has helped to modify Latin American life by bringing Dallas, Dynasty, Michael Jackson and Madonna into most front rooms. As a result, it has changed cultural expectations and stimulated new consumer tastes. It is estimated that in 1986 there were 26 million television sets in Brazil and 9.5 million in Mexico, the vast bulk in the urban areas.

Finally, Latin American cities are similar insofar as there is insufficient well-paid employment. As a result, large numbers of people in every city eke out a living in some part of the so-called "informal sector." The consequences of low pay, albeit usually much higher than rural incomes, are obvious in the dress, retail outlets and housing of the majority.

Every Latin American city is dominated by this mass of poor people and the contrast they make with the well-dressed, affluent minority. The colour of the faces of the poor may differ throughout the region, but their dress and work differ remarkably little. With the exception of Cuba, few governments have made a determined effort to rectify the inequalities in urban society. The divide between rich and poor remains great, and urban poverty casts a shadow across all of Latin America.

ECONOMIC DEVELOPMENT AND URBAN GROWTH

The period from 1940 to 1980 was both an intense phase of urban development and also a period of sustained economic growth throughout the region. When the economic crisis of the 1980s hit Latin America, urban growth began to slow. The nature of urban growth is integrally linked to the pace and form of economic development. Without understanding the link between the two, misleading conclusions may be drawn about the nature of the city.

First, urban growth has long contributed to economic development rather than acting as a drain on the economy. Since urban activities tend to be more productive than most rural activities, the shift from rural to urban production raised incomes. As a result, those moving to the city were less the victims of migration than its beneficiaries. They also contributed to economic development rather than creating a social problem which should have been stemmed at source.[4]

Second, because urban growth occurred during periods of economic expansion, governments could raise taxes and provide services and infrastructure for the burgeoning cities. Had governments not been able to extend water and electricity systems, bus routes and health care, the urban situation would have become dire. As it was, Latin American cities absorbed huge numbers of new inhabitants with relative ease. The history of the Latin American city between 1940 and 1980 is one of continuous improvement, if not for everyone, at least for the bulk of the population.

The 1980s, of course, saw the reversal of what had been assumed to be normal practice. Between 1980 and 1989, the overall gross national product of Latin America and the Caribbean declined by

TABLE 42–3 Population Growth of Selected Latin American Cities, 1960–1990 (percent per annum)

City	1960s	1970s	1980s
Mexico City	5.6	3.7	3.0
Bogota	6.2	4.1	3.2
Caracas	5.0	1.7	1.2
Santiago	4.2	2.9	2.4
Buenos Aires	2.1	1.8	1.5
São Paulo	5.5	4.1	3.7
Rio de Janeiro	3.7	2.2	2.2
Lima	7.3	5.1	4.1

Source: United Nations, Department of International Economic and Social Affairs (1991) and national censuses.

8.3 percent. Among Latin American countries, only Chile, Colombia and Cuba managed to grow. Most of the rest experienced major recessions, with per capita income in Argentina, Ecuador, Peru and Venezuela declining by around one-wuarter, and in Nicaragua by one-third. Not only did average incomes fall but the urban areas fared worse than the countryside. The cities suffered from rising unemployment as large numbers of industries went out of business because governments had reduced protection against imports and cut back on subsidies. Urban unemployment rose as governments laid off increasing numbers of workers. In some countries, urban unemployment rose to unprecedented levels: 20 percent in Chile in 1982 and 22 percent in Panama in 1989. The urban population also suffered as governments cut back on social expenditure. Social spending was severely reduced in most countries during the recession of the 1980s.

A clear consequence of the economic recession was a slowing in the pace of urban growth. The region's major cities grew much more slowly during the 1980s than they had previously.

URBAN PRIMACY AND THE GROWTH OF MEGACITIES

Despite the recent slowing of urban growth, Latin America still contains some of the world's largest metropolitan areas. However their urban areas are defined, Mexico City and São Paulo are certainly among the world's most populous cities. If fore-casts that Mexico City will have 30 million people by the year 2000 seem hugely wide of the mark, its population is clearly going to reach 20 million.

When compared with Mexico City or São Paulo, most of the region's other cities are relatively small. But by the standards of many other parts of the world, even these smaller cities are rather impressive. Apart from Rio de Janeiro and Buenos Aires, which both have over ten million inhabitants, even Latin American cities which most readers will have difficulty placing on a map, have several million inhabitants. As Table 42–4 shows, Latin America now has 11 cities with more than 3 million inhabitants. The region has 39 cities with more than one million people, and no fewer than 14 of these are in Brazil.

Not only are the metropolitan centres of Latin America enormous, but in many cases they are very much larger than any other city in the same country. Thus Lima is approximately ten times larger than Peru's second city, Arequipa, and Buenos Aires ten times larger than Córdoba. Certainly, Latin America tends to contain more primate cities than most other parts of the world. Among the twenty Latin American republics only Bolivia, Brazil,

TABLE 42–4 Latin America's Giant Cities, 1990

City	Population (millions)
Mexico City	20.19
São Paulo	17.40
Buenos Aires	11.51
Rio de Janeiro	10.71
Lima	6.25
Bogota	4.85
Santiago (Chile)	4.73
Caracas	4.10
Belo Horizonte	3.60
Guadalajara	3.16
Oirti Alegre	3.12
Monterrey	2.97
Recife	2.49
Brasilia	2.36
Santo Domingo	2.20
Havana	2.10
Fortaleza	2.09
Curitiba	2.03

Source: United Nations, Department of International Economic and Social Affairs, (1991).

Note: Some of the figures are clearly overestimates: e.g. Caracas, Mexico City and São Paulo, but for the sake of consistency have not been corrected.

FIGURE 42–2   Latin America's Giant Cities, 1990

Colombia, Ecuador, and Honduras do not have a primate city whose population exceeds that of the second city of the country by at least three times. Even among the exceptions, Brazil, Ecuador and Honduras hardly count since they contain two cities both of which greatly exceed the population of the third city in the country.

Urban primacy has long been present in Latin America. It was certainly encouraged by the political and administrative centralism instituted by Por-

tuguese and Spanish rule and which was accentuated after independence. It was encouraged further by the port locations of most of the capital cities, an advantage which allowed them to control the flows of most exports and imports. During the twentieth century, the strategy of encouraging industrial development behind high tariff walls and the active involvement of government in the process increased the advantages of the capital cities. As a result, most Latin American countries developed urban systems which became increasingly distorted. As an example, Santiago had 1.3 times as many people as Valparaíso in 1875, 2.8 times as many in 1920, and 7 times as many in 1971. Lima was 8 times larger than Arequipa in 1940 but 11 times larger in 1972.

NOTES

1. There are, of course, major exceptions, such as most of the cities in the Amazon area including such famous new cities as Brasília and Ciudad Guayana, Venezuela, yet such exceptions are surprisingly few in number.

2. Until the eighteenth century, most of the Spanish realm in North and Central America was administered as part of the Viceroyalty of Spain and most of South America (plus Panama) as part of the Viceroyalty of Peru.

3. The outbreak of cholera in Lima which was first announced in January 1991 was untypical by modern Latin American standards.

4. An argument put forward by many social scientists in the 1950s when they realised how rapidly Latin American cities were growing and when they saw that the process of economic development was different in important respects from that in the developed countries.

FURTHER READING

Good general introductions to Latin America's economic, social and historical background are given in Collier et al. (1985), Cubitt (1987), and Green (1991). Good accounts of the historical dimension of Latin American urbanisation are given by Hardoy (1975), Morse (1971), Newson (1987) and Sargent (1993).

For discussions of population growth, see Blouet and Blouet (1982), Sánchez-Albornoz (1974) and Merrick (1986). For information on urban primacy, see Gilbert and Gugler (1992) and Skeldon (1990).

REFERENCES

Cardoso, F. H. (1975) 'The city and politics,' in Hardoy, J. E. (ed.), 157–190.

Collier, S., Blakemore, H. and Skidmore, T. E. (eds.) (1985) *The Cambridge Encyclopedia of Latin America and the Caribbean,* Cambridge University Press.

Cordera Campos, R. and González Tiburcio, E. (1990) Crisis and transition in the Mexican economy, in González, M. and Escobar, A. (eds.) 19–56.

Cubitt, T. (1988) *Latin American society,* Longman.

Gilbert, A. G. and Gugler, J. (1992a) *Cities, poverty and development: urbanization in the Third World,* Oxford University Press (second edition).

Green, D. (1992) *Faces of Latin America,* Latin America Bureau.

Hardoy, J. E. (ed.) (1975) *Urbanization in Latin America: approaches and issues,* Anchor Books.

Merrick, T. W. (1986) 'Population pressures in Latin America', *Population Bulletin* 41, number 3.

Newson, L. (1987) 'The Latin American colonial experience', in Preston, D. (ed.) *Latin American development: geographical perspectives,* Longman, 7–33.

Sánchez-Albornoz, N. (1974) *The population of Latin America: a history,* University of California Press.

Sargent, C.S. (1993) 'The Latin American city' in Blouet, B. and blouet, O. (eds.) *Latin America and the Caribbean: a systematic and regional survey,* John Wiley, 172–216.

Skeldon, R. (1990) *Population mobility in developing countries,* Belhaven Press.

Tello, C. (1990) 'Combating poverty in Mexico', in González, M. and Escobar, A. (eds.) 19–56.

United Nations, Department of International Economic and Social Affairs (1991) *World urbanization prospects 1990,* New York.

Wilkie, J., Lorey, D. E. and Ochoa, E. (1988) *Statistical abstract for Latin America 26,* University of California, Los Angeles.

Wilkie, J., Ochoa, E. and Lorey, D. E. (1990) *Statistical abstract for Latin America 28,* University of California, Los Angeles.

43

Conclusion
Imagining a Postdevelopment Era

Arturo Escobar

We don't know exactly when we started to talk about cultural difference. But at some point we refused to go on building a strategy around a catalogue of "problems" and "needs." The government continues to bet on democracy and development; we respond by emphasizing cultural autonomy and the right to be who we are and have our own life project. To recognize the need to be different, to build an identity, are difficult tasks that demand persistent work among our communities, taking their very heterogeneity as a point of departure. However, the fact that we do not have worked out social and economic alternatives makes us vulnerable to the current onslaught by capital. This is one of our most important political tasks at present: to advance in the formulation and implementation of alternative social and economic proposals.

—Libia Grueso, Leyla Arroyo, and Carlos Rosero, the Organization of Black Communities of the Pacific Coast of Colombia, January 1994

From Arturo Escobar, "Conclusion: Imagining a Postdevelopment Era," *Encountering Development: The Making of the Third World*, pp. 213–226, 1995, Princeton University Press, Princeton, NJ.

STATISTICS (1980S)

The industrialized countries, with 26 percent of the population, account for 78 percent of world production of goods and services, 81 percent of energy consumption, 70 percent of chemical fertilizers, and 87 percent of world armaments. One U.S. resident spends as much energy as 7 Mexicans, 55 Indians, 168 Tanzanians, and 900 Nepalis. In many Third World countries, military expenditures exceed expenditures for health. The cost of one modern fighter plane can finance forty thousand rural health centers. In Brazil, the consumption of the 20 percent richest is thirty-three times that of the 20 percent poorest, and the gap between rich and poor is still growing. Forty-seven percent of the world's grain production is used for animal feed. The same amount of grain could feed more than 2 billion people. In Brazil the area planted with soybeans could feed 40 million people if sown with corn and beans. The world's six larger grain merchants control 90 percent of the global trade of grain, whereas several million people have died of hunger in the Sahel region as a result of famines during the 1980s alone. The tropical rain forest provides about 42 percent of the world's plant biomass and oxygen; 600,000 hectares of rain forest are destroyed annually in Mexico alone, 600,000 in Colombia. The amount of coffee that producing countries had to export to obtain one barrel of oil doubled between 1975 and 1982. Third World workers who are in the textile and electronic industries are paid up to twenty times less than their counterparts in Western Europe, the United States, or Japan for doing the same job with at least the same productivity. Since the Latin American debt crisis broke in 1982, Third World debtors have been paying their creditors an average of $30 billion more each year than they have received in new lending. In the same period, the food available to poor people in the Third World has fallen by about 30 percent. One more: the vast majority of the more than 150 wars that have been waged in the world since 1945 have taken place in the Third World, as reflections of superpower confrontations. Even those taking place since the end of the cold war continue to be a reflection of the effects of the struggle for power among the industrialized nations.

One could continue.[1] Statistics tell stories. They are techno-representations endowed with complex political and cultural histories. Within the politics of representation of the Third World, statistics such as these function to entrench the development discourse, often regardless of the political aim of those displaying them. Toward the end of this book, however, one should be able to draw a different reading from these figures: not the reading that reproduces the tale of populations in need of development and aid; nor the reductive interpretation of these figures in terms of pressing needs that call for the "liberation" at any cost of poor people from their suffering and misery; perhaps not even the narrative of exploitation of the South by the North, in the ways in which this story was told up to a decade ago. Instead, one should be able to analyze counting in terms of its political consequences, the way in which it reflects the crafting of subjectivities, the shaping of culture, and the construction of social power—including what these figures say about surplus material and symbolic consumption in those parts of the world that think of themselves as developed. Not the perverse reading, finally, of the International Monetary Fund insisting on "austerity measures" for the Third World, as if the majority of people in the Third World had known anything but material austerity as a fundamental fact of their daily existence—but a renewed awareness of the suffering of many, of the fact that "the modern world, including the modernized Third

World, is built on the suffering and brutalization of millions" (Nandy 1989, 269).

THE THIRD WORLD AND THE POLITICS OF REPRESENTATION

"Today something that we do will touch your life." This Union Carbide motto became ironically real after the December 1984 gas leak in Bhopal, India, which affected two hundred thousand people and left at least five thousand dead. Bhopal is not only a reminder of the connection between the choices and power of some and the chances of others, a connection firmly established by the global economy with a deadly appearance of normalcy; as Visvanathan (1986) has suggested, Bhopal is also a metaphor of development as a diaster of sorts which demands that the casualties be forgotten and dictates that a community that fails to develop is obsolescent. An entire structure of propaganda, erasure, and amnesia on Bhopal was orchestrated by science, government, and corporations which allowed the language of compensation as the only avenue of expression of outrage and injustice—and even compensation was precarious at best. If, as in the Sahelian famines, those affected cannot be accommodated within the languages of the market, salvation (by U.S. Marines or international troops), and semisecularized Christian hope, so much the worse for them. In these examples, the clinical, military, and corporate gazes join their efforts to launch allegedly beneficent and sanitized operations for the good of Mankind (with a capital *M,* that of Modern Man). Restore Hope, Desert Storm, Panama, and Granada are signs of a so-called new world order.[2]

The development discourse, as this book has shown, has been the central and most ubiquitous operator of the politics of representation and identity in much of Asia, Africa, and Latin America in the post–World War II period. Asia, Africa, and Latin America have witnessed a succession of regimes of representation—originating in colonialism and European modernity but often appropriated as national projects in postindependence Latin America and postcolonial Africa and Asia— each with its accompanying regime of violence. As places of encounter and suppression of local cultures, women, identities, and histories, these regimes of representation are originary sites of violence (Rojas de Ferro 1994). As a regime of representation of this sort, development has been linked to an economy of production and desire, but also of closure, difference, and violence. To be sure, this violence is also mimetic violence, a source of self-formation. Terror and violence circulate and become, themselves, spaces of cultural production (Girard 1977 and Taussig 1987). But the modernized violence introduced with colonialism and development is itself a source of identity. From the will to civilization in the nineteenth century to today, violence has been engendered through representation.

The very existence of the Third World has in fact been wagered, mamaged, and negotiated around this politics of representation. As an effect of the discursive practices of development, the Third World is a contested reality whose current status is up for scrutiny and negotiation. For some, the Third World "can be made a symbol of planetary intellectual responsibility . . . it can be read as a text of survival" (Nandy 1989, 275). After the demise of the Second World, the Third and First worlds necessarily have to realign their places and the space of ordering themselves. Yet it is clear that the Third World has become the other of the First with even greater poignancy.[3] "To survive, 'Third World' must necesarily have negative *and* positive connotations: negative when viewed in a vertical ranking system . . . positive when understood sociopolitically as a subversive, 'non-aligned' force" (Trinh 1989, 97). The term will continue to have currency for quite some time, because it is still an essential construct for those in power. But it can also be made the object of different reimaginings. "The Third World is what holds in trust the rejected selves of the First and the [formerly] Second Worlds . . . before envisioning the global civilization of the future, one must first own up the responsibility of creating a space at the margins of the present global civilization for a new, plural, political ecology of knowledge" (Nandy 1989, 266, 273).

As we will see, however, the Third World should in no way be seen as a reservoir of "traditions." The selves of the Third World are manifold and multiple, including selves that are becoming increasingly illegible according to any known idiom of modernity, given the growing fragmentation, polarization, violence, and uprootedness that are

taking hold of various social groups in a number of regions.[4] It is also possible, even likely, that radically reconstituted identities might emerge from some of those spaces that are traversed by the most disarticulating forces and tensions. But it is too soon even to imagine the forms of representation that this process might promote. Instead, at present one seems to be led to paying attention to forms of resistance to development that are more clearly legible, and to the reconstruction of cultural orders that might be happening at the level of popular groups and social movements.

Since the middle and late 1980s, for instance, a relatively coherent body of work has emerged which highlights the role of grassroots movements, local knowledge, and popular power in transforming development. The authors representing this trend state that they are interested not in development alternatives but in alternatives to development, that is, the rejection of the entire paradigm altogether. In spite of significant differences, the members of this group share certain preoccupations and interests;[5] an interest in local culture and knowledge; a critical stance with respect to established scientific discourses; and the defense and promotion of localized, pluralistic grassroots movements. The importance and impact of these movements are far from clear; yet, to use Sheth's (1987) expression, they provide an arena for the pursuit of "alternative development as political practice." Beyond, in spite of, against development: these are metaphors that a number of Third World authors and grassroots movements use to imagine alternatives to development and to "marginalize the economy"—another metaphor that speaks of strategies to contain the Western economy as a system of production, power, and signification.

The grassroots movements that emerged in opposition to development throughout the 1980s belong to the novel forms of collective action and social mobilization that characterized that decade. Some argue that the 1980s movements changed significantly the character of the political culture and political practice (Laclan and Mouffe 1985; Escobar and Alvarez 1992). Resistance to development was one of the ways in which Third World groups attempted to construct new identities. Far from the essentializing assumptions of previous political theory (for example, the mobilization was based on class, gender, or ethnicity as fixed catagories), these processes of identity construction were more flexible, modest, and mobile, relying on tactical articulations arising out of the conditions and practices of daily life. To this extent, these struggles were fundamentally cultural. Some of these forms and styles of protest will continue throughout the 1990s.

Imaging the end of development as a regime of representation raises all sorts of social, political, and theoretical questions. Let us start with this last aspect by recalling that discourse is not just words and that words are not "wind, an external whisper, a beating of wings that one has difficulty in hearing in the serious matter of history" (Foucault 1972, 209). Discourse is not the expression of thought; it is a practice, with conditions, rules, and historical transformations. To analyze development as a discourse is "to show that to speak is to do something—something other than to express what one thinks; . . . to show that to add a statement to a pre-existing series of statements is to perform a complicated and costly gesture" (1972, 209). I have shown how seemingly new statements about women and nature are "costly gestures" of this sort, ways of producing change without transforming the nature of the discourse as a whole.

Said differently, changing the order of discourse is a political question that entails the collective practice of social actors and the restructuring of existing political economies of truth.[6] In the case of development, this may require moving away from development sciences in particular and a partial, strategic move away from conventional Western modes of knowing in general in order to make room for other types of knowledge and experience. This transformation demands not only a change in ideas and statements but the formation of nuclei around which new forms of power and knowledge might converge. These new nuclei may come about in a "serial" manner.[7] Social movements and antidevelopment struggles may contribute to the formation of nuclei of problematized social relations around which novel cultural productions might emerge. The central requirement for a more lasting transformation in the order of discourse is the breakdown of the basic organization of the discourse, that is, the appearance of new rules of formation of statements and visibilities. This may or may not entail new objects and concepts; it may be marked by the reappearance of concepts and practices discarded long ago (new fundamentalisms are a case in point); it may be a slow process but it may also happen with relative rapidity. This transformation will also depend on how new historical situations—Such as the divisions of social labor based on high technology—alter what may be constituted as objects of discourse, as well as on the relation between development and other institutions and practices, such as the state, political parties, and the social sciences.

Challenges to development are multiplying, often in dialectical relation to the fragmentary attempts at control inherent in post-Fordist regimes of representation and accumulation; post-Fordism necessarily connects or disconnects selectively regions and communities from the world economy; although always partial, disconnection not infrequently presents attractive opportunities from poor people's perspectives. Some of this is going on in the so-called informal economies of the Third World (the label is an attempt by economic culture to maintain the hold on those realities that exist or emerge at its limits). As local communities in the West and the Third World struggle for incorporation into the world economy, they still might have to develop creative and more autonomous practices that could be more conducive to renegotiating class, gender, and ethnic relations at the local and regional levels.

The process of unmaking development, however, is slow and painful, and there are no easy solutions or prescriptions. From the West, it is much more difficult to perceive that development is at the same time self-destructing and being unmade by social action, even as it continues to destroy people and nature. The dialectic here tends to push for another round of solutions, even if conceived through more radical categories—cultural, ecological, politicoeconomic, and so on. This will not do. The emply defense of development must be left to the bureaucrats of the development apparatus and those who support it, such as the military and (not all of) the corporations. It is up to us, however, to make sure that the life span of the bureaucrats and the experts as producers and enforcers of costly gestures is limited. Development unmade means the inauguration of a discontinuity with the discursive practice of the last forty years, imagining the day when we will not be able to say or even entertain the thoughts that have led to forty years of incredibly irresponsible policies and programs. In some parts of the Third World, this possibility may already be (in some communities it always was) a social reality.

HYBRID CULTURES AND POSTDEVELOPMENT IN LATIN AMERICA

It is said that during the 1980s Latin American countries experienced the harshest social and economic conditions since the conquest. But the 1980s also witnessed unprecedented forms of collective mobilization and theoretical renewals of importance, particularly in social movements and in the analysis of modernity and postmodernity. The specificity of the Latin American contribution to the discussions of modernity stems from two main sources: the social and temporal heterogencity of Latin America modernity, that is, the coexistence—in a coeval way, even if emerging from different cultural temporalities—of premodern, modern, and even antimodern and amodern forms; and the urgency of social questions, coupled with a relatively close relation between intellectual and social life. This basis for critical intellectual work is reflected in the forms and products of analysis, particularly in the following areas: the linking of analyses of popular culture with social and political struggles, for instance in the literature on social movements; the willingness to take up the questions of social justice and of the construction of new social orders from the vantage point of postmodernity; a novel theorization of the political and its relation to both the cultural and the democratization of social and economic life; the reformulation of the question of cultural identity in nonessentialist ways; and a keen interest in the relation between aesthetics and society.

The point of departure is a challenging reinterpretation of modernity in Latin America. In Latin America, "where the traditions have not yet left and modernity has not settled in," people doubt whether "to modernize ourselves should be our principal objective, as politicians, economists and the publicists of the new technologies do not cease to tell us" (García Canclini 1990, 13). Neither on the way to the lamentable erradication of all traditions nor triumphantly marching toward progress and modernity, Latin America is seen as charac-

terized by complex processes of cultural hybridization encompassing manifold and multiple modernities and traditions. This hybridization, reflected in urban and peasant cultures composed of sociocultural mixtures that are difficult to discern, "determines the modern specificity of Latin America" (Calderón 1988, 11). Within this view, the distinctions between traditional and modern, rural and urban, high, mass, and popular cultures lose much of their sharpness and relevance. So does the intellectual division of labor, of anthropology as the science of stubborn traditions and sociology as the study of overpowering modernity, for instance. The hypothesis that emerges is no longer that of modernity-generating processes of modernization that operate by substituting the modern for the traditional but of a hybrid modernity characterized by continuous attempts at renovation, by a multiplicity of groups taking charge of the multitemporal heterogeneity precular to each sector and country.[8]

Accounts of successful hybrid experiences among popular groups are becoming numerous. These accounts reveal the incluctable traffic between the traditional and the modern that these groups have to practice and the growing importance of transnational visual archives for popular art and struggles. The Kayapo's use of video cameras and planes to defend their culture and ancestral lands in the Brazilian rain forest is already becoming legendary. Peasants in northern Peru are also found to combine, transforming and reinventing them, elements of long-standing peasant culture, modern urban culture, and translational culture in their process of political organization (Starn 1992). The study of this complex semiotics of protest and of the hybrid and inventive character of popular daily life presents challenging questions to anthropologists and others. The question that arises is how to understand the ways in which cultural actors—cultural producers, intermediaries, and the public—transform their practices in the face of modernity's contradictions. Needless to say, inequalities in access to forms of cultural production continue, yet these inequalities can no longer be confined within the simple polar terms of tradition and modernity, dominators and dominated.

The analysis in terms of hybrid cultures leads to a reconceptualization of a number of established views. Rather than being eliminated by development, many "traditional cultures" survive through their transformative engagement with modernity. It becomes more appropriate to speak of popular culture as a present-oriented process of invention through complex hybridizations that cut across class, ethnic, and national boundaries. Moreover, popular sectors rarely attempt to reproduce a normalized tradition; on the contrary, they often exhibit an openness toward modernity that is at times critical and at times transgressive and even humorous. Not infrequently, what looks like authentic practice or art hides, on close inspection, the commodification of types of "authenticity" that have long ceased to be sources of cultural insights. If we continue to speak of tradition and modernity, it is because we continually fall into the trap of not saying anything new because the language does not permit it. The concept of hybrid cultures provides an opening toward the invention of new languages.[9]

Several disclaimers must accompany this theorization of popular culture. First, it should not be imagined that these processes of hybridization necessarily unmake long-standing traditions of domination. In many cases, the harshness of conditions reduces hybridization to mundane adaptations to increasingly oppressive market conditions. Economic reconversion overdetermines cultural reconversions that are not always felicitous. Paradoxically, however, the groups with a higher degree of economic autonomy and "insertion" into the market have at times a better chance of successfully affirming their ways of life than those clinging to signs of identity the social force of which has been greatly diminished by adverse economic conditions (García Canclini 1990). What is essential in these cases—for example, musicians and producers of handicrafts such as weavers and potters who incorporate transnational motifs into traditional designs—is the mediation new elements effect between the familiar and the new, the local and that which comes from afar, which is even closer. This cultural hybridization results in negotiated realities in contexts shaped by traditions, capitalism, and modernity.

The second qualification is that the concept of hybridization should in no way be interpreted as the exhaustion of Third World imagery, cosmology, and mythical-cultural traditions; despite the pervasive influence of modern forms, the weighty presence of magic and myth in the social life of the Third World is still extremely significant, as

writers and artists continue to make patently clear. As Taussig (1987) suggests, the vitality, magic, wit, humor, and nonmodern ways of seeing that persist among popular groups can be best understood in terms of dialectical images produced in ongoing contexts of conquest and domination. At the level of daily life, these popular practices represent a counterhegemonic force that opposes the instrumentalizing and reactionary attempts of the church, the state, and modern science to domesticate popular culture. These practices resist narrative ordering, flashing back and forth between historical times, self and group, and alienation from and immersion in magic.[10]

This also means that cultural crossings "frequently involve a radical restructuring of the links between the traditional and the modern, the popular and the educated, the local and the foreign. . . . What is modern explodes and gets combined with what is not, is affirmed and challenged at one and the same time" (García Canclini 1990, 223, 331). Let us be sure about one thing: the notion of hybrid cultures—as a biological reading might suggest—does not imply the belief in pure strands of tradition and modernity that are combined to create a hybrid with a new essence; nor does it amount to the combination of discrete elements from tradition and modernity, or a "sell-out" of the traditional to the modern. Hybridity entails a cultural (re)creation that may or may not be (re)inscribed into hegemonic constellations. Hybridizations cannot be celebrated in and of themselves, to be sure; yet they might provide opportunities for maintaining and working out cultural differences as a social and political fact. By effecting displacements on the normal strategies of modernity, they contribute to the production of different subjectivities.

More than the biological metaphor, hybrid cultures call forth what Trinh T. Minh-ha calls the hyphenated condition. The hyphenated condition, she writes, "does not limit itself to a duality between two cultural heritages. . . . [it] requires a certain freedom to modify, appropriate, and reappropriate without being trapped in imitation" (1991, 159, 161). It is a "transcultural between-world reality" that requires traveling simultaneously backward—into cultural heritage, oneself, one's social group—and forward, cutting across social boundaries into progressive elements of other cultural formations. Again, it is necessary to point out that there is nothing here that speaks of the "preservation of tradition" in the abstract. Hybrid cultures are not about fixed identities, even if they entail a shifting between something that might be construed as a constant, long-standing presence (existing cultural practices) and something else construed as a transient, new, or incoming element (a transnational element or force). It is also necessary to point out that everything that is happening in the Third World can by no means be considered a hybrid culture in the terms just specified. In a similar vein, the progressive (or conservative) character of specific hybridizations is not given in advance; it rests on the articulations they may establish with other social struggles and discourses. Precisely, it is the task of critical research to learn to look at and recognize hybrid cultural differences of political relevance, a point to which I will return.[11]

Unlike major analytical tendencies in the West, the anthropology of modernity in terms of hybrid cultures does not intend to provide a solution to the philosophy of the subject and the problem of subject-centered reason—as Habermas (1987) defined the project of the critical discourses on modernity from Nietzsche to Heidegger, Derrida, Bataille, and Foucault—nor a recasting of the Enlightenment project, as in the case of Touraine (1988) and Giddens (1990) and Habermas's own project of communicative reason. In Habermas's account, the Third World will have no place, because sooner or later it too will be completely transformed by the pressures of reflexivity, universalism, and individualation that define modernity, and because sooner or later its "lifeworld" will be fully rationalized and its "traditional nuclei" will "shrink to abstract elements" (1987, 344) after being fully articulated and stabilized by and through modern discourses. In the Third World, modernity is not "an unfinished project of Enlightenment." Development is the last and failed attempt to complete the Enlightenment in Asia, Africa, and Latin America.[12]

Latin America's anthropology of modernity retakes the question of the reconstitution of social orders through collective political practice. For some, this process has to be based on the belief that Latin Americans "have to stop being what we have not been, what we will never be, and what we do not have to be," (strictly) modern (Quijano 1990, 37). In the face of worsening material conditions

for most people and the rising hegemony of technocratic and economic neoliberalism as the new dogma of modernity in the contenent, the call to resist modernization while acknowledging the existence of hybrid cultures that harbor modern forms seem utopian. There is, indeed, a utopian content to this admonition, but not without a theory of the history that makes it possible. This historical sense includes a cultural theory that confronts the logics of capital and instrumental reason.[13]

It is clear that the technological gap between rich and poor countries is growing in the wake of the global economic restructuring of the 1980s and the advent of cyberculture. Should this phenomenon be interpreted as a "new dependency" (Castells and Laserna 1989)? Is the choice really between a dynamic renegotiation of dependency—one that may allow Latin America to accede to the production of some of the new technologies—or the further marginalization from the world economy with the concomitant progressive decomposition of social and economic structures (Castells 1986; Castells and Laserna 1989)? If it is true, as Castells and Laserna state, that the Third World is more and more subjected to types of economic integration that are coupled with greater social disintegration; that entire regions in the Third World are in peril (is it necessarily a peril?) of becoming totally irrelevant to the world economy (marginalized from its benefits even if integrated into its effects); that, finally, this whole state of affairs seems to bring with it "sociocultural perversion" and political disarticulation; if all of these processes are taking place, in sum, can one accept, with these authors, that the answer should be "a policy capable of articulating social reform with technological modernization in the context of democracy and competitive participation in the world economy" (1989, 16)? Or are there other possible perspectives, other ways of participating in the conversations that are reshaping the world?

ETHNOGRAPHY, CULTURAL STUDIES, AND THE QUESTION OF ALTERNATIVES

One of the most common questions raised about a study of this kind is what it has to say about alternatives. By now it should be clear that there are no grand alternatives that can be applied to all places or all situations. To think about alternatives in the manner of sustainable development, for instance, is to remain within the same model of thought that produced development and kept it in place. One must then resist the desire to formulate alternatives at an abstract, macro level; one must also resist the idea that the articulation of alternatives will take place in intellectual and academic circles, without meaning by this that academic knowledge has no role in the politics of alterative thinking. It certainly does, as we will see shortly.

Where, then, lies "the alternative"? What instances must be interrogated concerning their relation to possible alternative practices? A first approach to these questions is to look for alternative practices in the resistance grassroots groups present to dominant interventions. This was the predominant approach to the question of alternatives during the 1980s, both in anthropology and critical development studies, even if the relationship between resistance and alternatives was not fully articulated as such. . . . Ethnography research might be taken as a point of departure for the investigation of alternatives from anthropological perspectives. In other words, ethnographies of the circulation of discourses and practices of modernity and development provide us, perhaps for the first time, with a view of where these communities are culturally in relation to development. This view may be taken as a basis for interrogating current practices in terms of their potential role in articulating alternatives. Notions of hybrid models and communities of modelers are ways of giving form to this research strategy.

Said differently, the nature of alternatives as a research question and a social practice can be most fruitfully gleaned frm the specific manifestations of such alternatives in concrete local settings. The alternative is, in a sense, always there. From this perspective, there is not surplus of meaning at the local level but meanings that have to be read with new senses, tools, and theories. The deconstruction of development, coupled with the local ethnographs just mentioned, can be important elements for a new type of visibility and audibility of forms of cultural difference and hybridization that researchers have generally glossed over until now. The subaltern do in fact speak, even if the audibility of their voices in the circles where "the West" is reflected upon and theorized is tenuous at best.

There is also the question of the translatability into theoretical and practical terms of what might be read, heard, smelled, felt, or intuited in Third World settings. This process of translation has to move back and forth between concrete proposals based on existing cultural differences—with the goal of strengthening those differences by inserting them into political strategies and self-defined and self-directed socioeconomic experiments—and the opening of spaces for destabilizing dominant modes of knowing, so that the need for the most violent forms of translation is diminished. In other words, the process must embrace the challenge of simultaneously seeing theory as a set of contested forms of knowledge—originating in many cultural matrices—and have that theory foster concrete interventions by the groups in question.[14]

The crisis in the regimes of representation of the Third World thus calls for new theories and research strategies; the crisis is a real conjunctional moment in the reconstruction of the connection between truth and reality, between words and things, one that demands new practices of seeing, knowing, and being. Ethnography is by no means the sole method of pursuing this goal; but given the need to unmake and unlearn development, and if one recognizes that the crucial insights for the pursuit of alternatives will be found not in academic circles—critical or conventional—or in the offices of institutions such as the World Bank but in a new reading of popular practices and of the reappropriation by popular actors of the space of hegemonic sociocultural production, then one must at least concede that the task of conceptualizing alternatives must include a significant contact with those whose "alternatives" research is supposed to illuminate. This is a conjunctural possibility that ethnography-oriented research might be able to fulfill, regardless of the discipline.

Can the project of cultural studies as political practice contribute to this project of figuration? If it is true, as Stuart Hall proposes, that "movements provoke theoretical moments" (1992, 283), it is clear that the movement for refiguring the Third World has generated neither the intellectual momentum nor the policital intention necessary for its proper theoretical moment to arise. This moment, moreover, can be crafted not merely as a moment pertaining to the Third World but as a global moment, the moment of cybercultures and hybrid reconstructions of modern and traditional orders, the moment of possible (truly) postmodern and posthumanist landscapes. The Third World has unique contributions to make to these figurations and intellectual and political efforts, to the extent that its hybrid cultures or "rejected selves" may provide a vital check and different sense of direction to the trends of cyberculture now dominant in the First World (Escobar 1994). The shifting project of cultural studies—its "arbitrary closure," to use Hall's expression—must begin to take into account the various ongoing attempts at refiguring the Third World.

Some of this is starting to happen. Critiques of development produced in the Third World are beginning to circulate in the West. This aspect deserves some attention, because it raises other complex questions, beginning with "what is the West?" As Ashis Nandy writes, the "West is now everywhere, within the West and outside: in structures and minds" (1983, xii). There is sometimes a reluctance on the part of some of the Third World authors who call for the dismantling of development to acknowledge this fact—that is, to keep on seeing strong traditions and radical resistance in places where perhaps there are other things going on as well. But there is also a reluctance on the part of academic audiences in the First World—particularly the progressive audiences who want to recognize the agency of Third World people—to think about how they appropriate and "consume" Third World voices for their own needs, whether it is to provide the expected difference, renew hope, or think through political directions.

If Third World intellectuals who travel to the West must position themselves in a more self-conscious manner vis-à-vis both their Third World constituencies and their First World audiences—that is, with respect to the political functions they take on—European and American audiences must be more self-critical of their practices of reading Third World voices. As Lata Mani (1989) suggests, we all have to be more reflective of the modes of knowing that are intensified because of our particular location (see also Chow 1992). This is doubly important because theory is no longer simply produced in one place and applied in another; in the post-Fordist world, theorists and theories travel across discontinuous terrains (Clifford 1989), even if, as this book has shown, there are identifiable centers of production of dominant knowledges. But even these knowledges are far from being just applied without substantial modifications, appropriations, and subversions. If one were to look for an image that describes the production of development knowledge today, one would use not epistemological centers and peripheries but a decentralized network of nodes in and through which theorists, theories, and multiple users move and meet, sharing and contesting the socioepistemological space.

At the bottom of the investigation of alternatives lies the sheer fact of cultural difference. Cultural differences embody—for better or for worse, this is relevant to the politics of research and intervention—possibilities for transforming the politics of representation, that is, for transforming social life itself. Out of hybrid or minority cultural situations might emerge other ways of building economies, of dealing with basic needs, of coming together into social groups. The greatest political promise of minority cultures is their potential for resisting and subverting the axiomatics of capitalism and modernity in their hegemonic form.[15] This is why cultural difference is one of the key political facts of our times. Because cultural difference is also at the root of postdevelopment, this makes the reconceptualization of what is happening in and to the Third World a key task at present. The unmaking of the Third World—as a challenge to the Western historical mode to which the entire globe seems to be captive—is in the balance.

Despite flexibility and contradictions, it is clear that capital and new technologies are not conducive to the defense of minority subjectivities—minority seen here not only as ethnicity but in relation to its opposition to the axiomatics of capitalism and modernity. Yet everything indicates at the same time that the resurgence and even reconstitution of subjectivities marked by multiple traditions is a distinct possibility. The informational coding of subjectivities in today's global ethnoscapes does not succeed in erasing completely singularity and difference. In fact, it relies more and more on the production of both homogeneity and difference. But the dispersion of social forms brought about by the deterritorialized information economy nevertheless makes modern forms of control difficult. This might offer unexpected opportunities that groups at the margin could seize to construct innovative visions and practices. At the same time, it must be recognized that this dispersal takes place at the cost of the living conditions of vast numbers of people in the Third World and, increasingly, in the West itself. This situation must be dealt with at many levels—economic, cultural, ecological, and political.[16]

Popular groups in many parts of the Third World seem to be increasingly aware of these dilemmas. Caught between conventional development strategies that refuse to die and the opening of spaces in the wake of ecological capital and discourses on cultural plurality, biodiversity, and ethnicity, some of these groups respond by attempting to craft unprecedented visions of themselves and the world around them. Urged by the need to come up with alternatives—lest they be swept away by another round of conventional development, capitalist greed, and violence—the organizing strategies of these groups begin to revolve more and more around two principles: the defense of cultural difference, not as a static but as a transformed and transformative force; and the valorization of economic needs and opportunities in terms that are not strictly those of profit and the market. The defense of the local as a prerequisite to engaging with the global; the critique of the group's own situation, values, and practices as a way of clarifying and strengthening identity; the opposition to modernizing development; and the formulation of visions and concrete proposals in the context of existing constraints, these seem to be the principal elements for the collective construction of alternatives that these groups seem to be pursuing.[17]

Postdevelopment and cyberculture thus become parallel and interrelated processes in the cultural politics of the late twentieth century. For what awaits both the First and the Third World, perhaps finally transcending the difference, is the possibility of learning to be human in posthumanist (postman and postmodern) landscapes. But we must be mindful that in many places there are worlds that development, even today and at this moment, is bent on destroying.

NOTES

1. Most of these figures from Strahm (1986). Some come from World Bank sources. On statistics as political technologies, see Urla (1993).

2. Generally speaking, "Attempts to introduce the language of liberation to those who do not speak it, as

a precondition for the latter qualifying for what the moderns call liberation, is a travesty of even the normatives of the modern concept of liberation. . . . To the lesser mortals, being constantly sought to be liberated by a minority within the modern world, the resistance to the categories imposed by the dominant language of dissent is part of the struggle for survival" (Nandy 1989, 269).

3. Here I am talking primarily about the geographical Third World, or South, but also the Third World within the First. The connection between the Third World within and without can be important in terms of building a cultural politics in the West.

4. I have in mind, for instance, the profound breakdown and reconstitution of identities and social practices fostered by drug money and drug-related violance in countries like Colombia and Peru, or the social geographies of many large Third World cities, with their fortified sectors for the rich—connected with a growing number of electronic media to transnational cyberspaces—and massively pauperized and eroded sectors for the poor. These social geographies resemble more and more *Blade Runner*–type science fiction scenarios.

5. Among the most visible members of this group are Ashis Nandy (1983, 1989); Vandana Shiva (1989); D. L. Sheth (1987); Shiv Visvanathan (1986, 1991); Majid Rahnema (1988a, 1988b); Orlando Eals Borda (1984, 1988; Fals Borda and Rahman (1991); Gustavo Esteva (1987); and Pramod Parajuli (1991). A more complete bibliography and treatment of the works of these authors is found in Escobar (1992b).

6. "A change in the order of discourse," wrote Foucault in the conclusion of *The Archaeology of Knowledge,* "does not presuppose 'new ideas,' a little invention and creativity, a different mentality, but transformations in a practice, perhaps also in neighbouring practices, and in their common articulation. I have not denied—far from it—the possibility of changing discourse: I have deprived the sovereignty of the subject of the exclusive and instantaneous right to it" (1972, 209).

7. "The substitution of one formation by another is not necessarily carried out at the level of the most general or most easily formalized statements. Only a serial method, as used today by historians, allows us to construct a series around a single point and to seek out other series which might prolong this point in different directions on the level of other points. There is always a point in space or time when series begin to diverge and become redistributed in a new space, and it is at this point that a break takes place. . . . And when a new formation appears, with new rules and series, it never comes all at once, in a single phrase or act of creation, but emerges

like a series of 'building blocks,' with gaps, traces and reactivations of former elements that survive under the new rules" (Delenze 1988, 21).

8. Although there are significant differences among the authors reviewed in this section, they share common themes and positions. The work of CLACSO's (Latin American Social Science Council) Working Group on Cultural Politics has been instrumental in advancing this line of research. The coordinator of this group, Néstor García Canclini, has produced what is perhaps the most important text in this regard, under the poetic title *Culturas Hibridas: Estrategias Para Entrar y Salir de la Modernidad.* Many of these debates are carried out in the journals *David y Goliath,* published by CLACSO in Buenos Aires, and *Nueva Socicdad,* published in Caracas. See also García Canclini, ed. (1987); Bartra (1987); Calderón, ed. (1988); Quijano (1988, 1990); Lechner (1988); Sarlo (1991); and Britto García (1991). Some of these texts are reviewed in Montaldo (1991). The only text available in English that deals with this literature is Yúdice, Franco, and Flores, eds. (1992).

9. Related theorizations of popular culture have appeared in the United States and Europe, chiefly in cultural studies. See particularly the works of de Certeau (1984), Fiske (1989a, 1989b), Willis (1990), and Angus and Jhally, eds. (1989).

10. García Marquez emphasizes that everything he has written is strictly real. "Daily life in Latin America shows us that reality is filled with extraordinary things. . . . It is sufficient to glance at the newspapers to realize that extraordinary events are always happening" (1982, 36). Neruda spoke of Mexico as the last magic country, in ways that apply to many places in the Third World.

11. Some of these points became clear to me in discussions with Trinh T. Minh-ha and Rey Chow at faculty seminars held in Northampton, Massachusetts, on January 20–22, 1993, and organized by the women's studies program at Smith College.

12. Habermas's tour de force (1987) shows the shortcomings of the various attempts since Nietzsche at overcoming subject-centered reason for relying on reason, even if he does it in order to prepare the ground for his own attempt (communicative action), probably no less flawed according to his own criteria than those he critiques. One quick note on Habermas's treatment of Foucault (1987, chs. 9 and 10); although Habermas is right in saying that Foucault does not succeed in providing a fully satisfactory account of the genealogy of the social, Foucault's (1986) notion of "problematizations of truth" (games of truth and power) as the source of specific con-

figurations of social life does not entail positing power as a transcendental that arrives from nowhere, as Habermas imputes to Foucault. Laclau and Mouffe's (1985) notion of "field of discursivity" from which all social reality emerges through articulations—derived from a reformulation of Foucault's notion of discursive formation—and Deleuze's interpretation of Foucault's work in terms of mathematical concepts such as strata, foldings, topology, and the outside are meant to give an idea of the sources of power.

13. "Utopia is what connects philosophy to its epoch . . . it is with utopia that philosophy becomes political, carrying to its extreme the critique of the epoch" (Delenze and Guattari 1993, 101; my translation from the Spanish version).

14. This is a risky question—one that oscillates between unreflective interventionism based on the belief that one can "liberate" others, on the one hand, and a total disregard for the role of intellecltual work in social life, on the other. There is also the danger, as bell hooks put it, that "cultural studies could easily become the space for the informers" (1990, 9). For hooks, only a significant exchange between the critic and the people he or she writes about "will insure that it [cultural studies] is a location that enables critical intervention" (9).

15. "The response of the States, or of the axiomatic, may obviously be to accord the minorities regional or federal or statutory autonomy, in short, to add axioms. But this is not the problem: this operation consists only in translating the minorities into denumerable sets or subsets, which would enter as elements into the majority, which could be counted among the majority. . . . What is proper to the minority is to assert a power of the nondenumerable, even if that minority is composed of a single member. This is the formula for multiplicities" (Delenze and Guattari 1987, 470).

16. A discussion of some of these questions is found in the visionary articles written by Guattari in the last months of his life. See Guattari (1993) for a Spanish-language collection of these works. In these writings, Guattari introduced the notion of ecosophy, an ethico-political perspective on diversity and alterity that requires economic, ecological, psychological, scientific, and social transformations. He spoke of the need to "construct new transcultural, transnational, and transversalist lands, and value universes freed from the allure of territorialized power" as the only way to overcome the current planetary predicament (1993, 208).

17. I have in mind, for instance, the organization of black communities in the Pacific Coast region of Colom-

bia, which are confronted by growing forces destructive to their culture and tropical rainforest environment. Their social movement is framed by large-scale government plans for the "sustainable development" of the region; projects for the conservation of the region's almost legendary biological diversity; capitalist pressures for the control of land; the integration of the country into the Pacific Basin economies; and a political opening for the defense of minority rights, territories, and cultures.

REFERENCES

Angus, Ian, and Sut Jhally, eds. 1989. Cultural Politics in Contemporary America. New York: Routledge.

Bartra, Roger. 1987. La Jaula de la Melancolía México, D. F.: Grijalbo.

Britto García, Luis. 1991. El Imperio Contracultural: Del Rock a la Postmodernidad. Caracas: Nueva Sociedad.

Calderón, Fernando, ed. 1988. Imágenes Desconocidas: La Modernidad en la Encrucijada Postmoderna. Buenos Aires: CLACSO.

Castells, Manual. 1986. High Technology, World Development, and Structural Transformations: The Trends and the Debates. Alternatives 11 (3): 297–344.

———, and Roberto Laserna. 1989. La Nueva Dependencia: Cambio Technológico y Reestructuración en Latinoamérica. David y Goliath 55:2–16.

Chow, Rey. 1992. Postmodern Automatons. In Feminists Theorize the Political, edited by Judith Butler and Joan Scott, 101–17. New York: Routledge.

Clifford, James.

——— 1989. Notes on Theory and Travel. Inscriptions 5:177–88.

De Certeau, Michel. 1984. The Practice of Everyday Life. Berkeley: University of California Press.

Deleuze, Gilles. 1988. Foucault. Minneapolis: University of Minnesota Press.

———, and Félix Guattari. 1987. A Thousand Plateaus. Minneapolis: University of Minnesota Press.

Escobar, Arturo.

———, 1992b. Reflections on "Development": Grassroots Approaches and Alternative Politics in the Third World. Futures 24 (5): 411–36.

———, 1994. Welcome to Cyberia: Notes on the Anthropology of Cyberculture. Current Anthropology, Forthcoming.

———, and Sonia E. Alvarez, eds. 1992. The Making of Social Movements in Latin America: Identity, Strategy, and Democracy. Boulder: Westview Press.

Esteva. Gustavo. 1987. Regenerating People's Space. Alternatives 12 (1): 125–52.

Fals Borda, Orlando.

———, 1984. Resistencia en el San Jorge. Bogotá: Carlos Valencia Editores.

———, and Anisur Rahman, eds. 1991. Action and Knowledge: Breaking the Monopoly with Participatory Action-Research. New York: Apex Press.

Fiske, John. 1989a. Understanding the Popular. Boston: Unwin Hyman.

———, 1989b. Reading the Popular. Boston: Unwin Hyman.

Foucault, Michel. 1972. The Archaeology of Knowledge. New York: Harper Colophon Books.

———, 1986. The Use of Pleasure. New York: Pantheon Books.

García Canclini, Néstor. 1990. Culturas Híbridas: Estrategias para Entrar y Salir de la Modernidad. México, D.F.: Grijalbo.

García Márquez, Gabriel. 1982. El Olor de la Guayaba. Bogotá: La Oveja Negra.

Giddens, Anthony. 1990. The Consequences of Modernity. Stanford: Stanford University Press.

Girard, René. 1977. Violence and the Sacred. Baltimore: Johns Hopkins University Press.

Guatari, Felix. 1993. El Constructivismo Guattariano. Cali: Universidad del Valle Press.

Habermas, Juürgen. 1987. The Philosophical Discourse of Modernity. Cambridge: MIT Press.

Hall, Stuart. 1992. Cultural Studies and Its Theoretical Legacies. In Cultural Studies, edited by Lawrence Grossberg, Cary Nelson, and Paula Treichler, 286–94. New York: Routledge.

hooks, bell. 1990. Yearning: Race, Gender, and Cultural Politics. Boston: South End Press.

Laclau, Ernesto, and Chantal Mouffe. 1985. Hegemony and Socialist Strategy. London: Verso.

Lechner, Norbert. 1988. Los Patios Interiores de la Democracia. Subjetividad y Política. Santiago: FLACSO.

Mani, Lata. 1989. Multiple Mediations: Feminist Scholarship in the Age of Multinational Reception. Inscriptions 5:1–24.

Montaldo, Graciela. 1991. Estrategias del Fin de Siglo. Nueva Sociedad, no. 116:75–87.

Nandy, Ashis. 1983. The Intimate Enemy: Loss and Recovery of Self under Colonialism. Delhi: Oxford University Press.

———, 1989. Shamans, Savages, and the Wilderness: On the Audibility of Dissent

Parajuli, Pramod. 1991. Power and Knowledge in Development Discourse. International Social Science Journal 127:173–90.

Quijano, Aníbal. 1988. Modernidad, Identidad y Utopía en América Latina. Lima: Sociedad y Política Ediciones.

Rahnema, Majid.

———, 1988a. Power and Regenerative Processes in

Micro-Spaces. International Social Science Journal 117:361–75.

———, 1988b. On a New Variety of AIDS and Its Pathogens: Homo Economicus, Development, and Aid. Alternatives 13 (1): 117–36.

Rojas de Ferro, María Cristina. 1994. A Political Economy of Violence. Ph.D. diss., Carleton University, Ottawa.

Sarlo, Beatriz. 1991. Un Debate Sobre la Cultura. Nueva Sociedad, no. 116:88–93.

Sheth, D. L. 1987. Alternative Development as Political Practice. Alternatives 12 (2): 155–71.

Shiva, Vandana. 1989. Staying Alive. Women, Ecology and Development. London: Zed Books.

Starn, Orin. 1992. "I Dreamed of Foxes and Hawks": Reflections on Peasant Protest, New Social Movements, and the *Rondas Campesinas* of Northern Peru. *In* The Making of Social Movements in Latin America: Identity, Strategy, and Democracy, edited by Arturo Escobar and Sonia Alvarez, 89–111. Boulder: Westview Press.

Strahm, Rudolf. 1986. Por Qué Somos Tan Pobres? México, D.F.: Secretaría de Educación Pública.

Taussig, Michael.

———, 1987. Shamanism, Colonialism, and the Wild Man. Chicago: University of Chicago Press.

Touraine, Alain. 1988. The Return of the Actor, Minneapolis: University of Minnesota Press.

Trinh T. Minh-ha. 1989. Woman, Native, Other. Bloomington: Indiana University Press.

———, 1991. When the Moon Waxes Red. New York: Routledge.

Urla, Jacqueline. 1993. Cultural Politics in the Age of Statistics: Numbers, Nations, and the Making of Basque Identities. American Ethnologist 20 (4): 818–43.

Visvanathan, Shiv. 1986. Bhopal: The Imagination of a Disaster. Alternatives 11 (1): 147–65.

———, 1991. Mrs. Bruntland's Disenchanted Cosmos. Alternatives 16 (3): 377–84.

Willis, Paul. 1990. Common Culture. Boulder: Westview Press.

Yúdice, George, Jean Franco, and Juan Flores, eds. 1992. On Edge: The Crisis of Contemporary Latin American Culture. Minneapolis: University of Minnesota Press.